P9-DMF-286

ABBREVIATIONS USED IN THE TEXT

kg kilogram
km/h kilometer per hour
k_p permeability constant

L liter, tube length
LDH lactate dehydrogenase
LDL low-density lipoprotein
LH luteinizing hormone
l_o optimal length
LSD lysergic acid diethylamide
LTP long-term potentiation

M molar
M myosin
M phase mitosis phase of cell cycle
MAC membrane attack complex
MAP mean arterial pressure
MES microsomal enzyme system
Mg magnesium
MHC major histocompatibility complex
mi mile
mi/h mile per hour
MIF Müllerian inhibiting factor
min minute
ml milliliter
mM millimolar
mm millimeter
mmHg millimeters of mercury
mmol millimol
$mOsm$ milliosmolar
mOsmol milliosmol
mRNA messenger RNA
ms millisecond
mV millivolt
μg microgram
μL microliter
μM micromolar
μm micrometer
μmol micromol
μV microvolt

n any whole number

Na sodium
NAD⁺ nictinamide adenine dinucleotide
NE norepinephrine
ng nanogram
NIDDM non-insulin-dependent diabetes mellitus
NK natural killer cell
nm nanometer
nM nanomolar
nmol nanomol
NO nitric oxide
NPY neuropeptide Y
NSAID nonsteroidal anti-inflammatory drug

Osm osmolar

P partial pressure, permeability
P_{alv} alveolar pressure
P_{atm} atmospheric pressure
P_c capillary hydrostatic pressure
PF platelet factor
PGA prostaglandin of the A type
PGE prostaglandin of the E type
PGE₂ prostaglandin E_2
PGI₂ prostacyclin, prostaglandin I_2
PHI peptide histidine isoleucine
PHM peptide histidine methionine
P_i inorganic phosphate
P_{IF} interstitial fluid hydrostatic pressure
P_{ip} intrapleural pressure
PIP₂ phosphatidylinositol bisphosphate
pM picomolar
PMS premenstrual syndrome
PRF prolactin releasing factor
π_C osmotic force due to plasma protein concentration
π_{IF} osmotic force due to interstitial fluid protein concentration

R remainder of molecule
R resistance

r inside radius of tube
RNA ribonucleic acid
RQ respiratory quotient
rRNA ribosomal RNA

s second
S phase synthesis phase of cell cycle
SA sinoatrial
SP systolic pressure
SR sarcoplasmic reticulum
SS somatostatin
STD sexually transmitted disease
SV stroke volume

T thymine
T₃ triiodothyronine
T₄ thyroxine
t-PA tissue plasminogen activator
T tubule transverse tubule
TBW total body water
TFPI tissue factor pathway inhibitor
TH thyroid hormones
TIA transient ischemic attack
T_m transport maximum
TNF tumor necrosis factor
TPR total peripheral resistance
TRH thyrotropin releasing hormone
tRNA transfer RNA
TSH thyroid-stimulating hormone

U uracil
U_x urine concentration of sustance x

V volume
VIP vasoactive intestinal peptide
VLDL very-low-density lipoprotein
V_{O_2}-max maximal oxygen consumption
vWF von Willebrand factor

W work

HUMAN PHYSIOLOGY
THE MECHANISMS OF BODY FUNCTION

McGRAW-HILL, INC.

New York   St. Louis   San Francisco
Auckland   Bogotá   Caracas   Lisbon   London   Madrid
Mexico City   Milan   Montreal   New Delhi   San Juan   Singapore
Sydney   Tokyo   Toronto

SIXTH EDITION

HUMAN PHYSIOLOGY

THE MECHANISMS OF BODY FUNCTION

ARTHUR J. VANDER, M.D.
Professor Emeritus of Physiology
University of Michigan

JAMES H. SHERMAN, PH.D.
Associate Professor of Physiology
University of Michigan

DOROTHY S. LUCIANO, PH.D.
Formerly of the Department of Physiology
University of Michigan

HUMAN PHYSIOLOGY
THE MECHANISMS OF BODY FUNCTION

4 5 6 7 8 9 0 VNH   VNH 9 0 9 8 7 6 5 4

ISBN 0-07-066992-9

This book was set in New Caledonia by York Graphic Services, Inc.
The editors were Kathi M. Prancan and James W. Bradley;
the designer was Jo Jones;
the production supervisor was Paula Keller.
The photo editor was Mira Schachne.
The art editor was Arthur Ciccone.
New drawings were done by York Graphic Services, Inc.
New anatomical drawings were done by BioGraphics.
Von Hoffmann Press, Inc., was printer and binder.

Cover photograph by © Don Mason/The Stock Market. Inset photographs, from top to bottom: © Scott Camazine/Photo Researchers, Inc.; Dr. Dennis Kunkel/PhotoTake, NYC, © Science Photo Library/Science Source; and © Teri J. McDermott, M.A./PhotoTake.

The following illustrations were rendered by Deanne McKeown, Uppercase Graphics, © 1990: Figures 1–1; 8–1; 8–35; 8–37; 8–38; 8–41; 9–6; 9–8; 9–12; 9–34; 9–37; 11–33; 11–34; 11–35; 11–36; 12–2A; 12–6; 12–8; 12–9; 12–10; 12–13; 13–7; 13–14B; 13–15; 14–13; 14–18; 14–19; 14–24; 14–30; 14–52; 14–54; 14–59; 15–4; 15–13; 15–26; 16–4; 17–14; 17–15; 17–16; 17–17; 17–31; and 19–12.

Library of Congress Cataloging-in-Publication Data

Vander, Arthur J., (date).
   Human physiology: the mechanisms of body function / Arthur J. Vander, James H. Sherman, Dorothy S. Luciano.—6th ed.
      p.   cm.
   Includes bibliographical references and index.
   ISBN 0-07-066992-9 (acid-free paper)
   1. Human physiology.   I. Sherman, James H., (date).
II. Luciano, Dorothy S.   III. Title.
QP34.5.V36   1994
612—dc24   93-15950

INTERNATIONAL EDITION

*To our parents,
and to Judy, Peggy, and Joe
without whose understanding
it would have been
impossible*

REFERENCES FOR FIGURE ADAPTATIONS

Berne, R. M., and N. M. Levy: "Cardiovascular Physiology," 6th edn., Mosby, St. Louis, 1992.

Bloom, F. E., A. Lazerson, and L. Hofstadter: "Brain, Mind, and Behaviour," Freeman, New York, 1985.

Carlson, B. M.: "Patten's Foundations of Embryology," 5th edn., McGraw-Hill, New York, 1988.

Chaffee, E. E., and I. M. Lytle: "Basic Physiology and Anatomy," 4th edn., Lippincott, Philadelphia, 1980.

Chapman, C. B., and J. H. Mitchell: *Sci. Amer.*, May, 1965.

Comroe, J. H.: "Physiology of Respiration," Year Book, Chicago, 1965.

Crosby, W. H.: *Hosp. Prac.*, February, 1987.

Curtis, B. A., S. Jacobson, and E. M. Marcus: "An Invitation to the Neurosciences," Saunders, Philadelphia, 1972.

Davis, H., and H. R. Silverman: "Hearing and Deafness," Holt, Rinehart, and Winston, New York, 1970.

Davson, H.: "The Eye," Vol. 1, 2d edn., Academic, New York, 1969.

Dowling, J. E., and B. B. Boycott: *Proc. R. Soc. Lond.*, **166**:80, 1966.

Erickson, G. F., D. A. Magoffin, C. A. Dyer, and C. Hofeditz: *Endocrine Reviews:* Summer, 1985.

Felig, P., and J. Wahren: *N. Eng. J. Med.*, **293**:1078 (1975).

Ganong, W. F.: "Review of Medical Physiology," 4th edn., Lange, Los Altos, Calif., 1969.

Gardner, E.: "Fundamentals of Neurology," 5th edn., Saunders, Philadelphia, 1968.

Golde, D. W., and Gasson, J. C.: *Sci. Amer.*, July, 1988.

Goodman, H. M.: "Basic Medical Endocrinology," Raven, New York, 1988.

Gray, H. M., A. Sette, and S. Buus (drawing by G. V. Kelvin): *Sci. Amer.*, November, 1989.

Guyton, A. C.: "Functions of the Human Body," 3d edn., Saunders, Philadelphia, 1969.

Hedge, G. A., H. D. Colby, and R. L. Goodman: "Clinical Endocrine Physiology," Saunders, Philadelphia, 1987.

Hoffman, B. F., and P. E. Cranefield: "Electrophysiology of the Heart," McGraw-Hill, New York, 1960.

Hubel, D. H., and T. N. Wiesel: *J. Physiol.*, **154**:572 (1960).

Hudspeth, A. J.: *Sci. Amer.*, January, 1983.

Kandel, E. R., and J. H. Schwartz: "Principles of Neural Science," 2d edn., Elsevier/North-Holland, New York, 1985.

Kappas, A., and A. P. Alvares: *Sci. Amer.*, June 1975.

Lambersten, C. J.: in P. Bard (ed.): "Medical Physiological Psychology," 11th edn., Mosby, St. Louis, 1961.

Lehninger, A. L.: "Biochemistry," Worth, New York, 1970.

Lentz, T. L.: "Cell Fine Structure," Saunders, Philadelphia, 1971.

Little, R. C.: "Physiology of the Heart and Circulation," 2d edn., Year Book, Chicago, 1981.

Maxwell, D. J., and M. Rethely: *TINS*, **10**:117 (1987).

Nauta, W. J. H., and M. Fiertag: "Fundamental Neuroanatomy," Freeman, New York, 1986.

Oldendorf, W. H.: *Hosp. Prac.*, **17**:143 (1982).

Olds, J.: *Sci. Am.*, October, 1956.

Pardo, J. V., P. J. Fox, and M. E. Raichle: *Nature*, **349**:61 (1991).

Patton, H. D., A. F. Fuchs, B. Hille, A. M. Scher, and R. Steiner: "Textbook of Physiology," Saunders, Philadelphia, 1989.

Rasmujssen, A. T.: "Outlines of Neuroanatomy," 2d edn., Wm. C. Brown, Dubuque, Ia., 1943.

Roberts, H. R., and J. N. Lozier (drawing by Ilil Arbil): *Hosp. Prac.* January, 1992.

Rushmer, R. F.: "Cardiovascular Dynamics," 2d edn., Saunders, Philadelphia, 1961.

Scales, W. E., A. J. Vander, M. B. Brown, and M. J. Kluger: *Am. J. Physiol.*, **65**:1840 (1988).

Snyder, S. H.: "Drugs and the Brain," Freeman, New York, 1986.

Tung, K.: Immunopathology and male infertility, *Hosp. Prac.*, June, 1988.

von Bekesy, G.: *Sci. Amer.*, August, 1957.

Wang, C. C., and M. I. Grossman: *Am. J. Physiol.*, **164**:527 (1951).

CONTENTS IN BRIEF

PART THREE
COORDINATED BODY FUNCTIONS

CONTENTS

4 MOLECULAR CONTROL MECHANISMS: PROTEINS AND DNA

55

5 ENERGY AND CELLULAR METABOLISM

83

PART THREE
COORDINATED BODY FUNCTIONS

19 REPRODUCTION 647

PREFACE

Because our text has worked well for so many through five editions, the fundamental purpose of this book has not changed in the sixth edition. Again, we have attempted to present the principles of human physiology in a format that is suitable for undergraduate students, regardless of academic background or field of study—liberal arts, biology, nursing, pharmacy, or other allied health professions. Many medical and dental students have also used previous editions to lay the foundation for the more detailed coverage they receive in their advanced courses.

The clear, up-to-date, and accurate explanations of mechanisms have always been and continue to be the most significant feature of this book. Our goal is to integrate and synthesize information rather than simply describe facts and events. We believe this will enable students to achieve a working knowledge of physiology, not just a memory bank of physiological facts.

ALTERNATIVE SEQUENCES

Given the inevitable restrictions of time, our organization permits a variety of sequences and approaches to be adopted. Chapter 1 should definitely be read first as it introduces the basic themes of the book. Depending on the time available, the instructor's goals, and the students' backgrounds in physical science and/or cellular biology, the chapters of Part I can either be worked through systematically at the outset or be used more selectively as background reading in the contexts of Parts 2 and 3.

In Part 2, the absolutely essential chapters are, in order, Chapters 7, 8, 10 and 11. They present the basic concepts and facts relevant to homeostasis, intercellular communication, signal transduction, the nervous and endocrine systems, and muscle. The material in Chapters 9, 12, and 13 could be skipped since they are not as critical for an understanding of later chapters.

The coordinated body functions of Part 3 are best introduced by covering circulation, Chapter 14, first. Otherwise, the chapters of Part 3, as well as Chapters 9, 12, and 13 of Part 2, can be rearranged and used or not to suit individual instructor's preferences and time available.

REVISION HIGHLIGHTS

(1) Our major goal for this revision was to update completely all material and assure the greatest accuracy possible. A large number of physiologists reviewed the manuscript (see list in the acknowledgements) to help assure not only accuracy but balance. The following is a partial list (in order of the chapters in which they appear) of topics that have either been significantly altered (and frequently expanded) or added for the first time:

imaging techniques
protein conformation
mitochondrial DNA
allosteric and covalent modulation
ribosomal RNA
regulation of protein synthesis
cell division cycle genes
alleles
homo- and heterozygosity
cancer
recombinant DNA
reversible and irreversible reactions
carbohydrate catabolism
glucose synthesis

diffusion
mediated transport
ion channels
nonsteroidal anti-inflammatory drugs (NSAIDs)
biochemical mechanism of G-protein activation
G-protein interaction with membrane effector proteins
set-point resetting
adaptation to night-shift work
biological rhythms in cancer therapy
synaptic effectiveness
gases (nitric oxide and carbon monoxide) as neurotransmitters
M- and P-type visual coding
short portal vessels and their role in prolactin secretion
dopamine and prolactin releasing factor as posterior pituitary hormones
excitation-contraction coupling in skeletal muscle
muscle fatigue
muscular dystrophy
nonpyramidal pathways
neural mechanisms for directed attention
neural mechanisms for conscious experiences
antidepressant drugs (for example Prozac)
cross-tolerance to drugs
possible roles of nitric oxide in long-term potentiation and memory
parallel processing of language functions
measurement of cardiac function—echocardiography and cardiac angiography
hematopoietic growth factors
SA node permeability changes
clinical use of pacemakers
excitation-contraction coupling in cardiac muscle
mechanism of Starling's law of the heart
ejection fraction and its clinical use
vascular influences of endothelin, prostacyclin, and nitric oxide
mechanism of lymph formation and flow
blood pressure measurements during everyday activities
causes of primary hypertension
use of vasodilator drugs in heart failure
transpulmonary pressure, lateral traction, and airway resistance
airway resistance in emphysema
treatment of asthma
role of the kidneys in high-altitude adaptation
renal clearance technique
new names for nephron segments
sodium cotransport and countertransport mechanisms
macula densa control of renin release
bone metabolism and bone diseases
integration of renal and respiratory function in acid-base balance

role of ammonium production and excretion in acid-base balance
bicarbonate secretory mechanisms
emulsification of fat and micelle formation
iron absorption
motilin
intestinal motility
ulcers and Helicobacter pyloris
insulin's effects and their biochemical mechanisms
pathophysiology of diabetes mellitus
apolipoproteins in lipoproteins
fatty acids and plasma cholesterol
oncogenes and growth factors
growth hormone and aging
bulimia
endogenous pyrogens in addition to IL-1
roles of Sertoli cells
impotence
inhibin
stages of oogenesis
feedback effects of pituitary and ovarian hormones
acrosome reaction
relationships between placenta and fetal adrenal glands
pregnancy sickness
control of prolactin secretion
RU 486, Norplant, and Depo-Provera
brain differences in homosexual and heterosexual men
immunogens and antigens
antigen processing and presentation to T cells
cytokines
NK cells
antibody dependent cellular cytotoxicity (ADCC)
defenses against cancer cells
immunotherapy against cancer
HIV infection, AIDS, and zidovudine
allergy and autoimmune disease

Despite many additions, careful editing and a ruthless removal of material no longer deemed essential have permitted us to maintain the text size essentially constant.

(2) In the previous edition, for the first time, full-color was employed in approximately half the figures. We found that this so enhanced these figures' educational value that we have extended the use of full-color to all figures in this edition.

(3) Several rearrangements have been made in the organization of the neurophysiology material. Former Chapter 20, Consciousness and Behavior, has been moved forward and is now Chapter 13. This places all the major neurophysiology material in Part 2 of the book. The sections of Chapter 8 have been reordered—membrane potentials and synapses before neuroanatomy–for better flow and to correspond to general teaching patterns. In

addition, the section on sensory receptors has been moved to Chapter 9, where it introduces sensory coding; therefore all information pertaining to sensory receptors is now in one chapter.

(4) The topic order of Chapter 5 has been extensively reorganized for greater clarity. The order of discussion is now glycolysis, Krebs cycle, and oxidative phosphorylation.

(5) Chapter section titles are now given in the Contents in Brief at the beginning of the book, and a comprehensive Contents has been added for the first time to facilitate students' reference to major topics

(6) In the previous edition, all study aids (summaries, key-term lists, review questions, and thought questions) were at the ends of the chapters. In this edition, the summaries, key-term definition lists, and review questions are given at the ends of individual sections in those chapters that are broken into sections. This permits more rapid feedback to the student and has the same effect as breaking the larger chapters into multiple chapters. (The thought questions continue to be at the ends of all chapters to permit integration of material across sections.)

(7) We have chosen to continue our practice of presenting exercise physiology where relevant throughout the book, rather than in a separate chapter, because we feel that the integrated tack provides an excellent way of summarizing and applying much of the material used in the individual chapters. However, to provide a rapid overview of this extensive coverage and a method for accessing it, we have added a new appendix at the back of the book—Appendix E: Outline of Exercise Physiology.

(8) Our coverage of clinical applications (pathophysiology) has again been expanded, but we continue our practice of using it mainly to illustrate basic physiological principles. Some of this material is embedded in the text (for example, a reference to cystic fibrosis when we discuss chloride channels) whereas much is in separate sections bearing the name of the disease process (for example, Heart Attacks). To draw the reader's attention to this highly interesting and relevant material we have adopted three new conventions for this edition: (a) All clinical terms appear in bold face italics; (b) a list of these clinical terms appears at the end of each chapter; and (3) an index of clinical applications appears at the back of the book in a new Appendix for easy reference.

STUDY AIDS

A variety of pedagogical aids are used in this edition:
(1) **Boldface key terms** throughout each chapter. (As noted above, clinical terms are designated by ***boldface italics.***)

(2) The **illustration program** is now in full-color. The extensive use of flow diagrams, which we introduced in 1970 (and which has been so widely imitated in other texts) has been continued. Certain conventions are used in these diagrams throughout the book to enhance learning. Look, for example, at Figure 18-10. The beginning and ending boxes of the flow-diagram are in light green, and the beginning is further clarified, when needed, by the use of a "Begin" logo. Blue three-dimensional boxes are used to denote events occurring inside organs and tissues (identified by boldface underlined labels in the upper right of the boxes), so that the reader can easily pick out the anatomic entities that participate in the sequences of events. Finally, the participation of hormones in the sequences stand out by the placing of changes in their plasma concentrations in orange boxes.

(3) **Summary tables.** We have again increased the number of reference and summary tables in this edition. Some summarize small amounts of information (for example, the summary of second messengers in Table 7-8), whereas others bring together large amounts of information that may be scattered throughout the book (for example the reference figure of liver functions in Chapter 17). In several places, mini-glossaries are included as reference tables in the text (for example, the list of immune-system cells and chemical mediators in Chapter 20). Because the tables complement the figures, these two learning aids taken together provide a rapid means of reviewing the most important material in a chapter.

(4) **End-of-section or -chapter study aids.** As already described, summaries, key-term definition lists, and review questions appear at the ends of the sections in those chapters that are broken into sections. These aids appear at the ends of non-sectioned chapters. The clinical-term lists and thought questions are always at the ends of chapters.

(a) **Extensive summaries** in outline form.

(b) **Key-term definition lists** of all boldfaced words in the section/chapter (excluding the clinical terms).

(c) **Comprehensive review questions** in essay format. These review questions, in essence, constitute a complete list of learning objectives.

(d) **Clinical-term lists** of all boldface italicized words in the chapter. This serves to remind the student of how the physiology has been applied to clinical examples in the chapter.

(e) **Thought questions** that challenge the student to go beyond memorization of facts to solve problems, often presented as case histories or experiments. Complete Answers to Thought Questions appear as Appendix A.

(5) **An extensive Glossary,** with pronunciation guides, is provided in Appendix B.

(6) **Additional Appendixes,** C and D, respectively, English-Metric Interconversions and Electrophysiology

Equations. Appendixes E and F, respectively, are an Outline of Exercise Physiology and Index of Clinical Applications in the Text.

(7) **Suggested readings** are presented in Appendix G.

(8) **Abbreviations** used in the text are alphabetized and are given on the endpapers.

SUPPLEMENTS

o accompany this edition, a **Study Manual** has been prepared by Donna Van Wynsberghe (University of Wisconsin-Milwaukee) to supplement the end-of-chapter study material already provided in the text. Students will have the opportunity to test and expand their knowledge of material through a variety of activities.

The **Test Bank** features more than 50 questions per chapter. Sandra Winicur (Indiana University at South Bend) has prepared a variety of question types including the more rote examples as well as problem-solving and conceptual examples. Graphics are used where appropriate. All answers are provided at the end of the manual. The questions are also available on diskette for IBM PC and Macintosh computers.

A set of 100 **Overhead Transparencies** of the most important illustrations and photographs from the text are available free to adopters.

Computer Software has been specifically designed by David J. Combs to accompany the text. It features five separate modules covering different systems and provides self-test material and animated presentations of difficult concepts such as the action potential. It is available for the Macintosh computer.

ACKNOWLEDGMENTS

e are very grateful to the many physiologists who read one or more chapters during various stages of this revision: D. Andy Anderson, Utah State University; Marjorie Anderson, University of Washington; Paul Bier-

suck, Nassau Community College; Stephen T. Bishoff, University of South Carolina at Sumter; T. Earle Bowen, Jr., University of Kentucky Medical Center; Kenneth Casey, University of Michigan Medical Center; David E. Cochrane, Tufts University; Annabelle Cohen, SUNY College of Staten Island; Susan Dougherty, Monroe Community College; Rita A. Garrick, Fordham University; H. Maurice Goodman, University of Massachusetts Medical School; Lois Jane Heller, University of Minnesota at Duluth Medical School; H. Rodney Holmes, University of Chicago; Hsiaolan S. Hsu, California Institute of Technology; John M. Johnson, University of Texas at San Antonio; Leonard R. Johnson, University of Tennessee College of Medicine; Fred J. Karsch, University of Michigan; Carolyn O. Kerr, Merced College; P. Landis Keyes, University of Michigan Medical School; T. Daniel Kimbrough, Virginia Commonwealth University; Barbara Klemenok, Napa Valley College; Jack L. Kostyo, University of Michigan; Steven L. Kunkel, University of Michigan; Michael G. Levitzky, Louisiana State University Medical Center; John H. Martin, Columbia University; E. Keith Michal, Ohio State University; Hylan C. Moises, University of Michigan; Annie Peterman, University of Washington School of Medicine; Stanley A. Schwartz, SUNY at Buffalo; Kathleen M. Susman, Vassar College; and Guy Van Cleave, Modesto Junior College. Their advice was extremely useful in helping us to be accurate and balanced in our coverage. We hope they will be understanding of the occasions when we did not heed their advice, and we are, of course, solely responsible for any errors that have crept in.

We would also like to thank our sponsoring editor, Kathi Prancan, for her patient and wise counsel, our art consultant, Arthur Ciccone, for his skillful and painstaking advice, our editing supervisor James W. Bradley, our production supervisor Paula Keller, our designer Jo Jones, and our photo editor Mira Schachne.

Arthur J. Vander

James H. Sherman

Dorothy S. Luciano

HUMAN PHYSIOLOGY
THE MECHANISMS OF BODY FUNCTION

CHAPTER

1

A FRAMEWORK
FOR HUMAN PHYSIOLOGY

One cannot meaningfully analyze the complex activities of the human body without a framework upon which to build, a set of viewpoints to guide one's thinking.

It is the purpose of this chapter to provide such an orientation to the subject of **human physiology**—the mechanisms by which the body functions.

MECHANISM AND CAUSALITY

The **mechanist view** of life holds that all phenomena, no matter how complex, are ultimately describable in terms of physical and chemical laws. In this view, which is that taken by physiologists, the human being is a machine—an enormously complex machine, but a machine nevertheless. In contrast, **vitalism** is the view that some "vital force" beyond physics and chemistry is required to explain life. The mechanist view has predominated in the twentieth century because virtually all information gathered from observation and experiment has agreed with it.

Physiologists should not be misunderstood when they sometimes say that "the whole is greater than the sum of its parts." This statement in no way implies a vital force but rather recognizes that *integration* of an enormous number of individual physical and chemical events occurring at all levels of organization is required for biological systems to function. Thus the scope of physiology is extremely broad. At one end of the spectrum, it includes the study of individual molecules—for example, how a particular protein's shape and electrical properties allow it to function as a channel for water movement into or out of a single cell. At the other end, it is concerned with complex processes that depend on the interplay of many widely separated organs in the body—for example, regulation of the amount of water in the entire body.

A common denominator of physiological processes is their contribution to survival. Unfortunately, it is easy to misunderstand the nature of this relationship. Consider, for example, the statement, "During exercise a person sweats because the body *needs* to get rid of the excess heat generated." This type of statement is an example of **teleology**, the explanation of events in terms of purpose, but it is not an explanation at all in the scientific sense of the word. It is somewhat like saying, "The furnace is on because the house needs to be heated." Clearly, the furnace is on not because it senses in some mystical manner the house's "needs," but because the temperature has fallen below the thermostat's set point and the electric current in the connecting wires has turned on the heater.

Is it not true that sweating serves a useful purpose because the excess heat, if not eliminated, might cause sickness or even death? Yes, it is, but this is totally different from stating that a need to avoid injury causes the sweating. The cause of the sweating is a sequence of events initiated by the increased heat generation: increased heat generation → increased blood temperature → increased activity of specific nerve cells in the brain → increased activity of a series of nerve cells → increased production of sweat by the sweat-gland cells. Each step occurs by means of physicochemical changes in the cells involved. In science, to explain a phenomenon is to reduce it to a causally linked sequence of physicochemical events. This is the scientific meaning of causality, of the word "because."

This is a good place to emphasize that causal chains can be not only long, as in the example just cited, but also multiple. In other words, one should not assume the simple relationship of one cause, one effect. We shall see that multiple factors often must interact to elicit a response. To take an example from medicine, cigarette smoking causes lung cancer, but the likelihood of cancer developing in a smoker depends on a variety of other factors, including the way that person's body processes the chemicals in cigarette smoke, the rate at which damaged molecules are repaired, and so on.

That a phenomenon is beneficial to a person, while not explaining the mechanism of the phenomenon, is of obvious interest and importance. Evolution is the key to understanding why most body activities do indeed appear to be purposeful, since those responses having survival value undergo natural selection. Throughout this book we emphasize how a particular process contributes to survival, but the reader must never confuse this survival value of a process with the explanation of the mechanisms by which the process occurs.

A SOCIETY OF CELLS

Cells: The Basic Units

The simplest structural units into which a complex multicellular organism can be divided and still retain the functions characteristic of life are called **cells**. One of the unifying generalizations of biology is that certain fundamental activities are common to almost all cells and represent the minimal requirements for maintaining cell integrity and life. Thus, a human liver cell and an amoeba are remarkably similar in their means of exchanging materials with their immediate environments, of obtaining energy from organic nutrients, of synthesizing complex molecules, and of duplicating themselves.

Each human organism begins as a single cell, the fertilized ovum, which divides to form two cells, each of which divides in turn, resulting in four cells, and so on. If cell multiplication were the only event occurring, the end result would be a spherical mass of identical cells. During development, however, each cell becomes specialized in the performance of a particular function, such as developing force and movement (muscle cells) or generating electric signals (nerve cells). The process of transforming an unspecialized cell into a specialized cell is known as **cell differentiation**.

In addition to differentiating, cells migrate to new locations during development and form selective adhesions with other cells to create multicellular structures. In this manner, the cells of the body are arranged in various combinations to form a hierarchy of organized structures. Differentiated cells with similar properties aggregate to form **tissues** (nerve tissue, muscle tissue, and so on), which combine with other types of tissues to form **organs** (the heart, lungs, kidneys, and so on), which are linked together to form **organ systems** (Figure 1-1).

About 200 distinct kinds of cells can be identified in the body in terms of differences in structure and function. When cells are classified according to the broad types of function they perform, however, four categories emerge: (1) muscle cells, (2) nerve cells, (3) epithelial cells, and (4) connective-tissue cells. In each of these functional categories, there are several cell types that perform variations of the specialized function. For example, there are three types of muscle cells—skeletal-, cardiac-, and smooth-muscle cells—all of which generate forces and produce movement but differ from each other in shape, in the mechanisms controlling their contractile activity, and in their location in the various organs of the body.

Muscle cells are specialized to generate the mechanical forces that produce force and movement. They may be attached to bones and produce movements of the limbs or trunk. They may be attached to skin, as for example, the muscles producing facial expressions, or they may enclose hollow cavities so that their contraction expels the contents of the cavity, as in the case of the pumping of the heart. Muscle cells also surround many of the tubes in the body—blood vessels, for example—and their contraction changes the diameter of these tubes.

Nerve cells are specialized to initiate and conduct electric signals, often over long distances. A signal may influence the initiation of new electric signals in other nerve cells, or it may influence secretion by a gland cell or contraction of a muscle cell. Thus, nerve cells provide a major means of controlling the activities of other cells.

FIGURE 1-1
Levels of cellular organization.

Their activity also underlies such phenomena as consciousness, perception, and cognition.

Epithelial cells are specialized for the selective secretion and absorption of ions and organic molecules. They are located mainly at the surfaces that either cover the body or individual organs or else line the walls of various tubular and hollow structures within the body. Epithelial cells, which rest on a homogeneous noncellular material called the **basement membrane**, form the boundaries between compartments and function as selective barriers regulating the exchange of molecules across them. For example, the epithelial cells at the surface of the skin form a barrier that prevents most substances in the external environment from entering the body through the skin. Epithelial cells are also found in glands that form from the invagination of epithelial surfaces.

Connective-tissue cells, as their name implies, have as their major function connecting, anchoring, and supporting the structures of the body. These cells typically have a large amount of extracellular material between them. The cells themselves include those in the loose meshwork of cells and fibers underlying most epithelial layers, plus other types as diverse as fat-storing cells, bone cells, and red and white blood cells. Many connective-tissue cells secrete into the fluid surrounding them molecules that form a matrix consisting of various types of protein **fibers** embedded in a **ground substance** made of complex sugars, protein, and crystallized minerals. This matrix may vary in consistency from a semifluid gel, in loose connective tissue, to the solid crystalline structure of bone. These extracellular fibers include ropelike **collagen fibers**, which have a high tensile strength and resist stretching, rubber-band-like **elastin fibers**, and fine, highly branched **reticular fibers**.

Tissues

Most specialized cells are associated with other cells of a similar kind to form tissues. Corresponding to the four general categories of differentiated cells, there are four general classes of tissues: (1) **muscle tissue**, (2) **nerve tissue**, (3) **epithelial tissue**, and (4) **connective tissue**. It should be noted that the term "tissue" is frequently used in several ways. It is formally defined as just described, that is, as an aggregate of a single type of specialized cell. However, it is also commonly used to denote the general cellular fabric of any organ or structure, for example, kidney tissue or lung tissue, each of which in fact usually contains all four classes of tissue.

Organs and Organ Systems

Organs are composed of the four kinds of tissues arranged in various proportions and patterns: sheets, tubes, layers, bundles, strips, and so on. For example, the kidneys consist of (1) a series of small tubes, each composed of a single layer of epithelial cells; (2) blood vessels, whose walls contain varying quantities of smooth muscle and connective tissue; (3) nerve-cell extensions that end near the muscle and epithelial cells; and (4) a loose network of connective-tissue elements that are interspersed throughout the kidneys and also form enclosing capsules.

Many organs are organized into small, similar subunits often referred to as **functional units**, each performing the function of the organ. For example, the kidneys' 2 million functional units are termed nephrons (which contain the small tubes mentioned in the previous paragraph), and the total production of urine by the kidneys is the sum of the amounts formed by the individual nephrons.

Finally, we have the organ system, a collection of organs that together perform an overall function. For example, the kidneys, the urinary bladder, the tubes leading from the kidneys to the bladder, and the tube leading from the bladder to the exterior constitute the urinary system. There are 10 organ systems in the body. Their components and functions are given in Table 1-1.

To sum up, the human body can be viewed as a complex society of differentiated cells structurally and functionally combined and interrelated to carry out the functions essential to the survival of the organism. The individual cells constitute the basic units of this society, and almost all of these cells individually exhibit the fundamental activities common to all forms of life. Indeed, many of the cells can be removed and maintained in test tubes as free-living organisms (this is termed "in vitro," literally "in glass," as opposed to "in vivo," meaning "within the body").

There is a paradox in this analysis. If each cell performs the fundamental activities required for its own survival, what contributions do the organ systems make? How is it that the functions of the organ systems are essential to the survival of the organism when each individual cell seems capable of performing its own fundamental activities? The resolution of this paradox is found in the isolation of most of the cells of a multicellular organism from the environment surrounding the organism—the **external environment**—and the presence of an internal environment.

THE INTERNAL ENVIRONMENT AND HOMEOSTASIS

An amoeba and a human liver cell both obtain their energy by breaking down certain organic nutrients. The chemical reactions involved in this intracellular process are remarkably similar in the two types of cells and involve the utilization of oxygen and the production of carbon dioxide. The amoeba picks up oxygen directly from the fluid surrounding it (its external environment) and eliminates carbon dioxide into the same fluid. But how can

TABLE 1-1   ORGAN SYSTEMS OF THE BODY

System	Major organs or tissues	Primary functions
Circulatory	Heart, blood vessels, blood (Some classifications also include lymphatic vessels and lymph in this system.)	Transport of blood throughout the body's tissues
Respiratory	Nose, pharynx, larynx, trachea, bronchi, lungs	Exchange of carbon dioxide and oxygen; regulation of hydrogen-ion concentration
Digestive	Mouth, pharynx, esophagus, stomach, intestines, salivary glands, pancreas, liver, gallbladder	Digestion and absorption of organic nutrients, salts, and water
Urinary	Kidneys, ureters, bladder, urethra	Regulation of plasma composition through controlled excretion of salts, water, and organic wastes
Musculoskeletal	Cartilage, bone, ligaments, tendons, joints, skeletal muscle	Support, protection, and movement of the body; production of blood cells
Immune	White blood cells, lymph vessels and nodes, spleen, thymus, and other lymphoid tissues	Defense against foreign invaders; return of extracellular fluid to blood; formation of white blood cells
Nervous	Brain, spinal cord, peripheral nerves and ganglia, special sense organs	Regulation and coordination of many activities in the body; detection of changes in the internal and external environments; states of consciousness; learning; cognition
Endocrine	All glands secreting hormones: Pancreas, testes, ovaries, hypothalamus, kidneys, pituitary, thyroid, parathyroid, adrenal, intestinal, thymus, heart, and pineal	Regulation and coordination of many activities in the body
Reproductive	Male: Testes, penis, and associated ducts and glands Female: Ovaries, uterine tubes, uterus, vagina, mammary glands	Production of sperm; transfer of sperm to female Production of eggs; provision of a nutritive environment for the developing embryo and fetus; nutrition of the infant
Integumentary	Skin	Protection against injury and dehydration; defense against foreign invaders; regulation of temperature

the liver cell and all other internal parts of the body obtain oxygen and eliminate carbon dioxide when, unlike the amoeba, they are not in direct contact with the external environment—the air surrounding the body?

Figure 1-2 summarizes the exchanges of matter that occur in a person. Supplying oxygen is the function both of the respiratory system, which takes up oxygen from the external environment, and of the circulatory system, which distributes the oxygen to all parts of the body. In addition, the circulatory system carries the carbon dioxide generated by all the cells of the body to the lungs, which eliminate it to the exterior. Similarly, the digestive and circulatory systems working together make nutrients from the external environment available to all the body's cells. Wastes other than carbon dioxide are carried by the circulatory system from the cells that produced them to the kidneys and liver, which excrete them from the body. The kidneys also regulate the concentrations of water and

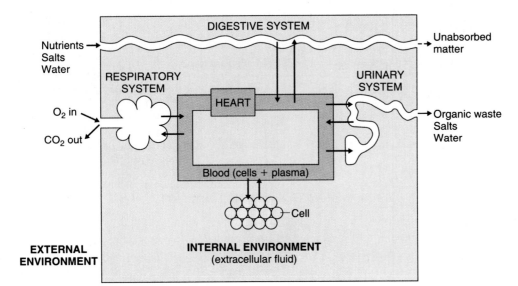

FIGURE 1-2
Exchanges of matter occur between the external environment and the circulatory system via the digestive, respiratory, and urinary systems. Extracellular fluid (plasma and interstitial fluid) is the internal environment of the body. The external environment is the air surrounding the body.

many essential minerals in the plasma. The nervous and hormonal systems coordinate and control the activities of all the other organ systems.

Thus the overall effect of the activities of organ systems is to create within the body an environment in which all cells can survive and function. This environment surrounding each cell is called the **internal environment**. The internal environment is not merely a theoretical physiological concept. It can be identified quite specifically in anatomical terms. The body's internal environment is the **extracellular fluid** (literally, "fluid outside the cells"), which bathes each cell (Figure 1-2).

In other words, the environment in which each cell lives is not the external environment surrounding the entire body but the local extracellular fluid surrounding that cell. It is from this fluid that the cells receive oxygen and nutrients and into which they excrete wastes. A multicellular organism can survive only as long as it is able to maintain the composition of its internal environment in a state compatible with the survival of its individual cells. In 1857, the French physiologist Claude Bernard clearly described the central importance of the extracellular fluid: "It is the fixity of the internal environment that is the condition of free and independent life. . . . All the vital mechanisms, however varied they may be, have only one object, that of preserving constant the conditions of life in the internal environment."

The concept that the composition of the internal environment is maintained relatively constant is known as **homeostasis**. Changes do occur, but the magnitudes of these changes are small and are kept within narrow limits. As emphasized by the twentieth-century American physiologist Walter B. Cannon, such stability can be achieved

only through the operation of carefully coordinated physiological processes. The activities of the cells, tissues, and organs must be regulated and integrated with each other in such a way that any change in the extracellular fluid initiates a reaction to minimize the change. A collection of body components that functions to maintain a physical or chemical property of the internal environment relatively constant is termed a **homeostatic control system**.

The description at the beginning of this chapter of how sweating is brought about in response to increased heat generation is an example of a homeostatic control system in operation. Here is another: When, for any reason, the concentration of oxygen in the blood significantly decreases below normal, the nervous system detects the change and increases its output to the skeletal muscles responsible for breathing movements. The result is a compensatory increase in oxygen uptake by the body and a restoration of normal internal oxygen concentration.

To summarize, the total activities of every individual cell in the body fall into two categories: (1) Each cell performs for itself all those fundamental basic cellular processes—movement of materials across its membrane, extraction of energy, protein synthesis, and so on—that represent the minimal requirements for maintaining its individual integrity and life; and (2) each cell simultaneously performs one or more specialized activities that, in concert with the activities performed by the other cells of its tissue or organ system, contribute to the survival of the organism by helping maintain the stable internal environment required by all cells.

One more point should be made concerning basic cell activities: Because of our emphasis on homeostasis, we have introduced the principle of biological control in the context of the total body. You must realize, however, that the fundamental processes performed by any single cell are also carefully regulated by purely intracellular mechanisms. These determine, for example, which proteins a cell is to synthesize, how large the cell is to grow, and when it is to divide. Thus, an understanding of cellular physiology requires knowledge not only of the basic processes but also of the intracellular mechanisms that control them.

BODY-FLUID COMPARTMENTS

To reiterate, the internal environment can be equated with the extracellular fluid. What was not stated earlier is that extracellular fluid exists in two locations—surrounding cells and inside blood vessels. Approximately 80 percent of the extracellular fluid surrounds all the body's cells except the blood cells. Because it lies between cells, this 80 percent of the extracellular fluid is known as **intercellular fluid** or, more often, **interstitial fluid**. The remaining 20 percent of the extracellular fluid is the fluid portion of the blood, the **plasma**, in which the various blood cells are suspended.

As the blood (plasma plus suspended blood cells) is continuously circulated by the action of the heart to all parts of the body, the plasma exchanges oxygen, nutrients, wastes, and other metabolic products with the interstitial fluid surrounding the smallest of the blood vessels. Be-

cause of the exchanges between plasma and interstitial fluid, concentrations of dissolved substances are virtually identical in the two fluids, except for protein concentration. With this major exception—higher protein concentration in plasma than in interstitial fluid—the entire extracellular fluid may be considered to have a homogeneous composition. In contrast, the composition of the extracellular fluid is very different from that of the **intracellular fluid**—the fluid inside the cells (the actual differences will be presented in Chapter 6, Table 6-1).

In essence, then, the fluids in the body are enclosed in "compartments." The volumes of the body-fluid compartments are summarized in Figure 1-3 in terms of water, since water is by far the major component of the fluids in each compartment. Water accounts for about 60 percent of normal body weight. Two-thirds of this water (28 L) is intracellular fluid. The remaining one-third (14 L) is extracellular, and as described above, 80 percent of this extracellular fluid is interstitial fluid (11 L) and 20 percent (3 L) is plasma.

Compartmentalization is an important general principle in physiology (we shall see in Chapter 2 that the inside of cells also is divided into compartments). Compartmentalization is achieved by barriers between the compartments, and the properties of the barriers determine the movements of substances between contiguous compartments. These movements in turn account for the differences in the compositions of the different compartments. In the case of the body-fluid compartments, the intracellu-

FIGURE 1-3

Fluid compartments of the body. Volumes are for a normal 70-kg man.

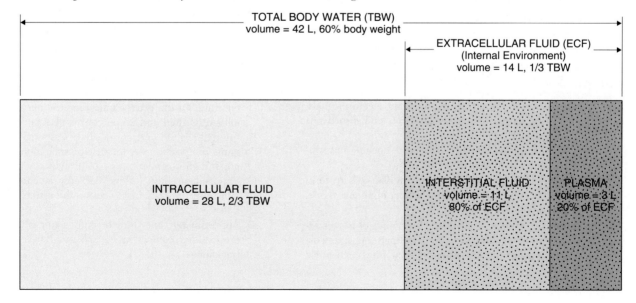

lar fluid is separated from the extracellular fluid by molecular membranes that surround the cells. The properties of these membranes and how they account for the profound differences between intracellular and extracellular fluid are described in Chapter 6. In contrast, the two components of extracellular fluid—the interstitial fluid and the blood plasma—are separated by the cellular wall of the smallest blood vessels, the capillaries. How this barrier normally keeps 80 percent of the extracellular fluid in the interstitial compartment and restricts proteins mainly to the plasma is described in Chapter 14.

This completes our introductory framework. With it in mind, the overall organization and approach of this book should easily be understood. Because the fundamental features of cell function are shared by virtually all cells and because these features constitute the foundation upon which specialization develops, we devote the first part of the book to an analysis of basic cell physiology.

At the other end of the organizational spectrum, the final part of the book describes how coordinated functions (circulation, respiration, and so on) result from the precisely controlled and integrated activities of specialized cells grouped together in tissues and organs. The theme of these descriptions is that each function, with the obvious exception of reproduction, serves to keep some important aspect of the body's internal environment relatively constant. Thus, homeostasis, achieved by homeostatic control systems, is the single most important unifying idea to be kept in mind in Part 3.

The middle part of the book provides the principles and information required to bridge the gap between these two organizational levels, the cell and the body. Chapter 7 describes the basic characteristics of homeostatic control systems and the required cellular communications. The other chapters of Part 2 deal with the specific components of the body's control systems: nerve cells, muscle cells, and gland cells. Once familiar with this cast of major characters and the theme—the maintenance of a stable internal environment—the reader will be free to follow the specific plot lines—circulation, respiration, and so on—of Part 3.

SUMMARY

MECHANISM AND CAUSALITY

I. The mechanist view of life, the view taken by physiologists, holds that all phenomena are describable in terms of physical and chemical laws.
II. Vitalism holds that some additional force is required to explain the function of living organisms.

A SOCIETY OF CELLS

I. Cells are the simplest structural units into which a complex multicellular organism can be divided and still retain the functions characteristic of life.
II. Cell differentiation results in the formation of four categories of specialized cells.
   A. Muscle cells generate the mechanical activities that produce force and movement.
   B. Nerve cells initiate and conduct electric signals.
   C. Epithelial cells selectively secrete and absorb ions and organic molecules.
   D. Connective-tissue cells connect, anchor, and support the structures of the body.
III. Specialized cells associate with similar cells to form tissues: muscle tissue, nerve tissue, epithelial tissue, and connective tissue.
IV. Organs are composed of the four kinds of tissues arranged in various proportions and patterns; many organs contain multiple small similar functional units.

V. An organ system is a collection of organs that together perform an overall function.

THE INTERNAL ENVIRONMENT AND HOMEOSTASIS

I. The extracellular fluid surrounding a cell is the cell's internal environment.
   A. The function of organ systems is to maintain the internal environment relatively constant—homeostasis. This is achieved by homeostatic control systems.
   B. Each cell performs the basic cellular processes required to maintain its own integrity, plus specialized activities that help achieve homeostasis.
II. The body fluids are enclosed in compartments.
   A. The extracellular fluid is composed of the blood plasma and the fluid between cells—the interstitial fluid. Of the extracellular fluid, 80 percent is interstitial fluid and 20 percent is plasma.
   B. Interstitial fluid and plasma have essentially the same composition except that plasma contains a much higher concentration of protein.
   C. Extracellular fluid differs markedly in composition from the fluid inside cells—the intracellular fluid.
   D. Approximately one-third of body water is in the extracellular compartment, and two-thirds is intracellular.

E. The compositions of the compartments reflect the activities of the barriers separating them.

extracellular fluid
homeostasis
homeostatic control system
intercellular fluid

interstitial fluid
plasma
intracellular fluid

KEY TERMS

human physiology
mechanist view
vitalism
teleology
cells
cell differentiation
tissues
organs
organ systems
muscle cells
nerve cells
epithelial cells
basement membrane

connective-tissue cells
fibers
ground substance
collagen fibers
elastin fibers
reticular fibers
muscle tissue
nerve tissue
epithelial tissue
connective tissue
functional units
external environment
internal environment

REVIEW QUESTIONS

1. Describe the levels of cellular differentiation and state the four types of specialized cells and tissues.

2. List the 10 organ systems of the body and give one-sentence descriptions of their functions.

3. Contrast the two categories of functions performed by every cell.

4. Name two fluids that constitute the extracellular fluid. What are their relative proportions, and in what way do they differ from each other in composition?

5. State the relative volumes of water in the body-fluid compartments.

PART

ONE

BASIC
CELL
FUNCTIONS

CHAPTER

2

CHEMICAL COMPOSITION OF THE BODY

Atoms and molecules are the chemical units of cell structure and function. In this chapter we describe the distinguishing characteristics of the major chemicals in the human body. The specific roles of these substances will be discussed in subsequent chapters. This chapter is, in essence, an expanded glossary of chemical terms and structures, and like a glossary, it should be consulted according to need.

ATOMS

The units of matter that form all chemical substances are called **atoms**. The smallest atom, hydrogen, is approximately 2.7 billionths of an inch in diameter. Each type of atom—carbon, hydrogen, oxygen, and so on—is called a **chemical element**. A one- or two-letter symbol is used as a shorthand identification of each chemical element. Although more than 100 chemical elements exist in the universe, only 24 (Table 2-1) are known to be essential for the structure and function of the human body.

The chemical properties of atoms can be described in terms of three subatomic particles—**protons, neutrons,** and **electrons** (Table 2-2). The protons and neutrons are confined to a very small volume at the center of an atom, the **atomic nucleus**, whereas the electrons revolve in orbits at various distances from the nucleus. This miniature-solar-system model of an atom is an oversimplification, but it is sufficient to provide a conceptual framework for understanding the chemical and physical interactions of atoms.

Each of these subatomic particles has a different electric charge: Protons have one unit of positive charge, electrons have one unit of negative charge, and neutrons are electrically neutral, having no electric charge. Since the protons are located in the atomic nucleus, the nucleus has a net positive charge equal to the number of protons it contains. The entire atom has no net electric charge however, because the number of negatively charged electrons orbiting the nucleus is equal to the number of positively charged protons in the nucleus.[1]

Protons and neutrons are approximately equal in mass and are about 1800 times heavier than an electron (Table 2-2). Thus, almost all the mass of an atom is located in its nucleus.

Atomic Number

Every atom of each chemical element contains a specific number of protons, and it is this number of protons that distinguishes one type of atom from another. This number is known as the **atomic number**. For example, hydrogen, the simplest atom, has an atomic number of 1, corresponding to its single proton, and calcium has an atomic number of 20, corresponding to its 20 protons. Since an atom is

TABLE 2-1 ESSENTIAL ELEMENTS IN THE BODY

Element	Symbol
Major elements: 99.3% of total atoms	
Hydrogen	H (63%)
Oxygen	O (26%)
Carbon	C (9%)
Nitrogen	N (1%)
Mineral elements: 0.7% of total atoms	
Calcium	Ca
Phosphorus	P
Potassium	K (Latin *kalium*)
Sulfur	S
Sodium	Na (Latin *natrium*)
Chlorine	Cl
Magnesium	Mg
Trace elements: less than 0.01% of total atoms	
Iron	Fe (Latin *ferrum*)
Iodine	I
Copper	Cu (Latin *cuprum*)
Zinc	Zn
Manganese	Mn
Cobalt	Co
Chromium	Cr
Selenium	Se
Molybdenum	Mo
Fluorine	F
Tin	Sn (Latin *stannum*)
Silicon	Si
Vanadium	V

---

[1]Although the number of neutrons in the nucleus of an atom is often equal to the number of protons, many chemical elements can exist in multiple forms—isotopes—distinguished by the number of neutrons they contain.

TABLE 2-2 CHARACTERISTICS OF MAJOR SUBATOMIC PARTICLES

Particle	Mass relative to electron mass	Electric charge	Location in atom
Electron	1	−1	Orbiting the nucleus
Proton	1836	+1	Nucleus
Neutron	1839	0	Nucleus

electrically neutral, the atomic number is also equal to the number of electrons in the atom.

Atomic Weight

Atoms have very little mass. A single hydrogen atom, for example, has a mass of only 1.67×10^{-24} g. The **atomic weight** scale is a scale that indicates an atom's mass relative to the mass of other atoms. This scale is based upon assigning the carbon atom a value of 12. On this scale a hydrogen atom has an atomic weight of approximately 1, indicating that it has one-twelfth the mass of a carbon atom; a magnesium atom, with an atomic weight of 24, has twice the mass of a carbon atom.[2] Since almost all the mass of an atom is due to its neutrons and protons, and since hydrogen, with a single proton, has an atomic weight of 1, the atomic weight of an atom is approximately equal to the sum of the number of protons and neutrons it contains. Its atomic weight is not exactly equal to this sum because electrons do have some mass and because protons and neutrons do not have exactly equal masses.

One **gram atomic mass** of a chemical element is the amount of the element in grams that is equal to the numerical value of its atomic weight. Thus, 12 g of carbon is 1 gram atomic mass of carbon, and 1 g of hydrogen is 1 gram atomic mass of hydrogen. *One gram atomic mass of any element contains the same number of atoms.* For example, 1 g of hydrogen contains 6×10^{23} atoms, and 12 g of carbon, whose atoms have 12 times the mass of a hydrogen atom, also has 6×10^{23} atoms.

Atomic Composition of the Body

Just four of the body's essential elements (Table 2-1)—hydrogen, oxygen, carbon, and nitrogen—account for over 99 percent of the atoms in the body.

---

[2]Since the atomic weight scale is a *ratio* of atomic masses, it has no units. The unit of atomic mass is known as a dalton [1 dalton (d) is equal to one-twelfth the mass of a single carbon atom]. Thus, carbon has an atomic weight of 12, and a single carbon atom has an atomic mass of 12 daltons.

The 7 essential mineral elements are the most abundant substances dissolved in the extracellular and intracellular fluids. Most of the body's calcium and phosphorus atoms, however, make up the solid matrix of bone tissue.

The 13 essential **trace elements** are present in extremely small quantities, but they are nonetheless essential for normal growth and function. For example, iron plays a critical role in the transport of oxygen by the blood. Additional trace elements will likely be added to this list as the chemistry of the body becomes better understood.

Many other elements, in addition to the 24 listed in Table 2-1, can be detected in the body. These elements enter through the foods we eat and the air we breathe but do not have any known essential chemical function. Some elements, for example, mercury, are not required for normal function and can be toxic.

MOLECULES

Two or more atoms bonded together make up a **molecule**. For example, a molecule of water contains two hydrogen atoms and one oxygen atom, which can be represented by H_2O. The atomic composition of glucose, a sugar, is $C_6H_{12}O_6$, indicating that the molecule contains 6 carbon atoms, 12 hydrogen atoms, and 6 oxygen atoms. Such formulas, however, do not indicate which atoms are linked to which in the molecule.

Covalent Chemical Bonds

The atoms in molecules are held together by chemical bonds, which are formed when electrons are transferred from one atom to another or are shared between two atoms. The strongest chemical bond between two atoms, a **covalent bond**, is formed when one electron in the outer electron orbit of each atom is shared between the two atoms. The atoms in most molecules found in the body are linked by covalent bonds.

The atoms of some elements can form more than one covalent bond and thus become linked simultaneously to two or more other atoms (Figure 2-1). Each type of atom has a characteristic number of covalent bonds it can form, which depends on the number of electrons present in its outermost electron orbit. The number of chemical bonds formed by the four most abundant atoms in the body are hydrogen, 1; oxygen, 2; nitrogen, 3; and carbon, 4. When the structure of a molecule is diagramed, each covalent bond is represented by a line indicating a pair of shared electrons. The covalent bonds of the four elements mentioned above can be represented as

$$ \text{H}- \qquad -\text{O}- \qquad -\overset{|}{\text{N}}- \qquad -\overset{|}{\underset{|}{\text{C}}}- $$

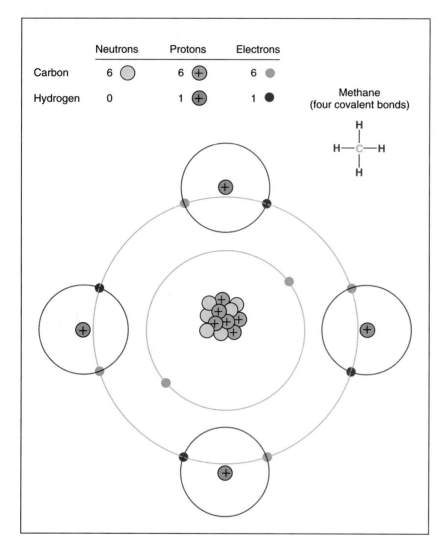

	Neutrons	Protons	Electrons
Carbon	6	6 ⊕	6
Hydrogen	0	1 ⊕	1

Methane
(four covalent bonds)

$$H-\underset{\underset{H}{|}}{\overset{\overset{H}{|}}{C}}-H$$

FIGURE 2-1
Each of the four hydrogen atoms in a molecule of methane, CH_4, forms a covalent bond with an atom of carbon by sharing its one electron with one of the electrons in the carbon atom. Each shared pair of electrons forms a covalent bond.

A molecule of water can be illustrated as

$$H-O-H$$

In some cases, two covalent bonds—a double bond—are formed between two atoms when two electrons from each atom are shared; an example of this is carbon dioxide (CO_2):

$$O=C=O$$

Note that in this molecule the carbon atom still forms four covalent bonds, and each oxygen atom only two.

Molecular Shape

When atoms are linked together, molecules with various shapes can be formed. Although we draw diagrammatic structures of molecules on flat sheets of paper, these molecules actually have a three-dimensional shape. When more than one covalent bond is formed with a given atom, the bonds are distributed about the atom in a pattern that may or may not be symmetrical (Figure 2-2).

Molecules are not rigid, inflexible structures. Within certain limits, the shape of a molecule can be changed without breaking the covalent bonds linking its atoms together. A covalent bond is like an axle around which the joined atoms can rotate. As illustrated in Figure 2-3, a sequence of six carbon atoms can assume a number of shapes as a result of rotations around various covalent bonds. As we shall see, the three-dimensional shape of molecules is one of the major factors governing molecular interactions.

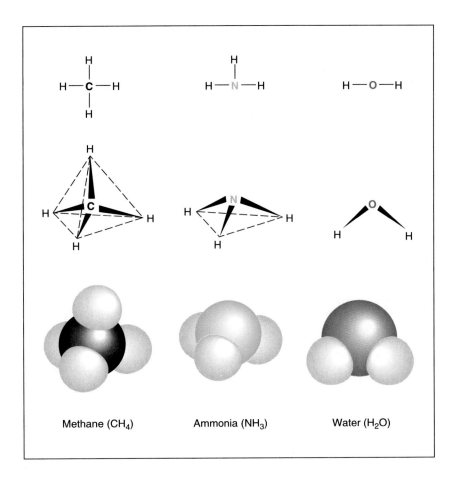

FIGURE 2-2

Geometrical configuration of covalent bonds around the carbon, nitrogen, and oxygen atoms bonded to hydrogen atoms.

Methane (CH_4)   Ammonia (NH_3)   Water (H_2O)

IONS

An atom is electrically neutral since it contains equal numbers of negative electrons and positive protons. If, however, an atom gains or loses one or more electrons, it acquires a net electric charge and becomes an **ion**. For example, when a sodium atom, which has 11 electrons, loses 1 electron, it becomes a sodium ion (Na^+) with a net positive charge; that is, it now has only 10 electrons but 11 protons. On the other hand, a chlorine atom, which has 17 electrons, can gain an electron and become a chloride ion (Cl^-) with a net negative charge—it now has 18 electrons but only 17 protons. Some atoms can gain or lose more than 1 electron to become ions with two or even three units of net electric charge, for example, calcium, Ca^{2+}.

Because of their ability to conduct electricity when dissolved in water, ions are collectively referred to as **electrolytes**. Hydrogen atoms and most mineral and trace element atoms readily form ions. The number of electrons an atom may gain or lose in becoming an ion is a specific characteristic of each type of atom. Table 2-3 lists the ionic forms of some of these elements. Ions that have a net

positive charge are called **cations**; negatively charged ions are called **anions**.

The process of ion formation, known as ionization, can occur in single atoms or in atoms that are covalently linked in molecules. Within molecules two commonly encountered groups of atoms that undergo ionization are the **carboxyl group** (—COOH) and the **amino group** (—NH₂). The formulas for molecules containing such groups are written as R—COOH or R—NH₂, where R signifies the remaining portion of the molecule. The carboxyl group ionizes when the oxygen atom linked to the hydrogen atom captures the hydrogen atom's only electron to form a carboxyl ion (R—COO⁻) and releases a hydrogen ion (H^+):

$$R\text{—COOH} \rightleftharpoons R\text{—COO}^- + H^+$$

The amino group can bind a hydrogen ion to form an ionized amino group (R—NH₃⁺):

$$R\text{—NH}_2 + H^+ \rightleftharpoons R\text{—NH}_3^+$$

The ionization of each of the above groups can be re-

TABLE 2-3   MOST FREQUENTLY ENCOUNTERED IONIC FORMS OF ELEMENTS

Atom	Chemical symbol	Ion	Chemical symbol	Electrons gained or lost
Hydrogen	H	Hydrogen ion	H^+	1 lost
Sodium	Na	Sodium ion	Na^+	1 lost
Potassium	K	Potassium ion	K^+	1 lost
Chlorine	Cl	Chloride ion	Cl^-	1 gained
Magnesium	Mg	Magnesium ion	Mg^{2+}	2 lost
Calcium	Ca	Calcium ion	Ca^{2+}	2 lost

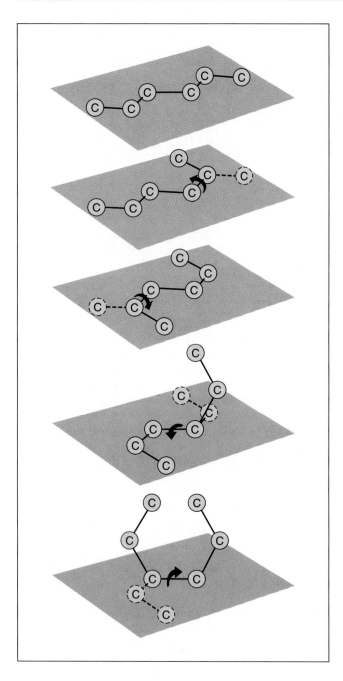

versed, as indicated by the double arrows; the ionized carboxyl group can combine with a hydrogen ion to form an un-ionized carboxyl group, and the ionized amino group can loose a hydrogen ion and become an un-ionized amino group.

POLAR MOLECULES

As we have seen, when the electrons of two atoms interact, the two atoms may share the electrons equally, forming an electrically neutral covalent bond, or one of the atoms may completely capture an electron from the other atom, forming an ion. Between these two extremes there exist covalent bonds in which the electrons are not shared equally between the two atoms but instead reside closer to one atom of the pair. This atom thus acquires a slight negative charge, while the other atom, having partly lost an electron, becomes slightly positive. Such bonds are known as **polar covalent bonds** (or, simply, polar bonds) since the atoms at each end of the bond have an opposite electric charge. Polar bonds do not have a *net* electric charge, as do ions, since they contain equal amounts of negative and positive charge. For example, the bond between hydrogen and oxygen in a **hydroxyl group** (—OH) is a polar covalent bond in which the oxygen is slightly negative and the hydrogen slightly positive.

$$\overset{(-)}{R-O}\overset{(+)}{-H}$$

The electric charge associated with the ends of a polar bond is considerably less than the charge of a fully ionized

FIGURE 2-3
Changes in molecular shape occur as portions of a molecule rotate around different carbon-carbon bonds, transforming the molecule's shape from a relatively straight chain into a ring.

TABLE 2-4   EXAMPLES OF NONPOLAR AND POLAR BONDS, AND IONIZED CHEMICAL GROUPS

Nonpolar bonds	$-\overset{\displaystyle |}{\underset{\displaystyle |}{C}}-H$	Carbon-hydrogen bond
	$-\overset{\displaystyle |}{\underset{\displaystyle |}{C}}-\overset{\displaystyle |}{\underset{\displaystyle |}{C}}-$	Carbon-carbon bond
Polar bonds	$\overset{(-)\quad(+)}{R-O\!-\!\!-\!H}$	Hydroxyl group (R—OH)
	$\overset{(-)\quad(+)}{R-S\!-\!\!-\!H}$	Sulfhydryl group (R—SH)
	$R-\overset{\displaystyle H\;(+)}{\underset{(-)}{N}}-R$	Nitrogen-hydrogen bond
Ionized groups	$R-\overset{\displaystyle O}{\overset{\displaystyle \|}{C}}-O^{\ominus}$	Carboxyl group ($R-COO^-$)
	$R-\overset{\displaystyle H}{\underset{\displaystyle H}{\overset{\displaystyle \|}{\underset{\displaystyle \|}{N}}}}\!\!\!\overset{\oplus}{}-H$	Amino group ($R-NH_3^+$)
	$R-O-\overset{\displaystyle O}{\underset{\displaystyle O}{\overset{\displaystyle \|}{\underset{\displaystyle \|}{P}}}}\!\!\!-O^{\ominus}\;\;{}_{\ominus}$	Phosphate group ($R-PO_4^{2-}$)

atom (for example, the oxygen in the polarized hydroxyl group has only about 13 percent of the negative charge associated with the oxygen in an ionized carboxyl group, $R-COO^-$).

Atoms of oxygen and nitrogen, which have a relatively strong attraction for electrons, form polar bonds with hydrogen atoms; in contrast, the bond between carbon and hydrogen atoms and that between two carbon atoms are electrically neutral (Table 2-4).

A single molecule may contain nonpolar, polarized, and ionized bonds in different regions of the molecule. Molecules containing significant numbers of polar bonds or ionized groups are known as **polar molecules**, whereas molecules composed predominantly of electrically neutral bonds are known as **nonpolar molecules**. As we shall see, the physical characteristics of these two classes of molecules, especially their solubility in water, are quite different.

Hydrogen Bonds

The electrical attraction between a hydrogen atom in one polarized bond and an oxygen or nitrogen atom in a polar-

ized bond of another molecule—or within the same molecule if the bonds are sufficiently separated from each other—forms a **hydrogen bond**. This type of bond is very weak, having only about 4 percent of the strength of the covalent bonds linking the hydrogen and oxygen within a water molecule (H_2O). These weak hydrogen bonds are represented in diagrams by dashed or dotted lines to distinguish them from stronger covalent bonds (Figure 2-4). Hydrogen bonds between and within molecules play an important role in molecular interactions and in determining the shape of large molecules.

Water

Hydrogen is the most numerous atom in the body, and water is the most numerous molecule. Out of every 100 molecules, 99 are water. The covalent bonds linking the two hydrogen atoms to the oxygen atom in a water molecule are polar. Therefore, the oxygen in water has a slight negative charge, and each hydrogen atom has a slight positive charge. The positively polarized regions near the hydrogen atoms of one water molecule are electrically attracted to the negatively polarized regions of the oxygen

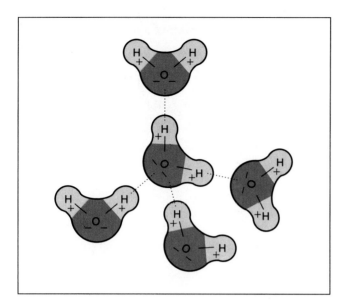

FIGURE 2-4

Five water molecules. Note that polarized covalent bonds link the hydrogen and oxygen atoms within each water molecule and that hydrogen bonds occur between adjacent water molecules. Hydrogen bonds are represented in diagrams by dashed or dotted lines, and covalent bonds by solid lines.

atoms in adjacent water molecules to form hydrogen bonds (Figure 2-4).

At body temperature, the hydrogen bonds between water molecules are continuously being formed and broken, accounting for the liquid state of water. If the temperature is lowered, hydrogen bonds are broken less frequently, and larger and larger clusters of water molecules are formed until at 0°C water freezes into a continuous crystalline matrix—ice.

Water molecules take part in many chemical reactions of the general type

$$R_1—R_2 \ + \ H—O—H \longrightarrow R_1—OH \ + \ H—R_2$$

In this reaction the covalent bond between R_1 and R_2 and the bond between a hydrogen atom and oxygen in water are broken and the hydroxyl group and hydrogen atom are transferred to R_1 and R_2, respectively. Reactions of this type are known as hydrolytic reactions or simply **hydrolysis**. Many large molecules in the body are broken down into smaller molecular units by hydrolysis.

SOLUTIONS

Substances dissolved in a liquid are known as **solutes**; the liquid in which they dissolve is the **solvent**. Solutes dissolve in a solvent to form a **solution**. Water is the most abundant solvent in the body, accounting for 60 percent of total body weight. A majority of the chemical reactions that occur in the body involve molecules that are dissolved in water—in either intracellular or extracellular fluid. But, not all molecules dissolve in water.

Molecular Solubility

In order to dissolve in water, a substance must be electrically attracted to water molecules. For example, table salt (NaCl) is a solid crystalline substance because of the strong electrical attraction between positive sodium ions and negative chloride ions. This strong attraction between two oppositely charged ions is known as an **ionic bond**. When a crystal of sodium chloride is placed in water, the polar water molecules are attracted to the charged sodium and chloride ions (Figure 2-5); the ions become surrounded by clusters of water molecules, allowing the sodium and chloride ions to separate from the salt crystal and enter the water, that is, to dissolve.

Molecules having a sufficient number of polar bonds and/or ionized groups will dissolve in water. Such molecules are said to be **hydrophilic**—water-loving. Thus, the presence in a molecule of ionized groups, such as carboxyl and amino groups, or of polar groups, such as hydroxyl groups, promotes solubility in water. In contrast, molecules composed predominantly of carbon and hydrogen are insoluble in water since their electrically neutral covalent bonds are not attracted to water molecules. These molecules are **hydrophobic**—water-fearing.

When nonpolar molecules are mixed with water, two phases are formed, as occurs when oil is mixed with water. The strong attraction between polar water molecules "squeezes" the nonpolar molecules out of the water phase. Such a separation is never 100 percent complete, however, and very small amounts of nonpolar solutes remain dissolved in the water phase. Although nonpolar molecules do not dissolve to any great extent in water, they do dissolve in nonpolar solvents, such as carbon tetrachloride.

Molecules that have a polar or ionized region at one end and a nonpolar region at the opposite end are called **amphipathic**—consisting of two parts. When mixed with water, amphipathic molecules form clusters, with their polar (hydrophilic) regions located at the surface of the cluster where they are attracted to the surrounding water molecules. The nonpolar (hydrophobic) ends are oriented toward the interior of the cluster (Figure 2-6). Such an arrangement provides the maximal interaction between water molecules and the polar ends of the amphipathic molecules. Nonpolar molecules can dissolve in the central nonpolar regions of these clusters and thus exist in aqueous solutions in far higher amounts than would otherwise be possible based on their low solubility in water. As we shall see, the orientation of amphipathic molecules plays an important role in the structure of cell membranes and in both the absorption of nonpolar molecules from the gastrointestinal tract and their transport in the blood.

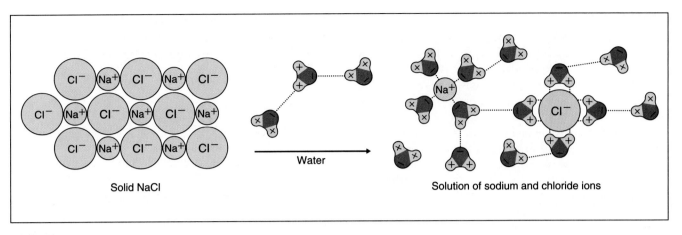

FIGURE 2-5

The ability of water to dissolve sodium chloride crystals depends upon the electrical attraction between the polar water molecules and the charged sodium and chloride ions.

FIGURE 2-6

In water, amphipathic molecules aggregate into spherical clusters. Their polar regions form hydrogen bonds with water molecules at the surface of the cluster.

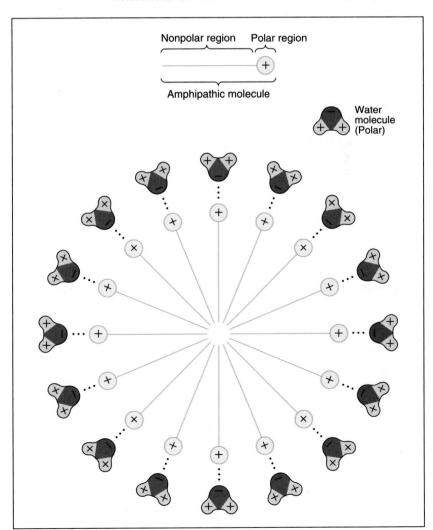

Concentration

Solute **concentration** is defined as the amount of the solute present in a unit volume of solution. The unit of volume in the metric system is a liter (L). (One liter equals 1.06 quarts. See Appendix C for English and metric units.) Smaller units are the milliliter (ml, or 0.001 liter) and the microliter (μl, or 0.001 ml). One measure of the amount of a substance is its mass given in grams. Its concentration in a solution can then be expressed as the number of grams of the substance present in one liter of solution (g/L).

A comparison of the concentrations of two different substances on the basis of the number of *grams* per liter of solution does not directly indicate how many *molecules* of each substance are present. For example, 10 g of compound X, whose molecules are heavier than those of compound Y, will contain fewer molecules than 10 g of compound Y. Concentrations in units of grams per liter are most often used when the chemical structure of the solute is unknown. When the structure of a molecule is known, concentrations are usually expressed as moles per liter, which provides a unit of concentration based upon the number of solute molecules in solution, as described next.

The **molecular weight** of a molecule is equal to the sum of the atomic weights of all the atoms in the molecule. For example, glucose ($C_6H_{12}O_6$) has a molecular weight of 180 ($6 \times 12 + 12 \times 1 + 6 \times 16 = 180$). One **mole** (mol) of a compound is the amount of the compound in grams equal to its molecular weight. A solution containing 180 g of glucose (1 mol) in 1 L of solution is said to be a 1 molar (abbreviated 1 M or 1 mol/L) solution of glucose. If 90 g of glucose is dissolved in enough water to produce 1 L of solution, the solution will have a concentration of 0.5 mol per liter (0.5 M). Just as 1 gram atomic mass of any element contains the same number of atoms, 1 mol (1 gram molecular mass) of any molecule has the same number of molecules—6×10^{23}. Thus, a 1 M solution of glucose contains the same number of solute molecules per liter as a 1 M solution of urea or any other substance.

The concentrations of solutes dissolved in the body fluids are much less than 1 M; many have concentrations in the range of millimoles per liter (1 mM = 0.001 M), while others are present at even smaller concentrations—micromoles per liter (1 μM = 0.000001 M) or nanomoles per liter (1 nM = 0.000000001 M).

Hydrogen Ions and Acidity

As mentioned earlier, a hydrogen atom consists of a single proton orbited by a single electron. A hydrogen ion (H^+), formed by the loss of the electron, is thus a single free proton. Hydrogen ions are formed when the proton of a hydrogen atom in a molecule is released, leaving behind its electron. Molecules that release hydrogen ions (protons) in solution are called **acids**, for example:

$$HCl \longrightarrow H^+ + Cl^-$$
Hydrochloric acid   Chloride

$$H_2CO_3 \rightleftharpoons H^+ + HCO_3^-$$
Carbonic acid   Bicarbonate

Lactic acid   Lactate

Conversely, any substance that can accept a hydrogen ion is termed a **base**. In the reactions above, bicarbonate and lactate are bases since they can combine with hydrogen ions (note the double arrows in the two reactions above). Bases will remove hydrogen ions from solution, lowering the hydrogen-ion concentration. It must be understood that the hydrogen-ion concentration of a solution refers only to the hydrogen ions that are free in solution and not to those that may be bound, for example, to amino groups ($R-NH_3^+$).

When hydrochloric acid is dissolved in water, 100 percent of its atoms separate to form hydrogen and chloride ions and do not recombine in solution (note the one-way arrow above). In the case of lactic acid, however, only a fraction of lactic acid molecules in solution release hydrogen ions at any instant. Therefore, if a 1 M solution of hydrochloric acid is compared with a 1 M solution of lactic acid, the hydrogen-ion concentration will be lower in the lactic acid solution than in the hydrochloric acid solution. Hydrochloric acid and other acids that are 100 percent ionized in solution are known as **strong acids**, whereas carbonic and lactic acids and other acids that do not completely ionize in solution are **weak acids**. The same principles apply to bases: Strong bases are 100 percent ionized in solution, whereas weak bases are only partially ionized.

The **acidity** of a solution refers to the *free* (unbound) hydrogen-ion concentration in the solution; the higher the hydrogen-ion concentration, the greater the acidity. The hydrogen-ion concentration is frequently expressed in terms of the **pH** of a solution, which is defined as the negative logarithm to the base 10 of the hydrogen-ion concentration (the brackets around the symbol for the hydrogen ion in the formula below indicate concentration):

$$pH = -\log [H^+]$$

Thus, a solution with a hydrogen-ion concentration of 10^{-7} M has a pH of 7, whereas a more acidic solution with a concentration of 10^{-6} M has a pH of 6. Note that as the acidity *increases,* the pH *decreases;* thus a change in pH from 7 to 6 represents a tenfold increase in the hydrogen-ion concentration.

Pure water has a hydrogen-ion concentration of $10^{-7}\,M$ (pH = 7.0) and is termed a **neutral solution**. **Alkaline solutions** have a lower hydrogen-ion concentration (a pH higher than 7.0), while those with a higher hydrogen-ion concentration (a pH lower than 7.0) are **acidic solutions**. The extracellular fluid of the body has a hydrogen-ion concentration of about $4 \times 10^{-8}\,M$ (pH = 7.4), with a normal range of about pH 7.35 to 7.45, and is thus slightly alkaline. Intracellular fluids have a slightly higher hydrogen-ion concentration than extracellular fluids.

As we saw earlier, the ionization of carboxyl and amino groups in various molecules in the body involves the release and uptake, respectively, of hydrogen ions. These groups behave as weak acids and bases. Increasing the free hydrogen-ion concentration decreases the number of ionized carboxyl groups since it increases the probability that an ionized carboxyl group will bump into a hydrogen ion and combine with it:

$$R\!-\!COOH \rightleftharpoons R\!-\!COO^- + H^+$$

Lowering the hydrogen-ion concentration has the opposite effect.

Changes in the acidity of solutions containing molecules with carboxyl and amino groups alters the net electric charge on these molecules by shifting the ionization reaction to the right or left, as illustrated for the carboxyl group above. If the electric charge on a molecule is altered, its interaction with other molecules or with other regions within the same molecule is altered, and thus its functional characteristics are altered. In the extracellular fluid, hydrogen-ion concentrations beyond the tenfold pH range of 7.8 to 6.8 are incompatible with life if maintained for more than a brief period of time. Even small changes in the hydrogen-ion concentration can produce large changes in the activities of cells, as we shall see.

CLASSES OF ORGANIC MOLECULES

Because most naturally occurring carbon-containing molecules are found in living organisms, the study of these compounds became known as organic chemistry. (Inorganic chemistry is the study of non-carbon-containing molecules.) However, the chemistry of living organisms, biochemistry, now forms only a portion of the broad field of organic chemistry.

One of the properties of the carbon atom that makes life possible is its ability to form four covalent bonds with other atoms, in particular with other carbon atoms. Since carbon atoms can also combine with hydrogen, oxygen,

TABLE 2-5   MAJOR CATEGORIES OF ORGANIC MOLECULES IN THE BODY

Category	Percent of body weight	Majority of atoms	Subclass	Subunits
Carbohydrates	1	C, H, O	Monosaccharides (sugars)	
			Polysaccharides	Monosaccharides
Lipids	15	C, H	Triacylglycerols	3 fatty acids + glycerol
			Phospholipids	2 fatty acids + glycerol + phosphate + small charged nitrogen molecule
			Steroids	
Proteins	17	C, H, O, N	Peptides	Amino acids
			Proteins	Amino acids
Nucleic acids	2	C, H, O, N	DNA	Nucleotides containing the bases adenine, cytosine, guanine, thymine, the sugar deoxyribose, and phosphate
			RNA	Nucleotides containing the bases adenine, cytosine, guanine, uracil, the sugar ribose, and phosphate

nitrogen, and sulfur atoms, a vast number of compounds can be formed with relatively few chemical elements. Some of these molecules are extremely large (**macromolecules**), being composed of thousands of atoms. Such large molecules are formed by linking together hundreds of smaller molecules (subunits) and are thus known as **polymers** (many small parts). The structure of macromolecules depends upon the structure of the subunits, the number of subunits linked together, and the position along the chain of each type of subunit.

Most of the organic molecules in the body can be classified into one of four groups: carbohydrates, lipids, proteins, and nucleic acids (Table 2-5).

Carbohydrates

Although carbohydrates account for only about 1 percent of the body weight, they play a central role in the chemical reactions that provide cells with energy. Carbohydrates are composed of carbon, hydrogen, and oxygen atoms in the proportions represented by the general formula $C_n(H_2O)_n$, where n is any whole number. It is from this formula that this class of molecules gets its name, **carbohydrate**—water-containing (hydrated) carbon atoms. Linked to most of the carbon atoms in a carbohydrate are a hydrogen atom and a hydroxyl group:

$$H-\overset{|}{\underset{|}{C}}-OH$$

Chemical groups containing nitrogen and phosphorus atoms may also be linked to this basic carbohydrate structure. The presence of numerous polar hydroxyl groups makes carbohydrates readily soluble in water.

Most carbohydrates taste sweet, and it is among the carbohydrates that we find the substances known as sugars. The simplest sugars are the **monosaccharides** (single-sweet), the most abundant of which is **glucose**, a six-carbon molecule ($C_6H_{12}O_6$) often called "blood sugar" because it is the major monosaccharide found in the blood.

There are two ways of representing the linkage between the atoms of a monosaccharide, as illustrated in Figure 2-7. The first is the conventional way of drawing the structure of organic molecules, but the second gives a better representation of the three-dimensional shape of monosaccharides. Five carbon atoms and an oxygen atom form a ring that lies in an essentially flat plane; the hydrogen and hydroxyl groups on each carbon lie above and below the plane of this ring. If one of the hydroxyl groups below the ring is shifted to a position above the ring, as shown in Figure 2-8, a different monosaccharide is produced.

FIGURE 2-7

Two ways of diagramming the structure of the monosaccharide glucose.

Most monosaccharides in the body contain five or six carbon atoms and are called **pentoses** and **hexoses**, respectively. Larger carbohydrate molecules can be formed by linking a number of monosaccharides together. Carbohydrate molecules composed of two monosaccharides are known as **disaccharides**. **Sucrose** (table sugar) (Figure 2-9) is composed of two monosaccharides, glucose and fructose. The linking together of most monosaccharides involves the removal of a hydroxyl group from one monosaccharide and of a hydrogen atom from the other, giving rise to a molecule of water and linking the two sugars together through an oxygen atom. Conversely, hydrolysis of the disaccharide breaks this linkage by adding back the water and thus uncoupling the two monosaccharides. Additional disaccharides frequently encountered are maltose

FIGURE 2-8

The difference between the monosaccharides glucose and galactose has to do with whether the hydroxyl group at the position indicated lies above or below the plane of the ring.

FIGURE 2-9
Sucrose (table sugar) is a disaccharide formed by the linking together of two monosaccharides, glucose and fructose.

(glucose-glucose), formed during the digestion of large carbohydrate molecules in the intestinal tract, and lactose (glucose-galactose), present in milk.

When many monosaccharides are linked together to form large polymers, the molecules are known as **polysaccharides**. Starch, found in plant cells, and **glycogen** (Figure 2-10), present in animal cells and often called "animal starch," are examples of polysaccharides. Both of these polysaccharides are composed of thousands of glucose molecules linked together in long chains. They differ only in the degree of branching along the chain. Hydrolysis of these polysaccharides leads to release of the glucose subunits.

Lipids

Lipids are molecules composed predominantly of hydrogen and carbon atoms. Since these atoms are linked by neutral covalent bonds, lipids are nonpolar molecules and thus insoluble in water. It is this physical property of insolubility in water that characterizes this class of organic molecules. The lipids, which account for about 40 percent of the organic matter in the average body (15 percent of the body weight), can be divided into four subclasses: fatty acids, triacylglycerols, phospholipids, and steroids.

Fatty Acids. A **fatty acid** consists of a chain of carbon atoms with a carboxyl group at one end. Because fatty acids are synthesized in the body by the linking together of 2-carbon fragments, most fatty acids have an even number of carbon atoms, 16- and 18-carbon fatty acids being the most common. When all the carbons in a fatty acid chain are linked by single covalent bonds, the fatty acid is said to be a **saturated fatty acid**. Some fatty acids contain one or more double bonds, and these are known as **unsaturated fatty acids**. If one double bond is present, the fatty acid is said to be **monounsaturated**, and if more than one double bond, **polyunsaturated** (Figure 2-11). As we shall see, fatty acids can be found as subunits of triacylglycerols or phospholipids.

Some fatty acids can be altered to produce a special class of molecules that regulate a number of cell functions. As described in more detail in Chapter 7, these modified fatty acids—collectively termed **eicosanoids**—are derived from the 20-carbon, polyunsaturated fatty acid **arachidonic acid**.

Triacylglycerols. The **triacylglycerols** (also known as triglycerides) constitute the majority of the lipids in the body, and it is these molecules that are generally referred to simply as "fat." Triacylglycerols are formed by the linking together of **glycerol**, a three-carbon carbohydrate, with three fatty acids (Figure 2-11). Each of the three hydroxyl groups in glycerol is linked to the carboxyl group of a fatty acid by the removal of a molecule of water to form a triacylglycerol molecule. Animal fats generally contain a high proportion of saturated fatty acids, whereas vegetable fats contain more unsaturated fatty acids.

The three fatty acids in a molecule of triacylglycerol need not be identical; therefore, a variety of fats can be formed with fatty acids of different chain lengths and de-

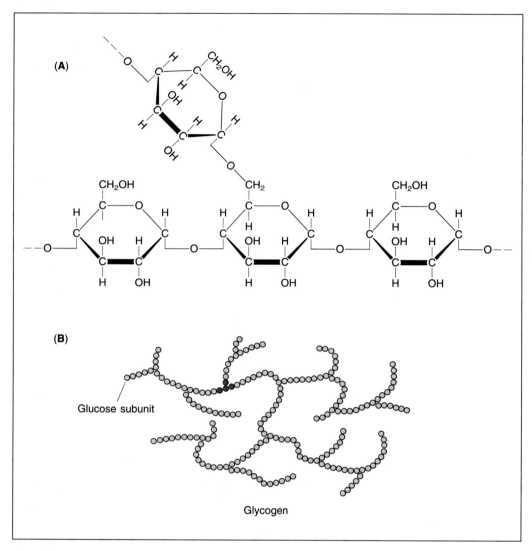

FIGURE 2-10
Many molecules of glucose linked end to end and at branch points form the branched-chain poly-saccharide glycogen (A), shown in diagrammatic form in B. The four red subunits in B correspond to the four glucose subunits in A.

grees of saturation. Hydrolysis of triacylglycerols releases the fatty acids from glycerol, and these products can then be utilized to provide energy for cell functions.

Phospholipids. **Phospholipids** are similar in overall structure to triacylglycerols, with one important differ-ence. The third hydroxyl group of glycerol, rather than being attached to a fatty acid, is linked to phosphate. In addition, a small polar or ionized nitrogen-containing mol-ecule is usually attached to this phosphate (Figure 2-11). These groups constitute a polar (hydrophilic) region at one end of the phospholipid molecule, whereas the fatty acid chains provide a nonpolar (hydrophobic) region at the

opposite end. Therefore, these molecules are amphi-pathic. In water they become organized into clusters, with their polar ends being attracted to the water molecules.

Steroids. **Steroids** have a distinctly different structure from that of the other subclasses of lipid molecules. Four interconnected rings of carbon atoms form the skeleton of all steroids (Figure 2-12). A few polar hydroxyl groups may be attached to this ring structure, but they are not numer-ous enough to make a steroid water-soluble. Examples of steroids are cholesterol, cortisol from the adrenal glands, and female (estrogen) and male (testosterone) sex hor-mones secreted by the gonads.

FIGURE 2-11

Glycerol and fatty acids are the major subunits that combine to form triacylglycerols and phospholipids.

FIGURE 2-12

Steroid ring structure, shown with all the carbon and hydrogen atoms in the rings and again without these atoms to emphasize the overall ring structure of this class of lipids. Different steroids have different types and numbers of chemical groups attached at various locations on the steroid ring, as shown by the example of the steroid cholesterol.

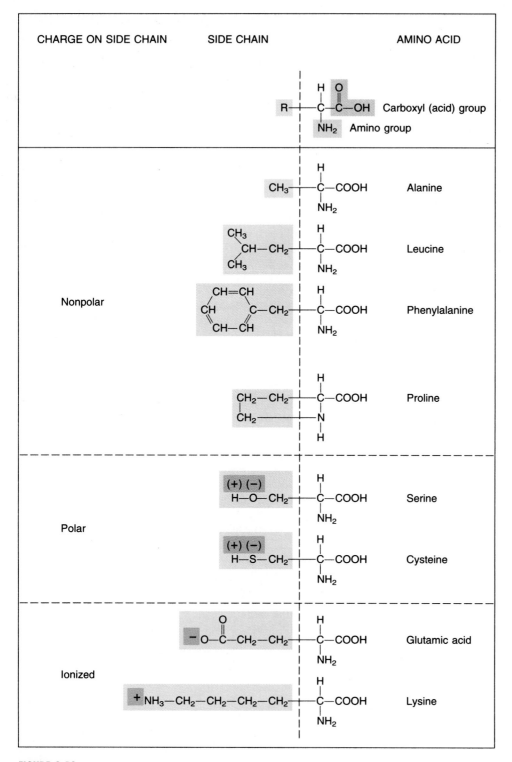

CHARGE ON SIDE CHAIN	SIDE CHAIN	AMINO ACID

FIGURE 2-13

Structures of 8 of the 20 amino acids found in proteins. Note that proline does not have a free amino group, but it can still form a peptide bond.

Proteins

The term "**protein**" comes from the Greek *proteios* (of the first rank), which aptly describes their importance. These molecules, which account for about 50 percent of the organic material in the body (17 percent of the body weight), play critical roles in almost every physiological process. Proteins are composed of atoms of carbon, hydrogen, oxygen, and nitrogen, and small amounts of other elements, notably sulfur. They are macromolecules, often containing thousands of atoms, and like most large molecules, they are formed by the linking together of a large number of small subunits to form long chains.

Amino Acid Subunits.   The subunit of protein structure is an **amino acid**; thus, proteins are polymers of amino acids. Every amino acid (except one—proline) has an amino (—NH_2) and a carboxyl (—COOH) group linked to the terminal carbon atom in the molecule:

$$
R-\overset{\overset{\displaystyle H}{|}}{\underset{\underset{\displaystyle NH_2}{|}}{C}}-COOH
$$

The third bond of this terminal carbon atom is linked to a hydrogen atom, and the fourth to the remainder of the molecule, which is known as the **amino acid side chain** (R in the formula). The proteins of all living organisms are composed of the same set of 20 different amino acids, corresponding to 20 different side chains. The side chains may be nonpolar (8 amino acids), polar (7 amino acids), or ionized (5 amino acids) (Figure 2-13).

FIGURE 2-14
Linkage of amino acids by peptide bonds to form a polypeptide.

Polypeptides. Amino acids are joined together by linking the carboxyl group of one amino acid to the amino group of another. In the process, a molecule of water is formed (Figure 2-14). The bond formed between the amino and carboxyl groups is called a **peptide bond**, and it is a polar covalent bond. Note that when two amino acids are linked together, one end of the resulting molecule has a free amino group and the other has a free carboxyl group. Additional amino acids can be linked by peptide bonds to these free ends. A sequence of amino acids linked by peptide bonds is known as a **polypeptide**. The peptide bonds form the backbone of the polypeptide, and the side chain of each amino acid sticks out from the side of the chain. If the number of amino acids in a polypeptide is 50 or less, the molecule is known as a **peptide**; if the sequence is more than 50 amino acid units long, the polypeptide is known as a protein. The number 50 is arbitrary and has become the convention for distinguishing between large and small polypeptides.

After certain proteins have been synthesized, one or

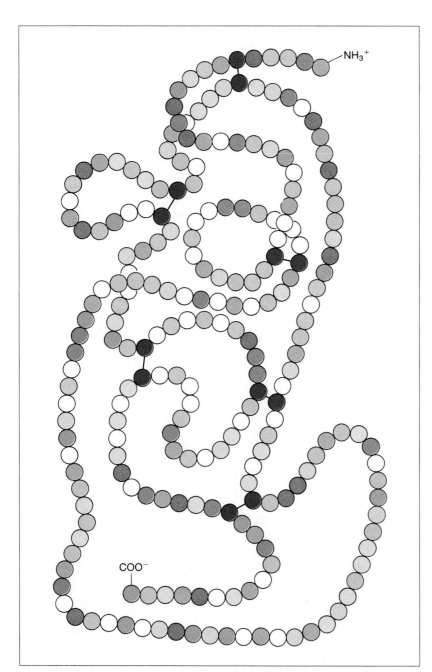

FIGURE 2-15

The position of each type of amino acid in a polypeptide chain and the total number of amino acids in the chain distinguish one polypeptide from another. The example shown above contains 223 amino acids; different types of amino acids are represented by different-colored circles. The bonds between different regions of the chain (red to red) represent covalent disulfide bonds between cysteine side chains.

FIGURE 2-16

Conformation of a protein molecule (myoglobin). Regions of alpha-helix conformation are interrupted at sites of bending by random coil conformations. (*Adapted from Albert L. Lehninger.*)

more monosaccharides are covalently attached to the side chains of specific amino acids (serine and threonine) to form a class of proteins known as **glycoproteins**.

Primary Protein Structure. Two variables determine the primary structure of a polypeptide: (1) the number of amino acids in the chain, and (2) the specific type of amino acid at each position along the chain (Figure 2-15). Each position along a polypeptide chain can be occupied by any one of the 20 different amino acids. Let us consider the number of different peptides that can be formed that have a sequence of three amino acids. Any one of the 20 different amino acids may occupy the first position in the sequence, any one of the 20 the second position, and any one of the 20 the third position, for a total of $20 \times 20 \times 20 = 20^3 = 8000$ possible sequences of three amino acids. If the peptide is 6 amino acids in length, $20^6 = 64,000,000$ possible combinations can be formed. Peptides that are only 6 amino acids long are still very small molecules compared to proteins, which may have sequences of 1000 or more amino acids. Thus, with 20 different amino acids an almost unlimited variety of polypeptides can be formed by altering both the amino acid sequence and the total number of amino acids in the chain.

Protein Conformation. The structure of a polypeptide is analogous to a string of beads, each bead representing a single amino acid (Figure 2-15). Moreover, since amino acids can rotate around their peptide bonds, a polypeptide chain is flexible and can be bent into a number of shapes, just as a string of beads can be twisted into many configurations. The three-dimensional shape of a molecule is known as its **conformation** (Figure 2-16). The conformations of peptides and proteins play a major role in the functioning of these molecules, as we shall see in Chapter 4.

Four factors determine the conformation of a polypeptide chain once the amino acid sequence has been formed: (1) hydrogen bonds between portions of the chain or with surrounding water molecules; (2) ionic bonds between polar and ionized regions along the polypeptide chain; (3) **van der Waals forces**, which are very weak forces of attraction between nonpolar (hydrophobic) regions in close proximity to each other; and (4) covalent bonds linking the side chains of two amino acids (Figure 2-17).

An example of the attractions between various regions along a polypeptide chain is the hydrogen bonds that can occur between the hydrogen linked to the nitrogen atom in one peptide bond and the double-bonded oxygen in

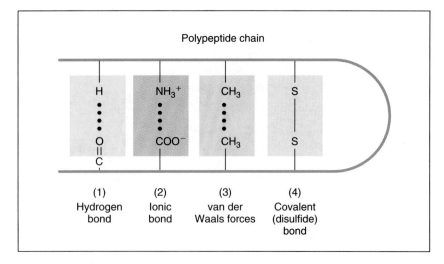

FIGURE 2-17
Factors that contribute to the folding of polypeptide chains and thus to their conformation are (1) hydrogen bonds between side chains or with surrounding water molecules, (2) ionic bonds between polar or ionized amino acid side chains, (3) weak van der Waals forces between nonpolar side chains, and (4) covalent bonds between side chains.

another peptide bond (Figure 2-18). Since peptide bonds occur at regular intervals along a polypeptide chain, the hydrogen bonds between them tend to force the polypeptide chain into a helical configuration known as an **alpha helix**. However, for several reasons, a given region of a polypeptide chain may not assume a helical shape. The sizes of the side chains and ionic bonds between oppositely charged ionized side chains can interfere with the coiling and distort the helix, producing shapes with no regularity. These uncoiled regions are known as **random coil** config-

urations and occur in regions where the polypeptide is bent (Figure 2-16).

Water plays an important role in determining the conformation of a polypeptide chain. When polypeptides are dissolved in water, the polarized and ionized regions of the molecule are attracted to the surrounding polar water molecules. This tends to force the polar and ionized side chains toward the surface of the molecule, orienting them toward the water, while the hydrophobic side chains tend to become located in the interior of the molecule, re-

FIGURE 2-18
Hydrogen bonds between regularly spaced peptide bonds can produce a helical configuration in a polypeptide chain.

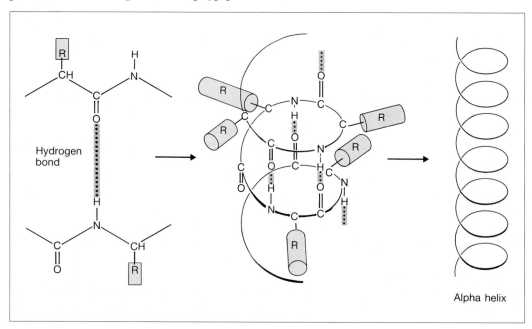

Alpha helix

FIGURE 2-19

Formation of a disulfide bond between the side chains of two cysteine amino acids links two regions of the polypeptide together. The hydrogen atoms on the sulfhydryl groups of the cysteines are transferred to another molecule, X, during formation of the disulfide bond.

moved from contact with water. If they come close to each other, the hydrophobic side chains located in the interior of the protein are attracted by van der Waals forces as a result of the weak electromagnetic field that surrounds electrically neutral atoms.

Covalent bonds between certain side chains can distort the regular pattern of the alpha-helix conformation and can be used to link two polypeptides together. The side chain of the amino acid cysteine contains a sulfhydryl group (R—SH), which can react with a sulfhydryl group in

another cysteine side chain to produce a **disulfide bond** (R—S—S—R), linking the two amino acid side chains together (Figure 2-19). Disulfide bonds form strong covalent bonds between portions of a polypeptide chain, in contrast to the weaker hydrogen and ionic bonds, which are more easily broken. Table 2-6 provides a summary of the types of bonding forces that contribute to the conformation of polypeptide chains. These same bonds are also involved in other intermolecular interactions, which will be described in later chapters.

TABLE 2-6 BONDING FORCES BETWEEN ATOMS AND MOLECULES

Bond	Strength	Characteristics	Examples
Hydrogen	Weak	Electrical attraction between polarized bonds, usually hydrogen and oxygen	Attractions between peptide bonds forming the alpha helix structure of proteins and between polar amino acid side chains contributing to protein conformation; attractions between water molecules
Ionic	Strong	Electrical attraction between oppositely charged ionized groups	Attractions between ionized groups in amino acid side chains contributing to protein conformation; attractions between ions in a salt
Van der Waals	Very weak	Attraction between nonpolar molecules and groups when very close to each other	Attractions between nonpolar amino acids in proteins contributing to protein conformation; attractions between lipid molecules
Covalent	Strong	Shared electrons between atoms	Most bonds linking atoms together to form molecules

A number of proteins contain more than one polypeptide chain. The same factors that influence the conformation of a single polypeptide also determine the interactions between the polypeptides in a multichain protein. Thus, the separate chains can be held together by interactions between various ionized, polar, and nonpolar side chains, as well as by disulfide covalent bonds between the chains. The polypeptide chains in a multichain protein may be identical or different. For example, hemoglobin, the protein that transports oxygen in the blood, is composed of four polypeptide chains, two of one kind and two of another.

The primary structures (amino acid sequences) of a large number of proteins are known, but three-dimensional conformations have been determined for only a few. Because of the multiple factors that can influence the folding of a polypeptide chain, it is not yet possible to predict accurately the conformation of a protein from its primary amino acid sequence.

Nucleic Acids

Nucleic acids account for only 2 percent of the body's weight, yet these molecules are extremely important because they are responsible for the storage, expression, and transmission of genetic information. It is the expression of genetic information that determines whether one is a human being or a mouse, or whether a cell is a muscle cell or a nerve cell.

There are two classes of nucleic acids, **deoxyribonucleic acid (DNA)** and **ribonucleic acid (RNA)**. DNA molecules store genetic information coded in terms of their repeating subunit structure, whereas RNA molecules are involved in the decoding of this information into instructions for linking together a specific sequence of amino acids to form a specific polypeptide chain. Both types of nucleic acids are polymers composed of linear sequences of repeating subunits. Each subunit, known as a **nucleotide**, has three components: a phosphate group, a sugar, and a ring of carbon and nitrogen atoms known as a base because it can accept hydrogen ions (Figure 2-20). The phosphate group of one nucleotide is linked to the sugar of the adjacent nucleotide to form a chain, with the bases sticking out from the side of the phosphate-sugar backbone (Figure 2-21).

DNA. The nucleotides in DNA contain the five-carbon sugar **deoxyribose**; hence the name "deoxyribonucleic acid." Four different nucleotides are present in DNA, corresponding to the four different bases that can be linked to deoxyribose. These bases are divided into two classes: (1) the **purine** bases, **adenine** and **guanine**, which have double (fused) rings of nitrogen and carbon atoms; and

FIGURE 2-20
Nucleotide subunits of DNA and RNA. Nucleotides are composed of a sugar, a base, and phosphate. Deoxyribonucleotides present in DNA contain the sugar deoxyribose. The sugar in ribonucleotides, present in RNA, is ribose, which has an OH at the position that lacks this group in deoxyribose.

(2) the **pyrimidine** bases, **cytosine** and **thymine**, which have only a single ring (Figure 2-21).

A DNA molecule consists of not one but two chains of nucleotides coiled around each other in the form of a double helix (Figure 2-22). The two chains are held together by hydrogen bonds between purine and pyrimidine bases. This base pairing maintains a constant distance between

FIGURE 2-21
Phosphate-sugar bonds link nucleotides in sequence to form nucleic acids. Note that the pyrimidine base thymine is found only in DNA and uracil is present only in RNA.

the sugar-phosphate backbones of the two chains as they coil around each other. Specificity is imposed on the base pairings by the location of the hydrogen-bonding groups in the four bases (Figure 2-22). Three hydrogen bonds are formed between the purine guanine and the pyrimidine cytosine (G-C pairing), while only two hydrogen bonds can be formed between the purine adenine and the pyrimidine thymine (A-T pairing). As a result, G is always paired with

C, and A with T. In Chapter 4 we shall see how this specificity in base pairing provides the mechanism for duplicating and transferring genetic information.

RNA. The structure of RNA molecules differs in only a few respects from that of DNA (Table 2-7): (1) RNA consists of a single (rather than a double) chain of nucleotides; (2) in RNA, the sugar in each nucleotide is **ribose** rather

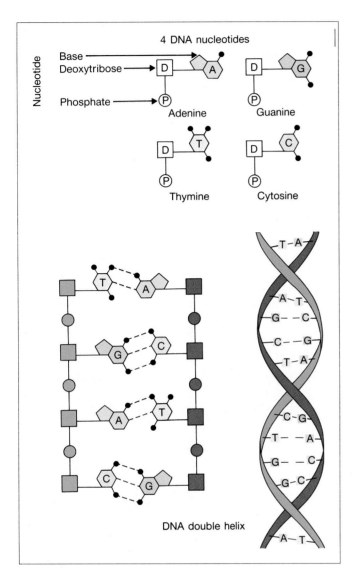

DNA double helix

FIGURE 2-22
Base pairings between two nucleotide chains form the double-helical structure of DNA. D and P represent deoxyribose and phosphate, which form the backbone of each polynucleotide chain. The four bases are indicated by A, T, C, and G.

than deoxyribose; and (3) the pyrimidine base thymine in DNA is replaced in RNA by the pyrimidine base **uracil** (U) (Figure 2-20), which can base-pair with the purine adenine (A-U pairing). The other three bases, adenine, guanine, and cytosine, are the same in both DNA and RNA. Although RNA contains only a single chain of nucleotides, portions of this chain can bend back upon itself and base-pair with other nucleotides in the same chain.

TABLE 2-7   COMPARISON OF DNA AND RNA COMPOSITION

	DNA	RNA
Nucleotide sugar	Deoxyribose	Ribose
Nucleotide bases		
Purines	Adenine	Adenine
	Guanine	Guanine
Pyrimidines	Cytosine	Cytosine
	Thymine	Uracil
Number of chains	Two	One

SUMMARY

ATOMS

I. Atoms are composed of three subatomic particles: positive protons and neutral neutrons, both located in the nucleus, and negative electrons revolving around the nucleus.

II. The atomic number is the number of protons in an atom, and because atoms are electrically neutral, it is also equal to the number of electrons.

III. The atomic weight of an atom is the ratio of an atom's mass relative to that of a carbon-12 atom. It is approximately equal to the number of protons plus neutrons.

IV. One gram atomic mass is the number of grams of an element equal to its atomic weight. One gram atomic mass of any element contains the same number of atoms—6×10^{23}.

V. The 24 elements essential for normal body function are listed in Table 2-1.

MOLECULES

I. Molecules are formed by linking atoms together.

II. A covalent bond is formed when two atoms share a pair of electrons. Each type of atom can form a characteristic number of covalent bonds: hydrogen forms one, oxygen two, nitrogen three, and carbon four.

III. Molecules have characteristic shapes, which can be altered within limits by the rotation of their atoms around covalent bonds.

IONS

I. When an atom gains or loses one or more electrons, it acquires a net electric charge and becomes an ion.

POLAR MOLECULES

I. In polar covalent bonds, one atom attracts the bonding electrons more than the other atom does.

II. The electrical attraction between hydrogen and the oxygen or nitrogen atom in a separate molecule or different region of the same molecule forms a hydrogen bond.

III. Water, a polar molecule, is attracted to other water molecules by hydrogen bonds.

SOLUTIONS

I. Substances dissolved in a liquid are solutes, and the liquid in which they are dissolved is the solvent. Water is the most abundant solvent in the body.

II. Substances that have polar or ionized groups dissolve in water by being electrically attracted to the polar water molecules.

III. In water, amphipathic molecules form clusters with the polar regions at the surface and the nonpolar regions in the interior of the cluster.

IV. The molecular weight of a molecule is the sum of the atomic weights of all its atoms. One mole of any substance is its weight in grams equal to its molecular weight and contains 6×10^{23} molecules.

V. Substances that release a hydrogen ion in solution are called acids. Those that accept a hydrogen ion are bases.
   A. The acidity of a solution is determined by its free hydrogen-ion concentration; the greater the hydrogen-ion concentration, the greater the acidity.
   B. The pH of a solution is the negative logarithm of the hydrogen-ion concentration. As the acidity of a solution increases, the pH decreases. Pure water has a pH of 7.0.

CLASSES OF ORGANIC MOLECULES

I. Carbohydrates are composed of carbon, hydrogen, and oxygen in the proportions $C_n(H_2O)_n$.
   A. The presence of the polar hydroxyl groups makes carbohydrates soluble in water.
   B. The most abundant monosaccharide in the body is glucose ($C_6H_{12}O_6$), which is stored in cells in the form of the polysaccharide glycogen.

II. Lipids lack polar and ionized groups, a characteristic that makes then insoluble in water.

A. Triacylglycerols are formed when fatty acids are linked to each of the three hydroxyl groups in glycerol.
B. Phospholipids contain two fatty acids linked to two of the hydroxyl groups in glycerol, with the third hydroxyl linked to phosphate, which in turn is linked to a small charged or polar compound. The polar and ionized groups at one end of phospholipids make these molecules amphipathic.
C. Steroids are composed of four interconnected rings, often containing a few polar hydroxyl groups.

III. Proteins, macromolecules composed primarily of carbon, hydrogen, oxygen, and nitrogen, are polymers of amino acids.
   A. Nineteen of the 20 amino acids have an amino ($—NH_2$) and a carboxyl ($—COOH$) group linked to their terminal carbon atom.
   B. Amino acids are linked together by peptide bonds between the carboxyl group of one amino acid and the amino group of the next.
   C. The primary structure of a polypeptide chain is determined by (1) the number of amino acids in sequence, and (2) the type of amino acid at each position.
   D. The factors that determine the conformation of a polypeptide chain are summarized in Figure 2-17.
   E. Hydrogen bonds between peptide bonds along a polypeptide chain force much of the chain into an alpha helix.
   F. The interactions of polar and ionized side chains with water tend to force these regions to the surface of the protein, leaving the nonpolar side chains to occupy the interior.
   G. Covalent disulfide bonds can form between the sulfhydryl groups of cysteine side chains to hold regions of a polypeptide chain close to each other.
   H. Some proteins have multiple polypeptide chains.

IV. Nucleic acids are responsible for the storage, expression, and transmission of genetic information.
   A. Deoxyribonucleic acid (DNA) stores genetic information.
   B. Ribonucleic acid (RNA) is involved in the decoding of the information coded in DNA into instructions for linking amino acids together to form proteins.
   C. Both types of nucleic acids are polymers of nucleotides, each containing a phosphate group, a sugar, and a base of carbon, hydrogen and nitrogen atoms.
   D. DNA contains the sugar deoxyribose and consists of two chains of nucleotides coiled around each other in a double helix. The chains are held together by hydrogen bonds between purine and pyrimidine bases in the two chains.

E. Base pairings in DNA always occur between guanine and cytosine and between adenine and thymine.

F. RNA consists of a single chain of nucleotides, containing the sugar ribose and three of the four bases found in DNA. The fourth base is the pyrimidine uracil rather than thymine. Uracil base-pairs with adenine.

KEY TERMS

atoms	neutral solution
chemical element	alkaline solutions
protons	acidic solutions
neutrons	macromolecules
electrons	polymers
atomic nucleus	carbohydrate
atomic number	monosaccharides
atomic weight	glucose
gram atomic mass	pentoses
trace elements	hexoses
molecule	disaccharides
covalent bond	sucrose
ion	polysaccharides
electrolytes	glycogen
cations	lipids
anions	fatty acid
carboxyl group	saturated fatty acid
amino group	unsaturated fatty acid
polar covalent bonds	monounsaturated fatty acid
hydroxyl group	polyunsaturated fatty acid
polar molecules	eicosanoids
nonpolar molecules	arachidonic acid
hydrogen bond	triacylglycerols
hydrolysis	glycerol
solutes	phospholipids
solvent	steroids
solution	protein
ionic bond	amino acid
hydrophilic	amino acid side chain
hydrophobic	peptide bond
amphipathic	polypeptide
concentration	peptide
molecular weight	glycoproteins
mole	conformation
acids	van der Waals forces
base	alpha helix
strong acids	random coil
weak acids	disulfide bond
acidity	nucleic acids
pH	deoxyribonucleic acid (DNA)

ribonucleic acid (RNA)	pyrimidine
nucleotide	cytosine
deoxyribose	thymine
purine	ribose
adenine	uracil
guanine	

REVIEW QUESTIONS

1. Describe the electric charge, mass, and location of the three major subatomic particles in an atom.

2. Which four atoms are the most abundant in the body?

3. Describe the distinguishing characteristics of the three classes of essential chemical elements found in the body.

4. How many covalent bonds can be formed by atoms of carbon, nitrogen, oxygen, and hydrogen?

5. What property of molecules allows them to change their three-dimensional shape?

6. Describe how an ion is formed.

7. Draw the structures of an ionized carboxyl group and an ionized amino group.

8. Describe the polar characteristics of a water molecule.

9. What determines a molecule's solubility or lack of solubility in water?

10. Describe the organization of amphipathic molecules in water.

11. What is the molar concentration of 80 g of glucose dissolved in sufficient water to make 2 L of solution?

12. What distinguishes a weak acid from a strong acid?

13. What effect does increasing the pH of a solution have upon the ionization of a carboxyl group? An amino group?

14. Name the four classes of organic molecules in the body.

15. Describe the three subclasses of carbohydrate molecules.

16. To which subclass of carbohydrates does each of the following molecules belong: glucose, sucrose, and glycogen?

17. What properties are characteristic of lipids?

18. Describe the subclasses of lipids.

19. Describe the linkage between amino acids to form a polypeptide chain.

20. What is the difference between a peptide and a protein?

21. What two factors determine the primary structure of a polypeptide chain?

22. Describe the types of interactions that determine the conformation of a polypeptide chain.

23. Describe the structure of DNA and of RNA.

24. Describe the characteristics of base pairings between nucleotide bases.

CHAPTER
3

CELL STRUCTURE

As we learned in Chapter 1, cells are the structural and functional units of all living organisms. The human body is composed of trillions of cells, each a microscopic compartment (Figure 3-1). In fact, the word "cell" means "a small chamber" (like a jail cell). In this chapter, we describe the structures present in most of the body's cells and state their functions. Subsequent chapters describe the mechanisms by which these structures perform their functions.

The cells of a mouse, a human being, and an elephant are all approximately the same size. An elephant is large because it has more cells, not because it has larger cells. A majority of the cells in a human being have diameters in the range of 10 to 20 μm, although cells as small as 2 μm and as large as 120 μm are present. A cell 10 μm in diameter is about one-tenth the size of the smallest object that can be seen with the naked eye; a microscope must therefore be used to observe cells and their internal structure.

MICROSCOPIC OBSERVATIONS OF CELLS

The smallest object that can be seen clearly under a microscope depends upon the wavelength of the radiation used to illuminate the specimen—the shorter the wavelength, the smaller the object that can be seen. With a **light microscope**, the smallest object that can be seen

clearly is about 0.2 μm in diameter, and so this instrument can be used to see individual cells as well as some intracellular structure. However, an **electron microscope** is necessary to make visible the finer details of cellular structure.

An electron microscope uses electrons instead of light rays to form an image of a specimen. A beam of electrons can be focused by electromagnetic lenses, just as glass

FIGURE 3-1
Cellular organization of tissues, as illustrated by a portion of spleen. Oval, clear spaces in the micrograph are blood vessels. (*From Johannes A. G. Rhodin, "Histology: A Text and Atlas,"* *Oxford University Press, New York, 1974.*)

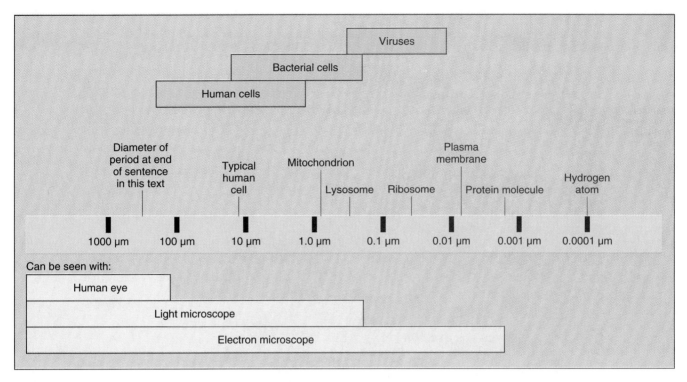

FIGURE 3-2

Size range of cell structures, plotted on a logarithmic scale. Typical sizes are given. Each component has a range of sizes around this typical value.

lenses focus a beam of light in a light microscope. A greater resolution is achieved by an electron microscope because electrons behave as waves with much shorter wavelengths than those of visible light. Cell structures as small as 0.002 μm can be resolved with an electron microscope. Very large molecules, such as proteins and nucleic acids, can be seen through an electron microscope, although the individual atoms that make up these large molecules are still beyond the limits of effective resolution. Typical sizes of cells and cellular components are illustrated in Figure 3-2.

Although *living* cells can be observed with a light microscope, this is not possible with an electron microscope. To form an image with an electron beam, most of the electrons must pass through the specimen, just as light passes through a specimen in a light microscope. However, electrons can penetrate only a short distance through matter; therefore, the observed specimen must be very thin. Cells must be specially prepared for observation in an electron microscope by being cut into thin sections, like slices of salami. Each section is on the order of 0.1 μm thick, which is about one-hundredth of the thickness of a typical cell.

Because electron micrographs (such as Figure 3-3) are images of very thin sections of a cell rather than of the whole cell, they can often be misleading. Structures that appear as separate objects in an electron micrograph may actually be continuous structures that are connected through a region lying outside the plane of the section. As an analogy, a thin section through a ball of string would appear as a collection of separate lines and disconnected dots even though the piece of string was originally continuous.

Cells have a variety of shapes. Most cells are surrounded by and anchored to neighboring cells, and such immobilized cells usually have a polyhedral shape (Figure 3-1). Specialized cells often have shapes that are related to the specific functions they perform. Extending from a nerve cell, for example, are one or more cylindrical processes, much like the branches of a tree, which are used to receive and transmit electric signals.

There are three types of biological units: **prokaryotic cells**, **eukaryotic cells**, and **viruses**. The cells in the human body, as well as in other multicellular animals and plants, are eukaryotic (true-nucleus) cells. These cells are distinguished by the presence of a nuclear membrane surrounding the cell nucleus and the presence of numerous membrane-bound organelles within the cell. Prokaryotic cells lack these membranous structures; bacteria make up the largest class of prokaryotic cells. Viruses have the simplest structure, consisting of only a nucleic acid molecule surrounded by a protein shell. Numerous infectious dis-

Granular endoplasmic reticulum

Nucleus

Mitochondria

Lysosomes

Golgi apparatus

Agranular endoplasmic reticulum

FIGURE 3-3

Electron micrograph of a thin section through a portion of a rat liver cell. [*From K. R. Porter, in T. W. Goodwin and O. Lindberg (eds.), "Biological Structure and Function," vol. 1, Academic Press, New York, 1961.*]

eases are caused by the invasion of multicellular organisms by prokaryotic cells and viruses (Chapter 20). This chapter describes the structure of eukaryotic cells only.

CELL COMPARTMENTS

Compare an electron micrograph of a section through a cell (Figure 3-3) with a diagrammatic illustration of a typical human cell (Figure 3-4). What is immediately obvious, from both the diagram and the electron micrograph, is the extensive structure inside the cell. A human

cell is not simply a chemical solution surrounded by a limiting barrier, the **plasma membrane**, which covers the cell surface. The cell interior is divided into a number of compartments also surrounded by membranes. These membrane-bound compartments, along with some particles and filaments, are known as **cell organelles** (little organs). Each cell organelle performs a specific function that contributes to the cell's survival.

The interior of a cell is divided into two regions: (1) the **nucleus**, a spherical or oval structure usually located near the center of the cell; and (2) the **cytoplasm**, the region that makes up all the interior of the cell except the nu-

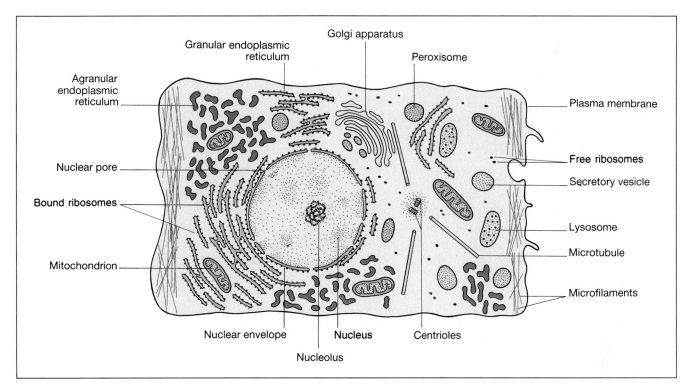

FIGURE 3-4
Structures found in most human cells.

cleus. The cytoplasm contains two components: (1) cell organelles other than the nucleus, and (2) the fluid surrounding these organelles and known as the **cytosol** (Figure 3-5). The term **intracellular fluid** refers to *all* the fluid inside a cell—in other words, cytosol plus the fluid inside all the organelles, including the nucleus. The chemical compositions of the fluids in these cell organelles differ from that of the cytosol. The cytosol is by far the largest intracellular fluid compartment.

Membranes

Membranes form a major structural element in human cells. They are found surrounding the entire cell (the plasma membrane) and enclosing most of the cell organelles. Although membranes perform a variety of functions, their most universal role is to act as a selective barrier to the passage of molecules, allowing some molecules to cross while excluding others. The plasma membrane regulates the passage of substances into and out of the cell, whereas the membranes surrounding cell organelles allow selective movement of substances between the organelles and the cytosol. One of the advantages of restricting the movements of molecules across membranes is that the products of chemical reactions can often be confined to specific cell organelles. As we shall see in Chapter 6, the hindrance offered by a membrane to the passage of sub-

stances can be altered to allow increased or decreased flow of molecules or ions across the membrane.

The plasma membrane, in addition to acting as a selective barrier, plays an important role in detecting chemical

FIGURE 3-5
Comparison of cytoplasm and cytosol. (A) Cytoplasm (the colored area) is the region that includes every point inside the cell except the interior of the nucleus. (B) Cytosol (the colored area) is the liquid that fills all of the cytoplasmic region except the interior of the cell organelles.

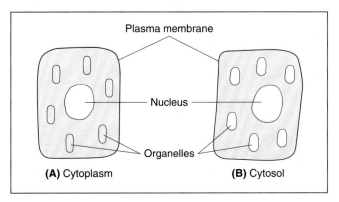

TABLE 3-1 FUNCTIONS OF PLASMA MEMBRANES

1. Regulate the passage of substances into and out of the cells
2. Detect chemical messengers arriving at the cell surface
3. Link adjacent cells together by membrane junctions
4. Anchor a variety of proteins, including intracellular and extracellular protein filaments involved in the generation and transmission of force, to the cell surface

signals from other cells, anchoring cells to adjacent cells, and providing sites for the attachment of protein filaments associated with the generation and transmission of force (Table 3-1).

Membrane Structure. All membranes consist of a double layer of lipid molecules in which proteins are embedded (Figure 3-6). The lipid layer prevents the movement of most polar or ionized molecules through the membrane, whereas the proteins provide pathways for the selective transfer of these substances through the lipid barrier.

The major membrane lipids are **phospholipids**. As described on page 26, these are amphipathic molecules.

One end has a charged region, and the remainder of the molecule, which consists of two long fatty acid chains, is nonpolar. The phospholipids in cell membranes are organized into a bimolecular layer with the nonpolar fatty acid chains located in the middle. The polar regions of the phospholipids are oriented toward the surfaces of the membrane as a result of their attraction to the polar water molecules in the extracellular fluid and cytosol.

There are no chemical bonds linking the phospholipids to each other or to the membrane proteins. Therefore, each molecule is free to move independently of the others. This results in considerable random lateral movement parallel to the surfaces of the bilayer. In addition, the long fatty acid chains can bend and wiggle back and forth. Thus, the lipid bilayer has the characteristics of a fluid, much like a thin layer of oil on a water surface. This fluidity makes the membrane quite flexible. Like a piece of cloth, membranes can be bent and folded but cannot be stretched without being torn. This flexibility, along with the fact that cells are filled with fluid, allows cells to undergo considerable changes in shape without disruption of their structural integrity.

The plasma membrane also contains **cholesterol** (about one molecule of cholesterol for each molecule of phospholipid), whereas intracellular membranes contain very little cholesterol. Cholesterol, a steroid, is slightly

FIGURE 3-6

(A) Electron micrograph of a human red-cell plasma membrane. Cell membranes are 6 to 10 nm thick, too thin to be seen without the aid of an electron microscope. In an electron micrograph a membrane appears as two dark lines separated by a light interspace. The dark lines correspond to the polar regions of the proteins and lipids, whereas the light interspace corresponds to the nonpolar regions of these molecules. [*From J. D. Robertson, in Michael Locke (ed.), "Cell Membranes in Development," Academic Press, New York, 1964.*] (B) Arrangement of the proteins and lipids in the membrane.

(A)

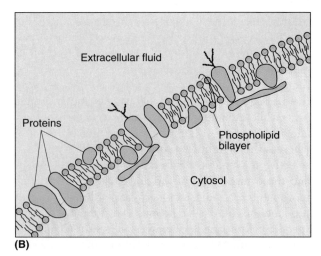

(B)

amphipathic because of a single polar hydroxyl group (Figure 2-12) on its nonpolar ring structure. Therefore, cholesterol, like the amphipathic phospholipids, is inserted into the lipid bilayer with its polar region at a bilayer surface and its nonpolar rings in the interior in association with the fatty acid chains. The cholesterol in the plasma membrane plays an important role in maintaining the fluidity of the lipid bilayer, preventing close association of the long fatty acid chains, which are attracted to each other by van der Waals forces (page 31). In the absence of cholesterol, these forces would tend to solidify the lipid bilayer.

There are two classes of membrane proteins: integral and peripheral membrane proteins. **Integral membrane proteins** are closely associated with the membrane lipids and cannot be extracted from the membrane without disrupting the lipid bilayer. Like the phospholipids, the integral proteins are amphipathic, having polar amino acid side chains located in one region of the molecule and nonpolar side chains clustered together in a separate region. Because they are amphipathic, integral proteins are arranged in the membrane with the same orientation as amphipathic lipids—the polar regions are at the surfaces in association with polar water molecules, and the nonpolar regions are in the interior in association with nonpolar fatty acid chains (Figure 3-7). Like the membrane lipids, many of the integral proteins can move laterally in the plane of the membrane, but others are immobilized because they are linked to a network of peripheral proteins located primarily at the cytoplasmic surface of the membrane.

Most integral proteins span the entire membrane and are referred to as "transmembrane" proteins. These proteins have two polar regions connected by a nonpolar segment that associates with the nonpolar regions of the lipids in the interior of the membrane. The polar regions of transmembrane proteins may extend far beyond the polar surface of the lipid bilayer. Some transmembrane integral proteins form channels through which ions or water can move across the membrane, whereas others are associated with the transmission of chemical signals across the membrane.

Peripheral membrane proteins are not amphipathic and do not associate with the nonpolar regions of the lipids in the interior of the membrane. They are located at the membrane surface where they are bound to the polar regions of the integral membrane proteins (Figure 3-7). Most of the peripheral proteins are located on the cytoplasmic surface of the plasma membrane rather than on the extracellular surface and are associated with such properties as cell shape and motility.

The plasma membrane also contains small amounts of carbohydrate covalently linked to some of the membrane lipids and proteins. These carbohydrates consist of short, branched chains of monosaccharides that extend from the cell surface into the extracellular fluid where they form a fuzzy, "sugar-coated" layer known as the **glycocalyx**. The carbohydrate portions of the membrane are all located at the extracellular surface. This is a second example of the asymmetrical distribution of membrane components, the first being the location of most peripheral proteins at the inner surface. In addition, the lipids in the outer half of the bilayer differ somewhat in kind and amount from those in the inner half, and, as we have seen, the proteins or portions of proteins on the outer surface differ from those on the inner surface. Many membrane functions are related to these asymmetries in chemical composition.

Although all membranes have the general structure described above, which has come to be known as the **fluid-mosaic model** (Figure 3-8), the proteins and, to a lesser extent, the lipids in the plasma membrane are dif-

FIGURE 3-7

Arrangement of integral and peripheral membrane proteins in association with a biomolecular layer of phospholipids. Dark-blue areas indicate the polar regions of integral membrane proteins.

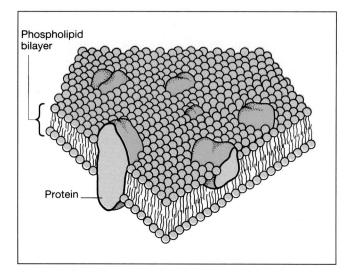

FIGURE 3-8

Fluid-mosaic model of cell membrane structure. (*Redrawn from S. J. Singer and G. L. Nicholson, Science, 175:723. Copyright 1972 by the American Association for the Advancement of Science.*)

ferent from those in organelle membranes. Thus, the special functions of membranes, which depend primarily on the membrane proteins, are different in the various membrane-bound organelles and in the plasma membranes of different types of cells.

Membrane Junctions.   In addition to providing a barrier to the movements of molecules between the intracellular and extracellular fluids, plasma membranes are involved in interactions between cells to form tissues. Some cells, particularly those of the blood, do not associate with other cells but remain as independent cells suspended in a fluid—the blood plasma in the case of blood cells. Most cells, however, are packaged into tissues and are not free to move around the body. But even the cells in a tissue are not packed so tightly that the adjacent cell surfaces are in direct contact with each other, except at certain specialized junctions. There usually exists a space of at least 20 nm between the opposing membranes of adjacent cells. This space is filled with extracellular fluid and provides the pathway for substances to pass between cells on their way to and from the blood.

The forces that organize cells into tissues and organs are poorly understood but depend, at least in part, on the ability of binding sites on the plasma membranes to recognize and associate with specific proteins that bind cells together.

Some tissues can be separated into individual cells by gentle procedures, such as shaking the tissues in a calcium-free medium. The absence of calcium ions decreases

the ability of the cells to stick together, suggesting that the doubly charged Ca^{2+} may act as a link between cells by combining with negatively charged groups on adjacent cell surfaces. Many types of cells, however, require more drastic chemical procedures to separate them from their neighbors.

The electron microscope has revealed that many cells are physically joined by specialized types of membrane junctions known as desmosomes, tight junctions, and gap junctions.

Desmosomes (Figure 3-9A) consist of a region between two adjacent cells where the two opposed plasma membranes are separated by about 20 nm and have a dense accumulation of protein at each cytoplasmic membrane surface and in the space between the two membranes. In addition, fibers extend from the cytoplasmic surface into the cell and are linked to other desmosomes on the opposite side of the cell. The function of the desmosome is to hold adjacent cells firmly together in areas that are subject to considerable stretching, such as in the skin. The specialized area of the membrane in the region of a desmosome is usually disk-shaped, and these membrane junctions could be likened to rivets or spot welds.

A second type of membrane junction, the **tight junction** (Figure 3-9B), is formed when the extracellular surfaces of two adjacent plasma membranes are joined together so that there is no extracellular space between the adjacent cells. Unlike the desmosome, which is limited to a disk-shaped area of the membrane, the tight junction occurs in a band around the entire circumference of the cell. Tight junctions greatly restrict the movement of most organic molecules through the extracellular space between the joined cells, but they have a variable leakiness to small ions and water.

Most epithelial cells are joined by tight junctions. For example, epithelial cells cover the inner surface of the intestinal tract, where they come in contact with the digestion products in the cavity of the tract. During absorption, the products of digestion move across the epithelium and enter the blood. This transfer could take place by movement either through the extracellular space between the epithelial cells or through the epithelial cells themselves. Movement through the extracellular space is blocked by the tight junctions that encircle the cells near their luminal border. Thus, absorption of organic nutrients requires them to pass through cells, rather than between them. In this way the selective barrier properties of the plasma membrane can be used to control the types and amounts of absorbed substances. Figure 3-9D shows both a tight junction and a desmosome near the luminal border between two epithelial cells.

A third type of junction, the **gap junction**, contains protein channels linking the cytoplasms of adjacent cells (Figure 3-9C). In the region of the gap junction, the two

FIGURE 3-9

Three types of specialized membrane junctions: (A) desmosome, (B) tight junction, and (C) gap junction. (D) Electron micrograph of two intestinal epithelial cells joined by a tight junction near the luminal surface and a desmosome below the tight junction. [*Electron micrograph from M. Farquhar and G. E. Palade, Journal of Cell Biology, 17:375–412 (1963).*]

opposing plasma membranes come within 2 to 4 nm of each other, allowing proteins from the two membranes to become joined, thereby forming the walls of small channels. These channels extend across the gap between the cells, linking the cytoplasms. The small diameter of these channels (about 1.5 nm) limits what can pass between the connected cells to small molecules and ions, such as sodium and potassium, and excludes the exchange of large protein molecules. A variety of cell types possess gap junctions, including the muscle cells of the heart and smooth-muscle cells. As we shall see in Chapter 11, these gap junctions play a very important role in the transmission of electrical activity between certain types of muscle cells. In other cases, gap junctions coordinate the activities of adjacent cells by allowing chemical messengers to move from one cell to another.

CELL ORGANELLES

Nucleus

Almost all cells contain a single nucleus. (A few specialized types, for example, skeletal-muscle cells, contain multiple nuclei, while the mature red blood cell has none.) The primary function of the nucleus is the storage, transmission, and expression of genetic information used to synthesize the proteins that determine the structure and function of the cell (Chapter 4).

Surrounding the nucleus is a barrier, the **nuclear envelope**, composed of two membranes. At regular intervals along the surface of the nuclear envelope, the two membranes become joined to each other, forming the rims of circular openings known as **nuclear pores** (Figure 3-10). Molecules that regulate the expression of genetic information move between the nucleus and cytoplasm through these nuclear pores. Very large molecules, such as RNA and proteins, can move through the nuclear pores, but such movement is selective, that is, restricted to specific macromolecules. An energy-dependent process that alters the diameter of the pore in response to specific signals is involved in the transfer process.

Within the nucleus, DNA, in association with proteins, forms a fine network of threads, known as **chromatin**, that are coiled to a greater or lesser degree, producing the variations in the density of the nuclear contents seen in electron micrographs (Figure 3-10). When a cell divides, the chromatin threads become highly condensed to form **chromosomes**.

The most prominent organelle in the nucleus is the **nucleolus**, a highly coiled structure associated with numerous particles but not surrounded by a membrane. The nucleolus is composed of RNA and proteins associated with specific regions of DNA that contain the genes for forming the RNA found in particular cytoplasmic organelles called ribosomes. It is in the nucleolus that the subunits of ribosomes are assembled. These ribosomal subunits are transferred to the cytoplasm, where they combine to form functional ribosomes.

Ribosomes

Ribosomes are the sites at which protein molecules are synthesized from amino acids, using genetic information sent by RNA messenger molecules from DNA in the nucleus. Ribosomes are large particles, about 20 nm in diameter, each of which is composed of a large number of proteins and several RNA molecules (Chapter 4). Ribosomes are either bound to the organelle called granular endoplasmic reticulum (described next) or are found free in the cytoplasm.

The proteins synthesized on the free ribosomes are released into the cytosol, where they perform their functions. The proteins synthesized by ribosomes attached to the granular endoplasmic reticulum pass into the lumen of the reticulum from which they are transferred to yet another organelle, the Golgi apparatus.

Endoplasmic Reticulum

The most extensive cytoplasmic organelle is the network of membranes that forms the **endoplasmic reticulum** (Figure 3-11). The membranes enclose a space that is continuous throughout the network. The continuity of the endoplasmic reticulum is not obvious when examining a single electron micrograph because only a portion of the network is present in any one section.

Two forms of endoplasmic reticulum can be distinguished: **granular** (rough-surfaced) and **agranular** (smooth-surfaced). As noted above, the granular endoplasmic reticulum has ribosomes bound to its cytosolic surface, and it has a flattened-sac appearance. The outer membrane of the nuclear envelope also has ribosomes on its surface, and the space between the two nuclear envelope membranes is continuous with that of the granular endoplasmic reticulum. The agranular endoplasmic reticulum has no ribosomal particles on its surface and has a branched, tubular structure.

Both granular and agranular endoplasmic reticulum exist in the same cell. The relative amounts of the two types vary in different types of cells and even within the same cell during different periods of cell activity. Granular endoplasmic reticulum is involved in the packaging of proteins that are to be secreted by cells or distributed to other cell organelles (Chapter 6). The agranular endoplasmic reticulum is the site at which lipid molecules are synthesized (Chapter 5), and it also stores and releases calcium

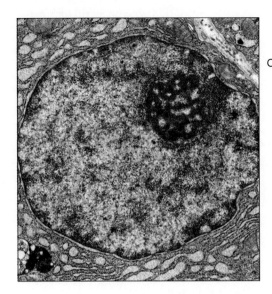

NUCLEUS

Structure: Largest organelle. Round or oval body located near cell center. Surrounded by nuclear envelope composed of two membranes. Envelope contains nuclear pores through which messenger molecules pass between the nucleus and the cytoplasm. No membrane-bound organelles are present in nucleus, which contains coiled strands of DNA known as chromatin, which condense to form chromosomes at the time of cell division.

Function: Stores and transmits genetic information in the form of DNA. Genetic information passes from the nucleus to the cytoplasm, where amino acids are assembled into proteins.

NUCLEOLUS

Structure: Densely stained filamentous structure within nucleus. Consists of proteins associated with DNA in regions where information concerning ribosomal proteins is being expressed.

Function: Forms subunits of ribosomal particles that move into the cytoplasm, where they function as sites of protein synthesis.

FIGURE 3-10
Components of cell nucleus. (*Electron micrograph courtesy of K. R. Porter.*)

ions involved in controlling various cell activities (Chapter 7).

Golgi Apparatus

The **Golgi apparatus** is a series of closely opposed, flattened membranous sacs that are slightly curved, forming a cup-shaped structure (Figure 3-12). Most cells have a single Golgi apparatus located near the nucleus, although some cells may have several. Associated with this organelle, particularly near its concave surface, are a number of approximately spherical, membrane-enclosed vesicles. The Golgi apparatus sorts the different types of proteins received from the granular endoplasmic reticulum into vesicles that will be delivered to various parts of the cell, including the plasma membrane where the protein contents of the vesicle are released to the outside of the cell. When proteins are secreted by cells, the vesicles that contain these proteins are known as **secretory vesicles**.

Mitochondria

Mitochondria (singular, *mitochondrion*) are primarily concerned with the chemical processes by which energy is made available to cells in the form of molecules of adenosine triphosphate (ATP) (Chapter 5). Most of the ATP

Granular endoplasmic
reticulum

Lysosome   Mitochondria   Agranular endoplasmic
reticulum

Granular endoplasmic reticulum   Agranular endoplasmic reticulum

Ribosomes

GRANULAR ENDOPLASMIC RETICULUM

Structure: Extensive membranous network of flattened sheets. Encloses a space that is continuous throughout the organelle and continuous with the space formed by the two nuclear-envelope membranes. Has ribosomal particles attached to its cytosolic surface.

Function: Proteins synthesized on the attached ribosomes are ultimately distributed to other organelles or secreted from cell.

AGRANULAR ENDOPLASMIC RETICULUM

Structure: Highly branched tubular network that does not have attached ribosomes but may be continuous with the granular endoplasmic reticulum.

Function: Contains enzymes for fatty acid and steroid synthesis. Stores and releases calcium, which controls various cell activities.

FIGURE 3-11
Endoplasmic reticulum. (*Electron micrograph from D. W. Fawcett, "The Cell: An Atlas of Fine Structure," W. B. Saunders, Philadelphia, 1966.*)

used by cells is formed in the mitochondria by a process that consumes oxygen and produces carbon dioxide.

Mitochondria are spherical or elongated, rodlike structures surrounded by an inner and an outer membrane (Figure 3-13). The outer membrane is smooth, whereas the inner membrane is folded into sheets or tubules, known as **cristae**, that extend into the inner compartment (**matrix**). Mitochondria are found throughout the cytoplasm. Large numbers of them, as many as 1000, are present in cells that utilize large amounts of energy, whereas less active cells contain fewer.

Mitochondria have small amounts of DNA that contain the genes for the synthesis of some of the mitochondrial proteins. This DNA, which uses a slightly different genetic code than nuclear DNA (Chapter 4), was apparently acquired millions of years ago when a bacteria-like organism was engulfed by another cell and, rather than being destroyed, remained as a symbiotic organism within the cell.

Lysosomes

Lysosomes are spherical or oval organelles surrounded by a single membrane (Figure 3-11). A typical cell may con-

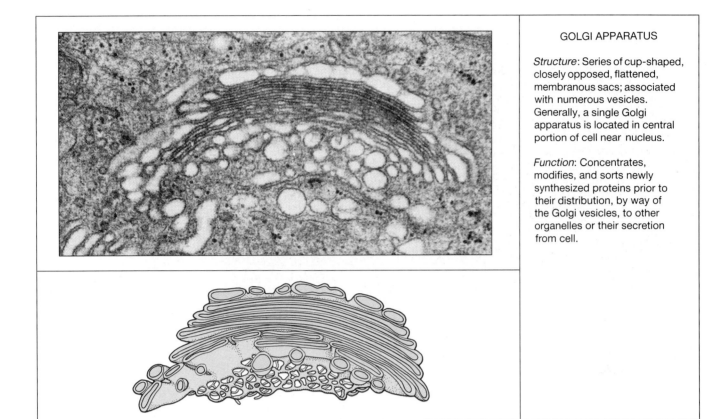

GOLGI APPARATUS

Structure: Series of cup-shaped, closely opposed, flattened, membranous sacs; associated with numerous vesicles. Generally, a single Golgi apparatus is located in central portion of cell near nucleus.

Function: Concentrates, modifies, and sorts newly synthesized proteins prior to their distribution, by way of the Golgi vesicles, to other organelles or their secretion from cell.

FIGURE 3-12

Golgi apparatus. (*Electron micrograph from W. Bloom and D. W. Fawcett, "Textbook of Histology," 9th ed. W. B. Saunders, Philadelphia, 1968.*)

tain several hundred lysosomes. The fluid within a lysosome is highly acidic and contains a variety of digestive enzymes. Lysosomes act as "cellular stomachs," breaking down bacteria and the debris from dead cells that have been engulfed by a cell. They may also break down cell organelles that have been damaged and are no longer functioning normally. They play an especially important role in the various specialized cells that make up the defense systems of the body (Chapter 20).

Peroxisomes

The structure of **peroxisomes** is similar to that of lysosomes, that is, oval bodies enclosed by a single membrane, but their chemical composition is quite different. Like mitochondria, peroxisomes consume oxygen, although in much smaller amounts, but this oxygen is not used in chemical reactions associated with ATP formation. Peroxisomes destroy certain products formed from oxygen, notably hydrogen peroxide, that can be quite toxic to cells—thus the organelles' name. In addition, the peroxisomes in

liver and kidney use the hydrogen peroxide formed to detoxify various ingested molecules.

Filaments

In addition to the membrane-enclosed organelles, the cytoplasm of most cells contains a variety of filaments. This filamentous network is referred to as the cell's **cytoskeleton** (Figure 3-14), and, like the bony skeleton of the body, it is associated with processes that maintain and change cell shape and produce cell movements.

There are four classes of filaments, based on their diameter and the types of protein they contain (Figure 3-15). In order of size, starting with the thinnest, they are (1) microfilaments, (2) intermediate filaments, (3) muscle thick filaments, and (4) microtubules. Microfilaments and microtubules can be rapidly assembled and disassembled, allowing a cell to change its cytoskeletal framework according to changing requirements. The other two types of filaments, once assembled, are less readily disassembled.

Microfilaments, which are composed of the contract-

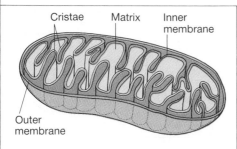

Cristae   Matrix   Inner membrane

Outer membrane

MITOCHONDRION

Structure: Rod- or oval-shaped body surrounded by two membranes. Inner membrane folds into matrix of the mitochondrion, forming cristae.

Function: Major site of ATP production, O_2 utilization, and CO_2 formation. Contains enzymes of Krebs cycle and oxidative phosphorylation.

FIGURE 3-13

Mitochondrion. (*Electron micrograph courtesy of K. R. Porter.*)

ile protein **actin**, make up a major portion of the cytoskeleton in all cells. **Intermediate filaments** are most extensively developed in regions of cells that are subject to mechanical stress. **Muscle thick filaments**, composed of the contractile protein **myosin**, are found only in muscle cells. Individual molecules of myosin, however, are present in most nonmuscle cells where they are involved in producing forces associated with various cell movements.

Microtubules, which are composed of helical arrangements of the protein **tubulin**, are hollow tubes about 25 nm in diameter. They are the most rigid of the cytoskeletal filaments and are present in the long processes of nerve cells, where they provide the framework that maintains the processes' cylindrical shape. Microtubules are also associated with movements of parts of cells. For example, the spindle fibers responsible for separation of the

FIGURE 3-14

Cells stained to show the intermediate filament components of the cytoskeleton. [*From Roy A. Quinlan et al., Annals of the New York Academy of Sciences, 455:282–306 (1985).*]

CYTOSKELETAL FILAMENTS	DIAMETER, nm	PROTEIN SUBUNIT
Microfilament	7	Actin
Intermediate filament	10	Several proteins
Muscle thick filament	15	Myosin
Microtubule	25	Tubulin

FIGURE 3-15
Cytoskeletal filaments associated with cell shape and motility.

chromosomes during cell division are composed of microtubules, as are the **centrioles**, which are the organelles that generate the spindle fibers at the time of cell division (Figure 3-4).

The hairlike extensions—**cilia**—on the surface of some epithelial cells have a central core of microtubules, which produce the movements of the cilia. In hollow organs that are lined with ciliated epithelium, the cilia wave back and forth, propelling the luminal contents along the surface of the epithelium. Microtubules have also been implicated in the movements of organelles within the cytoplasm. The microtubules form tracks along which organelles are propelled by contractile proteins attached to the surface of the organelles.

SUMMARY

I. All living matter is composed of cells.

CELL COMPARTMENTS

I. Every cell is surrounded by a plasma membrane.

II. Within each cell are numerous membrane-bound compartments, nonmembranous particles, and filaments, known collectively as cell organelles.

III. A cell is divided into two regions, the nucleus and the cytoplasm, the latter composed of the cytosol and cell organelles other than the nucleus.

IV. The membranes that surround the cell and cell organelles regulate the movements of molecules and ions into and out of the cell and its compartments.

A. Membranes consist of a bimolecular lipid layer, composed of phospholipids and cholesterol, in which proteins are embedded.

B. The lipid layer prevents the movement of most molecules through the membrane, while the proteins provide pathways for the selective entry of substances.

C. Integral membrane proteins are amphipathic proteins that often span the membrane, whereas peripheral membrane proteins are confined to the surfaces of the membrane.

V. Three types of membrane junctions link adjacent cells:
   A. Desmosomes link cells that are subject to considerable stretching.
   B. Tight junctions, found primarily in epithelial cells, limit the passage of molecules through the extracellular space between the cells.
   C. Gap junctions form channels between the cytoplasms of adjacent cells.

CELL ORGANELLES

I. The nucleus transmits and expresses genetic information.
   A. Threads of chromatin, composed of DNA and protein, condense to form chromosomes when a cell divides.
   B. The nucleolus is the site at which ribosomal subunits are formed.
II. Ribosomes, composed of RNA and protein, are the sites of protein synthesis.
III. The endoplasmic reticulum is a network of flattened sacs and tubules in the cytoplasm.
   A. Granular endoplasmic reticulum has attached ribosomes and is primarily involved in the packaging of proteins that are to be secreted by the cell.
   B. Agranular endoplasmic reticulum is tubular, lacks ribosomes, and is the site of lipid synthesis and calcium accumulation and release.
IV. The Golgi apparatus sorts the proteins that are synthesized on the rough endoplasmic reticulum and packages them into secretory vesicles.
V. Mitochondria are the major sites at which chemical energy is transferred to ATP.
VI. Lysosomes digest particulate matter that enters the cell.
VII. Peroxisomes break down certain toxic products formed from oxygen.
VIII. The cytoplasm contains a network of four types of filaments known as the cytoskeleton: (1) microfilaments, (2) intermediate filaments, (3) muscle thick filaments, and (4) microtubules.

KEY TERMS

light microscope	cell organelles
electron microscope	nucleus
prokarotic cells	cytoplasm
eukaryotic cells	cytosol
viruses	intracellular fluid
plasma membrane	phospholipids

cholesterol	Golgi apparatus
integral membrane proteins	secretory vesicles
peripheral membrane proteins	mitochondria
glycocalyx	mitochondrial cristae
fluid-mosaic model	mitochondrial matrix
desmosomes	lysosomes
tight junction	peroxisomes
gap junction	cytoskeleton
nuclear envelope	microfilaments
nuclear pores	actin
chromatin	intermediate filaments
chromosomes	muscle thick filaments
nucleolus	myosin
ribosomes	microtubules
endoplasmic reticulum	tubulin
granular endoplasmic reticulum	centrioles
agranular endoplasmic reticulum	cilia

REVIEW QUESTIONS

1. In terms of the size and number of cells, what makes an elephant larger than a mouse?
2. Identify the location of cytoplasm, cytosol, and intracellular fluid within a cell.
3. Identify the classes of organic molecules in cell membranes and describe the major contribution of each to membrane function.
4. Describe the orientation of the phospholipid molecules in a membrane.
5. Which plasma membrane components are responsible for membrane fluidity?
6. Describe the location and characteristics of integral and peripheral membrane proteins.
7. Describe the structure and function of the three types of junctions found between cells.
8. What function is performed by the nucleolus?
9. Describe the location and function of ribosomes.
10. Contrast the structure and functions of the granular and agranular endoplasmic reticulum.
11. What function is performed by the Golgi apparatus?
12. Describe the structure and primary function of mitochondria.
13. What functions are performed by lysosomes and peroxisomes?
14. List the four types of filaments associated with the cytoskeleton. Identify the structures in cells that are composed of microtubules.

CHAPTER

4

MOLECULAR CONTROL MECHANISMS: PROTEINS AND DNA

The outstanding accomplishment of twentieth-century biology has been the discovery of the chemical basis of heredity and its relationship to protein synthesis. Whether an organism is a human being or a mouse, has blue eyes or black, has light skin or dark, is determined by the proteins it possesses. Moreover, within an individual organism, muscle cells differ from nerve cells or epithelial cells or any other type of cell because of the types of proteins they contain and the functions performed by these proteins.

Crucial for an understanding of protein function is the fact that each protein has a unique shape, which determines its interaction with other molecules. In the first section of this chapter the relation between protein shape and function is described.

The hereditary information in each cell contains the instructions for synthesizing the cell's proteins. These instructions are coded into DNA molecules. The second section of this chapter describes the chemical basis of the genetic code and the decoding mechanisms that lead from DNA to protein synthesis.

Given that different cell types have different proteins and that the specifications for these proteins are coded in DNA, one might be led to conclude that different cell types contain different DNA molecules. However, such is not the case. All cells in the body, with the exception of sperm or eggs, receive the same genetic information when DNA molecules are duplicated and passed on to daughter cells at the time of cell division. Cells differ in structure and function because only a portion of the total genetic information common to all cells is used by any given cell to synthesize proteins. The last portion of this chapter describes some of the factors that govern the selective expression of genetic information, as well as the process by which DNA molecules are replicated and their genetic information passed on to daughter cells during cell division.

SECTION A

BINDING SITES ON PROTEINS

BINDING-SITE CHARACTERISTICS

The ability to bind various molecules and ions to specific sites on the surface of a protein forms the basis for the wide variety of functions performed by proteins. A **ligand** is any molecule or ion that is bound to the surface of a protein by forces other than covalent chemical bonds. These forces are either (1) attractions between oppositely charged ionic or polarized groups on the ligand and the protein, or (2) weaker attractions due to van der Waals forces between nonpolar regions on the two molecules (page 31). The region of a protein to which a ligand binds is known as a **binding site**. A protein may contain several binding sites, each specific for a particular ligand.

Chemical Specificity

The force of electrical attraction between oppositely charged regions on a protein and a ligand decreases markedly as the distance between them increases. The even weaker van der Waals forces act only between nonpolar groups that are very close to each other. Therefore, in order for a ligand to bind to a protein, the ligand must be close to the protein surface. This occurs when the shape of the ligand is complementary to the shape of the protein binding site, such that the two fit together like pieces of a jigsaw puzzle (Figure 4-1).

The binding between a ligand and a protein may be so specific that a binding site can bind only one type of ligand and no other. Such selectivity allows a protein to "identify" (by binding) one particular molecule in a solution containing hundreds of different molecules. This ability of a protein to bind specific ligands is known as **chemical specificity**, since the binding site determines the type of chemical that is bound.

In the previous chapter we described how the conformation of a protein is determined by the location of the various amino acids along the polypeptide chain. Accordingly, proteins with different amino acid sequences have different shapes and therefore differently shaped binding sites, each with its own chemical specificity. As illustrated in Figure 4-2, the amino acids that interact with a ligand at the binding site need not be adjacent to each other along the polypeptide chain since the folding of the protein may bring various segments of the molecule into juxtaposition.

Although some binding sites have a chemical specificity that allows them to bind only one type of ligand, other binding sites may be less specific and thus be able to bind a number of related ligands. For example, three different ligands can combine with the binding site of protein X in Figure 4-3 since a portion of each ligand is complementary to the shape of the binding site. In contrast, protein Y has a greater, that is, more limited, specificity and can bind only one of the three ligands.

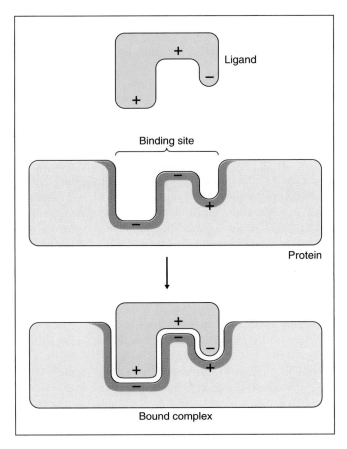

FIGURE 4-1
Complementary shapes of ligand and protein binding site determine the chemical specificity of binding.

Affinity

The strength of ligand-protein binding is a property of the binding site known as **affinity**. The affinity of a binding site for a ligand determines how likely it is that a bound ligand will leave the protein surface and return to its unbound state. Binding sites that tightly bind a ligand are called high-affinity binding sites; those to which the ligand is weakly bound are low-affinity binding sites.

Affinity and chemical specificity are two distinct, although closely related, properties of binding sites. Chemical specificity, as we have seen, depends only on the shape of the binding site, whereas affinity depends on the strength of the attraction between the protein and the ligand. Thus, different proteins may be able to bind the same ligand, that is, may have the same chemical specificity, but may have different affinities for that ligand. For example, a ligand may have a negatively charged ionized group that would bind strongly to a site containing a positively charged amino acid side chain but would bind less strongly (Figure 4-4) to a binding site having the same shape but no positive charge. In addition, the closer the

surfaces of the ligand and binding site to each other, the stronger the electrical or van der Waals attractions. Hence, the more closely the ligand shape matches the binding-site shape, the greater the affinity. In other words, shape can influence affinity as well as chemical specificity.

Saturation

In a solution containing both ligands and proteins, some ligands will bind to unoccupied binding sites on the proteins, while some of the bound ligands will come off. At any given time, a binding site will be either occupied or unoccupied. The term **saturation** refers to the fraction of binding sites that are occupied at any given time. When all the binding sites are occupied, the population of binding sites is 100 percent saturated. When half the available sites

FIGURE 4-2
Amino acids that interact with the ligand at a binding site need not be at adjacent sites along the polypeptide chain, as indicated in this model showing the three-dimensional folding of a protein. The unfolded polypeptide chain is shown below.

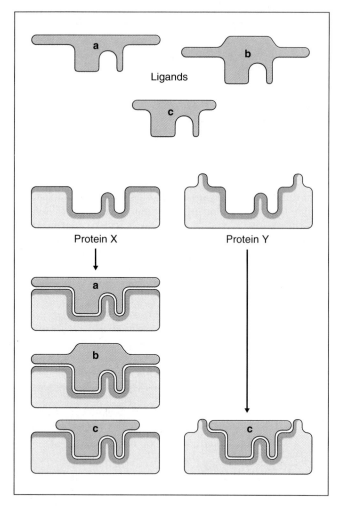

FIGURE 4-3

Protein X is able to bind all three ligands, which have similar chemical structures. Protein Y, because of the shape of its binding site, can bind only ligand c. Protein Y, therefore, has a greater chemical specificity than protein X.

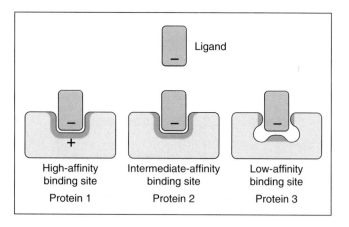

FIGURE 4-4

Three binding sites with the same chemical specificity for a ligand but different affinities.

are occupied, the system is 50 percent saturated, and so on. A *single* binding site would also be 50 percent saturated if it were occupied by a ligand 50 percent of the time.

The percent saturation of a binding site depends upon two factors: (1) the concentration of unbound ligand in the solution, and (2) the affinity of the binding site for the ligand.

The greater the ligand concentration, the greater the probability of a ligand molecule encountering an unoccupied binding site and becoming bound. Thus, the percent saturation of binding sites will increase with increasing ligand concentration until all the sites become occupied (Figure 4-5). Assuming that the ligand is a molecule that exerts a biological effect when it is bound to a protein, the magnitude of the effect would also increase with increasing numbers of bound ligands until all the binding sites were occupied. Further increases in ligand concentration would produce no further effect since there would be no additional sites to be occupied. To generalize, a continuous increase in the magnitude of a chemical stimulus (ligand concentration), which exerts its effects by binding to proteins, will produce an increased biological response up to the point where the protein binding sites become 100 percent saturated.

The second factor determining the percent of binding-site saturation is the affinity of the binding site. Collisions between molecules in a solution and a protein containing a bound ligand can dislodge a loosely bound ligand, just as tackling a football player may cause a fumble. If a binding site has a high affinity for a ligand, even a low ligand concentration will result in a high degree of saturation since, once bound to the site, the ligand is not easily dislodged. A low-affinity site, on the other hand, requires a much higher concentration of ligand to achieve the same degree of saturation (Figure 4-6) since any given ligand remains bound for a much shorter period of time, requiring more frequent encounters between unbound ligand and the binding site to keep the site occupied. One measure of binding-site affinity is the ligand concentration necessary to produce 50 percent saturation; the lower the ligand concentration required to produce 50 percent saturation, the greater the affinity of the binding site (Figure 4-6).

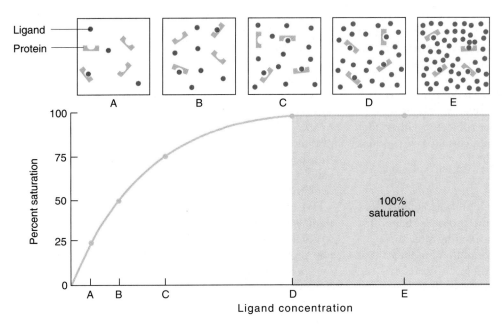

FIGURE 4-5
Increasing ligand concentration increases the number of binding sites occupied, that is, increases the percent saturation. At 100 percent saturation, all the binding sites are occupied, and further increases in ligand concentration do not increase the amount bound.

Competition

As we have seen, more than one type of ligand can bind to certain binding sites (Figure 4-3). In such cases **competition** occurs between the ligands for the same binding site.

FIGURE 4-6
When two different proteins, X and Y, are able to bind the same ligand, the protein with the higher-affinity binding site (protein Y) has more bound sites at any given ligand concentration until 100 percent saturation.

In other words, the presence of multiple ligands able to bind to the same binding site affects the percentage of binding sites occupied by any one ligand. If two competing ligands, A and B, are present, increasing the concentration of A will increase the amount of A that is bound, thereby decreasing the number of sites available for the binding of B and decreasing the amount of B that is bound.

As a result of competition, the biological effects of one ligand may be markedly diminished by the presence of another. For example, many drugs produce their effects by competing with the body's natural ligands for binding sites. By occupying the binding sites, the drug decreases the amount of natural ligand that can be bound.

REGULATION OF BINDING-SITE CHARACTERISTICS

Because proteins are associated with practically every cell function, the mechanisms for controlling these functions center on the control of protein activity. There are two ways of controlling protein activity: (1) Changing protein shape alters its binding of ligands; and (2) regulation of protein synthesis determines the types and amounts of proteins in a cell. The first type of regulation—control of protein shape—is discussed in this section, and the second—protein synthesis—in later sections.

Since a protein's shape depends on electrical attractions

between charged or polarized groups in various regions of a protein (page 31), a change in the charge distribution along a protein or in the polarity of the molecules immediately surrounding it will alter its shape. The two mechanisms used by cells to selectively alter protein shape are allosteric modulation and covalent modulation.[1] Before describing these mechanisms, however, it should be emphasized that most proteins are not subject to either allosteric or covalent modulation. Only certain key proteins are regulated by these mechanisms.

Allosteric Modulation

Whenever a ligand binds to a protein, the attracting forces between ligand and protein alter the protein's shape. For example, as a ligand approaches a binding site, these attracting forces can cause the surface of that binding site to bend into a shape that more closely approximates the shape of the ligand's surface.

Moreover, as the shape of a binding site changes during binding, it will produce changes in the shape of *other* regions of the protein outside that particular binding site, just as pulling on one end of a rope (the polypeptide chain) will cause the other end of the rope to move. Therefore, when a protein contains two binding sites, the binding of a ligand to one site can alter the shape of the second binding site and, hence, the binding characteristics of that site. This is termed **allosteric** (other shape) **modulation** (Figure 4-7), and such proteins are known as **allosteric proteins**.

One binding site on an allosteric protein, known as the **functional site** (also termed the active site), carries out the protein's physiological function. The other binding site is the **regulatory site**, and the ligand that binds to this site is known as a **modulator molecule** since its binding to the regulatory site allosterically modulates the shape and thus the activity of the functional site.

The regulatory site to which modulator molecules bind is the equivalent of a molecular switch that controls the functional site. In some allosteric proteins, the binding of the modulator molecule to the regulatory site turns *on* the functional site by changing its shape so that it can bind the functional ligand. In other cases, the binding of a modulator molecule turns *off* the functional site by preventing the functional site from bindings its ligand. In still other cases, binding of the modulator molecule may decrease or increase the affinity of the functional site. For example, if the functional site is 50 percent saturated at a particular ligand concentration, the binding of a modulatory ligand that increases the affinity of the functional site may increase its saturation to 75 percent.

To summarize, the activity of a protein can be increased without changing the concentration of either the protein or the functional ligand. By controlling the concentration of the regulatory ligand, and thus the percent saturation of the regulatory site, the functional activity of an allosterically regulated protein has the potential of being altered over the entire range from 0 to 100 percent activity.

We have spoken thus far only of interactions between regulatory and functional binding sites. There is, however, a way that functional sites can influence each other in certain proteins. These proteins are composed of more than one polypeptide chain held together by electrical attractions between the chains. There may be only one binding site, a functional binding site, on each chain. The binding of a functional ligand to one of the chains, however, can result in an alteration of the functional binding sites in the other chains. This happens because the change in shape of the chain to which the ligand is bound induces a change in the shape of the other chains. This interaction between the functional binding sites of a multimeric protein is known as **cooperativity**. It can result in a progressive increase in the affinity for ligand binding as more and more of the sites become occupied. This occurs, for example, in the binding of oxygen to hemoglobin, a protein composed of four polypeptide chains, each containing one binding site for oxygen.

Covalent Modulation

A second way to alter the shape and therefore the activity of a protein is to covalently bind charged chemical groups to some of the protein's side chains. This is known as **covalent modulation**. In most cases a phosphate group, which has a net negative charge, is covalently attached by a chemical reaction called **phosphorylation**.

When one of the side chains in certain amino acids in a protein is phosphorylated, a negative charge is introduced into this region of the protein. This alters the distribution of electric forces in the protein, producing a change in protein conformation (Figure 4-7). If this conformational change affects a binding site, it will change the binding site's properties. Although the mechanism is completely different, the *effects* produced by covalent modulation are the same as those of allosteric modulation; that is, a functional binding site may be turned on or off or the affinity of the site for its ligand may be altered.

To reiterate, unlike allosteric modulation, which involves simple *binding* of modulator molecules, covalent modulation requires chemical reactions in which covalent bonds are formed. Most chemical reactions in the body are

---

[1]Two additional nonspecific factors that alter protein shape are (1) temperature, which alters the amount of kinetic energy available for breaking the electrostatic attractions between various regions of a protein; and (2) acidity, which alters the ionization of amino acid side chains. Because both these factors are maintained relatively constant in the body, they are not usually used to selectively regulate protein activity. Should large changes in temperature or acidity occur, however, as in disease, they can produce marked alterations in protein shape and thus in protein activity.

FIGURE 4-7

(A) Allosteric modulation. Binding of a modulator molecule at a regulatory site alters the shape of the functional site. (B) Covalent modulation. Phosphorylation of a hydroxyl group on an amino acid side chain in one region of the protein alters the shape of the functional site located in another region of the protein. The enzyme protein kinase catalyzes the phosphorylation of the protein, whereas a second enzyme, phosphoprotein phosphatase, removes the phosphate group, returning the protein to its original shape.

mediated by a special class of proteins known as **enzymes**, whose properties will be discussed in Chapter 5. For now, suffice it to say that enzymes accelerate the rate at which molecules called substrates are converted to different molecules called products. Any enzyme that mediates protein phosphorylation is called a **protein kinase**. These enzymes catalyze the transfer of phosphate from a molecule of adenosine triphosphate (ATP) (see Chapter 5) to a hydroxyl group present on the side chain of certain amino acids:

$$\text{Protein} + \text{ATP} \xrightarrow{\substack{\text{Protein} \\ \text{kinase}}} \text{protein—PO}_4^{2-} + \text{ADP}$$

The protein and ATP are the substrates for protein kinase, and the phosphorylated protein and ADP are the products of the reaction.

There is also a mechanism for removing the phosphate group and returning the protein to its original shape. This dephosphorylation is accomplished by a second enzyme known as **phosphoprotein phosphatase**:

$$\text{Protein—PO}_4^{2-} + \text{H}_2\text{O} \xrightarrow{\substack{\text{Phosphoprotein} \\ \text{phosphatase}}} \text{protein} + \text{HPO}_4^{2-}$$

Thus, two enzymes control a protein's activity by covalent modulation: one that adds phosphate and one that removes it.

Although most proteins contain amino acids capable of being phosphorylated, only those proteins that are substrates for specific protein kinases are actually phosphorylated. There are many protein kinases, each with specificities for different proteins, and several kinases may be present in the same cell. The chemical specificities of the phosphoprotein phosphatases are broader, and a single enzyme can dephosphorylate many different phosphorylated proteins. Moreover, unlike protein kinases, phosphoprotein phosphatases tend to be continuously active.

When a particular protein kinase is active, the rate of phosphorylation of the protein it acts upon exceeds that of dephosphorylation, and most of the protein molecules being covalently modulated are maintained in the phosphorylated state. Dephosphorylating such protein mole-cules requires only stopping the kinase reaction since the continuously active phosphoprotein phosphatase will remove the phosphate groups.

An important interaction between allosteric and covalent modulation results from the fact that protein kinases are themselves allosteric proteins and so can be controlled by modulator molecules. Thus, the process of covalent modulation is itself indirectly regulated by allosteric mechanisms. In addition, some allosteric proteins can also be modified by covalent modulation.

SECTION A SUMMARY

BINDING-SITE CHARACTERISTICS

I. Ligands bind to proteins at sites that have shapes that are complementary to the ligand shape.

II. Protein binding sites have the properties of chemical specificity, affinity, saturation, and competition.

REGULATION OF BINDING-SITE CHARACTERISTICS

I. Protein activity in a cell can be controlled by regulating either the shape of the protein or the amount of protein synthesized.

II. The binding of a modulator molecule to the regulatory site on an allosteric protein alters the shape of the functional binding site, thereby altering its binding characteristics and the activity of the protein. The activity of allosteric proteins is regulated by varying the concentrations of their modulator molecules.

III. Protein kinase enzymes catalyze the addition of a phosphate group to the side chains of certain amino acids in a protein, changing the shape of the protein's binding site and thus altering the protein's activity by covalent modulation. A second enzyme is required to remove the phosphate group, returning the protein to its original state.

SECTION A KEY TERMS

ligand	binding site
chemical specificity	modulator molecule
affinity	cooperativity
saturation	covalent modulation
competition	phosphorylation
allosteric modulation	enzymes
allosteric proteins	protein kinase
functional site	phosphoprotein phosphatase
regulatory site	

SECTION A REVIEW QUESTIONS

1. List the four characteristics of a protein binding site.
2. List the types of forces that hold a ligand on a protein surface.
3. What characteristics of a binding site determine its chemical specificity?
4. Under what conditions can a single binding site have a chemical specificity for more than one type of ligand?
5. What characteristics of a binding site determine its affinity for a ligand?
6. What two factors determine the percent saturation of a binding site?
7. Describe the mechanism responsible for competition in terms of the properties of binding sites.
8. What are two ways of controlling protein activity in a cell?
9. How is the activity of an allosteric protein modulated?
10. How does regulation of protein activity by covalent modulation differ from that by allosteric modulation?

SECTION

B

GENETIC INFORMATION AND PROTEIN SYNTHESIS

GENETIC CODE

Molecules of DNA contain instructions, coded in the sequence of nucleotides, for the synthesis of proteins. A sequence of nucleotides containing the information that determines the amino acid sequence of a single polypeptide chain is known as a **gene**. A gene is thus a unit of hereditary information, and a single molecule of DNA contains many genes. The total collection of genes that specifies a particular organism's structure and function is known as its **genome**. The human genome contains between 50,000 and 100,000 genes.

As an example of the expression of genetic information, consider eye color, which is due to the presence of pigment molecules in certain cells in the eye. Sequences of enzyme-mediated reactions are required to synthesize these pigments, and the genes that determine eye color do so by coding for different enzymes in these pathways. Note that these genes do not contain any information about the chemical structure of the eye pigments. All they contain is the information required to synthesize the enzymes that mediate the formation of the pigments.

Within the human population a given gene exists in a number of slightly different nucleotide sequences that have resulted from mutations (see below). These variants of the same gene are known as **alleles**. At the time of conception the fertilized egg contains two copies of each of its genes,[2] one gene supplied by the mother's egg and the other allelic gene from the father's sperm. Both genes may have identical nucleotide sequences, in which case the individual is said to be **homozygous** for that particular gene, or the two genes may have slightly different nucleotide sequences (different alleles), in which case the individual is **heterozygous** for that gene.

The alleles of a particular gene can be classified as being either **dominant genes** or **recessive genes**, depending on the effects they have when present in a cell. A single copy of a dominant gene will cause the production of the protein coded for by that gene regardless of the protein coded for by its corresponding allelic gene. In the case of recessive genes, both alleles must code for the same protein (or no protein at all). For example, the gene that codes for the enzyme that leads to the production of black eye pigment is a dominant gene. If this gene is inherited from either the mother or the father, the child will have black eyes. In contrast, the gene for blue eyes is recessive, and a child must receive two copies of this gene, one from the mother and one from the father, to produce blue eyes.

Although DNA contains the information necessary for the synthesis of proteins, it does not itself participate *directly* in the assembly of protein molecules. Most of a cell's DNA is in the nucleus (a small amount is in the mitochondria), whereas most protein synthesis occurs in the cytoplasm. The transfer of information from DNA to the site of protein synthesis is the function of RNA molecules (page 35), whose synthesis is governed by the information in DNA. This mechanism for expressing genetic information occurs in all living organisms and is called the "central dogma" of molecular biology: Genetic information flows from DNA to RNA and then to protein:[3]

$$DNA \longrightarrow RNA \longrightarrow protein$$

Figure 4-8 summarizes the general pathway by which the information stored in DNA influences cell activity via protein synthesis.

As described on page 34, a molecule of DNA consists of two polynucleotide chains coiled around each other to form a double helix (see Figure 2-22). Each nucleotide contains one of four bases—adenine (A), guanine (G), cytosine (C), or thymine (T)—and each of these bases is specifically paired, A to T and G to C, with a base on the opposite chain of the double helix. Thus, both nucleotide chains contain a specifically ordered sequence of bases, one chain being complementary to the other.

The genetic language is similar in principle to a written

[2]Actually there are not two copies of every gene, only of most genes. Of the 23 pairs of chromosomes, one set, the sex chromosomes (see Chapter 19), do not contain corresponding copies of the same genes. In addition, some genes are present in multiple copies at different sites along a given DNA molecule.

[3]In some viruses, genetic information can be transferred from RNA to protein in the absence of DNA, while in other viruses the flow can be from RNA to DNA to RNA to protein.

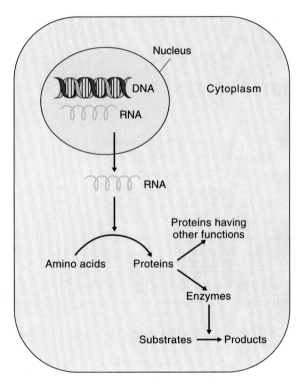

FIGURE 4-8

The expression of genetic information in a cell occurs through its transcription from DNA to RNA in the nucleus, followed by the translation of the RNA information into protein synthesis in the cytoplasm.

FIGURE 4-9

Relation between the sequence of triplet code words in one strand of DNA and the amino acid sequences of proteins that correspond to them. The names of the amino acids are abbreviated. Note that all three genes are part of the same DNA molecule, which may contain hundreds of genes in a linear sequence, each gene being composed of hundreds of sequential bases.

language, which consists of a set of symbols, such as α, β, δ, γ, forming an alphabet. The letters are arranged in specific sequences to form words, and the words are arranged in linear sequences to form sentences. The genetic language contains only four letters, corresponding to the four bases A, G, C, and T. The words are three-base sequences that specify particular amino acids; that is, each word in the genetic language is only three letters long. This is termed a triplet code. These triplets are arranged in a linear sequence along DNA, and the sequence of triplets specifying the structure of a single protein makes up a gene (Figure 4-9). A typical human gene may consist of a sequence of approximately 20,000 base pairs. Thus, a gene is equivalent to a sentence, and the entire collection of genes in a cell is equivalent to a book—the human genome.

The four bases in the DNA alphabet can be arranged in 64 different three-letter combinations ($4 \times 4 \times 4 = 64$). Thus, a triplet code actually provides more than enough words to code for 20 amino acids. It turns out, however, that not just 20, but 61 of the 64 possible triplets are used to specify amino acids. This means that a given amino acid is usually specified by more than one code word. For example, the four triplets C-C-A, C-C-G, C-C-T, and C-C-C all specify the same amino acid, glycine.

The three triplets that do not specify amino acids are known as **termination code words**. They perform the same function as does a period at the end of a sentence—they indicate that the end of a genetic message has been reached. The code word for the amino acid methionine does double duty by also indicating the beginning of the gene.

The **genetic code** is a universal language used by all living cells. For example, the code words for the amino acid tryptophan are the same in the DNA of a bacterium, an amoeba, a plant, and a human being. Although the same code words are used by all living cells, the messages

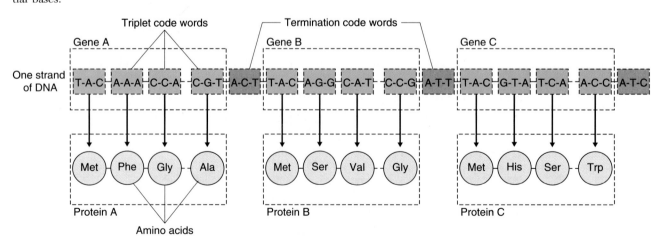

they spell out—the sequences of code words (the "sentences") that determine the amino acid sequences in proteins—are different in each organism. The universal nature of the genetic code supports the concept that all forms of life on earth evolved from a common ancestor.

PROTEIN SYNTHESIS

Molecules of DNA are too large to pass through the nuclear membrane into the cytoplasm. Yet it is in the cytoplasm, on ribosomes, that proteins are synthesized. Since DNA cannot leave the nucleus, a message carrying genetic information must pass from the nucleus to the cytoplasm. This message is carried by RNA molecules known as **messenger RNA (mRNA)**. The transfer of genetic information from DNA to protein thus occurs in two stages: First, the genetic message is passed from DNA to mRNA in the nucleus (**transcription**); second, the message in mRNA passes from the nucleus to the cytoplasm where it is used to direct the assembly of the specific sequence of amino acids to form a particular protein (**translation**).

Transcription: mRNA Synthesis

During transcription, the sequence of nucleotides in a gene in one of the DNA molecules is used to determine the sequence of nucleotides in mRNA corresponding to that gene. As described on page 35, ribonucleic acids are single-chain polynucleotides whose nucleotides differ

from DNA in that they contain the sugar ribose (rather than deoxyribose) and the base uracil (rather than thymine). The other three bases—adenine, guanine, and cytosine—occur in both DNA and RNA. The pool of subunits used to synthesize mRNA are free (uncombined) ribonucleotides, each containing three phosphate groups (ribonucleotide triphosphates): ATP, GTP, CTP, and UTP.

In DNA, the two polynucleotide chains are linked together by hydrogen bonds (page 35) between specific pairs of bases—A pairing with T, and G with C. Transcription begins with the breakage of these hydrogen bonds so that a portion of the two chains of the DNA double helix separates (Figure 4-10). The bases in the exposed DNA nucleotides are then able to pair with the bases in the free ribonucleotide triphosphates. Free ribonucleotides containing adenine pair with any exposed thymine base in DNA. Likewise, free ribonucleotides containing G, C, or U pair with the exposed DNA bases C, G, and A, respectively. (Note that uracil, which is present in RNA but not DNA, pairs with the base adenine in DNA.) In this way, the nucleotide sequence in DNA acts as a template that determines the sequence of nucleotides in mRNA.

The aligned ribonucleotides are joined together by the enzyme **RNA polymerase**. This enzyme, which binds to a specific site on DNA just ahead of the gene to be transcribed, catalyzes both the splitting off of two of the three phosphate groups from each nucleotide and the covalent linkage of the RNA ribonucleotide to the next one in the sequence. RNA polymerase is active only when bound to DNA and will not link free ribonucleotides together (in what would be a random sequence) when they are not

FIGURE 4-10
Transcription of a gene from a single strand of DNA to mRNA.

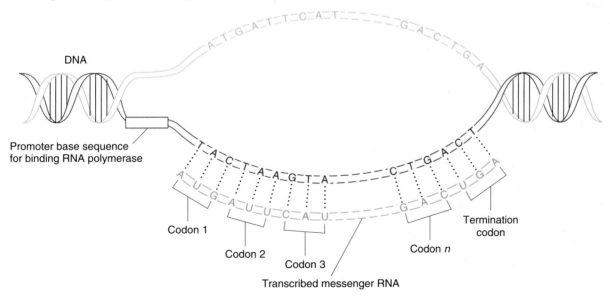

base-paired with DNA. DNA acts as a modulator molecule that allosterically activates RNA polymerase.

Since DNA consists of two strands of polynucleotides, both of which are exposed during transcription, it should theoretically be possible to form two different mRNA molecules, one from each strand. However, only one of the two potential mRNAs is ever formed. Which of the two DNA strands is used as the template for mRNA synthesis is determined by a specific sequence of nucleotides in DNA, called the **promoter**, located at the beginning of each gene (Figure 4-10). The promoter, to which RNA polymerase binds, is present in only one of the two DNA strands. Beginning at the promoter end of a gene, the RNA polymerase separates the two DNA strands as it moves along one strand, joining one ribonucleotide at a time to the growing mRNA chain until it reaches a termination code word at the end of the gene. This causes the RNA polymerase to release the newly formed mRNA.

In a given cell, the information in only a few of the thousands of genes present in DNA is transcribed into mRNA at any given time. Genes are transcribed only when RNA polymerase can bind to their promoter sites. Various mechanisms are used by cells either to block or to make accessible the promoter region of any particular gene. Such regulation of gene transcription provides a means of controlling the synthesis of specific proteins and thereby the activities of cells.

It must be emphasized that the base sequence in mRNA is not *identical* to that in the corresponding strand of DNA, since its formation depends on the pairing between complementary, not identical, bases (Figure 4-10). A three-base sequence in mRNA that specifies one amino acid is called a **codon**. Each codon is *complementary* to a three-base sequence in DNA. For example, the base sequence T-A-C in DNA corresponds to the codon A-U-G in mRNA.

Although the entire sequence of nucleotides in a gene is transcribed into a corresponding sequence of nucleotides in mRNA, only certain segments of the gene actually code for sequences of amino acids. These regions of the gene, known as **exons** (expression regions), are separated by noncoding sequences of nucleotides known as **introns** (intervening sequences). Before passing to the cytoplasm, a newly formed mRNA must undergo splicing (Figure 4-11) to remove the sequences that correspond to the DNA introns. Nuclear enzymes that identify specific nucleotide sequences at the beginning and end of each intron sequence remove the sequence from mRNA and splice the end of one exon-derived sequence to the beginning of another to form an mRNA with no intron-derived segments. In some cases, the exon-derived sequence from a single gene can be spliced together in several different ways, resulting in the formation of different mRNAs from the same gene and giving rise, in turn, to several different proteins.

The mRNAs formed as a result of RNA splicing are 75 to 90 percent shorter than the originally transcribed mRNA, meaning that 75 to 90 percent of the nucleotide

FIGURE 4-11

RNA splicing removes the noncoding sequences (corresponding to the introns in DNA) before the mRNA passes through the nuclear pores to the cytosol. The length of the intron and exon segments represent the relative lengths of the base sequences in these regions.

sequences in DNA are introns. What role such large amounts of "nonsense" DNA may perform is unclear.

Finally, it should be noted that not all genes give rise to mRNA and hence code for proteins. Some genes code for other RNA molecules that perform other functions in the process of protein synthesis, as described in the next sections.

Translation: Polypeptide Synthesis

Once transcribed and spliced, the mRNA moves through the pores in the nuclear envelope into the cytoplasm where it binds to a ribosome, the cell organelle that contains the enzymes and other components required for the translation of mRNA's coded message into protein. Before describing this assembly process, we must first present the structure of a ribosome as well as the characteristics of two additional types of RNA involved in protein synthesis.

Ribosomes. As described in Chapter 3, ribosomes are small granules (diameter about 23 nm) located in the cytoplasm, either suspended in the cytosol (free ribosomes) or attached to the surface of the endoplasmic reticulum (bound ribosomes). Proteins synthesized on free ribosomes are released into the cytosol, whereas those synthesized on bound ribosomes are inserted through the membrane of the endoplasmic reticulum and released into its lumen, from which they are either secreted by the cell or transferred to various other organelles (see below).

Each ribosome contains many proteins in association with a type of RNA known as **ribosomal RNA (rRNA)**. Ribosomal RNA is synthesized in the nucleus, with DNA again serving as a template for positioning the sequence of nucleotides in rRNA. The genes that code for rRNA, however, are associated with the nucleolus, which is also the site at which the protein and rRNA components of the ribosome are combined before passing into the cytoplasm.

Transfer RNA. How do individual amino acids identify the appropriate codons in mRNA during the process of translation? By themselves, free amino acids do not have the ability to bind to the bases in mRNA codons. This process of identification involves yet a third type of RNA, known as **transfer RNA (tRNA)**. Transfer RNA molecules are the smallest (about 80 nucleotides long) of the three types of RNA. The single chain of tRNA loops back upon itself, forming a structure resembling a cloverleaf with three loops (Figure 4-12).

Like mRNA and rRNA, tRNA is synthesized in the nucleus by base-pairing with DNA nucleotides at specific tRNA genes and then moves to the cytoplasm. The key to tRNA's role in protein synthesis is that it can combine with both a specific amino acid and a codon in ribosome-bound mRNA specific for that amino acid. This permits tRNA to

act as the link between an amino acid and the mRNA codon for that amino acid.

Transfer RNA is covalently linked to an amino acid by an enzyme known as aminoacyl-tRNA synthetase. There are at least 20 different aminoacyl-tRNA synthetases, each of which catalyzes the linkage of a specific amino acid to a particular type of tRNA. The next step is to link the tRNA, bearing its attached amino acid, to the mRNA codon for that amino acid. As one might predict, this is achieved by base-pairing between tRNA and mRNA. A three-nucleotide sequence at the end of one of the loops of tRNA can base-pair with a complementary codon in mRNA. This tRNA triplet sequence is appropriately termed an **anticodon**. Figure 4-13 illustrates the binding between mRNA and a tRNA specific for the amino acid alanine. Note that alanine is covalently linked to one end of tRNA and does not itself bind to the anticodon region.

Protein Assembly. The individual amino acids linked to mRNA by tRNA must now be bound to each other by peptide bonds. Several ribosomal proteins and rRNA interact in a complex manner to identify the initial codon sequence in mRNA and to catalyze the formation of a peptide bond between the first and second amino acids in the peptide chain being synthesized.[4] This initial step is the slowest step in protein assembly, and the rate of protein synthesis can be regulated by factors that influence this initiation process.

Following the initiation of a protein's synthesis, the polypeptide chain is elongated by the successive addition of amino acids (Figure 4-13). A ribosome has two binding sites for tRNA. One holds the tRNA attached to the most recently added amino acid, and the other holds the tRNA containing the next amino acid to be added to the chain. Ribosomal enzymes catalyze the formation of a peptide bond between these two amino acids. Following the formation of the peptide bond, the tRNA at the first binding site is released from the ribosome, and the tRNA at the second site—now linked to the peptide chain—is transferred to the first binding site. The ribosome moves one codon space along the mRNA, making room for the binding of the next amino acid–tRNA molecule. This process is repeated over and over as each amino acid is added in succession to the growing peptide chain, at an average rate of two to three amino acids per second. When the ribo-

---

[4]Although rRNA accounts for the major portion of a cell's RNA, its precise function in the process of protein synthesis is still unclear. It is thought by some to be the remnant of an earlier stage in our evolutionary past in which RNA molecules acted as the major catalysts of chemical reactions in cells before being superseded in this role by protein enzymes. This role may be retained in the ribosome, where rRNA appears to be able to catalyze the formation of peptide bonds between the incoming amino acids and the growing polypeptide chain.

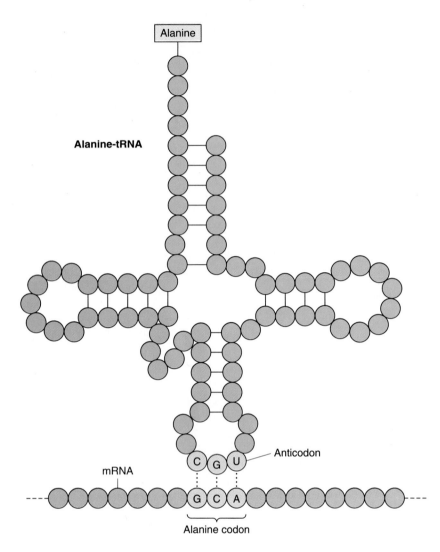

FIGURE 4-12

Base-pairing between the anticodon region of a tRNA molecule and the corresponding codon region of a mRNA molecule.

some reaches a termination codon in mRNA specifying the end of the protein, the link between the polypeptide chain and the last tRNA is broken, and the completed protein is released from the ribosome.

A single strand of mRNA can be used to synthesize many molecules of the protein because the mRNA is not destroyed during protein assembly. Moreover, while one ribosome is moving along a particular strand of mRNA, a second ribosome may become attached to the mRNA and begin the synthesis of a second identical protein molecule. Thus, a number of ribosomes, as many as 70, may be attached to the same strand of mRNA at any one time (Figure 4-14).

Molecules of mRNA do not, however, remain in the cytoplasm indefinitely. Eventually they are broken down into nucleotides by cytoplasmic enzymes. Therefore, if a gene corresponding to a particular protein ceases to be transcribed into mRNA, the synthesis of that protein will eventually slow down and cease as the mRNA is broken down.

The function of a protein, as we have noted, depends on its conformation, which determines its ability to bind specific ligands. A newly synthesized polypeptide comes off a ribosome as an essentially linear amino acid chain, which must then fold into its proper conformation. For some proteins this folding occurs spontaneously and is solely determined by the amino acid sequence of the proteins. For others, particularly large proteins, a number of other special proteins, known as **chaperones**, guide the folding of large segments of newly formed proteins into their proper conformations.

Finally, changes can occur in the structure of some polypeptide chains after their synthesis on a ribosome. Certain classes of proteins, the glycoproteins for example, are formed by the posttranslational addition of various carbohydrate groups to the protein. In other cases, specific peptide bonds in a large polypeptide are enzymatically broken to produce a number of shorter polypeptides, each of which may perform a different function. For example, as illustrated in Figure 4-15, five proteins can be derived

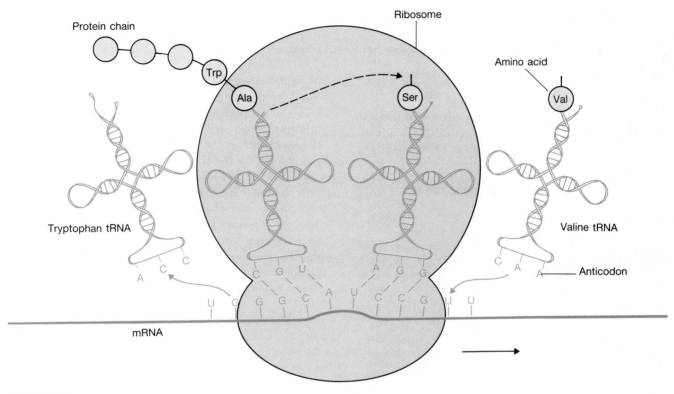

FIGURE 4-13

Sequence of events during the synthesis of a protein on the surface of a ribosome. The three-base anticodon of tRNA carrying one amino acid, for example, serine (ser), binds to the corresponding codon of mRNA, and the tRNA transfers its amino acid to the growing polypeptide chain. As the ribosome moves along the strand of mRNA, successive amino acids are added to the polypeptide chain.

FIGURE 4-14

Several ribosomes can simultaneously move along the same strand of messenger RNA, producing proteins in different states of assembly.

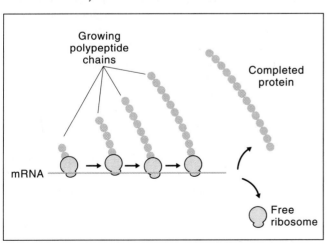

FIGURE 4-15

Posttranslational splitting of a protein can result in several proteins, each of which may perform a different function. All these proteins are derived from the same gene.

from the same mRNA as a result of posttranslational changes.

The steps leading from DNA to protein are summarized in Table 4-1.

Protein Secretion

A fact not stated earlier is that upon arriving in the cytoplasm from the nucleus, a molecule of mRNA binds to a *free* ribosome and begins the process of translating its

---

TABLE 4-1	EVENTS LEADING FROM DNA TO PROTEIN SYNTHESIS

Transcription

1. RNA polymerase binds to the promoter region of a gene and separates the two strands of the DNA double helix in the region of the gene to be transcribed.
2. Free ribonucleotide triphosphates base-pair with the deoxynucleotides in DNA.
3. The ribonucleotides paired with one strand of DNA are linked by RNA polymerase to form mRNA containing a sequence of bases complementary to one strand of the DNA base sequence.
4. mRNA splicing removes the intron regions of mRNA, which contain noncoding sequences, and splices together the exon regions, which code for specific amino acids.

Translation

5. Processed mRNA passes from the nucleus to the cytoplasm, where one end of the mRNA binds to a ribosome.
6. Free amino acids are linked to their corresponding tRNAs by aminoacyl-tRNA synthetase.
7. The three-base anticodon in an amino acid–tRNA complex pairs with the corresponding codon in the region of the mRNA bound to the ribosome.
8. The portion of the peptide that has already been synthesized (and is still attached to a tRNA bound to the ribosome) is now linked by a peptide bond to the amino acid on the tRNA next to it, thereby adding one more amino acid to the chain.
9. The tRNA that has been freed of the peptide chain is released from the ribosome.
10. The ribosome moves one codon step along mRNA.
11. Steps 7 to 10 are repeated over and over until the end of the mRNA message is reached.
12. The completed protein chain is released from the ribosome when the termination codon in mRNA is reached.
13. Chaperone proteins guide the folding of some proteins into their proper conformation.
14. In some cases, the protein undergoes posttranslational processing in which various chemical groups are attached to specific side chains or the protein is split into several smaller peptide chains.

---

message into a polypeptide chain. But during synthesis of the protein the ribosome may not remain free but may become attached to the endoplasmic reticulum. The first 15 to 30 amino acids to be linked together in the growing polypeptide chain determine the fate of the ribosome and where the protein's synthesis will be completed.

This initial portion of some protein chains is known as the **signal sequence** (or signal peptide). If there is no signal sequence at the beginning of the protein, synthesis is completed on the free ribosome and the protein is released into the cytosol. If there is a signal sequence, however, it acts as a ligand that binds to a site on the surface of the granular endoplasmic reticulum. By this mechanism ribosomes become attached to the reticulum. Once the mRNA, with its attached ribosome and growing polypeptide chain, is bound to the reticulum, the polypeptide chain is inserted through the reticulum membrane as additional amino acids are added to the polypeptide (Figure 4-16).

At the completion of its synthesis, the polypeptide with a signal sequence is either released into the lumen of the endoplasmic reticulum or remains inserted in the reticular membrane as a membrane protein. The mechanism by which the growing polypeptide chain passes through the reticulum membrane is unknown. This is the only stage along its route to the outside of the cell at which a protein that is to be secreted passes directly through a membrane.

Within the lumen of the endoplasmic reticulum, enzymes remove the signal sequence from most proteins, and so this portion is not present in the final protein. In addition, carbohydrate groups are added to these proteins by enzymes in the endoplasmic reticulum. Almost all proteins that are secreted are glycoproteins.

Following these modifications, portions of the reticulum membrane bud off, forming vesicles that contain the newly synthesized proteins. These vesicles migrate to the Golgi apparatus (Figure 4-16) and fuse with the Golgi membranes. Within the Golgi apparatus the protein undergoes still further modification. Some of the carbohydrates that were added in the granular endoplasmic reticulum are now removed and new groups added. These latter carbohydrate groups function as labels that can be recognized when the protein encounters various binding sites during the remainder of its trip through the cell.

While in the Golgi apparatus, the many different proteins that have been funneled into this organelle become sorted out according to their final destination. How this sorting takes place is largely unknown, but it involves selective binding of the proteins to different regions of the Golgi membrane.

Following modification and sorting, the proteins are packaged into vesicles that bud off the surface of the Golgi membrane. Some of the vesicles travel to the plasma membrane where they fuse with the membrane and release their contents to the extracellular fluid, a process

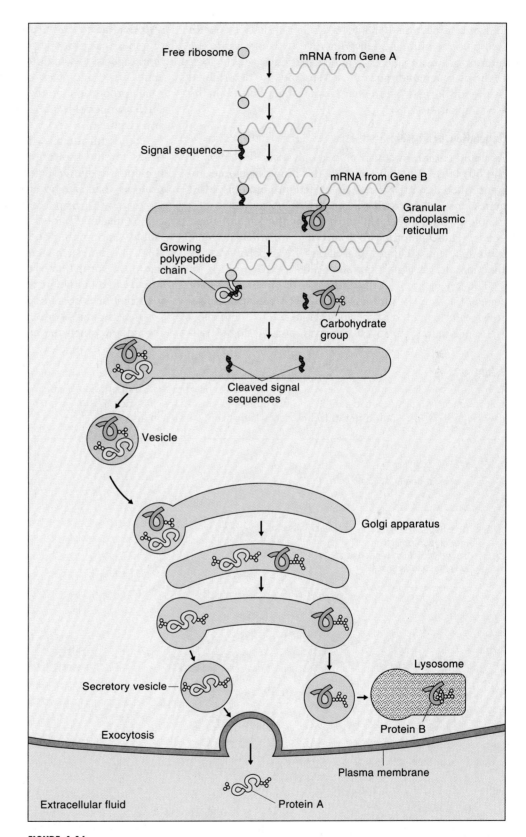

FIGURE 4-16

Pathway traveled by proteins that are to be secreted by cells or transferred to lysosomes.

known as exocytosis (Chapter 6). Other vesicles fuse with lysosome membranes, delivering digestive enzymes to the interior of this organelle. Where a particular vesicle goes, to the plasma membrane or to a lysosome, was determined by the sorting and "addressing" events that occurred in the Golgi apparatus.

Regulation of Protein Synthesis

As noted earlier, in any given cell only a small fraction of the 50,000 to 100,000 genes in the human genome are transcribed into mRNA and translated into proteins. Most genes are not transcribed because RNA polymerase is unable to bind effectively to the promoter sites of these genes. Thus, in order to transcribe a particular gene, something must happen that allows RNA polymerase to function at that gene's promoter site.

The key element in this process is the presence or absence of a group of proteins known as **transcription factors**, which can bind to specific regions of DNA and allow RNA polymerase to initiate transcription. A single tran-

scription factor can turn on the transcription of a number of genes that produce proteins related in function. Thus, there need not be a different transcription factor for each gene. Since any given cell is actively transcribing only a small proportion of the total genome, only a relatively small number of transcription factors need be produced by any given cell.

There still remains the problem of what turns on the genes for the transcription factors? Associated with the promoter regions of genes for transcription factors are proteins that can be activated by allosteric or covalent modulation in response to signals originating within the cell or reaching the cell via the extracellular fluid, for example, hormones. Modulation of these proteins allows RNA polymerase to initiate transcription of the gene leading to the formation of the particular transcription factor, which can then initiate the transcription of the other genes for which it is specific (Figure 4-17).

Once a gene's code has been transcribed into mRNA, the rate at which the corresponding protein is formed is

FIGURE 4-17

Control of gene transcription (gene A in diagram) by means of protein transcription factors that interact with RNA polymerase at specific promoter sites. A specific transcription factor may be formed in response to extracellular signals that initiate their transcription.

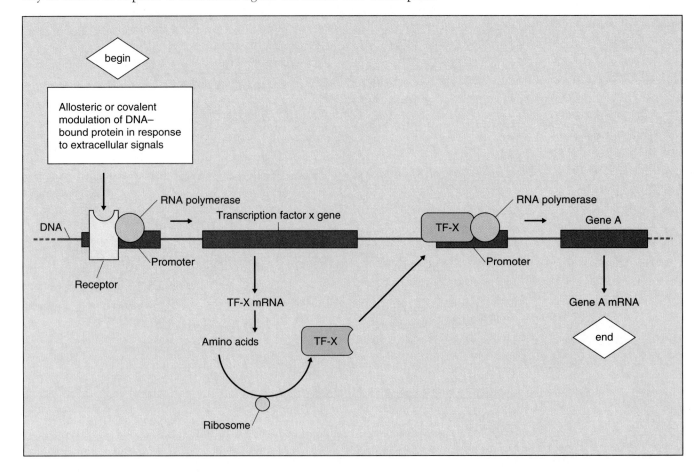

still subject to regulation at several stages between mRNA and the finished protein. For example, regulating the rate of mRNA breakdown will control the average time a molecule of mRNA remains in the cytoplasm and thus the number of protein molecules it forms. Finally, the translation process that occurs on the ribosome can be slowed down or speeded up. One or more of the above regulatory mechanisms may be involved in the synthesis of any given protein.

REPLICATION AND EXPRESSION OF GENETIC INFORMATION

The development of the human body from a single fertilized egg involves cell growth, division, and differentiation into specialized types such as nerve and muscle cells. The maintenance of structure and function in the adult also requires these same processes. Each process depends on the controlled synthesis of proteins, but cell division requires, in addition, the replication of DNA and the transmission of identical copies of this genetic information to each of the two resulting cells.

Replication of DNA

DNA is the only molecule in a cell able to duplicate itself without information from some other cell component. In contrast, as we have seen, RNA can only be formed using the information present in DNA, protein formation uses the information in mRNA, and all other molecules use the protein enzymes in metabolic pathways that determine the structure of the products formed.

DNA replication is, in principle, similar to the process whereby mRNA is synthesized. During DNA replication (Figure 4-18), the two strands of the double helix separate, but the exposed bases in *each* strand base-pair with free *deoxyribonucleotide* triphosphates present in the nucleus. The enzyme **DNA polymerase** then links the free nucleotides together, forming a new strand of DNA. The end result is two identical molecules of DNA, each called a "copy." In each copy, one strand of nucleotides is from the original DNA molecule and one strand has been newly synthesized.

Before cell division, the DNA molecules are replicated by the above process. One copy is passed on to each of the two new cells, termed **daughter cells**, when the cell divides. Thus, the daughter cells receive a copy of the same genetic information present in the parent cell.

Cell Division

Starting with a single fertilized egg, the first cell division produces 2 cells. When these daughter cells divide, they each produce 2 cells, giving a total of 4. These 4 cells

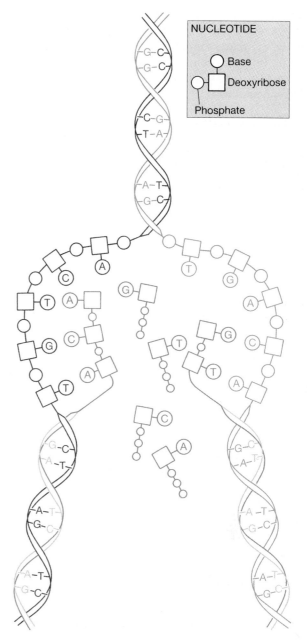

FIGURE 4-18
Replication of DNA involves the pairing of free deoxyribonucleotides with the bases of each DNA strand, giving rise to two new identical DNA molecules, each containing one old and one new polynucleotide strand.

produce a total of 8, and so on. Thus, starting from a single cell, 3 division cycles will produce 8 cells (2^3), 10 division cycles will produce $2^{10} = 1024$ cells, and 20 division cycles will produce $2^{20} = 1,048,576$ cells. If the development of the human body involved only cell division and growth without any cell death, only about 46 division cycles would be needed to produce all the cells in the adult body. However, large numbers of cells die during the course of development, and even in the adult many cells survive only a few days and are continually replaced by the division of existing cells.

The time between cell divisions varies considerably in different types of cells, and the most rapidly growing cells divide about once every 24 h. During most of this period, there is no visible evidence that the cell will divide. For example, in a 24-h division cycle, visible changes in cell structure begin to appear only 1 h before division. The period between the end of one division and the appearance of the structural changes that indicate the beginning of the next division is known as **interphase**. Since cell division takes only about 1 h, the cell spends most of its time in interphase, and most of the cell properties described in this book are properties of interphase cells.

One very important event related to subsequent cell division does occur during interphase, namely, the replication of DNA, which begins about 10 h before the first visible signs of division and lasts about 7 h. This period of the cell cycle is known as the S phase (synthesis) (Figure 4-19). Following the end of DNA synthesis there is a brief interval, G_2 (second gap), before the physical signs of cell division begin. The period from the end of cell division to the beginning of the S phase is the G_1 (first gap) phase of the cell cycle.

FIGURE 4-19

Phases of the cell cycle in a cell that divides every 24 h. A cell may leave the cell cycle and enter the G_0 phase in which division ceases unless it receives a specific signal to reenter the cycle.

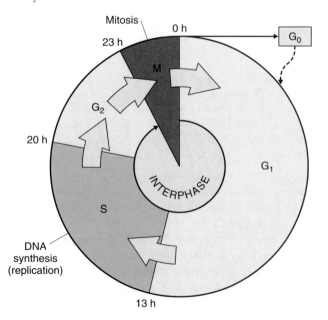

Cell division involves two processes: nuclear division (**mitosis**) and cytoplasmic division (**cytokinesis**). Although mitosis and cytokinesis are separate events, the term "mitosis" is often used in a broad sense to include the subsequent cytokinesis, and so the two events constitute the M phase (mitosis) of the cell cycle. Mitosis that is not followed by cytokinesis produces the multinucleated cells found in the liver, placenta, and some embryonic cells and cancer cells.

During most of interphase, DNA is dispersed throughout the nucleus in association with proteins called histones to form 46 extended nucleoprotein threads known as **chromatin** (Figure 4-20A). At the time of conception 23 of these chromatin threads were supplied by the mother's egg and 23 from one of the father's sperm. All 46 are duplicated during the S phase, and copies are passed on to each daughter cell during mitosis. When each of the 46 chromatin threads replicates, the result is two identical threads termed **sister chromatids**, which initially are joined together at one point known as the **centromere** (Figure 4-20B). In other words, there are now 46 pairs of sister chromatids. As a cell enters mitosis (Figure 4-20C), each chromatid pair becomes highly coiled and condensed, forming visible rod-shaped bodies known as **chromosomes** ("colored bodies," so named because of their intense staining by the dyes used to visualize structures under a microscope).

As the chromosomes condense, the nuclear membrane breaks down, and the chromosomes become linked, at their centromeres, to spindle fibers. The **spindle fibers**, composed of microtubules, generate the forces that divide the cell. Some of the spindle fibers extend between two **centrioles** (Figure 4-20C) located on opposite sides of the cell, while others connect the centrioles to the chromosomes. During the preceding interphase, at the time that DNA was replicating, the second centriole formed and the two centrioles moved to opposite sides of the nucleus and began to generate the spindle fibers. The spindle fibers and centrioles constitute the **mitotic apparatus**. A single centriole will pass to each of the daughter cells during cytokinesis.

As mitosis proceeds, the sister chromatids in each chromosome separate at the centromere and move toward the opposed centrioles (Figure 4-20D). Cytokinesis begins as the sister chromatids separate. The cell begins to constrict along a plane perpendicular to the axis of the mitotic apparatus, and constriction continues until the cell has been pinched in half, forming the two daughter cells (Figure 4-20E). Following cytokinesis, the spindle fibers dissolve, a nuclear envelope forms, and the chromatids uncoil in each daughter cell to form chromatin threads once again.

The forces producing the movements associated with mitosis and cytokinesis are generated by a family of contractile proteins similar to those producing the forces generated by muscle cells (see Chapter 11).

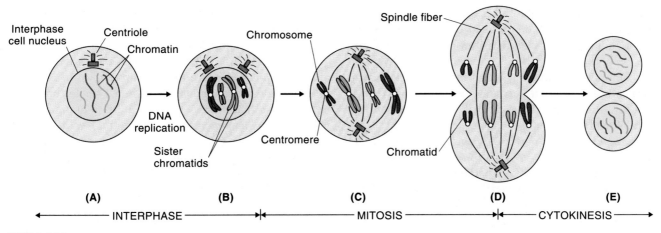

FIGURE 4-20

Mitosis and cytokinesis. (Only 4 of the 46 chromosomes in a human cell are illustrated.) (A) During interphase, chromatin exists in the nucleus as long, extended threads. (B) Prior to the onset of mitosis, DNA replicates, forming two sister chromatids that are joined at the centromere. A second centriole is also formed at this time. (C) As mitosis begins, the chromatids condense into chromosomes, which become attached to spindle fibers. (D) The two chromatids of each chromosome separate and move toward opposite poles of the cell as the cell divides (cytokinesis) into two daughter cells (E).

There are two classes of cells in the adult body with regard to the capacity to undergo cell division. Some cells proceed continuously through one cell cycle after another, while others do not normally divide. The first group constitutes the stem cells that provide a continuous supply of cells that differentiate into specialized cells to replace those that are continuously lost, such as blood cells, skin cells, and the cells lining the intestinal tract. The second class includes a number of differentiated, specialized cell types, such as nerve and striated muscle cells, that never divide once they have been formed. Such cells leave the cell cycle and enter a phase known as G_0 (Figure 4-19) in which they are prevented from progressing on to the next division. In some cases, however, a cell in the G_0 phase, upon receiving an appropriate signal, can reenter the cell cycle, begin replicating DNA, and proceed on to mitosis.

There are two critical control points in the cell cycle, at which special events must occur in order for a cell to progress to the next phase. One is at the boundary between G_1 and S, and again between G_2 and M. A group of **cell division cycle genes** (cdc genes) code for specific protein kinase enzymes that are essential for the cell to progress beyond its current phase in the cycle.

A protein, called **cyclin**, whose concentration progressively increases during interphase and then rapidly falls during mitosis, acts as a modulator molecule to activate the kinase enzymes produced by the cdc genes. Once activated, the kinase enzymes phosphorylate, and thus activate or inhibit, a variety of proteins involved in the division process, including an enzyme that digests cyclin and thus prepares the cell to begin the next division cycle.

Mutation

In order to form the 40 trillion cells of the adult human body, a minimum of 40 trillion individual cell divisions must occur.[5] Thus, the DNA in the original fertilized egg must be replicated at least 40 trillion times. Actually, many more than 40 trillion divisions occur during the growth of a fertilized egg into an adult human being since, as noted earlier, many cells die during development and are replaced by the division of existing cells.

If a secretary were to type the same manuscript 40 trillion times, one would expect to find some typing errors. Likewise, it is not surprising to find that during the duplication of DNA, errors occur that result in an altered sequence of bases and a change in the genetic message. What is amazing is that DNA can be duplicated so many times with relatively few errors.

A mechanism called **proofreading** corrects errors in the base sequence as it is being duplicated and is largely responsible for the low error rate observed during DNA replication. As described earlier, the replication process involves pairing between the base in a free deoxyribonucleotide and the appropriate complementary base in the old strand of DNA. DNA polymerase catalyzes the linking

---

[5]To be absolutely accurate, one less than 40 trillion cell divisions.

of the free nucleotide to the end of the new strand of DNA and then proceeds to the next nucleotide pair along the chain. If, however, an incorrect free nucleotide has become temporarily paired with a base in the old strand of DNA (for example, C pairing with A rather than its appropriate partner G), the DNA polymerase somehow "recognizes" this abnormal pairing and will not proceed in the linking of nucleotides until the abnormal pairing has been replaced. Note that in performing this proofreading, the DNA polymerase needs to identify only two configurations, the normal A-T and G-C pairing; any other combination halts polymerase activity. In this manner each nucleotide, as it is inserted into the new DNA chain, is checked for its appropriate complementarity to the base in the old chain.

Any alteration in the genetic message carried by DNA is known as a **mutation**. Factors in the environment that increase the mutation rate are known as **mutagens** and include certain chemicals and various forms of ionizing radiation, such as x-rays, cosmic rays, and atomic radiation. Most of these mutagens break chemical bonds in DNA so that incorrect pairing between bases occurs or the wrong base is incorporated when the broken bonds are reformed. Even in the absence of specific agents that increase the likelihood of mutations, the mutation rate is never zero.

The simplest type of mutation occurs when a single base is inserted at the wrong position in DNA. For example, the base sequence C-G-T forms the DNA code word for the amino acid alanine. If guanine (G) is replaced by adenine (A) in this sequence, it becomes C-A-T, which is the code word for valine.[6] It is during the replication of DNA, when free nucleotides are being incorporated into new strands of DNA, that incorrect base substitution is most likely to occur.

In a second type of mutation, large sections of DNA are deleted from the molecule or single bases are added or deleted. Such mutations may result in the loss of an entire gene or group of genes or may cause the misreading of a large sequence of bases. Figure 4-21 shows the effect of removing a single base on the reading of the genetic code. Since the code is read in sequences of three bases, the removal of one base not only alters the code word containing that base but also causes a misreading of all subsequent bases by shifting the reading sequence. Addition of

an extra base would cause a similar misreading. Such mutations result either in no protein being formed, if the gene has been deleted, or in the formation of a nonsense protein, a protein in which the amino acid sequence does not correspond to any functional protein.

Assume that a mutation has altered a single code word in a gene so that it now codes for a different amino acid, for example, alanine C-G-T changed to valine C-A-T. What effect does this mutation have upon the cell? The answer depends partly upon the type of gene and where in the gene the mutation has occurred. Although proteins are composed of many amino acids, the properties of a protein often depend upon only a very small region of the total molecule, such as the binding site of an enzyme. If the mutation does not alter the conformation of the binding site, there may be little or no change in the protein's properties. On the other hand, if the mutation alters the binding site, a marked change in the protein's properties may occur. Thus, if the protein is an enzyme, a mutation may change its affinity for a substrate or render it totally inactive.

If such a mutated enzyme is in a pathway supplying most of a cell's chemical energy, the loss of the enzyme *could* lead to the death of the cell. The story is more complex, however, since the cell contains a second gene for this enzyme, one which has not been mutated and is able to form an active enzyme. Thus, little or no change in cell function would result from this mutation. If both genes had mutations that rendered their products inactive, then no functional enzyme would be formed and the cell would die. In contrast, if the active enzyme were involved in the synthesis of a particular amino acid, and if the cell could obtain that amino acid from the extracellular fluid, the cell's functioning would not be impaired by the absence of the enzyme.

To generalize, a mutation may have any one of three effects upon a cell: (1) It may cause no noticeable change in the cell's functioning; (2) it may modify cell function but still be compatible with cell growth and replication; or (3) it may lead to cell death.

With one exception—cancer, to be described below—the malfunction of a single cell, other than a sperm or egg, as a result of a mutation usually has no significant effect because there are so many cells performing the same function in an organ. Unfortunately, the story is different when the mutation occurs in a sperm or egg since these cells combine to form the fertilized egg from which all the cells of a new individual will develop. In this case, the mutation will be passed on to *all* the cells in the body. Thus, mutations in the sperm or egg do not affect the individual in which they occur but do affect, often catastrophically, the child produced by these cells. Moreover, these mutations will also be passed on to some individuals in future generations descended from the individual carrying the original mutant gene.

---

[6]Because the genetic code has several different code words representing the same amino acid, a mutation in a single code word does not always alter the type of amino acid coded. We saw that substituting A for G in the alanine code word C-G-T produced the valine code word C-A-T. If, instead, the mutation caused cytosine C to be substituted for thymine T, the protein formed by the mutant gene would not be altered in amino acid sequence in spite of the change in base sequence because the new codon C-G-C is one of several that correspond to alanine.

FIGURE 4-21
A deletion mutation caused by the loss of a single base G in one of the two DNA strands causes a misreading of all code words beyond the point of the mutation.

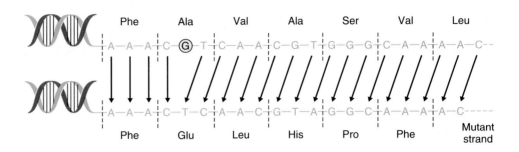

Inherited diseases resulting from gene mutation are termed ***inborn errors of metabolism***. An example is ***phenylketonuria***, a disorder that can lead to a form of mental retardation in children. Because of a single abnormal enzyme, these individuals are unable to convert the amino acid phenylalanine to the amino acid tyrosine at a normal rate. Phenylalanine is therefore diverted into other biochemical pathways in large amounts, giving rise to products that interfere with the normal activity of the nervous system. These products are also excreted in large amounts in the urine, accounting for the name of the disease. Fortunately, the symptoms of the disease can be prevented if the content of phenylalanine in the diet is restricted during childhood, thus preventing accumulation of the toxic products formed from phenylalanine.

Cells possess a number of enzymatic mechanisms for repairing DNA that has been damaged by chemical or physical trauma. Such abnormalities include breaks, loss of nucleotides, and formation of abnormal bases as a result of the loss or addition of chemical groups on the bases. These alterations result in abnormal molecular shapes that are recognized by the repair enzymes. These repair mechanisms all depend on the damage occurring in only one of the two DNA strands, so that the undamaged strand can provide the correct code for rebuilding the damaged strand. One set of repair enzymes identifies an abnormal region in one of the DNA strands. The enzymes then cut out the damaged segment, and DNA polymerase rebuilds the segment by base-pairing with the undamaged strand just as it did during DNA replication. Now, however, only a small segment of DNA is being replaced rather than the whole molecule. If adjacent regions in both strands of DNA are damaged, a permanent mutation is created which cannot be repaired by these mechanisms.

This repair mechanism is particularly important for long-lived cells, such as nerve and muscle cells, that do not divide and therefore do not replicate their DNA. This means that the same molecule of DNA in these cells must continue to function and maintain the stability of its genetic information for as long as the individual lives, which could be 100 years or even more.

Mutations contribute to evolution. Mutations may alter the activity of an enzyme in such a way that it is more, rather than less, active, or they may introduce an entirely new type of enzyme activity into a cell. If an organism carrying such a mutant gene is able to perform some function more effectively than an organism lacking the mutant gene, it has a better chance of surviving and passing the mutant gene on to its descendants. If the mutation produces an organism that functions less effectively than organisms lacking the mutation, the organism is less likely to survive and pass on the mutant gene. This is the principle of **natural selection**. Although any one mutation, if it is able to survive in the population, may cause only a very slight alteration in the properties of a cell, given enough time, a large number of small changes can accumulate to produce very large changes in the structure and function of an organism.

Recombinant DNA

Since a number of diseases are known to be the result of mutated genes, one approach to curing such diseases would be to replace the abnormal gene with a normal one. What was once a theoretical possibility is approaching the point of being a reality, at least under some circumstances. A tremendous number of technical problems must be solved before gene transfers become a practical approach to treating genetic diseases. First, the location of the normal gene on its chromosome must be identified, the gene isolated, its base sequence determined, and copies of the base sequence manufactured—a process known as **gene cloning**. Then a mechanism must be developed to insert copies of the normal gene into the DNA of mutated cells, forming **recombinant DNA**.

In the early 1970s, bacterial enzymes were discovered that split molecules of DNA in a unique manner. These enzymes, called **restriction nucleases**, identify specific nucleotide sequences, usually four to six nucleotides long, and in this region they cut DNA at a different site on each strand (Figure 4-22). Each of the cut strands has a short, exposed sequence of bases that are complementary to each other. If the DNA from two cells is cut by the same restriction nuclease, then a DNA fragment from one cell can base-pair with the complementary end of a DNA segment from a second cell. Another enzyme, known as a ligase, can then covalently link the two molecules of DNA

FIGURE 4-22

The basis of recombinant DNA. (A) Bacterial restriction enzymes break the two strands of DNA at different points, producing ends with exposed bases that are complementary to each other. (B) A segment of DNA containing one or more genes from one organism (donor) can be inserted into the DNA of another organism (host) by using these restriction enzymes to produce DNA segments whose ends can bind together.

together. By this procedure, DNA fragments (genes) from one cell can be inserted into the DNA from a second cell to form recombinant DNA.

The next step in replacing a mutated gene with a normal gene is to devise a means of inserting the recombinant DNA into a cell since a cell's plasma membrane is impermeable to these large DNA molecules. One method is to insert the gene into the nucleic acid of a virus and then infect cells with the altered virus. As will be described in Chapter 20, some viral nucleic acids become incorporated into the host's DNA and thus the virus acts as a carrier to get the recombinant DNA into the cell. When the recombinant DNA is inserted into a living cell, its genetic message is transcribed into mRNA along with the messages from the host's genes and then translated into protein.

It is hoped that techniques employing recombinant DNA may one day provide the ability to selectively replace mutant genes in humans with normal genes and thus provide a cure for genetic diseases. This recombinant DNA technology is already providing many practical benefits. For example, inserting the gene that codes for human insulin into bacterial DNA leads to the production of insulin

by the bacteria. Large amounts of this protein hormone can then be produced and used to treat diabetic patients who are unable to synthesize their own insulin.

On the other hand, this technology bears potential hazards. For example, it would be theoretically possible to insert a gene that codes for a toxic protein into a harmless bacterium that commonly inhabits the human gastrointestinal tract and thereby produce a widespread epidemic.

CANCER

n an adult, the rates at which new cells in a tissue are formed and old cells die are in balance, producing a steady state in which the tissue does not increase in size. If the mechanisms regulating cell division are not functioning properly, however, the affected cells may produce new cells faster than old cells are removed, forming a growing mass of tissue known as a *tumor*. If the tumor cells remain localized and do not invade surrounding tissues, the tumor is said to be a ***benign tumor***. If, however, the tumor cells grow into the surrounding tissues, disrupting their functions, and/or spread to other regions of the body, the tumor is said to be a ***malignant tumor*** and may lead to the death of the organism.

Malignant tumors are composed of ***cancer cells***, which are cells that have lost the ability to respond to the normal mechanisms that regulate cell growth. Cancer cells are characterized by their capacity for unlimited multiplication and for their ability to break away from the parent tumor. They spread by way of the circulatory system to other parts of the body, where they form multiple tumor sites, a process known as ***metastasis***.

Approximately 1200 Americans die each day from cancer. Fifty percent of all cancer deaths occur from cancers in three organs—the lung (28 percent), the colon (13 percent), and the breast (9 percent). About 90 percent of cancers develop in epithelial cells and are known as ***carcinomas***. Those derived from connective tissue and muscle are called ***sarcomas***, and those from blood cells are ***leukemias*** and ***lymphomas***.

If a cancer is detected in the early stages of its growth, before it has metastasized, the tumor may be removed by surgery. Once it has metastasized to many organs, surgery is no longer possible. Drugs and radiation can be used to inhibit cell multiplication and destroy malignant cells, both before and after metastasis. Unfortunately these treatments also damage the growth of normal cells. Other treatments, which utilize the body's own immune defenses against cancer, are described in Chapter 20.

Any normal cell in the body may at some point undergo transformation to a malignant cell. A number of agents known as ***carcinogens***, such as radiation, viruses, and certain chemicals, can induce the cancerous transformation of cells. These agents act mainly by altering or activating various genes associated with cell growth. Thus, mutagenic agents also tend to be carcinogenic. It is estimated that approximately 90 percent of all cancers are the result of environmental factors and life style.

The transformation of a normal cell into a cancer cell is a multistep process that involves altering not only the mechanisms that regulate cell replication but also those that control the invasiveness of the cell and its ability to subvert the body's defense mechanisms. (As will be discussed in Chapter 20, the body's defense system is normally able to detect and destroy most cancerous cells.) In most cases a cancer cell does not arise in its fully malignant form from a single mutation, but progresses through various stages from the benign to the malignant state as a result of successive mutations. The incidence of cancer increases with age as a result of the accumulation of these mutations. Some of the early stages of transformation result in changes in the cell's morphology, known as ***dysplasia***, a precancerous state that can be detected by microscopic examination. At this stage the cell has not yet

acquired a capacity for unlimited growth or an ability to invade surrounding tissues.

Over the last 20 years a growing number of genes have been identified that contribute to the cancerous state when they become mutated. These cancer-related genes fall into two classes: dominant and recessive. The dominant cancer-producing genes[7] are called ***oncogenes*** (Greek: *onkos*, mass, tumor—the branch of medicine that deals with cancer is known as oncology). Oncogenes arise as mutations of normal genes known as proto-oncogenes.

The second class of genes involved in cancer are recessive genes known as ***tumor suppressor genes***. In their unmutated state these genes prevent the cancerous transformations produced by oncogenes. Mutation of one of the allelic pair of tumor suppressor genes inactivates its function but leaves a normal gene on the homologous chromosome that can still function to suppress tumor development. It is only when both alleles of the tumor suppressor genes have been mutated that the cell becomes cancerous.

Although a number of proto-oncogenes and tumor suppressor genes have been identified, little is currently known about how they function or how their altered function leads to uncontrolled growth. Some produce protein kinases that modulate the functions of other proteins, others produce transcription factors that control the transcription of specific genes, while still others produce proteins that act as binding sites for various regulatory molecules, such as growth factors. Thus, all cancer-related genes do not produce products with similar functions.

In addition to the mutations occurring in proto-oncogenes and tumor suppressor genes, a number of additional factors not related to mutations can influence the development of cancer. The normal growth of many types of cells is stimulated by various hormones and growth factors. Many cancer cells retain the ability to respond to these growth-promoting signals. These stimulating agents may also contribute to the progression of the tumor to a more malignant stage since rapidly dividing cells are more susceptible to mutations, which often occur during the process of replicating DNA. Thus, removing or inhibiting the actions of these stimulating agents can reduce the growth rates and progression of certain tumors. An example is the effect of estrogen on some forms of breast cancer.

Through a better understanding of the molecular processes that control both normal and abnormal growth, the means of combating cancerous growths may be found.

---

[7]Although dominant, and only a single copy of the mutated gene must be present, the full cancerous effects of the gene will not be expressed unless several other genes in the cell have also been mutated.

SECTION B SUMMARY

GENETIC CODE

I. Each individual inherits two copies of each gene, one from the mother and one from the father. These allelic genes can be classified as either dominant or recessive.

II. Genetic information is coded in the nucleotide sequence of DNA. A single gene contains either (a) the information that, via mRNA, determines the amino acid sequence in a specific protein, or (b) the information for forming rRNA or tRNA, which assists in protein assembly.

III. Genetic information is transferred from DNA to mRNA in the nucleus, and then mRNA passes to the cytoplasm, where its information is used to synthesize protein.

IV. The words in the DNA genetic code consist of a sequence of three nucleotide bases that specify a single amino acid. The sequence of triplet code words along a gene determines the sequence of amino acids in a protein. There can be more than one code word specifying a given amino acid.

PROTEIN SYNTHESIS

I. Protein synthesis involves (a) transcription of genetic information from DNA to mRNA, which occurs in the nucleus, and (b) translation of the information in mRNA into protein, which occurs in the cytoplasm on the surface of ribosomes. Table 4-1 summarizes the steps leading from DNA to protein and the role of tRNA.

II. Proteins secreted by cells pass through the sequence of steps illustrated in Figure 4-16.

III. The rate of protein synthesis can be regulated by controlling (a) transcription of a gene into mRNA, (b) splicing of mRNA, (c) stability of mRNA, and (d) translation of mRNA by ribosomes.

REPLICATION AND EXPRESSION OF GENETIC INFORMATION

I. When DNA replicates, exposed bases in each of the two unwound strands base-pair with bases of free deoxyribonucleotide triphosphates. DNA polymerase joins the nucleotides together to form a new strand of DNA.

II. When a cell divides, one copy of DNA passes to each daughter cell, so that both receive the same set of genetic instructions.

III. Cell division, consisting of nuclear division—mitosis—and cytoplasmic division—cytokinesis—lasts about 1 h.

IV. During interphase, DNA replicates, forming two identical sister chromatids joined by a centromere.

V. The main events of mitosis are:
A. The chromatids condense into highly coiled chromosomes.
B. The centromeres of each chromosome become attached to spindle fibers extending from the centrioles, which have migrated to opposite poles of the nucleus.
C. The two chromatids of each chromosome separate and move toward opposite poles of the cell as the cell divides into two daughter cells. Following cell division, the condensed chromatids uncoil into their extended interphase form.

VI. Entry into the S and M phases of the cell cycle is dependent on the activity of enzymes coded by cell division cycle genes. These enzymes are activated by cyclin.

VII. Proofreading mechanisms help prevent the introduction of errors during DNA replication.

VIII. Mutations occur when incorrect bases are inserted into new strands of DNA during replication or when single bases or large sections of DNA are added or deleted.
A. A mutation may (a) cause no noticeable change in a cell's function, (b) modify cell function but still be compatible with cell growth and replication, or (c) lead to the death of the cell.
B. Mutations occurring in egg or sperm cells will be passed on to all the cells on a new individual and possibly to some of the individuals in future generations.

IX. DNA repair mechanisms are important in preventing the accumulation of mutations, particularly in long-lived cells that do not divide.

X. With the use of bacterial enzymes, segments of DNA can be cut from the DNA of one cell and inserted into the DNA of another cell to form recombinant DNA. The recombinant DNA will then direct the synthesis of proteins coded by the donor DNA in the host cell.

XI. Cancer cells are characterized by their capacity for unlimited multiplication and their ability to metastasize to other parts of the body, forming multiple tumor sites.
A. Mutations in proto-oncogenes and tumor suppressor genes lead to cancer.

B. More than one mutation is necessary to cause the transformation of a normal cell into a cancer cell.

SECTION B KEY TERMS

gene	signal sequence
genome	transcription factors
alleles	DNA polymerase
homozygous	daughter cells
heterozygous	interphase
dominant genes	mitosis
recessive genes	cytokinesis
termination code words	chromatin
genetic code	sister chromatids
messenger RNA (mRNA)	centromere
transcription	chromosomes
translation	spindle fibers
RNA polymerase	centrioles
promoter	mitotic apparatus
codon	cell division cycle genes
exons	cyclin
introns	proofreading
ribosomal RNA (rRNA)	natural selection
transfer RNA (tRNA)	gene cloning
anticodon	recombinant DNA
chaperones	restriction nucleases

SECTION B REVIEW QUESTIONS

1. Describe the differences between a dominant and a recessive gene.
2. Summarize the direction of information flow during protein synthesis.
3. Describe the way in which the genetic code in DNA specifies the amino acid sequence in a protein.
4. List the four nucleotides used to form mRNA.
5. Describe the main events that occur during the transcription of genetic information into mRNA.
6. List the components of a ribosome and identify the site of ribosomal subunit assembly.
7. Describe the role of tRNA in protein assembly.
8. Describe the events of protein translation that occur on the surface of a ribosome.
9. Describe the pathway that leads to the secretion of proteins from cells.
10. What is the function of the signal sequence of a protein?

11. List the ways in which regulation of protein synthesis can occur.
12. Describe the mechanism by which DNA is replicated.
13. Summarize the main events of mitosis and cytokinesis.
14. Describe the role of cell division cycle genes and the protein cyclin in controlling cell division.
15. How will the deletion of a single base in a gene affect the protein synthesized?
16. List the three effects that a mutation can have on a cell's function.
17. Describe the mechanism by which recombinant DNA is formed.
18. Describe the characteristics of a cancer cell.
19. Describe the difference between an oncogene and a tumor suppressor gene.
20. Describe how various environmental factors can increase the risk of cancer.

CHAPTER 4 CLINICAL TERMS

mutation	carcinomas
mutagens	sarcomas
inborn errors of metabolism	leukemias
phenylketonuria	lymphomas
tumor	carcinogens
benign tumor	dysplasia
malignant tumor	oncogenes
cancer cells	tumor suppressor genes
metastasis	

CHAPTER 4 THOUGHT QUESTIONS

(Answers are given in Appendix A.)

1. A variety of chemical messengers that normally regulate acid secretion in the stomach bind to proteins in the plasma membranes of the acid-secreting cells. Some of these binding reactions lead to increased acid secretion, and others inhibit its secretion. In what ways might a drug that inhibits acid secretion be acting on these cells?

2. In one type of diabetes the plasma concentration of the hormone insulin is normal, but the response of the cells to which insulin usually binds is markedly decreased. Suggest a reason for this in terms of the properties of protein binding sites.

3. Given the following substances in a cell and their effects on each other, predict the change in compound H that will result from an increase in compound A and diagram this sequence of changes.

Compound A is a modulator molecule that allosterically activates protein B.

Protein B is a protein kinase enzyme that activates protein C.

Protein C is an enzyme that converts substrate D to product E.

Compound E is a modulator molecule that allosterically inhibits protein F.

Protein F is an enzyme that converts substrate G to product H.

4. Shown below is the relation between the amount of acid secreted and the concentration of compound X, which stimulates acid secretion in the stomach by binding to a membrane protein. At a plasma concentration of 2 pM, compound X produces an acid secretion of 20 mmol/h.

a. Specify two ways in which acid secretion by compound X could be increased to 40 mmol/h.

b. Why will increasing the concentration of compound X to 28 pM not produce more acid secretion than increasing the concentration of X to 18 pM?

5. What would be the consequences for protein regulation of a mutation that has led to the loss of phosphoprotein phosphatase from cells?

6. A base sequence in a portion of one strand of DNA is A-G-T-G-C-A-A-G-T-C-T. Predict:

a. The base sequence in the corresponding strand of DNA.

b. The base sequence in mRNA transcribed from the sequence shown.

7. The triplet code in DNA for the amino acid histidine is G-T-A. Predict the mRNA codon for this amino acid and the tRNA anticodon.

8. If a protein contains 100 amino acids, how many nucleotides will be present in the gene that codes for this protein?

9. Why will chemical agents that inhibit the polymerization of tubulin (Chapter 3, page 50) inhibit cell division?

10. Why are drugs that inhibit the replication of DNA potentially useful in the treatment of cancer? What are some of the limitations of such drugs?

CHAPTER
5

ENERGY AND CELLULAR METABOLISM

Thousands of chemical reactions occur each instant throughout the body, this entire collection of reactions being termed **metabolism** (Greek: change). Metabolism includes the synthesis of the specific molecules required for cell structure and function, the breakdown of these molecules, and the provision of energy for cell functions. The synthesis of organic molecules by cells is called **anabolism**, and their breakdown, **catabolism**.

The body's organic molecules undergo continuous transformations as some molecules are broken down while others of the same type are being synthesized. Chemically, no person is the same at noon as at 8 o'clock in the morning since during even this short period much of the body's structure has been torn apart and replaced with newly synthesized molecules. In adults the body's composition is in a steady state in which the anabolic and catabolic rates for the synthesis and breakdown of most molecules are equal.

This chapter describes four aspects of metabolism: (1) the factors that determine the rates of chemical reactions; (2) the role of enzymes in accelerating chemical reactions and how enzyme activity can be controlled; (3) the biochemical pathways by which energy is obtained from the breakdown of carbohydrates, fats, and proteins; and (4) the pathways by which carbohydrates and fats are synthesized. (The pathway for protein synthesis was described in Chapter 4.) We begin by discussing the characteristics of chemical reactions because these concepts underlie all the other chapter topics.

CHEMICAL REACTIONS

Chemical reactions involve (1) the breaking of chemical bonds in reactant molecules, followed by (2) the making of new chemical bonds to form the product molecules. In the chemical reaction in which carbonic acid is transformed into carbon dioxide and water, for example, two of the chemical bonds in carbonic acid are broken and the product molecules are formed by establishing two new bonds between different pairs of atoms:

$$H-O-\overset{\overset{O}{\|}}{C}-O-H \longrightarrow O=\overset{\overset{O}{\|}}{C} + H-O-H$$

Broken   Broken   Formed   Formed

$$H_2CO_3 \longrightarrow CO_2 + H_2O$$

Carbonic   Carbon   Water
acid   dioxide

Since the energy contents of the reactants and products are usually different, and because energy can neither be created nor be destroyed, energy must either be added or released during a chemical reaction. For example, the reaction in which carbonic acid breaks down into carbon dioxide and water occurs with the release of 4 kcal of energy per mole of products formed since carbonic acid has a higher energy content (155 kcal/mol) than the sum of the energy contents of carbon dioxide and water (94 + 57 = 151 kcal/mol).

The energy that is released appears as heat, the energy of increased molecular motion, which is measured in units of calories. One **calorie** (1 cal) is the amount of heat required to raise the temperature of 1 g of water 1° on the Celsius scale. Energies associated with most chemical reactions are several thousand calories per mole and are reported as **kilocalories** (1 kcal = 1000 cal).

Determinants of Reaction Rates

The rate of a chemical reaction (in other words, how rapidly the products of the reaction are formed) can be determined by measuring the change in the concentration of reactants or products per unit of time. The faster the product concentration increases or the reactant concentration decreases, the greater the rate of the reaction. Four factors (Table 5-1) influence the reaction rate: reactant concentration, activation energy, temperature, and the presence of a catalyst.

The lower the concentration of reactants, the slower the reaction simply because there are fewer molecules available to react. Conversely, the higher the concentration of reactants, the faster the reaction rate.

Given the same initial concentrations of reactants, however, all reactions do not occur at the same rate. Each type of chemical reaction has its own characteristic rate, which depends upon what is called the activation energy for the

---

TABLE 5-1   DETERMINANTS OF CHEMICAL REACTION RATES

Reactant concentrations (higher concentrations:
   faster reaction rate)

Activation energy (higher activation energy:
   slower reaction rate)

Temperature (higher temperature: faster reaction rate)

Catalyst (increases reaction rate)

reaction. In order for a chemical reaction to occur, reactant molecules must acquire enough energy—the **activation energy**—to enter an activated state in which chemical bonds can be broken and formed. The activation energy does not alter the difference in energy content between the reactants and final products since this energy is released when the products are formed.

How do reactants acquire activation energy? In most of the metabolic reactions we will be considering, activation energy is obtained when reactants collide with other molecules. If the activation energy required for a reaction is large, then the probability of a given reactant molecule acquiring this amount of energy will be small, and the reaction rate will be slow. Thus, the higher the activation energy, the slower the rate of a chemical reaction.

Temperature is the third factor influencing reaction rates. The higher the temperature, the faster molecules move and thus the greater their impact when they collide. Therefore, one reason that increasing the temperature increases a reaction rate is that reactants have a better chance of acquiring sufficient activation energy from a collision. In addition, faster-moving molecules will collide more frequently.

A **catalyst** is a substance that interacts with a reactant in such a manner that it alters the distribution of energy between the chemical bonds of the reactant, the result being a decrease in the activation energy required to transform the reactant into product. Since less activation energy is required, a reaction will proceed at a faster rate in the presence of a catalyst. The chemical composition of a catalyst is not altered by the reaction, and thus a single catalyst molecule can be used over and over again to catalyze the conversion of many reactant molecules to products. Furthermore, a catalyst does not alter the difference in the energy contents of the reactants and products.

Reversible and Irreversible Reactions

Consider our previous example in which carbonic acid breaks down into carbon dioxide and water. The products of this reaction, carbon dioxide and water, can also recombine to form carbonic acid:

$$CO_2 \quad + \quad H_2O \quad + 4\,kcal/mol \quad \longrightarrow \quad H_2CO_3$$
$$\text{94 kcal/mol} \qquad \text{57 kcal/mol} \qquad\qquad\qquad \text{155 kcal/mol}$$

Since carbonic acid has a greater content than the sum of the energies contained in carbon dioxide and water, energy must be added to the latter molecules in order to form carbonic acid. (This 4 kcal of energy is *not* activation energy but is an integral part of the energy balance.) This energy can be obtained, along with the activation energy, through collisions with other molecules.

Thus, in every chemical reaction there are two reactions going on simultaneously: a reaction (we will call it

"forward") in which reactants are converted to products, and one (we will call it "reverse") in which products are converted to reactants. The overall reaction is said to be a **reversible reaction**:

$$\text{Reactants} \underset{\text{Reverse}}{\overset{\text{Forward}}{\rightleftharpoons}} \text{Products}$$

As a reaction progresses, the rate of the forward reaction will decrease as the concentration of reactants decreases. Simultaneously the rate of the reverse reaction will increase as the concentration of the product molecules increases. Eventually the reaction will reach a state of **chemical equilibrium** in which the forward and reverse reaction rates are equal. At this point there will be no further change in the concentrations of reactants or products even though reactants will continue to be converted into products and products converted to reactants.

When chemical equilibrium has been reached, the concentration of products need not be equal to the concentration of reactants even though the forward and reverse reaction rates are equal. The ratio of product concentration to reactant concentration at equilibrium depends upon the amount of energy released or added during the reaction. This is because the greater the energy released, the smaller the probability that the product molecules will be able to obtain this energy and undergo the reverse reaction to re-form reactants. Therefore, in this case, the ratio of product to reactant concentration at chemical equilibrium will be large.

To be specific, if there is no difference in the energy contents of reactants and products, their concentrations will be equal at equilibrium. If only a small amount of energy is released, on the order of 1 kcal or less, the product concentration at equilibrium will be between 1 and 10 times the reactant concentration. When larger amounts of energy are released, for example, 4 kcal, the ratio of product to reactant molecules at equilibrium is about 1000 to 1.

Thus, although all chemical reactions are reversible to some extent, reactions that release large quantities of energy are said to be **irreversible reactions** in the sense that almost all of the reactant molecules have been converted to product molecules when chemical equilibrium is reached. A single arrow is used to indicate an irreversible reaction, and a double arrow for a reversible reaction. It must be emphasized that the energy released in a reaction determines the degree to which the reaction is reversible or irreversible. This energy is *not* the activation energy and it does *not* determine the reaction rate, which is governed by the four factors discussed earlier. The characteristics of reversible and irreversible reactions are summarized in Table 5-2.

TABLE 5-2 CHARACTERISTICS OF REVERSIBLE AND IRREVERSIBLE CHEMICAL REACTIONS

Reversible reactions	$A + B \rightleftharpoons C + D$ + small amount of energy
	At chemical equilibrium, product concentrations are only slightly higher than reactant concentrations.
Irreversible reactions	$E + F \longrightarrow G + H$ + large amount of energy
	At chemical equilibrium, almost all reactant molecules have been converted to product.

Law of Mass Action

The concentrations of reactants and products play a very important role in determining not only the rates of the forward and reverse reactions but also the direction in which the *net* reaction proceeds—whether products are accumulating or reactants are accumulating at a given time.

Consider the following reversible reaction that has reached chemical equilibrium:

$$A + B \underset{\text{Reverse}}{\overset{\text{Forward}}{\rightleftharpoons}} C + D$$

$$\underbrace{}_{\text{Reactants}} \qquad \underbrace{}_{\text{Products}}$$

If at this point we increase the concentration of one of the reactants, the rate of the forward reaction will increase and lead to increased product formation. In contrast, increasing the concentration of one of the product molecules will drive the reaction in the reverse direction, increasing the formation of reactants. The direction in which the net reaction is proceeding can also be altered by *lowering* the concentration of one of the participants. Thus, lowering the concentration of one of the products will drive the net reaction in the forward direction since it will lower the rate of the reverse reaction without changing the rate of the forward reaction.

These effects of reactant and product concentrations on the direction in which the net reaction is proceeding are known as the **law of mass action**. Mass action is often a major determining factor controlling the direction in which metabolic pathways proceed.

ENZYMES

Most of the chemical reactions that occur in the body, if carried out in a test tube with only reactants and products present, would proceed at very low rates because they have high activation energies. In order to achieve the high reaction rates observed in living organisms, catalysts are required to lower the activation energy.

These particular catalysts are called enzymes (meaning "in yeast," since the first enzymes were discovered in yeast cells). Enzymes are protein molecules, and so an **enzyme** can be defined as a protein catalyst.[1]

To function, an enzyme must come into contact with reactants, which are called **substrates** in the case of enzyme-mediated reactions. The substrate becomes bound to the enzyme, forming an enzyme-substrate complex, which breaks down to release products and enzyme (Figure 5-1). The reaction between enzyme and substrate can be written:

$$\underset{\text{Substrate}}{S} + \underset{\text{Enzyme}}{E} \rightleftharpoons \underset{\substack{\text{Enzyme-}\\\text{substrate}\\\text{complex}}}{ES} \rightleftharpoons \underset{\text{Product}}{P} + \underset{\text{Enzyme}}{E}$$

At the end of the reaction, the enzyme is free to undergo the same reaction with additional substrate molecules. The overall effect is to accelerate the conversion of substrate into product, the enzyme acting as a catalyst.

The interaction between substrate and enzyme has all the characteristics described in Chapter 4 for the binding of a ligand to a binding site on a protein—specificity, affinity, competition, and saturation. The region of the enzyme to which the substrate binds is known as the enzyme's **active site** (a term equivalent to "binding site"). The shape of the enzyme in the region of the active site provides the basis for the enzyme's chemical specificity since the shape of the active site is complementary to the substrate's shape (Figure 5-1).

There are approximately 4000 different enzymes in a typical cell, each capable of catalyzing a different chemical reaction. Enzymes are generally named by adding the suffix *-ase* to the name of either the substrate or the type of reaction catalyzed by the enzyme. For example, the reaction in which carbonic acid is broken down into carbon dioxide and water is catalyzed by the enzyme carbonic anhydrase.

---

[1]Some RNA molecules possess catalytic activity, but the number of reactions they catalyze is very small, and so we shall restrict the term "enzyme" to protein catalysts.

FIGURE 5-1
Binding of substrate to the active site of an enzyme catalyzes the formation of products.

The catalytic activity of an enzyme can be extremely large. For example, a single molecule of carbonic anhydrase can catalyze the conversion of about 100,000 substrate molecules to products in 1 s.

The major characteristics of enzymes are listed in Table 5-3.

TABLE 5-3 CHARACTERISTICS OF ENZYMES

1. An enzyme undergoes no net chemical change as a consequence of the reaction it catalyzes.
2. The binding of substrate to an enzyme's active site has all the characteristics—chemical specificity, affinity, competition, and saturation—of a ligand binding to a protein.
3. An enzyme increases the rate of a chemical reaction but does not cause a reaction to occur that would not occur in its absence.
4. An enzyme increases both the forward and reverse rates of a chemical reaction and thus does not change the chemical equilibrium that is finally reached. It only increases the rate at which equilibrium is achieved.
5. An enzyme lowers the activation energy of a reaction but does not alter the net amount of energy that is added to or released by the reactants in the course of the reaction.

Cofactors

Many enzymes are inactive in the absence of small amounts of other substances known as **cofactors**. In some cases, the cofactor is a trace metal (Chapter 2), such as magnesium, iron, zinc, or copper, and its binding to an enzyme alters the conformation of the enzyme so that the enzyme can interact with the substrate. Since only a few enzyme molecules need be present to catalyze the conversion of large amounts of substrate to product, very small quantities of these trace metals are sufficient to maintain enzymatic activity.

In other cases the cofactor is an organic molecule that directly participates as one of the substrates in the reaction being catalyzed, in which case the cofactor is termed a **coenzyme**. Enzymes that require coenzymes catalyze reactions in which a few atoms, for example, hydrogen, acetyl, or methyl groups, are either removed from or added to a substrate. For example:

$$R—2H + coenzyme \underset{}{\overset{Enzyme}{\rightleftharpoons}} R + coenzyme—2H$$

What makes a coenzyme different from an ordinary substrate is the fate of the coenzyme. In our example, the two hydrogen atoms that are transferred to the coenzyme can then be transferred from the coenzyme to another substrate with the aid of a second enzyme. This second reaction converts the coenzyme back to its original form, which becomes available to accept two more hydrogen atoms (Figure 5-2). A single coenzyme molecule can be used over and over again to transfer molecular fragments from one reaction to another. Thus, as with metallic cofactors, only small quantities of coenzymes are necessary to maintain the enzymatic reactions in which they participate.

Coenzymes are derived from a special class of nutrients known as vitamins. **Vitamins** are organic substances that are required in small amounts for health but cannot be synthesized in the body from other nutrients and therefore must be supplied by the diet. The coenzymes nicotinamide adenine dinucleotide (**NAD$^+$**) and flavine adenine dinucleotide (**FAD**) (Figure 5-2) are derived from the B vitamins niacin and riboflavin, respectively, and as we shall see, play major roles in energy metabolism by transferring hydrogen from one substrate to another.

REGULATION OF ENZYME-MEDIATED REACTIONS

The rate of an enzyme-mediated reaction in the body depends on substrate concentration and on the concentration and activity (a term defined below) of the en-

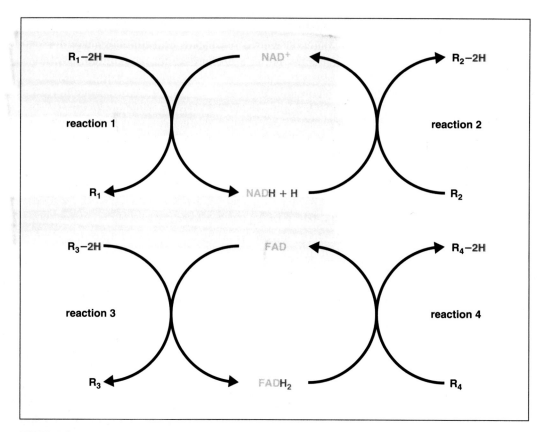

FIGURE 5-2

The coenzymes NAD^+ and FAD are used to transfer two hydrogen atoms from one reaction and donate them to a second reaction. In the process the hydrogen-free forms of the coenzymes are regenerated.

zyme that catalyzes the reaction. Since body temperature is normally maintained nearly constant, changes in temperature are not used directly to alter the rates of metabolic reactions. Increases in body temperature can occur during a fever, however, and around muscle tissue during exercise, and such increases in temperature increase the rates of all metabolic reactions in the affected tissues.

Substrate Concentration

Substrate concentration may be altered as a result of factors that alter the supply of a substrate from outside a cell. Thus, there may be changes in its blood concentration due, for example, to changes in diet or rate of substrate absorption from the intestinal tract. In addition, a substrate's entry into the cell through the plasma membrane can be controlled by mechanisms that will be discussed in Chapter 6. Intracellular substrate concentration can also be altered by reactions in a cell that either utilize the same substrate and thus tend to lower its concentration, or synthesize the substrate and thereby increase its intracellular concentration.

The rate of an enzyme-mediated reaction increases as the substrate concentration increases, as illustrated in Figure 5-3, until it reaches a maximal rate, which remains constant despite further increases in substrate concentration. The maximal rate is reached when the enzyme becomes saturated with substrate, that is, when the active site of every enzyme molecule is occupied by a substrate molecule.

Since coenzymes are substrates in certain enzyme reactions, changes in coenzyme concentration also affect reaction rates, as occurs with ordinary substrates.

Enzyme Concentration

At any substrate concentration, including saturating concentrations, the rate of an enzyme-mediated reaction can be increased by increasing the enzyme concentration. In most metabolic reactions, the substrate concentration is much greater than the small concentration of enzyme needed to catalyze the reaction. Therefore, if the number of enzyme molecules is doubled, twice as many active sites will be available to bind substrate, and twice as much sub-

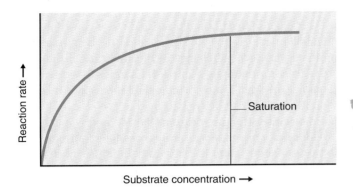

FIGURE 5-3

Rate of an enzyme-catalyzed reaction as a function of substrate concentration.

strate will be converted to product (Figure 5-4). Certain reactions proceed faster in some cells than in others because more enzyme molecules are present.

In order to change the concentration of an enzyme, either the rate of enzyme synthesis or the rate of enzyme breakdown must be altered. Since enzymes are proteins, this involves changing the rates of protein synthesis or breakdown. In Chapter 4 some of the mechanisms regulating protein synthesis were discussed; regulation of gene transcription is the primary mechanism for altering the synthesis and, hence, the concentrations of most enzymes. The substrate or product molecules of the reaction in which the enzyme takes part are often the molecules that lead to the activation or inhibition of gene transcription for the enzyme. Less is known about the factors controlling the selective breakdown of enzymes. Regardless of

whether altered synthesis or altered breakdown is involved, changing the concentration of enzymes is a relatively slow process, generally requiring several hours.

Enzyme Activity

In addition to changing the rate of enzyme-mediated reactions by changing the *concentration* of either substrate or enzyme, the rate can be altered by changing enzyme *activity*. Such a rate change occurs when the properties of the enzyme's active site are altered by either allosteric or covalent modulation (Chapter 4). Such modulation alters the rate at which the binding site converts substrate to product, or the affinity of the binding site for substrate, or both.

Figure 5-5 illustrates the effect of increasing the affinity of an enzyme's active site without changing the substrate (or enzyme) concentration. Provided the substrate concentration is less than the saturating concentration, the increased affinity of the enzyme's binding site will result in an increased number of active sites that contain bound substrate, and thus in the rate of the reaction.

The regulation of metabolism through the control of enzyme activity is an extremely complex process since, in many cases, the activity of an enzyme can be altered by more than one agent (Figure 5-6). The modulator molecules that *allosterically* alter enzyme activities are product molecules produced by other reactions in the cell. The result is that the overall rates of metabolism can be adjusted to meet various metabolic demands, as will be illustrated in the next section. In contrast, *covalent* modulation of enzyme activity is usually mediated by the activity of protein kinase enzymes (enzymes that phosphorylate specific proteins—Chapter 4) in response to various chemical signals received by a cell, for example, in response to a

FIGURE 5-4

Rate of an enzyme-catalyzed reaction as a function of substrate concentration at two enzyme concentrations: A and 2A. Enzyme concentration 2A is twice the enzyme concentration of A, resulting in a reaction that proceeds twice as fast at any substrate concentration.

FIGURE 5-5

At a constant substrate concentration, increasing the affinity of an enzyme for its substrate by allosteric or covalent modulation increases the rate of the enzyme-mediated reaction. Note that increasing the enzyme's affinity does not increase the *maximal* rate of the enzyme-mediated reaction.

FIGURE 5-6
On a single enzyme multiple sites can modulate the activity, and hence the reaction rate, either by increasing the affinity of the active site—allosteric and covalent activation—or by decreasing its affinity—allosteric and covalent inhibition.

hormone. (The mechanisms by which protein kinase enzymes are influenced by various messenger molecules will be described in Chapter 7.)

Figure 5-7 summarizes the factors that play a role in regulating the rate of an enzyme-mediated reaction.

MULTIENZYME METABOLIC PATHWAYS

he sequence of enzyme-mediated reactions leading to the formation of a particular product is known as a **metabolic pathway**. For example, the 19 reactions that

convert glucose to carbon dioxide and water constitute the metabolic pathway for glucose catabolism. Each reaction produces only a small change in the structure of the substrate (see, for example, Figures 5-12 and 5-14). By such a sequence of small steps, a complex chemical structure, such as glucose, can be transformed to the relatively simple molecular structures carbon dioxide and water.

Consider a metabolic pathway containing four enzymes (e_1, e_2, e_3, and e_4) and leading from an initial substrate A to the end product E, through a series of intermediates, B, C, and D:

$$A \xrightleftharpoons{e_1} B \xrightleftharpoons{e_2} C \xrightleftharpoons{e_3} D \xrightarrow{e_4} E$$

(The irreversibility of the last reaction is of no consequence for the moment.) By mass action, increasing the concentration of A will lead to an increase in the concentration of B (provided e_1 is not already saturated with substrate), and so on until eventually there is an increase in the concentration of the end product E. Since different enzymes have different activities and concentrations, it would be extremely unlikely that the reaction rates of all these steps would be exactly the same. Thus, one step is very likely to be slower than all the others. This step is known as the **rate-limiting reaction** in a metabolic pathway. None of the reactions that occur later in the sequence, including the formation of end product, can proceed more rapidly than the rate-limiting reaction since they depend upon the rate at which their substrates are being supplied by the previous steps. By regulating the concentration or activity of the rate-limiting enzyme, the rate of flow through the whole pathway can be increased

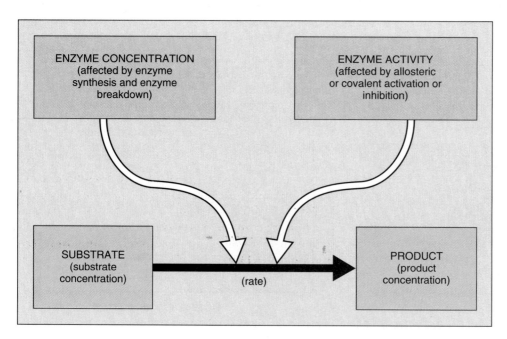

FIGURE 5-7
Factors that affect the rate of enzyme-mediated reactions.

or decreased. Thus, it is not necessary to alter all the enzymes in a metabolic pathway to control the rate at which the end product is produced.

Rate-limiting enzymes are often the sites of allosteric or covalent regulation. For example, if enzyme e_2 is rate-limiting in the pathway described above and is subject to allosteric inhibition by the end product E, **end-product inhibition** occurs. Such inhibition is frequently found in synthetic pathways where it effectively shuts down the formation of end product when the end product is not being utilized, preventing excessive accumulation of the end product. We thus have a metabolic pathway that is able to regulate itself (Figure 5-8).

Control of enzyme activity or concentration also can be critical for reversing a metabolic pathway. Consider the pathway we have been discussing, ignoring the presence of end-product inhibition of enzyme e_2. The pathway consists of three reversible reactions mediated by e_1, e_2, and e_3, followed by an irreversible reaction mediated by enzyme e_4. The last reaction is irreversible because a large amount of energy is released in it. E can be converted into D, however, if the reaction is coupled to the simultaneous breakdown of a molecule that releases large quantities of energy. In other words, an irreversible step can be "reversed" by an alternative route, using a second enzyme and its substrate to provide the required energy. Two such high-energy irreversible reactions are indicated by bowed arrows to emphasize that two separate enzymes are involved in the two directions:

$$A \underset{}{\overset{e_1}{\rightleftharpoons}} B \underset{}{\overset{e_2}{\rightleftharpoons}} C \underset{}{\overset{e_3}{\rightleftharpoons}} D \overset{e_4}{\underset{e_5}{\rightleftarrows}} E$$
$$Y \qquad X$$

FIGURE 5-8
End-product inhibition of the rate-limiting enzyme in a metabolic pathway. The end product E becomes the modulator molecule that produces allosteric inhibition of enzyme e_2.

Allosteric inhibition of e_2

$$A \overset{e_1}{\rightleftharpoons} B \overset{e_2}{\rightleftharpoons} C \overset{e_3}{\rightleftharpoons} D \overset{e_4}{\rightarrow} E$$

Rate-limiting enzyme   End product (modulator molecule)

By controlling the activities or concentrations of e_4 and e_5, the direction of flow through the pathway can be regulated. If e_4 is activated and e_5 inhibited, the flow will proceed from A to E, whereas inhibition of e_4 and activation of e_5 will produce flow from E to A.

Another situation involving the differential control of several enzymes arises when there is a branch in a metabolic pathway. A single metabolite, C, may be the substrate for more than one enzyme, as illustrated by the pathway

$$A \overset{e_1}{\rightleftharpoons} B \overset{e_2}{\rightleftharpoons} C \overset{e_3}{\nearrow} D \overset{e_4}{\rightleftharpoons} E$$
$$\qquad\qquad\qquad \overset{e_5}{\searrow} F \overset{e_6}{\rightleftharpoons} G$$

Altering the activities or concentrations of e_3 and e_5 regulates the flow of metabolites through the two branches of the pathway.

When one considers the thousands of reactions that occur in the body and the permutations and combinations of possible control points, the overall result is staggering. The details of metabolic regulation at the enzymatic level are beyond the scope of this book. In the remainder of this chapter, we consider only (1) the overall characteristics of the pathways by which cells obtain energy; and (2) the pathways by which carbohydrates, fats, and proteins are broken down and synthesized. As we shall see, the latter pathways also constitute crucial components of the former pathways.

ATP AND CELLULAR ENERGY TRANSFER

The Role of ATP

The functioning of a cell depends upon its ability to extract and use the chemical energy in organic molecules. When, in the presence of oxygen, a cell breaks down 1 mol of glucose to carbon dioxide and water, 686 kcal of energy is released. Some of this energy appears as heat, but a cell cannot use heat energy to perform its functions. The remainder of the energy is transferred to another molecule, which can in turn transfer it to yet another molecule or to energy-requiring processes. In all cells, from bacterial to human, the primary molecule to which energy from the breakdown of fuel molecules—carbohydrates, fats, and proteins—is transferred and which then transfers this energy to cell functions is the nucleotide **adenosine triphosphate (ATP)** (Figure 5-9). (As we shall see, other nucleotide triphosphates such as GTP, are also used to transfer energy in special cases.) For the moment we will disregard how ATP is formed from fuel molecules and focus on its energy release.

FIGURE 5-9

Chemical structure of ATP. Its breakdown into ADP and P_i is accompanied by the release of 7 kcal of energy per mol.

The chemical reaction (referred to as ATP hydrolysis) that removes the terminal phosphate group from ATP is accompanied by the release of a large amount of energy, 7 kcal/mol:

$$ATP + H_2O \longrightarrow ADP + P_i + 7 \text{ kcal/mol}$$

The products of the reaction are adenosine diphosphate (ADP) and inorganic phosphate (P_i). Note that 7 kcal of energy is released when *one mole* (6×10^{23} molecules) of ATP is hydrolyzed, not just one molecule.

The energy derived from the hydrolysis of ATP is used by energy-requiring processes in cells for (1) the production of force and movement as in muscle contraction (Chapter 11), (2) membrane active transport (Chapter 6),

and (3) synthesis of the organic molecules used for cell structure and function.

We must emphasize that cells use ATP not to *store* energy but rather to *transfer* it. ATP is an energy-carrying molecule which transfers relatively small amounts of energy from fuel molecules to the points in a cell that require energy. ATP is often referred to as the energy currency of the cell. By analogy, if the amount of usable energy released by the catabolism of one molecule of glucose were equivalent to a $10 bill, then the energy released by the hydrolysis of one molecule of ATP would be worth about a quarter. The energy-requiring machinery of the cell uses only quarters; it will not accept $10 bills. Transferring energy to ATP is the cell's way of making change.

Energy is continuously cycled through ATP molecules

FIGURE 5-10

Flow of chemical energy from fuel molecules to ATP and heat, and then from ATP to energy-requiring cell functions.

in a cell. A typical ATP molecule may exist for only a few seconds before it is broken down to ADP and P_i, with the released energy used to perform a cell function. Equally rapidly, the products of ATP hydrolysis, ADP and P_i, are converted back into ATP through coupling to reactions that release energy during the catabolism of carbohydrates, fats, or proteins (Figure 5-10). The total amount of ATP in the body is sufficient to maintain the resting functions of the tissues for only about 90 s. Thus, energy must be continuously transferred from fuel molecules to ATP:

$$ADP + P_i + 7 \text{ kcal/mol} \longrightarrow ATP + H_2O$$

(From catabolism
of fuel molecules)

Only about 40 percent of the energy released by the catabolism of fuel molecules is transferred to ATP, the remaining 60 percent appearing as heat.

Three distinct but linked metabolic pathways are used by cells to transfer the energy released from the breakdown of fuel molecules to ATP. They are known as **glycolysis**, the **Krebs cycle**, and **oxidative phosphorylation** (Figure 5-11). In the following sections we will describe the major characteristics of these three pathways in terms of the location of the enzymes for them in the cell, the relative contribution of each pathway to ATP production, the sites of carbon dioxide formation and oxygen utilization, and the key molecules that enter and leave each of the pathways. One important generalization to keep in mind is that glycolysis can occur in either the presence or absence of oxygen, whereas the other two pathways require oxygen to be present.

Glycolysis

Glycolysis (derived from the Greek words *glycos*, sugar, and *lysis*, breakdown) catabolizes carbohydrates exclusively, primarily glucose. It consists of 10 enzymatic reactions that convert a six-carbon molecule of glucose into two three-carbon molecules of **pyruvate**[2] (Figure 5-12) and in the process produce a net gain of two molecules of ATP:

anaerobic

$$\text{Glucose} + 2\,ADP + 2\,P_i + 2\,NAD^+ \longrightarrow$$
$$2\text{ pyruvate} + 2\,ATP + 2\,NADH + 2H^+ + 2\,H_2O \quad (5\text{-}1)$$

These reactions, *none of which utilizes oxygen*, take place in the cytosol, in contrast to the mitochondrial location of the enzymes for the Krebs cycle and oxidative phosphorylation. Note (Figure 5-12) that all of the intermediates between glucose and the end product pyruvate contain one or more ionized phosphate groups. As we shall learn in Chapter 6, plasma membranes are very impermeable to such highly ionized molecules, and thus these molecules remain trapped within the cell.

Note next that the early steps in glycolysis—steps 1 and 3—each *use*, rather than produce, one molecule of ATP, to form phosphorylated intermediates. Note in addition that reaction 4 splits a six-carbon intermediate into two three-carbon molecules—dihydroxyacetone phosphate and 3-phosphoglyceraldehyde—and that reaction 5 converts dihydroxyacetone phosphate into another molecule of 3-phosphoglyceraldehyde. Thus, at that point in the pathway we have two molecules of 3-phosphoglyceraldehyde derived from one molecule of glucose. Keep in mind, then, that from this point on, *two* molecules of each intermediate are involved.

[2]Actually, it is pyruvic acid that is directly formed but then ionizes to yield a hydrogen ion plus the anion pyruvate. The names of the ionized forms of weak acids end in *-ate*. Thus the ionized forms of pyruvic acid, lactic acid, and citric acid are pyruvate, lactate, and citrate. Since most of the intermediates in the pathways of fuel metabolism are weak acids that are ionized under the slightly alkaline conditions of the intracellular fluid, the names of the ionized forms of the molecules will be used in the text.

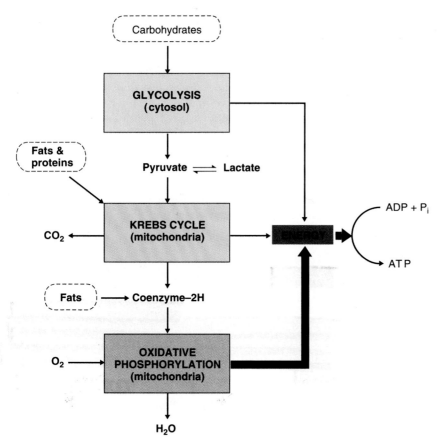

FIGURE 5-11

Pathways linking the energy released from the catabolism of fuel molecules to the formation of ATP. For simplicity, this figure does not show that glycolysis also provides some coenzyme-2H molecules to oxidative phosphorylation.

The first *formation* of ATP in glycolysis occurs during reaction 7 when a phosphate group is transferred from 1,3-bisphosphoglycerate to ADP to form ATP. This mechanism of forming ATP is known as **substrate level phosphorylation** since the phosphate group is transferred from a substrate molecule to ADP. Since, as stressed above, two intermediates exist at this step, reaction 7 produces two molecules of ATP, one from each of them. As we shall see, this mechanism is quite different from that used during oxidative phosphorylation in which *free* inorganic phosphate is coupled to ADP to form ATP.

A similar substrate level phosphorylation of ADP occurs during reaction 10, where again two molecules of ATP are formed. Thus, reactions 7 and 10 generate a total of four molecules of ATP for every molecule of glucose entering the pathway. There is a net gain, however, of only two molecules of ATP during glycolysis because of the two molecules of ATP used in the earlier reactions 1 and 3.

The end product of glycolysis, pyruvate, can proceed in one of two directions, depending on the availability of molecular oxygen, which, as we stressed earlier, is *not* utilized in any of the glycolytic reactions themselves. If oxygen is present, that is, if **aerobic** conditions exist, pyruvate enters the Krebs cycle and is broken down into carbon dioxide, as described in the next section. In contrast, in the absence of oxygen (**anaerobic** conditions), pyruvate is converted to **lactate** by a single enzyme-mediated reaction.[3] In this reaction (Figure 5-13) two hydrogen atoms derived from NADH + H$^+$ are transferred to pyruvate to form lactate. These hydrogens were originally added to NAD$^+$ during glycolysis in reaction 6, and so the coenzyme NAD$^+$ shuttles hydrogen between the two reactions during anaerobic glycolysis. The *overall* reaction, therefore, for anaerobic glycolysis is

$$\text{Glucose} + 2\,\text{ADP} + 2\,\text{P}_i \longrightarrow$$
$$2\,\text{lactate} + 2\,\text{ATP} + 2\,\text{H}_2\text{O} \quad (5\text{-}2)$$

Recall that under aerobic conditions pyruvate is not converted to lactate but rather enters the Krebs cycle. Therefore, the mechanism just described for regenerating NAD$^+$ from NADH + H$^+$ by forming lactate no longer occurs. Instead, as we shall see, the NADH + H$^+$ formed in reaction 6 is reconverted to NAD$^+$ by the transfer of its hydrogens to oxygen during oxidative phosphorylation.

---

[3]In some microorganisms, yeast cells for example, pyruvate is converted under anaerobic conditions to carbon dioxide and alcohol rather than to lactate. This process is known as fermentation and forms the basis for the production of alcohol from cereal grains that are rich in carbohydrates.

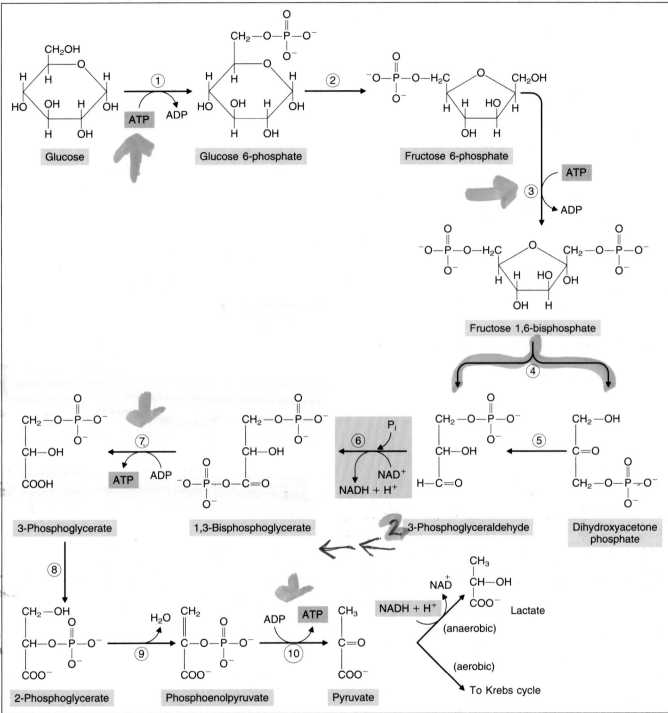

FIGURE 5-12 ✶

Glycolytic pathway. Under anaerobic conditions there is a net synthesis of two molecules of ATP for every molecule of glucose that enters the pathway. Two molecules of ATP are used in reactions 1 and 3. Reactions 4 and 5 combined produce two molecules of 3-phosphoglyceraldehyde, each of which yields two molecules of ATP, one at step 7 and one at step 10. Thus, in glycolysis, there is a total of four ATP produced and two consumed.

(handwritten notes:)

use up 2ATP's
make 4ATP's
NET: made 2ATP's

in cytosol

← 93

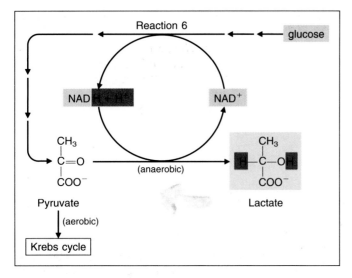

FIGURE 5-13
Under anaerobic conditions the coenzyme NAD^+ utilized in the glycolytic reaction 6 (Figure 5-12) is regenerated when it transfers its hydrogen atoms to pyruvate during the formation of lactate.

In most cells, the amount of ATP produced by glycolysis is much smaller than the amount formed by the other two ATP-generating pathways—the Krebs cycle and oxidative phosphorylation. There are special cases, however, in which glycolysis supplies most, and even all, of a cell's ATP. For example, erythrocytes contain the enzymes for glycolysis but have no mitochondria, which are required for the other pathways. All of their ATP production occurs, therefore, by glycolysis. Certain types of skeletal muscles contain considerable amounts of glycolytic enzymes but have few mitochondria. During intense muscle activity,

glycolysis provides most of the ATP in these cells and is associated with the production of large amounts of lactate. Despite these exceptions most cells do not have sufficient concentrations of glycolytic enzymes or enough glucose to provide, by glycolysis alone, the high rates of ATP production necessary to meet their energy requirements and thus are unable to function under anaerobic conditions.

Our discussion of glycolysis has focused upon glucose as the major carbohydrate entering the glycolytic pathway. However, other carbohydrates such as fructose, derived from the disaccharide sucrose (table sugar), and galactose, from the disaccharide lactose (milk sugar), can also be catabolized by glycolysis since these carbohydrates are converted into several intermediates that participate in the early portion of the glycolytic pathway.

Table 5-4 summarizes the major characteristics of glycolysis.

Krebs Cycle   *aerobic*

The Krebs cycle, named in honor of Hans Krebs who worked out the intermediate steps in this pathway (also known as the **citric acid cycle** or **tricarboxylic acid cycle**) is the second of the three pathways involved in fuel catabolism and ATP production. It utilizes molecular fragments formed during carbohydrate, protein, and fat breakdown, and it produces carbon dioxide, hydrogen atoms bound to coenzymes, and small amounts of ATP. The enzymes for this pathway are located in the mitochondria. Most of these enzymes are soluble enzymes in the inner mitochondrial compartment (the matrix—page 50).

The primary molecule entering at the beginning of the Krebs cycle is **acetyl coenzyme A** (acetyl CoA):

$$CH_3{-}\overset{\overset{\displaystyle O}{\|}}{C}{-}S{-}R$$

TABLE 5-4 CHARACTERISTICS OF GLYCOLYSIS	
Entering substrates	Glucose and other monosaccharides
Enzyme location	Cytosol
Net ATP production	2 ATP formed directly per molecule of glucose entering pathway
	Can be produced in the absence of oxygen (anaerobically)
Coenzyme production	2 NADH + H$^+$ formed under aerobic conditions
Final products	Pyruvate—under aerobic conditions
	Lactate—under anaerobic conditions
Net reaction	
Aerobic:	Glucose + 2 ADP + 2 P$_i$ + 2 NAD$^+$ $\longrightarrow$
	2 pyruvate + 2 ATP + 2 NADH + 2 H$^+$ + 2 H$_2$O
Anaerobic:	Glucose + 2 ADP + 2 P$_i$ $\longrightarrow$ 2 lactate + 2 ATP + 2 H$_2$O

Coenzyme A (CoA), a precursor of acetyl CoA, is derived from the B vitamin pantothenic acid, and its primary function is to transfer the two-carbon acetyl group from one molecule to another.[4] These acetyl groups come either from pyruvate, which as we have just seen is the end product of glycolysis, or from the breakdown of fatty acids and some amino acids, as we shall see in a later section. Pyruvate, upon entering mitochondria from the cytosol, undergoes the following reaction to produce acetyl CoA:

$$\text{Pyruvate} + \text{CoA} + \text{NAD}^+ \longrightarrow$$
$$\text{acetyl CoA} + \text{CO}_2 + \text{NADH} + \text{H}^+ \quad \text{(5-3)}$$

Note that this reaction produces the first molecule of CO_2 we have seen formed thus far in the pathways of fuel catabolism, and that hydrogen atoms have been transferred to NAD^+. We will make use of this latter fact later.

The Krebs cycle begins with the transfer of the acetyl group of acetyl CoA to the four-carbon molecule, oxaloacetate, to form the six-carbon molecule, citrate (Figure 5-14). At the third step in the cycle one molecule of CO_2 is produced, and again at the fourth step. Thus, two carbon atoms entered the cycle in the form of the acetyl group attached to CoA and now two carbons (although not the same ones) have left in the form of CO_2. Note also that the oxygen that appears in the CO_2 is not derived from molecular oxygen but from the carboxyl groups of Krebs-cycle intermediates.

In the remainder of the cycle, the four-carbon molecule formed in reaction 4 is modified through a series of reactions to produce the four-carbon molecule oxaloacetate, which becomes available to accept another acetyl group and repeat the cycle.

Now we come to a very crucial fact: In addition to producing carbon dioxide, intermediates in the Krebs cycle donate hydrogen atoms to the coenzymes NAD^+ and FAD. Two hydrogen atoms are transferred to NAD^+ in each of steps 3, 4, and 8, and to FAD in reaction 6. These hydrogens will be transferred from the coenzymes to oxygen in the next stage of fuel metabolism, oxidative phosphorylation. Since oxidative phosphorylation is necessary for regeneration of the hydrogen-free form of these coenzymes, the Krebs cycle can operate only under aerobic conditions. There is no pathway in the mitochondria that can remove the hydrogen from these coenzymes under anaerobic conditions.

So far we have said nothing of how the Krebs cycle contributes to the formation of ATP. In fact, the Krebs cycle directly produces only one high-energy nucleotide triphosphate. This occurs during reaction 5 in which inor-

ganic phosphate is transferred to guanosine diphosphate (GDP) to form guanosine triphosphate (GTP). The hydrolysis of GTP, like that of ATP, can provide energy for some energy-requiring reactions. In addition, the energy in GTP can be transferred to ATP by the reaction

$$\text{GTP} + \text{ADP} \rightleftharpoons \text{GDP} + \text{ATP}$$

This reaction is reversible, and the energy in ATP can be used to form GTP from GDP when additional GTP is required for this molecule's roles in protein synthesis and signal transduction (Chapter 7).

To reiterate, the formation of GTP is the only mechanism by which ATP is directly formed within the Krebs cycle. Why, then, is the Krebs cycle so important? Because the hydrogen atoms transferred in the cycle to the coenzymes are used in the next pathway, oxidative phosphorylation, to form large amounts of ATP. The net result of the catabolism of one acetyl group from acetyl CoA by way of the Krebs cycle can be written:

$$\text{Acetyl CoA} + 3\,\text{NAD}^+ + \text{FAD} + \text{GDP} +$$
$$\text{P}_i + 2\,\text{H}_2\text{O} \longrightarrow 2\,\text{CO}_2 + \text{CoA} + 3\,\text{NADH} +$$
$$3\,\text{H}^+ + \text{FADH}_2 + \text{GTP} \quad \text{(5-4)}$$

Table 5-5 summarizes the characteristics of the Krebs-cycle reactions.

One more point should be noted: Although the major function of the Krebs cycle is the provision of hydrogen atoms to the oxidative phosphorylation pathway, some of the intermediates in the cycle can be used to synthesize organic molecules, especially several types of amino acids, required by cells. Oxaloacetate is one of the intermediates used in this manner. When a molecule of oxaloacetate is removed from the Krebs cycle in the process of forming amino acids, it is not available to combine with the acetate fragment of acetyl CoA at the beginning of the cycle. Thus, there must be a way of replacing the oxaloacetate and other Krebs-cycle intermediates that are consumed in synthetic pathways. Carbohydrates provide one source of oxaloacetate replacement by the following reaction, which converts pyruvate into oxaloacetate (contrast this reaction to Equation 5-3):

$$\text{Pyruvate} + \text{CO}_2 + \text{ATP} \longrightarrow$$
$$\text{oxaloacetate} + \text{ADP} + \text{P}_i \quad \text{(5-5)}$$

Certain amino acid derivatives, as we shall see, also can be used to form oxaloacetate and other Krebs-cycle intermediates.

Oxidative Phosphorylation

Oxidative phosphorylation provides the third, and quantitatively most important, mechanism by which energy de-

---

[4]Coenzyme A can also transfer other small carbon fragments such as succinate, as occurs in reaction 5 of the Krebs cycle.

w/o much acetyl CoA's, slower cyclic mvmt.

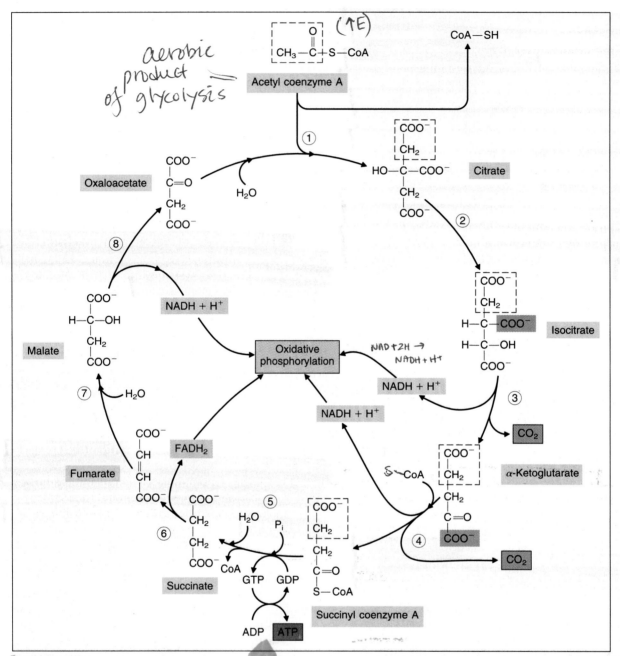

aerobic product of glycolysis =

★ **FIGURE 5-14**

The Krebs-cycle pathway begins with the entry of a two-carbon acetyl group from acetyl coenzyme A, and one turn of the cycle results in the production of $2\,CO_2 + 3\,NADH + 3\,H^+ + FADH_2 + GTP$. (Note that the carbon atoms of the two molecules of CO_2 produced are not the same two carbon atoms that entered the cycle as an acetyl group—identified by the dashed box throughout the figure.)

- *happens in mitochondrial matrix*

1 ATP made

rived from fuel molecules can be transferred to ATP. The basic principle behind this pathway is simple: The energy transferred to ATP is derived from the energy released when hydrogen combines with molecular oxygen to form water. The source of the hydrogen is the $NADH + H^+$ and $FADH_2$ coenzyme molecules. The net reaction involving $NADH + H^+$ is

$$\tfrac{1}{2}\,O_2 + NADH + H^+ \longrightarrow H_2O + NAD^+ + 53\ \text{kcal/mol}$$

Since only 7 kcal/mol of energy is required to synthesize

TABLE 5-5 CHARACTERISTICS OF THE KREBS CYCLE

Entering substrate	Acetyl coenzyme A—acetyl groups derived from pyruvate and fatty acids Some intermediates derived from amino acids
Enzyme location	Inner compartment of mitochondria (the mitochondrial matrix)
ATP production	1 GTP formed directly, which can be converted into ATP Operates only under aerobic conditions even though molecular oxygen is not used directly in this pathway
Coenzyme production	3 NADH + 3 H$^+$ and 1 FADH$_2$
Final products	2 CO$_2$ for each molecule of acetyl coenzyme A entering pathway Some intermediates used to synthesize amino acids and other organic molecules required for special cell functions
Net reaction	Acetyl CoA + 3 NAD$^+$ + FAD + GDP + P$_i$ + 2 H$_2$O $\longrightarrow$ 2 CO$_2$ + CoA + 3 NADH + 3 H$^+$ + FADH$_2$ + GTP

1 mol of ATP from ADP and P$_i$, there is enough energy released in the above reaction to form more than one molecule of ATP.

The proteins that mediate oxidative phosphorylation are located in the mitochondria, but unlike the enzymes of the Krebs cycle, which are soluble enzymes in the matrix compartment, the proteins that mediate oxidative phosphorylation are embedded in the inner mitochondrial membrane. These proteins can be divided into two groups: (1) those that mediate the series of reactions by which hydrogen is transferred to molecular oxygen, and (2) those that couple the energy released by these reactions to the synthesis of ATP.

Most of the first group of proteins contain iron and copper cofactors, forming proteins known as **cytochromes** because in pure form they are brightly colored. They resemble in their structure the red iron-containing hemoglobin molecule, which binds oxygen in the blood. The cytochromes form the components of the **electron transport chain**, in which two electrons from the hydrogen atoms are initially transferred either from NADH + H$^+$ or FADH$_2$ to one of the elements in the electron transport chain. These electrons are then successively transferred to other elements in the chain, often to or from an iron or copper ion, until the electrons are finally transferred to molecular oxygen, which then combines with hydrogen ions (protons) to form water. These hydrogen ions, like the electrons, come from the hydrogen-bearing coenzymes, having been released from them early in the transport chain when the electrons from the hydrogen atoms were transferred to the cytochromes.

In addition to transferring the coenzyme-hydrogens to water, this process regenerates the hydrogen-free form of the coenzymes, which then become available to accept two more hydrogens from intermediary reactions. Thus, the electron transport chain provides the aerobic mechanism for regenerating the hydrogen-free form of the coenzymes, whereas as described earlier the anaerobic mechanism is coupled to the formation of lactate.

At each step along the electron-transport chain small amounts of energy are released, which in total amount to the full 53 kcal/mol released from a direct reaction between hydrogen and oxygen. Because this energy is released in small steps, it can be linked to the synthesis of several molecules of ATP, each of which requires only 7 kcal/mol. Overall, 40 percent of the energy released from this chain of reactions is transferred to ATP, the remaining 60 percent appearing as heat.

At three points along the electron-transport chain ATP is formed. The mechanism by which this occurs is known as the **chemiosmotic hypothesis**. As electrons are transferred along the cytochrome chain, the energy released is used to move hydrogen ions (protons) from the matrix to the cytosolic side of the inner mitochondrial membrane, thus producing a source of potential energy in the form of a hydrogen-ion gradient across the membrane. At three points along the chain a complex of proteins forms a channel through which the highly concentrated hydrogen ions on the cytoplasmic side of the membrane can flow back to the matrix side and in the process transfer their potential energy to the formation of ATP from ADP and P$_i$ (Figure 5-15). The molecular details of this coupling process are still uncertain.

FADH$_2$, which is formed during one of the steps in the Krebs cycle, has a slightly lower chemical energy content than does NADH + H$^+$ and enters the electron-transport

FIGURE 5-15

ATP is formed during oxidative phosphorylation by the flow of hydrogen ions across the inner mitochondrial membrane. Two or three molecules of ATP are produced per pair of electrons donated, depending on the point at which a particular coenzyme enters the electron-transport chain.

chain at a point beyond the first site of ATP generation (Figure 5-15). Thus, the transfer of its electrons to oxygen produces only two ATP rather than the three formed from $NADH + H^+$.

To repeat, the majority of the ATP formed in the body is produced during oxidative phosphorylation as a result of the processing of hydrogen atoms provided, largely via the Krebs cycle, during the breakdown of carbohydrates, fats, and proteins. The mitochondria, where oxidative phosphorylation occurs, are thus considered the powerhouses of the cell. In addition, as we have just seen, it is within these organelles that the majority of the oxygen we breathe is consumed and the carbon dioxide we expire is produced.

Table 5-6 summarizes the key features of oxidative phosphorylation.

CARBOHYDRATE, FAT, AND PROTEIN METABOLISM

Having described the three pathways by which energy is transferred to ATP, we now consider how each of the three classes of fuel molecules enters the ATP-generating pathways. We also consider the synthesis of these fuel molecules and the pathways and restrictions governing their conversion from one class to another. These anabolic pathways are also used to synthesize molecules that have functions other than the storage and release of energy. For example, with the addition of a few enzymes, the pathway for fat synthesis is also used for synthesis of the phospholipids found in membranes.

TABLE 5-6   CHARACTERISTICS OF OXIDATIVE PHOSPHORYLATION

Entering substrates	Hydrogen atoms obtained from $NADH + H^+$ and $FADH_2$ formed (1) during glycolysis and (2) by the Krebs cycle during the breakdown of pyruvate and amino acids, and (3) during the breakdown of fatty acids
	Molecular oxygen
Enzyme location	Inner mitochondrial membrane
ATP production	3 ATP formed from each $NADH + H^+$
	2 ATP formed from each $FADH_2$
Final products	H_2O—one molecule for each pair of hydrogens entering pathway.
Net reaction	$\frac{1}{2} O_2 + NADH + H^+ + 3\ ADP + 3\ P_i \longrightarrow$
	$H_2O + NAD^+ + 3\ ATP$

Carbohydrate Metabolism

Carbohydrate Catabolism. In the previous sections we have described the major pathways of carbohydrate catabolism: the breakdown of glucose to pyruvate or lactate by way of the glycolytic pathway, and the metabolism of pyruvate to carbon dioxide and water by way of the Krebs cycle and oxidative phosphorylation.

The amount of energy released during the catabolism of glucose to carbon dioxide and water is 686 kcal/mol of glucose:

$$C_6H_{12}O_6 + 6\,O_2 \longrightarrow 6\,H_2O + 6\,CO_2 + 686 \text{ kcal/mol}$$

How much of this energy is transferred to ATP? Figure 5-16 illustrates the points at which ATP is formed during glucose catabolism. As we have seen, a net formation of two molecules of ATP occurs by substrate level phosphorylation during glycolysis, and two more are formed during the Krebs cycle from GTP, one from each of the two molecules of pyruvate entering the cycle. The major portion of the ATP is generated by oxidative phosphorylation from the hydrogens generated at various steps during glucose breakdown.

With the exception of the two NADH + H$^+$ formed during glycolysis, all the hydrogen-bound coenzymes are generated within the mitochondria and can therefore enter the oxidative phosphorylation pathway. The two molecules of NADH + H$^+$ generated during glycolysis, however, cannot cross the inner mitochondrial membrane. During anaerobic glycolysis these hydrogens are transferred to pyruvate to form lactate and regenerate the hydrogen-free form of the coenzyme, as was previously described. Under aerobic conditions these hydrogens are transferred to an intermediate in the cytosol that is able to cross the mitochondrial membrane. Once within the mitochondria, the hydrogens are transferred from this intermediate either to NAD$^+$ or to FAD, depending on the enzymes present in the mitochondria of different tissues. Thus, from the two cytosolic NADH + H$^+$ formed during aerobic glycolysis, either four or six ATP will be produced.

As summarized in Table 5-7, from the aerobic breakdown of one molecule of glucose, a total of either 36 or 38 ATP can be produced, depending on the fate of the cytosolic NADH + H$^+$ produced during glycoysis. Since 7 kcal is required to form 1 mol of ATP, and a total of 38 mol of ATP can be formed per mole of glucose catabolized, a total of 266 kcal (7 × 38) can be transferred from glucose to ATP. The remaining 420 kcal (686 − 266) is released as heat. Thus, approximately 40 percent of the energy in glucose is transferred to ATP under aerobic conditions.

FIGURE 5-16

Pathways of aerobic glucose catabolism and their linkage to ATP formation. Depending on the mechanism for transferring the hydrogen generated during glycolysis into the mitochondria, each molecule of NADH + H$^+$ gives rise to two or three ATP.

TABLE 5-7 AEROBIC YIELD OF ATP FROM GLUCOSE CATABOLISM

Pathway		ATP per glucose	Percent of total ATP
Glycolysis (cytosol), substrate phosphorylation		2	5
Krebs cycle (mitochondria), 2 GTP to 2 ATP		2	5
Oxidative phosphorylation (mitochondria)		32 or 34	90
1. 2 NADH + 2 H$^+$ from glycolysis:	4 or 6 ATP		
2. 2 NADH + 2 H$^+$ from pyruvate to acetyl CoA:	6 ATP		
3. 6 NADH + 6 H$^+$ from Krebs cycle:	18 ATP		
4. 2 FADH$_2$ from Krebs cycle:	4 ATP		
Total		36 or 38	100

In the absence of oxygen, only 2 molecules of ATP can be formed by the breakdown of glucose to lactate. This yield represents only 2 percent of the energy stored in glucose. Thus, the evolution of aerobic metabolic pathways greatly increased the amount of energy available to a cell from glucose catabolism. For example, if a muscle consumed 38 molecules of ATP during a contraction, this amount of ATP could be supplied by the breakdown of 1 molecule of glucose in the presence of oxygen or 19 molecules of glucose under anaerobic conditions.

It is important to note, however, that although only 2 molecules of ATP are formed per molecule of glucose under anaerobic conditions, large amounts of ATP can still be supplied by the glycolytic pathway if large amounts of glucose are broken down to lactate. This is not an efficient utilization of fuel energy, but it does permit continued ATP production under anaerobic conditions, such as occur during intense exercise (Chapter 9).

Glycogen Storage. A small amount of glucose can be stored in the body to provide a reserve supply for use during those periods when glucose is not being absorbed into the blood from the intestinal tract. It is stored in the form of the polysaccharide **glycogen**, mostly in skeletal muscles and the liver.

Glycogen is synthesized from glucose by the pathway illustrated in Figure 5-17. The enzymes for both glycogen synthesis and glycogen breakdown are located in the cytosol. The first step, the transfer of phosphate from a molecule of ATP to glucose, forming glucose 6-phosphate, is the same as the first step in glycolysis. Thus glucose 6-phosphate can either be broken down to pyruvate or be incorporated into glycogen.

Note that, as indicated by the bowed arrows in Figure 5-17, different enzymes are used to synthesize and break

down glycogen. The existence of two pathways containing enzymes that are subject to both covalent and allosteric modulation provides a mechanism for regulating the flow of glucose to and from glycogen. When an excess of glucose is available to a liver or muscle cell, the enzymes in

FIGURE 5-17

Pathways for glycogen synthesis and breakdown. Each bowed arrow indicates an irreversible reaction that requires one enzyme to catalyze the reaction in the forward direction and a separate enzyme (or enzymes) for the reverse reaction.

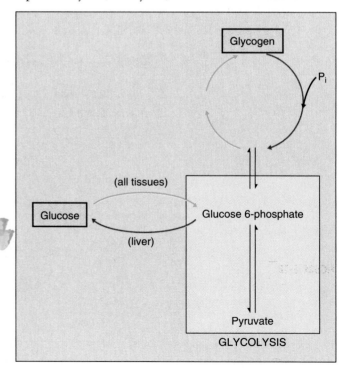

the glycogen synthesis pathway are activated, by the chemical signals described in Chapter 18, and the enzyme that breaks down glycogen is simultaneously inhibited. This combination leads to the net storage of glucose in the form of glycogen. When less glucose is available, the reverse combination of enzyme stimulation and inhibition occurs, and there is a net breakdown of glycogen to glucose 6-phosphate.

Two paths are available to the glucose 6-phosphate formed from the breakdown of glycogen: (1) In most cells, including skeletal muscle, glucose 6-phosphate enters the glycolytic pathway and, in the presence of oxygen, the pyruvate formed passes into the mitochondria where it is broken down into carbon dioxide and water; (2) in liver cells, glucose 6-phosphate can be converted to free glucose by removal of the phosphate group, and glucose is then able to pass out of the cell into the blood and become available to be used as fuel by other cells (Chapter 18).

Glucose Synthesis. In addition to being formed in the liver from the breakdown of glycogen, glucose can be synthesized in the liver and kidneys from intermediates derived from the breakdown of other classes of fuel molecules. This process of generating new molecules of glucose is known as **gluconeogenesis**. The major input to gluconeogenesis is pyruvate, formed from lactate and from several amino acids during protein breakdown. In addition, glycerol derived from the hydrolysis of triacylglycerols can be converted into glucose via a pathway that does not involve pyruvate.

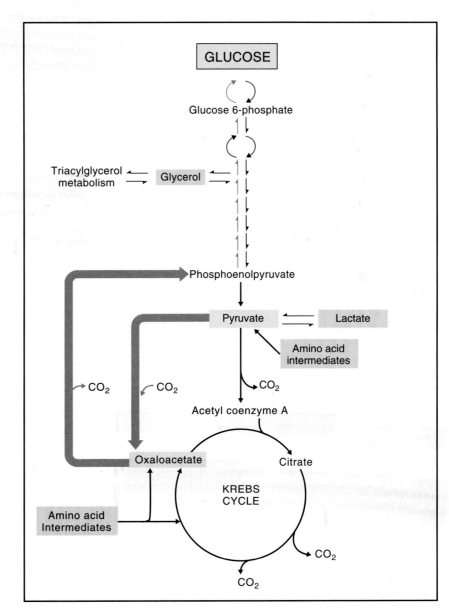

FIGURE 5-18
Gluconeogenic pathway by which pyruvate, lactate, glycerol, and various amino acid intermediates can be converted into glucose in the liver. Note the points at which each of these precursors, supplied by the blood, enters the pathway.

The pathway for gluconeogenesis in the liver and kidneys (Figure 5-18) makes use of many but not all of the enzymes used in glycolysis because most of these enzyme reactions are reversible. However, reactions 3 and 10 (Figure 5-12) are irreversible, and additional enzymes are required, therefore, to form glucose from pyruvate. Pyruvate is converted to phosphoenolpyruvate by a series of mitochondrial reactions in which CO_2 is added to pyruvate to form the four-carbon Krebs-cycle intermediate oxaloacetate. [In addition to being an important intermediary step in gluconeogenesis, this reaction (Equation 5-5) provides a pathway for replacing Krebs-cycle intermediates, as described earlier.] An additional series of reactions leads to the transfer of a four-carbon intermediate derived from oxaloacetate out of the mitochondria and its conversion to phosphoenolpyruvate in the cytosol. Phosphoenolpyruvate then reverses the steps taken in glycolysis back to the level of reaction 3, in which a different enzyme from that used in glycolysis is required to convert fructose 1,6-bisphosphate to fructose 6-phosphate. From this point on the reactions are again reversible, leading to glucose 6-phosphate, which can be converted to glucose or stored as glycogen.

Since energy is released during the glycolytic breakdown of glucose to pyruvate in the form of heat and ATP generation, energy must be added to reverse this pathway. A total of six ATP are consumed in the reactions of gluconeogenesis. Thus, as with most anabolic reactions, energy must be expended to synthesize glucose, whereas energy is released during glucose breakdown.

Since many of the same enzymes are used in glycolysis and gluconeogenesis, the question arises as to what controls the direction of metabolic flow through this series of enzymes. What conditions determine whether glucose is broken down to pyruvate or whether pyruvate is converted into glucose? The answer lies in the concentrations of glucose or pyruvate in a cell and in the allosteric control of the enzymes that occur at the irreversible steps in the pathway, a control exerted via various hormones (Chapter 18).

Fat Metabolism

Fat Catabolism. Triacylglycerol (fat) consists of three fatty acids linked to glycerol (page 25). Fat accounts for the major portion (approximately 80 percent) of the energy stored in the body (Table 5-8). Under resting conditions, approximately half the energy used by such tissues as muscle, liver, and kidneys is derived from the catabolism of fatty acids.

Although most cells store small amounts of fat, the majority of the body's fat is stored in specialized cells known as **adipocytes**. Almost the entire cytoplasm of these cells is filled with a single large fat droplet. Clusters of adipocytes form **adipose tissue**, most of which is located in

TABLE 5-8 FUEL CONTENT OF A 70-KG PERSON

	Total-body content, kg	Energy content, kcal/g	Total-body energy content kcal	%
Triacylglycerols	15.6	9	140,000	78
Proteins	9.5	9	38,000	21
Carbohydrates	0.5	4	2,000	1

deposits underlying the skin. The function of adipocytes is to synthesize and store triacylglycerols during periods of food uptake and then, when food is not being absorbed from the intestinal tract, to release fatty acids and glycerol into the blood from which they can be taken up and used by other cells to provide the energy for ATP formation. The factors controlling fat storage and release from adipocytes will be described in Chapter 18. Here we will emphasize the pathway by which fatty acids are catabolized by most cells to provide the energy for ATP synthesis, and the pathway for the synthesis of fatty acids from other fuel molecules.

Figure 5-19 shows the pathway for fatty acid catabolism, which is achieved by enzymes present in the mitochondrial matrix. The breakdown of a fatty acid is initiated by linking a molecule of coenzyme A to the carboxyl end of the fatty acid. This initial step is accompanied by the breakdown of ATP to AMP and two P_i. Since the terminal phosphates of both ATP and ADP are high-energy bonds, the energy released in this reaction is equivalent to that released when two ATP are hydrolyzed to two ADP and two P_i. Thus, although only one ATP is used in the reaction, the energy cost is equivalent to two ATP.

The coenzyme A derivative of the fatty acid then proceeds through a series of reactions, known as **beta oxidation**, which split off a molecule of acetyl coenzyme A from the end of the fatty acid and transfer two pairs of hydrogen atoms to coenzymes, one pair to FAD and the other to NAD^+. These coenzymes then enter the oxidative phosphorylation pathway, $NADH + H^+$ forming three molecules of ATP, and $FADH_2$ forming two, for a total of five ATP.

When the terminal acetyl coenzyme A is split from the fatty acid, another coenzyme A is added (ATP is not required for this step), and the sequence is repeated. Each passage through this sequence shortens the fatty acid chain by two carbon atoms until all the carbon atoms have been transferred to coenzyme A. As we saw on page 97, the acetyl coenzyme A molecules then enter the Krebs

9 acetyl Co-A's

in mito.
matrix

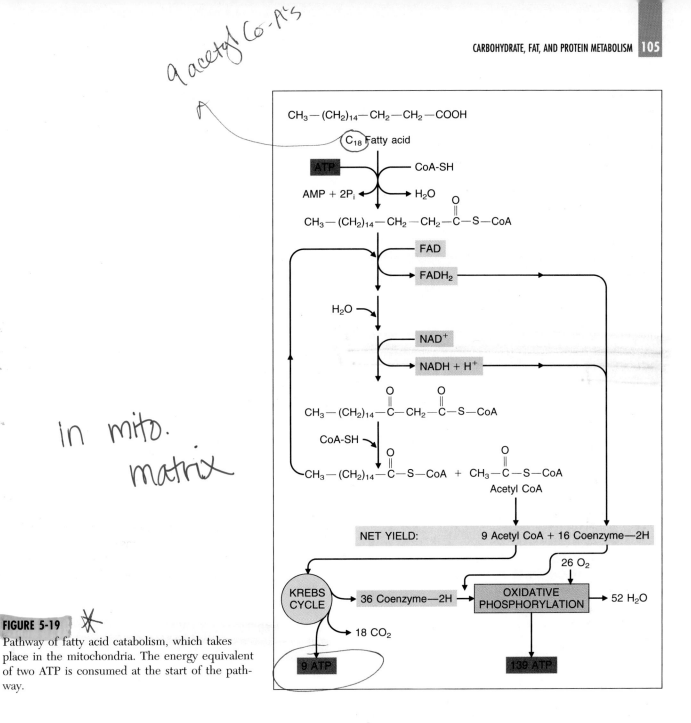

FIGURE 5-19 ✳
Pathway of fatty acid catabolism, which takes place in the mitochondria. The energy equivalent of two ATP is consumed at the start of the pathway.

cycle, each two-carbon fragment producing 2 molecules of CO_2 and ultimately 12 molecules of ATP via the Krebs cycle and oxidative phosphorylation.

How much ATP is formed as a result of the total catabolism of a fatty acid? Most fatty acids in the body contain 14 to 22 carbons, 16 and 18 being most common. The catabolism of one 18-carbon saturated fatty acid yields 146 ATP molecules (Table 5-9). In contrast, the catabolism of one glucose molecule yields a maximum of 38 ATP molecules. Thus, taking into account the difference in molecular weight of the fatty acid and glucose, it turns out that the amount of ATP formed from the catabolism of a gram of fat is about $2\frac{1}{2}$ times greater than the amount of ATP pro-

duced by catabolizing one gram of carbohydrate. If an average person stored most of his or her fuel as carbohydrate rather than as fat, body weight would have to be approximately 30 percent greater in order to store the same amount of usable energy, and the person would consume more energy moving this extra weight around. Thus, a major step in fuel economy occurred when animals evolved the ability to store fuel as fat. In contrast, plants store almost all their fuel as carbohydrate (starch).

Fat Synthesis. The synthesis of fatty acids occurs by reactions that are almost the reverse of those that degrade them. However, the enzymes in the synthetic pathway are

of fat

TABLE 5-9   ATP FORMED FROM CATABOLISM OF ONE 18-CARBON FATTY ACID

	Molecules of ATP
8 pairs of coenzyme—2H from beta oxidation (5 ATP formed per pair of coenzyme—2H)	$8 \times 5 = 40$
9 molecules of acetyl coenzyme A enter Krebs cycle (12 ATP formed per acetyl coenzyme A)	$9 \times 12 = 108$
	$\overline{148}$
Energy equivalent of 2 ATP used at start of pathway	$\underline{-2}$
	Total = 146

located in the cytosol, whereas (as we have just seen) the enzymes catalyzing fatty acid breakdown are located in the mitochondria. Fatty acid synthesis begins with acetyl coenzyme A, which, through a series of reactions requiring ATP and NADPH + H^+ (a phosphorylated form of NADH + H^+), transfers its acetyl group to another molecule of acetyl coenzyme A to form a 4-carbon chain. By repetition of this process, long-chain fatty acids are built up 2 carbons at a time, which accounts for the fact that all the fatty acids synthesized in the body contain an even number of carbon atoms. The overall reaction for the synthesis of an 18-carbon fatty acid can be written:

$$9 \ CH_3\overset{\displaystyle O}{\overset{\displaystyle \|}{C}}{-}S{-}CoA + 8 \ ATP + 16 \ NADPH +$$
$$16 \ H^+ \longrightarrow CH_3(CH_2)_{16}COOH + 8 \ ADP + 8 \ P_i +$$
$$16 \ NADP^+ + 7 \ H_2O + 9 \ CoA{-}SH$$

Once the fatty acids are formed, triacylglycerol can be synthesized by linking fatty acids to each of the three hydroxyl groups in glycerol, more specifically, to a phosphorylated form of glycerol called **α-glycerol phosphate**. The synthesis of triacylglycerol is carried out by enzymes associated with the membranes of the smooth endoplasmic reticulum.

Compare the molecules produced by glucose catabolism with those required for both fatty acid and α-glycerol phosphate synthesis. First, acetyl coenzyme A, the starting material for fatty acid synthesis, can be formed from pyruvate, the end product of glycolysis. Second, the other ingredients required for fatty acid synthesis—hydrogen-bound coenzymes and ATP—are produced during carbohydrate catabolism. Third, α-glycerol phosphate can be formed from a glucose intermediate. It should not be surprising, therefore, that much of the carbohydrate in food is converted into fat and stored in adipose tissue shortly after its absorption from the gastrointestinal tract. Mass action resulting from the increased concentration of

glucose intermediates, as well as the specific hormonal regulation of key enzymes, promotes this conversion, as will be described in Chapter 18.

It is very important to note that fatty acids, or more specifically the acetyl coenzyme A derived from fatty acid breakdown, cannot be used to synthesize new molecules of glucose. The reasons for this can be seen by examining the pathways for glucose synthesis (Figure 5-18). First, because the reaction in which pyruvate is broken down to acetyl coenzyme A and carbon dioxide is irreversible, acetyl coenzyme A cannot be converted into pyruvate, a molecule that can lead to the production of glucose. Second, the equivalent of the two carbon atoms in acetyl coenzyme A are converted into two molecules of carbon dioxide during their passage through the Krebs cycle before reaching oxaloacetate, another takeoff point for glucose synthesis, and therefore cannot be used to synthesize *net* amounts of oxaloacetate.

Thus, glucose can readily be converted into fat, but the fatty acid portion of fat cannot be converted to glucose. It is important to note, however, that the glycerol backbone of fat can be converted into an intermediate in the gluconeogenic pathway and thus give rise to glucose, as was mentioned earlier.

Protein and Amino Acid Metabolism

In the last chapter we described how amino acids are linked together to form proteins and how DNA and RNA direct this process. In contrast to the complexities of this synthetic pathway, protein catabolism requires only a few enzymes, termed **proteases**, to break the peptide bonds between amino acids. Some of these enzymes split off single amino acids, one at a time, from the ends of the protein chain, whereas others break peptide bonds between specific amino acids within the chain, forming peptides rather than free amino acids.

Amino acids can be catabolized to provide energy for ATP synthesis and can provide intermediates for the syn-

OXIDATIVE DEAMINATION

$$R-\underset{\underset{NH_2}{|}}{CH}-COOH + H_2O + coenzyme \longrightarrow R-\overset{\overset{O}{\|}}{C}-COOH + NH_3 + coenzyme-2H$$

Amino acid   Keto acid   Ammonia

TRANSAMINATION

$$R_1-\underset{\underset{NH_2}{|}}{CH}-COOH + R_2-\overset{\overset{O}{\|}}{C}-COOH \rightleftharpoons R_1-\overset{\overset{O}{\|}}{C}-COOH + R_2-\underset{\underset{NH_2}{|}}{CH}-COOH$$

Amino acid 1   Keto acid 2   Keto acid 1   Amino acid 2

FIGURE 5-20

Oxidative deamination and transamination of amino acids.

thesis of a number of molecules other than proteins. Since there are 20 different amino acids, a large number of intermediates can be formed and there are many pathways for processing them. A few basic types of reactions common to most of these pathways can provide an overview of amino acid catabolism.

Unlike carbohydrates and fats, amino acids contain nitrogen atoms (in their amino groups) in addition to carbon, hydrogen, and oxygen atoms. Once the nitrogen-containing amino group is removed, the remainder of most amino acids can be metabolized to intermediates capable of entering either the glycolytic or Krebs-cycle pathway.

The two types of reactions by which the amino group is removed are illustrated in Figure 5-20. In the first reaction

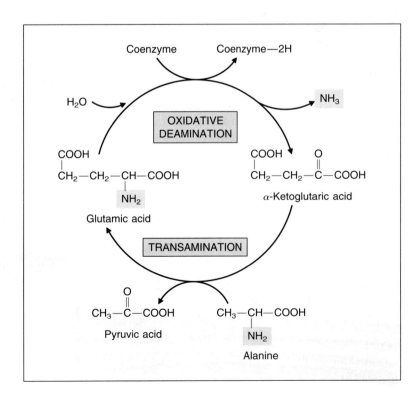

FIGURE 5-21

Oxidative deamination and transamination of the amino acids glutamate and alanine lead to keto acids that can enter the carbohydrate pathways.

illustrated, **oxidative deamination**, the amino group gives rise to a molecule of ammonia (NH_3) and is replaced by an oxygen atom, derived from water, to form a **keto acid**, a categorical name rather than the name of a specific molecule. The second means of removing an amino group is known as **transamination** and involves transfer of the amino group from an amino acid to a keto acid. Note that the keto acid to which the amino group is transferred becomes an amino acid. The nitrogen derived from amino groups can also be used by cells to synthesize other important nitrogen-containing molecules, such as the purine and pyrimidine bases found in nucleic acids.

Figure 5-21 illustrates the oxidative deamination of the amino acid glutamate and the transamination of the amino acid alanine. Note that the keto acids formed are intermediates either in the Krebs cycle (α-ketoglutarate) or glycolytic pathway (pyruvate). Once formed, these keto acids can be metabolized to produce carbon dioxide and form ATP, or they can be used as intermediates in the synthetic pathway leading to the formation of glucose. As a third alternative, they can be used to synthesize fatty acids after their conversion to acetyl coenzyme A by way of pyruvate. Thus, amino acids can be used as a source of energy, and some can be converted into carbohydrate and fat.

As we have seen, the oxidative deamination of amino acids yields ammonia. This substance, which is highly toxic to cells if allowed to accumulate, readily passes through cell membranes and enters the blood, which carries it to the liver (Figure 5-22). The liver contains enzymes that can link two molecules of ammonia with carbon dioxide to form **urea**. Thus, urea, which is relatively nontoxic, is the major nitrogenous waste product of protein catabolism. It leaves the liver and is excreted by the kidneys into the urine. Two of the 20 amino acids also contain atoms of sulfur, which can be converted to sulfate, SO_4^{2-}, and excreted in the urine.

Thus far, we have discussed mainly amino acid *catabolism*. The keto acids, pyruvic acid and α-ketoglutaric acid, can be derived from the breakdown of glucose and then be transaminated, as described above, to form glutamate and alanine. Thus glucose can be used to produce certain amino acids, provided other amino acids are available in the diet to supply amino groups for transamination. However, only 11 of the 20 amino acids can be formed by this process because 9 of the specific keto acids cannot be synthesized from other intermediates. The 9 amino acids corresponding to these keto acids must be obtained from the food we eat and are known as **essential amino acids**.

Figure 5-23 provides a summary of the multiple routes by which amino acids are handled by the body. The amino acid pools, which consist of the body's total free amino acids, are derived from (1) ingested protein, which is degraded to amino acids during digestion in the intestinal tract; (2) the synthesis of nonessential amino acids from

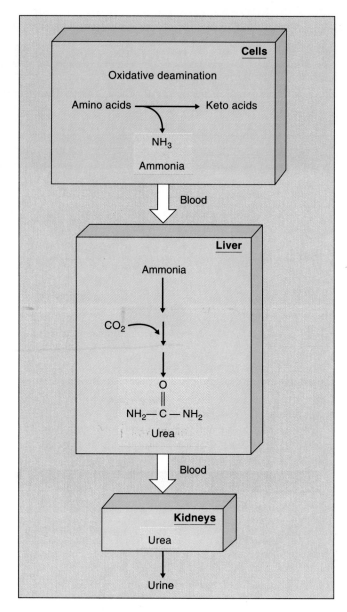

FIGURE 5-22

Formation and excretion of urea, the major nitrogenous waste product of protein catabolism.

the keto acids derived from carbohydrates and fat; and (3) the continuous breakdown of body protein. These pools are the source of amino acids for the resynthesis of body protein and a host of specialized amino acid derivatives, as well as for conversion to carbohydrate and fat. A very small quantity of amino acids and protein is lost from the body via the urine, skin, hair, fingernails, and in women, the menstrual fluid. The major route for the loss of amino acids from the body is not excretion of amino

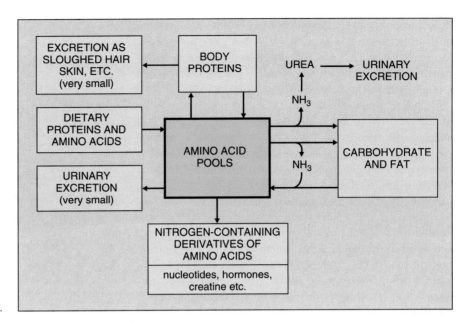

FIGURE 5-23

Pathways of amino acid metabolism.

FIGURE 5-24

Interrelations among the pathways for the metabolism of carbohydrates, fats, and proteins.

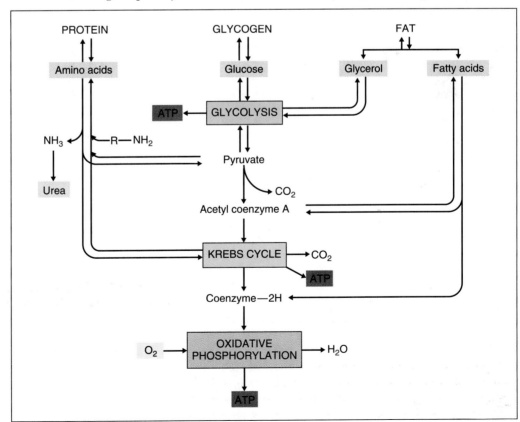

acids but rather their deamination, with ultimate excretion of the nitrogen atoms as urea in the urine. The terms **negative nitrogen balance** and **positive nitrogen balance** refer to whether there is a net loss or gain, respectively, of amino acids in the body over any period of time.

If any of the essential amino acids are missing from the diet, a negative nitrogen balance, that is, loss greater than gain, always results. The proteins that require a missing essential amino acid cannot be synthesized, and the other amino acids that would have been incorporated into these proteins are metabolized. This explains why a dietary requirement for protein cannot be specified without regard to the amino acid composition of that protein. Protein is graded in terms of how closely its relative proportions of essential amino acids approximate those in the average body protein. The highest-quality proteins are found in animal products, whereas the quality of most plant proteins is lower. Nevertheless, it is quite possible to obtain adequate quantities of all essential amino acids from a mixture of plant proteins alone.

Fuel Metabolism Summary

Having discussed the metabolism of the three major classes of organic molecules, we can now briefly review how each class is related to the others and to the process of synthesizing ATP. Figure 5-24 illustrates the major pathways we have discussed and the relations of the common intermediates. All three classes of molecules can enter the Krebs cycle through some intermediate, and thus all three can be used as a source of chemical energy for the synthesis of ATP in the cycle and, more importantly, by oxidative phosphorylation. Glucose can be converted into fat or into some amino acids by way of common intermediates such as pyruvate, oxaloacetate, and acetyl coenzyme A. Similarly, some amino acids can be converted into glucose and fat. Fatty acids cannot be converted into glucose because of the irreversibility of the reaction converting pyruvate to acetyl coenzyme A, but the glycerol portion of triacylglycerols can be converted into glucose. Fatty acids can be used to synthesize portions of the keto acids used to form some amino acids. Metabolism is thus a highly integrated process in which all classes of molecules can be used, if necessary, to provide energy, and in which each class of molecule can to a large extent provide the raw materials required to synthesize members of other classes.

ESSENTIAL NUTRIENTS

There are about 50 substances that are required for normal or optimal body function but that cannot be synthesized by the body or are synthesized in amounts inadequate to keep pace with the rates at which they are broken down or excreted. They are known as **essential nutrients** (Table 5-10). Because they are all removed at some finite rate, a continual new supply must be provided by the foods we eat.

TABLE 5-10 ESSENTIAL NUTRIENTS

Water

Mineral elements
 7 major mineral elements (Table 2-2)
 13 trace elements (Table 2-2)

Essential amino acids
 Isoleucine
 Leucine
 Lysine
 Methionine
 Phenylalanine
 Threonine
 Tryptophan
 Tyrosine
 Valine

Essential fatty acids
 Linoleic
 Linolenic

Vitamins
 Water-soluble vitamins
  B_1: thiamine
  B_2: riboflavin
  B_6: pyridoxine
  B_{12}: cobalamine
  Niacin
  Pantothenic acid
  Folic acid
  Biotin
  Lipoic acid
  Vitamin C
 Fat-soluble vitamins
  Vitamin A
  Vitamin D
  Vitamin E
  Vitamin K

Other essential nutrients
 Inositol
 Choline
 Carnitine

It must be emphasized that the term "essential nutrient" is reserved for substances that fulfill two criteria: (1) They must be essential for health, and (2) they must not be synthesized by the body in adequate amounts. Thus, glucose, although "essential" for normal metabolism, is not classified as an essential nutrient because the body normally can synthesize all it needs, from amino acids, for example. Furthermore, the quantity of an essential nutrient that must be present in the diet in order to maintain health is not a criterion for determining if the substance is essential. Approximately 1500 g of water, 2 g of the amino acid methionine, but only about 1 mg of the vitamin thiamine are required per day.

Water is an essential nutrient because far more of it is lost in the urine and from the skin and respiratory tract than can be synthesized by the body. (Recall that water is formed as an end product of oxidative phosphorylation as well as from several other metabolic reactions.) Therefore, to maintain water balance, an intake of water is essential.

The mineral elements provide an example of substances that are not metabolized but are continually lost from the body in the urine, feces, and various secretions. The major minerals must be supplied in fairly large amounts, whereas only small quantities of the trace elements are required.

We have already noted that 9 of the 20 amino acids are essential. Two fatty acids, linoleic and linolenic acid, which contain a number of double bonds and serve important roles in chemical messenger systems, are also essential nutrients. Three additional essential nutrients—inositol, choline, and carnitine—have functions that will be described in later chapters but do not fall into any common category other than being essential nutrients. Finally, the class of essential nutrients known as vitamins deserves special attention.

Vitamins

Fourteen vitamins have been shown to be essential for normal growth and health in humans. The exact chemical structures of the first vitamins to be discovered were unknown, and they were simply identified by letters of the alphabet. Vitamin B turned out to be composed of eight substances now known as the vitamin B complex. Plants and bacteria have the enzymes necessary for vitamin synthesis, and it is by eating either plants or meat from animals that have eaten plants that we get our vitamins.

The vitamins as a class have no particular chemical structure in common, but they can be divided into the **water-soluble vitamins** and the **fat-soluble vitamins**. The water-soluble vitamins form portions of coenzymes, such as NAD^+, FAD, and coenzyme A. The fat-soluble vitamins (A, D, E, and K) in general do not function as coenzymes. For example, vitamin A (retinol) is used to form the light-sensitive pigment in the eye, and lack of this vitamin leads to night blindness. The specific functions of each of the fat-soluble vitamins will be described in later chapters.

By themselves vitamins do not provide chemical energy, although they may participate as coenzymes in chemical reactions that release energy from other molecules. Increasing the amount of vitamins in the diet beyond a certain minimum does not necessarily increase the activity of the enzymes for which the vitamin functions as a coenzyme. Only very small quantities of coenzymes are necessary to saturate the binding sites for them on enzyme molecules, and increasing the concentration above this level does not increase the enzyme's activity.

The fate of large quantities of ingested vitamins varies, depending upon whether the vitamin is water-soluble or fat-soluble. As the amount of water-soluble vitamins in the diet is increased, so is the amount excreted in the urine, with the result that the accumulation of these vitamins in the body is relatively limited. On the other hand, fat-soluble vitamins can accumulate in the body because they are poorly excreted by the kidneys and because they dissolve in the fat stores in adipose tissue. The intake of very large quantities of fat-soluble vitamins can produce toxic effects.

SUMMARY

I. In adults the rates at which molecules are synthesized (anabolism) and broken down (catabolism) are approximately equal, and so the chemical composition of the body does not change appreciably.

CHEMICAL REACTIONS

I. The difference in the energy content of reactants and products is the amount of energy that is released or added during a reaction.

II. The energy released during a chemical reaction either is released as heat or is transferred to other molecules.

III. The four factors that can alter the rate of a chemical reaction are listed in Table 5-1.

IV. The activation energy required to initiate the breaking of chemical bonds in a reaction is usually acquired through collisions with other molecules.

V. Catalysts increase the rate of a reaction by lowering the activation energy.

VI. The characteristics of reversible and irreversible reactions are listed in Table 5-2.

VII. The net direction in which a reaction proceeds can be altered, according to the law of mass action, by increases or decreases in the concentrations of reactants or products.

ENZYMES

I. Nearly all chemical reactions in the body are catalyzed by enzymes, the characteristics of which are summarized in Table 5-3.

II. Some enzymes require small concentrations of cofactors for activity.

A. The binding of trace-metal cofactors maintains the conformation of the enzyme's binding site so that it is able to bind substrate.

B. Coenzymes, derived from vitamins, transfer small groups of atoms from one substrate to another. The coenzyme is regenerated in the course of these reactions and can be used over and over again.

REGULATION OF ENZYME-MEDIATED REACTIONS

I. The rates of enzyme-mediated reactions can be altered by changes in temperature, substrate concentration, enzyme concentration, and enzyme activity. Enzyme activity is altered by allosteric or covalent modulation.

MULTIENZYME METABOLIC PATHWAYS

I. The rate of product formation in a metabolic pathway can be controlled by allosteric or covalent modulation of the enzyme mediating the rate-limiting reaction in the pathway. The end product often acts as a modulator molecule, inhibiting the rate-limiting enzyme's activity.

II. An "irreversible" step in a metabolic pathway can be reversed by the use of two enzymes, one for the forward reaction and one for the reverse direction via another, energy-yielding reaction.

ATP AND CELLULAR ENERGY TRANSFER

I. In all cells, energy is transferred from the catabolism of fuel molecules to ATP. The hydrolysis of ATP to ADP and P_i then transfers this energy to cell functions. ATP is formed by substrate level phosphorylation and oxidative phosphorylation.

II. The end products of glycolysis under aerobic conditions are ATP and pyruvate, whereas ATP and lactate are the end products under anaerobic conditions.

A. Carbohydrates are the only fuel molecules that can enter the glycolytic pathway, enzymes for which are located in the cytosol.

B. During anaerobic glycolysis, hydrogen atoms are transferred to NAD^+ which then transfers them to pyruvate to form lactate, thus regenerating the original coenzyme molecule.

C. During aerobic glycolysis, $NADH + H^+$ transfers its hydrogen atoms to the oxidative phosphorylation pathway.

D. The formation of ATP in glycolysis is by substrate level phosphorylation, a process in which a phosphate group is transferred from a phosphorylated metabolic intermediate directly to ADP.

III. The Krebs cycle, the enzymes of which are located in the matrix of the mitochondria, catabolizes molecular fragments derived from fuel molecules and produces carbon dioxide, hydrogen atoms, and ATP.

A. Acetyl coenzyme A, the acetyl portion of which is derived from all three types of fuel molecules, is the major substrate entering the Krebs cycle. Amino acids can also enter at several other sites in the cycle by being converted to cycle intermediates.

B. During one rotation of the Krebs cycle two molecules of carbon dioxide are produced, and four pairs of hydrogen atoms are transferred to coenzymes. By substrate level phosphorylation one molecule of GTP is formed, which can be converted to ATP.

IV. Oxidative phosphorylation forms ATP from ADP and P_i, using the energy released when molecular oxygen ultimately combines with hydrogen atoms to form water.

A. The enzymes for oxidative phosphorylation are located on the inner membrane of mitochondria.

B. Hydrogen atoms derived from glycolysis, the Krebs cycle, and the breakdown of fatty acids to acetyl coA, are delivered to the electron transport chain, which regenerates the hydrogen-free forms of the coenzymes NAD^+ and FAD by transferring the hydrogens to molecular oxygen to form water.

C. The reactions of the electron-transport chain produce a hydrogen-ion gradient across the inner mitochondrial membrane, and this provides the energy for ATP synthesis as the hydrogen ions flow back across the membrane.

CARBOHYDRATE, FAT, AND PROTEIN METABOLISM

I. The aerobic catabolism of carbohydrates proceeds through the glycolytic pathway to pyruvate, which enters the Krebs cycle and is broken down to carbon dioxide.

   A. Under aerobic conditions, 38 molecules of ATP can be formed from 1 molecule of glucose: 34 from oxidative phosphorylation, 2 from glycolysis, and 2 from the Krebs cycle.

   B. Under anaerobic conditions, 2 molecules of ATP are formed from 1 molecule of glucose during glycolysis.

   C. About 40 percent of the chemical energy in glucose can be transferred to ATP under aerobic conditions, the rest appearing as heat.

II. Carbohydrates are stored as glycogen, primarily in the liver and skeletal muscles.

   A. Two different enzymes are used to synthesize and break down glycogen. The control of these enzymes regulates the flow of glucose to and from glycogen.

   B. In most cells glucose 6-phosphate is formed by glycogen breakdown and is catabolized to produce ATP. In liver cells, glucose can be derived from glycogen and can be released from the cells into the blood.

III. New glucose can be synthesized (gluconeogenesis) from some amino acids, lactate and glycerol via the enzymes that catalyze reversible reactions in the glycolytic pathway. Fatty acids cannot be used to synthesize glucose.

IV. Fat, stored primarily in adipose tissue, provides about 80 percent of the stored energy in the body.

   A. Fatty acids are broken down, two carbon atoms at a time, in the mitochondrial inner compartment by beta oxidation, to form acetyl coenzyme A and hydrogen atoms, which combine with coenzymes.

   B. The acetyl portion of acetyl coenzyme A is catabolized to carbon dioxide in the Krebs cycle, and the hydrogen atoms generated there plus those generated during beta oxidation are used by the oxidative phosphorylation pathway to form ATP.

   C. The amount of ATP formed by the catabolism of 1 g of fat is about $2\frac{1}{2}$ times greater than the amount formed from 1 g of carbohydrate.

   D. Fatty acids are synthesized from acetyl coenzyme A by enzymes located in the cytosol and are linked to α-glycerol phosphate, produced from carbohydrates, to form triacylglycerols by enzymes in the smooth endoplasmic reticulum.

V. Proteins are broken down to free amino acids by proteases.

   A. The amino groups of amino acids are removed, forming keto acids, which can either be catabolized via the Krebs cycle to provide energy for the synthesis of ATP or be converted into glucose and fatty acids.

   B. Amino groups are removed by (1) oxidative deamination, which gives rise to ammonia, or by (2) transamination, in which the amino group is transferred to a keto acid to form a new amino acid.

   C. The ammonia formed from the oxidative deamination of amino acids is converted to urea by enzymes in the liver and then excreted in the urine by the kidneys.

VI. Some amino acids can be synthesized from keto acids derived from glucose, while others cannot be synthesized by the body and must be provided in the diet.

ESSENTIAL NUTRIENTS

I. Approximately 50 essential nutrients, listed in Table 5-10, are necessary for health but cannot be synthesized in adequate amounts by the body and must therefore be provided in the diet.

II. A large intake of water-soluble vitamins leads to their rapid excretion in the urine, while large intakes of fat-soluble vitamins lead to their accumulation in adipose tissue and may produce toxic effects.

KEY TERMS

metabolism	active site
anabolism	cofactors
catabolism	coenzyme
calorie	vitamins
kilocalories	NAD$^+$
activation energy	FAD
catalyst	substrate level
reversible reactions	phosphorylation
chemical equilibrium	aerobic
irreversible reaction	anaerobic
law of mass action	lactate
enzyme	citric acid cycle
substrates	tricarboxylic acid cycle

acetyl coenzyme A
cytochromes
electron transport chain
chemiosmotic hypothesis
glycogen
gluconeogenesis
adipocytes
adipose tissue
beta oxidation
α-glycerol phosphate
proteases
oxidative deamination
metabolic pathway
rate-limiting reaction
end-product inhibition

adenosine triphosphate
  (ATP)
glycolysis
Krebs cycle
oxidative phosphorylation
pyruvate
keto acid
transamination
urea
essential amino acids
negative nitrogen balance
positive nitrogen balance
essential nutrients
water-soluble vitamins
fat-soluble vitamins

REVIEW QUESTIONS

1. How do molecules acquire the activation energy required for a chemical reaction?

2. List the four factors that influence the rate of a chemical reaction and state whether increasing the factor will increase or decrease the rate of the reaction.

3. What characteristics of a chemical reaction make it reversible or irreversible?

4. List five characteristics of enzymes.

5. What is the difference between a cofactor and a coenzyme?

6. From what class of nutrients are coenzymes derived?

7. Why are small concentrations of coenzymes sufficient to maintain enzyme activity?

8. List three ways in which the rate of an enzyme-mediated reaction can be altered?

9. How can an irreversible step in a metabolic pathway be reversed?

10. What is the function of ATP in metabolism?

11. Approximately how much of the energy released from the catabolism of fuel molecules is transferred to ATP? What happens to the rest?

12. What are the end products of glycolysis under aerobic and anaerobic conditions?

13. To which molecule are the hydrogen atoms in $NADH + H^+$ transferred during anaerobic glycolysis? During aerobic glycolysis?

14. What are the major substrates entering the Krebs cycle and what are the products formed?

15. Why will the Krebs cycle operate only under aerobic conditions even though molecular oxygen is not used in any of its reactions?

16. Identify the molecules that enter the oxidative phosphorylation pathway and the products that are formed.

17. Where are the enzymes for the Krebs cycle located? The enzymes for oxidative phosphorylation? The enzymes for glycolysis?

18. How many molecules of ATP can be formed from the breakdown of one molecule of glucose under aerobic conditions? Under anaerobic conditions?

19. Describe the pathways by which glycogen is synthesized and broken down by cells.

20. What molecules can be used to synthesize glucose?

21. Why can't fatty acids be used to synthesize glucose?

22. Describe the pathways used to catabolize fatty acids to carbon dioxide.

23. Why is it more efficient to store fuel as fat than as glycogen?

24. Describe the pathway by which glucose is converted into fat.

25. Describe the two processes by which amino groups are removed from amino acids.

26. What can keto acids be converted into?

27. What is the source of the nitrogen atoms in urea, and in what organ is urea synthesized?

28. Why is water considered an essential nutrient whereas glucose is not?

29. What is the consequence of ingesting large quantities of water-soluble vitamins? Fat-soluble vitamins?

THOUGHT QUESTIONS

(Answers are given in Appendix A).

1. How much energy is added to or released from a reaction in which reactants A and B are converted to products C and D if the energy content, in kilocalories per mole, of the participating molecule is A = 55, B = 93, C = 62, and D = 87? Is this reaction a reversible or an irreversible reaction? Explain.

2. In the following metabolic pathway, in which the maximal rates of the individual steps are indicated, what is the rate at which the end product E is formed if substrate A is present at a saturating concentration?

$$A \xrightarrow{30} B \xrightarrow{5} C \xrightarrow{20} D \xrightarrow{40} E$$

3. Under what conditions will increasing the concentration of oxygen at the level of the mitochondria lead to an increase in ATP production?

4. During a prolonged period of starvation, when glucose is not being absorbed from the gastrointestinal tract, what molecules can be used to synthesize new glucose?

5. Why does the catabolism of fatty acids occur only under aerobic conditions?

6. Why do certain forms of liver disease produce an increase in the blood levels of ammonia?

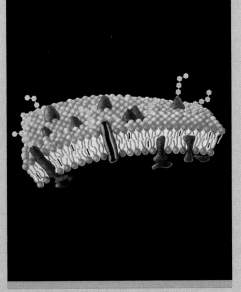

CHAPTER

6

MOVEMENT OF MOLECULES ACROSS CELL MEMBRANES

As we saw in Chapter 2, the contents of a cell are separated from the surrounding extracellular fluid by a thin layer of lipids and protein—the **plasma membrane**. In addition, membranes associated with mitochondria, endoplasmic reticulum, lysosomes, the Golgi apparatus, and the nucleus divide the intracellular fluid into separate compartments.

The contributions of this array of membranes to cell function fall into two categories: (1) The membranes act as barriers to the movements of certain molecules and ions both between the various cell organelles and the cytosol, and between the cytosol and the extracellular fluid; and (2) they provide a scaffolding to which various cell components are anchored, such as enzymes, contractile protein filaments, and binding sites for messenger molecules. This chapter focuses upon the barrier function of membranes, with emphasis on the plasma membrane.

We say that a membrane is *permeable* to any substance that can pass through it, regardless of the mechanism of permeation. If membranes were equally permeable to all substances, one would not expect the composition of the intracellular fluid to be much different from the extracellular fluid, whereas in fact (Table 6-1) there are large differences in the concentrations of most substances on the two sides of the plasma membrane. These differences in intracellular and extracellular composition result from two properties of membranes: (1) Membranes are selectively permeable, allowing some substances to pass but not others; and (2) the permeability of membranes to certain substances can be increased or decreased. This second property provides one of the mechanisms by which cells respond to signals from other cells, as will be described in Chapters 7 through 10.

There are several mechanisms by which substances pass through membranes, and we begin our discussion of membrane permeability with the physical process known as diffusion.

TABLE 6-1 COMPOSITION OF EXTRACELLULAR AND INTRACELLULAR FLUIDS

	Extracellular concentration, mM	Intracellular concentration,° mM
Na^+	145	15
K^+	4	150
Ca^{2+}	1	1.5
Mg^{2+}	1.5	12
Cl^-	110	10
HCO_3^-	24	10
P_i	2	40
Amino acids	2	8
Glucose	5.6	1
ATP	0	4
Protein	0.2	4

°The intracellular concentrations differ slightly from one tissue to another, but the concentrations shown above are typical of most cells. The intracellular concentrations listed above may not reflect the free concentration of the substance in the cytosol since some may be bound to proteins or confined within cell organelles. For example, the free cytosolic concentration of calcium is only about 0.0001 mM.

DIFFUSION

All molecules in any substance, be it solid, liquid, or gas, are in a continuous state of movement or vibration, and the warmer a substance is, the faster its molecules move. The average speed of this thermal motion also depends upon the mass of the molecule. At body temperature, a molecule of water moves at about 2500 km/h (1500 mi/h), whereas a molecule of glucose, which is 10 times heavier, moves at about 850 km/h. In solutions, such rapidly moving molecules cannot travel very far before colliding with other molecules. They bounce off each other like rubber balls, undergoing millions of collisions every

second. Each collision alters the direction of the molecule's movement, so that the path of any one molecule becomes unpredictable. Since any molecule may at any instant be moving in any direction, such movement is said to be "random," meaning that it has no preferred direction of movement.

The random thermal motion of molecules in a liquid or gas will eventually distribute them uniformly throughout the container. Thus, if we start with a solution in which a solute is more concentrated in one region than another (Figure 6-1A), random thermal motion will redistribute the solute from regions of high concentration to regions of lower concentration until the solute reaches a uniform concentration throughout the solution (Figure 6-1B). This net movement of molecules from regions of higher to

(A)   (B)

FIGURE 6-1
Molecules initially concentrated in one region of a solution (A) will, because of their random thermal motion, undergo a net movement from the region of higher to the region of lower concentration; that is, they will *diffuse* until they become uniformly distributed throughout the solution (B).

lower concentration as a result of their thermal motion is known as **diffusion**.

Many processes in living organisms are closely associated with diffusion. For example, oxygen, nutrients, and other molecules enter and leave the blood by diffusion, and the movement of many substances across the plasma membrane and organelle membranes occurs by diffusion.

Magnitude and Direction of Diffusion

The diffusion of glucose between two compartments of equal volume separated by a permeable barrier is illustrated in Figure 6-2. Initially glucose is present in compartment 1 at a concentration of 20 mmol/L, and there is no glucose in compartment 2. The random movements of the glucose molecules in compartment 1 carry some of them into compartment 2. The amount of material crossing a surface in a unit of time is known as a **flux**. This one-way flux of glucose from compartment 1 to compartment 2 depends on the concentration of glucose in compartment 1. If the number of molecules in a unit of volume is doubled, the flux of molecules across each surface of the unit will also be doubled, since twice as many molecules will be moving in any random direction at a given time.

After a short time, some of the glucose molecules that have entered compartment 2 will randomly move back into compartment 1 (Figure 6-2B). The magnitude of the one-way glucose flux from compartment 2 to compartment 1 depends upon the concentration of glucose in compartment 2 at any time. The **net flux** of glucose between the two compartments at any instant in time is the difference between the two one-way fluxes. It is the net flux that determines the net gain of molecules by compartment 2 and the net loss from compartment 1.

As the concentration of glucose in compartment 2 increases, the flux of glucose from 2 back into 1 increases. And as the concentration in compartment 1 decreases, the flux from 1 to 2 decreases. Eventually the concentrations of glucose in the two compartments become equal at 10 mmol/L. The two one-way fluxes are then equal in

magnitude but opposite in direction, and the net flux of glucose is zero (Figure 6-2C). The system has now reached **diffusion equilibrium**, and no further change in the glucose concentration of the two compartments will occur, although thermal motion will continue to move equal numbers of glucose molecules in both directions between the two compartments.

Several important properties of diffusion can be reemphasized using this example. Three fluxes can be identified at any surface—the two one-way fluxes occurring in opposite directions from one compartment to the other, and the net flux, which is the difference between them (Figure 6-3). It is the net flux that is the most important component in diffusion since it is the net amount of material transferred from one location to another. Although the movement of individual molecules is random, *the net flux always proceeds from regions of higher concentration to regions of lower concentration*. For this reason, we often say that substances move "downhill" by diffusion. The greater the difference in concentration between any two regions, the greater the magnitude of the net flux. Thus, both the direction and the magnitude of the net flux are determined by the concentration difference.

At any concentration difference, however, the magnitude of the net flux depends on several additional factors: (1) temperature—the higher the temperature, the greater the speed of molecular movement and the greater the net flux; (2) mass of the molecule—large molecules (for example, proteins) have a greater mass and lower speed than smaller molecules (for example, glucose) and thus have a smaller net flux; (3) surface area—the greater the surface area between two regions, the greater the space available for diffusion and thus the greater the net flux; (4) medium—molecules diffuse more rapidly in a gas phase than in water because collisions are less frequent in a gas phase.

Speed of Diffusion

The speed of diffusion is an important factor in determining the rate at which molecules can reach a cell from the

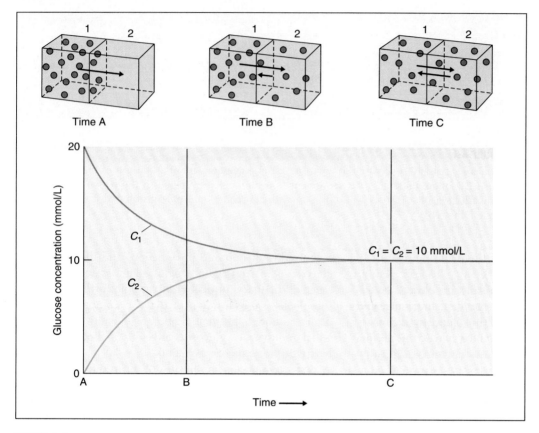

FIGURE 6-2

Diffusion of glucose between two compartments of equal volume separated by a permeable barrier. Initially, at time A, compartment 1 contains glucose at a concentration of 20 mmol/L, and no glucose is present in compartment 2. At time B, some glucose molecules have moved into compartment 2, and some are moving at random back into compartment 1. The lengths of the arrows represent the magnitude of the one-way movement. At time C, diffusion equilibrium has been reached, the concentration of glucose is equal in the two compartments (10 mmol/L), and the net movement is zero.

In the graph at the bottom of the figure, the red line represents the concentration in compartment 1 (C_1), and the blue line the concentration in compartment 2 (C_2).

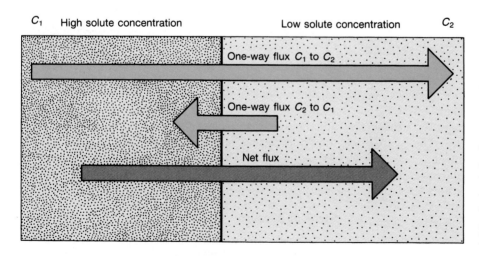

FIGURE 6-3

The three fluxes occurring during the diffusion of solute across a boundary: two one-way fluxes and the net flux (the difference between the two one-way fluxes). The net flux always occurs in the direction from higher to lower concentration.

blood or move throughout the interior of a cell after crossing the plasma membrane. Although individual molecules travel at high speeds, the number of collisions they undergo prevents them from traveling very far in a straight line. Diffusion times increase in proportion to the *square* of the distance over which the molecules diffuse. It is for this reason, for example, that it takes glucose approximately 3.5 s to reach 90 percent of diffusion equilibrium at a point 10 μm away form a source of glucose, such as the blood, but it would take over 11 years to reach the same concentration at a point 10 cm away from the source.

Thus, although diffusion can distribute molecules rapidly over distances of cellular dimensions, it takes a very long time when distances of a few centimeters or more are involved. For an organism as large as a person, the diffusion of oxygen and nutrients from the body surface to tissues located several centimeters below the surface would be far too slow to provide adequate nourishment. Accordingly, the circulatory system provides the mechanism for rapidly moving materials over large distances (by blood flow using a mechanical pump, the heart), with diffusion providing movement between the blood and tissue cells.

The rate at which diffusion is able to move molecules *within* a cell is one of the reasons that cells are so small. A cell would not have to be very large before diffusion failed to provide sufficient nutrients to the intracellular fluid. For example, the center of a 20-μm diameter cell reaches diffusion equilibrium with extracellular oxygen in about 15 ms, but it would take 265 days to reach equilibrium at the center of a cell the size of a basketball.

Diffusion Through Membranes

The rate at which a substance diffuses across the plasma membrane can be measured by monitoring the rate at which its intracellular concentration approaches diffusion equilibrium with its concentration in the extracellular fluid. If the volume of extracellular fluid is large, its solute concentration will remain essentially constant as the substance diffuses into the small intracellular volume (Figure 6-4). As with all diffusion processes, the net flux F of material across the membrane is from the region of higher concentration (the extracellular solution in this case) to the region of lower concentration (the intracellular fluid). The net flux is the difference between the two one-way fluxes, the influx f_i into the cell and the efflux f_e out of the cell. The magnitude of the net flux is directly proportional to the difference in concentration across the membrane $(C_o - C_i)$, the surface area of the membrane A, and the membrane **permeability constant k_p**:

$$\text{Influx: } f_i = k_p A C_o$$
$$\text{Efflux: } f_e = k_p A C_i$$
$$\text{Net flux: } F = k_p A (C_o - C_i) \qquad (6\text{-}1)$$

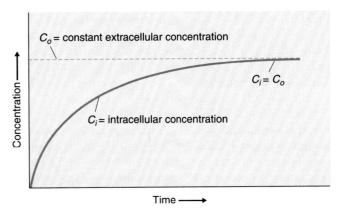

FIGURE 6-4

The increase in intracellular concentration as a substance diffuses from a constant extracellular concentration until diffusion equilibrium is reached across the plasma membrane of a cell.

The numerical value of the permeability constant k_p depends on the type of molecule, its molecular weight, the temperature, and the characteristics of the membrane through which the molecule is diffusing. It is an experimentally determined number for a given type of molecule at a given temperature, and it reflects the ease with which the molecule is able to move through a given membrane. In other words, the greater the permeability constant, the larger the net flux across the membrane for any given concentration difference and membrane area. Equation 6-1 also applies if diffusion is occurring out of a cell, for example, when a substance is synthesized within a cell and diffuses out, but then the net flux would be negative because C_i would be greater than C_o.

The rates of diffusion across membranes are a thousand to a million times smaller than the diffusion rates of the same molecules in water. In other words, a membrane acts as a barrier that considerably slows the diffusion of molecules across its surface. The major factor limiting diffusion across a membrane is its lipid bilayer.

Diffusion Through the Lipid Bilayer. When the permeability constants of different organic molecules are examined in relation to their molecular structures, a correlation emerges. Whereas most polar molecules diffuse into cells very slowly or not at all, nonpolar molecules diffuse rapidly across plasma membranes; that is, they have large permeability constants. The reason is that nonpolar molecules can dissolve in the nonpolar regions of the membrane—regions occupied by the fatty acid chains of the membrane phospholipids. In contrast, polar molecules have a much lower solubility in the membrane lipids. Increasing the lipid solubility of a substance (decreasing the number of polar or ionized groups it contains) will increase the number of molecules dissolved in the membrane lipids and thus increase its flux across the membrane. Oxygen, carbon dioxide, fatty acids, and steroid hormones are examples of nonpolar molecules that diffuse rapidly through the lipid portions of membranes.

That it is the lipid bilayer portion of the membrane, and not the membrane proteins, that provides the selective barrier is substantiated by experiments using artificial membranes consisting of a bimolecular layer of lipids but containing no protein. For most substances the rates of diffusion across these artificial lipid bilayers and their selectivity are very similar to those of plasma membranes. An apparent exception to this generalization, however, occurs in the case of ions, to which we now turn.

Diffusion of Ions Through Protein Channels. Ions such as Na^+, K^+, Cl^-, and Ca^{2+} diffuse across plasma membranes at rates that are much faster than would be predicted from their very low solubility in membrane lipids. Moreover, different cells have quite different permeabilities to these ions, whereas nonpolar substances have similar permeabilities when different cells are compared. The fact that artificial lipid bilayers containing no protein are practically impermeable to these ions, whereas plasma membranes have a considerable permeability to them, suggests that it is the protein component of the membrane that is responsible for these permeability differences.

As we have seen (page 45), integral membrane proteins can span the lipid bilayer. Such proteins can form **channels** through which ions can diffuse across the membrane (Figure 6-5). A single protein may have a conforma-

tion similar to that of a doughnut, with the hole in the middle providing the channel for ion movement. More often several proteins aggregate to form the walls of a channel (Figure 6-6). The diameters of protein channels are very small, only slightly larger than those of the ions that pass through them. The small size of the channels prevents larger, polar organic molecules from entering the channel. Only the mineral ions (and possibly water) are small enough to pass through these protein channels.

Very importantly, channels can exist in an open or closed state. The variation in membrane permeability to ions found in different cell membranes reflects differences in the number of open ion channels in the membranes. The greater the number of open channels, the greater the ion flux across the membrane for any given ion concentration difference. Furthermore, the ion channels show a selectivity for the type of ions that can pass through them. This selectivity is based partially on the channel diameter and partially on the charged and polar surfaces of the proteins that form the channel walls and that electrically attract or repel the ions. For example, some channels (K channels) will allow only potassium ions to pass, others are specific for sodium (Na channels), and still others allow both sodium and potassium ions to pass (Na,K channels). Two membranes that have the same permeability to potassium, because they have the same number of open K channels, may have quite different permeabilities to sodium because of differences in the number of Na channels.

Role of Electric Forces on Ion Movements. Thus far we have described the direction and magnitude of diffu-

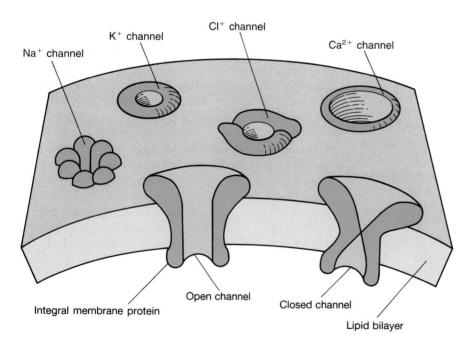

Na$^+$ channel
K$^+$ channel
Cl$^+$ channel
Ca^{2+} channel
Integral membrane protein
Open channel
Closed channel
Lipid bilayer

FIGURE 6-5

Hypothetical shapes of the integral membrane proteins that form the various channels through which ions diffuse across membranes. A single protein or a cluster of more than one protein forms the walls of a channel. A channel may be open or closed as a result of conformational changes in the channel proteins.

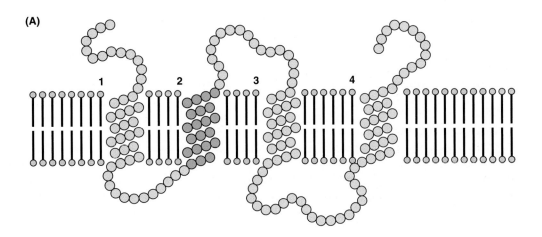

(A)

FIGURE 6-6

Model of an ion channel structure composed of five polypeptide subunits. (A) A channel subunit consisting of an integral membrane protein containing 4 transmembrane segments (1, 2, 3, and 4) each of which has an alpha-helical configuration within the membrane. Although we have illustrated only 4 transmembrane segments, some channel proteins have as many as 12. (B) The same subunit as in A shown in three dimensions within the membrane with the four transmembrane helices aggregated together. (C) The ion channel consists of 5 of the subunits illustrated in B, which form the sides of the channel. As shown in cross section, the helical transmembrane segment (2) of each subunit forms the walls of the channel, and the presence of ionized amino acid side chains along this region determines the selectivity of the channel to ions. Although this model shows 5 identical subunits, many ion channels are formed from the aggregation of several different types of subunit polypeptides.

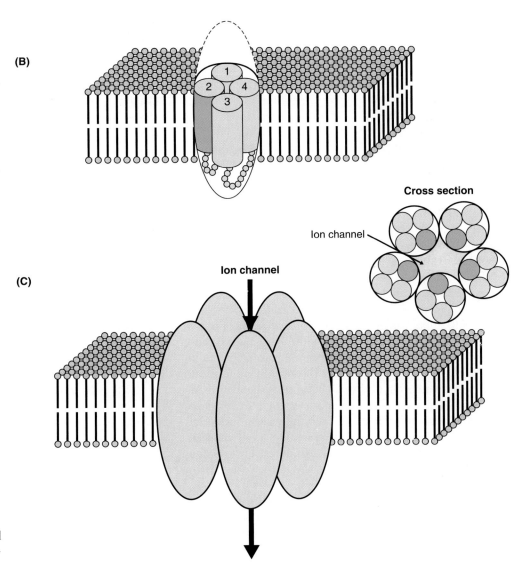

(B)

(C)

Cross section

Ion channel

Ion channel

FIGURE 6-7

The separation of electric charge across a plasma membrane (membrane potential) provides the electric force that drives positive ions into a cell and negative ions out of a cell.

sion across a membrane as being determined by the concentration difference across the membrane. When describing the diffusion of ions, however, one additional factor must be considered, the presence of electric forces acting upon the ions. There exists a separation of electric charge across plasma membranes (Figure 6-7), the origin of which will be described in Chapter 8. Such a charge separation, known as a **membrane potential**, affects the diffusion of ions across the membrane because ions are charged. For example, if the inside of a cell has a net negative charge with respect to the outside, as it does in most cells, there will be an electric force attracting positive ions into the cell and repelling negative ions. Even if there were no ion concentration difference across the membrane, there would still be a net flux of positive ions into and negative ions out of the cell because of the membrane potential. Thus, the direction and magnitude of *ion* fluxes across membranes depend on both the concentration difference and the electrical difference (the membrane potential). These two driving forces are collectively known as the **electrochemical difference**, also termed the electrochemical gradient, across a membrane.

It is worth noting that the two forces that make up the electrochemical difference may oppose each other. Thus, the *membrane potential* may be driving potassium ions, for example, in one direction across the membrane, while the *concentration difference* of potassium is driving these ions in the opposite direction. The net movement of potassium in this case would be determined by the magnitudes of the two opposing forces, that is, by the electrochemical difference across the membrane.

Regulation of Diffusion Through Membranes. The diffusion of a substance across a membrane may be altered by changes in one or more of the variables in Equation 6-1: (1) the surface area A, (2) the concentration difference for the substance, $C_o - C_i$, and the electrical difference in the case of ions, and (3) the membrane permeability constant k_p for the substance. Of these three, the membrane permeability constant is the one that can be altered to effect rapid changes in ion fluxes across the membrane.

Changes in a membrane's permeability to ions can occur rapidly as a result of the opening or closing of ion channels, which occurs when the channel proteins undergo a change in shape. The process of opening and closing ion channels is known as **channel gating**, like the opening and closing of a gate in a fence. A single ion channel may open and close many times in a single second, suggesting that the channel protein is fluctuating between two (or more) conformations, possibly as a result of random collisions with molecules in the surrounding medium. Over an extended period of time, at any given electrochemical difference, the total number of ions that pass through a single channel depends on how frequently the channel opens and how long it stays open.

Three factors can alter the stability of the channel protein conformations, producing changes in the opening frequency or the duration the channel remains open: (1) the binding of specific chemical "messengers" to the plama membrane (described in Chapter 7), (2) changes in the membrane potential—**voltage-sensitive channels**, and (3) distorting the membrane—**mechanosensitive channels**. A single channel may be affected by any number of these factors.

A particular type of ion may pass through several different types of channels. For example, a membrane may contain messenger-linked potassium channels, voltage-sensitive potassium channels, and mechanosensitive potassium channels. The same membrane may also have several types of voltage-sensitive potassium channels, each responding to a different range of membrane voltage, or several types of messenger-linked potassium channels, each responding to a different chemical messenger. The roles of these gated channels in cell communication and electrical activity will be discussed in Chapters 7 through 9.

MEDIATED-TRANSPORT SYSTEMS

Although diffusion accounts for some of the transmembrane movement of ions, it does not account for all. Moreover, there are a number of other molecules, including amino acids and glucose, that are able to cross membranes yet are too polar to diffuse through the lipid bilayer or too large to diffuse through protein channels. The passage of these molecules and the nondiffusional movements of ions through membranes are mediated by integral membrane proteins known as **transporters** (or carriers). Such **mediated-transport** systems are quite different from the passage of substances through membranes by diffusion.

A substance that crosses a membrane by mediated transport must first bind to a specific site on a transporter (see Figure 6-10), a site that is exposed to the substance on one surface of the membrane. A portion of the transport protein then undergoes a change in shape, exposing this same binding site to the solution on the opposite side of the membrane. The dissociation of the substance from the transporter binding site completes the process of moving the material through the membrane. Using this mechanism, molecules can move in either direction across the membrane, getting on the transporter at one side and off at the other.

The diagram of the transporter in Figure 6-8 is only a model, since we have little information concerning the specific conformational changes of any transport protein.[1] Transport proteins amount to less than 0.2 percent of the total membrane proteins, and the amino acid sequences of a number of transport proteins have been determined as a result of advances in the molecular biology of gene cloning. This information, however, does not yet allow determination of the conformation of the transport protein within the membrane.

There are many types of transport proteins in membranes, each type having binding sites that are specific for a particular substance or a specific class of related substances. For example, although both amino acids and sugars undergo mediated transport, a protein that transports amino acids does not transport sugars, and vice versa. Just as with ion channels, the plasma membranes of different cells may contain different types and numbers of transport proteins and thus exhibit differences in the types of substances transported and their rates of transport.

Three factors determine the magnitude of the solute flux through a mediated-transport system: (1) the extent to which the transporter binding site is saturated, which depends on both the solute concentration and the affinity of the transporter for the solute; (2) the number of transport proteins in the membrane—the greater the number of transporters, the greater the flux at any level of saturation; and (3) the rate at which the conformational change in the transport protein occurs. The flux through a mediated transport system can be altered by changing any of these three factors.

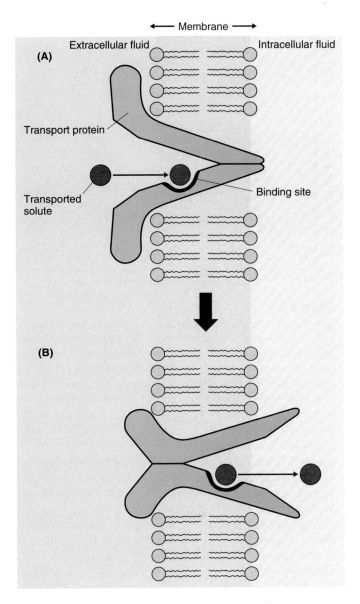

FIGURE 6-8

Model of mediated transport. A change in the conformation of the transport protein moves the transporter binding site from one surface of the membrane to the other, thereby transferring the bound solute from one side of the membrane to the other.

For any transported solute, there is a finite number of specific transport proteins in a given membrane at any particular moment. As with any binding site, as the concentration of the ligand (the solute to be transported in this case) is increased, the number of occupied binding sites increases until the transporters become saturated, that is, until all the sites become occupied. Beyond this point, further increases in solute concentration will not increase the transport flux (Figure 6-9). When the trans-

---

[1] It is assumed that these conformational changes are analogous to those undergone by channel proteins that spontaneously open and close.

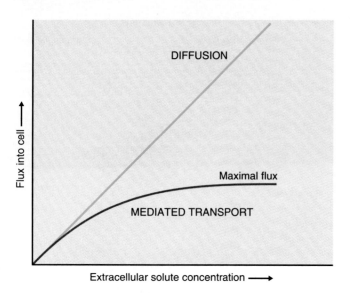

FIGURE 6-9

The flux of molecules diffusing across a plasma membrane (blue line) increases in proportion to the extracellular concentration, whereas the flux of molecules through a mediated-transport system (red line) reaches a maximal value. This maximal mediated-transport flux corresponds to the saturation of all the available transporters by the transported solute.

porters are saturated, the maximal transport flux depends upon the rate at which the conformational changes in the transport proteins can transfer the binding site from one surface to the other.

Contrast the saturation behavior of mediated-transport fluxes (Figure 6-9) with the fluxes produced by diffusion. A flux into a cell resulting from diffusion increases in direct proportion to the increase in extracellular concentration, and there is no maximal limit since diffusion does not involve binding to a fixed number of sites.

Two types of mediated transport can be distinguished— **facilitated diffusion** and **active transport**. Facilitated diffusion uses a transport protein to move solute from a higher to a lower concentration across a membrane, whereas active transport uses a transport protein that is coupled to an energy source to move solute "uphill" across a membrane from lower to higher concentration, that is, against its electrochemical difference.

Facilitated Diffusion

"Facilitated diffusion" is an unfortunate term since the process it denotes does not involve diffusion. The term arose because the end results of both diffusion and facilitated diffusion are the same. In both processes the net flux across a membrane always proceeds from higher to lower concentration and continues until the concentrations on the two sides of the membrane become equal. At this

point, in the case of facilitated diffusion, equal numbers of molecules are binding to the transporter at the outer surface of the cell and moving into the cell as are binding at the inner surface and moving out. When the transported-solute concentration is increased sufficiently, however, facilitated-diffusion systems reach a maximal flux that cannot be increased by further increases in concentration because the transport proteins become saturated, whereas fluxes due to diffusion do not saturate (Figure 6-10). Neither diffusion nor facilitated diffusion is coupled to energy derived from metabolism, and thus they are incapable of moving solute from a lower to a higher concentration across a membrane.

Among the most important facilitated-diffusion systems in the body are those that move glucose across most plasma membranes. Without such glucose transporters, cells would be impermeable to glucose, which is a relatively large, polar molecule. One might expect that as a result of facilitated diffusion the glucose concentration inside cells would become equal to the extracellular concentration. This does not occur in most cells, however, because glucose is metabolized almost as quickly as it enters. Thus, the intracellular glucose concentration remains lower than the extracellular concentration (Table 6-1), and there is a continuous net flux of glucose into most cells.

Four transport proteins are known to mediate the facilitated diffusion of glucose across cell membranes. Each transporter is coded by a different gene, and these genes are expressed in different types of cells. The transporters differ in the affinity of their binding sites for glucose, the maximal rates of transport when saturated (a measure of the rate at which the transporter undergoes a conformational change from one side of the membrane to another), and their ability to be modified by various chemical signals. As will be discussed in Chapter 18, the hormone insulin increases the number of glucose transport proteins found in the plasma membranes of muscle and adipose tissue cells and thereby increases the rate of glucose movement into these cells. Although glucose enters all cells by means of glucose transporters, insulin affects only the type of glucose transporter expressed in muscle and adipose tissue.

Active Transport

Active transport differs from facilitated diffusion in its use of energy to move substances *uphill*, that is, from a region of lower concentration to one of higher concentration across a membrane (Figure 6-11). Because active-transport processes move molecules *uphill*, they are often referred to as "pumps." Recall that with ions, the electrical difference as well as the concentration difference influences fluxes across a membrane. Thus, the active transport of ions can move ions against an electrochemical difference. To simplify our discussion, however, we shall refer

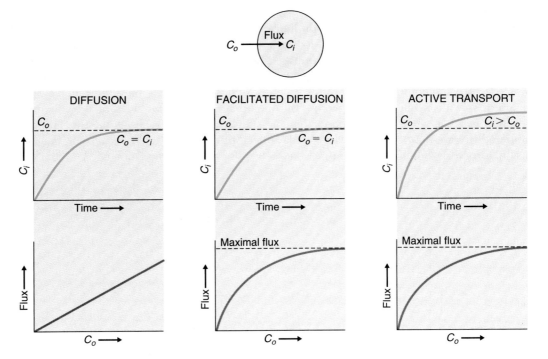

FIGURE 6-10

Comparison of diffusion, facilitated diffusion, and active transport in terms of the level of intracellular concentration reached relative to the extracellular concentration and the presence or absence of a limiting maximal flux due to saturation. (Note that the upper figures show the increase in the intracellular concentration as a function of *time* at one extracellular concentration, while the lower figures show the flux into the cell as a function of increasing extracellular *concentration*.) The steady-state intracellular concentration will not distinguish between diffusion and facilitated diffusion at a given extracellular concentration, nor will saturation distinguish facilitated diffusion from active transport with increasing extracellular concentrations.

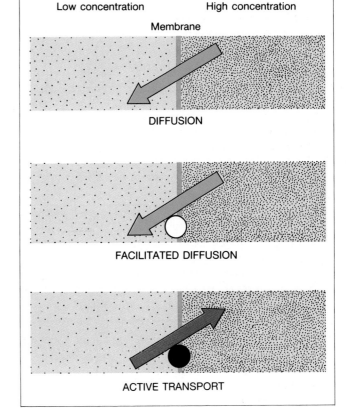

FIGURE 6-11

Direction of net solute flux crossing membrane by (1) diffusion—high to low concentration, (2) facilitated diffusion—high to low concentration, and (3) active transport—low to high concentration. (The symbols $\overset{\longrightarrow}{\bigcirc}$ and $\overset{\longrightarrow}{\bullet}$ will be used throughout this book to represent a transport protein in a membrane—an open circle for facilitated diffusion, and a solid circle for active transport. If a substance crosses a membrane by diffusion, no circle will be present.)

only to the concentration difference, by implication including the electrical difference when ions are involved.

As in facilitated diffusion, the active transport of a substance across a membrane requires binding to a transport protein in the membrane. The transport protein exhibits chemical specificity, and the flux across the membrane becomes maximal when the transporter binding sites are saturated (Figure 6-10). Recall that during facilitated diffusion, however, when the concentrations on the two sides

of a membrane become equal, the flux of substance into the cell through the transporter becomes equal to the flux out of the cell and there is no further change in the concentrations on the two sides of the membrane. In the case of active transport into a cell, when the concentrations on the two sides of the membrane become equal (Figure 6-12, time A), the flux into the cell remains greater than the flux out. As a result, there will continue to be a net flux into the cell, and the intracellular concentration will be-

Time A

Time B

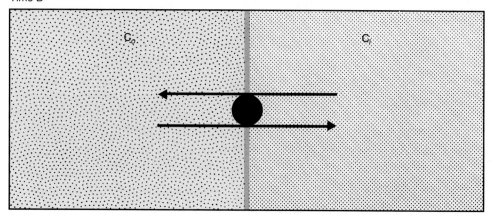

FIGURE 6-12

As the concentrations on the two sides of a membrane become equal (time A) during the active transport of a substance into a cell, the flux into the cell remains greater than the flux out, producing a net flux into the cell and a continued rise in intracellular concentration until a steady state is reached (time B). At this time the fluxes in the two directions become equal, and no further change in intracellular concentration occurs.

come greater than the extracellular concentration. As the intracellular concentration continues to increase, the flux out of the cell will increase until a steady state is reached in which the fluxes in the two directions become equal and there is no further change in the intracellular concentration with time (Figure 6-12, time B). Although the above description is in terms of the active transport of a substance *into* a cell, there are also active-transport processes that move a substance out of a cell from a lower intracellular to a higher extracellular concentration. In this case the fundamental mechanism is the same, and only the direction of net transport is reversed.

The net movement from lower to higher concentration and the maintenance of a higher steady-state concentration on one side of a membrane can be achieved only by a continuous input of energy into the active-transport process. The result of this energy input can (1) alter the affinity of the binding site on the transporter such that it has a higher affinity when facing one side of the membrane than when facing the other side, resulting in more binding and thus a greater flux from the high-affinity side to the low-affinity side; or (2) alter the rate at which the transport protein moves the binding site from one surface to the other.

The energy for active transport is ultimately derived from metabolism, since inhibition of ATP production in a cell will eventually result in a failure of membrane transporters to actively transport substances uphill. In order to move molecules from a lower concentration (lower energy state) to a higher concentration (higher energy state), energy must be added. Therefore, active transport must be coupled to the simultaneous flow of some energy source from a higher energy level to a lower energy level. Two means of coupling an energy flow to transport proteins are known: (1) the direct use of ATP in **primary active transport**, and (2) the use of an ion concentration difference across a membrane to drive the process in **secondary active transport**.

Primary Active Transport. The hydrolysis of ATP by a transport protein provides the energy for primary active transport by that protein. The transporter is an enzyme, an ATPase, that catalyzes the breakdown of ATP and in the process phosphorylates itself. In this case an enzyme and one of its substrates are the same molecule. Phosphorylation of the transporter (Figure 6-13) alters either the affinity of its binding site or the rate of conformational change, in either case producing an asymmetry in movements of the transported substance across the membrane. (Note that this is an example of covalent modulation, as discussed on page 60, in which the phosphorylation of a protein alters its properties.)

Four primary active-transport proteins have been iden-

FIGURE 6-13

Primary active transport. The hydrolysis of ATP by the transport protein leads to phosphorylation of the transporter, altering the translocation process (covalent modulation of the transport protein).

tified, each an ATPase and each involved in transporting ions: (1) One simultaneously pumps sodium and potassium ions (Na,K-ATPase); (2) one pumps calcium ions (Ca-ATPase); (3) one pumps hydrogen ions (H-ATPase); and (4) one pumps both hydrogen and potassium ions (H,K-ATPase).

The Na,K-ATPase is present in all cells. The pumping activity of this transport system leads to the characteristic

FIGURE 6-14

The primary active transport of sodium and potassium ions in opposite directions by the Na,K-ATPase in plasma membranes is responsible for the low sodium and high potassium intracellular concentrations. For each ATP hydrolyzed, three sodium ions are moved out of a cell and two potassium ions are moved in.

distribution of high intracellular potassium and low intracellular sodium relative to their respective extracellular concentrations (Figure 6-14). For each molecule of ATP that is hydrolyzed, this carrier moves three sodium ions *out* of a cell and two potassium ions *in.*

The Ca-ATPase is found in the plasma membrane and several organelle membranes, including the membranes of the endoplasmic reticulum and the mitochondria. In the plasma membrane, the direction of active calcium transport is from cytosol to extracellular fluid. In organelle membranes it is from cytosol into the organelle lumen. The active transport of calcium out of the cytosol, via the Ca-ATPase, is one reason that the cytosol of most cells has a very low calcium concentration, about 10^{-7} mol/L compared with an extracellular calcium concentration of 10^{-3} mol/L, 10,000 times greater (a second reason will be given below).

The H-ATPase is located in the plasma membrane and in several organelle membranes, including the inner mitochondrial and lysosomal membranes. In the plasma membrane the hydrogen transporter moves hydrogen ions out of cells. The H,K-ATPase is also located in the plasma membrane of some cells, where it pumps hydrogen ions out of the cell and moves potassium in. This transporter is responsible for the secretion of acid by the stomach, as we shall see in Chapter 17.

Secondary Active Transport. Secondary active transport is distinguished from primary active transport by its use of an ion concentration gradient across a membrane as the energy source. The flow of ions from a high concentration (high energy state) to a lower concentration (low energy state) provides energy for the uphill movement of the actively transported solute.[2] Like facilitated diffusion and primary active transport, secondary active transport requires binding of the transported solute (amino acids, for example) to a transport protein, which has the properties of chemical specificity, affinity and a limiting maximal-transport rate because of saturation of the transporter.

In addition to having a binding site for the actively transported solute, the transport protein in a secondary-active-transport system also has an additional binding site for an ion (Figure 6-15). This ion is usually sodium, but in some cases it can be another ion such as bicarbonate, chloride, or potassium. Examples of the use of other ions to drive secondary active transport will be illustrated in subsequent chapters.

The binding of an ion to the secondary-active-transport protein produces the same types of changes in a transport protein as occur in primary active transport, namely, (1) altering the affinity of the binding site for the transported solute, or (2) altering the rate at which the transport protein moves the binding site from one surface to the other. In the case of primary active transport the transport protein is altered by covalent modulation resulting from the covalent linkage of phosphate from ATP to the transport protein, whereas in the case of secondary active transport the changes are brought about through allosteric modulation as a result of ion binding.[3]

There is a very important indirect link between the secondary active transporters that utilize sodium and the primary active sodium transporter, the Na,K-ATPase. Recall that the intracellular concentration of sodium is much lower than the extracellular sodium concentration because of the primary active transport of sodium out of the cell by Na,K-ATPase. Because of the low intracellular sodium concentration few of the sodium binding sites on the secondary-active-transport protein are occupied at the intracellular surface of the transporter. Thus, the characteristics of this transport protein differ at the extracellular and intracellular surfaces depending on the presence or absence of a bound sodium ion. This difference provides the

---

[2]The energy stored in an ion concentration gradient across a membrane can also be used to synthesize ATP from ADP and P_i. Electron transport through the cytochrome chain produces a hydrogen-ion concentration gradient across the inner mitochondrial membrane. The movement of hydrogen ions down this gradient provides the energy that is coupled to the synthesis of ATP during oxidative phosphorylation—the chemiosmotic hypothesis discussed in Chapter 5.

[3]See Chapter 4 for a review of covalent and allosteric modulation mechanisms.

FIGURE 6-15

Secondary active transport. The binding of sodium ions to the transport protein produces an allosteric alteration of the transport protein at the outer surface of the membrane, while the absence of sodium binding at the inner surface, because of the low intracellular sodium concentration, reverses these changes, leading to the asymmetrical fluxes of the transported solute across the membrane.

The creation of a sodium concentration difference across the plasma membrane by the *primary* active transport of sodium is a means of indirectly "storing" energy that can then be used to drive *secondary*-active-transport pumps. Ultimately, however, the energy for secondary active transport is derived from metabolism in the form of the ATP that is used by the primary Na,K-ATPase to create the sodium concentration gradient. If the production of ATP were inhibited, the primary active transport of sodium would cease and the cell would no longer be able to maintain a sodium concentration gradient across the membrane. This in turn would lead to a failure of the secondary-active-transport systems that depend on the sodium gradient for their source of energy. Between 10 and 40 percent of the ATP produced by a cell, under rest-

FIGURE 6-16

During secondary active transport involving sodium, this ion always moves *down* its concentration gradient into a cell, and the transported solute always moves *up* its gradient. Both sodium and the transported solute X move in the same direction during cotransport but in opposite directions during countertransport.

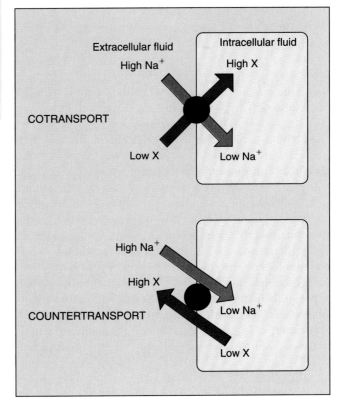

basis for the asymmetry in the transport fluxes, leading to the uphill movement of the transported solute. At the same time, the sodium ion that binds to the transporter at the extracellular surface moves *downhill* into the cell when the transporter undergoes its conformational change.

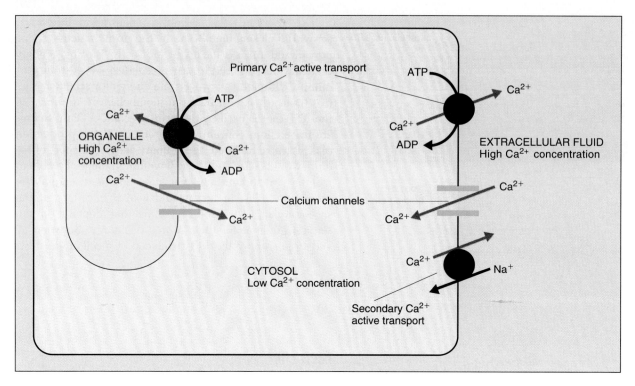

FIGURE 6-17

Pathways affecting cytosolic calcium concentration. The active transport of calcium, both by primary Ca-ATPase pumps and by secondary active calcium countertransport with sodium, moves calcium ions out of the cytosol. Calcium channels allow calcium to diffuse into the cytosol from either the extracellular fluid or the cell organelles. Cytosolic calcium concentration is the resultant of all these processes.

ing conditions, is used by the Na,K-ATPase to maintain the sodium gradient, which in turn drives a multitude of secondary-active-transport systems.

As noted earlier, the net movement of sodium by a secondary-active-transport protein is always from high extracellular concentration into the cell, where the concentration of sodium is lower. Thus, in secondary active transport, the movement of sodium is always downhill, while the net movement of the actively transported solute on the same transport protein is uphill, moving from lower to higher concentration. The movement of the actively transported solute can be either into the cell (in the same direction as sodium), in which case it is known as **cotransport**, or out of the cell (opposite the direction of sodium movement), which is called **countertransport**[4] (Figure 6-16).

A variety of organic molecules and a few ions are moved across membranes by sodium-coupled secondary active transport. For example, amino acids, in most cells, are actively transported into the cell by cotransport with sodium ions, attaining intracellular concentrations 2 to 20 times higher than in the extracellular fluid.

An example of the secondary active transport of ions is provided by calcium. In addition to the previously described primary active transport of calcium from cytosol to extracellular fluid via Ca-ATPase proteins, there also exists in many membranes a Na-Ca countertransport protein (or Na-Ca "exchanger")[5] that uses the downhill movement of sodium ions into a cell to pump calcium ions out by secondary active transport. Figure 6-17 illustrates the dependence of cytosolic calcium concentration on the several pathways that can move calcium ions into or out of the cytosol via calcium channels, a Ca-ATPase pump, and Na-Ca countertransport. Alterations in the movement of calcium through any of these pathways will lead to a

---

[4]The terms "symport" and "antiport" are also used to refer to the processes of cotransport and countertransport, respectively.

[5]Countertransport proteins that move one ion into a cell while moving another out of the cell are often referred to as *exchangers*.

TABLE 6-2   MAJOR CHARACTERISTICS OF PATHWAYS BY WHICH SUBSTANCES CROSS MEMBRANES

	Diffusion		Mediated Transport		
	Through lipid bilayer	Through protein channel	Facilitated diffusion	Primary active transport	Secondary active transport
Direction of net flux	High to low concentration	High to low concentration	High to low concentration	Low to high concentration	Low to high concentration
Equilibrium or steady state	$C_o = C_i$	$C_o = C_i°$	$C_o = C_i$	$C_o \neq C_i$	$C_o \neq C_i$
Use of integral membrane protein	No	Yes	Yes	Yes	Yes
Maximal flux at high concentration (saturation)	No	No	Yes	Yes	Yes
Chemical specificity	No	Yes	Yes	Yes	Yes
Use of energy and source	No	No	No	Yes; ATP	Yes; ion gradient (often Na)
Typical molecules using pathway	Nonpolar: O_2, CO_2, fatty acids	Ions: Na^+, K^+, Ca^{2+}	Polar: glucose	Ions: Na^+, K^+, Ca^{2+}, H^+	Polar: amino acids, glucose, some ions

°In the presence of a membrane potential, the intracellular and extracellular ion concentrations will not be equal at equilibrium.

change in cytosolic calcium concentration and, as a result, alter the cellular activities that are dependent on cytosolic calcium, as will be described in subsequent chapters.

Table 6-2 provides a summary of the major characteristics of the different pathways by which substances move through cell membranes.

OSMOSIS

Water is a small, polar molecule, about 0.3 nm in diameter, that diffuses across most cell membranes very rapidly. One might expect that, because of its polar structure, water would not penetrate the nonpolar lipid regions of membranes. However, artificial phospholipid bilayers also have a high permeability to water, indicating that water can diffuse through the membrane lipid layer. The very small size of the water molecule, plus the fact that it is polar rather than ionized, may contribute to its ability to do so. Because of its small size, water can also diffuse through some protein channels, but it does not cross membranes by mediated-transport systems.

Osmosis is the net diffusion of water from a region of higher water concentration to a region of lower water concentration. As with any diffusion process, there must be a concentration difference in order to produce a net flux. How can a difference in water concentration be established across a membrane?

The addition of a solute to water will lower the concentration of water in the solution compared to the concentration of water in pure water. Let us take an example. A liter of pure water weighs about 1000 g, and the molecular weight of water is 18. Thus, the concentration of water in pure water is 1000/18 = 55.5 *M*. However, if a solute such as glucose is dissolved in water, the concentration of water in the resulting solution is less than that of pure water. A given volume of a glucose solution will contain fewer water molecules than an equal volume of pure water since each glucose molecule in solution will occupy space formerly occupied by a water molecule (Figure 6-18). The decrease in water concentration in a solution is approximately equal to the concentration of added solute. In other words, one solute molecule will displace one water molecule.[6] The water concentration in a 1 *M* glucose solution is thus approximately 54.5 *M* rather than 55.5 *M*. Just as adding water to a solution will dilute the solute, adding solute to a solution will "dilute" the water. *The greater the solute concentration, the lower the water concentration.*

It is essential to recognize that the degree to which the water concentration is decreased by the addition of solute depends upon the *number* of particles (molecules or ions) of solute in solution (the solute concentration) and not upon the chemical nature of the solute. For example, 1 mol of glucose in 1 L of solution decreases the water concentration to approximately the same extent as does 1 mol of an amino acid, or 1 mol of urea, or 1 mol of any other molecule that exists as a single particle in solution. A molecule that ionizes in solution decreases the water concentration in proportion to the number of ions formed. Hence, 1 mol of sodium chloride in solution gives rise to 1 mol of sodium ions and 1 mol of chloride ions, producing 2 mol of solute particles, which lowers the water concentration twice as much as does 1 mol of glucose. By the

same reasoning, a 1 *M* $MgCl_2$ solution lowers the water concentration three times as much as does a 1 *M* glucose solution.

Since the water concentration in a solution depends upon the number of solute particles, it is useful to have a concentration term that refers to the total concentration of solute particles in a solution, regardless of their chemical composition. The total solute concentration of a solution is known as its **osmolarity**. One **osmole** is equal to 1 mol of solute particles. Thus, a 1 *M* solution of glucose has a concentration of 1 *Osm* (1 Osmol per liter), but a 1 *M* solution of sodium chloride contains 2 osmol of solute per liter of solution. A liter of solution containing 1 mol of glucose and 1 mol of sodium chloride has an osmolarity of 3 *Osm*. A solution with an osmolarity of 3 *Osm* may contain 1 mol of glucose and 1 mol of sodium chloride, or 3 mol of glucose, or 1.5 mol of sodium chloride, or any other combination of solutes as long as the total solute concentration is equal to 3 *Osm*.

It is essential to realize that although osmolarity refers to the concentration of solute particles, it also determines the *water concentration* in the solution since the *higher* the osmolarity, the *lower* the water concentration. The concentration of water in any two solutions having the same osmolarity is the same since the total number of solute particles per unit volume is the same.

Let us now apply these principles governing water concentration to the diffusion of water across membranes. Figure 6-19 shows two 1-L compartments separated by a membrane permeable to *both* solute and water. The concentration of solute is 2 *Osm* in compartment 1 and 4 *Osm* in compartment 2. This difference in solute concentration means there is also a difference in water concentration across the membrane: 53.5 *M* in compartment 1 and 51.5 *M* in compartment 2. Therefore, there will be a net diffusion of water from the higher concentration in 1 to the lower concentration in 2, and of solute in the opposite direction, from 2 to 1. When diffusion equilibrium is reached, both the solute and water concentrations will be equal in the two compartments, 3 *Osm* and 52.5 *M*, re-

---

[6]Because molecules have different sizes and may contain charged or polar groups that interact with the polar water molecules, there is not an exact one-to-one displacement of one water molecule for each solute molecule in solution, but for dilute solutions this generalization is approximately correct.

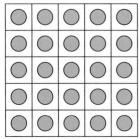

Pure water
(high water concentration)

◯ Water molecule

⬤ Solute molecule

Solution
(lower water concentration)

FIGURE 6-18
The addition of solute molecules to pure water lowers the water concentration in the solution.

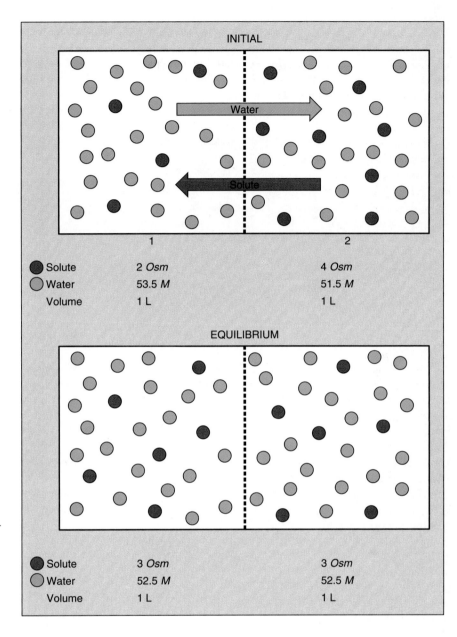

INITIAL

	1	2
● Solute	2 *Osm*	4 *Osm*
○ Water	53.5 *M*	51.5 *M*
Volume	1 L	1 L

EQUILIBRIUM

● Solute	3 *Osm*	3 *Osm*
○ Water	52.5 *M*	52.5 *M*
Volume	1 L	1 L

FIGURE 6-19
The net diffusion of water and solute between two compartments of equal volume, in opposite directions across a membrane permeable to both, leads to diffusion equilibrium of both water and solute, with no change in the volume of either compartment.

spectively. One mole of water will have diffused from compartment 1 to compartment 2, and 1 mol of solute will have diffused from 2 to 1. Since 1 mol of solute has replaced 1 mol of water in compartment 1, and vice versa in compartment 2, there is no change in the *volume* of either compartment.

If the membrane is now replaced by one that is permeable to water but impermeable to solute (Figure 6-20), the same *concentrations* of water and solute will be reached at equilibrium as before, but there will also be a change in the *volumes* of the compartments. Water will diffuse from 1 to 2, but there will be no solute diffusion in the opposite direction because the membrane is impermeable to solute.

Water will continue to diffuse into compartment 2, therefore, until the water concentrations on the two sides become equal. The solute concentration in compartment 2 will decrease as it is diluted by the incoming water, and the solute in compartment 1 will become more concentrated as water moves out. When the water has reached diffusion equilibrium, the osmolarities of the compartments will be equal, and thus the solute concentrations must also be equal. To reach this state of equilibrium, 18.5 mol (0.33 L)[7] of water must be transferred by osmosis from

[7]The 4 Osmol of solute initially present cannot leave compartment 1. The addition of 0.33 L of water (18.5 mol) to the liter of water already present will dilute the 4 Osmol of solute to (4 Osmol/1.33 L) = 3 *Osm*.

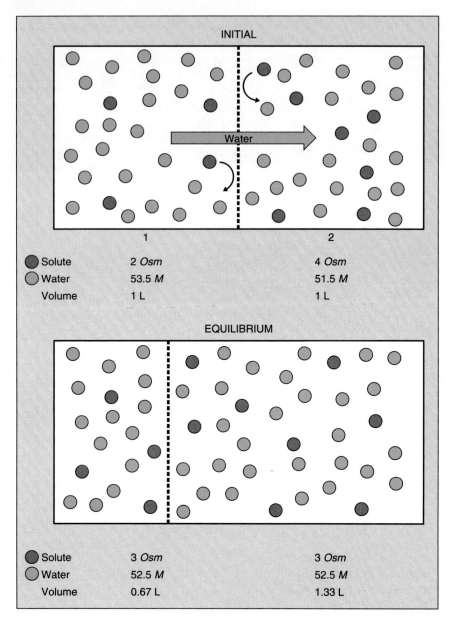

INITIAL

		1	2
●	Solute	2 *Osm*	4 *Osm*
○	Water	53.5 *M*	51.5 *M*
	Volume	1 L	1 L

EQUILIBRIUM

●	Solute	3 *Osm*	3 *Osm*
○	Water	52.5 *M*	52.5 *M*
	Volume	0.67 L	1.33 L

FIGURE 6-20

The movement of water across a membrane that is permeable to water but not permeable to solute leads to an equilibrium state in which there is a change in the initially equal volumes of the two compartments as a result of the net diffusion of water (0.33 L in this case) from compartment 1 to compartment 2. (The membrane in this example stretches as the volume of compartment 2 increases so that no significant change in intracellular pressure occurs.)

compartment 1 to compartment 2, increasing the volume of compartment 2 by one-third and decreasing the volume of compartment 1 by an equal amount. It is most important to realize that it is the presence of a membrane impermeable to solute that leads to the volume changes associated with osmosis.

We have treated the two compartments as if they were infinitely expandable, so that the net transfer of water does not create a pressure difference across the membrane. This is essentially the situation that occurs across plasma membranes. In contrast, if the walls of compartment 2 could not expand, the movement of water into compartment 2 would raise the pressure in compartment 2, which

would oppose further net water entry. If a solution containing nonpenetrating solutes is separated from pure water by a membrane, the pressure that must be applied to the solution to prevent the net flow of water across the membrane is a measure of a property of the solution known as its **osmotic pressure**. The greater the osmolarity of a solution, the greater its osmotic pressure. It is important to note that the osmotic pressure of a solution does not push water molecules into the solution. Rather it is equal to the amount of pressure that must be applied to the solution to *prevent* the net flow of water into the solution. Like osmolarity, osmotic pressure is an indirect measure of the water concentration since the higher the osmotic pressure, the lower the water concentration of the solution.

Extracellular Osmolarity and Cell Volume

We can now apply the principles learned about osmosis to cells, which meet all the criteria necessary to produce an osmotic flow of water across a membrane. Both the intracellular and extracellular fluids contain water, and cells are surrounded by a membrane that is very permeable to water but impermeable to many substances (**nonpenetrating solutes**).

About 85 percent of the extracellular solute particles are sodium and chloride ions, which can diffuse through protein channels in the plasma membrane or enter the cell during secondary active transport. As we have seen, however, the plasma membrane contains an active-transport system that pumps sodium ions out of the cell as rapidly as they enter. Sodium thus behaves as if it were a nonpenetrating solute confined to the extracellular fluid. Also, secondary-active-transport pumps and the membrane potential move chloride ions out of cells as rapidly as they enter, with the result that chloride ions also behave as if they were nonpenetrating solutes confined to the extracellular fluid.

Inside the cell, the major solute particles are potassium ions and a number of organic solutes. Most of the latter are unable to cross the plasma membrane. Although potassium ions can leak out of a cell through potassium channels, they are actively transported back by the Na,K-ATPase pump. The net effect, as with sodium, is that potassium behaves as if it were a nonpenetrating solute, in this case in the intracellular fluid. Thus, sodium and chloride outside the cell and potassium and organic solutes inside the cell behave as nonpenetrating solutes on the two sides of the plasma membrane.

The osmolarity of the extracellular fluid is normally about 300 mOsm. Since water can diffuse across plasma membranes, the water in the intracellular fluid will come to diffusion equilibrium with the water in the extracellular fluid. At equilibrium, therefore, the osmolarity of the intracellular fluid is the same—300 mOsm—as the osmolarity of the extracellular fluid.

Changes in extracellular osmolarity can cause cells to shrink or swell as a result of the changes produced in the extracellular water concentration. As we shall see in Chapter 16, one of the major functions of the kidneys is to regulate the excretion of water in the urine so that the osmolarity of the extracellular fluid remains nearly con-

FIGURE 6-21

Changes in cell volume produced by hypertonic, isotonic, and hypotonic solutions.

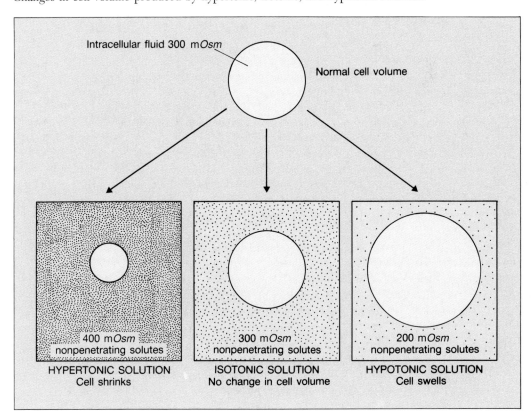

stant in spite of variations in salt and water intake and loss, thereby preventing damage to cells that would occur from excessive swelling or shrinkage.

If cells are placed in a solution of nonpenetrating solutes having an osmolarity of 300 m*Osm,* they will neither swell nor shrink since the water concentrations in the intra- and extracellular fluid are the same and the solutes cannot leave or enter. Such solutions are said to be **isotonic** (Figure 6-21), defined as having the same concentration of *nonpenetrating* solutes as normal extracellular fluid. Solutions containing less than 300 m*Osm* of nonpenetrating solutes (**hypotonic** solutions) will cause cells to swell because water will diffuse into the cell from its higher concentration in the extracellular fluid. Solutions containing greater than 300 m*Osm* of nonpenetrating solutes (**hypertonic** solutions) will cause cells to shrink as water diffuses out of the cell into the fluid with a lower water concentration. Note that the concentration of *nonpenetrating* solutes in a solution, not the total osmolarity, determines its tonicity—hypotonic, isotonic, or hypertonic.

In contrast, another set of terms—**isoosmotic**, **hyperosmotic**, and **hypoosmotic**—denotes simply the osmolarity of a solution relative to that of normal extracellular fluid without regard for whether the solute is penetrating or nonpenetrating. The two sets of terms are therefore not synonymous. For example, a 1-L solution containing 300 mOsmol of nonpenetrating NaCl and 100 mOsmol of urea, which can cross plasma membranes, would have a total osmolarity of 400 m*Osm* and would be hyperosmotic. It would, however, still be an isotonic solution, and so cells immersed in it would not shrink or swell. The reason is that urea will diffuse into the cells and reach the same concentration as the urea in the extracellular solution, and thus both the intracellular and extracellular solutions will have the same osmolarity (400 m*Osm*), and there will be no difference in the water concentration across the membrane and thus no change in cell volume.

Table 6-3 provides a comparison of the various terms used to describe the osmolarity of solutions. All hypoosmotic solutions are also hypotonic, whereas a hyperosmotic solution can be hypertonic, isotonic, or hypotonic.

The tonicity of solutions injected into the body is of great importance in medicine. Such solutions usually consist of an isotonic solution of NaCl (150 m*M* NaCl—isotonic saline) or an isotonic solution of glucose (5% dextrose solution). Injecting a drug dissolved in such solutions will not produce changes in cell volume, whereas injection

TABLE 6-3 TERMS REFERRING TO THE SOLUTE OSMOLARITY AND TONICITY OF SOLUTIONS

Isoosmotic	A solution containing 300 mOsmol/L of solute, regardless of its composition of membrane-penetrating and nonpenetrating solutes
Hyperosmotic	A solution containing greater than 300 mOsmol/L of solutes, regardless of the composition of membrane-penetrating and nonpenetrating solutes
Hypoosmotic	A solution containing less than 300 mOsmol/L of solutes, regardless of the composition of membrane-penetrating and nonpenetrating solutes
Isotonic	A solution containing 300 mOsmol/L of nonpenetrating solutes, regardless of the concentration of membrane-penetrating solutes that may be present
Hypertonic	A solution containing greater than 300 mOsmol/L of nonpenetrating solutes, regardless of the concentration of membrane-penetrating solutes that may be present
Hypotonic	A solution containing less than 300 mOsmol/L of nonpenetrating solutes, regardless of the concentration of membrane-penetrating solutes that may be present

of the same drug dissolved in pure water, a hypotonic solution, will produce cell swelling, perhaps to the point that plasma membranes will rupture, destroying cells.

ENDOCYTOSIS AND EXOCYTOSIS

In addition to diffusion and mediated transport, there is another pathway by which substances can enter or leave cells, one that does not require the molecules to pass through the structural matrix of the membrane. When living cells are observed under a light microscope, regions of the plasma membrane can be seen to fold into the cell, forming small pockets that pinch off to produce intracellular membrane-bound vesicles that enclose a small volume of extracellular fluid. This process is known as **endocytosis** (Figure 6-22). A similar process in the reverse direction, known as **exocytosis**, occurs when membrane-bound vesicles in the cytoplasm fuse with the plasma membrane and release their contents to the outside of the cell.

Endocytosis

Several varieties of endocytosis can be identified. When the vesicle simply encloses a small volume of extracellular fluid, as described above, the process is known as **fluid endocytosis**. In other cases, specific molecules in the extracellular fluid bind to the plasma membrane and are carried into the cell along with the extracellular fluid when the membrane invaginates. This is known as **adsorptive endocytosis**. In addition to taking in trapped extracellular fluid, adsorptive endocytosis leads to selective concentration in the vesicle of the material bound to the membrane. Both fluid and adsorptive endocytosis are often referred to as **pinocytosis** (cell drinking). A third type of endocytosis

FIGURE 6-22
Endocytosis and exocytosis.

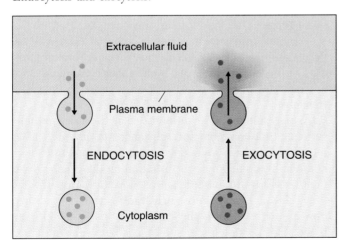

occurs when large particles, such as bacteria and debris from damaged tissues, are engulfed by the plasma membrane. In this form of endocytosis, known as **phagocytosis** (cell eating), the membrane folds around the surface of the particle so that little extracellular fluid is enclosed within the vesicle. While most cells undergo pinocytosis, only a few special cells carry out phagocytosis.

In most cells, fluid endocytosis occurs continuously, whereas adsorptive endocytosis and phagocytosis are stimulated by the binding of specific molecules or particles to the cell surface. Endocytosis of any kind requires metabolic energy in the form of ATP, although the molecular mechanisms by which this energy is coupled to membrane movements during endocytosis are unknown.

What is the fate of the endocytotic vesicles once they have entered the cell? In some cases they pass through the cytoplasm and fuse with the plasma membrane on the opposite side of the cell, releasing their contents to the extracellular space (Figure 6-23). This provides a pathway for transferring large molecules, such as proteins, across the cells that separate two compartments, for example, blood and interstitial fluid. A similar process allows small amounts of protein to be moved across the intestinal epithelium.

In most cells, however, endocytotic vesicles fuse with the membranes of lysosomes (Figure 6-23), organelles that contain digestive enzymes that break down large molecules such as proteins, polysaccharides, and nucleic acids. The fusion of the endocytotic vesicle with the lysosomal membrane exposes the contents of the vesicle to these digestive enzymes. The phagocytosis of bacteria and their destruction by the lysosomal digestive enzymes is one of the body's major defense mechanisms against germs (Chapter 20).

Endocytosis removes a small portion of the membrane from the cell surface. In cells that have a great deal of endocytotic activity, more than 100 percent of the plasma membrane may be internalized in an hour, yet the membrane surface area remains constant. This is because the membrane is replaced at about the same rate by vesicle membrane that fuses with the plasma membrane during exocytosis.

Exocytosis

Exocytosis performs two functions for cells: (1) It provides a way to replace portions of the plasma membrane that have been removed by endocytosis and, in the process, to add new membrane components; and (2) it provides a route by which membrane-impermeable molecules synthesized by cells can be released (secreted) into the extracellular fluid.

How are substances that are to be secreted by exocytosis packaged into vesicles? The story for protein synthesis and packaging into vesicles was described in Chapter 4.

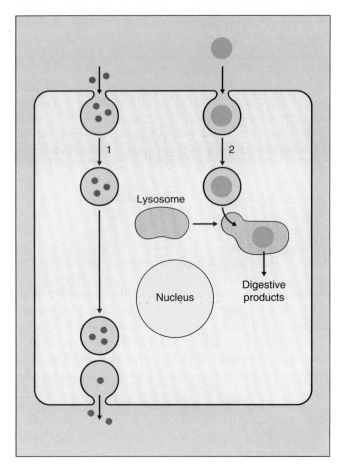

FIGURE 6-23

Fate of endocytotic vesicles. Pathway 1 transfers extracellular materials from one side of the cell to the other. Pathway 2 leads to fusion with lysosomes and digestion of the vesicle contents.

For nonproteins, in some cases the enzymes synthesizing a particular product to be secreted are located in the vesicles. In other cases, the vesicle membrane has mediated-transport systems that transport the product into the vesicle after it has been synthesized in the cytosol. Very high concentrations of certain products can be achieved within vesicles by a combination of mediated transport followed by their specific binding to proteins within the vesicle.

The secretion of substances by exocytosis is triggered in most cells by stimuli to the cell that lead to an increase in cytosolic calcium concentration. As described in Chapter 7, the stimuli do so by opening calcium channels in either the plasma membrane and/or the membranes of intracellular organelles. The resulting increase in cytosolic calcium concentration triggers the movement of vesicles by a process that may involve the activation of contractile proteins. These proteins move the vesicles along microtubules

toward the plasma membrane, leading to eventual fusion of the secretory vesicles with the membrane and the release of their contents. Material stored in secretory vesicles is available for rapid secretion in response to a stimulus, without delays that might occur if the material had to be synthesized after the arrival of the stimulus.

EPITHELIAL TRANSPORT

Epithelial cells (page 4) line hollow organs or tubes and regulate the movement of substances across these surfaces. One surface of the epithelium generally faces a hollow fluid-filled chamber, and the plasma membrane on this side is referred to as the **luminal membrane** (also the apical or mucosal membrane) of the epithelium. The plasma membrane on the opposite surface, which is usually adjacent to a network of blood vessels, is referred to as the **basolateral membrane** (also the serosal membrane).

There are two pathways by which a substance can cross an epithelial layer of cells: (1) by diffusion *between* the adjacent cells of the epithelium—the **paracellular pathway**, and (2) by movement into an epithelial cell across either the luminal or basolateral membrane, diffusion through the cytosol, and exit across the opposite membrane. This is termed the **transcellular pathway**. Diffusion through the paracellular pathway is limited by the presence of tight junctions between adjacent cells, since these junctions form a seal around the luminal end of the epithelial cells (page 46). Although small ions and water are able to diffuse to some degree through tight junctions, the amount of paracellular diffusion is limited by the tightness of the junctional seal and the relatively small area accessible for diffusion. The leakiness of the paracellular pathway varies in different types of epithelium, with some being very leaky and others very tight.

During transcellular transport the movements of molecules through the plasma membranes of epithelial cells occur through the kinds of pathways already described for movements across membranes in general. However, the permeabilities of the luminal and basolateral membranes are not the same. These two membranes contain different ion channels and different transport proteins for mediated transport.

As a result of these differences in the two epithelial surfaces, it is possible for substances to undergo a net movement from a low concentration on one side of an epithelium to a higher concentration on the other side, or in other words, to undergo active transport across the epithelial layer. Examples of such transport are the absorption of material from the gastrointestinal tract into the blood, the movements of substances between the kidney

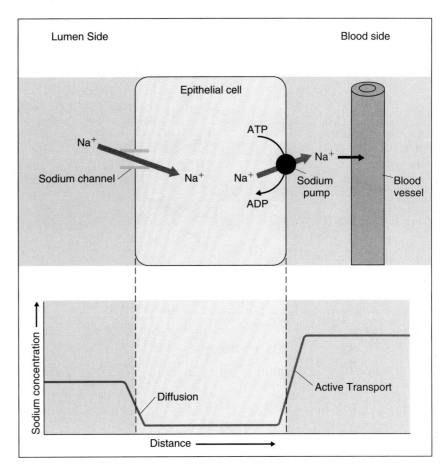

FIGURE 6-24

Active transport of sodium across an epithelial cell. The transepithelial transport of sodium involves, in this example, diffusion through channels at one surface followed by active transport out of the cell across the opposite surface. Shown below the cell is the concentration profile of the transported solute across the epithelium. In some epithelia, downhill sodium movement across the first membrane is by means of a secondary-active-transport protein rather than through channels.

tubules and the blood during urine formation, and the secretion of salts and fluid by glands.

Figures 6-24 and 6-25 illustrate two examples of active transport across an epithelium. Sodium is actively transported across most epithelia from lumen to blood side in absorptive processes, and from blood side to lumen during secretion. During absorption, the movement of sodium from a lumen into an epithelial cell often occurs by diffusion through sodium channels in the luminal membrane (Figure 6-24). Sodium diffuses into the cell because the intracellular concentration of sodium is kept low by the active transport of sodium out of the cell across the basolateral membrane on the opposite side, where all of the Na,K-ATPase pumps are located. In other words, sodium moves downhill into the cell and then uphill out of it. The net result is that sodium can be moved from lower to higher concentration across the epithelium.

Figure 6-25 illustrates the active absorption of organic molecules across an epithelium. In this case, entry of the organic molecule X across the luminal plasma membrane occurs via a secondary active cotransporter linked to the downhill movement of sodium into the cell. In the process, X moves from a lower concentration in the luminal fluid to a higher concentration in the cell. Exit of the substance across the basolateral membrane occurs by facilitated diffusion, which moves the material from its high concentration in the cell to a lower concentration in the extracellular fluid on the blood side. The concentration of the substance may be considerably higher on the blood side than in the lumen since the blood-side concentration can approach equilibrium with the high intracellular concentration.

Although water is not actively transported across cell membranes, a net movement of water across an epithelium can be achieved by osmosis as a result of the active transport of solutes, especially sodium, across the epithelium. The active transport of sodium across the epithelium as described above results in a decrease in the sodium concentration on one side and an increase on the other. These changes in solute concentration are accompanied by changes in the water concentration on the two sides since a change in solute concentration, as we have seen, produces a change in water concentration. The water concentration difference produced will cause water to move by osmosis from the low-sodium to the high-sodium side of the epithelium (Figure 6-26). Thus, net movement of sol-

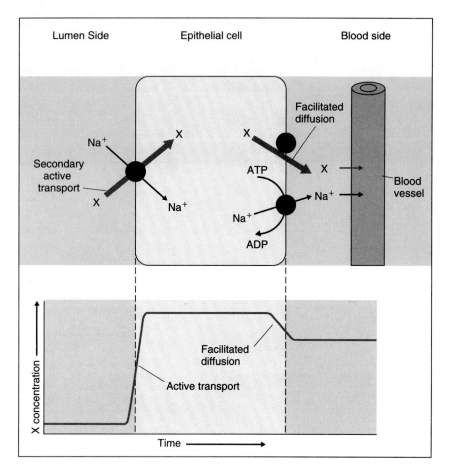

FIGURE 6-25

The transepithelial transport of most organic solutes (X) involves their movement into a cell through a secondary-active-transport pump coupled to sodium, followed by movement out of the cell and down a concentration gradient, by means of facilitated diffusion at the opposite surface. Shown below the cell is the concentration profile of the solute transported across the epithelium.

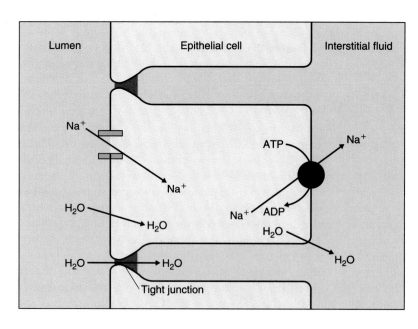

FIGURE 6-26

Movements of water across an epithelium. The active transport of sodium out of the cells, into the surrounding interstitial spaces, produces an elevated osmolarity in this region, leading to the osmotic flow of water across the epithelium.

ute across an epithelium is accompanied by a flow of water in the same direction.

Glands

The function of glands is to secrete substances into hollow organs, into the blood, or onto the surface of the skin in response to appropriate stimuli. The mechanisms of glandular secretion depend upon the principles of membrane permeability and transport described in this chapter.

Glands are formed during embryonic development by the infolding of the epithelial layer of an organ's surface. Many of these glands remain connected by ducts to the epithelial surfaces from which they were formed, while others lose this connection and become isolated clusters of cells. The first type of gland is known as an **exocrine gland**, and its secretions flow through ducts and are discharged into the lumen of an organ or, in the case of the skin glands, onto the surface of the skin (Figure 6-27). Sweat glands and salivary glands are examples of exocrine glands.

In the second type of gland, known as an **endocrine gland** or a ductless gland, secretions are released directly into the interstitial fluid surrounding the gland cells (Figure 6-27). From this point, the material diffuses into the blood, which carries it throughout the body. The endocrine glands secrete a major class of chemical messengers—the **hormones**—and in practical usage the term "endocrine gland" has come to be synonymous with "hormone-secreting gland." However, it should be noted that there are "ductless glands" that secrete nonhormonal, organic substances into the blood. For example, fat cells secrete fatty acids and glycerol, and liver cells secrete glucose, amino acids, fats, and proteins. These substances serve as nutrients for other cells or perform special functions in the

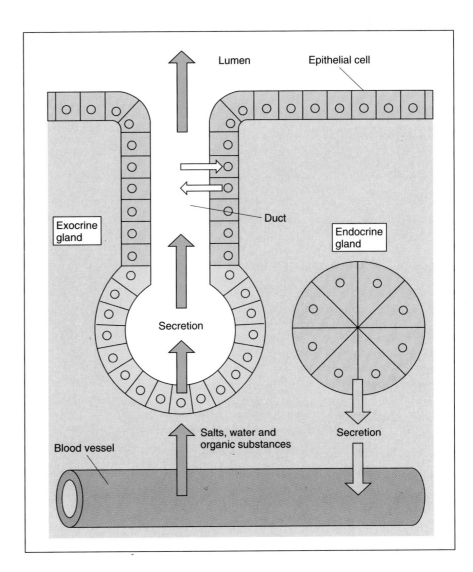

FIGURE 6-27

Glands are composed of epithelial cells. Exocrine-gland secretions enter ducts, whereas hormones or other substances secreted by endocrine (ductless) glands diffuse into the blood.

blood, but they do not act as messengers and therefore are not hormones.

The substances secreted by glands fall into two chemical categories: (1) organic materials that are, for the most part, synthesized by the gland cells; and (2) salts and water, which are simply moved from one extracellular compartment to another across the glandular epithelium.

Organic molecules are secreted by gland cells via all the pathways already described: diffusion in the case of lipid-soluble materials, mediated transport for some polar materials, and exocytosis for very large molecules such as proteins. Salts are actively transported across glandular epithelia, producing changes in the extracellular osmolarity, which in turn causes the osmotic flow of water. In exocrine glands, as the secreted fluid passes along the ducts connecting the gland to the luminal surface, the composition of the fluid originally secreted may be altered as a result of absorption or secretion by the duct cells. Often the composition of the secreted material at the end of the duct will vary with the rate of secretion, reflecting the amount of

time the fluid remains in the duct where it can be modified.

Most glands undergo a low, basal rate of secretion, which can be greatly augmented in response to the appropriate signal, usually a nerve impulse or a hormone. The mechanism of the increased secretion is again one of altering some portion of the secretory pathway. This may involve (1) increasing the rate at which a secreted organic substance is synthesized by activating the appropriate enzymes, (2) providing the calcium signal for exocytosis of already synthesized material, or (3) altering the pumping rates of transport proteins or opening ion channels.

The volume of fluid secreted by an exocrine gland can be increased by increasing the sodium pump activity or, more often, by controlling the opening of sodium channels in the plasma membrane. The increased flow of sodium across the epithelium increases the sodium concentration in the lumen, which in turn increases the flow of water by osmosis. The greater the solute transfer, the greater the water flow.

SUMMARY

DIFFUSION

I. Diffusion is the movement of molecules from one location to another by random thermal motion.
   A. The net flux between two compartments always proceeds from higher to lower concentration of the diffusing substance.
   B. Diffusion equilibrium is reached when the concentrations in the two compartments become equal, resulting in zero net flux.
II. The magnitude of the net flux F across a plasma membrane is directly proportional to the concentration difference across the membrane, $C_o - C_i$, the surface area of the membrane A, and the membrane permeability constant k_p.
III. Nonpolar molecules diffuse through the lipid portions of membranes much more rapidly than do polar or ionized molecules because nonpolar molecules can dissolve in the nonpolar lipids in the membrane.
IV. Mineral ions diffuse across membranes by passing through ion channels formed by integral membrane proteins.
   A. The net diffusion of ions across a membrane depends on the concentration gradient and the membrane potential.

B. The flux of ions across a membrane can be altered by opening or closing ion channels.

MEDIATED-TRANSPORT SYSTEMS

I. The mediated transport of molecules or ions across a membrane involves binding of the transported solute to a transport protein in the membrane. Changes in the conformation of the transporter move the binding site to the opposite side of the membrane, where the solute dissociates from the protein.
   A. The binding sites on transport proteins exhibit chemical specificity, affinity and saturation.
   B. The magnitude of the flux through a mediated-transport system depends on the degree of transporter saturation, the number of transport proteins in the membrane, and the rate at which the conformational change in the transporter occurs.
II. Facilitated diffusion is a mediated-transport process that moves molecules from higher to lower concentration across a membrane by means of a transport protein until the two concentrations become equal. Metabolic energy is not required for this process.
III. Active transport is a mediated-transport process that moves molecules against an electrochemical differ-

ence across a membrane by means of a transport protein and requires an input of energy.

A. Active transport is achieved either by altering the affinity of the binding site so that it differs on the two sides of the membrane or by altering the rate at which the protein changes its conformation from one side of the membrane to the other.

B. Primary active transport directly uses the phosphorylation of the transporter by ATP to alter the transport process.

C. Secondary active transport uses the binding of ions (often sodium) to the transporter to alter the transport process.

D. In secondary active transport the downhill flow of an ion is linked to the uphill movement of a second solute either in the same direction as the ion—cotransport, or in the opposite direction of the ion—countertransport.

OSMOSIS

I. Osmosis is the diffusion of water from a region of higher water concentration to a region of lower water concentration. The osmolarity—the total solute concentration in a solution—determines the water concentration. The higher the osmolarity of a solution, the lower the water concentration.

II. Osmosis across a membrane that is permeable to water but impermeable to solute leads to an increase in the volume of the compartment on the initially high-osmolarity side and a decrease in the volume on the initially low-osmolarity side.

III. Application of pressure to a solution equal to the osmotic pressure of the solution will prevent the osmotic flow of water into the solution from a compartment of pure water. The greater the osmolarity of a solution, the greater its osmotic pressure.

IV. The osmolarity of the extracellular fluid is about 300 mOsm. Since water is in diffusion equilibrium across cell membranes, the intracellular fluid also has an osmolarity of 300 mOsm.

A. Na^+ and Cl^- ions are the major effectively nonpenetrating solutes in the extracellular fluid, while K^+ ions and the organic solutes are the major nonpenetrating solutes in the intracellular fluid.

B. The terms used to describe the osmolarity of solutions containing different compositions of penetrating and nonpenetrating solutes are given in Table 6-3.

C. Cells placed in hypotonic solutions swell, whereas cells placed in hypertonic solutions shrink.

ENDOCYTOSIS AND EXOCYTOSIS

I. During endocytosis, regions of the plasma membrane invaginate and pinch off to form vesicles that enclose a small volume of extracellular material.

A. The three classes of endocytosis are (1) fluid endocytosis, (2) adsorptive endocytosis, and (3) phagocytosis.

B. In most cells, endocytotic vesicles fuse with the membranes of lysosomes, in which the vesicle contents are digested by lysosomal enzymes.

II. Exocytosis, which occurs when intracellular vesicles fuse with the plasma membrane, provides a route by which membrane-impermeable molecules synthesized by cells, such as proteins, can be released into the extracellular fluid.

EPITHELIAL TRANSPORT

I. Molecules can cross an epithelial layer of cells by two pathways: (1) through the extracellular spaces between the cells—the paracellular pathway; and (2) by the transcellular pathway, in which the substance must cross both the luminal and basolateral membranes as well as the cell's cytoplasm.

II. In epithelial cells, the permeability and transport characteristics of the luminal and basolateral plasma membranes differ, resulting in the ability of the cells to actively transport a substance between the fluid on one side of the cell and the fluid on the opposite side of the cell.

III. The active transport of sodium through an epithelium increases the osmolarity on one side of the cell and decreases it on the other, causing water to move by osmosis in the same direction as the transported sodium.

IV. Glands are composed of epithelial cells that secrete water and solutes in response to stimulation.

A. There are two categories of glands: (1) exocrine glands, which secrete into ducts; and (2) endocrine glands (ductless glands), which secrete hormones and other substances into the extracellular fluid, from which they diffuse into the blood.

B. The secretions of glands consist of (1) organic substances that have been synthesized by the gland; and (2) salts and water, which have been transported across the gland cells from the blood.

KEY TERMS

plasma membrane	osmole
diffusion	osmotic pressure
flux	nonpenetrating solutes
net flux	isotonic
diffusion equilibrium	hypotonic
permeability constant k_p	hypertonic
channels	isoosmotic
membrane potential	hyperosmotic
electrochemical difference	hypoosmotic
channel gating	endocytosis
voltage-sensitive channels	exocytosis
mechanosensitive channels	fluid endocytosis
transporters	adsorptive endocytosis
mediated transport	pinocytosis
facilitated diffusion	phagocytosis
active transport	luminal membrane
primary active transport	basolateral membrane
secondary active transport	paracellular pathway
cotransport	transcellular pathway
countertransport	exocrine gland
osmosis	endocrine gland
osmolarity	hormones

REVIEW QUESTIONS

1. What determines the direction in which net diffusion of a nonpolar molecule will occur?

2. In what ways can the net solute flux between two compartments separated by a permeable membrane be increased?

3. Why are membranes more permeable to nonpolar molecules than to most polar and ionized molecules?

4. Ions diffuse across cell membranes by what pathway?

5. When considering the diffusion of ions across a membrane, what driving force, in addition to the ion concentration gradient, must be considered?

6. What factors can alter the opening and closing of protein channels in a membrane?

7. Describe the mechanism by which a mediated-transport protein moves a solute from one side of a membrane to the other.

8. What determines the magnitude of a mediated-transport flux across a membrane?

9. What characteristics distinguish diffusion from facilitated diffusion?

10. What characteristics distinguish facilitated diffusion from active transport?

11. Contrast the mechanism by which energy is coupled to a transport protein during (a) primary active transport, and (b) secondary active transport.

12. Describe the direction in which sodium ions and a transported solute move during cotransport and countertransport.

13. How can the concentration of water in a solution be decreased?

14. If two solutions having different osmolarities are separated by a water-permeable membrane, why will there be a change in the volumes of the two compartments if the membrane is impermeable to the solutes, but no change in volume if the membrane is permeable to solute?

15. To which solution must pressure be applied to prevent the osmotic flow of water across a membrane separating a solution of high osmolarity and a solution of lower osmolarity?

16. Why do sodium and chloride ions in the extracellular fluid and potassium ions in the intracellular fluid behave as if they are nonpenetrating solutes?

17. What is the osmolarity of the extracellular fluid? Of the intracellular fluid?

18. What change in cell volume will occur when a cell is placed in a hypotonic solution? In a hypertonic solution?

19. Under what conditions will a hyperosmotic solution be isotonic?

20. Endocytotic vesicles deliver their contents to which parts of a cell?

21. How do the mechanisms for actively transporting glucose and sodium across an epithelium differ?

22. By what mechanism does the active transport of sodium lead to the osmotic flow of water across an epithelium?

23. What is the difference between an endocrine gland and an exocrine gland?

THOUGHT QUESTIONS

(Answers are given in Appendix A.)

1. In two cases (A and B), the concentrations of solute X in two 1-L compartments separated by a membrane through which X can diffuse are

	Concentration of X, mM	
Case	Compartment 1	Compartment 2
A	3	5
B	32	30

a. In what direction will the net flux take place in case A and in case B?

b. When diffusion equilibrium is reached, what will be the concentration of solute in each compartment in case A and in case B?

c. Will A reach diffusion equilibrium faster, slower, or at the same rate as B?

2. When the extracellular concentration of the amino acid alanine is increased, the flux of the amino acid leucine into a cell is decreased. How might this observation be explained?

3. If an active-transport protein has a lower affinity for the transported solute on the extracellular surface of the plasma membrane than on the intracellular surface, in what direction will there be a net transport of the solute across the membrane? (Assume that the rate of protein conformational change is the same in both directions.)

4. Why will inhibition of ATP synthesis by a cell lead to a decrease in secondary active transport?

5. Given the following solutions, which has the lowest water concentration? Which two are isoosmotic?

| | Concentration, mM | | | |
Solution	Glucose	Urea	NaCl	CaCl$_2$
A	20	30	150	10
B	10	100	20	50
C	100	200	10	20
D	30	10	60	100

6. Assume that a membrane separating two compartments is permeable to urea but not permeable to NaCl. If compartment 1 contains 200 mmol/L of NaCl and 100 mmol/L of urea and compartment 2 contains 100 mmol/L of NaCl and 300 mmol/L of urea, which compartment will have increased in volume when osmotic equilibrium is reached?

7. What will happen to cell volume if a cell is placed in each of the following solutions?

| | Concentration, mM | |
Solution	NaCl (nonpenetrating)	Urea (penetrating)
A	150	100
B	100	150
C	200	100
D	100	50

8. Characterize each of the solutions in question 7 as to whether it is isotonic, hypotonic, hypertonic, hypoosmotic, or hyperosmotic.

9. By what mechanism might an increase in intracellular sodium concentration lead to an increase in exocytosis?

P A R T

TWO

BIOLOGICAL CONTROL SYSTEMS

CHAPTER

7

HOMEOSTATIC MECHANISMS AND CELLULAR COMMUNICATION

Part 2 provides the information needed to bridge the gap between the cell physiology discussed in Part 1 and the coordinated body functions described in Part 3. This chapter begins that process by amplifying the concept of homeostasis first presented in Chapter 1 and describing the general characteristics of homeostatic control systems. The operation of these systems requires that cells be able to communicate with each other, often over long distances. We shall see that much of this intercellular communication is mediated by chemical messengers that interact with their target cells by means of specific proteins—receptors—on the cells. Finally, these interactions trigger, *within* the target cells, sequences of chemical events that culminate in the cells' response to the messenger.

GENERAL CHARACTERISTICS OF HOMEOSTATIC CONTROL SYSTEMS

As described in Chapter 1, the activities of cells, tissues, and organs must be regulated and integrated with each other in such a way that any change in the extracellular fluid initiates a reaction to minimize the change. **Homeostasis** denotes the relatively stable conditions of the internal environment that result from these compensating regulatory responses performed by **homeostatic control systems**.

Consider the regulation of body temperature. Our subject is a resting, lightly clad man in a room having a temperature of 20°C and moderate humidity. His internal body temperature is 37°C, and he is losing heat to the external environment because it is at a lower temperature. However, the chemical reactions occurring within the cells of his body are producing heat at a rate equal to the rate of heat loss. Under these conditions, the body undergoes no net gain or loss of heat and the body temperature remains constant. The system is said to be in a **steady state**, defined as a system in which a particular variable (temperature, in this case) is not changing, but energy (in this case, heat) must be added continuously to maintain the variable constant. Steady states differ from equilibria, in which a particular variable is not changing but no input of energy is required to maintain the constancy. The steady-state temperature in our example is known as the **operating point** (also termed the set point) of the thermoregulatory system.

This example illustrates a crucial generalization about homeostasis: Stability of an internal environmental variable is achieved by the balancing of inputs and outputs. In this case, the variable—body temperature—remains constant because metabolic heat production (input) equals heat loss from the body (output).

Now we lower the temperature of the room rapidly, say to 5°C, and keep it there. This immediately increases the loss of heat from our subject's warm skin, upsetting the dynamic balance between heat gain and loss. The body temperature therefore starts to fall. Very rapidly, however, a variety of homeostatic responses occur to limit the fall (Figure 7-1). First, the blood vessels to the skin narrow, reducing the amount of warm blood flowing through the skin and thus reducing heat loss. At a room temperature of 5°C, however, blood vessel constriction is not able to eliminate completely the extra heat loss from the skin. Our subject curls up in order to reduce the surface area of skin available for heat loss. This helps a bit, but excessive heat loss still continues and body temperature keeps falling, although at a slower rate. He has a strong desire to put on more clothing, for "voluntary" behavioral responses are often crucial components in homeostasis, but no clothing is available. Clearly, then, if excessive heat loss (output) cannot be prevented, the only way of restoring the balance between heat input and output is to increase input, and this is precisely what occurs. He begins to shiver, and the chemical reactions responsible for the muscular contractions that constitute shivering produce large quantities of heat.

Indeed, heat production may transiently exceed heat loss so that body temperature begins to go back toward the value existing before the room temperature was lowered. It eventually stabilizes at a temperature *a bit below this original value*; at this new steady state, heat input and heat output are again equal to each other. Here is another crucial generalization about homeostasis: Stability of an internal environmental variable depends not upon the absolute magnitudes of opposing inputs and outputs, but only upon the balance between them.

The thermoregulatory system just described is an example of a **negative-feedback** system, in which an increase or decrease in the variable being regulated brings about responses that tend to move the variable in the direction opposite ("negative" to) the direction of the original change. Thus, in our example, the *decrease* in body temperature led to responses that tended to *increase* the body temperature, that is, move it toward its original value.

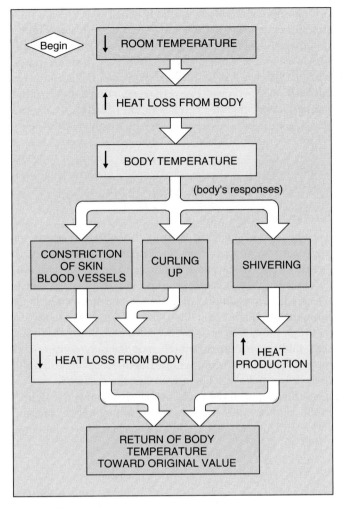

FIGURE 7-1

A homeostatic control system. This system maintains body temperature relatively constant when room temperature decreases. This diagram is typical of those used throughout the remainder of this book to illustrate homeostatic systems, and several conventions should be noted. The "begin" sign indicates where to start. The arrows next to each term denote increases or decreases. The arrows connecting any two terms in the figure denote cause and effect; that is, an arrow can be read as "causes" or "leads to" (for example, decreased room temperature "leads to" increased heat loss from the body). In general, one should add the words "tends to" in thinking about these cause-and-effect relationships. For example, decreased room temperature tends to cause an increase in heat loss from the body, and curling up tends to cause a decrease in heat loss from the body. Qualifying the relationship in this way is necessary because variables like heat production and heat loss are under the influence of many factors, some of which oppose each other.

Negative-feedback control systems are the most common homeostatic mechanisms in the body, but there is another type of feedback known as **positive feedback** in which an initial disturbance in a system sets off a train of events that increase the disturbance even further. Thus positive feedback does not favor stability and often abruptly displaces a system away from its steady-state operating point. As we shall see, several important positive-feedback relationships occur in the body, blood clotting being one example.

Much of the sequence of events shown in Figure 7-1 is familiar, of course, since the ultimate responses—decreased skin temperature, curling up, and shivering—are visible. But what about the internal workings underlying them? First, what initiated the signals in the nerves to the blood vessels and the muscles that shiver? These nerves are controlled by centers in the brain, which are in turn controlled by signals coming from small groups of temperature-sensitive nerve cells in various parts of the body. The chain of events can be summarized: Decreased internal body temperature → increased activity of temperature-sensitive nerve cells → increased activity of a series of nerve cells in the central nervous system, the last of which stimulate contraction of skeletal muscles (to produce shivering) and smooth muscles in the skin blood vessels (to reduce skin blood flow).

A third generalization about homeostasis follows from the preceding description of system components and the nature of negative feedback: Homeostatic control systems cannot maintain *complete* constancy of the internal environment in the face of persistent change in the external environment but can only minimize changes (Figure 7-2). Imagine for the moment that the body's responses to a cold environment really did return body temperature completely to 37°C. What would happen to the output of the first component, the temperature-sensitive nerve cells—the "detectors"? Recall that it was the drop in internal body temperature that elicited the change in output from these detectors in the first place. If the body temperature were to return completely to its original value, so would the output of the detectors, and the entire sequence of events would stop. The blood vessels would stop constricting, shivering would cease, and body temperature would once again fall since the compensations would no longer be present. In other words, as long as the exposure to cold continues, some decrease in body temperature must persist to serve as a signal to maintain the responses. Such a signal is termed an **error signal**.

Just how big the error signal is in a control system depends on the magnitude of the external change, the sensitivity of the detectors, the efficiency of the connections between the system's components, and the responsiveness of the final apparatus in the control system. The temperature-regulating systems of the body are extremely sensitive, so that body temperature normally varies by only about 1°C even in the face of marked changes in the external environment.

FIGURE 7-2

Negative-feedback control systems cannot return the regulated variable to its original value as long as the environmental perturbation persists. The deviation from the original value is called the error signal.

Inherent in the last sentence is another generalization about homeostasis: Even in reference to one individual, thus ignoring variation among persons, any regulated variable in the body cannot be assigned a single "normal" value but has a more-or-less narrow range of normal values, depending on external conditions. The more precise the homeostatic mechanisms for regulating a variable are, the narrower is the range. Thus, the concept of homeostasis is an ideal, since total constancy of the internal environment can never be achieved.

As we have seen, perturbations in the external environment can displace a variable from its preexisting operating point. In addition, we now recognize that the operating points for many regulated variables can be physiologically altered or *reset*; that is, the values which the homeostatic control systems are "trying" to maintain relatively constant can be altered. A common example is fever, the increase in body temperature that occurs in response to infection and which is analogous to raising the setting of your house's thermostat. The homeostatic control systems regulating body temperature are still functioning during a fever, but they maintain the temperature at a higher value. We shall see in Chapter 20 that this regulated rise in body temperature is adaptive for fighting the infection. The resetting of a set point that occurs for other variables is also adaptive in some cases, but in others it reflects the clashing demands of different regulatory systems.

The example of fever may have left the impression that operating points are reset only in response to external stimuli, in this case the presence of bacteria, but such is not the case. Indeed, as described in the next section, the operating points for many regulated variables change on a rhythmical basis every day; for example, the operating point for body temperature is higher during the day than at night.

One more generalization should be noted: It is not possible for everything to be maintained relatively constant by homeostatic mechanisms. In our example, body temperature was maintained constant, but only because large changes occurred in skin blood flow and skeletal-muscle contraction. Moreover, because so many properties of the internal environment are closely interrelated, it is often possible to maintain one property relatively constant only by moving others farther from their usual values. This is what we meant earlier by "clashing demands."

The generalizations we have given concerning homeostatic control systems are summarized in Table 7-1.

Feedforward Regulation

Another type of regulatory process frequently used in conjunction with negative-feedback systems is feedforward. Let us give an example of feedforward and then define it. The temperature-sensitive nerve cells that trigger negative-feedback regulation of body temperature when body temperature begins to fall are located *inside* the body. In addition, there are temperature-sensitive nerve cells in the skin, and these cells, in effect, monitor *outside* temperature. When outside temperature falls, as in our example, these nerve cells immediately detect the change and relay this information to the brain, which then sends out signals to the blood vessels and muscles, resulting in heat conservation and increased heat production. In this manner com-

---

TABLE 7-1 SOME IMPORTANT GENERALIZATIONS ABOUT HOMEOSTATIC CONTROL SYSTEMS

1. Stability of an internal-environmental variable is achieved by balancing inputs and outputs. It is not the absolute magnitudes of the inputs and outputs that matter but the balance between them.

2. In negative-feedback systems, a change in the variable being regulated brings about responses that tend to move the variable in the direction opposite the original change, that is, back toward the initial value.

3. Homeostatic control systems cannot maintain complete constancy of any given feature of the internal environment. Therefore, any regulated variable will have a more-or-less narrow range of normal values depending on the external-environmental conditions.

4. The operating point of some variables regulated by homeostatic control systems can be reset, that is, physiologically raised or lowered.

5. It is not possible for everything to be maintained relatively constant by homeostatic control systems. There is a hierarchy of importance, such that the constancy of certain variables is altered markedly to maintain others relatively constant.

pensatory thermoregulatory responses are activated *before* the colder outside temperature can cause the internal body temperature to fall. Thus, **feedforward** regulation anticipates changes in a regulated variable (internal body temperature in the example), improves the speed of the body's homeostatic responses, and minimizes fluctuations in the level of the variable being regulated.

Acclimatization

The term **adaptation** denotes a characteristic that favors survival in specific environments. Homeostatic control systems are inherited biological adaptations. An individual's ability to adapt to a particular environmental stress is not fixed, however, but can be enhanced, with no change in genetic endowment, by prolonged exposure to that stress. This type of adaptation is known as **acclimatization**.

Let us take sweating in response to heat exposure as an example and perform a simple experiment. On day 1 we expose a person for 30 min to a high temperature and ask her to do a standardized exercise test. Body temperature rises, and sweating begins after a certain period of time. The sweating provides a mechanism for increasing heat loss from the body and thus tends to minimize the rise in body temperature in a hot environment. The volume of sweat produced under these conditions is measured. Then, for a week, our subject enters the heat chamber for 1 or 2 h per day and exercises. On day 8, the sweating rate is again measured during the same exercise test performed on day 1; the striking finding is that the subject begins to sweat earlier and much more profusely than she did on day 1. Accordingly, her body temperature does not rise to nearly the same degree.

The subject has become acclimatized to the heat; that is, she has undergone an adaptive change induced by exposure to the heat and is now better adapted to heat exposure. In a sense, acclimatization may be viewed as an environmentally induced improvement in the functioning of an already existing genetically based homeostatic system. Up to some maximal limit, repeated or prolonged exposure to a particular environmental stress enhances the responsiveness of the system to that type of stress.

Heat acclimatization is completely reversible. If the daily exposures to heat are discontinued, the sweating rate of our subject will revert to the preacclimatized value within a relatively short time. If an acclimatization is induced very early in life, however, at the **critical period** for development of a structure or response, it is termed a **developmental acclimatization** and may be irreversible. For example, the barrel-shaped chests of natives of the Andes Mountains represent not a genetic difference between them and their lowland compatriots but rather an irreversible acclimatization induced during the first few years of their lives by their exposure to the low-oxygen environment of high altitude. The altered chest size remains even though the individual moves to a lowland environment later in life and stays there. Lowland persons who have suffered oxygen deprivation from heart or lung disease during their early years show precisely the same chest shape.

Biological Rhythms

A striking characteristic of many body functions is the rhythmical changes they manifest. The most common type is the **circadian rhythm**, which cycles approximately once every 24 h. Waking and sleeping, body temperature, hormone concentrations in the blood, the excretion of ions into the urine, and many other functions undergo circadian variation (Figure 7-3). Other cycles have much longer periods, the menstrual cycle (approximately 28 days) being the most well known.

A crucial point concerning most body rhythms is that they are *internally* driven. Environmental factors do not drive the rhythm but rather provide the timing cues important for **entrainment** (that is, setting of the actual hours) of the rhythm. A classic experiment will clarify this distinction.

Subjects were put in experimental chambers that completely isolated them from the external environment. For the first few days, they were exposed to a 24-h rest-activity cycle in which the room lights were turned on and off at the same time each day. Under these conditions, their sleep-wake cycles were 24 h long. Then, all environmental time cues were eliminated, and the individuals were allowed to control the lights themselves. Immediately, their sleep-wake patterns began to change. On the average, bedtime began about 30 min later *each day* and so did wake-up time. Thus a sleep-wake cycle persisted in the complete absence of environmental cues, and such a rhythm is called a **free-running rhythm**. In this case it was approximately 25 h rather than 24; that is, cues are required to entrain a circadian rhythm to 24 h.

One more point should be mentioned: By altering the duration of the light-dark cycles, sleep-wake cycles can be entrained to any value between 23 and 27 h, but shorter or longer durations cannot be entrained; instead, the rhythm continues to free-run. Because of this, the bodies of people whose work causes them to adopt sleep-wake cycles longer than 27 h are never able to make the proper adjustments and achieve stable rhythms. The result is symptoms similar to those of jet lag, to be described later.

The light-dark cycle is the most important environmental time cue in our lives but not the only one. Others include external environmental temperature, meal timing, and many social cues. Thus, if several people were undergoing the experiment just described in isolation from each other, their free-runs would be different, but if they were all in the same room, one person would be dominant and set the cycle for the others.

Environmental time cues also function to phase-shift rhythms, in other words, to reset the internal clock. Thus if

FIGURE 7-3

Circadian rhythms of several physiological variables in a human subject with room lights on (open bars at top) for 16 h and off (black bars at top) for 8 h. As is usual in dealing with rhythms, we have used a 24-h clock in which both 0 and 24 designate midnight and 12 designates noon. Cortisol is a hormone secreted by the adrenal glands. *(Adapted from Moore-Ede and Sulzman.)*

one jets west or east to a different time zone, the sleep-wake cycle and other circadian rhythms slowly shift to the new light-dark cycle. These shifts take time, however, and the disparity between external time and internal time is one of the causes of the symptoms of *jet lag*—disruption of sleep, gastrointestinal disturbances, decreased vigilance and attention span, and a general feeling of malaise. Similar symptoms occur in workers on permanent or rotating night shifts. Such individuals generally do not adapt to these schedules even after several years because they are exposed to the usual outdoor light-dark cycle (normal indoor lighting is too dim to function as a good entrainer). In recent experiments, night-shift workers were exposed to extremely bright indoor lighting while they worked and 8 h of total darkness during the day while they slept. This schedule produced total adaptation to the night-shift work within 5 days.

What is the neural basis of body rhythms? In the part of the brain called the hypothalamus are several specific collections of nerve cells that function as the principal **pacemaker** (time clock) for circadian rhythms. How they "keep time" independent of any external environmental cues is not really understood. The input the pacemaker receives from the eyes and many other parts of the nervous system mediates the entrainment effects exerted by the external environment.

What have biological rhythms to do with homeostasis? They add a "predictive" component to homeostatic control systems, in effect a feedforward response operating without detectors. The negative-feedback homeostatic responses we described earlier in this chapter are corrective responses, in that they are initiated *after* the steady state of the individual has been perturbed. In contrast, biological rhythms enable homeostatic mechanisms to be utilized immediately and automatically by activating them at times when a challenge is *likely* to occur but before it actually does occur. For example, there is a rhythm in the urinary excretion of potassium such that excretion is high during the day and low at night; this makes sense since we ingest potassium in our food during the day, not at night when we are asleep. Therefore, the total amount of potassium in the body fluctuates less than if the rhythm did not exist.

It should not be surprising that rhythms have effects on the body's resistance to various **stresses**. Indeed, certain diseases have characteristic rhythms. For example, heart attacks are almost twice as common in the first hours after waking, and asthma frequently flares at night. Insights about these rhythms have already been incorporated into therapy; for example, once-a-day timed-release pills for asthma are taken at night and deliver a high dose of medication between midnight and 8 A.M. Perhaps the most striking application in medicine of the growing information about rhythms is in the treatment of **cancer**. Many drugs used in cancer chemotherapy kill only dividing cells; since cancer cells generally divide rapidly, they are preferentially destroyed. However, the drugs also injure normal tissues and organs consisting of cells that divide rapidly, leading to toxic side effects such as diarrhea caused by damage to the intestinal lining. It is known that intestinal cells divide most slowly during the evening, and so by delivering the drug only at this time a much larger dose of drug can be given with less toxicity to these normal cells.

Aging and Homeostasis

Aging represents the operation of a distinct process that is distinguishable from those diseases such as heart disease frequently associated with aging. Whether these diseases are themselves promoted by the aging process or simply occur over the same time frame is not known.

Aging is associated with a decrease in the number of cells in the body, due to some combination of decreased

THE BALANCE CONCEPT AND CHEMICAL HOMEOSTASIS

THE BALANCE CONCEPT AND CHEMICAL HOMEOSTASIS **155**

cell division and increased cell death, and to malfunction of many of the cells that remain. The immediate cause of these changes is probably an interference in the function of the cells' macromolecules—DNA, RNA, and cell proteins—and in the flow of information between these macromolecules. The crucial question, unanswered at present, concerns what causes these changes. One theory places the blame on progressive accumulation of damage to the macromolecules, while the other hypothesizes that cellular senescence is actually programmed in our genes; that is, that certain genes responsible for the aging process become activated as one grows older.

The physiological manifestations of aging are a gradual deterioration in the function of virtually all tissues and organ systems and in the capacity of the body's homeostatic systems to respond to environmental stresses. However, it is difficult to sort out the extent to which any particular age-related change is due to aging itself and the extent to which it is secondary to disease and lifestyle changes. For example, until recently it was believed that the functioning of the nervous system markedly deteriorates as a result of aging per se, but this view is now being seriously questioned. It seems to have been based on studies of the performance of individuals with age-related diseases. More recent studies of people without such diseases do document changes—loss of memory, increased difficulty in learning new tasks, a decrease in the speed of processing by the brain, loss of brain mass—but these changes are modest, and most brain functions considered to underlie intelligence seem to remain relatively intact.

To take another example, a similar reevaluation of changes in heart function with age has suggested that much of the decrease in the ability of the heart to pump blood at rest and during exercise in older people may be the result of disease and lifestyle changes (decreased phys-

ical activity, for example) rather than to the aging process itself. In contrast, the 30 to 40 percent decrease (somewhat less in women) in the mass and strength of limb muscles that occurs in men between 30 and 80 years of age is due to aging changes per se. Physically active individuals have greater strength at any given age, compared to inactive persons, but the rate of decline with age is similar.

THE BALANCE CONCEPT AND CHEMICAL HOMEOSTASIS

Many homeostatic systems are concerned with the balance of a chemical component. Figure 7-4 is a generalized schema of the possible pathways involved in the balance of a chemical substance. The **pool** occupies a position of central importance in the balance sheet. It is the body's readily available quantity of the particular substance and is frequently identical to the amount present in the extracellular fluid. The pool receives substances from and contributes them to all the pathways.

The pathways on the left of the figure are sources of net gain to the body. A substance may enter the body through the gastrointestinal (GI) tract or the lungs. Alternatively, a substance may be synthesized by cells within the body from other materials.

The pathways on the right of the figure are causes of net loss from the body. A substance may be lost in the urine, feces, expired air, or menstrual fluid, as well as from the surface of the body as skin, hair, nails, sweat, and tears. The substance may also be chemically altered and thus removed by metabolism.

The central portion of the figure illustrates the distribution of the substance within the body. The substance may

FIGURE 7-4

Balance diagram for a chemical substance.

be taken from the pool and accumulated in storage depots, as for example the accumulation of fat in adipose tissue. Conversely, it may leave the storage depots to reenter the pool. Finally, the substance may be incorporated reversibly into some other molecular structure such as fatty acids into membranes or iodine into thyroxine. Incorporation is reversible in that the substance is liberated again whenever the more complex molecule is broken down. This pathway is also distinguished from storage in that the latter has no function other than the passive one of storage, whereas the incorporation of the substance into other molecules produces new molecules with specific functions.

It should be recognized that not every pathway of this generalized schema is applicable to every substance. For example, mineral electrolytes such as sodium cannot be synthesized, do not normally enter through the lungs, and cannot be removed by metabolism.

The orientation of Figure 7-4 illustrates two important generalizations concerning the balance concept: (1) Total-body balance depends upon the rates of net gain and net loss to the body; and (2) the pool concentration depends not only upon total-body balance but also upon exchanges of the substance within the body.

For any chemical, three states of total-body balance are possible (Table 7-2): (1) Loss exceeds gain, so that the total amount of the substance in the body decreases and the person is said to be in **negative balance**; (2) gain exceeds loss, so that the total amount of the substance in the body increases and the person is said to be in **positive balance**; and (3) gain equals loss, and the person is in **stable balance**.

Clearly a stable balance can be upset by alteration of the amount being gained or lost in any single pathway in the schema; for example, severe negative water balance can be caused by increased sweating. Conversely, stable balance can be restored by homeostatic control of water intake and output.

Let us take sodium as an example. The control systems for sodium balance have as their targets the kidneys, and

TABLE 7-2	THREE STATES OF TOTAL-BODY BALANCE OF A CHEMICAL SUBSTANCE
Negative balance:	Loss exceeds gain
Positive balance:	Gain exceeds loss
Stable balance:	Loss equals gain

the systems operate by inducing the kidneys to excrete into the urine an amount of sodium approximately equal to the amount ingested daily. In this example, we assume for simplicity that all sodium loss from the body occurs via the urine. Now imagine a person with a daily intake and excretion of 7 g of sodium and a stable amount of sodium in her body (Figure 7-5). On day 2 of our experiment, the subject changes her diet so that her daily sodium consumption rises to 15 g and remains there indefinitely. On this same day, the kidneys excrete into the urine somewhat more than 7 g of sodium but certainly not all the ingested 15 g. The result is that some excess sodium is retained in the body on that day; that is, the person goes into *positive* sodium balance. The kidneys do somewhat better on day 3, but it is probably not until day 4 or 5 that they are excreting 15 g. From this time on, output from the body once again equals input and sodium balance is once again *stable*.

But, and this is an important point, although again in stable balance, the woman has perhaps 2 to 3 percent more sodium in her body than was the case when she was in stable balance ingesting 7 g.[1] It is this 2 to 3 percent extra sodium that constitutes the continuous error signal to the control systems driving the kidneys to excrete 15 g/day

---

[1] Note that a large percentage change in intake (>100 percent) causes only a small change (2 to 3 percent) in total body content before the new steady state is reached. In other words, the percentage change in the regulated variable is small compared to the percentage change in the altered input.

FIGURE 7-5

Effects of a continued change in the amount of sodium ingested on sodium excretion and total-body sodium balance. A stable sodium balance is reattained by day 4 but with some gain of total-body sodium.

rather than 7 g/day. An increase of 2 to 3 percent does not seem large, but it has been hypothesized that this small gain might facilitate the development of high blood pressure in some persons.

COMPONENTS OF HOMEOSTATIC SYSTEMS

Reflexes

The thermoregulatory systems we used as an example earlier in the chapter and many of the body's other homeostatic control systems belong to the general category of stimulus-response sequences known as reflexes. Although in some reflexes we are aware of the stimulus and/or the response, many reflexes regulating the internal environment occur without any conscious awareness.

In the most narrow sense of the word, a **reflex** is an involuntary, unpremeditated, unlearned "built-in" response to a stimulus. Examples of such reflexes include pulling one's hand away from a hot object or shutting one's eyes as an object rapidly approaches the face. There are also many responses, however, that appear to be automatic and stereotyped but are actually the result of learning and practice. For example, an experienced driver performs many complicated acts in operating a car. To the driver these motions are, in large part, automatic, stereotyped, and unpremeditated, but they occur only because a great deal of conscious effort was spent learning them. We shall refer to such reflexes as **learned** or **acquired**. In general, most reflexes, no matter how basic they may appear to be, are subject to alteration by learning; that is, there is often no clear distinction between a basic reflex and one with a learned component.

The pathway mediating a reflex is known as the **reflex arc**, and its components are shown in Figure 7-6.

A **stimulus** is defined as a detectable change in the internal or external environment, such as a change in temperature, potassium concentration, or blood pressure. A **receptor** detects the environmental change; we referred to the receptor as a detector earlier. A stimulus acts upon a receptor to produce a signal that is relayed to an **integrating center**. The pathway traveled by the signal between the receptor and the integrating center is known as the **afferent pathway** (the general term afferent means "to carry to," in this case the integrating center).

An integrating center often receives signals from many receptors, some of which may be responding to quite different types of stimuli. Thus, the output of an integrating center reflects the net effect of the total afferent input; that is, it represents an integration of numerous bits of information.

The output of an integrating center is sent to the last component of the system, a device whose change in activ-

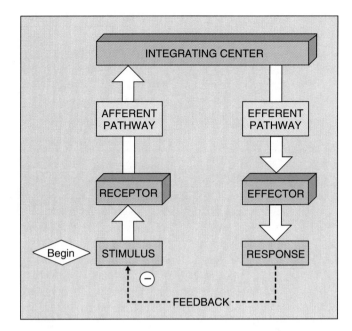

FIGURE 7-6

General components of a reflex arc that functions as a negative-feedback control system. The response of the system has the effect of counteracting or eliminating the stimulus. This phenomenon of negative feedback is emphasized by the minus sign in the feedback loop.

ity constitutes the overall response of the system. This component is known as an **effector**. The information going from an integrating center to an effector is like a command directing the effector to alter its activity. The pathway along which this information travels is known as the **efferent pathway** (the general term "efferent" means "to carry away from," in this case away from the integrating center).

Thus far we have described the reflex arc as the sequence of events linking a stimulus to a response. If the response produced by the effector causes a decrease in the magnitude of the stimulus that triggered the sequence of events, then the reflex incorporates negative feedback and we have a typical homeostatic control system. Not all reflexes incorporate such feedback. For example, the smell of food stimulates the secretion of a hormone by the stomach, but this hormone does not eliminate the smell of food (the stimulus).

To illustrate the components of a homeostatic reflex arc, let us use Figure 7-7 to apply these terms to thermoregulation. The temperature receptors are the endings of certain nerve cells in various parts of the body. They generate electric signals in the nerve cells at a rate determined by the temperature. These electric signals are conducted by the nerve fibers—the afferent pathway—to a specific part of the brain—the integrating center—which in turn

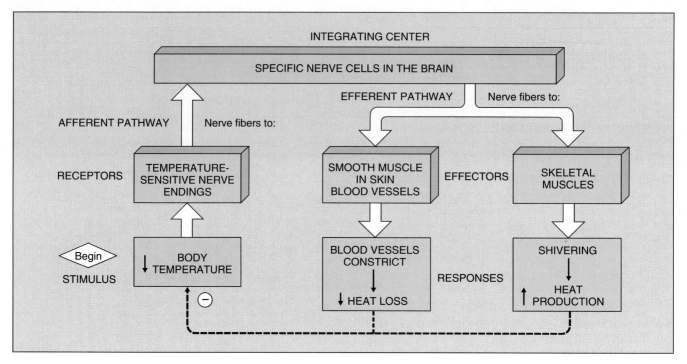

FIGURE 7-7

Reflex for minimizing the decrease in body temperature that occurs on exposure to a reduced external environmental temperature. This figure provides the internal components for the reflex shown in Figure 7-1. Another skeletal-muscle response to cold is curling up, which reduces heat loss. The dashed arrow indicates the negative-feedback nature of the reflex.

determines the signals sent out along those nerve cells that cause skeletal muscles and the muscles in skin blood vessels to contract. The latter nerve fibers are the efferent pathway, and the muscles they innervate are the effectors.

Traditionally, the term "reflex" was restricted to situations in which the receptors, afferent pathway, integrating center, and efferent pathway are all parts of the nervous system, as in the thermoregulatory reflex. Present usage is not so restrictive, however, and recognizes that the principles are essentially the same when a blood-borne messenger known as a **hormone**, rather than a nerve fiber, serves as the efferent pathway, or when a hormone-secreting gland (termed an **endocrine gland**) serves as the integrating center. Thus, in the thermoregulation example, the integrating center in the brain not only sends signals by way of nerve fibers but also causes the release of several hormones that travel via the blood to many cells, where they produce an increase in the amount of heat produced by these cells. These hormones therefore also serve as an efferent pathway in thermoregulatory reflexes.

Accordingly, in our use of the term "reflex," we include hormones as reflex components. Moreover, depending on the specific nature of the reflex, the integrating center may reside either in the nervous system or in an endocrine gland.

Finally, to complete our illustration of the components of a reflex arc, we must identify the effectors, the cells whose outputs constitute the ultimate responses in the reflexes. Almost all body cells can act as effectors in that their activity is subject to control by nerves or hormones. There are, however, two specialized classes of tissues—muscle and gland tissues—that are the major effectors of biological control systems. Muscle cells are specialized for the generation of force and movement, and their physiology is described in Chapter 11. Glands consist of epithelial cells specialized for the function of secretion (Chapter 6).

To summarize, many reflexes function in a homeostatic manner to keep a physical or chemical variable of the body relatively constant. One can analyze any such system by answering the questions listed in Table 7-3.

Local Homeostatic Responses

In addition to reflexes, another group of biological responses is of great importance for homeostasis. We shall call them **local homeostatic responses**. They are initiated by a change in the external or internal environment, that is, a stimulus, and they induce an alteration of cell activity with the net effect of counteracting the stimulus. Like a reflex, a local response is a sequence of events proceeding from stimulus to response. Unlike a reflex, how-

TABLE 7-3   QUESTIONS TO BE ASKED ABOUT ANY HOMEOSTATIC REFLEXES

1. What is the variable (for example, plasma potassium concentration, body temperature, blood pressure) that is maintained relatively constant in the face of changing conditions?

2. Where are the receptors that detect changes in the state of this variable?

3. Where is the integrating center to which these receptors send information and from which information is sent out to the effectors, and what is the nature of these afferent and efferent pathways?

4. What are the effectors, and how do they alter their activities so as to maintain the regulated variable near the operating point of the system?

cals that help the local defense against further injury; and (2) an exercising muscle liberates into the extracellular fluid chemicals that act locally to dilate the blood vessels in the area, thereby permitting the required inflow of additional blood to the muscle. The signficance of such local responses is that they provide individual areas of the body with mechanisms for local self-regulation.

Intercellular Chemical Messengers

Essential to reflexes and local homeostatic responses, and therefore to homeostasis, is the ability of cells to communicate with one another. In most cases, this communication *between* cells—*inter*cellular communication—is performed by chemical messengers. Thus, a hormone functions as a chemical messenger communicating between the hormone-secreting cell and the cell acted upon by the hormone—its **target cell**, with the blood acting as the delivery service. Most nerve cells also communicate with each other or with effector cells by means of chemical messengers called **neurotransmitters**. Thus, one nerve cell alters the activity of the next nerve cell by releasing from its ending a neurotransmitter which diffuses through the extracellular fluid separating the two nerve cells and acts upon the second (Figure 7-8). Similarly, neurotrans-

ever, the entire sequence occurs only in the area of the stimulus.

Two examples should help clarify the nature and significance of local responses: (1) Damage to an area of skin causes cells in the damaged area to release certain chemi-

FIGURE 7-8

Categories of chemical messengers. A neurohormone is the product of a nerve cell but is secreted into the blood; the latter characteristic makes it a hormone. An autocrine agent acts on the cell that secreted it. With the exception of autocrine agents, all other messengers act between cells, that is, *inter*cellularly.

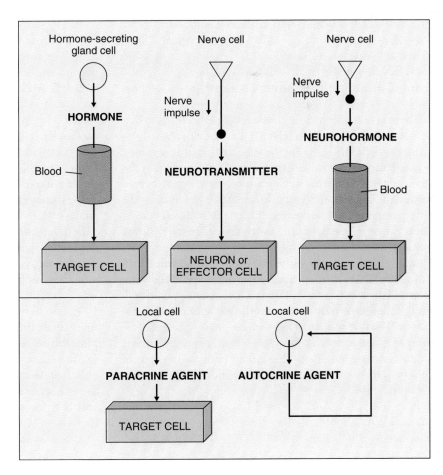

mitters released from nerve cells going to effector cells constitute the immediate signal, or input, to the effector cells.

As described more fully in Chapter 10, the chemical messengers released by certain nerve cells do not act on adjacent nerve cells or effector cells but rather enter the bloodstream to act on target cells elsewhere in the body. These messengers therefore are properly termed hormones, not neurotransmitters. They are often called **neurohormones** (Figure 7-8) in recognition of their secretion by nerve cells.

Chemical messengers participate not only in reflexes but also in local responses, as the examples above illustrate. The chemical messengers, known as **paracrine agents**, involved in local responses are synthesized by cells and released, once given the appropriate stimulus, into the extracellular fluid. They then diffuse to neighboring cells and exert their particular effects on target cells.[2] Note that, given this broad definition, neurotransmitters could be classified as a subgroup of paracrine agents, but by convention they are not. Paracrine agents are generally inactivated rapidly by locally existing enzymes so that they do not enter the bloodstream in large quantities.

Paracrine agents are chemical substances synthesized and secreted *specifically* for the purpose of regulating local cells. During the course of metabolism, many substances, such as potassium and hydrogen ions, are released from cells and produce responses in neighboring cells, particularly smooth muscle cells of blood vessels. Such substances serve to regulate local responses, but they are secondary by-products of cellular activity, not specific chemical messengers, and so are not classified as paracine agents.

There is one category of local chemical messengers that are not *inter*cellular messengers at all, that is, do not communicate *between* cells. Rather, the chemical is secreted by a cell into the extracellular fluid and then acts upon the very cell that secreted it. Such messengers are termed **autocrine agents**. Frequently a messenger may serve both paracrine and autocrine functions simultaneously, that is, some molecules of the messenger released by a cell may act locally on adjacent cells while other molecules released by the same cell are acting on that cell itself.

A point of great importance must be emphasized here to avoid later confusion: A nerve cell, endocrine gland cell, or other cell type may all secrete the same chemical messenger. Thus, a particular messenger may sometimes be referred to as a neurotransmitter, as a hormone, or as a paracrine/autocrine agent, depending both on the type of cell doing the secreting and on the location of the messenger's target cells.

All the types of intercellular communication described in this section involve secretion of a chemical messenger into the extracellular fluid. However, there are two important types of chemical communication between cells that do not require such secretion. In the first type, which occurs via gap junctions (Chapter 3), chemicals move from one cell to an adjacent cell without ever entering the extracellular fluid. In the second type, the chemical messenger is not actually released from the cell producing it but rather is located in the outer plasma membrane of that cell. In this case, the cell links up with its target cell via the membrane-bound messenger. This type of signaling is of particular importance in the functioning of the cells that protect the body against microbes and other foreign cells (Chapter 20).

Eicosanoids. The general approach of this text is to describe specific chemical messengers in the context of the functions they influence. However, one set of local chemical messengers exerts such a wide variety of effects that it is best described separately at this point. These are the **eicosanoids**, a family of substances produced from the polyunsaturated fatty acid **arachidonic acid**, which is present in plasma-membrane phospholipids. The eicosanoids include the **cyclic endoperoxides**, the **prostaglandins**, the **thromboxanes**, and the **leukotrienes** (Figure 7-9).

As shown in Figure 7-9, the appropriate stimulus— hormone, neurotransmitter, paracrine agent, drug, or toxic agent—activates an enzyme, **phospholipase A_2**, in the plasma membrane of the stimulated cell. This enzyme splits off arachidonic acid from the phospholipid, and the arachidonic acid is then metabolized by several enzyme-mediated steps to yield the specific eicosanoids. There are two major branches from arachidonic acid. One branch is catalyzed by the enzyme **cyclooxygenase** and leads to formation of the cyclic endoperoxides, prostaglandins, and thromboxanes. The other branch is catalyzed by the enzyme **lipoxygenase** and leads to formation of the leukotrienes. Within both of these branches, synthesis of the various specific eicosanoids is also enzyme-mediated. Accordingly, beyond phospholipase A_2, the eicosanoid-pathway enzymes a particular cell has determine the specific eicosanoids the cell synthesizes in response to a stimulus.

Each of the major eicosanoid subdivisions contains more than one member, as indicated by the use of the plural in referring to them (prostaglandins, for example). On the basis of structural differences, the different molecules within each subdivision are designated by a letter— for example, PGA and PGE for prostaglandins of the A and E types, which then may be further subdivided—for example, PGE_2 (Figure 7-10).

Once synthesized in response to a stimulus, the

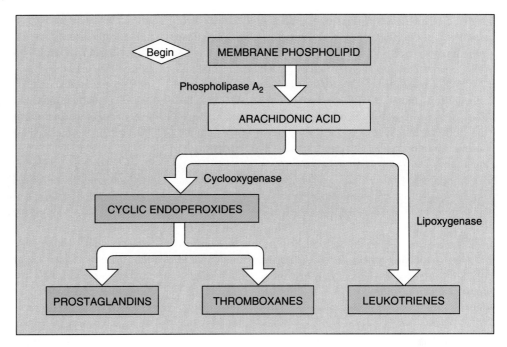

FIGURE 7-9

Pathways for the synthesis of eicosanoids. Phospholipase A_2 is the one enzyme common to the formation of all the eicosanoids; it is the site at which stimuli act. Different enzymes mediate each of the next steps, and because various cell types in the body possess different enzyme profiles, they produce different final substances in response to a stimulus. The step mediated by cyclooxygenase is inhibited by aspirin and other nonsteroidal anti-inflammatory drugs (termed NSAIDs). Anti-inflammatory steroids inhibit phospholipase A_2.

eicosanoids are not stored to any extent but are released immediately and act locally; accordingly, the eicosanoids are categorized as paracine and autocrine agents. After they act, they are quickly metabolized by local enzymes to inactive forms. Whether certain eicosanoids can also function as hormones, that is, can be carried by the blood to exert effects on sites distant from their tissues of origin, remains unsettled.

The eicosanoids exert a bewildering array of effects. For example, they are important in blood clotting, in regulation of smooth muscle contraction, in the modulation of neurotransmitter release and action, in multiple processes in the reproductive system, in the control of hormone secretion, in the generation of pain and fever, and in inflammation—the body's local response to injury and infection. We shall describe many of these specific effects in future chapters.

Finally, a word about drugs that influence the eicosanoid pathways since these are perhaps the most commonly used drugs in the world today. At the top of the list must come *aspirin*, which inhibits cyclooxygenase and, therefore, blocks the synthesis of the endoperoxides, prostaglandins, and thromboxanes. It and the newer drugs that also block cyclooxygenase are collectively termed *nonste-*

FIGURE 7-10

Structure of arachidonic acid and PGE_2. The subscript denotes the number of double bonds in the fatty acid portion of a prostaglandin molecule.

roidal anti-inflammatory drugs (NSAIDs). Their major uses are to reduce pain, fever, and inflammation. The term "nonsteroidal" distinguishes them from the steroid hormones, produced by the adrenal gland (Chapters 10 and 20), that are used in large doses as anti-inflammatory drugs; these steroids inhibit phospholipase A_2 and thus block the production of all eicosanoids. (It should be noted that both the NSAIDs and the steroids have other clinical actions in addition to their effects on the eicosanoids.)

RECEPTORS

To reiterate, most homeostatic systems require cell-to-cell communication via chemical messengers. The first step in the action of any intercellular chemical messenger on its target cell is the binding of the messenger to specific target-cell protein molecules. These molecules are known as **receptors**; in the general language of Chapter 4, the chemical messenger is a "ligand" and the receptor is a "binding site." The term "receptor" can be the source of confusion because the same word is used to denote the detectors in a reflex arc, as described earlier in this chapter. The reader must keep in mind the fact that "receptor" has two totally distinct meanings, but the context in which the term is used usually makes it quite clear which is meant.

What is the nature of the receptors with which chemical messengers combine? They are proteins (or glycoproteins) located either in the cell's plasma membrane or inside the cell. The plasma membrane is the much more common location, the major exceptions being the receptors for lipid-soluble hormones, which all readily traverse the lipid-rich plasma membranes of cells and combine with receptors inside the cells. Plasma-membrane receptors span the entire membrane thickness and are often composed of two or more nonidentical subunits. Recep-

TABLE 7-4   A GLOSSARY OF TERMS CONCERNING RECEPTORS

Receptor	A specific protein in either the plasma membrane or interior of a target cell with which a chemical messenger combines to exert its effects.
Specificity	Selectivity; the ability of a receptor to react with only one type or a limited number of structurally related types of molecule.
Saturation	The degree to which receptors are occupied by a messenger. If all are occupied, the receptors are fully saturated; if half are occupied, the saturation is 50 percent, and so on.
Affinity	The strength with which a chemical messenger binds to its receptor.
Competition	The ability of different molecules very similar in structure to combine with the same receptor.
Antagonist	A molecule that competes for a receptor with a chemical messenger normally present in the body. The antagonist binds to the receptor but does not trigger the cell's response.
Agonist	A chemical messenger that binds to a receptor and triggers the cell's response; often refers to a drug that mimics a normal messenger's action.
Down-regulation	A decrease in the total number of target-cell receptors for a given messenger in response to chronic high extracellular concentration of the messenger.
Up-regulation	An increase in the total number of target-cell receptors for a given messenger in response to a chronic low extracellular concentration of the messenger.
Supersensitivity	The increased responsiveness of a target cell to a given messenger, resulting from up-regulation.

tors may be distributed over the entire surface of the cell or confined to a particular region.

It is the combination of chemical messenger and receptor that initiates the events leading to the cell's response. The existence of receptors explains a very important characteristic of intercellular communication—**specificity** (see Table 7-4 for a glossary of terms concerning receptors). Although a chemical messenger—be it hormone, neurotransmitter, or paracrine agent—may come into contact with many different cells, it influences only certain cells and not others. The explanation is that cells differ in the types of receptors they contain. Accordingly, only certain cell types, frequently just one, possess the receptor required for combination with a given chemical messenger (Figure 7-11).

It is important to realize that, in the many cases where different cell types possess the same receptor type for a particular messenger, the responses of the various cell types to that messenger may differ from each other. For example, the neurotransmitter norepinephrine causes blood-vessel smooth muscle to contract, but via the same receptor type, norepinephrine causes cells in the pancreas to secrete less insulin. In essence, then, the receptor functions as a molecular "switch" that when "switched on" by the messenger binding to it, elicits the cell's response. Just as identical types of switches can be used to turn on a light or a radio, a single type of receptor can be used to produce quite different responses in different cell types.

Similar reasoning explains perhaps a more surprising phenomenon: A single cell may contain several different receptor types for a single messenger. Combination of the messenger with one of these receptor types may produce a

FIGURE 7-11

Specificity of receptors for chemical messengers.

cellular response quite different from, indeed sometimes opposite, that produced when the messenger combines with the other receptor type. The degree to which the messenger molecules combine with the different receptor types in a single cell is determined by such factors as the affinity of the different receptor types for the messenger.

It should not be inferred from these descriptions that a cell has receptors for only one messenger. In fact, a single cell usually contains many different receptor types, that is, distinct receptors for different chemical messengers.

Other characteristics of messenger-receptor interactions are **saturation** and **competition**. These phenomena were described in Chapter 4 for ligands binding to binding sites on proteins and are fully applicable here. In most systems, a cell's response to a messenger increases as the extracellular concentration of messenger increases, because the number of receptors occupied by messenger increases. There is an upper limit to this responsiveness, however, because only a finite number of receptors are available, and they become saturated at some point.

Competition is the ability of different messenger molecules very similar in structure to compete with each other for a receptor. Competition occurs physiologically with closely related messengers and also underlies the action of many drugs. If researchers or physicians wish to interfere with the action of a particular messenger, they can administer competing molecules, if available, that bind to the receptors for that messenger. This prevents the messenger from doing so but does not trigger the cell's response. Such drugs are known as **antagonists** with regard to the usual chemical messenger. On the other hand, some drugs that bind to a particular receptor type do trigger the cell's response exactly as if the true chemical messenger had combined with the receptor; such drugs are known as **agonists** and are used to mimic the messenger's action.

Regulation of Receptors

Receptors are themselves subject to physiological regulation. The number of receptors a cell has and the affinity of the receptors for their specific messenger can be increased or decreased, at least in certain systems. An important example of such regulation is the phenomenon of **down-regulation**. When a high extracellular concentration of a messenger is maintained for some time, the total number of receptors for that messenger may decrease—be down-regulated. Down-regulation has the effect of reducing the target cells' responsiveness to frequent or intense stimulation by a messenger and thus represents a local negative-feedback mechanism. For example, a prolonged high concentration of the hormone insulin, which stimulates glucose uptake by its target cells, causes down-regulation of its receptors, and this acts to dampen the ability of insulin to cause glucose uptake.

Change in the opposite direction (**up-regulation**) also

occurs. Cells exposed for a prolonged period to very low concentrations of a messenger may come to have many more receptors for that messenger, thereby developing increased sensitivity to it. For example, days after the nerves to a muscle are cut, thereby eliminating the neurotransmitter released by those nerves, the muscle will contract in response to amounts of experimentally injected neurotransmitter much smaller than those to which an innervated muscle can respond.

Up-regulation and down-regulation are made possible because there is a continuous degradation and synthesis of receptors. The main cause of down-regulation of plasma-membrane receptors is as follows: The binding of a messenger to its receptor stimulates the internalization of the complex; that is, the complex is taken into the cell by endocytosis (an example of receptor-mediated endocytosis, Chapter 6); this increases the rate of receptor degradation inside the cell. Thus, at high hormone concentrations, the number of plasma-membrane receptors of that type gradually decreases.

The opposite events also occur. The cell may contain stores of receptors bound in intracellular vesicles, and these are available for insertion into the plasma membrane via exocytosis (Chapter 6).

Down-regulation and up-regulation are physiological responses, but there also are many disease processes in which the number of receptors or their affinity for messenger becomes abnormal. The result is unusually large or small responses to any given level of messenger. For example, the disease called *myasthenia gravis* is due to destruction of the skeletal muscle receptors for acetylcholine, the neurotransmitter that normally causes contraction of the muscle in response to nerve stimulation; the result is muscle weakness or paralysis.

SIGNAL TRANSDUCTION MECHANISMS FOR PLASMA-MEMBRANE RECEPTORS

We have moved, in this chapter, from the broad organismic concept of homeostasis to the mechanisms by which cells communicate with one another. Now we move into the cell and describe the mechanisms by which the binding of a chemical messenger—hormone, neurotransmitter, or paracrine agent—to a receptor causes the cell to respond to the messenger. A note on terminology is appropriate here: For reasons that will be clear very soon, all these messengers, which reach the cell from the extracellular fluid, are termed **first messengers.**

The combination of messenger with receptor causes a change in the conformation of the receptor. This event, known as **receptor activation**, is always the initial step

leading to the cell's ultimate responses to the messenger, which can be (1) changes in the permeability, transport properties, or electrical state of the cell's plasma membrane; (2) changes in the cell's metabolism; (3) changes in the cell's secretory activity; and (4) changes in the contractile activity, if the cell is a muscle cell.

Despite the seeming variety of these ultimate responses, there is a common denominator: They are all due directly to alterations of particular cell proteins. Let us take a few examples of messenger-induced responses, all of which are described fully in subsequent chapters. Generation of electric signals in nerve cells reflects the altered conformation of membrane proteins constituting ion channels through which substances can diffuse between extracellular fluid and intracellular fluid. Changes in the rate of glucose secretion by the liver reflect the altered activity and concentration of enzymes in the metabolic pathways for glucose synthesis. Muscle contraction results from the altered conformation of contractile proteins.

To repeat, receptor activation by a messenger is only the first step leading to the cell's ultimate response (contraction, secretion, and so on) to that messenger. The sequences of events, however, between receptor activation and the responses may be very complicated and are termed **signal transduction mechanisms**. The "signal" is the receptor activation, and "transduction" denotes the process by which a stimulus is transformed into a response. The question is: How does receptor activation influence the cell's internal components, which may be located far from the receptor?

Signal transduction mechanisms differ at the very outset for the lipid-soluble and lipid-insoluble messengers since, as described earlier, the receptors for these two broad chemical classes of messenger are in different locations. The receptors for lipid-soluble messengers are intracellular; when activated, these receptors act in the nucleus as modulators of gene transcription. Because lipid-soluble messengers are all hormones, we shall delay further description of this mechanism to Chapter 10 and restrict the present discussion to the much larger number of messengers that are lipid-insoluble and bind to receptors on the cell's plasma membrane. On the basis of the signal transduction mechanisms used, plasma-membrane receptors can be classified into the types listed in Table 7-5.

The first type of plasma-membrane receptor signal transduction mechanism listed in Table 7-5 is the simplest mechanism since no molecules other than the receptor are involved. The protein complex that acts as receptor forms an ion channel, and activation of the receptor by a messenger causes the channel to open. The opening results in an increase in the net diffusion across the plasma membrane of the ion or ions specific to the channel (Figure 7-12). As we shall see in Chapter 8, such a change in ion diffusion is associated with an electric signal in the membrane, and

TABLE 7-5   CLASSIFICATION OF PLASMA-MEMBRANE RECEPTORS BASED ON THE SIGNAL TRANSDUCTION MECHANISMS THEY USE

1. Receptors that themselves function as ion channels
2. Receptors that themselves function as protein kinases, specifically as tyrosine kinases
3. Receptors that activate G proteins, which in turn act upon effector proteins in the plasma membrane. The effector proteins include:
    a. Adenylyl cyclase (leads to the formation of cyclic AMP)
    b. Guanylyl cyclase (leads to the formation of cyclic GMP)
    c. Phospholipase C (leads to the formation of diacylglycerol and inositol trisphosphate)
    d. Ion channels

FIGURE 7-13

Signal transduction mechanism in which the receptor complex itself can function as a protein kinase, specifically as a tyrosine kinase. Activation of the receptor activates the tyrosine kinase, which then phosphorylates cellular proteins, and these proteins participate in reactions leading to the cell's response.

this signal is an essential event in the cell's response to the messenger.

The second plasma-membrane signal transduction mechanism listed in Table 7-5, like the first, has the receptor playing a dual role, in this case functioning as an enzyme (rather than an ion channel) as well as a receptor. A portion of the protein complex that constitutes the receptor has the ability to function as a **protein kinase**, the general term for any enzyme that phosphorylates other proteins by transferring to them a phosphate group from ATP. As described in Chapter 4, introduction of the phosphate group changes the activity of the protein, often itself an enzyme. Accordingly, the sequence of events is as follows: A messenger binds to the extracellular surface of the

receptor, and this changes the conformation of the receptor so that its enzyme portion, located at its cytoplasmic surface, is activated and phosphorylates specific cytosolic and plasma-membrane proteins, including itself (Figure 7-13). Phosphorylation causes these proteins to alter their activity, and this brings about the response of the cell.[3]

Now for a very important point: As we shall see in the rest of this chapter, there are many different types of protein kinases involved in signal transduction mechanisms, each protein kinase being able to phosphorylate only certain proteins. It will be necessary to keep these different protein kinases straight. The receptors we described in the previous paragraph all function as **tyrosine kinases**, protein kinases that phosphorylate specifically the tyrosine portions of proteins. The messengers that use these receptors are almost all involved in growth and development.

The third category of plasma-membrane receptors listed in Table 7-5 is by far the largest, including approximately 100 distinct receptors. These receptors, upon activation, interact with one or more plasma-membrane proteins belonging to the family known as **G proteins**. (The term "G protein" includes all those proteins, regardless of location, that avidly bind guanine nucleotides with high affinity, and the plasma-membrane G proteins therefore encompass only a subset of G proteins.) The mechanism by which receptor activation leads to plasma-membrane G-protein activation is illustrated in Figure 7-14.

To repeat, in G-protein-dependent signal transduction, all the activated receptor does is activate a G protein, and

FIGURE 7-12

Signal transduction mechanism in which the receptor complex itself contains an ion channel. The first messenger, which reaches the cell from the extracellular fluid, is a hormone, neurotransmitter, paracrine agent, or autocrine agent. Activation of the receptor causes the ion channel portion of the receptor to open.

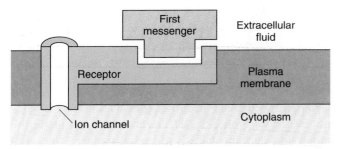

---

[3]As described in Chapter 4, protein phosphatases do the reverse of protein kinases. These enzymes also participate in signal transduction mechanisms, but their roles are much less understood than those of the protein kinases.

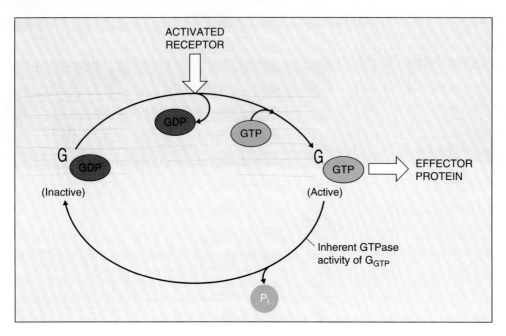

FIGURE 7-14

Biochemistry of plasma-membrane G proteins (the GTPase cycle). G proteins bind guanine nucleotides—both guanosine diphosphate (GDP) and guanosine triphosphate (GTP)—with high affinity, and the conformation of the G protein is different, depending upon which of the two nucleotides is bound to it. In the basal or inactive state, G proteins bind GDP. When a receptor that can couple to a G protein is activated by a first messenger, the receptor interacts with the G protein, causing the G protein to give up its bound GDP and bind GTP instead. This binding of GTP activates the G protein, which allows the G protein to interact in turn with effector proteins in the membrane and modulate these proteins' activity (Figure 7-15). This entire sequence is transient since the activated G protein has GTPase activity and splits off inorganic phosphate from itself to return to its GDP-bound inactive state, ready to reenter the cycle again by interacting with activated receptor.

the G protein takes over from there (Figure 7-15). It interacts with still other plasma-membrane proteins, called **effector proteins**, which are either ion channels or enzymes, and these effector proteins mediate the next step in the sequence of events leading to the cell's response (secretion, contraction, and so on). In essence, then, the G protein serves to "couple" a receptor to an effector protein in the plasma membrane, and the effector protein then takes over. We shall see in subsequent sections that the action of the effector protein is to cause a change in membrane potential and/or to yield **second messengers**, substances that serve as a direct relay from *the plasma membrane*—where the entire receptor, G protein, effector protein sequence has occurred—to the biochemical machinery *inside* the cell. Now you can see why the term "first messenger" is used to denote the original chemical messenger—hormone, neurotransmitter, or paracrine agent—that combines with the receptor.

Several features of the G-protein system help explain how a single first messenger can initiate a very complex cellular response. First, there are at least 16 distinct plasma-membrane G proteins, and a single receptor type may be associated with more than one type of G protein. Second, each of these G proteins may couple to more than one type of the many plasma-membrane effector proteins. Thus, a messenger-activated receptor, via its G-protein couplings, can call into action a variety of effector proteins, which in turn induce a variety of cellular events, to which we now turn. We will present only those pathways considered most important at present.

Adenylyl Cyclase and Cyclic AMP

The sequence of events for the most widely distributed plasma-membrane effector protein and its second messenger is illustrated in Figure 7-16. Activation of the receptor by the binding of first messenger allows the receptor to couple to a G protein known as **G$_s$ protein** (the subscript s denotes "stimulatory"; for orientation, we give the actual names of the involved G proteins in this system but will abandon this practice in subsequent sections). This binding causes G$_s$ protein to activate its effector protein, the membrane enzyme called **adenylyl cyclase**. The acti-

FIGURE 7-15

Flow of information in G-protein-dependent signal transduction. Subsequent sections of this chapter describe the specific effector proteins and second messengers. For simplicity, this figure does not show that a receptor can interact with more than a single type of G protein and that a G protein can interact with more than a single type of effector protein.

FIGURE 7-16

Cyclic-AMP second-messenger system. Combination of the first messenger—hormone, neurotransmitter, or paracrine agent—with its specific receptor permits the receptor to bind to the membrane G protein termed G_s. This protein in turn binds to adenylyl cyclase, activating it and causing it to catalyze the formation of cyclic AMP (cAMP) inside the cell. This cAMP activates cAMP-dependent protein kinase, which then phosphorylates specific proteins in the cell, thereby triggering the biochemical reactions leading ultimately to the cell's response. Not shown in the figure is the existence of another regulatory protein, G_i, with which certain receptors can react to cause inhibition of adenylyl cyclase.

vated adenylyl cyclase, whose catalytic site is located on the cytosolic surface of the plasma membrane, then catalyzes the conversion of some cytosolic ATP molecules to **cyclic 3′,5′-adenosine monophosphate**, called simply **cyclic AMP (cAMP)**. Cyclic AMP then diffuses throughout the cell to trigger the sequences of events leading to the cell's ultimate response to the first messenger. In this manner, cAMP is acting as a second messenger. Its action is terminated by its breakdown to noncyclic AMP, a reaction catalyzed by the enzyme **phosphodiesterase** (Figure 7-17).

What does cyclic AMP actually do inside the cell? It activates an enzyme known as **cAMP-dependent protein kinase** (also termed protein kinase A). In other words, the event common to the sequences initiated by cAMP is acti-

FIGURE 7-17

Structure of ATP, cAMP, and AMP, the last resulting from enzymatic alteration of cAMP.

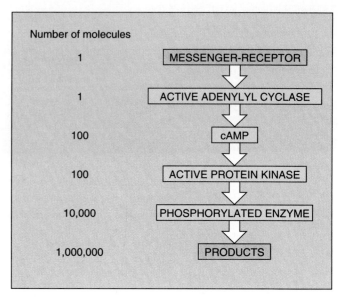

FIGURE 7-18

Example of amplification in the cAMP system. By means of an enzyme cascade, a single messenger-receptor complex ultimately leads to the generation of a very large number of product molecules. (Actually, there is another amplification step not shown in the figure, namely, the ability of a single activated receptor to activate more than one G_s protein, the G protein that will activate adenylyl cyclase.)

vation of this particular protein kinase. As defined above, protein kinases phosphorylate other proteins—often enzymes—by transferring a phosphate group to them. The change in the activity of the protein owing to its phosphorylation by cAMP-dependent protein kinase brings about the response of the cell (secretion, contraction, and so on). This is the second time—and it will not be the last—that we have invoked a protein kinase in the action of a receptor; earlier we pointed out how some receptors can themselves act as protein kinases of the tyrosine kinase type. The cAMP-dependent protein kinase is completely distinct from these tyrosine kinases and has different protein substrates.

In essence, then, the activation of adenylyl cyclase by G_s protein initiates a chain, or "cascade," of events in which proteins are converted in sequence from inactive to active forms. Figure 7-18 illustrates the benefit of such a cascade. While it is active, a single enzyme molecule is capable of transforming into product not one but many substrate molecules, let us say 100. Therefore, one active molecule of adenylyl cyclase may catalyze the generation of 100 cAMP molecules. At each of the two subsequent enzyme-activation steps in our example, another hundredfold amplification occurs. Therefore, the end result is that a single molecule of the first messenger could theoretically trigger the generation of 1 million product molecules. This fact helps to explain how hormones and other messengers can be effective at extremely low extracellular concentrations.

How can activation of a single molecule, cAMP-dependent protein kinase, by cAMP be an event common to the great variety of biochemical sequences and cell responses initiated by cAMP-generating messengers? The answer is that cAMP-dependent protein kinase has a large number of distinct substrates; that is, it can phosphorylate a large number of different proteins (Figure 7-19). This allows activated cAMP-dependent protein kinase to have multiple actions within a single cell and different actions in different cells. For example, epinephrine, a hormone that utilizes the cAMP pathway, acts on fat cells to cause both glycogen breakdown (mediated by one phosphorylated enzyme) and triacylglycerol breakdown (mediated by another phosphorylated enzyme). In other cells, in contrast, there are other substrates for cAMP-dependent protein kinase, and so cAMP generation in these cells induced by a first messenger will yield responses different from those of fat cells.

Another source of variety is that, whereas phosphorylation mediated by cAMP-dependent protein kinase *activates* certain enzymes, it *inhibits* others. For example, the enzyme catalyzing the rate-limiting step in glycogen synthesis is inhibited by phosphorylation, which explains how epinephrine inhibits glycogen synthesis at the same time that it stimulates glycogen breakdown (Figure 7-20).

In summary, the biochemistry of cAMP-dependent protein kinase and its substrates (the proteins it phosphorylates) explains how a single molecule, cAMP, can produce so many different effects. It must be reemphasized that the ability of a cell to respond at all to a cAMP-generating first messenger depends upon the presence of specific receptors for that messenger in the plasma membrane and upon the presence within the cell of proteins that can be phosphorylated by cAMP-dependent protein kinase.

Not mentioned previously is the fact that receptors for some first messengers, upon activation by their messengers, cause adenylyl cyclase to be *inhibited*, resulting in less, rather than more, generation of cAMP. This occurs because these receptors interact with a different G protein, known as **G_i protein** (the subscript i denotes "inhibitory"), and activation of G_i protein causes inhibition of adenylyl cyclase. The result is to decrease the concentration of cAMP in the cell and thereby to decrease the phosphorylation of key proteins inside the cell.

FIGURE 7-19

The variety of cellular responses induced by cAMP is due to the fact that cAMP-dependent protein kinase can phosphorylate many different proteins, activating them or inhibiting them. Our designations of the proteins being phosphorylated as 1, 2, and so on, are arbitrary. For clarity, the generation of cAMP and its activation of cAMP-dependent kinase are not shown in this figure (see Figure 7-16).

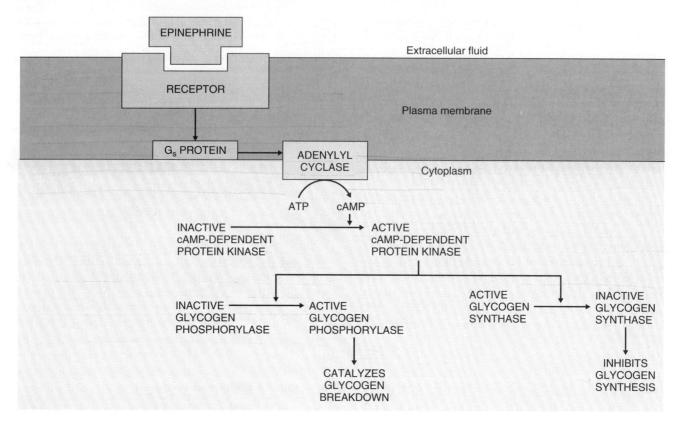

FIGURE 7-20

Coordinated stimulation of glycogen breakdown and inhibition of glycogen synthesis by epi-nephrine-induced generation of cAMP in liver cells. The cAMP activates cAMP-dependent protein kinase, which catalyzes the addition of phosphate to both the enzyme phosphorylase and the enzyme glycogen synthase. This addition *activates* the phosphorylase but *inhibits* the glycogen synthase.

Guanylyl Cyclase and Cyclic GMP

This system is analagous to the adenylyl cyclase–cAMP system. In this system, activated receptors, via a G protein, activate the membrane effector enzyme **guanylyl cyclase**, which then catalyzes the generation, in the cytosol, of a cyclic nucleotide—**cyclic 3′,5′-guanosine monophosphate (cGMP)**. In turn, cGMP acts as a second messenger to activate **cGMP-dependent protein kinase** (also called protein kinase G), which phosphorylates proteins. These proteins then elicit the cell's ultimate responses. The guanylyl cyclase-cGMP system is not coupled to nearly as many different receptors as is the adenylyl cyclase–cAMP system.

Phospholipase C, Diacylglycerol, and Inositol Trisphosphate

In this system, the activated receptor stimulates, via a G protein, a plasma-membrane effector enzyme called **phospholipase C** (don't confuse this phospholipase with phospholipase A_2, the enzyme that initiates the eicosanoid pathways). This enzyme catalyzes the breakdown of a plasma-membrane phospholipid (see Figure 2-11) known as **phosphatidylinositol bisphosphate**, abbreviated **PIP_2**, to **diacylglycerol (DAG)** and **inositol tris-phosphate (IP_3)** (Figure 7-21). Both DAG and IP_3 then function as second messengers but in very different ways.

DAG activates a particular protein kinase known as **protein kinase C**, which then phosphorylates a large number of other proteins leading to the cell's response. In particular, protein kinase C plays an important role, via phosphorylation, in the regulation of proteins associated with the plasma membrane.

IP_3, in contrast to DAG (as well as cAMP and cGMP), does not exert its second-messenger role by directly activating a protein kinase. Rather, IP_3, after entering the cytosol, acts upon the outer membranes of the endoplasmic reticulum (termed the sarcoplasmic reticulum in muscle), making them leaky to calcium (Figure 7-21). The concentration of calcium is much higher in the endoplasmic reticulum than in the cytosol, and so calcium diffuses out of this organelle into the cytosol, significantly increasing the

FIGURE 7-21

Mechanism by which an activated receptor stimulates the enzymatically mediated breakdown of PIP$_2$ to yield IP$_3$ and DAG. IP$_3$ then causes the release of calcium ions from the endoplasmic reticulum, and DAG activates a particular protein kinase known as protein kinase C.

cytosolic calcium concentration.[4] This increased calcium concentration then continues the sequence of events leading to the cell's response to the first messenger. We will pick up this thread after we present, in the next section, the last of the signal transduction mechanisms.

---

[4]It is also likely that IP$_3$ opens calcium channels in other intracellular organelles and possibly even in the plasma membrane as well.

Ion Channels Controlled by G Proteins

The first receptor signal transduction pathway we described (Table 7-5) is the case in which the receptor itself is an ion channel, which is opened when the receptor is activated. Now we deal with the situation in which the ion channel is not part of the receptor but is directly coupled to it by a G protein. Such ion channels are, therefore, plasma-membrane effector proteins, just as are the enzymes we have been discussing—adenylyl cyclase,

FIGURE 7-22

An example of how a single first messenger can cause an increase in cytosolic calcium concentration via several signal transduction pathways acting simultaneously. For simplicity, the calcium channel is shown as directly gated by the G protein, but indirect gating via a second messenger is also a possibility. Also for simplicity, a single G protein is shown mediating both the opening of the channel and the activation of phospholipase C; two different G proteins might actually be involved.

guanylyl cyclase, and phospholipase C. A receptor, once activated by a first messenger, activates in turn a particular G protein, which then interacts with an ion channel, causing it to open or close and thereby altering the net diffusion across the plasma membrane of the ion or ions specific to that channel (Figure 7-22). The overall result is an electric signal in the plasma membrane, that is, a change in the membrane potential. In addition, when calcium channels are opened, there occurs a significant increase in cytosolic calcium concentration, with consequences to be described in the subsequent section on calcium.

The situation described in the previous paragraph is known as *direct* G-protein gating of plasma-membrane ion channels because the G protein interacts directly with the channel (the term "gating" denotes control of the opening or closing of a channel). All the events occur in the plasma membrane and are independent of second messengers. Now we emphasize how this phenomenon differs from *indirect* gating of plasma-membrane ion channels by G proteins. Look back at Figure 7-19, and you will see that cAMP-dependent protein kinase can phosphorylate a plasma-membrane ion channel, thereby causing it to open. Since, as we have seen, the sequence of events leading to activation of cAMP-dependent protein kinase proceeds through G_s protein, it should be clear that the opening of this channel is *indirectly* dependent on that G protein. To generalize, the indirect gating of ion channels by G proteins utilizes a second-messenger pathway (cAMP, DAG, and so on) for the opening (or closing) of the channel.

Table 7-6 lists the three ways we have described by which receptor activation by a first messenger leads to opening or closing of ion channels. You might be wondering at this point what the adaptive value is of having multiple pathways. One thing that is affected is the time required for the response: When the channel is part of the receptor, the channel will open most rapidly (in about 1 ms), direct gating by G proteins takes longer (about 300 ms), and indirect gating by G proteins takes still longer (seconds) because of the required second-messenger processes. These time differences are particularly important for the functioning of the nervous system, as we shall see in Chapters 8 and 9.

TABLE 7-6   SUMMARY OF MECHANISMS BY WHICH RECEPTOR ACTIVATION INFLUENCES CHANNELS

1. The ion channel is part of the receptor.
2. A G protein directly gates the channel.
3. A G protein gates the channel indirectly via a second messenger.

Calcium as a Second Messenger

In our descriptions of the signal transduction pathways involving either IP_3 or gating of calcium channels by G proteins, we ended up with an increase in cytosolic calcium and stated that we would eventually describe the signficance of this increase for the rest of the signal transduction pathway. That is the subject of this section—how the calcium ion (Ca^{2+}) functions as a second messenger in a great variety of cellular responses to stimuli, both chemical (first messenger) and electrical.

The physiology of calcium as a second messenger requires an analysis of two broad questions: (1) How do stimuli cause the cytosolic calcium concentration to increase? and (2) How does the increased calcium concentration elicit the cells' responses? Note that, for simplicity, our two questions are phrased in terms of an *increase* in cytosolic concentration. There are, in fact, first messengers that elicit a *decrease* in cytosolic calcium concentration and therefore a decrease in calcium's second-messenger effects. As you read the next paragraph, therefore, keep in mind that cytosolic calcium concentration can be decreased by an event opposite that being described (for example, closing a calcium channel rather than opening it). Now for the answer to the first question.

The regulation of cytosolic calcium concentration is described in Chapter 6. In brief, by means of active-transport systems in the plasma membrane and cell organelles, this ion is maintained at an extremely low concentration in the cytosol. Accordingly, there is always a large electrochemical difference favoring diffusion of calcium into the cytosol via calcium channels in both the plasma membrane and endoplasmic reticulum. A stimulus to the cell can alter this steady state by influencing the active transport systems and/or the ion channels, resulting in a change in cytosolic calcium concentration.

The three ways that receptor activation by a first messenger can do this are summarized in the top part of Table 7-7. (1) The receptor activates a G protein that either directly or indirectly, via a second messenger, opens a *plasma-membrane* calcium channel; (2) via the phospholipase C pathway, IP_3 is generated and opens calcium channels in the membranes of the *endoplasmic reticulum*. (Note that in this last sequence IP_3 is acting as a second messenger to mobilize yet another second messenger—calcium); (3) a second messenger (cAMP, for example) is generated that leads to inhibition of the active transport of calcium out of the cytosol. These three mechanisms for increasing cytosolic calcium concentration, which all depend on receptor activation by a first messenger, are not mutually exclusive. On the contrary, several are often triggered simultaneously by the same first messenger (Figure 7-22).

This section has thus far dealt exclusively with receptor-initiated sequences of events. This is a good place, how-

TABLE 7-7 CALCIUM AS A SECOND MESSENGER

Mechanisms by which stimulation of a cell leads to an increase in cytosolic Ca^{2+} concentration:

1. Receptor activation by a first messenger
   a. Plasma-membrane calcium channels open as a result of direct or indirect gating by G proteins.
   b. Calcium is released from the endoplasmic reticulum; this is mediated by inositol trisphosphate (IP_3) generated from the breakdown of membrane phospholipid.
   c. Active calcium transport out of the cell is inhibited by a second messenger.
2. Opening of voltage-sensitive calcium channels

Mechanisms by which an increase in cytosolic Ca^{2+} concentration induces the cell's responses:

1. Calcium binds to calmodulin. On binding calcium, the calmodulin changes shape, which allows it to combine with a large variety of enzymes and other proteins, activating them or inhibiting them in turn. Many of these enzymes are protein kinases.
2. Calcium combines with calcium-binding intermediary proteins other than calmodulin. These proteins then act in a manner analogous to calmodulin.
3. Calcium combines with and alters response proteins directly, without the intermediation of any specific calcium-binding protein.

ever, to emphasize that there are calcium channels in the plasma membrane that are opened directly by an *electric* stimulus to the membrane (Chapter 6). Calcium can act as a second messenger, therefore, in response not only to chemical stimuli acting via receptors, but to electric stimuli acting via voltage-sensitive calcium channels as well. →Now we turn to the second question posed in the second paragraph of this section: How does the increased cytosolic calcium concentration elicit the cell's responses (bottom of Table 7-7)? The common denominator of calcium's actions is its ability to bind tightly and specifically to various cytosolic calcium-binding proteins. One of the most important of these is a protein found in virtually all cells and known as **calmodulin** (Figure 7-23). On binding with calcium, calmodulin changes shape, and this allows it to combine with a large variety of enzymes and other proteins, activating them or inhibiting them. At this point, the story for calcium-activated calmodulin becomes, at least in part, analogous to that for cAMP, cGMP, and DAG, in that several of the many proteins influenced by calmodulin are protein kinases. Activation or inhibition of **calmodulin-**

dependent protein kinases leads, via phosphorylation, to activation or inhibition of proteins involved in the cell's ultimate responses to the first messenger—contraction, secretion, and so on.

Calmodulin is not, however, the only intracellular protein that is influenced by calcium. Several other proteins bind calcium and then influence other proteins in turn. In still other cases, the calcium binds to proteins immediately involved in the cell's responses, without the intermediation of any other calcium-binding protein.

This concludes our description of signal transduction mechanisms, and Tables 7-5 through 7-8 together present an overview of these mechanisms. The five second mes-

FIGURE 7-23

Calcium, calmodulin, and the calmodulin-dependent protein kinase system. The mechanisms for increasing cytosolic calcium concentration are summarized in Figure 7-22 and the top of Table 7-7.

TABLE 7-8 SECOND MESSENGERS

Substance	Effects
Cyclic AMP	Activates cAMP-dependent protein kinase (protein kinase A).
Cyclic GMP	Activates cGMP-dependent protein kinase (protein kinase G).
Diacylglycerol (DAG)	Activates protein kinase C.
Inositol trisphosphate (IP$_3$)	Releases calcium from endoplasmic reticulum.
Calcium ion	Activates calmodulin and other calcium-binding proteins; calcium-calmodulin activates calmodulin-dependent protein kinases.

sengers we have described are summarized in Table 7-8, along with the four types of protein kinases activated by them. Note that each of the second messengers participates in the activation of a protein kinase. Cyclic AMP, cGMP, and DAG do so directly; IP$_3$ and calcium do so indirectly, calcium via calmodulin activation and IP$_3$ by increasing calcium.

Finally, a word is needed about how signal transduction mechanisms are shut off. A key event is the cessation of receptor activation. This occurs either when the extracellular concentration of the first messenger falls, causing the bound first messenger to come off the receptor, or as we have seen, when the combination of first messenger and receptor is taken into the cell by endocytosis. Because all the organic second messengers are continuously being broken down inside the cell and because calcium is continuously being pumped out of the cell or back into the endoplasmic reticulum, the increase in the concentrations of all the second messengers is a transient event and continues only as long as the receptor is activated by first messenger. This is also true for the opening of any channels that are part of receptors or directly gated by G proteins.

SUMMARY

GENERAL CHARACTERISTICS OF HOMEOSTATIC CONTROL SYSTEMS

I. Homeostasis denotes the stable conditions of the internal environment that result from the operation of compensatory homeostatic control systems.
  A. In a negative-feedback control system, a change in the variable being regulated brings about responses that tend to push the variable in the direction opposite the original change. Negative feedback minimizes changes from the operating point of the system, leading to stability.
  B. In a positive-feedback system, an initial disturbance in the system sets off a train of events that increases the disturbance even further.
  C. Homeostatic control systems minimize changes in the internal environment but cannot maintain complete constancy because of the need for error signals to drive the system.
  D. Feedforward regulation anticipates changes in a regulated variable, improves the speed of the body's homeostatic responses, and minimizes fluctuations in the level of the variable being regulated.
II. Acclimatization is an improved ability to respond to an environmental stress.
  A. The improvement is induced by prolonged exposure to the stress with no change in genetic endowment.
  B. If acclimatization occurs early in life, it may be irreversible and is known as a developmental acclimatization.
III. Biological rhythms are internally driven by brain pacemakers.
  A. The rhythms are entrained by environmental

cues, such as time, which also serve to phase-shift (reset) the rhythms when necessary.

    B. In the absence of cues, rhythms free-run.

IV. Aging is associated with a decrease in the number of cells in the body and with a disordered functioning of many of the cells that remain.

    A. It is a process distinct from the diseases associated with aging.

    B. Its physiological manifestations are a deterioration in organ-system function and in the capacity to respond homeostatically to environmental stresses.

THE BALANCE CONCEPT AND CHEMICAL HOMEOSTASIS

I. The balance of substances in the body is achieved by a matching of inputs and outputs.

II. Total-body balance of a substance may be negative, positive, or stable.

COMPONENTS OF HOMEOSTATIC SYSTEMS

I. The components of a reflex arc are receptor, afferent pathway, integrating center, efferent pathway, and effector. The pathways may be neural or hormonal.

II. Local homeostatic responses are also stimulus-response sequences, but they occur only in the area of the stimulus, neither nerves nor hormones being involved.

III. Intercellular communication is essential to reflexes and local responses and is achieved by neurotransmitters, hormones, and paracrine agents. Less common is intercellular communication through either gap junctions or cell-bound messengers.

IV. The eicosanoids are a widespread family of messenger molecules derived from arachidonic acid. They function mainly as paracrine and autocrine agents in local responses.

    A. The first step in production of the eicosanoids is the splitting off of arachidonic acid from plasma membrane phospholipids by the action of phospholipase A_2.

    B. There are two pathways from arachidonic acid, one mediated by cyclooxygenase and leading to the formation of prostaglandins and thromboxanes, and the other mediated by lipoxygenase and leading to the formation of leukotrienes.

RECEPTORS

I. Receptors for chemical messengers are proteins located either inside the cell or, much more com-

monly, in the plasma membrane. The binding of a messenger by a receptor manifests specificity, saturation, and competition.

II. Receptors are subject to physiological regulation by their own messengers. This includes down-regulation and up-regulation.

SIGNAL TRANSDUCTION MECHANISMS FOR PLASMA-MEMBRANE RECEPTORS

I. Binding a chemical messenger activates a receptor, and this initiates one or more signal transduction mechanisms leading to the cell's response.

    A. The receptor may contain an ion channel, which opens, resulting in an electric signal in the membrane.

    B. The receptor may itself act as a protein kinase, specifically a tyrosine kinase.

    C. The receptor may interact with a plasma-membrane G protein, which in turn interacts with plasma-membrane effector proteins—ion channels or enzymes. The effector protein's action usually involves second messengers, which function as a direct relay to the rest of the cell.

II. Very commonly, the receptor may activate, via a G_s protein, or inhibit, via a G_i protein, the membrane effector enzyme adenylyl cyclase, which catalyzes the conversion of cytosolic ATP to cyclic AMP.

    A. Cyclic AMP acts as a second messenger to activate intracellular cAMP-dependent protein kinase.

    B. This protein kinase phosphorylates proteins that mediate the cell's ultimate responses to the first messenger.

III. The receptor may activate, via a G protein, the membrane effector enzyme guanylyl cyclase, which catalyzes the formation of cyclic GMP, which then functions as a second messenger to activate a cGMP-dependent protein kinase.

IV. The receptor may activate, via a G protein, the membrane effector enzyme phospholipase C, which catalyzes the formation of diacylglycerol (DAG) and inositol trisphosphate (IP_3). DAG activates protein kinase C, and IP_3 acts as a second messenger to release calcium from the endoplasmic reticulum.

V. The receptor, via a G protein, may directly open or close an adjacent ion channel. This differs from indirect G-protein gating of channels, in which a second messenger acts upon the channel.

VI. The calcium ion is one of the most widespread second messengers.

    A. An activated receptor can increase cytosolic calcium concentration by the three ways summarized in Table 7-7. In addition, voltage-sensitive

calcium channels can influence cytosolic calcium concentration.
B. Calcium binds to one of several intracellular proteins, most often calmodulin. Calcium-activated calmodulin activates or inhibits many proteins, including calmodulin-dependent protein kinases.

KEY TERMS

homeostasis
homeostatic control systems
steady state
operating point
negative feedback
positive feedback
error signal
feedforward
adaptation
acclimatization
critical period
developmental acclimatization
circadian rhythm
entrainment
free-running rhythms
pacemaker
pool
negative balance
positive balance
stable balance
reflex
learned reflex
acquired reflex
reflex arc
stimulus
receptor (in reflex)
integrating center
afferent pathway
effector
efferent pathway
hormone
endocrine gland
local homeostatic response
target cell
neurotransmitter
neurohormone
paracrine agents
autocrine agents
eicosanoids
arachidonic acid
cyclic endoperoxides
prostaglandins
thromboxanes
leukotrienes
phospholipase A_2

cyclooxygenase
lipoxygenase
receptors (for messengers)
specificity
saturation
competition
antagonists
agonists
down-regulation
up-regulation
first messengers
receptor activation
signal transduction mechanisms
protein kinase
tyrosine kinases
G proteins
effector proteins
second messengers
G_s protein
adenylyl cyclase
cyclic 3′,5′-adenosine monophosphate
cyclic AMP (cAMP)
phosphodiesterase
cAMP-dependent protein kinase
G_i protein
guanylyl cyclase
cyclic 3′,5′-guanosine monophosphate (cGMP)
cGMP-dependent protein kinase
phospholipase C
phophatidylinositol bisphosphate (PIP_2)
diacylglycerol (DAG)
inositol trisphosphate (IP_3)
protein kinase C
calmodulin
calmodulin-dependent protein kinases

REVIEW QUESTIONS

1. Describe five important generalizations about homeostatic control systems.
2. Contrast negative-feedback systems and positive-feedback systems.
3. Contrast feedforward and negative feedback.
4. How do error signals develop and why are they essential for maintaining homeostasis?
5. Describe the conditions under which acclimatization occurs. In what period of life might an acclimatization be irreversible? Are acclimatizations passed on to a person's offspring?
6. Under what conditions do circadian rhythms become free-running?
7. How do phase shifts occur?
8. What are the important environmental time cues for entrainment of body rhythms?
9. What are the physiological manifestations of aging?
10. Draw a figure illustrating the balance concept in homeostasis.
11. What are the three possible states of total-body balance of any chemical?
12. List the components of a reflex arc.
13. What is the basic difference between a local homeostatic response and a reflex?
14. List the general categories of intercellular messengers.
15. Describe two types of intercellular communication that do not depend on chemical messengers.
16. Draw a figure illustrating the various pathways for eicosanoid synthesis.
17. What is the chemical nature of receptors? Where are they located?
18. Explain why different types of cells may respond differently to the same chemical messenger.
19. Describe how the metabolism of receptors can lead to down-regulation or up-regulation.
20. What is the first step in the action of a messenger on a cell?
21. Classify plasma-membrane receptors according to the signal transduction mechanisms they use.
22. What is the result of opening a membrane ion channel?
23. What kind of protein kinase activity is expressed by some receptors upon activation?
24. Describe the functioning of plasma-membrane G proteins and their relationship to membrane effector proteins and second messengers.
25. Draw a diagram describing the adenylyl cyclase–cAMP system.
26. What are the analogies between the cAMP and cGMP systems?
27. What are the two products released from PIP_2 by the action of phospholipase C? Contrast their actions.

28. Contrast direct and indirect gating of ion channels by G proteins.

29. What are the four mechanisms by which first messengers elicit an increase in cytosolic calcium concentration? What are the sources of the calcium in each mechanism?

30. How does the calcium-calmodulin system function?

31. List five second messengers and four types of protein kinases that participate in signal transduction. Which second messenger influences which protein kinase, directly or indirectly?

CLINICAL TERMS

jet lag	nonsteroidal anti-inflammatory drugs
stresses	(NSAIDs)
cancer	myasthenia gravis
aspirin	

THOUGHT QUESTIONS

(Answers are given in Appendix A.)

1. A person's plasma potassium concentration (a homeostatically regulated variable) is 4 mmol/L when she is eating 150 mmol of potassium per day. One day she doubles her potassium intake and continues to eat that amount indefinitely. At the new steady state, do you think her plasma potassium concentration is more likely to be 8, 4.4, or 4 mmol/L? (The answer to this question requires no knowledge about potassium, only the ability to reason about homeostatic control systems.)

2. Eskimos have a remarkable ability to work in the cold without gloves and not suffer decreased skin blood flow. Does this prove that there is a genetic difference between Eskimos and other people with regard to this characteristic?

3. Patient A is given a drug that blocks the synthesis of all eicosanoids, whereas patient B is given a drug that blocks the synthesis of leukotrienes but none of the other eicosanoids. What are the enzymes most likely blocked by these drugs?

4. Certain nerves to the heart release the neurotransmitter norepinephrine. If these nerves are removed in experimental animals, the heart becomes extremely sensitive to the administration of a drug that is an agonist of norepinephrine. Explain why in terms of receptor physiology.

5. A particular hormone is known to elicit, completely by way of the cyclic AMP system, six different responses in its target cell. A drug is found that eliminates one of these responses but not the other five. Which of the following, if any, could the drug be blocking: the hormone's receptors, G_s protein, adenylyl cyclase, or cyclic AMP?

6. If a drug were found that blocked all calcium channels directly linked to G proteins, would this eliminate the role of calcium as a second messenger?

7. What are DAG and calcium-activated calmodulin analogous to in the cAMP system?

C H A P T E R

8

NEURAL CONTROL MECHANISMS

Somatic nervous system

Autonomic nervous system

**BLOOD SUPPLY, BLOOD-BRAIN BARRIER
PHENOMENA, AND CEREBROSPINAL FLUID**

SECTION D SUMMARY

SECTION D KEY TERMS

SECTION D REVIEW QUESTIONS

CHAPTER 8 CLINICAL TERMS

CHAPTER 8 THOUGHT QUESTIONS

A long with the body's other communication system, the endocrine system, the nervous system regulates many internal functions and also organizes and controls the activities we know collectively as human behavior. These activities include not only such easily observed acts as smiling and walking but also experiences such as feeling angry, being motivated, having an idea, or remembering a long-past event. These experiences, which we attribute to the "mind," are related to the integrated activities of nerve cells in as yet unidentified ways.

The various parts of the nervous system are interconnected, but for convenience they can be divided into two parts: (1) the **central nervous system (CNS)**, composed of the brain and spinal cord; and (2) the **peripheral nervous system**, consisting of the nerves, which extend from the brain and spinal cord out to all points of the body (Figure 8-1). For example, branches of the peripheral nervous system go from the base of the spine to the tips of the toes and, although they are not shown in Figure 8-1, from the base of the brain to the internal organs.

In this chapter we are concerned with the components common to all neural mechanisms: the structure of individual nerve cells, the mechanisms underlying neural function, and the basic organization and major divisions of the nervous system.

FIGURE 8-1

The central nervous system (violet) and the peripheral nervous system (blue). Some of the peripheral nerves connect with the brain (these nerves are not shown) and others with the spinal cord.

he basic unit of the nervous system is the individual nerve cell—the **neuron**. Nerve cells operate by generating electric signals and passing them from one part of the cell to another and by releasing chemical messengers to communicate with other cells.

Neurons occur in a variety of sizes and shapes; nevertheless, as shown in Figure 8-2, most of them contain four parts: (1) the cell body, (2) the dendrites, (3) the axon, and (4) the axon terminals.

As in other types of cells, a neuron's **cell body** contains the nucleus and ribosomes and thus has the genetic information and machinery necessary for protein synthesis. The **dendrites** form a series of highly branched outgrowths from the cell body. They and the cell body are the sites of most of the specialized junctions where signals are received from other neurons, the dendrites being vastly more important in this role than the cell body. The dendrites (an average neuron may have as many as 10,000) increase the cell's receptive surface area and thereby increase its capacity to communicate with other neurons.

The **axon**, sometimes also called a **nerve fiber**, is a single long extension from the cell body. The portion of the axon closest to the cell body plus the part of the cell body where the axon is joined is known as the **initial segment**. The initial segment is where the electric signals are generated that then propagate away from the cell body along the axon. The axon may have branches, called **collaterals**, along its course, and near their ends both the axon and the collaterals undergo further branching. The greater the degree of branching of the axon, the greater the cell's sphere of influence. Each branch ends in an **axon terminal**, which is responsible for releasing chemical messengers from the axon. These messengers diffuse to the cell contacted by the terminal. In addition, some neurons release their chemical messengers from a series of bulging areas along the axon known as **varicosities**.

FIGURE 8-2

(A) Diagrammatic representation of a neuron. The proportions shown here are misleading because the axon may be 5000 to 10,000 times longer than the cell body is wide. The neuron shown here is a multipolar neuron, but there are several other types, one of which has no axons. (B) A neuron as observed through a microscope. The axon terminals cannot be seen at this magnification.

Cytoplasm

Nucleus

Myelin sheath

(A)

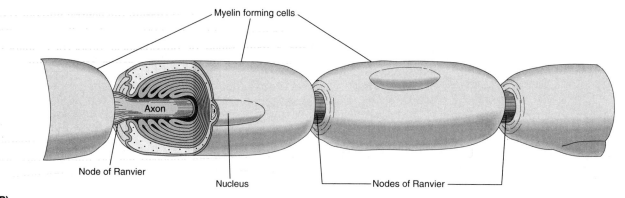

Myelin forming cells

Axon

Node of Ranvier

Nucleus

Nodes of Ranvier

(B)

FIGURE 8-3

(A) Cross section of an axon in successive stages of myelinization. The myelin-forming cell may migrate around the axon, trailing successive layers of its plasma membrane (red arrows). Alternatively, it may add to its tip, which lies against the axon, so that the tip is pushed around the axon, burrowing under the layers of myelin that are already formed (green arrows). The latter process must be used in the central nervous system where each myelin-forming cell may send branches to as many as 40 axons. (B) The myelin-forming cells are separated by a small space, the node of Ranvier (also called neurofibril node).

The axons of some neurons are covered by **myelin** (Figure 8-3), a fatty, membranous sheath consisting of layers of plasma membrane and formed by nearby supporting cells which wrap their plasma membranes around the axon. In the central nervous system these cells are the oligodendroglia, and in the peripheral nervous system they are the **Schwann cells**. The spaces between the myelin-forming cells where the axon's plasma membrane is exposed to extracellular fluid are the **nodes of Ranvier**. Myelin speeds up passage of the electric signal along the axon and conserves energy, as will be discussed later.

In order to maintain the structure and function of the cell axon, particularly when it is long, diverse organelles and materials must be moved from the cell body, where they are made, to the axon and its terminals. This movement is termed **axon transport**.

Axon transport of certain materials also occurs in the opposite direction, from the axon terminals to the cell body. This permits growth factors and other chemical signals picked up at the terminals to affect the neuron's morphology, biochemistry, and connectivity. This is also the route by which toxins, such as tetanus toxin, and herpes and polio viruses taken up by the peripheral nerve terminals enter the central nervous system.

Neurons can be divided into three functional classes: afferent neurons, efferent neurons, and interneurons. **Afferent neurons** convey information from the tissues and organs of the body *into* the central nervous system, **effer-**

ent neurons transmit electric signals *from* the central nervous system out to effector cells (muscle or gland cells), and **interneurons** connect afferent and efferent neurons within the central nervous system[1] (Figure 8-4).

At their ends farthest from the central nervous system, afferent neurons have receptors that respond to various physical or chemical changes in their environment by causing electric signals to be generated in the neuron. The receptor may be a specialized ending of the neuron or a separate cell closely associated with it. The afferent neurons propagate these electric signals from the receptors into the brain or spinal cord. (Recall from Chapter 7 that the term "receptor" has two totally distinct meanings, the one defined here and the other referring to the specific proteins with which a chemical messenger combines to exert its effects on a target cell; both types of receptors will be referred to frequently in this chapter.)

Afferent neurons are atypical in that they have no dendrites and only a single process, considered to be an axon.

---

[1]We use the term "interneuron" in its broadest sense. Some authors, however, limit its use to those nerve cells that have only a local action because they have a relatively short axon that remains in a given part of the nervous system. In that scheme, neurons within the central nervous system that have long axons are called projection neurons.

Shortly after leaving the cell body, the axon divides. One branch, the peripheral process, ends at the receptors, and the other branch, the central process, enters the central nervous system to form junctions with other neurons. Note in Figure 8-4 that both the cell body and the long peripheral process of the axon are *outside* the central nervous system and that only part of the relatively short central process enters the brain or spinal cord.

The cell bodies and dendrites of efferent neurons are within the central nervous system, but the axons extend out into the periphery. The axons of both the afferent and efferent neurons, except for the small part in the brain or spinal cord, form the **nerves** of the peripheral nervous system.

Interneurons lie entirely within the central nervous system. They account for about 99 percent of all neurons and have a wide range of physiological properties, shapes, chemistries, and functions. As a rough estimate, for each afferent neuron entering the central nervous system, there are about 10 efferent neurons and about 200,000 interneurons. The number of interneurons interposed between certain afferent and efferent neurons varies according to the complexity of the action. The knee-jerk reflex elicited by tapping below the kneecap has no interneurons, for there the afferent neurons end directly on the efferent

FIGURE 8-4

Three classes of neurons. Note that the interneurons form the connections between afferent and efferent neurons and lie entirely within the CNS. The dendrites, which function as an extension of the neuron cell body, are not shown. The arrows indicate the direction of transmission of neural activity. The stylized neurons in this figure show the conventions that we will use throughout this book for the different parts of neurons.

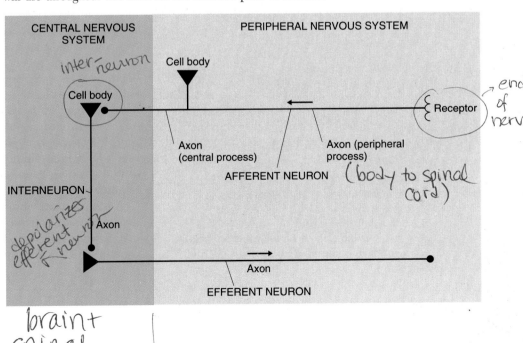

neurons. In contrast, stimuli invoking memory or language may involve millions of interneurons.

Interneurons serve as integrators within networks of neurons because their output reflects the balance of inputs they receive from the thousands of active neurons that impinge upon them. Interneurons also serve as signal changers or gatekeepers, changing, for example, an excitatory input into a inhibitory output or into no output at all. The mechanisms used by interneurons to achieve these functions will be discussed at length throughout this chapter.

Characteristics of the three functional classes of neurons are summarized in Table 8-1.

The anatomically specialized junction between two neurons where one neuron alters the activity of another is called a **synapse**.[2] At most synapses, a signal is transmitted from one neuron to another by chemical messengers known as **neurotransmitters**, a term that also includes the chemicals by which efferent neurons communicate

---

[2]The term "synapse" is also used sometimes for the junction between a neuron and an effector (muscle or gland) cell. In this book, we use the term "neuroeffector junction" for this site.

TABLE 8-1   THREE CLASSES OF NEURONS

I. Afferent neurons
  A. Transmit information into the central nervous system from receptors at their peripheral endings
  B. Are mostly (that is, the cell body and the long peripheral process of the axon) outside the central nervous system; only the short central process of the axon enters the central nervous system
  C. Have no dendrites

II. Efferent neurons
  A. Transmit information out of the central nervous system to effector cells (muscles or glands)
  B. Are mostly (that is, the cell body, dendrites, and a small segment of the axon) in the central nervous system; most of the axon is outside the central nervous system

III. Interneurons
  A. Function as integrators and signal changers
  B. Integrate groups of afferent and efferent neurons into reflex circuits
  C. Lie entirely within the central nervous system
  D. Account for 99 percent of all neurons

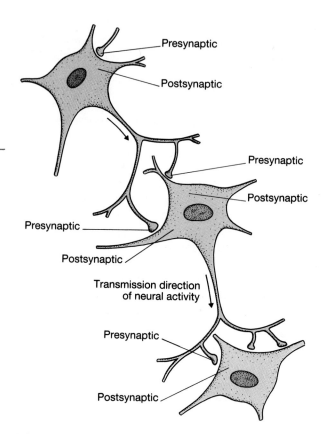

FIGURE 8-5

A neuron postsynaptic to one cell can be presynaptic to another.

with effector cells. The neurotransmitter released from one neuron alters the receiving neuron by binding with a specific membrane receptor on the receiving neuron. (The reader is cautioned one last time not to confuse this use of the term "receptor" with the receptors mentioned above that are on or associated with afferent neurons.)

Synapses generally occur between the axon terminal of one neuron and the dendrite or cell body of a second. In certain areas, however, synapses also occur between two dendrites, between a dendrite and a cell body, or between an axon terminal and a second axon terminal. A neuron conducting signals toward a synapse is called a **presynaptic neuron**, whereas a neuron conducting signals away from a synapse is a **postsynaptic neuron**. Figure 8-5 shows how, in a multineuronal pathway, a single neuron can be postsynaptic to one group of cells and presynaptic to another.

A postsynaptic neuron may have thousands of synaptic junctions on the surface of its dendrites and cell body, so that signals from many presynaptic neurons can affect it. Certain neurons in the brain receive more than 100,000 synaptic inputs.

NEURAL GROWTH AND REGENERATION **185**

Only about 10 percent of the cells in the central nervous system are neurons, and the neurons occupy about 50 percent of the volume of the central nervous system. The remainder are **glial cells** (also termed neuroglia). Glial cells branch but not as extensively as the neurons do.

As noted earlier, one type of glial cell, the oligodendroglia, forms the myelin covering of axons in the central nervous system.

A second type of glial cell, the astroglia, has multiple functions. They help regulate the composition of the extracellular fluid in the central nervous system because they remove potassium ions and neurotransmitters from the extracellular fluid around synapses. They also help sustain the neurons metabolically—for example, by providing glucose and removing ammonia. In the embryo, astroglia guide neurons as they migrate during neural development, and they stimulate the neurons' growth and the formation of their axons and dendrites by secreting growth factors. In addition, astroglia have many neuron-like characteristics, such as receptors for certain neurotransmitters, ion channels, and the capability of generating electrical responses. Thus, it has been suggested that glia take part in information signaling in the brain.

NEURAL GROWTH AND REGENERATION

The elaborate networks of nerve-cell processes that characterize the nervous system are remarkably similar in all human beings and depend upon the outgrowth of specific axons to specific targets. The mechanisms that guide the development of the brain and spinal cord are today under intense investigation by neuroscientists.

Development of the nervous system in the embryo begins with a series of divisions of precursor cells termed neuroblasts. After the last cell division, each cell, now called a neuron, migrates to its final location and begins to develop a spatial orientation, sending out processes that will become the axon and dendrites. A specialized enlargement, the growth cone, forms the tip of each extending process and is involved in finding the correct route and final target for the process.

As the cell process grows, it is guided along the surfaces of other cells, most commonly glial cells. Which particular route is followed depends in part on the presence of glycoproteins, known as cell adhesion molecules (CAMs), that provide recognition markers on the membranes of early neurons and other embryonic cells. Neuronal development is also influenced by chemical messengers that affect growth, such as **nerve growth factor**, in the extracellular region immediately surrounding the growth cone.

Once the target of the advancing growth cone is reached, synapses are formed. The synapses must be used, however, to transmit activity before their final maturation occurs. During these intricate early stages of neural development, alcohol and other drugs, radiation, and viruses can exert effects that cause permanent damage to the fetal nervous system.

A normal—although unexpected—aspect of development of the nervous system occurs after growth and projection of the axons. Many of the newly formed neurons and synapses are *destroyed*. In fact, as many as 50 to 70 percent of neurons die in some regions of the developing nervous system! Why this seemingly wasteful process occurs is unknown.

Although the basic shape of existing neurons in the mature central nervous system does not change, the creation and removal of synaptic contacts begun during fetal development continues at a slower pace throughout life as part of normal growth, learning, and aging.

Division of neuron precursors is essentially complete before birth, and no new neurons are formed to replace those that die. Damaged neurons can repair themselves, however, and significant function may be regained, provided that the damage occurs outside the central nervous system and does not affect the neuron cell body. After repairable injury, the segment of the axon now separated from the cell body degenerates. The proximal part of the axon (the stump still attached to the cell body) then gives rise to a growth cone, which grows out to the effector organ so that in some cases function is restored.

In contrast, damage to axons within the central nervous system is followed by attempts at sprouting, but no significant regeneration of the axon occurs across the damaged site, and there are no well-documented reports of function return. Mature neurons of the central nervous system are capable of regrowing processes when isolated in tissue culture, but some property of their environment in vivo, such as inhibitory factors from nearby oligodendroglia, prevents this from happening in the body.

Researchers are attempting to create artificial tubes of Schwann-cell membrane or even fetal amniotic membrane to provide an environment that will support axonal regeneration in the central nervous system. Attempts are also being made to restore function to damaged or diseased brains by the implantation of pieces of fetal brain or of tissues, such as the patient's own adrenal medulla (part of the adrenal glands, which are situated above the kidneys), that synthesize and secrete neurotransmitters.

This completes our discussion of neural tissue. We now turn to the mechanisms by which neurons and synapses function, beginning with the electrical properties that underlie all these events.

SECTION A SUMMARY

The nervous system is divided into two parts: The central nervous system comprises the brain and spinal cord, and the peripheral nervous system consists of nerves extending from the CNS.

I. The basic unit of the nervous system is the nerve cell, or neuron.
  A. The cell body and dendrites receive information from other neurons.
  B. The axon (nerve fiber), which may be covered with sections of myelin separated by nodes of Ranvier, transmits information to other neurons or effector cells.
II. Neurons are classified in three ways:
  A. Afferent neurons transmit information *into* the CNS from receptors at their peripheral endings.
  B. Efferent neurons transmit information *out of* the CNS to effector cells.
  C. Interneurons lie entirely within the CNS and form circuits with other interneurons or connect afferent and efferent neurons.
III. Information is transmitted across a synapse by a neurotransmitter, which is released by a presynaptic neuron and combines with receptors on a postsynaptic neuron.
IV. The CNS also contains glial cells, which sustain the neurons metabolically, form myelin, and serve as guides for the neurons during development.

NEURAL GROWTH AND REGENERATION

I. Neurons develop from precursor cells, migrate to their final location, and send out processes to their target cells.

II. Cell division to form new neurons is completed by birth.
III. After degeneration of a severed axon, damaged peripheral neurons can regrow the axon to their target organ. Damaged neurons of the CNS do not regenerate or restore function.

SECTION A KEY TERMS

central nervous system (CNS)	nodes of Ranvier
peripheral nervous system	axon transport
neuron	afferent neurons
cell body	efferent neurons
dendrites	interneurons
axon	nerves
nerve fiber	synapse
initial segment	neurotransmitters
collaterals	presynaptic neuron
axon terminal	postsynaptic neuron
varicosities	glial cells
myelin	nerve growth factor
Schwann cells	

SECTION A REVIEW QUESTIONS

1. Describe the direction of information flow through a neuron; through a network consisting of afferent neurons, efferent neurons, and interneurons.
2. Contrast the two uses of the word "receptor."

SECTION

B

MEMBRANE POTENTIALS

BASIC PRINCIPLES OF ELECTRICITY

As we have seen, many molecules have a net electric charge due to such components as the negative carboxyl group $RCOO^-$ and the positive amino group RNH_3^+. Moreover, most of the mineral elements, such as sodium, potassium, and chloride, are present in solution as ions (Na^+, K^+, and Cl^-).

With the exception of water, the major chemical substances in the extracellular fluid are, as discussed in Chapter 6, sodium and chloride ions, whereas the intracellular fluid contains high concentrations of potassium ions and ionized organic molecules, particularly proteins and phosphate compounds. Since many charged particles are found both inside and outside cells, it is not surprising that electrical phenomena resulting from the distribution of these charged particles play a significant role in cell function.

Like charges repel each other; that is, positive charge repels positive charge, and negative charge repels negative charge. In contrast, an electric force draws positively and negatively charged substances together.

When oppositely charged particles come together, the electric force of attraction moving them can be used to perform work. Conversely, to separate opposite charges, energy must be used to overcome this attractive force. Thus, separated electric charges of opposite sign have the potential of doing work if they are allowed to come together. This potential is called an **electric potential** or, because it is determined by the difference in charge between two points, a **potential difference**, which we shall often shorten to **potential**. The units of electric potential are volts, but since the total charge that can be separated in most biological systems is very small, the potential differences are small and are measured in millivolts (1 mV = 0.001 V).

The movement of electric charge is called a **current**. The electric force between charges tends to make them flow, producing a current. If the charges are of opposite sign, the current brings them toward each other; if the charges are alike, the current increases the separation between them. The amount of charge that moves—in other words, the current—depends on the potential difference between the charges and on the nature of the material through which they are moving. The hindrance to electric charge movement is known as the **resistance**. The relationship between current I, voltage E (for electric potential difference), and resistance R is given by **Ohm's law**:

$$I = \frac{E}{R}$$

Materials that have a high electrical resistance are known as insulators, whereas materials having a low resistance are conductors.

Water that contains dissolved ions is a relatively good conductor of electricity because the ions can carry the current. As we have seen, the intracellular and extracellular fluids contain numerous ions and can therefore carry current. Lipids, however, contain very few charged groups and cannot carry current. Therefore, the lipid layers of the plasma membrane are regions of high electrical resistance separating two water compartments—the intracellular fluid and the extracellular fluid—of low resistance.

THE RESTING MEMBRANE POTENTIAL

All cells under resting conditions have a potential difference across their plasma membranes oriented with the inside of the cell negatively charged with respect

FIGURE 8-6

The potential difference across a plasma membrane as measured by an intracellular microelectrode.

to the outside (Figure 8-6). This potential is the **resting membrane potential**.

By convention, extracellular fluid is assigned a voltage of zero, and the polarity (positive or negative) of the membrane potential is stated in terms of the sign of the excess charge on the inside of the cell. For example, if the intracellular fluid has an excess of negative charge and the potential difference across the membrane has a magnitude of 70 mV, we say that the membrane potential is −70 mV.

The magnitude of the resting membrane potential varies from about −5 to −100 mV, depending upon the type of cell (in neurons, it is generally in the range of −40 to −75 mV). As we shall see, the membrane potential of some cells can change rapidly in response to stimulation, an ability of key importance in their functioning.

The resting membrane potential can be accounted for by the fact that there is a small excess of negative ions inside the cell and an excess of positive ions outside. The excess negative charges inside are electrically attracted to the excess positive charges outside the cell, and vice versa. Thus, the excess charges (ions) collect in a thin shell at the inner and outer surfaces of the plasma membrane (Figure 8-7), whereas the bulk of the intracellular and extracellular fluids are electrically neutral. Unlike the diagrammatic representation in Figure 8-7, the number of positive and negative charges that have to be separated across a membrane to account for the potential is an infinitesimal fraction of the total number of charges within the cell.

The magnitude of the resting membrane potential is determined mainly by two factors: (1) the difference in ion concentrations of the intracellular and extracellular fluids,

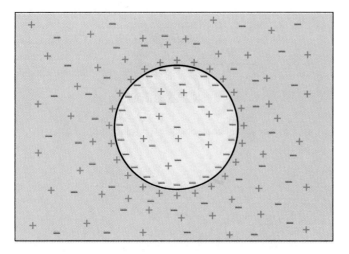

FIGURE 8-7
The excess of positive charges outside the cell and the excess of negative charges inside collect close to the plasma membrane. In reality, these excess charges are only a very small fraction of the total number of ions inside and outside the cell.

and (2) differences in membrane permeability to the different ions, which reflect the number of open channels for the different ions in the plasma membrane. The rest of this section analyzes how these two factors operate.

The concentrations of sodium, potassium, and chloride ions in the extracellular and intracellular fluids of a nerve cell are listed in Table 8-2. Although this table appears to contradict our earlier assertion that the bulk of the intra- and extracellular fluids are electrically neutral, there are many other ions, such as Mg^{2+}, Ca^{2+}, H^+, HCO_3^-, HPO_4^{2-}, SO_4^{2-}, amino acids, and proteins, in both fluid compartments. Sodium, potassium, and chloride ions, however, are present in the highest concentrations and therefore generally play the most important roles in generation of the resting membrane potential. Note that the sodium and chloride concentrations are lower inside the cell than outside, and that the potassium concentration is

greater inside. As we mentioned in Chapter 6, the concentration differences for sodium and potassium are due to the action of a plasma-membrane active-transport system, which pumps sodium out of the cell and potassium into it. We will see later the reason for the chloride distribution.

To understand how such concentration differences for sodium and potassium create membrane potentials, let us consider the situation in Figure 8-8. The assumption in this model is that the membrane contains potassium channels but no sodium channels. *Initially*, compartment 1 contains 0.15 M NaCl and compartment 2 contains 0.15 M KCl. There is no potential difference across the membrane because the two compartments contain equal numbers of positive and negative ions; that is, they are electrically neutral. The positive ions are different—sodium versus potassium—but the *total* numbers of positive ions in the two compartments are the same, and each positive ion is balanced by a chloride ion.

The initial state will not, however, last. Because of the potassium channels, potassium will diffuse down its concentration gradient from compartment 2 into compartment 1. After a few potassium ions have moved into compartment 1, that compartment will have an excess of positive charge, and compartment 2 will have an excess of

FIGURE 8-8
Generation of a diffusion potential across a membrane that contains only potassium channels. Arrows represent ion movements.

Compartment 1	Compartment 2
0.15 M NaCl	0.15 M KCl

TABLE 8-2	DISTRIBUTION OF MAJOR IONS ACROSS THE PLASMA MEMBRANE OF A TYPICAL NERVE CELL	
	Concentration, mmol/L	
Ion	**Extracellular**	**Intracellular**
Na^+	150	15
Cl^-	110	10
K^+	5	150

negative charge. Thus, a potential difference will exist across the membrane.

Now we introduce a second factor that can cause net movement of ions across a membrane: an electric potential. As compartment 1 becomes increasingly positive and compartment 2 increasingly negative, the membrane potential difference begins to influence the movement of the potassium ions. They are attracted by the negative charge of compartment 2 and repulsed by the positive charge of compartment 1.

As long as the flux due to the potassium concentration gradient is greater than the flux due to the membrane potential, there will be net movement of potassium from compartment 2 to compartment 1, and the membrane potential will increase. Compartment 1 will become more and more positive until the potential eventually produces a flux equal but opposite the flux due to the concentration gradient. The membrane potential at which these two fluxes become equal in magnitude but opposite in direction is called the **equilibrium potential** for that type of ion. At the equilibrium potential for an ion there is no net movement of the ion because the opposing fluxes are equal, and the potential will undergo no further change.

The value of the equilibrium potential for any type of ion depends on the concentration gradient for that ion across the membrane. If the concentrations on the two sides were equal, the flux due to the concentration gradient would be zero and the equilibrium potential would also be zero. The larger the concentration gradient, the larger the equilibrium potential since a larger electrically driven movement of ions would be required to balance the larger movement due to the concentration difference.

If the membrane separating the two compartments is replaced with one that contains only sodium channels, a parallel situation will occur (Figure 8-9). A sodium equilibrium potential will eventually be established, but compartment 2 will be *positive* with respect to compartment 1, at which point net movement will cease.

Thus, the equilibrium potential for one ion species can be different in magnitude and sometimes even in direction from those for other ion species, depending on the concentration gradients for each ion. Given the concentration gradient, the equilibrium potential for any ion can be calculated (by means of the Nernst equation, Appendix D).

When more than one ion species can diffuse across the membrane, the permeabilities and concentration gradients for all the ions must be considered when accounting for the membrane potential. For a given concentration gradient, the greater the membrane permeability to an ion species, the greater the contribution that ion species will make to the membrane potential. Given the concentration gradients and membrane permeabilities for several ion species, the potential of a membrane permeable to these species can be calculated (by the Goldman equation, Appendix D).

It is not difficult to move from these hypothetical examples to a nerve cell at rest where (1) the potassium concentration is much greater inside the nerve cell than outside (Figure 8-10A) and the sodium concentration profile is just the opposite (Figure 8-11A); and (2) the plasma membrane contains about 50 to 75 times more open potassium channels than open sodium channels. Given the actual potassium and sodium concentration differences, one can calculate that the potassium equilibrium potential will be approximately −90 mV (Figure 8-10B) and the sodium equilibrium potential about +60 mV (Figure 8-11B).

Since the membrane is permeable, to some extent, to both potassium and sodium, the resting membrane potential cannot be equal to either of these two equilibrium potentials. Because the membrane is so much more permeable to potassium than to sodium, however, the resting potential will be much closer to the potassium equilibrium potential.

In other words, a potential is generated across the plasma membrane largely because of the movement of potassium down its concentration gradient through open potassium channels, so that the inside of the cell becomes negative with respect to the outside. The experimentally measured resting membrane potential is *not* equal to the potassium equilibrium potential, however, because a small number of sodium channels are open in the resting state, and some sodium ions continually move into the cell, canceling the effect of an equivalent number of potassium ions simultaneously moving out.

Thus, at a resting potential of −70 mV, a typical value for neurons, neither sodium nor potassium is at its equilibrium potential, and so there is net movement through ion channels of sodium into the cell and potassium out. If such net ion movements occur, why does the concentration of

FIGURE 8-9

Generation of a diffusion potential across a membrane that contains only sodium channels. Arrows represent ion movements.

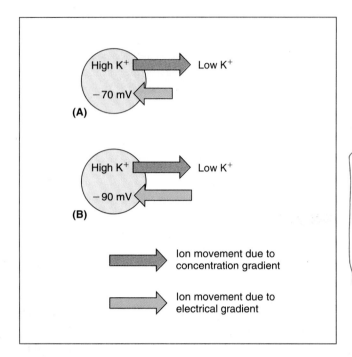

FIGURE 8-10

Forces acting on potassium when the membrane of a neuron is at (A) the resting potential (-70 mV, inside negative), and (B) the potassium equilibrium potential (-90 mV, inside negative).

FIGURE 8-11

Forces acting on sodium when the membrane of a neuron is at (A) the resting potential (-70 mV, inside negative), and (B) the sodium equilibrium potential ($+60$ mV, inside positive).

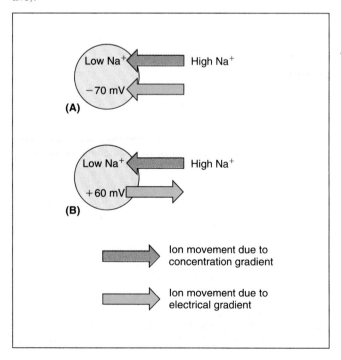

intracellular sodium not progressively increase and that of intracellular potassium decrease? The reason is that active-transport mechanisms in the plasma membrane utilize energy derived from cellular metabolism to pump the sodium back out of the cell and the potassium back in. Actually, the pumping of these ions is linked because they are both transported by the Na,K-ATPase pumps in the membrane (page 127).

In a resting cell, the number of ions moved by the pump equals the number of ions that move in the opposite direction through channels in the membrane down their concentration and/or electrical gradients (Figure 8-12), and therefore the concentrations of sodium and potassium in the cell do not change. As long as the concentration gradients remain fixed and the ion permeabilities of the plasma membrane do not change, the electric potential across the resting membrane will remain constant.

Thus far, we have described the membrane potential as due purely and directly to the passive movement of ions down their electrical and concentration gradients, the concentration gradients having been established by membrane pumps. There is, however, another component to the membrane potential, reflecting the *direct* separation of charge across the membrane by the transport of ions by the membrane Na,K-ATPase pump. If the pump were to move equal numbers of sodium and potassium ions across the membrane in opposite directions, it would not contribute directly to the separation of charge and all the charge separation would result from ion diffusion. If equal numbers of ions are not moved, however, the pump does separate charge and contributes directly to the membrane potential. It is known in this case as an **electrogenic pump**.

The Na,K-ATPase pump is, in fact, electrogenic since it moves three sodium ions out of the cell for every two potassium ions that it brings in. This unequal transport of positive ions directly makes the inside of the cell more negative than it would be from ion diffusion alone. In most cells (but by no means all), however, the electrogenic contribution to the membrane potential is quite small. It must be reemphasized that, even when the electrogenic contribution of the Na,K-ATPase pump is small, the pump makes an essential *indirect* contribution to the membrane potential because it maintains the concentration gradients down which the ions diffuse to produce most of the charge separation that makes up the potential.

We have not yet dealt with chloride ions. The plasma membranes of many cells have chloride channels and do not contain chloride-ion pumps. Therefore, in these cells the membrane potential, set up by all the interactions just described, acts on chloride ions. The inside negativity moves chloride out of the cell, and the chloride concentration outside the cell becomes higher than that inside. This concentration gradient, however, produces a diffusion of chloride back into the cell that exactly opposes the move-

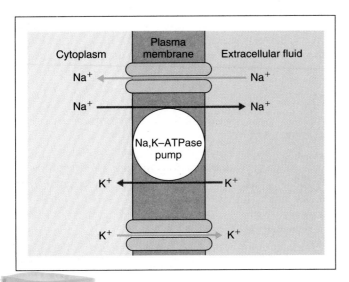

FIGURE 8-12

Movements of sodium and potassium ions across the plasma membrane of a resting neuron. The passive movements (blue arrows) are exactly balanced by the active transport (red arrows) of the ions in the opposite direction.

FIGURE 8-13

Depolarizing, repolarizing, hyperpolarizing, and overshoot changes in membrane potential.

ment out because of the electric potential. Thus, chloride concentrations shift until the equilibrium potential for chloride is equal to the resting membrane potential, and chloride makes no contribution to the magnitude of the membrane potential.

In contrast, some cells have an active-transport system that moves chloride out of the cell. In these cells, the membrane potential is not at the chloride equilibrium potential, and net chloride diffusion *into* the cell contributes to the excess negative charge inside the cell; that is, it increases the magnitude of the membrane potential.

Most of the negative charge in neurons is accounted for, however, not by chloride ions but by negatively charged organic molecules, such as proteins. Unlike chloride, these molecules do not readily cross the plasma membrane but remain inside the cell, where their charge contributes to the total negative charge within the cell.

GRADED POTENTIALS AND ACTION POTENTIALS

ransient changes in the membrane potential from its resting level produce electric signals that can alter cell activities. Such changes are the most important way that nerve cells process and transmit information. These signals occur in two forms: graded potentials and action potentials. Graded potentials are important in signaling over short distances, whereas action potentials are the long-distance signals of nerve and muscle membranes.

Adjectives such as "membrane," "resting," "action," and "graded" define the conditions under which the potential is measured or the way it develops (Table 8-3).

The terms "depolarize," "hyperpolarize," and "repolarize" will be used to describe the direction of changes in the membrane potential relative to the resting potential (Figure 8-13). The membrane is said to be **depolarized** when its potential is less negative (closer to zero) than the resting level. The membrane is **hyperpolarized** when the potential is more negative than the resting level. When a membrane potential that has been either depolarized or hyperpolarized returns toward the resting value, it is said to be **repolarizing**. **Overshoot** refers to a reversal of the membrane-potential polarity, that is, when the inside of a cell becomes positive.

Graded Potentials

Graded potentials are changes in membrane potential that are confined to a relatively small region of the plasma membrane and die out within 1 to 2 mm of their site of origin. They can occur in either a depolarizing or hyperpolarizing direction (Figure 8-14A), and they are usually produced by some stimulus, that is, by a specific change in the cell's environment acting on a specialized region of the membrane. They are called "graded potentials" because the magnitude of the potential change is variable (graded) and is related to the magnitude of the stimulus (Figure 8-14B). We shall encounter a number of graded potentials, which are given various names related to the location of the potential or to the function it performs: receptor potentials, synaptic potentials, end-plate potentials, pacemaker potentials.

Whenever a graded potential occurs, charge flows between the place of origin of the potential and adjacent regions of the plasma membrane, which are at the resting

TABLE 8-3   A MINIGLOSSARY

Potential = potential difference	The voltage difference between two points.
Membrane potential = transmembrane potential	The voltage difference between the inside and outside of a cell.
Equilibrium potential	The voltage difference across a membrane that produces a flux of a given ion species that is equal but opposite the flux due to the concentration gradient affecting that same ion species.
Resting membrane potential = resting potential	The steady transmembrane potential of a cell that is not producing an electric signal.
Graded potential	A potential change of variable amplitude and duration that is conducted decrementally; it has no threshold or refractory period.
Action potential	A brief all-or-none depolarization of the membrane, reversing polarity in neurons; it has a threshold and refractory period and is conducted without decrement.
Postsynaptic potential	A graded potential change produced in the postsynaptic neuron in response to release of a neurotransmitter by a presynaptic terminal; it may be depolarizing (an **excitatory postsynaptic potential** or **EPSP**) or hyperpolarizing (an **inhibitory postsynaptic potential** or **IPSP**).
Receptor potential	A graded potential produced at the peripheral endings of afferent neurons (or in separate receptor cells) in response to a stimulus.
Pacemaker potential	A spontaneously occurring graded potential change that occurs in certain specialized cells.

potential. In Figure 8-15A, a small region of a membrane has been depolarized by a stimulus and therefore has a potential less negative than that of adjacent areas. Inside the cell (Figure 8-15B), positive charge (positive ions) will flow through the intracellular fluid away from the depolarized region and toward the more negative, resting regions of the membrane. Simultaneously, outside the cell, positive charge will flow from the more positive region of the resting membrane toward the less positive region just created by the depolarization. The greater the potential change, the greater the currents. By convention, the direction in which positive ions move is designated the direc-

tion of the current, although negatively charged ions simultaneously move in the opposite direction.

Note that this local current removes positive charges from regions adjacent to the depolarization site along the outside of the membrane and adds positive charge to regions adjacent to the depolarization site along the inside of the membrane. Thus it produces a decrease in the amount of charge separation (depolarization) in the membrane sites adjacent to the originally depolarized region. The local current is carried by ions such as K^+, Na^+, Cl^-, and HCO_3^-.

Local current flows much like water flows through a

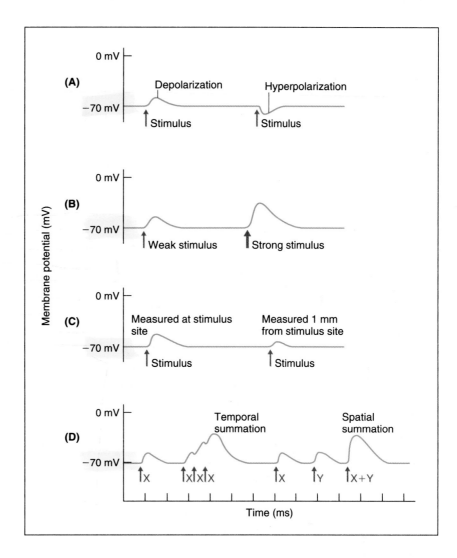

FIGURE 8-14

Graded potentials (A) can be depolarizing or hyperpolarizing, (B) can vary in size, (C) are conducted decrementally, and (D) can be summed. Temporal and spatial summation will be discussed later in the chapter.

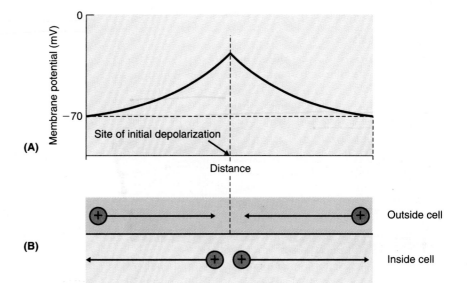

FIGURE 8-15

(A) Potential changes around a depolarization site. (B) Local current surrounding a depolarized region of a membrane produces a depolarization of adjacent regions.

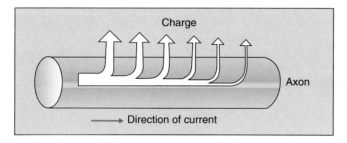

FIGURE 8-16
Leakage of charge across the plasma membrane reduces the local current at sites farther along the membrane.

leaky hose. Charge is lost across the membrane because the membrane is permeable to ions, just as water is lost from the leaky hose. The result is that the magnitude of the current decreases with the distance from the initial site of the potential change, just as water flow decreases the farther along the leaky hose you are from the faucet (Figure 8-16). In fact, plasma membranes are so leaky to ions that local currents die out almost completely within a few millimeters of their point of origin. There is another way of saying the same thing: Local current is **decremental**; that is, its amplitude decreases with increasing distance from the site of origin of the potential. The resulting change in membrane potential from resting level therefore also decreases with the distance from the potential's site of origin (Figures 8-14C and 8-15A).

Because the electric signal decreases with distance, graded potentials (and the local current they generate) can function as signals only over very short distances (a few millimeters). Nevertheless, graded potentials are the only means of communication used by some neurons and, as we shall see, play very important roles in the initiation and integration of signals by neurons and some other cells.

Action Potentials

Action potentials are very different from graded potentials (Table 8-4). They are rapid alterations in the membrane potential that may last only 1 ms, during which time the membrane potential may change 100 mV, from −70 mV to +30 mV, and then repolarize to its resting membrane potential (Figure 8-17). Nerve and muscle cells as well as some endocrine, immune, and reproductive cells have plasma membranes capable of producing action potentials. These membranes are called **excitable membranes**, and their ability to generate action potentials is known as **excitability**. The propagation of action potentials is the mechanism used by the nervous system to communicate over long distances.

How does an excitable membrane make rapid changes in its membrane potential? How is an action potential propagated along an excitable membrane? These questions will be discussed in the following sections.

Ionic Basis of the Action Potential. Action potentials can be explained by the concepts already developed for describing the origins of resting membrane potentials. We have seen that the magnitude of the resting membrane potential depends upon the concentration gradients of and membrane permeabilities to different ions, particularly sodium and potassium. This dependence is true for the period of the action potential as well: The action potential results from a transient change in membrane ion permeability, whereas concentration gradients remain unchanged. In the resting state the open channels in the plasma membrane are predominantly those that are permeable to potassium and chloride ions. Almost all the sodium-ion channels are closed, and the resting potential is therefore much closer to the potassium equilibrium potential than to the sodium equilibrium potential. During an action potential, however, the membrane permeabilities to sodium and potassium ions are markedly altered.

The depolarizing phase of the action potential is due to the opening of sodium channels, increasing the membrane permeability to sodium ions several hundredfold. This allows some sodium ions to rush into the cell. During this period, therefore, more positive charge enters the cell in the form of sodium ions than leaves in the form of potassium ions, and the membrane potential depolarizes. It may even overshoot, becoming positive on the inside and negative on the outside of the membrane. In this phase the

FIGURE 8-17
Changes in membrane potential and changes in the membrane permeability (P) to sodium and potassium ions during an action potential.

TABLE 8-4 DIFFERENCES BETWEEN GRADED POTENTIALS AND ACTION POTENTIALS

Graded potentials	Action potentials
Graded response; amplitude varies with conditions of the initiating event	All-or-none response; once membrane is depolarized to threshold, amplitude is independent of initiating event
Graded response; can be summed	All-or-none response; cannot be summed
Has no threshold	Has a threshold that is usually about 15 mV depolarized relative to the resting potential
Has no refractory period	Has a refractory period
Is conducted decrementally; that is, amplitude decreases with distance	Is conducted without decrement; the amplitude is constant
Duration varies with initiating conditions	Duration constant for a given cell type under constant conditions
Can be a depolarization or a hyperpolarization	Is a depolarization (with overshoot in neurons)
Initiated by environmental stimulus (receptor), by neurotransmitter (synapse), or spontaneously	Initiated by membrane depolarization
Dominated by receptor-operated channels or other chemical changes	Dominated by voltage-sensitive channels

membrane potential approaches but does not quite reach the sodium equilibrium potential.

Action potentials in nerve cells last about 1 ms and typically show an overshoot. (They may last much longer in certain types of muscle cells.) What causes the membrane potential to return so rapidly to its resting level? The answer to this question is twofold: (1) The sodium channels that opened during the depolarization phase undergo inactivation, which causes them to close; and (2) a special set of potassium channels begins to open, albeit more slowly. The timing of these two events can be seen in Figure 8-17.

Closure of the sodium channels alone would restore the membrane potential to its resting level since potassium flux out would then exceed sodium flux in. However, the process is speeded up by the simultaneous increase in potassium permeability. These two events, inactivation of the sodium channels and opening of additional potassium channels, lead to a potassium diffusion out of the cell that is much greater than the sodium diffusion in, rapidly re-

turning the membrane potential to its resting level. In fact, after the sodium channels have closed, at least some of the additional potassium channels are still open, and there is generally a small hyperpolarizing overshoot of the membrane potential in nerve cells (**afterhyperpolarization**, Figure 8-17).

One might think that large movements of ions across the membrane would be required to produce such large changes in membrane potential. Actually, only about 1 of every 100,000 sodium ions enters the cell during an action potential, and approximately the same number of potassium ions diffuses out to return the membrane potential to its resting level. These ion movements are so small that they produce only infinitesimal changes in the intracellular ion concentrations, and that is why we said earlier that the action potential is *not* associated with changes in ionic concentrations. Yet if this tiny number of ions crossing the membrane with each action potential were not eventually moved back across the membrane, the concentration gradients of sodium and potassium would gradually disappear and action potentials could no longer be generated. As might be expected, cellular accumulation of sodium and loss of potassium are prevented by the continuous action of the membrane Na,K-ATPase pumps.

It may seem foolish to let sodium move into the neuron and then pump it back out, but sodium movement into the cell creates the electric signal necessary for communication between parts of the cell, and pumping sodium out restores the concentration gradient so that, in response to a new stimulus, sodium will enter the cell and create another signal.

Mechanism of Ion-channel Changes. In the above section, we described the various phases of the action potential as due to the opening and/or closing of ion channels. What causes these changes? The very first part of the depolarization, as we shall see later, is due to local current. Once depolarization starts, the depolarization itself causes sodium channels to open. In light of our discussion of the ionic basis of membrane potentials, it is very easy to confuse the cause-and-effect relationships of this last statement. Earlier we pointed out that an increase in sodium permeability *causes* membrane depolarization; now we are saying that depolarization *causes* an increase in sodium permeability. Combining these two distinct causal relationships yields the positive-feedback cycle (Figure 8-18) responsible for the depolarizing phase of the action potential: Depolarization opens sodium channels so that the membrane permeability to sodium increases. Because of increased sodium permeability, sodium diffuses into the cell; this addition of positive charge to the cell further depolarizes the membrane, which in turn produces a still greater increase in sodium permeability, which in turn causes. . . .

Ion channels, such as these sodium channels, that can be opened or closed by changes in membrane potential are called voltage-sensitive ion channels (page 122). The potassium channels that open during an action potential are also voltage-sensitive. In fact, their opening is triggered by the same depolarization that opens the sodium channels, but the potassium-channel opening is slightly delayed.

What about the inactivation of the voltage-sensitive sodium channels that opened during the rising phase of the action potential? This is the result of a change in the conformation of the proteins that constitute the channel.

The generation of action potentials is prevented by **local anesthetics** such as procaine hydrochloride (Novocaine) and lidocaine (Xylocaine) because these drugs prevent opening of the sodium channels in response to depolarization. Without action potentials, afferent signals generated in the periphery—in response to injury, for example—cannot reach the brain and give rise to the sensation of pain.

Although we have discussed only sodium and potassium channels, in some regions of nerve-cell membrane and in various nonneural cells calcium channels open in response to membrane depolarization. In these cases, calcium diffusion into the cell through these voltage-sensitive channels is responsible for generating action potentials. These are generally prolonged action potentials, and the inward calcium diffusion couples membrane excitability to events within the cell, explaining some of the special properties of these cells.

Threshold. Not all stimulus-induced depolarizations trigger the positive-feedback relationship that leads to an action potential. Action potentials occur only when the membrane is depolarized enough (and therefore enough sodium channels are open) so that sodium entry exceeds potassium exit. In other words, action potentials occur only when the *net* movement of positive charge through ion channels is inward. The membrane potential at which the *net* movement of ions through the ion channels first changes from outward to inward is the **threshold**, and stimuli that are just strong enough to depolarize the membrane to this level are **threshold stimuli** (Figure 8-19).

The threshold of most excitable membranes is about 15 mV less negative inside than the resting membrane potential. Thus, if the resting potential of a neuron is −70 mV, the threshold potential may be −55 mV. Stimuli must depolarize the membrane by at least 15 mV in order to initiate the positive feedback that produces an action potential. At depolarizations less than threshold, outward potassium movement still exceeds sodium entry and the positive-feedback cycle cannot get started despite the increase in sodium entry. In such cases, the membrane will return to its resting level as soon as the stimulus is removed, and no action potential is generated. These weak depolarizations are **subthreshold potentials**, and the stimuli that cause them are **subthreshold stimuli**.

FIGURE 8-18
Positive-feedback relation between membrane depolarization and increased sodium permeability, which leads to the rapid depolarizing phase of the action potential.

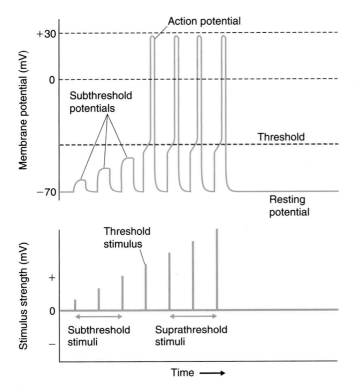

FIGURE 8-19

Changes in the membrane potential with increasing strength of depolarizing stimulus. When the membrane potential reaches threshold, action potentials are generated. Increasing the stimulus strength above threshold level does not cause larger action potentials. (The afterhyperpolarization has been omitted from this figure for clarity.)

Just like threshold stimuli, stimuli of more than threshold magnitude (**suprathreshold stimuli**) also elicit action potentials, but as can be seen in Figure 8-19, the action potentials resulting from such stimuli have exactly the same amplitude as those caused by threshold stimuli. This is explained by the fact that once threshold is reached, membrane events are no longer dependent upon stimulus strength. The depolarization continues on to generate an action potential because the positive-feedback cycle is operating. Action potentials either occur maximally or do not occur at all. Another way of saying this is that action potentials are **all-or-none**.[3]

The firing of a gun is a mechanical analogy that shows the principle of all-or-none behavior characteristic of nerve axons. The magnitude of the explosion and the velocity at which the bullet leaves the gun do not depend on how hard the trigger is squeezed. Either the trigger is pulled hard enough to fire the gun, or it is not; one cannot fire a gun halfway.

Because of this all-or-none nature, a single action potential cannot convey information about the magnitude of the stimulus that initiated it. How then does one distinguish between a loud noise and a whisper, a light touch and a pinch? This information, as we shall see, depends in part upon the number of action potentials transmitted per unit of time, that is, frequency, and not upon their size.

Refractory Periods. How soon after firing an action potential can an excitable membrane fire a second one? During the action potential, a second stimulus—no matter how strong—will not produce a second action potential, and the membrane is said to be in its **absolute refractory period**. Following this period, there is an interval during which a second action potential can be produced, but only if the stimulus strength is considerably greater than threshold. This is the **relative refractory period**, which can last 10 to 15 ms or longer. If a threshold depolarization outlasts the relative refractory period, an additional action potential will be fired.

Refractory periods reflect the fact that after an action potential, time is required to restore the proteins of the voltage-sensitive ion channels to their original resting conformation. Both refractory periods correspond to times of residual sodium inactivation and increased potassium permeability. A suprathreshold stimulus can cause an action potential during the relative refractory period when a threshold stimulus cannot because the suprathreshold stimulus opens more sodium channels so there is a greater chance that sodium entry will exceed potassium exit, triggering the positive feedback cycle illustrated in Figure 8-18.

The refractory periods limit the number of action potentials that can be produced by an excitable membrane in a given period of time. Most nerve cells respond at frequencies of up to 100 action potentials per second, and some may produce much higher frequencies for brief periods of time.

Action-potential Propagation. Once generated, one particular action potential does not itself travel along the membrane. Rather, the local current produced by one action potential is great enough to serve as the stimulus that depolarizes the adjacent membrane to its threshold potential. The sodium positive-feedback cycle takes over, and a new action potential occurs there.

The new action potential then produces local currents of its own, which depolarize the region adjacent to it, producing yet another action potential at the next site, and so on to cause **action-potential propagation** along the length of the membrane. Because each action potential depends on the sodium-feedback cycle of the membrane

---

[3]There is a qualification: The action potential fires maximally if it fires at all, but its maximal amplitude depends on the electrical and chemical conditions across the membrane and upon the state of the membrane. For example, if extracellular sodium concentration is reduced, the action potential will be smaller than usual because of the reduced concentration gradient that drives sodium into the cell.

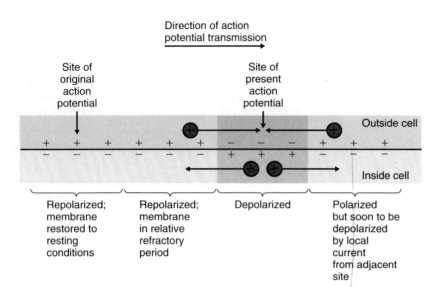

Direction of action
potential transmission

Site of
original
action
potential

Site of
present
action
potential

Outside cell

Inside cell

Repolarized;
membrane
restored to
resting
conditions

Repolarized;
membrane
in relative
refractory
period

Depolarized

Polarized
but soon to be
depolarized
by local
current
from adjacent
site

FIGURE 8-20

Propagation of an action potential along a
plasma membrane.

where the action potential is occurring, the action potential arriving at the end of the membrane is virtually identical in form to the initial one. Thus, action potentials are not conducted decrementally as are graded potentials.

Because the membrane areas that have just undergone an action potential are refractory and cannot immediately undergo another, the only direction of action-potential propagation is away from a region of membrane that has recently been active (Figure 8-20).

If the membrane through which the action potential must travel is not refractory, excitable membranes are able to conduct action potentials in either direction, the direction of propagation being determined by the stimulus location. For example, the action potentials in skeletal muscle cells are initiated near the middle of these cylindrical cells and propagate toward the two ends. In most nerve cells, however, action potentials are initiated at one end of the cell and propagate toward the other end, for reasons to be described in the next section. The propagation ceases when the action potential reaches the end of an axon.

The velocity with which an action potential propagates along a membrane depends upon fiber diameter and whether or not the fiber is myelinated. The larger the fiber diameter, the faster the action potential propagates. This is because a larger fiber offers less resistance to local current, and so adjacent regions of the membrane are brought to threshold faster.

Myelin is an insulator that makes it more difficult for charge to flow between intra- and extracellular fluid compartments. Moreover, the concentration of sodium channels in the myelinated region of axons is low. Therefore, action potentials do not occur along the sections of membrane covered by myelin. Rather, they occur only at the nodes of Ranvier where the myelin coating is interrupted and the concentration of sodium channels is high. Thus,

action potentials literally jump from one node to the next as they propagate along a myelinated fiber, and for this reason this method of propagation is called **saltatory conduction** (Latin *saltare*, to leap).

Propagation via saltatory conduction is faster than propagation in nonmyelinated fibers of the same axon diameter because less charge leaks out through the myelin-covered section of the membrane (Figure 8-21). Thus, more charge arrives at the node adjacent to the active node, and an action potential is generated there sooner than if the myelin were not present.

Conduction velocities range from about 0.5 m/s (1 mi/h) for small-diameter, unmyelinated fibers to about 100 m/s (225 mi/h) for large-diameter, myelinated fibers. At 0.5 m/s, an action potential travels from the head to the toe of an average-size person in about 4 s; at a velocity of 100 m/s, it would take about 0.02 s.[4]

Initiation of Action Potential. In afferent neurons, the initial depolarization to threshold is achieved by a graded potential generated in the receptors at the peripheral ends of the neurons, in other words, at the ends farthest from the central nervous system, and where the nervous system functionally encounters the outside world. In all other neurons, the depolarization to threshold is due either to a graded potential generated by synaptic input to the neuron or to a spontaneous change in the neuron's membrane potential, known as a **pacemaker potential**. How synaptic potentials are produced is the subject of the next sec-

---

[4]The actual time required for a signal to travel from the head to the toe is slightly longer because there are no single nerve fibers leading from the head to the toe. Synapses must be crossed, each synapse contributing a slight delay.

FIGURE 8-21

Current direction during an action potential in (A) a myelinated and (B) an unmyelinated axon.

tion. The production of receptor potentials is discussed in Chapter 9.

Spontaneous generation by pacemaker potentials occurs in the absence of any identifiable external stimulus and is an inherent property of certain neurons (and other excitable cells, including certain smooth-muscle and cardiac-muscle cells). In these cells, the ion channels in the plasma membrane open and close by intrinsic mechanisms,[5] the net effect being a graded depolarization of the membrane—the pacemaker potential. If threshold is reached, an action potential occurs; the membrane then repolarizes and again begins to depolarize (Figure 8-22). There is no stable, resting membrane potential in such cells because of the continuous change in membrane per-

meability. The rate at which the membrane depolarizes to threshold determines the action-potential frequency. Pacemaker potentials are implicated in many rhythmical behaviors, such as breathing, the heartbeat, and movements within the walls of the stomach and intestines.

FIGURE 8-22

Action potentials resulting from pacemaker potentials.

---

[5]For example, in one case, the depolarizing phase of the pacemaker potential occurs because calcium enters the cell through voltage-sensitive calcium channels, some of which are open at the cell's resting potential. The cytosolic calcium concentration rises, and this causes calcium-sensitive potassium channels to open. As potassium flows out through these channels, the membrane repolarizes and most of the calcium channels close. As the membrane calcium pumps restore cytosolic calcium to resting levels, the potassium channels close. Once the resting state is achieved, the cycle begins anew.

SECTION B SUMMARY

THE RESTING POTENTIAL

I. Membrane potentials are generated by the diffusion of ions and are determined by (a) the ionic concentration differences across the membrane, and (b) the membrane's relative permeability to ions.

A. Plasma membrane Na,K-ATPase pumps maintain intracellular sodium concentration low and potassium high.

B. In almost all resting cells, the plasma membrane is much more permeable to potassium than to sodium, and so the membrane potential is close to the potassium equilibrium potential, that is, the inside is negative relative to the outside.

    C. The Na,K-ATPase pumps also contribute directly a small component of the potential because they are electrogenic.

GRADED POTENTIALS AND ACTION POTENTIALS

  I. Neurons signal information by graded potentials and action potentials.

  II. Graded potentials are local potentials whose magnitude can vary and that die out within 1 or 2 mm of their site of origin.

  III. An action potential (AP) is a rapid change in the membrane potential during which the potential rapidly depolarizes and repolarizes. In neurons the potential reverses and the membrane becomes positive inside. APs provide long-distance transmission of information through the nervous system.

    A. APs occur in excitable membranes because these membranes contain voltage-sensitive sodium channels, which open as the membrane depolarizes, causing a positive feedback toward the sodium equilibrium potential.

    B. The action potential is ended as the sodium channels close and additional potassium channels open, which restores the resting conditions.

    C. Depolarization of excitable membranes triggers action potentials only when the membrane potential exceeds a threshold potential.

    D. Regardless of the size of the stimulus, if the membrane reaches threshold, the APs generated are all the same size.

    E. A membrane is refractory for a brief time even though stimuli that were previous effective are applied.

    F. APs are propagated from one site to another along a membrane without any change in size.

    G. In a myelinated nerve fiber, action potentials manifest saltatory conduction.

    H. APs can be initiated by receptors at the ends of afferent neurons, by synapses, or in some cells, by pacemaker potentials.

SECTION B KEY TERMS

electric potential	action potentials
potential difference	excitable membranes
potential	excitability
current	afterhyperpolarization
resistance	threshold
Ohm's law	threshold stimuli
resting membrane	subthreshold potentials
potential	subthreshold stimuli
equilibrium potential	suprathreshold stimuli
electrogenic pump	all-or-none
depolarized	absolute refractory period
hyperpolarized	relative refractory period
repolarizing	action-potential
overshoot	propagation
graded potentials	saltatory conduction
decremental	pacemaker potential

SECTION B REVIEW QUESTIONS

1. Describe the way that negative and positive charges interact and the potential that exists between separated charges.

2. Contrast the abilities of intracellular and extracellular fluids and membrane lipid to conduct electric current.

3. Draw a simple cell; indicate where the concentrations of Na^+, K^+, and Cl^- are high and low and the electric potential difference across the membrane when the cell is at rest.

4. Explain the conditions that give rise to the resting membrane potential. What effect does membrane permeability have on this potential? What is the role of the Na,K-ATPase membrane pumps on the membrane potential? Is this role direct or indirect?

5. Which two factors determine the magnitude of the resting membrane potential?

6. Explain why the resting membrane potential is not equal to the potassium equilibrium potential.

7. Draw a graded potential and an action potential on a graph of membrane potential versus time. Indicate zero membrane potential, resting membrane potential, and threshold potential; indicate when the membrane is depolarized, hyperpolarized, and repolarizing.

8. List at least eight differences between graded potentials and action potentials.

9. Describe the ionic basis of an action potential; include the role of voltage-sensitive channels and the positive-feedback cycle.

10. Explain threshold and the relative and absolute refractory periods in terms of the ionic basis of the action potential.

11. Describe the propagation of an action potential. Contrast this event in myelinated and unmyelinated axons.

12. List three ways in which action potentials can be initiated in neurons.

As defined earlier, a synapse is an anatomically specialized junction between two neurons, at which the electrical activity in one neuron, the presynaptic neuron, influences the electrical activity in the second, postsynaptic cell. Anatomically, synapses include parts of the presynaptic and postsynaptic neurons and, for most synapses, the extracellular space between these two cells.

When active, synapses can increase or decrease the activity in a postsynaptic neuron by producing a brief, graded potential there. The membrane potential of a postsynaptic neuron is brought closer to threshold at an **excitatory synapse**, and it is either driven farther from threshold or stabilized at its present level at an **inhibitory synapse**.

Thousands of synapses from many different presynaptic cells can affect a single postsynaptic cell (**convergence**), and a single presynaptic cell can send branches to affect many other postsynaptic cells (**divergence**, Figure 8-23).

The level of excitability of a postsynaptic cell at any moment, that is, how close its membrane potential is to threshold, depends on the number of synapses active at any one time and the number that are excitatory or inhibitory. If the membrane of the postsynaptic neuron reaches threshold, it will generate an action potential that is propagated along the axon to the terminal branches, which diverge to influence the excitability of other neurons. Because the output of a neuron reflects the sum of all the incoming signals arriving in the form of excitatory and in-

hibitory synaptic inputs, neurons function as integrators, as described in Chapter 7.

FUNCTIONAL ANATOMY OF SYNAPSES

There are two types of synapses: **electric** and **chemical**. At electric synapses, the plasma membranes of the pre- and postsynaptic cells are joined by gap junctions (page 46). These allow the local currents resulting from action potentials in the presynaptic neuron to flow directly into the postsynaptic cell, depolarizing the membrane to threshold and thus initiating an action potential in the postsynaptic cell. Electric synapses are rare in the mammalian nervous system, and we shall discuss the much more common chemical synapse.

Figure 8-24 shows the structure of a single typical chemical synapse. Note that in actuality the size and shape

FIGURE 8-24

Diagram of a synapse. The "dust" in the synaptic cleft represents not neurotransmitters but rather a fibrillar substance that lies within the cleft.

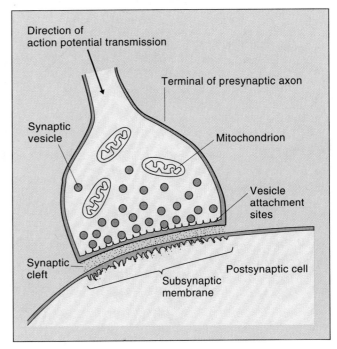

FIGURE 8-23

Convergence of neural input from many neurons onto a single neuron and divergence of output from a single neuron onto many others. Presynaptic neurons are shown in orange, and postsynaptic neurons in brown.

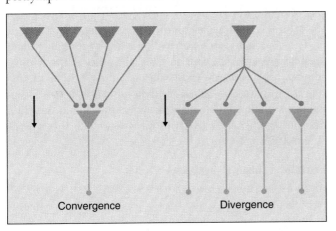

of the pre- and postsynaptic elements can vary greatly (Figure 8-25). The axon of the presynaptic neuron ends in a slight swelling, the axon terminal, and the postsynaptic membrane under the axon terminal is usually thickened. A 10- to 20-nm extracellular space, the **synaptic cleft**, separates the pre- and postsynaptic neurons and prevents *direct* propagation of the current from the presynaptic neuron to the postsynaptic cell. Instead, signals are transmitted across the synaptic cleft by means of a chemical messenger—a neurotransmitter—released from the presynaptic axon terminal. Sometimes, more than one neurotransmitter may be simultaneously released from an axon, in which case the additional neurotransmitter is called a **cotransmitter**.

The neurotransmitter in terminals is stored in membrane-bound **synaptic vesicles**. When an action potential in the presynaptic neuron reaches the end of the axon and depolarizes the axon terminal, voltage-sensitive calcium channels in the membrane open, and calcium diffuses into the axon terminal from the extracellular fluid. The increase in calcium ions in the terminal causes some of the synaptic vesicles to fuse with specific vesicle-attachment sites on the inner surface of the presynaptic plasma membrane and liberate the vesicle contents into the synaptic cleft by the process of exocytosis.

Once released from the axon terminal, small quantities of neurotransmitter—and cotransmitter, if there is one—diffuse across the cleft, and a fraction of these molecules bind to receptor sites on the plasma membrane of the postsynaptic cell (the fate of the others will be described later). The activated receptor may itself contain an ion channel, or it may act indirectly, via a G protein, on ion channels. In either case, the result of the binding of neurotransmitter to receptor is the opening or closing of specific ion channels in the postsynaptic plasma membrane. These channels belong, therefore, to the classes of channels whose function is controlled by receptors, as discussed in Chapter 7 and are distinct from voltage-sensitive channels.

Although Figure 8-25 shows a few exceptions, in general the neurotransmitter is stored on the presynaptic side of the synaptic cleft, whereas receptor sites are on the postsynaptic side. Therefore, chemical synapses operate in only one direction. One-way conduction across synapses causes action potentials to be transmitted along a given multineuronal pathway in one direction.

There is a delay between the arrival of an action potential at a presynaptic terminal and the membrane-potential changes in the postsynaptic cell. It lasts about 1 ms and is called the **synaptic delay**. It can be accounted for by the time required for calcium to enter the axon terminal, for the synaptic vesicles to fuse with the plasma membrane and release their neurotransmitter, and for the neurotransmitter to diffuse across the synaptic cleft.

The ion channels in the postsynaptic membrane return to their resting state when the neurotransmitter is no longer bound to the receptor. Neurotransmitters may be removed because (1) they are chemically transformed into an ineffective substance; (2) they diffuse away from the receptor site; or (3) they are actively transported back into the axon terminal or, in some cases, into nearby glial cells.

The two kinds of chemical synapses—excitatory and inhibitory—are differentiated by the effects the neurotransmitter has on the postsynaptic cell. Whether the effect is inhibitory or excitatory depends on the type of signal transduction mechanism brought into operation when the neurotransmitter binds to a receptor and the type of channel the receptor influences.

Excitatory Chemical Synapses

At an excitatory synapse, the postsynaptic response to the neurotransmitter is a depolarization, bringing the mem-

FIGURE 8-25

Variety of synaptic associations made upon a fiber of an ascending pathway in the spinal cord. Dendrites are shaded green, and axon terminals purple. (A) Simple axodendritic connection, which may include (B) one or more presynaptic synapses or (C) an arrangement known as a synaptic triad. (D) Synaptic arrangement ending on a spine extending from the postsynaptic cell. Such spines are common in the CNS and are thought to play a role in learning. The arrows indicate the direction of synaptic transmission. (*Redrawn from Maxwell and Rethelyi.*)

FIGURE 8-26
Excitatory postsynaptic potential (EPSP). Stimulation of the presynaptic neuron is marked by the arrow.

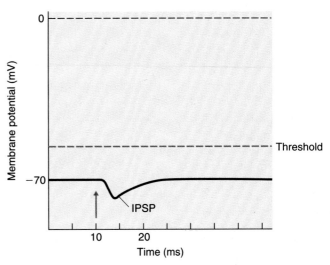

FIGURE 8-27
Inhibitory postsynaptic potential (IPSP). Stimulation of the presynaptic neuron is marked by the arrow.

brane potential closer to threshold. Here the usual effect of the activated receptor on the postsynaptic membrane is to open postsynaptic-membrane ion channels that are permeable to sodium, potassium, and other small, positively charged ions. These ions then are free to move according to the electrical and chemical gradients across the membrane.

Recall that there is both an electrical and a concentration gradient driving sodium into the cell, whereas in the case of potassium, the electrical gradient is opposed by the concentration gradient. Opening channels to all small positively charged ions, therefore, results in the simultaneous movement of a relatively small number of potassium ions out of the cell and a larger number of sodium ions into the cell. Thus, the *net* movement of positive ions is into the postsynaptic cell, and this slightly depolarizes it. This potential change is called an **excitatory postsynaptic potential** (**EPSP**, Figure 8-26).

The EPSP is a graded potential that spreads decrementally away from the synapse by local current. Its only function is to bring the membrane potential of the postsynaptic neuron closer to threshold.

Inhibitory Chemical Synapses

At inhibitory synapses, any potential change in the postsynaptic neuron is a hyperpolarizing graded potential called an **inhibitory postsynaptic potential** (**IPSP**, Figure 8-27). Alternatively, there may be no IPSP but rather *stabilization* of the membrane potential at its existing value. In either case, activation of an inhibitory synapse lessens the likelihood that the cell will depolarize to threshold and generate an action potential.

At an inhibitory synapse the activated receptors on the postsynaptic membrane open chloride or, sometimes, potassium channels; sodium channels are not affected. In cells that actively transport chloride ions out of the cell, the chloride equilibrium potential (-80 mV) is more negative than the resting potential. As chloride channels open, chloride enters the cell, producing a hyperpolarization; that is, an IPSP. In cells in which the equilibrium potential for chloride is equal to the resting membrane potential, a rise in chloride ion permeability increases chloride's influence on the membrane potential. This in turn makes it more difficult for other ion types to affect the potential and results in a stabilization of the membrane at the resting level without producing a hyperpolarization.

Increased potassium permeability also produces an IPSP. On page 189 it was noted that if a cell membrane were permeable only to potassium ions, the resting membrane potential would equal the potassium equilibrium potential; that is, the resting membrane potential would be -90 mV instead of -70 mV. Thus, with an increased potassium permeability, more potassium ions leave the cell and cause a hyperpolarization.

ACTIVATION OF THE POSTSYNAPTIC CELL

A feature that makes postsynaptic integration possible is that, in most neurons, one excitatory synaptic event by itself is not enough to cause threshold to be reached in the postsynaptic neuron. For example, a single EPSP in a neuron that goes to skeletal muscle is estimated

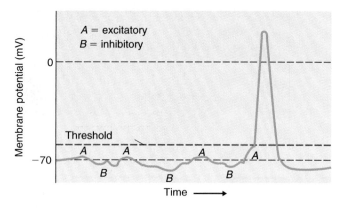

FIGURE 8-28

Intracellular recording from a postsynaptic cell during episodes when (A) excitatory synaptic activity predominates and the cell is facilitated, and (B) inhibitory synaptic activity dominates.

to be only 0.5 mV, whereas changes of about 15 mV are necessary to depolarize the membrane to threshold. This being the case, an action potential can be initiated only by the combined effects of many excitatory synapses.

Of the thousands of synapses on any one neuron, probably hundreds are active simultaneously or close enough in time so that the effects can add together. The membrane potential of the neuron at any moment is, therefore, the resultant of all the synaptic activity affecting it at that time. There is a depolarization of the membrane toward threshold when excitatory synaptic input predominates, and either a hyperpolarization or stabilization when inhibitory input predominates (Figure 8-28).

Let us perform a simple experiment to see how two EPSPs, two IPSPs, or an EPSP plus an IPSP interact (Figure 8-29). Assume there are three synaptic inputs to the postsynaptic cell: The synapses from axons A and B are

excitatory, and the synapse from axon C is inhibitory. There are laboratory stimulators on axons A, B, and C so that each can be activated individually. An electrode is placed in the cell body of the postsynaptic neuron and connected to record the membrane potential. In part 1 of the experiment, we shall test the interaction of two EPSPs by stimulating axon A and then, after a short time, stimulating it again. Part 1 of Figure 8-29 shows that no interaction occurs between the two EPSPs. The reason is that the change in membrane potential associated with an EPSP is fairly short-lived. Within a few milliseconds (by the time we stimulate axon A for the second time), the postsynaptic cell has returned to its resting condition.

In part 2, we stimulate axon A for the second time *before* the first EPSP has died away; the second synaptic potential adds to the previous one and creates a greater depolarization than from one synapse alone. This is called **temporal summation** since the input signals arrive at the same cell at different times. The potentials summate because there are a greater number of open ion channels and, therefore, a greater flow of positive ions into the cell. In part 3, axon B is stimulated alone to determine its response, and then axons A and B are stimulated simultaneously. The two EPSPs that result also summate in the postsynaptic neuron; this is called **spatial summation** since the two inputs occurred at different locations on the same cell. The interaction of multiple EPSPs through ongoing spatial and temporal summation can increase the inward flow of positive ions and bring the membrane to threshold so that action potentials are initiated (part 4).

So far we have tested only the patterns of interaction of excitatory synapses. What happens if an excitatory and an inhibitory synapse are activated so that their effects occur in the postsynaptic cell simultaneously? Since EPSPs and IPSPs are due to oppositely directed local currents, they tend to cancel each other, and there is little or no change

FIGURE 8-29

Interaction of EPSPs and IPSPs at the postsynaptic neuron. Arrows indicate time of stimulation.

in membrane potential (Figure 8-29, part 5). Inhibitory potentials can also show spatial and temporal summation.

As described above, the postsynaptic membrane is depolarized at an activated excitatory synapse and either hyperpolarized or stabilized at an activated inhibitory synapse. Via the local-current mechanisms described earlier, the plasma membrane of the entire postsynaptic cell body and the initial segment reflect these changes. It becomes slightly depolarized during activation of an excitatory synapse and slightly hyperpolarized or stabilized during activation of an inhibitory synapse (Figure 8-30).

In the above examples, we referred to the threshold of the postsynaptic neuron as though it were the same for all parts of the cell. However, different parts of the neuron have different thresholds. In many cells the initial segment has a threshold that is lower, that is, much closer to the resting potential than the threshold of the cell body and dendrites. In these cells the initial segment reaches

threshold first whenever enough EPSPs summate, and the resulting action potential is initiated and then propagated from this point down the axon.

The fact that the initial segment usually has the lowest threshold explains why the location of individual synapses on the postsynaptic cell is important. A synapse located near the initial segment will produce a greater voltage change there than will a synapse on the outermost branch of a dendrite because it will expose the initial segment to a larger local current. In fact, some dendrites are so long that they use propagated action potentials over portions of their length to convey information about the synaptic events occurring at their endings to the initial segment of the cell.

Postsynaptic potentials last much longer than action potentials do. In the event that cumulative EPSPs cause the initial segment to still be depolarized to threshold after an action potential has been fired and the refractory period is over, a second action potential will occur. In fact, as long as the membrane is depolarized to threshold, action potentials will continue to fire. Neuronal responses almost always occur in bursts of action potentials rather than as single isolated events.

This discussion has no doubt left the impression that one neuron can influence another only at a synapse. This view requires qualification. Under certain circumstances, local currents from one neuron may directly affect the membrane potential of nearby neurons. This phenomenon is particularly important in areas of the central nervous system that contain a high density of unmyelinated neuronal processes.

SYNAPTIC EFFECTIVENESS

Individual synaptic events—whether excitatory or inhibitory—have been presented as though their effects are constant and reproducible. Actually, the variability in postsynaptic potentials following any particular presynaptic input is enormous. The effect of a given synapse can be influenced by both presynaptic and postsynaptic mechanisms (Table 8-5), as described in the next section.

A presynaptic terminal does not secrete a constant amount of neurotransmitter every time it is activated. One reason for this is as follows. Calcium that has entered the terminal during previous action potentials is normally removed by being pumped out of the cell or (temporarily) into intracellular organelles. If the calcium removal systems are not able to keep up with entry, as can occur during high-frequency stimulation, calcium concentration in the terminal and hence the amount of neurotransmitter released upon subsequent stimulation will be greater than normal. The greater the amount of neurotransmitter re-

FIGURE 8-30
Comparison of excitatory and inhibitory synapses, showing current direction through the postsynaptic cell following synaptic activation. (A) Current through the postsynaptic cell is away from the excitatory synapse, depolarizing the cell. (B) Current through the postsynaptic cell is toward an inhibitory synapse, hyperpolarizing the cell.

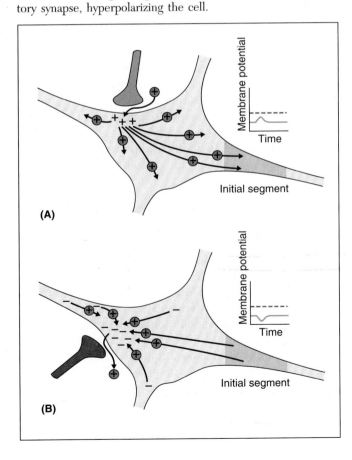

TABLE 8-5   FACTORS THAT DETERMINE SYNAPTIC EFFECTIVENESS

I. Presynaptic factors
  A. Availability of neurotransmitter
    1. Availability of precursor molecules
    2. Amount (or activity) of the rate-limiting enzyme in the pathway for neurotransmitter synthesis
  B. Axon terminal membrane potential
  C. Axon terminal residual calcium
  D. Activation of membrane receptors on presynaptic terminal
    1. Presynaptic (axon-axon) synapses
    2. Autoreceptors
    3. Other receptors
  E. Certain drugs and diseases
II. Postsynaptic factors
  A. Immediate past history of electrical state of postsynaptic membrane, that is, facilitation or inhibition from temporal or spatial summation
  B. Effects of other neurotransmitters or neuromodulators acting on postsynaptic neuron
  C. Certain drugs and diseases

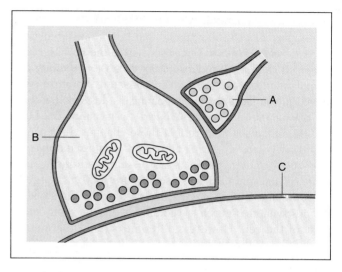

FIGURE 8-31

A presynaptic (axon-axon) synapse between axon terminal A and axon terminal B. C is the final postsynaptic cell body.

leased, the greater the number of ion channels opened in the postsynaptic membrane, and the larger the amplitude of the EPSP or IPSP in the postsynaptic cell.

In addition, presynaptic terminals have membrane receptors—much as the postsynaptic cells do—and input to these receptors alters the neurotransmitter output of the terminals. These receptors are often associated with a second synaptic ending known as an axon-axon or **presynaptic synapse**, in which an axon terminal of one neuron ends on an axon terminal of another. For example, in Figure 8-31 the neurotransmitter released by A combines with receptor sites on B, resulting in a change in the amount of neurotransmitter released from B in response to action potentials. Thus, neuron A has no *direct* effect on neuron C but has an important influence on the ability of B to influence C. Neuron A is said to be exerting a *presynaptic* effect on the synapse between B and C. Depending upon the nature of the neurotransmitter released from A and the type of receptor sites on B, the presynaptic effect may decrease the amount of neurotransmitter released from B (**presynaptic inhibition**) or increase it (**presynaptic facilitation**).

The presynaptic synapse (A in Figure 8-31) works by altering the calcium concentration in axon terminal B. If the calcium concentration increases, the amount of neurotransmitter released from B increases; decreased calcium reduces the amount of transmitter released. Presynaptic synapses are important because they control one specific

input to the postsynaptic neuron (C). In contrast, direct inhibition of the postsynaptic neuron, that is, an IPSP in neuron C, is averaged in with all the other inputs and is not specific.

Receptors on the presynaptic terminal need not be associated with axon-axon synapses, in which case they are activated by transmitters released by nearby neurons or glia, distant tissues, or the axon terminal itself. In the last case, the receptors are called **autoreceptors** and provide an important feedback mechanism by which the neuron can regulate its own neurotransmitter output.

Many of the *postsynaptic* mechanisms for varying synaptic effectiveness were presented in Chapter 7 in the discussion of receptors. In addition, experiments with drugs that stimulate or block specific receptors have shown that there are several types of receptors for each type of neurotransmitter and that many of these receptor types can be further categorized into subtypes. All the different receptors and their various subtypes correspond to differences in the receptor proteins. The different receptor types operate by different signal transduction mechanisms and have different—sometimes even opposite—results on the channels they influence. Moreover, a given signal transduction mechanism may be regulated by different neurotransmitters, and the various second-messenger systems affecting a channel may interact with each other.

Recall, too, from Chapter 7 that the number of receptors is not constant, varying with up- and down-regulation, for example. Also, the ability of a given receptor to respond to its neurotransmitter can change. Thus, in many systems a receptor responds once and then temporarily fails to respond despite the continued presence of the receptor's neurotransmitter, a phenomenon known as receptor desensitization.

Imagine the complexity when a cotransmitter (or several cotransmitters) is released with the neurotransmitter to act upon postsynaptic receptors and maybe upon presynaptic receptors as well! Clearly, the possible variations in transmission at even a single synapse are enormous.

Modification of Synaptic Transmission by Drugs and Disease

Most drugs act on the nervous system by altering synaptic mechanisms and thus synaptic effectiveness. The synaptic mechanisms labeled in Figure 8-32 are vulnerable.

FIGURE 8-32

Drug actions at synapses. (A) Increase leakage of neurotransmitter to cytoplasm, (B) increase and (C) block transmitter release, (D) inhibit transmitter synthesis, (E) block transmitter reuptake, (F) block enzymes that metabolize transmitter, (G) bind to receptor to block (antagonist) or mimic (agonist) transmitter action, and (H) inhibit or facilitate second-messenger activity. (Redrawn from DRUGS AND THE BRAIN by Solomon H. Snyder. Copyright © 1986 by Scientific American Books, Inc. Reprinted by permission of W. H. Freeman and Co.)

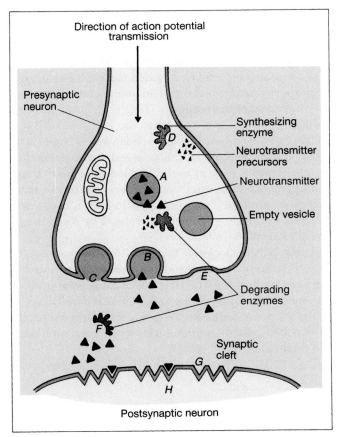

The long-term effects of drugs are sometimes difficult to predict because the imbalances produced by the initial drug action are soon counteracted by feedback mechanisms that normally regulate the processes. For example, if a drug interferes with the action of a neurotransmitter by inhibiting the rate-limiting enzyme in its synthetic pathway, the neurons may respond by increasing the rate of precursor transport into the axon terminals to maximize the use of any enzyme that is available.

Recall from Chapter 7 that drugs that bind to a receptor and produce a response similar to the normal activation of that receptor are called **agonists**, and drugs that bind to the receptor but are unable to activate it are **antagonists**. By occupying the receptors, antagonists prevent binding of the normal neurotransmitter when it is released at the synapse. Specific agonists and antagonists can affect receptors on both pre- and postsynaptic membranes.

Diseases can also affect synaptic mechanisms. For example, a toxin produced by the **tetanus** bacillus interferes with inhibitory synaptic input to the neurons—motor neurons—supplying skeletal muscles. This elimination of inhibitory input to the motor neurons leaves unchecked the excitatory inputs, resulting in excessive motor neuron activity, which leads to involuntary contraction of the skeletal muscles. The spasms of the jaw muscles appearing early in the disease are responsible for the common name of the condition, lockjaw.

NEUROTRANSMITTERS AND NEUROMODULATORS

We emphasized the role of neurotransmitters in eliciting EPSPs and IPSPs. Some chemical messengers elicit in neurons complex responses that cannot be simply described as EPSPs or IPSPs. The word "modulation" is used for these complex responses, and the messengers that cause them are called **neuromodulators**. The distinctions between neuromodulators and neurotransmitters are, however, far from clear. In fact, certain neuromodulators are often synthesized by the presynaptic cell and released with the neurotransmitter. To add to the complexity, certain hormones, paracrine agents, and messengers used by the immune system may serve as neuromodulators.

Neuromodulators often modify the *postsynaptic* cell's response to specific neurotransmitters, amplifying or dampening the effectiveness of ongoing synaptic activity. Alternatively, they may change the *presynaptic* cell's synthesis, release, reuptake, or metabolism of a transmitter.

In general, the receptors for neurotransmitters influence ion channels that are part of the receptor or are influenced directly by G proteins. These mechanisms operate within milliseconds. Receptors for neuromodulators, on the other hand, more often bring about biochemical changes in neurons, often via G proteins coupled to second-messenger systems. These changes, which can occur over minutes, hours, or even days, include alterations in enzyme activity or, by way of influences on RNA transcription, in protein synthesis. Thus, neurotransmitters are involved in rapid communication, whereas neuromodulators tend to be associated with slower events such as learning, development, motivation states, or even some sensory or motor activities.

Table 8-6 lists some substances generally accepted as neurotransmitters or neuromodulators.[6] In Chapter 10 you will see that some of these substances also are secreted by endocrine glands and function as hormones.

For simplicity's sake, in the following discussion of several major chemical messengers in the nervous system, we use the term "neurotransmitter" in a general sense, realizing that sometimes the messenger may more appropriately be described as a neuromodulator. A note on terminology should be included here: Neurons are often referred to as _____ergic, where the blank is the type of neurotransmitter released by the neuron. For example, "dopaminergic" applies to neurons that release the neurotransmitter dopamine, and "cholinergic" to those that release acetylcholine.

Acetylcholine

Acetylcholine (ACh) is synthesized from choline and acetyl coenzyme A in the cytoplasm of synaptic terminals and is stored in synaptic vesicles. After it is released and activates receptors on the postsynaptic membrane, the concentration of ACh at the postsynaptic membrane is reduced (thereby stopping receptor activation) by an enzyme, **acetylcholinesterase**. This enzyme is located on the pre- and postsynaptic membranes and rapidly destroys ACh, releasing choline. The choline is then actively transported back into the axon terminals where it is reused in the synthesis of new ACh. The acetylcholine concentration at the receptors is also reduced by simple diffusion away from the site and eventual breakdown of the molecule by an enzyme in the blood.

Some acetylcholine receptors respond to the drug nicotine and, therefore, have come to be known as **nicotinic receptors**. Others are stimulated by the mushroom poison muscarine; they are called **muscarinic receptors**.

Acetylcholine is a major neurotransmitter in the peripheral nervous system (page 180) and is also present in the brain. The cell bodies of the brain's cholinergic neurons are concentrated in relatively few areas, but their axons are widely distributed. Fibers that release acetylcholine are called **cholinergic** fibers.

One cholinergic system in the brain (Figure 8-33) plays a major role in learning and memory. Neurons associated with this system degenerate in people with **Alzheimer's disease**, a brain disease that is usually age-related and is the most common cause of declining intellectual function in late life, affecting 10 to 15 percent of people over age 65 and 50 percent of people over age 85. Because of the degeneration of cholinergic neurons, this disease is associated with a decreased amount of ACh in certain areas of the brain and a loss of the postsynaptic neurons that would have responded to it.[7] These defects are presumably related to the declining language and perceptual abilities, confusion, and memory loss that characterize Alzheimer's victims. The exact causes of this disease are unknown.

Biogenic Amines

The **biogenic amines** are neurotransmitters that are synthesized from amino acids and contain an amino group ($R—NH_2$). Amino acids themselves also function as neurotransmitters and fit this chemical type, but neurophysiologists traditionally put them into a category of their own. The most common biogenic amines in the nervous system are dopamine, norepinephrine, serotonin, and histamine. Epinephrine, another biogenic amine, is not a common neurotransmitter in the nervous system but is the major *hormone* secreted by the adrenal medulla, a gland that is activated by the peripheral nervous system, as will be discussed later.

Dopamine, **norepinephrine**, and **epinephrine** all contain a catechol ring (a six-sided carbon ring with two adjacent hydroxyl groups) and an amine group; thus they are called **catecholamines**. The catecholamines are formed from the amino acid tyrosine and share the synthetic pathway shown in Figure 8-34, which begins with the uptake of tyrosine by the axon terminals. Depending on the enzymes present in the terminals, the neurotransmitter ultimately released may be any one of the three catecholamines. Release of catecholamines from the presynaptic terminals is strongly modulated by receptors on the presynaptic terminals.

After activation of the receptors on the postsynaptic cell, the catecholamine concentration in the synaptic cleft declines mainly because the catecholamine is actively transported back into the axon terminal. As we shall see in Chapter 13, the drug cocaine interferes with the reuptake of dopamine and, therefore, increases its concentration in the synaptic cleft.

---

[6]All these substances have not met all the criteria to be classified as "established" neurotransmitters or neuromodulators, and some are more properly considered "candidates." We shall not distinguish between them.

[7]The loss of ACh-containing neurons in the base of the forebrain is one of the most consistent characteristics of Alzheimer's disease, but many other neurotransmitter systems also degenerate.

TABLE 8-6   CLASSES OF SOME OF THE CHEMICALS KNOWN OR PRESUMED TO BE NEUROTRANSMITTERS OR NEUROMODULATORS

1. Acetylcholine (ACh)

2. Biogenic amines
   Catecholamines
      Dopamine (DA)
      Norepinephrine (NE)
      Epinephrine (Epi)
   Serotonin (5-hydroxytryptamine, 5-HT)
   Histamine

3. Amino acids
   Excitatory amino acids
      Glutamate
      Aspartate
   Inhibitory amino acids
      Gamma-aminobutyric acid (GABA)
      Glycine
      Taurine

4. Neuropeptides
   Endogenous opioids (endorphin, enkephalins, dynorphins)
   Substance P
   Somatostatin
   Vasoactive intestinal peptide (VIP)
   Cholecystokinin
   Neurotensin
   Insulin
   Gastrin
   Glucagon
   Thyrotropin releasing hormone (TRH)
   Gonadotropin releasing hormone (GnRH)
   Adrenocorticotropic hormone (ACTH)
   Angiotensin II
   Bradykinin
   Vasopressin (antidiuretic hormone, ADH)
   Oxytocin
   Epidermal growth factor
   Prolactin
   Bombesin
   Motilin
   Peptide histidine isoleucine (PHI)
   Peptide histidine methionine (PHM)
   Secretin
   Neuropeptide Y (NPY)
   Peptide YY
   Pancreatic polypeptide
   Growth hormone releasing hormone (GHRH)
   Neurokinin A (substance K)
   Neurokinin B
   Interferon
   Interleukin 1 (IL-1)
   Thymosin
   Galanin
   Calcitonin gene-related peptide (CGRP)

5. Miscellaneous
   Gases
      Nitric oxide
      Carbon monoxide
   Nucleotides
      Adenosine
      Adenosine triphosphate (ATP)
   Steroids
      Aldosterone
      Cortisol and other glucocorticoids
      Progesterone
      Estrogens (17β-estriol)
      Testosterone
   Prostaglandins (prostaglandin E)

FIGURE 8-33

The major cholinergic pathways implicated in Alzheimer's disease. As will be seen in Figure 8-42, the violet structure is the limbic system. (*Adapted from BRAIN, MIND AND BEHAVIOR by Floyd E. Bloom and Arlyne Lazerson. Copyright © 1985, 1988 by Educational Broadcasting Corporation. Reprinted by permission of W. H. Freeman and Company.*)

FIGURE 8-34

Catecholamine biosynthetic pathway. The asterisk indicates the site of action of tyrosine hydroxylase, the rate-limiting enzyme; the colored screen indicates the more common CNS catecholamine neurotransmitters.

Tyrosine   L-Dopa   Dopamine   Norepinephrine   Epinephrine

The catecholamine neurotransmitters are broken down by the enzymes monoamine oxidase and catechol-*O*-methyltransferase, which occur in both the extracellular fluid and the axon terminal. The intracellular enzymes play a larger role in catecholamine breakdown.

The cell bodies of the catecholamine releasing neurons lie in the part of the brain called the brainstem, and although relatively few in number, their axons branch greatly and go to virtually all parts of the brain and spinal cord. The catecholamines exert a much greater influence in the central nervous system than the number of neurons alone would suggest, possibly because of their neuromodulator-like effects on postsynaptic neurons. Their receptor action is linked, via G proteins, to the second messengers cAMP and phosphatidylinositol metabolites and to ion channels.

Norepinephrine and Epinephrine. Norepinephrine plays an important role in the central nervous system and, as we shall see, in the peripheral nervous system as well. In the central nervous system, norepinephrine is thought to be important in setting levels of neural activity that underlie different behavioral states. We remind the reader that epinephrine serves most importantly as a hormone, and it will be discussed later in this role.

During the early experiments on these two neurotransmitters, norepinephrine was mistakenly taken to be epinephrine, and epinephrine was called by its British name "adrenaline." Consequently, nerve fibers that release epinephrine or norepinephrine came to be called **adrenergic** fibers. Norepinephrine releasing fibers are also called **noradrenergic**.

There are two major classes of receptors for norepinephrine and epinephrine: **alpha-adrenergic receptors** and **beta-adrenergic receptors** (these are also called **alpha-adrenoceptors** and **beta-adrenoceptors**). The major way of distinguishing the two classes of receptors is that they are influenced by different drugs. Both alpha- and beta-adrenergic receptors can be subdivided still further (alpha$_1$ and alpha$_2$, for example), again according to the drugs that influence them. Another difference between the two is that they use different second-messenger systems: Activation of beta-adrenergic receptors results in the generation of cAMP, whereas stimulation of alpha-adrenergic receptors results in the activation of phospholipase C or cAMP second messenger systems or directly affects calcium and potassium channels (Chapter 7).

Serotonin. While not a catecholamine, **serotonin** (5-hydroxytryptamine, 5-HT) is an important biogenic amine. It is produced from tryptophan, an essential amino acid, and is metabolized by monoamine oxidase. Its effects generally have a slow onset, indicating that it works as a neuromodulator. It is contained mainly in brainstem neurons

that innervate virtually all other areas of the central nervous system. In general, serotonin has an excitatory effect on pathways that are involved in the control of muscles, and an inhibitory effect on pathways that mediate sensations. The activity of serotonergic neurons is lowest or absent during sleep and highest during states of alert wakefulness.

Serotonin may also be important in the neural pathways controlling mood. Several substances chemically related to it, for example, psilocybin, a hallucinogenic agent found in some mushrooms, have potent psychic effects. Moreover, LSD (lysergic acid diethylamide), the most potent hallucinogenic drug known, inhibits serotonergic neurons. Antidepressants such as Prozac enhance serotonin's actions.

Serotonergic pathways also function in the regulation of food intake and certain other homeostatic systems, and they have been implicated in alcoholism and other obsessive-compulsive disorders. Serotonin is also present in many nonneural cells, for example, blood platelets, mast cells, and specialized cells lining the digestive tract. In fact, the brain contains only 1 to 2 percent of the body's serotonin.

Amino Acid Neurotransmitters

As we have just seen, a number of neurotransmitters are synthesized from amino acids; in addition, several amino acids function directly as neurotransmitters. Two so-called **excitatory amino acids**, **glutamate** and **aspartate**, are used as neurotransmitters by the vast majority of excitatory synapses in the central nervous system, and most central nervous system neurons respond to them. The receptors for these substances function either as ion channels for calcium and sodium or activate the phospholipase C second-messenger system.

The excitatory amino acids function in learning, memory, and neural development. They are also implicated in epilepsy, Alzheimer's and Parkinson's diseases, and the neural damage that follows strokes, brain trauma, and other conditions of low oxygen availability. One of the family of glutamate receptors is the site of action of a number of mind-altering drugs such as phencyclidine ("angel dust").

GABA (gamma-aminobutyric acid) and the amino acid **glycine** are the major inhibitory neurotransmitters in the central nervous system. (GABA is not the same type of amino acid as the other amino acid neurotransmitters, but it is a modified form of glutamic acid, which is an amino acid, and GABA is classified with the amino acids.) GABA receptors are present on most neurons in the central nervous system. Receptors for GABA and glycine are inhibitory because they either function themselves as chloride channels or, via a G protein, open potassium channels. The result is that the membrane is hyperpolarized or stabilized at its present level. Drugs, such as Valium, that reduce anxiety enhance the action of GABA.

Neuropeptides

The **neuropeptides** are composed of two or more amino acids linked together by peptide bonds and are synthesized in neural tissue. More than 50 neuropeptides have been found, though the physiological roles are not known for many of them. It seems that evolution has selected the same chemical messengers for use in widely differing circumstances, and many of the neuropeptides had been previously identified in nonneural tissue where they function as hormones or paracrine agents. Thus, many of the peptides function in communication networks within the neural, endocrine, and immune systems. They generally retain the name they were given when first discovered in the nonneural tissue.

The neuropeptides are formed differently from the other neurotransmitters, which are synthesized in the axon terminals via a very few enzyme-mediated steps. The neuropeptides, in contrast, are derived from large precursor molecules called prohormones or preprohormones (the term "hormone" is used even when referring to peptide neurotransmitters), which in themselves have little, if any, inherent biological activity. The synthesis of these precursors is directed by mRNA and occurs on ribosomes, which exist only in the cell body and large dendrites of the neuron, often a considerable distance from axon terminals or varicosities where the peptides are released.

In the cell body, the prohormone is packaged into vesicles, which are then moved by way of axon transport into the terminals or varicosities where the vesicle contents are cleaved by specific peptidases. Many of the prohormones and preprohormones are actually "polyproteins" in that they contain multiple copies of peptides. These copies may be of the same or different peptides. Neurons that release one or more of the peptide neurotransmitters are collectively called **peptidergic**. In many cases neuropeptides are cosecreted with another type of neurotransmitter.

Certain neuropeptides, termed **endogenous opioids—endorphin**, the **dynorphins**, and the **enkephalins—**have attracted much interest since their discovery because receptors for these neurotransmitters are the sites of action of the opiate drugs such as morphine and codeine. No physiological function of any of the opioid peptides has been demonstrated conclusively, but they are powerful **analgesics** (that is, they relieve pain without loss of consciousness). There is also evidence that they play a role in regulating pain, in eating and drinking behavior, in central regulation of the cardiovascular system, and in mood and emotion.

Substance P, another of the neuropeptides, is a neurotransmitter for afferent neurons that relay sensory information into the central nervous system. It is involved in the transmission of pain-producing stimuli and serves as a link between the immune system and the nervous system. In addition to being widely distributed in the central nervous system, substance P and certain other peptides are released from the *peripheral* endings of afferent neurons out in the tissues near the neurons' receptor endings. When an afferent ending is activated by sensory stimuli, peptides are released from the peripheral branches of that same afferent neuron to exert effects on nearby smooth-muscle cells, epithelial cells, and agents of the immune system. The release of substance P from afferent-neuron endings in joints and the local enzyme changes stimulated by the substance P have been implicated in the joint deterioration associated with arthritis.

Gases

Surprisingly, some gases serve as neurotransmitters, albeit unusual ones. Gases are not released from presynaptic vesicles, nor do they activate postsynaptic receptors. They simply diffuse from their sites of origin in one cell to nearby cells.

Nitric oxide, which is actually a poisonous gas, serves as an intercellular messenger between neurons and between neurons and effector cells. It is produced from the amino acid arginine in one cell, and it activates guanylyl cyclase in the recipient cell, thereby increasing the concentration of the second-messenger cyclic GMP in that cell.

Nitric oxide is thought to play a role in learning (Chapter 13). Paradoxically, it is also implicated in neural damage that results, for example, from the stoppage of blood flow to the brain or a head injury. In later chapters we shall see that nitric oxide is produced by a variety of nonneural cells and plays an important paracrine role in the cardiovascular and immune systems, among others.

Carbon monoxide, which is also suspected of serving as a transmitter with a role in learning, also stimulates guanylyl cyclase.

NEUROEFFECTOR COMMUNICATION

Thus far we have described the effects of neurotransmitters released from synapses. Many neurons of the peripheral nervous system end, however, not on other neurons but on muscle and gland cells. The neurotransmitters released by these efferent neurons' terminals or varicosities provide the link by which electrical activity of the nervous system is able to regulate effector cell activity.

As mentioned previously, these junctions between efferent neurons and effector cells are called neuroeffector junctions, and the events that occur there are similar to those at a synapse. The neurotransmitter is released from the efferent neurons upon the arrival of an action potential at the neuron's axon terminals or varicosities, and the neurotransmitter then diffuses to the surface of the effector cell, where it binds to receptors on that cell's plasma membrane. The receptors may be directly under the axon terminal or varicosity, or they may be some distance away so that the diffusion path that must be followed by the neurotransmitter is tortuous and long. The receptor of the effec-

tor cell may be associated with ion channels that alter the membrane potential of the cell, or it may be associated with an enzyme that results in the formation of a second messenger in the effector cell. The response (muscle contraction or glandular secretion) of the effector cell to these changes will be described in later chapters. The major neurotransmitters released at neuroeffector junctions are acetylcholine and norepinephrine.

SECTION C SUMMARY

I. An excitatory synapse brings the membrane of the postsynaptic cell closer to threshold. An inhibitory synapse hyperpolarizes the postsynaptic cell or stabilizes it at its resting level.

II. Whether a postsynaptic cell fires action potentials depends on the number of synapses that are active and whether they are excitatory or inhibitory.

FUNCTIONAL ANATOMY OF SYNAPSES

I. The signal from a pre- to a postsynaptic neuron is a neurotransmitter stored in synaptic vesicles in the presynaptic axon terminal. Depolarization of the axon terminal, which raises the calcium concentration within the terminal, causes the release of neurotransmitter into the synaptic cleft.

II. The neurotransmitter diffuses across the synaptic cleft and binds to receptors on the postsynaptic cell; the activated receptors usually open ion channels.
   A. At an excitatory synapse the electrical response in the postsynaptic cell is called an excitatory postsynaptic potential (EPSP). At an inhibitory synapse, it is an inhibitory postsynaptic potential (IPSP).
   B. Usually at an excitatory synapse, channels in the postsynaptic cell that are permeable to sodium, potassium, and other small positive ions are opened; at inhibitory synapses, channels to chloride and/or potassium are opened.
   C. The postsynaptic cell's membrane potential is the result of temporal and spatial summation of the EPSPs and IPSPs at the many active excitatory and inhibitory synapses on the cell.

SYNAPTIC EFFECTIVENESS

Synaptic effects are influenced by pre- and postsynaptic events, drugs, and diseases (Table 8-5).

NEUROTRANSMITTERS AND NEUROMODULATORS

I. In general, neurotransmitters cause EPSPs and IPSPs, and neuromodulators cause more complex metabolic effects in the postsynaptic cell.

II. The actions of neurotransmitters are usually faster than those of neuromodulators.

III. A substance can act as a neurotransmitter at one receptor type and as a neuromodulator at another.

IV. The known or suspected neurotransmitters and neuromodulators are listed in Table 8-6.

NEUROEFFECTOR COMMUNICATION

I. The junction between a neuron and an effector cell is called a neuroeffector junction.

II. The events at a neuroeffector junction—release of neurotransmitter into an extracellular space, diffusion of neurotransmitter to the effector cell, and binding with a receptor on the effector cell—are similar to those at a synapse.

SECTION C KEY TERMS

excitatory synapse
inhibitory synapse
convergence
divergence
electric synapse
chemical synapse
synaptic cleft
cotransmitter
synaptic vesicles
synaptic delay
excitatory postsynaptic potential (EPSP)
inhibitory postsynaptic potential (IPSP)
temporal summation
spatial summation
presynaptic synapse
presynaptic inhibition
presynaptic facilitation
autoreceptors
neuromodulators
acetylcholine
acetylcholinesterase
nicotinic receptors
muscarinic receptors
cholinergic
biogenic amines
dopamine

norepinephrine
epinephrine
catecholamines
adrenergic
noradrenergic
alpha-adrenergic receptors
beta-adrenergic receptors
alpha-adrenoceptors
beta-adrenoceptors
serotonin
excitatory amino acids
glutamate
aspartate

GABA (gamma-
    aminobutyric acid)
glycine
neuropeptides
peptidergic
endogenous opioids
endorphin
dynorphins
enkephalins
analgesics
substance P
nitric oxide
carbon monoxide

SECTION C REVIEW QUESTIONS

1. Contrast the postsynaptic mechanisms of excitatory and inhibitory synapses.
2. Explain how synapses allow neurons to act as integrators; include the concepts of facilitation, temporal and spatial summation, and convergence in your explanation.
3. List at least eight ways in which the effectiveness of synapses may be altered.
4. Discuss differences between neurotransmitters and neuromodulators.
5. Discuss the relationship among dopamine, norepinephrine, and epinephrine.

SECTION

STRUCTURE OF THE NERVOUS SYSTEM

We shall now survey the anatomy and broad functions of the major structures of the nervous system; future chapters will describe these functions in more detail. First, we must deal with some potentially confusing terminology. Recall that a long extension from a *single* neuron is called an axon or a nerve fiber. The term **nerve** refers to a group of *many* nerve fibers that are traveling together to the same general location in the peripheral nervous system. There are no nerves in the central nervous system. A group of nerve fibers traveling together in the central nervous system is called a **pathway**, a **tract**, or, when it links the right and left halves of the central nervous system, a **commissure**.

The cell bodies of neurons having similar functions also are often clustered together. Groups of neuron cell bodies in the peripheral nervous system are called **ganglia** (singular *ganglion*), but in the central nervous system they are usually called **nuclei** (singular *nucleus*).

The brain lies within the skull, and the spinal cord within the vertebral column. Between the soft neural tissues and the protective bones that house them are three protective membranous coverings, or **meninges**: the dura mater next to the bone, the arachnoid in the middle, and the pia mater next to the nervous tissue. A space, the subarachnoid space, between the arachnoid and pia is filled with **cerebrospinal fluid**.

CENTRAL NERVOUS SYSTEM: SPINAL CORD

The spinal cord (Figure 8-35) is a slender cylinder of soft tissue about as big around as the little finger. The central butterfly-shaped area of **gray matter** is composed of interneurons, the cell bodies and dendrites of efferent neurons, the entering fibers of afferent neurons, and glial cells. It is called gray matter because the structures there lack myelin, which is whitish.

The gray matter is surrounded by **white matter**, which consists largely of groups of the myelinated axons of interneurons. These groups of axons, that is, the pathways, run longitudinally through the cord, some descending to convey information from the brain to the spinal cord or from upper levels of the spinal cord to lower levels, others ascending to transmit information to the brain.

Groups of afferent fibers that enter the spinal cord from the peripheral nerves enter on the dorsal side of the cord (the side nearest the back of the body) via the **dorsal roots**. Small bumps on the dorsal roots, the **dorsal root ganglia**, contain the cell bodies of the afferent neurons. The axons of efferent neurons leave the spinal cord on the ventral side (nearest the front surface of the body) via the **ventral roots**. A short distance from the cord, the dorsal and ventral roots from the same level combine to form a

afferent fibers
attaching to
inter-neurons,
which are
connected to
ventral horn
cells
glial cell

PNS axon goes in dorsal
root
CNS inter-neuron
goes out ventral
root

★ **FIGURE 8-35**
Section of the spinal cord, ventral view.
The arrows indicate the direction of trans-
mission of neural activity.

pair of **spinal nerves**, one on each side of the spinal cord. The spinal nerves are organized into four levels: cervical, thoracic, lumbar, and sacral (Figure 8-36).

CENTRAL NERVOUS SYSTEM: BRAIN

The brain is composed of six subdivisions: **cerebrum, diencephalon, midbrain, pons, medulla oblongata**, and **cerebellum** (Figure 8-37). The cerebrum and diencephalon together constitute the **forebrain**. The midbrain, pons, and medulla together form the **brainstem**.

The brain also contains four interconnected cavities, the **cerebral ventricles**, which contain cerebrospinal fluid (Figure 8-38).

Brainstem

The brainstem is literally the stalk of the brain. Through it pass all the nerve fibers that relay signals between the spinal cord and the forebrain or cerebellum. Information

is transmitted between the brainstem and cerebellum by three large bundles of nerve fibers, the cerebellar peduncles.

Running through the core of the brainstem and consisting of loosely arranged neuron cell bodies intermingled with bundles of axons is the **reticular formation**, which is the one part of the brain absolutely essential for life. It receives and integrates input from all regions of the central nervous system and is also responsible for the *output* of a great deal of neural information. Most reticular formation neurons send axons for considerable distances up or down the brainstem and beyond, to most regions of the brain and spinal cord. This pattern indicates the very large scope of influence the reticular formation has over other parts of the central nervous system.

The pathways that convey information from the reticular formation to the upper portions of the brain divide near the junction of the brainstem and forebrain. One branch goes to the thalamus, a large sensory way station in the forebrain, and a second branch goes to regions in the base of the forebrain, including the hypothalamus, a center crit-

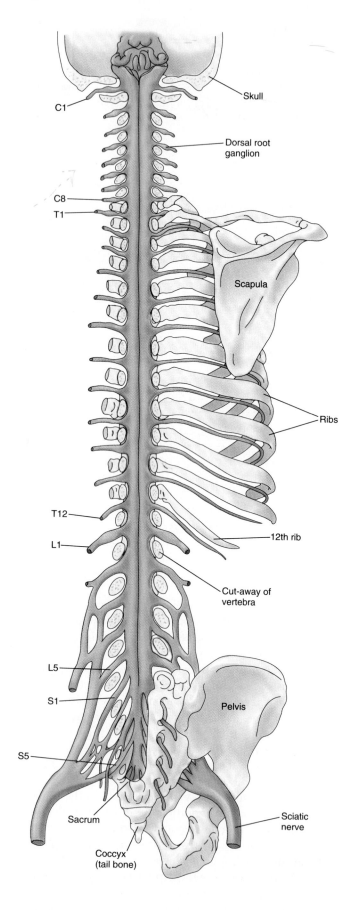

C1

Skull

Dorsal root
ganglion

C8

T1

Scapula

Ribs

T12

12th rib

L1

Cut-away of
vertebra

L5

S1

Pelvis

S5

Sacrum

Sciatic
nerve

Coccyx
(tail bone)

FIGURE 8-36

Dorsal view of the spinal cord. Parts of the skull and vertebrae have been cut away. In general, the 8 cervical nerves (C) control the muscles and glands and receive sensory input from the neck, shoulder, arm, and hand. The 12 thoracic nerves (T) are associated with the chest and abdominal walls. The 5 lumbar nerves (L) are associated with the hip and leg, and the 5 sacral nerves (S) are associated with the genitals and lower digestive tract. (*Redrawn from FUNDAMENTAL NEUROANATOMY by Walle J. H. Nauta and Michael Fiertag. Copyright © 1986 by W. H. Freeman and Co. Reprinted by permission.*)

ical for regulation of the internal environment. Some of the fibers from these two branches continue to the cerebral cortex, which is thought to be that part of the brain having the greatest mental capacity and influence over social behavior. These ascending reticular pathways affect such things as wakefulness and the direction of attention to specific events.

The reticular formation also gives rise to connections with the cerebellum and the spinal cord. The fibers that descend to the spinal cord form the reticulospinal pathways. They influence activity in both the efferent and afferent neurons. There is considerable interaction between the reticular pathways that go up to the forebrain, down to the spinal cord, and to the cerebellum. For example, all three components function in controlling muscle activity.

Some reticular-formation neurons are clustered together, forming certain of the brainstem nuclei and integrating centers. These include the cardiovascular, respiratory, swallowing, and vomiting centers, all of which are discussed in subsequent chapters. The reticular formation also has nuclei important in eye-movement control and the reflex orientation of the body in space.

In addition, the brainstem contains nuclei involved in processing information for 10 of the 12 pairs of **cranial nerves**. These are the peripheral nerves that connect with the brain and innervate the muscles, glands, and sensory receptors of the head as well as many organs in the thoracic and abdominal cavities (Table 8-7).

Information can pass through the brainstem in two ways: (1) **long neural pathways**, which carry information directly between the brain and spinal cord or between the forebrain and brainstem; and (2) **multineuronal** or **multisynaptic pathways** (Figure 8-39). As their name suggests, the multineuronal pathways are made up of many neurons and many synaptic connections. Since synapses are the sites where new information can be integrated into neural messages, there are many opportunities for neural processing along the multineuronal pathways. The long pathways, on the other hand, consist of chains of only a few sequentially connected neurons. Because the long pathways contain few synapses, there is little opportunity for alteration in the information they transmit.

FIGURE 8-37

The spinal cord and six divisions of the brain.

Forebrain { Cerebrum
            Diencephalon

Midbrain

Brainstem { Pons

Medulla oblongata

Cerebellum

Spinal cord

FIGURE 8-38

The four interconnected ventricles of the brain.

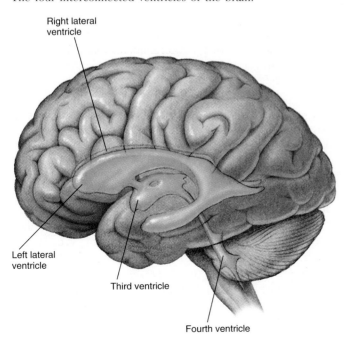

Right lateral ventricle

Left lateral ventricle

Third ventricle

Fourth ventricle

Cerebellum

The cerebellum, chiefly involved with the control of skeletal muscle functions, consists of an outer layer of cells, the cerebellar cortex, and several deeper cell clusters, the cerebellar nuclei. It is connected to the brainstem by the cerebellar peduncles. Although the cerebellum does not initiate voluntary movements, it is an important center for coordinating and learning movements and for controlling posture and balance. In order to carry out these functions, the cerebellum receives information from the muscles and joints, skin, eyes and ears, viscera, and the parts of the brain involved in control of movement.

Forebrain

The central core of the forebrain is formed by the diencephalon. It is covered by the second component of the forebrain, the cerebrum, which consists of the right and left **cerebral hemispheres** and certain other structures on the underside of the brain.

The cerebral hemispheres (Figure 8-40) consist of the

TABLE 8-7   THE CRANIAL NERVES

Name	Fibers	Comments
I. Olfactory nerve	Afferent	Tract of brain; not true nerve. Carries input from receptors in olfactory (smell) epithelium.
II. Optic nerve	Afferent	Tract of brain; not true nerve. Carries input from receptors in eye.
III. Oculomotor nerve	Efferent	Innervates skeletal muscles that move eyeball up, down, and medially and raise upper eyelid; innervates smooth muscles that constrict pupil and alter lens shape for near and far vision.
	Afferent	Transmits information from receptors in muscles.
IV. Trochlear nerve	Efferent	Innervates skeletal muscles that move eyeball downward and laterally.
	Afferent	Transmits information from receptors in muscle.
V. Trigeminal nerve	Efferent	Innervates skeletal chewing muscles.
	Afferent	Transmits information from receptors in skin; skeletal muscles of face, nose, and mouth; and teeth sockets.
VI. Abducens nerve	Efferent	Innervates skeletal muscles that move eyeball laterally.
	Afferent	Transmits information from receptors in muscle.
VII. Facial nerve	Efferent	Innervates skeletal muscles of facial expression and swallowing; innervates nose, palate, and lacrimal and salivary glands.
	Afferent	Transmits information from taste buds in front of tongue and mouth.
VIII. Vestibulocochlear nerve	Afferent	Transmits information from receptors in ear.
IX. Glossopharyngeal nerve	Efferent	Innervates skeletal muscles involved in swallowing and parotid salivary gland.
	Afferent	Transmits information from taste buds at back of tongue and receptors in auditory-tube skin.
X. Vagus nerve	Efferent	Innervates skeletal muscles of pharynx and larynx and smooth muscle and glands of thorax and abdomen.
	Afferent	Transmits information from receptors in thorax and abdomen.
XI. Accessory nerve	Efferent	Innervates neck skeletal muscles.
XII. Hypoglossal nerve	Efferent	Innervates tongue skeletal muscles.

pyramidal cells form the major output cells of the cortex, sending their axons to other parts of the cortex and to other parts of the central nervous system.

The cerebral cortex is the most complex integrating area of the nervous system. It is necessary for the bringing together of basic afferent information into meaningful

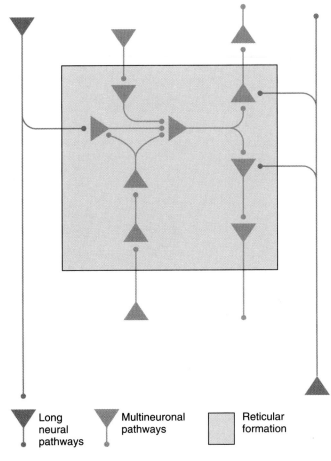

Long neural pathways   Multineuronal pathways   Reticular formation

FIGURE 8-39
Relationship of long neural pathways and multineuronal (multisynaptic) pathways to the reticular formation.

cerebral cortex, an outer shell of gray matter, plus underlying nuclei and the many nerve fibers that bring information into the cerebrum, carry information out, and interconnect the neurons in the cerebrum. The hemispheres, although largely separated by a longitudinal division, are connected to each other by bundles of nerve fibers known as commissures, the **corpus callosum** being the largest (Figure 8-40). Areas within a hemisphere are connected to each other by association fibers, not shown in the figure.

The cortex of each hemisphere is divided into four **lobes**: the **frontal**, **parietal**, **occipital**, and **temporal** (Figure 8-41). It averages only 3 mm in thickness but accounts for 46 percent of the cerebrum's volume. The cortex is highly folded, which increases the area available for cortical neurons without increasing appreciably the volume of the brain. Its cells are arranged most often in six layers, a distinguishing trait of the cortex. The cortical neurons are of two basic types: pyramidal cells (named for the shape of their cell bodies) and nonpyramidal cells. The

TABLE 8-8 SUMMARY OF FUNCTIONS OF THE MAJOR PARTS OF THE BRAIN

I. Brainstem
   A. Contains fibers passing between spinal cord, forebrain, and cerebellum
   B. Contains the reticular formation and its integrating centers for cardiovascular and respiratory activity (Chapters 14 and 15)
   C. Contains nuclei for most of the cranial nerves
II. Cerebellum
   A. Coordinates movements, including those for posture and balance (Chapter 12)
   B. Participates in some forms of learning (Chapter 13)
III. Cerebral hemispheres
   A. Contains the cerebral cortex, which participates in perception (Chapter 9), the generation of skilled movements (Chapter 12), reasoning, learning, and memory (Chapter 13)
   B. Contains subcortical nuclei, which participate in coordination of skeletal-muscle activity (Chapter 12)
   C. Contains interconnecting fiber pathways
IV. Thalamus
   A. Is a synaptic relay station for sensory pathways on their way to the cerebral cortex (Chapter 9)
   B. Participates in control of skeletal-muscle coordination (Chapter 12)
V. Hypothalamus
   A. Regulates anterior pituitary gland (Chapter 10)
   B. Regulates water balance (Chapter 16)
   C. Participates in regulation of autonomic nervous system (Chapters 8 and 18)
   D. Regulates eating and drinking behavior (Chapter 18)
   E. Regulates reproductive system (Chapters 10 and 19)
   F. Reinforces certain behaviors (Chapter 13)
   G. Generates and regulates circadian rhythms (Chapters 7, 9, 10, and 18)
   H. Regulates body temperature (Chapter 18)
   I. Participates in generation of emotional behavior (Chapter 13)
VI. Limbic system
   A. Participates in generation of emotions and emotional behavior (Chapter 13)
   B. Plays essential role in most kinds of learning (Chapter 13)

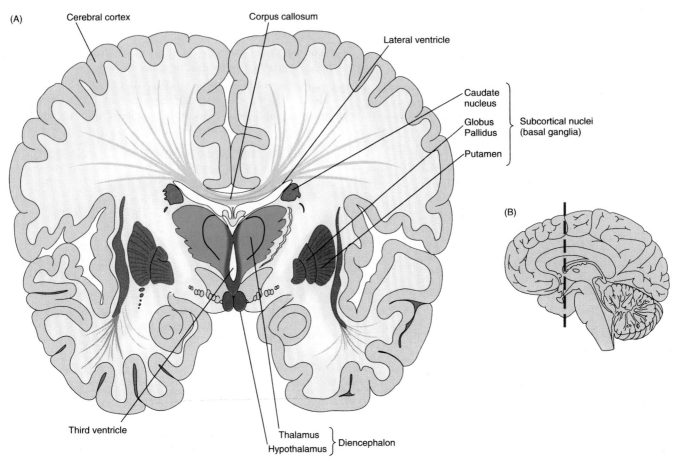

(A) Cerebral cortex

Corpus callosum

Lateral ventricle

Caudate nucleus

Globus Pallidus

Putamen

Subcortical nuclei (basal ganglia)

(B)

Third ventricle

Thalamus
Hypothalamus
Diencephalon

FIGURE 8-40

(A) Coronal (side-to-side) section of the brain, with the thalamus shaded in blue–green and the hypothalamus shaded in violet. (B) The dashed line indicates the location of the cross section in A.

Frontal lobe

Parietal lobe

Occipital lobe

Temporal lobe

FIGURE 8-41

A lateral view of the brain. The outer layer of the forebrain (the cortex) is divided into four lobes, as shown.

perceptual images and for the ultimate refinement of control over the systems that govern the movement of the skeletal muscles. Nerve fibers enter the cortex from a variety of places but particularly from the thalamus, from other regions of the cortex, and from the brainstem reticular formation. Some of the input fibers convey information about specific events in the environment, whereas others are more concerned with controlling levels of cortical excitability, determining states of arousal, and directing attention to specific stimuli.

The **subcortical nuclei** form other areas of gray matter that lie deep within the cerebral hemispheres. Predominant among them are the **basal ganglia**, which play an important role in the control of movement and posture and in more complex aspects of behavior. In other parts of the forebrain, axons predominate, their whitish myelin coating distinguishing them as white matter.

The diencephalon, the second component of the forebrain, contains two major parts: the thalamus and the hypothalamus (Figure 8-40). The **thalamus**, which lies at the center of the brain, is a large cluster of nuclei that serves as a synaptic relay station and important integrating center for most inputs to the cortex.

The **hypothalamus** (Figure 8-40), which lies below the thalamus, is a tiny region that accounts for less than 1 percent of the brain's weight. Yet it is crucial to homeostatic regulation and is a principal site for regulating the behavior essential to the survival of the individual and the species. The integration achieved by the hypothalamus often involves correlation of neural and endocrine functions. Indeed, the hypothalamus appears to be the single most important control area for regulation of the internal environment. It lies directly above the pituitary gland, an important endocrine structure, attached to it by a stalk.

An area of the forebrain that includes both gray and white matter is the **limbic system**. This is an interconnected group of brain structures, taking in portions of frontal-lobe cortex, temporal lobe, thalamus, and hypothalamus, as well as the circuitous fiber pathways that connect them (Figure 8-42). The limbic system is associated with learning, emotional experience and behavior, and a wide variety of visceral and endocrine functions. Besides being connected with each other, the parts of the limbic system are connected with many other parts of the central nervous system.

The functions of the major parts of the brain are listed in Table 8-8 on page 219.

PERIPHERAL NERVOUS SYSTEM

Nerve fibers in the peripheral nervous system transmit signals between the central nervous system and

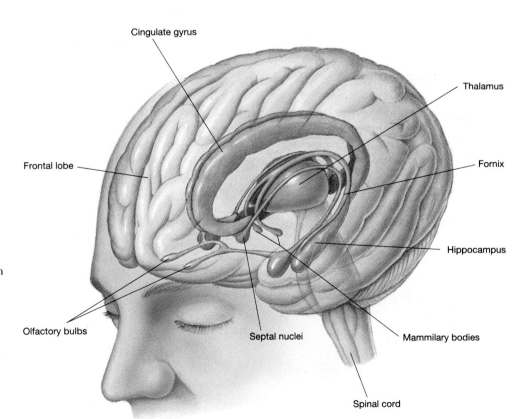

FIGURE 8-42

Structures of the limbic system are shown shaded in violet in this partially transparent view of the brain. *(Redrawn from BRAIN, MIND AND BEHAVIOR by Floyd E. Bloom and Arlyne Lazerson. Copyright © 1985, 1988 by Educational Broadcasting Corporation. Reprinted by permission of W. H. Freeman and Co.)*

Cingulate gyrus

Thalamus

Frontal lobe

Fornix

Hippocampus

Olfactory bulbs

Septal nuclei

Mammilary bodies

Spinal cord

all other parts of the body. As noted earlier, the nerve fibers are grouped into bundles called nerves. The peripheral nervous system consists of 43 pairs of nerves: 12 pairs of cranial nerves and 31 pairs that connect with the spinal cord as the spinal nerves. The cranial nerves and a summary of the information they transmit were listed in Table 8-7.

Each nerve fiber is surrounded by a Schwann cell. Some of the fibers are wrapped in layers of Schwann-cell membrane, and these tightly wrapped membranes form a myelin sheath (Figure 8-3). Other fibers are unmyelinated.

A nerve contains nerve fibers that are the axons of efferent neurons or afferent neurons. Accordingly, fibers in a nerve may be classified as belonging to the **efferent** or the **afferent division** of the peripheral nervous system (Table 8-9). All the spinal nerves contain both afferent and efferent fibers, whereas some of the cranial nerves (the optic nerves from the eyes, for example) contain only afferent fibers.

Peripheral Nervous System: Afferent Division

As noted earlier, afferent neurons convey information from receptors at their peripheral endings to the central nervous system. The long part of their axon is outside the central nervous system and is part of the peripheral nervous system. Afferent neurons are sometimes called primary afferents or first-order neurons because they are the first cells entering the central nervous system in the synaptically linked chains of neurons that handle incoming information.

Peripheral Nervous System: Efferent Division

Recall that efferent neurons carry signals from the central nervous system out to muscles or glands. The efferent division of the peripheral nervous system is more complicated than the afferent, being subdivided into a **somatic nervous system** and an **autonomic nervous system**. These terms are somewhat misleading because they suggest additional nervous systems distinct from the central and peripheral systems. Keep in mind that the terms refer simply to the efferent division of the peripheral nervous system.

TABLE 8-9 DIVISIONS OF THE PERIPHERAL NERVOUS SYSTEM

I. Afferent division
II. Efferent division
  A. Somatic nervous system
  B. Autonomic nervous system
    1. Sympathetic division
    2. Parasympathetic division

TABLE 8-10 DIFFERENCES BETWEEN SOMATIC AND AUTONOMIC NERVOUS SYSTEMS

Somatic
1. Consists of a single neuron between central nervous system and effector organ
2. Innervates skeletal muscle
3. Can lead only to muscle excitation

Autonomic
1. Has two-neuron chain (connected by synapse) between central nervous system and effector organ
2. Innervates smooth and cardiac muscle, glands, and GI neurons
3. Can lead to excitation or inhibition of effector cells

The simplest distinction between the somatic and autonomic systems is that the neurons of the somatic division innervate skeletal muscle, whereas the autonomic neurons innervate smooth and cardiac muscle, glands, and neurons in the gastrointestinal tract. Other differences are listed in Table 8-10.

Somatic Nervous System. The somatic portion of the efferent division of the peripheral nervous system is made up of all the nerve fibers going from the central nervous system to skeletal-muscle cells. The cell bodies of these neurons are located in groups in the brainstem or spinal cord. Their large-diameter, myelinated axons leave the central nervous system and pass without any synapses to skeletal-muscle cells. The neurotransmitter released by these neurons is acetylcholine. Because activity in the somatic neurons leads to contraction of the innervated skeletal-muscle cells, these neurons are often called **motor neurons**. Excitation of motor neurons leads only to the *contraction* of skeletal-muscle cells; there are no somatic neurons that inhibit the muscles.

Autonomic Nervous System. The efferent innervation of all tissues other than skeletal muscle is by way of the autonomic nervous system. In the case of the gastrointestinal tract, the autonomic nervous system innervates the neurons that are part of the **enteric nervous system**, a specialized nerve network in the wall of the intestinal tract, which regulates the glands and smooth muscles found there. The enteric nervous system is considered by some to be a specialized part of the autonomic nervous system and does not have all of the characteristics discussed below. It will be discussed in Chapter 17.

In the autonomic nervous system, the groups of axons between the central nervous system and the effector cells

(voluntary)

1 neuron

2 neuron

sympathetic = norepinephrine
para: AcH)

why 2? Control; involuntary

FIGURE 8-43
Efferent division of the peripheral nervous system. Overall plan of the somatic and autonomic nervous systems.

consist of two neurons and one synapse (Figure 8-43). (This is in contrast to the single neuron of the somatic system.) The first neuron has its cell body in the central nervous system. The synapse between the two neurons is outside the central nervous system, in a cell cluster called an **autonomic ganglion**. The nerve fibers passing between the central nervous system and the ganglia are called **preganglionic fibers**; those passing between the ganglia and the effector cells are **postganglionic fibers**.

Anatomical and physiological differences within the autonomic nervous system are the basis for its further subdivision into **sympathetic** and **parasympathetic** components. The nerve fibers of these components leave the central nervous system at different levels—the sympathetic fibers from the thoracic and lumbar (chest) regions of the spinal cord and the parasympathetic fibers from the brain and the sacral portion of the spinal cord (lower back, Figure 8-44). Therefore, the sympathetic division is also called the thoracolumbar division, and the parasympathetic, the craniosacral division.

The two divisions of the autonomic nervous system also differ in the location of ganglia. Most of the sympathetic ganglia lie close to the spinal cord and form the two chains of ganglia—one on each side of the cord—known as the **sympathetic trunks** (Figure 8-44). Other sympathetic ganglia, called collateral ganglia—the celiac, superior mesenteric, and inferior mesenteric ganglia—lie far away from the spinal cord, closer to the innervated organ (Figure 8-44). In contrast, the parasympathetic ganglia lie within the organs innervated by the postganglionic neurons.

The anatomy of the sympathetic nervous system can be confusing. Preganglionic sympathetic *fibers* leave the spinal cord only between the first thoracic and third lumbar segments, whereas sympathetic *trunks* extend the entire length of the cord—from the cervical levels high in the neck down to the sacral levels. The "extra" ganglia in the sympathetic trunks receive preganglionic fibers from the thoracolumbar regions because some of the preganglionic fibers, once in the sympathetic trunks, turn to travel up-

ward or downward for several segments before forming synapses with postganglionic neurons (Figure 8-45, numbers 1 and 4). The ganglia at the cervical levels are the superior cervical, middle cervical, and stellate ganglia (Figure 8-44). Other possible paths taken by the sympathetic fibers are shown in Figure 8-45, numbers 2, 3, and 5.

The anatomical arrangements in the sympathetic nervous system to some extent tie the entire system together so it can act as a single unit, although small segments of the system can still be regulated independently. Furthermore, the ganglia can act either as automatic relay stations with practically no change in the information they transmit to the effector organ or as important integrating centers capable of generating individualized responses. The parasympathetic system, in contrast, is made up of relatively independent components. Thus, overall autonomic responses, made up of many small parts, are quite variable and finely tailored to the specific demands of any given situation.

In both sympathetic and parasympathetic divisions, the major neurotransmitter released between pre- and postganglionic fibers is acetylcholine (Figure 8-46). In the parasympathetic division, the major neurotransmitter between the postganglionic fiber and the effector cell is also acetylcholine. In the sympathetic division, the major transmitter between the postganglionic fiber and the effector cell is usually norepinephrine. We stress "major" and "usually" because acetylcholine is released by some sympathetic postganglionic endings. Moreover, one or more cotransmitters are usually stored and released with the autonomic transmitters; these include ATP, dopamine, and several of the neuropeptides. These substances, however, play a smaller role in sympathetic nervous system activity than norepinephrine does.

Recall that the somatic efferent nerve fibers are also cholinergic. Thus, the neurons in the entire efferent nervous system are either cholinergic or adrenergic (Figure 8-46).

Many of the drugs that stimulate or inhibit various com-

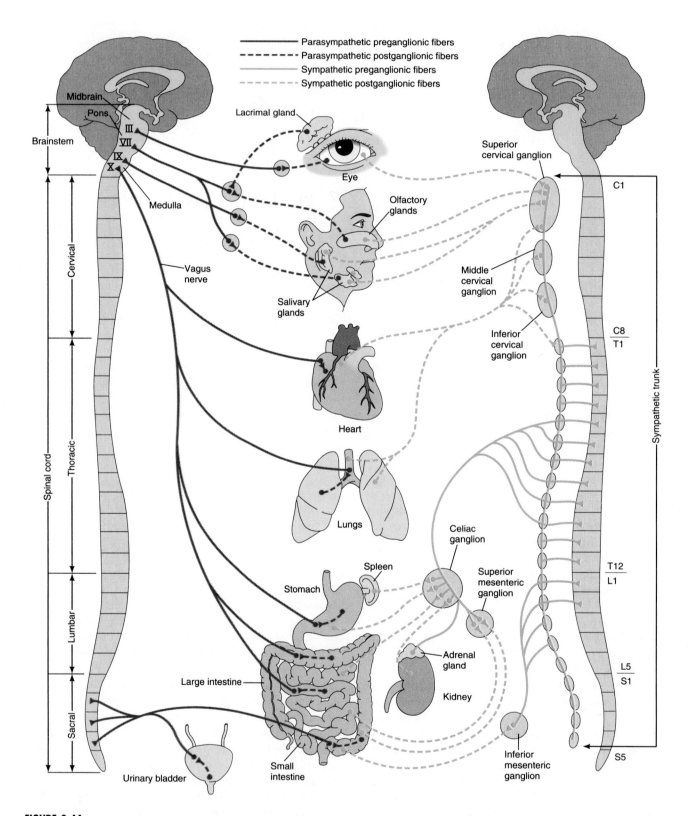

FIGURE 8-44

The parasympathetic (left) and sympathetic (right) divisions of the autonomic nervous system. The celiac, superior mesenteric, and inferior mesenteric ganglia are collateral ganglia. Only the sympathetic trunk on the right side of the spinal cord is shown, although another exists on the left. Not shown are the fibers passing to the liver, blood vessels, and skin glands from the sympathetic trunk.

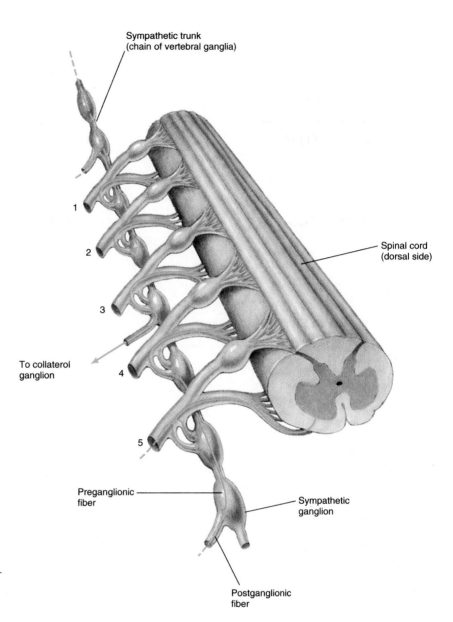

Sympathetic trunk
(chain of vertebral ganglia)

1

2

3

To collaterol
ganglion

4

5

Spinal cord
(dorsal side)

Preganglionic
fiber

Sympathetic
ganglion

Postganglionic
fiber

FIGURE 8-45

Relationship between a sympathetic trunk
and the spinal cord. (1 through 5) Various
courses that preganglionic sympathetic fibers
(solid lines) may take through the sympathetic trunk. Dashed lines represent postganglionic fibers. A mirror image of this exists
on the opposite side of the spinal cord.

ponents of the autonomic nervous system affect receptors
for acetylcholine and norepinephrine. Recall that there are
several types of receptors for each neurotransmitter (Table
8-11). The great majority of acetylcholine receptors on
autonomic postganglionic neurons are nicotinic receptors.
In contrast, the acetylcholine receptors on smooth-muscle,
cardiac-muscle, and gland cells are muscarinic receptors.
To complete the story of the peripheral cholinergic receptors, it should be emphasized that the cholinergic receptors on the neuromuscular junctions of skeletal-muscle
fibers, innervated by the *somatic* motor neurons, not autonomic neurons, are nicotinic receptors.

One set of postganglionic neurons in the sympathetic
division never develops axons; instead, upon activation by
preganglionic axons, the cells of this "ganglion" release
their transmitters into the bloodstream (Figure 8-46). This

"ganglion," called the **adrenal medulla**, therefore functions as an endocrine gland whose secretion is controlled
by the sympathetic preganglionic nerve fibers. It releases a
mixture of about 80 percent epinephrine and 20 percent
norepinephrine into the blood (plus small amounts of
other substances, such as dopamine, ATP, and some of the
neuropeptides). These substances, properly called hormones rather than neurotransmitters in this circumstance,
are transported via the blood to receptor sites on effector
cells sensitive to them. The receptor sites may be the same
adrenergic receptors that are located near the release sites
of sympathetic postganglionic neurons and that are normally activated by the norepinephrine released from these
neurons, or the receptor sites may be located at places that
are not near the neurons and therefore activated only by
the circulating epinephrine or norepinephrine.

FIGURE 8-46

Transmitters used in the various components of the peripheral nervous system. In a few cases (to be described later) sympathetic neurons release a transmitter other than norepinephrine. ACh, Acetylcholine; NE, norepinephrine; Epi, epinephrine, DA, dopamine.

TABLE 8-11   CLASSES OF RECEPTORS FOR ACETYLCHOLINE, NOREPINEPHRINE, AND EPINEPHRINE

I. Receptors for acetylcholine
  A. Nicotinic receptors
    On postganglionic neurons in the autonomic ganglia
    At neuromuscular junctions of skeletal muscle
    On some central nervous system neurons
  B. Muscarinic receptors
    On smooth muscle
    On cardiac muscle
    On gland cells
    On some central nervous system neurons
    On some neurons of autonomic ganglia (although the great majority of receptors at this site are nicotinic)

II. Receptors for norepinephrine and epinephrine
    On smooth muscle
    On cardiac muscle
    On gland cells
    On some central nervous system neurons

Table 8-12 is a reference list of the effects of the autonomic nervous system, which will be described in subsequent chapters. Note that the heart and many glands and smooth muscles are innervated by both sympathetic and parasympathetic fibers; that is, they receive **dual innervation**. Whatever effect one division has on the effector cells, the other division frequently (but not always) has the opposite effect.

Dual innervation by nerve fibers that cause opposite responses provides a very fine degree of control over the effector organ—it is like equipping a car with both an accelerator and a brake. One can slow the car simply by decreasing the pressure on the accelerator; however, the combined effects of releasing the accelerator and applying the brake provide faster and more accurate control. Analogously, the sympathetic and parasympathetic divisions are usually activated reciprocally; that is, as the activity of one division is increased, the activity of the other is decreased.

A helpful generalization is that the sympathetic system increases its response under conditions of stress. Indeed, a full-blown sympathetic response is called the **fight-or-flight response**, describing the situation of an animal forced to challenge an attacker or run from it. Activity of the parasympathetic system, on the other hand, increases with vegetative, housekeeping functions, such as digestion.

Autonomic responses usually occur without conscious control or awareness, as though they were indeed autonomous (in fact, the autonomic nervous system has been called the "involuntary" nervous system). However, it is wrong to assume that this is always the case, for it has been shown that discrete visceral or glandular responses can be learned and thus, to this extent, voluntarily controlled.

Opposite functions (ex: dilate vs. constricts)

TABLE 8-12 SOME EFFECTS OF AUTONOMIC NERVOUS SYSTEM ACTIVITY

Effector organ	Sympathetic effect		Parasympathetic effect[†]
	Receptor type[°]		
Eyes			
Iris muscles	Alpha$_1$	Contracts radial muscle (widens pupil)	Contracts sphincter muscle (makes pupil smaller)
Ciliary muscle	Beta$_2$	Relaxes (flattens lens for far vision)	Contracts (allows lens to become more convex for near vision)
Heart			
SA node	Beta$_1$	Increases heart rate	Decreases heart rate
Atria	Beta$_1$	Increases contractility	Decreases contractility
AV node	Beta$_1$	Increases conduction velocity	Decreases conduction velocity
Ventricles	Beta$_1$	Increases contractility	Decreases contractility slightly
Arterioles			
Coronary	Alpha$_{1,2}$	Constricts	Dilates
	Beta$_2$	Dilates	
Skin	Alpha$_{1,2}$	Constricts	—[†]
Skeletal muscle	Alpha[§]	Constricts	—
	Beta$_2$	Dilates	
Abdominal viscera	Alpha$_1$	Constricts	—
	Beta$_2$	Dilates	
Salivary glands	Alpha$_{1,2}$	Constricts	Dilates
Veins	Alpha$_1$	Constricts	
	Beta$_2$	Dilates	
Lungs			
Bronchial muscle	Beta$_2$	Relaxes	Contracts
Bronchial glands	Alpha$_1$	Inhibits secretion	Stimulates secretion
	Beta$_2$	Stimulates secretion	
Salivary glands	Alpha$_1$	Stimulates K$^+$ and H$_2$O secretion	Stimulates K$^+$ and H$_2$O secretion
	Beta[§]	Stimulates enzyme secretion	
Stomach			
Motility, tone	Alpha$_{1,2}$ Beta$_2$	Decreases	Increases
Sphincters	Alpha$_1$	Contracts	Relaxes
Secretion	§	Inhibits (?)	Stimulates

(continued)

TABLE 8-12 *(continued)*

Effector organ	Sympathetic effect		Parasympathetic effect[†]
	Receptor type[°]		
Intestine			
Motility	Alpha$_{1,2}$	Decreases	Increases
	Beta$_{1,2}$	Decreases	
Sphincters	Alpha$_1$	Contracts (usually)	Relaxes (usually)
Secretion	Alpha$_2$	Inhibits	Stimulates
Gallbladder	Beta$_2$	Relaxes	Contracts
Liver	[§]	Glycogenolysis Gluconeogenesis	—
Pancreas			
Exocrine glands	Alpha[§]	Inhibits secretion	Stimulates secretion
Endocrine glands	Alpha$_2$	Inhibits insulin secretion	Stimulates insulin secretion
Fat cells	Alpha[§] Beta$_1$	Increases fat breakdown	
Kidneys	Beta$_1$	Increases renin secretion	—
Urinary bladder			
Bladder wall	Beta$_2$	Relaxes	Contracts
Sphincter	Alpha$_1$	Contracts	Relaxes
Uterus	Alpha$_1$	Contracts in pregnancy	Variable
	Beta$_2$	Relaxes	
Reproductive tract (male)	Alpha$_1$	Ejaculation	Erection
Skin			
Muscles causing hairs to stand erect	Alpha$_1$	Contracts	—
Sweat glands	Alpha$_1$	Localized secretion	Generalized secretion
Lacrimal glands	Alpha[§]	Secretion	Secretion

[°]Note that in many effector organs, there are both alpha-adrenergic and beta-adrenergic receptors. Activation of these receptors may produce either the same or opposing effects. For simplicity, except for the arterioles and a few other cases, only the dominant sympathetic effect is given when the two receptors oppose each other.
[†]These effects are all mediated by muscarinic receptors.
[‡]A dash means these cells are not innervated by this branch of the autonomic nervous system.
[§]The specific receptor type is undetermined.
Table adapted from "Goodman and Gilman's The Pharmacological Basis of Therapeutics," Alfred Goodman Gilman, Theodore W. Rall, Alan S. Nies, and Palmer Taylor, eds., 8th edn., Pergamon Press, New York, 1990.

BLOOD SUPPLY, BLOOD-BRAIN BARRIER PHENOMENA, AND CEREBROSPINAL FLUID

Usually, glucose is the only substrate metabolized by the brain to supply its energy requirements, and most of the energy from the oxidative breakdown of glucose is transferred to ATP. The brain's glycogen stores being negligible, it is completely dependent upon a continuous blood supply of glucose. Also essential is a blood supply of oxygen for oxidative phosphorylation. Although the adult brain is only 2 percent of the body weight, it receives 15 percent of the total blood supply to support its high oxygen utilization. If the oxygen supply is cut off for 4 to 5 min or if the glucose supply is cut off for 10 to 15 min, brain damage will occur. In fact, the most common form of brain damage is caused by a stoppage of the blood supply to a region of the brain, which results in a *stroke*. The cells in the region deprived of nutrients cease to function and die.

The exchange of substances between blood and extracellular fluid in the central nervous system is different from the more-or-less unrestricted diffusion of nonprotein substances from blood to extracellular fluid in the other organs of the body. A complex group of **blood-brain barrier** mechanisms closely controls both the kinds of substances that enter the extracellular fluid of the brain and the rate at which they enter. These mechanisms regulate the chemical composition of the extracellular fluid of the brain and minimize the ability of many harmful substances to reach the neurons.

The blood-brain barrier resides within the cells—endothelial cells—that line the brain capillaries (capillaries are the smallest blood vessels and the major vessels across which substances pass between the blood and tissue fluids). In brain capillaries the edges of adjacent endothelial cells abut against each other, and the cells are completely sealed together by continuous tight junctions. This means that all substances entering or leaving the brain must pass through the two plasma membranes and cytoplasm of the endothelial cells (Figure 8-47) rather than between the cells. Capillaries in certain areas of the brain lack a blood-brain barrier, but these areas account for less than 1 percent of the brain volume.

The blood-brain barrier has both anatomical structures and physiological transport systems that handle different classes of substances in different ways; thus, the barrier is said to be selective. For example, substances that dissolve readily in the lipid components of the plasma membranes enter the brain quickly. This characteristic of the blood-brain barrier explains some drug actions, as can be seen from the following scenario: Morphine differs chemically from heroin only in that morphine has two hydroxyl

FIGURE 8-47

A diagram of the blood-brain barrier, which is formed by the endothelial cells that line the brain capillaries. (*Redrawn from Oldendorf.*)

groups where heroin has two acetyl groups ($-COCH_3$). This small difference renders morphine highly lipid-insoluble and heroin highly lipid-soluble. Thus, heroin crosses the blood-brain barrier more readily than morphine. As soon as heroin enters the brain, however, enzymes remove the acetyl groups from heroin and change it to morphine. The morphine, highly insoluble in lipid, is then effectively trapped in the brain where it continues to exert its effect. Some other drugs that have rapid effects in the central nervous system because of their high lipid solubility are the barbiturates, nicotine, caffeine, and alcohol.

Many substances that do not dissolve readily in lipids, such as glucose and other important substrates of brain metabolism, nonetheless enter the brain quite rapidly, by combining with membrane transport proteins. Similar transport systems also move surplus substances out of the brain and into the blood, preventing the buildup of molecules that could interfere with brain function.

In addition to its blood supply, the central nervous system is perfused by a second fluid, the cerebrospinal fluid. This clear fluid fills the cerebral ventricles and the subarachnoid space, which surrounds the brain and spinal cord (Figure 8-48). Thus, the central nervous system literally floats in a cushion of cerebrospinal fluid. Since the brain and spinal cord are very soft, delicate tissues with about the consistency of Jello, they are protected by the fluid from sudden and jarring movements.

Most of the cerebrospinal fluid is secreted into the ventricles by the **choroid plexuses**, which form part of the lining of the four ventricles. A barrier is present here, too, between the blood in the capillaries of the choroid plexuses and the cerebrospinal fluid that flows next to the neural tissue. Consistent with the barrier mechanisms, cerebrospinal fluid is a selective secretion, not a simple filtrate of plasma. For example, potassium and calcium concentrations are slightly lower in cerebrospinal fluid than in plasma, whereas the sodium and chloride concentrations are slightly higher.

The cerebrospinal fluid circulates through the interconnected ventricular system to the brainstem, where it passes through small openings out to the surface of the brain and spinal cord. Aided by circulatory, respiratory, and postural pressure changes, the fluid ultimately flows to the top of the outer surface of the brain, where most of it is reabsorbed into the bloodstream through one-way valves in large veins. If the flow is obstructed at any point, cerebrospinal fluid accumulates, causing hydrocephalus ("water on the brain"). In severe untreated cases, the resulting elevation of pressure in the ventricles may damage the brain and cause mental retardation.

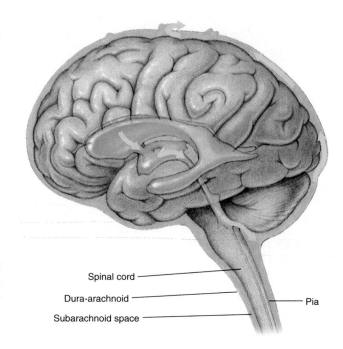

Spinal cord —
Dura-arachnoid —
Subarachnoid space —
— Pia

FIGURE 8-48
The ventricular system of the brain and the distribution of the cerebrospinal fluid, shown in green. Cerebrospinal fluid is formed in the ventricles, passes to the subarachnoid space outside the brain and spinal cord, and then moves through small valvelike structures into the large veins of the head.

SECTION D SUMMARY

I. Inside the skull and vertebral column, the brain and spinal cord are enclosed in and protected by the meninges.

CENTRAL NERVOUS SYSTEM: SPINAL CORD

I. The spinal cord is divided into two areas: central gray matter, which contains nerve cell bodies and dendrites; and white matter, which surrounds the gray matter and contains myelinated axons organized into ascending or descending tracts.

II. The axons of the afferent and efferent neurons form the spinal nerves.

CENTRAL NERVOUS SYSTEM: BRAIN

I. The brain is divided into six regions: cerebrum, diencephalon, midbrain, pons, medulla oblongata, and cerebellum.

II. The midbrain, pons, and medulla oblongata form the brainstem, which contains the reticular formation.

III. The cerebellum plays a role in posture, movement, and some kinds of memory.

IV. The cerebrum, made up of right and left cerebral hemispheres, and the diencephalon together form the forebrain. The cerebral cortex forms the outer shell of the cerebrum and is divided into parietal, frontal, occipital, and temporal lobes.

V. The diencephalon contains the thalamus and hypothalamus.

VI. The limbic system is a set of deep-forebrain structures associated with learning and emotions.

PERIPHERAL NERVOUS SYSTEM

I. The peripheral nervous system consists of 43 paired nerves: 12 pairs of cranial nerves and 31 pairs of spinal nerves. Most nerves contain axons of both afferent and efferent neurons.

II. The efferent division of the peripheral nervous system is divided into somatic and autonomic parts. The somatic fibers innervate skeletal muscle cells and release the neurotransmitter acetylcholine.

III. The autonomic nervous system innervates cardiac and smooth muscle, glands, and gastrointestinal-tract neurons. Each autonomic pathway consists of a preganglionic neuron with its cell body in the CNS and a postganglionic neuron with its cell body in an autonomic ganglion outside the CNS.

   A. The autonomic nervous system is divided into sympathetic and parasympathetic components. The preganglionic neurons in both sympathetic and parasympathetic divisions release acetylcholine; the postganglionic parasympathetic neurons release mainly acetylcholine, and the postganglionic sympathetics release norepinephrine.

   B. The receptors that respond to acetylcholine are classified as nicotinic and muscarinic, and those that respond to norepinephrine and epinephrine as alpha- and beta-adrenergic types.

   C. The adrenal medulla is a hormone-secreting part of the sympathetic nervous system and secretes mainly epinephrine.

   D. Effector organs innervated by the autonomic nervous system generally receive dual innervation.

BLOOD SUPPLY, BLOOD-BRAIN BARRIER PHENOMENA, AND CEREBROSPINAL FLUID

   I. Brain tissue depends on a continuous supply of glucose and oxygen for metabolism.

   II. The chemical composition of the extracellular fluid of the CNS is closely regulated by the blood-brain barrier.

   III. The brain ventricles and the space within the meninges are filled with cerebrospinal fluid, which is formed in the ventricles.

SECTION D KEY TERMS

nerve	white matter
pathway	dorsal roots
tract	dorsal root ganglia
commissure	ventral roots
ganglia	spinal nerves
nuclei	cerebrum
meninges	diencephalon
cerebrospinal fluid	midbrain
gray matter	pons

medulla oblongata	efferent division of the peripheral nervous system
cerebellum	
forebrain	afferent division of the peripheral nervous system
brainstem	
cerebral ventricles	somatic nervous system
reticular formation	autonomic nervous system
cranial nerves	motor neurons
long neural pathways	enteric nervous system
multineuronal pathways	autonomic ganglion
multisynaptic pathways	preganglionic fibers
cerebral hemispheres	postganglionic fibers
cerebral cortex	sympathetic division of the autonomic nervous system
corpus callosum	
frontal lobe	parasympathetic division of the autonomic nervous system
parietal lobe	
occipital lobe	
temporal lobe	sympathetic trunks
subcortical nuclei	adrenal medulla
basal ganglia	dual innervation
thalamus	fight-or-flight response
hypothalamus	blood-brain barrier
limbic system	choroid plexuses

SECTION D REVIEW QUESTIONS

1. Draw an organizational chart showing the central nervous system, peripheral nervous system, brain, spinal cord, spinal nerves, cranial nerves, forebrain, brainstem, cerebrum, diencephalon, midbrain, pons, medulla oblongata, and cerebellum.

2. Draw a cross section of the spinal cord showing the gray and white matter, dorsal and ventral roots, dorsal root ganglion, and spinal nerve. Indicate the general location of pathways.

3. List two functions of the thalamus.

4. List seven functions of the hypothalamus.

5. Draw a peripheral nervous system chart indicating the relationships among afferent and efferent divisions, somatic and autonomic nervous systems, and sympathetic and parasympathetic divisions.

6. Contrast the somatic and autonomic nervous systems; mention at least three characteristics of each.

7. Name the neurotransmitter released at each synapse or neuroeffector junction in the somatic and autonomic systems.

8. Contrast the sympathetic and parasympathetic divisions; mention at least four characteristics of each.

9. Explain how the adrenal medulla can affect receptors on various effector organs despite the fact that its cells have no axons.

10. The chemical composition of the CNS extracellular fluid is different from that of blood. Explain how this difference is achieved.

CHAPTER 8 CLINICAL TERMS

local anesthetics
agonists
antagonists
tetanus
Alzheimer's disease
stroke

CHAPTER 8 THOUGHT QUESTIONS

(Answers are given in Appendix A.)

1. Neurons are treated with a drug that instantly and permanently stops the Na,K-ATPase pumps. Assume for this question that the pumps are not electrogenic. What happens to the resting membrane potential immediately and over time?

2. Extracellular potassium concentration in a person is increased with no change in intracellular potassium concentration. What happens to the resting potential and the action potential?

3. A person has received a severe blow to the head but appears to be all right. Over the next weeks, however, he develops loss of appetite, thirst, and sexual capacity but no loss in sensory or motor function. What part of the brain do you think may have been damaged?

4. A person is taking a drug that causes, among other things, dryness of the mouth and speeding of the heart rate but no impairment of the ability to use the skeletal muscles. What type of receptor does this drug probably block? (Table 8-11 will help you answer this.)

5. Some cells are treated with a drug that blocks chloride channels, and the membrane potential of these cells becomes slightly depolarized (less negative). From these facts, predict whether the plasma membrane of these cells actively transports chloride and in what direction.

6. If the enzyme acetylcholinesterase were blocked with a drug, what malfunctions would occur?

7. The compound tetraethylammonium (TEA) blocks the voltage-sensitive changes in potassium permeability that occur during an action potential. After administration of TEA, what changes would you expect in the action potential? In the afterhyperpolarization?

CHAPTER

9

THE SENSORY SYSTEMS

A person's awareness of the world is determined by the neural mechanisms that process afferent information. The initial step of this processing is the transformation of stimulus energy first into receptor potentials and then into action potentials in nerve fibers. The pattern of action potentials in particular nerve fibers is a code that provides information about the world even though, as is frequently the case with symbols, the action potentials differ vastly from what they represent.

A **sensory system** is a part of the nervous system that consists of sensory receptors that receive stimuli from the external or internal environment, the neural pathways that conduct information from the receptors to the brain, and those parts of the brain that deal primarily with processing the information.

Information processed by a sensory system may or may not lead to conscious awareness of the stimulus. Regardless of whether the information reaches consciousness, it is called **sensory information**. If the information reaches consciousness, it can also be called a **sensation**. The understanding of the sensation's meaning is called **perception**. For example, feeling pain is a sensation, but the awareness I have that my tooth hurts is a perception. Perceptions occur by means of the neural processing of sensory information. At present we have little understanding of the final stages in this processing by which patterns of action potentials become sensations or perceptions.

Intuitively, it might seem that sensory systems operate like familiar electrical equipment, but this is true only up to a point. As an example, let us compare telephone transmission with our auditory (hearing) sensory system. The telephone changes sound waves into electric impulses, which are then transmitted along wires to the receiver. Thus far the analogy holds. (Of course, the mechanisms by which electric currents and action potentials are transmitted are quite different, but this does not affect our argument.) The telephone then changes the coded electric impulses *back into sound waves.* Here is the crucial difference, for our brain does not physically translate the code into sound. Rather, the coded information itself or some correlate of it is what we perceive as sound.

RECEPTORS

Neural activity is initiated at the border between the nervous system and the world outside it by **sensory receptors** (recall again the two different meanings of "receptor" described in Chapter 7). Since some receptors respond to changes in the internal environment, the "outside world" in this sense can also mean, for example, distension of a blood vessel in our body.

Information about the external world and about the body's internal environment exists in different energy forms—pressure, temperature, light, sound waves, and so on. Receptors at the ends of afferent neurons translate these energy forms into graded potentials that can initiate action potentials, which travel into the central nervous system. (Again, we mean the end farthest from the central nervous system.) The receptors are either specialized endings of afferent neurons (Figure 9-1A) or separate cells that affect the ends of afferent neurons (Figure 9-1B).

Regardless of the original form of the energy, information from receptors linking the nervous system with the outside world must be translated into the language of graded potentials or action potentials. The energy form that impinges upon and activates a receptor is known as a **stimulus**. The process by which a stimulus—a photon of light, say, or the stretch of a muscle—is transformed into an electrical response at a receptor is known as **transduction**.

There are many types of receptors, each of which is specific; that is, each responds much more readily to one form of energy than to others. The type of energy to which a receptor responds in normal functioning is known as its **adequate stimulus**. Specificity exists at still another level. Each receptor responds best, that is, at lowest threshold, to only a very narrow band of stimulus energy. For example, individual receptors in the ear respond best to one particular tone. Thus, each receptor is "tuned" to respond

FIGURE 9-1

Afferent receptors. The sensitive membrane that responds to a stimulus is either (A) an ending of the afferent neuron or (B) on a separate cell adjacent to the afferent neuron (highly schematized).

most readily to a very specific energy range. The receptors *will* respond, however, to a wide range of tones if the stimulus energy is great enough.

We have been addressing receptor responses to one energy form, for example, only light or only sound. In addition, virtually all receptors can be activated by several forms of energy if the intensity is sufficiently high. For example, the receptors of the eye normally respond to light, but they can be activated by an intense mechanical stimulus, like a poke in the eye. Regardless of how the receptor is stimulated, any given receptor gives rise to only one sensation. This concept, that for every kind of sensation there is a special type of receptor whose activation always gives rise to that sensation, is stated as the **doctrine of specific nerve energies**.

Most receptors are exquisitely sensitive to their specific energy forms. For example, olfactory receptors can respond to as few as three or four odorous molecules in the inspired air, and visual receptors can respond to a single photon, the smallest quantity of light.

The Receptor Potential

The transduction process in all receptors involves the opening or closing of ion channels in a specialized receptor membrane that receives information about the outside world. These special ion channels do not occur on ordinary axonal membrane. The altered ion channels allow a change in the ion fluxes across the receptor membrane, which in turn produces a change in the membrane potential there. This change in potential is a graded potential called a **receptor potential**, sometimes called a generator potential. The different mechanisms by which ion channels are affected in the various types of sensory receptors will be presented throughout this chapter.

The specialized receptor membrane where the initial ion-channel changes occur, unlike ordinary axonal membrane, does not generate action potentials. Instead, in the case where the sensitive membrane is on the ending of the afferent neuron itself, local current flows from the receptor membrane a short distance along the axon to a region where the membrane threshold for generating action potentials is lower. In myelinated afferent neurons, this region is usually at the first node of Ranvier of the myelin sheath (Figure 9-2).

In the case where the sensitive membrane is on a separate cell, the receptor potential there causes the release of a neurotransmitter that diffuses across the extracellular cleft between the receptor cell and the afferent neuron and binds to specific sites on the afferent neuron as at a synapse. The combination of neurotransmitter with plasma-membrane receptors (here we are using the term in the sense of binding site) on the afferent neuron generates a graded potential in this neuron's end analagous to an excitatory postsynaptic potential.

As is true of all graded potentials, the magnitude of a receptor potential or, in the case just described, a graded potential in the axon adjacent to the receptor cell, decreases with distance from its origin, but if the amount of depolarization that reaches the first node in the afferent neuron is large enough to bring the membrane there to threshold, action potentials are initiated. The action potentials then propagate along the nerve fiber; the only

FIGURE 9-2
An afferent neuron with a receptor ending. The receptor potential arises at the nerve ending 1, and the action potential arises at the first node of the myelin sheath 2.

function of the graded potential is to trigger action potentials. (Turn to Figure 8-14 to review the properties of graded potentials.)

As long as the afferent neuron remains depolarized to threshold, action potentials continue to fire and propagate along the afferent neuron. With greater depolarizations, threshold is reached faster and the frequency of action potentials is greater, up to a limit.[1] Therefore, the magnitude of the graded potential determines the action-potential frequency in the afferent neuron. Although the graded-potential amplitude is a determinant of action-potential *frequency,* it does not determine action-potential *magnitude.* Since the action potential is all-or-none, its magnitude is independent of the strength of the initiating stimulus.

Factors that control the magnitude of the receptor potential include stimulus strength, rate of change of stimulus application, temporal summation of successive receptor potentials (Figure 8-14), and **adaptation**, which is a decrease in the frequency of action potentials in an afferent neuron despite maintenance of the stimulus at constant strength.

Adaptation of an afferent neuron can be seen in Figure 9-3. We shall see the significance of adaptation later when we discuss the coding of stimulus duration.

NEURAL PATHWAYS IN SENSORY SYSTEMS

The afferent neurons form the first link in a sensory pathway. A **sensory pathway** is made up of a group of neuron chains, each chain consisting of three or more neurons connected end to end by synapses. The chains in a given pathway run parallel to each other in the central nervous system and carry information to that part of the brain responsible for conscious recognition of the informa-

---

[1] The action-potential frequency is limited by the refractory period. Recall from Chapter 8 that during the absolute refractory period, no further action potentials can be generated, and during the relative refractory period, threshold is raised and the membrane must be depolarized more than usual to generate action potentials.

FIGURE 9-3
Action potentials in a single afferent nerve fiber showing adaptation to a stimulus of constant strength.

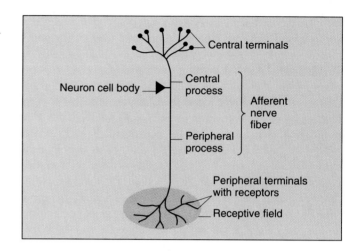

FIGURE 9-4
Sensory unit and receptive field.

tion, generally accepted to be the cerebral cortex. Sensory pathways are called **ascending pathways** because they go to the brain.

Sensory Units

A single afferent neuron with all its receptor endings makes up a **sensory unit**. In a few cases, the afferent neuron has a single receptor, but generally the peripheral end of an afferent neuron divides into many fine branches, each terminating at a receptor.

The portion of the body that, when stimulated, leads to activity in a particular afferent neuron is called the **receptive field** for that neuron (Figure 9-4). Receptive fields of neighboring afferent neurons overlap so that stimulation of a single point activates several sensory units; activation of a single sensory unit almost never occurs. As we shall see, the degree of overlap varies in different parts of the body.

Ascending Pathways

The central processes of the afferent neurons synapse upon interneurons in the brain or spinal cord. The central processes diverge to terminate on several, or many, interneurons (Figure 9-5A) and converge so that the processes of many afferent neurons terminate upon a single interneuron (Figure 9-5B). The interneurons upon which the afferent neurons synapse are termed second-order neurons, and these in turn synapse with third-order neurons, and so on, until the information reaches the cerebral cortex.

Some of the pathways convey information about only a single type of sensory information. Thus, one pathway may be influenced only by information from mechanoreceptors, whereas another may be influenced only by information from thermoreceptors. The ascending pathways in the

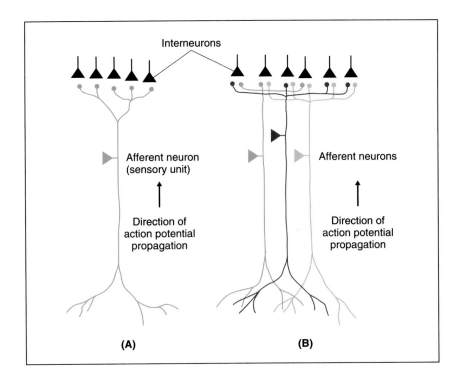

FIGURE 9-5

(A) Divergence of afferent neuron terminals. (B) Convergence of input from several afferent neurons onto single interneurons.

spinal cord and brain that carry information about single types of stimuli are known as the **specific ascending pathways**. The specific pathways, except for the olfactory pathways (which go to parts of the limbic system), pass to the brainstem and thalamus, and the final neurons in the pathways go from there to different areas of the cerebral cortex.

The specific ascending pathways that transmit information from **somatic receptors**, that is, the receptors in the framework or outer walls of the body, including skin, skeletal muscle, tendons, and joints, go to the **somatosensory cortex**, a strip of cortex that lies in the parietal lobe of the brain just behind the junction of the parietal and frontal lobes (Figure 9-6). The specific pathways from the eyes go

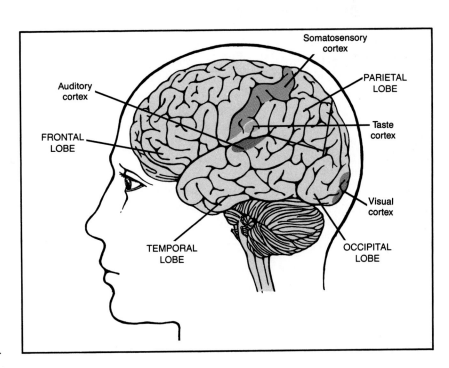

FIGURE 9-6

Primary sensory areas of the cerebral cortex.

to another primary cortical receiving area, the **visual cortex**, which is in the occipital lobe, and the specific pathways from the ears go to the **auditory cortex**, which is in the temporal lobe (Figure 9-6). Specific pathways from the taste buds pass to a cortical area adjacent to the face region of the somatosensory cortex. The pathways serving olfaction have no representation in the cerebral cortex.

In contrast to the specific ascending pathways, neurons in the **nonspecific ascending pathways** are activated by sensory units of several different types (Figure 9-7) and therefore signal only general information. In other words, they indicate that *something* is happening, without specifying just what or where. A given neuron in the nonspecific pathways may respond, for example, to input from several afferent neurons each activated by a different stimulus, such as maintained skin pressure, heating, cooling, and skin stretch. Such pathway neurons are called **polymodal neurons**. The nonspecific pathways—as well as collaterals from the specific pathways—feed into the brainstem reticular formation and regions of the thalamus and cerebral cortex that are not highly discriminative but are important in the control of alertness and arousal.

Finally, the processing of afferent information does not end in the primary cortical receiving areas but continues from these areas to association areas of the cerebral cortex.

ASSOCIATION CORTEX AND PERCEPTUAL PROCESSING

The **cortical association areas** (Figure 9-8) are brain areas that lie outside the primary cortical sensory or motor areas but are connected to them. The association areas are not considered part of the sensory pathways but rather play a role in the progressively more complex analysis of incoming information. They also serve integrative functions and are implicated in many forms of behavior.

The more central regions of association cortex receive information only after it has undergone initial processing by the association region closest to the primary receiving area. Some of the neurons in these central regions receive input concerning two or even three of the different types of sensory stimuli. These regions of association cortex are assumed to serve more complex functions. Thus, a neuron receiving input from both the visual cortex and the "neck" region of the somatosensory cortex might be concerned with integrating visual information with sensory information about head position so that, for example, a tree is understood to be vertical even though the viewer's head is tipped sideways.

Fibers from neurons of the posterior parietal lobe go to association areas in the frontal lobes that are part of the limbic system. Through these connections sensory infor-

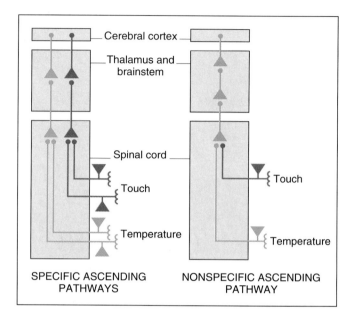

FIGURE 9-7
Diagrammatic representation of two specific sensory pathways and a nonspecific sensory pathway.

mation can be invested with emotional and motivational significance. Further perceptual processing involves not only arousal, attention, learning, memory, language, and emotions but also comparing the information presented via one type of sensation with that of another. For example, we may hear a growling dog, but our perception of the event varies markedly, depending upon whether our visual system detects that the sound source is an angry animal or a loudspeaker.

Factors That Distort Perception

We put great trust in our sensory-perceptual processes despite the inevitable modifications we know to exist. Some factors known to distort our perceptions of the real world are as follows:

1. Afferent information is distorted by receptor mechanisms, for example by adaptation, and by processing of the information along afferent pathways.
2. Factors such as emotions, personality, experience, and social background can influence perceptions so that two people can witness the same events and yet perceive them differently.
3. Not all information entering the central nervous system gives rise to conscious sensation. Actually, this is a very good thing because many unwanted signals are generated by the extreme sensitivity of our receptors. For example, under ideal conditions the rods of the eye can detect the flame of a candle 17 mi away. The hair cells of the ear can detect vibrations of an amplitude much

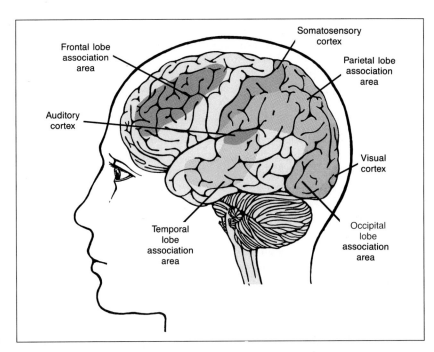

FIGURE 9-8

Areas of association cortex.

lower than those caused by blood flow through the ears' blood vessels and can even detect molecules in random motion bumping against the ear drum. Olfactory receptors respond to the presence of only four to eight odorous molecules. It is possible to detect one action potential generated by a certain type of mechanoreceptor. If no mechanisms existed to select, restrain, and organize the barrage of impulses from the periphery, life would be unbearable. Moreover, information in some receptors' afferent pathways is not canceled out—it simply does not give rise to a conscious sensation. For example, stretch receptors in the walls of some of the largest blood vessels effectively monitor both absolute blood pressure and its rate of change, but people have no conscious awareness of their blood pressure.

4. We lack suitable receptors for many energy forms. For example, we cannot directly detect ionizing radiation and radio or television waves.

5. Damaged neural networks may give faulty perceptions.

6. Some drugs alter perceptions.

Another example of distorted perception is the bizarre phenomenon known as ***phantom limb***, in which a limb that has been lost by accident or amputation is experienced as though it were still in place. The missing limb can be the "site" of tingling, touch, pressure, warmth, itch, wetness, pain, and even fatigue, and it is felt as though it were still a part of "self." It seems that the sensory neural networks in the central nervous system that exist genetically in everyone and are normally triggered by receptor activation are, instead, in the case of phantom limb, activated independently of peripheral input. The activated neural networks generate the usual sensations, which are perceived as arising from the missing receptors.

However, the most dramatic examples of a clear difference between the real world and our perceptual world can be found in illusions and drug- and disease-induced hallucinations, where whole worlds can be created.

Much can be learned about the processing of sensory experiences by studying the ways in which perceptions become distorted.

In summary, for perception to occur, three processes—transducing stimulus energy to action potentials by the receptor, transmitting data through the nervous system, and interpreting it—cannot be separated. Sensory information is processed at each synapse along the afferent pathways and at many levels of the central nervous system, with the more complex stages receiving input only after it has been processed by the more elementary systems. This hierarchical processing of afferent information along individual pathways is an important organizational principle of sensory systems. A second important principle is that information is processed by *parallel* pathways, each of which handles a limited aspect of the neural signals generated by the sensory transducers. Every synapse along the afferent pathways adds an element of organization and contributes to the sensory experience.

We turn now to the way a particular stimulus type, intensity, location, and duration are coded by the various receptors and sensory pathways.

PRIMARY SENSORY CODING

The sensory systems code four aspects of a stimulus: stimulus type, intensity, location, and duration.

Stimulus Type

Another term for stimulus type, that is, heat, cold, sound, or pressure, for example, is stimulus **modality**. Modalities can be divided into submodalities: Cold and warm are submodalities of temperature, whereas salt, sweet, bitter, and sour are submodalities of taste. The specific receptor type activated by a stimulus plays the primary role in coding the stimulus modality.

As mentioned earlier, a given receptor type is particularly sensitive to one stimulus modality because of the signal transduction mechanisms and ion channels incorporated in the receptor's plasma membrane. For example, receptors for vision, which contain pigment molecules whose shape is transformed by light, have intracellular mechanisms by which changes in the pigment molecules alter the activity of membrane ion channels and generate a neural signal. Receptors in the skin have neither light-sensitive molecules nor plasma-membrane ion channels that can be affected by them; thus, receptors in the eyes respond to light and those in the skin do not.

All the receptors of an afferent neuron are preferentially sensitive to the same type of stimulus. For example, they are all sensitive to cold or all to pressure. Adjacent sensory units may be sensitive to different types of stimuli. Since the receptive fields for different modalities overlap, a single stimulus—let us say an ice cube on the skin—can give rise simultaneously to the sensations of touch and temperature.

Regardless of the stimulus type and the receptors that respond to that particular stimulus, however, all information from receptors is transmitted in afferent neurons and throughout the central nervous system in the form of graded potentials and action potentials.

Stimulus Intensity

How is a strong stimulus distinguished from a weak one when the information about both stimuli is relayed by action potentials, which are all the same size? Action-potential *frequency* in a single afferent nerve fiber is one way, since increased stimulus strength means a larger receptor potential and a higher frequency of action-potential firing. A record of an experiment in which increased stimulus intensity is reflected in increased action-potential frequency in a single afferent nerve fiber is shown in Figure 9-9.

As stimulus strength increases, receptors on other branches of the same afferent neuron also begin to respond. The action potentials generated by these receptors propagate along the branches to the main afferent nerve fiber and add to the train of action potentials there (Figure 9-10).

In addition to increasing the firing frequency in a single afferent neuron, stronger stimuli usually affect a larger area and activate similar receptors on the endings of *other* afferent neurons. For example, when one touches a surface lightly with a finger, the area of skin in contact with the surface is small, and only receptors in that skin area are stimulated. Pressing down firmly increases the area of skin

FIGURE 9-9

Action potentials from the afferent fiber leading from a pressure receptor as the receptor is subjected to pressures of different magnitudes.

FIGURE 9-10

Simultaneous activation of two receptors in a sensory unit increases the number of action potentials transmitted along the afferent neuron. If, however, the main branch of the neuron is refractory because of just having transmitted an action potential, the transmission of further action potentials may be blocked for a brief time.

stimulated. This "calling in" of receptors on additional afferent neurons is known as **recruitment** or, sometimes, as spatial summation (*not* synaptic spatial summation).

Stimulus Location

A third type of information to be signaled is the location of the stimulus, in other words, where the stimulus is being applied. (It should be noted that in vision, hearing, and smell, stimulus location is interpreted as arising from the site from which the stimulus *originated* rather than the place on our body where the stimulus was actually *applied*. For example, we interpret the sight and sound of a barking dog as occurring in that furry thing on the other side of the fence rather than to a specific region of our eyes and ears. More will be said of this later; we deal here with the senses in which the stimulus is located to a site on the body.)

The main factor coding stimulus location is the site of the stimulated receptor. The precision (**acuity**) with which one stimulus can be located and differentiated from an adjacent one depends upon the amount of convergence of neuronal input in the specific ascending pathways. The greater the convergence, the less the acuity. Other factors affecting acuity are the size of the receptive field covered by the single sensory unit and the amount of overlap of nearby receptive fields. For example, it is easy to discriminate between two adjacent stimuli (two-point discrimination) applied to the skin on a finger, where the sensory units are small and the overlap considerable. It is harder to do so on the back, where the sensory units are large and widely spaced. Locating sensations from the internal organs is less precise than from the skin because there are fewer afferent neurons in the internal organs and each has a larger receptive field.

It is fairly simple to see why a stimulus to a neuron that has a small receptive field can be located more precisely than a stimulus to a neuron with a large receptive field (Figure 9-11). The fact is, however, that even in the

former case one cannot distinguish exactly where within a receptive field a stimulus has been applied. One can only tell that the afferent neuron has been activated. This is where receptive-field overlap aids stimulus localization even though, intuitively, overlap would seem to "muddy" the image. Let us examine more closely how overlap improves stimulus localization.

An afferent neuron responds most vigorously to stimuli applied at the center of its receptive field because the receptor density, that is, the number of receptors in a

FIGURE 9-11

The information from neuron A indicates the stimulus location more precisely than does that from neuron B because A's receptive field is smaller.

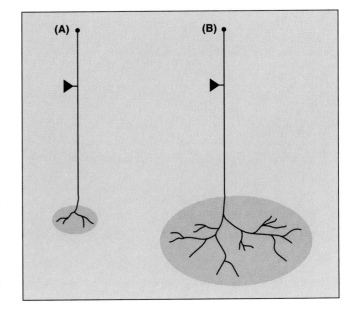

given area, is greatest there. The response decreases as the stimulus is moved toward the receptive-field periphery. Thus, a stimulus activates more receptors and generates more action potentials if it occurs at the center of the receptive field (point A in Figure 9-12). The firing frequency of the afferent neuron is also related to stimulus strength, however, and a high frequency of impulses in the single afferent nerve fiber of Figure 9-12 could mean either that a moderately intense stimulus was applied at A or that a strong stimulus was applied at B. Thus, neither the intensity nor the location of the stimulus can be detected precisely with a single afferent neuron.

Since the receptor endings of different afferent neurons overlap, however, a stimulus will trigger activity in more than one sensory unit. In Figure 9-13, neurons A and C, stimulated near the edge of their receptive fields where the receptor density is low, fire at a lower frequency than neuron B, stimulated at the center of its receptive field. In the group of sensory units in Figure 9-13, a high action-potential frequency in neuron B occurring simultaneously with a lower frequency in A and C permits a more accurate localization of the stimulus near the center of neuron B's receptive field. Once this location is known, the firing frequency of neuron B can be used to indicate stimulus intensity.

Lateral Inhibition. Far more important in localization of the stimulus site than the different sensitivity of receptors throughout the receptive field is the phenomenon of **lateral inhibition**. In lateral inhibition, information from receptors at the edge of a stimulus is inhibited, while information from the stimulus's center is enhanced. Figure

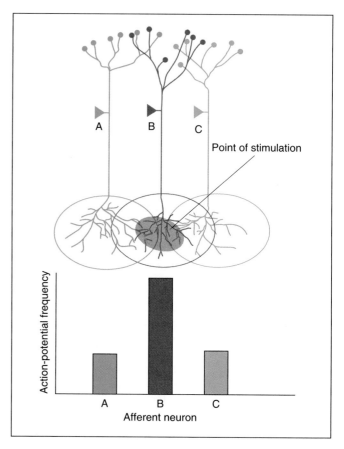

FIGURE 9-13

A stimulus point falls within the overlapping receptive fields of three afferent neurons. Note the difference in receptor response, that is, the action-potential frequency in the three neurons, due to the difference in receptor distribution under the stimulus (low receptor density in A and C, high in B).

FIGURE 9-12

Two stimulus points, A and B, in the receptive field of a single afferent neuron. The density of nerve endings in area A is greater than in B, and therefore the frequency of action-potentials to a stimulus in area A will be greater.

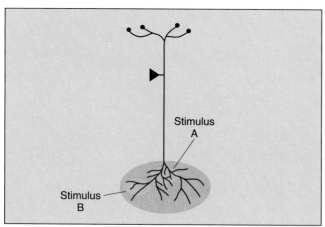

9-14 shows one neuronal arrangement that accomplishes lateral inhibition. Lateral inhibition can occur at different levels of the sensory pathways but typically happens at an early stage.

Lateral inhibition can be demonstrated in the following way. While pressing the tip of a pencil against your finger with your eyes closed, you can localize the pencil point precisely, even though the region around the pencil tip is also indented and mechanoreceptors within this region are activated (Figure 9-15). Exact localization occurs because the information from the peripheral regions is removed by lateral inhibition. Thus, lateral inhibition increases the contrast between "wanted" and "unwanted" information, thereby increasing the effectiveness of selected pathways and focusing sensory-processing mechanisms on "important" messages.

Lateral inhibition is utilized to the greatest degree in the pathways providing the most accurate localization. For

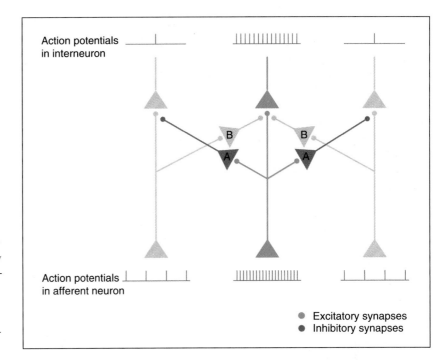

FIGURE 9-14

Afferent pathways showing lateral inhibition. The central fiber at the beginning of the pathway (bottom of figure) is firing at the highest frequency and inhibits, via inhibitory neurons A, the lateral neurons more strongly than the lateral pathways inhibit it, via inhibitory neurons B. Thus, because of lateral inhibition, the lateral pathways are inhibited more strongly than the central pathway and the contrast between the activity in the adjacent pathways is enhanced.

example, movement of skin hairs, which we can locate quite well, activates pathways that have significant lateral inhibition, but temperature and pain, which we can locate only poorly, activate pathways that use lateral inhibition to a lesser degree.

Stimulus Duration

Receptors differ in the way they respond to a constantly maintained stimulus. The response—that is, the action-potential frequency—at the beginning of the stimulus indicates the stimulus strength, but after this initial response, the frequency differs widely in different types of receptors. Some receptors respond very rapidly at the stimulus onset and, after their initial burst of activity, fire only very slowly or stop firing all together during the remainder of the stimulus. These are the **rapidly adapting receptors** (or phasic receptors), and they are important in signaling change, for example, vibrating or moving stimuli. (Recall that adaptation is a decline in a receptor's response despite the continued application of a constant stimulus.)

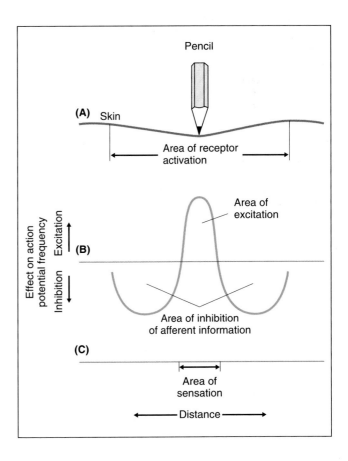

FIGURE 9-15

(A) A pencil tip pressed against the skin depresses the surrounding tissue. Receptors are activated under the pencil tip and in the adjacent tissue. (B) Because of lateral inhibition, the central area of excitation is surrounded by an area where the afferent information is inhibited. (C) The sensation is localized to a more restricted region than that in which mechanoreceptors were actually stimulated.

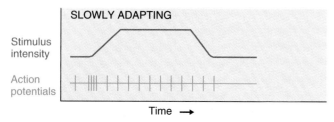

FIGURE 9-16

Rapidly and slowly adapting receptors. The top line (red) indicates application of the stimulus, and the bottom line (green), the action potential firing of the afferent nerve fiber from the receptor.

Some receptors adapt so rapidly that they fire only a single action potential at the onset of a stimulus, while others respond at the beginning of the stimulus and again at its removal. The rapid fading of the sensation of our clothes pressing on our skin is due to rapidly adapting receptors.

Slowly adapting receptors (or tonic receptors) maintain their response at or near the initial level of firing regardless of the stimulus duration (Figure 9-16). These receptors signal slow changes or prolonged events, such as occur in the joint and muscle receptors that participate in the maintenance of upright posture when we are standing or sitting for long periods of time.

Central Control of Afferent Information

All sensory information is subject to extensive control at the various synaptic junctions along the ascending pathways before it reaches higher levels of the central nervous system. Much of the incoming information is reduced or even abolished by inhibition from collaterals from other neurons in ascending pathways—an example being lateral inhibition, discussed earlier—or by pathways descending downward from higher regions. The reticular formation and cerebral cortex in particular control much afferent information via descending pathways. The inhibitory controls may be exerted directly by synapses on the axon terminals of the primary afferent neurons (an example of presynaptic inhibition, introduced in Chapter 8) or indirectly via interneurons that affect other neurons in the sensory pathways via inhibitory synapses (Figure 9-17).

In some cases, for example pain pathways, the afferent input is continuously, that is, tonically, inhibited to some degree. This provides the flexibility of either removing the inhibition (disinhibition) so as to allow a greater degree of signal transmission or of increasing the inhibition so as to block the signal more completely.

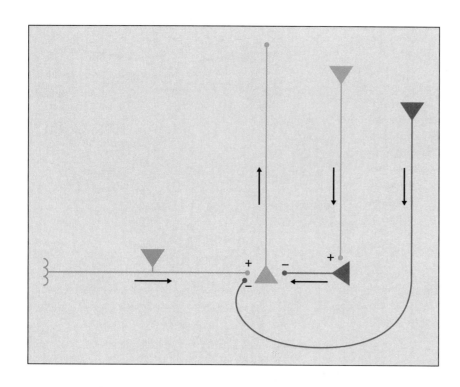

FIGURE 9-17

Descending pathways may control sensory information by directly inhibiting the central terminals of the afferent neuron (an example of presynaptic inhibition) or via an interneuron that affects the ascending pathway by inhibitory synapses. Neurons ending in excitatory synapses are green; those ending in inhibitory synapses are red. Arrows indicate the direction of action-potential transmission.

This completes our general introduction to sensory system pathways and coding. We now present the individual systems, covering the somatic sensations and vision in greater detail than the others because they serve as good models for the principles of sensory system organization that appear in all the sensory systems. These principles are (1) a specific sensory pathway codes for the particular modality being discussed; (2) information is organized such that initial processing of the various modalities occurs in different parts of the brain; (3) the ascending pathways are crossed so that sensory information is processed by the side of the brain opposite the side of the body that was stimulated; and (4) in addition to other synaptic relay points, all ascending pathways, except for those involved in taste, synapse in the thalamus.

SOMATIC SENSATION

Sensation from the skin, body walls, muscles, bones, tendons, and joints is termed **somatic sensation** and is initiated by a variety of somatic receptors (Figure 9-18). Some respond to mechanical stimulation of the skin, hairs,

and underlying tissues, whereas others respond to temperature changes and some chemical changes. Activation of somatic receptors gives rise to the sensations of touch, pressure, warmth, cold, pain, and awareness of the position of the body parts and their movement. (Visceral sensations, which arise in the organs of the thoracic and abdominal cavities, originate in the same kinds of receptors that give rise to somatic sensations. Only the receptor locations differ.)

Each sensation is associated with a specific receptor type. In other words, there are distinct receptors for heat, cold, touch, pressure, limb position or movement, and pain. After entering the central nervous system, the afferent nerve fibers from the somatic receptors synapse on neurons that form the specific ascending pathways going primarily to the somatosensory cortex via the brainstem and thalamus. They also synapse on interneurons that give rise to the nonspecific pathways. The location of some important ascending pathways is shown in a cross section of the spinal cord (Figure 9-19A), and two are diagrammed in Figure 9-19B and C.

Note that the pathways cross from the side at which the afferent neurons enter the central nervous system to the opposite side in the spinal cord (Figure 9-19B) or brain-

FIGURE 9-18

Skin receptors. Some nerve fibers, usually those with little or no myelin, have free nerve terminals not related to any apparent receptor structures. These terminals are sensitive to stimuli that give rise to pain and temperature. Thicker, myelinated axons, on the other hand, end in receptors that can be quite complex, for example, the lamellated (Pacinian) corpuscle, the tactile (Meissner's and Merkel's) corpuscles, and the corpuscle of Ruffini. These are all mechanoreceptors, sensitive to displacement of the skin: The Pacinian corpuscles are especially sensitive to vibration and other rapid changes, the Meissner corpuscle to slow flutter, and the corpuscles of Ruffini and Merkel disks to sustained pressure. One afferent fiber connects to only one type of receptor so that the information coded by the different receptor types is kept separate.

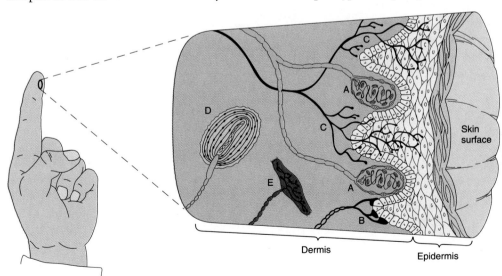

A – Tactile (Meissner's) corpuscle
B – Tactile (Merkle's) corpuscles
C – Free terminal
D – Lamellated (Pacinian) corpuscle
E – Ruffini corpuscle

(A)

(C)

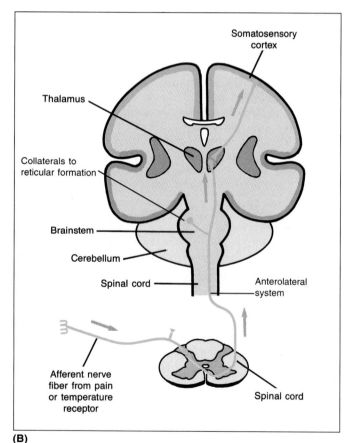

(B)

FIGURE 9-19

(A) A cross section of the spinal cord, showing the relative locations of the major ascending fiber tracts. Two pathways, the fasciculus gracilis and the fasciculus cuneatus, make up the dorsal columns. The dorsal (posterior) and ventral (anterior) spinocerebellar tracts carry information from the muscles or tendons. (B) The anterolateral system conveys information associated primarily with pain and temperature. The three pathways that constitute this system each convey information about a different component of pain. (C) The posterior (dorsal) columns, which relay information related to vibration, joint position, and the ability to discriminate between two points placed near each other on the skin. Information carried over collaterals to the reticular formation in B and C contribute to alertness and arousal mechanisms. (*Parts B and C adapted from Gardner.*)

In the somatosensory cortex, the axonal endings of the individual fibers of the specific somatic pathways are grouped according to the location of the receptors giving rise to the pathways (Figure 9-20). The parts of the body that are most densely innervated—fingers, thumb, and lips—are represented by the largest areas of the somatosensory cortex.

Touch-Pressure

Stimulation of the variety of mechanoreceptors in the skin (Figure 9-18) leads to a wide range of touch-pressure ex-

stem (Figure 9-19C). Thus, the sensory pathways from somatic receptors on the left side of the body go to the somatosensory cortex of the right cerebral hemisphere, and vice versa.

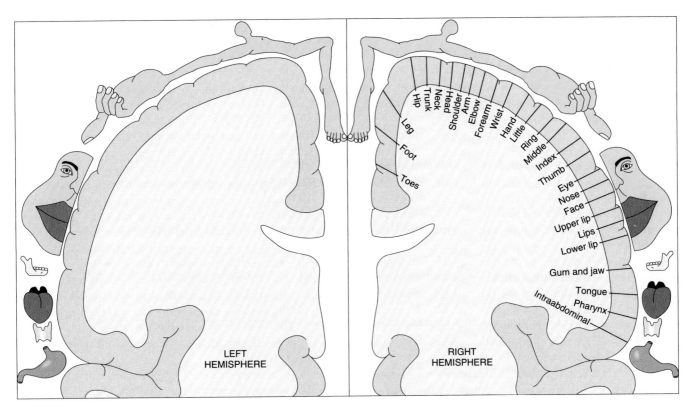

FIGURE 9-20
Location of pathway terminations for different parts of the body in the somatosensory cortex.
The left half of the body is represented on the right hemisphere of the brain, and the right
half of the body is represented on the left hemisphere.

periences—hair bending, deep pressure, and superficial touch, for example. The skin mechanoreceptors adapt at different rates, about half adapting rapidly (that is, they fire only when the stimulus is changing), and the others adapting slowly. Activation of rapidly adapting receptors gives rise to the sensations of touch, movement, and vibration, whereas slowly adapting receptors give rise to the sensation of pressure.

In both categories, some receptors have small, well-defined receptive fields and are able to provide precise information about the contours of objects indenting the skin. As might be expected, these receptors are concentrated at the fingertips. In contrast, other receptors have large receptive fields with obscure boundaries, sometimes covering a whole finger or a large part of the palm. These receptors are not involved in detailed spatial discrimination but signal information about vibration, skin stretch, and joint movement.

It is probable that the receptor mechanisms for the senses of touch and pressure depend on mechanosensitive ion channels, which open (or close) when pressure applied to the plasma membrane increases the tension in the membrane. The tension is transmitted to the channels via elements of the cytoskeleton that are attached to the membrane.

Sense of Posture and Movement

The senses of posture and movement are complex. The major receptors responsible for these senses are the muscle-spindle stretch receptors, which occur in skeletal muscles and respond both to the absolute magnitude of muscle stretch and to the rate at which the stretch occurs (Chapter 12). The senses of posture and movement are also supported by vision and the vestibular organs (the "sense organs of balance," to be described below). Mechanoreceptors in the joints, tendons, ligaments, and skin also play a role. The term **kinesthesia** is often used for the sense of movement at a joint.[2]

Temperature

There are two types of thermoreceptors in the skin, each of which responds to a limited range of temperature.

---

[2]The term "proprioception" is sometimes used for the sense of the body's position in space, but this term is not well defined and we have chosen not to use it.

Warmth receptors respond to temperatures between 30 and 43°C with an increased discharge rate upon warming, whereas receptors for cold are stimulated by temperatures between 35 and 20°C and increase their discharge rate upon cooling. It is not known how heat or cold alters the endings of the thermosensitive afferent neurons to generate receptor potentials.

Pain

A stimulus that causes (or is on the verge of causing) tissue damage usually elicits a sensation of pain. Pain differs from the other somatosensory modalities in that such emotions as fear and anxiety and feelings of unpleasantness are experienced along with the perceived sensation. Also, a painful stimulus can evoke a reflex escape or withdrawal response as well as a gamut of physiological changes similar to those elicited during fear, rage, and aggression. These changes, mediated by the sympathetic nervous system, include increased heart rate and blood pressure, greater secretion of epinephrine into the bloodstream, increased blood glucose concentration, decreased gastric motility, decreased blood flow to the viscera and skin, dilation of the pupils, and sweating. In other words, the stimuli that give rise to pain result in a sensory experience *plus* a reaction to it.

Probably more than any other type of sensation, pain can be altered by past experiences, suggestion, emotions (particularly anxiety), and the simultaneous activation of other sensory modalities. Thus, the level of pain is not solely a physical property of the stimulus as, for example, shape is. Instead, painfulness depends in part on the subjective opinion of the person receiving the stimulus.

The receptors, known as **nociceptors**, whose stimulation gives rise to pain are located at the ends of small unmyelinated or lightly myelinated afferent neurons. These receptors have high thresholds and respond to intense mechanical and thermal stimulation or to irritant chemicals. Chemicals such as H^+, K^+, histamine, bradykinin, and prostaglandins released from nearby damaged tissue may depolarize nociceptor nerve endings, initiating action potentials in the afferent nerve fibers.

In addition, these chemicals may alter the nociceptors themselves so that their threshold is decreased and their response to later painful stimuli is increased. They may even fire spontaneously. This increase in sensitivity to painful stimuli, known as *hyperalgesia*, can last hours after the original stimulus is over. Inhibition of prostaglandin production at the stimulation site by aspirin and aspirin-like drugs (Chapter 7) partially accounts for their effectiveness in the relief of hyperalgesia.

The primary afferents coming from nociceptors synapse on interneurons after entering the central nervous system. Substance P is one of the transmitters released at this site. Pain information is mediated by three ascending pathways that together are known as the **anterolateral system**. They convey information that leads to both the localization of pain and its affective component.

Reflecting the diverse influences on pain perception, neurons in the central-nervous-system pain pathways are subject to both short- and long-term changes in excitability and show a high degree of plasticity, or alterability. Thus, a neuron may or may not respond to a given nociceptive input, depending on the circumstances, and stimuli that are not normally painful may become so.

The activation of interneurons by incoming nociceptive afferents may lead to the phenomenon of *referred pain*, in which the sensation of pain is experienced at a site other than the injured or diseased part. For example, during a heart attack, pain is often experienced in the left arm. This type of referred pain occurs because both visceral and somatic afferents often converge on the same interneurons in the pain pathways. Excitation of the somatic afferent fibers is the more usual source of afferent discharge, so we "refer" the location of receptor activation to the somatic source even though, in the case of visceral pain, the perception is incorrect.

Electrical stimulation of specific areas of the central nervous system can produce a profound reduction in pain, a phenomenon called *stimulation-produced analgesia*, by inhibiting pain pathways. Parts of the thalamus, central region of the brainstem, and spinal cord at the level of entry of the active nociceptor afferents have all been electrically stimulated with some success in alleviating pain.

Analgesia occurs from such stimulation because descending pathways that originate in these brain areas selectively inhibit the transmission of information originating in nociceptors. The descending axons end at lower brainstem and spinal levels on interneurons in the pain pathways as well as on the synaptic terminals of the afferent nociceptor neurons themselves. Some of the neurons in these inhibitory pathways release or are sensitive to certain endogenous opioids (Chapter 8). Thus, infusion of morphine, which stimulates opioid receptors, into the spinal cord at the level of entry of the active nociceptor fibers can provide relief in many cases of intractable pain. This is separate from morphine's effect on the brain.

Transcutaneous electric nerve stimulation, or *TENS*, in which the painful site itself or the nerves leading from it are stimulated by electrodes placed on the surface of the skin, is often useful in lessening pain. TENS works because the stimulation of nonpain, low-threshold afferent fibers (for example, the fibers from touch receptors) leads to inhibition of neurons in the pain pathways. We often apply our own type of TENS therapy when we rub or press hard on a painful area, utilizing the fact that pathways activated by the touch receptors add inhibitory synaptic input to the pain pathways.

Under certain circumstances *acupuncture* prevents or

alleviates pain. During acupuncture analgesia, needles are introduced into specific parts of the body to stimulate afferent fibers, which causes analgesia in the same way as TENS. The endogenous opioid neurotransmitters may be involved in acupuncture analgesia.

Stimulation-produced analgesia, TENS, and acupuncture work by exploiting the body's built-in mechanisms that control pain.

VISION

The eyes are composed of an optical portion, which focuses the visual image on the receptor cells, and a neural component, which transforms the visual image into a pattern of neural discharges. The receptors of the eye are sensitive only to that tiny portion of the vast spectrum of electromagnetic radiation that we call visible light (Figure 9-21).

Light

Radiant energy is described in terms of wavelengths and frequencies. The **wavelength** is the distance between two successive wave peaks of the electromagnetic radiation (Figure 9-22). Wavelengths can vary from several kilometers at the long-wave radio end of the spectrum to minute fractions of a millimeter at the γ-ray end. The **frequency**, or the number of cycles per second, of the radiation wave varies inversely with wavelength. Those wavelengths capable of stimulating the receptors of the eye—the **visible spectrum**—are between 400 and 700 nm. Light of different wavelengths in this band is perceived as having different colors.

The Optics of Vision

A light wave can be represented by a line drawn in the direction in which the wave is traveling. Light waves are propagated in all directions from every point of a visible object. Before an accurate image of the object is achieved, these divergent light waves must pass through an optical system that focuses them back into a point. In the eye, the image of the object being viewed is focused upon the **retina**, a thin layer of neural tissue lining the back of the eyeball (Figure 9-23). The retina contains the light-sensitive receptor cells of the eye.

The **lens** and **cornea** of the eye are the optical systems that focus an image upon the retina. At a boundary between two substances, such as the cornea and the air, light rays are bent so that they travel in a new direction. The cornea plays a larger role than the lens in focusing light rays because the rays are bent more in passing from air into the cornea than they are when passing into and out of the lens or any other transparent structure of the eye.

FIGURE 9-21

Electromagnetic spectrum.

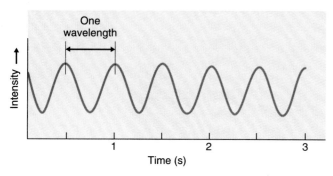

FIGURE 9-22

Properties of a wave. The frequency of this wave is 2 Hz (cycles/s).

The surface of the cornea is curved so that light rays coming from a single point source hit the cornea at different angles and are bent different amounts, directing the light rays back to a point after emerging from the lens. The image on the retina is upside-down relative to the original light source (Figure 9-24), and it is also reversed right to left.

Light rays from objects close to the eye strike the cornea at greater angles and must be bent more in order to reconverge on the retina. Although, as noted above, the cornea performs the greater part quantitatively of focusing the visual image on the retina, all *adjustments* for distance are made by changes in lens shape. Such changes are part of the process known as **accommodation**.

The shape of the lens is controlled by the **ciliary muscle** and the tension it applies to the **zonular fibers**, which attach this smooth muscle to the lens (Figure 9-25). The zonular fibers pull the lens into a flattened, oval shape, and when their pull is removed, the natural elasticity of the lens causes it to become more spherical. This more spherical shape provides additional bending of the light rays, which is important when near objects are viewed. The ciliary muscle, which is controlled by parasympathetic nerves, is circular, like a sphincter, so that it draws nearer to the lens as it contracts and therefore removes tension on the zonular fibers. Accommodation for viewing near objects (Figure 9-26) also includes moving the lens slightly toward the back of the eye, turning the eyes inward toward the nose (convergence), and constricting the pupil. The sequence of events for accommodation is reversed when distant objects are viewed.

The cells that make up most of the lens lose all their internal membranous structures early in life and are thus transparent, but they lack the ability to replicate. The only lens cells that retain the capacity to divide are on the surface of the lens, and as new cells are formed, older cells come to lie deeper within the lens. With increasing age, the central part of the lens becomes increasingly dense and stiff and acquires a coloration that progresses from yellow to black.

Since the lens must be elastic to assume a rounder shape during accommodation for near vision, the increasing stiffness of the lens that occurs with aging makes accommodation for near vision increasingly difficult. This

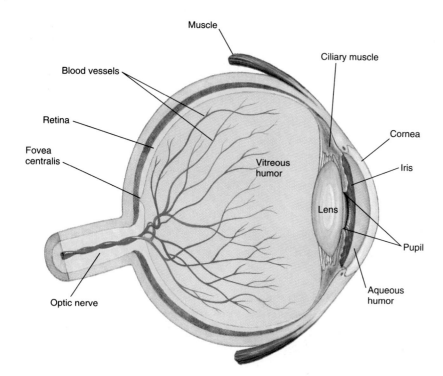

FIGURE 9-23

The human eye. The blood vessels depicted run along the back of the eye between the retina and the vitreous humor, not through the vitreous humor.

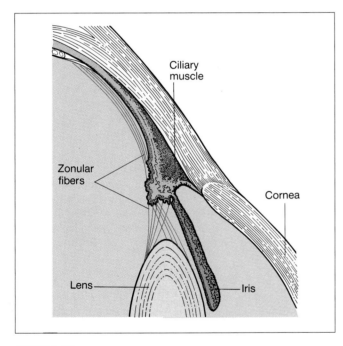

FIGURE 9-24

Refraction (bending) of light by the lens system of the eye. The focusing of light rays from a single point, for example, a, forms a single point, a′, on the retina. The focusing of light rays from more than one point forms an image that is inverted and, not shown here, reversed right to left. In reality, the image is not focused where the optic nerve leaves the eye, which is a "blind spot." Rather, the image is focused on the fovea centralis, the area of the retina with greatest clarity, which is near the exit of the nerve. In this figure and in Figure 9-26, for simplicity we show light refraction at the cornea where the greatest effect occurs. Refraction actually occurs at multiple sites in the eye.

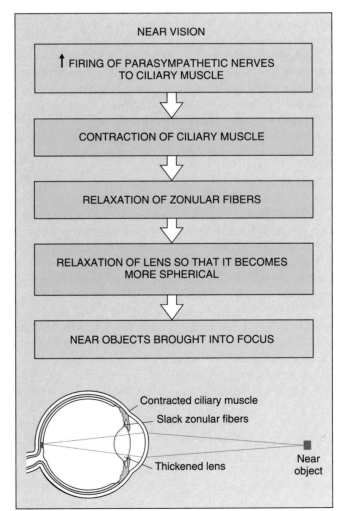

FIGURE 9-25

Ciliary muscle, zonular fibers, and lens of the eye. (*Redrawn from Davson.*)

FIGURE 9-26

Accommodation of the lens for near vision. Again, for simplicity, refraction is shown only at the cornea even though it occurs at several sites and the change in refraction during accommodation is a function of the lens.

condition, known as ***presbyopia***, is a normal part of the aging process and is the reason that people around 45 years of age may have to begin wearing reading glasses or bifocals for close work.

The changes in lens color that occur with aging are responsible for ***cataract***, which is an opacity of the lens and one of the most common eye disorders. Early changes in lens color do not interfere with vision, but vision is impaired as the process slowly continues. The opaque lens can be removed surgically. With the aid of compensating eyeglasses, contact lenses, or even an implanted artificial lens, effective vision can then be restored, although the ability to accommodate will be lost.

Cornea and lens shape and eyeball length determine the point where light rays reconverge. Defects in vision occur if the eyeball is too long in relation to the lens size. In this case, the images of near objects fall on the retina but the images of far objects focus at a point in front of the retina. This is a ***nearsighted***, or ***myopic***, eye, which is unable to see distant objects clearly. If the eye is too short for the lens, images of distant objects are focused on the retina but those of near objects are focused behind it. This eye is ***farsighted***, or ***hyperopic***, and near vision is poor. The use of corrective lenses for near- and farsighted vision is shown in Figure 9-27.

Defects in vision also occur where the lens or cornea does not have a smoothly spherical surface, a condition known as ***astigmatism***. These surface imperfections can usually be compensated for by eyeglasses.

The lens separates two fluid-filled chambers in the eye, the anterior chamber, which contains aqueous humor, and the posterior chamber, which contains the more viscous vitreous humor (Figure 9-23). These two substances are colorless and permit the transmission of light from the front of the eye to the retina. The aqueous humor is formed by special vascular tissue that overlies the ciliary muscle. In some instances the aqueous humor is formed faster than it is removed, which results in increased pressure within the eye, a condition known as ***glaucoma***. This can be associated with damage to nerve fibers of the eye and loss of vision.

The amount of light entering the eye is controlled by a ringlike pigmented muscle known as the **iris** (Figure 9-23), the color being of no importance as long as the tissue is sufficiently opaque to prevent the passage of light. The hole in the center of the iris through which light enters the eye is the **pupil**. The iris is composed of smooth muscles, which are innervated by autonomic nerves. Stimulation of sympathetic nerves to the iris causes the radially arranged muscle fibers to contract and enlarges the pupil. Stimulation of parasympathetic fibers to the iris causes the sphincter muscle fibers, which circle around the pupil, to contract and to make the pupil smaller.

These neurally induced changes occur in response to

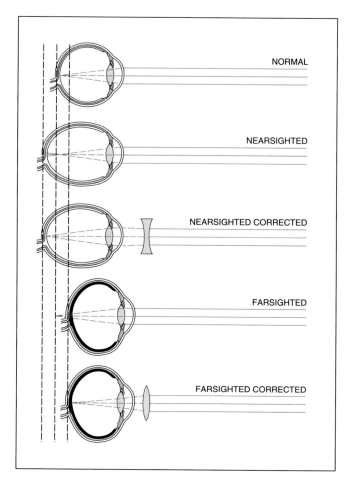

FIGURE 9-27

In the nearsighted eye, light rays from a distant source are focused in front of the retina. A concave (cupping inward) lens placed before the eye bends the light rays out sufficiently to move the focused image back onto the retina. In contrast, in the farsighted eye, near objects are focused behind the retina, and they are blurred. A convex—bulging outward—lens converges light rays before they enter the eye so that images of near objects can be focused on the retina. (*Redrawn from Patton et al.*)

light-sensitive reflexes. Bright light causes a decrease in the diameter of the pupil, which not only reduces the amount of light entering the eye but, more important, directs the light to the central part of the lens for more accurate vision. Conversely, the sphincter fibers relax in dim light, when maximal illumination is needed.

Receptor Cells

The photoreceptor cells in the retina are called **rods** and **cones** because of the shapes of their light-sensitive tips (Figure 9-28). Note in Figures 9-28 and 9-29 that the light-sensitive portion of the photoreceptor cells faces *away* from the incoming light. The rods are extremely sen-

FIGURE 9-28

Organization of the retina. Light enters the eye through the lens and passes through the vitreous humor and the front surface of the retina. Since the tips of the rods and cones are on the side of the retina opposite the light entry, the light must pass through all the retinal cell layers before reaching the photoreceptors and stimulating them. The pigmented layer of the eye (the choroid), which lies behind the retina, absorbs light and prevents light reflection back to the rods and cones. Reflection of this light would cause the visual image to be blurred. *(Redrawn from Dowling and Boycott.)*

sitive and respond to very low levels of illumination, whereas the cones are considerably less sensitive and respond only when the light is brighter than, for example, twilight.

Photoreceptors contain molecules called **photopigments**, which absorb light. There are four different photopigments in the retina, one **(rhodopsin)** in the rods and one in each of the three cone types. Each photopigment contains one of a group of integral proteins collectively known as **opsin**, which surrounds and binds a **chromo-**

phore molecule (Figure 9-29). The chromophore, which is the actual light-sensitive part of the photopigment, is the same in each of the four photopigments and is **retinal**, a slight variant of vitamin A. The opsin, which filters the light reaching the retinal, differs in each of the four types. The different opsins cause each of the four photopigments to absorb light most effectively at a different part of the visible spectrum. For example, one photopigment absorbs wavelengths in the range of red light best, whereas another absorbs green light best.

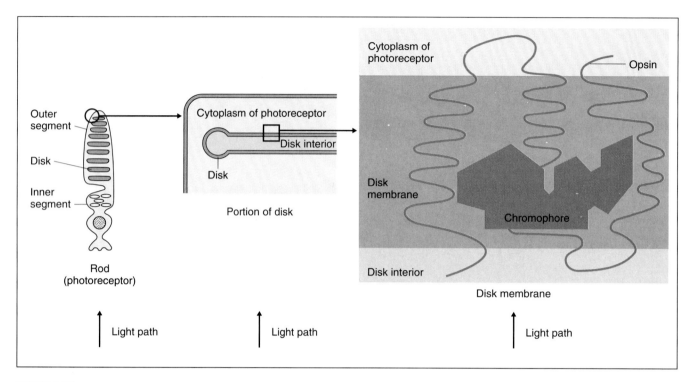

FIGURE 9-29

The arrangement of opsin and chromophore in the membrane of the photoreceptor disks. The opsin actually crosses the membrane seven times, not three as shown here. Note that the chromophore is perpendicular to the incoming light rays so that its ability to "catch" light is maximal.

Within the photoreceptor cells the photopigments lie in specialized membranes that are arranged in highly ordered stacks, or disks, parallel to the retina (Figure 9-29). The repeated layers of membranes in each photoreceptor may contain over a billion molecules of photopigment, providing an effective trap for light.

Light activates a molecule of retinal and causes it to change shape (Figure 9-30). This change facilitates the binding of opsin to a G protein, which activates the enzyme phosphodiesterase. This enzyme in turn hydrolyzes cyclic GMP, thereby decreasing its concentration. Thus, in light, photoreceptor cyclic GMP concentrations are low, and plasma-membrane ion channels controlled by this second messenger are closed. Plasma-membrane pumps continue to pump Ca^{2+} out of the photoreceptor and the cell *hyperpolarizes*. The hyperpolarization is conducted passively to the end of the photorecepter cell where it *decreases* the rate of neurotransmitter release from the cell. The decreased neurotransmitter concentration signals those neurons that synapse with the photoreceptor that light has been absorbed by the receptor. Note that in the case of photoreceptors, the receptor potential is a *hyperpolarization*.

In darkness, the cyclic GMP in the photoreceptors is high. The plasma-membrane ion channels are open, permitting Na^+ and Ca^{2+} to enter the cell and *depolarize* the membrane, and transmitter release is therefore high in the dark.

After its activation by light, the retinal changes shape back to its resting shape by several mechanisms that do not depend on light but are enzyme-mediated.

High sensitivity of the visual receptors is not always an advantage. If the receptor is saturated by high light levels, it cannot respond to information about further small increases or decreases. Light exposure, however, in addition to altering the cyclic GMP cascade, also initiates a sequence of events that decrease the sensitivity of the photo-transduction process to further light stimulation. This altered sensitivity, known as **light adaptation**, is achieved by control of cyclic GMP levels by intracellular Ca^{2+}.

Neural Pathways of Vision

The neural pathways of vision begin with the rods and cones. These photoreceptors interact with each other and with second-order neurons, one of which is the **bipolar**

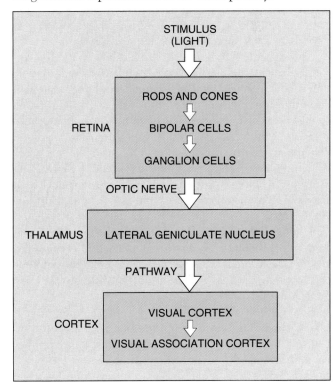

FIGURE 9-30
The change in retinal, the chromophore portion of the photopigment, in response to light.

cell (Figures 9-28 and 9-31). The bipolar cells respond differentially to the various characteristics of visual images, such as color, intensity, form, depth, and movement. These distinct characteristics are transmitted through the visual system along multiple, parallel pathways. This parallel processing of information continues all the way to the cerebral cortex, to the highest stages of visual neural networks.

The bipolar cells synapse (still within the retina) both upon neurons that pass information horizontally from one part of the retina to another and upon the **ganglion cells**. A great deal of information processing takes place at this early stage of the sensory pathway.

Ganglion cells are of two types, so-called magnocellular (M) and parvocellular (P) cells, each of which is concerned with different aspects of the visual stimulus. (It must be noted that in this discussion of the visual pathway, the term "response" denotes not a direct response to a light stimulus—only the rods and cones show such responses—but rather to the synaptic input reaching the relevant pathway neuron as a consequence of the original stimulus to the rods and cones.) The P cells respond best to small, stationary stimuli in the center of the visual image and are suited to deal with fine details. M cells, on the other hand, respond best to larger, moving stimuli at the edge of the visual image and are best suited to analyzing the gross features of a stimulus and to detecting motion. The P cells, as we shall see, also transmit information about color.

Ganglion cells respond to activation by producing action potentials, whereas the rods and cones and almost

FIGURE 9-31
Diagrammatic representation of the visual pathway.

all other retinal neurons produce only graded potentials. The axons of the ganglion cells form the output from the retina—the optic nerve, or cranial nerve II—which leads into the brain. The two optic nerves meet at the base of the brain to form the optic chiasm, where some of the fibers cross to the opposite side of the brain, providing both cerebral hemispheres with input from each eye.

Optic nerve fibers project to several structures in the brain, the largest number passing to the **lateral geniculate nucleus** in the thalamus (Figure 9-31), where the information from P and M ganglion cells is kept distinct. In addition to the input from the retina, many neurons of the lateral geniculate nucleus also receive input from the brainstem reticular formation and input relayed back from the visual cortex. These nonretinal inputs can control the transmission of information from the retina to the visual cortex and may be involved in the ability to shift attention between vision and the other sensory modalities or between different objects in the visual field.

The lateral geniculate nucleus sends action potentials on to the visual cortex, the primary visual area of cerebral cortex (Figure 9-6). The visual cortex has several subdivisions, each representing the complete **visual field**, that part of the visual world that stimulates the retina at any given time. Just as in the somatosensory system, the visual cortex on one side of the brain receives input from the opposite visual field. For example, the visual cortex in the left cerebral hemisphere receives information about what is out in the visual world on the right side of the head. The relay of information from the retina to the various areas of the visual cortex follows a precise point-to-point projection pattern so that adjacent retinal regions project to adjacent regions in each subdivision of the visual cortex.

The separate functions of cells, which began in the retina, are maintained in the visual cortex. In fact, an important aspect of lateral geniculate function is to separate and relay different kinds of visual information from the retina to different cortical zones. Thus, most neurons in one subdivision of the visual cortex are responsive only to stimuli oriented in a particular direction in the visual field, a property important in elaboration of the form of an object. The neurons in another subdivision are most responsive to movement of an object across the visual field. Furthermore, other neuronal groups may respond best to color, and others only to input from both eyes, an important clue to depth perception. Again, the functional differences between various areas of the visual cortex are determined by the input these areas receive from the distinct classes of ganglion cells.

Some of the information is kept separate even after it leaves the visual cortex. For example, some pathways transmit information from the visual cortex to the temporal lobe, where the identification of objects in the visual field is processed—analyzing the "what" of the visual stimulus. Other pathways travel to the parietal lobe, where information about the location of objects in the visual field is processed—analyzing the "where" of the visual stimulus. Output from both the temporal and parietal lobes then passes to the frontal cortex, which uses the visual information, for example, in directing actions. Thus, different aspects of visual information are carried in parallel pathways and are processed simultaneously in a number of independent ways in different parts of the cerebral cortex before they are reintegrated to produce the conscious sensation of sight.

Note that the cells of the visual pathways are organized to handle information about line, contrast, movement, and color. They do not, however, form a picture in the brain. Rather, they form a spatial and temporal pattern of electrical activity.

We mentioned that a substantial number of fibers of the visual pathway project to regions of the brain other than the visual cortex. For example, visual information is transmitted to the **suprachiasmatic nucleus**, which lies just above the optic chiasm and plays a major role in a variety of circadian behaviors, as described in Chapter 7. This nucleus functions as a "biological clock," and information about diurnal cycles of light intensity is used to synchronize this neuronal clock. Other visual information is passed to the brainstem and cerebellum, where it is used in the coordination of eye and head movements, fixation of gaze, and constriction of the pupils.

Color Vision

The colors we perceive are related to the wavelengths of light that are reflected, absorbed, or transmitted by the pigments in the objects of our visual world. For example, an object appears red because shorter wavelengths, which would be perceived as blue, are absorbed by the object, while the longer wavelengths, perceived as red, are reflected to excite the photopigment of the retina most sensitive to red. Light perceived as white is a mixture of all wavelengths, and black is the absence of all light.

Color vision begins with activation of the photopigments in the cone receptor cells. Human retinas have three kinds of cones, which contain red-, green-, or blue-sensitive photopigments. As their names imply, these pigments absorb and hence respond optimally to light of different wavelengths. Because the red pigment is actually more sensitive to the wavelengths that correspond to yellow, this pigment is sometimes called the yellow photopigment.

Although each type of cone is excited most effectively by light of one particular wavelength, it responds to other wavelengths as well. Thus, for any given wavelength, the three cone types are excited to different degrees (Figure 9-32). For example, in response to light of 530-nm wavelength, the green cones respond maximally, the red cones less, and the blue cones not at all. Our sensation of color

FIGURE 9-32
The sensitivities of the photopigments in the three types of cones in the normal human retina. Action potential frequency in the optic nerve is directly related to absorption of light by a photopigment.

depends upon the relative outputs of these three types of cone cells and their comparison by higher-order cells in the visual system.

The pathways for color vision follow those described in Figure 9-31. The M-type ganglion cells respond to a broad band of wavelengths. In other words, they receive input from all three types of cones, and they signal not specific color but general brightness. P-type ganglion cells code

FIGURE 9-33
Response of a single opponent color ganglion cell to blue, red, and white lights. (*Redrawn from Hubel and Wiesel.*)

specific colors. These latter cells are also called **opponent color cells** because they have an excitatory input from one type of cone receptor and an inhibitory input from another. For example, the cell in Figure 9-33 increases its rate of firing when the retina is stimulated by a blue light but decreases it when a red light replaces the blue. The cell gives a weak response when stimulated with a white light because the light contains both blue and red wavelengths. Other more complicated patterns also exist. Opponent cells are also found in the lateral geniculate nucleus and visual cortex.

At high light intensities, as in daylight vision, most people—92 percent of the male population and over 99 percent of the female population—have normal color vision. People with the most common kind of *color blindness* lack either the red or green cone pigments and, as a result, have trouble perceiving red versus green.

Eye Movement

The cones are most concentrated in a specialized area of the retina known as the **fovea centralis** (Figure 9-23), and images focused there are seen with the greatest acuity. In order to focus the most important point in the visual image, the fixation point, on the fovea and keep it there, the eyeball must be able to move. Six skeletal muscles attached to the outside of each eyeball (Figure 9-34) control its movement. These muscles perform two basic movements, fast and slow.

The fast movements, called **saccades**, are small, jerking movements that rapidly bring the eye from one fixation point to another to allow a sweeping search of the visual field. In addition, saccades move the visual image over the receptors, thereby preventing adaptation. Saccades also occur during certain periods of sleep when the eyes are closed and may be associated with "watching" the visual imagery of dreams.

Slow eye movements are involved both in tracking visual objects as they move through the visual field and during compensation for movements of the head. The control centers for these compensating movements obtain their information about head movement from the vestibular system, which will be described shortly. Control systems for the other slow movements of the eyes require the continuous feedback of visual information about the moving object.

HEARING

The sense of hearing is based on the physics of sound and the physiology of the external, middle, and inner ear, the nerves to the brain, and the brain parts involved in processing acoustic information.

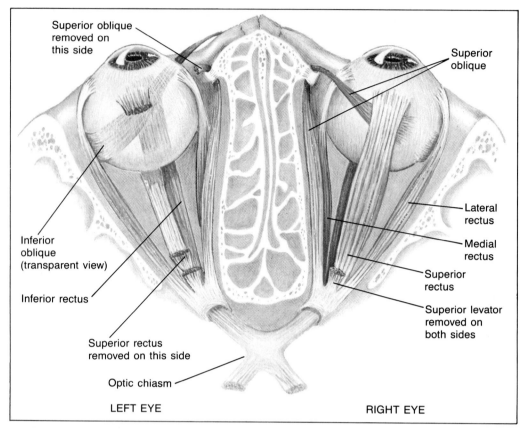

Superior oblique
removed on
this side

Superior
oblique

Inferior
oblique
(transparent view)

Inferior rectus

Lateral
rectus

Medial
rectus

Superior
rectus

Superior levator
removed on
both sides

Superior rectus
removed on this side

Optic chiasm

LEFT EYE

RIGHT EYE

FIGURE 9-34

A superior view of the muscles that move the eye to direct the gaze and give convergence.

Sound

Sound energy is transmitted through a medium by a vibration of the medium's molecules, air being the most common medium for sound transmission. When there are no molecules, as in a vacuum, there can be no sound. Anything capable of creating a disturbance of air molecules can serve as a sound source, but a common one is a vibrating object such as a tuning fork (Figure 9-35). The disturbance of air molecules that makes up a sound wave consists of zones of compression, in which the air molecules are close together and the pressure is high, alternating with zones of rarefaction, where the molecules are farther apart and the pressure is lower (Figure 9-35A through D).

A sound wave measured over time (Figure 9-35E) consists of rapidly alternating pressures that vary continuously from a high during compression of air molecules, to a low during rarefaction, and back again. The difference between the pressure of air molecules in zones of compression and rarefaction determines the wave's amplitude, which is related to the loudness of the sound; the greater the amplitude, the louder the sound. The frequency of vibration of the sound source determines the pitch we hear; the faster the vibration, the higher the pitch. The sounds heard most keenly by human ears are those from sources vibrating at frequencies between 1000 and 4000 Hz, but the entire range of frequencies audible to human beings extends from 20 to 20,000 Hz. Sound waves with repeating patterns are generally perceived as musical, the complexity of the individual waves giving the sound its characteristic quality, or timbre. Sound waves without repeating patterns are generally perceived as noise.

We can distinguish about 400,000 different sounds. For example, we can distinguish the note A played on a piano from the same note on a violin. We can also selectively *not* hear sounds, tuning out the babble of a party to concentrate on a single voice.

Sound Transmission in the Ear

The first step in hearing is the entrance of sound waves into the **external auditory canal** (Figure 9-36). The shapes of the outer ear (the pinna, or auricle) and the external auditory canal help to amplify and direct the sound. The sound waves reverberate from the sides and end of the external auditory canal, filling it with the continuous vibrations of pressure waves.

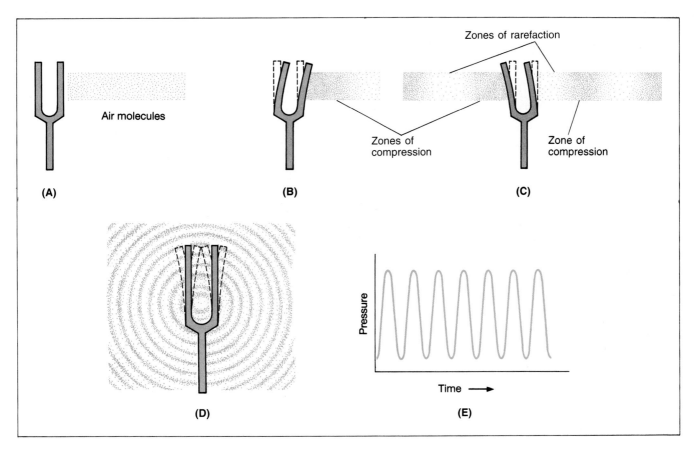

FIGURE 9-35
Formation of sound waves from a vibrating tuning fork.

The **tympanic membrane** (eardrum) is stretched across the end of the external auditory canal, and air molecules push against the membrane, causing it to vibrate at the same frequency as the sound wave. Under higher pressure during a zone of compression, the tympanic membrane bows inward. The distance the membrane moves, although always very small, is a function of the force with which the air molecules hit it and is related to the sound pressure and therefore its loudness. During the following zone of rarefaction, the membrane returns to its original position. The exquisitely sensitive tympanic membrane responds to all the varying pressures of the sound waves, vibrating slowly in response to low-frequency sounds and rapidly in response to high-frequency ones.

The tympanic membrane separates the external auditory canal from the **middle-ear cavity**, an air-filled cavity in the temporal bone of the skull. The pressures in these two spaces are normally equal to atmospheric pressure. The middle ear is exposed to atmospheric pressure through the **auditory** (eustachian) **tube**, which connects the middle ear to the pharynx. The slitlike ending of this tube in the pharynx is normally closed, but muscle move-

ments open the tubes during yawning, swallowing, or sneezing, and the pressure in the middle ear equilibrates with atmospheric pressure. A difference in pressure can be produced with sudden changes in altitude (as in an ascending or descending elevator or airplane), when the pressure outside the ear and in the ear canal changes while the pressure in the middle ear remains constant because of the closed auditory tube. This pressure difference can excessively stretch the tympanic membrane and cause pain.

The second step in hearing is the transmission of sound energy from the tympanic membrane through the middle-ear cavity to the **inner ear**. The inner ear, called the **cochlea**, is a fluid-filled, spiral-shaped passage in the temporal bone. The temporal bone also houses other passages, including the semicircular canals, which contain the sensory organs for equilibrium and movement, to be discussed later. Because liquid is more difficult to move than air, the sound pressure transmitted to the inner ear must be amplified. This is achieved by a movable chain of three small bones, the **malleus**, **incus**, and **stapes** (Figure 9-37), which acts as a piston and couples the motions of the tympanic membrane to a membrane-covered opening

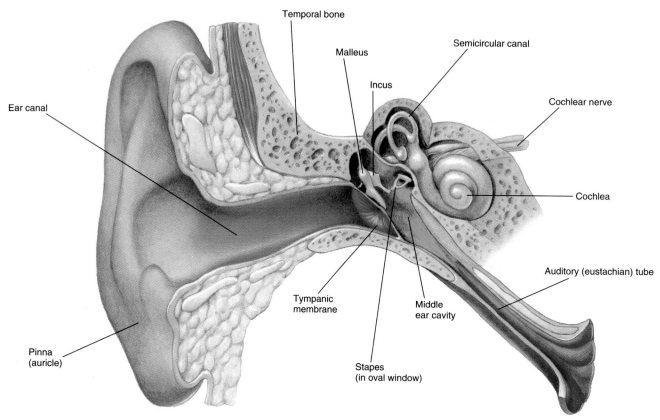

FIGURE 9-36

The human ear. In this and the following drawing, violet indicates the outer ear, green the middle ear, and blue the inner ear. The malleus, incus, and stapes are bones even though they are colored green in this figure to indicate that they are components of the middle ear compartment. The end of the auditory tube is normally closed, but it opens temporarily during muscle movements of the pharynx.

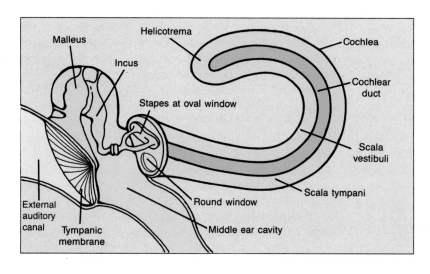

FIGURE 9-37

Relationship between the middle ear bones and the cochlea. Movement of the stapes against the membrane covering the oval window sets up pressure waves in the fluid-filled scala vestibuli. These waves cause vibration of the cochlear duct and the basilar membrane. Some of the pressure is transmitted around the helicotrema directly into the scala tympani.

(the **oval window**) separating the middle and inner ear (Figure 9-38).

The *total* force of a sound wave applied to the tympanic membrane is transferred to the oval window, but because the oval window is so much smaller than the tympanic membrane, the *force per unit area* (that is, the pressure) is increased 15 to 20 times. Additional advantage is gained through the lever action of the middle-ear bones. The amount of energy transmitted to the inner ear can be lessened by the contraction of two small muscles in the middle ear that alter the tension of the tympanic membrane and the position of the stapes in the oval window. These muscles help to protect the delicate receptor apparatus of the inner ear from continuous intense sound stimuli and improve hearing over certain frequency ranges.

The entire system described thus far has been concerned with the transmission of sound energy into the cochlea, where the receptor cells are located. The cochlea is almost completely divided lengthwise by a fluid-filled membranous tube, the **cochlear duct**, which follows the cochlear spiral (Figure 9-37).

On either side of the cochlear duct are fluid-filled compartments: the **scala vestibuli**, which is on the side of the cochlear duct that ends at the oval window; and the **scala tympani**, which is below the cochlear duct and ends in a second membrane-covered opening to the middle ear, the round window. The scala vestibuli and scala tympani meet at the end of the cochlear duct at the helicotrema (Figure 9-37).

As the sound waves in the ear canal push on the tympanic membrane, the chain of middle-ear bones presses the stapes against the membrane covering the oval window, causing it to bow into the scala vestibuli and back out

FIGURE 9-38
Diagrammatic representation showing that the middle ear bones act as a piston against the fluid of the inner ear. (*Redrawn from von Bekesy.*)

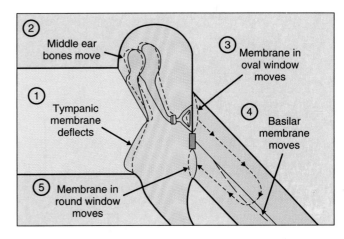

FIGURE 9-39
Transmission of sound vibrations through the middle and inner ear. (*Redrawn from Davis and Silverman.*)

(Figure 9-39), creating waves of pressure there. The wall of the scala vestibuli is largely bone, but there are two paths by which the pressure waves can be dissipated. One path is to the helicotrema, where the waves pass around the end of the cochlear duct into the scala tympani and back to the round-window membrane, which is then bowed out into the middle-ear cavity. However, most of the pressure is transmitted from the scala vestibuli across the cochlear duct.

One side of the cochlear duct is formed by the **basilar membrane** (Figure 9-40), to which is attached the **organ of Corti** (also called the spiral organ), which contains the ear's sensitive receptor cells. Pressure waves crossing the cochlear duct cause the basilar membrane to vibrate.

The region of maximal displacement of the basilar membrane varies with the frequency of the sound source. The properties of the membrane nearest the middle ear are such that this region vibrates most easily, that is, undergoes the greatest movement, in response to high-frequency (high-pitched) tones. As the frequency of the sound is lowered, vibration waves travel out along the membrane for greater distances. Progressively more distant regions of the basilar membrane vibrate maximally in response to progressively lower tones.

Hair Cells of the Organ of Corti

The receptor cells of the organ of Corti, the **hair cells**, are mechanoreceptors that have hairlike **stereocilia** protruding from one end (Figure 9-40C). The hair cells transform the pressure waves in the cochlea into receptor potentials. Movements of the basilar membrane stimulate the hair cells because they are attached to the membrane. The greatest stimulation of the hair cells occurs wherever displacement of the basilar membrane is greatest. Thus, indi-

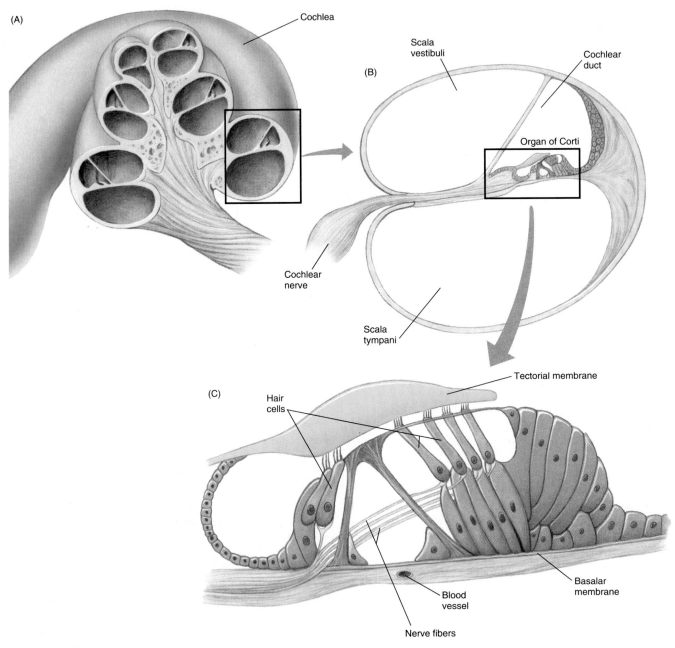

(A)

Cochlea

Scala
vestibuli

(B)

Cochlear
duct

Organ of Corti

Cochlear
nerve

Scala
tympani

Tectorial membrane

(C)

Hair
cells

Basalar
membrane

Blood
vessel

Nerve fibers

FIGURE 9-40

Cross section of the membranes and compartments of the inner ear with detailed view of the hair cells and other structures on the basilar membrane as shown with increasing magnifications in views (A), (B), and (C). Although not shown here, the stereocilia are actually inserted into the tectorial membrane. (*Redrawn from Rasmussen.*)

vidual hair cells develop a maximal receptor potential for a particular frequency of stimulation. The frequencies of the incoming sound waves are, in effect, sorted out along the length of the basilar membrane, and certain hair cells respond maximally to a particular frequency of stimulation.

Each individual stereocilia is a bundle of cross-linked actin microfilaments covered by plasma membrane. The stereocilia are in contact with the overhanging **tectorial membrane** (Figure 9-40), which projects inward from the side of the cochlea. As the basilar membrane is displaced by pressure waves, the hair cells move in relation to the tectorial membrane, and, consequently, the stereocilia are bent. Whenever the stereocilia bend, ion channels in the plasma membrane of the hair cell open, and the resulting ion movements depolarize the membrane and create a receptor potential.

The hair cells are easily damaged by exposure to high-intensity noises such as amplified rock music concerts, engines of jet planes, and revved-up motorcycles. The damaged sensory hairs form abnormal hair structures or are lost altogether. With chronic exposure to loud sounds, some hair cells completely degenerate. Much lesser noise levels also cause damage if exposure is chronic.

Hair cell depolarization leads to release from the cell of a chemical transmitter (probably glutamate) that activates receptor sites on the terminals of about 20 afferent neurons that contact each hair cell. This causes the generation of action potentials in the neurons, the axons of which form the cochlear nerve, a component of cranial nerve VIII. The greater the energy (loudness) of the sound wave, the greater the frequency of action potentials generated in the afferent nerve fiber. Each nerve fiber responds within a limited range of sound frequency and intensity, but it responds best to a single frequency, known as its best frequency.

Efferent fibers coming from the brainstem end on hair cells and on the ends of the afferent neurons. Efferent control of the organ of Corti by these fibers is thought to alter its sensitivity to sound pressure.

Neural Pathways in Hearing

Cochlear nerve fibers enter the brainstem and synapse with interneurons there, fibers from both ears often converging on the same neuron. Many of these neurons are sensitive to the different arrival times and intensities of the input from the two ears. The different arrival times of low-frequency sounds and the difference in intensities of high-frequency sounds are used to determine the source of a sound. If, for example, a sound is louder in the right ear or arrives at the right ear slightly earlier than at the left, we assume that the sound source is on the right.

From the brainstem, the information is transmitted via a multineuron pathway to the thalamus and on to the auditory cortex (Figure 9-6). Neuron pathways from different parts of the basilar membrane are connected to specific sites along the strips of auditory cortex in an orderly manner, according to the pitch of the sound, in much the same way that signals from different regions of the body are represented at different sites in the somatosensory cortex.

VESTIBULAR SYSTEM

Changes in the motion and position of the head are detected by hair cells in the **vestibular apparatus** of the inner ear (Figure 9-41), a series of fluid-filled membranous tubes that connect with each other and with the

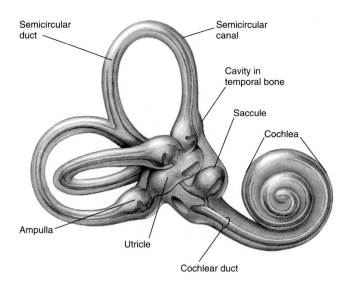

FIGURE 9-41

A tunnel in the temporal bone contains a fluid-filled membranous duct system, part of which can be seen in this cutaway view. The semicircular duct, utricle, and saccule make up the vestibular apparatus. The vestibular duct is connected to the cochlear duct. The purple region on the ducts indicates the positions of hair (receptor) cells. (*Redrawn from Hudspeth.*)

cochlear duct. The vestibular apparatus consists of three **semicircular ducts** and two saclike swellings, the **utricle** and **saccule**, all of which lie in tunnels in the temporal bone on each side of the head. The bony canals of the inner ear in which the vestibular apparatus and cochlea are housed have such a complicated shape that they are sometimes called the **labyrinth**.

The Semicircular Canals

The bony **semicircular canals** house the membranous semicircular ducts, which detect angular acceleration during *rotation* of the head along three perpendicular axes. (The term "semicircular canal" is often also used to denote the semicircular ducts.) The three axes of the semicircular canals are those activated while nodding the head up and down as in signifying "yes," shaking the head from side to side as in signifying "no," and tipping the head so the ear touches the shoulder (Figure 9-42).

Receptor cells of the semicircular canals, like those of the organ of Corti, contain cilia, or hairs. These cilia are closely ensheathed by a gelatinous mass, the **cupula**, which extends across the lumen of each semicircular duct at the **ampulla**, a slight bulge in the wall of each duct (Figure 9-43). Whenever the head is moved, the bony semicircular canal, its enclosed duct, and the attached bodies of the hair cells all turn with it. The fluid filling the duct, however, is not attached to the skull, and because of

FIGURE 9-42
Relation of the two sets of semicircular canals.

FIGURE 9-43
(A) Organization of a cupula and ampulla. (B) Relation of the cupula to the ampulla when the head is at rest and when it is accelerating.

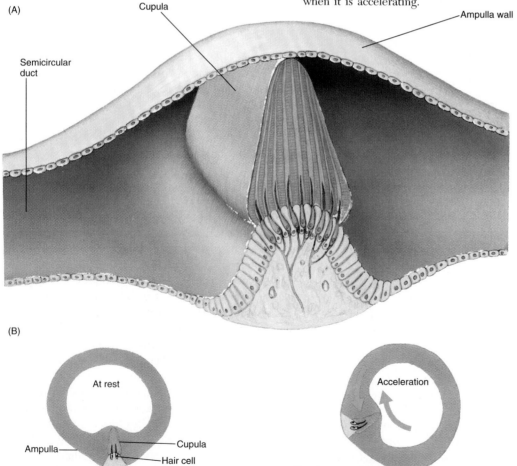

(A)

Cupula

Ampulla wall

Semicircular duct

(B)

At rest

Ampulla

Cupula

Hair cell

Acceleration

Rotation of head

inertia tends to retain its original position, that is, to be "left behind." Thus, the moving ampulla is pushed against the stationary fluid, which causes bending of the cilia, stimulation of the hair cells, and release of a chemical transmitter that activates the nerve terminals synapsing with the hair cells.

At a constant velocity, the duct fluid begins to move at the same rate as the rest of the head, and the cilia slowly return to their resting position. For this reason, the hair cells are stimulated only during *changes* in the rate of motion, that is, during acceleration or deceleration, of the head.

The speed and magnitude of rotational head movements determine the way in which the cilia are bent and the hair cells stimulated. Each receptor has one direction of maximum sensitivity, and when its cilia are bent in this direction, the receptor cell depolarizes. When the cilia are bent in the opposite direction, the cell hyperpolarizes (Figure 9-44). The frequency of action potentials in the afferent nerve fibers that synapse with the hair cells is related to both the amount of force bending the cilia on the receptor cells and to the direction in which this force is applied.

The Utricle and Saccule

The utricle and saccule provide information about *linear* acceleration and changes in head position relative to the forces of gravity. The receptor cells here, too, are mechanoreceptors sensitive to the displacement of projecting hairs. The patch of hair cells in the utricle is nearly horizontal in a standing person, and that in the saccule is vertical.

The cilia are covered by a gelatinous substance in which tiny stones, or otoliths, made up of calcium carbonate crystals are embedded, making the gelatinous substance heavier than the surrounding fluid. In response to any linear acceleration, the gelatinous-otolithic material changes its position, pulled by gravitational forces against the hair cells so that the cilia are bent and the receptor cells stimulated.

Vestibular Information and Dysfunction

Information about hair-cell stimulation is relayed from the vestibular apparatus to the brainstem via cranial nerve VIII, the same nerve that carries acoustic information. It is transmitted via a multineuronal pathway to the parietal lobe to an area adjacent to the somatosensory cortex. Vestibular information is integrated with information from the joints, tendons, and skin, leading to the sense of posture and movement.

Vestibular information is used in three ways. One is to control eye muscles so that, in spite of changes in head position, the eyes can remain fixed on the same point. *Nystagmus*, a repetitive, back-and-forth movement of the

FIGURE 9-44
Relationship between position of hairs and activity in afferent neurons. (A) Resting activity. (B) Movement of hairs in one direction increases the action potential frequency in the afferent nerve activated by the hair cell. (C) Movement in the opposite direction decreases the rate relative to the resting state. (*Redrawn from Wersall, Gleisner, and Lundquist.*)

eyes, can occur in response to vestibular input in normal people but can also be a pathological sign.

The second use of vestibular information is in reflex mechanisms for maintaining upright posture. The vestibular apparatus plays a role in the support of the head during movement, orientation of the head in space, and reflexes accompanying locomotion. Very few postural reflexes depend primarily on input from the vestibular system, however, despite the fact that the vestibular organs are sometimes called the sense organs of balance.

The third use of vestibular information is, after relay via the thalamus to the cortex, in providing conscious awareness of the position and acceleration of the body.

An unexpected combination of inputs from the vestibular system and other sensory systems can induce **vertigo**, defined as an illusion of movement, which is often accompanied by feelings of nausea and lightheadedness. Some people, for example, experience the sensation of falling, nausea, and dizziness when they are in high places looking down to the ground. **Motion sickness** also involves the vestibular system, as when one is on a boat in rough weather and linear and rotational accelerations occur in an unpredicted way.

Ménière's disease is a disorder involving the vestibular system and is associated with episodes of abrupt and often severe dizziness, ringing in the ears, and bouts of hearing loss. It is due to an increased pressure of the fluid in the membranous duct system of the inner ear. The dizziness occurs because the inputs from the two ears are not bal-

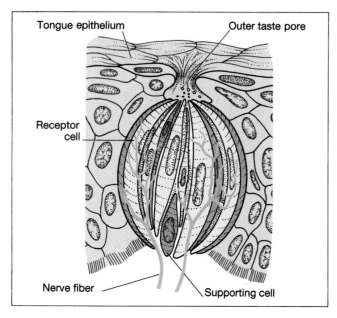

FIGURE 9-45

Structure and innervation of a taste bud. Unlike the taste bud here, each taste bud actually contains 100 or so receptor cells.

anced, either because only one ear is affected or because the two are affected to different degrees.

CHEMICAL SENSES

Receptors sensitive to specific chemicals are **chemoreceptors**. Some of these respond to chemical changes in the internal environment, two examples being the oxygen and hydrogen-ion receptors in certain large blood vessels. Others respond to external chemical changes, and in this category are the receptors for taste and smell, which affect a person's appetite, saliva flow, gastric secretions, and avoidance of harmful substances.

Taste

The specialized sense organs for taste are the 10,000 or so **taste buds** that are found primarily on the tongue. In the taste buds, the receptor cells and the adjacent cells that support them are arranged like the segments of an orange (Figure 9-45). The multifolded upper surfaces of the receptor cells extend into a small pore at the surface of the taste bud, where they are bathed by the fluids of the mouth.

Taste sensations are traditionally divided into four basic groups: sweet, sour, salty, and bitter. Each group seems to have its own transduction mechanism. For example, salt taste occurs by direct membrane depolarization as sodium

FIGURE 9-46

(A) Location and (B) enlargement of a portion of the mucosa, showing the structure of the olfactory receptors.

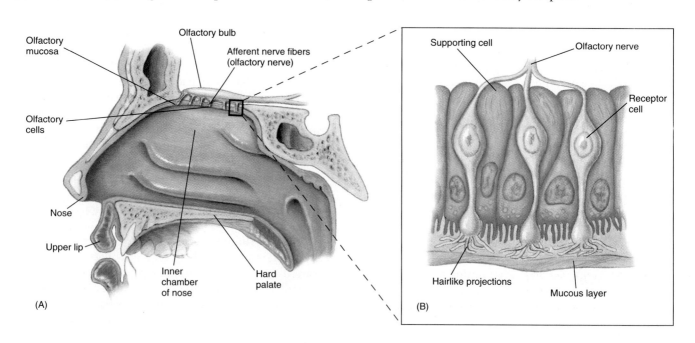

enters the cell through open channels. Single receptor cells have multiple sensibilities and can respond in varying degrees to substances that fall into more than one taste category.

Afferent nerve fibers synapse with the receptor cells and are activated by a neurotransmitter released from these cells. More than one afferent fiber synapses with each receptor cell, and there is clearly no one-to-one relationship between single receptor cells and the nervous system. Awareness of the specific taste of a substance probably depends, therefore, upon the pattern of firing in a group of neurons rather than the firing of a specific neuron. The pathways for taste in the central nervous system project to the parietal cortex, near the "mouth" region of the somatosensory cortex.

It is not known how we can distinguish so many different taste sensations when the receptor cells lack specificity both in terms of the kind of chemical to which they respond and the way in which they are connected to the brain. The odor of the substance clearly helps to identify it, as is attested by the common experience that food lacks taste when one has a head cold.

Smell

The olfactory receptor cells, which give rise to the sense of smell, lie in a small patch of mucus-secreting membrane (the **olfactory mucosa**) in the upper part of the nasal cavity (Figure 9-46A). The olfactory receptors are not separate cells but are specialized afferent neurons. The cell bodies of these neurons have an enlarged extension, analogous to a dendrite, from which several long, hairlike processes extend out to the surface of the olfactory mucosa (Figure 9-46B). The hairlike cilia are the primary sites of sensory transduction by olfactory stimuli. The axons of these neurons project to the brain as the olfactory nerve, which is cranial nerve I.

For an odorous substance, that is, an **odorant**, to be detected, molecules of the substance must diffuse into the air and pass into the nose to the region of the olfactory mucosa. Once there, the odorant molecules first dissolve in a layer of mucus that covers the receptor cells and then bind to receptor sites on the hairlike processes. **Odorant-binding proteins** in the mucus covering the olfactory receptors may interact with the odorant molecules, transport them to the receptors, and facilitate the binding of the odorant to specific receptors on the olfactory neurons. Any given receptor cell is responsive to many different compounds.

The number of distinct receptors that underlie odor recognition has not been determined. As with taste, odor information seems to be signaled in part by the activity distributed across many neurons.

Olfactory discrimination varies with attentiveness, state of the olfactory mucosa—the sense of smell decreases when the mucosa is congested, as in a head cold; hunger—sensitivity is greater in hungry subjects; gender—women in general have keener olfactory sensitivities than men; smoking—decreased sensitivity has been repeatedly associated with smoking; and age—the ability to identify odors decreases with age, and a large percentage of elderly persons cannot detect odors at all.

Olfactory pathways go to the olfactory bulbs, which lie on the undersurface of the frontal lobes of the brain. Some olfactory processing occurs in the limbic system (see Figure 8-42), the part of the brain most intimately associated with neuroendocrine regulation and emotional, food-getting, and sexual behavior. There are also olfactory sensory processing regions distinct from the limbic system.

SUMMARY

I. Sensory processing begins with the transformation of stimulus energy into receptor potentials and then into action potentials in nerve fibers.

II. Information carried in a sensory system may or may not lead to a conscious awareness of the stimulus.

RECEPTORS

I. Receptors translate information from the external world and internal environment into graded potentials, which then generate action potentials.

A. Receptors may be either specialized endings of afferent neurons or separate cells at the end of the neurons.

B. Receptors respond best to one form of stimulus energy, but they may respond to other energy forms if the stimulus intensity is abnormally high.

C. Regardless of how a specific receptor is stimulated, activation of that receptor always leads to perception of one sensation (the doctrine of specific nerve energies). Not all receptor activations lead, however, to conscious sensations.

II. The transduction process in all sensory receptors involves the opening or closing of ion channels in the receptor. Ions then flow across the membrane, causing a receptor potential.
  A. Receptor-potential magnitude and action-potential frequency increase as stimulus strength increases.
  B. Receptor-potential magnitude varies with stimulus strength, rate of change of stimulus application, temporal summation of successive receptor potentials, and adaptation.

NEURAL PATHWAYS IN SENSORY SYSTEMS

I. A single afferent neuron with all its receptor endings is a sensory unit.
  A. Afferent neurons, which usually have more than one receptor of the same type, are the first neurons in sensory pathways.
  B. The area of the body that, when stimulated, causes activity in a sensory unit or other neuron in the afferent pathway is called the receptive field for that neuron.
II. The specific ascending pathways convey information to specific primary receiving areas of the cerebral cortex about only a single type of stimulus.
III. Nonspecific ascending pathways convey information from more than one type of sensory unit to the brainstem reticular formation and regions of the thalamus not part of the specific ascending pathways.

ASSOCIATION CORTEX AND PERCEPTUAL PROCESSING

I. Information from the primary sensory cortical areas is elaborated after it is relayed to a cortical association area.
  A. The region of association cortex closest to the primary sensory cortical area processes the information in fairly simple ways and serves basic sensory-related functions.
  B. Regions of association cortex farther from the primary sensory areas process the sensory information in more complicated ways.
  C. Processing in the association cortex includes input from areas of the brain serving arousal, attention, memory, language, and emotions.

PRIMARY SENSORY CODING

I. The type of stimulus perceived is determined primarily by the type of receptor activated. All receptors of a given sensory unit respond to the same stimulus modality.
II. Stimulus intensity is coded by the rate of firing of individual sensory units and by the number of sensory units activated.
III. Perception of the stimulus location depends on the size of the receptive field covered by a single sensory unit and on the overlap of nearby receptive fields. Lateral inhibition is a means by which ascending pathways emphasize wanted information and increase sensory acuity.
IV. Stimulus duration is coded by slowly adapting receptors.
V. Information coming into the nervous system is subject to control by both ascending and descending pathways.

SOMATIC SENSATION

I. Sensory function of the skin and underlying tissues is served by a variety of receptors sensitive to one (or a few) stimulus types.
II. Information about somatic sensation enters both specific and nonspecific ascending pathways. The specific pathways cross to the opposite side of the brain.
III. The somatic sensations include touch-pressure, the senses of posture and movement, temperature, and pain.
  A. Rapidly adapting mechanoreceptors of the skin give rise to sensations such as vibration, touch, and movement, whereas slowly adapting ones give rise to the sensation of pressure.
  B. Skin receptors having small receptive fields are involved in fine spatial discrimination, whereas receptors having larger receptive fields signal less spatially precise touch-pressure sensations.
  C. The major receptor type responsible for the senses of posture and kinesthesia is the muscle-spindle stretch receptor.
  D. Cold receptors are sensitive to decreasing temperature; warm receptors signal information about increasing temperature.
  E. Tissue damage stimulates specific receptors that give rise to the sensation of pain, which may also induce emotional and reflex responses.
  F. Stimulation-produced analgesia, transcutaneous nerve stimulation (TENS), and acupuncture control pain by blocking transmission in the pain pathways.

VISION

I. Light is described by its wavelength or frequency.
II. The light that falls on the retina must be focused by the cornea and lens.
  A. Lens shape is changed in response to viewing

near or distant objects (accommodation) so that both are focused on the retina.

B. Presbyopia interferes with accommodation. Cataract decreases the amount of light reaching the retina.

C. An eyeball too long or too short relative to the focusing power of the lens causes nearsighted or farsighted vision, respectively.

III. The photopigments of the rods and cones are made up of a protein component (opsin) and a chromophore (retinal).

A. The rods and each of the three cone types have different opsins, which make each of the four receptor types sensitive to a different wavelength of light.

B. When light falls upon the chromophore, the photic energy causes the chromophore to change shape, which triggers a cascade of events involving the second-messenger cyclic GMP.

C. This leads to hyperpolarization of the photoreceptors and decreased neurotransmitter release from them. When exposed to darkness, the rods and cones are depolarized and release more neurotransmitter.

IV. The rods and cones synapse on bipolar cells, which synapse on ganglion cells.

A. Ganglion-cell axons form the optic nerves, which lead into the brain.

B. Half the optic nerve fibers cross to the opposite side of the brain in the optic chiasm. The fibers from the optic nerves terminate in the lateral geniculate nuclei of the thalamus, which send fibers to visual cortex.

C. Visual information is also relayed to areas of the brain dealing with biological rhythms.

V. Coding in the visual system occurs along parallel pathways, in which different aspects of visual information, such as color, form, movement, and depth, are kept separate from each other.

VI. The colors we perceive are related to the wavelength of light. Different wavelengths excite one of the three cone photopigments most strongly.

A. Certain ganglion cells are excited by input from one type of cone cell and inhibited by input from a different cone type.

B. Our sensation of color depends on the output of the various opponent-color cells and the processing of this output by brain areas involved in color vision.

VII. Six skeletal muscles control eye movement to scan the visual field for objects of interest, keep the fixation point focused on the fovea centralis despite movements of the object or the head, prevent adaptation, and move the eyes during accommodation.

HEARING

I. Sound energy is transmitted by movements of pressure waves.

A. The sound wave frequency determines pitch.

B. The sound wave amplitude determines loudness.

II. The sound transmission sequence is as follows:

A. Sound waves enter the external auditory canal and press against the tympanic membrane, causing it to vibrate.

B. The vibrating membrane causes movement of the three small middle-ear bones, and the stapes vibrates against the oval-window membrane.

C. Movements of this membrane set up pressure waves in the fluid-filled scala vestibuli, which cause vibrations in the cochlear duct wall, setting up pressure waves in the fluid there.

D. These pressure waves cause vibrations in the basilar membrane, located on one side of the cochlear duct.

E. As this membrane vibrates, the hair cells of the organ of Corti move in relation to the tectorial membrane.

F. Movement of the hair cells' stereocilia stimulates them to release neurotransmitter, which activates receptors on the peripheral ends of the afferent nerve fibers.

III. Each part of the basilar membrane vibrates maximally in response to one particular sound frequency.

VESTIBULAR SYSTEM

I. A vestibular apparatus lies in the temporal bone on each side of the head and consists of three semicircular ducts, a utricle, and a saccule.

II. The semicircular ducts detect angular acceleration during rotation of the head, which causes bending of the stereocilia on their hair cells.

III. Otoliths in the gelatinous substance of the utricle and saccule move in response to changes in linear acceleration and the position of the head relative to gravity and stimulate the stereocilia on the hair cells.

CHEMICAL SENSES

I. The receptors for taste lie in taste buds throughout the mouth, principally on the tongue, and can respond to many different substances. Different types of taste receptors operate by different mechanisms.

II. Olfactory receptors, which are part of the afferent olfactory neurons, lie in the mucosa in the upper nasal cavity.

A. Odorant molecules, once dissolved in the mucus that bathes the olfactory receptors, are transported to the receptors by odorant-binding proteins.

B. Olfactory pathways go to the limbic system.

KEY TERMS

sensory system	rhodopsin
sensory information	opsin
sensation	chromophore
perception	retinal
sensory receptors	light adaptation
stimulus	bipolar cell
transduction	ganglion cells
adequate stimulus	lateral geniculate
doctrine of specific	nucleus
nerve energies	visual field
receptor potential	suprachiasmatic
adaptation	nucleus
sensory pathway	opponent color cells
ascending pathways	fovea centralis
sensory unit	saccades
receptive field	external auditory
specific ascending pathways	canal
somatic receptors	tympanic membrane
somatosensory cortex	middle-ear cavity
visual cortex	auditory tube
auditory cortex	inner ear
nonspecific ascending pathways	cochlea
polymodal neurons	malleus
cortical association areas	incus
modality	stapes
recruitment	oval window
acuity	cochlear duct
lateral inhibition	scala vestibuli
rapidly adapting receptors	scala tympani
slowly adapting receptors	basilar membrane
somatic sensation	organ of Corti
kinesthesia	hair cells
nociceptors	stereocilia
anterolateral system	tectorial membrane
wavelength	vestibular apparatus
frequency	semicircular ducts
visible spectrum	utricle
retina	saccule
lens	labyrinth
cornea	semicircular canals
accommodation	cupula
ciliary muscle	ampulla
zonular fibers	chemoreceptors
iris	taste buds
pupil	olfactory mucosa
rods	odorant
cones	odorant-binding
photopigments	proteins

REVIEW QUESTIONS

1. Distinguish between a sensation and a perception.
2. Describe the general process of transduction in a re-ceptor that is a cell separate from the afferent neuron. Include in your description the terms specificity, stimulus, receptor potential, neurotransmitter, graded potential, action potential.

3. List four ways in which the magnitude of a receptor potential can be varied.

4. Describe the relationship between sensory information processing in the primary cortical sensory areas and in the cortical association areas.

5. List four ways in which sensory information can be distorted.

6. How does the nervous system distinguish between stimuli of different types?

7. How is information about stimulus intensity coded by the nervous system?

8. Diagram a specific ascending pathway that relays information from nociceptors. Diagram a nonspecific ascending pathway that relays information from mechanoreceptors and nociceptors.

9. Describe the similarities between pain and the other somatic sensations. Describe the differences.

10. List the structures through which light must pass before it reaches the photopigment in the rods and cones.

11. Describe the events that take place during accommodation for far vision.

12. What changes take place in neurotransmitter release from the rods or cones when they are exposed to light?

13. Beginning with the ganglion cells of the retina, describe the visual pathway.

14. List the sequence of events that occur between entry of a sound wave into the ear canal and the firing of action potentials in the cochlear nerve.

15. Describe the anatomical relationship between the cochlea and the cochlear duct.

16. What is the relationship between head movement and cupula movement in a semicircular canal?

17. What causes the release of neurotransmitter from the utricle and saccule receptor cells?

18. In what ways are the sensory systems for taste and olfaction similar? In what ways are they different?

CLINICAL TERMS

phantom limb	myopic
hyperalgesia	farsighted
referred pain	hyperopic
stimulation-produced analgesia	astigmatism
transcutaneous electric nerve	glaucoma
stimulation (TENS)	color blindness
acupuncture	nystagmus
presbyopia	vertigo
cataract	motion sickness
nearsighted	Ménière's disease

THOUGHT QUESTIONS

(Answers are given in Appendix A.)

1. Describe eight mechanisms by which pain could theoretically be controlled medically or surgically.

2. At what two sites would central nervous system injuries interfere with the perception of heat applied to the right side of the body? At what single site would a central nervous system injury interfere with the perception of heat applied to either side of the body?

3. What would vision be like after a drug has destroyed all the cones in the retina?

4. Damage to what parts of the cerebral cortex could explain the following behaviors? (a) A person walks into a chair placed in her path. (b) The person does not walk into the chair but does not know what the chair can be used for.

CHAPTER

10

HORMONAL CONTROL MECHANISMS

The endocrine system is one of the body's two major communication systems, the nervous system being the other. The **endocrine system** consists of all those glands, termed **endocrine glands**, that secrete hormones. **Hormones**, as noted in Chapter 7, are chemical messengers that are carried *by the blood* from endocrine glands to the cells upon which they act. The cells influenced by a particular hormone are termed the **target cells** (or effector cells) for that hormone.

Table 10-1 summarizes, for reference and orientation, the endocrine glands, the hormones they secrete, and the major functions the hormones control. The endocrine system differs from most of the other organ systems of the body in that the various glands are not in anatomical conti-

MEMORIZE

TABLE 10-1   SUMMARY OF THE HORMONES

Site produced (endocrine gland)	Hormone	Major function° is control of:
Hypothalamus	Hypophysiotropic hormones	Secretion of hormones by the anterior pituitary
	Posterior pituitary hormones	See posterior pituitary
Anterior pituitary	Growth hormone (somatotropin, GH)†	Growth via secretion of IGF-I; protein, carbohydrate, and lipid metabolism
	Thyroid-stimulating hormone (TSH, thyrotropin)	Thyroid gland
	Adrenocorticotropic hormone (ACTH, corticotropin)	Adrenal cortex
	Prolactin	Breast growth and milk synthesis; permissive for certain reproductive functions in the male
	Gonadotropic hormones: Follicle-stimulating hormone (FSH) Luteinizing hormone (LH)	Gonads (gamete production and sex hormone secretion)
	β-lipotropin and β-endorphin	Unknown
Posterior pituitary‡	Oxytocin	Milk let-down; uterine motility
	Vasopressin (antidiuretic hormone, ADH)	Water excretion by the kidneys; blood pressure
	Dopamine	Prolactin secretion inhibition
	Prolactin releasing factor	Prolactin secretion
Adrenal cortex	Cortisol	Organic metabolism; response to stresses; immune system
	Androgens	Sex drive in women
	Aldosterone	Sodium, potassium, and acid excretion by kidneys
Adrenal medulla	Epinephrine Norepinephrine	Organic metabolism; cardiovascular function; response to stress
Thyroid	Thyroxine (T_4) Triiodothyronine (T_3)	Metabolic rate; growth; brain development and function
	Calcitonin	? Plasma calcium
Parathyroids	Parathyroid hormone (parathormone, PTH, PH)	Plasma calcium and phosphate

TABLE 10-1 (*continued*)

Site produced (endocrine gland)	Hormone	Major function° is control of:
Gonads:		
Female: ovaries	Estrogen	Reproductive system; breasts; growth
	Progesterone	and development
	Inhibin	FSH secretion
	Relaxin	? Relaxation of cervix and pubic ligaments
Male: testes	Testosterone	Reproductive system; growth and development
	Inhibin	FSH secretion
	Müllerian-inhibiting hormone	Regression of Müllerian ducts
Pancreas	Insulin	Organic metabolism; plasma glucose
	Glucagon	
	Somatostatin	
	Pancreatic polypeptide	
Kidneys	Renin (→angiotensin II)§	Aldosterone secretion; blood pressure
	Erythropoietin	Erythrocyte production
	1,25-dihydroxyvitamin D_3	Plasma calcium
Gastrointestinal tract	Gastrin	Gastrointestinal tract; liver; pancreas; gallbladder
	Secretin	
	Cholecystokinin	
	Glucose-dependent insulinotropic peptide (GIP)	
	Somatostatin	
Liver (and other cells)	Insulin-like growth factors (IGF-I and II)	Growth
Thymus	Thymopoietin	T-lymphocyte function
Pineal	Melatonin	? Sexual maturity; body rhythms
Placenta	Chorionic gonadotropin (CG)	Secretion by corpus luteum
	Estrogens	See ovaries
	Progesterone	See ovaries
	Placental lactogen	Breast development; organic metabolism
Heart	Atrial natriuretic factor (ANF, atriopeptin, auriculin)	Sodium excretion by kidneys; blood pressure
Leukocytes, macrophages, endothelial cells, and fibroblasts	Cytokines¶ (these include the interleukins, colony-stimulating factors, interferons, tumor necrosis factors)	Immune defenses (see Chapter 20)
Multiple cell types	Growth factors¶ (e.g., epidermal growth factor)	Growth and proliferation of specific cell types

°This table does not list all functions of the hormones.
†The names and abbreviations in parentheses are synonyms.
‡The posterior pituitary stores and secretes these hormones; they are made in the hypothalamus.
§Renin is an enzyme that initiates reactions in blood that generate angiotensin II.
¶Some classifications include the cytokines under the category of growth factors.

nuity with each other; however, they do form a system in the functional sense. The reader may be puzzled to see listed as endocrine glands some organs—the heart, for instance—that clearly have other functions. The explanation is that, in addition to the cells that carry out the organ's other functions, the organ also contains cells that secrete hormones.

Note also in Table 10-1 that the hypothalamus, a part of the brain, is considered part of the endocrine system too. This is because the chemical messengers released by certain neuron terminals in both the hypothalamus and its extension, the posterior pituitary, do not function as neurotransmitters affecting adjacent cells but rather enter the blood and are carried to sites of action elsewhere. As pointed out in Chapter 7, hormones released from neuron terminals are referred to as **neurohormones**.

Table 10-1 demonstrates that there are a large number of endocrine glands and hormones. One way of describing the physiology of the individual hormones is to present all relevant material, gland by gland, in a single chapter. In keeping with our emphasis on hormones as messengers in homeostatic control mechanisms, however, we have chosen to describe the physiology of specific hormones and the glands that secrete them in subsequent chapters, in the context of the control systems in which they participate. For example, pancreatic hormones are described in Chapter 18 on organic metabolism, parathyroid hormone

in Chapter 16 in the context of calcium metabolism, and so on.

The aims of the present chapter are therefore limited to presenting (1) the general principles of endocrinology, that is, a structural and functional analysis of hormones in general that transcends individual glands; and (2) an analysis of the hypothalamus-pituitary hormonal system. The control systems for the hormones of this particular system are so interconnected that they are best described as a unit to lay the foundation for subsequent descriptions in other chapters.

Before we turn to these analyses, however, several additional general points should be made concerning Table 10-1. One phenomenon evident from this table is that a single gland may secrete multiple hormones. The usual pattern in such cases is that a single cell type secretes only one hormone, so that multiple hormone secretion reflects the presence of different endocrine cell types in the same gland. In a few cases, however, a single cell may secrete more than one hormone.

Another point of interest illustrated by Table 10-1 is that a particular hormone may be produced by more than one type of endocrine gland. For example, somatostatin is secreted by endocrine cells in both the gastrointestinal tract and the pancreas and is also one of the hormones secreted by the hypothalamus.

HORMONE STRUCTURES AND SYNTHESIS

Hormones fall into three chemical classes: (1) amines, (2) peptides and proteins, and (3) steroids.

Amine Hormones

The **amine hormones** are all derivatives of the amino acid tyrosine. They include the thyroid hormones, epinephrine and norepinephrine (produced by the adrenal medulla), and dopamine (produced by the hypothalamus and posterior pituitary).

Thyroid Hormones. The **thyroid gland** is located in the lower part of the neck wrapped around the front of the trachea (windpipe). It secretes three hormones, but the two iodine-containing amine hormones shown in Figure 10-1—**thyroxine (T_4)** and **triiodothyronine (T_3)**—are collectively known as the **thyroid hormones (TH)**. The third hormone, a peptide called calcitonin, is not included in subsequent references to thyroid hormones.

Iodine is an essential element that functions as a component of T_4 and T_3. Most of the iodine ingested in food is absorbed, by active transport, into the blood from the gastrointestinal tract, in the process being converted to the ionized form, iodide. Iodide then leaves the blood and is actively transported into the thyroid cells. Once in the gland, the iodide is converted back to iodine, which is then used, along with tyrosine, for hormone synthesis.

The thyroid hormones are stored in the thyroid gland, incorporated by peptide bonds into molecules of the protein called **thyroglobulin**. Hormone secretion occurs by enzymatic splitting of T_4 and T_3 from the thyroglobulin and the entry of the freed hormones into the blood. T_4 is secreted in much larger amounts than is T_3. However, a variety of tissues, particularly the liver and kidneys, convert most of this T_4 into T_3 by enzymatic removal of one iodine atom, and this constitutes the major source of plasma T_3. This is an important point because T_3 is a much more active hormone than is T_4.

Virtually every tissue in the body is affected by the thyroid hormones. These effects, which are described in

FIGURE 10-1
Chemical structures of the thyroid hormones, thyroxine and triiodothyronine. The two molecules differ by only one iodine atom, a difference noted in the abbreviations T_3 and T_4.

Chapter 18, include regulation of metabolic rate, growth, and brain development and function.

Adrenal Medullary Hormones and Dopamine. There are two adrenal glands, one on the top of each kidney. Each **adrenal gland** constitutes two distinct endocrine glands, an inner **adrenal medulla**, which secretes amine hormones, and a surrounding **adrenal cortex**, which secretes steroid hormones. As described in Chapter 8, the adrenal medulla is really a modified sympathetic ganglion whose cell bodies do not send out nerve fibers but instead release their secretions into the blood, thereby fulfilling a criterion for an endocrine gland.

The adrenal medulla secretes mainly two amine hormones, **epinephrine (E)** and **norepinephrine (NE)**, which constitute, with **dopamine (DA)**, the chemical family of **catecholamines**. The structures and pathways for synthesis of the catecholamines were described in Chapter 8, when these three substances were dealt with as neurotransmitters. In humans, the adrenal medulla secretes approximately four times more epinephrine than norepinephrine.[1] Epinephrine and norepinephrine exert actions similar to those of the sympathetic nerves. These effects are described in various chapters and summarized in Chapter 20 in the section on stress.

The adrenal medulla also secretes small amounts of dopamine and several substances other than catechol-

amines, but whether any of these adrenal secretions other than epinephrine and norepinephrine actually serve hormonal functions is unknown.

In contrast, as described below, the dopamine secreted by cells in two other sites—the hypothalamus and the posterior pituitary—does function as a hormone.

Peptide Hormones

The great majority of all hormones are either peptides or proteins. They range in size from small peptides having only three amino acids to small proteins (some of which are glycoproteins). For convenience, we shall follow a common practice of endocrinologists and refer to all these hormones as **peptide hormones**.

In many cases, they are initially synthesized, on the ribosomes of the endocrine cells, as larger proteins known as preprohormones, which are then cleaved to **prohormones** by proteolytic enzymes in the granular endoplasmic reticulum of the cell (Figure 10-2). The prohormone is then packaged into secretory vesicles by the Golgi apparatus of the cell. In this process, the prohormone is cleaved to yield the active hormone and other peptide chains found in the prohormone. Therefore, when the cell is stimulated to release the contents of the secretory vesicles by exocytosis, the other peptides are cosecreted with the hormone. In certain cases they, too, may exert hormonal effects. In other words, instead of just one peptide hormone, the cell may be secreting multiple peptide hormones that differ in their effects on target cells.

The direct stimulus of secretory-vesicle exocytosis in peptide-producing endocrine cells, as in neurons, is an increase in cytosolic calcium concentration. The source of the calcium during cell stimulation is either the extracellular fluid or the agranular endoplasmic reticulum. Many of the stimuli directly or indirectly cause some degree of plasma-membrane depolarization—sometimes even action potentials—which opens voltage-sensitive calcium channels in the plasma membrane and allows diffusion of calcium into the cell.

Capillaries supplying peptide-secreting endocrine glands are generally quite leaky to proteins, and so, once released into the extracellular fluid by exocytosis, peptide hormones diffuse between the capillary endothelial cells to enter the blood.

One more point about peptide hormones: As mentioned in Chapters 7 and 8, many peptides serve as both neurotransmitters (or neuromodulators) and as hormones. For example, most of the hormones secreted by the endocrine glands in the gastrointestinal tract are also produced by neurons in the brain where they function as neurotransmitters. It is important to recognize the separation of function here: Because of the blood-brain barrier, the gastrointestinal hormones circulating in the blood cannot gain entry to the brain and activate the receptors normally acti-

---

[1]Yet under basal conditions, the plasma concentration of norepinephrine is much higher than that of epinephrine; the source of most of this circulating norepinephrine is not the adrenal medulla but neurotransmitter that has been released from postganglionic sympathetic neurons and entered the blood.

SYNTHESIS | PACKAGING | STORAGE | SECRETION

Preprohormone → Prohormone → Hormone → Hormone (and any "pro" fragments)
↓
Prohormone → Hormone

FIGURE 10-2

Typical synthesis and secretion of peptide hormones. Some peptide hormones do not go through all these stages. In some cells the calcium that causes exocytosis is released from intracellular sites rather than entering from the extracellular fluid. *(Adapted from Hedge et al.)*

vated when these same molecules are released from neurons.

Steroid Hormones

The third family of hormones is the steroids, the lipids whose ringlike structure was described on page 26. **Steroid hormones** are produced by the adrenal cortex and the **gonads** (testes and ovaries), as well as by the placenta during pregnancy. Examples are shown in Figure 10-3. In addition, the hormone, 1,25-dihydroxyvitamin D_3, the active form of vitamin D, is a steroid derivative.

Cholesterol is the precursor of all steroid hormones. Although steroid-producing endocrine glands synthesize some of their own cholesterol, their major source is the cholesterol delivered to the cells by plasma lipoproteins that are made in the liver and circulate in the blood. The many biochemical steps in steroid synthesis beyond cholesterol involve small changes in the molecules and are mediated by specific enzymes. The steroids that a particular cell produces depend therefore on the types and concentrations of the enzymes the cell has. Because steroids are highly lipid-soluble, once they are synthesized they simply diffuse across the plasma membrane of the steroid-producing cell and enter the interstitial fluid and then the blood.

The next sections describe the pathways for steroid synthesis by the adrenal cortex and gonads. Those for the placenta are somewhat unusual and are discussed in Chapter 19.

Hormones of the Adrenal Cortex. Steroid synthesis by the adrenal cortex is illustrated in Figure 10-4. The five

hormones normally secreted in physiologically significant amounts by the adrenal cortex are aldosterone, cortisol, corticosterone, dehydroepiandrosterone, and androstenedione. **Aldosterone** is known as a **mineralocorticoid** because its effects are on salt (mineral) metabolism, mainly on the kidneys' handling of sodium, potassium, and hydrogen ions. **Cortisol** and corticosterone are called **glucocorticoids** because they have important effects on the

FIGURE 10-3

Structures of representative steroid hormones.

Cortisol

Aldosterone

Testosterone

Estradiol

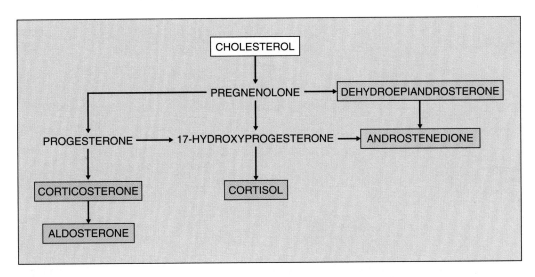

FIGURE 10-4

Simplified flow sheet for synthesis of steroid hormones by the adrenal cortex; many intermediate steps have been left out. The various steps are mediated by specific enzymes. The five hormones in colored boxes are the major steroid hormones secreted. Dehydroepiandrosterone and androstenedione are androgens, that is, testosterone-like hormones. Cortisol and corticosterone are glucocorticoids, and aldosterone is a mineralocorticoid.

metabolism of glucose and other organic nutrients.[2] Cortisol is by far the more important of the two glucocorticoids in humans, and so we shall deal only with it in future discussions. In addition to its effects on organic metabolism (described in Chapter 18), cortisol exerts many other effects, including facilitation of the body's responses to stress and regulation of the immune system (Chapter 20).

Dehydroepiandrosterone and androstenedione belong to the class of hormones known as **androgens**, which includes the male sex hormone, testosterone, produced by the testes. All androgens have actions similar to those of testosterone. Because the adrenal androgens are much less potent than testosterone, they are of little physiological significance in the male; they do, however, play roles in the female, as described in Chapter 19.

The adrenal cortex is not a homogeneous gland but is composed of three distinct layers (Figure 10-5). The outer layer—the zona glomerulosa—possesses very high concentrations of the enzymes required to convert corticosterone to aldosterone but lacks the enzymes required for the formation of cortisol and androgens. Accordingly, this layer synthesizes and secretes aldosterone but not the other major adrenal cortical hormones. In contrast, the zona fasciculata and zona reticularis have just the opposite enzyme profile. They, therefore, secrete no aldosterone but much cortisol and androgen.

In certain disease states, the adrenal cortex may secrete decreased or increased amounts of various steroids. For example, an absence of the enzymes for the formation of cortisol by the adrenal can result in the shunting of the cortisol precursors into the androgen pathway. In a woman, the result of the large increase in androgen secretion would be masculinization.

Hormones of the Gonads Compared to the adrenal cortex, the gonads have very different concentrations of key enzymes in their steroid pathways. Endocrine cells in both testes and ovaries lack the enzymes needed to produce aldosterone and cortisol. They possess high concentrations of enzymes in the androgen pathways leading to androstenedione, as in the adrenal cortex. In addition, however, the cells in the testes contain a high concentration of the enzyme that converts androstenedione to **testosterone**, which is therefore the major androgen secreted by the testes. The ovarian cells that synthesize the major female sex hormone, **estradiol**, have a high concentration of the enzyme required to go one step further, that is, to transform testosterone to estradiol. Accordingly, estradiol, rather than testosterone, is secreted by the ovaries. Ovarian cells also secrete a second major steroid hormone, **progesterone**.

Very small amounts of testosterone do leak out of ovarian endocrine cells, however, and very small amounts of

---

[2]In very high concentrations glucocorticoids also exert some mineralocorticoid effects and mineralocorticoids exert some glucocorticoid effects.

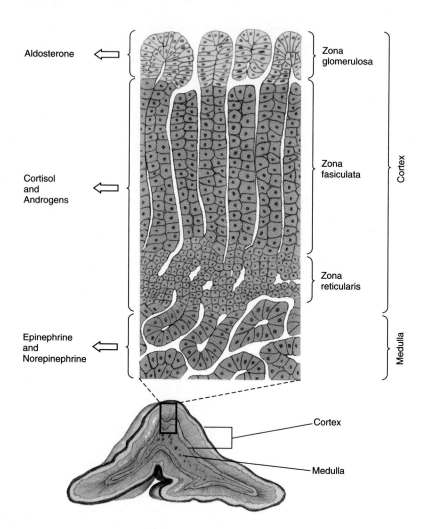

Aldosterone ⇐ Zona glomerulosa

Cortisol and Androgens ⇐ Zona fasiculata

Zona reticularis

Cortex

Epinephrine and Norepinephrine ⇐ Medulla

Cortex

Medulla

FIGURE 10-5

Section through an adrenal gland showing both adrenal medulla and adrenal cortex, as well as the hormones they secrete.

estradiol are produced from testosterone in the testes. Moreover, following their secretion into the blood by the gonads and the adrenal cortex, steroid hormones may undergo further interconversion in either the blood or other organs. For example, testosterone is converted to estradiol in some of its target cells. Indeed, we shall see, in Chapter 19, that in males such conversion is critical for testosterone's effects on the brain. Thus, the major male and female sex hormones—testosterone and estradiol, respectively—are not unique to males and females, although, of course, the relative concentrations of the hormones are quite different in the two sexes.

HORMONE TRANSPORT IN THE BLOOD

Peptide and catecholamine hormones are water-soluble. Therefore, with the exception of a few peptides, these hormones are carried in plasma simply dis-solved in the plasma water (Table 10-2). In contrast, the steroid hormones and the thyroid hormones circulate in the blood largely bound to plasma proteins.

Even though the steroid and thyroid hormones exist in plasma mainly bound to proteins, small concentrations of these hormones do exist dissolved in the plasma. The dis-solved, or free, hormone is in equilibrium with the bound hormone:

Free hormone + binding protein ⇌
hormone-protein complex

The total hormone concentration in plasma is the sum of the free and bound hormone. It is important to realize, however, that only the *free* hormone can diffuse across capillary walls and encounter its target cells. Accordingly, the concentration of the free hormone is what is physio-logically important rather than the concentration of the total hormone, most of which is bound. For example, less than 1 percent of plasma thyroid hormone is free, that is,

TABLE 10-2   CATEGORIES OF HORMONES

Types	Form in plasma	Location of receptors	Signal transduction mechanisms	Rate of excretion

Peptides and catecholamines	Free	Plasma membrane	Receptor channels
			Channels gated by
			  G proteins
			Cyclic AMP
			Cyclic GMP
			Ca^{2+}, IP_3, DAG
				Fast (minutes to
				  a few hours)

Steroids and thyroid hormones	Protein- bound	Cell interior	Activates genes	Slow (hours to days)

not bound to plasma proteins. As we shall see, the degree of protein binding also influences the rate of metabolism and the excretion of the hormone.

HORMONE METABOLISM AND EXCRETION

A hormone's concentration in the plasma depends not only upon its rate of secretion by the endocrine gland but also upon its rate of .removal from the blood, either by excretion or by metabolic transformation. The liver and the kidneys are the most important organs that excrete or metabolize hormones. Because for many hormones and their metabolites the rate of urinary excretion is directly proportional to the original rate of secretion, the excretion rate can be used as an indicator of the secretory rate.

The liver and kidneys are not the only routes for eliminating hormones. Sometimes the hormone is metabolized by the cells upon which it acts. For example, endocytosis of plasma-membrane hormone-receptor complexes enables cells to remove peptide hormones rapidly from their surfaces and catabolize them intracellularly—the receptors are then often recycled to the plasma membrane.

In general, catecholamine and peptide hormones, which circulate mainly free in the plasma, are comparatively easily excreted or attacked by enzymes in the blood and tissues. These hormones therefore tend to remain in the bloodstream for only brief periods—minutes to a few hours. In contrast, because protein-bound hormones are less vulnerable to excretion or metabolism by enzymes,

FIGURE 10-6
Possible fates and actions of a hormone following its secretion by an endocrine cell. Not all paths apply to all hormones.

removal of the circulating steroid and thyroid hormones generally takes many hours or even several days.

In some cases, metabolism of the hormone after its secretion *activates* the hormone rather than inactivates it. In other words, the secreted hormone may be relatively or completely unable to act upon a target cell until metabolism elsewhere in the body transforms it into a substance that can act. We have already seen one example of hormone activation—the conversion of circulating T_4 to the far more active T_3 by various organs. Another example is provided by testosterone, which is converted to dihydrotestosterone in certain of its target cells. This latter steroid, rather than testosterone itself, then elicits the response of the target cell.

There is another kind of activation that applies to a few hormones. Instead of the hormone itself being activated after secretion, it acts enzymatically on another plasma protein to split off a peptide that functions as the active hormone. The best known example of this is the renin-angiotensin system, described in Chapters 14 and 16.

Figure 10-6 summarizes the fates of hormones after their secretion.

MECHANISMS OF HORMONE ACTION

Hormone Receptors

Because they travel in the blood, hormones are able to reach virtually all tissues. Yet the body's response to a hormone is not all-inclusive but highly specific, involving only the target cells for that hormone. The ability to respond depends upon the presence on (or in) the target cells of specific receptors for those hormones.

As emphasized in Chapter 7, the response of a target cell to a chemical messenger is only the final event in a sequence that begins when the messenger binds to specific cell receptors. Where in the target cells are the hormone receptors located? The receptors for steroid hormones and the thyroid hormones are proteins *inside* the target cells. Because these hormones are lipid-soluble, they readily cross the plasma membrane and combine with their specific intracellular receptors.

In contrast, the receptors for the peptide hormones and catecholamines are proteins located on the plasma membranes of the target cells. However, many peptide hormones do in fact gain entry to the interior of cells by endocytosis of the plasma-membrane hormone-receptor complex (this is an example of receptor-mediated endocytosis, described in Chapter 6). It is likely that most of the hormone-receptor complexes internalized in this way simply undergo catabolism, but it is also possible that either they or the peptide fragments resulting from their catabolism exert additional effects upon the target cell.

Hormones can influence the ability of target cells to respond to them by regulating hormone receptors. Basic concepts of receptor modulation (up-regulation and down-regulation) were described in Chapter 7. In the context of hormones, **up-regulation** is an increase in the number of a hormone's receptors on a target cell resulting from prolonged exposure to a low concentration of the hormone. **Down-regulation** is a decrease in receptor number resulting from exposure to high concentrations of the hormone.

Hormones can down-regulate or up-regulate not only their own receptors but the receptors for other hormones as well. If one hormone induces a loss of a second hormone's receptors, the result will be a reduction of the second hormone's effectiveness. On the other hand, a hormone may induce an increase in the number of receptors for a second hormone. In this case the effectiveness of the second hormone is increased.

This last phenomenon, in some cases, underlies the important hormone-hormone interaction known as permissiveness. In general terms, **permissiveness** means that hormone A must be present for the full exertion of hormone B's effect. A low concentration of hormone A is usually all that is needed for this permissive effect, which is due to A's positive effect on B's receptors. For example, as shown in Figure 10-7, epinephrine causes the release of fatty acids from adipose tissue, but only in the presence of permissive amounts of thyroid hormone because thyroid hormone facilitates the synthesis of receptors for epinephrine in adipose tissue. It should be noted, however, that receptor alteration does not explain all cases of permissiveness; often the explanation is not known.

FIGURE 10-7

Ability of thyroid hormone to "permit" epinephrine-induced release of fatty acids from adipose-tissue cells. The thyroid hormones exert this effect by causing an increased number of epinephrine receptors on the cell.

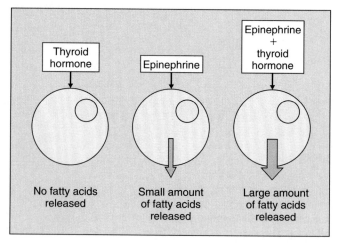

Events Elicited by Hormone-Receptor Binding

Effects of Peptide Hormones and Catecholamines.
As described above, the receptors for peptide hormones and the catecholamine hormones are located on the outer surface of the target cell's plasma membrane. Most of these receptors utilize one or more of the signal transduction mechanisms and second messengers described in Chapter 7: channels that are part of receptors, channels gated by G proteins, cyclic AMP, cyclic GMP, calcium, and the phosphatidylinositol system. Again as described in Chapter 7, all these signal transduction mechanisms result in alterations of protein activity, leading to the cell's ultimate response to the hormones.

Effects of Steroid and Thyroid Hormones.
The common denominator of the effects of the steroid and thyroid hormones is a change in the rate of synthesis of specific proteins—enzymes, structural proteins, and so on—by their target cells. These hormones increase or decrease protein synthesis by stimulating or inhibiting the production of mRNA via the following sequence of events (Figure 10-8). The receptors for steroid and thyroid hormones are synthesized in the cytosol and then move into the nu-

cleus. In most cases, therefore, the hormone diffuses first across the cell's plasma membrane and then the nuclear membrane and binds to its specific receptor in the nucleus. However, in some cases, the hormone combines with receptor still in the cytosol, and the entire complex then moves into the nucleus. In all cases, the receptor, activated by the binding of hormone to it, binds in the nucleus to segments of DNA specific for it. This binding to DNA occurs in the promoter region of a gene in that section of DNA and results in a change in the rate of its transcription. That is, the activated receptor stimulates or inhibits the synthesis of particular molecules of mRNA, which then enter the cytosol and serve as templates for synthesis of specific proteins. More than one gene may be activated by a given hormone-receptor complex.

Pharmacological Effects of Hormones

Administration of very large quantities of a hormone for medical purposes may have effects that are never seen in a normal person. They are called ***pharmacological effects***, and they can also occur in diseases when excessive amounts of hormones are secreted. Pharmacological effects are of great importance in medicine, since hormones are often used in large doses as therapeutic agents. Per-

FIGURE 10-8

Steroid and thyroid hormones enter the target cell and bind to their specific receptors, usually in the nucleus. For some hormones (not shown) the binding takes place in the cytosol rather than the nucleus, and the hormone-receptor complex then moves into the nucleus. The activated receptor interacts with specific genes in DNA and stimulates (or, in some cases, inhibits) the transcription of mRNA, which directs the synthesis of the proteins that mediate the cell's response.

haps the most common example is that of the adrenal cortical hormone cortisol, which is administered in large amounts to suppress allergic and inflammatory reactions.

TYPES OF INPUTS THAT CONTROL HORMONE SECRETION

Most hormones are released in short bursts, with little or no release occurring between bursts. Accordingly, the plasma concentrations of hormones may fluctuate rapidly over brief time periods. Hormones also manifest 24-h cyclical variations in their secretory rates, the circadian patterns being different for different hormones. Some are clearly linked to sleep. For example, Figure 10-9 illustrates how growth hormone's secretion is markedly increased during the early period of sleep. The mechanisms underlying these cycles are ultimately traceable to cyclical variations in the activity of neural pathways involved in the hormone's release.

Hormone secretion is controlled mainly by four types of inputs to endocrine cells (Figure 10-10): (1) changes in the plasma concentrations of mineral ions; (2) changes in the plasma concentrations of organic nutrients; (3) neurotransmitters released from neurons impinging on the endocrine cell; and (4) another hormone (or, in some cases, a paracrine agent) acting on the endocrine cell. There is actually a fifth type of input—chemical and physical factors in the lumen of the gastrointestinal tract—but it applies only to the hormones secreted by the gastrointestinal tract and will be described in Chapter 17.

Before we look more closely at each category, it must be stressed that, in many cases, hormone secretion is influenced by more than one input. For example, insulin secretion is controlled by the extracellular concentrations of glucose and other nutrients, by both sympathetic and parasympathetic neurons to the insulin-secreting endocrine cells and by several hormones acting on these cells. Thus, endocrine cells, like neurons, may be subject to multiple, simultaneous, often opposing inputs, and the resulting output—the rate of hormone secretion—reflects the integration of all these inputs.

One more point should be made to avoid misunderstanding. The term "secretion" applied to a hormone denotes its synthesis and release from the cell. Some inputs to endocrine cells specifically stimulate or inhibit only synthesis, for example, by altering the expression of the gene for that hormone, with changes in release occurring as a secondary result. In contrast, other inputs directly influence only the actual release of the hormone from the cell, and some inputs influence both synthesis and release. For simplicity in this chapter and hereafter, we will generally not distinguish between these possibilities when we refer to stimulation or inhibition of hormone "secretion."

Control by Plasma Concentrations of Mineral Ions or Organic Nutrients

There are at least five hormones whose secretion is directly controlled, at least in part, by the plasma concentrations of specific mineral ions or organic nutrients. In each case, a major function of the hormone is to regulate, in a negative-feedback manner, the plasma concentration of the ion or nutrient controlling its secretion. For example, insulin secretion is stimulated by an elevated plasma glucose concentration, and the additional insulin then causes, by several actions, the plasma glucose concentration to decrease (Figure 10-11).

Control by Neurons

The adrenal medulla behaves like a sympathetic ganglion and thus is stimulated by sympathetic preganglionic fibers. In addition to its control of the adrenal medulla, the autonomic nervous system has other influences on the endocrine system (Figure 10-12). Various endocrine glands receive a rich supply of sympathetic and, in some cases, parasympathetic neurons, whose activity influences the glands' rates of hormone secretion. Examples are the secretion of insulin and the gastrointestinal hormones. In most cases studied, the autonomic input serves not as the sole regulator of the hormone's secretion but rather as one of multiple inputs.

Thus far, our discussion of neural control of hormone release has been limited to the role of the *autonomic* ner-

FIGURE 10-9

Plasma growth hormone concentrations in a normal 23-year-old male over 24 h. [*Adapted from Sassin et al. (1972).*]

FIGURE 10-10 (*Above*)

Types of inputs that act directly on endocrine-gland cells to stimulate or inhibit hormone secretion.

FIGURE 10-11 (*Left*)

Example of how the direct control of hormone secretion by the plasma concentration of a substance, either organic nutrient or mineral ion, results in the negative-feedback control of that substance's plasma concentration.

FIGURE 10-12 (*Below*)

Pathways by which the nervous system influences hormone secretion. (A) Neurons in the hypothalamus, some of which terminate in the posterior pituitary, themselves secrete hormones. (B) The autonomic nervous system controls hormone secretion by the adrenal medulla and many other endocrine glands; both parasympathetic and sympathetic inputs to these other glands may occur, some inhibitory and some stimulatory. Not shown is that each neuron in the central nervous system is under the influence of the many other neurons synapsing upon it.

vous system. However, one large group of hormones—those secreted by the hypothalamus and its extension, the posterior pituitary—are under the direct control not of autonomic neurons but of neurons in the brain itself (Figure 10-12). This category will be described in detail later in this chapter.

Control by Other Hormones

In many cases, the secretion of a particular hormone is directly controlled by the blood concentration of another hormone. As we shall see, there are often complex sequences in which the only function of the first few hormones in the sequence is to stimulate the secretion of the next one. A hormone that stimulates the secretion of another hormone is often referred to as a **tropic hormone**. The tropic hormones usually stimulate not only secretion but the growth of the gland as well.

CONTROL SYSTEMS INVOLVING THE HYPOTHALAMUS AND PITUITARY

The **pituitary gland** (or hypophysis) lies in a pocket of bone at the base of the brain (Figure 10-13), just below the brain area called the **hypothalamus**. The pituitary is connected to the hypothalamus by a stalk (the infundibulum) containing nerve fibers and small blood vessels. In adult human beings, the pituitary gland is composed of two adjacent lobes—the **anterior pituitary** (toward the front of the head) and the **posterior pituitary** (toward the back of the head)—each of which is a more-or-less distinct gland.[3] The anterior pituitary and its part of the stalk are termed the adenohypophysis, and the posterior pituitary with its part of the stalk is the neurohypophysis.

The posterior pituitary is an outgrowth of the hypothalamus and is neural tissue. The axons of two well-defined clusters of hypothalamic neurons pass down the infundibulum and end within the posterior pituitary in close proximity to capillaries (the smallest of blood vessels) (Figure 10-13).

In contrast to the neural connections between the hypothalamus and *posterior* pituitary, there are no important neural connections between the hypothalamus and *anterior* pituitary. There is, however, an unusual *blood-vessel* connection (Figure 10-13B). The capillaries at the base of the hypothalamus (the **median eminence**) recombine into the **hypothalamo-pituitary portal vessels**—the

term "portal" denotes vessels that connect distinct capillary beds. The hypothalamo-pituitary portal vessels pass down the stalk connecting the hypothalamus and pituitary and enter the anterior pituitary where they drain into a second capillary bed, the anterior pituitary capillaries. Thus, the hypothalamo-pituitary portal vessels offer a local route for blood flow directly from the hypothalamus to the anterior pituitary.

As shown in Figure 10-13B, the hypothalamo-pituitary portal vessels are not the only portal-type vessels involving the anterior pituitary. A second group—termed the short portal vessels—carries some blood directly from the posterior pituitary to the anterior pituitary. It must be emphasized that the short portal vessels carry only a small portion of the blood leaving the posterior pituitary, the rest going by a different set of vessels directly to the heart. With one important exception to be described in the next section, the short portal vessels will not be mentioned again in this book.

Posterior Pituitary Hormones

Earlier we stressed that the posterior pituitary is really a neural extension of the hypothalamus (Figure 10-13). The term "posterior pituitary hormones" is somewhat of a misnomer, therefore, since the hormones are not synthesized in the posterior pituitary itself but in the hypothalamus, specifically in the cell bodies of the hypothalamic neurons whose axons pass through the infundibulum and end in the posterior pituitary. Only one hormone is produced by any particular neuron. Enclosed in small vesicles, the hormone moves down the neural axons to accumulate at the axon terminals in the posterior pituitary. In response to an action potential in the axon, the hormone is released into the capillaries and carried away by the blood returning to the heart.

The two well-established posterior pituitary hormones are **oxytocin** and **vasopressin** (the latter is also known as **antidiuretic hormone**, or **ADH**). Vasopressin participates in the control of water excretion by the kidneys and of blood pressure (Chapters 14 and 16). Oxytocin acts on the breasts and uterus (Chapter 19).

Recent studies indicate that there are probably two other posterior pituitary hormones—the catecholamine dopamine and an as yet unidentified substance termed **prolactin releasing factor (PRF)**. Dopamine and PRF help control secretion of a hormone—prolactin—from the *anterior* pituitary (see below); this is the one case in which the short portal vessels described in the previous section are known to be important—they provide a route directly from the posterior pituitary to the anterior pituitary.

Vasopressin, oxytocin, and dopamine are also produced in other areas of the brain and serve in these locations as neurotransmitters or neuromodulators.

---

[3]In many mammalian species an intermediate lobe is found between the anterior and posterior portions of the pituitary, but this is not the case in humans.

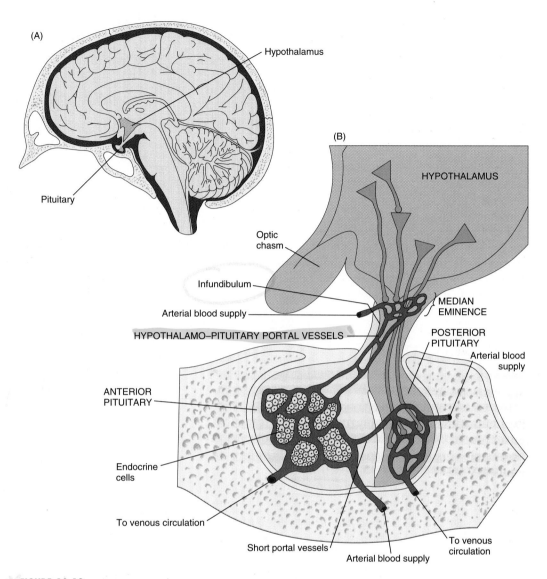

FIGURE 10-13

(A) Relation of the pituitary gland to the brain and hypothalamus. (B) Neural and vascular connections between the hypothalamus and pituitary. Some hypothalamic neurons run down the infindibulum to end in the posterior pituitary, whereas others end in the median eminence. Almost the entire blood supply of the anterior pituitary comes via the hypothalamo-pituitary portal vessels, which originate in the median eminence. The short portal vessels, which originate in the posterior pituitary, carry only a small fraction of the blood leaving the posterior pituitary and supply only a small fraction of the blood supplying the anterior pituitary.

The Hypothalamus and Anterior Pituitary

Hypothalamic neurons, in addition to producing the hormones released from the *posterior* pituitary, secrete other hormones that control, in large part, the secretion of all the *anterior* pituitary hormones. These other hypothalamic hormones are collectively termed **hypophysio-** **tropic hormones** (recall that another name for the pituitary is hypophysis); they are also commonly called hypothalamic releasing hormones. One more word about terminology is appropriate: "Hypophysiotropic hormones" denotes only those hormones from the *hypothalamus* that influence the anterior pituitary. We shall see later that nonhypothalamic hormones also can influence the anterior pituitary, but they are not categorized as hypophysiotropic hormones.

With one exception, each of the hypophysiotropic hormones is the beginning of a sequence of three hormones: (1) A hypophysiotropic hormone controls the secretion of (2) an anterior pituitary hormone, which controls the secretion of (3) a hormone from some other endocrine gland (Figure 10-14). This last hormone then acts on its target cells. We begin our description of these sequences in the middle, that is, with the anterior pituitary hormones, because the names and actions of the hypophysiotropic hormones are all based on the names of the anterior pituitary hormones.

Before proceeding, however, we must emphasize that the hypophysiotropic hormones are the *major* but not the *sole* controllers of anterior pituitary function. Hormones produced in locations other than the hypothalamus also exert important effects on hormone secretion by the anterior pituitary.

Anterior Pituitary Hormones. As shown in Table 10-1, the anterior pituitary secretes at least eight hormones, but only six have well-established functions. All peptides, these six "classical" hormones are **follicle-stimulating hormone (FSH), luteinizing hormone (LH), growth hormone (GH), thyroid-stimulating hormone (TSH,** thyrotropin), **prolactin,** and **adrenocorticotropic hormone (ACTH,** corticotropin). Each of the last four is probably secreted by a distinct cell type in the anterior pituitary, whereas FSH and LH, collectively termed **gonadotropic hormones** because they stimulate the gonads, are both secreted by the same cells.

What about the other two peptides—β-lipotropin and β-endorphin—secreted by the anterior pituitary? They are initially synthesized as part of the large **pro-opiomelanocortin** molecule (Figure 10-15), which is then cleaved in the cell to form ACTH and other peptides, including **β-lipotropin**. The latter molecule is cleaved, in turn, to form the powerful opioid **β-endorphin**. Then β-lipotropin and β-endorphin, and perhaps other cleavage products as well, are cosecreted from the anterior pituitary along with ACTH. The functions of circulating β-lipotropin and β-endorphin are not presently known, but some possibilities are described in Chapters 9 and 13.

The target organs and major functions of the six classical anterior pituitary hormones are summarized in Figure 10-16. Note that the only major function of two of the six is to stimulate secretion of other hormones: Thyroid-stimulating hormone induces secretion of thyroid hormones—thyroxine and triiodothyronine—from the thyroid; adrenocorticotropic hormone, meaning "hormone that stimulates the adrenal cortex," stimulates the secretion of cortisol by that gland.

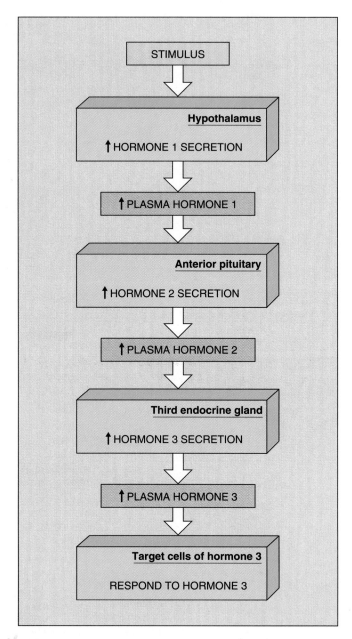

FIGURE 10-14

Typical sequential pattern by which a hypothalamic hormone controls the secretion of an anterior pituitary hormone, which in turn controls the secretion of a hormone by a third endocrine gland. As will be described later (Figures 10-20 through 10-23), the second and third hormones in the sequence usually also exert feedback effects on the sequence.

Three other anterior pituitary hormones also stimulate secretion of another hormone but have an additional function as well: Follicle-stimulating hormone and luteinizing hormone stimulate secretion of the sex hormones—

FIGURE 10-15

After its synthesis in the anterior pituitary, the pro-opiomelanocortin molecule is successively cleaved to yield ACTH and other peptides, the most important of which is β-endorphin, an endogenous opiod. The other peptides are cosecreted with ACTH. For simplicity, several of the peptides resulting from the cleavages have not been named in the figure; they are represented by empty boxes.

estradiol, progesterone, and testosterone—by the gonads and, in addition, regulate the growth and development of sperm and ova. Growth hormone stimulates the liver and many other body cells to secrete a growth-promoting peptide hormone known as **insulin-like growth factor I** (**IGF-I**, also called somatomedin C) and, in addition, exerts direct effects on the metabolism of protein, carbohydrate, and lipid by various organs and tissues (Chapter 18).

Prolactin is unique among the anterior pituitary hormones in that it does not exert major control over the secretion of a hormone by another endocrine gland. Rather, its most important action is to stimulate development of the mammary glands and milk production by direct effects upon the breasts. In the male, prolactin may facilitate several components of reproductive function.

It should be emphasized that many, perhaps all, of the anterior pituitary hormones are also secreted by cells elsewhere in the body and may, in those other sites, exert functions (as neurotransmitters, neuromodulators, or paracrine agents) quite different from those summarized in Figure 10-16.

Hypophysiotropic Hormones. As stated above, secretion of the anterior pituitary hormones is largely regulated

FIGURE 10-16

Targets and major functions of the six classical anterior pituitary hormones.

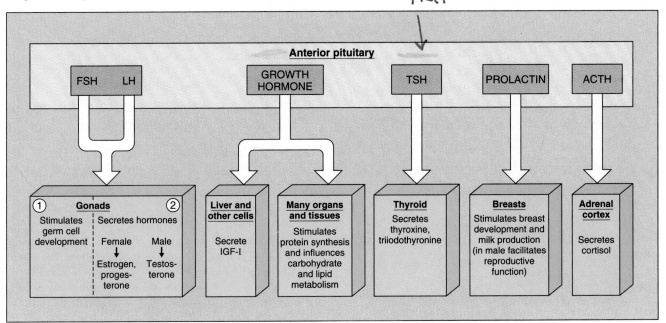

by hormones produced by the hypothalamus and collectively called hypophysiotropic hormones. These hormones are secreted by neurons that originate in diverse areas of the hypothalamus and terminate in the median eminence around the capillaries that are the origins of the hypothalamo-pituitary portal vessels. The generation of action potentials in these neurons causes them to release their hormones, which enter the capillaries and are carried to the anterior pituitary by the hypothalamo-pituitary portal vessels (Figure 10-17). There they act upon the various anterior pituitary cells to control their hormone secretions.

Thus, these hypothalamic neurons secrete hormones in a manner identical to that described previously for the hypothalamic neurons whose axons end in the posterior pituitary. In both cases the hormones are made in hypothalamic neurons, pass down axons to the neuron terminals, and are released in response to action potentials in the neurons. The crucial differences, however, between the two systems need emphasizing: (1) The axons of the hypothalamic neurons that secrete the posterior pituitary hormones leave the hypothalamus and end in the posterior pituitary, whereas those that secrete the hypophysiotropic hormones remain in the hypothalamus, ending in its median eminence. (2) Most of the posterior pituitary capillaries, into which the posterior pituitary hormones are secreted, immediately drain into the main bloodstream, which carries the hormones to the heart to be distributed to the entire body.[4] In contrast, the capillaries entered by the hypophysiotropic hormones in the median eminence of the hypothalamus do not directly join the main bloodstream but empty into the hypothalamo-pituitary portal vessels, which provide a direct route to the anterior pituitary (from which the blood then returns to the heart). Thus, the anterior pituitary is uniquely exposed to plasma concentrations of the hypophysiotropic hormones much higher than those existing in systemic arterial plasma.

There are multiple discrete hypophysiotropic hormones, each secreted by a particular group of hypotha-

---

[4]Some blood, as described earlier in the text, does go directly to the anterior pituitary via a set of "short portal vessels" connecting the posterior and anterior pituitaries.

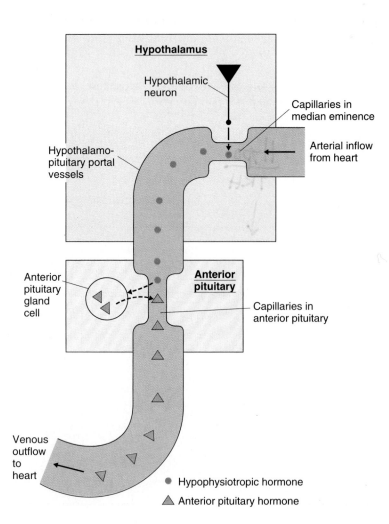

FIGURE 10-17

Hormone secretion by the anterior pituitary is controlled by hypophysiotropic hormones released by hypothalamic neurons and reaching the anterior pituitary by way of the hypothalamo-pituitary portal vessels.

lamic neurons and influencing the release of one or more of the anterior pituitary hormones. For simplicity, Figure 10-18 and this chapter summarize only those hypophysiotropic hormones that are known to play important roles and whose structures have been identified.[5] Each is named according to an anterior pituitary hormone whose secretion it controls; for example, the secretion of growth hormone is stimulated by **growth hormone releasing hormone (GHRH)**, and the secretion of ACTH is stimulated by **corticotropin releasing hormone (CRH)**.[6]

_____

[5]A variety of other substances, some of which have not yet been identified, very likely function as hypophysiotropic hormones, but their precise contributions remain to be determined.

[6]Interestingly, the hypothalamic neurons that secrete CRH cosecrete vasopressin, which also stimulates ACTH secretion. Thus vasopressin is secreted not only by neurons that end in the posterior pituitary but also by neurons that end in the median eminence.

As shown in Figure 10-18, at least two of the hypophysiotropic hormones do not cause _release_ of anterior pituitary hormones but rather _inhibit_ their release. One of them inhibits secretion of growth hormone and is most commonly called **somatostatin (SS)**. The other— dopamine (also termed, in this location, prolactin inhibiting hormone)—inhibits secretion of prolactin. Here is a potential source of confusion: We mentioned earlier in this chapter that dopamine is released from the _posterior pituitary_ and is therefore a posterior pituitary hormone; now we have stated that dopamine is also released from the median eminence of the hypothalamus and is therefore also a hypophysiotropic hormone. This should reinforce the generalization, made several times already, that a single hormone is often produced in multiple sites.

As also shown in Figure 10-18, there is not a strict one-to-one correspondence of hypophysiotropic hormone and anterior pituitary hormone. For one thing, in at least three

FIGURE 10-18

Major known hypophysiotropic hormones and their effects on the anterior pituitary.

Major, known hypophysiotropic hormones	Effect on anterior pituitary
Corticotropin releasing hormone (CRH)	Stimulates secretion of ACTH
Thyrotropin releasing hormone (TRH)	Stimulates secretion of TSH and prolactin
Growth hormone releasing hormone (GHRH)	Stimulates secretion of GH
Somatostatin (SS, also known as growth hormone release inhibiting hormone, GIH)	Inhibits secretion of GH and TSH (and possibly several other hormones)
Gonadotropin releasing hormone (GnRH)	Stimulates secretion of LH and FSH
Dopamine (DA, also known as prolactin release inhibiting hormone, PIH)°	Inhibits secretion of prolactin

°Dopamine is a catecholamine; all the other hypophysiotropic hormones are peptides.

cases, a hypophysiotropic hormone influences the secretion of more than one anterior pituitary hormone: (1) **gonadotropin releasing hormone (GnRH)** stimulates the secretion of both FSH and LH, (2) **thyrotropin releasing hormone (TRH)** stimulates the secretion not only of TSH but of prolactin as well, and (3) somatostatin inhibits the secretion not only of growth hormone but also of TSH.[7]

The cases described in the previous paragraph are of a single hypophysiotropic hormone controlling more than one anterior pituitary hormone, but Figure 10-18 also shows that in at least three cases—growth hormone, TSH and prolactin—secretion of a single anterior pituitary hormone is controlled by more than one hypophysiotropic hormone. Moreover, the several hypophysiotropic hormones involved may exert opposing effects. Thus, as we have seen, the secretion of growth hormone is controlled by two hypophysiotropic hormones—somatostatin, which inhibits its release, and growth hormone releasing hormone, which stimulates it. In such multiple-control cases, the anterior pituitary response depends upon the relative amounts of the opposing hormones released by the hypothalamic neurons, as well as upon the relative sensitivities of the anterior pituitary to them.

Control of prolactin secretion offers a further example of this generalization. As shown in Figure 10-18, the hypothalamus secretes two established hypophysiotropic hormones—TRH and dopamine—that influence prolactin secretion. TRH stimulates prolactin secretion (just as it does TSH secretion), whereas dopamine inhibits it. In addition, not shown in the figure, there is evidence for at least one other, as-yet-unidentified, hypophysiotropic hormone, distinct from TRH, that stimulates prolactin secretion. The important point is that under basal conditions the inhibitory hormone—dopamine—is dominant over all stimulatory inputs from the hypothalamus (and elsewhere), and so prolactin secretion is quite low. As described in Chapter 19, this balance changes during pregnancy and lactation, and prolactin secretion increases markedly.

With one exception, all the known hypophysiotropic hormones are peptides. These peptides all also occur in locations other than the hypothalamus, particularly in other areas of the central nervous system, where they function as neurotransmitters or neuromodulators, and in the gastrointestinal tract. The one hypophysiotropic hormone that is not a peptide is dopamine. As described earlier, this substance is a member of the catecholamine family.

---

[7]Somatostatin can also inhibit several other anterior pituitary hormones, although whether these inhibitory effects are physiological is still not clear.

Figure 10-19 summarizes the information presented in Figures 10-16 and 10-18 to demonstrate the full sequences controlled by the hypothalamus.

Given that the hypophysiotropic hormones control anterior pituitary function, we must now ask: What controls secretion of the hypophysiotropic hormones? Some of the neurons that secrete hypophysiotropic hormones may possess spontaneous activity, but the firing of most of them requires neuronal and hormonal input. First, let us deal with the neuronal input.

Neural Control of Hypophysiotropic Hormones. The hypothalamus receives synaptic input, both stimulatory and inhibitory, from virtually all areas of the central nervous system, and specific neural pathways influence secretion of the individual releasing hormones. A large number of neurotransmitters, including the catecholamines, acetylcholine, and β-endorphin, are used at the synapses on the hormone-secreting hypothalamic neurons, and this explains why the secretion of the hypophysiotropic hormones can be altered by drugs that influence these neurotransmitters.

Figure 10-20 illustrates one example of the role of neural input to the hypothalamus. Corticotropin releasing hormone (CRH), secreted by the hypothalamus, stimulates the anterior pituitary to secrete ACTH, which in turn stimulates the adrenal cortex to secrete cortisol. A wide variety of stresses, both physical and emotional, act via neural pathways to the hypothalamus to increase CRH secretion and, hence, ACTH and cortisol secretion, markedly above basal values. Thus, stress is the common denominator of reflexes leading to increased cortisol secretion. Cortisol then functions to facilitate an individual's response to stress. Even in an unstressed person, however, the secretion of cortisol varies in a highly stereotyped manner during a 24-h period because neural rhythms within the central nervous system also impinge upon the hypothalamic neurons that secrete CRH.

Hormonal Feedback Control of the Hypothalamus and Anterior Pituitary. A prominent feature of each of the hormonal sequences initiated by the hypophysiotropic hormones is negative feedback exerted upon the hypothalamo-pituitary system by one or more of the hormones in the sequence. For example, in the CRH-ACTH-cortisol sequence (Figure 10-20), the final hormone—cortisol—acts upon the hypothalamus to reduce secretion of CRH by causing a decrease in the frequency of action potentials in the neurons secreting CRH. In addition, cortisol acts directly on the anterior pituitary to reduce the response of the ACTH-secreting cells to CRH. Thus, by a double-barreled action, cortisol exerts a negative-feedback control over its own secretion.

Such a system is effective in dampening hormonal re-

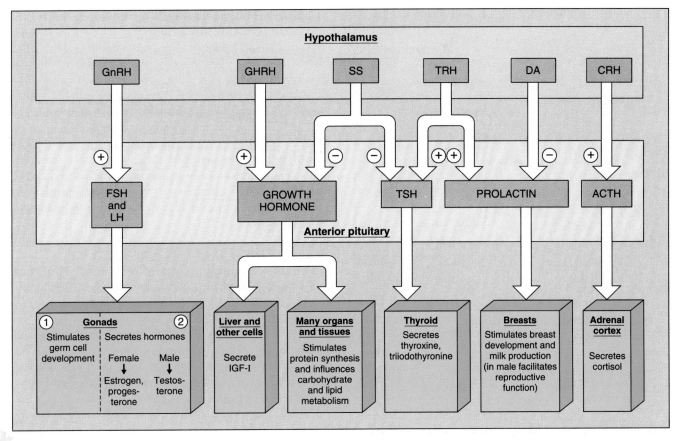

FIGURE 10-19

A combination of Figures 10-16 and 10-18 summarizes the hypothalamic-anterior-pituitary system.

sponses, that is, in limiting the extremes of hormone secretory rates. For example, when a painful stimulus elicits increased secretion of CRH, ACTH, and cortisol, the resulting elevation in plasma cortisol concentration feeds back to inhibit the hypothalamus and anterior pituitary. Therefore, cortisol secretion does not rise as much as it would without these negative feedbacks.

Another adaptive function of these negative feedbacks is that they maintain the plasma concentration of the final hormone in a sequence relatively constant whenever a primary change occurs in the metabolism of that hormone. An example of this is shown in Figure 10-21 for cortisol.

Another example is provided by the TRH-TSH-TH system. The thyroid hormones (TH) exert a feedback inhibition on the hypothalamo-pituitary system, mainly by decreasing the response of TSH-secreting cells to the stimulatory effects of TRH. Since iodine is essential for the synthesis of TH, individuals with iodine deficiencies tend to have a deficient production of TH. The resulting decrease in plasma TH concentration relieves some of the feedback inhibition TH exerts on the pituitary. Therefore, more TSH is secreted in response to the TRH coming from the hypothalamus, and the increased plasma TSH

stimulates the thyroid gland to enlarge and to utilize more efficiently whatever iodine is available (the enlarged gland is known as *iodine-deficient goiter*). In this manner, plasma TH concentration can be kept quite close to normal.

The situations described above for cortisol and the thyroid hormones, in which the hormone secreted by the third endocrine gland in a sequence exerts a negative-feedback effect over the anterior pituitary and/or hypothalamus, is known as a **long-loop negative feedback** (Figure 10-22). This type of feedback exists for each of the five three-hormone sequences initiated by a hypophysiotropic hormone.

Long-loop feedback cannot exist for prolactin since this is the one anterior pituitary hormone that does not have major control over another endocrine gland; that is, it does not participate in a three-hormone sequence. Nonetheless, there is negative feedback in the prolactin system, for this hormone itself acts upon the hypothalamus to influence the secretion of at least one—dopamine—of the hypothalamic hormones that control its secretion. This influence of an anterior pituitary hormone on the hypothalamus is known as a **short-loop negative feedback** (Figure

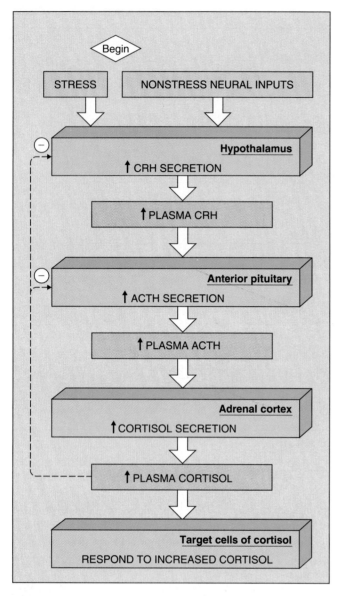

FIGURE 10-20

CRH-ACTH-cortisol sequence. The "stress" input to the hypothalamus is via neural pathways. Cortisol exerts a negative feedback control over the system by acting on (1) the hypothalamus to inhibit CRH secretion and (2) the anterior pituitary to reduce responsiveness to CRH. Not shown is that vasopressin and other messengers released both by hypothalamic neurons and by peripheral tissues also act on the anterior pituitary to stimulate ACTH secretion. The common denominator of many of the effects of cortisol is to increase plasma glucose concentration and to facilitate a person's responses to stress (Chapters 18 and 20).

10-22). Several anterior pituitary hormones (growth hormone, for example) other than prolactin also exert such feedback on the hypothalamus.

The Role of "Nonsequence" Hormones on the Hypothalamus and Anterior Pituitary. It must be emphasized that there are many hormonal influences, both stimulatory and inhibitory, on the secretion of hormones by the hypothalamus and/or anterior pituitary other than those that fit the feedback patterns just described. In other words, a hormone that is not itself in a particular hormonal sequence may nevertheless exert important influences on the secretion of the hypothalamic or anterior pituitary hormones in that sequence. For example, estrogen markedly enhances the secretion of prolactin by the anterior pituitary, even though estrogen secretion is not controlled by prolactin. Thus, one should not view these sequences as isolated units.

A Summary Example: Control of Growth Hormone Secretion. The three-hormone sequences beginning in the hypothalamus can be extremely complex, incorporating multiple sites of feedback, both long-loop and short-loop, as well as other hormones not in the sequence. Purely for the sake of illustrating this complexity, we describe here the control of growth hormone secretion (Figure 10-23), building upon the information already presented in this chapter.

Recall from Figure 10-18 that the secretion of GH by the anterior pituitary is controlled mainly by two hormones from the hypothalamus: (1) somatostatin, which inhibits GH secretion; and (2) GHRH, which stimulates it. With such a dual control system, the rate of GH secretion at any moment reflects the relative amounts of simultaneous stimulation by GHRH and inhibition by somatostatin. For example, as shown in Figure 10-9, very little growth hormone is secreted during the day in nonstressed persons who are eating normally, and whether this reflects a very low secretion of GHRH or a very high secretion of somatostatin is not yet clear. Similarly, a large number of physiological states (exercise, stress, fasting, a low plasma glucose concentration, and sleep) stimulate growth hormone secretion by decreasing the secretion of somatostatin and/or increasing that of GHRH.

As shown in Figures 10-16 and 10-19, growth hormone stimulates the secretion of another hormone, IGF-I, from the liver and many other target cells of GH. This makes possible a variety of feedbacks by which an increase in plasma GH results in inhibition of GH secretion (Figure 10-23): (1) a short-loop negative feedback exerted by GH on the hypothalamus, and (2) a long-loop negative feedback exerted by IGF-I on the hypothalamus. Both of these feedbacks operate by inhibiting secretion of GHRH and/or stimulating secretion of somatostatin, the result in either case being less stimulation of GH secretion. In addition, (3) IGF-I also acts directly on the pituitary to inhibit the stimulatory effect of GHRH on GH secretion; again, the result is decreased GH secretion.

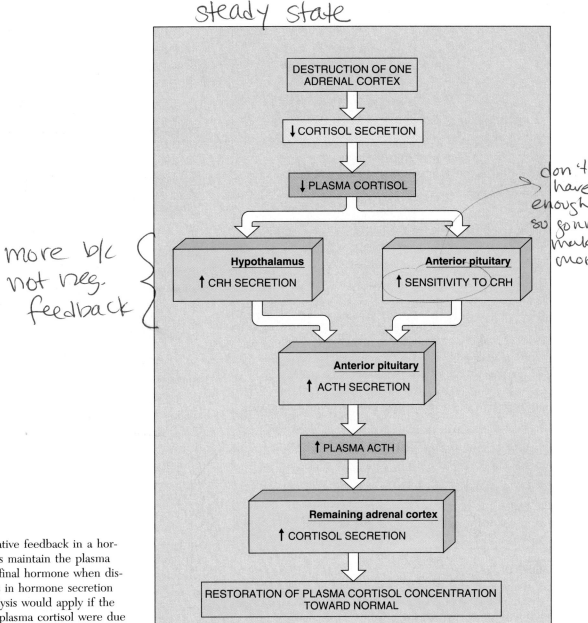

steady state

more b/c not neg. feedback

don't have enough so gonna make more

FIGURE 10-21

Example of how negative feedback in a hormonal sequence helps maintain the plasma concentration of the final hormone when disease-induced changes in hormone secretion occur. The same analysis would apply if the original reduction in plasma cortisol were due to excessive metabolism of cortisol rather than deficient secretion.

Finally, the secretion of growth hormone is influenced by several other hormones not in the sequence, for example, by the sex hormones. Some of these hormones may affect the sequence indirectly by altering the release of somatostatin and/or GHRH from the hypothalamus, whereas others may act directly upon the anterior pituitary.

CANDIDATE HORMONES

Many substances, termed **candidate hormones**, are suspected of being hormones in humans but are not considered classical hormones for one of two rea-

sons: Either (1) their functions have not been conclusively documented; or (2) they have well-documented functions as paracrine and autocrine agents, but it is not certain that they ever reach additional target cells via the blood, an essential criterion for classification as a hormone. This second category includes certain of the eicosanoids (Chapter 7) and a large number of what are called growth factors (Chapter 18) that are secreted by multiple cell types and stimulate specific cells to differentiate and undergo cell division.

A substance that fits the first category described above is the amino acid derivative **melatonin**, which is synthesized from serotonin. This candidate hormone is produced by the **pineal gland** (also known as the pineal body), an

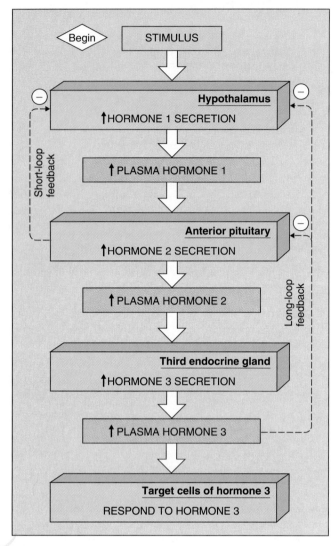

FIGURE 10-22

Short-loop and long-loop feedbacks. Long-loop feedback is exerted on the hypothalamus and/or anterior pituitary by the third hormone in the sequence. Short-loop feedback is exerted by the anterior pituitary hormone on the hypothalamus. A third type of negative feedback, not shown in the figure, is that the action of hormone 3 may eliminate the original stimulus for the secretion of hormone 1.

outgrowth from the roof of the diencephalon of the brain (see Figure 8-37). The function of melatonin and the pineal gland in humans, in contrast to several other animals, is uncertain. Its secretion is stimulated by sympathetic postganglionic neurons that constitute the last link in a neuronal chain primarily triggered by receptors in the eyes responding to the prevailing light-dark environment. Melatonin secretion, therefore, undergoes a marked 24-h cycle, being high at night and low during the day, and melatonin probably influences a variety of body rhythms.

Its relationship to **seasonal affective disorder** ("winter depression"), its ability to reduce the symptoms of jet lag, and its possible role in the onset of puberty are all being studied.

TYPES OF ENDOCRINE DISORDERS

Most endocrine disorders fall into one of three categories: (1) too little hormone (**hyposecretion**), (2) too much hormone (**hypersecretion**), and (3) reduced response of the target cells (**hyporesponsiveness**). The phrases "too little hormone" and "too much hormone" here mean "too little" or "too much" for any given physiological situation. For example, as we shall see, insulin secretion decreases during fasting, and this decrease is an adaptive physiological response, not too little insulin. In contrast, insulin secretion should increase after eating, and if its increase is less than normal, this is too little hormone secretion.

Hyposecretion

An endocrine gland may be secreting too little hormone because the gland is not able to function normally. This is termed **primary hyposecretion**. Examples of primary hyposecretion include (1) genetic absence of a steroid-forming enzyme, leading to decreased cortisol secretion, and (2) dietary deficiency of iodine, leading to decreased secretion of thyroid hormones. There are many other causes—infections, toxic chemicals, and so on—all having the common denominator of damaging the endocrine gland.

In contrast to primary hyposecretion, a gland may be secreting too little hormone not because the gland is abnormal but because there is not enough of its tropic hormone. This is termed **secondary hyposecretion**. For example, there may be nothing wrong with the thyroid gland, but it may be secreting too little thyroid hormone because the secretion of TSH by the anterior pituitary is abnormally low. Thus, the hyposecretion by the thyroid gland in this case is secondary to inadequate secretion by the anterior pituitary.

This example raises the next question applicable to any of the other anterior pituitary hormones as well: Is the hyposecretion of TSH primary, that is, due to a defect in the anterior pituitary, or is it secondary to a hypothalamic defect causing too little secretion of TRH? If the latter were true, then we would have the following sequence: primary hyposecretion of TRH leading to secondary hyposecretion of TSH leading to secondary hyposecretion of TH.

In diagnosing the presence of hyposecretion, a basic measurement to be made is the concentration of the

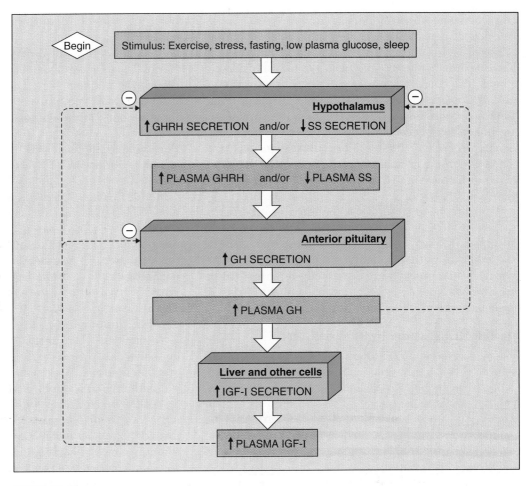

FIGURE 10-23

Hormonal pathways controlling the secretion of growth hormone (GH) and insulin-like growth factor I (IGF-I). At the hypothalamus, the minus sign (−) denotes that the input inhibits the secretion of growth hormone releasing hormone (GHRH) and/or stimulates the release of somatostatin (SS). Not shown in the figure is that several hormones (for example, the thyroid hormones) influence growth hormone secretion via effects on the hypothalamus and/or anterior pituitary.

hormone in either plasma or urine. The finding of a low concentration will not distinguish between primary and secondary hyposecretion, however. To do this, the concentration of the relevant tropic hormone must also be measured. Thus, in our example, if the hyposecretion of TH is secondary to hyposecretion of TSH, then the plasma concentrations of both will be decreased. If the hyposecretion of TH is primary, then TH concentration will be decreased and TSH concentration will be increased because of less negative-feedback inhibition by TH over TSH secretion.

Another diagnostic approach is to attempt to stimulate the gland in question by administering either its tropic hormone or some other substance known to elicit increased secretion. The increase in hormone secretion elicited by the stimulus will be normal if the original hyposecretion is secondary, but less than normal if primary hyposecretion is the problem.

The most common means of treating hormone hyposecretion is to administer the hormone that is missing or present in too small amounts. In cases of secondary hyposecretion, there is a choice since at least two hormones are involved. In our example, the TH deficiency could theoretically be eliminated by administering either TH or TSH.

Hypersecretion

A hormone can also undergo either ***primary hypersecretion*** (the gland is secreting too much of the hormone on its own) or ***secondary hypersecretion*** (there is excessive stimulation of the gland by its tropic hormone). One of the most common causes of primary hypersecretion is the presence of a hormone-secreting endocrine-cell tumor.

The diagnosis of primary versus secondary hypersecretion of a particular hormone is analogous to that of hyposecretion. The concentrations of the hormone and, if relevant, its tropic hormone are measured in plasma or urine. If both concentrations are elevated, then the hormone in question is being secondarily hypersecreted. If the hypersecretion is primary, there will be a decreased concentration of the tropic hormone because of negative feedback by the high concentration of the hormone being hypersecreted.

When an endocrine tumor is the cause of hypersecretion, it can often be removed surgically or destroyed with radiation. In many cases hypersecretion can also be blocked by drugs that inhibit the hormone's synthesis. Alternatively, the situation can be treated with drugs that do not alter the hormone's secretion but instead block the hormone's actions on its target cells.

Hyporesponsiveness and Hyperresponsiveness

In some cases, the endocrine system may be dysfunctioning even though there is nothing wrong with hormone secretion. The problem is that the target cells do not respond normally to the hormone. This condition is termed hyporesponsiveness. An important example of a disease resulting from hyporesponsiveness, in this case to insulin, is the major form of diabetes mellitus ("sugar diabetes").

One cause of hyporesponsiveness is either a lack or deficiency of receptors for the hormone. For example, certain men have a genetic defect manifested by the absence of receptors for dihydrotestosterone, the form of testosterone active in many target cells. In such men, these cells are unable to bind dihydrotestosterone, and the result is lack of development of certain male characteristics, just as though the hormone were not being produced.

In a second type of hyporesponsiveness the receptors for a hormone may be normal, but some event occurring after the hormone binds to receptors may be defective. For example, the activated receptor might be unable to stimulate formation of cyclic AMP or open a plasma-membrane channel.

A third cause of hyporesponsiveness applies to hormones that require metabolic activation by some other tissue after secretion. There may be a lack or deficiency of the enzymes that catalyze the activation. For example, some men secrete testosterone normally and have normal receptors for dihydrotestosterone but are missing the enzyme that converts testosterone to dihydrotestosterone. The result is the same as in the case in which there are no dihydrotestosterone receptors.

In situations characterized by hyporesponsiveness to a hormone, the plasma concentration of the hormone in question is normal or elevated, but the response to administered hormone is diminished.

Finally, in a few cases *hyperresponsiveness* to a hormone can occur and cause problems. For example, the thyroid hormones cause an up-regulation of the beta-adrenergic receptors for epinephrine, and so a primary or secondary hyperthyroidism causes in turn a hyperresponsiveness to epinephrine.

SUMMARY

I. The endocrine system is one of the body's two major communications systems. It consists of all the glands that secrete hormones, which are chemical messengers carried by the blood from the endocrine glands to target cells elsewhere in the body.

HORMONE STRUCTURES AND SYNTHESIS
I. The amine hormones are the iodine-containing thyroid hormones—thyroxine and triiodothyronine—and the catecholamines secreted by the adrenal medulla, the hypothalamus, and the posterior pituitary.
II. The majority of hormones are peptides, many of which are synthesized as larger molecules, which are then cleaved.
III. Steroid hormones are produced from cholesterol by the adrenal cortex and the gonads, and by the placenta during pregnancy.
   A. The most important steroid hormones produced by the adrenal cortex are the mineralocorticoid aldosterone, the glucocorticoid cortisol, and two androgens.
   B. The ovaries produce mainly estradiol and progesterone, and the testes mainly testosterone.

HORMONE TRANSPORT IN THE BLOOD
I. Peptide hormones and catecholamines circulate dissolved in the plasma water, but steroid and thyroid hormones circulate mainly bound to plasma proteins.

HORMONE METABOLISM AND EXCRETION
I. The liver and kidneys are the major organs that re-

move hormones from the plasma by metabolizing or excreting them.

II. The peptide hormones and catecholamines are rapidly removed from the blood, whereas the steroid and thyroid hormones are removed more slowly.

III. After their secretion, some hormones are metabolized to more active molecules in their target cells or other organs.

MECHANISMS OF HORMONE ACTION

I. The receptors for steroid and thyroid hormones are inside the target cells; those for the peptide hormones and catecholamines are on the plasma membrane.

II. Hormones can cause up-regulation and down-regulation of their own receptors and those of other hormones. The induction of one hormone's receptors by another hormone increases the first hormone's effectiveness and may be essential to permit the first hormone to exert its effects.

III. Receptors activated by peptide hormones and catecholamines utilize one or more of the signal transduction mechanisms available to plasma membrane receptors; the result is altered activity of proteins in the cell.

IV. Intracellular receptors activated by steroid and thyroid hormones combine with DNA in the nucleus and induce the transcription of DNA into mRNA; the result is increased synthesis of particular proteins.

V. In pharmacological doses, hormones can have effects not seen under ordinary circumstances.

TYPES OF INPUTS THAT CONTROL HORMONE SECRETION

I. The secretion of a hormone may be controlled by the plasma concentration of an ion or nutrient that the hormone regulates, by neural input to the endocrine cells, and by a tropic hormone.

II. The autonomic nervous system is the neural input controlling many hormones, but the hypothalamic and posterior pituitary hormones are controlled by neurons in the brain.

CONTROL SYSTEMS INVOLVING THE HYPOTHALAMUS AND PITUITARY

I. The pituitary gland, comprising the anterior pituitary and the posterior pituitary, is connected to the hypothalamus by a stalk containing nerve fibers and blood vessels.

II. The nerve fibers, which originate in the hypothalamus and terminate in the posterior pituitary, secrete oxytocin, vasopressin, dopamine, and a prolactin releasing factor.

III. The anterior pituitary secretes growth hormone (GH), thyroid-stimulating hormone (TSH), adrenocorticotropic hormone (ACTH), prolactin, and two gonadotropic hormones—follicle-stimulating hormone (FSH) and luteinizing hormone (LH). The functions of these hormones are summarized in Figure 10-16.

IV. The anterior pituitary also produces β-lipotropin and β-endorphin along with ACTH, all being portions of the parent pro-opiomelanocortin molecule.

V. Secretion of the anterior pituitary hormones is controlled mainly by hypophysiotropic hormones secreted into capillaries in the median eminence of the hypothalamus and reaching the anterior pituitary via the portal vessels connecting the hypothalamus and anterior pituitary. The actions of the hypophysiotropic hormones on the anterior pituitary are summarized in Figure 10-18.

VI. The secretion of each hypophysiotropic hormone is controlled by neuronal and hormonal input to the hypothalamic neurons producing it.

A. In each of the three-hormone sequences beginning with a hypophysiotropic hormone, the third hormone exerts a long-loop, negative-feedback effect on the secretion of the hypothalamic and/or anterior pituitary hormone.

B. The anterior pituitary hormone may exert a short-loop, negative-feedback inhibition of the hypothalamic releasing hormone(s) controlling it.

C. Hormones not in a particular sequence can also influence secretion of the hypothalamic and/or anterior pituitary hormones in that sequence.

CANDIDATE HORMONES

I. Substances that are suspected of functioning as hormones but have not yet been proven to do so are called candidate hormones.

II. Melatonin is a hormone secreted with a 24-h rhythm by the pineal gland, an outgrowth of the diencephalon, but its functions in humans are uncertain.

TYPES OF ENDOCRINE DISORDERS

I. Endocrine disorders may be classified as hyposecretion, hypersecretion, and target-cell hyporesponsiveness or hyperresponsiveness.

A. Primary disorders are those in which the defect is in the cells that secrete the hormone.

B. Secondary disorders are those in which there is too much or too little tropic hormone.

C. Hyporesponsiveness is due to an alteration in the receptors for the hormone, to disordered postreceptor events, or to failure of normal metabolic activation of the hormone in those cases requiring such activation.

II. These disorders can be distinguished by measurements of the hormone and any tropic hormones under both basal conditions and during experimental stimulation or suppression of the hormone's secretion.

KEY TERMS

endocrine system
endocrine glands
hormones
target cells
neurohormones
amine hormones
thyroid gland
thyroxine (T$_4$)
triiodothyronine (T$_3$)
thyroid hormones (TH)
iodine
thyroglobulin
adrenal gland
adrenal medulla
adrenal cortex
epinephrine (E)
norepinephrine (NE)
dopamine (DA)
catecholamines
peptide hormones
prohormones
steroid hormones
gonads
aldosterone
mineralocorticoid
cortisol
glucocorticoids
androgens
testosterone
estradiol
progesterone
up-regulation
down-regulation
permissiveness
tropic hormone
pituitary gland
hypothalamus
anterior pituitary
posterior pituitary

median eminence
hypothalamo-pituitary portal
    vessels
oxytocin
vasopressin
antidiuretic hormone (ADH)
prolactin releasing factor
    (PRF)
hypophysiotropic hormones
follicle-stimulating hormone
    (FSH)
luteinizing hormone (LH)
growth hormone (GH)
thyroid-stimulating hormone
    (TSH)
prolactin
adrenocorticotropic hormone
    (ACTH)
gonadotropic hormones
pro-opiomelanocortin
β-lipotropin
β-endorphin
insulin-like growth factor I
    (IGF-I)
growth hormone releasing
    hormone (GHRH)
corticotropin releasing
    hormone (CRH)
somatostatin (SS)
gonadotropin releasing
    hormone (GnRH)
thyrotropin releasing
    hormone (TRH)
long-loop negative feedback
short-loop negative feedback
candidate hormones
melatonin
pineal gland

REVIEW QUESTIONS

1. What are three general chemical classes of hormones?

2. What essential nutrient is needed for synthesis of the thyroid hormones?

3. Which catecholamine is secreted in the largest amount by the adrenal medulla?

4. What are the major hormones produced by the adrenal cortex? By the testes? By the ovaries?

5. Which classes of hormones are carried in the blood mainly as unbound, dissolved hormone? Mainly bound to plasma proteins?

6. Do protein-bound hormones cross capillary walls?

7. Which organs are the major sites of hormone excretion and metabolic transformation?

8. How do the rates of metabolism and excretion differ for the various classes of hormones?

9. What must some hormones undergo after their secretion to become activated?

10. Contrast the locations of receptors for the various classes of hormones.

11. How do hormones influence the concentrations of their own receptors and those of other hormones? How does this explain permissiveness in hormone action?

12. Describe the sequence of events when steroid or thyroid hormones bind to their receptors.

13. Describe the sequence of events when peptide or catecholamine hormones bind to their receptors.

14. What are the four types of direct inputs to endocrine glands controlling hormone secretion?

15. How does control of hormone secretion by plasma mineral ions and nutrients achieve negative-feedback control of these substances?

16. What roles does the autonomic nervous system play in controlling hormone secretion?

17. What groups of hormones receive input from neurons located in the brain rather than in the autonomic nervous system?

18. Describe the anatomical relationships between the hypothalamus and the pituitary.

19. Name the two well-established posterior pituitary hormones and describe their site of synthesis and mechanism of release. Name two other posterior pituitary hormones.

20. List the six well-established anterior pituitary hormones and their functions; list two other anterior pituitary hormones and their biochemical origin.

21. List the major hypophysiotropic hormones and the hormone(s) whose release each controls.

22. What kinds of inputs control secretion of the hypophysiotropic hormones?

23. Diagram the CRH-ACTH-cortisol system.

24. What is the difference between long-loop and short-loop negative feedback in the hypothalamo-anterior pituitary system?

25. How would you distinguish between primary and secondary hyposecretion of a hormone? Between hyposecretion and hyporesponsiveness?

CLINICAL TERMS

pharmacological effects
iodine-deficient goiter
seasonal affective disorder
hyposecretion
hypersecretion
hyporesponsiveness

primary hyposecretion
secondary hyposecretion
primary hypersecretion
secondary hypersecretion
hyperresponsiveness

THOUGHT QUESTIONS

(Answers are given in Appendix A.)

1. In an experimental animal the sympathetic preganglionic fibers to the adrenal medulla are cut. What happens to the plasma concentration of epinephrine at rest and during stress?

2. During pregnancy there is an increase in both the production (by the liver) and the plasma concentration of the major plasma binding protein for the thyroid hormones (TH). This causes a sequence of events involving feedback that results in an increase in the plasma concentration of TH but no evidence of hyperthyroidism. Describe the sequence of events.

3. A child shows the following symptoms: deficient growth, failure to show sexual development, decreased ability to respond to stress. What is the most likely source of all these symptoms?

4. If all the neural connections between the hypothalamus and pituitary were severed, the secretion of which pituitary hormones would be affected? Which pituitary hormones would not be affected?

5. An antibody to a peptide combines with the peptide and renders it nonfunctional. If an animal were given an antibody to somatostatin, the secretion of which anterior pituitary hormones would change and in what direction?

6. A drug that blocks the action of norepinephrine is injected directly into the hypothalamus of an experimental animal, and the secretion rates of several anterior pituitary hormones are observed to change. How is this possible, since norepinephrine is not a hypophysiotropic hormone?

7. A person is receiving very large doses of a cortisol-like drug to treat her arthritis. What happens to her secretion of cortisol?

8. A person with symptoms of hypothyroidism (for example, sluggishness and intolerance to cold) is found to have abnormally low plasma concentrations of T_4, T_3, and TSH. After an injection of TRH the plasma concentrations of all three hormones increase. Where is the site of the defect leading to the hypothyroidism?

CHAPTER

11

MUSCLE

The ability to use chemical energy to produce force and movement is present to a limited extent in most living cells. It is, however, in muscle cells that this process has its greatest development. The primary function of these specialized cells is to generate the forces and movements used by multicellular organisms in the regulation of the internal environment and to produce the movements of the entire organism in its external environment. In the case of humans, speech and the ability to manipulate objects in the environment are also the result of muscle contractions. Indeed, it is only by controlling the activity of muscles that the human mind ultimately expresses itself.

Three types of muscle can be identified on the basis of their structures, contractile properties, and control mechanisms: (1) **skeletal muscle**, (2) **smooth muscle**, and (3) **cardiac muscle**. Most skeletal muscle, as the name implies, is attached to bone, and its contraction is responsible for supporting and moving the skeleton. The contraction of skeletal muscle is initiated by impulses in the motor neurons to the muscle and is usually under voluntary control.

Sheets of smooth muscle surround various hollow organs and tubes, including the stomach, intestinal tract, urinary bladder, uterus, blood vessels, and airways in the lungs. Single smooth-muscle cells are also found distributed throughout organs and in small bundles of cells attached to the hairs in the skin and the iris of the eye. Contraction of the smooth muscle surrounding hollow organs may propel the luminal contents through the organ, or it may regulate internal flow by changing the tube diameter. Smooth-muscle contraction is controlled by the autonomic nervous system, hormones, paracrine agents, and other local chemical signals. Some smooth muscles contract spontaneously, however, even in the absence of such signals.

Cardiac muscle is the muscle of the heart. Its contraction propels blood through the circulatory system. Like smooth muscle, it is regulated by the autonomic nervous system and hormones, and portions of it can undergo spontaneous contractions.

Although there are significant differences in these three types of muscle, the force-generating mechanism is similar in all of them. Skeletal muscle will be described first, followed by a discussion of smooth muscle. Cardiac muscle, which combines some of the properties of both skeletal and smooth muscle, will be described in Chapter 14 in association with its role in the circulatory system.

SECTION

SKELETAL MUSCLE

STRUCTURE

A single skeletal-muscle cell is known as a **muscle fiber**. Each muscle fiber is formed during development by the fusion of a number of undifferentiated, mononucleated cells, known as **myoblasts**, into a single cylindrical, multinucleated muscle fiber. This stage of muscle differentiation is completed around the time of birth, and the differentiated fibers continue to increase in size with the growth of the child. If skeletal-muscle fibers are destroyed after birth as a result of injury, they cannot be replaced by the division of other existing muscle fibers. New fibers can be formed, however, from undifferentiated cells known as **satellite cells**, which are located adjacent to the muscle fibers. This capacity for forming new skeletal-muscle fibers is considerable but will not restore a severely damaged muscle to full strength. Much of the compensation for a loss of muscle tissue occurs through increased growth in the size of the remaining muscle fibers. As we will see, satellite cells do not contribute to the increased muscle strength that can be produced by exercising.

Muscle fibers have diameters between 10 and 100 μm and a length that may extend up to 20 cm. The term **muscle** refers to a number of muscle fibers bound together by connective tissue (Figure 11-1) and usually linked to bones by bundles of collagen fibers, known as **tendons**, located at each end of the muscle. The relationship between a single muscle fiber and a muscle is analogous to that between a single neuron and a nerve, which is composed of the axons of many neurons.

In some muscles, the individual fibers extend the entire length of the muscle, but in most the fibers are shorter, often oriented at an angle to the longitudinal axis of the muscle. These short fibers are anchored to the connective-tissue network surrounding the muscle fibers. The transmission of force from muscle to bone is like a number of people pulling on a rope, each person corresponding to a single muscle fiber and the rope corresponding to the connective tissue and tendons.

Some tendons are very long, with the site of tendon

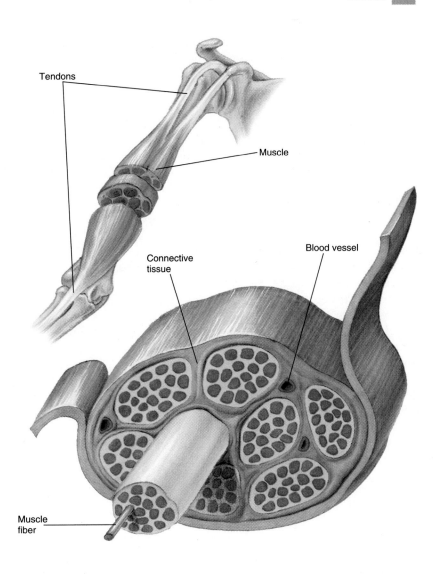

handout →

FIGURE 11-1

Organization of cylindrical muscle fibers in a muscle that is attached to bones by tendons.

attachment to bone far removed from the end of the muscle. For example, some of the muscles that move the fingers are located in the forearm, as one can observe by wiggling one's fingers and feeling the movement of the muscles in the lower arm. These muscles are connected to the fingers by long tendons. If the muscles that move the fingers were located in the fingers themselves, we would have very thick fingers.

The most striking feature seen when observing a muscle fiber through a light microscope (Figure 11-2) is a series of light and dark bands perpendicular to the long axis of the fiber. Both skeletal- and cardiac-muscle fibers (Figure 11-3) have this characteristic banding and are known as **striated muscles**. Smooth-muscle cells do not show a banding pattern. The striated pattern in skeletal and cardiac fibers results from the presence of numerous thick and thin filaments in the cytoplasm that are organized into approximately cylindrical bundles (1 to 2 μm in diameter)

known as **myofibrils** (Figure 11-4). Most of the cytoplasm is filled with myofibrils, each of which extends from one end of a fiber to the other.

Each myofibril is composed of thick and thin filaments (Figure 11-5) arranged in a repeating pattern along the length of the myofibril. One unit of this repeating pattern is known as a **sarcomere** (*sarco*, muscle; *mere*, small). The **thick filaments** are composed almost entirely of the contractile protein **myosin**. The **thin filaments** (about half the diameter of the thick filaments) contain the contractile protein **actin** as well as two other proteins—troponin and tropomyosin—that play important roles in regulating contraction, as we shall see.

The thick filaments are located in the middle of each sarcomere, where their orderly parallel arrangement produces the wide, dark band known as the **A band** (Figure 11-4). Each sarcomere contains two sets of thin filaments, one at each end. One end of each thin filament in a set is

FIGURE 11-2

Skeletal-muscle fibers in a muscle viewed through a light microscope. Arrow indicates a blood vessel containing erythrocytes. (*From Edward K. Keith and Michael H. Ross, "Atlas of Descriptive Histology," Harper & Row, New York, 1968.*)

FIGURE 11-3

The three types of muscle fibers. Note the difference in their sizes. (The single nucleus in the center of the cardiac muscle fiber is not shown.)

anchored to a network of interconnecting proteins known as the **Z line**, whereas the other end overlaps a portion of the thick filaments. Two successive Z lines define the limits of one sarcomere. Thus, thin filaments from two adjacent sarcomeres are anchored to each Z line.

The light band, known as the **I band** (Figure 11-4), lies between the ends of the A bands of two adjacent sarcomeres and contains those portions of the thin filaments that do not overlap the thick filaments. It is bisected by the Z line.

Two additional bands are present in the A-band region of each sarcomere (Figure 11-5). The **H zone** is a relatively light band in the center of the A band. It corresponds to the space between the ends of the two sets of thin filaments in each sarcomere; hence, only thick filaments, specifically their central parts, are found in the H zone. The narrow, dark band in the center of the H zone is known as the **M line** and corresponds to proteins that link together the central region of the thick filaments. In addition, filaments composed of the protein **titin** extend from the Z lines and are linked to the ends of the thick filaments. Thus, neither the thick nor the thin filaments are free-floating, since the thin filaments are anchored to the Z line, and the thick filaments are linked together by the M line and to the Z line by the titin filaments.

A cross section through the A bands of six adjacent myofibrils shows the regular, almost crystalline, arrangement of the thick and thin filaments (Figure 11-6). Each thick filament is surrounded by a hexagonal array of six thin filaments, and each thin filament is surrounded by a

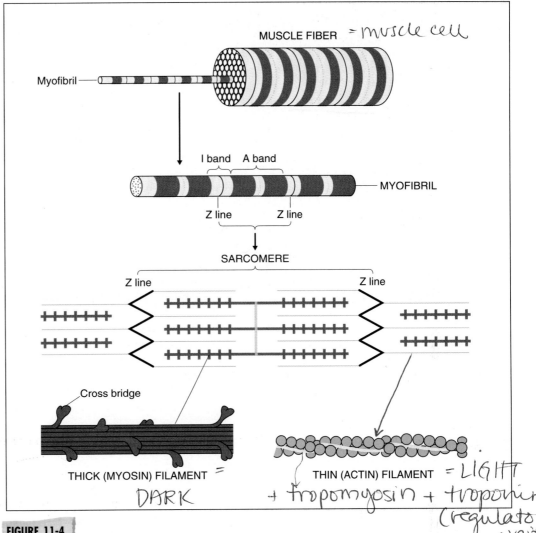

MUSCLE FIBER = muscle cell

Myofibril

I band · A band

MYOFIBRIL

Z line · Z line

SARCOMERE

Z line · Z line

Cross bridge

THICK (MYOSIN) FILAMENT = DARK

THIN (ACTIN) FILAMENT = LIGHT + tropomyosin + troponin (regulatory unit)

FIGURE 11-4

Arrangement of filaments in a skeletal muscle fiber that produce the striated banding pattern.

triangular arrangement of three thick filaments. Altogether there are twice as many thin as thick filaments in the region of filament overlap.

The space between adjacent thick and thin filaments is bridged by projections known as **cross bridges**, portions of myosin molecules that extend from the surface of the thick filaments toward the thin filaments (Figures 11-4 and 11-7). During muscle contraction, these cross bridges make contact with the thin filaments and exert force on them. Thus, the cross bridges are the force-generating structures in muscle cells.

MOLECULAR MECHANISMS OF CONTRACTION

The term **contraction**, as used in muscle physiology, does not necessarily mean "shortening"; rather it refers only to the turning on of the force-generating sites—the cross bridges—in a muscle fiber. In order for shortening to occur, the forces exerted on the thin filaments by the cross bridges must be greater than the force opposing shortening. Following contraction, the mechanisms that initiate force generation are turned off, and tension generation declines, producing **relaxation** of the muscle fiber.

Sliding-Filament Mechanism

When force generation produces shortening of a skeletal muscle fiber, the overlapping thick and thin filaments in each sarcomere move past each other, propelled by movements of the cross bridges. During this movement, there is no change in the lengths of either the thick or thin filaments (Figure 11-8). This is known as the **sliding-filament mechanism** of muscle contraction.

During shortening, each cross bridge attached to a thin filament moves in an arc much like the oars on a boat. This swiveling motion forces the thin filaments at either end of

Myofibrils

Z lines

(A)

(B)

A band

Z line

H zone

Z line

Titin filament   Thin filament   M line   Thick filament

(C)   SARCOMERE

FIGURE 11-5

(A) Numerous myofibrils in a single skeletal-muscle fiber (arrows in upper right corner indicate mitochondria located between the myofibrils). (B) High magnification of a single sarcomere within a single myofibril (arrow at the right of A band indicates end of a thick filament). (C) Arrangement of the thick and thin filaments in the single sarcomere shown in B.

(A)

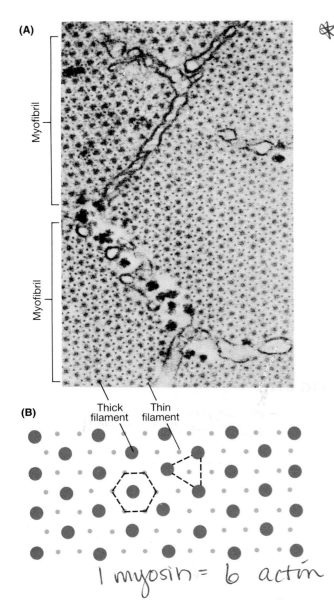

Myofibril

Myofibril

(B)

Thick filament Thin filament

I myosin = 6 actin

FIGURE 11-6

(A) Electron micrograph of a cross section through six myofibrils in a single skeletal-muscle fiber. [*From H. E. Huxley, J. Mol. Biol., 37:507–520 (1968).*] (B) Hexagonal arrangements of the thick and thin filaments in the overlap region in a single myofibril. Six thin filaments surround each thick filament and three thick filaments surround each thin filament.

the A band toward the center of the sarcomere, thereby shortening the sarcomere (Figure 11-9). One stroke of a cross bridge produces only a very small movement of a thin filament relative to a thick filament. While the force-generating mechanism remains active, however, the cross bridges repeat their swiveling motion many times, resulting in large displacements of the filaments, each displacement being made up of a series of the small steps.

Let us look more closely at these events. A muscle fiber's ability to generate force and movement depends on the interactions of the two so-called contractile proteins—myosin in the thick filaments and actin in the thin filaments—and the energy provided by ATP. Actin is a globular protein that polymerizes to form the two intertwined helical chains (Figure 11-10) that make up the core of the thin filaments. Myosin has a globular end attached to a long tail (Figure 11-11). The tails lie along the axis of the thick filament, and the globular heads extend out to the sides, forming the cross bridges. Each globular head contains a binding site for actin and an enzymatic site—an ATPase—that catalyzes the hydrolysis of ATP to ADP and inorganic phosphate, releasing the chemical energy stored in ATP.

FIGURE 11-7

High-magnification electron micrograph in the filament-overlap region near the middle of a sarcomere. Cross bridges between the thick and thin filaments can be seen at regular intervals along the filaments. [*From H. E. Huxley and J. Hanson, in G. H. Bourne (ed.), "The Structure and Function of Muscle," Vol. 1, Academic Press, New York, 1960.*]

M line

Thin filaments

Thick filaments

bridges

H zone

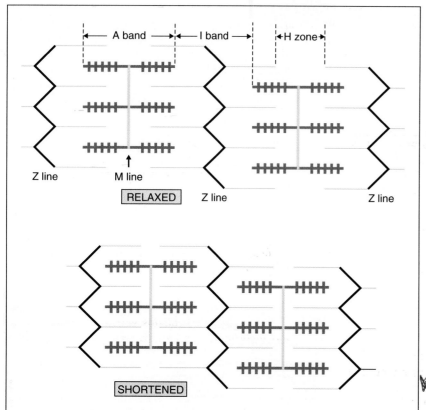

FIGURE 11-8
Changes in thick- and thin-filament alignment as a result of myofibril shortening.

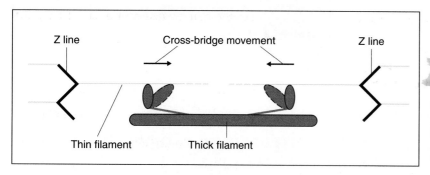

FIGURE 11-9
Cross bridges in the thick filaments bind to actin in the thin filaments and undergo a conformational change that propels the thin filaments toward the center of a sarcomere. (Only 2 of the approximately 200 cross bridges in each thick filament are shown.)

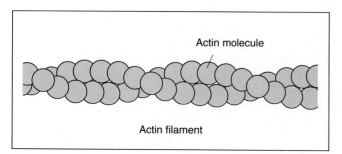

FIGURE 11-10
Two intertwined helical chains of actin molecules form the primary structure of the thin filaments.

[handwritten margin notes at top of page, partly illegible]

enzymes activate things (phys.)

[handwritten note: ATP →(ATPase) ADP + Pi → energy here]

[handwritten left margin: ATP →ˣ ADP + Pi ATPase myosin head (sticks onto myosin head)]

✳ FIGURE 11-11

Orientation of myosin molecules in one thick filament. The globular heads of myosin form cross bridges and the myosin tails are located in the core of the filament.

The myosin molecules in the two halves of each thick filament are oriented in opposite directions, such that all their tail ends are directed toward the center of the filament (Figure 11-11). Because of this arrangement, the power strokes of the cross bridges in the two halves of each thick filament are directed toward the center, thereby moving the attached thin filaments at the two ends of the sarcomere toward the center during shortening (Figure 11-9).

The sequence of events that occurs between the time a cross bridge binds to a thin filament, moves, and then begins to repeat the process is known as a **cross-bridge cycle**. Each cycle consists of four steps: (1) attachment of the cross bridge to a thin filament, (2) movement of the cross bridge, producing movement of the thin filament, (3) detachment of the cross bridge from the thin filament, and (4) movement of the cross bridge into a position where it can again reattach to a thin filament and repeat the cycle. Each cross bridge undergoes its own cycle of movements independently of the other cross bridges, and at any one instant during contraction only about 50 percent of the cross bridges overlapping a thin filament are attached to the thin filaments and are producing movement.

The chemical and physical events occurring during the four steps of a cross-bridge cycle are illustrated in Figure 11-12. At the conclusion (step 4) of the preceding cycle, the ATP bound to myosin is split, releasing chemical energy. This energy is transferred to myosin (M), producing an energized form of myosin (M*) to which the products of ATP hydrolysis, ADP and inorganic phosphate (P_i), are still bound.

Step 4: $M \cdot ATP \xrightarrow{\text{ATP hydrolysis}} M^* \cdot ADP \cdot P_i$

A new cross-bridge cycle begins with the binding of an energized myosin cross bridge to actin (A) in a thin-filament (step 1):

Step 1:

$$A + M^* \cdot ADP \cdot P_i \xrightarrow[\text{Actin binding}]{} A \cdot M^* \cdot ADP \cdot P_i$$

The binding of this energized myosin to actin triggers the discharge of energy stored in myosin, with the resulting movement of the bound cross bridge (step 2) and the release of ADP and P_i:

Step 2:

$$A \cdot M^* \cdot ADP \cdot P_i \xrightarrow[\substack{\text{Cross-bridge}\\\text{movement}}]{} A \cdot M + ADP + P_i$$

This sequence of energy storage and release by myosin is analogous to the operation of a mousetrap: Energy is stored in the trap by cocking the spring (ATP hydrolysis in the previous step 4) and released by springing the trap (binding to actin).

During the cross-bridge movement, myosin binds very firmly to actin, and this linkage must be broken in order to allow the cross bridge to reattach to a new actin site and repeat the cycle. The binding of a molecule of ATP to myosin is responsible for breaking the link between actin and myosin (step 3):

Step 3:

$$A \cdot M + ATP \xrightarrow[\substack{\text{Cross-bridge}\\\text{dissociation from actin}}]{} A + M \cdot ATP$$

[handwritten annotations:]
relaxed state
contraction
isometric mvmt. (sitting there)
ADP + Pi on myosin head
Energized cross bridge
gotten enough energy to move up
A + M* · ADP · Pi — stuck together — not on it / on it
mvmt.
the ATP that caused relaxation is here "same as time as relax"
isotonic mvmt. (actual mvmt.)
Contraction
A · M — energy is gone → ADP + Pi fell off
— until more ATP put on, stuck here
when ATP binds to myosin, contraction released

FIGURE 11-12

Chemical and mechanical changes during the four stages of a cross-bridge cycle. In a resting muscle fiber, contraction begins with the binding of a cross bridge to actin in a thin filament—step 1. (M° represents an energized myosin cross bridge.)

The dissociation of actin and myosin by ATP is an example of allosteric regulation of protein activity. The binding of ATP at one site on myosin decreases the affinity of myosin for actin bound at another site on myosin. Thus, ATP is acting as a modulator molecule controlling the binding of actin to myosin. Note that ATP is not split in this step.

Following the dissociation of actin and myosin, the ATP bound to myosin is split (step 4), thereby re-forming the energized state of myosin, which can now reattach to a new site on the actin filament and repeat the cycle.

To summarize, ATP performs two distinct roles in the cross-bridge cycle: (1) The energy released from ATP *hydrolysis* ultimately provides the energy for cross-bridge movement, and (2) the *binding* (not hydrolysis) of ATP to myosin breaks the link formed between actin and myosin during the cycle, allowing the cycle to be repeated. Note that the release of energy by the hydrolysis of ATP (step 4) and the movement of the cross bridge (step 2) are not simultaneous events.

The importance of ATP in dissociating actin and myosin

during step 3 of a cross-bridge cycle is illustrated by **rigor mortis**, the stiffening of skeletal muscles that begins several hours after death and is complete after about 12 h. The ATP concentration in cells, including muscle cells, declines after death because the nutrients and oxygen required by the metabolic pathways to form ATP are no longer supplied by the circulation. In the absence of ATP, nonenergized cross bridges can bind to actin, but the subsequent movement of the cross bridge and the breakage of the link between actin and myosin do not occur because these events require the binding of ATP. The thick and thin filaments become bound to each other by immobilized cross bridges, producing a rigid condition. The stiffness of rigor mortis disappears about 48 to 60 h after death as a result of the disintegration of muscle tissue.

Role of Troponin, Tropomyosin, and Calcium in Contraction

Since every muscle fiber contains all the ingredients necessary for cross-bridge activity—actin, myosin, and ATP—the question arises: Why are muscles not in a continuous

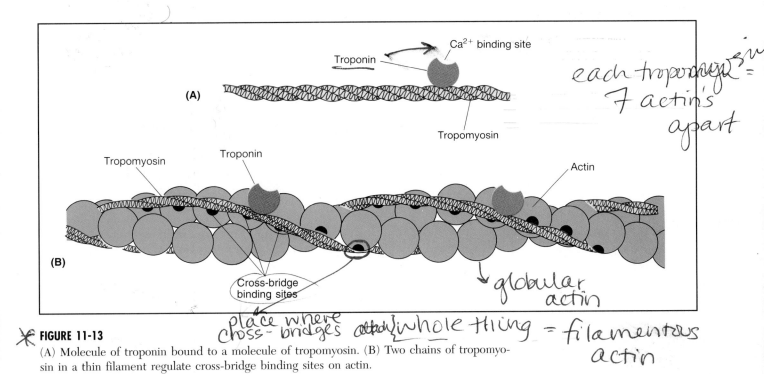

each tropomyosin = 7 actins apart

globular actin

place where cross-bridges attach *whole thing = filamentous actin*

FIGURE 11-13

(A) Molecule of troponin bound to a molecule of tropomyosin. (B) Two chains of tropomyosin in a thin filament regulate cross-bridge binding sites on actin.

state of contractile activity? The answer is that in a resting muscle fiber, the cross bridges are prevented from interacting with actin by two regulator proteins, **troponin** and **tropomyosin**, which, as noted earlier, are located on the thin filaments (Figure 11-13).

Tropomyosin is a rod-shaped molecule composed of two intertwined polypeptides with a length approximately equal to that of seven actin molecules. Chains of tropomyosin molecules are arranged end to end along the actin double helix. Present theory holds that these tropomyosin molecules partially cover the myosin-binding site on each actin, thereby preventing the cross bridges from making contact with actin. Each tropomyosin molecule is held in this blocking position by troponin, a smaller, globular protein that is bound to both tropomyosin and actin. One molecule of troponin binds to each molecule of tropomyosin and regulates the myosin-binding sites on the seven actin molecules in contact with this one molecule of tropomyosin.[1]

Having described the system that prevents cross-bridge activity and thus keeps a muscle fiber in a resting state, we can now ask what triggers a contraction, that is: What allows cross-bridge activity to occur? In order for the cross bridges to bind to actin, the tropomyosin molecules must be moved away from their blocking positions on actin. This occurs when calcium binds to specific binding sites on troponin. The binding of calcium produces a change in the shape of troponin, which through troponin's effects on tropomyosin, exposes the myosin-binding site on each of the actin monomers in contact with the tropomyosin molecule. Conversely, removal of calcium from troponin reverses the process, turning off contractile activity.

Thus, cytosolic calcium-ion concentration determines the number of troponin sites occupied by calcium, which in turn determines the number of actin sites to which cross bridges can bind and exert force on the thin filaments. These changes in cytosolic calcium concentration are controlled by electrical events occurring in the muscle plasma membrane, which we will now discuss.

Excitation-Contraction Coupling

Excitation-contraction coupling refers to the sequence of events by which an action potential in the plasma membrane of a muscle fiber leads to cross-bridge activity by the mechanisms just described. The skeletal-muscle plasma membrane is an excitable membrane capable of generating and propagating action potentials by mechanisms similar to those described for nerve cells (Chapter 8). An action potential in a skeletal-muscle fiber lasts 1 to 2 ms and is completed before any signs of mechanical activity begin (Figure 11-14). Once begun, the mechanical activity following a single action potential may last 100 ms or more. Hence, the electrical activity in the plasma mem-

---

[1] There is also evidence to suggest that in addition to physically blocking the myosin-binding site on actin, the troponin-tropomyosin complex may also modulate the affinity of this binding site for the myosin cross bridge.

FIGURE 11-14

Time relations between a skeletal-muscle fiber action potential and the resulting shortening and relaxation of the muscle fiber.

brane does not *directly* act upon the contractile proteins but instead produces a state (increased cytosolic calcium concentration) that continues to activate the contractile apparatus long after the electrical activity in the membrane has ceased.

In a resting muscle fiber, the concentration of free ionized calcium in the cytosol surrounding the thick and thin filaments is very low, about 10^{-7} mol/L. At this low calcium concentration, very few of the calcium-binding sites on troponin are occupied, and thus cross-bridge activity is blocked by tropomyosin. Following an action potential, there is a rapid increase in cytosolic calcium concentration and calcium binds to troponin, removing the blocking effect of tropomyosin and allowing cross-bridge cycling. The source of the increased calcium is the **sarcoplasmic reticulum** within the muscle fiber.

Sarcoplasmic Reticulum. The sarcoplasmic reticulum in muscle is homologous to the endoplasmic reticulum found in most other cells and forms a series of sleevelike structures around each myofibril (Figure 11-15), one portion surrounding the A band and another the I band. There are two enlarged regions at each end of the sarcoplasmic reticulum, known as **lateral sacs** (also known as terminal cisternae), which are connected by a series of smaller tubular elements. The lateral sacs store calcium, which is then released following membrane excitation.

A separate tubular structure, the **transverse tubule** (T tubule) crosses the muscle fiber at the level of each A-I junction, passing between adjacent lateral sacs and eventually joining the plasma membrane. The lumen of the T tubule is continuous with the extracellular fluid sur-

rounding the muscle fiber. The membrane of the T tubule, like the plasma membrane, is able to propagate action potentials. Once initiated in the plasma membrane, an action potential is rapidly conducted over the surface of the membrane and into the interior of the muscle fiber by way of the T tubules. As the action potential in a T tubule passes near the sarcoplasmic reticulum, it triggers the opening of some of the calcium channels in the lateral sacs, allowing calcium to diffuse from the calcium-rich lumen of the lateral sacs into the cytosol. The mechanism by which an electrical event in one membrane—the T tubule—triggers the opening of calcium channels in another membrane—the sarcoplasmic reticulum—remains a major unanswered question in muscle physiology.

The initial calcium released from the sarcoplasmic reticulum can bind to still closed calcium channels there, opening them and producing a positive-feedback rapid rise in the cytosolic calcium concentration. As the concentration of cytosolic calcium rises to even higher levels, however, calcium becomes bound to low-affinity sites on the calcium channels, and this causes the channels to close and end calcium release.

As stated above, contraction will not cease until calcium is removed from troponin, and this is achieved by a lowering of the calcium concentration in the cytosol. The membranes of the sarcoplasmic reticulum contain primary-active-transport proteins (Ca-ATPases) that pump calcium ions from the cytosol back into the lumen of the reticulum. As we just saw, calcium is rapidly released from the reticulum upon arrival of an action potential, but the pumping of the released calcium back into the reticulum requires a much longer time. Therefore, the cytosolic calcium concentration remains elevated, and the contraction continues for some time after one action potential.

To reiterate, just as contraction results from the release of calcium ions stored in the sarcoplasmic reticulum, so contraction ends and relaxation begins as calcium is pumped back into the reticulum (Figure 11-16). ATP is

---

TABLE 11-1 FUNCTIONS OF ATP IN SKELETAL-MUSCLE CONTRACTION

1. Hydrolysis of ATP by myosin energizes the cross bridges, providing the energy for force generation.
2. Binding of ATP to myosin dissociates cross bridges bound to actin, allowing the bridges to repeat their cycle of activity.
3. Hydrolysis of ATP by the Ca-ATPase in the sarcoplasmic reticulum provides the energy for the active transport of calcium ions into the lateral sacs of the reticulum, lowering cytosolic calcium, ending the contraction, and allowing the muscle fiber to relax.

FIGURE 11-15

(A) Diagrammatic representation of the sarcoplasmic reticulum, transverse tubules, and myofibrils. (B) Three-dimensional view of the transverse tubules and sarcoplasmic reticulum in a single skeletal-muscle fiber.

required to provide the energy for the calcium pump, and this is the third major role of ATP in muscle contraction (Table 11-1).

Membrane Excitation: The Neuromuscular Junction

We have just seen that an action potential in the plasma membrane of a skeletal-muscle fiber is the signal that triggers contraction. The next question we must ask then is: How are these action potentials initiated? Stimulation of the nerve fibers to a skeletal muscle is the only mechanism by which this type of muscle is normally activated. As we shall learn, there are additional mechanisms for activating cardiac- and smooth-muscle contraction.

The nerve cells whose axons innervate skeletal muscle

[handwritten annotations: Muscle plasma membrane = Sarcolemma; quick spreading of depolarization; Active transport (going against gradient)*]*

FIGURE 11-16

Release and uptake of calcium by the sarcoplasmic reticulum during contraction and relaxation of a skeletal-muscle fiber.

fibers are known as **motor neurons** (or somatic efferent neurons), and their cell bodies are located in either the brainstem or the spinal cord. The axons of motor neurons are myelinated and are the largest-diameter axons in the body. They are therefore able to propagate action potentials at high velocities, allowing signals from the central nervous system to be transmitted to skeletal-muscle fibers with minimal delay.

Upon reaching a muscle, the axon of a motor neuron divides into many branches, each branch forming a single junction with a muscle fiber. Thus, a single motor neuron innervates many muscle fibers, but each muscle fiber is controlled by only one motor neuron. A motor neuron plus the muscle fibers it innervates is called a **motor unit** (Figure 11-17A). The muscle fibers in a single motor unit are all located in one muscle, but they are scattered throughout the muscle and do not all lie adjacent to each other (Figure 11-17B). When an action potential is produced in

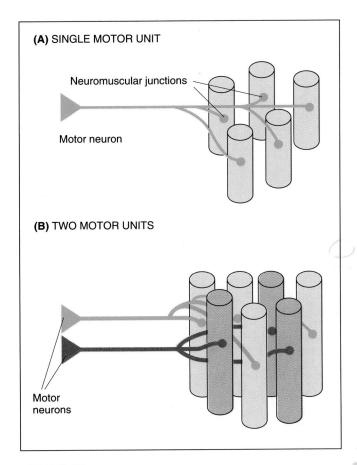

(A) SINGLE MOTOR UNIT

Neuromuscular junctions

Motor neuron

(B) TWO MOTOR UNITS

Motor neurons

FIGURE 11-17

(A) Single motor unit consisting of one motor neuron and the muscle fibers it innervates. (B) Two motor units and their intermingled fibers in a muscle.

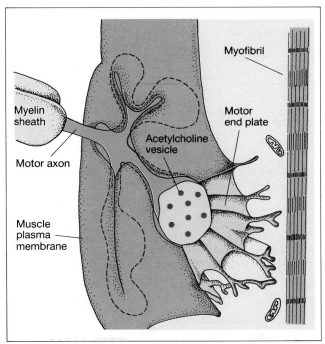

Myofibril

Myelin sheath

Motor end plate

Acetylcholine vesicle

Motor axon

Muscle plasma membrane

FIGURE 11-18

Neuromuscular junction. The motor axon terminals are embedded in grooves in the muscle fiber's surface.

a motor neuron, all the muscle fibers in its motor unit contract.

The myelin sheath surrounding the axon of a motor neuron ends near the surface of a muscle fiber, and the axon divides into a number of short processes that lie embedded in grooves on the muscle-fiber surface. The region of the muscle-fiber plasma membrane that lies directly under the terminal portion of the axon has special properties and is known as the **motor end plate**. The junction of an axon terminal with the motor end plate is known as a **neuromuscular junction** (Figure 11-18).

The axon terminals of a motor neuron contain membrane-bound vesicles resembling the vesicles found at synaptic junctions, that is, junctions between two neurons. The vesicles contain the chemical transmitter **acetylcholine (ACh)**. When an action potential in a motor neuron arrives at an axon terminal, it depolarizes the nerve plasma membrane, opening voltage-sensitive calcium channels and thus allowing calcium ions to diffuse into the axon terminal from the extracellular fluid. This calcium triggers

the release, by exocytosis, of acetylcholine from the vesicles into the extracellular cleft separating the axon terminal and the motor end plate.

The acetylcholine diffuses across this cleft and binds to receptor sites [of the nicotinic type (page 208)] on the motor end plate. The binding of ACh opens ion channels in the receptor proteins. Both sodium and potassium ions can pass through these channels. Because of the differences in electrochemical gradients across the plasma membrane (Chapter 8), more sodium moves in than potassium out, producing a local depolarization of the motor end plate known as an **end-plate potential (EPP)**. Thus, an EPP is analogous to an EPSP (excitatory postsynaptic potential) at a synapse (page 203).

The magnitude of a single EPP is, however, much larger than that of an EPSP because in the former much larger amounts of neurotransmitter are released over a larger surface area, opening many more ion channels. For this reason, an EPP is normally sufficient to depolarize the adjacent plasma membrane, by local current flow, to its threshold potential, initiating an action potential in the muscle plasma membrane. This action potential is then propagated over the surface of the muscle fiber by the same mechanism described in Chapter 8 for the propagation of action potentials along axon membranes (Figure 11-19). Most neuromuscular junctions are located in the middle of a muscle fiber, and newly generated muscle

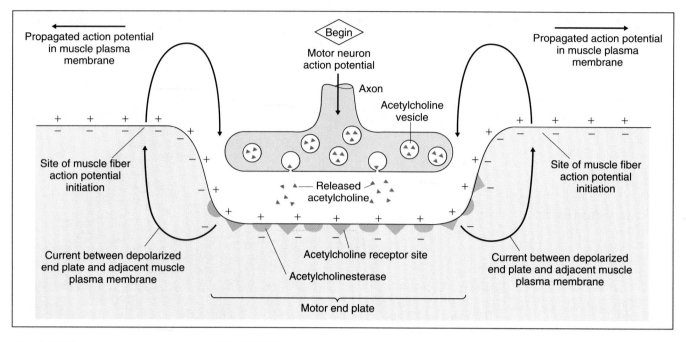

FIGURE 11-19

Events occurring at a neuromuscular junction that lead to an action potential in the muscle fiber plasma membrane.

action potentials are propagated from this region in both directions toward the ends of the fiber.

Actually the magnitude of an EPP elicited by a single nerve action potential is not only sufficient but is considerably larger than that required to reach the threshold for producing a muscle action potential. With repeated nerve stimulation the amount of ACh released from the nerve terminals declines, producing progressively smaller EPPs. The large size of each EPP, however, provides a safety factor so that even with the decline in its magnitude, these smaller EPPs are sufficient to reach threshold and fire a muscle action potential. To repeat, every action potential in a motor neuron normally produces an action potential in each muscle fiber in its motor unit. This is quite different from synaptic junctions, where multiple EPSPs must occur, undergoing temporal and spatial summation, in order for threshold to be reached and an action potential elicited in the postsynaptic membrane.

A second difference between synaptic and neuromuscular junctions should be noted. As we saw in Chapter 8, at some synaptic junctions, IPSPs (inhibitory postsynaptic potentials) are produced. They hyperpolarize or stabilize the postsynaptic membrane and decrease the probability of its firing an action potential. Inhibitory potentials are not found in human skeletal muscle; all neuromuscular junctions are excitatory.

In addition to receptor sites for ACh, the motor end plate contains the enzyme **acetylcholinesterase** at its surface. This enzyme breaks down ACh, just as occurs at ACh-mediated synapses in the nervous system. ACh bound to receptor sites is in equilibrium with free ACh in the cleft between the nerve and muscle membranes. As the concentration of free ACh falls because of its breakdown by acetylcholinesterase, less ACh is available to bind to the receptor sites. When the receptor sites no longer contain bound ACh, the ion channels in the end plate close. The depolarized end plate returns to its resting potential and can respond to the arrival of a new burst of ACh released by another nerve action potential.

Table 11-2 summarizes the sequence of events that lead from an action potential in a motor neuron to the contraction and relaxation of a skeletal-muscle fiber.

There are many ways events at the neuromuscular junction can be modified by disease or drugs. For example, the deadly South American arrowhead poison **curare** binds strongly to the ACh receptor site, but it does not open ion channels and is not destroyed by acetylcholinesterase. When a receptor site is occupied by curare, ACh cannot bind to the receptor. Therefore, although the motor nerves still conduct normal action potentials and release ACh, there is no resulting EPP in the motor end plate and hence no contraction. Since the skeletal muscles responsible for breathing, like all skeletal muscles, depend upon neuromuscular transmission to initiate their contraction, curare poisoning can lead to death by asphyxiation. Curare and similar drugs are used in small amounts to prevent

TABLE 11-2   SEQUENCE OF EVENTS BETWEEN A MOTOR NEURON ACTION POTENTIAL AND SKELETAL-MUSCLE FIBER CONTRACTION

1. Action potential is initiated and propagates in motor neuron axon.
2. Action potential triggers release of ACh from axon terminals at neuromuscular junction.
3. ACh diffuses from axon terminals to motor end plate in muscle fiber.
4. ACh binds to receptor sites on motor end plate, opening Na^+, K^+ ion channels.
5. More Na^+ moves into the fiber at the motor end plate than K^+ moves out, depolarizing the membrane, producing the end-plate potential (EPP).
6. Local currents depolarize the adjacent plasma membrane to its threshold potential, generating an action potential that propagates over the muscle fiber surface and into the fiber along the transverse tubules.
7. Action potential in transverse tubules triggers release of Ca^{2+} from lateral sacs of sarcoplasmic reticulum.
8. Ca^{2+} binds to troponin on the thin filaments, causing tropomyosin to move away from its blocking position and thus uncovering cross-bridge binding sites on actin.
9. Energized myosin cross bridges on the thick filaments bind to actin:

$$A + M^\circ \cdot ADP \cdot P_i \longrightarrow A \cdot M^\circ \cdot ADP \cdot P_i$$

10. Cross-bridge binding triggers release of energy stored in myosin, producing an angular movement of each cross bridge:

$$A \cdot M^\circ \cdot ADP \cdot P_i \longrightarrow A \cdot M + ADP + P_i$$

11. ATP binds to myosin, breaking linkage between actin and myosin and thereby allowing cross bridges to dissociate from actin:

$$A \cdot M + ATP \longrightarrow A + M \cdot ATP$$

12. ATP bound to myosin is split, transferring energy to myosin cross bridge:

$$M \cdot ATP \longrightarrow M^\circ \cdot ADP \cdot P_i$$

13. Cross bridges repeat steps 9 to 12, producing movement of thin filaments past thick filaments. Cycles of cross-bridge movement continue as long as Ca^{2+} remains bound to troponin.
14. Cytosolic Ca^{2+} concentration decreases as Ca^{2+} is actively transported into sarcoplasmic reticulum by Ca-ATPase.
15. Removal of Ca^{2+} from troponin restores blocking action of tropomyosin, the cross-bridge cycle ceases, and the muscle fiber relaxes.

muscular contractions during certain types of surgical procedures when it is necessary to immobilize the surgical field. Patients are artificially ventilated in order to maintain respiration until the drug has been removed from the system.

Neuromuscular transmission can also be blocked by inhibiting acetylcholinesterase. Some organophosphates, which are the main ingredients in certain pesticides and "nerve gases" (the latter developed for biological warfare), inhibit this enzyme. In the presence of such agents, ACh is released normally upon the arrival of an action potential at the axon terminal and binds to the end-plate receptors. The ACh is not destroyed, however, because the acetylcholinesterase is inhibited. The ion channels in the end plate therefore remain open, producing a maintained de-

polarization of the end plate and the muscle plasma membrane adjacent to the end plate. A skeletal-muscle membrane maintained in a depolarized state cannot generate action potentials because the voltage-sensitive sodium channels in the membrane have entered a refractory state, which requires repolarization to remove. Thus, the muscle does not contract in response to subsequent nerve stimulation, and the result is skeletal-muscle paralysis and death from asphyxiation.

A third group of substances, including the toxin produced by the bacterium *Clostridium botulinum*, blocks the release of acetylcholine from nerve terminals, preventing transmission of the chemical signal from the nerve to the muscle fiber. This toxin, which produces ***botulism***, a type of food poisoning, is one of the most deadly poisons known.

MECHANICS OF SINGLE-FIBER CONTRACTION

The force exerted on an object by a contracting muscle is known as muscle **tension**, and the force exerted on the muscle by the weight of an object is the **load**. Muscle tension and load are opposing forces. Whether or not force generation leads to fiber shortening depends on the relative magnitudes of the tension and the load. In order for muscle fibers to shorten and therefore move a load, muscle tension must become and remain slightly greater than the opposing load.

When a muscle develops tension but does not shorten (or lengthen), the contraction is said to be **isometric** (constant length). Such contractions occur when the muscle supports a load in a constant position or attempts to move an otherwise supported load that is greater than the tension developed by the muscle. A contraction in which the load on a muscle remains constant but the muscle is shortening is said to be **isotonic** (constant tension).

A third type of contraction is a **lengthening contraction.** This occurs when an unsupported load on a muscle is greater than the tension being generated by the cross bridges. In this situation, the load pulls the muscle to a longer length in spite of the opposing force being produced by the cross bridges. Such lengthening contractions occur when an object being supported by muscle contractions is lowered, such as occurs when you sit down from a standing position or walk down a flight of stairs. It must be emphasized that in these situations the lengthening of muscle fibers is not an active process produced by the contractile proteins but a consequence of the external forces being applied to the muscle. In the absence of external forces, a fiber will only *shorten* when stimulated; it will never lengthen. All three types of contractions—isometric, isotonic, and lengthening—occur in the natural course of muscle activity in the body.

During each type of contraction the cross bridges repeatedly go through the four steps of the cross-bridge cycle illustrated in Figure 11-12. During step 2 of an isotonic contraction, the cross bridges bound to actin move to their angled positions, causing shortening of the sarcomeres. In contrast, during an isometric contraction, the bound cross bridges are unable to move the thin filaments because of the load on the muscle fiber, but they do exert a force on the thin filaments—isometric tension. During a lengthening contraction, the cross bridges in step 2 are pulled toward the Z lines by the load while still bound to actin. The events of steps 1, 3, and 4 are the same in all three types of contractions. Thus, the chemical changes in the contractile proteins during each type of contraction are the same. The end result of shortening, no length change, or lengthening is determined by the magnitude of the load on the muscle.

Figure 11-20 illustrates the general method of recording isotonic and isometric contractions. During an isotonic contraction, the distance the muscle shortens as a function of time is recorded. The shortening distance is measured by a pen attached to the muscle and leaves a trace on a moving strip of paper as the muscle contracts and relaxes. During an isometric contraction, the force (tension) generated by the muscle as a function of time is measured by attaching the muscle at one end to a rigid support and at the other end to an electronic force-sensing device that controls the movement of a pen in proportion to the force exerted.

FIGURE 11-20

Methods of recording (A) isotonic and (B) isometric muscle contractions.

(A) ISOTONIC CONTRACTION

(B) ISOMETRIC CONTRACTION

Contraction terminology and recording methods apply to both single fibers and whole muscles. We first describe the mechanics of single-fiber contractions and later discuss the factors controlling the mechanics of whole-muscle contraction.

Twitch Contractions

The mechanical response of a muscle fiber to a single action potential is known as a **twitch**. Figure 11-21 shows the main features of an isometric twitch. Following the action potential, there is an interval of a few milliseconds, known as the **latent period**, before the tension in the muscle fiber begins to increase. During this latent period, the processes associated with excitation-contraction coupling (page 313) are occurring. The time interval from the beginning of tension development at the end of the latent period to the peak tension in an isometric contraction is the **contraction time**. Not all skeletal-muscle fibers have the same contraction time. Some fast fibers have contraction times as short as 10 ms, whereas slower fibers may take 100 ms or longer.

Comparing an isotonic twitch with an isometric twitch in the same muscle fiber, one can see from Figure 11-22 that the time between the action potential and the beginning of shortening in an isotonic twitch is longer than the latent period in an isometric contraction, while the duration of the mechanical event—shortening—is briefer than the duration of force generation in an isometric twitch. Moreover, the characteristics of an isotonic twitch depend upon the magnitude of the load being lifted (Figure 11-23). At heavier loads the delay before shortening is longer, but the velocity of shortening (distance shortened per unit of time), the duration of the twitch, and the distance shortened all decrease.

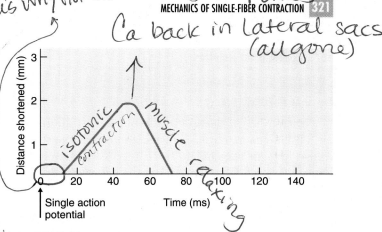

(handwritten: Ca going out + cross-bridges attaching (this why not start at zero); LATENCY PERIOD   Ca back in lateral sacs (all gone)   isotonic contraction   muscle relaxing)

FIGURE 11-22

An isotonic twitch of a skeletal-muscle fiber following a single action potential.

Let us look more closely at the sequence of events in an isotonic contraction. Following excitation the cross bridges begin to develop force, but shortening does not begin until the muscle tension just exceeds the load on the fiber. Thus, before shortening, there is a period of isometric contraction during which the tension increases. (A similar period of isometric contraction occurs at the end of an isotonic contraction, as the tension becomes less than the load.) The heavier the load, the longer it takes for the tension to increase to the value of the load, where shortening will begin. If the load on a fiber is increased, eventually a load will be reached that the muscle is unable to lift, the velocity and distance of shortening will be zero, and the contraction will become completely isometric. At still higher loads, if the load is otherwise unsupported, the muscle fiber will lengthen, in spite of maximal cross-bridge force—a lengthening contraction.

(handwritten: LATERAL SACS INSTANTLY CONNECTED TO CROSS-BRIDGES)

FIGURE 11-21

An isometric twitch of a skeletal-muscle fiber following a single action potential.

(handwritten: = cross-bridges attach but can't go anywhere!)

(handwritten: Ca pumped back into sacs; actin/myosin slowly disconnected)

FIGURE 11-23

Isotonic twitches with different loads. The distance shortened, velocity of shortening, and duration of shortening all decrease with increased load, whereas the latent period increases with increasing load.

(handwritten: Heavy load = longer latent pd- b/c need more actin-myosin attachments   distance not so shortened b/c muscle can't go further)

(handwritten: - more gradual decline → lasts longer   - latent pd- shorter)

Frequency-Tension Relation

Since a single action potential in a skeletal-muscle fiber lasts 1 to 2 ms but the twitch may last for 100 ms, it is possible for a second action potential to be initiated during the period of mechanical activity. Figure 11-24 illustrates the tension generated during isometric contractions of a muscle fiber in response to three successive stimuli. In Figure 11-24A, the isometric twitch following the first stimulus S_1 lasts 150 ms. The second stimulus S_2, applied to the muscle fiber 200 ms after S_1 when the fiber has completely relaxed, causes a second identical twitch, and a third stimulus S_3, equally timed, produces a third identical twitch. In Figure 11-24B, the interval between S_1 and S_2 remains 200 ms, but a third stimulus is applied 60 ms after S_2, when the mechanical response resulting from S_2 is beginning to decrease. Stimulus S_3 induces a contractile response whose peak tension is greater than that produced by S_2. In Figure 11-24C, the interval between S_2 and S_3 is further reduced to 10 ms, and the resulting peak tension is even greater. Indeed, the mechanical response to S_3 is a smooth continuation of the mechanical response already induced by S_2.

FIGURE 11-24

Summation of isometric contractions produced by shortening the time between stimuli S_2 and S_3.

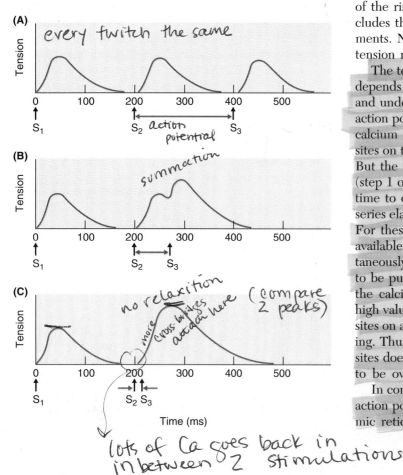

The increase in the mechanical response of a muscle fiber to successive action potentials occurring during the phase of mechanical activity is known as **summation**. Contractile activity can be sustained (in the absence of fatigue) if a fiber is repeatedly stimulated at a frequency sufficient to prevent complete relaxation between stimuli. A maintained contraction in response to repetitive stimulation is known as a **tetanus**. At low stimulation frequencies, the tension may oscillate as the muscle fiber partially relaxes between stimuli, producing an unfused tetanus. A fused tetanus, with no oscillations, is produced at higher stimulation frequencies (Figure 11-25).

As the frequency of action potentials increases, the level of sustained tension also increases until a maximal tetanic tension is reached, beyond which tension no longer increases with further increases in stimulation frequency. This maximal tetanic tension is about three to five times greater than the isometric twitch tension. Since different muscle fibers have different contraction times, the stimulus frequency that will produce a maximal tetanic tension also differs from fiber to fiber.

The increased tension produced by increased stimulus frequency can be explained by events occurring in the muscle fiber. The explanation requires one new piece of information: A muscle contains elastic elements that are in series with the contractile elements and transmit the tension to the ends of the fibers. Therefore, the time course of the rise in tension during an isometric contraction includes the time required to stretch the series elastic elements. Now we turn to an explanation of the frequency-tension relationship.

The tension produced by each sarcomere at any instant depends upon the number of cross bridges bound to actin and undergoing step 2 of the cross-bridge cycle. A single action potential in a skeletal-muscle fiber releases enough calcium to saturate troponin, and all the myosin-binding sites on the thin filaments are therefore *initially* available. But the binding of energized cross bridges to these sites (step 1 of the cross-bridge cycle) takes a finite amount of time to occur and, as noted above, the stretching of the series elastic elements by the cross bridges also takes time. For these reasons, even though all the binding sites are available initially, maximal tension is not developed instantaneously. Almost immediately, however, calcium begins to be pumped back into the sarcoplasmic reticulum, and the calcium concentration begins to fall from its initial high value, causing more and more of the myosin-binding sites on actin to become unavailable for cross-bridge binding. Thus, during a single twitch, the maximal number of sites does not stay available long enough for the time lags to be overcome and maximal tension to be developed.

In contrast, during a tetanic contraction, the successive action potentials each release calcium from the sarcoplasmic reticulum before all the calcium from the previous

more Ca out there, so greater tension

not allowing Ca to go back in, so fused so back in,

FIGURE 11-25

Isometric contractions produced by multiple stimuli of 10 stimuli per second (unfused tetanus) and 100 stimuli per second (fused tetanus), as compared with a single twitch.

high-freq. stimulus

isotonic → isometric contractions

action potential has been pumped back into the reticulum. This results in a maintained elevated cytosolic calcium concentration and prevents a decline in the number of available binding sites on the thin filaments. Under these conditions, the maximum number of binding sites remains available and the tension has time to rise to its maximal level.

Length-Tension Relation

The amount of tension developed by a muscle fiber and thus its strength can be altered not only by changing the frequency of stimulation but also by changing the length of the fiber before contraction. One can stretch a muscle fiber to various lengths and measure the magnitude of the maximal isometric tetanic tension generated in response to stimulation at each length (Figure 11-26). The length at which the fiber develops the greatest tension is termed the **optimal length**, l_o. When muscle fiber length is 60 percent of l_o, the fiber develops no tension when stimulated. As length is increased from this point, the isometric tension is increased up to a maximum at l_o, and further lengthening leads to a drop in tension. At lengths of 175 percent l_o or beyond, the fiber develops no tension when stimulated.

The lengths of most fibers when all the skeletal muscles in the body are relaxed are near l_o and thus near the optimal lengths for force generation. The length of a relaxed fiber can be altered by the load on the muscle or the contraction of other muscles that stretch the relaxed fibers, but the extent to which the relaxed length can be changed is limited by the muscle's attachments to bones. It rarely exceeds a 30 percent change from l_o and is often much less. Over this range of lengths, the ability to develop tension never falls below about half of the tension that can be developed at l_o (Figure 11-26).

The relationship between fiber length and the fiber's capacity to develop tension can be mainly explained in terms of the sliding-filament mechanism. Stretching a relaxed muscle fiber pulls the thin filaments past the thick filaments, changing the amount of overlap between them. Stretching a fiber to 1.75 l_o pulls the filaments apart to the point where there is no overlap. At this point there can be no cross-bridge binding to actin and no development of tension. Between 1.75 l_o and l_o, there is more and more filament overlap, and the tension developed upon stimulation increases in proportion to the increased number of cross bridges in the overlap region. Filament overlap is greatest at l_o, allowing the maximal number of cross bridges to bind to the thin filaments, thereby producing

FIGURE 11-26

Variation in isometric tetanic tension with muscle fiber length. The shaded band represents the range of length changes that can occur physiologically in the body while muscles are attached to bones.

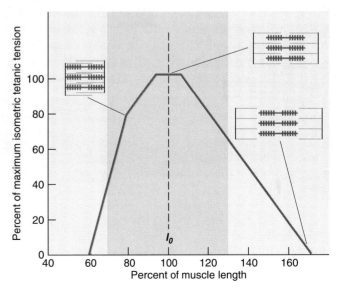

maximal tension. At lengths less than l_o, tension declines because the overlapping of the two sets of thin filaments from opposite ends of the sarcomere interfere with the cross bridges' ability to bind and exert force in the regions of double overlap.[2]

Load-Velocity Relation

It is a common experience that light objects can be moved faster than heavy objects. The velocity at which a muscle fiber shortens while undergoing maximal tetanic stimulation decreases with increasing loads (Figure 11-27). The shortening velocity is maximal at zero load and is zero when the load is equal to the maximal isometric tension. At loads greater than the maximal isometric tension, the fiber will *lengthen* at a velocity that increases with load, and at very high loads the fiber will break.

The shortening velocity is determined by the rate at which individual cross bridges undergo their cyclical activity. For complex reasons, increasing the load on a cross bridge decreases the rate at which the bridge proceeds through step 2, the force-generating step in the cross-bridge cycle. The slower the rate of cross-bridge cycling, the slower the shortening velocity.

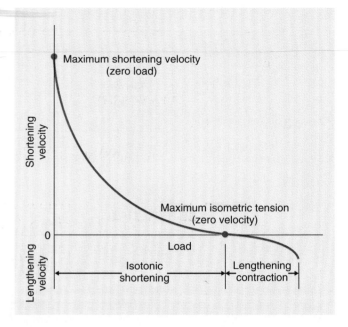

FIGURE 11-27

Velocity of skeletal-muscle fiber shortening and lengthening as a function of load. Note that the force being sustained by cross bridges during a lengthening contraction is greater than the maximum isometric tension.

SKELETAL-MUSCLE ENERGY METABOLISM

As we have seen, ATP performs three functions directly related to muscle fiber contraction and relaxation (Table 11-1). In no other cell type does the rate of ATP breakdown increase so much from one moment to the next as in a skeletal-muscle fiber (20 to several hundredfold depending on the type of muscle fiber) when it goes from rest to a state of contractile activity. If a fiber is to sustain contractile activity, molecules of ATP must be supplied by metabolism as rapidly as they are broken down during the contractile process. The small supply of preformed ATP that exists at the start of contractile activity is consumed within a few twitches. If this were the only source of energy, the muscle cross bridges would rapidly become locked in a state equivalent to rigor mortis as the ATP is depleted.

There are three ways a muscle fiber can form ATP during contractile activity (Figure 11-28): (1) phosphorylation of ADP by **creatine phosphate**; (2) oxidative phosphorylation of ADP, in the mitochondria; and (3) substrate level phosphorylation of ADP by the glycolytic pathway in the cytosol.

Phosphorylation of ADP by the cell's creatine phosphate (CP) provides a very rapid means of forming ATP at the onset of contractile activity. When the chemical bond between creatine (C) and phosphate is broken, the amount of energy released is about the same as that released when the terminal phosphate bond in ATP is broken. This energy, along with the phosphate group, can be transferred to ADP to form ATP in a reversible reaction catalyzed by creatine kinase:

$$CP + ADP \underset{\substack{\text{Creatine} \\ \text{kinase}}}{\rightleftharpoons} C + ATP$$

In a resting muscle fiber, the concentration of ATP is much greater than that of ADP, leading by mass action to the formation of creatine phosphate. During periods of rest, muscle fibers build up a concentration of creatine phosphate to a level approximately five times that of ATP. At the beginning of contraction, when the concentration of ATP begins to fall and that of ADP to rise owing to the increased rate of ATP breakdown, mass action favors the formation of ATP from creatine phosphate. This transfer of energy from creatine phosphate to ATP is so rapid that the concentration of ATP in a muscle fiber changes very little at the start of contraction, whereas the concentration of creatine phosphate falls rapidly.

---

[2]In addition, at these shorter fiber lengths, for reasons that are not clear, less calcium is released from the sarcoplasmic reticulum and the affinity of troponin for calcium is decreased.

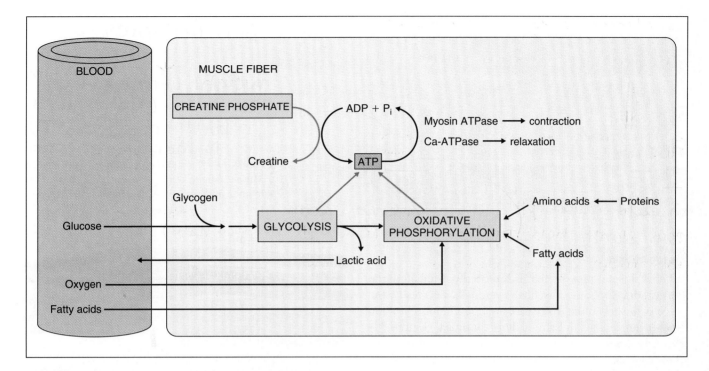

FIGURE 11-28

The three sources of ATP production during muscle contraction: (1) creatine phosphate, (2) oxidative phosphorylation, and (3) glycolysis.

Although the formation of ATP from creatine phosphate is very rapid, requiring only a single enzymatic reaction, the amount of ATP that can be formed by this process is limited by the initial concentration of creatine phosphate in the cell. If contractile activity is to be continued for more than a few seconds, the muscle must be able to form ATP from the other sources listed above. The use of creatine phosphate at the start of contractile activity provides the few seconds necessary for the slower, multienzyme pathways of oxidative phosphorylation and glycolysis to increase their rates of ATP formation to levels that match the rates of ATP breakdown.

At moderate levels of muscular activity (moderate rates of ATP breakdown), most of the ATP used for muscle contraction is formed by oxidative phosphorylation. During the first 5 to 10 min of exercise, muscle glycogen is the major fuel contributing to oxidative phosphorylation. For the next 30 min or so, blood-borne fuels become dominant, blood glucose and fatty acids contributing approximately equally to oxidative phosphorylation of the muscle. Beyond this period, fatty acids become progressively more important and glucose utilization decreases.

If the intensity of exercise exceeds about 70 percent of the maximal rate of ATP breakdown, glycolysis contributes an increasingly significant fraction of the total ATP generated by the muscle. The glycolytic pathway, although producing only small quantities of ATP from each molecule of glucose metabolized, can produce large quantities of ATP when enough enzymes and substrate are available, and it can do so in the absence of oxygen. The glucose for glycolysis can be obtained from two sources: the blood or the stores of glycogen within the muscle fibers. As the intensity of muscle activity increases, more and more of the ATP is formed by anaerobic glycolysis, with a corresponding increase in the production of lactic acid (which dissociates to yield lactate ions and hydrogen ions).

At the end of muscle activity, creatine phosphate and glycogen levels in the muscle have decreased. To return a muscle fiber to its original state, these energy-storing compounds must be replaced. Both processes require energy, and so a muscle continues to consume increased amounts of oxygen for some time after it has ceased to contract, as evidenced by the fact that one continues to breathe deeply and rapidly for a period of time immediately following intense exercise. This elevated consumption of oxygen following exercise repays the **oxygen debt** that was incurred during the previous contractile activity when ATP was being utilized faster than it could be generated by oxidative phosphorylation. The longer and more intense the exercise, the longer it takes to restore the glycogen and creatine phosphate (energy stores) in a muscle fiber to their original concentrations.

Why fatigue quicker 2nd time around? ATP not cause of fatigue; instead, use up glucose, then use up glycogen, then fat stores

↓

weight lifting = Ca out/in aerobics (lactic acid build-up → need O₂ to make pyruvic acid → microtears in muscles)

high-freq.

FIGURE 11-29
Muscle fatigue during a maintained isometric tetanus and recovery following a period of rest.

lactic acid causes pH change; actin + myosin don't hold together well (acidic pH not good here)

Muscle Fatigue

When a skeletal-muscle fiber is repeatedly stimulated, the tension developed by the fiber eventually decreases, the velocity of shortening decreases, and the rate of relaxation slows even though the stimulation continues (Figure 11-29). This decline in muscle tension as a result of previous contractile activity is known as **muscle fatigue**. The onset of fatigue and its rate of development depend on the type of skeletal muscle fiber and on the intensity and duration of contractile activity.

If a muscle is allowed to rest after the onset of fatigue, it can recover its ability to contract upon restimulation (Figure 11-29). The rate of recovery depends upon the duration and intensity of the previous activity. Some muscle fibers fatigue fairly rapidly if continuously stimulated at a high frequency but also recover rapidly. This is the type of fatigue that accompanies short-duration, high-intensity exercise, such as weight lifting. Fatigue that develops more slowly with low-intensity, long-duration exercise, such as long-distance running, during which there are cyclical periods of contraction and relaxation, requires much longer periods of rest, often up to 24 h, before the muscle achieves complete recovery.

It might seem logical that depletion of available ATP would account for fatigue, but the ATP concentration in fatigued muscle is found to be only slightly lower than in a resting muscle, and other factors are responsible for the fatigue process. Although the onset of fatigue during low-intensity, long-duration exercise is correlated with the depletion of muscle glycogen—the larger the glycogen content of a muscle, the longer the duration of activity before fatigue sets in—the molecular mechanism linking glycogen depletion and muscle fatigue is unknown.

During continuous high-frequency stimulation of a muscle, there is a rapid rise in hydrogen-ion concentration due to the production of lactic acid by glycolysis, and inorganic phosphate concentration rises as ATP is split to produce ADP and P_i. The increased hydrogen-ion and inorganic phosphate concentrations inhibit portions of the cross-bridge cycle, leading to decreased force production. However, these chemical changes account for only about 50 percent of decreased force production. The additional contributing factor in this type of fatigue is a decreased release of calcium from the sarcoplasmic reticulum in response to electrical stimulation.[3]

A different set of factors contributes to the slower-developing, longer-lasting fatigue that occurs with prolonged periods of cyclical activity.[4] They reflect changes in the activity of various muscle proteins—calcium channels, the Ca-ATPase pumps in the sarcoplasmic reticulum, troponin, tropomyosin, actin, and myosin.

Although not directly caused by a decrease in ATP concentration, fatigue does occur at a time when ATP breakdown is beginning to exceed its production. If contractile activity were to continue without fatigue, the ATP concentration would decrease to the point that the cross bridges would become linked in a rigor configuration. Thus, muscle fatigue may have evolved as a mechanism for preventing the onset of rigor, which is very damaging to muscle fibers.

---

[3]The mechanisms responsible for this failure in excitation-contraction coupling may involve failure of the action potential to be conducted along the T tubule to the sarcoplasmic reticulum or the failure of this signal to open the calcium-release channels in the sarcoplasmic reticulum membrane. Recall that each action potential is produced by the flow of sodium ions into the fiber and potassium ions out. These ion fluxes lead to the accumulation of potassium and depletion of sodium in the small volume of the T tubule during high-frequency stimulation. These changes in ion concentrations lead to an inactivation of the channel processes involved in generating action potentials and thus to the failure of action potential generation along the T tubule. Recovery from this form of fatigue occurs rapidly as the ion concentrations in the T tubules are restored during periods of rest by diffusion of ions between the lumen of the T tubule and the rest of the extracellular fluid.

[4]These factors include (1) reduced storage and release of calcium by the sarcoplasmic reticulum, (2) reduced sensitivity of the troponin-tropomyosin system to cytosolic calcium, and (3) reduced ability of each cross bridge to develop tension. The effect of these factors, which differ in degree between different fiber types and with the duration of the fatigue, is to decrease the number of active cross bridges and to decrease the force generated by each bridge.

There is another type of fatigue quite different from muscle fatigue. Failure of the appropriate regions of the cerebral cortex to send excitatory signals to the motor neurons can also lead to the failure of muscle fibers to contract. This is called **central command fatigue**, and it may cause an individual to stop exercising even though the muscles are not fatigued. An athlete's performance depends not only on the physical state of the appropriate muscles but also upon the "will to win," the ability to initiate central commands to muscles during a period of increasingly distressful sensations.

TYPES OF SKELETAL-MUSCLE FIBERS

All skeletal-muscle fibers do not have the same mechanical and metabolic characteristics. Different types of fibers can be identified on the basis of (1) their maximal velocities of shortening—fast and slow fibers—and (2) the major pathway used to form ATP—oxidative and glycolytic fibers.

Fast and slow fibers contain myosin isozymes (Chapter 4) that differ in the maximal rates at which they split ATP, which in turn determine the maximal rate of cross-bridge cycling and hence the fibers' maximal shortening velocity. Fibers containing myosin with high ATPase activity are classified as **fast fibers**, and those containing myosin with lower ATPase activity are **slow fibers**.

The second means of classifying skeletal-muscle fibers is according to the type of enzymatic machinery available for synthesizing ATP. Some fibers contain numerous mitochondria and thus have a high capacity for oxidative phosphorylation. These fibers are classified as **oxidative fibers**. Most of the ATP produced by such fibers is dependent upon blood flow to deliver oxygen and fuel molecules to the muscle, and these fibers are surrounded by numerous small blood vessels. They also contain large amounts of an oxygen-binding protein known as **myoglobin**, which increases the rate of oxygen diffusion within the fiber in addition to providing a small store of oxygen. The large amounts of myoglobin present in oxidative fibers give the muscle a dark-red color, and thus oxidative fibers are often referred to as **red muscle** fibers.

In contrast, **glycolytic fibers** have few mitochondria but possess a high concentration of glycolytic enzymes and a large store of glycogen. Corresponding to their limited use of oxygen, these fibers are surrounded by relatively few blood vessels and contain little myoglobin. The lack of myoglobin is responsible for the pale color of glycolytic fibers and their frequent designation as **white muscle** fibers.

On the basis of these two general characteristics, three types of skeletal-muscle fibers can be distinguished:[5]

1. **Slow-oxidative fibers** combine low myosin-ATPase activity with high oxidative capacity.
2. **Fast-oxidative fibers** combine high myosin-ATPase activity with high oxidative capacity.
3. **Fast-glycolytic fibers** combine high myosin-ATPase activity with high glycolytic capacity.

In addition to these biochemical differences, there are also size differences, glycolytic fibers generally having much larger diameters than oxidative fibers (Figure 11-30). This fact has significance for tension development. The density of thick and thin filaments per unit of cross-sectional area is about the same in all types of skeletal-muscle fibers. The larger the diameter of a muscle fiber, therefore, the greater the maximum tension it can develop (the greater its strength) because there are more thick and thin filaments acting in parallel to produce force. Accordingly, the average glycolytic fiber develops more tension when it contracts than does an oxidative fiber.

These three types of fibers also differ in their capacity to resist fatigue. Fast-glycolytic fibers fatigue rapidly, whereas slow-oxidative fibers are very resistant to fatigue, which allows them to maintain contractile activity for long periods with little loss of tension. Fast-oxidative fibers have an intermediate capacity to resist fatigue (Figure 11-31).

The characteristics of the three types of skeletal-muscle fibers are summarized in Table 11-3.

WHOLE-MUSCLE CONTRACTION

As described earlier, whole muscles are made up of many muscle fibers organized into motor units. All the muscle fibers in a single motor unit are of the same fiber type. Thus, one can apply the fiber type designation to the whole motor unit and refer to slow-oxidative motor units, fast-glycolytic motor units, and fast-oxidative motor units.

Most muscles are composed of all three motor unit types interspersed with each other (Figure 11-30). Depending on the proportions of the three fiber types pres-

[5]Additional designations for these three fiber types are slow-oxidative fibers [SO, type I, S (slow)], fast-oxidative fibers [FOG, type IIa, FR (fatigue-resistant)], and fast-glycolytic fibers [FG, type IIb, FF (fast fatigable)].

(A) Capillary blood vessels

Glycolytic fibers large diameter

(B) Oxidative fibers small diameter

�ⁱ**FIGURE 11-30**

Cross sections of skeletal muscle. (A) The capillaries surrounding the muscle fibers have been stained. Note the large number of capillaries surrounding the small-diameter oxidative fibers. (B) The mitochondria have been stained. Fibers containing a high concentration of stained material indicate the large numbers of mitochondria in the small-diameter oxidative fibers. (*Courtesy of John A. Faulkner.*)

MEMORIZE

Largest diameter (most tension)

TABLE 11-3   CHARACTERISTICS OF THE THREE TYPES OF SKELETAL MUSCLE FIBERS

	Slow-oxidative fibers	**Fast-oxidative fibers**	**Fast-glycolytic fibers**
Primary source of ATP production	Oxidative phosphorylation =ETC	Oxidative phosphorylation	Glycolysis.
Mitochondria	Many	Many	Few
Capillaries	Many	Many	Few
Myoglobin content	High (red muscle)	High (red muscle)	Low (white muscle)
Glycolytic enzyme activity	Low	Intermediate	High
Glycogen content	Low	Intermediate	High
Rate of fatigue	Slow / low	Intermediate	Fast / high
Myosin-ATPase activity	Low	High	High
Contraction velocity	Slow	Fast	Fast
Fiber diameter	Small	Intermediate	Large
Motor unit size	Small	Intermediate	Large
Size of motor neuron innervating fiber	Small	Intermediate	Large

(swinging around)

Fast-glycolytic fibers

Fast-oxidative fibers

Slow-oxidative fibers

FIGURE 11-31

The rate of fatigue development in the three fiber types. Each vertical line is the contractile response to a brief tetanic stimulus and relaxation that is then repeated again and again for 60 minutes. The contractile responses occurring between about 9 min and 60 minutes are not shown on the figure.

ent, muscles can differ considerably in their maximal contraction speed, strength, and fatigability. For example, the muscles of the back and legs must be able to maintain their activity for long periods of time without fatigue while supporting an upright posture. These muscles contain

large numbers of slow-oxidative fibers, which are resistant to fatigue. In contrast, the muscles in the arms may be called upon to produce large amounts of tension over a short time period, as when lifting a heavy object, and these muscles have a greater proportion of fast-glycolytic fibers.

We will now use the characteristics of single fibers to describe whole-muscle contraction and its control.

Control of Muscle Tension

The total tension a muscle can develop depends upon two factors (Table 11-4): (1) the amount of tension developed by each fiber, and (2) the number of fibers contracting at any time. By controlling these two factors, the nervous system controls whole-muscle tension as well as shortening velocity. The conditions that determine the amount of tension developed in a single fiber have been discussed previously and are summarized in I of Table 11-4.

The number of fibers contracting at any time—the second factor determining total muscle tension—depends on (1) the number of fibers in each motor unit, and (2) the number of active motor units.

The number of muscle fibers in a motor unit (motor unit size) varies considerably from one muscle to another. The muscles in the hand and eye, which produce very delicate movements, contain small motor units. For example, one motor neuron innervates only about 13 fibers in an eye muscle. In contrast, in the more coarsely controlled muscles of the back and legs, each motor unit contains hundreds and in some cases several thousand fibers. When a muscle is composed of small motor units, the total tension produced by the muscle can be increased in small steps by activating additional motor units in the muscle. If the motor units are large, large increases in tension will occur as each additional motor unit is activated. Thus, finer control of muscle tension is possible in muscles with small motor units.

The force produced by a single fiber, as we have seen (page 320), depends in part on the fiber diameter—the greater the diameter, the greater the force. We have also noted that fast-glycolytic fibers have the largest diameters. Thus, a motor unit composed of 100 fast-glycolytic fibers

TABLE 11-4 FACTORS DETERMINING MUSCLE TENSION

I. Tension developed by each individual fiber
   A. Action-potential frequency (frequency-tension relation)
   B. Fiber length (length-tension relation)
   C. Fiber diameter
   D. Fatigue
II. Number of active fibers
   A. Number of fibers per motor unit
   B. Number of active motor units

produces more force than a motor unit composed of 100 slow-oxidative fibers. In addition, fast-glycolytic motor units tend to have more muscle fibers. For both of these reasons, activating a single fast-glycolytic motor unit will produce more force than activating a single slow-oxidative motor unit.

The process of increasing the number of motor units that are active in a muscle at any given time is called **recruitment**. It is achieved by increasing the excitatory synaptic input to the motor neurons. The greater the number of active motor neurons, and hence motor units recruited, the greater the muscle tension.

Motor neuron size plays an important role in the recruitment of motor units (the size of a motor neuron refers to the diameter of the nerve cell body, which is usually correlated with the diameter of its axon, and does not refer to the size of the motor unit the neuron controls). Given the same number of sodium ions entering a cell during synaptic activity in a large and in a small motor neuron, the small neuron will undergo a greater depolarization because these ions will be distributed over a smaller membrane surface area. Accordingly, the smallest neurons are recruited first and cause contraction of these motor units. Then the larger neurons are recruited, and the strength of the contraction increases. Since the smallest motor neurons are part of the slow-oxidative motor units (Table 11-3), these motor units are recruited first, followed by fast-oxidative motor units, and finally, during very strong contractions, by fast-glycolytic motor units (Figure 11-32).

Thus, during moderate-strength contractions, such as are used in most endurance types of exercise, relatively few fast-glycolytic motor units are recruited, and most of the activity occurs in oxidative fibers, which are more resistant to fatigue. The large fast-glycolytic motor units, which fatigue rapidly, begin to be recruited when the intensity of contraction exceeds about 40 percent of the maximal tension producible by the muscle.

In conclusion, the neural control of whole-muscle tension involves both the frequency of action potentials in individual motor units (to vary the tension generated by the fibers in that unit) and the recruitment of motor units (to vary the number of active fibers). Most motor neuron activity occurs in bursts of action potentials, which produce tetanic contractions rather than single twitches. Recall from page 322 that the tension of a single fiber increases only three- to fivefold when going from a twitch to a maximal tetanic contraction. Therefore, varying the frequency of action potentials in the neurons supplying them provides a way to make only three- to fivefold adjustments in the tension of the recruited motor units. The force a whole muscle exerts can be varied over a much wider range than this, from very delicate movements to extremely powerful contractions, by the recruitment of motor units. Thus, recruitment provides the primary

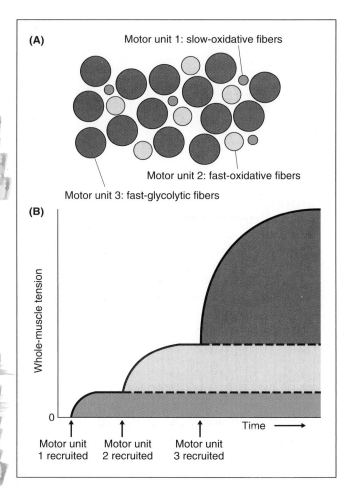

FIGURE 11-32

(A) Diagram of a cross section through a muscle composed of three types of motor units. (B) Tetanic muscle tension resulting from the successive recruitment of the three motor units. Note that motor unit 3, composed of fast-glycolytic fibers, produces the greatest rise in tension because it is composed of the largest-diameter fibers and contains the largest number of fibers per motor unit.

means of varying tension in a whole muscle. Recruitment is controlled by the central commands from the cerebral cortex to the various motor neurons.

Control of Shortening Velocity

As we saw earlier, the velocity at which a *single* muscle fiber shortens is determined by (1) the load on the fiber (page 324), and (2) whether the fiber is a fast fiber or a slow fiber (page 327). Translated to a *whole* muscle, these characteristics become (1) the load on the whole muscle, and (2) the types of motor units in the muscle. For the whole muscle, however, recruitment becomes a third very important factor so that the shortening velocity can be varied from very fast to very slow even though the load on the muscle remains constant. Consider, for the sake of illustration, a muscle composed of only two motor units of the same size and fiber type. One motor unit by itself will lift a 4-g load more slowly than a 2-g load because the shortening velocity decreases with increasing load. When both units are active and a 4-g load is lifted, each motor unit bears only half the load, and its fibers will shorten as if it were lifting only a 2-g load. Thus, the muscle will lift the 4-g load at a higher velocity when both motor units are active.

Muscle Adaptation to Exercise

The regularity with which a muscle is used, as well as the duration and intensity of its activity, affects the properties of the muscle. If the neurons to a skeletal muscle are severed or otherwise destroyed, the denervated muscle fibers will become progressively smaller in diameter, and the amount of contractile proteins they contain will decrease. This condition is known as **denervation atrophy**. A muscle can also atrophy with its nerve supply intact if the muscle is not used for a long period of time, as when a broken arm or leg is immobilized in a cast. This condition is known as **disuse atrophy**.

In contrast to the decrease in muscle mass that results from a lack of neural stimulation, increased amounts of contractile activity—in other words, exercise—can produce an increase in the size (**hypertrophy**) of muscle fibers as well as changes in their chemical composition. Since the number of fibers in a muscle remains essentially constant throughout adult life, the changes in muscle size with atrophy and hypertrophy do not result from changes in the *number* of muscle fibers but in the metabolic capacity and size of each fiber.

Exercise that is of relatively low intensity but of long duration (popularly called "aerobic exercise"), such as long-distance running and swimming, produces increases in the number of mitochondria in the fast- and slow-oxidative fibers, which are recruited in this type of activity. In addition, there is an increase in the number of capillaries around these fibers. All these changes lead to an increase in the capacity for endurance activity with a minimum of fatigue. (Surprisingly, fiber diameter decreases slightly, and thus there is a small decrease in the strength of muscles as a result of endurance exercise.) As we shall see in later chapters, endurance exercise produces changes not only in the skeletal muscles but also in the respiratory and circulatory systems, changes that improve the delivery of oxygen and fuel molecules to the muscle.

In contrast, short-duration, high-intensity exercise (popularly called "strength training"), such as weight lifting, affects primarily the fast-glycolytic fibers, which are briefly recruited during strong contractions. These fibers undergo an increase in fiber diameter resulting from the increased synthesis of actin and myosin filaments, which form more myofibrils. In addition, the glycolytic activity is increased because of the increased synthesis of glycolytic enzymes. The result of such high-intensity exercise is an increase in the strength of the muscle, producing the bulging muscles of a conditioned weight lifter. Such muscles, although very powerful, have little capacity for endurance and fatigue rapidly.

Exercise produces little change in the types of myosin formed by the fibers and thus little change in the proportions of fast and slow fibers in a muscle. As described above, however, exercise does change the rates at which metabolic enzymes are synthesized, leading to changes in the proportion of oxidative and glycolytic fibers within a muscle.

The signals responsible for all these changes in muscle with different types of activity are unknown. They are related to the frequency and intensity of the contractile activity in the muscle fibers and thus to the pattern of action potentials produced in the muscle over an extended period of time. Similar adaptive changes in cell size, number, or capacity for functional activity are seen in many other organs in the body in response to increased demands on the tissue.

Because different types of exercise produce quite different changes in the strength and endurance capacity of a muscle, an individual performing regular exercises to improve muscle performance must choose a type of exercise that is compatible with the type of activity he or she ultimately wishes to perform. Thus, lifting weights will not improve the endurance of a long-distance runner, and jogging will not produce the increased strength desired by a weight lifter. Most exercises have some effect on both strength and endurance.

The changes in muscle occur slowly over a period of weeks in response to repeated periods of exercise. If exercise is stopped, the changes in the muscle that occurred as a result of the exercise will slowly revert to their state before exercise began.

The maximum force generated by a muscle decreases by 30 to 40 percent between the ages of 30 and 80. This decrease in tension-generating capacity is due primarily to a decrease in average fiber diameter. Some of the change is simply the result of diminishing physical activity with age and can be prevented by exercise programs. The ability of a muscle to adapt to exercise, however, decreases with age: The same intensity and duration of exercise in an older individual will not produce the same amount of change (adaptation) as in a younger person. This decreased ability to adapt to increased activity is seen in most organs as one ages (Chapter 7). The precise cause is unknown but probably involves impairment of the mechanisms by which genes are transcribed and translated into proteins.

This effect of aging, however, is only partial, and there is no question that even in the elderly, exercise can produce significant adaptation. Until recently, aerobic training received major attention because of its effect on the cardiovascular system (Chapter 14). More recently, however, strength training of a modest degree has also become strongly recommended because it can partially prevent the loss of muscle tissue that occurs with aging. [Moreover, it also helps maintain stronger bones (Chapter 18).]

Extensive exercise by an individual whose muscles have not adapted to the particular type of exercise leads to muscle soreness the next day. This soreness is the result of a mild inflammation of the muscle, which occurs whenever tissues are damaged (Chapter 20). The most severe inflammation occurs following a period of lengthening contractions, suggesting that the lengthening of a muscle fiber by an external force produces greater muscle damage than do either isotonic or isometric contractions. Thus, exercising by gradually lowering weights will produce greater muscle soreness than an equivalent amount of weight lifting.

Finally, the effects of anabolic steroids on skeletal muscle growth and strength are described in Chapter 18.

Lever Action of Muscles and Bones

A contracting muscle exerts a force on bones through its connecting tendons. When the force is great enough, the bone moves as the muscle shortens. A contracting muscle exerts only a pulling force, so that as the muscle shortens, the bones to which it is attached are pulled toward each other. **Flexion** refers to the *bending* of a limb at a joint, thereby decreasing the angle around the joint, whereas **extension** is the *straightening* of a limb, which increases the angle around a joint (Figure 11-33). These opposing motions require at least two muscles, one to cause flexion and the other extension. Groups of muscles that produce

FIGURE 11-33

Antagonistic muscles for flexion and extension of the forearm.

oppositely directed movements at a joint are known as **antagonists**. From Figure 11-33 it can be seen that contraction of the biceps causes flexion of the arm at the elbow, whereas contraction of the antagonistic muscle, the triceps, causes the arm to extend. Both muscles exert only a pulling force upon the forearm when they contract.

Sets of antagonistic muscles are required not only for flexion-extension, but also for side-to-side movements or

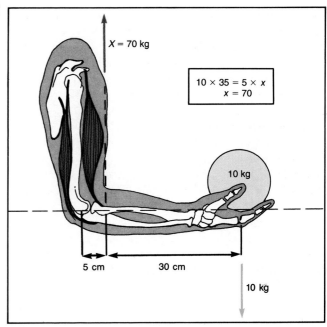

FIGURE 11-35
Mechanical equilibrium of forces acting on the forearm while supporting a 10-kg load.

FIGURE 11-34
Contraction of the gastrocnemius muscle in the calf can lead either to flexion of the leg, if the quadriceps femoris muscle is relaxed, or to extension of the foot, if the quadriceps is contracting, preventing bending of the knee joint.

rotation of a limb. The contraction of some muscles leads to two types of limb movement, depending on the contractile state of other muscles acting on the same limb. For example, contraction of the gastrocnemius muscle in the leg causes a flexion of the leg at the knee, as in walking (Figure 11-34). However, contraction of the gastrocnemius muscle with the simultaneous contraction of the quadriceps femoris (which causes extension of the lower leg) prevents the knee joint from bending, leaving only the ankle joint capable of moving. The foot is extended, and the body rises on tiptoe.

The muscles, bones, and joints in the body are arranged in lever systems. The basic principle of a lever is illustrated by the flexion of the arm by the biceps muscle (Figure 11-35), which exerts an upward pulling force on the forearm about 5 cm away from the elbow. In this example, a 10-kg weight held in the hand exerts a downward force of 10 kg about 35 cm from the elbow. A law of physics tells us that the forearm is in mechanical equilibrium (no net forces acting on the system) when the product of the downward force (10 kg) and its distance from the elbow (35 cm) is equal to the product of the isometric tension exerted by the muscle (X) and its distance from the elbow (5 cm); that is, $10 \times 35 = 5 \times X$. Thus $X = 70$ kg. Note that this system is working at a mechanical disadvantage since the force exerted by the muscle (70 kg) is considerably greater than the load (10 kg) it is supporting.

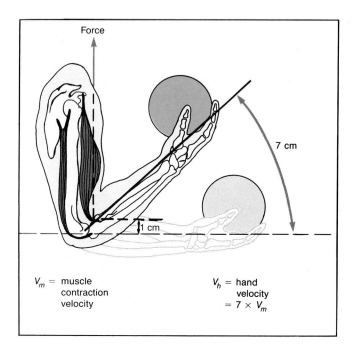

V_m = muscle contraction velocity

V_h = hand velocity = $7 \times V_m$

FIGURE 11-36

Velocity of the biceps muscle is amplified by the lever system of the arm, producing a greater velocity of the hand. The range of movement is also amplified (1 cm of shortening by the muscle produces 7 cm of movement by the hand).

However, the mechanical disadvantage under which most muscle lever systems operate is offset by increased maneuverability. In Figure 11-36, when the biceps shortens 1 cm, the hand moves through a distance of 7 cm. Since the muscle shortens 1 cm in the same amount of time that the hand moves 7 cm, the velocity at which the hand moves is seven times greater than the rate of muscle shortening. The lever system amplifies the velocity of muscle shortening so that short, relatively slow movements of the muscle produce faster movements of the hand. Thus, a pitcher can throw a baseball at 90 to 100 mi/h even though his muscles shorten at only a small fraction of this velocity.

Skeletal-Muscle Disease

A number of diseases can affect the contraction of skeletal muscle. Many of them are due to defects in the parts of the nervous system that control contraction of the muscle fibers, however, rather than to defects in the muscle fibers themselves. For example, polio is a viral disease that destroys motor neurons, leading to the paralysis of skeletal muscle, and may result in death due to respiratory failure.

Muscle Cramps. Involuntary tetanic contraction of skeletal muscles produces *muscle cramps*. During cramping, action potentials fire at rates as high as 300/s, a much greater rate than occurs during maximal voluntary con-

traction. The specific cause of this high activity is unknown but is probably related to electrolyte imbalances in the extracellular fluid surrounding both the muscle and nerve fibers and changes in extracellular osmolarity, especially hypoosmolarity.

Hypocalcemic Tetany. Similar in symptoms to muscular cramping is the involuntary tetanic contraction of skeletal muscles, *hypocalcemic tetany*, that occurs when the extracellular calcium concentration falls to about 40 percent of its normal value. This may seem surprising since we have seen that calcium is required for muscle contraction. The effect of altered extracellular calcium is exerted not on the intracellular proteins, however, but on the plasma membrane. Low extracellular calcium (hypocalcemia) increases the opening of sodium channels in excitable membranes, leading to membrane depolarization and the spontaneous firing of action potentials. The mechanisms controlling the extracellular concentration of calcium ions are discussed in Chapter 16.

Muscular Dystrophy. This disease is one of the most frequently encountered genetic diseases, affecting one in every 4000 boys (but much less commonly girls) born in America. *Muscular dystrophy* results in the progressive degeneration of skeletal- and cardiac-muscle fibers, weakening the muscle and leading ultimately to death from respiratory or cardiac failure. While exercise strengthens normal skeletal muscle, it weakens dystrophic muscle. The symptoms become evident at about 2 to 6 years of age, and most affected individuals do not survive much beyond the age of 20. In addition, about one-third of dystrophic patients show signs of mental retardation.

The gene responsible for a major form of muscular dystrophy has been identified on the X chromosome. (As described in Chapter 19, girls have two X chromosomes and boys only one. Accordingly, a girl with one abnormal X chromosome and one normal one will not develop the disease. This is why the disease is so much more common in boys.) This gene codes for a protein known as dystrophin, which is absent or present in a nonfunctional form in patients with the disease. Dystrophin is located on the inner surface of the plasma membrane in normal muscle. It resembles other known cytoskeletal proteins and may be involved in maintaining the structural integrity of the plasma membrane or of elements within the membrane, such as ion channels, in a cell subjected to repeated structural deformation during contraction. Preliminary attempts are being made to treat the disease by inserting the normal gene into dystrophic muscle cells.

Myasthenia Gravis. *Myasthenia gravis*, which is characterized by muscle fatigue and weakness, progressively worsens as the muscle is used. It affects about 12,000

Americans. The symptoms result from a decrease in the number of ACh receptors on the motor end plate. The release of ACh from the nerve terminals is normal, but the magnitude of the muscle end-plate potential is markedly reduced because of the decreased number of receptor sites for ACh. After a few motor nerve impulses, the magnitude of the EPP falls below the threshold for initiating a muscle action potential. As described in Chapter 20, the destruction of the ACh receptors is brought about by the body's own defense mechanisms gone awry, specifically because of the formation of antibodies to the ACh-receptor proteins.

SECTION A SUMMARY

I. There are three types of muscle—skeletal, smooth, and cardiac. Skeletal muscle is attached to bones and moves and supports the skeleton. Smooth muscle surrounds hollow cavities and tubes. Cardiac muscle is the muscle of the heart.

STRUCTURE

I. Skeletal muscles, composed of cylindrical muscle fibers (cells), are linked to bones by tendons at each end of the muscle.

II. Skeletal-muscle fibers have a repeating, striated pattern of light and dark bands, due to the location of the thick and thin filaments within the myofibrils.

III. Actin-containing thin filaments are anchored to the Z lines at each end of a sarcomere, while their free ends partially overlap the myosin-containing thick filaments in the A band.

MOLECULAR MECHANISMS OF CONTRACTION

I. When a skeletal-muscle fiber actively shortens, the thin filaments are propelled toward the center of their sarcomere by movements of the myosin cross bridges that bind to actin.
   A. The globular head of each myosin molecule contains a binding site for actin and an enzymatic site that splits ATP.
   B. The four steps occurring during each cross-bridge cycle are summarized in Figure 11-12. The cross bridges undergo repeated cycles during a contraction, each producing only a small increment of movement.
   C. The three functions of ATP in muscle contraction are summarized in Table 11-1.

II. In a resting muscle, attachment of cross bridges to actin is prevented by tropomyosin molecules that are in contact with the actin subunits of the thin filaments.

III. Contraction is initiated by an increase in cytosolic calcium concentration. The calcium ions bind to troponin on the thin filaments, producing a change in its shape that is transmitted via tropomyosin to the binding sites on actin, allowing the cross bridges to bind to the thin filaments.
   A. The rise in cytosolic calcium concentration is triggered by an action potential in the plasma membrane. The action potential is propagated into the interior of the fiber along the transverse tubules to the region of the sarcoplasmic reticulum, where it produces a release of calcium ions from the reticulum.
   B. Relaxation of a contracting muscle fiber is achieved by actively transporting the cytosolic calcium ions back into the sarcoplasmic reticulum.

IV. Branches of a motor neuron axon form neuromuscular junctions with many muscle fibers in a muscle. Each muscle fiber is innervated by a branch from only one motor neuron. A motor unit consists of a single motor neuron and the muscle fibers it innervates.
   A. Acetylcholine released by an action potential in a motor neuron binds to receptors on the motor end plate of the muscle membrane, opening ion channels that allow the passage of sodium and potassium ions, which results in depolarization of the end-plate membrane.
   B. A single action potential in a motor neuron is sufficient to produce an action potential in a skeletal-muscle fiber.

V. Table 11-2 summarizes the events leading to the contraction of a skeletal-muscle fiber.

MECHANICS OF SINGLE-FIBER CONTRACTION

I. Contraction refers to the turning on of the cross-bridge cycle. Whether there is an accompanying change in muscle length depends upon the external forces acting on the muscle.

II. Three types of contractions can occur following activation of a muscle fiber: an isometric contraction—the muscle generates tension but does not change length; an isotonic contraction—the muscle shortens, moving a load; and a lengthening contraction—the external load on the muscle is greater than the muscle tension, causing the muscle to lengthen during the period of contractile activity.

III. Increasing the frequency of action potentials in a muscle fiber increases the mechanical response (tension or shortening), up to the level of maximal tetanic tension.

IV. Maximum isometric tetanic tension is produced when there is a maximal overlap of thick and thin filaments, that is, at the optimal length l_o. Stretching a fiber beyond its optimal length decreases the filament overlap and decreases the tension produced, whereas decreasing the fiber length below l_o also decreases the tension generated as a result of interference with cross-bridge binding.

V. The velocity of muscle fiber shortening decreases with increases in load. Maximum velocity occurs at zero load.

SKELETAL-MUSCLE ENERGY METABOLISM

I. Muscle fibers form ATP by the transfer of phosphate from creatine phosphate to ADP, by oxidative phosphorylation of ADP in mitochondria, and by substrate level phosphorylation of ADP in the glycolytic pathway.

II. At the beginning of exercise, muscle glycogen is the major fuel consumed. As the exercise proceeds, glucose and fatty acids from the blood provide most of the fuel, fatty acids becoming progressively more important during prolonged exercise. When the intensity of exercise exceeds about 70 percent of maximum, glycolysis begins to contribute an increasing fraction of the total ATP generated.

III. Muscle fatigue is caused by a variety of factors, including internal changes in acidity, phosphate concentration, glycogen depletion, and excitation-contraction coupling failure, not by a lack of ATP.

TYPES OF SKELETAL-MUSCLE FIBERS

I. Three types of skeletal-muscle fibers—slow-oxidative, fast-oxidative, and fast-glycolytic fibers—can be distinguished by their maximal shortening velocities and the predominate pathway used to form ATP.

A. Differences in maximal shortening velocities are the result of different myosin isozymes with high or low ATPase activities, giving rise to fast and slow fibers.

B. Fast-glycolytic fibers have a larger average diameter than oxidative fibers and therefore produce greater tension, but they also fatigue more rapidly.

II. All the muscle fibers in a single motor unit belong to the same fiber type, and most muscles contain all three types.

III. Table 11-3 summarizes the characteristics of the three types of skeletal-muscle fibers.

WHOLE-MUSCLE CONTRACTION

I. The tension produced by whole-muscle contraction depends on the amount of tension developed by each fiber and the number of active fibers in the muscle (Table 11-4).

II. Muscles that produce delicate movements have a small number of fibers per motor unit, whereas postural muscles have much larger motor units.

III. Fast-glycolytic motor units not only have large-diameter fibers but also tend to have large numbers of fibers per motor unit.

IV. Increases in muscle tension are controlled primarily by increasing the number of active motor units in a muscle—a process known as recruitment. Slow-oxidative motor units are recruited first during weak contractions, then fast-oxidative motor units, and finally fast-glycolytic motor units during very strong contractions.

V. Increasing motor unit recruitment increases the velocity at which a muscle will move a given load.

VI. The strength and susceptibility to fatigue of a muscle can be altered by exercise.

A. Long-duration, low-intensity exercise increases a fiber's capacity for oxidative ATP production by increasing the number of mitochondria and blood vessels in the muscle, resulting in increased endurance.

B. Short-duration, high-intensity exercise increases fiber diameter as a result of increased synthesis of actin and myosin, resulting in increased strength.

VII. Movement around a joint requires two antagonistic groups of muscles: One flexes the limb at the joint, and the other extends the limb.

VIII. The lever system of muscles and bones requires muscle tensions far greater than the load in order to sustain a load in an isometric contraction. This disadvantage is offset because the lever system produces a shortening velocity at the end of the lever arm that is greater than the muscle-shortening velocity.

SECTION A KEY TERMS

skeletal muscle	neuromuscular
smooth muscle	junction
cardiac muscle	acetylcholine (ACh)
muscle fiber	end-plate potential
myoblasts	(EPP)
satellite cells	acetylcholinesterase
muscle	tension
tendons	load
striated muscles	isometric contraction
myofibrils	isotonic contraction
sarcomere	lengthening
thick filaments	contraction
myosin	twitch
thin filaments	latent period
actin	contraction time
A band	summation
Z line	tetanus
I band	optimal length (l_o)
H zone	creatine phosphate
M line	oxygen debt
titin	muscle fatigue
cross bridges	central command
contraction	fatigue
relaxation	fast fibers
sliding-filament mechanism	slow fibers
cross-bridge cycle	oxidative fibers
rigor mortis	myoglobin
troponin	red muscle
tropomyosin	glycolytic fibers
excitation-contraction	white muscle
coupling	slow-oxidative fibers
sarcoplasmic reticulum	fast-oxidative fibers
lateral sacs	fast-glycolytic fibers
transverse tubule	recruitment
(T tubule)	hypertrophy
motor neurons	flexion
motor unit	extension
motor end plate	antagonists

SECTION A REVIEW QUESTIONS

1. List the three types of muscle cells and where they are located.

2. Draw a diagram of the arrangement of thick and thin filaments in a striated-muscle sarcomere and label the major bands that give rise to the striated pattern.

3. Describe the organization of myosin and actin molecules in the thick and thin filaments.

4. Describe the four steps of one cross-bridge cycle.

5. Describe the physical state of a muscle fiber in rigor mortis and the conditions that produce this state.

6. What three events in skeletal-muscle contraction and relaxation are dependent on ATP?

7. What prevents cross bridges from attaching to sites on the thin filaments in a resting skeletal muscle?

8. Describe the role of calcium ions in initiating contraction in skeletal muscle.

9. Describe the location, structure, and function of the sarcoplasmic reticulum in skeletal-muscle fibers.

10. Describe the structure and function of the transverse tubules.

11. Describe the events that result in the relaxation of skeletal-muscle fiber.

12. Define a motor unit and describe its structure.

13. Describe the sequence of events by which an action potential in a motor neuron produces an action potential in the plasma membrane of a skeletal-muscle fiber.

14. What is an end-plate potential and what ions are involved in producing it?

15. Compare and contrast the transmission of electrical activity at a neuromuscular junction with that at a synapse.

16. Describe isometric, isotonic, and lengthening contractions.

17. What factors determine the duration of an isotonic twitch in skeletal muscle? An isometric twitch?

18. What effect does increasing the frequency of action potentials in a skeletal-muscle fiber have upon the force of contraction? Explain the mechanism responsible for this effect.

19. Describe the length-tension relationship in striated-muscle fibers.

20. Describe the effect of increasing the load on a skeletal-muscle fiber on the velocity of shortening.

21. What is the function of creatine phosphate in skeletal-muscle contraction?

22. What fuel molecules are metabolized to produce ATP during skeletal-muscle activity?

23. What factors are responsible for skeletal-muscle fatigue?

24. What component of skeletal-muscle fibers accounts for the differences in their maximal shortening velocities?

25. Summarize the characteristics of the three types of skeletal-muscle fibers.

26. Upon what two factors does the amount of tension developed by a whole skeletal muscle depend?

27. Describe the process of motor unit recruitment in controlling (a) whole-muscle tension, and (b) velocity of whole-muscle shortening.

28. During voluntary increases in the force of skeletal-muscle contraction, what is the order of recruitment of the different types of motor units?

29. What happens to skeletal-muscle fibers when the motor neuron to the muscle is destroyed?

30. Describe the changes that occur in skeletal muscles following a period of (a) long-duration, low-intensity exercise training; and (b) short-duration, high-intensity exercise training.

31. How are skeletal muscles arranged around joints so that a limb can push or pull?

32. What are the advantages and disadvantages of the muscle-bone-joint lever system?

SECTION

SMOOTH MUSCLE

Having described the properties and control of skeletal muscle, we now examine the second of the three types of muscle found in the body—smooth muscle. Two characteristics are common to all smooth muscles: They lack the cross-striated banding pattern found in skeletal and cardiac fibers (hence the name "smooth muscle"), and the nerves to them are derived from the autonomic division of the nervous system rather than the somatic division. Thus, smooth muscle is not under direct voluntary control.

Smooth muscle, like skeletal muscle, uses cross-bridge movements between actin and myosin filaments to generate force, and calcium ions to control cross-bridge activity. However, the organization of the contractile filaments and the process of excitation-contraction coupling are quite different in these two types of muscle. Furthermore, there is considerable diversity among various smooth muscles with respect to the mechanism of excitation-contraction coupling.

STRUCTURE

Each smooth-muscle fiber is a spindle-shaped cell with a diameter ranging from 2 to 10 μm, as compared to a range of 10 to 100 μm for skeletal-muscle fibers (Figure 11-3). Unlike skeletal-muscle fibers, the precursor cells of smooth-muscle fibers do not fuse during embryological development. While skeletal-muscle fibers are multinucleate cells that are unable to divide, smooth-muscle fibers contain only a single nucleus and can divide.

Two types of filaments are present in the cytoplasm of smooth-muscle fibers (Figure 11-37): thick myosin-containing filaments and thin actin-containing filaments. The latter are anchored either to the plasma membrane or to cytoplasmic structures known as **dense bodies**, which are functionally similar to the Z lines in skeletal-muscle fibers. Note in Figure 11-37 that the filaments are oriented slightly diagonally to the long axis of the cell. When the fiber shortens, the regions of the plasma membrane between the points where actin is attached to the membrane balloon out. The thick and thin filaments are not organized into myofibrils, as is the case in striated muscles, and there is no regular alignment of these filaments into sarcomeres, which accounts for the absence of a banding pattern in smooth-muscle fibers (Figure 11-38).

The concentration of myosin in smooth muscle is only about one-third that in striated muscle, whereas the actin content can be twice as great. In spite of these differences, the maximal tension per unit of cross-sectional area developed by smooth muscles is similar to that developed by skeletal muscle.

The tension produced by smooth-muscle fibers varies with muscle length in a manner qualitatively similar to that observed in skeletal muscle. There is an optimal length at which tension development is maximal, and less tension is generated at lengths shorter or longer than this optimal length. The range of muscle lengths over which smooth muscle is able to develop tension is greater, however, than it is in skeletal muscle. This property is highly adaptive since most smooth muscle surrounds hollow organs that undergo changes in volume with accompanying changes in the lengths of the smooth-muscle fibers in their walls. Even with relatively large increases in volume, as during the accumulation of large amounts of urine in the bladder, the smooth-muscle fibers in the wall retain some ability to develop tension, whereas such distortion might stretch

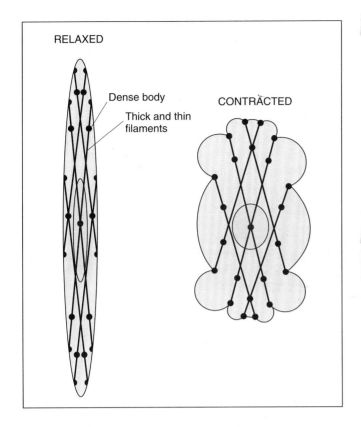

RELAXED

Dense body

Thick and thin
filaments

CONTRACTED

FIGURE 11-37
Thick and thin filaments in smooth muscle are arranged in
slightly diagonal chains that are anchored to the plasma membrane and to dense bodies within the cytoplasm. When activated, the thick and thin filaments slide past each other causing the smooth-muscle fiber to shorten and thicken.

skeletal-muscle fibers beyond the point of thick- and thin-
filament overlap.

The presence of actin and myosin, overlapping thick
and thin filaments with cross bridges, and the length-
tension relationship all provide evidence that smooth-
muscle contraction occurs by a sliding-filament mechanism similar to that in skeletal and cardiac muscle.

FIGURE 11-38
Electron micrograph of portions of three smooth-muscle fibers. Higher magnification of thick filaments (insert) with arrows indicating cross bridges connecting adjacent thin filaments. [*From A. P. Somlyo, C. E. Devine, Avril V. Somlyo,
and R. V. Rice, Phil. Trans. R. Soc. Lond. B, 265:223–229
(1973).*]

Fiber 1

Fiber 2

Fiber 3

CONTRACTION AND ITS CONTROL

Changes in cytosolic calcium concentration control the contractile activity in smooth-muscle fibers, as in striated muscle. However, there are significant differences between the two types of muscle in the way in which calcium exerts its effects on cross-bridge activity and in the mechanisms by which stimulation leads to alterations in calcium concentration.

Cross-Bridge Activation

The thin filaments in smooth muscle do not have the calcium-binding protein troponin that mediates calcium-triggered cross-bridge activity in both skeletal and cardiac muscle. Instead, cross-bridge cycling in smooth muscle is controlled by a calcium-regulated enzyme that phospho-rylates myosin. Only the phosphorylated form of smooth-muscle myosin is able to bind to actin and undergo cross-bridge cycling.

The following sequence of events occurs after a rise in cytosolic calcium in a smooth-muscle fiber (Figure 11-39): (1) Calcium binds to calmodulin, a calcium-binding protein that is present in most cells (Chapter 7) and whose structure is related to that of troponin; (2) the calcium-calmodulin complex binds to a protein kinase, **myosin light-chain kinase**, thereby activating the enzyme; (3) the active protein kinase then uses ATP to phosphorylate myosin. Hence, cross-bridge activity in smooth muscle is turned on by calcium-mediated changes in the thick filaments, whereas in skeletal and cardiac muscle, calcium mediates changes in the thin filaments.

The smooth-muscle myosin isozyme has a very low maximal rate of ATPase activity, on the order of 10 to 100

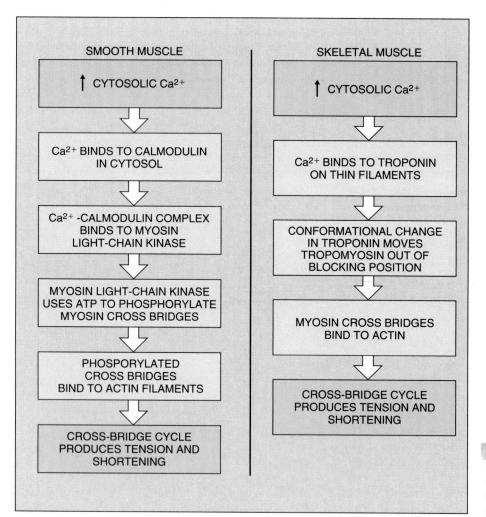

FIGURE 11-39

Pathways leading from increased cytoplasmic calcium to cross-bridge cycling in smooth- and skeletal-muscle fibers.

times less than that of skeletal-muscle myosin. Since the rate of ATP splitting determines the rate of cross-bridge cycling and thus shortening, smooth-muscle shortening is much slower than that of skeletal muscle. The overall low rate of ATP utilization may contribute to the fact that smooth muscle does not undergo fatigue during prolonged periods of activity.

In addition, if the cytosolic calcium concentration remains elevated, the rate of ATP splitting by the cross bridges declines even though isometric tension is maintained. The cross bridges enter a state similar to rigor, in which they are attached to the thin filaments, maintaining tension, but are cycling at a very slow rate. This provides a very economical means of maintaining tension since it uses only small amounts of ATP.

To relax a contracted smooth muscle, the phosphorylated myosin must be dephosphorylated by a phosphatase enzyme. This enzyme is always present in its active form, even during contraction. When cytosolic calcium rises, the rate of myosin phosphorylation by the activated kinase exceeds the rate of dephosphorylation, and the amount of phosphorylated myosin in the cell increases. Then, when the cytosolic calcium concentration decreases, the rate of dephosphorylation exceeds the rate of phosphorylation, and the amount of phosphorylated myosin decreases, producing relaxation.

Sources of Cytosolic Calcium

Two sources of calcium contribute to the rise in cytosolic calcium that initiates smooth-muscle contraction: (1) the sarcoplasmic reticulum, and (2) extracellular calcium entering the cell through plasma-membrane calcium channels. The amount of calcium contributed by each of these two sources differs among various smooth muscles, some being more dependent on extracellular calcium than the internal stores of calcium in the sarcoplasmic reticulum, and vice versa.

Let us look first at the sarcoplasmic reticulum. The total quantity of this organelle in smooth muscle is smaller than in skeletal muscle, and it is not arranged in any specific pattern in relation to the thick and thin filaments. There are no T tubules connected to the plasma membrane in smooth muscle. The small fiber diameter and the slow rate of contraction do not require such a mechanism of getting an excitatory signal rapidly into the muscle fiber, in contrast to the case in skeletal muscle. Portions of the sarcoplasmic reticulum are located near the plasma membrane, forming associations similar to those between T tubules and the lateral sacs in skeletal muscle, and action potentials in the plasma membrane may be coupled to the release of calcium from these portions. In addition, second messengers, such as inositol trisphosphate (page 170), re-leased from the plasma membrane in response to the binding of chemical messengers to plasma-membrane receptors, can trigger the release of calcium from the sarcoplasmic reticulum.

What about extracellular calcium in excitation-contraction coupling? Since the concentration of calcium in the extracellular fluid is 10,000 times greater than cytosolic calcium concentration (page 314), the opening of calcium channels in the plasma membrane results in an increased flow of calcium into the cell. There are voltage-sensitive calcium channels in the plasma membrane of smooth muscles, as well as calcium channels controlled by extracellular chemical messengers.

As in the case of striated muscle, an initial rise in cytosolic calcium can trigger the release of additional calcium from the sarcoplasmic reticulum, amplifying the calcium-triggered contractile activity in smooth muscle.

Removal of calcium from the cytosol, to bring about relaxation, is achieved by the active transport of calcium back into the sarcoplasmic reticulum as well as out of the cell across the plasma membrane. The rate of calcium removal in smooth muscle is much slower than in skeletal muscle, with the result that a single twitch lasts only a fraction of a second in skeletal muscle but may last several seconds in smooth muscle.

Again unlike the situation in skeletal muscle, in which a single action potential releases sufficient calcium to turn on all the cross bridges in a fiber, only a portion of the cross bridges are activated in a smooth-muscle fiber in response to most stimuli. Therefore, the tension generated by smooth muscle can be graded by varying the magnitude of the changes in cytosolic calcium concentration. The greater the increase in calcium concentration, the greater the number of cross bridges activated and the greater the tension.

In some smooth muscles, the cytosolic calcium concentration is sufficient to maintain a low level of cross-bridge activity in the absence of external stimuli. This activity is known as **smooth-muscle tone**. Its intensity can be varied by factors that alter the cytosolic calcium concentration.

In a sense, we have approached the question of excitation-contraction coupling in smooth muscle backward by first describing the coupling (the changes in cytosolic calcium), but now we must ask what constitutes the excitation that elicits these changes in calcium concentration.

Membrane Activation

In contrast to skeletal muscle, in which membrane activation is dependent on a single input—the somatic neurons to the muscle—many inputs to the smooth-muscle plasma membrane can alter the contractile activity of the muscle

TABLE 11-5 INPUTS INFLUENCING SMOOTH-MUSCLE CONTRACTILE ACTIVITY

1. Spontaneous electrical activity in the fiber plasma membrane
2. Neurotransmitters released by autonomic neurons
3. Hormones
4. Locally induced changes in the chemical composition (paracrine agents, acidity, oxygen, osmolarity, and ion concentrations) of the extracellular fluid surrounding the fiber
5. Stretch

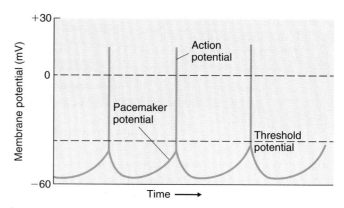

FIGURE 11-40

Generation of action potentials in a smooth-muscle fiber resulting from spontaneous depolarizations of the membrane (pacemaker potentials).

(Table 11-5). All these inputs have the ultimate effect of altering cytosolic calcium concentration as described in the previous section.

As we shall see, most smooth muscles are capable of producing action potentials, but some are not. In those smooth muscles in which action potentials occur, calcium ions, rather than sodium ions, carry positive charge into the cell during the rising phase of the action potential; that is, depolarization of the membrane opens voltage-sensitive calcium channels, producing calcium action potentials rather than sodium action potentials.

Another very important point needs to be made about electrical activity and cytosolic calcium concentration in smooth muscle. Unlike the situation in striated muscle, in smooth muscle cytosolic calcium concentration can be increased (or decreased) by *graded* changes in membrane potential, not just by action potentials.

Finally, we shall see that, again in contrast to the situation in skeletal muscle, membrane stimulation of smooth muscle can sometimes be achieved with no change at all in the plasma-membrane potential.

Spontaneous Electrical Activity. Some types of smooth-muscle fibers generate action potentials spontaneously in the absence of any neural or hormonal input. The plasma membrane in these fibers does not maintain a constant resting potential. Instead, it gradually depolarizes until it reaches the threshold potential and produces an action potential. Following repolarization, the membrane again begins to depolarize (Figure 11-40), so that a sequence of action potentials occurs, producing a tonic state of contractile activity. The potential change occurring during the spontaneous depolarization to threshold is known as a **pacemaker potential**. (As described in other chapters, some cardiac-muscle fibers and a few neurons in the central nervous system also have pacemaker potentials and can spontaneously generate action potentials in the absence of external stimuli.)

Nerves and Hormones. The contractile activity of smooth muscles is influenced by neurotransmitters released by autonomic nerve endings. Unlike skeletal-muscle fibers, smooth-muscle fibers do not have a specialized motor end-plate region. As the axon of a postganglionic autonomic neuron enters the region of smooth-muscle fibers, it divides into numerous branches, each branch containing a series of swollen regions known as **varicosities**. Each varicosity contains numerous vesicles filled with neurotransmitter, which is released when an action potential conducted along the axon passes the varicosity. Varicosities from a single axon may be located along several muscle fibers, and a single muscle fiber may be located near varicosities belonging to postganglionic fibers of both sympathetic and parasympathetic neurons (Figure 11-41). Therefore, a number of smooth-muscle fibers are influenced by neurotransmitter released by a single nerve fiber, and a single smooth-muscle fiber may be influenced by neurotransmitter from more than one neuron.

Whereas some neurotransmitters depolarize smooth-muscle membranes, others produce a *hyperpolarization*, which leads to decreased cytosolic calcium concentration, producing a *lessening* of contractile activity. Thus, in contrast to skeletal muscle, which receives only excitatory input from its motor neurons, smooth-muscle tension can be either increased or decreased by neural activity.

Moreover, a given neurotransmitter may produce opposite effects in different smooth-muscle tissues. For example, norepinephrine, the neurotransmitter released from most postganglionic sympathetic neurons, depolar-

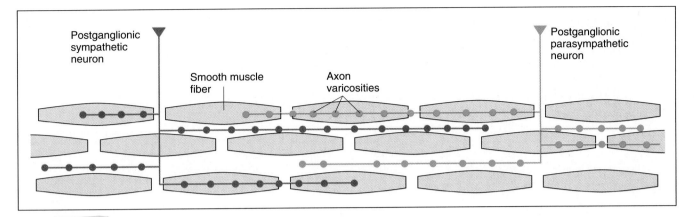

FIGURE 11-41

Innervation of smooth muscle by postganglionic autonomic neurons. Neurotransmitter is released from the varicosities along the branched axons and diffuses to receptors on muscle fiber plasma membranes.

izes certain types of blood-vessel smooth muscle, thereby initiating action potentials and contraction of the muscle. In contrast, the same neurotransmitter inhibits spontaneous activity in intestinal smooth muscle and produces a relaxation. Thus, the type of response (excitatory or inhibitory) depends not on the chemical messenger per se but on the receptor to which the chemical messenger binds in the membrane.

In addition to receptors for neurotransmitters, the plasma membrane of smooth-muscle cells contains receptors for a variety of hormones. Binding of a hormone to its receptor may lead to a change in membrane potential as a result of opening or closing of ion channels and/or to the release of a second messenger that affects the release of calcium from the sarcoplasmic reticulum. The result can be either increased or decreased contractile activity.

Although most changes in smooth-muscle contractile activity induced by chemical messengers are accompanied by a change in membrane potential, this is not always the case. Second messengers, released in response to the binding of a chemical messenger to a receptor, can cause the release of calcium from the sarcoplasmic reticulum, producing a contraction, without a change in membrane potential.

Local Factors. Local factors, including paracrine agents, acidity, oxygen concentration, osmolarity, and the ion composition of the extracellular fluid, can also alter smooth-muscle tension by affecting cytosolic calcium concentration. The specific mechanisms by which many of these local factors act on a smooth-muscle fiber to bring about changes in contraction are generally unknown.

Some smooth muscles respond by contracting when they are stretched. Stretching opens mechanosensitive ion channels, leading to membrane depolarization, which induces contraction. The resulting contraction opposes the forces acting to stretch the muscle.

All these responses to local factors provide a means for altering smooth-muscle contraction in response to changes in the muscle's immediate internal environment, which can lead to regulation that is independent of long-distance signals from nerves and hormones.

Types of Smooth Muscle

The great diversity of the factors that can influence the contractile activity of smooth muscles from various organs has made it difficult to classify smooth-muscle fibers. Many smooth muscles can be placed, however, into one of two groups, based on the excitability characteristics of the plasma membrane and on the conduction of electrical activity from fiber to fiber within the muscle tissue: (1) **single-unit smooth muscles**, whose membranes are capable of propagating action potentials from cell to cell through gap junctions and may manifest spontaneous action potentials, and (2) **multiunit smooth muscles**, which exhibit little, if any, propagation of electrical activity from fiber to fiber and whose contractile activity is closely coupled to the neural activity to them.

It must be emphasized that most smooth muscles do not show all the characteristics of either single-unit or

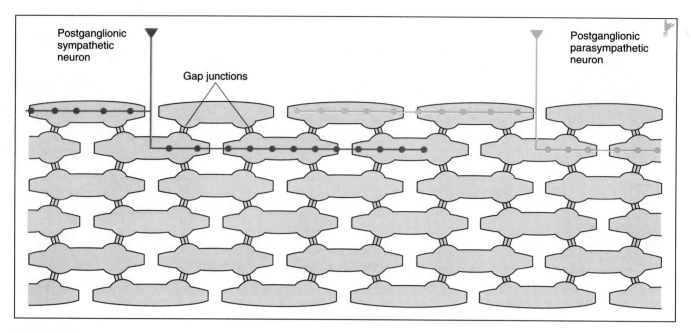

FIGURE 11-42

Innervation of a single-unit smooth muscle is often restricted to only a few fibers in the muscle. Electrical activity is conducted from fiber to fiber throughout the muscle by way of the gap junctions between the fibers.

multiunit smooth muscles. These two prototypes represent the two extremes in smooth-muscle characteristics, with many smooth muscles having characteristics that overlap the two groups.

Single-Unit Smooth Muscle. The smooth muscles of the intestinal tract, the uterus, and small-diameter blood vessels are examples of single-unit smooth muscles. All the muscle fibers in a single-unit smooth muscle undergo synchronous activity, both electrical and mechanical; that is, the whole muscle responds to stimulation as a single unit. This occurs because each muscle fiber is linked to adjacent fibers by gap junctions, through which action potentials occurring in one cell are propagated to other cells by local currents. Therefore, electrical activity occurring anywhere within a group of single-unit smooth-muscle fibers can be conducted to all the other cells (Figure 11-42).

Some of the fibers in a single-unit muscle are pacemaker cells that spontaneously generate action potentials, which are conducted by way of gap junctions into fibers that do not spontaneously generate action potentials. The majority of cells in the muscle are nonpacemaker cells.

The contractile activity of single-unit smooth muscles can be altered by nerves, hormones, and local factors, using the variety of mechanisms described previously for smooth muscles in general. The extent to which these muscles are innervated varies considerably in different organs. The nerve terminals are often restricted to the small regions of the muscle that contain pacemaker cells. By regulating the activity of the pacemaker cells, the activity of the entire muscle can be controlled.

One additional characteristic of single-unit smooth muscles is that a contractile response can often be induced by stretching the muscle. In several hollow organs—the uterus for example—stretching of the smooth muscles in the walls of the organ as a result of increases in the volume of material in the lumen initiates a contractile response that opposes the increase in volume.

Multiunit Smooth Muscle. The smooth muscle in the large airways to the lungs, in large arteries, and attached to the hairs in the skin are examples of multiunit smooth muscles. Because these smooth muscles have few gap junctions, each muscle fiber responds independently of its neighbors, and the muscle behaves as multiple units. Multiunit smooth muscles are richly innervated by branches of the autonomic nervous system. The contractile response of the whole muscle depends on the number of muscle fibers that are activated and on the frequency of nerve stimulation. Although stimulation of the nerve fibers to the mus-

TABLE 11-6 CHARACTERISTICS OF MUSCLE FIBERS

| Characteristic | Skeletal muscle | Smooth muscle | | Cardiac muscle |
		Single unit	Multiunit	
Thick and thin filaments	Yes	Yes	Yes	Yes
Sarcomeres—banding pattern	Yes	No	No	Yes
Transverse tubules	Yes	No	No	Yes
Sarcoplasmic reticulum (SR)°	++++	+	+	++
Gap junctions between fibers	No	Yes	Few	Yes
Source of activating calcium	SR	SR and extracellular	SR and extracellular	SR and extracellular
Site of calcium regulation	Troponin	Myosin	Myosin	Troponin
Speed of contraction	Fast-slow	Very slow	Very slow	Slow
Spontaneous production of action potentials by pacemakers	No	Yes	No	Yes; most are not spontaneously active
Tone (low levels of maintained tension in the absence of external stimuli)	No	Yes	No	No
Effect of nerve stimulation	Excitation	Excitation or inhibition	Excitation or inhibition	Excitation or inhibition
Physiological effects of hormones on excitability and contraction	No	Yes	Yes	Yes
Stretch of fiber produces contraction	No	Yes	No	No

°Number of plus signs (+) indicates the relative amount of sarcoplasmic reticulum present in a given muscle type.

cle leads to a depolarization and a contractile response, action potentials do not occur in most multiunit smooth muscles. Circulating hormones can also increase or decrease contractile activity in multiunit smooth muscle, but stretching does not induce contraction in this type of mus-

cle, nor does the membrane spontaneously generate action potentials.

Table 11-6 compares the properties of the different types of muscle. Cardiac muscle has been included for completeness; its properties are discussed in Chapter 14.

SECTION B SUMMARY

STRUCTURE

I. Smooth-muscle fibers are spindle-shaped cells that lack striations, have a single nucleus, and are capable of cell division. They contain actin and myosin filaments and contract by the sliding-filament mechanism.

CONTRACTION AND ITS CONTROL

I. An increase in cytosolic calcium leads to the binding of calcium by calmodulin. The calcium-calmodulin complex then binds to myosin light-chain kinase, activating the enzyme, which uses ATP to phosphorylate smooth-muscle myosin. In smooth muscle only phosphorylated myosin is able to bind to actin and undergo cross-bridge cycling.

II. Smooth-muscle myosin has a low rate of ATP splitting, and as a result the velocity of contraction is much slower than that of striated muscles. However, the tension produced per unit cross-sectional area is equivalent to that of skeletal muscle.

III. The two sources of the cytosolic calcium ions that initiate smooth-muscle contraction are the sarcoplasmic reticulum and extracellular calcium. The opening of calcium channels in the smooth-muscle plasma membrane allows extracellular calcium ions to enter the cell.

IV. The increase in cytosolic calcium resulting from most stimuli does not activate all the cross bridges in smooth muscle. Therefore smooth-muscle tension can be increased by agents that increase the concentration of cytosolic calcium ions.

V. Table 11-5 summarizes the types of stimuli that can initiate smooth-muscle contraction.

VI. Most, but not all, smooth-muscle cells can generate action potentials in their plasma membrane upon membrane depolarization. The rising phase of the smooth-muscle action potential is due to the influx of calcium ions into the cell through open calcium channels.

VII. Some smooth muscles generate action potentials spontaneously, in the absence of any external input, because of pacemaker potentials in the plasma membrane that repeatedly depolarize the membrane to threshold.

VIII. Smooth-muscle cells do not have a specialized endplate region. A number of smooth-muscle fibers may be influenced by neurotransmitters released by a single nerve ending, and a single smooth-muscle fiber may be influenced by neurotransmitters from more than one neuron. Neurotransmitters may have either excitatory or inhibitory effects on smooth-muscle contraction.

IX. Smooth muscles can be classified broadly as single-unit or multiunit smooth muscle (Table 11-6).

SECTION B KEY TERMS

dense bodies	varicosities
myosin light-chain kinase	single-unit smooth muscles
smooth-muscle tone	multiunit smooth muscles
pacemaker potential	

SECTION B REVIEW QUESTIONS

1. How does the organization of thick and thin filaments in smooth-muscle fibers differ from that in striated-muscle fibers?

2. Compare the mechanisms by which a rise in cytosolic calcium concentration initiates contractile activity in skeletal- and smooth-muscle fibers.

3. What are the two sources of calcium that lead to the increase in cytosolic calcium that triggers contraction in smooth muscle?

4. What types of stimuli can trigger a rise in cytosolic calcium in smooth-muscle fibers?

5. What effect does a pacemaker potential have on a smooth-muscle cell?

6. In what ways does the neural control of smooth-muscle activity differ from that of skeletal muscle?

7. Describe how a stimulus may lead to the contraction of a smooth-muscle cell without a change in the plasma membrane potential.

8. Describe the differences between single-unit and multiunit smooth muscles.

CHAPTER 11 CLINICAL TERMS

curare	muscle cramps
botulism	hypocalcemic tetany
denervation atrophy	muscular dystrophy
disuse atrophy	myasthenia gravis

CHAPTER 11 THOUGHT QUESTIONS

(Answers are given in Appendix A.)

1. Myosin is in which of the following states: (a) $M \cdot ATP$, (b) $M^{\circ} \cdot ADP \cdot P_i$, (c) $A \cdot M^{\circ} \cdot ADP \cdot P_i$, (d) $A \cdot M$ under resting conditions? In rigor mortis?

2. If the transverse tubules of a skeletal muscle are disconnected from the plasma membrane, will action potentials trigger a contraction? Give reasons.

3. If a small load is attached to a muscle that is then tetanically stimulated, the muscle will lift the load in an isotonic contraction over a certain distance and then stop shortening and enter a state of isometric contraction. If a heavier load is used, the distance shortened before entering an isometric contraction is shorter. Explain these shortening limits in terms of the sliding-filament model of contraction and the length-tension relation.

4. What conditions produce the maximum tension from any given skeletal-muscle fiber?

5. A skeletal muscle can often maintain a moderate level of active tension for long periods of time, even though many of its fibers become fatigued. Explain.

6. If the blood flow to a skeletal muscle were markedly decreased, which types of motor units would most rapidly have their ability to produce ATP for muscle contraction severely reduced? Why?

7. As a result of an automobile accident, 50 percent of the muscle fibers in the biceps muscle of a patient were destroyed. Ten months later, the biceps muscle was able to generate 80 percent of its original force. Describe the changes that took place in the damaged muscle that enabled it to recover.

8. In the laboratory, if an isolated skeletal muscle is placed in a solution that contains no calcium ions, will the muscle contract when it is stimulated (a) directly by depolarizing its membrane, or (b) by stimulating the nerve to the muscle? What would happen if it was a smooth muscle?

9. The following experiments were performed on a single-unit smooth muscle in the gastrointestinal tract.

(a) Stimulating the parasympathetic nerves to the muscle produced a contraction.

(b) Injecting a nonmetabolized form of acetylcholine into the blood vessels to the muscle produced a contraction.

(c) Applying a drug that blocks the voltage-sensitive sodium channels in most plasma membranes led to a failure to contract upon stimulating the parasympathetic nerves but did not prevent the muscle from contracting in response to the nonmetabolized form of acetylcholine.

(d) Applying a drug that binds to muscarinic receptors (Chapter 8, page 208), and hence blocks the action of ACh at these receptors, prevented the smooth muscle from contracting when the nonmetabolized form of ACh was injected but did not prevent the muscle from contracting when the parasympathetic nerve was stimulated. From these observations, what might one conclude about the mechanism by which parasympathetic nerve stimulation produces a contraction of the smooth muscle?

CHAPTER

12

CONTROL OF BODY MOVEMENT

Carrying out a coordinated movement is a complicated process involving nerves, muscles, and bones. Consider the events associated with reaching out and grasping an object. The fingers are first *extended* (straightened) to reach around the object, and then *flexed* (bent) to grasp it. The degree of extension will depend upon the size of the object (Is it a golf ball or a soccer ball?), and the force of flexion will depend upon its weight and consistency (A bowling ball or a balloon?). Simultaneously, the wrist, elbow, and shoulder are extended, and the trunk is inclined forward, the exact movements depending upon the object's position relative to the person doing the lifting. The shoulder, elbow, and wrist are also stabilized to support first the weight of the arm and hand and then the added weight of the object. Through all this, upright posture is maintained despite the body's continuously shifting balance.

The building blocks for all movements are **motor units**, each comprising one motor neuron together with all the skeletal-muscle fibers that this neuron innervates (page 316). It is through the stimulation of individual motor units that all skeletal muscle contraction in the body is controlled.

All the motor neurons for a given muscle make up the **motor neuron pool** for the muscle. The pool for a given muscle is located either in the ventral horn of the spinal cord (see Figure 8-35) or in the parts of the brainstem where the nerves for that muscle leave the central nervous system.

The axons of many neurons synapse on a motor neuron to control its activity. Although no single input to a motor unit is essential for movement, a balanced input from all sources is necessary to provide the precision and speed of normally coordinated actions. For example, if an inhibitory system synapsing on a given motor neuron is altered so that inhibitory input is decreased, the still-normal excitatory input to the neuron will be unopposed and the motor neuron will fire excessively. This, you will recall from page 207, is what happens in the disease **tetanus (lockjaw)**.

Each of the myriad coordinated body movements of which a person is capable is achieved by many motor units of various muscles activated in a precise temporal order. It is important to realize that movements—even simple movements such as reaching and grasping—are rarely achieved by just one muscle.

This chapter deals with the interrelated neural inputs that converge upon the motor neurons to control their activity. We present first a summary of a model of motor system functioning and then describe each component of the model in detail.

MOTOR CONTROL HIERARCHY

Throughout the CNS, the neurons involved in controlling skeletal muscles are organized in a hierarchical fashion—the **motor control hierarchy** (Figure 12-1)—each level having a limited task in motor control. It is important to realize that we are speaking of a *functional* hierarchy, not an anatomical one. The areas of the central nervous system that are involved in the control of movement and posture, however, have so many reciprocal connections that it is nearly impossible to assign a specific function to a given brain area. Thus, the following hierarchical model is meant to be only a guide.

Note that many contractions executed by skeletal muscles—particularly the muscles involved in postural support—are isometric, and even though the muscle is active during these contractions, no movement occurs. In the following discussions the general term "muscle movement" includes these isometric contractions. In addition, keep in mind throughout this section that all "information" in the nervous system is transmitted in the form of graded potentials or action potentials.

To begin a movement, a general "intention" such as "pick up sweater" or "write signature" or "answer telephone" is generated at the highest level of the motor-control hierarchy. This highest level encompasses many regions of the brain, including those involved in memory and emotions. Very little is known, however, as to exactly where intentions for movements are formed in the brain, despite the critical importance of this question and the research efforts spent upon it.

Information is relayed from hypothesized neural networks, referred to as the "command" neurons, at the highest hierarchical level to parts of the brain that make up the middle level of the motor control hierarchy. The middle-level structures specify the postures and movements needed to carry out the intended action. In our example of picking up a sweater, structures of the middle hierarchical level coordinate the commands that tilt the body and extend the arm and hand toward the sweater and shift the body's weight to maintain balance. The middle hierarchi-

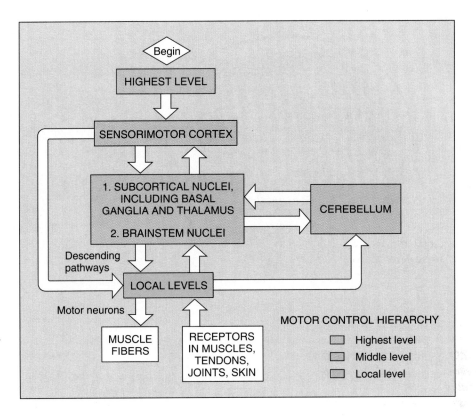

FIGURE 12-1

The hierarchical organization of the neural system controlling body movement. All the skeletal muscles of the body are controlled by motor neurons. Sensorimotor cortex includes those parts of the cerebral cortex that act together to control skeletal-muscle activity.

cal structures are located in parts of the cerebral cortex and in the cerebellum, subcortical nuclei, and brainstem (Figure 12-2A and B). These structures have extensive interconnections.

As the neurons in the middle level of the hierarchy are receiving input from the command neurons, they simultaneously receive afferent information (from receptors in the muscles, tendons, joints, skin, vestibular apparatus, and eyes) about the starting position of the body part that is to be "commanded" to move. This afferent information is integrated by neurons of the middle level of the hierarchy with the signals from the command neurons, and the middle level of the hierarchy creates a **motor program**, that is, the pattern of neural activity required to perform the desired movement.

The information determined by that motor program is then transmitted via **descending pathways** to the lowest level of the motor control hierarchy, the **local level**, at which the motor neurons to the muscles exit the brainstem or spinal cord. This level of the hierarchy is the final determinant of exactly which motor neurons will be activated.

The motor programs are continuously adjusted during the course of most movements. As the initial motor program is implemented and the action gets underway, those brain regions concerned with motor control at the middle level of the hierarchy continue to receive a constant stream of updated information from receptors in the pe-

riphery, eyes, and vestibular apparatus about the movements taking place. Say, for example, that the sweater being picked up is wet and heavier than expected so that the initially determined amount of muscle contraction is not sufficient to lift it. Any discrepancies between the intended and actual movements are detected, program corrections are determined, and the corrections are relayed via the lowest level of the hierarchy to the motor neurons.

When learning has taken place and a movement becomes skilled, the initial information from the middle hierarchical level is more accurate and fewer corrections need be made. Also, movements performed at high speed without concern for fine control are made solely according to the initial motor program.

The structures and functions of the motor control hierarchy are summarized in Table 12-1.

Voluntary and Involuntary Actions

Given such a hierarchical model, it is difficult to use the phrase **voluntary movement** with any real precision. We shall use it, however, to refer to those actions that have the following characteristics: (1) The movement is accompanied by a conscious awareness of what we are doing and why we are doing it rather than the feeling that it "just happened," and (2) our attention is directed toward the action or its purpose.

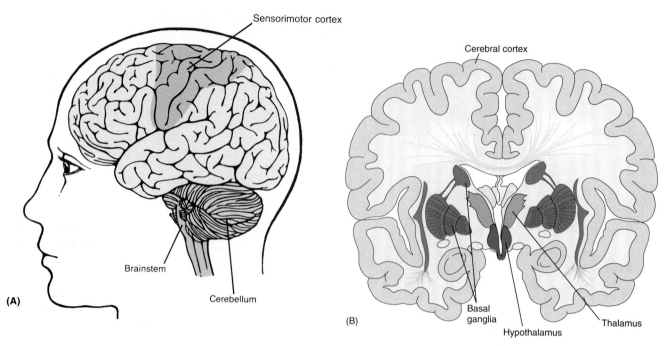

FIGURE 12-2

(A) Side view of brain showing three of the four components of the middle level of the motor control hierarchy. (B) Cross section of brain showing the parts of the basal ganglia, the fourth important component of the hierarchy's middle level.

The term "involuntary," on the other hand, describes actions that do not have these characteristics. "Unconscious," "automatic," and "reflex" are often taken to be synonyms for "involuntary," although in the motor system the term "reflex" has a more precise meaning. Motor reflexes are indeed involuntary, but they are also rapid, indicating the involvement of relatively few neurons, and they are unlearned.

Despite our attempts to distinguish between voluntary and involuntary actions, almost all motor behavior involves both components, and the distinction between the two cannot be made easily. Even such a highly conscious act as threading a needle involves the unconscious postural support of the hand and forearm and inhibition of the antagonistic muscles—those muscles whose activity would oppose the intended action, in this case, the muscles that straighten the fingers.

Most motor behavior is neither purely voluntary nor purely involuntary but falls somewhere between these two extremes. Moreover, actions shift along the spectrum according to the frequency with which they are performed. When a person first learns to drive a car with a standard transmission, for example, shifting gears is a fairly complicated process and requires a great deal of conscious attention. With practice, the same actions become automatic, and a complicated pattern of muscle movements is shifted from the highly conscious end of the spectrum toward the

involuntary end by the process of learning. And reflex behaviors, which are all the way at the involuntary end of the spectrum, can with special effort be modified or even prevented.

We now turn to an analysis of the individual components of the motor control hierarchy, beginning with local control mechanisms because their activity serves as a base upon which the pathways descending from the brain exert their influence.

LOCAL CONTROL OF MOTOR NEURONS

n describing local control, we must add one more element to our motor control system. Afferent fibers in the muscles, tendons, joints, and skin of the body part to be moved enter the central nervous system and transmit information not only to higher levels of the hierarchy, as noted earlier, but also to the local level as well.

Interneurons

Most of the synaptic input to motor neurons from the descending pathways and afferent neurons, described in our hierarchical model, does not go *directly* to motor neurons but rather to interneurons that synapse with the motor neurons. These interneurons are of several types. Some

TABLE 12-1   MOTOR CONTROL HIERARCHY FOR VOLUNTARY MOVEMENTS

I. The highest level
   A. Function: forms complex plans according to individual's intention and communicates with the middle level via "command neurons."
   B. Structures: areas involved with memory and emotions; supplementary motor area; and association cortex. All these structures receive and correlate input from many other brain structures.

II. The middle level
   A. Function: converts complex plans received from highest level to a number of smaller motor programs, which determine the pattern of neural activation required to perform the movement. These programs are broken down into subprograms that determine the movements of individual joints. The programs and subprograms are transmitted, often via the cerebral cortex, through descending pathways to the lowest control level.
   B. Structures: sensorimotor cortex, cerebellum, parts of basal ganglia, some brainstem nuclei.

III. The lowest level (the local level)
   A. Function: specifies tension of particular muscles and angle of specific joints necessary to carry out the programs and subprograms transmitted from the middle-control levels.
   B. Structures: levels of brainstem or spinal cord from which motor neurons exit.

interneurons are confined to the general region of the motor neuron upon which they synapse and thus are called local interneurons. Others have processes that extend up or down short distances in the spinal cord and brainstem, whereas still others have very long processes that can extend throughout much of the length of the CNS. The interneurons with longer processes are important in movements that involve the coordinated interaction of, let us say, an arm and a leg, whereas the interneurons with shorter processes are activated in movements that involve a smaller region of the body, for example, only a shoulder and arm.

The local interneurons are important integrative elements of the lowest level of the motor control hierarchy. Inputs converge upon them from higher centers, peripheral receptors, and other interneurons (Figure 12-3A). They can act as "switches" that enable a movement to be turned on or off under the command of higher motor centers. For example, if we pick up a hot object, a local reflex arc will be activated normally, resulting in our dropping the object. But if it were something we had spent a great deal of effort to prepare, descending commands could in-

fluence the local activity, and we would continue to hold onto the object until we could put it down safely.

Also, an interneuron that receives excitatory input from descending pathways may itself make inhibitory synapses on motor neurons so that the descending influence is converted from excitatory to inhibitory (Figure 12-3B), or vice versa.

Local Afferent Input

As noted earlier, local afferent fibers usually impinge upon the local interneurons (in one case, they synapse directly on the motor neuron). The afferent fibers bring information from receptors in three areas: (1) the very muscles controlled by the motor neurons, (2) other nearby muscles, and (3) the tendons, joints, and skin surrounding the muscle.

The receptors at the peripheral ends of these afferent fibers monitor the length and tension of the muscles and movement of the joints. As we shall see next, their input

FIGURE 12-3

(A) Convergence of axons onto a local interneuron. (B) An inhibitory interneuron reverses the action of an excitatory descending pathway.

FIGURE 12-4

(A) Diagrammatic and (B) anatomic views of a muscle spindle. Note in B that the muscle spindle is parallel to the extrafusal muscle fibers. [(B) *Adapted from Elias, Pauly, and Burns.*]

provides negative-feedback control over the muscles and contributes to the conscious awareness of limb position.

Length-Monitoring Systems and the Stretch Reflex.
Absolute muscle length and changes in muscle length are monitored by stretch receptors embedded within the muscle. These receptors consist of endings of afferent nerve fibers that are wrapped around modified muscle fibers, several of which are enclosed in a connective-tissue capsule. The entire structure is called a **muscle spindle** (Figure 12-4A and B). The modified muscle fibers within the spindle are known as **intrafusal** (or spindle) **fibers**, whereas the skeletal-muscle fibers that form the bulk of the muscle are the **extrafusal** (or skeletomotor) **fibers** (Figure 12-4B).

Within a given spindle, there are two kinds of stretch receptors: One responds best to how much the muscle has been stretched, the other to both the magnitude of the stretch and the speed with which it occurs. Although the two kinds of stretch receptors are separate entities, they will be referred to collectively as the **muscle-spindle stretch receptors**.

The muscle spindles are parallel to the extrafusal fibers such that stretch of the muscle by an *external* force pulls on the intrafusal fibers, stretching them and activating their receptor endings (Figure 12-5A). The greater the stretch, the greater the rate of receptor firing. In contrast, *contraction* of the extrafusal fibers and the resultant shortening of the muscle remove tension on the spindle and slow down the rate of firing of the stretch receptor (Figure 12-5B).

FIGURE 12-5

(A) Passive stretch of the muscle activates the spindle stretch receptors and causes an increased rate of action potential firing in the afferent nerve. (B) Contraction of the muscle removes tension on the stretch receptors and lowers the rate of action potential firing. Blue arrows indicate direction of force on the muscle spindles.

When the afferent fibers from the muscle spindle enter the central nervous system, they divide into branches that take several different paths. One path (A in Figure 12-6) directly stimulates motor neurons going back to the muscle that was stretched, thereby completing a reflex arc known as the **stretch** (or myotatic) **reflex**.

This reflex is probably most familiar in the form of the **knee jerk**, part of a routine medical examination. The examiner taps the patellar tendon (Figure 12-6), which passes over the knee and connects extensor muscles in the thigh to the tibia in the lower leg. As the tendon is pushed in by tapping, the thigh muscles to which it is attached are stretched, and all the stretch receptors within these muscles are activated. More action potentials are generated in the afferent nerve fibers from the stretch receptors to the motor neurons that control these same muscles. The motor units are stimulated, the thigh muscles shorten, and the patient's lower leg is extended to give the knee jerk. The proper performance of the knee jerk tells the physician that the stretch receptors, the afferent fibers, the balance of synaptic input to the motor neurons, the motor neurons themselves, the neuromuscular junctions, and the muscles are all functioning normally.

During normal movement, in contrast to the knee jerk reflex, the stretch receptors are rarely all activated at the same time, nor are they activated so strongly. Consequently, the response to the stretching that occurs physiologically is a smooth, ongoing (tonic) contraction rather than a jerk.

Because the afferent nerve fibers mediating the stretch reflex synapse *directly* with the motor neurons without the interposition of any interneurons, the stretch reflex is called **monosynaptic**. Stretch reflexes are the only known monosynaptic reflex arcs. All other reflex arcs are **polysynaptic**, having at least one interneuron, and usually many, between the afferent and efferent neurons.

A second path for the branches of the afferent nerve fibers from stretch receptors (B in Figure 12-6) ends on interneurons that, when activated, inhibit the motor neurons controlling antagonistic muscles, whose contraction would interfere with the reflex response (in the knee jerk, for example, the flexor muscles of the knee are inhibited). The activation of one muscle and the simultaneous inhibition of its antagonistic muscle are called **reciprocal innervation** and are characteristic of many movements, not just the stretch reflex.

A third path (C in Figure 12-6) ends on other motor neurons that go the same muscle and to **synergistic muscles**, that is, muscles whose contraction assists the intended motion (in our example, other leg extensor muscles). The muscles activated are on the same side of the body as the receptors, and the response is therefore **ipsilateral**; a response on the opposite side of the body would be **contralateral**.

A fourth path (D in Figure 12-6) synapses with interneurons that convey information about the muscle length to areas of the brain dealing with motor control, information that is especially important during slow, controlled movements such as the performance of an unfamiliar action. Ascending paths also provide information that contributes to the conscious perception of the position of a limb.

[Handwritten notes at top of page: excitatory afferent ← inhibitory neuron → out of it = gabba (when depolarized), binds to gabba receptor on neuron also hyperpolarized ∴ inhibited b/c by a⁻ no AP]

[Handwritten annotations around Figure 12-6: "(other stuff already happ.)", "inh neuron", "afferent", "afferent nerve (naked nerve)", "in addition to stretching extensor, have to relax flexor → inhibition", "fibers stretched & made LONGER b/c bump in"]

FIGURE 12-6

Neural pathways involved in the knee jerk reflex. Tapping the patellar tendon stretches the extensor muscle causing (A and C) compensatory contraction of this and other extensor muscles, (B) relaxation of the flexor muscle, and (D) information about muscle length to be sent to the brain. Arrows indicate direction of action potential propagation.

Alpha-Gamma Coactivation.

As indicated in Figure 12-5B, stretch on the intrafusal fibers decreases when the muscle shortens. In this example, the spindle stretch receptors go completely slack at this time, and they stop firing action potentials. In this situation, there is no indication of any further changes in muscle length the whole

time the muscle is contracting. Physiologically, to prevent this loss of information, the two ends of each intrafusal fiber are also stimulated to contract during the shortening of the extrafusal fibers, thus maintaining tension in the central region of the intrafusal fiber, where the stretch receptors are located (Figure 12-7). It must be emphasized that the intrafusal fibers are not large enough or strong enough to shorten whole muscle and move joints; their sole job is to maintain tension on the spindle stretch receptors.

The intrafusal fibers contract in response to activation by motor neurons to them, but the motor neurons supplying them are usually not those that activate the extrafusal muscle fibers. The motor neurons controlling the extrafusal muscle fibers are larger and are classified as **alpha motor neurons**, whereas the smaller motor neurons whose axons innervate the intrafusal fibers are known as **gamma motor neurons** (Figure 12-7).

FIGURE 12-7

As the muscles at the two ends of an intrafusal fiber contract in response to gamma motor neuron activation, they pull on the center of the fiber and stretch the receptor. The thin arrows beside the nerve fibers indicate direction of action potential transmission.

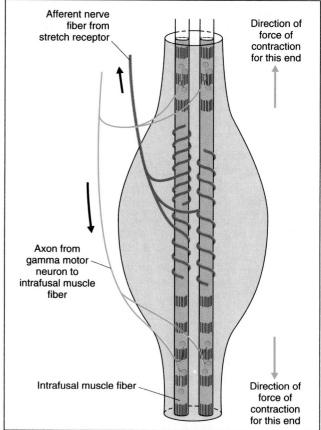

Alpha and gamma motor neurons are activated both by interneurons in their immediate vicinity and by neurons of the descending pathways. In fact, as described above, they are often **coactivated**, that is, excited at almost the same time during many voluntary and involuntary movements. Coactivation ensures that information about muscle length will be continuously available to provide for moment-to-moment adjustment during ongoing actions and to plan and program future movements.

Tension-Monitoring Systems. Any given set of inputs to a given set of motor neurons can lead to various degrees of tension in the muscles they innervate, depending on muscle length, the load on the muscles, and the degree of muscle fatigue. Therefore, feedback is necessary to inform the motor control systems of the tension actually achieved. Such feedback is provided by a second component of the local motor control apparatus, which monitors how much tension is being exerted by the contracting motor units (or imposed on the muscle by external forces if the muscle is being stretched).

The receptors employed in the tension-monitoring system are the **Golgi tendon organs**, which are located in the tendons near their junction with the muscle (Figure 12-4B). Endings of afferent nerve fibers are wrapped around collagen bundles in the tendon, bundles that are slightly bowed in the resting state. When the attached extrafusal muscle fibers contract, they pull on the tendon, which straightens the collagen bundles and distorts the receptor endings. Thus, the Golgi tendon organs discharge in response to the tension generated by the contracting muscle and initiate action potentials that are transmitted to the central nervous system.

Branches of the afferent neuron inhibit, via interneurons, the motor neurons of the contracting muscle (A in Figure 12-8). They also *activate* the motor neurons of the antagonistic muscle (B in Figure 12-8). Note that this reciprocal innervation is the opposite of that produced by the muscle spindle afferents.

The activity of afferent fibers from the Golgi tendon organ supplies the motor control systems (both locally and in the brain) with continuous information about the muscle's tension.

Other Local Afferent Input. In addition to the afferent information from the spindle stretch receptors and Golgi tendon organs of the activated muscle, other input is fed into the local motor control systems. For example, stimulation of the skin, particularly painful stimulation, activates the ipsilateral flexor motor neurons and inhibits the ipsilateral extensor motor neurons, moving the body part away from the stimulus. This is called the **flexion**, or withdrawal, **reflex** (Figure 12-9). The same stimulus causes just the opposite response on the contralateral side of the

FIGURE 12-8

Neural pathways underlying the Golgi tendon organ component of the local control system. In this diagram, contraction of the extensor muscle causes tension in the Golgi tendon organ and increases the firing rate of action potentials in the afferent nerve fiber. By way of interneurons, this increased activity results in (A) inhibition of the extensor muscle's motor neuron and (B) excitation of the flexor muscle's motor neuron. Arrows indicate direction of action potential propagation.

body—activation of the extensor motor neurons and inhibition of the flexor motor neurons (the **crossed-extensor reflex**). In the example in Figure 12-9, the strengthened extension of the contralateral leg means that this leg can

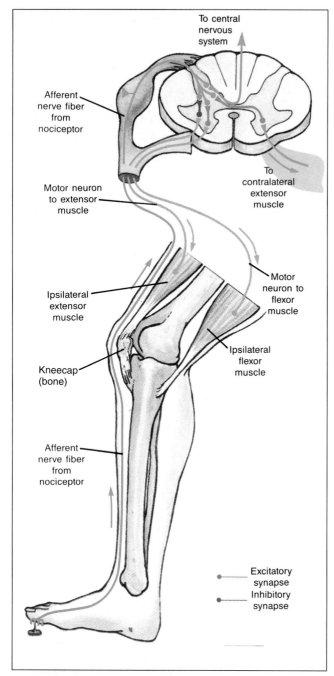

FIGURE 12-9

In response to pain, the ipsilateral flexor's motor neuron is stimulated (flexion reflex). In the case illustrated, the opposite limb is extended (crossed-extensor reflex) to support the body's weight. Arrows indicate direction of action potential transmission.

support more of the body's weight as the hurt foot is raised from the ground by flexion.

The local motor control systems are also affected by information from joint receptors. These inputs are all polysynaptic.

THE BRAIN MOTOR CENTERS AND THE DESCENDING PATHWAYS THEY CONTROL

As emphasized in our model, the motor neurons and interneurons at the local levels of motor control are influenced by descending pathways, and these pathways are themselves controlled by various motor centers in the brain (Figure 12-1).

Cerebral Cortex

The cerebral cortex plays a critical role in both the planning and ongoing control of normal voluntary movements, functioning in both the highest and middle levels of the motor control hierarchy. The term **sensorimotor cortex** is used to include all those parts of the cerebral cortex that act together in the control of muscle movement. A large number of nerve fibers that give rise to some of the descending pathways come from two areas of sensorimotor cortex on the posterior part of the frontal lobe: the **primary motor cortex** (sometimes called simply the **motor cortex**) and the **premotor area** (Figure 12-10). Other areas of sensorimotor cortex are the **supplementary motor cortex**, which lies on the surface of the frontal lobe where the cortex folds down between the two hemispheres (Figure 12-10B), the **somatosensory cortex**, and parts of the **parietal-lobe association cortex** (Figure 12-10A and B).

Neurons in the primary motor cortex mainly contribute directly to movements involving the use of individual muscle groups, such as those that move a single finger. In general, the location of the neurons in the motor cortex varies with the parts of the body they serve. As one starts at the top of the brain and moves down along the side (A to B in Figure 12-11), the cortical neurons affecting movements of the toes and feet are at the top, followed by neurons controlling leg, trunk, arm, hand, fingers, neck, and face.

The size of the representation of each of the individual body parts in Figure 12-12 is proportional to the amount of cortex devoted to its control. Clearly, the cortical areas representing the hand and face are the largest. The great number of cortical neurons for innervation of the hand and face is one factor responsible for the fine degree of motor control that can be exerted over those parts. The more delicate the function of any muscle, the more nearly one-to-one the relationship between cortical neurons and the muscle's motor units. Even with the finest control, however, there is still much convergence of input onto each motor neuron so that losing one cortical neuron never causes the loss of control of a motor neuron.

Moving anteriorly (C to D in Figure 12-11) in the cortex, primary motor cortex gives way to the premotor area,

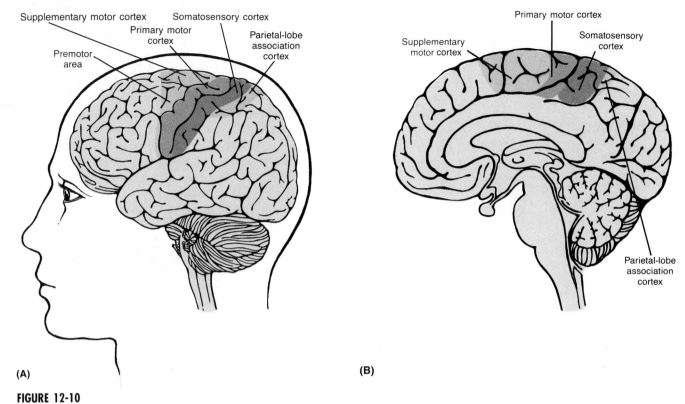

FIGURE 12-10
(A) The major motor areas of cerebral cortex. (B) Midline view of the brain showing the supplementary motor cortex, which lies in the part of the cerebral cortex that is folded down between the two cerebral hemispheres. Other cortical motor areas also extend onto this area. The premotor, supplementary motor, primary motor, somatosensory, and parietal-lobe association cortexes together make up the sensorimotor cortex.

whose neurons are involved in more complicated motor functions such as a change in the force or velocity of a movement, a change from one task to another, a movement made in response to visual control or a spoken command, two-handed coordination, and postural support for a wide variety of detailed movements.

The premotor area is also an important gateway for relaying processed information from other regions of the cerebral cortex and from other parts of the brain to the primary motor cortex or directly to the descending pathways. Some of this relayed information comes, for example, from the parietal-lobe association areas that process signals from sensory systems to indicate the body's position in space and the direction in which the body must be moved to achieve the desired goal.

We have described the primary motor cortex and premotor areas as giving rise, either directly or indirectly, to pathways descending to the motor neurons. As we have stated, however, these neurons are part of the middle hierarchical level and are not the prime *initiators* of movement. They are simply a tremendously important relay and integrative station.

Starting about 55 ms before voluntary muscle activity begins, a distinct wave of electrical activity, known as the **motor potential**, occurs within the primary motor cortex, signifying neuronal excitement there. About 800 ms before this, however, a different wave, the **readiness potential**, can be recorded from electrodes on the scalp. It arises in the supplementary motor cortex (Figure 12-10B), although other brain regions, particularly the association areas of the parietal and frontal lobes, also contribute to it. The readiness potential is the earliest detectable sign of "getting ready" to make a voluntary motion and is an indication of activity at the highest hierarchical level.

In the short time between the termination of the readiness potential and the beginning of the motor potential, subcortical mechanisms become active, and it is to these areas of the middle-level motor control system that we now turn.

Subcortical and Brainstem Nuclei

A dozen or so highly interconnected structures lie within the cerebrum beneath the cerebral cortex and in the brainstem, and they interact with the cortex to control movements. Their influence is transmitted to the motor neurons both by pathways that go back to the cerebral cortex and by descending pathways that arise directly from some of the brainstem nuclei.

Premotor area — Primary motor cortex

FIGURE 12-11

Primary motor cortex and the premotor area. Arrows A-B and C-D are explained in the text.

FIGURE 12-12

Representation of the body in primary motor cortex. Note the disproportionately large areas devoted to control of the hands and facial muscles. Within the hand area, however, no one area exclusively controls the movement of a single finger, and there is much overlap between adjacent finger regions.

It is not known to what extent, if any, these structures act at the highest level of the motor control hierarchy, but they definitely play a prominent role in the hierarchy's middle level. They convert the overall plan or goal of an action into programs that determine the specific movements needed to accomplish that action.

Prominent among the subcortical nuclei are the paired **basal ganglia** (Figure 12-2B). In contrast to most other components of the motor control system, which transmit via excitatory synapses, the basal ganglia are characterized by their inhibitory influences. They seem to select appropriate components from the excitatory repertoire and suppress antagonistic or unwanted behaviors so that desired patterns of motor activity can be maintained.

This role explains the defects in motor control associated with individuals who have the inadequately functioning basal ganglia of *Parkinson's disease*. These individuals have difficulty establishing new behaviors because it is difficult for them to stop ongoing activity. Thus, if walking, they tend to keep walking; if seated, they tend to remain seated. A common set of other symptoms evolve, including a tremor that is most prominent at rest; a change in facial

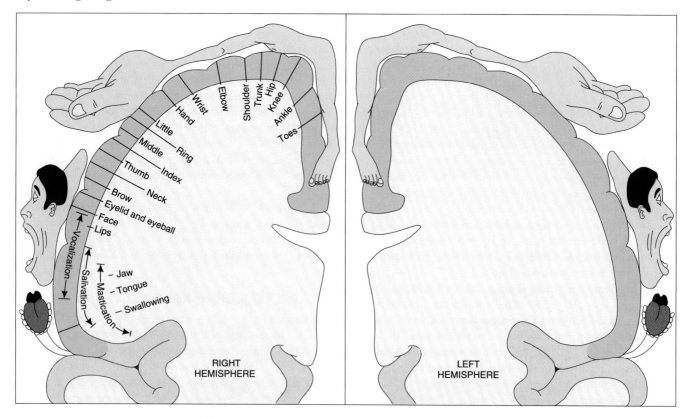

RIGHT HEMISPHERE

LEFT HEMISPHERE

expression resulting in a masklike, unemotional appearance; muscular rigidity; a shuffling gait with loss of arm swing; and a stooped and unstable posture.

Although the symptoms of Parkinson's disease reflect inadequate functioning of the basal ganglia, the initial defect arises in neurons of the **substantia nigra** ("black substance"), a subcortical nucleus that gets its name from the dark pigment in its cells. These neurons, which degenerate in Parkinson's disease, project to the basal ganglia where they normally liberate the neurotransmitter dopamine from their axon terminals. As substantia nigra neurons degenerate, the amount of dopamine they deliver to the basal ganglia is reduced and the basal ganglia function decreases.

One drug used to treat Parkinson's disease is L-dopa, a precursor of dopamine. L-Dopa enters the bloodstream, crosses the blood-brain barrier, and is converted to dopamine (dopamine itself is not used as medication because it cannot cross the blood-brain barrier). The newly formed dopamine activates the receptors in the basal ganglia and relieves the symptoms of the disease. Another drug used to slow the progress of the disease is deprenyl, which inhibits the brain enzyme that breaks down dopamine so that more of the neurotransmitter reaches the neurons in the basal ganglia. Still highly controversial is an experimental treatment for Parkinson's disease that involves the transplantation into (or onto) the basal ganglia of either fetal neurons that synthesize dopamine or genetically engineered cells that form tyrosine hydroxylase, the enzyme that drives dopamine production (see Figure 8-34).

In addition to the role played by the basal ganglia in posture and movement, they serve in intellectual function and possibly in learning motor tasks.

Cerebellum

The cerebellum is behind the brainstem, as can be seen in Figure 12-2A. It exerts a very important influence on posture and movement, but it does not exert this influence *directly* by pathways that descend to the motor neurons. Rather, the cerebellum affects motor behavior by means of input to brainstem nuclei and (by way of the thalamus) to regions of the sensorimotor cortex.

The cerebellum's role in motor functioning, at least in part, is to perform the critical task of comparing information about what the muscles *should* be doing with information about what they actually *are* doing. To achieve this, the cerebellum receives information both from the sensorimotor cortex (relayed via brainstem nuclei) and from the vestibular system, eyes, ears, skin, muscles, joints, and tendons, that is, from the major receptors affected by movement. If there is a discrepancy between the intended movement and the actual one, the cerebellum sends an error signal to the motor cortex and subcortical centers to modify the central motor programs, correct the ongoing

movement, and ensure that future movements of the same kind will be performed more accurately. In fact, the cerebellum plays an important role in the learning of motor skills. The cerebellum serves another crucial function, that of regulating the timing of the complex muscle actions required for even the simplest motor act.

The role of the cerebellum in programming movements can best be appreciated when seeing the absence of this function in individuals with cerebellar disease who cannot perform movements smoothly. If they try to touch an object, their movements are jerky and accompanied by oscillating, to-and-fro tremors that become more marked as the hand approaches the object and continue for a few moments after the object has been reached (called **dysmetria**). They cannot start or stop movements quickly or easily. If, for example, they are asked to rotate the wrist over and back rapidly, their motions are slow and irregular. Moreover, they cannot easily combine the movements of several joints into a single smooth, coordinated motion. To move the arm, they might first move the shoulder, then the elbow, and finally the wrist.

Unstable posture is another symptom characteristic of cerebellar dysfunction. For example, persons with cerebellar damage walk awkwardly, with the feet well apart, and they have such difficulty maintaining balance that their gait appears drunken. A final symptom involves difficulty in learning new motor skills, and individuals with cerebellar dysfunction find it hard to modify movements in response to new situations. Cerebellar damage does not cause paralysis, which indicates that the cerebellum is not responsible for *initiating* movements.

Descending Pathways

The influence exerted by the various brain regions on posture and movement has to be relayed by descending pathways to the motor neurons and the interneurons that affect them. The pathways are of two types: the corticospinal pathways which, as their name implies, originate in the cerebral cortex; and a second group which we shall call the noncorticospinal pathways, which originate in the brainstem.

Descending fibers from both types of descending pathways may end at synapses on alpha and gamma motor neurons, but most end on interneurons that affect the alpha motor neurons either directly or via still other interneurons. Sometimes, as mentioned earlier, these are the same interneurons that are used by reflex arcs, thereby ensuring that the descending signals are fully integrated with local information before the activity of the motor neurons is altered. The ultimate effect of the descending pathways on the alpha motor neurons may be excitatory or inhibitory.

Some of the descending fibers affect *afferent* systems. They do this via (1) presynaptic synapses on the terminals of afferent neurons as these fibers enter the central nervous system, or (2) synapses on interneurons in the ascending pathways. The overall effect of this descending input to afferent systems is to limit their influence on either the local or brain motor control areas, thereby altering the importance of a particular bit of afferent information or sharpening its focus. Because of this descending (motor) control over ascending (sensory) information, there is clearly no real functional separation of the motor and sensory systems.

Corticospinal Pathway. The nerve fibers of the **corticospinal pathways**, as mentioned before, have their cell bodies in the cerebral cortex, specifically, in the sensorimotor regions, and terminate in the spinal cord. The corticospinal pathways are also called the **pyramidal tracts**, or **pyramidal system** (perhaps because of their shape as they pass along the surface of the medulla oblongata or because they were formerly thought to arise solely from the pyramidal cells of the motor cortex). In the medulla oblongata, near the junction of the spinal cord and brain-

stem, most of the corticospinal fibers cross the spinal cord to descend on the opposite side (Figure 12-13). Thus, the skeletal muscles on the left side of the body are controlled largely by neurons in the right half of the brain, and vice versa.

As the corticospinal fibers descend through the brain from the cerebral cortex, they are accompanied by fibers of the **corticobulbar pathway** (bulbar means "pertaining to the brainstem"), a pathway that begins in the sensorimotor cortex and ends in the brainstem. The corticobulbar fibers control, directly or indirectly via interneurons, the motor neurons that innervate muscles of the eye, face, tongue, and throat. These fibers are the main source of control for voluntary movement of the muscles of the head and neck, whereas the corticospinal fibers serve this function for the muscles of the rest of the body. For convenience, we shall henceforth include the corticobulbar pathway in the general term "corticospinal pathways."

Axons of single corticospinal neurons influence motor neurons of several muscles, and neurons from a wide area of the sensorimotor cortex converge (page 201) on a single motor neuron. The extensive convergence suggests that the activity of each motor neuron is influenced by more than one of the brain motor control centers.

The corticospinal pathways serve rapid, fine movements of the distal extremities, such as those made when an object is manipulated by the fingers. After damage to the corticospinal pathways, all movements are slower and weaker, individual finger movements are absent, and it is difficult to release a grip.

FIGURE 12-13

The corticospinal pathway. Most of these fibers cross in the brainstem to descend in the opposite side of the spinal cord. Arrows indicate direction of action potential propagation. *(Adapted from Gardner.)*

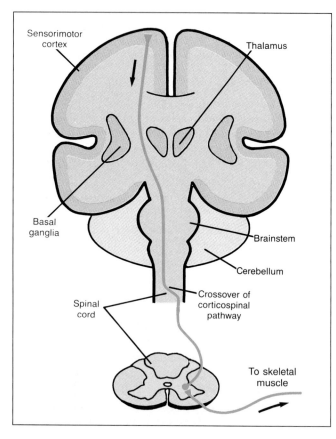

Noncorticospinal Pathways. Axons descending from neurons in the brainstem also form pathways that descend into the spinal cord to influence motor neurons. These pathways were previously referred to as the extrapyramidal system to distinguish them from the corticospinal (pyramidal) pathways, but this is now in disfavor. No new general term has been adopted for these pathways that descend from the brainstem, and for convenience we shall refer to them collectively as the noncorticospinal pathways.

Axons of some of the noncorticospinal pathways cross from their side of origin in the brainstem to affect muscles on the opposite side of the body, and others remain uncrossed. In the spinal cord the fibers of the noncorticospinal pathways form distinct clusters, named according to their sites of origin. For example, the vestibulospinal pathway descends to the spinal cord from the vestibular nuclei in the brainstem, whereas the reticulospinal pathway descends from neurons in the brainstem reticular formation.

The noncorticospinal pathways are especially important in the control of upright posture, balance, and walking. These pathways are anatomically suited to invoke the large groups of muscles characteristic of postural support in three ways: (1) They generally exert greater influence on motor neurons that control muscles in the neck, trunk, and upper part of the limbs than on motor neurons that control muscles in the fingers and toes; (2) as they descend through the spinal cord, they give rise to collateral branches that affect motor neurons at many levels of the cord; and (3) rather than ending on interneurons that are part of the local reflex arcs, as corticospinal neurons generally do, fibers of the noncorticospinal descending pathways are apt to end on interneurons that send long branches that interconnect different levels of the spinal cord.

Summary Comments on the Descending Pathways. In general, the corticospinal neurons have greater influ-

ence over motor neurons that control muscles involved in fine, isolated movements, particularly those of the fingers and hands. The noncorticospinal descending pathways are more involved with coordination of the large muscle groups used in the maintenance of upright posture, in locomotion, and in head and body movements when turning toward a specific stimulus.

There is, however, much interaction between the descending pathways. For example, some fibers of the corticospinal pathway end on interneurons that play important roles in posture, whereas fibers of the noncorticospinal descending pathways sometimes end directly on the alpha motor neurons to control discrete muscle movements. Because of this redundancy, loss of function resulting from

---

TABLE 12-2 SOME CHARACTERISTICS OF MOTOR CONTROL SYSTEMS

1. Even though it seems obvious to think of the motor system as controlling the contraction of *muscles*, much of the motor system functions more in determining the components of *actions* as they are needed to achieve a purpose or goal. This can be said in another way: The central nervous system knows more about movements than it knows about muscles. Thus, to take a book from a shelf, more of the motor control system is involved with calculating the direction the arm must move and how far than with selecting which motor neurons to activate and when.

2. Before descending pathways can activate specific motor neurons, a great deal of neural activity takes place in the brain. Whether the intention of an action arises from within the brain (I think I'll study now so I won't have to do it later) or as an outside stimulus (the telephone rings and I answer it), the intention has to be translated into the direction and distance the body must be moved. This translation process is completed gradually by many components of the brain's motor system acting simultaneously, each component adding a special contribution.

3. The motor control system must select from a variety of ways of achieving the purpose, since most motor acts can be executed in many ways with different sets of muscles. A simple example of this is a rat trained to press a lever whenever a light flashes. Depending upon its original position in the cage, its movements can be quite varied. If the rat is to the left of the lever, it moves to the right; if it is to the right, it moves to the left. If its paw is on the floor, it raises the paw; if its paw is above the lever, it lowers the paw.

4. The brain operates pretty much as a whole in producing movement; that is, many brain structures are involved.

5. The motor cortex is unable to generate coordinated voluntary movements without input from the subcortical motor centers.

6. Not all voluntary movements are channeled through the motor cortex. For example, tongue movements during speech are controlled by special speech areas (Chapter 13).

7. A given set of muscles can be controlled by several neural systems, and the central nervous system can select from them to execute a movement.

8. Movements that involve learning, movements to be made in response to an expected signal, highly skilled movements that have become almost automatic—all these are controlled by different components of the motor control systems.

9. The limbic system (emotion and motivation) plays an important role in motor control (we are all aware that it is usually difficult to make well-controlled, detailed movements when in a highly emotional state).

10. The motor cortex is more important in controlling skilled, accurate movements than in producing automatic or rhythmical ones.

11. Movements performed to achieve a specific task are variable and seemingly inconsequential. For example, it usually does not matter whether you comb your hair with the right or left hand. It is the end result that matters, but only the intervening acts or movements can be programmed by the nervous system

12. In certain circumstances a spinal reflex, for example, the flexion reflex, can override a command from a higher hierarchical level, for example, "extend leg to bear body's weight."

13. Movements are generally accompanied by changes in posture and alterations in sensory input. Anticipatory adjustments are made to prevent loss of balance and to compensate for the changed sensory information.

damage to one system may be compensated for by the remaining system, although the compensation is generally not complete.

Thus, the distinctions between the corticospinal and noncorticospinal descending pathways are not clear-cut. It is incorrect to imagine a total separation of function between them since all movements, whether automatic or voluntary, require the continuous coordinated interaction of both types of pathways.

In conclusion, the complete control of any movement—complex or simple—is presently understood only imperfectly. Some interesting additional features of motor control that are, however, becoming clear are listed in Table 12-2.

MUSCLE TONE

The resistance of skeletal muscle to passive stretch when a person is attempting to relax is known as **muscle tone**. It is usually tested as the examiner moves the relaxed limb or neck of the subject. Under such circumstances in a normal person, the resistance to passive movement is slight and uniform, regardless of the speed of the movement.

Muscle tone is due both to the viscoelastic properties of the muscles and joints and to whatever degree of alpha motor neuron activity exists. When a person is deeply relaxed, the alpha motor neuron activity probably makes no contribution to the resistance to stretch. As the person becomes increasingly alert, some activation of the alpha (and gamma) motor neurons occurs and muscle tone increases. Active motor neurons play an ever-increasing role until they—or rather the myofibrillar cross-bridge activity they stimulate—account for much of the resistance to stretch.

Abnormal Muscle Tone

Abnormally high muscle tone, seen particularly clearly when a joint is moved passively at high speeds, is called **hypertonia**. The increased resistance is due to a greater-than-normal level of alpha motor neuron activity that keeps a muscle contracted despite the individual's attempt to relax it. Hypertonia is usually found when there are disorders of the descending pathways[1] that result in de-

creased inhibitory influences exerted by them on the motor neurons.

Spasticity is a form of hypertonia in which the muscles do not develop increased tone until they are stretched a bit; after a brief increase in tone, the contraction subsides for a short time. The period of "give" occurring after a time of resistance is called the clasp-knife phenomenon. Spasticity is accompanied by increased responses of motor reflexes such as the knee jerk, and by decreased coordination and strength of voluntary actions. **Rigidity** is a form of hypertonia in which the increased muscle contraction is continual and the resistance to passive stretch is constant. The rigidity of a person with Parkinson's disease is the most familiar example. Two other forms of hypertonia that can occur suddenly in individual or multiple muscles are **spasms**, which are brief contractions, and **cramps**, which are prolonged and painful.

Hypotonia is a condition of abnormally low muscle tone, accompanied by weakness, atrophy (a decrease in muscle bulk), and decreased or absent reflex responses. Dexterity and coordination are generally preserved unless profound weakness is present. While hypotonia may develop after cerebellar disease, it more frequently accompanies disorders of the alpha motor neurons, neuromuscular junctions, or muscles. The term **flaccid**, which means "weak" or "soft," is often used to describe hypotonic muscles.

MAINTENANCE OF UPRIGHT POSTURE AND BALANCE

The skeleton supporting the body is a system of long bones and a many-jointed spine, which cannot stand erect against the forces of gravity without the support given by coordinated muscle activity. The muscles that maintain upright posture, that is, support the body's weight against gravity, are controlled by the brain and by reflex mechanisms that are "wired into" the neural networks of the brainstem and spinal cord. Many of the reflex pathways previously introduced, for example, the stretch and crossed-extensor reflexes, are used in posture control.

Added to the problem of maintaining upright posture is that of maintaining balance. A human being is a very tall structure balanced on a relatively small base, and its center of gravity is quite high, being situated just above the pelvis. For stability, the center of gravity must be kept within the base of support provided by the feet (Figure 12-14). Once the center of gravity has moved beyond this base, the body will fall unless one foot is rapidly shifted to broaden the base of support. Yet people often operate under conditions of unstable equilibrium and would topple easily if their

---

[1] Clinically, the descending pathways, primarily the corticospinal pathways, and neurons of the motor cortex are called the upper motor neurons (a serious misnomer because they are not really motor neurons at all). Abnormalities due to their dysfunction are classed as upper motor neuron disorders. Thus, hypertonia indicates an upper motor neuron disorder. In this classification, the alpha motor neurons are termed lower motor neurons.

FIGURE 12-14
The center of gravity is the point in an object at which, if a string were attached to the object at this point and pulled up, all the downward force due to gravity would be exactly balanced. (A) The center of gravity must remain within the upward vertical projections of the object's base (the tall box outlined in the drawing) if stability is to be maintained. (B) Stable conditions: Box tilts a bit, but the center of gravity remains within the base area and so the box will return to its upright position. (C) Unstable conditions: The box tilts so far that its center of gravity is not above any part of the object's base—the dashed rectangle on the floor—and the object will fall.

balance were not protected by complex interacting **postural reflexes**, all the components of which we have met previously.

The afferent pathways of the postural reflexes come from three sources: the eyes, the vestibular apparatus, and the somatic receptors. The efferent pathways are the alpha motor neurons to the skeletal muscles. The integrating centers are neuron networks in the brainstem and spinal cord.

There are many familiar examples of postural reflexes. The stretch reflex is activated, for example, when the knees begin to buckle, stretching the spindle receptors in the thigh muscles. Although the input from the muscle-spindle afferent fibers onto the alpha motor neurons does not exert a powerful effect, it is thought to be useful for small adjustments of posture. The crossed-extensor reflex is clearly used to maintain postural support. As one leg is flexed, the other is extended more strongly to support the added weight of the body, and the positions of various parts of the body are shifted to move the center of gravity over the single, weight-bearing leg. This shift in the center of gravity, demonstrated in Figure 12-15, is an important component in the stepping mechanism of locomotion.

It is clear that afferent input from several sources is necessary for effective postural adjustments, yet interfering with any one of these inputs alone does not cause a person to topple over. Blind people maintain their balance quite well with only a slight loss of precision, and people whose vestibular mechanisms have been destroyed have very little disability in everyday life as long as their visual system and somatic receptors are functioning.

The conclusion to be drawn from such examples is that the sensory information received by postural control mechanisms is redundant and that one particular type of information becomes critically important only when all the other inputs have been lost.

WALKING

The cyclical, alternating movements of walking are controlled by **central pattern generators** in the spinal cord at the level of the motor neurons. The central pattern generators are networks of interneurons that coordinate the output of the various motor neuron pools controlling muscles of the arms, shoulders, trunk, hips, and legs. In addition to activating those alpha motor neurons necessary for locomotion, the central pattern generators regulate the afferent input so that it does not hinder the motor neurons' activity.

Walking is initiated by allowing the body to fall forward to an unstable position and then moving one leg forward to regain equilibrium. The legs may be activated out of phase

FIGURE 12-15
Postural changes with stepping. (Left) Normal standing posture. The line of the center of gravity falls directly between the two feet. (Right) As the left foot is raised, the whole body leans to the right so that the center of gravity shifts over the right foot.

with each other, as in walking or running. In such cases, spinal pattern generators utilize reciprocal innervation so that when the extensor muscles are activated on one side of the body, to bear the body's weight, the contralateral extensors are inhibited to allow that limb to flex and swing forward.

Although the central pattern generators can bring about the rhythmical movement of a limb in the absence of afferent information, such input normally does contribute substantially to locomotion by acting on the generators and indirectly on the motor neurons themselves. This afferent information ensures that the output of the central pattern generator is optimally adapted to the environment. For example, if the limb movement should be slowed by

external factors, as in wading through water, the afferent signals prevent a premature flexion of the limb.

The central pattern generators are also affected by the descending pathways, both during the initiation of activity and during ongoing activity. Such input helps adjust the movement to the person's goals and to the environment, adding influence from the eyes, vestibular apparatus, and ears. For example, depending upon commands from the descending pathways, the two limbs may be operated together, as in jumping, instead of reciprocally. One attractive hypothesis is that the brain can control stereotyped behaviors such as locomotion simply by activating the appropriate central pattern generators by way of the descending pathways.

SUMMARY

Skeletal muscles are controlled by their motor neurons. All the motor neurons that control a given muscle form a motor neuron pool.

MOTOR CONTROL HIERARCHY

The neural systems that control body movements are arranged in a motor control hierarchy.

I. The highest level determines the general intention of an action.

II. The middle level specifies the postures and movements needed to carry out the intended action and, taking account of sensory information that indicates the body's position, establishes a motor program.

III. The lowest level determines which motor neurons will be activated.

IV. As the movement progresses, information about what the muscles are doing is fed back to the motor control centers, which make any needed program corrections.

V. Actions are voluntary when we are aware of what we are doing and why, or when we are paying attention to the action or its purpose.

VI. Almost all actions have conscious and unconscious components.

LOCAL CONTROL OF MOTOR NEURONS

I. Most input to motor neurons is from local interneurons, which themselves receive input from peripheral receptors, descending pathways, and other interneurons.

II. Muscle length and changes in length are monitored by muscle-spindle stretch receptors.
   A. Activation of these receptors initiates the stretch reflex, in which motor neurons of ipsilateral antagonists are inhibited and those of synergists are activated.
   B. Tension on the stretch receptors is maintained during muscle contraction by gamma efferent activation of the spindle muscle fibers.
   C. Alpha and gamma motor neurons are often coactivated.

III. Muscle tension is monitored by Golgi tendon organs, which, via interneurons, activate inhibitory synapses on motor neurons of the contracting muscle and excitatory synapses on motor neurons of ipsilateral antagonists.

IV. The flexion reflex excites the ipsilateral flexor muscles and inhibits the ipsilateral extensors. The

crossed-extensor reflex excites the contralateral extensor muscles during excitation of the ipsilateral flexors.

THE BRAIN MOTOR CENTERS AND THE DESCENDING PATHWAYS THEY CONTROL

I. The location of the neurons in the motor cortex varies with the part of the body the neurons serve.

II. A motor potential occurs in the motor cortex before muscle activation occurs. This is preceded by a readiness potential produced by the supplementary motor cortex 800 ms before any electrical activity in the motor cortex begins.

III. The basal ganglia help determine the direction, force, and speed of movements.

IV. The cerebellum coordinates posture and movement and plays a role in motor learning.

V. The corticospinal pathways pass directly from the sensorimotor cortex to motor neurons in the spinal cord (or in the brainstem, in the case of the corticobulbar pathways) or to nearby interneurons.
   A. In general, neurons on one side of the brain control muscles on the other side of the body.
   B. Corticospinal pathways serve predominately fine, precise movements.
   C. Some corticospinal fibers affect the transmission of information in afferent pathways.

VI. Other (noncorticospinal) pathways arise in the brainstem and are involved in the coordination of large groups of muscles used in posture and locomotion.

VII. There is some duplication of function between the two descending pathways.

MUSCLE TONE

I. Hypertonia, as seen in spasticity, rigidity, spasms, and cramps, usually occurs with disorders of the descending pathways.

II. Hypotonia can be seen with cerebellar disease or, more commonly, with disease of the alpha motor neurons or muscle.

MAINTENANCE OF UPRIGHT POSTURE AND BALANCE

I. To maintain balance, the body's center of gravity must be kept over the body's base.

II. The stretch and crossed-extensor reflexes are postural reflexes.

WALKING

I. Central pattern generators bring about the cyclical, alternating movements of locomotion.

II. The pattern generators are affected by feedback and motor programs.

KEY TERMS

motor units	alpha motor neurons
motor neuron pool	gamma motor neurons
coactivated	flexion reflex
Golgi tendon organs	crossed-extensor reflex
motor control hierarchy	sensorimotor cortex
motor program	primary motor cortex
descending pathways	motor cortex
local level	premotor area
voluntary movement	supplementary motor
muscle spindle	cortex
intrafusal fibers	somatosensory cortex
extrafusal fibers	parietal-lobe association
muscle-spindle stretch	cortex
receptors	motor potential
stretch reflex	readiness potential
knee jerk	basal ganglia
monosynaptic	substantia nigra
polysynaptic	corticospinal pathways
reciprocal innervation	pyramidal tracts
synergistic muscles	pyramidal system
ipsilateral	corticobulbar pathway
contralateral	postural reflexes
	central pattern generators

REVIEW QUESTIONS

1. Describe motor control in terms of the motor control hierarchy, using the following terms: highest, middle, and lowest levels; motor program; descending pathways; and motor neuron.

2. List the characteristics of voluntary actions.

3. Picking up a book, for example, has both voluntary and involuntary components. List six components of this action and indicate whether each is voluntary or involuntary.

4. List the inputs that can converge on the interneurons active in local motor control.

5. Draw a muscle spindle within a muscle, labeling the spindle, intrafusal and extrafusal muscle fibers, stretch receptors, afferent fibers, and alpha and gamma efferent fibers.

6. Describe the components of the knee jerk (stimulus, receptor, afferent pathway, integrating center, efferent pathway, effector, and response).

7. Describe the major function of alpha-gamma coactivation.

8. Distinguish among the following areas of the cerebral cortex: sensorimotor, primary motor, premotor, and supplementary motor.

9. Contrast the two major types of descending pathways in terms of structure and function.

10. Describe the roles that the basal ganglia and cerebellum play in motor control.

11. Explain how hypertonia might result from disease of the descending motor pathways.

12. Explain how hypotonia might result from disease of the alpha motor neurons.

13. Explain the role played by the stretch reflex in postural stability.

14. Explain the role played by the crossed-extensor reflex in postural stability.

15. Explain the role of the central pattern generators in walking, incorporating in your discussion the following terms: interneuron, reciprocal innervation, synergist, antagonist, and feedback.

CLINICAL TERMS

tetanus (lockjaw)	rigidity
Parkinson's disease	spasms
dysmetria	cramps
muscle tone	hypotonia
hypertonia	flaccid
spasticity	

THOUGHT QUESTIONS

(Answers are given in Appendix A.)

1. What changes would occur in the knee jerk reflex after destruction of the gamma motor neurons?

2. What changes would occur in the knee jerk reflex after destruction of the alpha motor neurons?

3. Draw a cross section of the spinal cord and a portion of the thigh (similar to Figure 12-6) and "wire up" and activate the neurons so the leg becomes a stiff pillar, that is, the knee does not bend.

4. We have said that hypertonia is usually considered a sign of disease of the descending motor pathways, but how might it result from abnormal function of the alpha motor neurons?

C H A P T E R

13

CONSCIOUSNESS AND BEHAVIOR

The term "consciousness" includes two distinct concepts: **states of consciousness** and **conscious experiences**. The first concept refers to whether a person is awake, asleep, drowsy, and so on. "Conscious experiences" refers to those things a person is aware of—thoughts, feelings, perceptions, ideas, dreams, reasoning—during any of the states of consciousness.

STATES OF CONSCIOUSNESS

A person's state of consciousness is defined in two ways: (1) by behavior, covering the spectrum from maximum attentiveness to coma; and (2) by the pattern of brain activity that can be recorded electrically. This record, known as the **electroencephalogram (EEG)**, portrays the electric-potential difference between two points on the surface of the scalp. The EEG is such an important tool in identifying the different states of consciousness that we begin with it.

Electroencephalogram

When neurons are functioning, their activity is indicated by the electric signals known as graded potentials and action potentials (Chapter 8). The electrical activity that is going on in the brain's neurons, particularly those near the surface, can be recorded from the outside of the head. Electrodes, which are wires attached to the head by a salty paste that conducts electricity, pick up electric signals generated by neurons in the brain and transmit them to a machine that transforms them into the EEG.

While we often think of neural activity in terms of action potentials, they usually contribute little to the EEG. Rather, EEG patterns are largely due to graded potentials, in this case summed postsynaptic potentials (Chapter 8) in the many hundreds of thousands of brain neurons that underlie the recording electrode.

EEG patterns, such as that shown in Figure 13-1, are waves, albeit complex ones, with large variations in both amplitude and frequency. The wave's amplitude (Figure 13-2) indicates how much electrical activity of a similar type is going on beneath the recording electrodes at any given time. The amplitude is measured in volts or, because the amplitudes are so small, in microvolts. The amplitude may range from 0.5 to 100 μV. Note that EEG amplitudes are about 1000 times smaller than an action potential recorded from inside a cell. This difference in amplitude occurs partly because the EEG indicates *extracellular* potentials, partly because the EEG is recorded through the skull and other brain coverings, and partly because even when recorded under the same conditions, postsynaptic potentials are of lower amplitude than action potentials.

The wave's frequency indicates how often the wave cycles from its maximal amplitude to its minimal amplitude and back. The frequency is measured in hertz (Hz), or cycles per second, and may vary from 1 to 30 Hz. Four major frequency ranges are found in EEG patterns. In general, lower EEG frequencies indicate less responsive behaviors, such as sleep, whereas higher frequencies indicate states of increased alertness.

The cause of the wavelike nature, or rhythmicity, of the EEG is not certain. It is currently thought that clusters of neurons in the thalamus are the rhythm generators. They provide a fluctuating output through nerve fibers leading from the thalamus to the cortex. This output causes, in turn, a rhythmical pattern of activity in the neurons of the cortex. The cortical activity—not the activity of the deep thalamic structures—comprises most of the EEG signal that one records.

The EEG is a useful clinical tool because the normal patterns are altered over brain areas that are diseased or damaged, for example, by tumors, blood clots, hemorrhage, regions of dead tissue, and high or low blood sugar. *Epilepsy* is a common neurological disease associated with EEG changes, the waves having distinctive high amplitudes (up to 1000 μV) and individual spikes or combinations of spikes and waves (Figure 13-3). This disease is also associated with stereotyped changes in behavior that vary according to the part of the brain affected and can include a temporary loss of consciousness. The EEG can also be

FIGURE 13-1
EEG patterns are wavelike. This represents a typical EEG recorded from the parietal or occipital lobes of an awake, relaxed person.

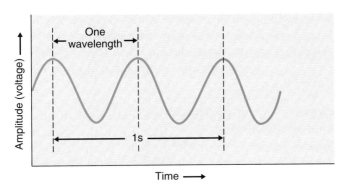

FIGURE 13-2

Characteristics of an EEG wave. The wave amplitude is also called the wave voltage. The frequency of this wave pattern is 2 cycles per second (Hz).

FIGURE 13-4

The (A) alpha and (B) beta rhythms of the EEG.

helpful in distinguishing confusion caused by overmedication from that caused by a degenerative disease, such as Alzheimer's.

The Waking State

Behaviorally, the waking state is far from homogeneous, comprising the infinite variety of things one can be doing. The most prominent EEG wave pattern of an awake, relaxed adult whose eyes are closed is a slow oscillation of 8 to 13 Hz, known as the **alpha rhythm** (Figure 13-4). The alpha rhythm is recorded best over the parietal and occipital lobes and is associated with decreased levels of attention. When alpha rhythms are being generated, subjects commonly report that they feel relaxed and happy. However, people who normally experience more alpha rhythm have not been shown to be psychologically different from those with less.

When people are attentive to an external stimulus or are thinking hard about something, the alpha rhythm is replaced by lower-amplitude, higher-frequency oscillations, the **beta rhythm** (Figure 13-4). This transformation is known as **EEG arousal** and is associated with the act of paying attention to a stimulus rather than with the act of perception. For example, if people open their eyes in a completely dark room and try to see, EEG arousal occurs even though they are able to perceive nothing. With decreasing attention to repeated stimuli, the EEG pattern reverts to the alpha rhythm.

Sleep

The EEG pattern changes profoundly in sleep. As a person becomes increasingly drowsy, there is a decrease in alpha-wave amplitude and frequency. When he or she actually falls asleep, the alpha rhythm shifts toward slower-frequency, higher-amplitude wave patterns (Figure 13-5). These EEG changes are accompanied by complex behavioral, psychological, and physiological events.

Neurophysiologists recognize two phases of sleep—slow-wave sleep and paradoxical sleep. The initial phase, called **slow-wave sleep**, itself is divided into four stages, each successive stage having an EEG pattern characterized by a slower frequency and higher amplitude than the preceding one (Figure 13-5A). Initially there is considerable tension in the postural muscles, but the muscles become progressively more relaxed as slow-wave sleep progresses. The eyes begin slow, rolling movements that finally stop in stage 4 (deep sleep) with the eyes turned upward. If the sleeper is awakened during stage 4 or other stages of slow-wave sleep, he or she rarely reports dreaming.

Sleep always begins with the slow-wave sleep progression just described, from stage 1 to stage 4. This progression normally takes 30 to 45 min, and then the process reverses itself, the EEG ultimately resuming the low-voltage, high-frequency pattern characteristic of the alert, awake state (Figure 13-5B). Instead of the person waking, however, the behavioral characteristics of sleep continue at this time.

FIGURE 13-3

Spike and wave pattern in the EEG of a patient during an epileptic seizure.

FIGURE 13-5

The EEG record of a person (A) passing from the awake state to deep sleep (stage 4) and (B) during paradoxical (REM) sleep.

Rapid eye movement is so characteristic of this last state of sleep that the state is often called **REM** (rapid eye movement) **sleep**. It is also called **paradoxical sleep** because the sleeper is difficult to arouse despite having an EEG that is characteristic of the alert, awake state. Even though difficult for someone else to rouse, a sleeper is more apt to awaken spontaneously during REM sleep than during slow-wave sleep. When awakened during REM sleep, subjects report, 80 to 90 percent of the time, that they have been dreaming. This is true even in people who do not remember dreaming when they awaken later spontaneously.

With several exceptions, skeletal-muscle tension, already decreased during slow-wave sleep, is markedly inhibited during REM sleep. One exception, as we have seen, is the eye muscles, where rapid bursts of saccade-like eye movements occur (page 257). The motor neurons to the muscles of respiration also normally escape the generalized inhibition. In the disease known as **sleep apnea**, however, the respiratory muscles are also inhibited, sometimes hundreds of times during a night. This disease, which affects more men than women, leads to excessive sleepiness during the day.

If uninterrupted, sleep continues in this cyclical fashion, beginning with slow-wave sleep and punctuated at regular intervals by episodes of REM sleep. Continuous recordings of adults show that the average total sleep period comprises four or five such cycles, each lasting 90 to

100 min (Figure 13-6). Slow-wave sleep constitutes 75 to 80 percent of the total sleeping time in young adults; the remainder is spent in paradoxical sleep. The time spent in paradoxical sleep increases toward the end of an undisturbed night.

During the sleep cycle, there are many changes, in addition to altered muscle tension, throughout the body. During slow-wave sleep, there are pulsatile releases of growth hormone (page 153) and the gonadotropic hormones from the anterior pituitary, as well as decreases in blood pressure, heart rate, and respiratory rate. Based on these changes, some researchers speculate that slow-wave sleep may serve as a time of the body's rest and metabolic restoration.

REM sleep is associated with an increase and irregularity in blood pressure, heart rate, and respiratory rate. Moreover, erection of the penis, engorgement of the clitoris, and twitches of the facial or limb muscles occur (despite the generalized lack of skeletal-muscle tone).

Although adults spend about one-third of their time sleeping, physiologists know little about the functions served by it. Both slow-wave sleep and REM sleep are, however, active functional states of the brain. For example, REM sleep may allow for the expression, through dreams, of concerns in the "subconscious" and for the long-term chemical and structural changes that the brain must undergo to make learning and memory possible.

The sleep stages are summarized in Table 13-1.

Neural Substrates of States of Consciousness

Periods of sleep and wakefulness alternate about once a day; that is, they manifest a circadian rhythm consisting

FIGURE 13-6

A typical night's sleep in an average young adult. The lavender-colored lines indicate periods of paradoxical sleep, which are characterized by EEG patterns similar to an alert, awake state and the presence of rapid eye movements. (*Adapted from Nicholi.*)

TABLE 13-1   SLEEP-WAKEFULNESS STAGES

Stage	Behavior	EEG (see Figures 13-4 and 13-5)
Alert wakefulness	Awake, alert with eyes open.	Beta rhythm (faster than 13 Hz).
Relaxed wakefulness	Awake, relaxed with eyes closed.	Mainly alpha rhythm (8–13 Hz) over the parietal and occipital lobes. Changes to beta rhythm in response to internal or external stimuli.
Relaxed drowsiness	Fatigued, tired, or bored; eyelids may narrow and close; head may start to droop; momentary lapses of attention and alertness. Sleepy but not asleep.	Decrease in alpha-wave amplitude and frequency.
Slow-wave sleep		
Stage 1	Light sleep; easily aroused by moderate stimuli or even by neck muscle jerks triggered by muscle stretch receptors as head nods; continuous lack of awareness.	Alpha waves reduced in frequency, amplitude, and percentage of time present; gaps in alpha rhythm filled with theta (4–8 Hz) and delta (slower than than 4 Hz) activity.
Stage 2	Further lack of sensivity to activation and arousal.	Alpha waves replaced by random waves of greater amplitude.
Stages 3 and 4	Deep sleep; in stage 4, activation and arousal occur only with vigorous stimulation.	Much theta and delta activity, predominant delta in stage 4.
Paradoxical (REM) sleep	Deepest sleep; greatest relaxation and difficulty of arousal; begins 50–90 min after sleep onset, episodes are repeated every 60–90 min, each episode lasting about 10 min; dreaming occurs, rapid eye movements behind closed eyelids; marked increase in brain O_2 consumption.	EEG resembles that of alert awake state.

typically of 8 h asleep and 16 h awake. This basic rhythm is controlled by the biological-clock functions of the suprachiasmatic nucleus in the hypothalamus (Figure 13-7 and page 256). Within the sleep portion of this circadian cycle, slow-wave sleep and REM sleep alternate, as we have seen.

Two other hypothalamic areas affect sleep (Figure 13-7). One, the **preoptic area**, promotes sleep, whereas increased activity of the other, in the posterior hypothalamus, leads to wakefulness. These two areas use prostaglandins as neurotransmitters, one type of prostaglandin in the preoptic area and a different type in the posterior hypothalamus. *Narcolepsy*, a genetic disorder characterized by sudden muscle weakness and brief periods of REM sleep during normal waking hours, and the disease *African sleeping sickness* have both been associated with elevated levels of the sleep-promoting prostaglandin.

Also active in the sleep-wake rhythms are two interacting systems in the brainstem, one an arousal system and the other (with several components) a sleep-producing system (Figure 13-7). Thus, neurons in some brainstem regions are most active during waking and are inhibited during sleep, while neurons in other regions show the opposite activity pattern. A separate cluster of brainstem neurons is responsible for the cyclical imposition of REM sleep upon slow-wave sleep. Nerve pathways connect these brainstem centers with those in the hypothalamus. (As we shall see below, the brainstem centers also connect to the thalamus.) The neurotransmitters norepinephrine, serotonin, dopamine, and acetylcholine all play a role in the brainstem centers for alternating states of consciousness.

In addition to these neurotransmitters, over 30 other chemical substances that affect sleep have been found in blood, urine, cerebrospinal fluid, and brain tissue. For example, one of the cytokines, which is a family of intercellular messengers having an important role in the body's immune defense system (Chapter 20), also affects sleep. Cerebrospinal fluid concentrations of this cytokine, known as interleukin 1, fluctuate in parallel with normal sleep-wake cycles. Levels of interleukin 1 increase during infections, possibly explaining why we sleep more when we are sick.

The changes in activity of the cerebral cortex, as reflected in EEG changes during waking and the two phases of sleep, are mediated by pathways passing from the brainstem to neurons in the thalamus and then from the thalamic neurons to the cortex. The EEG of REM sleep, even though it is similar to the awake EEG, is mediated by different pathways, which include the norepinephrine releasing neurons of the locus coeruleus to be described later.

FIGURE 13-7

Brain structures involved in sleep-wakefulness cycles. The circadian rhythm of sleep-wakefulness is controlled by the suprachiasmatic nucleus, sleep being promoted by the preoptic area and wakefulness by the posterior hypothalamus. Brainstem centers are concerned with arousal, paradoxical sleep, and slow-wave sleep.

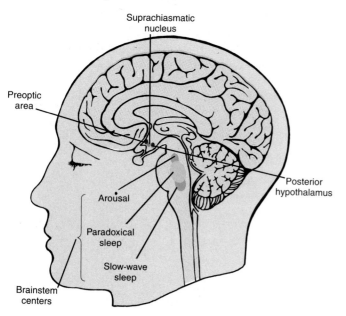

Coma and Brain Death

The term *coma* describes a severe or total decrease in mental function due to structural, physiological, or metabolic impairment of the brain. A person in a coma is characterized by a sustained loss of the capacity for arousal even in response to vigorous stimulation. There is no outward behavioral expression of any mental function, the eyes are closed, and sleep-wake cycles disappear. Coma can result from extensive damage to the cerebral cortex; damage to the brainstem arousal mechanisms; interruptions of the connections between the brainstem and cortical areas; metabolic dysfunctions; brain infections; or an overdose of certain drugs, such as sedatives, sleeping pills, and, in some cases, narcotics.

But a coma—even an irreversible coma—is not equivalent to death. We are left, then, with the question: When is a person actually dead? And this question often has urgent medical, legal, and social consequences. For example, with the advent of organ transplantation and the need for viable tissues, it became imperative to know just when a person was "dead" so that organs for transplant could be removed as soon after death as possible.

Brain death is widely accepted by doctors and lawyers as the criterion for death, despite the viability of other organs. Brain death describes the irreversible loss of all brain function. In other words, the brain no longer functions and has no possibility of functioning again.

TABLE 13-2   CRITERIA FOR BRAIN DEATH

   I. The nature and duration of the coma must be known.
      A. Known structural damage to brain or irreversible systemic metabolic disease.
      B. No chance of drug intoxication, especially from paralyzing or sedative drugs.
      C. No sign of brain function for 6 h in cases of known structural cause and when no drugs or alcohol is involved; otherwise, 12–24 h without signs of brain function plus a negative drug screen.
  II. Cerebral and brainstem function are absent.
      A. No response to painful stimuli administered above the spinal cord.
      B. Pupils unresponsive to light.
      C. No eye movement in response to ice-water stimulation of the vestibular reflex.
      D. Apnea (no spontaneous breathing) for 10 min.
      E. Systemic circulation may be intact.
      F. Purely spinal reflexes may be retained.
 III. Supplementary (optional) criteria.
      A. Flat EEG (wave amplitudes less than 2 μV).
      B. Responses absent in vital brainstem structures.
      C. No cerebral circulation.

The problem now becomes practical: How does one know when a person in a coma is considered brain dead? There is general agreement that the criteria listed in Table 13-2, if met, denote brain death. Notice that the cause of a coma must be known because comas due to drug poisoning are usually reversible. Also, the criteria specify that there be no evidence of functioning neural tissues *above* the spinal cord because fragments of spinal reflexes may remain for several hours or longer after the brain is dead. The criterion for lack of spontaneous respiration (apnea) can be difficult to test because once a patient is on a respirator, it is of course inadvisable to remove him or her for the 10-min test because of the danger of further brain damage due to oxygen lack. Therefore, apnea is diagnosed if there is no spontaneous attempt to "fight" the respirator; that is, the patient's reflexes do not drive respiration at a rate or depth different from those of the respirator.

CONSCIOUS EXPERIENCES

Having run the gamut of the states of consciousness from the awake, alert state to coma and brain death, we turn now to the conscious experiences during the awake state. We begin with the subject of how we pay attention because we are aware of (that is, we experience) only those ideas, perceptions, and actions to which we pay some degree of attention. For instance, I am aware of the weight of my glasses resting on my nose only when I think about it. It is believed that the amount of attention that can be paid to different events at any one time is limited, thus limiting the number of things we can consciously experience at one time.

Directed Attention

The term **directed attention** means the avoidance of distraction by irrelevant stimuli while seeking out and focusing on stimuli that are momentarily important. An example familiar to students is ignoring distracting events in a busy library while studying there.

Presentation of a novel stimulus to a relaxed subject showing an alpha EEG pattern causes EEG arousal (if the subject is already concentrating on something, the EEG is already in the beta rhythm). If the stimulus has meaning for the individual, behavioral changes occur. The person stops what he or she is doing and looks around, listening intently and orienting toward the stimulus source. This behavior is called the **orienting response**. If the person is concentrating hard and is not distracted by the novel stimulus, the orienting response does not occur.

For attention to be directed only toward stimuli that are meaningful, the nervous system must have the means to evaluate the importance of the incoming sensory information. Even before we focus attention on an object in our sensory world and become aware of it, a certain amount of processing has occurred. This so-called **preattentive processing** serves to direct our attention toward the part of the sensory world that is of particular interest and prepares the brain's perceptual processes that function as we direct our attention to the object.

If a stimulus is repeated but is irrelevant, there is a progressive behavioral decrease in response to the stimulus **(habituation)**. For example, when a loud bell is sounded for the first time, it may evoke an orienting response because the person might be frightened by or curious about the novel stimulus. After several ringings, however, the individual makes progressively less response and eventually may ignore the bell altogether. An extraneous stimulus of another type or the same stimulus at a different intensity restores the orienting response.

Habituation is not due to receptor fatigue or adaptation. Rather, it involves a depression of synaptic transmission in the involved pathways, possibly related to prolonged inactivation of calcium channels in presynaptic axon terminals. Such inactivation results in a decreased calcium influx during depolarization and, hence, a decrease in the amount of neurotransmitter released in response to action potentials that carry information about the stimulus.

Neural Mechanisms for Directed Attention.   Directing our attention to an object involves at least three distinct neurological processes. First, our attention must be disengaged from its present focus. Then, attention must be moved to the new focus. And, finally, attention must be engaged at the new focus. Evidence from brain-damaged people indicates that the three steps are the result of events that occur at separate places in the brain. For example, patients with damage in their parietal lobes have difficulty disengaging their attention from one focus to pay attention to a new object. If the damage is restricted to the parietal lobe of one hemisphere, they often neglect, that is they fail to pay attention to, anything on the side of their body opposite the damaged side. (Recall from Chapter 9 that the sensory pathways are crossed, those from the right side of the body going to the left half of the brain, and vice versa.)

Such neglect is always more severe if the damage occurs in the right half of the brain, indicating that the right hemisphere plays a special role in focusing attention. Supporting the theory of right-hemisphere importance are blood flow studies that show increased metabolic activity in specific regions of the right frontal and parietal lobes (Figure 13-8) when an experimental subject pays vigilant attention to an object in the visual field or a touch on the skin. Blood flow increases in these areas in the right hemisphere regardless of whether the stimulus is presented on the right or the left side of the body.

The locus coeruleus, a nucleus in the brainstem pons, which projects to the parietal cortex and to many other parts of the central nervous system as well, is also implicated in directed attention. According to one view, the system of fibers leading from the locus coeruleus determines which brain area is to gain temporary predominance

FIGURE 13-8

Areas of increased blood flow and, therefore, increased activity in the frontal and parietal lobes in response to paying close attention to a stimulus. *(Data from Pardo et al.)*

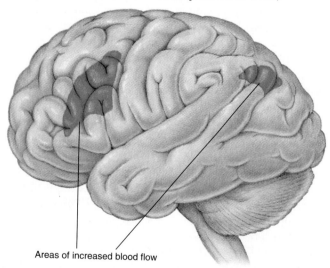

Areas of increased blood flow

in the ongoing stream of the conscious experience. Norepinephrine, the transmitter released by these neurons, acts as a neuromodulator to enhance the signals transmitted by certain sensory inputs so the difference between them and weaker signals is increased. Thus, neurons of the locus coeruleus seem to improve information processing during directed attention.

Neural Mechanisms for Conscious Experiences

Finding the neural substrate of conscious experience begins with the question: Which neural actions are specifically required for conscious experiences to occur? Certainly, there can be neural responses to stimulation without any accompanying conscious experience of the event. For example, stimulation of the cerebral cortex surface exposed during neurosurgery performed under local anesthesia can produce large neural responses but no awareness of the event by a conscious, alert subject. To take another example, stimulation of peripheral nerves does not always lead to conscious sensation. From these observations, we conclude that certain specific kinds of neural activity must be present in the brain if conscious experiences are to occur.

All conscious experiences are popularly attributed to the workings of the "mind," a word that conjures up the image of a nonneural "me," a phantom interposed between afferent and efferent impulses, with the implication that a mind is something more than neural activity. Most neuroscientists agree that the mind represents the summed total of all neural activity in the brain at any given moment and does not require anything more than the brain.

Although a good definition of "mind" is not possible at this time, the term includes such actions as thinking, perceiving, making decisions, feeling, and imagining. Thus, we can conclude that "mind" refers to a "process" that gives rise to and includes conscious experiences. The truth of the matter is, however, that physiologists have only a minimal understanding of the brain mechanisms that give rise to mind or to conscious experiences.

Let us see in the rest of this section how two prominent neuroscientists, Francis Crick and Christof Koch, have speculated about this problem. They begin with the assumption that conscious experience requires neural processes—either graded potentials or action potentials—somewhere in the brain. We are certainly not conscious, however, of all the different processes that go on there. At any moment, certain of these processes are correlated with conscious awareness, and others are not. A key question here is: What is different about such processes that we are aware of?

A further assumption is that the neural activity that corresponds to conscious experience resides not in a single anatomical cluster of "consciousness neurons" but rather in a set of neurons that are temporarily functioning together in a specific way. And since we can become aware of many different things, we further assume that this particular set of neurons can vary, shifting, for example, among parts of the brain that deal with visual or auditory stimuli, memories or new ideas, and emotions or language.

Consider perception of a visual object. As was discussed in Chapter 9, different aspects of something we see are processed by different areas of the visual cortex—the object's color by one part, its motion by another, its location in the visual field by another, and its shape by still another—but we see *one* object. Not only do we perceive it; we may also know its name and function. Moreover, an object that can be seen can sometimes be heard or smelled, which requires participation of brain areas other than the visual cortex.

Neurons from the various parts of the brain that synchronously process different aspects of the information related to the object that we see are said to form a "temporary set" of neurons. It is suggested that the synchronous activity of the neurons in the temporary set leads to conscious awareness of the object we are seeing. (Instead of "leads to," perhaps we should say "corresponds to" or "is." We don't even know the appropriate term here.)

As we become aware of still other events—perhaps a memory related to this object—the set of neurons involved in the synchronous activity shifts, and a different temporary set forms. In other words, it is suggested that specific relevant neurons in many areas of the brain function together to form the unified activity that corresponds to awareness.

It is possible to record neuronal activity pulsing at a frequency of 40 to 70 Hz—faster even than the beta waves of the EEG. These waves may be the electrical record of a synchronous neural set.

One important question is: What parts of the brain might be involved in such a neuronal set? Clearly the cerebral cortex is involved, although not all parts at once, since removal of specific areas of the cortex abolish awareness of only specific types of consciousness. An example was mentioned previously: Damage to parts of the parietal lobe causes one to neglect parts of the body as though they do not exist. Some subcortical areas, for example, the thalamus and basal ganglia, may also be directly involved in conscious experience, but it seems that the hippocampus and cerebellum are not.

Another critical question is: What binds together the functions of first one set of neurons and then another? How this happens is not known. By experience, we know that the binding must occur rapidly and that it can be very short-lived. Moreover, although its capacity at any one time may be limited, there is a huge range of combinations possible. In other words, we must postulate a mechanism that can focus our attention on a limited number of things at any one time but, over time, can bring an enormous number of things into conscious awareness.

Saying that we can bind together the activity of one set of neurons and shift the binding to a new set at a later time may be the same as saying we can focus attention on—that is, bring into conscious awareness—one object or event and then shift our focus of attention to another object or event at a later time. In other words, the mechanisms of conscious awareness and attention must be intimately related.

MOTIVATION AND EMOTION

Motivation is a factor in most, if not all, behaviors, while emotions accompany many of our conscious experiences.

Motivation

Those processes responsible for the goal-directed quality of behavior are the **motivations**, or "drives," for that behavior. **Primary motivated behavior** is behavior related directly to homeostasis, that is, the maintenance of a relatively stable internal environment, an example being getting something to drink when one is thirsty. In such homeostatic goal-directed behavior, specific body needs are satisfied. Thus, in our example the correlate of need is a drop in body water concentration, and the correlate of need satisfaction is the return of the body water concentration to normal. The neurophysiological integration of much homeostatic goal-directed behavior will be discussed later (thirst and drinking, Chapter 16; food intake and temperature regulation, Chapter 18; reproduction, Chapter 19).

In many kinds of behavior, however, the relation between the behavior and the primary goal is indirect. For example, the selection of a particular drink—water or soda pop, for example—has little if any apparent relation to homeostasis. The motivation in this case is called secondary. Much of human behavior fits into this latter category and is influenced by habit, learning, experience, and emotions. These factors as well as the actual homeostatically related "needs" are thought to determine the degree of motivation, or drive, behind a particular behavior.

The concepts of reward and punishment are inseparable from motivation. Rewards are things that organisms work for or things that make the behavior that leads to them occur more often, and punishments are the opposite.

Much of the available information concerning the neural substrates of motivation has been obtained by studying behavioral responses of animals—and, in some cases, people—to rewarding or punishing stimuli. One way in which this can be done is by using the technique of **brain self-stimulation**. In this technique, an unanesthetized experimental animal (or a human undergoing neurosurgery for other reasons) regulates the rate at which electric stimuli are delivered through electrodes implanted in discrete brain areas. The experimental animal is placed in a box containing a lever it can press (Figure 13-9). If no stimulus is delivered to the brain when the bar is pressed, the animal usually presses it occasionally at random.

If, in contrast, a stimulus is delivered to the brain as a result of a bar press, a different behavior occurs, depending on the location of the electrodes. If the animal increases the bar-pressing rate above the level of random presses in the absence of a stimulus, the electric stimulus is by definition rewarding. If the animal decreases the press rate below the random level, the stimulus is punishing.

Thus, the rate of bar pressing with the electrode in different brain areas is taken to be a measure of the effectiveness of the reward or punishment. Different pressing rates are found in different brain regions.

Scientists expected the hypothalamus to play a role in motivation because the neural centers for the regulation of eating, drinking, temperature control, and sexual behavior are there (Chapter 8). They found that brain self-stimulation of the lateral regions of the hypothalamus serves as a positive reward. Animals with electrodes in these areas have been known to bar-press to stimulate their brains 2000 times per hour continuously for 24 h until they drop from exhaustion! In fact, electric stimulation of the lateral hypothalamus is more rewarding than external rewards in that hungry rats, for example, often ignore available food

FIGURE 13-9

Apparatus for self-stimulation experiments. (*Adapted from Olds.*)

for the sake of electrically stimulating their brains at that location.

Although the rewarding sites are more densely packed in the lateral hypothalamus than anywhere else in the brain, self-stimulation can be obtained from a large number of other brain areas. It is thought that self-stimulation in these brain areas triggers such behaviors as feeding, drinking, and sexual behavior. Consistent with this is the fact that the animal's rate of self-stimulation in some areas increases when it is deprived of food. In other areas, it is decreased by castration and restored by the administration of sex hormones. Thus, neurons controlling homeostatic goal-directed behavior are themselves intimately involved in the reinforcing effects of reward and punishment. Self-stimulation in the nucleus accumbens (Figure 13-10) which, as we shall see, is implicated in drug addiction, is also rewarding.

Chemical Mediators. Two catecholamines, norepinephrine and dopamine, are transmitters in the pathways that mediate the brain reward systems and motivation. For this reason, drugs that increase synaptic activity in the catecholamine pathways—amphetamines, for example—increase self-stimulation rates. Conversely, drugs such as chlorpromazine, an antipsychotic agent, that lower activity in the catecholamine pathways, decrease self-stimulation.

In addition to the catecholamine pathways, a system of neurons activated by morphine and enkephalin is involved in motivation. The catecholamines and enkephalin are also, as we shall see, implicated in the pathways subserving learning. This is not unexpected since rewards and punishments are believed to constitute incentives for learning.

Emotion

Emotions are complex feeling states that have mental, physical, and behavioral components. Pervasive and sustained emotions are called moods.

Emotions are related to motivation in that they lend strength or intensity to an action. For purposes of this discussion, we distinguish two aspects of emotion: (1) **inner emotions**, such as the feelings of fear, love, anger, joy, anxiety, hope, and so on, that are entirely within a person; and (2) the outward expressions and displays of **emotional behavior**. Emotional behavior includes such complex behaviors as attack and such simple actions as laughing, sweating, crying, or blushing. Emotional behavior is achieved by integrated activity of the autonomic nervous and somatic efferent systems and provides an outward sign that an inner emotion has occurred.

Inner emotions involve the amygdala, a nucleus at the tip of the temporal lobe (Figure 13-10), and the region of association cortex on the lower surface of the frontal lobe, although there is ample reason to believe that the generation of our emotions is not limited to these two areas. Emotional behavior, on the other hand, is centered in the hypothalamus. All three of these areas are part of the lim-

FIGURE 13-10

Brain structures involved in directed attention, emotion, motivation, and the affective disorders. The limbic system is shaded purple. *From BRAIN, MIND AND BEHAVIOR by Floyd E. Bloom and Arlyne Lazerson. Copyright © 1985, 1988 by Educational Broadcasting Corporation. Reprinted by permission of W.H. Freeman and Company.*

bic system. Limbic structures other than the hypothalamus play a role in a wide variety of complex emotional behaviors that receive their final coordination by the hypothalamus.

Emotional behavior, unlike inner emotions, can be studied reasonably well because it includes responses that are easily measured. For example, stimulation of the lateral hypothalamus caused an experimental animal to arch its back, puff out the fur on its tail, hiss, snarl, bare its claws and teeth, flatten its ears, and strike. Simultaneously, its heart rate, blood pressure, respiration, salivation, and concentrations of plasma epinephrine and fatty acids all increased. Clearly, this behavior typified that of an enraged or threatened animal. Moreover, the animal's behavior could be changed from savage to docile and back again simply by stimulating different areas of the limbic system, such as parts of the amygdala.

Limbic areas have been stimulated in awake human beings undergoing neurosurgery. These patients reported vague feelings of fear or anxiety during periods of stimulation to certain areas. Stimulation of other areas induced pleasurable sensations that the subjects found hard to define precisely.

The models presently available to explain inner emotions and emotional behavior are far from complete. It seems that nonhypothalamic parts of the limbic system receive information from cortical association areas, particularly those in the frontal lobe, and send output directly to the hypothalamus. Thus, the limbic system serves as the route by which information about the emotional meaning of an external stimulus (for example, whether it is threatening or friendly), including information gleaned from memory and understanding, is passed to the hypothalamus. The hypothalamus then integrates the endocrine and autonomic behaviors and even influences some of the motor activities that form appropriate emotional behavior.

In addition to its role in elaborating the conscious experience of emotional feelings, the cerebral cortex provides the neural mechanisms that direct the motor responses to the external event during emotional behavior, for example, to approach or avoid a situation. Moreover, it is forebrain structures, including the cerebral cortex, that account for the modulation, direction, understanding, or even inhibition of emotional behaviors.

ALTERED STATES OF CONSCIOUSNESS

The state of consciousness may be different from the commonly experienced wakefulness, drowsiness, and so on. Other, more bizarre situations, such as those occurring with hypnosis, mind-altering drugs, and certain diseases, are referred to as *altered states of consciousness*.

Schizophrenia

One of the diseases that induces altered states of consciousness is *schizophrenia*. The key symptoms include hallucinations, especially "hearing" voices, and delusions, such as the belief that one has been chosen for a special mission or is being persecuted by others. Schizophrenics become withdrawn, show little empathy for others, and experience inappropriate moods. They also experience abnormal motor behavior, which can range from total immobilization (catatonia) to wild, purposeless activity.

Two patterns of the disease exist, one in which the patients have mainly so-called positive symptoms (delusions and hallucinations, for example), and the other in which they show mainly negative symptoms (emotional unresponsiveness, withdrawal, few movements or gestures, loss of drive, depressed mood). Those with the positive symptoms respond better to drug therapy, and those having negative symptoms are apt to show more abnormalities in brain structure.

As compared to normal people, some schizophrenics have smaller brains and a decreased number of neurons, particularly in the frontal lobes and the part of the temporal lobes that houses the hippocampus and amygdala (Figure 13-10). These abnormalities are usually greater in the left hemisphere of the brain.

Schizophrenia is a fairly common disease. It can appear gradually, often during adolescence in an otherwise bright and normal person, or it can occur suddenly after a single precipitating event. Despite extensive research, the causes of schizophrenia remain unclear, although the disease is known to have a genetic component: Whereas 1 percent of the general population will develop the disease, 10 to 16 percent of people having a schizophrenic parent will themselves become schizophrenic.

The most widely accepted explanation for schizophrenia is the *dopamine hypothesis*, which suggests that increased stimulation of dopamine receptors at least partially explains the symptoms of the disease. This hypothesis is supported by the fact that drugs that alter schizophrenia influence transmission at dopamine-mediated synapses. Thus, the symptoms are made worse by amphetamine-like drugs, which are dopamine agonists, and the most therapeutically beneficial drugs used in treating schizophrenia block dopamine receptors.

Abnormalities in neurotransmitter function in the brains of schizophrenics are, however, not *directly* due to dopamine. Rather, in some schizophrenics at least, abnormalities are found in the glutamate systems, which are closely related to dopaminergic systems, and in serotonin levels.

The Affective Disorders: Depressions and Manias

The term **affect** refers to the external expression of inner emotions. Whereas schizophrenia is largely a disease with disordered thought, the *affective disorders* are characterized by serious, prolonged disturbances of mood. The affective disorders include the *depressions*, the *manias*, and swings between these two states, the *bipolar affec-* *tive disorders*. In the depressive disorders, the prominent feature is a pervasive sadness, loss of interest or pleasure, and feelings of worthlessness. The essential features of the manias are elated mood, sometimes with euphoria (that is, an exaggerated sense of well being), overconfidence, and irritability. Along with schizophrenia, the affective disorders form the major psychiatric illnesses today. The causes of mood disorders are not known.

Depression can be triggered by stressful events, it can accompany other mental or medical disorders, or it can arise spontaneously. Although the biochemical basis of depression is unknown, it is associated with abnormally low levels of certain neurotransmitters in the brain. Serotonin is the major neurotransmitter implicated, although norepinephrine may be involved as well, and the major antidepressant drugs alter the functioning of one or the other of these substances or both of them.

The classical antidepressant drugs are of two types. The *tricyclic antidepressant drugs*, such as Elavil and Pamelor, interfere with serotonin and/or norepinephrine uptake by presynaptic endings. The *monoamine oxidase inhibitors* interfere with the enzyme responsible for the breakdown of these same two neurotransmitters. A newer class of antidepressant drugs, of which Prozac is an example, selectively inhibits serotonin reuptake by presynaptic terminals. In all three cases, the result is an *increased* concentration of serotonin and/or norepinephrine in the extracellular fluid at synapses. Since the reuptake inhibitors show beneficial effects only after several weeks of treatment, their therapeutic effects must be due to a compensatory change in response to the elevated levels of transmitter and not directly to the increased neurotransmitter levels.

In depressed (or manic) persons for whom drug therapy has proved ineffective or is contraindicated, *electroconvulsive therapy (ECT)* is often effective. As the name suggests, electricity is used to induce a convulsion, or seizure, the patient being under anesthesia and prepared with a muscle relaxant to minimize convulsions. A series of ECT treatments alters neurotransmitter function, for example, by causing a down-regulation of certain postsynaptic receptors. It is unclear whether serotonin receptors are involved in these changes. The finding that beta-adrenergic and muscarinic acetylcholine receptors are also down-regulated after ECT raises the possibility that it might be the *balance* between the various transmitter systems that is important in depression rather than functional alterations involving only a single transmitter.

The major drug used in treating manic or bipolar affective disorder is lithium carbonate. It is highly specific, normalizing both the manic and depressing moods of bipolar disorders and slowing down thinking and motor behavior without causing sedation. In addition, it decreases the severity of the swings between mania and depression that occur in the bipolar disorders. In some cases, lithium is even effective in depression not associated with manias.

Lithium is thought to interfere with the formation of members of the inositol phosphate family and, therefore to decrease the postsynaptic neurons' response to neurotransmitters that utilize this second-messenger pathway (Chapter 7).

Psychoactive Drugs, Dependence, and Tolerance

In the previous sections, we mentioned several drugs used to combat altered states of consciousness. Psychoactive drugs are also used as "street drugs" in a deliberate attempt to elevate mood (euphorigens) and produce unusual states of consciousness ranging from meditational states to hallucinations. Virtually all the psychoactive drugs exert their actions either directly or indirectly by altering neurotransmitter-receptor interactions. For example, cocaine blocks the reuptake of serotonin and the catecholamine neurotransmitters, particularly dopamine, into the presynaptic axon terminal. As mentioned on page 211, psychoactive drugs are often chemically similar to neurotransmitters such as serotonin, dopamine (Figure 13-11), and

norepinephrine, and they interact with the receptors activated by these transmitters.

Dependence. *Drug dependence*, the term now preferred for addiction, has two facets that may occur either together or independently: (1) a psychological dependence that is experienced as a craving for a drug and an inability to stop using the substance at will; and (2) a physical dependence that requires one to take the drug to avoid *withdrawal*, that is, the unpleasant symptoms that occur with cessation of drug use.

Drug dependence has not been defined to everyone's satisfaction. Regardless, most agree that the definition should include the following concepts: (1) Drug dependence is characterized by the tendency toward a progressive increase in consumption of the drug; and (2) it is characterized by a persistent tendency to relapse to use of the substance even after abstinence has been achieved and withdrawal symptoms are no longer in evidence.

Different substances have different potentials for pro-

FIGURE 13-11
Molecular similarities between neurotransmitters (blue type) and some euphorigens (black type). At high doses, these euphorigens can cause hallucinations.

ducing dependence. Thus, just because a person can drink or not drink beer as he chooses, it does not follow that that same person will be able to use or not use cocaine or heroin as he or she chooses.

The chemical basis for dependence and the parts of the brain involved in it are not fully known. The brain reward system, mentioned earlier in the contexts of motivation and emotion, allows a person to experience pleasure in response to pleasurable events or in response to certain drugs. Apparently, drugs that lead to dependence act on these neural pathways to increase drug-taking behavior. The nucleus accumbens (Figure 13-10), a structure that lies in the lower part of the forebrain and is part of the reward system is probably involved in addictive behavior. Three major neurotransmitter systems—dopamine, opioid, and GABA—are strongly implicated in addiction, but other transmitters—including glutamate—are being investigated.

According to popular opinion, people take drugs primarily to feel pleasure, but some researchers are presenting a different view. They believe that in people who are prone to drug dependence the neurotransmitters may be handled abnormally in the nerve pathways that are involved in depression, anger, or anxiety. By using drugs, addicts are self-medicating in an attempt to stabilize their emotions so they can feel normal and relaxed. In other cases, people take drugs primarily to avoid the discomfort of withdrawal. The underlying mechanism of withdrawal is still unknown, but one theory is described in the next section.

Tolerance. *Tolerance* to a drug occurs when increasing doses of the drug are required to achieve effects that initially occurred in response to a smaller dose; that is, it takes more of the drug to do the same job. Tolerance can develop to one drug as a result of taking another drug. In this case, it is called **cross-tolerance**. The word "tolerance" is also used loosely to refer to the individual variation in the amount of a substance a person can use before feeling ill effects. This type of tolerance appears to be inborn and is independent of the person's past history of drug use.

Tolerance that depends on previous drug usage may develop because the presence of the drug stimulates the synthesis, especially in the microsomal enzyme system (Chapter 20), of the enzymes that degrade it. As drug concentrations increase, so do the concentrations of the enzymes that degrade it. Thus, more of the drug must be administered to produce the same plasma concentrations of the drug and hence the same initial effect.

It has been hypothesized that tolerance can also develop as a result of changes in the number and/or sensitivity of receptors that respond to the drug. For example, the drug's effects might add to those of the normally occurring neurotransmitter, thereby producing an increased response that, by feedback mechanisms, decreases the release of the neurotransmitter. Let us use enkephalin—one of the endogenous opioids—and morphine to show how this theory might work.

Normally, enkephalin, which is a neurotransmitter in central nervous system pathways involved both in pain inhibition and in a sense of well-being, is continually released, at least to some degree, by the neurons that use it as their neurotransmitter. Accordingly, the enkephalin receptors are always exposed to a certain amount of stimulation (Figure 13-12). When morphine, an opiate drug that reacts with some of the receptors normally activated by enkephalin, is present, it binds to receptors not already occupied by enkephalin and thereby increases the analgesic-euphorigenic effects of the enkephalin pathways. As the enkephalin receptors in the postsynaptic neuron are stimulated more and more strongly, a feedback system acts on the *presynaptic* neuron, thereby decreasing its synthesis and release of enkephalin. The postsynaptic receptors, no longer receiving their usual amount of enkephalin, can therefore accept more morphine. In other words, to regain the previous analgesic-euphorigenic effects of full receptor activation, increased amounts of morphine are required.

FIGURE 13-12

Hypothesized steps in the production of morphine dependence in a person.

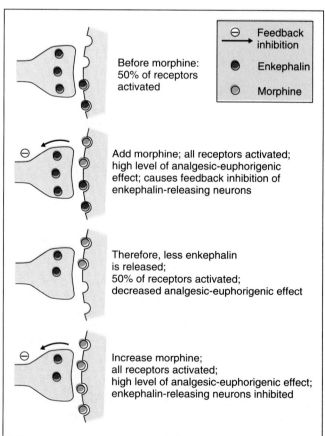

Before morphine: 50% of receptors activated

⊖ Feedback inhibition

● Enkephalin

○ Morphine

Add morphine; all receptors activated; high level of analgesic-euphorigenic effect; causes feedback inhibition of enkephalin-releasing neurons

Therefore, less enkephalin is released; 50% of receptors activated; decreased analgesic-euphorigenic effect

Increase morphine; all receptors activated; high level of analgesic-euphorigenic effect; enkephalin-releasing neurons inhibited

ESSAY

ALCOHOL: AN EXAMPLE

Medically, central nervous system depressants, such as alcohol, are used to produce sedation, sleep, and anesthesia. Nonmedicinally, these drugs are used for relaxation and relief from anxiety, to produce a mild euphoria, and to promote sleep. With repeated usage, they result in tolerance and both the physical and psychological forms of dependence.

Excess ingestion of alcohol causes a variety of central nervous system symptoms, for example, poor coordination, sluggish reflexes, emotional instability, and out-of-character behavior such as belligerence and aggression in a person typically shy, retiring, and mild-mannered. Sometimes, amnesia for events that happen during the intoxicated period (blackout) occurs.

The degree of intoxication relates to body size, amount of alcohol consumed, rapidity of drinking, tolerance, the presence or absence of food in the stomach, and many other factors. Individual response to alcohol consumption varies greatly, but signs of intoxication are almost always present at blood levels of 2000 mg/L, unconsciousness usually occurs when blood levels exceed 4000 mg/L, and death frequently occurs at concentrations above 5000 mg/L. A blood alcohol level of 1000 mg/L, or 0.1 g/dl, is the legal upper limit for driving a car in most states. Unconsciousness usually occurs before the person can drink enough to die, but the rapid consumption of large amounts of alcohol can cause death either by depression of the medullary respiratory center or by vomiting followed by aspiration of vomitus into the respiratory tract.

The length of the intoxication period ranges from several hours to 8 to 12 h or longer after alcohol consumption stops. More than 95 percent of the alcohol consumed is metabolized in the liver by oxidation to acetaldehyde and coenzyme A, and this occurs at a relatively slow rate. For example, it takes 5 to 6 h for the blood of an average-sized person to be cleared of the alcohol in 120 ml (4 oz) of whisky or 1.2 L (1.25 qt) of beer, and it takes up to 14 h for the ability to make accurate skilled maneuvers and sound judgments to return.

Withdrawal symptoms following cessation of prolonged, heavy drinking are tremors, nausea and vomiting, a dry mouth, headache and muscular weakness, nightmares, and feelings of anxiety, guilt, and irritability. Hallucinations and seizures can also occur. Withdrawal symptoms disappear in 5 to 7 days.

Alcohol produces a variety of central nervous system effects, and it is unclear which, if any, are related to the drug's behavioral effects. It is generally accepted that alcohol interacts with plasma membranes of neurons not by way of receptors but by causing nonspecific changes in the membranes' lipids and proteins. These nonspecific changes seem, however, to cause specific indirect changes in membrane receptors that are coupled to adenylyl cyclase or ion channels. In particular, alcohol increases the movement of chloride ions through GABA receptors, thereby increasing the effectiveness of the brain's major inhibitory neurotransmitter.

The benzodiazepines, such as Librium and Valium, and the barbiturates also interact with GABA receptors. This probably explains why drugs of these two classes and alcohol produce cross-tolerance and cross-dependence. Because of such interactions, the withdrawal symptoms suffered by a person who is addicted to alcohol, for example, can be relieved by taking either benzodiazepines or barbiturates.

These events could also explain withdrawal symptoms. When the drug is stopped (abstinence), the receptors receive neither the drug nor the normal neurotransmitter for some time since the neurotransmitter synthesis and release have been inhibited by previous prolonged drug use. This results in the physical symptoms of withdrawal. Withdrawal symptoms disappear as neurotransmitter release returns to normal levels.

Tolerance may also be due to changes in the postsynaptic cells. For example, concentrations of calcium and cAMP may change in response to continued drug usage.

LEARNING AND MEMORY

Learning is the acquisition and storage of information as a consequence of experience. It is measured by an increase in the likelihood of a particular behavioral response to a stimulus. Generally, rewards or punishments, as mentioned earlier, are crucial ingredients of learning, as is contact with and manipulation of the environment. **Memory** is the relatively permanent storage form of the learned information.

The neural circuits that connect a sensory event with a learned behavioral response to that event must have been altered in some way to support the learning. This change is called the **memory trace**. For example, if an animal learns to blink its eye in response to a tone, the learning can only be explained by some molecular or cellular change in the neural circuits between the ear and the motor neurons that control the eye muscles. It is important to note that the memory trace is the only part of those circuits that shows the training-induced behavioral changes. Just where the memory trace occurs and what form it takes are the paramount questions in the study of learning. We shall discuss them after a brief description of memory itself.

Memory

Depending on how long a memory lasts, it is designated as either **working memory**, a limited-capacity, short-term memory that lasts seconds to minutes, or **long-term memory**, which lasts hours, days, or years. The process of transferring memories from the working to the long-term form is called **memory consolidation** (Figure 13-13). When stored information suddenly becomes relevant and is retrieved from long-term memory, it returns to working memory, where it is accessed.

Working Memory. Working memory consists of the set of things we are paying attention to at any one time. It incorporates (1) the attention-focusing mechanisms that have been directed to a specific object, (2) the visual image or language-based information that is associated with that object, and (3) relevant stored data that have been retrieved from long-term memory. In working memory, information is simultaneously processed and stored.

The operations of working memory are carried out in the frontal lobes of the cerebral cortex, where discrete regions seem to be specialized for dealing with specific kinds of information. Thus, one area of the frontal cortex encodes information about the location of objects, whereas a different area encodes information about the objects' color, size, and shape.

Dopamine is one of the most important neurotransmitters in the operation of working memory.

The component of working memory that focuses attention is essential for many memory-based skills. The longer the span of attention in working memory, the better the chess player, the greater the ability to reason, and the better a student is at understanding complicated sentences and drawing inferences from texts. Conversely, the specific memory deficit in victims of Alzheimer's disease, a condition marked by serious memory losses, may be in this attention-focusing component of working memory.

Long-Term Memory. After their existence in working memory, memories may either fade away or be consolidated into long-term memories. Which of these two events happens depends on factors such as attention, motivation, and the levels of various neurotransmitters and hormones. For example, at specific synaptic sites within the brain, increasing levels of GABA decreases memory consolidation, whereas increasing brain levels of glutamate, acetylcholine, and norepinephrine enhance it. The hormones epinephrine, ACTH, and vasopressin also affect the retention of learned experiences. These hormones are normally released in response to stressful or even mildly stimulating experiences, suggesting that the hormonal consequences of our experiences affect our memories of them.

Two of the opioid peptides, enkephalin and endorphin, interfere with learning and memory, particularly when the lesson involves a painful stimulus. They may inhibit learning simply because they decrease the emotional (fear, anxiety) component of the painful experience associated with the learning situation, thereby decreasing the motivation necessary for learning to occur.

Memories can be consolidated very rapidly, sometimes after just one trial, and they can be retained over extended periods. Information can be retrieved from long-term memory stores after long periods of disuse, and the common notion that memory, like muscle, atrophies with lack of use is not always true. Also, unlike working memory, long-term memory has a seemingly unlimited capacity because people's memories never seem to be so full that they cannot learn something new.

Long-term memories are of two kinds: procedural and declarative. **Procedural memories** are those involved in

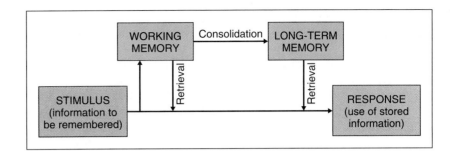

FIGURE 13-13

Events involved in learning and retrieving information.

remembering how to do something, such as ride a bike, whereas **declarative memories** are involved in remembering facts and events, for example, someone's name. Individuals can suffer from severe deficits in declarative memory but have intact procedural memory. One case study describes a pianist who learned a new piece to accompany a singer at a concert but had no recollection the following morning of having performed the composition. He could remember *how* to play the music but could not remember having done so.

The Location of Memory

Most researchers agree that memory traces are laid down in specific neural systems throughout the brain and that different types of memory tasks utilize different systems. For even a simple memory task, such as trying to recall a certain word from a previously seen word list, different specific parts of the brain are activated in sequence. It is as though there are several small "processors" linked together in a memory system for that type of memory task.

The structures most involved in declarative memories are the hippocampus (Figure 13-10) and the areas of the cerebral cortex that are closely associated with the limbic system. The cerebral cortex is essential for declarative memories. The hippocampus and the cerebral cortex that overlies it pull information together from the individual sites activated in the cerebral cortex during the working-memory phase that together represents an entire memory episode. The finding that people in whom the hippocampus has been destroyed are unable to form new declarative memories supports the importance of the hippocampus in memory functions.

Although the hippocampus is essential during early phases of learning, its role is temporary. Eventually, declarative memories are stored at other sites that are independent of the hippocampus.

The cerebellum is necessary for procedural learning, and the amygdala seems to be necessary for learning to avoid pain.

The Neural Basis of Learning and Memory

Working memory and long-term memory have different neural mechanisms. Conditions such as coma, deep anesthesia, electroconvulsive shock, and insufficient blood sup-

ply to the brain, all of which interfere with the electrical activity of the brain, interfere with working memory. Thus, it is assumed that working memory exists in the form of ongoing graded or action potentials. Working memory is interrupted when a person becomes unconscious from a blow on the head, and memories are abolished for all that happened for a variable period of time before the blow, so-called *retrograde amnesia*. (*Amnesia* is defined as the loss of memory.) Working memory is also susceptible to external interference, such as an attempt to learn conflicting information. On the other hand, long-term memory can survive deep anesthesia, trauma, or electroconvulsive shock, all of which disrupt the normal patterns of neural conduction in the brain.

As stated earlier, memory consolidation involves cellular or molecular changes in one or more neurons, and these changes constitute the memory trace. The changes are initiated by electrical activity in the neurons during working memory. This activity, in turn, causes alterations in synaptic effectiveness (pages 205–207) or even in the formation of new synapses.

One model for memory consolidation is **long-term potentiation (LTP)**, in which certain synapses undergo a long-lasting increase in their effectiveness when they are heavily used. This increased efficacy, which results in increased firing in the *postsynaptic* cell, can last minutes, hours, or even weeks. Although LTP occurs at many excitatory synapses in the central nervous system, it takes place most prominently in the hippocampus which, as we have just seen, is essential during the early phases of learning.

Learning is also associated with increased transmitter release from the *presynaptic* neuron. The postsynaptic cell must therefore inform the presynaptic cell in some way about its increased activity; in other words, information must move backward across the synapse. Candidates for this retrograde messenger are arachidonic acid, nitric oxide, and carbon monoxide because these compounds readily cross cell membranes and can diffuse back to the presynaptic neuron. Resulting changes in Ca^{2+} permeability alter the amount of neurotransmitter released from the presynaptic terminal in response to action potentials in the terminal. These changes can be long-lasting. Such changes occur in invertebrate systems during memory formation and probably occur in the human brain as well.

In contrast to working memory, long-term memory is associated with anatomical changes in the brain. Exposing experimental animals to enriched environments—ones containing toys, social situations, physical challenges, and so on—improved long-term memory. The enriched environments induced dramatic anatomical changes in the subjects' brains, particularly the cerebral cortex, hippocampus, and cerebellum. Compared to the brains of animals raised in isolation (an impoverished environment), the brains of animals in an enriched environment had more neuroglial cells, a more complex branching of neuron dendrites, an increase in the spines on nerve-cell processes, which serve as sites for synapses, and a change in the synapse structure. This ability of neural tissue to change because of its activation is known as **plasticity**.

When the isolated animals and enriched animals were later tested and compared in learning ability, the enriched animals learned faster. When the animals' brains were examined, a direct correlation was found between learning ability and the brain structural changes induced by the enriched environment: The greater the capability for learning, the greater the brain changes. Thus, structural changes may be associated with learning.

Plasticity occurs even when the enriched environment begins at middle or old age. This suggests that the patterns by which neurons are connected during youth continue to change throughout life.

CEREBRAL DOMINANCE AND LANGUAGE

The two cerebral hemispheres appear to be nearly symmetrical, but each has anatomical, chemical, and functional specializations. For example, in 90 percent of the population the left hemisphere is specialized to produce language—the conceptualization of what one wants to say or write, the neural control of the act of speaking or writing, and recent verbal memory. This is even true of the sign language used by deaf people.

Within the left cerebral cortex, the frontal, parietal, and temporal lobes all contain areas involved in language, but the areas are compartmentalized into distinct functional systems, each of which deals with a separate aspect of language. For example, there are distinct areas of the cerebral cortex that are specialized for hearing words, seeing words, speaking words, and generating words (Figure 13-14). Language usage, therefore, requires continual shifting between cortical systems depending on whether one is talking or reading, using verbs or nouns, or speaking English or French.

The cortical system for each particular language function consists of both an essential discrete area and neurons that are widely dispersed—even to the opposite hemisphere. The components of a given system, including the widespread neurons, function simultaneously (that is, in parallel) rather than one after another. This parallel activation of the systems may be controlled by the thalamus. The cerebellum is also important in speaking and writing, which involve coordinated muscle contractions.

Such neural specialization is demonstrated by the *aphasias*, specific language defects not due to mental retardation or paralysis of the muscles involved in speech. For example, in most people, damage to the left cerebral hemisphere, but not to the right, interferes with the capacity for language manipulation, and damage to different areas of the left cerebral hemisphere affects language use differently.

Many of the essential components of the various language systems are clustered within the frontal and temporal lobes, and damage to one or the other of these areas causes two main types of aphasia. Damage to the temporal region, known as **Wernicke's area** (Figure 13-15), results in aphasias that are more closely related to comprehension—the individuals have difficulty understanding spoken or written language even though their hearing and vision are unimpaired. In contrast, damage to **Broca's area**, the language area in the frontal cortex responsible for the articulation of speech, results in expressive aphasias—the individuals have difficulty carrying out the coordinated respiratory and oral movements necessary for language even though they can move their lips and tongues. They understand spoken language and know what they want to say but have trouble forming words and putting them into grammatical order. Although Wernicke's and Broca's areas are important language-processing regions, the functional language systems extend to many additional areas.

The anatomical and physiological asymmetries in the two hemispheres are present at birth but are fairly flexible in the early years of life. For example, after accidental damage to the left hemisphere of children under the age of 2, adequate (though perhaps not equal) language develops in the intact right hemisphere. In these children, however, defects occur in those functions, such as spatial localization, in which the right hemisphere normally plays a role; that is, language develops at the expense of usual right-hemisphere functions.

Even if the left hemisphere is traumatized in children after the onset of language development, functional language ability is reestablished to some extent in the right hemisphere after variable periods of loss. The transfer of language functions to the right hemisphere becomes rapidly worse as the age at which the damage occurs increases, so that after the early teens, language development in the right hemisphere is interfered with permanently.

The dramatic change in the teens in the possibility of learning language, or the ease of learning a second language, may be related to the fact that the brain attains its

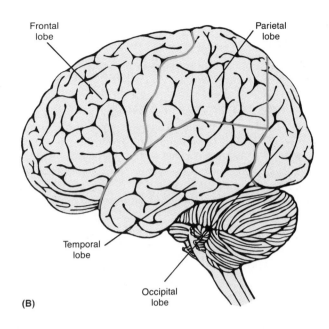

FIGURE 13-14 **(A)**

(A) PET scans reveal changes in blood flow during various language-based activities. *(Courtesy of Dr. Marcus E. Raichle.)* (B) An anatomical key for (A). Blue lines indicate divisions of the cortex into frontal, parietal, temporal, and occipital lobes.

structural, biochemical, and functional maturity at that time. Apparently, with brain maturation, language functions are irrevocably assigned, and for people with language specialization in the left hemisphere, utilization of the language propensities of the right hemisphere is no longer possible.

The left hemisphere is dominant for events that occur in sequences over time, such as those seen in language usage as, for example, speaking the first part of a word before the last. The right hemisphere, on the other hand, is thought to be specialized for processing information that is treated as a unified block, where occurrence over time is less important, such as the perception of faces and other three-dimensional objects.

Memories are handled differently in the two hemispheres, too, with verbal memories more apt to be associated with the left hemisphere, and nonverbal memories, for example, visual patterns, with the right. Even the emotional responses of the two hemispheres seem to be different. Thus, when electroconvulsive therapy is administered in the treatment of depression, better effects are often obtained when the electrodes are placed over the right hemisphere. The two sides of the brain also differ in their sensitivity to psychoactive drugs.

CONCLUSION

Until relatively recently it was thought that most complex mental acts are handled almost exclusively by specific limited regions of the cerebral cortex. Now it is understood that mental tasks are the result of synchro-nized activity in vast neuronal networks made up of many functional regions of the cerebral cortex and subcortical nuclei. Also important are the pathways that reciprocally connect these sites and orchestrate their performance during specific tasks. In fact, the nervous system is so abundantly interconnected that it is difficult to know where any particular subsystem begins or ends.

FIGURE 13-15

Areas found clinically to be involved in the comprehension (Wernicke's area) and motor (Broca's area) aspects of language. Blue lines indicate divisions of the cortex into frontal, parietal, temporal, and occipital lobes.

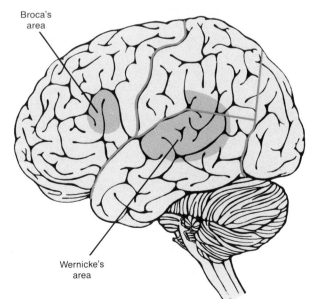

SUMMARY

Consciousness includes states of consciousness and conscious experiences.

STATES OF CONSCIOUSNESS

I. The electroencephalogram provides one means of defining the state of consciousness.

   A. Electric currents in the cerebral cortex due predominately to summed postsynaptic potentials are recorded as the EEG.

   B. Slower EEG waves correlate with less responsive behaviors.

   C. Rhythm generators in the thalamus are probably responsible for the wavelike nature of the EEG.

   D. EEG is used to diagnose brain disease and damage.

II. Alpha rhythms and, during EEG arousal, beta rhythms characterize the EEG of an awake person.

III. Slow-wave sleep progresses from stage 1 (faster, lower-amplitude waves) through stage 4 (slower, higher-amplitude waves) and then back again, followed by an episode of REM (paradoxical) sleep. There are generally four or five of these cycles per night.

IV. In the hypothalamus and brainstem, sleep-producing and arousal centers interact to cause the progressive sleep phases. The overall sleep-wake cycling is controlled by the suprachiasmatic nucleus in the hypothalamus. The hypothalamic centers use prostaglandins as neurotransmitters, whereas the brainstem centers use norepinephrine, serotonin, dopamine, and acetylcholine.

CONSCIOUS EXPERIENCES

I. Brain structures involved in directed attention determine which brain areas gain temporary predominance in the ongoing stream of conscious experience.

II. Conscious experiences might occur because a set of neurons temporarily functions together, the neurons comprising the set changing as the focus of attention changes.

MOTIVATION AND EMOTION

I. Behaviors that satisfy homeostatic needs are primary motivated behaviors. Behavior not related to homeostasis is a result of secondary motivation.

   A. Repetition of a behavior indicates that it is rewarding, and avoidance of a behavior indicates it is punishing.

   B. Lateral portions of the hypothalamus are involved in reward.

   C. Norepinephrine, dopamine, and enkephalin are transmitters in the brain pathways that mediate motivation and reward.

II. Two aspects of emotion, inner emotions and emotional behavior, can be distinguished. The limbic system integrates inner emotions and behavior.

ALTERED STATES OF CONSCIOUSNESS

I. Schizophrenics manifest either mainly positive or negative symptoms. Hyperactivity in brain dopaminergic systems is implicated in the disease.

II. The affective disorders are caused, at least in part, by disturbances in transmission at brain synapses mediated by dopamine or norepinephrine.

III. Many psychoactive drugs, which are often chemically related to neurotransmitters, result in drug dependence, withdrawal, and tolerance. These drug use patterns may result from homeostatic attempts to keep the transmitter-receptor interaction at a constant level.

LEARNING AND MEMORY

I. Depending on how long it lasts, memory is designated as working or long-term memory.

   A. Working memory has limited capacity, is short term, and depends on functioning brain electrical activity.

   B. After registering in working memory, facts either fade away or are consolidated in long-term memory, depending on attention, motivation, and various hormones.

   C. Long-term memory, of which there are two forms—procedural and declarative—has an unlimited capacity and is not destroyed by procedures that temporarily interrupt ongoing brain electrical activity.

II. Memory traces are cellular or molecular changes specific to different memories.

III. Learning is enhanced after subjects are exposed to enriched environments. The enhancement is presumably due to the brain neural and chemical development that follows such exposure.

CEREBRAL DOMINANCE AND LANGUAGE

I. The two cerebral hemispheres differ anatomically, chemically, and functionally. In 90 percent of the population, the left hemisphere is superior at producing language and in performing other tasks that require rapid changes over time.

II. After damage to the dominant hemisphere, some language function can be acquired by the opposite hemisphere—the younger the patient, the greater the transfer of function.

CONCLUSION

I. Many brain units are involved in the performance of even simple mental tasks.

II. Each unit is localized to a specific brain area, but, because many units are involved, widely distributed brain areas take part in mental tasks.

KEY TERMS

states of consciousness
conscious experiences
electroencephalogram (EEG)
alpha rhythm
beta rhythm
EEG arousal
slow-wave sleep
REM sleep
paradoxical sleep
preoptic area
directed attention
orienting response
preattentive processing
habituation
motivations
primary motivated behavior
brain self-stimulation

emotions
inner emotions
emotional behavior
affect
learning
memory
memory trace
working memory
long-term memory
memory consolidation
procedural memories
declarative memories
long-term potentiation
plasticity
Wernicke's area
Broca's area

REVIEW QUESTIONS

1. State the two criteria used to define one's state of consciousness.
2. What type of neural activity is recorded as the EEG?
3. Draw EEG records that show alpha and beta rhythms, the stages of slow-wave sleep, and REM sleep. Indicate the characteristic wave frequencies of each.
4. Using four characteristics, distinguish slow-wave sleep from REM sleep.
5. Briefly describe the neural mechanisms that determine the states of consciousness.
6. Name the criteria used to distinguish brain death from coma.
7. Describe the orienting response as a form of directed attention.
8. State two criteria that determine whether an experience will be conscious.
9. List the effects that unconscious processes can have on mental experiences.
10. Distinguish primary from secondary motivated behavior.
11. Explain how rewards and punishments are anatomically related to emotions.

12. Explain what brain self-stimulation can tell about emotions and rewards and punishments.
13. Name two neurotransmitters that mediate the brain reward systems.
14. Distinguish inner emotions from emotional behavior. Name the brain areas involved in each.
15. Describe the role of the limbic system in emotions.
16. Name the neurotransmitters involved in schizophrenia and the affective disorders.
17. Describe a mechanism that could explain tolerance and withdrawal.
18. Distinguish working memory from long-term memory and explain the relationship between them.
19. Name three factors that influence memory consolidation.
20. Explain how we can say that basic neural units are "strictly localized to specific parts of the brain" and yet say that "mental tasks are not performed by any single area of the brain."

CLINICAL TERMS

epilepsy
sleep apnea
narcolepsy
African sleeping sickness
brain death
altered states of
   consciousness
schizophrenia
catatonia
dopamine hypothesis
affective disorders
depressions
manias
bipolar affective disorders

tricyclic antidepressant
   drugs
monoamine oxidase
   inhibitors
electroconvulsive
   therapy (ECT)
drug dependence
withdrawal
tolerance
cross-tolerance
retrograde amnesia
amnesia
aphasias

THOUGHT QUESTIONS

(Answers are given in Appendix A.)

1. Explain why patients given drugs to treat Parkinson's disease (pages 360–361) sometimes develop symptoms similar to those of schizophrenia.
2. Explain how clinical observations of individuals with various aphasias help physiologists understand the neural basis of language.

THREE

COORDINATED BODY FUNCTIONS

CHAPTER
14

CIRCULATION

Beyond a distance of a few cell diameters, diffusion—the random movement of substances from a region of high concentration to one of low concentration—is not sufficiently rapid to meet the metabolic requirements of cells. For multicellular organisms to evolve to a size larger than a microscopic cluster of cells, some mechanism other than diffusion was needed to transport molecules rapidly over the long distances between internal cells and the body's surface and between the various specialized tissues and organs. This problem was solved in the animal kingdom by the **circulatory system**, which comprises the blood, the set of interconnected tubes (**blood vessels** or **vascular system**) through which the blood flows, and a pump (the **heart**) that produces this flow. The heart and blood vessels together are termed the **cardiovascular system**.

SECTION

BLOOD

Blood is composed of cells and a liquid, **plasma**, in which they are suspended. The cells are the **erythrocytes** (red blood cells), the **leukocytes** (white blood cells), and the **platelets**, which are not complete cells but cell fragments. More than 99 percent of the cells are erythrocytes, which are the oxygen-carrying cells of the blood. The leukocytes protect against infection and cancer. The platelets function in blood clotting. In the cardiovascular system, the constant motion of the blood keeps all the cells well dispersed throughout the plasma.

The **hematocrit** is defined as the percentage of total blood volume that is erythrocytes. It is determined by centrifuging (spinning at high speed) a sample of blood, the erythrocytes being forced to the bottom of the centrifuge tube and the plasma to the top, the leukocytes and platelets forming a very thin layer between them (Figure 14-1). The normal hematocrit is approximately 45 percent in men and 42 percent in women.

The total blood volume of an average person is approximately 5.5 L. If we take the hematocrit to be 45 percent, then

$$\text{Total erythrocyte volume} = 0.45 \times 5.5 \text{ L} = 2.5 \text{ L}$$

Therefore,

$$\text{Plasma volume} = 5.5 \text{ L} - 2.5 \text{ L} = 3.0 \text{ L}$$

This last calculation ignores the volume occupied by the leukocytes and platelets because it is normally so small.

anemic = RBC count ↓ though same volume

infection = WBC count ↑

serum = plasma − fibrinogen

Plasma = 55%

Leukocytes and platelets *(reflects light differently)* *↓ for clotting*

Erythrocytes = 45% (hematocrit = 45%)

FIGURE 14-1

If a blood-filled capillary tube is centrifuged, the erythrocytes become packed in the lower portion, and the percentage of blood that is erythrocytes can be determined. This is called the hematocrit. The leukocytes and platelets form a very thin layer, known as a buffy coat, between the plasma and red cells. Its presence explains why, in this example, the value for plasma determined by this method is actually slightly less than 55 percent.

PLASMA

Plasma, the liquid portion of the blood, consists of a large number of organic and inorganic substances dissolved in water (Table 14-1). Most **plasma proteins** can be classified, according to certain physical and chemical reactions, into three broad groups: the **albumins** and **globulins**, which have many overlapping functions summarized in Table 14-1 and described in relevant chapters, and **fibrinogen**, which functions in blood clotting (Chapter 20). The albumins are by far the most abundant of these three groups and are synthesized by the liver.

It must be emphasized that the plasma proteins normally are not taken up by cells. Cells use plasma amino acids, not plasma proteins, to make their own proteins. Accordingly, plasma proteins must be viewed quite differently from most of the other organic constituents of plasma, which use the plasma as a vehicle for transport but are used by cells. The plasma proteins perform their functions in the plasma itself or in the interstitial fluid.

Serum is plasma from which fibrinogen and other proteins involved in clotting have been removed as a result of clotting.

In addition to the organic solutes—proteins, nutrients, and metabolic waste products—plasma contains a variety of mineral electrolytes. Note in Table 14-1 that these ions constitute much less of the weight of plasma than the proteins do but in most cases have much higher molar concentrations. This is because molarity is a measure not of *weight* but of *number* of molecules or ions per unit volume. Thus, there are many more ions than protein molecules, but the protein molecules are so large that a very small number of them greatly outweighs the much larger number of ions.

The characteristic straw color of plasma is due largely to a waste product of hemoglobin breakdown called **bilirubin**, which will be described in a later section.

THE BLOOD CELLS

Erythrocytes

Erythrocytes have the shape of a biconcave disk, that is, a disk thicker at the edge than in the middle, like a doughnut with a center depression on each side instead of a hole (Figure 14-2). Their shape and small size (7 μm in diameter) impart to them a high surface-to-volume ratio, so that oxygen and carbon dioxide can rapidly diffuse to and from the interior of the cell. The plasma membrane of erythrocytes contains specific polysaccharides and proteins that differ from person to person, and these confer upon the blood its so-called type, or group. Our description of blood groups is best delayed until Chapter 20, where it can be

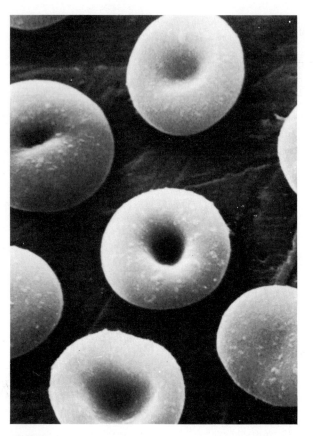

FIGURE 14-2

Scanning electron micrograph of erythrocytes. (*From R. G. Kessel and C. Y. Shih, "Scanning Electron Microscopy in Biology," Springer-Verlag, New York, 1974, p. 265.*)

[handwritten annotations:]
- *easier diapodesis = when get bumped against arteries/-ioles, not shatter*
- *O₂ gets in very quickly b/c w/o dead cntr*

done in the context of the immune responses that occur in so-called transfusion reactions.

Erythrocytes contain the protein **hemoglobin**, which binds oxygen taken in by the lungs. Each erythrocyte contains 200 to 300 million hemoglobin molecules, which constitute approximately one-third of the total weight of the erythrocyte. Each hemoglobin molecule is made up of four subunits bound together. Each subunit consists of a molecular group known as **heme** and a polypeptide attached to the heme. The four polypeptides of a hemoglobin molecule are collectively called **globin**. Each of the four heme groups in a hemoglobin molecule (Figure 14-3) contains one atom of iron (Fe), which can bind one molecule of oxygen. Thus, a single hemoglobin molecule can bind four molecules of oxygen. The average concentration of hemoglobin in blood is 14 g/dl in women and 16 g/dl in men. Hemoglobin is not the only heme-containing protein in the body; the other major ones are the cytochromes (Chapter 5).

The site of erythrocyte production is the soft interior of bones called **bone marrow**, specifically the "red" bone

TABLE 14-1 CONSTITUENTS OF PLASMA

Constituent	Amount/concentration	Major functions
Water	93% of plasma weight	Medium for carrying all other constituents
Electrolytes (inorganic)	Total < 1% of plasma weight	Keep H_2O in extracellular compartment; act as buffers; function in membrane excitability and blood clotting
Na^+	145 mM	
K^+	4 mM	
Ca^{2+}	2.5 mM	
Mg^{2+}	1.5 mM	
Cl^-	103 mM	
HCO_3^-	24 mM	
Phosphate (mostly HPO_4^{2-})	1 mM	
SO_4^{2-}	0.5 mM	
Proteins	Total = 7% of plasma weight, 7.3 g/100 ml (2.5 mM)	Provide nonpenetrating solutes of plasma; act as buffers; bind and transport other plasma constituents (lipids, hormones, vitamins, metals, etc.); clotting factors; enzymes; enzyme precursors; antibodies (immune globulins); hormones
Albumins	4.5 g/100 ml	
Globulins	2.5 g/100 ml	
Fibrinogen	0.3 g/100 ml	Blood clotting
Gases		
CO_2	2 ml/100 ml (1 mM)	No function; a waste product
O_2	0.2 ml/100 ml (0.1 mM)	Oxidative metabolism
N_2	0.9 ml/100 ml (0.5 mM)	No function
Nutrients		
Glucose and other carbohydrates	100 mg/100 ml (5.6 mM)	
Total amino acids	40 mg/100 ml (2 mM)	
Total lipids	500 mg/100 ml (7.5 mM)	
Cholesterol	150–250 mg/100 ml (4–7 mM)	
Individual vitamins	0.0001–2.5 mg/100 ml (0.00005–0.1 mM)	
Individual trace elements	0.001–0.3 mg/100 ml (0.0001–0.01 mM)	
Waste products		
Urea (from protein)	34 mg/100 ml (5.7 mM)	
Creatinine (from creatine)	1 mg/100 ml (0.09 mM)	
Uric acid (from nucleic acids)	5 mg/100 ml (0.3 mM)	
Bilirubin (from heme)	0.2–1.2 mg/100 ml (0.003–0.018 mM)	
Individual hormones	0.000001–0.05 mg/100 ml (10^{-9}–10^{-6} mM)	

(handwritten note: Albumins, Globulins — made in liver; act as acidity buffers)

marrow. As differentiation occurs, these cells begin to produce hemoglobin but then ultimately lose their nuclei and organelles. Young erythrocytes in the bone marrow still contain a few ribosomes, which produce a weblike (reticular) appearance when treated with special stains, an appearance that gives these young erythrocytes the name **reticulocyte**. Normally, only mature erythrocytes, which have lost these ribosomes, leave the bone marrow and enter the general circulation. In the presence of unusually rapid erythrocyte production, however, many reticulocytes do enter the blood.

Because erythrocytes lack nuclei and organelles, they can neither reproduce themselves nor maintain their normal structure for very long. The average life span of an

1 hemoglobin = 1 globin + 4 heme's (ie, 4 Fe's)

FIGURE 14-3
Heme. Oxygen binds to the iron atom (Fe). Heme attaches to a polypeptide chain by a nitrogen atom to form one subunit of hemoglobin. Four of these subunits bind to each other to make a single hemoglobin molecule.

erythrocyte is approximately 120 days, which means that almost 1 percent of the body's erythrocytes are destroyed and must be replaced every day. This amounts to 100 billion cells per day! Erythrocyte destruction normally occurs in the spleen and the liver. As will be described below, most of the iron released in the process is conserved. The major breakdown product of heme is bilirubin, which, as noted above, gives plasma its color (the fate of this substance will be described in Chapter 17).

The production of erythrocytes requires the usual nutrients needed to synthesize any cell: amino acids, lipids, and carbohydrates. In addition, both iron and certain growth factors, including folic acid and vitamin B_{12}, are essential.

Iron. As noted above, **iron** is the element to which oxygen binds within an erythrocyte. Small amounts of iron are lost via the urine, feces, sweat, and cells sloughed from the skin. In addition, women lose a similar amount via menstrual blood. In order to remain in iron balance, the amount of iron lost from the body must be replaced by ingestion of iron-containing foods—particularly rich sources are meat, liver, shellfish, egg yolk, beans, nuts, and cereals. A significant upset of iron balance can result either in **iron deficiency**, leading to inadequate hemoglobin production, or in an excess of iron in the body, with serious toxic effects.

The homeostatic control of iron balance resides primarily in the intestinal epithelium, which actively absorbs iron from ingested food. Only a small fraction of ingested iron is normally absorbed, but what is more important, this

fraction is increased or decreased, in a negative-feedback manner, depending upon the state of the body's iron balance. These fluctuations are mediated by changes in the iron content of the intestinal epithelium (Chapter 17): The more iron in the body, the more in the intestinal epithelium, and the less new iron will be absorbed.

A buffer against iron deficiency is the considerable body store of iron, mainly in the liver, bound up in a protein called **ferritin**. About 50 percent of the total body iron is in hemoglobin, 25 percent is in heme-containing proteins (mainly the cytochromes) in other cells of the body, and 25 percent is in liver ferritin. Moreover, the recycling of iron is very efficient (Figure 14-4): As old erythrocytes are destroyed in the spleen and liver, their iron is released into the plasma and bound to an iron-transport protein called **transferrin**. Almost all of this iron is delivered by transferrin to the bone marrow to be incorporated into new erythrocytes. On a much lesser scale, other organs and tissues, some cells of which are continuously dying and being replaced, release iron from their cytochromes into the plasma and take up iron from it, transferrin serving as the carrier.

Folic Acid and Vitamin B_{12}. **Folic acid**, a vitamin found in large amounts in leafy plants, yeast, and liver, is required for synthesis of the pyrimidine thymine. It is, therefore, essential for the formation of DNA, and hence for normal cell division. When this vitamin is not present in adequate amounts, impairment of cell division occurs throughout the body but is most striking in rapidly proliferating cells, including erythrocyte precursors. Thus, fewer erythrocytes are produced when folic acid is deficient.

Production of normal erythrocyte numbers also requires extremely small quantities (one-millionth of a gram per day) of a cobalt-containing molecule, **vitamin B_{12}** (also called **cobalamin**), since this vitamin is required for the action of folic acid. Vitamin B_{12} is found only in animal products, and strictly vegetarian diets may be deficient in it. Also, as described in Chapter 17, the absorption of vitamin B_{12} from the gastrointestinal tract requires a protein, called **intrinsic factor**, which is secreted by the stomach; lack of this protein also causes vitamin B_{12} deficiency. Unlike folic acid, vitamin B_{12} is also needed for myelin formation, so a variety of neurological symptoms may accompany the poor erythrocyte production when vitamin B_{12} is deficient.

Regulation of Erythrocyte Production. In a normal person, the total volume of circulating erythrocytes remains remarkably constant because of reflexes that regulate the bone marrow's production of these cells. In the previous section, we stated that iron, folic acid, and vitamin B_{12} must be present for normal erythrocyte produc-

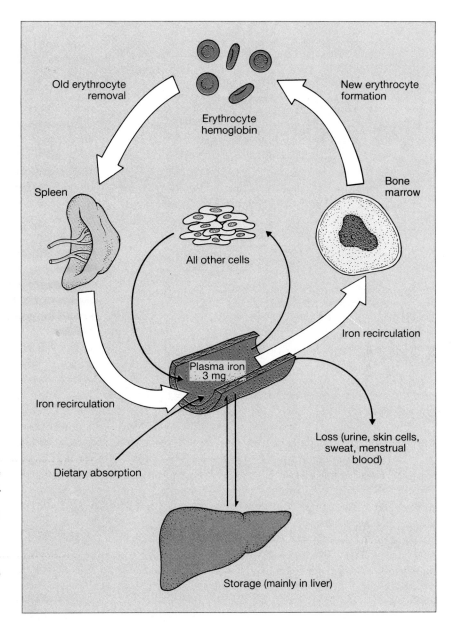

FIGURE 14-4

Summary of iron balance. The thickness of the arrows corresponds approximately to the amount of iron involved. In the steady state, the rate of gastrointestinal iron absorption and the rate of iron loss via urine, skin, and menstrual flow are equal. The rate of absorption is the major homeostatically controlled process. Recirculation of erythrocyte iron is very important because it involves 20 times more iron per day than is absorbed and excreted. (*Adapted from Crosby.*)

tion. However, none of these substances constitutes the signal that *regulates* production rate.

The direct control of erythrocyte production (erythropoiesis) is exerted mainly by a hormone called **erythropoietin**, which is secreted into the blood by capillary endothelial cells in the kidneys (and, to a much lesser extent, the liver). Erythropoietin acts on the bone marrow to stimulate the proliferation of erythrocyte progenitor cells and their differentiation into erythrocytes.

Erythropoietin is normally secreted in relatively small amounts, which stimulate the bone marrow to produce erythrocytes at a rate adequate to replace the usual loss. The erythropoietin secretion rate can be increased markedly above basal values, the stimulus being a decreased oxygen delivery to the kidneys. As a result of the increase

in erythropoietin secretion, plasma erythropoietin concentration, erythrocyte production, and the oxygen-carrying capacity of the blood all increase; therefore, oxygen delivery to the tissues returns toward normal (Figure 14-5).

Testosterone also stimulates the release of erythropoietin. This may account, at least in part, for the higher hemoglobin concentration in men than in women.

Anemia. Defined as (1) a decrease in the total number of erythrocytes, each having a normal quantity of hemoglobin, or (2) a diminished concentration of hemoglobin per erythrocyte, or (3) a combination of both, *anemia* has a wide variety of causes, summarized in Table 14-2.

The last disease—*sickle-cell anemia*—mentioned in Table 14-2 is due to a genetic mutation that causes substi-

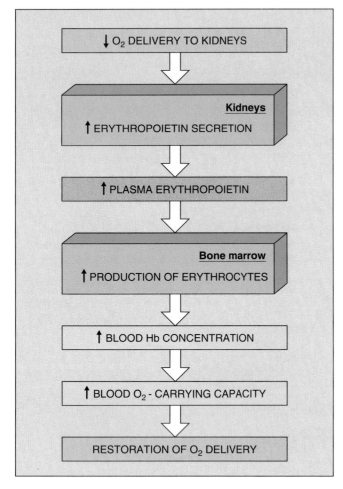

↓ O₂ DELIVERY TO KIDNEYS

Kidneys
↑ ERYTHROPOIETIN SECRETION

↑ PLASMA ERYTHROPOIETIN

Bone marrow
↑ PRODUCTION OF ERYTHROCYTES

↑ BLOOD Hb CONCENTRATION

↑ BLOOD O₂ - CARRYING CAPACITY

RESTORATION OF O₂ DELIVERY

FIGURE 14-5

Reflex by which a decreased oxygen delivery to the kidneys increases erythrocyte production via increased erythropoietin secretion. Situations that trigger this reflex include insufficient pumping of blood by the heart, lung disease, anemia (a decrease in number of erythrocytes or in hemoglobin concentration), and exposure to high altitude. The exact mechanism by which a decreased oxygen delivery stimulates erythropoietin secretion by the renal endothelial cells is unclear.

TABLE 14-2 MAJOR CAUSES OF ANEMIA

1. Dietary deficiencies of iron, vitamin B₁₂ (***pernicious anemia***), or folic acid
2. Bone marrow failure due to toxic drugs or cancer
3. Blood loss from the body (***hemorrhage***) leading to iron deficiency
4. Inadequate secretion of erythropoietin in kidney disease
5. Excessive destruction of erythrocytes (for example, ***sickle-cell anemia***)

---

tution of one wrong amino acid in a particular portion of globin. At the low oxygen concentrations existing in many capillaries, the abnormal hemoglobin molecules interact with each other to form fiber-like structures that distort the erythrocyte membrane and cause the cell to form sickle shapes or other bizarre forms. This results both in the blockage of capillaries, with consequent tissue damage and pain, and in the destruction of the deformed erythrocytes, with consequent anemia.

Laboratory evaluation of anemia starts with analysis of a blood sample for the concentration of hemoglobin, the number of erythrocytes, and the average cell size. Average cell size is particularly useful since it correlates well with several common types of anemia. For example, ***microcytosis*** (small cells) most commonly occurs in iron deficiency, ***normocytosis*** (normal-sized cells) accompanies acute blood loss, and ***macrocytosis*** (large cells) is characteristic of vitamin B₁₂ or folic acid deficiency. Macrocytosis is due to delayed cell division because of a DNA deficiency.

Finally, there also exist conditions in which the problem is just the opposite of anemia, namely, too many erythrocytes; this is termed ***polycythemia***.

Leukocytes

If one adds appropriate dyes to a drop of blood and examines it under a microscope, the various leukocyte types (Table 14-3) can be seen clearly (Figure 14-6). They are classified according to their structure and affinity for various dyes.

TABLE 14-3 NUMBERS AND DISTRIBUTIONS OF ERYTHROCYTES, LEUKOCYTES, AND PLATELETS IN NORMAL HUMAN BLOOD

Total erythrocytes = 5,000,000 per mm³ of blood

Total leukocytes = 7000 per mm³ of blood

Percent of total leukocytes:
Polymorphonuclear granulocytes
Neutrophils 50–70
Eosinophils 1–4
Basophils 0.1
Monocytes 2–8
Lymphocytes 20–40

Total platelets = 250,000 per mm³ of blood

The name **polymorphonuclear granulocytes** refers to the three types of leukocytes with multilobed nuclei and abundant membrane-bound granules. The granules of one group take up the red dye eosin, thus giving the cells their name **eosinophils**. Cells of a second group have an affinity for a blue dye termed a "basic" dye and are called

Erythrocytes	Leukocytes					Platelets
	Polymorphonuclear granulocytes			Monocytes	Lymphocytes	
	Neutrophils	Eosinophils	Basophils			
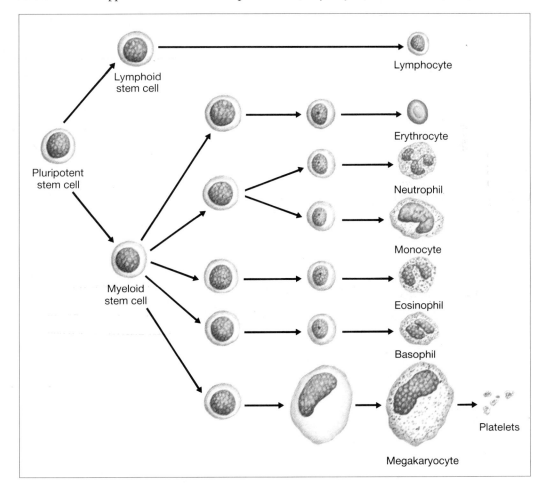	most common	red	blue			

FIGURE 14-6

Normal blood cell types.

basophils. The granules of the third group have only little affinity for either dye and are therefore called **neutrophils**. Neutrophils are by far the most abundant type of leukocyte.

A fourth type of leukocyte is the **monocyte**, which is somewhat larger than the granulocyte and has an oval or horseshoe-shaped nucleus and relatively few cytoplasmic granules. The final class of leukocytes is the **lymphocyte**, which contains scanty cytoplasm and, like the monocyte, a relatively large nucleus.

Like the erythrocytes, all types of leukocytes are produced in the bone marrow. In addition, monocytes and

 FIGURE 14-7

Production of blood cells by the bone marrow. For simplicity, no attempt has been made to differentiate the appearance of the various precursors. (*Adapted from Golde and Gasson.*)

many lymphocytes undergo further development and cell division in tissues outside the bone marrow, as described in Chapter 20. These events and the specific leukocyte functions in the body's defenses are discussed in Chapter 20.

Platelets

The circulating platelets are colorless cell fragments that contain numerous granules and are much smaller than erythrocytes. Platelets are produced when the cytoplasm of large bone marrow cells, termed **megakaryocytes**, becomes pinched off and enters the circulation. Platelet functions in blood clotting are described in Chapter 20.

Regulation of Blood Cell Production

In children, the marrow of most bones produces blood cells. By adulthood, however, only the bones of the chest, the base of the skull, and the upper portions of the limbs remain active. The bone marrow in an adult weighs almost as much as the liver, and it produces cells at an enormous rate.

All blood cell types are descended from a single population of bone marrow cells called **pluripotent stem cells**, which are undifferentiated cells capable of giving rise to precursors (progenitors) of any of the individual cell types (Figure 14-7). When a pluripotent stem cell divides, its two daughter cells either remain pluripotent stem cells or become committed to a particular developmental pathway—what governs this "decision" is not known. The first branching yields lymphoid stem cells, which give rise to the lymphocytes, and myeloid stem cells, the progenitors of all the other types. At some point, the proliferating offspring of the myeloid stem cells become committed to differentiate along only one path, for example, into erythrocytes.

Production of the various cells is stimulated at multiple points by at least 12 protein hormones collectively termed **hematopoietic growth factors (HGFs)**. Erythropoietin, described above, is one such hormone. Another group of HGFs are called **colony-stimulating factors (CSFs)** because they were originally discovered to stimulate the formation of colonies derived from individual bone marrow progenitors. The major effects of the CSFs are to stimulate the cell lines leading to granulocytes and monocytes. Still another group of HGFs belong to the family of hormones called **interleukins** for their ability to mediate communication between leukocytes, as described in Chapter 20.

The physiology of the HGFs is very complex since there are so many of them and since any given HGF often is produced by a variety of cell types throughout the body and exerts actions other than stimulating blood-cell production in the bone marrow. There are, moreover, many interactions of the HGFs on particular bone marrow cells and processes. For example, although erythropoietin is the major stimulator of erythropoiesis, at least 10 other HGFs cooperate in the process. Finally, the HGFs also enhance the function of blood cells after these cells' release from the bone marrow into the blood.

The administration of specific HGFs is proving to be of considerable clinical importance. Examples are the use of erythropoietin in persons with a deficiency of this hormone due to kidney disease, and the use of granulocyte CSF to stimulate granulocyte production in individuals whose bone marrow has been damaged.

SECTION A SUMMARY

I. Blood is composed of cells (erythrocytes, leukocytes, and platelets) and plasma, the liquid in which the cells are suspended.

II. Plasma contains proteins (albumins, globulins, and fibrinogen), nutrients, metabolic end products, hormones, and mineral electrolytes.

III. Erythrocytes, which make up more than 99 percent of blood cells, contain hemoglobin, an oxygen-binding protein consisting of heme and globin. Oxygen binds to the iron in heme.
   A. Erythrocytes are produced in the bone marrow and destroyed in the spleen and liver.
   B. Iron, folic acid, and vitamin B_{12} are essential for erythrocyte formation.
   C. The hormone erythropoietin, which is produced by the kidneys in response to low oxygen supply, stimulates erythrocyte differentiation and production by the bone marrow.
   D. Anemia can be caused not only by a deficiency of iron, vitamin B_{12}, or folic acid but also by bone marrow failure, excessive blood loss, excessive destruction of erythrocytes, and an erythropoietin deficiency.

IV. The leukocytes include three types of polymorphonuclear granulocytes (neutrophils, eosinophils, and basophils), monocytes, and lymphocytes.

V. Platelets are cell fragments essential for blood clotting.

VI. Blood cells are descended from stem cells in the bone marrow. Their production is controlled by hematopoietic growth factors.

SECTION A KEY TERMS

circulatory system	iron
blood vessels	ferritin
vascular system	transferrin
heart	folic acid
cardiovascular system	vitamin B_{12}
blood	cobalamin
plasma	intrinsic factor
erythrocytes	erythropoietin
leukocytes	polymorphonuclear
platelets	granulocytes
hematocrit	eosinophils
plasma proteins	basophils
albumins	neutrophils
globulins	monocytes
fibrinogen	lymphocytes
serum	megakaryocytes
bilirubin	pluripotent stem cells
hemoglobin	hematopoietic growth factors
heme	(HGFs)
globin	colony-stimulating factors
bone marrow	(CSFs)
reticulocytes	interleukins

SECTION A REVIEW QUESTIONS

1. Give average values for total blood volume, erythrocyte volume, plasma volume, and hematocrit.
2. Which is the most abundant class of plasma protein?
3. Which solute has the highest concentration in plasma?
4. Describe the structure of hemoglobin.
5. Summarize the production, life span, and destruction of erythrocytes.
6. What are the routes of iron gain, loss, and distribution, and how is iron recycled when erythrocytes are destroyed?
7. Describe the control of erythropoietin secretion and the effect of this hormone.
8. State the relative proportions of erythrocytes and leukocytes in blood.
9. Diagram the derivation of the different blood cell lines.
10. List the different hematopoietic growth factors.

SECTION

B

OVERALL DESIGN OF THE CARDIOVASCULAR SYSTEM

The rapid flow of blood throughout the body is produced by pressures created by the pumping action of the heart. This type of flow is known as **bulk flow** because all constituents of the blood move in one direction together. The extraordinary degree of branching of blood vessels ensures that almost all cells in the body are within a few cell diameters of at least one of the smallest branches, the capillaries. Nutrients and metabolic end products move between capillary blood and the interstitial fluid by diffusion. Movements between the interstitial fluid and cell interior are by diffusion and medicated transport.

At any given moment, approximately 5 percent of the total circulating blood is flowing through the capillaries. Yet it is this 5 percent that is performing the ultimate functions of the entire cardiovascular system: the supplying of nutrients and the removal of metabolic end products. All

other components of the system subserve the overall aim of getting adequate blood flow through the capillaries. This point should be kept in mind as we describe these components.

As discovered by the British physiologist William Harvey in 1628, the cardiovascular system forms a circle, so that blood pumped out of the heart through one set of vessels returns to the heart via a different set. There are actually two circuits (Figure 14-8), both originating and terminating in the heart, which is divided longitudinally into two functional halves. Each half contains two chambers: an **atrium** and a **ventricle**. The atrium on each side empties into the ventricle on that side, but there is no direct communication between the two atria or the two ventricles.

Blood is pumped via one circuit (the **pulmonary cir-**

O₂ lost from RBC's via diffusion.
arteries = thick-walled, so no diffusion
of materials; low resistance

arterioles =
↑ resistance

veins = low
resistance

LUNGS

BODY

✗ **FIGURE 14-8**

The systemic and pulmonary circulations. The pulmonary circulation pumps blood through
the lungs, and the systemic circulation supplies all other organs and tissues. As depicted by
the color change from blue to red, blood is fully oxygenated as it flows through the lungs
and then loses some oxygen (red to blue) as it flows through the other organs and tissues.
For simplicity, the arteries and veins leaving and entering the heart are depicted as single
vessels; in reality, this is true for the arteries but not for the veins (see Figure 14-9).

culation) from the right ventricle through the lungs and
then to the left atrium. It is then pumped through the
systemic circulation, from the left ventricle through all

the tissues of the body except the lungs and then to the
right atrium. In both circuits, the vessels carrying blood
away from the heart are called **arteries**, and those carry-

ing blood from either the lungs or all other parts of the body (peripheral organs and tissues) back to the heart are called **veins**.

In the systemic circuit, blood leaves the left ventricle via a single large artery, the **aorta** (Figure 14-9). The systemic arteries come off the aorta, dividing into progressively smaller branches. The smallest arteries branch into **arterioles**, which branch into a huge number of very small vessels—the **capillaries**, which unite to form larger-diameter vessels—**venules**. The arterioles, capillaries, and venules are collectively termed the **microcirculation**.

The venules in the systemic circulation then unite to form larger vessels, the veins. The veins from the various peripheral organs and tissues unite to produce two large veins, the **inferior vena cava**, which collects blood from the lower portion of the body, and the **superior vena cava**, which collects blood from the upper half of the body. It is via these two veins that blood is returned to the right atrium.

The pulmonary circulation is composed of a similar circuit. Blood leaves the right ventricle via a single large artery, the **pulmonary trunk**, which divides into two **pulmonary arteries**, one supplying the right lung and the other the left. In the lungs, the arteries continue to branch, ultimately forming capillaries that unite into venules and then veins. The blood leaves the lungs via four **pulmonary veins**, which empty into the left atrium.

As blood flows through the lung capillaries, it picks up oxygen supplied to the adjacent lung air sacs by breathing. Therefore, the blood in the pulmonary veins, left heart, and systemic arteries has a high oxygen content. As this blood flows through the capillaries of peripheral tissues

FIGURE 14-9

Blood leaves each of the ventricles via a single artery, the pulmonary trunk from the right ventricle and the aorta from the left ventricle. [Because the aorta and pulmonary trunk cross each other before emerging from the heart (Figure 14-13), one gets the mistaken impression that the aorta arises from the right ventricle and pulmonary trunk from the left ventricle.] Blood enters the right atrium via two large veins, the superior vena cava and inferior vena cava; it enters the left atrium via four pulmonary veins.

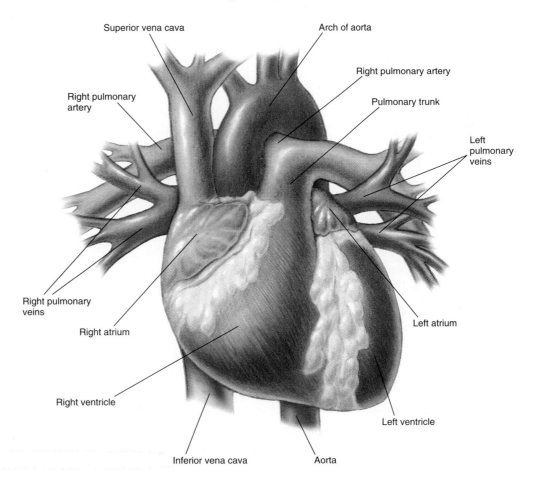

	Rest ml/min
Brain	750 (13%)
Heart	250 (4%)
Muscle	1200 (20%)
Skin	500 (9%)
Kidney	1100 (20%)
Abdominal organs	1400 (24%)
Other	600 (10%)
Total	5800

FIGURE 14-10

Distribution of systemic blood flow to the various organs and tissues of the body at rest. (*Adapted from Chapman and Mitchell.*)

and organs, some of this oxygen leaves the blood to enter and be used by cells, resulting in the lower oxygen content of systemic venous blood.

As shown in Figure 14-8, blood can pass from the systemic veins to the systemic arteries only by first being pumped through the lungs. Thus all the blood returning from the body's peripheral organs and tissues via the systemic veins is oxygenated before it is pumped back to them.

It must be emphasized that the lungs receive all the blood pumped by the right heart, whereas each of the peripheral organs and tissues receives only a fraction of the blood pumped by the left ventricle. For reference, the typical distribution of the blood pumped by the left ventricle in an adult at rest is given in Figure 14-10.

Finally, there are several exceptions, notably the liver and kidneys, to the usual anatomical pattern described in this section for the systemic circulation, and these will be presented in the relevant chapters dealing with those organs.

PRESSURE, FLOW, AND RESISTANCE

The last task in this survey of the design of the cardiovascular system is to introduce the concepts of pressure, flow, and resistance. Throughout the system, blood flow (*F*) is always from a region of higher pressure to one of lower pressure. The term "pressure" refers to the force exerted by the blood. The pressure exerted by a fluid is often termed a **hydrostatic pressure**. The units for the rate of flow are volume per unit time, usually liters per minute (L/min). The units for the pressure difference (ΔP) driving the flow are millimeters of mercury (mmHg) because historically blood pressure was measured by determining how high a column of mercury could be driven by the blood pressure.

It must be emphasized that it is not the absolute pressure at any point in the cardiovascular system that determines flow rate, but the *difference* in pressure between the relevant points (Figure 14-11).

Knowing only the pressure difference between two points will not tell you the flow rate, however. For this, you also need to know the **resistance (*R*)** to flow, that is, how difficult it is for blood to flow between two points at any given pressure difference. Resistance is the measure of the friction that impedes flow. The basic equation relating these variables is

$$F = \frac{\Delta P}{R} \qquad (14\text{-}1)$$

FIGURE 14-11

Flow between two points within a tube is proportional to the pressure difference between the points. The flows in these two identical tubes are the same because the pressure differences are the same.

In words, flow rate is directly proportional to pressure difference and inversely proportional to resistance. This equation applies not only to the cardiovascular system but to any system in which liquid or air flows through tubes.

Resistance cannot be directly measured but is calculated from the directly measured F and ΔP. For example, in Figure 14-11 the resistances in both examples can be calculated to be 90 mmHg ÷ 10 ml per minute = 9 mmHg/ml per minute.

This example illustrates how resistance can be *calculated*, but what is it that actually *determines* the resistance?[1] One determinant is the fluid property known as **viscosity**, which is a measure of the friction between adjacent layers of a flowing fluid; the greater the friction, the greater the viscosity. The other determinants of resistance are the tube's length and radius, which determine the amount of friction between the fluid and the tube wall. The following equation defines the contributions of these three determinants:

$$R = \frac{\eta L}{r^4}\frac{8}{\pi} \qquad (14\text{-}2)$$

where η = fluid viscosity
L = tube length
r = inside radius of the tube
$8/\pi$ = a constant

In other words, resistance is directly proportional to both the fluid viscosity and tube length, and inversely proportional to the fourth power of the radius, that is, the radius multiplied by itself four times.[2]

Blood viscosity is not fixed but increases as hematocrit increases, and changes in hematocrit, therefore, can have important effects on the resistance to flow in certain situations. Under most physiological conditions, however, the hematocrit and, hence, viscosity of blood is relatively constant and does not play a role in the *control* of resistance.

Similarly, since the lengths of the blood vessels remain constant in the body, length is also not a factor in the control of resistance. In contrast, as we shall see, tube radius does not remain constant, and so tube radius—the $1/r^4$ term in our equation—is the most important determinant of changes in resistance. Just how important changes in radius can be is illustrated in Figure 14-12: Decreasing

---

[1]This distinction between how a thing is measured (or calculated) and its determinants may seem confusing to the reader. By standing on a scale you *measure* your weight, but your weight is not *determined* by the scale but rather by how much you eat, exercise, and so on.

[2]Substituting the determinants of R, as given in Equation 14-2, for R in Equation 14-1 gives the so-called Poiseuille equation, the full expression of the determinants of flow.

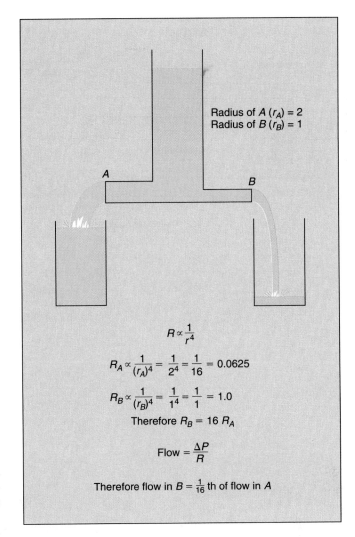

FIGURE 14-12
Effect of tube radius (r) on resistance (R) and flow.

the radius of a tube *twofold* increases its resistance *sixteenfold*. If ΔP is held constant in this example, flow through the tube decreases sixteenfold since $F = \Delta P/R$.

This completes our introductory survey of the cardiovascular system. We now turn to a description of its components and their control. In so doing, we might very easily lose sight of the forest for the trees if we do not persistently ask of each section: How does this component of the circulation contribute to adequate blood flow through the capillaries of the various organs or to an adequate exchange of materials between blood and cells? Referring to the summary in Table 14-4 as you read the description of each component will help you keep focused on this question.

TABLE 14-4   THE CARDIOVASCULAR SYSTEM

Component	Function
Heart	
Atria	Chambers through which blood flows from veins to ventricles. Atrial contraction adds to ventricular filling but is not essential.
Ventricles	Chambers whose contractions produce the pressures that drive blood through the pulmonary and systemic vascular systems and back to the heart.
Vascular system	
Arteries	Low-resistance tubes conducting blood to the various organs with little loss in pressure. They also act as pressure reservoirs for maintaining blood flow during ventricular relaxation.
Arterioles	Major sites of resistance to flow; responsible for the pattern of blood-flow distribution to the various organs; participate in the regulation of arterial blood pressure.
Capillaries	Sites of nutrient, waste product, and fluid exchange between blood and tissues.
Venules	Sites of nutrient, waste product, and fluid exchange between blood and tissues.
Veins	Low-resistance conduits for blood flow back to the heart. Their capacity for blood is adjusted so as to facilitate this flow.

SECTION B SUMMARY

I. The cardiovascular system consists of two circuits: the pulmonary circulation, from the right ventricle to the lungs and then to the left atrium; and the systemic circulation, from the left ventricle to all organs and tissues other than the lungs and then to the right atrium.

II. Arteries carry blood away from the heart, and veins carry blood to the heart.
   A. In the systemic circuit, the large artery leaving the left heart is the aorta, and the large veins emptying into the right heart are the superior and inferior venae cavae. The analogous vessels in the pulmonary circulation are the pulmonary trunk and the four pulmonary veins.
   B. The microcirculation consists of the vessels between arteries and veins—the arterioles, capillaries, and venules.

III. Flow between two points in the cardiovascular system is directly proportional to the pressure difference between the points and inversely proportional to the resistance: $F = \Delta P/R$

IV. Resistance is directly proportional to the viscosity of a fluid and to the length of the tube. It is inversely proportional to the fourth power of the tube's radius, which is the major variable controlling changes in resistance.

SECTION B KEY TERMS

bulk flow	venules
atrium	microcirculation
ventricle	inferior vena cava
pulmonary circulation	superior vena cava
systemic circulation	pulmonary trunk
arteries	pulmonary arteries
veins	pulmonary veins
aorta	hydrostatic pressure
arterioles	resistance (R)
capillaries	viscosity

SECTION B REVIEW QUESTIONS

1. State the formula relating flow, pressure difference, and resistance.
2. What are the three determinants of resistance?

ANATOMY

The heart is a muscular organ enclosed in a fibrous sac, the **pericardium**, and located in the chest (thorax). The narrow space between the pericardium and the heart is filled with a watery fluid that serves as a lubricant as the heart moves within the sac.

The walls of the heart are composed primarily of cardiac-muscle cells and are termed the **myocardium**. The inner surface of the walls, that is, the surface in contact with the blood within the cardiac chambers, is lined by a thin layer of cells known as **endothelial cells** or **endothelium**. (As we shall see, endothelial cells line not only the heart chambers but the entire vascular system as well.)

As noted earlier, the human heart is divided into right and left halves, each consisting of an atrium and a ventricle. Located between the atrium and ventricle in each half of the heart are the **atrioventricular (AV) valves**, which permit blood to flow from atrium to ventricle but not from ventricle to atrium (Figure 14-13). The right AV valve is called the **tricuspid valve**, and the left is called the **mitral valve**.

The opening and closing of the AV valves is a passive process resulting from pressure differences across the valves. When the blood is moving from atrium to ventricle, the valves are pushed open, but when a ventricle contracts, its AV valve is forced closed when the pressure of the blood in the ventricle becomes greater than that in the atrium. Blood is therefore forced into the pulmonary trunk from the right ventricle and into the aorta from the left ventricle, but blood does not normally move back into the atria.

To prevent the AV valves from being pushed up into the atrium, the valves are fastened to muscular projections **(papillary muscles)** of the ventricular walls by fibrous strands (chordae tendinae). The papillary muscles do *not* open or close the valves. They act only to limit the valves' movements and prevent them from being everted.

The opening of the right ventricle into the pulmonary trunk and of the left ventricle into the aorta are also regulated by valves, the **pulmonary** and **aortic valves** (Figure 14-13). These valves permit blood to flow into the arteries during ventricular contraction but prevent blood from moving in the opposite direction during ventricular relaxation. Like the AV valves, these valves act in a purely pas-

atria contract fairly simultaneously ventricles also beat = depolar.

FIGURE 14-13

Diagrammatic section of the heart. The arrows indicate the direction of blood flow.

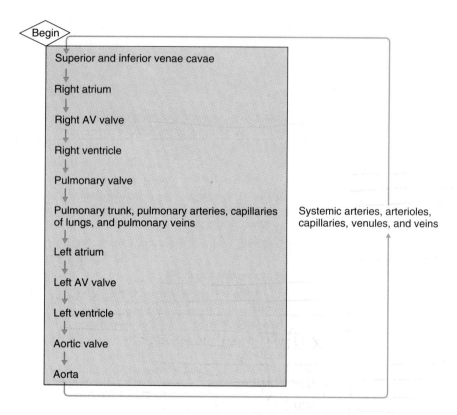

Begin

Superior and inferior venae cavae
↓
Right atrium
↓
Right AV valve
↓
Right ventricle
↓
Pulmonary valve
↓
Pulmonary trunk, pulmonary arteries, capillaries
of lungs, and pulmonary veins
↓
Left atrium
↓
Left AV valve
↓
Left ventricle
↓
Aortic valve
↓
Aorta

Systemic arteries, arterioles,
capillaries, venules, and veins

FIGURE 14-14
Path of blood flow through the entire cardiovascular system. All the
structures within the colored box are
located in the chest.

sive manner. Their being open or closed depends upon the pressure differences across them.

There are no valves at the entrances of the superior and inferior venae cavae (plural of vena cava) into the right atrium, and of the pulmonary veins into the left atrium. However, atrial contraction pumps very little blood back into the veins because atrial contraction compresses the veins at their site of entry into the atria, increasing the resistance to backflow. Actually, a little blood is ejected back into the veins, and this accounts for the venous pulse that can often be seen in the neck veins when the atria are contracting.

Figure 14-14 summarizes the path of blood flow through the entire cardiovascular system.

Cardiac Muscle

The cardiac-muscle cells of the myocardium are arranged in layers that are tightly bound together and completely encircle the blood-filled chambers. When the walls of a chamber contract, they come together like a squeezing fist and exert pressure on the blood they enclose.

Cardiac muscle combines properties of both skeletal and smooth muscle (Chapter 11). The cells are striated (Figure 14-15) as the result of an arrangement of thick myosin and thin actin filaments similar to that of skeletal muscle. Cardiac-muscle cells are considerably shorter than

skeletal-muscle fibers, however, and have several branching processes. Adjacent cells are joined end to end at structures called intercalated disks, within which are desmosomes that hold the cells together and to which the myofibrils are attached. Adjacent to the intercalated disks are gap junctions, similar to those in many smooth muscles.

Approximately 1 percent of the cardiac-muscle fibers have specialized features that are essential for normal heart excitation. They constitute a network known as the **conducting system** of the heart and are in contact with the other cardiac-muscle fibers via gap junctions. The conducting system initiates the heartbeat and helps spread the impulse rapidly throughout the heart.

One final point about the cardiac-muscle cells should be noted: Certain cells in the atria secrete the family of peptide hormones collectively called atrial natriuretic factor, described in Chapter 16.

Innervation. The heart receives a rich supply of sympathetic and parasympathetic nerve fibers, the latter contained in the vagus nerves. The sympathetic postganglionic fibers release primarily norepinephrine, and the parasympathetics release primarily acetylcholine. The receptors for norepinephrine on cardiac muscle are mainly beta-adrenergic (of the beta$_1$ subtype). The hormone epinephrine, from the adrenal medulla, combines with the same

striated muscle

A band

I band

Invagination of
sarcolemma by
transverse tubule

Transverse
tubule

Mitochondria

M line in
H zone

Z line

Sarcomere

Red cell in
capillary = *brings O₂
to heart (big
ETZ
agui)*

Capillary
endothelium

Connective
tissue

Intercalated
disk

Gap junction = *commu-
nication
between
actin +
myosin
filaments*

Sarcolemma

Sarcoplasmic
reticulum

*brings about
depolarized
ions to depol.
membranes*

FIGURE 14-15
Diagram of an electron micrograph of cardiac muscle. (*From R. M. Berne and M. N. Levy.*)

receptors as norepinephrine and exerts the same actions on the heart. The receptors for acetylcholine are of the muscarinic type.

Blood Supply. The blood being pumped through the heart chambers does not exchange nutrients and metabolic end products with the myocardial cells. They, like the cells of all other organs, receive their blood supply via arteries that branch from the aorta. The arteries supplying the myocardium are the **coronary arteries**, and the blood flowing through them is termed the **coronary blood flow**. The coronary arteries exit from the very first part of the aorta and lead to a branching network of small arteries, arterioles, capillaries, venules, and veins similar to those in all other organs.

HEARTBEAT COORDINATION

Contraction of cardiac muscle, like that of other muscle types, is triggered by depolarization of the plasma membrane of the cells making up the muscle. As described earlier, myocardial cells are connected to each other by gap junctions. These allow action potentials to spread from one cell to another. Thus, the initial excitation of one myocardial cell results in excitation of all cells. This initial depolarization normally arises in a small group of conducting-system cells, the **sinoatrial (SA) node**, located in the right atrium near the entrance of the superior vena cava. The action potential then spreads from the SA node throughout the heart in a manner that causes first the atria and then the ventricles to contract.

How does the action potential arise in the SA node, and what is the path and sequence of excitation? To answer these questions, we must first describe cardiac action potentials.

Cardiac Action Potentials

A typical ventricular action potential is illustrated in Figure 14-16A. The membrane permeability changes that underlie it are shown in Figure 14-16B. As in skeletal-muscle cells and neurons, the resting membrane is much more permeable to potassium than to sodium. Therefore, the resting membrane potential is much closer to the potassium equilibrium potential (−90 mV) than to the so-

dium equilibrium potential (+60 mV). Similarly, the depolarizing phase of the action potential is due mainly to a positive-feedback increase in sodium permeability caused by the opening of voltage-sensitive sodium channels. At almost the same time, the permeability to potassium decreases as potassium channels close, and this also contributes to the membrane depolarization.

Again as in skeletal-muscle cells and neurons, the increased sodium permeability is very transient since the sodium channels quickly close again. Unlike the case in these other excitable tissues, however, in cardiac muscle the return of sodium permeability toward its resting value is *not* accompanied by membrane repolarization. The membrane remains depolarized at a plateau of about 0 mV. The reasons for this continued depolarization are: (1) Potassium permeability stays below the resting value, and (2) there is a marked increase in the membrane permeability to calcium. The second reason is the more important of the two, and the explanation for it is as follows.

In myocardial cells, the original membrane depolarization causes voltage-sensitive calcium channels in the plasma membrane to open, which results in a flow of calcium ions down their electrochemical gradient into the cell. These channels are referred to as **slow channels** because there is a delay in their opening. The flow of positive calcium ions into the cell just balances the flow of positive potassium charge out of the cell and keeps the membrane depolarized at the plateau value.

Ultimately, repolarization does occur when the permeabilities of calcium and potassium return to their original state, that is, when the slow channels close and the potassium channels reopen.

The action potentials of atrial cells other than those of the SA node are similar in shape to those just described for ventricular cells, but the duration of their plateau phase is shorter.

In contrast, there are extremely important differences between action potentials of the vast majority of the myocardial cells, as just described—whether atrial or ventricular—and those in the conducting system. Figure 14-17B illustrates the action potential of a cell from the SA node. Note that the resting potential of the SA-node cell is not steady but instead manifests a slow depolarization. This gradual depolarization is known as a **pacemaker potential**; it brings the membrane potential to threshold, at which point an action potential occurs. Following the peak of the action potential, the membrane repolarizes, and the gradual depolarization begins again.

Thus, the pacemaker potential provides the SA node with **automaticity**, the capacity for spontaneous rhythmical self-excitation. The slope of the pacemaker potential, that is, how quickly the membrane potential changes per unit time, determines how quickly threshold is reached and the next action potential elicited. The inherent rate of

FIGURE 14-16

(A) Membrane potential recording from a ventricular muscle cell. (B) Simultaneously measured permeabilities *P* to potassium, sodium, and calcium during the action potential of (A).

FIGURE 14-17

Comparison of action potentials in a ventricular muscle cell (A, from Figure 14-16) and (B) a sinoatrial (SA)-nodal cell. The most important difference is the presence of the pacemaker potential in the SA node. The SA node action potential, in contrast to that of the ventricular muscle cell, is due to calcium influx through "slow" voltage-sensitive calcium channels; the SA node cells contain no voltage-sensitive sodium channels.

(and on and on . . .)

the SA node, that is, the rate exhibited in the total absence of any neural or hormonal input to the node, is approximately 100 depolarizations per minute.

What is responsible for the pacemaker potential? A major cause of this gradual depolarization is a progressive, "spontaneous" reduction in membrane permeability of the SA-node cells to potassium. There are also small progressive increases in the permeabilities to sodium and calcium. All these changes reflect the closing or opening of channels specific for these ions.

Several other portions of the conducting system are capable of generating pacemaker potentials, but the inherent rate of these other areas is slower than that of the SA node. In contrast, those cardiac-muscle cells not part of the conducting system are normally not capable of generating pacemaker potentials.

We can now apply this information concerning cardiac action potentials to understanding the origin of the heartbeat and the spread of excitation throughout the myocardium.

Sequence of Excitation

To reiterate, the SA node, having the fastest inherent discharge rate of any of the myocardial cells with pacemaker activity, is the normal pacemaker for the entire heart. Its depolarization normally generates the current that leads to depolarization of all other cardiac-muscle cells, and so its discharge rate determines the **heart rate**, the number of times the heart contracts per minute. If the activity of the SA node is depressed or conduction from it is blocked, another portion of the conducting system can take over as pacemaker and set the heart rate.

The action potential initiated in the SA node spreads throughout the myocardium, passing from cell to cell by way of gap junctions. The spread throughout the right atrium and from the right atrium to the left atrium does not depend on fibers of the conducting system. The spread is rapid enough that the two atria are depolarized and contract at essentially the same time.

The spread of the action potential to the ventricles is more complicated and involves the rest of the conducting system (Figures 14-18 and 14-19). The link between atrial depolarization and ventricular depolarization is a portion of the conducting system called the **atrioventricular (AV) node**, located at the base of the right atrium. The action potential spreading through the right atrium causes depolarization of the AV node. This node manifests a particularly important characteristic: For several reasons related to the electrical properties of the AV-node cells, the propagation of action potentials through the AV node is relatively slow (requiring approximately 0.1 s). This delay allows atrial contraction to add additional blood to the ventricles before ventricular excitation occurs.

After leaving the AV node, the impulse enters the wall between the two ventricles (the interventricular septum) via the conducting-system fibers termed the **bundle of His** (or atrioventricular bundle) after its discoverer (pronounced "hiss"). The bundle of His then divides within the septum into **right** and **left bundle branches**, which eventually leave the septum to enter the walls of both ventricles. These fibers in turn make contact with **Purkinje fibers** (also termed cardiac conducting myofibers), large conducting cells that rapidly distribute the impulse throughout much of the ventricles. Finally, the Purkinje fibers make contact with non-conducting-system ventricular cells, through which the impulse spreads through the rest of the ventricles.

The rapid conduction along the Purkinje fibers and the diffuse distribution of these fibers cause depolarization of all right and left ventricular cells more-or-less simultaneously and ensure a single coordinated contraction. Actually depolarization and contraction begin slightly earlier in the bottom (apex) of the ventricles and spread upward. The result is a more efficient contraction, like squeezing a tube of toothpaste from the bottom up.

It should be emphasized that the AV node and the bundle of His constitute the only electrical link between the atria and the ventricles. There are no others because a

VAP allows Ca into cell.

depolar. → gap junction →
heart tissue → AV node depolar.
→ bundle of his + fibers →
Purk.
fibers

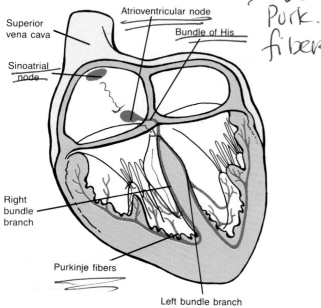

Superior
vena cava

Sinoatrial
node

Atrioventricular node

Bundle of His

Right
bundle
branch

Purkinje fibers

Left bundle branch

⋆ **FIGURE 14-18**
Conducting system of the heart.

only through the AV node, but it also means that drug- or disease-induced malfunction of the AV node may partially or completely block the transmission of action potentials from the atria to the ventricles.

If this occurs, autorhythmical cells in the bundle of His, no longer driven by the SA node, begin to initiate excitation at their own inherent rate and become the pacemaker for the ventricles. Their rate is quite slow, generally 25 to 40 beats/min, and it is completely out of synchrony with the atrial contractions, which continue at the normal higher rate of the SA node. Under such conditions, the atria are totally ineffective as pumps since they are often contracting against closed AV valves. Fortunately, atrial pumping, as we shall see, is relatively unimportant for cardiac function except during relatively strenuous exercise. The current treatment for all severe **AV conduction disorders** is permanent surgical implantation of an electrical device, a pacemaker, that stimulates the ventricular cells at a normal rate.

The Electrocardiogram

The **electrocardiogram** (**ECG** or **EKG**[3]) is primarily a tool for evaluating the *electrical* events within the heart. The action potentials of cardiac-muscle cells can be

---

[3]The k is from the German *kardio,* heart.

layer of nonconducting connective tissue, pierced by the bundle of His, completely separates each atrium from its ventricle. This anatomical pattern ensures that excitation will travel from the SA node to both ventricles

⋆ **FIGURE 14-19**
Sequence of cardiac excitation. The blue color denotes areas that are depolarized. Impulse spread from right atrium to left atrium is via the atrial muscle cells where the atria contact each other in their shared wall. (*Adapted from Rushmer.*)

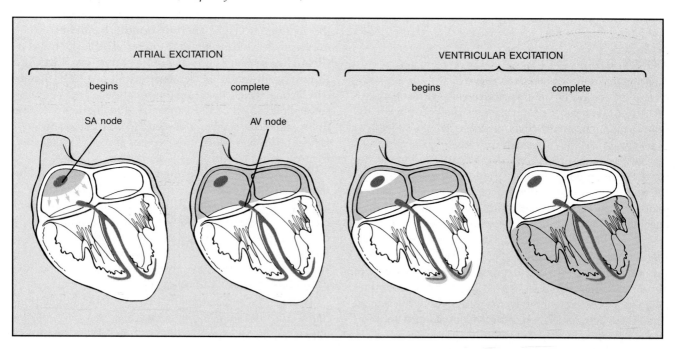

ATRIAL EXCITATION

begins   complete

SA node   AV node

VENTRICULAR EXCITATION

begins   complete

only measures currents, not ability to contract

SA node

ventricular depolar.

ECG

ventricular repolar.

atrial depolar.

Ventricular action potential

0.3
Time (s)

FIGURE 14-20

(Top) Typical electrocardiogram recorded from electrodes connecting the arms. P, atrial depolarization; QRS, ventricular depolarization; T, ventricular repolarization. (Bottom) Ventricular action potential recorded from a single ventricular muscle cell. Note the correspondence of the QRS complex with depolarization and the correspondence of the T wave with repolarization.

viewed as batteries that cause charge to move throughout the body fluids. These moving charges—currents, in other words—represent the sum of the action potentials occurring simultaneously in many individual cells and can be detected by recording electrodes at the surface of the skin. Figure 14-20 illustrates a typical normal ECG recorded as the potential difference between the right and left wrists. The first deflection, the **P wave**, corresponds to current flows during atrial depolarization. The second deflection, the **QRS complex**, occurring approximately 0.15 s later, is the result of ventricular depolarization. It is a complex deflection because the paths taken by the wave of depolarization through the thick ventricular walls differ from instant to instant, and the currents generated in the body fluids change direction accordingly. Regardless of its form, for example, the Q and/or S portions may be absent, the deflection is still called a QRS complex. The final deflection, the **T wave**, is the result of ventricular repolarization. Atrial repolarization is usually not evident on the ECG because it occurs at the same time as the QRS complex.

A typical clinical ECG makes use of 12 combinations of recording locations on the limbs and chest so as to obtain as much information as possible concerning different areas of the heart. The shapes and sizes of the P wave, QRS complex, and T wave vary with the electrode locations.

To reiterate, the ECG is not a *direct* record of the changes in membrane potential across individual cardiac-muscle cells but is rather a measure of the currents generated in the extracellular fluid by the changes occurring in many cells. To emphasize this point, Figure 14-20 shows, in addition to an ECG, the simultaneously occurring changes in membrane potential in a single ventricular cell.

Because many myocardial defects alter normal impulse propagation, and thereby the shapes and timing of the waves, the ECG is a powerful tool for diagnosing certain types of heart disease. Figure 14-21 gives one example. It must be emphasized, however, that the ECG provides information concerning only the electrical activity of the heart. Thus, if something is wrong with the heart's mechanical activity, but this defect does not give rise to altered electrical activity, then the ECG will not be of diagnostic value.

Excitation-Contraction Coupling

An action potential ("excitation") in the plasma membrane of cardiac-muscle cells triggers the cells' contraction. As is

FIGURE 14-21

Electrocardiograms from a healthy person and from two persons suffering from atrioventricular block. (A) A normal ECG. (B) Partial block. Damage to the AV node permits only one-half of the atrial impulses to be transmitted to the ventricles. Note that every second P wave is not followed by a QRS and T. (C) Complete block. There is absolutely no synchrony between atrial and ventricular electrical activities. The ventricles are being driven by a pacemaker in the bundle of His.

true for skeletal muscle, the action potential causes, by a sequence of events, an increase in cytosolic calcium concentration due mainly to release of calcium from the sarcoplasmic reticulum. Also as in skeletal muscle, this calcium combines with the regulator protein troponin, and cross-bridge formation between actin and myosin is initiated.

What is the sequence of events by which the action potential causes increased release of calcium from the sarcoplasmic reticulum? As in skeletal muscle, the plasma-membrane action potential spreads into the interior of cardiac-muscle cells via the T tubules. In skeletal muscle, as we saw in Chapter 11, the action potential itself causes the release of calcium from the adjacent sarcoplasmic reticulum. In cardiac muscle, however, the story is more complicated: The depolarizing phase of the action potential opens voltage-sensitive calcium channels in the T-tubule membrane, and calcium diffuses from the extracellular fluid through these channels into the cells. This calcium then acts on the adjacent sarcoplasmic reticulum to stimulate release of a much larger amount of calcium from this organelle, and it is mainly this calcium that causes the contraction. Thus, we have here an amplification effect (Figure 14-22): The entering extracellular calcium *directly* causes a *small* rise in the cytosolic concentration, and this small rise then induces a much larger rise by stimulating the release of calcium from the sarcoplasmic reticulum.

Contraction ends when the cytosolic calcium concentration is restored to its original extremely low value by active transport of calcium back into the sarcoplasmic reticulum. Also, an amount of calcium equal to what entered the cell from the extracellular fluid during excitation is transported out of the cell, so that the total cellular calcium content remains constant.

As we shall see, how much cytosolic calcium concentration increases during excitation is a major determinant of the strength of cardiac-muscle contraction. In this regard, cardiac muscle differs from skeletal muscle, in which the increase in cytosolic calcium occurring during membrane excitation is always adequate to produce maximal "turning-on" of cross bridges by calcium binding to all troponin sites. In cardiac muscle, the amount of calcium released is not usually sufficient to saturate all troponin sites. Therefore, the number of active cross bridges and thus the strength of contraction can be increased if cytosolic calcium is increased still further.

Refractory Period of the Heart

Ventricular muscle, unlike skeletal muscle, is incapable of any significant degree of summation of contractions, and this is a very good thing. Imagine that cardiac muscle is able to undergo a prolonged tetanic contraction. During this period no ventricular filling could occur since filling

FIGURE 14-22

Excitation-contraction coupling in cardiac muscle. Calcium released from the sarcoplasmic reticulum is the major source of the increased cytosolic calcium. The signal for this release is extracellular calcium diffusing into the cell across voltage-sensitive calcium channels. (These channels are located in the T tubules.)

can occur only when the ventricular muscle is relaxed, and the heart would therefore cease to function as a pump.

The inability of the heart to generate tetanic contractions is the result of the long **refractory period** of cardiac muscle, defined as the period during and following an action potential during which an excitable membrane cannot be reexcited. As described in Chapter 11, the absolute refractory periods of skeletal muscle are much shorter (1 to 2 ms) than the duration of contraction (20 to 100 ms), and a second contraction can therefore be elicited before the first is over (summation of contractions). In contrast, because of the long plateau in the cardiac-muscle action potential, the absolute refractory period of cardiac muscle lasts almost as long as the contraction (250 ms), and the muscle cannot be reexcited in time to produce summation (Figure 14-23).

SA node

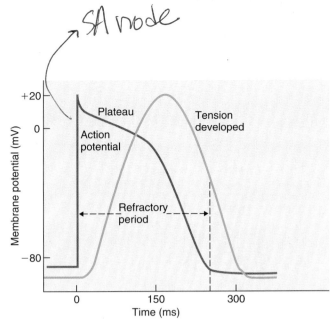

✗ **FIGURE 14-23**

Relationship between membrane potential changes and contraction in a ventricular muscle cell. The refractory period lasts almost as long as the contraction.

MECHANICAL EVENTS OF THE CARDIAC CYCLE

The orderly process of depolarization described in the previous sections triggers a recurring **cardiac cycle** of atrial and ventricular contractions and relaxations (Figure 14-24). For orientation, we shall first merely name the parts of this cycle and their key events. Then we shall go through the cycle again, this time describing the pressure and volume changes that cause the events.

The cycle is divided into two major phases, both named for events in the ventricle: the period of ventricular contraction and blood ejection, **systole**, followed by the period of ventricular relaxation and blood filling, **diastole**. At an average heart rate of 72 beats/min, each cardiac cycle lasts approximately 0.8 s, with 0.3 s in systole and 0.5 s in diastole.

As illustrated in Figure 14-24, both systole and diastole can be subdivided into several discrete phases. During the very first part of systole, the ventricles are contracting but all valves in the heart are closed and so no blood can be ejected. This period is termed **isovolumetric ventricular contraction** because the ventricular volume is constant. The ventricular walls are developing tension and squeezing on the blood they encircle, but because the volume of blood in the ventricles is constant and because blood, like water, is essentially incompressible, the ventricular muscle fibers cannot shorten. Thus, isovolumetric ventricular contraction is analogous to an isometric skeletal-muscle contraction: The muscle develops tension but does not shorten.

Once the rising pressure in the ventricles becomes great enough to open the aortic and pulmonary valves, the **ventricular ejection** period of systole occurs. Blood is forced into the aorta or pulmonary trunk as the contracting ventricular muscle fibers shorten. The volume of blood ejected from a ventricle during systole is termed the **stroke volume**.

During the very first part of diastole, the ventricles begin to relax, and the aortic and pulmonary valves close. No blood is entering or leaving the ventricles since once again all the valves are closed. Accordingly, ventricular volume is not changing, and this period is termed **isovolumetric ventricular relaxation**.[4] The AV valves then open, and **ventricular filling** occurs as blood flows in from the atria. Atrial contraction occurs at the very end of diastole, after most of the ventricular filling has taken place. This is an important point: The ventricle receives blood throughout most of diastole, not just when the atrium contracts. Indeed, in a person at rest, approximately 80 percent of ventricular filling occurs *before* atrial contraction.

This completes the basic orientation. We now analyze, using Figure 14-25, the pressure and volume changes that occur in the left ventricle and aorta during the cardiac cycle. Events on the right side are described later. Electrical events (ECG) and heart sounds, described in a subsequent section, are at the top of the figure so that their timing can be correlated with the phases of the cycle.

Mid-Diastole to Late Diastole

We begin our analysis at the far left of Figure 14-25 with the events of mid-diastole to late diastole. The left atrium and ventricle are both relaxed, and atrial pressure (not shown) is very slightly higher than ventricular pressure. Because of the pressure difference, the AV valve is open, and blood entering the atrium from the pulmonary veins continues on into the ventricle. Note that during diastole the aortic valve is closed because the aortic pressure is higher than the ventricular pressure.

Throughout diastole, the aortic pressure is slowly falling because blood is moving out of the arteries and through the vascular system. In contrast, ventricular pressure is rising slightly because blood is entering the relaxed ventricle from the atrium, thereby expanding the ventricular volume.

At the very end of diastole, the SA node discharges, the atrium depolarizes (as signified by the P wave of the ECG) and contracts, and a small volume of blood is added to the ventricle (note the small rise in ventricular pressure and blood volume). The amount of blood in the ventricle at the end of diastole is called the **end-diastolic volume**.

---

[4]Physiologists and clinical cardiologists do not all agree on the dividing line between systole and diastole. As presented here, this dividing line is the point at which ventricular contraction stops and the pulmonary and aortic valves close. In some definitions, systole includes isovolumetric ventricular relaxation, whereas still other definitions break the cycle up in other ways.

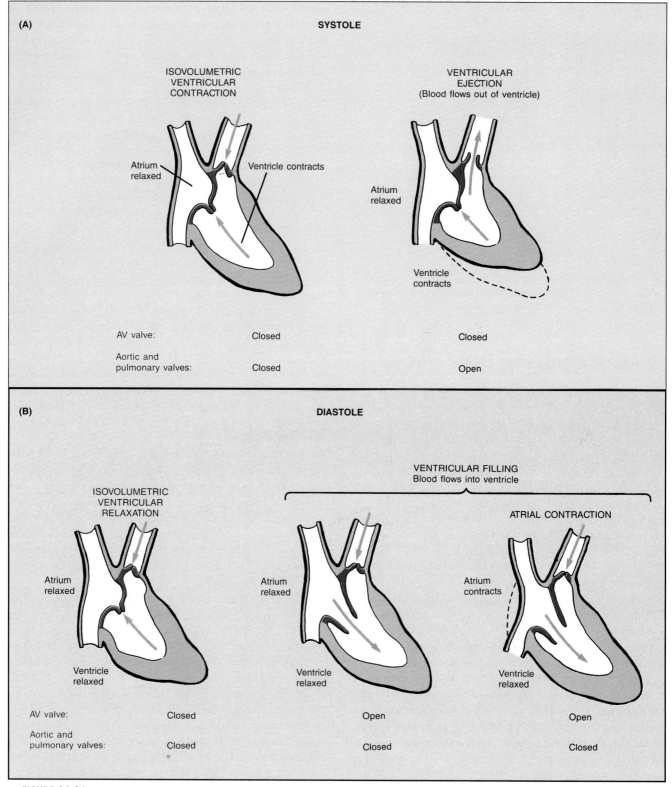

FIGURE 14-24

Divisions of the cardiac cycle: (A) systole; (B) diastole. For simplicity, only one atrium and ventricle are shown. The phases of the cycle are identical in both halves of the heart. The direction in which the pressure difference *favors* flow is denoted by the arrow; note, however, that flow, although favored by a pressure difference, will not actually occur if a valve prevents it.

FIGURE 14-25
Summary of events in the left ventricle and aorta during the cardiac cycle.

1 = VENTRICULAR FILLING
2 = ISOVOLUMETRIC VENTRICULAR CONTRACTION
3 = VENTRICULAR EJECTION
4 = ISOVOLUMETRIC VENTRICULAR RELAXATION

Systole

From the AV node, the wave of depolarization passes through the ventricle (as signified by the QRS complex of the ECG) and triggers ventricular contraction. Remember that just before the contraction the aortic valve is closed and the AV valve is open. As the ventricle contracts, ventricular pressure rises steeply, and almost immediately this pressure exceeds the atrial pressure, closing the AV valve and thus preventing backflow of blood into the atrium. Since the aortic pressure still exceeds the ventricular pressure, the aortic valve remains closed and the ventricle cannot empty despite its contraction.

This brief phase of isovolumetric ventricular contraction ends when the rising ventricular pressure exceeds aortic pressure. The aortic valve opens, and ventricular ejection occurs. The ventricular volume curve shows that ejection is rapid at first and then tapers off. Note that the ventricle does not empty completely. The amount of blood remaining after ejection is called the **end-systolic volume**. Thus,

Stroke volume = end-diastolic volume −
end-systolic volume

As shown in Figure 14-25, normal values for an adult at rest are stroke volume = 70 ml, end-diastolic volume = 135 ml, and end-systolic volume = 65 ml.

As blood flows into the aorta, the aortic pressure rises along with the ventricular pressure. Throughout ejection, only very small pressure differences exist between the ventricle and aorta because the aortic valve-opening offers little resistance to flow.

Note that peak ventricular and aortic pressures are reached before the end of ventricular ejection; that is, these pressures start to fall during the last part of systole despite continued ventricular contraction. This is because the strength of ventricular contraction and rate of blood ejection diminish during the last part of systole as shown by the ventricular volume curve, and the ejection rate is less than the rate at which blood is leaving the aorta. Accordingly, the volume and therefore the pressure in the aorta begin to decrease.

Early Diastole

Diastole begins as ventricular contraction and ejection stop and the ventricular muscle begins to relax. Immediately, ventricular pressure falls significantly[5] below aortic pressure, and the aortic valve closes. However, at this time, ventricular pressure still exceeds atrial pressure, so that the AV valve also remains closed. This early diastolic phase—isovolumetric ventricular relaxation—ends as ventricular pressure falls below atrial pressure, the AV valve opens, and rapid ventricular filling begins.

The ventricle's previous contraction compressed the elastic elements of this chamber in such a way that the ventricle actually tends to recoil outward once systole is over. This expansion, in turn, lowers ventricular pressure more rapidly than would otherwise occur—and may even create a negative pressure in the ventricle—which enhances filling. Thus, some energy is stored within the myocardium during contraction, and its release during the subsequent relaxation aids filling.

The fact that ventricular filling is almost complete during early diastole is of the greatest importance. It ensures that filling is not seriously impaired during periods when the heart is beating very rapidly and the duration of diastole and therefore total filling time are reduced. However, when rates of approximately 200 beats/min or more are reached, filling time does become inadequate, and the volume of blood pumped during each beat is decreased. The significance of this will be described in the section on exercise.

Early ventricular filling also explains why the conduction defects that eliminate the atria as efficient pumps do not seriously impair ventricular filling, at least in otherwise normal individuals at rest. One example of this is **atrial fibrillation**, a state in which the atria contract in a continuous and completely disordered manner and so fail to serve as effective pumps. Thus, the atrium may be conveniently viewed as merely a continuation of the large veins.

---

[5]The word "significantly" is used in this sentence because, in reality, left ventricular pressure is already slightly less than aortic pressure during late systole, despite the fact that ejection is still occurring. The physical explanation of this pressure "reversal" in late systole is beyond the scope of this book.

Pulmonary Circulation Pressures

The pressure changes in the right ventricle and pulmonary arteries are qualitatively similar to those just described for the left ventricle and aorta (Figure 14-26). There are striking quantitative differences, however. Typical pulmonary artery systolic and diastolic pressures are 24 and 8 mmHg, respectively, compared to systemic arterial pressures of 120 and 70 mmHg. Thus, the pulmonary circulation is a low-pressure system, for reasons to be described in a later section. This difference is clearly reflected in the ventricular architecture, the right ventricular wall being much thinner than the left (Figure 14-27). Despite its lower pressure during contraction, however, the right ventricle ejects the same amount of blood as the left.

Heart Sounds

Two sounds, termed **heart sounds**, stemming from cardiac contraction are normally heard through a stethoscope placed on the chest wall. The first sound, a soft low-pitched *lub*, is associated with closure of the AV valves at the onset of systole (Figure 14-25); the second, a louder *dup*, is associated with closure of the pulmonary and aortic valves at the onset of diastole. These sounds, which result from vibrations caused by the closing valves, are perfectly normal, but other sounds, known as **heart murmurs**, are frequently a sign of heart disease.

Murmurs can be produced by blood flowing rapidly in the usual direction through an abnormally narrowed valve (**stenosis**), by blood flowing backward through a damaged leaky valve (**insufficiency**), or by blood flowing between

FIGURE 14-26

Pressures in the right ventricle and pulmonary artery during the cardiac cycle. This figure is done on the same scale as Figure 14-25 to facilitate comparison. The pressure profiles are qualitatively identical in the pulmonary and systemic circuits, but the pressures are much lower in the former.

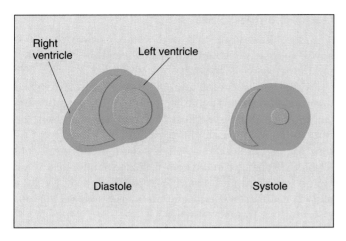

FIGURE 14-27
Cross section of the ventricular walls to illustrate the changes that occur during contraction. The view is from above, with the atria removed.

the two atria or two ventricles via a small hole in the wall separating them.

The exact timing and location of the murmur provide the physician with a powerful diagnostic clue. For example, a murmur heard throughout systole suggests a stenotic pulmonary or aortic valve, an insufficient AV valve, or a hole in the interventricular septum. In contrast, a murmur heard during diastole suggests a stenotic AV valve or an insufficient pulmonary or aortic valve.

THE CARDIAC OUTPUT

The volume of blood pumped by *each* ventricle per minute is called the **cardiac output (CO)**, usually expressed as liters per minute. It is also the volume of blood flowing through *either* the systemic *or* the pulmonary circuit per minute.

The cardiac output is determined by multiplying the heart rate (HR)—the number of beats per minute—and the stroke volume (SV), the blood volume ejected by each ventricle with each beat:

$$CO = HR \times SV$$

Thus, if each ventricle has a rate of 72 beats/min and ejects 70 ml of blood with each beat, the cardiac output is

$$CO = 72 \text{ beats/min} \times 0.07 \text{ L/beat} = 5.0 \text{ L/min}$$

These values are approximately normal for a resting adult. Since, by coincidence, total blood volume is also approximately 5 L, this means that essentially all the blood is

pumped around the circuit once each minute. During periods of exercise in well-trained athletes, the cardiac output may reach 35 L/min.

The following description of the factors that alter the two determinants of cardiac output—heart rate and stroke volume—applies in all respects to both the right and left heart since stroke volume and heart rate are the same for both under steady-state conditions. It must also be emphasized that heart rate and stroke volume do not always change in the same direction. For example, as we shall see, stroke volume decreases following blood loss while heart rate increases. These changes produce opposing effects on cardiac output.

Control of Heart Rate

Rhythmical beating of the heart at a rate of approximately 100 beats/min will occur in the complete absence of any nervous or hormonal influences on the SA node. This is the inherent autonomous discharge rate of the SA node. The heart rate may be much lower or higher than this, however, since the SA node is normally under the constant influence of nerves and hormones.

As mentioned earlier, a large number of parasympathetic and sympathetic postganglionic fibers end on the SA node. Activity in the parasympathetic (vagus) nerves causes the heart rate to decrease, whereas activity in the sympathetic nerves increases the heart rate. In the resting state, there is considerably more parasympathetic activity to the heart than sympathetic, and so the normal resting heart rate is well below the inherent rate of 100 beats/min.

Figure 14-28 illustrates how sympathetic and parasympathetic activity influences SA-node function. Sympathetic stimulation increases the slope of the pacemaker potential,

FIGURE 14-28
Effects of sympathetic and parasympathetic nerve stimulation on the slope of the pacemaker potential of an SA-nodal cell. Note that parasympathetic stimulation not only reduces the slope of the pacemaker potential but also causes the membrane potential to be more negative before the pacemaker potential begins. (*Adapted from Hoffman and Cranefield.*)

causing the SA-node cells to reach threshold more rapidly and the heart rate to increase. Stimulation of the parasympathetics has the opposite effect: The slope of the pacemaker potential decreases, threshold is reached more slowly, and heart rate decreases. Parasympathetic stimulation also hyperpolarizes the plasma membrane of the SA-node cells so that the pacemaker potential starts from a lower value.

How do the neurotransmitters released by the autonomic neurons cause these changes in the pacemaker potential? They do so by opening or closing ion channels for sodium and potassium. For example, one action of acetylcholine, the parasympathetic neurotransmitter, is to increase the number of open potassium channels, which tends to hold the membrane potential closer to the potassium equilibrium potential.

Factors other than the cardiac nerves can also alter heart rate. Epinephrine, the main hormone liberated from the adrenal medulla, speeds the heart by acting on the same beta-adrenergic receptors in the SA node as does neurally released norepinephrine. The heart rate is also sensitive to changes in body temperature, plasma electrolyte concentrations, and hormones other than epinephrine. These factors are normally of lesser importance, however. Figure 14-29 summarizes the major determinants of heart rate.

As stated in the section on innervation, sympathetic and parasympathetic neurons innervate other parts of the conducting system as well as the SA node. Thus, sympathetic stimulation not only speeds the SA node but increases conduction through the AV node. Parasympathetic stimulation, in contrast, decreases the rate of spread of excitation along almost the entire conducting system of the heart.

Control of Stroke Volume

The second variable that determines cardiac output is stroke volume, the volume of blood ejected by each ventricle during each contraction. As emphasized earlier, the ventricles never completely empty themselves of blood during contraction. Therefore, a more forceful contraction can produce an increase in stroke volume. Changes in the force of contraction can be produced by a variety of factors, but two are dominant under most physiological conditions: (1) changes in the end-diastolic volume, that is, the volume of blood in the ventricles just before contraction; and (2) changes in the magnitude of sympathetic nervous system input to the ventricles.

Relationship Between End-diastolic Volume and Stroke Volume: Starling's Law of the Heart. It is possible to study the characteristics of an isolated heart by using what is called a heart-lung preparation (Figure 14-30). Tubes are placed in the heart and blood vessels of an anesthetized animal so that blood flows from the first part of the aorta into a blood-filled reservoir and from there into the right atrium. The blood is then pumped by the right heart via the lungs into the left heart, from which it is returned to the reservoir.

A key feature of this preparation is that the pressure causing blood flow *into* the heart can be altered simply by raising or lowering the reservoir. This is analogous to altering the systemic venous and right atrial pressures to cause changes in the quantity of blood entering the right ventricle during diastole. Thus, when the reservoir is raised, the pressure is raised, and ventricular filling increases, thereby increasing end-diastolic volume. The important finding is that the ventricle, now distended with more blood, re-

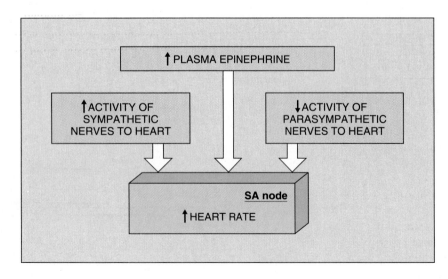

FIGURE 14-29

Major factors that influence heart rate. All effects are exerted upon the SA node. The figure shows how heart rate is increased; reversal of all the arrows in the boxes would illustrate how heart rate is decreased.

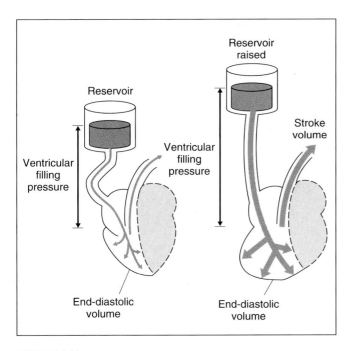

FIGURE 14-30

Experiment for demonstrating the relationship between ventricular end-diastolic volume and stroke volume (Starling's law of the heart). When the reservoir is raised, the pressure that causes ventricular filling is increased, and more blood enters the ventricle. This stretches the ventricular muscle, which responds with a stronger contraction.

sponds with a more forceful contraction. The net result is a new steady state in which end-diastolic volume and stroke volume are both increased. The British physiologist Ernest Henry Starling described this relationship between end-diastolic volume and force of contraction, and it is termed **Starling's law of the heart**.[6] A typical response curve obtained by progressively increasing end-diastolic volume is shown in Figure 14-31.

This characteristic of cardiac muscle is analogous to the length-tension relationship described for skeletal muscle in Chapter 11. End-diastolic volume acts as the preload for ventricular muscle, determining how stretched the ventricular sarcomeres are just before contraction. However, the major mechanism accounting for the increased contraction with increasing stretch is different for cardiac muscle than for skeletal muscle. For as yet unclear reasons, the affinity of troponin for calcium is increased with increasing length of the cardiac-muscle cells. Thus, at any given cytosolic calcium concentration, more calcium will

---

[6]It is also called the Frank-Starling mechanism in recognition of Otto Frank, who was one of the first to identify the relationship.

FIGURE 14-31

Relationship between ventricular end-diastolic volume and stroke volume (Starling's law of the heart). The data were obtained by progressively increasing ventricular filling pressure with a heart-lung preparation. The horizontal axis could have been labeled "sarcomere length," and the vertical "contractile force." In other words, this is a length-tension curve.

bind to troponin as the muscle is stretched, thereby leading to a stronger contraction.

The significance of the intrinsic mechanism represented by Starling's law of the heart should be apparent: When the flow of blood from the veins into the heart, termed **venous return**, increases, this automatically forces an increase in cardiac output by distending the ventricle and increasing stroke volume. One important function of this relationship is maintaining the equality of right and left cardiac outputs. Should the right heart, for example, suddenly begin to pump more blood than the left, the increased blood flow to the left ventricle would automatically produce an equivalent increase in left ventricular output. This ensures that blood will not accumulate in the lungs.

The Sympathetic Nerves. Sympathetic nerves are distributed not only to the conducting system but to the entire myocardium. The effect of the sympathetic mediator norepinephrine, acting on beta-adrenergic receptors, is to increase ventricular **contractility**, defined as the strength of contraction *at any given end-diastolic volume*. Plasma epinephrine, acting on these same receptors, also increases myocardial contractility. Thus, the increased force of contraction and stroke volume resulting from sympathetic-nerve stimulation or epinephrine is *independent* of a change in end-diastolic ventricular volume.

Note that a change in contraction force due to increased end-diastolic volume (Starling's law) does *not* reflect increased contractility. Increased contractility is specifically defined as an increased contraction force *at any given* end-diastolic volume.

The relationship between Starling's law and the cardiac sympathetic nerves as measured in a heart-lung prepara-

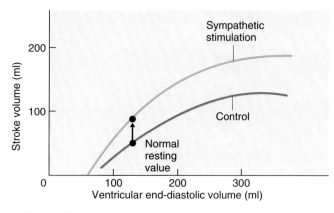

FIGURE 14-32

Effects on stroke volume of stimulating the sympathetic nerves to the heart. Stroke volume is increased at any given end-diastolic volume; that is, the sympathetic stimulation has increased ventricular contractility.

tion is illustrated in Figure 14-32. The red line is the same as the line shown in Figure 14-31. The blue line was obtained for the same heart during sympathetic-nerve stimulation. Starling's law still applies, but during nerve stimulation the stroke volume is greater at any given end-diastolic volume. In other words, the increased contractility leads to a more complete ejection of the end-diastolic ventricular volume.

FIGURE 14-33

Effects of sympathetic stimulation on ventricular contraction and relaxation. Note that both the rate of force development and the rate of relaxation are increased, as is the maximal force developed. All these changes reflect an increased contractility.

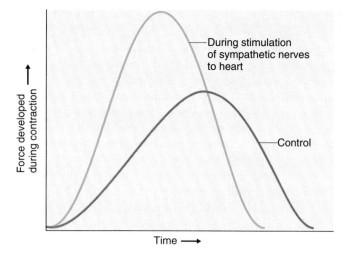

One way of quantitating contractility is as the **ejection fraction (EF)**, defined as the ratio of stroke volume (SV) to end-diastolic volume (EDV):

$$EF = \frac{SV}{EDV}$$

Expressed as a percentage, the ejection fraction normally averages 67 percent under resting conditions. Increased contractility causes an increased ejection fraction.

Not only does enhanced sympathetic-nerve activity to the myocardium cause the contraction to be more powerful, it also causes both the contraction and relaxation of the ventricles to occur more quickly (Figure 14-33). These latter effects are quite important since, as described earlier, increased sympathetic activity to the heart also increases heart rate. As heart rate increases, the time available for diastolic filling decreases, but the quicker contraction and relaxation induced simultaneously by the sympathetic neurons partially compensate for this problem by permitting a larger fraction of the cardiac cycle to be available for filling.

At the level of the contractile apparatus, two processes account for the increased contractility induced by norepinephrine and epinephrine. One is an increase in the number of actin-myosin cross-bridge attachments, resulting from an increased cytosolic calcium concentration. The other is an increase in the rate of cross-bridge cycling during a contraction. The cellular mechanisms by which these changes are brought about are summarized in Figure 14-34. This figure also describes the cause of the increased rate of relaxation associated with increased contractility.

In contrast to the sympathetic nerves, the parasympathetic nerves to the ventricles normally have only a small effect on contractility.

Table 14-5 summarizes the effects of the autonomic nerves on cardiac function.

In summary (Figure 14-35), the two major controllers of stroke volume are a mechanism (Starling's law) dependent upon changes in end-diastolic volume and a mechanism that is mediated by the cardiac sympathetic nerves and circulating epinephrine and that causes increased ventricular contractility. The contribution of each of these two mechanisms in specific physiological situations is described in later sections.

A summary of the major factors that determine cardiac output is presented in Figure 14-36, which combines the information of Figures 14-29 and 14-35.

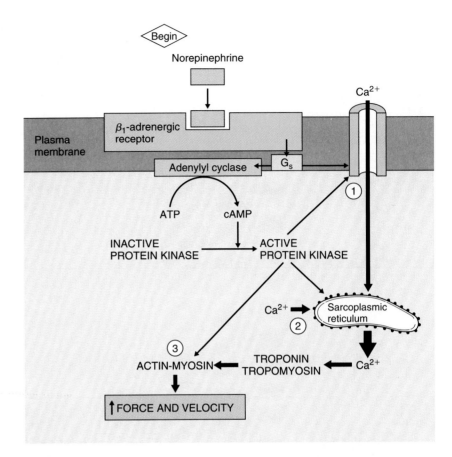

FIGURE 14-34

Mechanisms by which norepinephrine and epinephrine alter cardiac contractility and relaxation. Norepinephrine binds to beta$_1$-adrenergic receptors in the plasma membrane of the myocardial cells, and this causes the receptor to activate a G_s protein. This G protein has two distinct effects: it directly opens slow calcium channels in the plasma membrane, and it activates membrane-bound adenylyl cyclase. The latter effect results in an increase in intracellular cAMP, which activates cAMP-dependent protein kinase, which in turn phosphorylates and thereby activates at least three proteins: (1) a plasma-membrane protein that opens slow calcium channels; (2) a sarcoplasmic-reticulum protein that stimulates the ATP-dependent calcium-uptake pump in this organelle; and (3) myosin. These three phosphorylated proteins plus the direct G-protein opening of calcium channels then mediate the observed effects: (1) In the plasma membrane a greater number of slow calcium channels open during excitation, which permits more calcium to enter the cell and stimulate the sarcoplasmic reticulum to release still more calcium—the result is an increase in the number of actin-myosin cross-bridge attachments leading to more force development. (2) The sarcoplasmic reticulum protein stimulates the active transport of calcium into the sarcoplasmic reticulum, thereby increasing this organelle's calcium stores and the amount of calcium released into the cytosol during subsequent excitations. The increased rate of calcium pumping from the cytosol back into the sarcoplasmic reticulum after contraction is over also explains why norepinephrine speeds cardiac relaxation. (3) Phosphorylation of myosin causes an increase in the rate at which the cross bridges cycle. The result is an increase in the velocity of the contraction, that is, the rate of tension development per unit time.

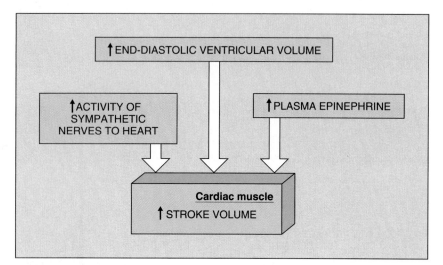

FIGURE 14-35
Major factors that directly influence stroke volume. The figure as drawn shows how stroke volume is increased. A reversal of all arrows in the boxes would illustrate how stroke volume is decreased.

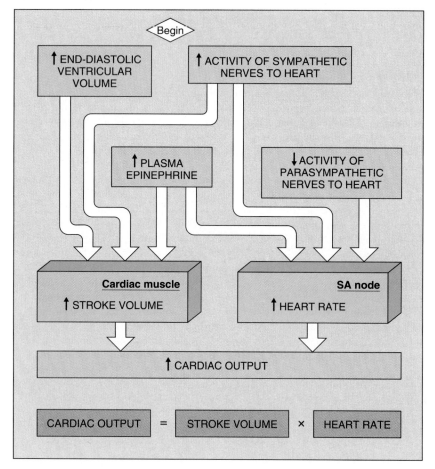

FIGURE 14-36
Major factors determining cardiac output (an amalgamation of Figures 14-29 and 14-35).

TABLE 14-5 EFFECTS OF AUTONOMIC NERVES ON THE HEART

Area affected	Sympathetic nerves	Parasympathetic nerves
SA node	Increased heart rate	Decreased heart rate
AV node	Increased conduction rate	Decreased conduction rate
Atrial muscle	Increased contractility	Decreased contractility
Ventricular muscle	Increased contractility	Decreased contractility (minor)

MEASUREMENT OF CARDIAC FUNCTION

Cardiac output in human beings can be measured by a variety of methods. Moreover, recent advances now make possible two- and three-dimensional images of the heart throughout the entire cardiac cycle. For example, in *echocardiography*, the most commonly used visualization technique, ultrasonic sound is beamed at the heart and returning echos are electronically plotted by computer to produce continuous images of the heart. This technique can detect abnormal functioning of cardiac valves or contractions of the cardiac walls and can be used to measure ejection fraction.

Echocardiography is a noninvasive technique because everything used remains external to the body. Other visualization techniques are invasive. One, *cardiac angiography*, requires the temporary placement of a thin flexible tube (catheter) into the heart, via an artery or vein, under fluoroscopy. A dye is then injected through the catheter during high-speed x-ray filming. This technique is useful not only for evaluating cardiac function but also for identifying narrowed coronary arteries.

SECTION C SUMMARY

ANATOMY

I. The atrioventricular (AV) valves prevent flow from the ventricles back into the atria.

II. The pulmonary and aortic valves prevent backflow from the pulmonary trunk into the right ventricle and from the aorta into the left ventricle.

III. Cardiac-muscle cells are joined by gap junctions that permit action potentials to be conducted from cell to cell.

IV. The myocardium also contains specialized muscle cells that constitute the conducting system of the heart, initiating the cardiac action potentials and speeding their spread through the heart.

HEARTBEAT COORDINATION

I. Cardiac-muscle cells must undergo action potentials for contraction to occur.

A. The rapid depolarization of the action potential in atrial and ventricular cells (other than those in the conducting system) is due mainly to a positive-feedback increase in sodium permeability.

B. Following the initial rapid depolarization, the membrane remains depolarized (the plateau phase) almost the entire duration of the contraction because of prolonged entry of calcium into the cell through slow plasma-membrane channels.

II. The SA node generates the current that leads to depolarization of all other cardiac-muscle cells.

A. The SA node manifests a pacemaker potential, which brings its membrane potential to threshold and initiates an action potential.

B. The impulse spreads from the SA node throughout both atria and to the AV node, where a small delay occurs. The impulse then passes in turn into the bundle of His, right and left bundle branches, Purkinje fibers, and non-conducting-system ventricular fibers.

III. Calcium, mainly released from the sarcoplasmic reticulum (SR), functions as the excitation-contraction coupler in cardiac muscle, as in skeletal muscle, by combining with troponin.

A. The major signal for calcium release from the SR

is calcium entering across the plasma membrane during the action potential.

B. The amount of calcium released does not usually saturate all troponin binding sites, and so the number of active cross bridges can be increased if cytosolic calcium is increased still further.

IV. Cardiac muscle cannot undergo summation of contractions because it has a very long refractory period.

MECHANICAL EVENTS OF THE CARDIAC CYCLE

I. The cardiac cycle is divided into systole (ventricular contraction) and diastole (ventricular relaxation).

A. At the onset of systole, ventricular pressure rapidly exceeds atrial pressure, and the AV valves close. The aortic and pulmonary valves are not yet open, however, and so no ejection occurs during this isovolumetric ventricular contraction.

B. When ventricular pressures exceed aortic and pulmonary trunk pressures, the aortic and pulmonary valves open, and ventricular ejection of blood occurs.

C. When the ventricles relax at the beginning of diastole, the ventricular pressures fall significantly below those in the aorta and pulmonary trunk, and the aortic and pulmonary valves close. Because the AV valves are also still closed, no change in ventricular volume occurs during this isovolumetric ventricular relaxation.

D. When ventricular pressures fall below the pressures in the right and the left atria, the AV valves open, and the ventricular filling phase of diastole begins.

E. Filling occurs very rapidly at first so that atrial contraction, which occurs at the very end of diastole, usually adds only a small amount of additional blood to the ventricles.

II. The amount of blood in the ventricles just before systole is the end-diastolic volume. The volume remaining after ejection is the end-systolic volume, and the volume ejected is the stroke volume.

III. Pressure changes in the systemic and pulmonary circulations have similar patterns, but the pulmonary pressures are much lower.

IV. The first heart sound is due to the closing of the AV valves, and the second to the closing of the aortic and pulmonary valves.

THE CARDIAC OUTPUT

I. The cardiac output is the volume of blood pumped by each ventricle and equals the product of heart rate and stroke volume.

A. Heart rate is increased by stimulation of the sympathetic nerves to the heart and by epinephrine; it is decreased by stimulation of the parasympathetic nerves to the heart.

B. Stroke volume is increased by an increase in end-diastolic volume (Starling's law of the heart) and by an increase in contractility due to sympathetic-nerve stimulation or to epinephrine.

SECTION C KEY TERMS

pericardium	P wave
myocardium	QRS complex
endothelial cells	T wave
endothelium	refractory period
atrioventricular (AV) valves	cardiac cycle
tricuspid valve	systole
mitral valve	diastole
papillary muscles	isovolumetric ventricular
pulmonary valve	contraction
aortic valve	ventricular ejection
conducting system	stroke volume
coronary arteries	isovolumetric ventricular
coronary blood flow	relaxation
sinoatrial (SA) node	ventricular filling
slow channels	end-diastolic volume
pacemaker potential	end-systolic volume
automaticity	heart sounds
heart rate	cardiac output (CO)
atrioventricular (AV) node	Starling's law of
bundle of His	the heart
right and left bundle	venous return
branches	contractility
Purkinje fibers	ejection fraction (EF)
electrocardiogram (ECG)	

SECTION C REVIEW QUESTIONS

1. List the structures through which blood passes from the systemic veins to the systemic arteries.

2. Contrast and compare cardiac muscle with skeletal and smooth muscle.

3. Describe the autonomic innervation of the heart, including the types of receptors involved.

4. Draw a ventricular action potential. Describe the changes in membrane permeability that underlie the potential changes.

5. Contrast action potentials in ventricular cells with SA-node action potentials. What is the pacemaker potential due to, and what is its inherent rate? By what mechanism does the SA node function as the pacemaker for the entire heart?

6. Describe the spread of excitation from the SA node through the rest of the heart.

7. Draw and label a normal ECG. Relate the P, QRS, and T waves to the ventricular action potential.

8. Describe the sequence of events leading to excitation-contraction coupling in cardiac muscle.

9. What prevents the heart from undergoing summation of contractions?

10. Draw a diagram of the pressure changes in the left ventricle and aorta throughout the cardiac cycle. Show when the valves open and close, when the heart sounds occur, and the pattern of ventricular ejection.

11. Contrast the pressures in the right ventricle and pulmonary trunk with those in the left ventricle and aorta.

12. What causes heart murmurs in diastole? In systole?

13. Write the formula relating cardiac output, heart rate, and stroke volume; give normal values for a resting adult.

14. Describe the effects of the sympathetic and parasympathetic nerves on heart rate. Which is dominant at rest?

15. What are the two major factors influencing force of contraction?

16. Draw a curve illustrating Starling's law of the heart.

17. Describe the effects of the sympathetic nerves on cardiac muscle during contraction and relaxation.

18. Draw a family of curves relating end-diastolic volume and stroke volume during different levels of sympathetic stimulation.

19. Summarize the effects of the autonomic nerves on the heart.

20. Draw a flow diagram summarizing the factors determining cardiac output.

SECTION

D

THE VASCULAR SYSTEM

The functional and structural characteristics of the blood vessels change with successive branching. Yet the entire cardiovascular system, from the heart to the smallest capillary, has one structural component in common, a smooth, single-celled layer of endothelial cells, or endothelium, which lines the inner (blood-contacting) surface of the vessels. Capillaries consist only of endothelium, whereas all other vessels have, in addition, layers of connective tissue and smooth muscle. Endothelial cells have a large number of active functions. These are summarized for reference in Table 14-6 and are described in relevant sections of this chapter or subsequent chapters.

We have previously described the pressures in the aorta and pulmonary arteries during the cardiac cycle. Figure 14-37 illustrates the pressure changes that occur along the rest of the systemic and pulmonary vascular systems. Text sections below dealing with the individual vascular segments will describe the reasons for these changes in pressure. For the moment, note only that by the time the blood has completed its journey back to the atrium in each circuit, virtually all the pressure originally generated by the ventricular contraction has been dissipated. The reason pressure at any point in the vascular system is less than that at an earlier point is that the blood vessels offer resistance to the flow from one point to the next.

TABLE 14-6   FUNCTIONS OF ENDOTHELIAL CELLS

1. Serve as a physical lining of heart and blood vessels

2. Secrete substances that act on adjacent vascular smooth muscle; these include the vasodilators, prostacyclin and endothelium-derived relaxing factor (EDRF), and the vasoconstrictor endothelin-1

3. Mediate angiogenesis (new capillary growth)

4. Regulate transport of macromolecules and other substances between plasma and interstitial fluid

5. Undergo contractile activity, which regulates capillary permeability

6. Influence vascular smooth-muscle proliferation in the disease atherosclerosis

7. Secrete substances that regulate platelet clumping, clotting, and anticlotting (Chapter 20)

8. Synthesize active hormones from inactive precursors (Chapter 16)

9. Extract or degrade hormones and other mediators (Chapter 15)

10. Function similarly to macrophages during immune responses (Chapter 20)

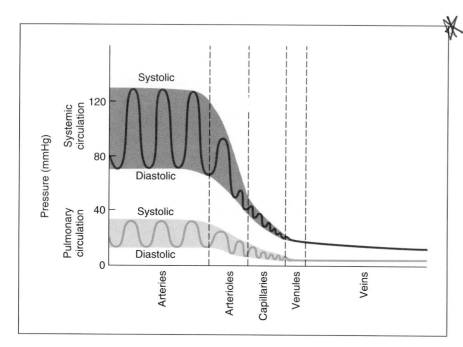

FIGURE 14-37
Pressures in the vascular system.

FIGURE 14-38
Movement of blood into and out of the arteries during the cardiac cycle. The lengths of the arrows denote relative quantities flowing into and out of the arteries and remaining in the arteries during systole. During systole, less blood leaves the arteries than enters from the heart, and so blood is retained in the arteries, stretching their walls. During diastole, the stretched walls recoil passively, and the blood retained in the arteries during the previous systole is driven out of the arteries.

ARTERIES

The aorta and other systemic arteries have thick walls containing large quantities of elastic tissue. Although they also have smooth muscle, arteries can be viewed most conveniently as elastic tubes. Because the arteries have large radii, they serve as low-resistance tubes conducting blood to the various organs. Their second major function, related to their elasticity, is to act as a "pressure reservoir" for maintaining blood flow through the tissues during diastole, as described below.

Arterial Blood Pressure

What are the factors determining the pressure within an elastic container, such as a balloon filled with water? The pressure inside the balloon depends on (1) the volume of water, and (2) how easily the balloon walls can be stretched. If the walls are very stretchable, large quantities of water can be added with only a small rise in pressure. Conversely, the addition of a small quantity of water causes a large pressure rise in a balloon that is difficult to stretch. The term used to denote how easily a structure can be stretched is **compliance**:

$$\text{Compliance} = \frac{\Delta \text{ volume}}{\Delta \text{ pressure}}$$

The *higher* the compliance of a structure, the *more easily* it can be stretched.

These principles can be applied to an analysis of arterial blood pressure. The contraction of the ventricles ejects

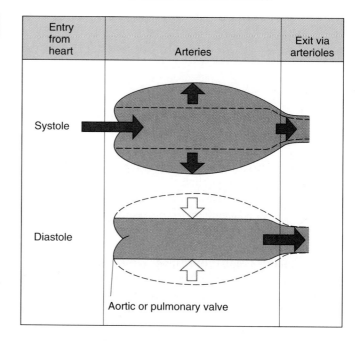

blood into the pulmonary and systemic arteries during systole. If a precisely equal quantity of blood were to flow simultaneously out of the arteries, the total volume of blood in the arteries would remain constant and arterial pressure would not change. Such is not the case, however. As shown in Figure 14-38, a volume of blood equal to only about one-third the stroke volume leaves the arteries during systole. The rest of the stroke volume remains in the arteries during systole, distending them and raising the arterial pressure. When ventricular contraction ends, the stretched arterial walls recoil passively, like a stretched

(A)

(B)

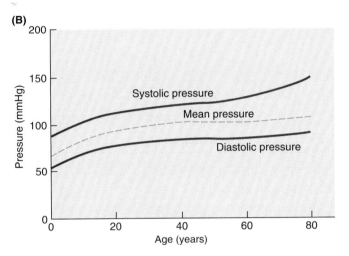

FIGURE 14-39

(A) Typical arterial pressure fluctuations during the cardiac cycle. (B) Changes in arterial pressure with age. (*Adapted from Guyton.*)

the **pulse pressure**. It can be felt as a pulsation or throb in the arteries of the wrist or neck with each heartbeat. During diastole, nothing is felt over the artery, but the rapid rise in pressure at the next systole pushes out the artery wall, and it is this expansion of the vessel that produces the detectable throb.

The two most important factors determining the magnitude of the pulse pressure, that is, how much greater systolic pressure is than diastolic, are (1) stroke volume, and (2) arterial compliance. Specifically, the pulse pressure produced by a ventricular ejection will be greater if the volume of blood ejected is increased or if the arteries are less compliant. This last phenomenon occurs in arteriosclerosis, the "hardening" of the arteries that progresses with age and accounts for the increasing pulse pressure seen so often in older people.

It is evident from Figure 14-39A that arterial pressure is continuously changing throughout the cardiac cycle. The *average* pressure (**mean arterial pressure, MAP**) in the cycle is not merely the value halfway between systolic pressure and diastolic pressure because diastole usually lasts longer than systole. The true mean arterial pressure can be obtained by complex methods, but for most purposes it is approximately equal to the diastolic pressure plus one-third of the pulse pressure (SP − DP):

$$MAP = DP + \tfrac{1}{3}(SP - DP)$$

Thus, in our example, MAP = 75 + $\tfrac{1}{3}$(50) = 92 mmHg. The MAP is the most important of the pressures described because it is the pressure driving blood into the tissues averaged over the entire cardiac cycle. We can say mean "arterial" pressure without specifying to which artery we are referring because the aorta and other large arteries have such large diameters that they offer only negligible resistance to flow, and the mean pressures are therefore similar everywhere in the large arteries.

One additional important point should be made: We have stated that arterial compliance is an important determinant of *pulse* pressure, but for complex reasons, compliance does *not* influence the *mean* arterial pressure. Thus, for example, a person with a low arterial compliance (due to atherosclerosis) but an otherwise normal cardiovascular system will have a large pulse pressure but a normal mean arterial pressure.

Measurement of Arterial Pressure

Both systolic and diastolic blood pressure are readily measured in human beings with the use of a sphygmomanometer. An inflatable cuff is wrapped around the upper arm, and a stethoscope is placed in a spot on the arm just below the cuff and beneath which the major artery to the lower arm runs.

rubber band being released, and blood continues to be driven into the arterioles during diastole. As blood leaves the arteries, the arterial volume and therefore the arterial pressure slowly fall, but the next ventricular contraction occurs while there is still adequate blood in the arteries to stretch them partially. Therefore, the arterial pressure does not fall to zero.

The aortic pressure pattern shown in Figure 14-39A is typical of the pressure changes that occur in all the large systemic arteries. The maximum pressure reached during peak ventricular ejection is called **systolic pressure (SP)**. The minimum pressure occurs just before ventricular ejection begins and is called **diastolic pressure (DP)**. Arterial pressure is generally recorded as systolic/diastolic, that is, 125/75 mmHg in our example (see Figure 14-39B for average values in people of different ages).

The difference between systolic pressure and diastolic pressure (125 − 75 = 50 mmHg in the example) is called

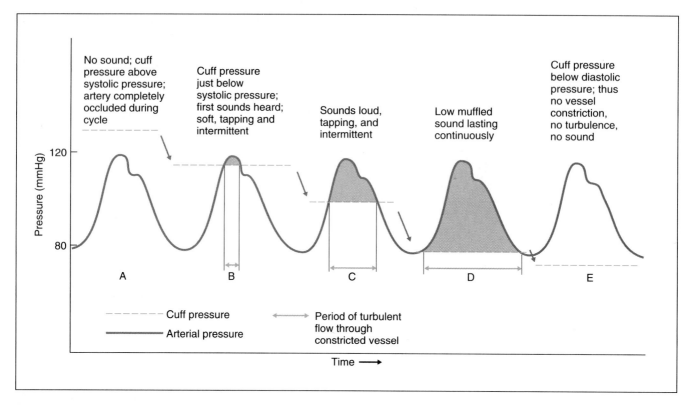

FIGURE 14-40
Sounds heard through a stethoscope while the cuff pressure of a sphygmomanometer is gradually lowered. Sounds are first heard at systolic pressure, and they disappear at diastolic pressure.

The cuff is then inflated with air to a pressure greater than systolic blood pressure (Figure 14-40). The high pressure in the cuff is transmitted through the tissue of the arm and completely compresses the artery under the cuff, thereby preventing blood flow through the artery. The air in the cuff is then slowly released, causing the pressure in the cuff and on the artery to drop. When cuff pressure has fallen to a value just below the systolic pressure, the artery opens slightly and allows blood flow for this brief time. During this interval, the blood flow through the partially compressed artery occurs at a very high velocity because of the small opening and the large pressure difference across the opening. The high-velocity blood flow is turbulent and produces vibrations that can be heard through the stethoscope. Thus, the pressure, measured on the manometer attached to the cuff, at which sounds are first heard as the cuff pressure is lowered is identified as the systolic blood pressure.

As the pressure in the cuff is lowered further, the duration of blood flow through the artery in each cycle becomes longer. When the cuff pressure reaches the diastolic blood pressure, all sound stops, because flow is now continuous and nonturbulent through the open artery.

Thus, diastolic pressure is identified as the cuff pressure at which sounds disappear.

It should be clear from this description that the sounds heard during measurement of blood pressure are *not* the same as the heart sounds described earlier, which are due to closing of cardiac valves.

ARTERIOLES

The arterioles play two major roles: (1) The arterioles in individual organs are responsible for determining the relative blood flows to those organs, and (2) the arterioles, as a whole, are a major factor in determining mean arterial pressure. The first function will be described in this section, and the second in the section on control of blood pressure.

Figure 14-41 illustrates the major principles of blood-flow distribution in terms of a simple model, a fluid-filled tank with a series of compressible outflow tubes. What determines the rate of flow through each exit tube? As stated in Section B of this chapter,

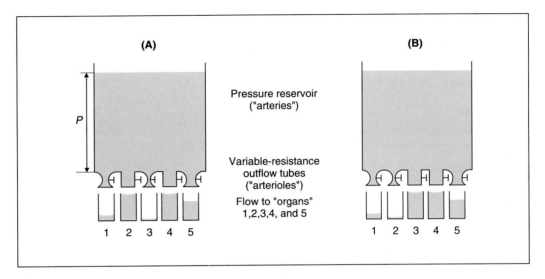

FIGURE 14-41

Physical model of the relationship between arterial pressure, arteriolar radius in different organs, and blood-flow distribution. In (A), blood flow is high through tube 2 and low through tube 3, whereas just the opposite is true for (B). This shift in blood flow was achieved by constricting tube 2 and dilating tube 3.

$$F = \frac{\Delta P}{R}$$

Since the driving pressure (the height of the fluid column in the tank) is identical for each tube, differences in flow are completely determined by differences in the resistance to flow offered by each tube. The lengths of the tubes are approximately the same, and the viscosity of the fluid is constant; therefore, differences in resistance offered by the tubes are due solely to differences in their radii. Obviously, the widest tubes have the greatest flows. If we equip each outflow tube with an adjustable cuff, we can obtain various combinations of flows.

This analysis can now be applied to the cardiovascular system. The tank is analogous to the arteries, which serve as a pressure reservoir, the major arteries themselves being so large that they contribute little resistance to flow. Therefore, all the large arteries of the body can be considered a single pressure reservoir.

The arteries branch within each organ into progressively smaller arteries, which then branch into arterioles. The smallest arteries are narrow enough to offer significant resistance to flow, but the still narrower arterioles are the major sites of resistance in the vascular tree and are therefore analogous to the outflow tubes in the model. This explains the large decrease in mean pressure—from about 90 mmHg to 35 mmHg—as blood flows through the arterioles (Figure 14-37). Pulse pressure also diminishes to the point that flow beyond the arterioles, that is, through capillaries and veins, is no longer pulsatile.

Like the model's outflow tubes, the arteriolar radii in individual organs are subject to independent adjustment. The blood flow through any organ is given by the following equation, assuming for simplicity that the venous pressure, the other component of the pressure gradient, is zero:

$$F_{\text{organ}} = \frac{\text{MAP}}{R_{\text{organ}}}$$

Since the MAP, the driving force for flow through each organ, is identical throughout the body, differences in flows between organs depend entirely on the relative resistances offered by the arterioles of each organ. Arterioles contain smooth muscle, which can either relax and cause the vessel radius to increase (**vasodilation**) or contract and decrease the vessel radius (**vasoconstriction**). Thus the pattern of blood-flow distribution depends upon the degree of arteriolar smooth-muscle contraction within each organ and tissue.

Arteriolar smooth muscle possesses a large degree of spontaneous activity, that is, contraction independent of any neural, hormonal, or paracrine input. This spontaneous contractile activity, which is submaximal, is called **myogenic tone** (also termed intrinsic or basal tone). It sets a baseline level of contraction that can be increased or decreased by external signals, such as neurotransmitters. These signals act by inducing changes in the muscle cell's cytosolic calcium concentration (see Chapter 11 for a description of excitation-contraction coupling in smooth muscle). An increase in contractile force above the vessel's myogenic tone causes vasoconstriction, whereas a decrease in contractile force causes vasodilation. The mechanisms controlling these changes in arteriolar resistance fall into two general categories: (1) local controls, and (2) extrinsic (or reflex) controls.

Local Controls

The term **local controls** denotes mechanisms independent of nerves or hormones by which organs and tissues alter their own arteriolar resistances, thereby self-regulating their blood flows. This self-regulation includes the phenomena of active hyperemia, flow autoregulation, reactive hyperemia, and local responses to injury.

Active Hyperemia.   Most organs and tissues manifest an increased blood flow (**hyperemia**) when their metabolic activity is increased (Figure 14-42); this is termed **active hyperemia**. For example, the blood flow to exercising skeletal muscle increases in direct proportion to the increased activity of the muscle. Active hyperemia is the direct result of arteriolar dilation in the more active organ or tissue. The vasodilation does not depend upon the presence of nerves or hormones but is a locally mediated response by which an increased rate of activity in an organ or tissue automatically produces an increased blood flow to that organ or tissue.

The factors acting upon arteriolar smooth muscle in active hyperemia to cause it to relax are local chemical changes in the extracellular fluid surrounding the arterioles. These result from the increased metabolic activity in the cells near the arterioles. The relative contributions of the various factors implicated vary, depending upon the organs involved and on the duration of the increased activity. Therefore, we shall only name but not quantify some of these local chemical changes that occur in the extracellular fluid: decreased oxygen concentration; increased concentrations of carbon dioxide, hydrogen ion, and metabolites such as adenosine; increased concentration of potassium as a result of enhanced potassium movement out of muscle cells during the more frequent action potentials; increased osmolarity resulting from the increased breakdown of high-molecular-weight substances; increased concentrations of eicosanoids (Chapter 7); and, in some glands, increased concentration of a peptide known as **bradykinin**. This last substance is generated locally from a circulating protein, **kininogen**, by the action of an enzyme, **kallikrein**, secreted by the active gland cells.

Changes in all these chemical factors have been shown to cause arteriolar dilation under controlled experimental conditions, and they all probably contribute to the active-hyperemia response in one or more organs. It is likely, moreover, that additional important local factors remain to be discovered. It must be emphasized once more that all these chemical changes in the extracellular fluid act locally upon the arteriolar smooth muscle, causing it to relax. No nerves or hormones are involved.

It should not be too surprising that active hyperemia is most highly developed in muscle and glands, which show the widest range of normal metabolic activities in the body. It is highly efficient, therefore, that their supply of

FIGURE 14-42

Local control of organ blood flow. Decreases in metabolic activity or increases in blood pressure would produce changes opposite those shown here.

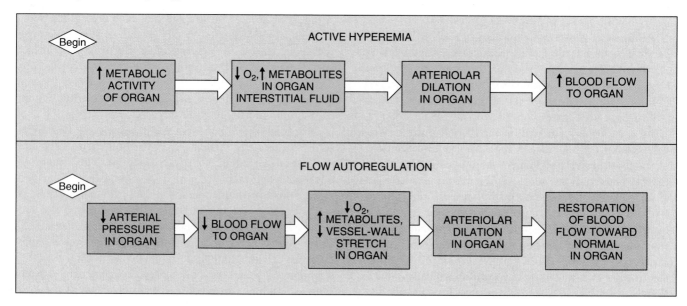

blood be primarily determined locally. Active hyperemia also provides a local mechanism for adjusting flow *within* an organ when different regions of the organ undergo different degrees of metabolic activity.

Flow Autoregulation. During active hyperemia, increased metabolic activity of the tissue or organ is the initial event leading to local vasodilation. However, locally mediated changes in arteriolar resistance may also occur when a tissue or organ suffers a change in its blood supply resulting from a change in blood pressure (Figure 14-42). The change in resistance is in the direction of maintaining blood flow nearly constant in the face of the pressure change and is therefore termed **flow autoregulation**. For example, when arterial pressure in an organ is reduced, say, because of a partial occlusion in the artery supplying the organ, local controls cause arteriolar vasodilation, which tends to maintain flow relatively constant.

What is the mechanism of flow autoregulation? One mechanism is the same metabolic factors described for active hyperemia. When an arterial pressure reduction lowers blood flow to an organ, the supply of oxygen to the organ is diminished and the local extracellular oxygen concentration decreases. Simultaneously, the extracellular concentrations of carbon dioxide, hydrogen ion, and metabolites all increase because they are not removed by the blood as fast as they are produced. Also, eicosanoid synthesis is increased by still unclear stimuli. Thus, the local metabolic changes occurring during decreased blood supply at constant metabolic activity are similar to those that occur during increased metabolic activity. This is because both situations reflect an initial imbalance between blood supply and level of cellular metabolic activity. Note then that the vasodilations of active hyperemia and of flow autoregulation in response to low arterial pressure differ not in their major mechanisms—local metabolic factors—but in the event—altered metabolism or altered blood pressure—that brings these mechanisms into play.

Flow autoregulation is not limited to circumstances in which arterial pressure goes down. The opposite events may occur when, for various reasons, arterial pressure increases: The initial increase in flow due to the increase in pressure removes the local vasodilator chemical factors faster than they are produced and increases the local concentration of oxygen. This causes the arterioles to constrict, thereby maintaining local flow relatively constant in the face of the increased pressure.

Although our description has emphasized the role of local *chemical* factors in flow autoregulation, it should be noted that another mechanism also participates in this phenomenon in certain tissues and organs. Some arteriolar smooth muscle responds directly to increased stretch, caused by increased arterial pressure, by contracting to a greater extent. Conversely, decreased stretch, due to de-

creased arterial pressure, causes this vascular smooth muscle to decrease its tone. These direct responses of arteriolar smooth muscle to stretch are termed **myogenic responses**. They are due to stretch-dependent changes in calcium movement into the smooth-muscle cells.

Reactive Hyperemia. When an organ or tissue has had its blood supply completely occluded, a profound transient increase in its blood flow occurs as soon as the occlusion is released. This phenomenon, known as **reactive hyperemia**, is essentially an extreme form of flow autoregulation. During the period of no blood flow, the arterioles in the affected organ or tissue dilate, owing to the local factors described above. Blood flow, therefore, is very great through these wide-open arterioles as soon as the occlusion to arterial inflow is removed.

Response to Injury. Tissue injury causes a variety of substances to be released locally from cells or generated from plasma precursors. These substances make arteriolar smooth muscle relax and cause vasodilation in an injured area. This phenomenon, part of the general process known as inflammation, will be described in detail in Chapter 20.

Extrinsic Controls

Sympathetic Nerves. Most arterioles receive a rich supply of sympathetic postganglionic nerve fibers. These neurons release norepinephrine,[7] which combines with alpha-adrenergic receptors on the vascular smooth muscle to cause vasoconstriction.

Note that the receptors for norepinephrine on arterioles are alpha-adrenergic, whereas those for norepinephrine on heart muscle, including the conducting system, are mainly beta-adrenergic. This permits the use of beta-adrenergic antagonists to block the actions of norepinephrine on the heart but not the arterioles, and vice versa for alpha-adrenergic antagonists.

Control of the sympathetic nerves can also be used to produce vasodilation. Since the sympathetic nerves are seldom completely quiescent but discharge at some finite rate, which varies from organ to organ, they always cause some degree of tonic constriction in addition to the vessels' myogenic tone. Dilation can be achieved by *decreasing* the rate of sympathetic activity below the basal level.

The skin offers an excellent example of the processes. At room temperature, skin arterioles are already under the

---

[7]There is one possible exception to the generalization that sympathetic nerves to arterioles release norepinephrine. In some mammalian species, a second group of sympathetic (not parasympathetic) nerves to the arterioles in skeletal muscle release acetylcholine, which causes arteriolar dilation and increased blood flow. The only known function of these vasodilator fibers is in the response to exercise or stress. Because their existence in human beings is questionable, we shall not deal with them here.

influence of a moderate rate of sympathetic discharge. An appropriate stimulus—fear or loss of blood, for example—causes reflex enhancement of this sympathetic discharge, and the arterioles constrict further. In contrast, an increased body temperature reflexly inhibits the sympathetic nerves to the skin, the arterioles dilate, and the skin flushes. This generalization cannot be stressed too strongly: Control of the sympathetic constrictor nerves to arteriolar smooth muscle can accomplish either vasodilation or vasoconstriction.

In contrast to active hyperemia and flow autoregulation, the primary functions of sympathetic nerves to blood vessels are concerned not with the coordination of local metabolic needs and blood flow but with reflexes. The most common reflex employing these nerves, as we shall see, is that which regulates arterial blood pressure by influencing arteriolar resistance throughout the body. Other reflexes redistribute blood flow to achieve a specific function (for example, to increase heat loss from the skin).

Parasympathetic Nerves and Other Vasodilator Nerves. Acetylcholine, the major parasympathetic neurotransmitter, is a vasodilator, but with few exceptions—notably the blood vessels supplying the external genitals—there is little important parasympathetic innervation of arterioles. Under study, however, are the possible physiological roles of a group of autonomic nerves that release neurotransmitters other than norepinephrine or acetylcholine and cause vasodilation.

Hormones. Epinephrine, like norepinephrine released from sympathetic nerves, can combine with alpha-adrenergic receptors on arteriolar smooth muscle and cause vas-

oconstriction. The story is more complex, however, because many arteriolar smooth-muscle cells possess beta-adrenergic receptors as well as alpha-adrenergic receptors, and combination of epinephrine with these beta-adrenergic receptors causes the muscle cells to relax rather than contract (Figure 14-43).

In most vascular beds, the existence of beta-adrenergic receptors is of little if any importance since they are greatly outnumbered by the alpha-adrenergic receptors. The arterioles in skeletal muscle are an important exception, however, because they have large numbers of beta-adrenergic receptors. Circulating epinephrine therefore usually causes dilation in this vascular bed.

Another hormone important for arteriolar control is angiotensin II, which directly constricts most arterioles and also increases the activity of the sympathetic nervous system. This peptide is part of the renin-angiotensin system, which will be described fully in Chapter 16.

Yet another important hormone that causes arteriolar constriction is vasopressin, which, as described in Chapter 10, is released into the blood by the posterior pituitary gland. The functions of vasopressin will also be described more fully in Chapter 16.

Finally, the hormone secreted by the atria—atrial natriuretic factor—is a potent vasodilator. Whether this hormone, whose actions on the kidneys are described in Chapter 16, plays a widespread role in control of arterioles is unsettled.

Endothelial Cells and Vascular Smooth Muscle

It should be clear from the preceding discussion that a large number of substances can induce the contraction or relaxation of vascular smooth muscle. Many substances do

FIGURE 14-43

Effects of sympathetic nerves and plasma epinephrine on the arterioles in skeletal muscle. After its release from neuron terminals, norepinephrine diffuses to the arterioles, whereas epinephrine—a hormone—is blood-borne. Note that activation of alpha-adrenergic receptors and beta-adrenergic receptors produces opposing effects. For simplicity, norepinephrine is shown binding only to alpha-adrenergic receptors; it also can bind to beta-adrenergic receptors on the arterioles, but this occurs to a lesser extent.

so by acting *directly* on the smooth muscle, but others act *indirectly* via the endothelial cells adjacent to the smooth muscle. Endothelial cells, in response to these latter substances as well as certain mechanical stimuli, secrete several paracrine agents, which then diffuse to the adjacent vascular smooth muscle and induce either relaxation or contraction, resulting in vasodilation or vasoconstriction, respectively.

One vasodilator released by endothelial cells is the eicosanoid **prostacyclin**, the actions of which will be described further in Chapter 20 in the context of blood clotting. A second, very important vasodilator released by endothelial cells is **endothelium-derived relaxing factor (EDRF)**, which is actually nitric oxide (formed in the endothelial cells from arginine). EDRF is released continuously in significant amounts by endothelial cells in the arterioles and contributes to arteriolar vasodilation in the basal state, but its secretion is rapidly and markedly increased in response to a large number of the chemical mediators involved in both reflex and local control of arterioles. For example, EDRF release is stimulated by bradykinin and histamine, substances produced locally during inflammation.

Endothelial cells in *arteries* can also secrete EDRF, in response to the mechanical shear stress that accompanies high blood-flow rate. The EDRF causes the arterial vascular smooth muscle to relax and the artery to dilate. This "flow-induced arterial vasodilation," which is independent of internal pressure and should be distinguished from *arteriolar* flow autoregulation, may be important in optimizing the supply of blood to tissues.

One of the *vasoconstrictor* substances released by endothelial cells in response to certain mechanical and chemical stimuli is **endothelin-1**, which belongs to a family of peptide paracrine agents secreted in various organs

and tissues. The physiological role of this potent vasoconstrictor is presently unknown.

Arteriolar Control in Specific Organs

Figure 14-44 summarizes the factors that determine arteriolar radius. The importance of local and reflex controls varies from organ to organ, and Table 14-7 lists for reference the key features of arteriolar control in specific organs.

CAPILLARIES

As mentioned at the beginning of Section B, at any given moment, approximately 5 percent of the total circulating blood is flowing through the capillaries, and it is this 5 percent that is performing the ultimate function of the entire cardiovascular system—the exchange of nutrients and metabolic end products. (Some exchange also occurs in the venules, which can be viewed as extensions of capillaries.)

The capillaries permeate almost every tissue of the body. Since most cells are no more than 0.01 cm from a capillary, diffusion distances are very small, and exchange is highly efficient. There are an estimated 25,000 mi of capillaries in an adult, each individual capillary being only about 1 mm long with an inner diameter of 5 μm, just wide enough for an erythrocyte to squeeze through. (For comparison, a human hair is about 100 μm in diameter.)

The essential role of capillaries in tissue function has stimulated many questions concerning how capillaries develop and grow (**angiogenesis**). For example, how do tumors stimulate growth of new capillaries, and what turns

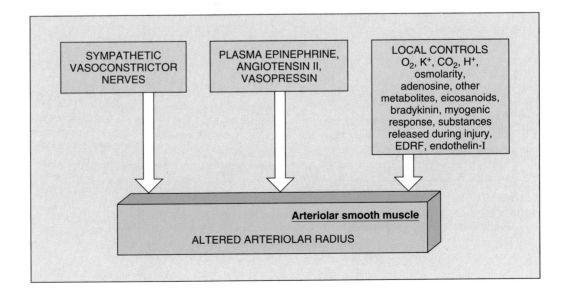

FIGURE 14-44
Major factors affecting arteriolar radius.

TABLE 14-7   VASCULAR CONTROL IN SPECIFIC ORGANS

Heart

High intrinsic tone; oxygen extraction is very high at rest and flow must increase when oxygen consumption increases.

Controlled mainly by local metabolic factors and flow autoregulation; direct sympathetic influences are minor and normally overridden by local factors.

Vessels are compressed during systole, and so coronary flow occurs mainly during diastole.

Skeletal Muscle

Controlled by local metabolic factors during exercise.

Sympathetic nerves cause vasoconstriction (mediated by alpha-adrenergic receptors) in reflex response to decreased arterial pressure.

Epinephrine causes vasodilation, via beta-adrenergic receptors, when present in low concentration and vasoconstriction, via alpha-adrenergic receptors, when present in high concentration.

GI Tract, Spleen, Pancreas, and Liver

Actually two capillary beds partially in series with each other; blood from the capillaries of the GI tract, spleen, and pancreas flows via the portal vein to the liver. In addition, the liver also receives a separate arterial blood supply.

Sympathetic nerves cause vasoconstriction, mediated by alpha-adrenergic receptors, in reflex response to decreased arterial pressure and during stress. The venous constriction causes displacement of a large volume of blood from the liver to the central venous pool.

Active hyperemia occurs following ingestion of a meal and is mediated by local metabolic factors and hormones secreted by the GI tract.

Kidneys

Flow autoregulation is a major factor.

Sympathetic nerves cause vasoconstriction, mediated by alpha-adrenergic receptors, in reflex response to decreased arterial pressure and during stress. Angiotensin II is also a major vasoconstrictor. These reflexes help conserve sodium and water.

Brain

Excellent flow autoregulation.

Distribution of blood within the brain is controlled by local metabolic factors.

Vasodilation occurs in response to increased concentration of carbon dioxide in arterial blood.

Influenced very little by the autonomic nervous system.

Skin

Controlled mainly by sympathetic nerves, mediated by alpha-adrenergic receptors; reflex vasoconstriction occurs in response to decreased arterial pressure and cold, whereas vasodilation occurs in response to heat.

Substances released from sweat glands and/or as yet uncharacterized nerves also cause vasodilation.

Venous plexus contains large volume of blood which contributes to skin color.

Lungs

Very low resistance compared to systemic circulation.

Controlled mainly by gravitational forces and passive physical forces within the lung.

Constriction, mediated by local factors, occurs in response to low oxygen concentration—just opposite that which occurs in the systemic circulation.

FIGURE 14-45

Capillary cross section. There are two endothelial cells in the figure, but the nucleus of only one is seen because the other is out of the plane of section. The fused-vesicle channel is part of endothelial cell 2. (*Adapted from Lentz.*)

on angiogenesis during wound healing? The vascular endothelial cells contain all the information needed to build an entire new capillary network by cell locomotion and cell division. They are stimulated to do so by a variety of **angiogenic factors** secreted locally by various tissue cells and the endothelial cells themselves. Tumor cells also secrete angiogenic factors.

Anatomy of the Capillary Network

Capillary structure varies considerably from organ to organ, but the typical capillary (Figure 14-45) is a thin-walled tube of endothelial cells one layer thick resting on a basement membrane, without any surrounding smooth-muscle or elastic tissue. Capillaries in several organs have a second set of cells that adhere to the opposite side of the basement membrane and influence the ability of substances to penetrate the endothelial layer.

The flat cells that constitute the endothelial tube are not attached tightly to each other but are separated by narrow water-filled spaces termed **intercellular clefts**. The endothelial cells generally contain large numbers of endocytotic and exocytotic vesicles, and sometimes these fuse to form continuous **fused-vesicle channels** across the cell (Figure 14-45).

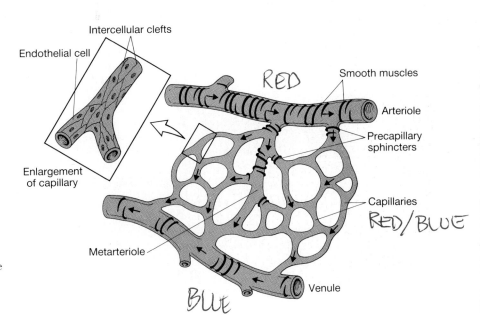

FIGURE 14-46

Diagram of microcirculation. Note the absence of smooth muscle in the capillaries. (*Adapted from Chaffee and Lytle.*)

Blood flow through capillaries depends very much on the state of the other vessels that constitute the microcirculation (Figure 14-46). Thus, vasodilation of the arterioles supplying the capillaries causes increased capillary flow, whereas arteriolar vasoconstriction reduces capillary flow. In addition, in some tissues and organs blood does not enter capillaries directly from arterioles but from vessels, called **metarterioles**, which connect arterioles to venules. Metarterioles are transitional vessels in that they retain, like arterioles, scattered smooth-muscle cells. The site at which a capillary exits from a metarteriole is surrounded by a ring of smooth muscle, the **precapillary sphincter**, which relaxes or contracts in response to local metabolic factors. When contracted, the precapillary sphincter closes the entry to the capillary completely. The more active the tissue, the more precapillary sphincters are open at any moment and the more capillaries in the network are receiving blood. Precapillary sphincters may also exist at the site of capillary exit from arterioles.

Velocity of Capillary Blood Flow

Figure 14-47 illustrates a simple mechanical model of a series of 1-cm-diameter balls being pushed down a single tube that branches into narrower tubes. Although each tributary tube has a smaller cross section than the wide tube, the sum of the tributary cross sections is much greater than that of the wide tube. Let us assume that in the wide tube each ball moves 3 cm/min. If the balls are 1 cm in diameter and they move two abreast, six balls leave the wide tube per minute and enter the narrow tubes, and six balls leave the narrow tubes per minute. At what speed does each ball move in the small tubes? The answer is *1 cm/min.*

This example illustrates the following important principle: When a continuous stream moves through consecutive sets of tubes, the velocity of flow decreases as the sum of the cross-sectional areas of the tubes increases. This is precisely the case in the cardiovascular system (Figure 14-48). The blood velocity is very great in the aorta, slows progressively in the arteries and arterioles, and then slows markedly as the blood passes through the huge cross-sectional area of the capillaries. The velocity of flow then progressively increases in the venules and veins because the cross-sectional area decreases.

Diffusion Across the Capillary Wall: Exchanges of Nutrients and Metabolic End Products

There are three basic mechanisms by which substances move across the capillary walls in most organs and tissues to enter or leave the interstitial fluid: diffusion, vesicle transport, and bulk flow. Mediated transport constitutes a fourth mechanism in the capillaries of the brain.

FIGURE 14-47

Relationship between total cross-sectional area and flow velocity. The total cross-sectional area of the small tubes is three times greater than that of the large tube. Accordingly, velocity of flow is one-third as great in the small tubes.

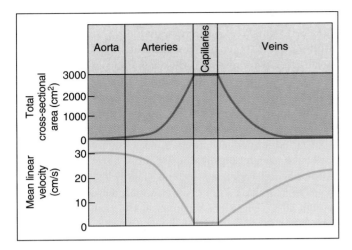

FIGURE 14-48

Relationship between total cross-sectional area and flow velocity in the systemic circulation (*Adapted from Lytle.*)

In all capillaries, excluding those in the brain, the first of these mechanisms—diffusion—constitutes the only important means by which net movement of nutrients, oxygen, and metabolic end products occurs across capillary walls. As described in the next section, there is some movement of these substances by bulk flow, but it is of negligible importance.

The factors determining diffusion rates were described in Chapter 6. Lipid-soluble substances, including oxygen and carbon dioxide, easily diffuse through the plasma membranes of the capillary endothelial cells. In contrast, ions and polar molecules are poorly soluble in lipid and must pass through small water-filled channels in the endothelial lining. One location of these channels is the intercellular clefts, that is, the narrow water-filled spaces between adjacent cells.[8] Another set of water-filled channels is provided by the fused-vesicle channels that penetrate the endothelial cells. The presence of water-filled channels in the capillary walls causes the permeability of ions and small polar molecules to be quite high, although still much lower than that of lipid-soluble molecules.

The intercellular clefts are, however, too small to allow the passage of proteins, but some protein can diffuse through the fused-vesicle channels, which are larger. Protein may also cross by endocytosis of plasma at the luminal border and movement of the vesicle across the endothelial cell, with exocytosis of its contents at the interstitial side. Although these various mechanisms do provide a means

for protein movement from plasma to interstitial fluid, such movement is quite small in most organs.

Variations in the size of the water-filled channels account for the great differences in the "leakiness" of capillaries in different organs. At one extreme are the "tight" capillaries of the brain, which have no intercellular clefts, only tight junctions. Therefore, water-soluble substances, even those of low molecular weight, can gain access to or exit from brain interstitial space only by carrier-mediated transport through the blood-brain barrier (Chapter 8).

At the other end of the spectrum are liver capillaries, which have large intercellular clefts as well as holes within the endothelial cells so that even protein molecules can readily pass. This is important because one of the major functions of the liver is the synthesis of plasma proteins and the metabolism of protein-bound substances, both of which must be able to enter or leave the blood.

The leakiness of capillaries in most organs and tissues lies between these extremes of brain and liver capillaries.

What is the sequence of events involved in transfers of materials between capillaries and cells? Tissue cells do not exchange material *directly* with blood; the fluid surrounding the cells—the interstitial fluid—acts as intermediary. Therefore, nutrients diffuse first across the capillary wall into the interstitial fluid, from which they gain entry to cells. Conversely, metabolic end products move across the tissue cells' plasma membranes into interstitial fluid, from which they diffuse into the plasma.

Transcapillary diffusion gradients for oxygen, nutrients, and metabolic end products occur as a result of cellular utilization or production of the substance. Let us take two examples: glucose and carbon dioxide in muscle. Glucose is continuously transported from interstitial fluid into the muscle cells by carrier-mediated transport mechanisms and utilized there. The removal of glucose from interstitial fluid lowers the interstitial-fluid glucose concentration below the glucose concentration in capillary plasma and creates the gradient for diffusion of glucose from the capillary into the interstitial fluid.

Simultaneously, carbon dioxide is continuously produced by muscle cells and diffuses into the interstitial fluid. This causes the carbon dioxide concentration in interstitial fluid to be greater than that in capillary plasma, producing a gradient for carbon dioxide diffusion from the interstitial fluid into the capillary. Note that in both examples metabolism of the substance is the event that ultimately establishes the transcapillary diffusion gradients.

If a tissue is to increase its metabolic rate, it must obtain more nutrients from the blood and eliminate more metabolic end products. One mechanism for achieving this is active hyperemia. The second important mechanism is to increase diffusion gradients between plasma and tissue: Increased cellular utilization of oxygen and nutrients lowers their tissue concentrations, while increased produc-

---

[8]Except in the kidney, the basement membrane offers no diffusion barrier, and so we ignore it in this discussion of diffusion.

tion of carbon dioxide and other end products raises their tissue concentrations. In both cases the substance's transcapillary concentration difference is increased, which increases the rate of diffusion.

Bulk Flow Across the Capillary Wall: Distribution of the Extracellular Fluid

To repeat, the exchange of nutrients, oxygen, and metabolic end products across most capillaries occurs almost entirely by diffusion. At the same time these diffusional exchanges are occurring, another completely distinct process is taking place across the capillary: the bulk flow of protein-free plasma. The function of this process is *not* exchange of materials but rather distribution of the extracellular fluid. As described in Chapter 1, extracellular fluid comprises the blood plasma and the interstitial fluid. Normally, there is approximately three times more interstitial fluid than plasma, 10 L vs. 3 L in a 70-kg person. This distribution is not fixed, however, and the interstitial fluid functions as a reservoir that can supply fluid to the plasma or receive fluid from it.

As described in the previous section, the capillary wall is highly permeable to water and to almost all plasma solutes, except plasma proteins. Therefore, in the presence of a hydrostatic pressure difference across it, the capillary wall behaves like a porous filter through which protein-free plasma (**ultrafiltrate**) moves by bulk flow from capillary plasma to interstitial fluid through the water-filled channels. The concentrations of all the plasma solutes except protein are virtually the same in the filtering fluid as in plasma.

The magnitude of the bulk flow is directly proportional to the difference between the capillary blood pressure and the interstitial-fluid pressure. Normally, the former is much larger than the latter. Therefore, a considerable hydrostatic pressure difference exists to filter protein-free plasma out of the capillaries into the interstitial fluid, the protein remaining behind in the plasma.

Why then does all the plasma not filter out into the interstitial space? The explanation was first presented by Starling—the same scientist who expounded the law of the heart that bears his name—and depends upon the principle of osmosis. In Chapter 6 we described how a net movement of water occurs across a semipermeable membrane from a solution of high water concentration to a solution of low water concentration, that is, from a region with a low concentration of solute to which the membrane is impermeable (nonpermeating solute) to a region of high nonpermeating solute concentration. Moreover, this osmotic flow of water "drags" along with it any dissolved solutes to which the membrane is highly permeable (permeating solute). Thus, a difference in water concentration secondary to different concentrations of *nonpermeating*

solute on the two sides of a membrane can result in the movement of a solution containing both water and permeating solutes in a manner similar to the bulk flow produced by a hydrostatic pressure difference. Units of pressure can be used in expressing this osmotic flow across a membrane.

This analysis can now be applied to capillary-fluid movements. The plasma within the capillary and the interstitial fluid outside it contain large quantities of low-molecular-weight permeating solutes (also termed **crystalloids**), for example, sodium, chloride, and glucose. Since the capillary lining is highly permeable to all these crystalloids, their concentrations in the two solutions are essentially identical.[9] Accordingly, no significant water concentration difference is caused by the presence of the crystalloids. In contrast, the plasma proteins (also termed **colloids**), being essentially nonpermeating, have a very low concentration in the interstitial fluid. This difference in protein concentration between plasma and interstitial fluid means that the water concentration of the plasma is lower than that of interstitial fluid, inducing an osmotic flow of water from the interstitial compartment into the capillary. Since the crystalloids in the interstitial fluid move along with the water, osmotic flow of fluid, like flow driven by a hydrostatic pressure difference, does not alter their concentrations in either plasma or interstitial fluid.

A key word in this last sentence is "concentrations." Because the interstitial fluid and plasma have identical crystalloid concentrations to start with, a transfer of fluid across the capillary wall does not change the crystalloid concentrations in either location. However, the *amount* of water (the *volume*) and the *amount* of crystalloids in the two locations do change. Thus, an increased filtration of fluid from plasma to interstitial fluid increases the volume of the interstitial fluid and decreases the volume of the plasma, even though no changes in crystalloid concentrations occur.

In summary (Figure 14-49A), two opposing forces act to move fluid across the capillary wall: (1) The difference between capillary blood hydrostatic pressure and interstitial-fluid hydrostatic pressure favors the filtration out of the capillary, and (2) the water concentration difference between plasma and interstitial fluid, which results from differences in protein concentration, favors the flow of interstitial fluid into the capillary. Accordingly, the movements of fluid depend directly upon four variables: capillary hydrostatic pressure, interstitial hydrostatic pressure, plasma protein concentration, and interstitial-fluid protein concentration. These four factors are termed the **Starling forces**.

---

[9]As we have seen, there are small concentration differences for substances that are consumed or produced by the cells. These tend, however, to cancel each other out.

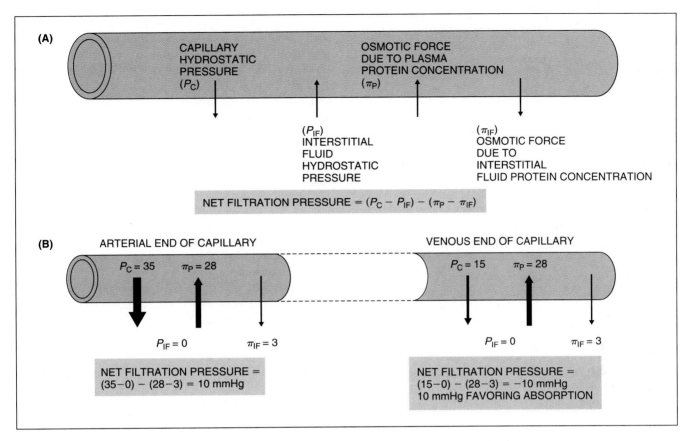

FIGURE 14-49

(A) The four factors determining fluid movement across capillaries. (B) Quantitation of forces causing filtration at the arteriolar end of the capillary and absorption at the venous end. Arrows in (B) denote magnitude of forces. No arrow is shown for interstitial fluid hydrostatic pressure (P_{IF}) because it is zero.

We may now consider this movement quantitatively in the systemic circulation (Figure 14-49B). Much of the arterial blood pressure has already been dissipated as the blood flows through the arterioles, so that pressure at the beginning of the capillary (the part closest to the arteriole) is about 35 mmHg. Since the capillary also offers resistance to flow, the pressure continuously decreases to approximately 15 mmHg at the end of the capillary (the part farthest from the arteriole). The interstitial pressure is very low, and we shall assume it to be zero.[10] The plasma protein concentration would produce an osmotic flow of water equivalent to that produced by a hydrostatic pressure of 28 mmHg. The interstitial protein concentration would produce a flow of water equivalent to that produced by a hydrostatic pressure of 3 mmHg. Therefore, the difference in protein concentrations induces a flow of fluid into the capillary equivalent to that produced by a hydrostatic pressure difference of $28 - 3 = 25$ mmHg.

Thus, in the beginning of the capillary the hydrostatic pressure difference across the capillary wall (35 mmHg) is greater than the opposing osmotic force (25 mmHg), and a net movement of fluid out of the capillary (**filtration**) occurs. In the end of the capillary, however, the osmotic force (25 mmHg) is greater than the hydrostatic pressure difference (15 mmHg), and fluid moves into the capillary (**absorption**). The result is that the early and late capillary events tend to cancel each other out. For the aggregate of capillaries in the body, however, there is a small net filtration of approximately 4 L/day (this number does not include the capillaries in the kidneys). The fate of this fluid will be described in the section on the lymphatic system.

This analysis of capillary fluid dynamics at the arterial and venous ends of the capillary has been somewhat oversimplified. It is very likely that many individual capillaries manifest only net filtration or net absorption along their

---

[10]The exact value of interstitial hydrostatic pressure remains highly controversial. Many physiologists believe that it is not zero but is actually subatmospheric. The outcome of this controversy will not, however, alter the basic concepts being presented here.

FIGURE 14-50

Effects of arteriolar vasodilation or vasoconstriction in an organ on capillary blood pressure in that organ.

entire lengths because the arterioles supplying them are either so dilated or so constricted that a capillary hydrostatic pressure above or below 25 mmHg exists along the entire length of the capillary.

The last paragraph illustrates the very important point that capillary pressure in any vascular bed is subject to physiological regulation, mediated mainly by changes in the resistance of the arterioles in that bed. As shown in Figure 14-50, dilating the arterioles in a particular vascular bed raises capillary pressure because less pressure is lost overcoming resistance between the arteries and the capillaries. Because of the increased capillary pressure, filtration is increased, and more protein-free fluid is lost to the interstitial fluid. In contrast, marked arteriolar constriction produces decreased capillary pressure and hence net movement of interstitial fluid into the vascular compartment.

It is this ability to change capillary pressure that determines the distribution of the extracellular-fluid volume between the cardiovascular and interstitial compartments. For example, when blood volume is low, as following a hemorrhage, the resulting decrease in capillary pressure causes net movement of interstitial fluid into the capillaries and helps expand the blood volume.

It should be stated again that capillary filtration and absorption play no significant role in the exchange of nutrients and metabolic end products between capillary and tissues. The reason is that the total quantity of a substance, such as glucose or carbon dioxide, moving into or out of a capillary as a result of net bulk flow is extremely small in comparison with the quantities moving by net diffusion.

Finally, this analysis of capillary fluid dynamics has been in terms of the systemic circulation. Precisely the same Starling forces apply to the capillaries in the pulmonary circulation, but the values of the four variables differ. In particular, because the pulmonary circulation is a low-resistance, low-pressure circuit, the normal pulmonary capillary pressure—the major force favoring movement of fluid out of the pulmonary capillaries into the interstitium—is only 15 mmHg. Therefore, normally net absorption of fluid occurs all along lung capillaries.

VEINS

Blood flows from capillaries into venules and then into veins. Some exchange of materials occurs between the interstitial fluid and the venules. Indeed, permeability to macromolecules is often greater for venules than for capillaries, particularly in damaged areas.

The veins outside the chest, the **peripheral veins**, contain valves that permit flow only toward the heart. Why are these valves necessary if the pressure gradient created by cardiac contraction pushes blood only toward the heart anyway? The answer will be given below.

The veins are the last set of tubes through which blood flows on its way back to the heart. In the systemic circulation the force driving this venous return is the pressure difference between the peripheral veins and the right atrium.[11] Most of the pressure imparted to the blood by the heart is dissipated by resistance as blood flows through the arterioles, capillaries, and venules so that pressure in the first portion of the peripheral veins is only 5 to 10 mmHg. The right atrial pressure is close to 0 mmHg, so that the total driving pressure for flow from the peripheral veins to the right atrium is only 5 to 10 mmHg. This is adequate because of the low resistance to flow offered by the veins, which have large diameters. Thus, a major function of the veins is to act as low-resistance conduits for blood flow from the tissues to the heart.

In addition to their function as low-resistance conduits, the veins perform a second important function: Their diameters are reflexly altered in response to changes in blood volume, thereby maintaining peripheral venous pressure and venous return to the heart. In a previous section, we emphasized that the rate of venous return to the heart is a major determinant of end-diastolic ventricular volume and thereby stroke volume. Thus, we now see that peripheral venous pressure is an important determinant of stroke volume.

---

[11]The blood in the right atrium and large veins of the thorax constitutes a single "pool"—the central venous pool. The pressure in this pool—the central venous pressure—is easily measured, and it is customary to substitute this pressure for right atrial pressure when dealing with venous return. However, to avoid potential confusion, we have not adopted this convention.

most volume of blood in veins
veins don't add resistance (b/c not enough
smooth muscle) - just expands

VEINS 445

Determinants of Venous Pressure

The factors determining pressure in any elastic tube are, as we know, the volume of fluid within it and the compliance of its wall. Accordingly, total blood volume is one important determinant of venous pressure since, at any given moment, most blood is in the veins. The walls of veins are thinner and much more compliant than those of arteries. Thus, veins can accommodate large volumes of blood with a relatively small increase in internal pressure. Approximately 60 percent of the total blood volume is present in the systemic veins at any given moment (Figure 14-51), but the venous pressure averages less than 10 mmHg. In contrast, the systemic arteries contain less than 15 percent of the blood, at a pressure of approximately 100 mmHg.

The walls of the veins contain smooth muscle innervated by sympathetic neurons. Stimulation of these neurons releases norepinephrine, which causes contraction of the venous smooth muscle, decreasing the diameter and compliance of the vessels and raising the pressure within

FIGURE 14-51

Distribution of the total blood volume in different parts of the cardiovascular system. (*Adapted from Guyton.*)

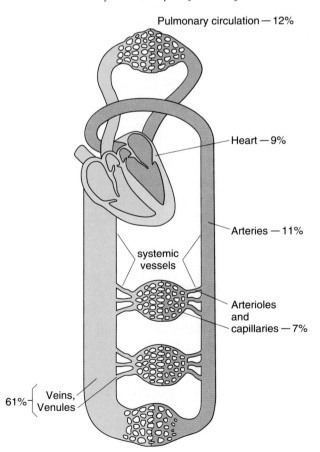

Pulmonary circulation — 12%

Heart — 9%

Arteries — 11%

systemic vessels

Arterioles and capillaries — 7%

61% { Veins, Venules

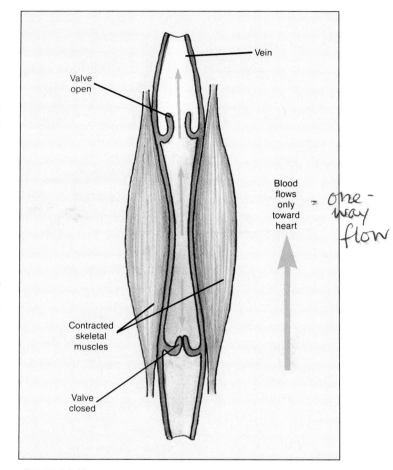

Vein

Valve open

Blood flows only toward heart

= one-way flow

Contracted skeletal muscles

Valve closed

FIGURE 14-52

The skeletal muscle pump. During muscle contraction, venous diameter decreases and venous pressure rises. The resulting increase in blood flow can occur only toward the heart because the valves in the veins are forced closed by any backward flow.

them. Increased venous pressure drives more blood out of the veins into the right heart.

Two other mechanisms, in addition to contraction of venous smooth muscle, can increase venous pressure and facilitate venous return. These mechanisms are the **skeletal-muscle pump** and the **respiratory pump**. During skeletal-muscle contraction, the veins running through the muscle are partially compressed, which reduces their diameter and forces more blood back to the heart. Now we can describe a major function of the peripheral-vein valves: When the skeletal-muscle pump raises venous pressure locally, the valves permit blood flow only toward the heart and prevent flow back toward the tissues (Figure 14-52).

The respiratory pump is somewhat more difficult to visualize. As will be described in Chapter 15, during inspira-

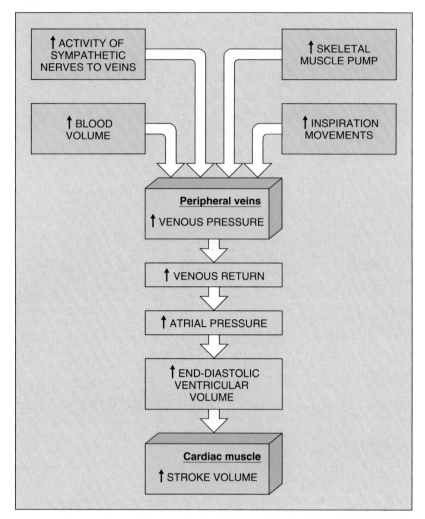

FIGURE 14-53

Major factors determining peripheral venous pressure and, hence, venous return and stroke volume. The figure shows how venous pressure and stroke volume are increased. Reversing the arrows in the boxes would indicate how these can be decreased. The effects of increased inspiration on end-diastolic ventricular volume are actually quite complex, and for the sake of simplicity, they are shown only as increasing venous pressure.

tion of air, the diaphragm descends, pushes on the abdominal contents, and increases abdominal pressure. This pressure increase is transmitted passively to the intraabdominal veins. Simultaneously, the pressure in the thorax *decreases,* thereby decreasing the pressure in the intrathoracic veins and right atrium. The net effect of the pressure changes in the abdomen and thorax is to increase the pressure difference between the peripheral veins and the heart. Accordingly, venous return is enhanced during inspiration (expiration would reverse this effect if it were not for the venous valves). The larger the inspiration, the greater the effect. Thus, breathing deeply and frequently, as in exercise, helps blood flow from the peripheral veins to the heart.

One might get the (incorrect) impression from these descriptions that venous return and cardiac output are independent entities. However, any change in venous return, due say to the skeletal-muscle pump, almost immediately causes equivalent changes in cardiac output, largely through the operation of Starling's law. Venous return and

cardiac output therefore must be identical except for very brief periods of time.

In summary (Figure 14-53), the effects of venous smooth-muscle contraction, the skeletal-muscle pump, and the respiratory pump are to facilitate return of blood to the heart and thereby to enhance cardiac output.

THE LYMPHATIC SYSTEM

The **lymphatic system** is a network of small organs (lymph nodes) and tubes (**lymphatic vessels** or simply "lymphatics") through which **lymph**—a fluid derived from interstitial fluid—flows. The lymphatic system is not technically part of the cardiovascular system, but it is described in this chapter because its vessels constitute a route for the movement of interstitial fluid to the cardiovascular system (Figure 14-54).

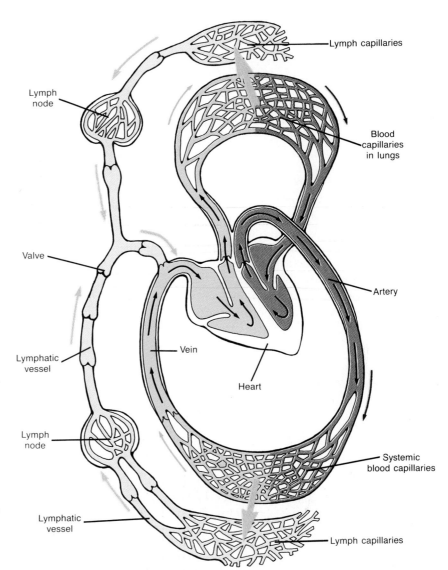

Lymph capillaries

Lymph node

Blood capillaries in lungs

Valve

Artery

Lymphatic vessel

Vein

Lymph node

Heart

Systemic blood capillaries

Lymphatic vessel

Lymph capillaries

FIGURE 14-54

The lymphatic system (yellow) in relation to the cardiovascular system (blue and red). The lymphatic system is a one-way system from interstitial fluid to the cardiovascular system. The excess fluid that filters from the blood capillaries into the interstitial fluid enters the lymph capillaries and flows through the lymphatic vessels and the nodes along them. Many lymphatic vessels arise in the systemic organs and the lungs, and each has multiple lymph nodes. All the lymphatic vessels converge into large lymphatic vessels that empty into the systemic circulation via the systemic veins.

Present in the interstitium of virtually all organs and tissues are numerous **lymphatic capillaries** that are completely distinct from blood vessel capillaries. Like the latter, they are tubes made of only a single layer of endothelial cells, but they have large water-filled channels that are permeable to all interstitial-fluid constituents, including protein. The lymphatic capillaries are the first of the lymphatic vessels, for unlike the blood vessel capillaries, no tubes flow into them.

Small amounts of interstitial fluid continuously enter the lymphatic capillaries at rates determined by the interstitial pressure. Now known as lymph, the fluid flows from the lymphatic capillaries into the next set of lymphatic vessels, which converge to form larger and larger lymphatic vessels. Ultimately, the entire network ends in two large lymphatic vessels that drain into veins in the lower neck. Valves at these junctions permit only one-way flow from

lymphatic vessels into veins. Thus, the lymphatic vessels carry interstitial fluid to the cardiovascular system. At various points, the lymph flows through lymph nodes, the function of which is described in Chapter 20.

The movement of interstitial fluid to the cardiovascular system via the lymphatics is very important because, as noted earlier, the amount of fluid filtered out of all the blood vessel capillaries (except those in the kidneys) exceeds that reabsorbed by approximately 4 L each day. This 4 L is returned to the blood via the lymphatic system. In the process, the small amounts of protein that leak out of blood vessel capillaries into the interstitial fluid are also returned to the cardiovascular system.

Failure of the lymphatic system, due for example to occlusion by infectious organisms (as in the disease *elephantiasis*) allows the accumulation of excessive interstitial fluid. The result can be massive swelling of the involved area. The accumulation of interstitial fluid for whatever cause (others are described in the section on heart failure) is termed *edema*.

As will be described in Chapter 17, the lymphatic system also provides the pathway by which fat absorbed from the gastrointestinal tract reaches the blood. The lymphatics also, unfortunately, are often the route by which cancer cells spread from their area of origin to other parts of the body.

Mechanism of Lymph Flow

In large part, the lymphatic vessels propel the lymph within them by their own contractions. The smooth muscle in the wall of the lymphatics exerts a pumplike action by inherent rhythmical contractions. Since the lymphatic vessels have valves similar to those in veins, these contractions produce a one-way flow toward the points at which the lymphatics enter the circulatory system. The lymphatic vessel smooth muscle is responsive to stretch, so when there is no accumulation of interstitial fluid, and hence no entry of lymph into the lymphatics, the smooth muscle is inactive. As lymph formation increases, however, say as a result of increased fluid filtration out of blood vessel capillaries, the increased lymph entering the lymphatics stretches the walls and triggers rhythmical contractions of the smooth muscle, the rate and force of which depend on the degree of stretch. This constitutes a negative-feedback mechanism for adjusting the rate of lymph flow to the rate of lymph formation and thereby helps prevent edema formation.

Moreover, the smooth muscle of the lymphatic vessels is innervated by sympathetic neurons, and excitation of these neurons in various physiological states such as exercise may contribute to increased lymph flow.

Lymph flow can also be enhanced by forces external to the lymphatic vessels. These include the same external forces we described for veins—the skeletal-muscle and respiratory pumps.

SECTION D SUMMARY

ARTERIES

I. The arteries function as low-resistance conduits and as pressure reservoirs for maintaining blood flow to the tissues during ventricular relaxation.

II. The difference between maximal arterial pressure (systolic pressure) and minimal arterial pressure (diastolic pressure) during a cardiac cycle is the pulse pressure.

III. Mean arterial pressure can be estimated as diastolic pressure plus one-third pulse pressure.

ARTERIOLES

I. Arterioles, the major site of resistance to flow in the vascular system, play a major role in determining both mean arterial pressure and the distribution of flows to the various organs and tissues.

II. Arteriolar resistance is determined by local factors and by reflex neural and hormonal input.

A. Local factors that change with the degree of metabolic activity cause the arteriolar vasodilation and increased flow of active hyperemia.

B. Flow autoregulation, a change in resistance that maintains flow constant in the face of a change in blood pressure, is due to local metabolic factors and to arteriolar myogenic responses to stretch.

C. The sympathetic nerves are the only innervation of most arterioles and cause vasoconstriction via alpha-adrenergic receptors.

D. Epinephrine causes vasoconstriction or vasodilation, depending on the proportion of alpha- and beta-adrenergic receptors in the organ.

E. Angiotensin II and vasopressin cause vasoconstriction.

F. Some vasodilator inputs act by releasing endothelium-derived relaxing factor from endothelial cells.

III. Arteriolar control in specific organs is summarized in Table 14-7.

CAPILLARIES

I. Capillaries are the site of exchange of nutrients and waste products between blood and tissues.

II. Capillary blood flow is determined by the resistance of the arterioles supplying the capillaries and by the number of open precapillary sphincters.

III. Blood flows through the capillaries more slowly than in any other part of the vascular system because of the huge cross-sectional area of the capillaries.

IV. Diffusion is the mechanism by which nutrients and waste products exchange between capillary plasma and interstitial fluid.

A. Lipid-soluble substances move across the entire endothelial wall, whereas ions and polar molecules move through water-filled intercellular clefts or fused-vesicle channels.

B. Plasma proteins move across most capillaries only very slowly, either by diffusion or vesicle transport.

C. The diffusion gradient for a substance across capillaries arises as a result of cell utilization or production of the substance. Increased metabolism increases the diffusion gradient and increases the rate of diffusion.

V. Bulk flow of protein-free plasma or interstitial fluid across capillaries determines the distribution of extracellular fluid between these two fluid compartments.
  A. Filtration from plasma to interstitial fluid is favored by the hydrostatic pressure difference between the capillary and the interstitial fluid. Absorption from interstitial fluid to plasma is favored by the plasma protein concentration difference between the plasma and the interstitial fluid.
  B. Filtration and absorption do not change the concentrations of crystalloids in the plasma and interstitial fluid because these substances move together with water.
  C. There is normally a small excess of filtration over absorption.

VEINS

I. Veins serve as low-resistance conduits for venous return.
II. Veins are very compliant and contain most of the blood in the vascular system.
  A. Their diameters are reflexly altered by sympathetically mediated vasoconstriction or vasodilation so as to maintain venous pressure and venous return.
  B. The skeletal-muscle pump and respiratory pump increase venous pressure locally and enhance venous return. Venous valves permit the pressure to produce only flow toward the heart.

THE LYMPHATIC SYSTEM

I. The lymphatic system provides a one-way route for movement of interstitial fluid to the cardiovascular system.
II. Lymph returns the excess fluid filtered from the blood vessel capillaries, as well as the protein that leaks out of the blood vessel capillaries.
III. Lymph flow is driven mainly by contraction of smooth muscle in the lymphatic vessels but also by the skeletal-muscle pump and the respiratory pump.

SECTION D KEY TERMS

compliance	kallikrein
systolic pressure (SP)	flow autoregulation
diastolic pressure (DP)	myogenic responses
pulse pressure	reactive hyperemia
mean arterial pressure (MAP)	prostacyclin
vasodilation	endothelium-derived
vasoconstriction	relaxing factor
myogenic tone	(EDRF)
local controls	endothelin-1
hyperemia	metarterioles
active hyperemia	angiogenesis
bradykinin	angiogenic factors
kininogen	intercellular clefts

fused-vesicle channels	peripheral veins
precapillary sphincter	skeletal-muscle pump
ultrafiltrate	respiratory pump
crystalloids	lymphatic system
colloids	lymphatic vessels
Starling forces	lymph
filtration	lymphatic capillaries
absorption	

SECTION D REVIEW QUESTIONS

1. Draw the pressure changes along the systemic and pulmonary vascular systems during the cardiac cycle.
2. What are the two functions of the arteries?
3. What are normal values for systolic, diastolic, and mean arterial pressures? How is mean arterial pressure estimated?
4. What are the three factors that determine pulse pressure?
5. What denotes systolic and diastolic pressure in the measurement of arterial pressure with a sphygmomanometer?
6. What are the major sites of resistance in the systemic vascular system?
7. What are two functions of arterioles?
8. Write the formula relating flow through an organ to (a) mean arterial pressure, and (b) the resistance to flow offered by that organ.
9. List the chemical factors thought to mediate active hyperemia.
10. Name the mechanism other than chemical factors that contributes to flow autoregulation.
11. What is the only autonomic innervation of most arterioles? What are the major adrenergic receptors influenced by these nerves? How can control of sympathetic nerves to arterioles achieve either dilation or constriction?
12. Name three hormones that influence arterioles and describe their effects.
13. Draw a flow diagram summarizing the factors affecting arteriolar radius.
14. What are the relative velocities of flow through the various segments of the vascular system?
15. Contrast diffusion and bulk flow. Which is the mechanism of exchange of nutrients, oxygen, and metabolic end products across the capillary wall?
16. What is the only solute to have significant concentration differences across the capillary wall? How does this difference influence water concentration?
17. What four variables determine flow of fluid across the capillary wall? Give representative values for each of them in the systemic capillaries.
18. How do changes in local arteriolar resistance influence local capillary pressure?
19. What is the relationship between cardiac output and venous return in the steady state? What is the force driving venous return?

20. Contrast the compliances and blood volumes of the veins and arteries.
21. What three factors influence venous pressure?

22. Approximately how much fluid is returned to the blood by the lymphatics each day?
23. Describe the forces that cause lymph flow.

SECTION

INTEGRATION OF CARDIOVASCULAR FUNCTION: REGULATION OF SYSTEMIC ARTERIAL PRESSURE

In Chapter 7 we described the fundamental ingredients of all reflex control systems: (1) the internal-environmental variable being maintained relatively constant, (2) receptors sensitive to changes in this variable, (3) afferent pathways from the receptors, (4) an integrating center that receives and integrates the afferent inputs, (5) efferent pathways from the control center, (6) effectors "directed" by the efferent pathways to alter their activities. The result is a change in the level of the regulated variable. The control and integration of cardiovascular function will be described in these terms.

The major cardiovascular variable being regulated is the mean arterial blood pressure in the systemic circulation. This should not be surprising since this pressure is the driving force for blood flow through all the organs except the lungs. Maintaining it is therefore a prerequisite for ensuring adequate blood flow to these organs.

The mean systemic arterial pressure is the arithmetic product of two factors: (1) the cardiac output and (2) the **total peripheral resistance (TPR)**, which is the sum of the resistances to flow offered by all the systemic blood vessels:

Mean systemic arterial pressure
          (MAP)
     = cardiac output × total peripheral resistance
          (CO)   (TPR)

The reason these two factors set the mean systemic arterial pressure is because they determine the average volume of blood in the systemic arteries over time, and it is this blood volume that causes the pressure.

That the volume of blood pumped into the arteries per unit time—the cardiac output—is one of the two direct determinants of mean arterial blood volume and hence mean arterial pressure should come as no surprise. That the total resistance of the blood vessels to flow—the TPR—is the other determinant may not be so intuitively obvious

but can be illustrated by using the model introduced in Figure 14-41.

As shown in Figure 14-55 a pump pushes fluid into a container at the rate of 1 L/min. At steady state, fluid also leaves the container via outflow tubes at a total rate of 1 L/min. Therefore, the height of the fluid column (ΔP), which is the driving pressure for outflow, remains stable. We then disturb the steady state by loosening the cuff on outflow tube 1, increasing its radius, reducing its resistance, and increasing its flow. The total outflow for the system immediately becomes greater than 1 L/min, and more fluid leaves the reservoir than enters from the pump. Therefore, the volume and hence the height of the fluid column begin to decrease until a new steady state between inflow and outflow is reached. In other words, at any given pump input, a change in *total* outflow resistance must produce changes in the volume and hence the height (pressure) in the reservoir.

This analysis can be applied to the cardiovascular system by again equating the pump with the heart, the reservoir with the arteries, and the outflow tubes with various arteriolar beds. As described earlier, most of the vascular resistance in the systemic circulation is supplied by the arterioles, and so we usually equate total peripheral resistance with arteriolar resistance. An analogy to opening outflow tube 1 is exercise: During exercise, the skeletal-muscle arterioles dilate, thereby decreasing resistance. If the cardiac output and the arteriolar diameters of all other vascular beds were to remain unchanged, the increased runoff through the skeletal-muscle arterioles would cause a decrease in systemic arterial pressure.

It must be reemphasized that it is the *total* arteriolar resistance that influences systemic arterial blood pressure. The *distribution* of resistances among organs is irrelevant in this regard. Figure 14-56 illustrates this point. On the right, outflow tube 1 has been opened, as in the previous example, while tubes 2 to 4 have been simultaneously tightened. The increased resistance offered by tubes 2 to 4 compensates for the decreased resistance offered by tube

FIGURE 14-55

Dependence of arterial blood pressure upon total arteriolar resistance. Dilating one arteriolar bed affects arterial pressure and organ blood flow if no compensatory adjustments occur. The middle panel is a transient state before the new steady state occurs.

1; therefore total resistance remains unchanged, and reservoir pressure is unchanged. Total outflow remains 1 L/min, although the distribution of flows is such that flow through tube 1 is increased, that of tubes 2 to 4 is decreased, and that of tube 5 is unchanged.

Applied to the systemic circulation, this process is analogous to altering the distribution of systemic vascular resistances. When the skeletal-muscle arterioles (tube 1) dilate during exercise, the *total* resistance of the systemic circulation can still be maintained if arterioles constrict in other organs, such as the kidneys, gastrointestinal tract, and skin (tubes 2 to 4). In contrast, the brain arterioles

FIGURE 14-56

Compensation for dilation in one bed by constriction in others. When outflow tube 1 is opened, outflow tubes 2 to 4 are simultaneously tightened so that total outflow resistance, total runoff rate, and reservoir pressure all remain constant.

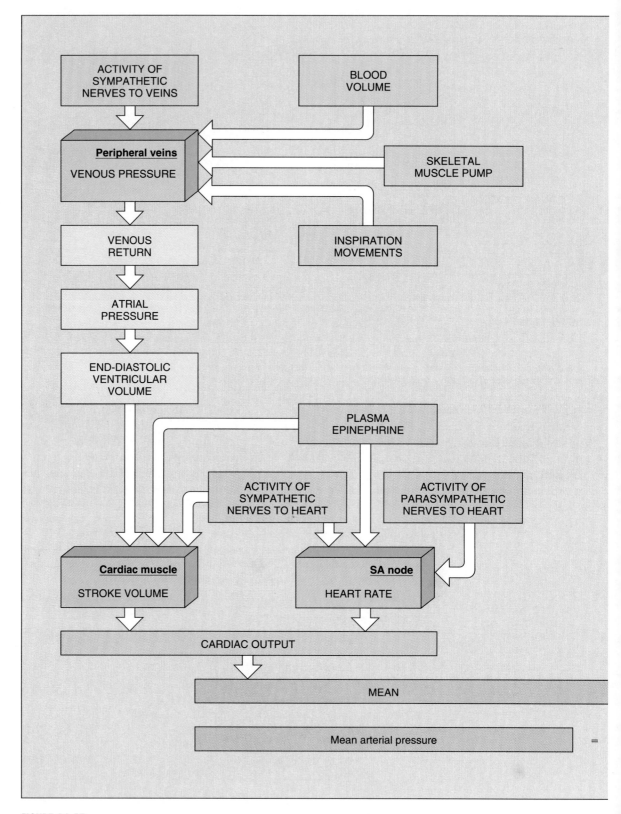

FIGURE 14-57

Summary of factors that determine systemic arterial pressure, an amalgamation of Figures 14-36, 14-44, and

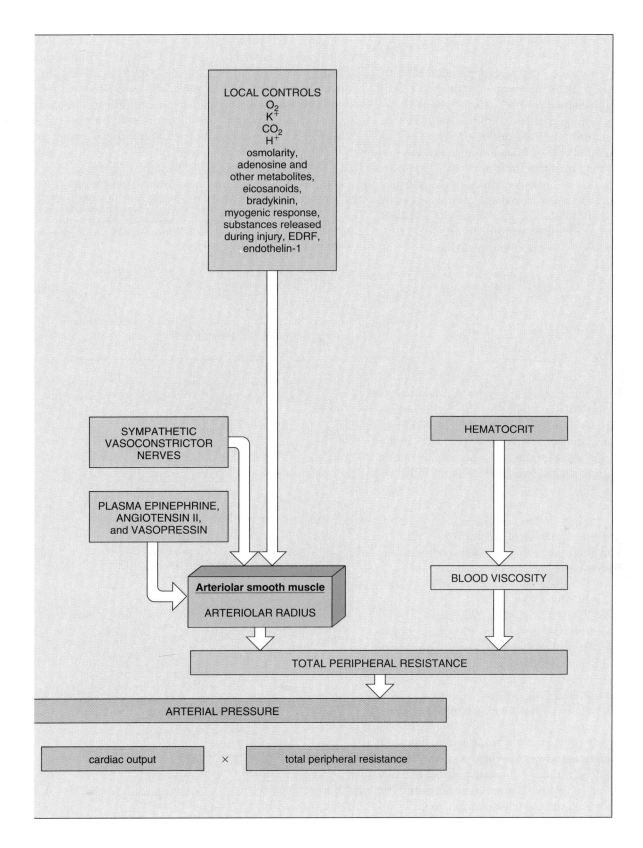

14-53, with the addition of the effect of hematocrit on resistance.

Cardiac output = heart rate ×
Stroke volume

(tube 5) remain unchanged, ensuring constant brain blood supply.

This type of resistance juggling can maintain total resistance only within limits, however. Obviously if tube 1 opens very wide, even total closure of the other tubes cannot prevent total outflow resistance from falling. We shall see that this is actually the case during exercise.

We have thus far explained in an intuitive way why cardiac output (CO) and total peripheral resistance (TPR) are the two variables that set mean systemic arterial pressure. This intuitive approach, however, does not explain specifically why MAP is the *arithmetic product* of CO and TPR. This relationship can be derived formally from the basic equation relating flow, pressure, and resistance:

$$F = \frac{\Delta P}{R}$$

Rearranging terms algebraically, we have

$$\Delta P = FR$$

Because the systemic vascular system is a continuous series of tubes, this equation holds for the entire system, that is, from the arteries to the right atrium. Therefore, the ΔP term is mean systemic arterial pressure (MAP) minus the pressure in the right atrium, F is the cardiac output (CO), and R is the total peripheral resistance (TPR):

$$MAP - \text{right atrial pressure} = CO \times TPR$$

Since the pressure in the right atrium is very close to 0 mmHg, we can drop this term and we are left with the equation presented earlier:

$$MAP = CO \times TPR$$

This equation is the fundamental equation of cardiovascular physiology. An analogous equation can also be applied to the pulmonary circulation:

Mean pulmonary arterial pressure
$$= CO \times \text{total pulmonary vascular resistance}$$

These equations provide a way to integrate almost all the information presented in this chapter. For example, we can now explain why mean pulmonary arterial pressure is much lower than mean systemic arterial pressure. The cardiac output through the pulmonary and systemic arteries is, of course, the same. Therefore, the pressures can differ only if the resistances differ. Thus, the pulmonary vessels offer much less resistance to flow than do the systemic vessels. In other words, the total pulmonary vascular resistance is lower than the total peripheral resistance.

Figure 14-57 presents the grand scheme of factors that determine mean systemic arterial pressure.[12] None of this information is new, all of it having been presented in previous figures. A change in only a single variable will produce a change in mean systemic arterial pressure by altering either cardiac output or total peripheral resistance. For example, Figure 14-58 illustrates how the decrease in

---

[12]Any model of a system as complex as the circulatory system must, of necessity, be an oversimplification. One basic deficiency in our model is that its chain of causal links is entirely unidirectional (from top to bottom in Figure 14-57), whereas in fact there are also important causal interactions in the reverse direction. A reader interested in delving further into these complex interactions and feedback loops should consult the more advanced works listed in Appendix G.

FIGURE 14-58

Sequence of events by which a decrease in blood volume leads to a decrease in mean arterial pressure.

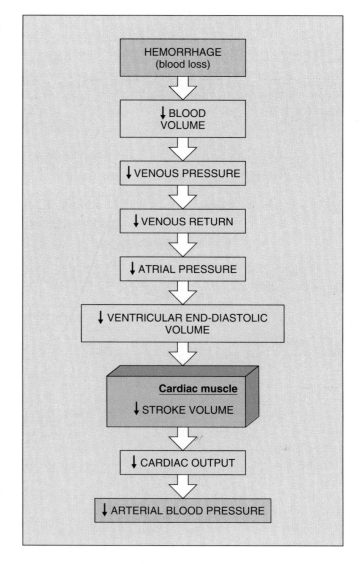

blood volume occurring during hemorrhage leads to a decrease in mean arterial pressure.

Conversely, any deviation in arterial pressure, such as that occurring during hemorrhage, will elicit reflexes so that cardiac output and/or total peripheral resistance will be changed in the direction required to minimize the initial change in arterial pressure.

In the short term—seconds to hours—these homeostatic adjustments are brought about by reflexes termed the baroreceptor reflexes. They utilize mainly changes in the activity of the autonomic nerves supplying the heart and blood vessels, as well as changes in the secretion of the hormones—epinephrine, angiotensin II, and vasopressin—that influence these structures. Over longer time spans, the baroreceptor reflexes become less important, and factors controlling blood volume play a dominant role in determining blood pressure.

BARORECEPTOR REFLEXES

Arterial Baroreceptors

It is only logical that the reflexes that homeostatically regulate arterial pressure originate primarily with arterial receptors that respond to changes in pressure. High in the neck, each of the two major vessels supplying the head, the common carotid arteries, divides into two smaller arteries. At this division, the wall of the artery is thinner than usual and contains a large number of branching, vinelike nerve endings (Figure 14-59). This portion of the artery is called the **carotid sinus**. Its nerve endings are highly sensitive to stretch or distortion. Since the degree of wall stretching is directly related to the pressure within the artery, the carotid sinuses serve as pressure receptors (**baroreceptors**). An area functionally similar to the carotid sinuses is found in the arch of the aorta and is termed the **aortic arch baroreceptor**. The two carotid sinuses and the aortic arch baroreceptor constitute the **arterial baroreceptors**. Afferent neurons from them travel to the brain and provide input to the neurons of cardiovascular control centers there.

Action potentials recorded in single afferent fibers from the carotid sinus demonstrate the pattern of baroreceptor response (Figure 14-60). In this experiment the pressure in the carotid sinus is artificially controlled so that the pressure is either steady or pulsatile, that is, varying as usual between systolic and diastolic pressure. At a particular steady pressure, for example, 100 mmHg, there is a certain rate of discharge by the neuron. This rate can be increased by raising the arterial pressure, or it can be decreased by lowering the pressure. Thus, the rate of discharge of the carotid sinus is directly proportional to the mean arterial pressure.

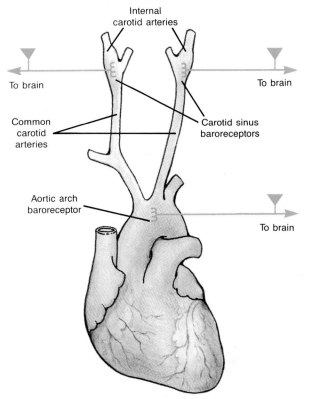

FIGURE 14-59
Locations of arterial baroreceptors.

If the experiment is repeated using the same mean pressures as before but allowing pressure pulsations, it is found that at any given mean pressure, the larger the pulse pressure, the faster the rate of firing by the carotid sinus. This responsiveness to pulse pressure adds a further ele-

FIGURE 14-60
Effect of changing mean arterial pressure (MAP) on the firing of action potentials by afferent neurons from the carotid sinus. This experiment is done by pumping blood through an isolated carotid sinus so as to be able to set the pressure inside it at any value desired.

ment of information to blood pressure regulation, since small changes in factors such as blood volume may cause changes in arterial pulse pressure with little or no change in mean arterial pressure.

Other Baroreceptors

The large systemic veins, the pulmonary vessels, and the walls of the heart also contain baroreceptors, most of which function in a manner analogous to the arterial baroreceptors. By keeping brain cardiovascular control centers constantly informed about changes in the systemic venous, pulmonary, atrial, and ventricular pressures, these other baroreceptors provide feedforward and a further degree of regulatory sensitivity. Thus, a slight decrease in ventricular pressure may reflexly increase the activity of the sympathetic nervous system even before the change lowers cardiac output and arterial pressure far enough to be detected by the arterial baroreceptors.[13]

The Medullary Cardiovascular Center

The primary integrating center for the baroreceptor reflexes is a diffuse network of highly interconnected neurons in the brainstem medulla oblongata called the **medullary cardiovascular center**. The neurons in this center receive input from the various baroreceptors. This input determines the outflow from the center along axons that terminate upon the cell bodies and dendrites of the vagus (parasympathetic) neurons to the heart and the sympathetic neurons to the heart, arterioles, and veins. When the arterial baroreceptors *increase* their rate of discharge, the result is a *decrease* in sympathetic outflow to the heart, arterioles, and veins, and an *increase* in parasympathetic outflow to the heart (Figure 14-61). A decrease in baroreceptor firing rate results in just the opposite pattern.

As parts of the baroreceptor reflexes, angiotensin II generation and vasopressin secretion are also altered so as to help restore blood pressure. Thus, a decreased pressure elicits increased plasma concentrations of both these hormones, which raise arterial pressure by constricting arterioles. For simplicity, however, we focus in the rest of this chapter only on the sympathetic nervous system when discussing reflex control of arterioles. The roles of angiotensin II and vasopressin will be described in Chapter 16.

Operation of the Baroreceptor Reflex

Our description of the baroreceptor reflex is now complete. If arterial pressure decreases as during a hemorrhage (Figure 14-62), this causes the discharge rate of the carotid sinus and aortic arch baroreceptors to decrease. Fewer impulses travel up the afferent nerves to the medullary cardiovascular center, and this induces (1) increased heart rate because of increased sympathetic activity to the

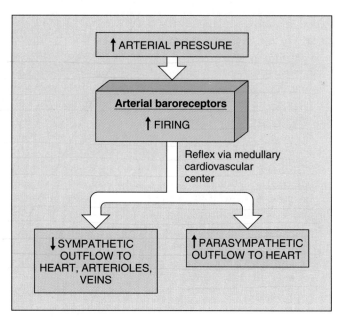

FIGURE 14-61

Neural components of the arterial baroreceptor reflex. When the initial change is a decrease in arterial pressure, all the arrows in the boxes would be reversed.

heart and decreased parasympathetic activity, (2) increased myocardial contractility because of increased sympathetic activity to the heart, (3) arteriolar constriction because of increased sympathetic activity to the arterioles and increased plasma concentrations of angiotensin II and vasopressin, and (4) increased venous constriction because of increased sympathetic activity to the veins. The net result is an increased cardiac output (increased heart rate and stroke volume), increased total peripheral resistance (arteriolar constriction), and return of blood pressure toward normal.

An increase in arterial blood pressure for any reason causes *increased* firing of the arterial baroreceptors, which reflexly induces a compensatory *decrease* in cardiac output and total peripheral resistance.

Having emphasized the great importance of this baroreceptor reflex, we must now add an equally important qualification. The baroreceptor reflex functions primarily as a *short-term* regulator of arterial blood pressure. It is activated instantly by any blood pressure *change* and attempts to restore blood pressure rapidly toward normal. Yet, if arterial pressure deviates from its normal operating point for more than a few days—recent experiments suggest even less time may be required—the arterial baroreceptors adapt to this new pressure, that is, they have a decreased frequency of action-potential firing at any given pressure. Thus, in patients who have chronically elevated blood pressure, the baroreceptors continue to oppose minute-to-minute changes in blood pressure, but at the higher level.

---

[13]One of these reflexes, termed the Bainbridge reflex, works in the opposite direction. By this reflex, an increased atrial pressure reflexly elicits an increased heart rate.

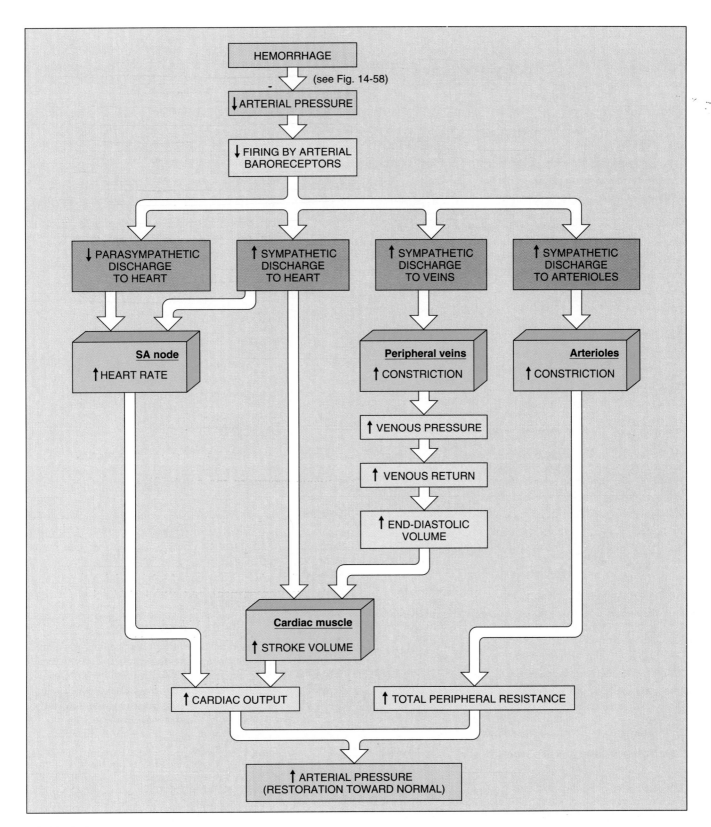

FIGURE 14-62

Arterial baroreceptor reflex compensation for hemorrhage. Hemorrhage causes a decrease in arterial pressure by causing decreases, in turn, of blood volume, venous pressure, venous return, atrial pressure, ventricular end-diastolic pressure, stroke volume, and cardiac output. The compensatory mechanisms do not restore arterial pressure completely to normal. Beyond the initial decrease in arterial pressure, all arrows signifying increases or decreases are relative to the state immediately following the hemorrhage but before reflex compensation begins. For simplicity, we have not shown the fact that plasma angiotensin II and vasopressin are also reflexly increased and help constrict arterioles.

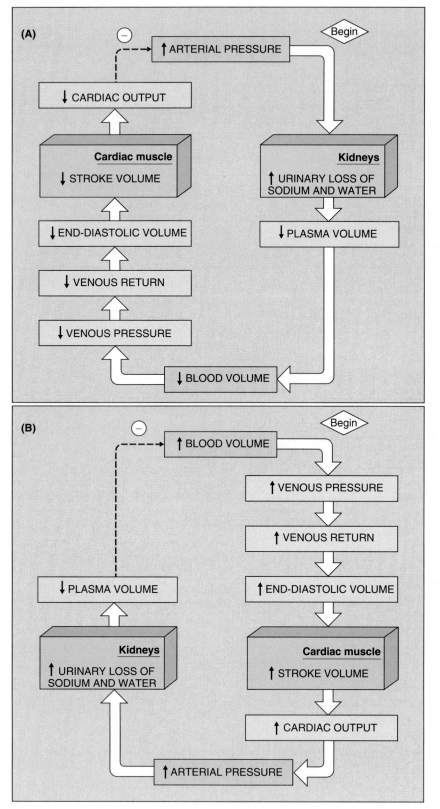

FIGURE 14-63

Causal reciprocal relationships between arterial pressure and blood volume. (A) An increase in arterial pressure due, for example, to an increased cardiac output induces a decrease in blood volume by promoting fluid excretion by the kidneys, which tends to restore arterial pressure to its original value. (B) An increase in blood volume due, for example, to altered kidney function induces an increase in arterial pressure, which tends to restore blood volume to its original value by promoting fluid excretion by the kidneys. Because of these relationships, blood volume is a major determinant of arterial pressure.

BLOOD VOLUME AND LONG-TERM REGULATION OF ARTERIAL PRESSURE

The fact that the baroreceptors adapt to prolonged changes in arterial pressure means that the baroreceptor reflex cannot *set* long-term arterial pressure. The major factor for long-term regulation is the blood volume. As described earlier, blood volume is a major determinant of arterial pressure because it influences in turn venous pressure, venous return, end-diastolic volume, stroke volume, and cardiac output. Thus, an increased blood volume increases arterial pressure. But the opposite causal chain also exists—an increased arterial pressure reduces blood volume (more specifically, the plasma component of the blood volume) by increasing the excretion of salt and water by the kidneys.

Figure 14-63 illustrates how these two causal chains constitute a negative-feedback loop that determines both blood volume and arterial pressure. If, for whatever reason, the blood *pressure* goes up as the initial event, this will cause a decreased blood volume, which will tend to bring the blood pressure back down. If, for whatever reason, the blood *volume* goes up as the initial event, this will raise the blood pressure, which will tend to bring the blood volume back down. The important point is this: Because arterial pressure influences blood volume but blood volume also influences arterial pressure, blood pressure can stabilize, in the long run, only at a value at which blood volume is also stable. Accordingly, blood volume changes are the single most important determinant, long term, of blood pressure.

OTHER CARDIOVASCULAR REFLEXES AND RESPONSES

Stimuli acting upon receptors other than baroreceptors can initiate reflexes that cause changes in arterial pressure. For example, the following stimuli all cause an increase in blood pressure: decreased arterial oxygen concentration, increased arterial carbon dioxide concentration, decreased brain blood flow, increased intracranial pressure, and pain originating in the skin (in contrast, pain originating in the viscera or joints may cause marked *decreases* in arterial pressure).

Many physiological states such as eating and sexual activity are also associated with changes in blood pressure. New techniques of noninvasive monitoring have allowed blood pressure to be taken while people go about normal daily activities. For example, attending business meetings raises mean blood pressure by 20 mmHg, walking increases it 10 mmHg, and sleeping lowers it 10 mmHg. Mood also has a significant effect on blood pressure, which tends to be lower when people reported that they are happy than when they are angry or anxious.

These changes are triggered by input from receptors or higher brain centers to the medullary cardiovascular center or, in some cases, to pathways distinct from these centers. For example, certain neurons in the cerebral cortex and hypothalamus synapse directly on the sympathetic neurons in the spinal cord, bypassing the medullary center altogether.

Thus, there is a marked degree of flexibility and integration in the control of blood pressure. For example, by stimulating electrically a discrete area of the hypothalamus of an experimental animal, all the usually observed neurally mediated cardiovascular responses to an acute emotional situation can be elicited. Stimulation of other brain sites elicits cardiovascular changes appropriate to the maintenance of body temperature, feeding, or sleeping. It seems that such outputs are "preprogrammed." The complete pattern can be released by a natural stimulus that initiates the flow of information to the appropriate controlling brain center.

SECTION E SUMMARY

I. Mean arterial pressure, the primary regulated variable in the cardiovascular system, equals the product of cardiac output and total peripheral resistance.

II. The factors that determine cardiac output and total peripheral resistance are summarized in Figure 14-57.

BARORECEPTOR REFLEXES

I. The primary baroreceptors are the arterial baroreceptors—the two carotid sinuses and the aortic arch. Nonarterial baroreceptors are located in the systemic veins, pulmonary vessels, and walls of the heart.

II. The firing rates of the arterial baroreceptors are proportional to mean arterial pressure and to pulse pressure.

III. An increase in firing of the arterial baroreceptors due to an increase in pressure causes, by way of the medullary cardiovascular center, an increase in parasympathetic outflow to the heart and a decrease in sympathetic outflow to the heart, arterioles, and veins. The result is a decrease in cardiac output and total peripheral resistance and, hence, a decrease in mean arterial pressure. The opposite occurs when the initial change is a decrease in arterial pressure.

BLOOD VOLUME AND LONG-TERM REGULATION OF ARTERIAL PRESSURE

I. The baroreceptor reflexes are short-term regulators of arterial pressure but adapt to a maintained change in pressure.

II. The most important long-term regulator of arterial pressure is the blood volume

SECTION E KEY TERMS

total peripheral resistance (TPR)
carotid sinus baroreceptors

aortic arch baroreceptor
arterial baroreceptors
medullary cardiovascular center

SECTION E REVIEW QUESTIONS

1. Write the equation relating mean arterial pressure to cardiac output and total peripheral resistance.
2. What variable accounts for mean pulmonary arterial pressure being lower than mean systemic arterial pressure?
3. Draw a flow diagram illustrating the factors that determine mean arterial pressure.
4. Identify the receptors, afferent pathways, integrating center, efferent pathways, and effectors in the arterial baroreceptor reflex.
5. When the arterial baroreceptors decrease or increase their rate of firing, what changes in autonomic outflow and cardiovascular function occur?
6. Describe the role of blood volume in the long-term regulation of arterial pressure.

SECTION

CARDIOVASCULAR PATTERNS IN HEALTH AND DISEASE

HEMORRHAGE AND OTHER CAUSES OF HYPOTENSION

The term *hypotension* means a low blood pressure, regardless of cause. The decrease in blood volume caused by hemorrhage produces hypotension by the sequence of events shown previously in Figure 14-58. The most serious consequences of hypotension are reduced blood flow to the brain and cardiac muscle.

The immediate counteracting response to hemorrhage is the baroreceptor reflex, previously summarized in Figure 14-62. Figure 14-64, which shows how five variables change over time when there is a decrease in blood volume, adds a further degree of clarification. The values of factors changed as a *direct* result of the hemorrhage—stroke volume, cardiac output, and mean arterial pressure—are restored by the baroreceptor reflex *toward*, but not *to* normal. In contrast, values not altered directly by the hemorrhage but only by the *reflex response* to hemorrhage—heart rate and total peripheral resistance—are increased above their prehemorrhage values. The increased peripheral resistance results from increases in sympathetic outflow to the arterioles in many vascular beds but not those of the heart and brain. Thus, skin blood flow may decrease markedly because of arteriolar vasocon-

striction—this is why the skin becomes cold and pale. Kidney and intestinal blood flow also decrease.

A second important type of compensatory mechanism (one not shown in Figure 14-62) involves the movement of interstitial fluid into capillaries. This occurs because both the drop in blood pressure and the increase in arteriolar constriction decrease capillary hydrostatic pressure, thereby favoring absorption of interstitial fluid (Figure 14-65). Thus, the initial event—blood loss and decreased

TABLE 14-8   FLUID SHIFTS AFTER HEMORRHAGE

| | | Percent of normal value | |
	Normal	Immediately after hemorrhage	18 h after hemorrhage
Total blood volume, ml	5000	80	98
Erythrocyte volume, ml	2300	80	80
Plasma volume, ml	2700	80	113

FIGURE 14-64

Five simultaneous graphs showing the time course of cardiovascular effects of hemorrhage. Note that the entire decrease in arterial pressure immediately following hemorrhage is secondary to the decrease in stroke volume and, hence, cardiac output. This figure emphasizes the relativeness of the "increase" and "decrease" arrows of Figure 14-62. All variables shown are increased relative to the state immediately following the hemorrhage, but not necessarily to the state prior to the hemorrhage.

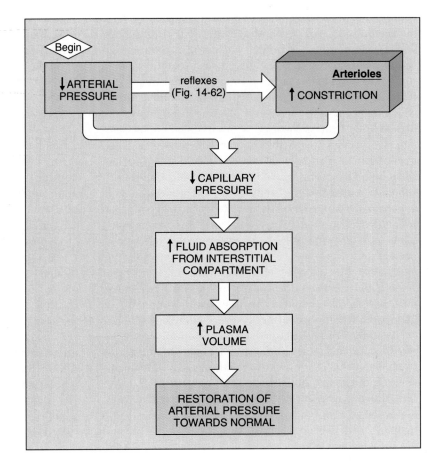

FIGURE 14-65

Mechanisms compensating for blood loss by movement of interstitial fluid into the capillaries.

blood volume—is in large part compensated for by the movement of interstitial fluid into the vascular system. Indeed, 12 to 24 h after a moderate hemorrhage, the blood volume may be restored virtually to normal by this mechanism (Table 14-8). At this time the entire restoration of blood volume is due to expansion of the plasma volume.

The early compensatory mechanisms for hemorrhage, the baroreceptor reflexes and interstitial fluid absorption, are highly efficient, so that losses of as much as 1.5 L of blood—approximately 30 percent of total blood volume—can be sustained with only slight reductions of mean arterial pressure or cardiac output.

We must emphasize that absorption of interstitial fluid only *redistributes* the extracellular fluid. Ultimate *replacement* of the fluid lost involves the control of fluid ingestion and kidney function. Both processes are described in Chapter 16. Replacement of the lost erythrocytes requires stimulation of erythropoiesis by erythropoietin. These replacement processes require days to weeks in contrast to the rapidly occurring reflex compensations described in Figure 14-62.

Loss of large quantities of cell-free extracellular fluid rather than whole blood can also cause hypotension. This type of fluid loss may occur via the skin, as in severe sweating or burns, via the gastrointestinal tract, as in diarrhea or vomiting, or via unusually large urinary losses. Regardless of the route, the loss of fluid decreases circulating blood volume and produces symptoms and compensatory cardiovascular changes similar to those seen in hemorrhage.

Hypotension may be caused by events other than blood or fluid loss. One such cause is strong emotion, during which hypotension can cause fainting. Somehow, the higher brain centers involved with emotions inhibit sympathetic activity and enhance parasympathetic activity, resulting in a markedly decreased arterial pressure and brain blood flow. This whole process is usually transient. It should be noted that the fainting that sometimes occurs in a person donating blood is usually due to hypotension brought on by emotion, not the blood loss, since losing 0.5 L of blood will not itself cause serious hypotension in normal individuals.

Massive liberation of chemicals that relax arteriolar smooth muscle may also cause hypotension by reducing total peripheral resistance. An important example is the hypotension that occurs during severe allergic responses.

Treatment of patients with hypotension in ways commonly favored by the uninformed, namely, administering alcohol and covering the person with mounds of blankets, is not appropriate. Both alcohol and excessive body heat cause dilation of skin arterioles, thus lowering total peripheral resistance and decreasing arterial blood pressure still further.

Shock

The term *shock* denotes any situation in which a decrease in blood flow to the organs and tissues damages them. The most common cause of shock is severe hemorrhage, and arterial pressure is usually, but not always, low in shock. The cardiovascular system, especially the heart, suffers damage if shock is prolonged. As the heart deteriorates, cardiac output declines even more and shock becomes progressively worse and ultimately irreversible, even though blood transfusions and other appropriate therapy may temporarily restore blood pressure.

Just as hemorrhage is not the only cause of hypotension and decreased cardiac output, so it is not the only cause of shock. Loss of fluid other than blood, excessive release of vasodilators as in allergy and infection, loss of neural tone to the cardiovascular system, and extensive bodily damage can all lead to severe reductions of tissue blood flow and the positive-feedback cycles culminating in irreversible shock.

THE UPRIGHT POSTURE

A decrease in the *effective* circulating blood volume occurs in the circulatory system when going from a lying, horizontal position to a standing, vertical one. Why this is so requires an understanding of the action of gravity upon the long, continuous columns of blood in the vessels between the heart and the feet.

The pressures we have given in previous sections of this chapter are for an individual in the horizontal position, in which all blood vessels are at approximately the same level as the heart. In this position, the weight of the blood produces negligible pressure. In contrast, when a person is vertical, the intravascular pressure everywhere becomes equal to the pressure generated by cardiac contraction *plus* an additional pressure equal to the weight of a column of blood from the heart to the point of measurement. In an average adult, for example, the weight of a column of blood extending from the heart to the feet amounts to 80 mmHg. In a foot capillary, therefore, the pressure increases from 25 (the pressure resulting from cardiac contraction) to 105 mmHg, the extra 80 mmHg being due to the weight of the column of blood.

This increase in pressure due to gravity influences the effective circulating blood volume. The increased hydrostatic pressure that occurs in the legs when a person is quietly standing pushes outward on the highly distensible vein walls, causing marked distension. The result is pooling of blood in the veins; that is, much of the blood emerging from the capillaries simply goes into expanding the veins rather than returning to the heart. Simultaneously, the increase in capillary pressure caused by the gravitational force produces increased filtration of fluid out of the capillaries into the interstitial space. This accounts for the fact that our feet swell during prolonged standing. The combined effects of venous pooling and increased capillary filtration reduce the *effective* circulating blood volume very similarly to the effects caused by a mild hemorrhage. The ensuing decrease in arterial pressure causes reflex compensatory adjustments similar to those shown in Figure 14-62 for hemorrhage.

One way to offset the effects of gravity is to contract the skeletal muscles in the legs. These contractions produce intermittent, complete emptying of the leg veins so that uninterrupted columns of venous blood from the heart to the feet no longer exist (Figure 14-66). The result is a decrease in both venous distension and pooling plus a marked reduction in capillary hydrostatic pressure and fluid filtration out of the capillaries.

Soldiers may faint while standing at attention for long periods of time because they have minimal contractions of the leg muscles. Here fainting may be considered adaptive in that the venous and capillary pressure changes induced by gravity are eliminated once the person is prone. The pooled venous blood is mobilized, and the filtered fluid is absorbed back into the capillaries. Thus, the wrong thing to do to a person who has fainted for whatever reason is to hold him or her upright.

EXERCISE

During exercise, cardiac output may increase from a resting value of 5 L/min to a maximal value of 35 L/min in trained athletes. The distribution of this cardiac output during strenuous exercise is illustrated in Figure 14-67. As expected, most of the increase in cardiac output goes to the exercising muscles, but there are also increases in flow to skin, required for dissipation of heat, and to the heart, required for the additional work performed by the heart in pumping the increased cardiac output. The increases in flow through these three vascular beds are the result of arteriolar dilation in them. In both skeletal and cardiac muscle, the dilation is mediated by local metabolic factors, whereas the dilation in skin is achieved by a decrease in the firing of the sympathetic neurons to the skin. At the same time that arteriolar dilation is occurring in these beds, arteriolar constriction—manifested as decreased blood flow in Figure 14-67—is occurring in the kidneys and gastrointestinal organs, secondary to increased activity of the sympathetic neurons supplying them.

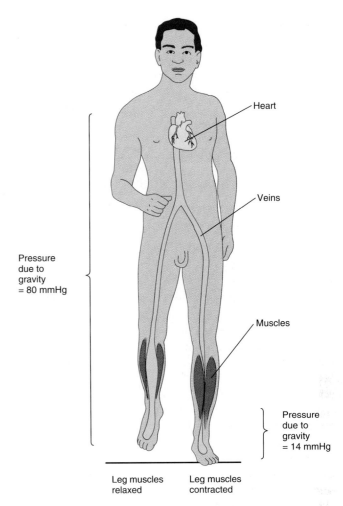

FIGURE 14-66

Role of contraction of the leg skeletal muscles in reducing capillary pressure and filtration in the upright position. The skeletal muscle contraction compresses the veins, causing intermittent emptying so that the columns of blood are interrupted. The venous pooling is exaggerated in this figure for purposes of illustration.

Dilation of arterioles in skeletal muscle, cardiac muscle, and skin causes a decrease in total peripheral resistance to blood flow. This decrease is partially offset by constriction of arterioles in other organs. Such "resistance juggling," however, is quite incapable of compensating for the huge dilation of the muscle arterioles, and the net result is a marked decrease in total peripheral resistance.

What happens to arterial blood pressure during exercise? As always, the mean arterial pressure is simply the arithmetic product of cardiac output and total peripheral resistance. During most forms of exercise (Figure 14-68 illustrates the case for mild exercise), the cardiac output tends to increase somewhat more than the total peripheral

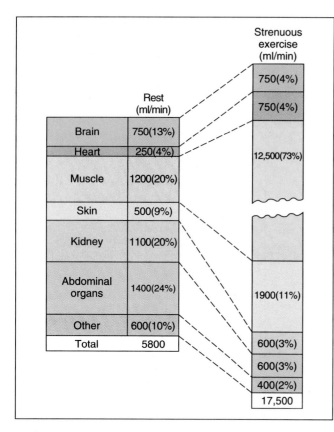

FIGURE 14-67

Distribution of the systemic cardiac output at rest and during strenuous exercise. The values at rest were previously presented in Figure 14-10. (*Adapted from Chapman and Mitchell.*)

lower end-diastolic volume and stroke volume (Starling's law). Therefore, factors promoting venous return during exercise are extremely important. They are (1) increased activity of the skeletal-muscle pump, (2) increased depth and frequency of inspiration, (3) sympathetically mediated increase in venous tone, and (4) greater ease of blood flow from arteries to veins through the dilated skeletal-muscle arterioles.

During vigorous exercise, in contrast to the mild exercise illustrated in Figure 14-68, these four factors may be so powerful that venous return is enhanced enough to cause an *increase* in end-diastolic ventricular volume. Under such conditions, stroke volume is further enhanced above what it would have been from increased contractility alone.

What are the control mechanisms by which the cardiovascular changes in exercise are elicited? As described previously, dilation of arterioles in skeletal and cardiac muscle once exercise is underway represents active hyperemia secondary to local metabolic factors within the muscle. But what drives the enhanced sympathetic outflow to most

FIGURE 14-68

Summary of cardiovascular changes during mild exercise.

resistance decreases, so that mean arterial pressure usually increases slightly.

The cardiac output increase during exercise is caused by a combination of greater sympathetic activity and less parasympathetic activity to the heart (which of these two autonomic changes is more important varies in different types of exercise). The increases in heart rate are usually much greater than those of stroke volume. Note in Figure 14-68 that, in our example, the increased stroke volume occurs without change in end-diastolic ventricular volume. Accordingly, the increased stroke volume in this case cannot be ascribed to Starling's law but is due completely to the increased contractility induced by the cardiac sympathetic nerves.

It would be incorrect to leave the impression that altered autonomic activity to the heart is sufficient to account for the elevated cardiac output that occurs in exercise. The fact is that cardiac output can be increased to high levels only if venous return to the heart is simultaneously increased to the same degree. Otherwise, the shortened filling time resulting from the high heart rate would other arterioles, the heart, and the veins and the decreased parasympathetic outflow to the heart? The control of this autonomic outflow during exercise offers an excellent example of what we earlier referred to as a preprogrammed pattern, modified by continuous afferent input. One or more discrete control centers in the brain are activated during exercise, and according to this "central command," descending pathways from these centers to the appropriate autonomic preganglionic neurons elicit the firing pattern typical of exercise. Indeed, these centers begin to "direct traffic" even before the exercise begins, since a person just about to begin exercising already manifests many of the changes in cardiac and vascular function.

Once exercise is underway, local chemical changes in the muscle develop unless there is a perfect matching between flow and metabolic demands, and these changes activate chemoreceptors in the muscle. Afferent input from these receptors goes to the medullary cardiovascular center and facilitates the output reaching the autonomic neurons from higher brain centers (Figure 14-69). The result is a further increase in heart rate, myocardial contractility, and vascular resistance in the nonactive organs. Such a system permits a fine degree of matching between cardiac pumping and total oxygen and nutrients required by the exercising muscles. Mechanoreceptors in the exercising muscles are also stimulated and provide input to the medullary cardiovascular center.

Finally, what role do the arterial baroreceptors play? Knowing that the mean and pulsatile pressures rise during exercise, you might assume that these baroreceptors would try to lower them by eliciting a pattern of autonomic responses opposite that coming from central command and the muscle chemoreceptors. This does not occur, however, because another component of the central neural command is to "reset" the arterial baroreceptors upward as exercise begins.

Table 14-9 summarizes the changes that occur during moderate endurance exercise, that is, exercise that involves large muscle groups for an extended period of time.

Maximal Oxygen Consumption and Training

As the magnitude of any endurance exercise increases, oxygen consumption also increases in exact proportion until a point is reached when it fails to rise despite a further increment in work load. This is known as **maximal oxygen consumption** ($\dot{V}_{O_2max}$). After $\dot{V}_{O_2max}$ has been reached, work can be increased and sustained only very briefly by anaerobic metabolism in the exercising muscles.

Theoretically, $\dot{V}_{O_2max}$ could be limited by the cardiac output, the respiratory system's ability to deliver oxygen to the blood, or the exercising muscle's ability to use oxygen. In fact, in normal people, cardiac output is the factor that determines $\dot{V}_{O_2max}$. With increasing work load (Figure 14-

FIGURE 14-69

Control of the autonomic nervous system during exercise. The primary outflow to the sympathetic and parasympathetic neurons is via pathways from "exercise centers" in the brain, pathways parallel to those going to the exercising muscles. Afferent input from chemoreceptors in these muscles also influences the autonomic neurons by way of the medullary cardiovascular center.

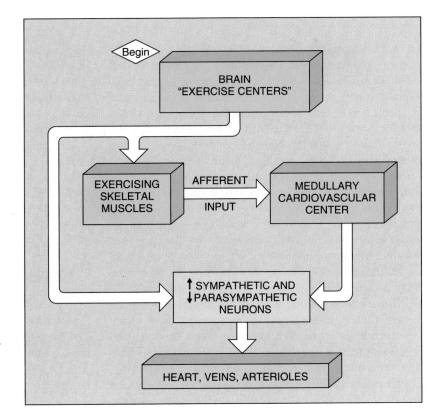

TABLE 14-9 CARDIOVASCULAR CHANGES IN MODERATE ENDURANCE EXERCISE

Variable	Change	Explanation
Cardiac output	Increases	Heart rate and stroke volume both increase.
Heart rate	Increases	Sympathetic-nerve activity to the SA node increases, and parasympathetic nerve activity decreases.
Stroke volume	Increases	Contractility increases due to increased sympathetic-nerve activity to the ventricular myocardium.
Total peripheral resistance	Decreases	Resistance in heart and skeletal muscles decreases more than resistance in other vascular beds increases.
Mean arterial pressure	Increases	Cardiac output increases more than total peripheral resistance decreases.
Pulse pressure	Increases	Stroke volume and velocity of ejection of the stroke volume increase.
End-diastolic volume	Unchanged	Filling time is decreased by the high heart rates, but this is compensated for by the factors favoring venous return—venoconstriction, skeletal-muscle pump, and increased inspiratory movements.
Blood flow to heart and skeletal muscle	Increases	Active hyperemia occurs in both vascular beds, mediated by local metabolic factors.
Blood flow to skin	Increases	Sympathetic nerves to skin vessels are inhibited reflexly by the increase in body temperature.
Blood flow to viscera	Decreases	Sympathetic nerves to the abdominal organs and the kidneys are stimulated.
Blood flow to brain	Unchanged	Autoregulation of brain arterioles maintains constant flow despite the increased mean arterial pressure.

70) heart rate increases progressively and markedly until it reaches a maximum. Stroke volume increases much less and tends to level off when 75 percent of $\dot{V}_{O_2max}$ has been reached (it actually starts to go back down in elderly people). The major factors responsible for limiting the rise in stroke volume are (1) the very rapid heart rate, which decreases diastolic filling time, and (2) inability of the peripheral factors favoring venous return—skeletal-muscle pump, respiratory pump, venoconstriction, arteriolar dilation—to increase ventricular filling further during the very short time available.

A person's $\dot{V}_{O_2max}$ is not fixed at any given value but can be altered by the habitual level of physical activity. For example, prolonged bed rest may decrease maximal exercise capacity by 25 percent, whereas intense long-term physical training may increase it by a similar amount. To be effective, the training must be of an endurance type. We are still uncertain of the most effective relative combinations of intensity and duration, but, as an example, jogging 20 to 30 min three times weekly at 5 to 8 mi/h definitely produces some training effect in most people.

This training effect is manifested at rest as an increased stroke volume and decreased heart rate with no change in cardiac output. At $\dot{V}_{O_2max}$, the trained individual has an increased cardiac output due entirely to an increased maximal stroke volume, since maximal heart rate is not altered by training (Figure 14-70). The increase in stroke volume is due to a combination of (1) effects on the heart—increased cardiac muscle mass and increased ventricular contractility, and (2) peripheral effects—increased blood volume and increases in the number of blood vessels in skeletal muscle, which increase muscle blood flow and venous return. Training also increases the concentrations of oxidative enzymes and mitochondria in the exercised muscles.

HYPERTENSION

Hypertension is defined as a chronically increased systemic arterial pressure. The dividing line between normal pressure and hypertension is set at approximately 140/90 mmHg.

Theoretically, hypertension could result from an increase in cardiac output or in total peripheral resistance,

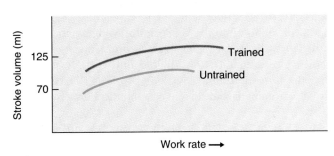

FIGURE 14-70

Changes in cardiac output, heart rate, and stroke volume with increasing work in untrained and trained persons.

or both. In reality, however, the major abnormality in most cases of well-established hypertension is increased total peripheral resistance, caused by abnormally reduced arteriolar radius.

What causes the arteriolar constriction? In only a small fraction of cases is the cause known. For example, diseases that damage a kidney or decrease its blood supply are often associated with **renal hypertension**; the cause of the hypertension may be increased release of renin from the kidney, with subsequent increased generation of the potent vasoconstrictor angiotensin II. However, for more than 95 percent of individuals with hypertension, the cause of the arteriolar constriction is unknown. Hypertension of unknown cause is called **primary hypertension** (formerly essential hypertension).

Many hypotheses have been proposed to explain the increased arteriolar constriction of primary hypertension. At present, much evidence suggests that excessive sodium

retention is a contributing factor in genetically predisposed persons. Although this relationship remains controversial, it is certainly true that many individuals with hypertension show a drop in blood pressure after being on low-sodium diets or receiving drugs, termed **diuretics**, that cause increased sodium loss via the urine. Low dietary intake of calcium has also been implicated as a possible contributor to primary hypertension, but this, too, remains controversial. Obesity is a definite risk factor for primary hypertension, and weight reduction and exercise are frequently effective in causing some reduction of blood pressure in overweight sedentary persons with hypertension. Cigarette smoking, too, is a definite risk factor.

Hypertension causes a variety of problems. One of the organs most affected is the heart. Because the left ventricle in a hypertensive person must chronically pump against an increased arterial pressure, it develops an adaptive increase in muscle mass. In the early phases of the disease, this helps maintain the heart's function as a pump. With time, however, changes in the organization and properties of myocardial cells occur, and these result in diminished contractile function and heart failure. The presence of hypertension also enhances the development of atherosclerosis and heart attacks (see below), kidney damage, and rupture of a cerebral blood vessel, which causes localized brain damage—a **stroke**.

In addition to diuretics, four other classes of drugs, all of which reduce peripheral resistance, are in common use for treating hypertension: (1) blockers of beta-adrenergic receptors, (2) blockers of calcium channels, (3) blockers of the formation of angiotensin II, and (4) drugs that act either on the brain or outside the brain to antagonize the sympathetic nervous system.

That drugs that block beta-adrenergic receptors *reduce* total peripheral resistance by *dilating* arterioles should come as a surprise to the reader: Since beta-adrenergic receptors in the arterioles mediate dilation, one would deduce that blockage of these receptors should cause arteriolar constriction. Clearly, the beta-adrenergic receptors on the *blood vessels* are not the critical ones being blocked in the treatment of hypertension, and the explanation of the decrease in resistance is uncertain.[14]

The calcium-channel blockers reduce the entry of calcium into vascular smooth-muscle cells, causing them to contract less strongly.

As will be described in Chapter 16, the final step in the formation of angiotensin II, a vasoconstrictor, is mediated by an enzyme called angiotensin-converting enzyme.

---

[14]One hypothesis is as follows. As described in Chapter 16, sympathetic nerves act via beta-adrenergic receptors to stimulate the secretion of renin, with subsequent generation in the plasma of angiotensin II. Blockade of these receptors would therefore result in a lower plasma concentration of this potent vasoconstrictor.

Drugs that block this enzyme therefore reduce the concentration of angiotensin II in plasma, which causes arteriolar dilation.

The antagonists of the sympathetic nervous system reduce sympathetically mediated stimulation of arteriolar smooth muscle.

HEART FAILURE

The heart may fail as a pump for many reasons. Two examples are pumping against a chronically elevated arterial pressure in hypertension and structural damage due to decreased coronary blood flow. It has become standard practice to separate persons with **heart failure** (also termed congestive heart failure) into two categories: (1) those with systolic dysfunction (problems with ventricular ejection), and (2) those with diastolic dysfunction (problems with ventricular filling). In fact, however, most persons with heart failure have elements of both categories.

A decreased contractility is often the hallmark of heart failure. As shown in Figure 14-71, the failing heart shifts downward to a lower Starling curve, that is, to a lower stroke volume at any given end-diastolic volume. When this occurs, a number of compensatory mechanisms come into play; these are quite similar to the reflex responses generated by a fall in blood pressure. For one thing, a reflex increase in sympathetic outflow to the heart helps to increase contractility back toward normal and also raises

heart rate, both of which contribute to a restoration of cardiac output.

A second reflex compensation is to increase ventricular end-diastolic volume. The sequence of events is as follows: Decreased cardiac output causes a decrease in mean and pulsatile arterial pressure. This triggers reflexes, including the baroreceptor reflexes, that induce the kidneys to reduce their excretion of sodium and water. The retained fluid then causes expansion of the extracellular volume, increasing venous pressure, venous return, and end-diastolic ventricular volume—thus tending to restore stroke volume toward normal. Thus, the heart in failure is generally distended with blood, as are the veins and capillaries, the major cause being an increase, sometimes massive, in plasma volume. It must be recognized, however, that if the ventricle becomes too distended, its force of contraction decreases and the situation worsens.

Even before this overdistension is reached, however, there is an undesirable result of the elevated venous pressure: the formation of edema. Why does an increased venous pressure cause edema? The capillaries, of course, drain via venules into the veins, and so when venous pressure increases, the capillary pressure also increases and causes increased filtration of fluid out of the capillaries into the interstitial fluid. Swelling of the legs and feet is usually prominent, but the engorgement occurs elsewhere as well.

Failure of the left ventricle leads to **pulmonary edema**, which is the accumulation of fluid in the interstitial spaces of the lung or in the air spaces themselves. This impairs gas exchange. The reason for such accumulation is that the relatively ineffective left ventricle *temporarily* fails to pump blood to the same extent as the right ventricle, and so the volume of blood in all the pulmonary vessels increases. The resulting engorgement of pulmonary capillaries raises the capillary pressure above its normally very low value, causing increased filtration out of the capillaries. This situation usually worsens at night: During the day, because of the patient's upright posture, fluid accumulates in the legs; then the fluid is slowly absorbed when the patient lies down at night, thus expanding the plasma volume and precipitating an attack of pulmonary edema.

The treatment for heart failure is easily understood in terms of its pathophysiology: (1) The precipitating cause, for example, hypertension, should be corrected if possible; (2) ventricular contractility can be increased by a drug known as **digitalis**, which acts by increasing cytosolic calcium in the myocardial cells; (3) fluid accumulation contributing to edema can be minimized by salt restriction and the use of diuretics; (4) vasodilator drugs can be used to lower peripheral resistance and hence the arterial blood pressure (afterload) against which the failing heart must pump. (Peripheral resistance is usually excessively elevated in heart failure because of reflex increases in both

FIGURE 14-71

Relationship between end-diastolic ventricular volume and stroke volume in normal and failing hearts. The normal curve is that shown previously in Figure 14-31. The failing heart can still eject an adequate stroke volume if the sympathetic activity to it is increased or if the end-diastolic volume increases, that is, if the ventricle becomes more distended.

TABLE 14-10   MAJOR CAUSES OF EDEMA

Physiological Event	Cause of edema
Increased arterial pressure secondary to increased cardiac output°	Increased capillary pressure, leading to increased filtration
Local arteriolar dilation, as in exercise or inflammation	Increased capillary pressure, leading to increased filtration.
Increased venous pressure, as in heart failure or venous obstruction	Increased capillary pressure, leading to increased filtration
Decreased plasma protein concentration, as in liver disease (decreased protein production), kidney disease (loss of protein in the urine), or protein malnutrition	Decreased force for osmotic absorption across capillary. Therefore, *net* filtration is increased.
Increased interstitial fluid protein concentration resulting from increased capillary permeability to protein (as in inflammation)	Decreased force for osmotic absorption across capillary. Therefore, *net* filtration is increased.
Obstruction of lymphatic vessels, as in infection by filaria roundworms (elephantiasis)	Fluid filtered from the blood capillaries into the interstitial compartment is not carried away. Protein also accumulates in the interstitial fluid.

°In contrast, if arterial pressure is elevated because of increased total peripheral resistance, edema may not occur; the capillary pressure may not be elevated because the increased arteriolar resistance causing the increased arterial pressure will prevent most of that increase in pressure from reaching the capillaries.

sympathetic outflow to arterioles and in the plasma concentrations of the two major hormonal vasoconstrictors—angiotensin II and vasopressin.)

The mechanism of action of digitalis offers an excellent review of cellular calcium metabolism. Digitalis inhibits Na,K-ATPase in the myocardial plasma membranes, leading to an increase in cytosolic sodium concentration. This decreases the gradient for sodium-calcium exchange across the plasma membranes, thereby decreasing calcium exit and increasing cytosolic calcium concentration.

In closing this section it should be emphasized that there are causes of edema other than heart failure and lymphatic malfunction described earlier. They are all understandable as imbalances in the Starling forces and are listed in Table 14-10.

CORONARY ARTERY DISEASE

We have seen that the myocardium does not extract oxygen and nutrients from the blood within the atria and ventricles but depends upon its own blood supply via the coronary arteries. In **coronary artery disease**, changes (to be described below) in one or more of the coronary arteries causes insufficient coronary blood flow. The result may be myocardial damage in the affected region and, if severe enough, death of that portion of the heart—a **myocardial infarction (heart attack)**. Many patients with coronary artery disease experience recurrent short-lived episodes of inadequate coronary blood flow, usually during exertion or emotional tension, before ultimately suffering a heart attack. The chest pain associated with these episodes is called **angina pectoris** (or, more commonly, simply angina).

The symptoms of myocardial infarction include prolonged chest pain, often radiating to the left arm, nausea, vomiting, sweating, weakness, and shortness of breath. Diagnosis is made by ECG changes typical of infarction and by measurement of certain enzymes in plasma. These enzymes are present in cardiac muscle and leak out into the blood when the muscle is damaged; they include particular variants of creatine phosphokinase (CPK) and lactate dehydrogenase (LDH).

Of the approximately 1.5 million heart attack victims in the United States each year, three-fourths are admitted to a hospital, where they can be given advanced care, and more than 80 percent of these people survive the attack and are discharged. Unfortunately, the other one-fourth of heart attacks occur with so little immediate warning that the victim has no opportunity to reach a hospital before the heart stops. These sudden cardiac deaths are due mainly to *ventricular fibrillation*, an abnormality in impulse condition triggered by the damaged myocardial cells and resulting in continuous disorganized ventricular contractions that are ineffective in producing flow. (Note that ventricular fibrillation is fatal, whereas atrial fibrillation, as described earlier in this chapter, generally causes only minor problems.) Many of these individuals can be saved if modern emergency resuscitation procedures are applied immediately after the attack. This treatment is *cardiopulmonary resuscitation (CPR)*, a repeated series of mouth-to-mouth respirations and chest compressions that circulate a small amount of blood to the brain, heart, and other vital organs when the heart has stopped. CPR is then followed by definitive treatment, including defibrillation, a procedure in which electric current is passed through the heart to try to halt the abnormal electrical activity causing the fibrillation. CPR is a potentially life-saving procedure that is easily learned in a few hours of training at readily available courses sponsored by the Red Cross and other groups.

The major cause of coronary artery disease is the presence of atherosclerosis in these vessels. *Atherosclerosis* is a disease characterized by a thickening of the portion of the arterial vessel wall closest to the lumen with (1) large numbers of abnormal smooth-muscle cells and (2) deposits of cholesterol and other substances. The mechanisms by which atherosclerosis reduces coronary blood flow is as follows: The extra muscle cells and various deposits in the wall bulge into the lumen of the vessel and increase resistance to flow. This is progressive, sometimes leading ultimately to complete occlusion. Total occlusion is usually caused, however, by the formation of a blood clot *(coronary thrombosis)* in the narrowed atherosclerotic artery, and this triggers the heart attack.

The processes that lead to atherosclerosis are complex and still not completely understood. But it is known that cigarette smoking, high plasma cholesterol concentration, hypertension, diabetes, a sedentary life style, and stress can increase the incidence and the severity of the atherosclerotic process. These are all termed, therefore, "risk factors" for coronary artery disease, and prevention of this disease focuses on eliminating or minimizing them.[15] The

control of plasma cholesterol concentration is described in Chapter 18.

The chronic treatment of coronary artery disease and angina with drugs can be understood in terms of physiological concepts described in this chapter. First, vasodilator drugs such as nitroglycerin[16] help in the following way: They dilate the coronary arteries and the systemic arterioles; the arteriolar effect lowers total peripheral resistance, thereby lowering arterial blood pressure and the work the heart must expend in ejecting blood. Second, beta-adrenergic blocking agents may be used to lower the arterial pressure, but more importantly, they block the effects of the sympathetic nerves on the heart; the result is reduced myocardial work, and hence oxygen demand because both heart rate and contractility are reduced. Third, calcium-channel blockers also reduce myocardial work by reducing myocardial contractility. Calcium-channel blockers are also coronary and general vasodilators, and they prevent abnormal electrical rhythms that can lead to ventricular fibrillation. How a blockage of calcium channels may achieve each of these effects should be understandable from previous descriptions of the roles of calcium in excitation-contraction coupling in cardiac and smooth muscle. Fourth, drugs that prevent or reverse clotting are also very important in the treatment (and prevention) of heart attacks. Use of these drugs is described in Chapter 20.

There are several surgical treatments for coronary artery disease after the area of narrowing or occlusion is identified by cardiac angiography (described earlier in this chapter). *Coronary angioplasty* is the passing of a catheter with a balloon at its tip into the occluded artery and then expanding the balloon. This enlarges the lumen by stretching the vessel and breaking up abnormal tissue deposits. A second surgical technique is *coronary bypass*, in which an area of occluded coronary artery is removed and replaced with a new vessel, often a vein taken from elsewhere in the patient's body. Tubes made of synthetic materials may also be used.

We do not wish to leave the impression that atherosclerosis attacks only the coronary vessels, for such is not the case. Many arteries of the body are subject to this same occluding process, and whenever the atherosclerosis becomes severe, the resulting symptoms reflect the decrease in blood flow to the specific area. For example, occlusion of a cerebral artery due to atherosclerosis and its associated blood clotting can cause localized brain damage—a stroke (recall that rupture of a cerebral vessel, as in hypertension, is the other cause of stroke). Persons with atherosclerotic cerebral vessels may also suffer reversible neurologic deficits, known as *transient ischemic attacks*

---

[15]Regular exercise is protective against heart attacks for a variety of reasons. It induces (1) increased diameter of coronary arteries, (2) decreased severity of hypertension and diabetes, (3) decreased plasma cholesterol concentration with simultaneous increase in the plasma concentration of a cholesterol-carrying lipoprotein thought to be protective against atherosclerosis, and (4) improved ability to dissolve blood clots.

[16]Nitroglycerin is a vasodilator because it is converted to nitric oxide, which as described in the text is actually EDRF.

(TIAs), lasting minutes to hours, without actually experiencing a stroke at the time.

Finally, it should be noted that both myocardial infarcts and strokes due to occlusion may result from the breaking off of a fragment of a blood clot or fatty deposit that then lodges downstream, completely blocking a smaller vessel. The fragment is termed an ***embolus***, and the process is ***embolism***.

SECTION F SUMMARY

HEMORRHAGE AND OTHER CAUSES OF HYPOTENSION

I. The physiological responses to hemorrhage are summarized in Figures 14-62, 14-64, and 14-65.

II. Hypotension can be caused by loss of body fluids, by strong emotion, and by liberation of vasodilator chemicals.

III. Shock is any situation in which blood flow to the tissues is low enough to cause damage to them.

THE UPRIGHT POSTURE

I. In the upright posture, gravity acting upon unbroken columns of blood reduces venous return by increasing vascular pressures in the veins and capillaries in the limbs.

  A. The increased venous pressure distends the veins, causing venous pooling, and the increased capillary pressure causes increased filtration out of the capillaries.

  B. These effects are minimized by contraction of the skeletal muscles in the legs.

EXERCISE

I. The cardiovascular changes that occur in endurance-type exercise are illustrated in Figures 14-67 and 14-68.

II. The changes are due to active hyperemia in the exercising skeletal muscles and heart, to increased sympathetic outflow to the heart, arterioles, and veins, and to decreased parasympathetic outflow to the heart.

III. The increase in cardiac output depends not only on the autonomic influences on the heart but on factors that help increase venous return.

IV. Training can increase a person's maximal oxygen consumption by increasing maximal stroke volume and hence cardiac output.

HYPERTENSION

I. Hypertension is usually due to increased total peripheral resistance resulting from increased arteriolar constriction.

II. More than 95 percent of hypertension is termed primary in that the cause of the increased arteriolar constriction is unknown.

HEART FAILURE

I. Heart failure can occur when a decreased cardiac contractility causes cardiac output to be inadequate.

II. This leads to fluid retention by the kidneys and formation of edema because of increased capillary pressure.

III. Pulmonary edema can occur when the left ventricle fails.

CORONARY ARTERY DISEASE

I. Insufficient coronary blood flow can cause damage to the heart.

II. Acute death from a heart attack is usually due to ventricular fibrillation.

III. The major cause of reduced coronary blood flow is atherosclerosis, an occlusive disease of arteries.

IV. Persons may suffer intermittent attacks of angina pectoris without actually suffering a heart attack at the time of the pain.

V. Atherosclerosis can also cause strokes and symptoms of inadequate blood flow in other areas.

SECTION F KEY TERMS

maximal oxygen consumption ($\dot{V}_{O_2max}$)

SECTION F REVIEW QUESTIONS

1. Draw a flow diagram illustrating the reflex compensation for hemorrhage.

2. What happens to plasma volume and interstitial-fluid volume following a hemorrhage?

3. What causes hypotension during a severe allergic response?

4. How does gravity influence effective blood volume?

5. Describe the role of the skeletal-muscle pump in decreasing capillary filtration.

6. List the directional changes that occur during exercise for all relevant cardiovascular variables. What are the specific efferent mechanisms that bring about these changes?

7. What factors enhance venous return during exercise?

8. Diagram the control of autonomic outflow during exercise.

9. What is the limiting cardiovascular factor in endurance exercise?

10. What changes in cardiac function occur at rest and during exercise as a result of endurance training?

11. What is the abnormality in most cases of established hypertension?

12. Describe two mechanisms for raising stroke volume in heart failure.

13. How does heart failure lead to edema?

14. Name four risk factors for atherosclerosis.

CHAPTER 14 CLINICAL TERMS

iron deficiency	renal hypertension
anemia	primary hypertension
pernicious anemia	diuretics
hemorrhage	stroke
sickle-cell anemia	heart failure
microcytosis	pulmonary edema
normocytosis	digitalis
macrocytosis	coronary artery disease
polycythemia	myocardial infarction
AV conduction	heart attack
disorders	angina pectoris
atrial fibrillation	ventricular fibrillation
heart murmurs	cardiopulmonary resuscitation
stenosis	(CPR)
insufficiency	atherosclerosis
echocardiography	coronary thrombosis
cardiac angiography	coronary angioplasty
elephantiasis	coronary bypass
edema	transient ischemic attacks
hypotension	(TIAs)
shock	embolus
hypertension	embolism

CHAPTER 14 THOUGHT QUESTIONS

(Answers are given in Appendix A.)

1. A person is found to have a hematocrit of 35 percent. Can you conclude from this that there is a decreased volume of erythrocytes in the blood?

2. Which would cause a greater increase in resistance to flow—a doubling of blood viscosity or a halving of tube radius?

3. If all plasma-membrane calcium channels in contractile cardiac-muscle cells were blocked with a drug, what would happen to the muscle's action potentials and contraction?

4. A person with a heart rate of 40 has no P waves but normal QRS complexes on the ECG. What is the explanation?

5. A person has a left ventricular systolic pressure of 180 mmHg and an aortic systolic pressure of 110 mmHg. What is the explanation?

6. A person has a left atrial pressure of 20 mmHg and a left ventricular pressure of 5 mmHg during ventricular filling. What is the explanation.

7. A patient is taking a drug that blocks beta-adrenergic receptors. What changes in cardiac function will the drug cause?

8. What is the mean arterial pressure in a person whose diastolic and systolic pressure are, respectively, 160 and 100 mmHg?

9. A person is given a drug that doubles the blood flow to her kidneys but does not change the mean arterial pressure. What must the drug be doing?

10. A blood vessel removed from an experimental animal dilates when exposed to acetylcholine. After the endothelium is scraped from the lumen of the vessel, it no longer dilates in response to this mediator. Explain.

11. A person is accumulating edema throughout the body. Average capillary pressure is 25 mmHg, and lymphatic function is normal. What is the most likely cause of the edema.

12. A person's cardiac output is 7 L/min and mean arterial pressure is 140 mmHg. What is the person's total peripheral resistance?

13. The following data are obtained for an experimental animal before and after a drug. Before: heart rate = 80 beats/min, and stroke volume = 80 ml/beat. After: heart rate = 100 beats/min, and stroke volume = 64 ml/beat. Total peripheral resistance remains unchanged. What has the drug done to mean arterial pressure?

14. When the nerves from all the arterial baroreceptors are cut in an experimental animal, what happens to mean arterial pressure?

15. What happens to the hematocrit within several hours after a hemorrhage?

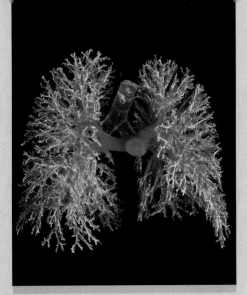

C H A P T E R

15

RESPIRATION

Respiration has two quite different meanings: (1) utilization of oxygen in the metabolism of organic molecules by cells, as described in Chapter 5, and (2) the exchanges of oxygen and carbon dioxide between an organism and the external environment. The second meaning is the subject of this chapter.

Our cells obtain most of their energy from chemical reactions involving oxygen. In addition, cells must be able to eliminate carbon dioxide, the major end product of oxidative metabolism. A unicellular organism can exchange oxygen and carbon dioxide directly with the external environment, but this is obviously impossible for most cells of a complex organism like a human being. Therefore, the evolution of large animals required the development of a specialized system—the respiratory system—to exchange oxygen and carbon dioxide for the entire animal with the external environment.

The **respiratory system** comprises those structures involved in the exchange of gases between the blood and external environment: the lungs (**pulmonary** is the adjectival form of "lungs"), the series of tubes leading to the lungs, and the chest structures responsible for moving air into and out of the lungs during breathing.

In addition to the provision of oxygen and elimination of carbon dioxide, the respiratory system serves other functions, as listed in Table 15-1 and discussed in this chapter.

TABLE 15-1 FUNCTIONS OF THE RESPIRATORY SYSTEM

1. Provides oxygen
2. Eliminates carbon dioxide
3. Regulates the blood's hydrogen-ion concentration (pH)
4. Forms speech sounds (phonation)
5. Defends against microbes
6. Influences arterial concentrations of chemical messengers by removing some from pulmonary capillary blood and producing and adding others to this blood
7. Traps and dissolves blood clots

ORGANIZATION OF THE RESPIRATORY SYSTEM

There are two lungs, the right and left, each divided into several lobes. The lungs of an adult consist mainly of tiny air-containing sacs called **alveoli** (singular, **alveolus**), which number approximately 300 million and are the sites of gas exchange with the blood. The **airways** are all the tubes through which air flows between the external environment and the alveoli.

Inspiration is the movement of air from the external environment through the airways into the alveoli during breathing. **Expiration** is movement in the opposite direction. An inspiration and an expiration constitute a respiratory cycle. During the entire respiratory cycle, the right ventricle of the heart pumps blood through the capillaries surrounding each alveolus. At rest, in a normal adult, approximately 4 L of environmental air enters and leaves the alveoli per minute, while 5 L of blood, the entire cardiac output, flows through the pulmonary capillaries. During heavy exercise, the air flow can increase thirty- to fortyfold, and the blood flow five- to sixfold. The alveolar air and capillary blood are separated from each other by extremely thin membranes, across which oxygen and carbon dioxide diffuse.

The Airways

During inspiration air passes through either the nose (the most common site) or mouth into the **pharynx** (throat), a passage common to the routes followed by air and food (Figure 15-1). The pharynx branches into two tubes, one (the esophagus) through which food passes to the stomach, and the other, the **larynx,** which is part of the airways. The larynx houses the **vocal cords,** two folds of elastic tissue stretched horizontally across its lumen. The flow of air past the vocal cords causes them to vibrate,

TABLE 15-2 FUNCTIONS OF THE CONDUCTING ZONE OF THE AIRWAYS

1. Provides a low-resistance pathway for air flow; resistance is physiologically regulated by changes in contraction of airway smooth muscle and by physical forces acting upon the airways.
2. Defends against microbes and other toxic chemicals and foreign matter; cilia, mucus, and phagocytes perform this function.
3. Warms and moistens the air.
4. Phonates (vocal cords).

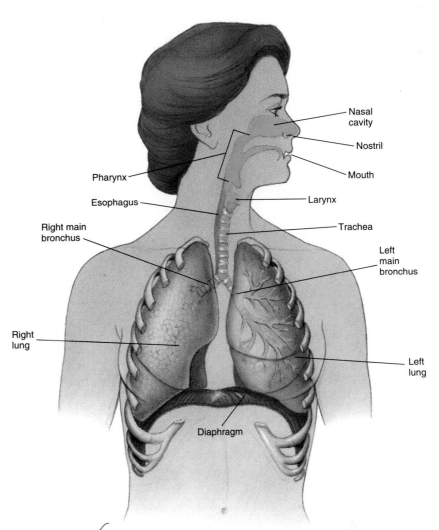

Nasal cavity

Nostril

Mouth

Pharynx

Esophagus

Larynx

Right main bronchus

Trachea

Left main bronchus

Right lung

Left lung

Diaphragm

FIGURE 15-1

Organization of the respiratory system. The ribs have been removed in front, and the left lung is shown in cross-section.

producing sounds. The nose, mouth, pharynx, and larynx are termed the upper airways.

The larynx opens into a long tube, the **trachea,** which in turn branches into two **bronchi** (singular, **bronchus**), one of which enters each lung. Within the lungs, there are more than 20 generations of branchings, each resulting in narrower, shorter, and more numerous tubes, the names of which are summarized in Figure 15-2. The walls of the trachea and bronchi contain cartilage, which gives them their cylindrical shape and supports them. The first airway branches that no longer contain cartilage are termed **bronchioles.** Alveoli first begin to appear, attached to the walls, in the bronchioles called respiratory bronchioles, and their number increases in the alveolar ducts (Figure 15-2) until the airways end in grapelike clusters of alveoli (Figure 15-3).

The airways beyond the larynx can be divided into two zones: (1) the **conducting zone**—from the top of the trachea to the beginning of the respiratory bronchioles—which contains no alveoli and across which gas exchange with the blood does not occur (Table 15-2); and (2) the **respiratory zone**—from the respiratory bronchioles on

down—which contains alveoli and across which gas exchange occurs.

The blood vessels supplying the lung generally accompany the airways and also undergo numerous branchings. The smallest of these vessels branch into networks of capillaries that richly supply the alveoli (Figure 15-3).

The epithelial surfaces of the airways, to the end of the respiratory bronchioles, contain cilia that constantly beat toward the pharynx. They also contain glands and individual epithelial cells that secrete mucus. Particulate matter, such as dust contained in the inspired air, sticks to the mucus, which is continually and slowly moved by the cilia to the pharynx and then swallowed. This mucus escalator is important to keep the lungs clear of particulate matter and the many bacteria that enter the body on dust particles. Ciliary activity can be inhibited by many noxious agents. For example, smoking a single cigarette can immobilize the cilia for several hours.

Adequate function of the mucus escalator depends not only on ciliary action but also on the secretion by the airway epithelium of a watery fluid upon which the mucus can ride freely. The production of this fluid requires active

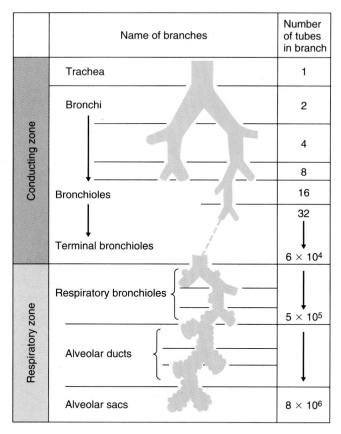

Name of branches	Number of tubes in branch
Trachea	1
Bronchi	2
	4
	8
Bronchioles	16
	32
Terminal bronchioles	6×10^4
Respiratory bronchioles	5×10^5
Alveolar ducts	
Alveolar sacs	8×10^6

(Conducting zone covers Trachea through Terminal bronchioles; Respiratory zone covers Respiratory bronchioles through Alveolar sacs.)

FIGURE 15-2

Airway branching.

secretion of chloride into the lumen of the airways, and this process is impaired in the genetic disease called *cystic fibrosis,* which is the most common lethal genetic disease of Caucasians and is characterized by the presence of a thick, dehydrated mucus layer. The impaired chloride secretion is due to a defect in the activation of chloride channels.

A second protective mechanism against infection is provided by cells, present in the airways (and alveoli) and termed macrophages, that engulf inhaled particles and bacteria and thus keep them from gaining access to other lung cells or from entering the blood. These cells are also injured by cigarette smoke and air pollutants.

Site of Gas Exchange: The Alveoli

The alveoli are tiny hollow sacs whose open ends are continuous with the lumens of the airways (Figures 15-2 and 15-4A). Typically, the air in two alveoli is separated by a single alveolar wall (Figure 15-4A). The air-facing surface(s) of the wall are lined by a continuous layer, one cell thick, of epithelial cells, most of which are the flat **type I alveolar cells.**

The alveolar walls contain capillaries, the endothelial linings of which are separated from the alveolar epithelial lining by only a basement membrane and a very thin interstitial space containing interstitial fluid and a loose meshwork of connective tissue (Figure 15-4B). Indeed, in places, the interstitial space may be absent altogether, and the basement membranes of the alveolar-surface epithelium and the capillary-wall endothelium may fuse. Thus the blood within an alveolar-wall capillary is separated from the air within the alveolus by only an extremely thin barrier (0.2 μm, compared with the 7-μm diameter of an average red blood cell). The total surface area of alveoli in contact with capillaries is approximately 75 m^2 (roughly the size of a tennis court and 40 times greater than the external body surface area). This extensive area, as well as the thinness of the barrier, permits the rapid exchange of large quantities of oxygen and carbon dioxide.

In addition to the type I alveolar cells, the alveolar epithelium contains smaller numbers of thicker specialized cells **(type II alveolar cells)** (Figure 15-4B) that produce a detergent-like substance, surfactant, to be discussed below. The alveolar walls also contain macrophages and other connective-tissue cells that function in the lung's defense mechanisms. Finally, the alveolar surfaces in contact with the air are moist.

In some of the alveolar walls there are pores that permit the flow of air between alveoli. This route can be very important when the airway leading to an alveolus is occluded by disease, since some air can still enter the alveolus by way of the pores between it and adjacent alveoli.

Relation of the Lungs to the Thoracic (Chest) Wall

The lungs, like the heart, are situated in the **thorax,** the compartment of the body between the neck and abdomen. "Thorax" and "chest" are synonyms, even though common usage often assumes that "chest" refers only to the front of the thorax. The thorax is a closed compartment, bounded at the neck by muscles and connective tissue and completely separated from the abdomen by a large dome-shaped sheet of skeletal muscle, the **diaphragm.** The wall of the thorax is formed by the spinal column, the ribs, the breastbone (sternum), and the muscles that lie between the ribs (the **intercostal muscles**). The thoracic wall also contains large amounts of elastic connective tissue.

Each lung is surrounded by a completely closed sac, the **pleural sac,** consisting of a thin sheet of cells called **pleura.** The two pleural sacs, one on each side of the midline, are completely separate from each other. The relationship between a lung and its pleural sac can be visualized by imagining what happens when one pushes a fist into a balloon (Figure 15-5): The arm represents the major bronchus leading to the lung, the fist is the lung, and the balloon is the pleural sac. The fist becomes coated by one surface of the balloon. In addition, the balloon is pushed back upon itself so that its opposite surfaces lie close together. The pleural surface coating the lung (the visceral

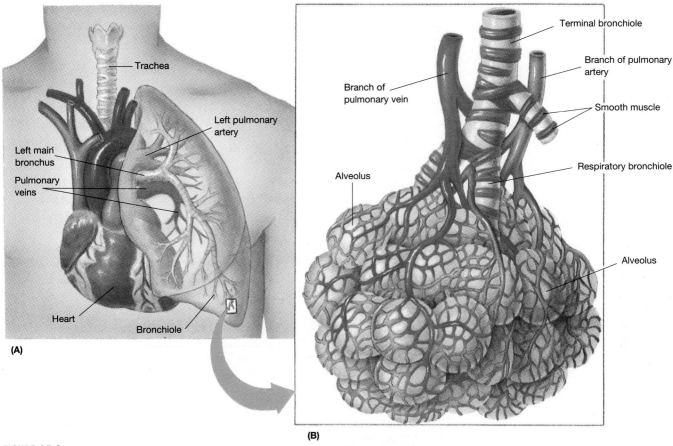

FIGURE 15-3

Relationships between blood vessels and airways. (A) The lung appears transparent so that
the relationships can be seen. The airways beyond the bronchiole are too small to be seen.
(B) An enlargement of a small section of 15-3A to show the continuation of the airways and
the clusters of alveoli at their ends. Virtually the entire lung, not just the surface, consists of
such clusters.

pleura) is firmly attached to the lung. Similarly, the outer
layer (parietal pleura) is attached to and lines the interior
thoracic wall and diaphragm. The two layers of pleura are
so close to each other that normally they are always in
virtual contact, but they are *not* attached to each other.
Rather, they are separated by an extremely thin layer of
intrapleural fluid, the total volume of which is only a few
milliliters. The intrapleural fluid lubricates the outer surface of the lungs. More important, as we shall see, pressure changes in the intrapleural fluid cause the lung surface and thoracic wall to move in and out together during
breathing.

Pulmonary Pressures

An important point for the discussion that follows is that
both the lungs and the thoracic wall are elastic structures.
If they are either stretched or compressed by some force,
they will recoil, that is, return to their original sizes and
positions when the force is removed.

The volume of the lungs and thorax at the end of an
unforced expiration is determined only by passive elastic
forces since no significant contractions of the respiratory
muscles are occurring. The volume of air in the lungs at
this time is known as the **functional residual capacity.**
The following simple observation reveals that this position
reflects a balance point between opposed forces.

In certain kinds of surgery, the chest wall ("chest wall"
and "thoracic wall" are synonyms) is opened and the parietal pleura cut, exposing the fluid-filled intrapleural space.
The lung is not cut, yet on the side of the incision the lung
collapses immediately to a smaller volume. Simultaneously, the chest wall on that side moves outward. The behavior of the lung shows that as long as the chest wall is
intact, some force must be acting to stretch the lung and
that this force is eliminated when the chest is opened. The
observations also show that the intact chest wall is normally partially pulled inward (compressed) by some force
resulting from the presence of the lung within it. In other

FIGURE 15-4

(A) Cross section through an area of the respiratory zone. There are 18 alveoli in this figure, only 4 of which are labelled. Two frequently share a common wall. (*From R. O. Greep and L. Weiss, "Histology," 3d edn., McGraw-Hill, New York, 1973.*) (B) Schematic enlargement of a portion of an alveolar wall. I = nucleus of a type I cell; II = nucleus of a type II cell. (*Adapted from Gong and Drage.*)

words, the lungs and chest wall would move away from each other, the lungs to recoil inward and the chest wall to pop outward, except that forces exist that keep them from doing so. We now turn to the nature of these forces and how they result in a stable equilibrium when the lung is at functional residual capacity.

Figure 15-6 illustrates the situation that normally exists at the end of an unforced expiration, when no respiratory muscle contraction is occurring and no air is flowing. All pressures in the respiratory system, as in the cardiovascular system, are given relative to **atmospheric pressure**—the pressure of the air surrounding the body (760 mmHg at sea level). The pressure within the alveoli is the **alveolar pressure** (P_{alv}, also termed intrapulmonary pressure).

FIGURE 15-5

Relationship of lungs, pleura, and thoracic wall, shown as analogous to pushing a fist into a fluid-filled balloon. Note that there is no communication between the right and left intrapleural fluids. For purposes of illustration, in this figure and other similar ones in this chapter, the volume of intrapleural fluid is greatly exaggerated; it normally consists of an extremely thin layer of fluid between the pleura membrane lining the inner surface of the thoracic wall and that lining the surface of the lungs.

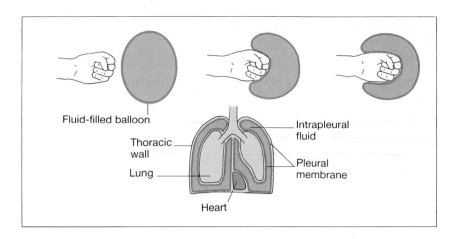

Between breaths it is 0 mmHg; that is, it is the same as atmospheric pressure. The pressure in the intrapleural fluid is the **intrapleural pressure (P_{ip})** or intrathoracic pressure. Between breaths it is approximately 4 mmHg less than atmospheric pressure, that is, −4 mmHg.[1] There is therefore a pressure difference of 4 mmHg [0 − (−4) = 4] across the lung wall. This pressure difference is known as the **transpulmonary pressure,** and it is the force that

---

[1] Physiologists usually express pressures in the respiratory system in cmH_2O rather than mmHg; we have chosen, for simplicity, not to do this (for reference, 1 cmH_2O = 1.3 mmHg).

FIGURE 15-6

Alveolar (P_{alv}), intrapleural (P_{ip}), and transpulmonary ($P_{alv} - P_{ip}$) pressures at the end of an unforced expiration. The transpulmonary pressure exactly opposes the elastic recoil of the lung, and the lung volume (and chest wall) remain stable. The lung volume at this time is the functional residual capacity.

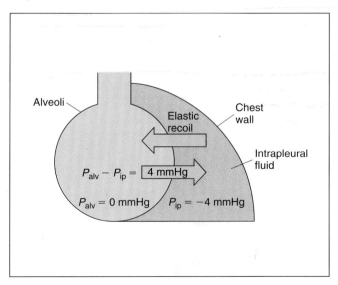

holds the *lungs* open, that is, keeps the stretched lungs from collapsing.

At the same time there is also a pressure difference of 4 mmHg keeping the *chest wall* from moving out: The atmospheric pressure against the outside of the wall is 0 mmHg, and the intrapleural pressure against the inside of the wall is −4 mmHg; the difference is 4 mmHg directed inward and opposing the tendency of the compressed thoracic wall to move outward.

We have so far not described how it is that the intrapleural pressure is subatmospheric. As the lungs (tending to move inward from their stretched position) and the thoracic wall (tending to move outward from its compressed position) move ever so slightly away from each other, there occurs an infinitesimal enlargement of the fluid-filled intrapleural space between them. But fluid cannot expand the way air can, and so even this tiny enlargement of the intrapleural space—so small that the pleural surfaces still remain in contact with each other—drops the intrapleural pressure below atmospheric pressure. In this way, the elastic recoil of both the lung and chest wall creates the subatmospheric intrapleural pressure that keeps them from moving apart more than a tiny amount.

Why the lung collapses when the chest wall is opened should now be apparent. When the chest wall is pierced, atmospheric air rushes through the wound into the intrapleural space (a phenomenon called **pneumothorax**), and the intrapleural pressure goes from −4 mmHg to 0 mmHg. The transpulmonary pressure acting to hold the lung open is thus eliminated, and the stretched lung collapses. At the same time, the chest wall moves outward because there is no longer a difference in pressure between the external environment and the intrapleural space to keep the chest wall compressed.

As we shall see in the next section, the magnitudes of the alveolar, intrapleural, and transpulmonary pressures vary during breathing and directly cause the changes in lung size that occur during inspiration and expiration.

VENTILATION AND LUNG MECHANICS

An inventory of steps involved in respiration (Figure 15-7) is provided for orientation before beginning the detailed descriptions of each step.

Ventilation is defined as the exchange of air between the atmosphere and alveoli. Like blood, air moves by *bulk flow*, from a region of high pressure to one of low pressure. We saw in Chapter 14 that bulk flow can be described by the equation

$$F = \frac{\Delta P}{R}$$

That is, flow (F) is proportional to the pressure difference (ΔP) between two points and inversely proportional to the resistance (R). For air flow into or out of the lungs, the relevant pressures are the alveolar pressure and the pressure at the nose and mouth, normally atmospheric pressure (P_{atm}):

$$F = \frac{P_{atm} - P_{alv}}{R}$$

Air moves into and out of the lungs because the alveolar pressure is made alternately less than and greater than atmospheric pressure (Figure 15-8). These alveolar pressure changes are caused, as we shall see, by changes in the dimensions of the lungs. To describe these changes, we need to learn one more basic concept. As stated by **Boyle's law** (Figure 15-9), at constant temperature the relationship between the pressure exerted by a fixed number of gas molecules in a container and the volume of the

① Ventilation: Exchange of air between atmosphere and alveoli by *bulk flow*
② Exchange of O_2 and CO_2 between alveolar air and blood in lung capillaries by *diffusion*
③ Transport of O_2 and CO_2 through pulmonary and systemic circulation by *bulk flow*
④ Exchange of O_2 and CO_2 between blood in tissue capillaries and cells in tissues by *diffusion*
⑤ Cellular utilization of O_2 and production of CO_2

FIGURE 15-7
The steps of respiration.

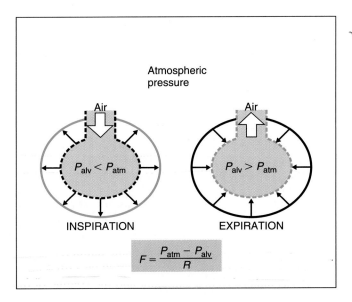

FIGURE 15-8

Relationships required for ventilation. When the alveolar pressure (P_{alv}) is less than atmospheric pressure (P_{atm}), air enters the lungs. Flow (F) is directly proportional to the pressure difference and inversely proportional to airway resistance (R). Black lines show lung's position at beginning of inspiration or expiration, and blue lines at end.

FIGURE 15-9

Boyle's law: The pressure exerted by a constant number of gas molecules in a container is inversely proportional to the volume of the container, that is, P is proportional to $1/V$.

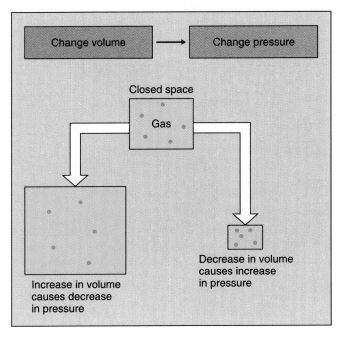

container is as follows: An increase in the volume of the container decreases the pressure of the gas, whereas a decrease in container volume increases the pressure.

Inspiration

Figures 15-10 and 15-11 summarize the events during normal inspiration at rest. Just before inspiration begins, that is, at functional residual capacity, the respiratory muscles are relaxed, and no air is flowing because the alveolar pressure is 0 mmHg, that is, the same as atmospheric pressure. As described earlier, the intrapleural pressure at this point is subatmospheric (-4 mmHg), and the transpulmonary pressure ($P_{alv} - P_{ip}$) is 4 mmHg.

Inspiration is initiated by the neurally induced contraction of the diaphragm and the inspiratory intercostal muscles.[2] The diaphragm is the most important inspiratory muscle during normal quiet breathing. When activation of the nerves to it causes it to contract, its dome moves downward into the abdomen, enlarging the thorax. Simultaneously, activation of the nerves to the inspiratory intercostal muscles causes them to contract, leading to an upward and outward movement of the ribs and a further increase in thoracic size. As the thorax enlarges, the thoracic wall moves ever so slightly further away from the lung surface, and the intrapleural fluid pressure becomes even more subatmospheric than it was between breaths. This increases the transpulmonary pressure, which forces the lung to expand.

Thus, when the inspiratory muscles increase the thoracic dimensions, the lungs are also forced to enlarge virtually to the same degree because of the change in intrapleural pressure. The enlargement of the lung causes an increase in the sizes of the alveoli throughout the lung. Therefore, by Boyle's law, the pressure within the alveoli drops to less than atmospheric. This produces the difference in pressure ($P_{alv} < P_{atm}$) that causes a bulk flow of air from the atmosphere through the airways into the alveoli. By the end of the inspiration, the pressure in the alveoli again equals atmospheric pressure.[3]

_____

[2] It has generally been assumed that the intercostal muscles involved in inspiration are the external intercostal muscles, whereas the internal intercostals are used in active expiration. However, because there is some controversy over this view, we shall simply refer to inspiratory and expiratory intercostals; that is, we shall use functional rather than anatomical terms. It should also be noted that additional muscles, termed the accessory muscles of inspiration, may be brought into play during labored inspiration. These muscles act both on the upper ribs to enlarge the upper thorax and on the sternum to move it forward and upward.

[3] It should be noted that the analysis of Figure 15-11 treats the lungs as a single alveolus. The fact is that there are significant regional differences in alveolar, intrapleural, and transpulmonary pressures throughout the lungs and thoracic cavity. These differences are due mainly to the effects of gravity. They are of great importance in determining the distribution of inspired air throughout the lung.

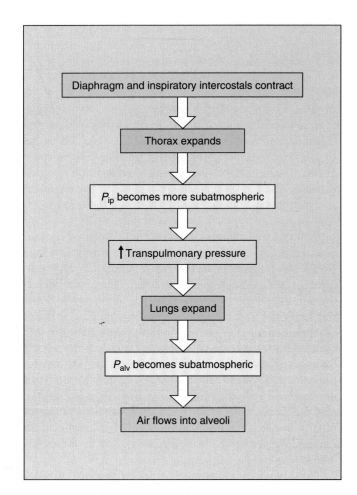

FIGURE 15-10

Sequence of events during inspiration. Figure 15-11 illustrates these events quantitatively.

Expiration

Figures 15-11 and 15-12 summarize the sequence of events during expiration. At the end of inspiration, the nerves to the diaphragm and inspiratory intercostal muscles cease firing, and so these muscles relax. The lungs and chest wall *passively* return to their original dimensions. As the lungs shrink, air in the alveoli becomes temporarily compressed so that, by Boyle's law, alveolar pressure exceeds atmospheric. Therefore, air flows from the alveoli through the airways out into the atmosphere. Thus, expiration at rest is completely passive, depending only upon the relaxation of the inspiratory muscles and recoil of the stretched lungs.

FIGURE 15-11

Summary of alveolar, intrapleural, and transpulmonary pressure changes and air flow during inspiration and expiration of 500 ml of air. The transpulmonary pressure is the gray area between the alveolar pressure and intrapleural pressure. Note that normal atmospheric pressure (760 mmHg) has a value of zero on the respiratory pressure scale. Note also that the transpulmonary pressure exactly opposes the elastic recoil of the lungs at the end of both inspiration and expiration.

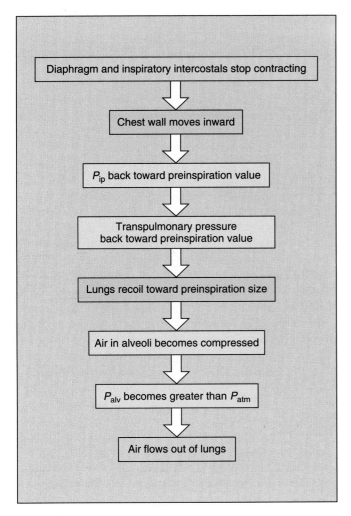

FIGURE 15-12
Sequence of events during expiration.

$$C_L = \frac{\Delta V_L}{\Delta(P_{alv} - P_{ip})}$$

Thus, the higher the lung compliance, the easier it is to expand the lungs at any given transpulmonary pressure. A low lung compliance means that a greater-than-normal transpulmonary pressure must be developed across the lung wall to produce a given amount of lung expansion. In other words, when lung compliance is low, intrapleural pressure must be made more subatmospheric than usual during inspiration to achieve lung expansion. This requires more vigorous contractions of the diaphragm and inspiratory intercostal muscles. Thus, the less compliant the lung, the more energy is required for a given amount of expansion. Persons with low lung compliance therefore tend to breathe shallowly and must compensate by breathing rapidly.

Determinants of Lung Compliance. There are two major determinants of lung compliance. One is the stretchability of the lung tissues, particularly its elastic connective tissues. Thus a thickening of the lung tissues decreases lung compliance. However, the single most important determinant of lung compliance is not the stretchability of the lung *tissues*, but the surface tension at the air-water interfaces within the alveoli. As noted earlier, the surfaces of the alveolar cells are moist, and so they can be pictured as air-filled sacs lined with water. At an air-water interface, the attractive forces between the water molecules, known as **surface tension,** make the water lining like a stretched balloon that constantly tries to shrink and resists further stretching. Thus, expansion of the lung requires energy not only to stretch the connective tissue of the lung but also to overcome the surface tension of the water layer lining the alveoli.

Indeed, the surface tension of pure water is so great that were the alveoli lined with pure water, lung expansion would require exhausting muscular effort and the lungs would tend to collapse. It is extremely important, therefore, that the type II alveolar cells produce a detergent-like substance known as pulmonary **surfactant,** which markedly reduces the cohesive forces between water molecules on the alveolar surface. Therefore, surfactant lowers the surface tension and increases lung compliance (Table 15-3).

Surfactant is a complex of both lipids and proteins, but its major component is a phospholipid, which forms a monomolecular layer between the air and water at the alveolar surface. The amount tends to decrease when breaths are small and constant. A deep breath, which people normally intersperse frequently in their breathing pattern, stimulates the type II cells to replenish the surfactant. This is why patients who have had thoracic or abdominal surgery and are breathing shallowly because of the pain must be urged to take occasional deep breaths.

Under certain conditions, during exercise, for example, expiration of larger volumes is achieved by contraction of the expiratory intercostal muscles and the abdominal muscles, which *actively* decreases thoracic dimensions. The expiratory intercostal muscles insert on the ribs in such a way that their contraction pulls the chest wall in. Contraction of the abdominal muscles increases intraabdominal pressure and forces the diaphragm up into the thorax.

Lung Compliance

To reiterate, the degree of lung expansion at any instant is proportional to the transpulmonary pressure, that is, the difference between the alveolar pressure and the intrapleural pressure. But just how much any given transpulmonary pressure expands the lung depends upon the stretchability, or compliance, of the lung. **Lung compliance (C_L)** is defined as the magnitude of the change in lung volume (ΔV_L) produced by a given change in the transpulmonary pressure:

TABLE 15-3   SOME IMPORTANT FACTS ABOUT PULMONARY SURFACTANT

1. Pulmonary surfactant is a phospholipid bound to a protein.
2. It is secreted by type II alveolar cells.
3. It lowers surface tension of the water layer at the alveolar surface, which increases lung compliance, that is, makes the lungs easier to expand.
4. Its concentration decreases when breaths are small and constant.

A striking example of what occurs when surfactant is deficient is the disease known as **respiratory-distress syndrome of the newborn,** which is the second leading cause of death in premature infants, in whom the surfactant-synthesizing cells may be too immature to function adequately. Because of low lung compliance, the infant is able to inspire only by the most strenuous efforts, which may ultimately cause complete exhaustion, inability to breathe, lung collapse, and death. Normal maturation of the surfactant-synthesizing apparatus is facilitated by several hormones, particularly cortisol, the secretion of which is increased late in pregnancy. Accordingly, administration of cortisol late in pregnancy to a woman who is likely to deliver prematurely provides an important means of preventing this disease. Another important therapy is the administration of exogenous surfactant to the newborn infant via the trachea.

Airway Resistance

As previously stated, the volume of air that flows into or out of the alveoli per unit time is directly proportional to the pressure difference between the atmosphere and alveoli and inversely proportional to the resistance to flow offered by the airways:

$$F = \frac{P_{atm} - P_{alv}}{R}$$

What factors determine airway resistance? Resistance is (1) directly proportional to the magnitude of the frictional interactions between the flowing gas molecules, that is, the viscosity of the air, which is much less than that of blood; (2) directly proportional to the length of the airway; and (3) inversely proportional to the fourth power of the airway radius. These factors are analogous to those determining resistance in the circulatory system. Resistance in the respiratory tree, just as in the circulatory tree, is largely controlled by the radius of the airways.

Resistance to air flow is normally so small that very small pressure differences suffice to produce large vol-

umes of air flow. As we have seen (Figure 15-11), the average atmosphere-to-alveoli pressure difference during a normal breath at rest is less than 1 mmHg; yet, approximately 500 ml of air is moved by this tiny difference.

Airway radii and therefore resistance are affected by physical, neural, and chemical factors. One important physical factor is the transpulmonary pressure, which exerts a distending force on the airways, just as on the alveoli. This is a major factor keeping the smaller airways—those without cartilage to support them—from collapsing. Because, as we have seen, transpulmonary pressure increases during inspiration, airway radius is larger and airway resistance is smaller when the lungs are expanded than when they are at functional residual capacity.

A second physical factor holding the airways open is the connective tissue fibers that attach to the airway exteriors and, because of their arrangement, continuously pull outward on the sides of the airways. This is termed **lateral traction**. Since these fibers become stretched as the lungs expand, they help pull the airways open even more during inspiration. Thus, both the transpulmonary pressure and lateral traction act in the same direction.

Such physical factors also explain why the airways become narrower and airway resistance increases during a forced expiration. Indeed, because of increased airway resistance, there is a limit as to how much one can increase the air flow rate during a forced expiration no matter how intense the effort.

In addition to these physical factors, a variety of chemical factors can influence airway smooth muscle and thereby airway resistance. The most important of these, along with the physical factors, are summarized in Table 15-4.

One might wonder why we have presented all these physical and chemical factors that *can* influence airway resistance when we earlier stated that airway resistance is *normally* so low that it is no impediment to air flow. The reason is that, under *abnormal* circumstances, changes in these factors may cause serious increases in airway resistance. Asthma and chronic obstructive pulmonary disease provide important examples.

Asthma. *Asthma* is a disease characterized by intermittent attacks in which airway smooth muscle contracts, increasing airway resistance enough to impair ventilation. More mucus may also be secreted by the airways, and this mucus may be abnormally thick, leading to a further increase in airway resistance secondary to mucous plugs. The basic defect in asthma is inflammation of the airways, the causes of which vary from person to person and include, among others, allergy and virus infections. The important point is that the underlying inflammation causes the airway smooth muscle to be hyperresponsive and to contract strongly when, depending upon the individual, he

TABLE 15-4 MAJOR FACTORS INFLUENCING THE AIRWAY RESISTANCE
Physical factors
Airways are held open by transpulmonary pressure and by lateral traction. Because of these factors, they open wider during inspiration and may collapse during forced expiration.
Airways may be partially or totally occluded by mucus accumulation.
Neuroendocrine agents
Parasympathetic nerves constrict (neurotransmitter = acetylcholine).
Circulating epinephrine dilates (action is on beta-adrenergic receptors).
Noncholinergic, nonadrenergic nerves dilate (neurotransmitter = vasoactive intestinal peptide).
Paracrine agents
Histamine constricts.
Several eicosanoids, notably the leukotrienes, constrict.
Several eicosanoids dilate.

or she exercises, is under emotional stress, is exposed to cold air, cigarette smoke, inhaled irritants, and certain drugs. The therapy for asthma is twofold—to reduce the inflammation with so-called anti-inflammatory drugs (such as adrenal glucocorticoids, Chapter 20), and to overcome the excessive airway smooth-muscle contraction with bronchodilator drugs, that is, drugs that relax the airways. The latter drugs work by influencing the neuroendocrine and paracrine effects on the airways summarized in Table 15-4. For example, some bronchodilator drugs mimic the action of epinephrine on beta-adrenergic receptors.

Chronic Obstructive Pulmonary Disease. The term *chronic obstructive pulmonary disease* refers to emphysema or chronic bronchitis or a combination of the two. These diseases, which cause severe difficulties not only in breathing but in oxygenation of the blood, are among the major causes of disability and death in the United States. In contrast to asthma, increased smooth-muscle contraction is *not* the cause of airway obstruction in these diseases.

Emphysema is characterized by destruction of the alveolar walls and consequently a marked enlargement of the alveolar air spaces and loss of pulmonary capillaries. These changes impair gas exchange, as will be described later. In addition, the small airways—those from the terminal bronchioles on down—are reduced in number and have atrophied walls. How all these changes occur is still poorly understood, but it is hypothesized that the lung undergoes self-destruction by proteolytic enzymes secreted by leukocytes in the lung. Cigarette smoking, perhaps by stimulating the release of these enzymes, is by far the most important cause of emphysema. Air pollution and hereditary factors also play a role in some patients.

The airway obstruction in emphysema is due to collapse of the airways. To understand this, recall that two physical factors passively holding the airways open are the transpulmonary pressure and the lateral traction of connective-tissue fibers attached to the airway exteriors. Both of these factors are diminished in emphysema because of the destruction of the lung elastic tissues, and so the airways collapse.

Chronic bronchitis is characterized by excessive mucus production in the bronchi and chronic inflammatory changes in the small airways. The cause of obstruction is accumulation of mucus in the airways and thickening of the inflamed airways. The same agents listed above—smoking, for example—that cause emphysema also cause chronic bronchitis. That is why the two diseases frequently coexist.

The Heimlich Maneuver. The *Heimlich maneuver* is used to aid persons choking on foreign matter caught in the upper airways. A sudden increase in abdominal pressure is produced as the rescuer's fists, placed against the victim's abdomen slightly above the navel and well below the tip of the sternum, are pressed into the abdomen with a quick upward thrust (Figure 15-13). The increased abdominal pressure forces the diaphragm upward into the thorax, reducing thoracic size and, by Boyle's law, increasing alveolar pressure. The forceful expiration produced by the increased alveolar pressure expels the object caught in the respiratory tract.

Lung Volumes and Capacities

The volume of air entering the lungs during a single inspiration is normally approximately equal to the volume leaving on the subsequent expiration and is called the **tidal volume**. The tidal volume during normal quiet breathing—termed the resting tidal volume—is approximately 500 ml.

After expiration of a resting tidal volume, the lungs still contain air. Recall that this volume is termed the functional residual capacity; it amounts to approximately 2500 ml (Figure 15-14). In other words, at rest, the 500 ml of air inspired with each breath adds to and mixes with 2500 ml of air already in the lungs, and then 500 ml of the total is expired. Through maximal active contraction of the expiratory muscles, it is possible to expire 1500 ml of the 2500 ml remaining after the resting tidal volume has been expired; this additional volume is termed the **expiratory reserve volume**. Even after a maximal active expiration, approximately 1000 ml of air still remains in the lungs and is termed the **residual volume**.

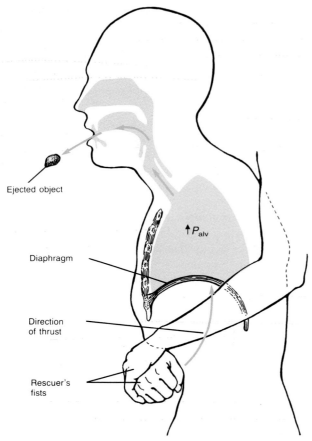

FIGURE 15-13

The Heimlich maneuver. The rescuer's fists are placed against the victim's abdomen. A quick upward thrust of the fists causes elevation of the diaphragm and a forceful expiration because of an increased P_{alv}. As this expired air is forced through the trachea and larynx, the foreign object in the airway is expelled.

Let us return to the situation in which a person is breathing at rest and see how much inspiration can be increased from this point. The volume of air that can be inspired over and above the resting tidal volume is called the **inspiratory reserve volume** and amounts to approximately 3000 ml of air (Figure 15-14). Thus, someone inspiring maximally after a resting expiration will inspire 500 ml, the resting tidal volume, plus another 3000 ml, the inspiratory reserve volume, for a total of 3500 ml. On the subsequent expiration, this air is all expelled.

A useful clinical measurement is the **vital capacity**, the maximal volume of air that a person can expire after a maximal inspiration. Under these conditions, the person is expiring the resting tidal volume and inspiratory reserve volume just inspired, followed by the expiratory reserve volume (Figure 15-14). In other words, the vital capacity is the sum of these three volumes.

A variant on this method is the ***forced vital capacity (FVC)***, in which the person takes a maximal inspiration and then exhales maximally *as fast as possible;* thus the name, "forced" vital capacity. For several reasons the FVC may differ somewhat from the value obtained in an "unforced" vital capacity measurement. But, most important, the apparatus used to measure FVC also measures the volume expired after 1 s [the ***forced expiratory volume in 1 s (FEV₁)***]. Normal individuals can expire approximately 80 percent of the FVC in 1 s.

These measurements are useful diagnostic tools. For example, people with obstructive lung diseases (increased airway resistance) typically have a FEV_1 which is less than 80 percent of the FVC because it is difficult for them to expire air rapidly through the narrowed airways. In contrast to obstructive lung diseases, ***restrictive lung diseases*** are characterized by normal airway resistance but

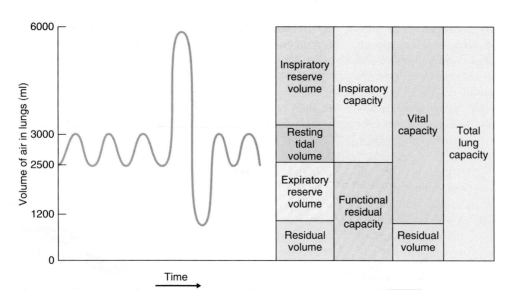

FIGURE 15-14

Lung volumes and capacities recorded on a spirometer, an apparatus for measuring inspired and expired volumes. When the subject inspires, the pen moves up; with expiration, it moves down. The capacities are the sums of two or more lung volumes. The lung volumes are the four distinct components of total lung capacity. (Note that residual volume and total lung capacity cannot be measured with a spirometer.)

impaired respiratory movements because of abnormalities in the lung tissue, the pleura, the chest wall, or the neuromuscular machinery. Restrictive lung diseases are characterized by a reduced vital capacity but a normal FEV_1/FVC ratio.

Alveolar Ventilation

The total ventilation per minute, termed the **minute ventilation**, is equal to the tidal volume multiplied by the respiratory rate:

Minute ventilation (ml/min) =
tidal volume (ml/breath) × respiratory rate (breaths/min)

For example, at rest, a normal person moves approximately 500 ml of air in and out of the lungs with each breath and takes 10 breaths each minute. The minute ventilation is therefore 500 ml/breath × 10 breaths/min = 5000 ml of air per minute. However, because of dead space, not all this air is available for exchange with the blood.

Dead Space. The conducting airways have a volume of about 150 ml. Exchanges of gases with the blood occur only in the alveoli and not in this 150 ml of the airways. Picture, then, what occurs during expiration of a tidal volume, which in this instance is 450 ml: The 450 ml of air is forced out of the alveoli and through the airways. Approximately 300 ml of this alveolar air is exhaled at the nose or mouth, but approximately 150 ml still remains in the airways at the end of expiration. During the next inspiration (Figure 15-15), 450 ml of air flows into the alveoli, but the first 150 ml entering the alveoli is not atmospheric air but

the 150 ml left behind from the last breath. Thus, only 300 ml of new atmospheric air enters the alveoli during the inspiration. At the end of inspiration, 150 ml of fresh air fills the conducting airways, but no gas exchange with the blood can occur there. At the next expiration, this fresh air will be washed out and again replaced by old alveolar air, thus completing the cycle. The end result is that 150 ml of the 450 ml of atmospheric air entering the respiratory system during each inspiration never reaches the alveoli but is merely moved in and out of the airways. Because these airways do not permit gas exchange with the blood, the space within them is termed the **anatomic dead space**.

Thus the volume of fresh air entering the alveoli during each inspiration equals the tidal volume minus the volume of air in the anatomic dead space. For the previous example:

Tidal volume = 450 ml

Anatomic dead space = 150 ml

Fresh air entering alveoli in one inspiration =
450 ml − 150 ml = 300 ml

To determine how much fresh air enters the alveoli per minute, we simply multiply the volume of fresh air entering the alveoli per breath by the breathing frequency (set at 12 breaths/min in our example):

300 ml/breath × 12 breaths/min = 3600 ml/min

This total, the volume of fresh air entering the alveoli per minute, is called the **alveolar ventilation**:

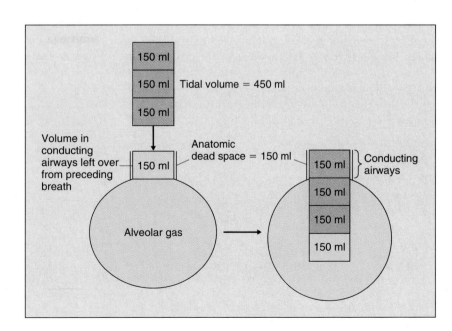

FIGURE 15-15
Effects of anatomic dead space on alveolar ventilation. Anatomic dead space is the volume of the conducting airways.

Alveolar ventilation =
$$\text{(tidal volume} - \text{dead space)} \times \text{frequency}$$

The value calculated for alveolar ventilation may be somewhat confusing because it seems to indicate that, in our example, only 3600 ml of gas enters and leaves the alveoli in each minute. This is not true—the total is 5400 ml (12 × 450), but only 3600 ml is fresh air; the rest, of course, is the air from the anatomic dead space.

What is the significance of the anatomic dead space and alveolar ventilation? Since only that portion of inspired air that enters the alveoli, that is, the alveolar ventilation, is useful for gas exchange with the blood, the magnitude of the alveolar ventilation is of much greater significance than is the minute ventilation, as can be demonstrated readily by data in Table 15-5.

In this experiment, subject A breathes rapidly and shallowly, B normally, and C slowly and deeply. Each subject has exactly the same minute ventilation; that is, each is moving the same amount of air in and out of the lungs per minute. Yet, when we subtract the anatomic-dead-space ventilation from the minute ventilation, we find marked differences in alveolar ventilation. Subject A has no alveolar ventilation and would become unconscious in several minutes, whereas C has a considerably greater alveolar ventilation than B, who is breathing normally. The important deduction to be drawn from this example is that increased *depth* of breathing is far more effective in elevating alveolar ventilation than is an equivalent increase in breathing *rate*. Conversely, a decrease in depth can lead to a critical reduction in alveolar ventilation. This is because a fixed volume of *each* tidal volume goes to the dead space. If the tidal volume decreases, the fraction of the tidal volume going to the dead space increases until, as in subject A, it may represent the entire tidal volume. On the other hand, any increase in tidal volume goes entirely toward increasing alveolar ventilation. These concepts have important physiological implications. Most situations that produce an increased ventilation, such as exercise, reflexly call forth a relatively greater increase in breathing depth than rate.

The anatomic dead space is not the only type of dead space. Some fresh inspired air is not used for gas exchange with the blood even though it reaches the alveoli because some alveoli, for various reasons, have little or no blood supply. This volume of air is known as **alveolar dead space**. It is quite small in normal persons but may be very large in several kinds of lung disease. As we shall see, it is minimized by local mechanisms that match air and blood flows. The sum of the anatomic and alveolar dead space is known as the **physiologic dead space**.

EXCHANGE OF GASES IN ALVEOLI AND TISSUES

We have now completed our discussion of the lung mechanics that produce alveolar ventilation, but this is only the first step in the respiratory process. Oxygen must move across the alveolar membranes into the pulmonary capillaries, be transported by the blood to the tissues, leave the tissue capillaries and enter the extracellular fluid, and finally cross plasma membranes to gain entry into cells. Carbon dioxide must follow a similar path in reverse.

In the steady state, the volume of oxygen that leaves the tissue capillaries and is consumed by the body cells per unit time is exactly equal to the volume of oxygen added to the blood in the lungs during the same time period. Similarly, the rate at which carbon dioxide is produced by the body cells and enters the systemic blood is identical to the rate at which carbon dioxide leaves the blood in the lungs and is expired.

The relative amounts of oxygen consumed by cells and carbon dioxide produced depend primarily upon which nutrients are being used for energy. The ratio CO_2 produced/O_2 consumed is known as the **respiratory quotient (RQ)**. On a mixed diet the RQ is approximately 0.8, that is, 8 molecules of CO_2 are produced for every 10 molecules of O_2 consumed.[4]

---

[4]The RQ is 1 for carbohydrate, 0.7 for fat, and 0.8 for protein.

TABLE 15-5 EFFECT OF BREATHING PATTERNS ON ALVEOLAR VENTILATION

Subject	Tidal volume, ml/breath	×	Frequency, breaths/min	=	Minute ventilation, ml/min	Anatomic dead-space ventilation, ml/min	Alveolar ventilation, ml/min
A	150		40		6000	150 × 40 = 6000	0
B	500		12		6000	150 × 12 = 1800	4200
C	1000		6		6000	150 × 6 = 900	5100

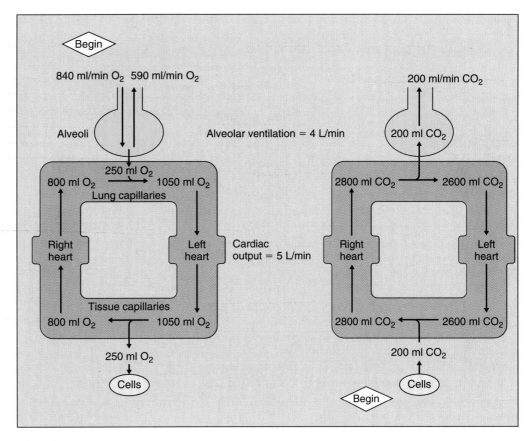

FIGURE 15-16

Summary of oxygen and carbon dioxide exchanges between atmosphere, lungs, blood, and tissues during 1 min. It is assumed that RQ = 0.8. Note that the values for oxygen and carbon dioxide in blood are *not* the values per liter of blood but rather the amounts transported per minute in the cardiac output (5 L normally). Thus, the volume of oxygen in 1 L of arterial blood is approximately 1000 ml O_2 divided by 5 L of blood = 200 ml O_2/L.

Figure 15-16 presents typical exchange values during 1 min for a person at rest, assuming a cellular oxygen consumption of 250 ml/min, a carbon dioxide production of 200 ml/min, an alveolar ventilation (supply of fresh air to the alveoli) of 4000 ml/min, and a cardiac output of 5000 ml/min.

Since only 21 percent of the atmospheric air is oxygen, the total oxygen entering the alveoli is 21 percent of 4000 ml, or 840 ml/min. Of this inspired oxygen, 250 ml crosses the alveoli into the pulmonary capillaries, and the remaining 590 ml is exhaled. This 250 ml of oxygen is carried away by 5 L of blood per minute—the cardiac output. Note, however, in Figure 15-16 that blood entering the lungs already contains large quantities of oxygen (the adaptive value of this seeming inefficiency will be described later), to which the new 250 ml is added. The blood then flows from the lungs to the left heart and is pumped by the left ventricle through the tissue capillaries, where 250 ml of oxygen leaves the blood to be taken up and utilized by cells. The quantities of oxygen added to the blood in the lungs and removed in the tissues are identical.

As shown by Figure 15-16, the story reads in reverse for carbon dioxide. There is already a good deal of carbon dioxide in systemic arterial blood; to this is added an additional 200 ml, the amount produced by the cells, as blood flows through tissue capillaries. This additional amount is eliminated as blood flows through the lungs.

Blood pumped by the heart carries oxygen and carbon dioxide between the lungs and tissues by bulk flow, but diffusion is responsible for the net movement of these molecules between the alveoli and blood, and between the blood and the cells of the body. Understanding the mechanisms involved in these diffusional exchanges depends upon some basic chemical and physical properties of gases, which we will now discuss.

Partial Pressures of Gases

Gas molecules undergo continuous random motion. These rapidly moving molecules exert a pressure, the magnitude of which is increased by anything that increases the rate of movement. The pressure a gas exerts is proportional to (1) the temperature (because heat increases the speed at which molecules move) and (2) the concentration of the gas, that is, the number of molecules per unit volume.

As stated by **Dalton's law**, in a mixture of gases, the pressure exerted by each gas is independent of the pressure exerted by the others. This is because gas molecules are normally so far apart that they do not interfere with each other. Since each gas in a mixture behaves as though no other gases are present, the total pressure of the mixture is simply the sum of the individual pressures. These individual pressures, termed **partial pressures**, are denoted by a P in front of the symbol for the gas. For example, the partial pressure of oxygen is represented by P_{O_2}. Net diffusion of a gas will occur from a region where its partial pressure is high to a region where it is low.

Atmospheric air consists primarily of nitrogen (approximately 79 percent) and oxygen (approximately 21 percent), with very small quantities of water vapor, carbon dioxide, and inert gases. The sum of the partial pressures of all these gases is termed atmospheric pressure or barometric pressure. It varies in different parts of the world as a result of differences in altitude (it also varies with local weather conditions), but at sea level it is 760 mmHg. Since the partial pressure of any gas in a mixture is the fractional concentration of that gas times the total pressure of all the gases, the P_{O_2} of atmospheric air is 0.21×760 mmHg = 160 mmHg at sea level.

Diffusion of Gases in Liquids. When a liquid is exposed to air containing a particular gas, molecules of the gas will enter the liquid and dissolve in it. Suppose, for example, that a closed container contains both water and gaseous oxygen. Oxygen molecules from the gas phase constantly bombard the surface of the water, some entering the water and dissolving. Since the number of molecules striking the surface is directly proportional to the P_{O_2} of the gas phase, the number of molecules entering the water is also directly proportional to the P_{O_2}. As long as the P_{O_2} in the gas phase is higher than the P_{O_2} in the liquid, there will be a net diffusion of oxygen into the liquid. Diffusion equilibrium will be reached when the P_{O_2} in the liquid is equal to the P_{O_2} in the gas phase, and there will be no further net diffusion between the two phases.

Conversely, if a liquid containing a dissolved gas at high partial pressure is exposed to a lower partial pressure of that same gas in a gas phase, gas molecules will diffuse from the liquid into the gas phase until the partial pressures in the two phases become equal.

The exchanges *between* gas and liquid phases described in the last two paragraphs are precisely the phenomena occurring between alveolar air and pulmonary capillary blood. In addition, dissolved gas molecules also diffuse *within* a liquid from a region of higher partial pressure to a region of lower partial pressure, an effect that underlies

partial pressure measures free O₂

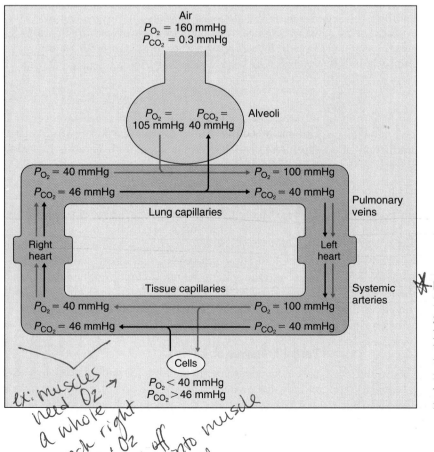

ex: muscles need O2 → a whole bunch right now. O2 diffuses off RBC into muscle cell

FIGURE 15-17

Partial pressures of carbon dioxide and oxygen in inspired air at sea level and various places in the body. Note that the P_{O_2} in the systemic arteries is shown as identical to that in the pulmonary veins; actually, for reasons described in the text, the arterial value should be slightly less, but we have ignored this for the sake of clarity.

the exchange of gases between cells, extracellular fluid, and capillary blood throughout the body.[5]

With these basic gas properties as the foundation, we can now discuss the diffusion of oxygen and carbon dioxide across alveolar, capillary, and plasma membranes. The pressures of these gases in air and in various sites of the body are given in Figure 15-17 for a resting person at sea level. We start our discussion with the *alveolar* gas pressures because their values set those of systemic arterial blood. This fact cannot be emphasized too strongly: In normal persons, the alveolar P_{O_2} and P_{CO_2} determine the systemic arterial P_{O_2} and P_{CO_2}.

Alveolar Gas Pressures

Normal alveolar gas pressures are $P_{O_2} = 105$ mmHg and $P_{CO_2} = 40$ mmHg. (We do not deal with nitrogen, even though it is the most abundant gas in the alveoli, because nitrogen is biologically inert under normal conditions and does not undergo any net exchange across the lung walls.) Compare these values with the gas pressures in the air being breathed: $P_{O_2} = 160$ mmHg and $P_{CO_2} = 0.3$ mmHg, a value so low that we will simply assume it to be zero. The alveolar P_{O_2} is lower than atmospheric P_{O_2} because some of the oxygen in the air entering the alveoli leaves them to enter the pulmonary capillaries. Alveolar P_{CO_2} is higher than atmospheric P_{CO_2} because carbon dioxide enters the alveoli from the pulmonary capillaries.

The factors that determine the precise value of alveolar P_{O_2} are (1) the P_{O_2} of atmospheric air, (2) the rate of cellular oxygen consumption, and (3) the alveolar ventilation. Although there are equations for calculating the alveolar

---

[5]The *concentration* of a gas in a liquid is proportional not only to the partial pressure of the gas but also to the solubility of the gas in the liquid; the more soluble the gas, the greater will be its concentration at any given partial pressure. Thus, if a liquid is exposed to two different gases at the same partial pressures, at equilibrium the *partial pressures* of the two gases will be identical in the liquid but the *concentrations* of the gases in the liquid will differ, depending upon their solubilities in that liquid.

gas pressures from these variables, we will describe the interactions in a more qualitative manner (Table 15-6).

First, breathing air having a low P_{O_2}, as at a high altitude, results in a low alveolar P_{O_2} since fewer molecules of oxygen are present in the air flowing into the alveoli. In contrast, administration of a high-oxygen gas mixture to a person increases alveolar P_{O_2}.

Next, consider the effects on the alveolar gas pressures of changing the alveolar ventilation but not the oxygen consumption (Figure 15-18). Suppose that the alveolar ventilation is larger than the usual 4 L/min because a resting person is deliberately breathing rapidly and deeply, but that the cellular oxygen utilization is unchanged at 250 ml/min. Under these conditions, the 250 ml of oxygen that leaves the alveoli each minute to enter the blood and be supplied to cells is a smaller fraction of the oxygen supplied by the alveolar ventilation. Therefore, steady-state alveolar P_{O_2} is higher; that is, it more closely approximates atmospheric air than usual. At the same time, the alveolar P_{CO_2} is lower than usual because the still normal amount of carbon dioxide (200 ml) entering the alveoli from the blood is diluted more than usual by the larger alveolar ventilation.

In contrast, a reduced alveolar ventilation in a person with normal cellular oxygen utilization and carbon dioxide production will result in a lower alveolar P_{O_2} and a higher alveolar P_{CO_2}.

Next, consider the effects of increasing cellular oxygen utilization and carbon dioxide production at constant alveolar ventilation. In this case, a larger fraction of the oxygen in the alveolar ventilation will leave the alveoli to enter the pulmonary capillaries; therefore, alveolar P_{O_2} will decrease. At the same time, the larger amount of carbon dioxide entering the alveoli from the blood will be diluted less than usual by the alveolar ventilation; therefore, the alveolar P_{CO_2} will increase.

Finally, consider the effects on the alveolar gas pressures of increasing cellular oxygen utilization and carbon

---

TABLE 15-6 EFFECTS OF VARIOUS CONDITIONS ON ALVEOLAR GAS PRESSURES

Condition	Alveolar P_{O_2}	Alveolar P_{CO_2}
Breathing air with low P_{O_2}	Decreases	No change°
↑Alveolar ventilation and unchanged metabolism	Increases	Decreases
↓Alveolar ventilation and unchanged metabolism	Decreases	Increases
↑Metabolism and unchanged alveolar ventilation	Decreases	Increases
Proportional increases in metabolism and alveolar ventilation	No change	No change

°Breathing air with low P_{O_2} has no direct effect on alveolar P_{CO_2}. However, as described later in the text, people in this situation will reflexly increase their ventilation and that will lower P_{CO_2}.

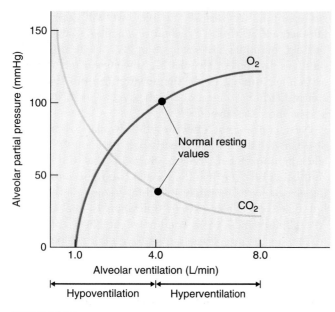

FIGURE 15-18

Effects of increasing or decreasing alveolar ventilation on alveolar partial pressures in a person having a constant metabolic rate (cellular oxygen consumption and carbon dioxide production). Note that alveolar P_{O_2} approaches zero when alveolar ventilation is about 1 L/min. At this point all the oxygen entering the alveoli crosses into the blood, leaving virtually no oxygen in the alveoli.

dioxide production while simultaneously increasing alveolar ventilation in an exact proportion. The result is that the gas pressures remain unchanged. This is the situation in modest exercise.

This last example emphasizes that, at any particular atmospheric P_{O_2}, it is the *ratio* of oxygen consumption to alveolar ventilation (that is, O_2 consumption/alveolar ventilation) that determines alveolar P_{O_2}—the *higher* the ratio, the *lower* the alveolar P_{O_2}. Alveolar P_{CO_2} is also determined by the ratio of carbon dioxide production to alveolar ventilation (that is, CO_2 production/alveolar ventilation); the *higher* the ratio, the *higher* the alveolar P_{CO_2}.

Two terms that denote the relationship between alveolar ventilation and metabolism can now be defined. For reasons that need not concern us here, these definitions are in terms of carbon dioxide rather than oxygen. **Hypoventilation** exists when there is an *increase in the ratio* of CO_2 production to alveolar ventilation. In other words, a person is said to be hypoventilating if his alveolar ventilation cannot keep pace with his carbon dioxide production. The result is that alveolar P_{CO_2} increases. **Hyperventilation** exists when there is a *decrease in the ratio* of CO_2 production to alveolar ventilation, that is, when alveolar ventilation is actually too great for the amount of carbon dioxide being produced. The result is that alveolar P_{CO_2} decreases.

Alveolar-Blood Gas Exchange

The blood that enters the pulmonary capillaries is, of course, systemic venous blood pumped to the lungs via the pulmonary arteries. Having come from the tissues, it has a high P_{CO_2} (46 mmHg in a normal person at rest) and a low P_{O_2} (40 mmHg) (Table 15-7). The differences in the partial pressures of oxygen and carbon dioxide on the two sides of the alveolar-capillary membrane result in the net diffusion of oxygen from alveoli to blood and of carbon dioxide from blood to alveoli. As this diffusion occurs, the capillary blood P_{O_2} rises and its P_{CO_2} falls. The net diffusion of these gases ceases when the capillary partial pressures become essentially equal to those in the alveoli.

In a normal person, the rates at which oxygen and carbon dioxide diffuse are so rapid and the blood flow through the capillaries so slow that complete equilibrium is reached well before the end of the capillaries (Figure 15-19). Only during the most strenuous exercise, when blood flows through the lung capillaries very rapidly, is there insufficient time for complete equilibration.

Thus, the blood that leaves the pulmonary capillaries to return to the heart and be pumped into the systemic arteries has essentially the same P_{O_2} and P_{CO_2} as alveolar air. (They are not exactly the same, for reasons given later.) Accordingly, the factors described in the previous section—atmospheric P_{O_2}, cellular oxygen consumption and carbon dioxide production, and alveolar ventilation—determine the alveolar gas pressures, which then determine the systemic arterial gas pressures.

Given that diffusion between alveoli and pulmonary capillaries normally achieves complete equilibrium, the more capillaries participating in this process, the more total oxygen and carbon dioxide can be exchanged. Many of the pulmonary capillaries are normally closed at rest. During exercise, these capillaries open and receive blood, thereby enhancing gas exchange. The mechanism by which this occurs is a simple physical one; the pulmonary circulation at rest is at such a low pressure that the pressure in many capillaries is inadequate to keep them open, but the increased cardiac output of exercise raises pulmonary vascular pressures, which opens these capillaries.

The diffusion of gases between alveoli and capillaries may be impaired in a number of ways, resulting in inade-

TABLE 15-7 NORMAL GAS PRESSURES IN SYSTEMIC BLOOD

	Venous	Arterial	Alveoli
P_{O_2}	40 mmHg	100 mmHg°	105 mmHg°
P_{CO_2}	46 mmHg	40 mmHg	40 mmHg

°The reason that the arterial P_{O_2} and alveolar P_{O_2} are not exactly the same is described later in the text.

FIGURE 15-19

Complete equilibration of blood P_{O_2} with alveolar P_{O_2} along the length of the pulmonary capillaries.

quate oxygen diffusion into the blood, particularly during exercise when the time for equilibration is reduced. For one thing, the surface area of the alveoli in contact with pulmonary capillaries may be decreased. In lung infections or pulmonary edema, for example, some of the alveoli may become filled with fluid. Diffusion may also be impaired if the alveolar walls become thickened, as for example in the disease (of unknown cause) called ***diffuse interstitial fibrosis***. Very importantly, diffusion problems in the lung are restricted to oxygen and do not affect elimination of carbon dioxide, which is much more diffusible than oxygen.

Matching of Ventilation and Blood Flow in Alveoli

The major disease-induced cause of inadequate oxygen movement between alveoli and pulmonary capillary blood is mismatching of the air supply and blood supply in individual alveoli.

The lungs are composed of approximately 300 million discrete alveoli, each capable of receiving carbon dioxide from, and supplying oxygen to, the pulmonary capillary blood. To be most efficient, the right proportion of alveolar air flow (ventilation) and capillary blood flow (perfusion) should be available to each alveolus. Any mismatching is termed ***ventilation-perfusion inequality.***

Even in normal persons there are factors, the most important of which is gravity, that cause ventilation and perfusion to be somewhat out of proportion to each other in parts of the lung. In disease states, regional changes in lung compliance, airway resistance, and vascular resistance can cause marked ventilation-perfusion inequalities. The extremes of this phenomenon are easy to visualize: (1) There may be ventilated alveoli with no blood supply at all (as defined earlier, this is alveolar dead space), or

(2) there may be blood flowing through areas of lung that have no ventilation (this is termed a **shunt**). But the inequality need not be all-or-none to be quite significant.

A striking example of ventilation-perfusion inequality is provided by emphysema. First, because of the destruction of lung tissue in this disease, as well as the obstruction of airways, some areas of lung may receive large amounts of air while others receive little or none. Second, there is also a maldistribution of blood flow because capillaries are lost when the alveolar walls are destroyed.

What is the effect of ventilation-perfusion inequalities on gas exchange? The major effect is to lower the P_{O_2} of systemic arterial blood. Indeed, there is enough ventilation-perfusion inequality in normal people to cause the arterial P_{O_2} to be about 5 mmHg less than it would otherwise be. (This is the major explanation of the fact, given earlier, that the P_{O_2} of systemic arterial blood is normally 5 mmHg less than that of average alveolar air.)

Carbon dioxide elimination is also impaired by ventilation-perfusion inequality but, for complex reasons, not to the same degree as oxygen uptake. Nevertheless, severe ventilation-perfusion inequalities in disease can lead to some elevation of arterial P_{CO_2}.

There are several local homeostatic responses within the lungs to minimize the mismatching of ventilation and blood flow. One of the most important operates on the blood vessels to alter blood-flow distribution. If an alveolus is receiving too little air relative to its blood supply, the P_{O_2} in the alveolus and its surrounding area will be low. This decreased P_{O_2} causes vasoconstriction of the small pulmonary blood vessels. (Note that this local effect of oxygen on *pulmonary* blood vessels is precisely the opposite of that exerted on *systemic* arterioles.) The net effect is to supply less blood to poorly ventilated areas and more blood to well-ventilated areas.

Gas Exchange in the Tissues

As the systemic arterial blood enters capillaries throughout the body, it is separated from the interstitial fluid by only the thin capillary wall, which is highly permeable to both oxygen and carbon dioxide. The interstitial fluid in turn is separated from intracellular fluid by cells' plasma membranes, which are also quite permeable to oxygen and carbon dioxide. Metabolic reactions occurring within cells are constantly consuming oxygen and producing carbon dioxide. Therefore, as shown in Figure 15-17, intracellular P_{O_2} is lower and P_{CO_2} higher than in blood. As a result, there is a net diffusion of oxygen from blood into cells and a net diffusion of carbon dioxide from cells into blood. In this manner, as blood flows through systemic capillaries, its P_{O_2} decreases and its P_{CO_2} increases. This accounts for the systemic venous blood values shown in Figure 15-17 and Table 15-7.

The mechanisms that enhance diffusion of oxygen and

carbon dioxide between cells and blood when a tissue increases its metabolic activity were discussed in Chapter 14.

In summary, the supply of new oxygen to the alveoli and the consumption of oxygen in the cells create P_{O_2} gradients that produce net diffusion of oxygen from alveoli to blood in the lungs and from blood to cells in the rest of the body. Conversely, the production of carbon dioxide by cells and its elimination from the alveoli via expiration create P_{CO_2} gradients that produce net diffusion of carbon dioxide from cells to blood in the rest of the body and from blood to alveoli in the lungs.

TRANSPORT OF OXYGEN IN BLOOD

Table 15-8 summarizes the oxygen content of systemic arterial blood (we shall henceforth refer to systemic arterial blood simply as arterial blood). Each liter normally contains the number of oxygen molecules equivalent to 200 ml of pure gaseous oxygen at atmospheric pressure. The oxygen is present in two forms: (1) dissolved in the plasma and erythrocyte water, and (2) reversibly combined with hemoglobin molecules.

The amount of oxygen dissolved in blood is directly proportional to the P_{O_2} of the blood. Because oxygen is relatively insoluble in water, only 3 ml can be dissolved in 1 L of blood at the normal arterial P_{O_2} of 100 mmHg. The other 197 ml of oxygen in a liter of arterial blood, more than 98 percent of the oxygen content in the liter, is carried in the erythrocytes reversibly bound to hemoglobin.

As described in Chapter 14, hemoglobin is a protein composed of four polypeptide chains, each of which contains a single atom of iron. It is the iron atom to which a molecule of oxygen binds. Thus, each hemoglobin molecule can bind four molecules of oxygen. However, for simplicity, the equation for the reaction between oxygen and hemoglobin is usually written in terms of a single polypeptide-heme chain of a hemoglobin molecule:

$$O_2 + Hb \rightleftharpoons HbO_2 \qquad (15\text{-}1)$$

Thus this chain can exist in one of two forms—**deoxyhemoglobin (Hb)** and **oxyhemoglobin (HbO_2)**. In a blood sample containing many hemoglobin molecules, the fraction of all the hemoglobin in the form of oxyhemoglobin is expressed as the **percent hemoglobin saturation**:

$$\text{Percent saturation} = \frac{\text{amount of } O_2 \text{ on Hb}}{\text{maximal possible amount}} \times 100$$

For example, if 40 percent of all the hemoglobin in a blood sample is oxyhemoglobin, the sample is said to be 40 percent saturated.

What factors determine the percent hemoglobin saturation? By far the most important is the blood P_{O_2}. Thus, the P_{O_2} determines not only the concentration of oxygen dissolved in the blood but also the amount that binds to hemoglobin. In this regard one more point deserves strong emphasis: The total amount of oxygen carried by hemoglobin in blood depends not only on the percent saturation of hemoglobin but also on how much hemoglobin is in each liter of blood. For example, if a person's blood contained only half as much hemoglobin per liter as normal, then at any given P_{O_2} the oxygen content of the blood would be only half as much. Thus, in the equation above, the denominator—"maximal possible amount"—is determined by the concentration of hemoglobin and is called the **oxygen-carrying capacity** of the blood.

Effect of P_{O_2} on Hemoglobin Saturation

From inspection of Equation 15-1 and the law of mass action, one can see that raising the blood P_{O_2} should increase the combination of oxygen with hemoglobin. The quantitative relationship between these variables is shown in Figure 15-20, which is called an **oxygen-hemoglobin dissociation curve**. (The term "dissociate" means "to separate," in this case oxygen from hemoglobin; it could just as well have been called an oxygen hemoglobin association curve.) The curve is S-shaped because, as stated earlier, each hemoglobin molecule contains four subunits; each subunit can combine with one molecule of oxygen, and the reactions of the four subunits occur sequentially, with each combination facilitating the next one. This is an example of cooperativity, as described in Chapter 4. Note that the curve has a steep slope between 10 and 60 mmHg P_{O_2} and a relatively flat portion (or plateau) between 70 and 100 mmHg P_{O_2}. Thus, the extent to which hemoglobin combines with oxygen increases very rapidly from 10 to 60 mmHg, so that at a P_{O_2} of 60 mmHg, 90 percent of the total hemoglobin is combined with oxygen. From this point on, a further increase in P_{O_2} produces only a small increase in oxygen binding.

TABLE 15-8 OXYGEN CONTENT OF SYSTEMIC ARTERIAL BLOOD AT SEA LEVEL

1 liter (L) arterial blood contains
  3 ml O_2 physically dissolved (1.5%)
  197 ml O_2 bound to hemoglobin (98.5%)
Total 200 ml O_2

Cardiac output = 5 L/min

O_2 carried to tissues/min = 5 L/min × 200 ml O_2/L
   = 1000 ml O_2/min

*how much hemoglobin actually saturated in systemic arterial? ~ 100%, but only need @ 65-70 mmHg in RBC to have ~100% RBC saturation

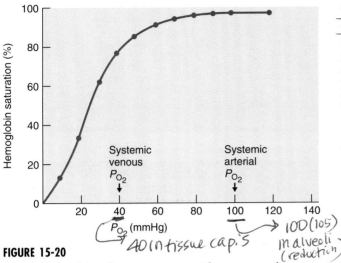

FIGURE 15-20

Oxygen-hemoglobin dissociation curve. This curve applies to blood at 37°C and a normal arterial hydrogen-ion concentration. At any given blood hemoglobin concentration, the vertical axis could also have plotted oxygen content, in milliliters of oxygen. At 100 percent saturation, the amount of hemoglobin in normal blood carries 200 ml of oxygen. (*Adapted from Comroe.*)

40 in tissue cap.s   100 (105) in alveoli (reduction)

The importance of this plateau at higher P_{O_2} values is as follows. Many situations, including high altitude and cardiac or pulmonary disease, are characterized by a moderate reduction in alveolar and therefore arterial P_{O_2}. Even if the P_{O_2} fell from the normal value of 100 to 60 mmHg, the total quantity of oxygen carried by hemoglobin would decrease by only 10 percent since hemoglobin saturation is still close to 90 percent at a P_{O_2} of 60 mmHg. The plateau therefore provides an excellent safety factor in the supply of oxygen to the tissues.

The plateau also explains another fact: In a normal person at sea level, raising the alveolar (and therefore the arterial) P_{O_2} either by hyperventilating or by breathing 100 percent oxygen adds very little additional oxygen to the blood. A small additional amount dissolves, but because hemoglobin is already almost completely saturated with oxygen at the normal arterial P_{O_2} of 100 mmHg, it simply cannot pick up any more oxygen when the P_{O_2} is elevated beyond this point. (This applies only to normal people at sea level. If the person initially has a low arterial P_{O_2} because of lung disease or high altitude, then there would be a great deal of deoxyhemoglobin initially present in the arterial blood. Therefore, raising the alveolar and thereby the arterial P_{O_2} would result in significantly more oxygen carriage.)

We now retrace our steps and reconsider the movement of oxygen across the various membranes, this time including hemoglobin in our analysis. It is essential to recognize that the oxygen bound to hemoglobin does ~~not con-~~

tribute directly to the P_{O_2} of the blood. Only dissolved oxygen does so. Therefore, oxygen diffusion is governed only by the dissolved portion, a fact that permitted us to ignore hemoglobin in discussing transmembrane partial pressure gradients. However, the presence of hemoglobin plays a critical role in determining the *total amount* of oxygen that will diffuse, as illustrated by a simple example (Figure 15-21).

Two solutions separated by a semipermeable membrane contain equal quantities of oxygen, the gas pressures are equal, and no net diffusion occurs. Addition of hemoglobin to compartment B destroys this equilibrium because much of the oxygen combines with hemoglobin. Despite the fact that the total quantity of oxygen in compartment B is still the same, the number of dissolved oxygen molecules has decreased. Therefore, the P_{O_2} of compartment B is less than that of A, and so net diffusion of oxygen occurs from A to B. At the new equilibrium, the oxygen pressures are once again equal, but almost all the oxygen is in compartment B and is combined with hemoglobin.

Let us now apply this analysis to capillaries of the lungs and tissues (Figure 15-22). The plasma and erythrocytes entering the lungs have a P_{O_2} of 40 mmHg. As we can see from Figure 15-20, hemoglobin saturation at this P_{O_2} is 75 percent. Oxygen then diffuses from the alveoli, because of its higher P_{O_2} (105 mmHg), into the plasma. This increases plasma P_{O_2} and induces diffusion of oxygen into the erythrocytes, elevating erythrocyte P_{O_2} and causing increased combination of oxygen and hemoglobin. The vast prepon-

O_2 # still there but only count FREE O_2 when talking about partial pressure

FIGURE 15-21

Effect of added hemoglobin on oxygen distribution between two compartments containing a fixed number of oxygen molecules and separated by a semipermeable membrane. At the new equilibrium, the P_{O_2} values are again equal to each other but lower than before the hemoglobin was added. However, the total oxygen, in other words, that dissolved plus that combined with hemoglobin, is now much higher on the right side of the membrane. (*Adapted from Comroe.*)

$8 O_2$, $8 O_2$ $8 O_2$, $2 O_2$ $2 O_2$, $2 O_2$

105 mmHg   105 mmHg   105 mmHg

40 mmHg   105 mmHg   105 mmHg

FIGURE 15-22

Oxygen movement in the lungs and tissues. Movement of inspired air into the alveoli is by bulk flow; all movement across membranes is by diffusion.

mitochondrea = 5 mmHg

(uses up O₂ quick b/c O₂ "runs" ETC; O₂ pushed into ↑er pressure in cell to ↓er pressure in mitochondrie

derance of the oxygen diffusing into the blood from the alveoli does not remain dissolved but combines with hemoglobin. Therefore, the blood P_{O_2} normally remains less than the alveolar P_{O_2} until hemoglobin is virtually 100 percent saturated. Thus the diffusion gradient favoring oxygen movement into the blood is maintained despite the very large transfer of oxygen.

In the tissue capillaries, the procedure is reversed: As the blood enters the capillaries, plasma P_{O_2} is greater than interstitial fluid P_{O_2}, and net oxygen diffusion occurs out of the capillary from the plasma. Plasma P_{O_2} is now lower than erythrocyte P_{O_2}, and oxygen diffuses out of the erythrocyte into the plasma. The lowering of erythrocyte P_{O_2} causes the dissociation of some of the oxygen from hemoglobin, thereby liberating oxygen. Simultaneously, the oxygen that had diffused into the interstitial fluid is moving into cells along the concentration gradient generated by cellular utilization of oxygen. The net result is a transfer of large quantities of oxygen from hemoglobin into cells purely by diffusion.

To repeat, in most tissues under resting conditions, hemoglobin is still 75 percent saturated as the blood leaves the tissue capillaries. This fact underlies an important automatic mechanism by which cells can obtain more oxygen whenever they increase their activity. An exercising muscle consumes more oxygen, thereby lowering its tissue P_{O_2}. This increases the blood-to-tissue P_{O_2} gradient and hence the diffusion of oxygen from blood to cell. In turn, the resulting reduction in erythrocyte P_{O_2} causes additional dissociation of hemoglobin and oxygen. Because of these

gradient changes, an exercising muscle can extract almost all the oxygen from its blood supply. This process is so effective because it takes place in the steep portion of the oxygen-hemoglobin dissociation curve. Of course, an increased blood flow to the muscles also contributes greatly to the increased oxygen supply.

Effects of Blood P_{CO_2}, H⁺ Concentration, Temperature, and DPG Concentration on Hemoglobin Saturation

At any given P_{O_2}, a variety of other factors influence the degree of hemoglobin saturation: blood P_{CO_2}, H⁺ concentration, temperature, and the concentration of a substance—DPG—produced by the erythrocytes. As illustrated in Figure 15-23, an increase in any of these factors causes the dissociation curve to shift to the right, which means that at any given P_{O_2} hemoglobin has less affinity for oxygen. In contrast, a decrease in any of these factors causes the dissociation curve to shift to the left, which means that, at any given P_{O_2}, hemoglobin has a greater affinity for oxygen.

The effects of increased P_{CO_2}, H⁺ concentration, and temperature are continuously exerted on the blood in tissue capillaries, because each of these factors is higher in tissue-capillary blood than in arterial blood. The P_{CO_2} is increased because of the carbon dioxide entering the blood from the tissues. For reasons to be described later, the H⁺ concentration is elevated because of the elevated P_{CO_2}. The temperature is increased because of the heat produced by tissue metabolism. Therefore, hemoglobin exposed to this elevated blood P_{CO_2}, H⁺ concentration,

Effect of DPG concentration

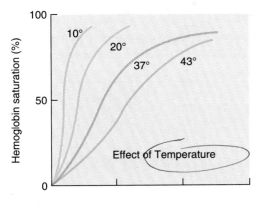

Effect of Temperature

HB DISASSOC CURVE

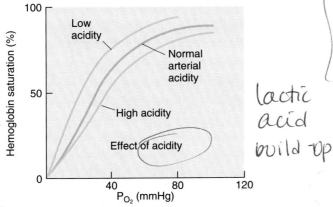

Effect of acidity

lactic acid build up

✱ **FIGURE 15-23** — *Imp. !!!*

Effects of DPG concentration, temperature, and acidity on the relationship between P_{O_2} and hemoglobin saturation. (*Adapted from Comroe.*)

EFFECTS OF EXERCISE

and temperature as it passes through the tissue capillaries has its affinity for oxygen decreased and therefore it gives up even more oxygen than it would have if the decreased tissue-capillary P_{O_2} had been the only operating factor.

The more active a tissue is, the greater its P_{CO_2}, H^+ concentration, and temperature. This causes hemoglobin to release more oxygen, at any given P_{O_2}, during passage through the tissue's capillaries, thereby providing the more active cells with additional oxygen.

What is the mechanism by which these factors influence hemoglobin's affinity for oxygen? Carbon dioxide and hydrogen ions do so by combining with the hemoglobin and altering its molecular configuration. Thus, these effects are a form of allosteric modulation, described in Chapter 4. An elevated temperature also decreases hemoglobin's affinity for oxygen by altering its molecular configuration.

Erythrocytes contain large quantities of the substance **2,3-diphosphoglycerate (DPG)**, which is present in only trace amounts in other mammalian cells. DPG, which is produced by the erythrocytes during glycolysis, binds reversibly with hemoglobin, causing it to have a lower affinity for oxygen (Figure 15-23). The net result is that whenever DPG levels are increased, there is enhanced unloading of oxygen from hemoglobin as blood flows through the tissues. Such an increase in DPG concentration is triggered by a variety of conditions associated with inadequate oxygen supply to the tissues and helps to maintain oxygen delivery. Examples include anemia and exposure to high altitude.

massage = ↑ microcirculation in area, so lactic acid "squeezed" out

TRANSPORT OF CARBON DIOXIDE IN BLOOD

As noted earlier, carbon dioxide is much more soluble in water than is oxygen, and so more dissolved carbon dioxide than dissolved oxygen is carried in blood. Even so, only a small amount of blood carbon dioxide is transported in this way.

Some of the carbon dioxide molecules, after dissolving in the blood, can also react reversibly with the amino groups of proteins, particularly hemoglobin, to form **carbamino compounds**:

$$RNH_2 + CO_2 \rightleftharpoons RNHCOOH$$

For simplicity, this reaction with hemoglobin is often written as

$$CO_2 + Hb \rightleftharpoons HbCO_2 \qquad (15\text{-}2)$$

But most of the carbon dioxide molecules, after dissolving in the blood, are converted to bicarbonate:

$$CO_2 + H_2O \underset{}{\overset{\text{Carbonic anhydrase}}{\rightleftharpoons}} \underset{\text{Carbonic acid}}{H_2CO_3} \rightleftharpoons \underset{\text{Bicarbonate}}{HCO_3^- + H^+}$$
$$(15\text{-}3)$$

The first reaction in Equation 15-3 is rate-limiting and is catalyzed by the enzyme **carbonic anhydrase**, which is present in the erythrocytes but not in the plasma. Car-

In tissue capillaries

In pulmonary capillaries

Hb + CO₂

① > P_{CO_2}

② > acidity

③ > temp.

(during exercise)

✗ **FIGURE 15-24**

Summary of CO₂ movement. All movement across membranes is by diffusion. Note that most of the CO₂ entering the blood in the tissues ultimately is converted to HCO_3^-. This occurs almost entirely in the erythrocytes because the carbonic anhydrase is located there, but most of the HCO_3^- then moves out of the erythrocytes into the plasma in exchange for chloride ions (the "chloride shift"). See Figure 15-25 for the fate of the hydrogen ions generated in the erythrocytes.

46

bonic acid dissociates into a bicarbonate ion and a hydrogen very rapidly without any enzyme assistance.

Because carbon dioxide undergoes these various reactions in blood, it is customary to add up the amounts of dissolved carbon dioxide, bicarbonate, and carbon dioxide in carbamino form and call this sum the **total blood carbon dioxide**.

Metabolism, in a resting person, generates about 200 ml of carbon dioxide per minute. When arterial blood flows through tissue capillaries, this volume of carbon dioxide diffuses from the tissues into the blood. Let us review, with the addition of a few more important facts, the reactions that this carbon dioxide undergoes after it enters the blood (Figure 15-24).

1. A small fraction (10 percent) of the carbon dioxide entering the blood remains physically dissolved in the plasma and erythrocytes.

2. Another fraction (30 percent) reacts directly with hemoglobin to form the carbamino compound, $HbCO_2$. This process is facilitated because much of the oxyhemoglobin becomes deoxyhemoglobin as blood flows through the tissues, and deoxyhemoglobin reacts more readily with carbon dioxide than does oxyhemoglobin.

3. Most of the carbon dioxide (60 percent) is converted to bicarbonate and hydrogen ions (Equation 15-3).[6] This occurs mainly in the erythrocytes because they contain the carbonic anhydrase required for the reactions to go

---

[6]The 60 percent figure might seem to conflict with the fact that bicarbonate constitutes 90 percent of the carbon dioxide content of arterial blood. There is no conflict, however. The *new* carbon dioxide added to blood in tissue capillaries does not distribute among carbamino and bicarbonate in the same proportions as those already present in *arterial blood*. The reason is that the concentration of deoxyhemoglobin is much higher in the *tissue capillary blood* than arterial blood and is available for binding carbon dioxide to form carbamino.

quickly. Once formed, most of the bicarbonate moves out of the erythrocytes into the plasma via a transporter that exchanges one bicarbonate for one chloride ion (this is called the "chloride shift"). The reactions described in Equation 15-3 also explain why, as mentioned earlier, the H^+ concentration in tissue capillary blood and systemic venous blood is higher than that of the arterial blood and increases as metabolic activity increases. The fate of these hydrogen ions will be discussed in the next section.

Just the opposite events occur as systemic venous blood flows through the lung capillaries (Figure 15-24). Because the blood P_{CO_2} is higher than alveolar P_{CO_2}, a net diffusion of CO_2 from blood into alveoli occurs. This loss of carbon dioxide from the blood lowers the blood P_{CO_2} and drives these reactions to the left: HCO_3^- and H^+ combine to give H_2CO_3, which then dissociates to CO_2 and H_2O. Similarly, $HbCO_2$ generates Hb and free CO_2. Normally, as fast as this CO_2 is generated from HCO_3^- and H^+ and from $HbCO_2$, it diffuses into the alveoli. In this manner, all the CO_2 delivered into the blood in the tissues now is delivered into the alveoli, from which it is eliminated from the body during expiration.

TRANSPORT OF HYDROGEN IONS BETWEEN TISSUES AND LUNGS

To repeat, as blood flows through the tissues, a fraction of oxyhemoglobin loses its oxygen to become deoxyhemoglobin, while simultaneously a large quantity of carbon dioxide enters the blood and undergoes the reactions that generate bicarbonate and hydrogen ions. What happens to these hydrogen ions? Deoxyhemoglobin has a much greater affinity for H^+ than does oxyhemoglobin, and so it binds (buffers) most of the hydrogen ions (Figure 15-25). Indeed, deoxyhemoglobin is often abbreviated HbH rather than Hb to denote its binding of H^+. In effect, the reaction is $HbO_2 + H^+ = HbH + O_2$.

In this manner only a small number of the hydrogen ions generated in the blood remain free. This explains why the acidity of venous blood is only slightly greater than that of arterial blood. The pH of arterial blood is 7.4, and that of venous blood is 7.36. (Remember than pH goes down as H^+ concentration goes up.) Thus, hemoglobin's ability to buffer hydrogen ions is crucial for preventing large and potentially damaging changes in blood acidity.

As the venous blood passes through the lungs, all these reactions are reversed. Deoxyhemoglobin becomes converted to oxyhemoglobin and, in the process, releases the hydrogen ions it had picked up in the tissues. The hydrogen ions react with bicarbonate to give carbon dioxide and water, and the carbon dioxide diffuses into the alveoli to

FIGURE 15-25

Binding of hydrogen ions by hemoglobin as blood flows through tissue capillaries. This reaction is facilitated because deoxyhemoglobin, formed as oxygen comes off hemoglobin, has a greater affinity for hydrogen ions than does oxyhemoglobin. For this reason, Hb and HbH are both abbreviations for deoxyhemoglobin.

be expired. Normally all the hydrogen ions that are generated from the reaction of carbon dioxide and water in the tissue capillaries recombine with bicarbonate to form carbon dioxide and water in the pulmonary capillaries. Therefore, none of these hydrogen ions appear in the arterial blood.

But what if the person is hypoventilating or has a lung disease that prevents normal elimination of carbon dioxide? Not only would arterial P_{CO_2} rise as a result but so would arterial H^+ concentration. Increased arterial H^+ concentration due to carbon dioxide retention is termed ***respiratory acidosis***. Conversely, hyperventilation would lower the arterial values of both P_{CO_2} and H^+ concentration—a ***respiratory alkalosis***.

In the course of describing the transport of oxygen, carbon dioxide, and H^+ in blood, we have presented multiple factors that influence the binding of these substances by hemoglobin. They are all sumarized in Table 15-9.

TABLE 15-9 EFFECTS OF VARIOUS FACTORS ON HEMOGLOBIN

The affinity of hemoglobin for oxygen is decreased by:

1. Increased hydrogen-ion concentration
2. Increased P_{CO_2}
3. Increased temperature
4. Increased DPG concentration

The affinity of hemoglobin for both hydrogen ions and carbon dioxide is decreased by increased P_{O_2}.

CONTROL OF RESPIRATION

Neural Generation of Rhythmical Breathing

Like cardiac muscle, the inspiratory muscles normally contract rhythmically, that is, alternately contract and relax. The origins of these contractions, however, are quite different. Certain cardiac-muscle cells have automaticity, and the nerves to the heart merely alter this inherent rate but are not required for cardiac contraction. In contrast, the diaphragm and intercostal muscles consist of skeletal muscle, which cannot contract unless stimulated to do so by nerves. Thus, breathing depends entirely upon cyclical respiratory muscle excitation by the motor nerves to the diaphragm and the intercostal muscles. Destruction of these nerves or the areas from which they originate, as in *poliomyelitis*, for example, results in paralysis of the respiratory muscles and death, unless some form of artificial respiration can be instituted.

Inspiration is initiated by a burst of action potentials in the nerves to the inspiratory muscles. Then the action potentials cease, the inspiratory muscles relax, and expiration occurs as the elastic lungs recoil. In situations when expiration is facilitated by contraction of expiratory muscles, the nerves to these muscles, which were quiescent during inspiration, begin firing during expiration.

By what mechanism are nerve impulses to the respiratory muscles alternately increased and decreased? Automatic control of this neural activity resides primarily in neurons in the medulla oblongata, the same area of brain that contains the major cardiovascular control centers. (For the rest of this chapter we shall refer to the medulla oblongata simply as the medulla.) In several areas of the medulla, clusters of neurons discharge in synchrony with inspiration and cease discharging during expiration. These neurons are called **medullary inspiratory neurons**. They provide, through either direct or interneuronal connections, the rhythmical input to the motor neurons innervating the inspiratory muscles.

Just how the brain generates alternating cycles of firing and quiescence in the medullary inspiratory neurons remains unclear. It is possible that the inspiratory neurons, or neurons that synapse upon them, are pacemaker neurons, that is, that they have inherent automaticity and rhythmicity. However, most experts believe that even though such pacemakers might play a role, a much more complex model is required to explain the on-off cycle of the neuronal output.

The medullary inspiratory neurons also receive a rich synaptic input from neurons in various areas of the pons, the part of the brainstem just above the medulla. This input modulates the output of the medullary inspiratory neurons and may help terminate inspiration by inhibiting them.

Another cutoff signal for inspiration comes from **pulmonary stretch receptors**, which lie in the airway smooth-muscle layer and are activated by lung inflation. Action potentials in the afferent nerve fibers from them travel to the brain and inhibit the medullary inspiratory neurons. This is known as the Hering-Breuer inflation reflex. Thus, feedback from the lungs helps to terminate inspiration. However, the threshold of these receptors in human beings is very high, and this pulmonary stretch receptor reflex plays a role in setting respiratory rhythm only under conditions of very large tidal volumes, as in exercise.

One last point about the medullary inspiratory neurons should be made: They are quite sensitive to depression by drugs, especially barbiturates and morphine, and death from an overdose of these drugs is often secondary to a cessation of ventilation.

Control of Ventilation by P_{O_2}, P_{CO_2}, and H^+ Concentration

Respiratory rate and tidal volume are not fixed but can be increased or decreased over a wide range. For simplicity, we shall describe the control of total ventilation without discussing whether rate or depth makes the greater contribution to the change.

There are many inputs to the medullary inspiratory neurons, but the most important for the involuntary control of ventilation are from peripheral chemoreceptors and central chemoreceptors.

The **peripheral chemoreceptors**, located high in the neck at the bifurcation of the common carotid arteries and in the thorax on the arch of the aorta (Figure 15-26), are called the **carotid and aortic bodies.** In both locations they are quite close to, but distinct from, the arterial baroreceptors described in Chapter 14. Of the two groups of peripheral chemoreceptors, the carotid bodies are by far the more important. They are composed of epithelium-like cells and neuron terminals in intimate contact with the arterial blood. Afferent nerve fibers arising from these terminals pass to the brainstem, where they influence ultimately the medullary inspiratory neurons. The peripheral chemoreceptors are sensitive to changes in the arterial P_{O_2}, H^+ concentration, and P_{CO_2}.

The **central chemoreceptors** are located in the medulla and provide synaptic input to the medullary inspiratory neurons. They respond to changes in the H^+ concentration of the brain's extracellular fluid. As we shall see, such changes occur particularly when the blood P_{CO_2} is altered.

The stimuli for the central and peripheral chemoreceptors are summarized in Table 15-10.

Control by P_{O_2}. Figure 15-27 illustrates an experiment in which healthy subjects breath low-P_{O_2} gas mixtures for several minutes. The experiment is performed in a way

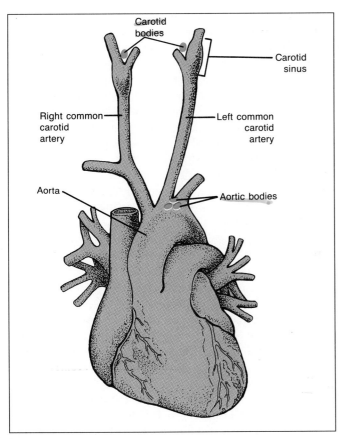

FIGURE 15-26

Location of the carotid and aortic bodies. Note that the carotid body is quite close to the carotid sinus, the major arterial baroreceptor. Both right and left common carotid bifurcations contain a carotid sinus and a carotid body.

breathing: 2 sets =
inspiration
exspiration

regulation: stretch receptor

TABLE 15-10   STIMULI FOR THE CENTRAL AND PERIPHERAL CHEMORECEPTORS

Peripheral chemoreceptors—that is, carotid bodies and aortic bodies—respond to changes in the *arterial blood.* They are stimulated by:

1. Decreased P_{O_2} $\downarrow O_2 \rightarrow$ *fires*
2. Increased hydrogen-ion concentration   *(buffer)*
3. Increased P_{CO_2}, mainly via associated changes in hydrogen-ion concentration

Central chemoreceptors—that is, located in the medulla oblongata—respond to changes in the *brain interstitial fluid.* They are stimulated by increased P_{CO_2}, via associated changes in hydrogen-ion concentration. (See Equation 15-3.)

FIGURE 15-27

The effect on ventilation of breathing low-oxygen mixtures. The arterial P_{CO_2} was maintained at 40 mmHg throughout the experiment.

FIGURE 15-28

Sequence of events by which a low arterial P_{O_2} causes hyperventilation, which maintains alveolar (and, hence, arterial) P_{O_2} at a value higher than would exist if the ventilation had remained unchanged.

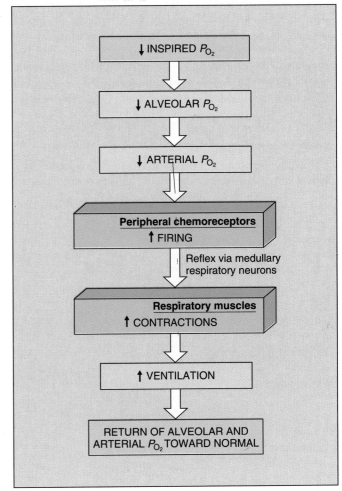

that keeps arterial P_{CO_2} constant so that the pure effects of changing only P_{O_2} can be studied. Little increase in ventilation is observed until the oxygen content of the inspired air is reduced enough to lower arterial P_{O_2} to 60 mmHg. Beyond this point, any further reduction in arterial P_{O_2} causes a marked reflex hyperventilation.

This reflex is mediated by the peripheral chemoreceptors (Figure 15-28). The low arterial P_{O_2} increases the rate at which the receptors discharge, resulting in an increased number of action potentials traveling up the afferent nerve fibers and stimulating the medullary inspiratory neurons. The resulting increase in ventilation provides more oxygen to the alveoli and minimizes the drop in alveolar and arterial P_{O_2} produced by the low-P_{O_2} gas mixture.

It may seem surprising that we are so insensitive to smaller reductions in arterial P_{O_2}, but look again at the oxygen-hemoglobin dissociation curve (Figure 15-20). Total oxygen carriage by the blood is not really reduced very much until the arterial P_{O_2} falls below 60 mmHg. Therefore, increased ventilation would not result in very much more oxygen being added to the blood until that point is reached.

To reiterate, the peripheral chemoreceptors respond to decreases in arterial P_{O_2}, as occurs in lung disease or exposure to high altitude. However, the peripheral chemoreceptors are *not* stimulated in situations in which there are modest reductions in the *oxygen content* of the blood but no change in arterial P_{O_2}. An example of this is anemia, where there is a decrease in the amount of hemoglobin present in the blood (Chapter 14) but no decrease in arterial P_{O_2} because the concentration of dissolved oxygen in the blood is normal. This same analysis holds true when oxygen content is reduced by the presence of carbon monoxide, a gas that has an extremely high affinity for the oxygen binding sites in hemoglobin and reduces the amount of oxygen combined with hemoglobin by competing for these sites. Since carbon monoxide does not affect the amount of oxygen that can dissolve in blood, the arterial P_{O_2} is unaltered, and no increase in peripheral chemoreceptor output occurs.

Control by P_{CO_2} That an increase in arterial P_{CO_2} plays an important role in the control of ventilation can be demonstrated by a simple experiment in which subjects breathe air containing variable quantities of carbon dioxide. The presence of carbon dioxide in the inspired air causes an elevation of alveolar P_{CO_2} and thereby an elevation of arterial P_{CO_2}. As can be seen in Figure 15-29, increased P_{CO_2} markedly stimulates ventilation, an increase of 2 to 5 mmHg in alveolar P_{CO_2} causing a 100 percent increase in ventilation.

Thus, unlike the case for lowered P_{O_2}, even the slightest change in arterial P_{CO_2} is associated with a significant reflex change in ventilation. Experiments like this have documented that small changes in arterial P_{CO_2} are resisted by the reflex mechanisms controlling ventilation to a greater degree than are equivalent changes in arterial P_{O_2}. An increase in arterial P_{CO_2} due, say, to lung disease results in stimulation of ventilation to promote the elimination of carbon dioxide. Conversely, a decrease in arterial P_{CO_2} below normal levels removes some of the stimulus for ventilation, thereby reducing ventilation and allowing metabolically produced carbon dioxide to accumulate and return the P_{CO_2} to normal. In this manner, the arterial P_{CO_2} is stabilized at the normal value of 40 mmHg.

The pathways by which changes in the arterial P_{CO_2} result in changes in ventilation include both the peripheral and central chemoreceptors. Before looking at the specific reflexes, we must emphasize that the ability of changes in arterial P_{CO_2} to control ventilation reflexly is largely due to associated changes in H^+ concentration (Equation 15-3).[7]

Figure 15-30 summarizes the pathways by which increased arterial P_{CO_2} stimulates ventilation. For one thing, the peripheral chemoreceptors are stimulated by the increased arterial H^+ concentration resulting from the increased P_{CO_2}. At the same time, because carbon dioxide diffuses rapidly across the membranes separating capillary blood and brain tissue, the increase in arterial P_{CO_2} causes a rapid identical increase in brain extracellular fluid P_{CO_2}. This increased P_{CO_2} increases brain extracellular fluid

FIGURE 15-29

Effects on respiration of increasing arterial P_{CO_2} achieved by adding carbon dioxide to inspired air.

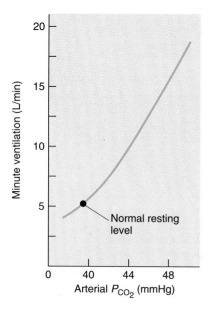

---

[7]An increased P_{CO_2} exerts some direct stimulation of the peripheral chemoreceptors, but this is very small compared to its indirect effects via changes in hydrogen-ion concentration.

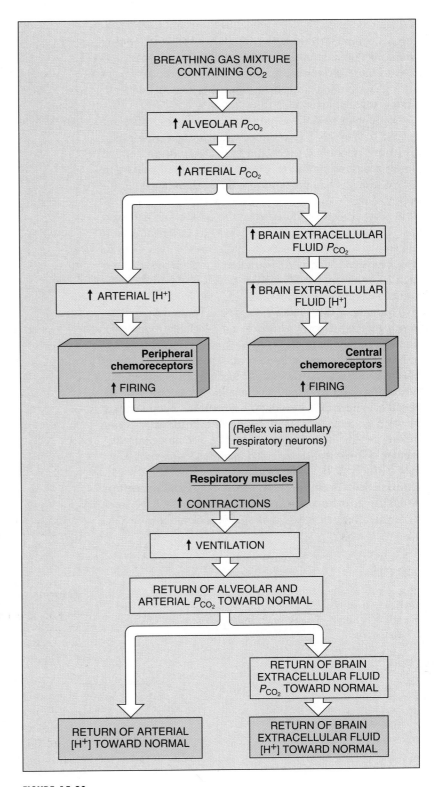

FIGURE 15-30

Pathways by which increased arterial P_{CO_2} stimulates ventilation. Note that the peripheral chemoreceptors are stimulated by an *increase* in H^+ concentration, whereas they are stimulated by a *decrease* in P_{O_2} (Fig. 15-28).

H^+ concentration, which stimulates the central chemoreceptors. Inputs from both the peripheral and central chemoreceptors stimulate the medullary inspiratory neurons to increase ventilation. The end result is a return of arterial and brain extracellular fluid P_{CO_2} and H^+ concentration toward normal.

Of the two sets of receptors involved in this reflex response to elevated P_{CO_2}, the central chemoreceptors are the more important, accounting for about 70 percent of the stimulus to ventilation. Contrast this to the low-oxygen reflex, which is mediated only by the peripheral chemoreceptors.

It should also be noted that the effects of increased P_{CO_2} and decreased P_{O_2} not only exist as independent inputs to the medulla but manifest synergistic interactions as well. Acute ventilatory response to combined low P_{O_2} and high P_{CO_2} is considerably greater than the sum of the individual responses.

Throughout this section, we have described the *stimulatory* effects of carbon dioxide on ventilation via *reflex* input to the medulla, but *very high* levels of carbon dioxide have just the opposite effect and may be lethal. This is because such concentrations of carbon dioxide act *directly* on the medulla to *inhibit* the respiratory neurons by an anesthesia-like effect. Symptoms caused by increased blood P_{CO_2} include severe headaches, restlessness, and dulling or loss of consciousness. The accompanying increased H^+ concentration also causes serious problems.

Control by Changes in Arterial H^+ Concentration Not Due to Altered Carbon Dioxide. We have seen that retention or excessive elimination of carbon dioxide

FIGURE 15-31

Changes in ventilation in response to an elevation of plasma hydrogen-ion concentration, produced by the administration of lactic acid. (*Adapted from Lambertsen.*)

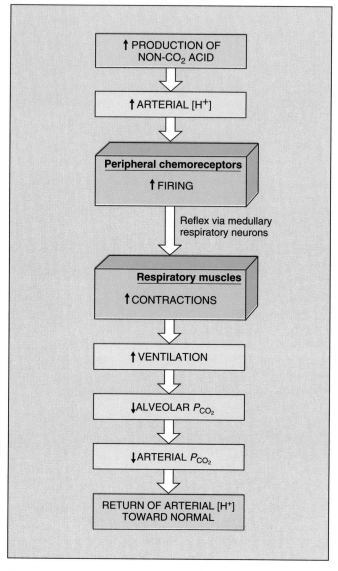

FIGURE 15-32

Reflexly induced hyperventilation minimizes the change in arterial hydrogen-ion concentration when acids are produced in excess in the body. Note that under such conditions, arterial P_{CO_2} is reflexly reduced below its normal value.

causes respiratory acidosis and respiratory alkalosis, respectively. There are, however, many normal and pathological situations in which a change in arterial H^+ concentration is due to some cause other than a primary change in P_{CO_2}. These are termed ***metabolic acidosis*** when H^+ concentration is increased, and ***metabolic alkalosis*** when it is decreased. In such cases, the peripheral chemoreceptors play the major role in altering ventilation.

For example, increased addition of lactic acid to the blood, as in strenuous exercise, causes hyperventilation almost entirely by stimulation of the peripheral chemoreceptors (Figures 15-31 and 15-32). The central chemoreceptors are only minimally stimulated in this case because brain H$^+$ concentration is increased to only a small extent, at least early on, by the hydrogen ions generated from the lactic acid. This is because hydrogen ions penetrate the blood-brain barrier very slowly. Contrast this with how easily carbon dioxide penetrates the blood-brain barrier and changes brain H$^+$ concentration.

The converse of the above situation is also true: When arterial H$^+$ concentration is lowered by any means other than by a reduction in P_{CO_2} (for example, by loss of hydrogen ions from the stomach in vomiting), ventilation is reflexly depressed because of decreased peripheral chemoreceptor output.

The adaptive value such reflexes have in regulating arterial H$^+$ concentration should be evident (Figure 15-32). The hyperventilation induced by a metabolic acidosis lowers arterial P_{CO_2}, which lowers arterial H$^+$ concentration back toward normal. Similarly, hypoventilation induced by a metabolic alkalosis results in an elevated arterial P_{CO_2} and a restoration of H$^+$ concentration toward normal. Notice that when a change in arterial H$^+$ concentration due to some acid unrelated to carbon dioxide influences ventilation via the peripheral chemoreceptors, P_{CO_2} is displaced from normal. This is a reflex that regulates arterial H$^+$ concentration at the expense of changes in arterial P_{CO_2}.

Figure 15-33 summarizes the control of ventilation by P_{O_2}, P_{CO_2}, and H$^+$ concentration.

Control of Ventilation During Exercise

During exercise, the alveolar ventilation may increase as much as twentyfold. On the basis of our three variables— P_{O_2}, P_{CO_2}, and H$^+$ concentration—it might seem easy to explain the mechanism that induces this increased ventilation. Unhappily, such is not the case.

Increased P_{CO_2} as the Stimulus? It would seem logical that, as the exercising muscles produce more carbon dioxide, blood P_{CO_2} would increase. This is true, however, only for systemic *venous* blood but not for arterial blood. Therefore, the reflex mechanisms by which increased arterial P_{CO_2} increases ventilation are *not* brought into play.

The reader might well wonder why arterial P_{CO_2} does not increase during exercise. Recall two facts from the section on alveolar gas pressures: (1) Alveolar P_{CO_2} sets arterial P_{CO_2}, and (2) alveolar P_{CO_2} is determined by the *ratio* of carbon dioxide production to alveolar ventilation. During exercise, the alveolar ventilation increases in exact proportion to the increased carbon dioxide production, and so alveolar and therefore arterial P_{CO_2} do not change. Indeed, for reasons described below, in very strenuous exercise the alveolar ventilation increases relatively more

than carbon dioxide production. In other words, the person hyperventilates, and thus alveolar and systemic arterial P_{CO_2} actually decrease (Figure 15-34).

Decreased P_{O_2} as the Stimulus? The story is similar for oxygen: although systemic venous P_{O_2} decreases during exercise, alveolar P_{O_2} and hence systemic arterial P_{O_2} usually remain unchanged. This is because cellular oxygen consumption and alveolar ventilation increase in exact proportion to each other (Figure 15-34).[8]

This is a good place to remind you of an important point made in Chapter 14: In normal individuals, ventilation is not the limiting factor in endurance exercise, cardiac output is. Ventilation can, as we have just seen, increase enough to maintain arterial P_{O_2}.

Increased H$^+$ Concentration as the Stimulus? Since the arterial P_{CO_2} does not change during moderate exercise and decreases in severe exercise, there is no accumulation of excess H$^+$ resulting from carbon dioxide accumulation. However, during strenuous exercise, there *is* an increase in arterial H$^+$ concentration (Figure 15-34), but for quite a different reason, namely, generation and release of lactic acid into the blood. This change in H$^+$ concentration is responsible, in part, for stimulating the hyperventilation of severe exercise.

We are left with the fact that we do not know what input stimulates ventilation during most exercise. Our "big three"—decreased arterial P_{O_2}, increased arterial P_{CO_2}, and increased arterial H$^+$ concentration do not occur and, therefore, cannot be the stimuli.

Other Factors. Many receptors in joints and muscles are stimulated by the physical movements that accompany muscle contraction. It is quite likely that afferent pathways from these receptors play a significant role in stimulating respiration during exercise. Thus, the mechanical events of exercise help to coordinate alveolar ventilation with the metabolic requirements of the tissues.

An increase in body temperature also frequently occurs as a result of increased physical activity and contributes to stimulation of alveolar ventilation. Body temperature also increases in many situations other than exercise, and when it does, it stimulates ventilation. Thus, people with fever show increased ventilation.

Epinephrine and norepinephrine are also respiratory stimulants. The increased plasma concentrations of these

---

[8]The hyperventilation of very strenuous exercise *raises* alveolar P_{O_2}, just as it lowers alveolar P_{CO_2}, but for a variety of reasons, the increase in alveolar P_{O_2} is not accompanied by an increase in arterial P_{O_2}. Indeed, especially in highly conditioned athletes, the arterial P_{O_2} may decrease somewhat during strenuous exercise and may also contribute to stimulation of ventilation.

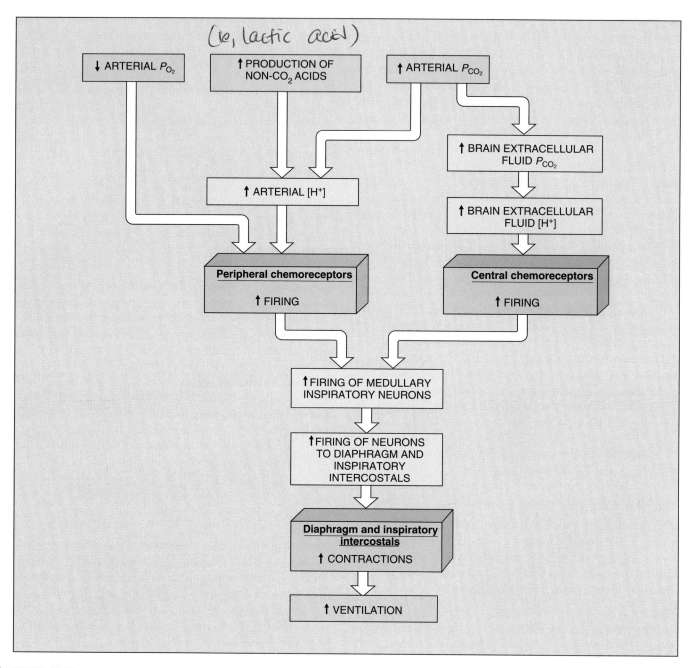

FIGURE 15-33

This is a combination of portions of Figures 15-28, 15-30, and 15-32, in order to summarize the chemical inputs that stimulate ventilation. When arterial P_{O_2} increases or when P_{CO_2} or hydrogen-ion concentration decreases, ventilation is reflexly decreased.

catecholamines with exercise probably contributes to the increased ventilation.[9]

Higher brain centers also influence ventilation during

exercise. Branches come off the axons descending from the brain to motor neurons supplying exercising muscles, and these branches influence the neurons that control the respiratory muscles.

Finally, there may be an important learned component to the ventilatory response to exercise. As shown in Figure 15-35, there is an abrupt increase—within seconds—in ventilation at the onset of exercise and an equally abrupt decrease at the end. Clearly, these changes occur too rap-

---

[9]Another plasma constituent, the concentration of which increases during exercise, is potassium, because of leakage from the exercising muscles. It is possible, though unproven, that this increased plasma potassium concentration stimulates ventilation, acting via the peripheral chemoreceptors.

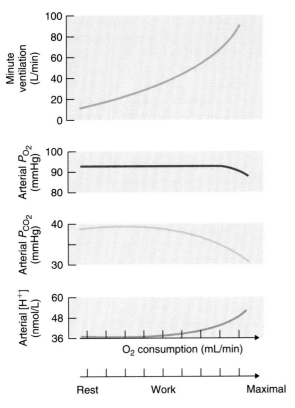

FIGURE 15-34

The effect of exercise on ventilation, arterial gas pressures, and hydrogen-ion concentration. (*Adapted from Comroe.*)

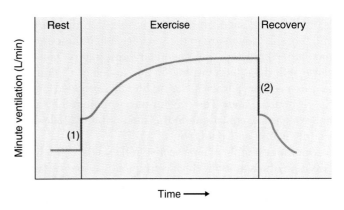

FIGURE 15-35

Ventilation changes during exercise. Note (1) the abrupt increase at the onset of exercise and (2) the equally abrupt but larger decrease at the end of the exercise.

idly to be explained by alteration of chemical constituents of the blood or altered body temperature. They probably represent a conditioned response mediated by neural input to the respiratory centers.

Figure 15-36 summarizes various factors that influence ventilation during exercise.

Other Ventilatory Responses

Protective Reflexes. A group of responses protect the respiratory system against irritant materials. Most familiar are the cough and the sneeze reflexes which originate in receptors located between airway epithelial cells. The re-

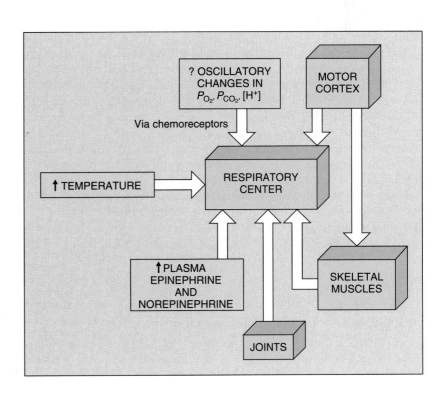

FIGURE 15-36

Summary of factors that stimulate ventilation during exercise. The possibility that *oscillatory* changes in P_{O_2}, P_{CO_2}, or H^+ concentration occur, in the absence of unchanged levels of these variables, and play a role has been proposed but remains unproven. Presently unknown factors also play important roles.

ceptors for the sneeze reflex are in the nose or pharynx, and those for cough are in the trachea. When these receptors are stimulated, the medullary respiratory neurons cause reflexly a deep inspiration and a violent expiration. In this manner, particles can be literally exploded out of the respiratory tract. The cough reflex is inhibited by alcohol, which may contribute to the susceptibility of alcoholics to choking and pneumonia.

Another example of a protective reflex is the immediate cessation of respiration which is frequently triggered when noxious agents are inhaled. Chronic smoking causes a loss of this reflex.

Pain and Emotion. Painful stimuli anywhere in the body can produce reflex stimulation of the respiratory neurons. Emotional states are also often accompanied by marked alterations in respiration, as evidenced by the rapid breathing that characterizes fright, anxiety, and many similar emotions. In addition, movement of air in or out of the lungs is required for such involuntary expressions of emotion as laughing and crying. In such situations, the descending pathways from higher brain centers are the controlling input.

Voluntary Control of Breathing. Although we have discussed in detail the involuntary nature of most respiratory reflexes, it is quite obvious that considerable voluntary control of respiratory movements exists. Voluntary control is accomplished by descending pathways from the cerebral cortex to the motor neurons of the respiratory muscles. This voluntary control of respiration cannot be maintained when the involuntary stimuli, such as an elevated P_{CO_2} or H^+ concentration, become intense. An example is the inability to hold one's breath for very long.

The opposite of breath-holding—deliberate hyperventilation—lowers alveolar and arterial P_{CO_2} and increases P_{O_2}. Unfortunately, swimmers sometimes voluntarily hyperventilate immediately before underwater swimming to be able to hold their breath longer. We say "unfortunately" because the low P_{CO_2} may still permit breath-holding at a time when the exertion is lowering the arterial P_{O_2} to levels that can cause unconsciousness and lead to drowning.

Besides the obvious forms of voluntary control, respiration must also be controlled during such complex actions as speaking and singing.

HYPOXIA

Hypoxia is defined as a deficiency of oxygen at the tissue level. There are many potential causes of hypoxia, but they can be classed in four general categories:

(1) *hypoxic hypoxia* (also termed *hypoxemia*), in which the arterial P_{O_2} is reduced; (2) *anemic hypoxia,* in which the arterial P_{O_2} is normal but the total oxygen *content* of the blood is reduced because of inadequate numbers of erythrocytes, deficient or abnormal hemoglobin, or competition for the hemoglobin molecule by carbon monoxide; (3) *ischemic hypoxia* (also called hypoperfusion hypoxia), in which blood flow to the tissues is too low; and (4) *histotoxic hypoxia*, in which the quantity of oxygen reaching the tissues is normal but the cell is unable to utilize the oxygen because a toxic agent—cyanide, for example—has interfered with the cell's metabolic machinery.

The primary causes of hypoxic hypoxia in disease are listed in Table 15-11. Exposure to the reduced P_{O_2} of high altitude also causes hypoxia but is not a "disease." The brief summaries in Table 15-11 provide a review of many of the key aspects of respiratory physiology and pathophysiology described in this chapter.

This table also emphasizes that some of the diseases that produce hypoxia also produce carbon dioxide retention and an increased arterial P_{CO_2} (**hypercapnea**). In such cases, treating only the oxygen deficit by administering oxygen may constitute inadequate therapy because it does nothing about the hypercapnea.[10]

Acclimatization to High Altitude

Atmospheric pressure progressively decreases as altitude increases. Thus, at the top of Mt. Everest (approximately 29,000 ft or 9000 m), the atmospheric pressure is 253 mmHg (recall that it is 760 mmHg at sea level). The air is still 21 percent oxygen, which means that the P_{O_2} is 53 mmHg, that is, 0.21 × 253 mmHg. Obviously, the alveolar and arterial P_{O_2} must decrease as one ascends unless pure oxygen is breathed.

The effects of oxygen lack vary from one individual to another, but most people who ascend rapidly to altitudes above 10,000 ft experience some degree of **mountain sickness.** This disorder consists of breathlessness, heart palpitations, headache, nausea, vomiting, insomnia, fatigue, and impairment of mental processes. Much more serious is the appearance, in some individuals, of life-threatening pulmonary edema.[11]

Over the course of several days, the symptoms of mountain sickness disappear, although maximal physical

---

[10]Indeed, such therapy may be dangerous. The primary respiratory drive in such patients is the hypoxia, since for several reasons the response to an increased P_{CO_2} may be lost in chronic situations; the administration of pure oxygen may cause such patients to stop breathing entirely.

[11]The cause of the pulmonary edema is still unclear. It may be due to increased permeability to protein and/or increased hydrostatic pressure in the pulmonary capillaries. Decreased active fluid absorption by the alveolar epithelial cells may also play a role.

TABLE 15-11 CAUSES OF A DECREASED ARTERIAL P_{O_2} (HYPOXIC HYPOXIA) IN DISEASE

1. *Hypoventilation* may be caused (a) by a defect anywhere along the respiratory control pathway, from the medulla through the respiratory muscles, (b) by severe thoracic cage abnormalities, and (c) by major obstruction of the upper airway. The hypoxemia of hypoventilation is always accompanied by an increased arterial P_{CO_2}.

2. *Diffusion impairment* results from thickening of the alveolar membranes or a decrease in their surface area. In turn, it causes failure of equilibration of blood P_{O_2} with alveolar P_{O_2}. Often it is apparent only during exercise. Arterial P_{CO_2} is either normal, since carbon dioxide diffuses more readily than oxygen, or reduced, if the hypoxemia reflexly stimulates ventilation.

3. A *Shunt* is an abnormality of the cardiovascular system or lungs that causes blood to bypass ventilated alveoli in passing from the right heart to the left heart. The most common causes are cardiac defects that permit blood to flow directly from the right heart to the left heart. Arterial P_{CO_2} generally does not rise since the effect of the shunt on it is counterbalanced by the increased ventilation reflexly stimulated by the hypoxemia.

4. *Ventilation-perfusion inequality* is by far the most common cause of hypoxemia. It occurs in chronic obstructive lung diseases and many other lung diseases. Arterial P_{CO_2} may be normal or increased, depending upon how much ventilation is reflexly stimulated.

TABLE 15-12 ACCLIMATIZATION TO THE HYPOXIA OF HIGH ALTITUDE

1. The peripheral chemoreceptors stimulate ventilation.

2. Erythropoietin, secreted by the kidneys, stimulates erythrocyte synthesis, resulting in increased erythrocyte and hemoglobin concentration of blood.

3. DPG increases and shifts the hemoglobin dissociation curve to the right, facilitating oxygen unloading in the tissues.

4. Increases in capillary density, mitochondria, and muscle myoglobin occur, all of which increase oxygen transfer.

5. The peripheral chemoreceptors stimulate an increased loss of sodium and water in the urine. This reduces plasma volume, resulting in a concentration of the erythrocytes and hemoglobin in the blood.

capacity remains reduced. Acclimatization to high altitude is achieved by the compensatory mechanisms given below. The highest villages permanently inhabited by people are in the Andes at 19,000 ft (5700 m). These villagers work quite normally, and the only major precaution they take is that the women come down to lower altitudes during late pregnancy.

In response to hypoxia, oxygen supply to the tissues is maintained in the five ways summarized in Table 15-12. It should be noted that the DPG effect is not always adaptive and may be maladaptive. This is because, at very high altitudes, a right shift in the curve impairs oxygen *loading* in the lungs, an effect that outweighs any benefit from facilitation of *unloading* in the tissues. Indeed, many high-altitude species such as the llama have a left-shifted curve, indicating an adaptive value for this factor.

Finally, it should be noted that the responses to high altitude are essentially the same as the responses to hypoxia from any other cause. Thus, a person with severe hypoxia from lung disease may show many of the same changes—increased hematocrit, for example—as a high-altitude sojourner.

NONRESPIRATORY FUNCTIONS OF THE LUNGS

The lungs have a variety of functions in addition to their roles in gas exchange and regulation of H^+ concentration. Most notable are the influences they have on the arterial concentrations of a large number of biologically active substances. Many substances—neurotransmitters and paracrine agents, for example—released locally into interstitial fluid may diffuse into capillaries and thus make their way into the systemic venous system. The lungs partially or completely remove some of these substances from the blood and thereby prevent them from reaching other locations in the body via the arteries. The cells that perform this function are the endothelial cells lining the pulmonary capillaries.

In contrast, the lungs may also produce and add new substances to the blood. Some of these substances play local regulatory roles within the lungs, but if produced in large enough quantity, they may diffuse into the pulmonary capillaries and be carried to the rest of the body. For example, inflammatory responses (Chapter 20) in the lung may lead, via excessive release of potent chemicals such as histamine, to profound alterations of systemic blood pressure or flow. In at least one case, the lungs contribute a hormone, angiotensin II, to the blood (Chapter 16).

Finally, the lungs also act as a "sieve" that traps and dissolves small blood clots generated in the systemic circulation, thereby preventing them from reaching the systemic arterial blood where they could occlude blood vessels in other organs.

SUMMARY

ORGANIZATION OF THE RESPIRATORY SYSTEM

I. The respiratory system comprises the lungs, the airways leading to them, and the chest structures responsible for movement of air into and out of them.
   A. The conducting zone of the airways consists of the trachea, bronchi, and terminal bronchioles.
   B. The respiratory zone of the airways consists of the alveoli, which are the sites of gas exchange, and those airways to which alveoli are attached.
   C. The alveoli are lined by type I cells with some type II cells, which produce surfactant.
   D. The lungs and interior of the thorax are covered by pleura between the surfaces of which is an extremely thin layer of intrapleural fluid.

II. The volume of air in the lungs at the end of an unforced expiration is the functional residual capacity (FRC). At this volume, only passive forces of the lungs and chest wall are acting.
   A. At FRC, the lungs are stretched and are attempting to recoil, whereas the chest wall is compressed and attempting to move outward. This creates a subatmospheric intrapleural pressure.
   B. The difference between the alveolar pressure and the intrapleural pressure is the transpulmonary pressure, which is the force acting to hold the lungs open.

SUMMARY OF STEPS INVOLVED IN RESPIRATION

I. The steps involved in respiration are summarized in Figure 15-7. In the steady state, the net volumes of oxygen and carbon dioxide exchanged in the lungs per unit time are equal to the net volumes exchanged in the tissues. Typical volumes per minute are 250 ml for oxygen consumption and 200 ml for carbon dioxide production.

VENTILATION AND LUNG MECHANICS

I. Bulk flow of air between the atmosphere and alveoli is proportional to the difference between the atmospheric and alveolar pressures and inversely proportional to the airway resistance: $F = (P_{atm} - P_{alv})/R$.

II. During inspiration, the contractions of the diaphragm and inspiratory intercostal muscles increase the volume of the thoracic cage.
   A. This makes intrapleural pressure more subatmospheric, increases transpulmonary pressure, and causes the lungs to expand.
   B. This expansion initially makes alveolar pressure subatmospheric, which creates the pressure difference between atmosphere and alveoli to drive air flow into the lungs.

III. During expiration, the inspiratory muscles cease contracting, allowing the lungs and chest wall to return passively to their original size.
   A. This initially compresses the alveolar air, raising alveolar pressure above atmospheric pressure and driving air out of the lungs.
   B. In forced expirations, the contraction of expiratory intercostal muscles and abdominal muscles actively decreases thoracic dimensions.

IV. Lung compliance is determined by the elastic connective tissues of the lungs and the surface tension of the fluid lining the alveoli. The latter is greatly reduced, and compliance increased, by surfactant, produced by the type II cells of the alveoli.

V. Airway resistance determines how much air flows into the lungs at any given pressure difference between atmosphere and alveolus. The major determinant of airway resistance is the radii of the airways, which are influenced by physical and chemical factors, summarized in Table 15-4.

VI. The vital capacity is the sum of resting tidal volume, inspiratory reserve volume, and expiratory reserve volume. The volume expired during the first second of a forced vital capacity (FVC) measurement is the FEV_1 and normally averages 80 percent of FVC.

VII. Minute ventilation is the product of tidal volume and respiratory rate; alveolar ventilation = (tidal volume minus anatomic dead space) × (respiratory rate).

EXCHANGE OF GASES IN ALVEOLI AND TISSUES

I. Exchange of gases in lungs and tissues is by diffusion, as a result of differences in partial pressures.

II. Normal alveolar gas pressure for oxygen is 105 mmHg, and for carbon dioxide 40 mmHg.
   A. At any given inspired P_{O_2}, the ratio of oxygen consumption to alveolar ventilation determines alveolar P_{O_2}—the higher the ratio, the lower the alveolar P_{O_2}.
   B. The higher the ratio of carbon dioxide production to alveolar ventilation, the higher the alveolar P_{CO_2}.

III. The average value at rest for systemic venous P_{O_2} is 40 mmHg, and for P_{CO_2} 46 mmHg.

IV. As systemic venous blood flows through the pulmonary capillaries, there is net diffusion of oxygen from alveoli to blood and of carbon dioxide from blood to alveoli.
   A. By the end of the pulmonary capillaries, the blood gas pressures have become equal to those in the alveoli.

B. Therefore, the P_{O_2} and P_{CO_2} in the systemic arterial blood are similar to those in the alveoli.

V. Inadequate gas exchange between alveoli and pulmonary capillaries may occur when the alveolus-capillary surface area is decreased, when the alveolar walls thicken, and when there are ventilation-perfusion inequalities.

VI. Significant ventilation-perfusion inequalities cause the systemic arterial P_{O_2} to be reduced. An important mechanism for opposing mismatching is that a low local P_{O_2} causes local vasoconstriction, thereby shunting blood from poorly ventilated areas.

VII. In the tissues, net diffusion of oxygen occurs from blood to cells, and net diffusion of carbon dioxide from cells to blood.

TRANSPORT OF OXYGEN IN THE BLOOD

I. Each liter of systemic arterial blood normally contains 200 ml of oxygen, more than 98 percent of which is bound to hemoglobin and the rest of which is dissolved.

II. The major determinant of the degree to which hemoglobin is saturated with oxygen is blood P_{O_2}.

A. Hemoglobin is almost 100 percent saturated at the normal systemic arterial P_{O_2} of 100 mmHg. The fact that saturation is already more than 90 percent at a P_{O_2} of 60 mmHg permits relatively normal uptake of oxygen by the blood even when alveolar P_{O_2} is moderately reduced.

B. Hemoglobin is 75 percent saturated at the normal systemic venous P_{O_2} of 40 mmHg. Thus, only 25 percent of the oxygen has dissociated from hemoglobin and entered the tissues.

III. The affinity of hemoglobin for oxygen is decreased by an increase in P_{CO_2}, hydrogen-ion concentration, and temperature. All these conditions exist in the tissues and facilitate the dissociation of oxygen from hemoglobin.

IV. The affinity of hemoglobin for oxygen is also decreased by erythrocyte DPG, which increases in situations associated with inadequate oxygen supply and helps maintain oxygen delivery to the tissues.

TRANSPORT OF CARBON DIOXIDE BY THE BLOOD

I. Each liter of systemic arterial blood contains approximately 550 ml of "total" carbon dioxide, 90 percent of which is bicarbonate.

II. When carbon dioxide molecules diffuse from the tissues into the blood, 10 percent remains dissolved in plasma and erythrocytes, 30 percent combines in the erythrocytes with deoxyhemoglobin to form carbamino compounds, and 60 percent combines in the erythrocytes with water to form carbonic acid, which then dissociates to yield bicarbonate and hydrogen ions. Most of the bicarbonate then moves out of the erythrocytes into the plasma in exchange for chloride ions.

III. As venous blood flows through lung capillaries, P_{CO_2} decreases because of diffusion of carbon dioxide out of the blood into the alveoli, and all these reactions are reversed.

TRANSPORT OF HYDROGEN IONS BETWEEN TISSUES AND LUNGS

I. Most of the hydrogen ions generated in the erythrocytes from carbonic acid during blood passage through tissue capillaries bind to deoxyhemoglobin because deoxyhemoglobin formed as oxygen unloads from oxyhemoglobin has a high affinity for hydrogen ions.

II. As the blood flows through the lung capillaries, hydrogen ions bound to deoxyhemoglobin are released and combine with bicarbonate to yield carbon dioxide and water.

CONTROL OF RESPIRATION

I. Breathing depends upon cyclical inspiratory muscle excitation by the nerves to the diaphragm and intercostal muscles. This neural activity is triggered by the medullary inspiratory neurons.

II. The most important inputs to the medullary inspiratory neurons for the involuntary control of minute ventilation are from the peripheral chemoreceptors—the carotid and aortic bodies—and the central chemoreceptors.

III. Ventilation is reflexly stimulated, via the peripheral chemoreceptors, by a decrease in arterial P_{O_2}, but only when the decrease is large.

IV. Ventilation is reflexly stimulated, via both the peripheral and central chemoreceptors, when the arterial P_{CO_2} goes up even a slight amount. The stimulus for this reflex is not the increased P_{CO_2} itself, but the concomitant increased hydrogen-ion concentration in arterial blood and brain extracellular fluid.

V. Ventilation is also stimulated, mainly via the peripheral chemoreceptors, by an increase in arterial hydrogen-ion concentration resulting from causes other than an increase in P_{CO_2}. The result of this reflex is to restore hydrogen-ion concentration toward normal by lowering P_{CO_2}.

VI. Ventilation is reflexly inhibited by an increase in arterial P_{O_2} and by a decrease in arterial P_{CO_2} or hydrogen-ion concentration.

VII. During moderate exercise, ventilation increases in exact proportion to metabolism, but the signals causing this are not known. During very strenuous exercise, ventilation increases more than metabolism.

A. The proportional increases in ventilation and metabolism during moderate exercise cause the arterial P_{O_2}, P_{CO_2}, and hydrogen-ion concentration to remain unchanged.

B. Arterial hydrogen-ion concentration increases during very strenuous exercise because of increased lactic acid production. This accounts for some of the hyperventilation seen in that situation.

VIII. Ventilation is also controlled by reflexes originating in airway receptors, by painful and emotional stimuli, and by conscious intent.

HYPOXIA

I. Causes of hypoxic hypoxia are listed in Table 15-11.

II. During exposure to hypoxia, as at high altitude, oxygen supply to the tissues is maintained by the five responses listed in Table 15-12.

NONRESPIRATORY FUNCTIONS OF THE LUNGS

I. The lungs influence arterial blood concentrations of biologically active substances by removing some from systemic venous blood and adding others to systemic arterial blood.

II. The lungs also act as sieves that dissolve small clots formed in the tissues.

KEY TERMS

respiration (two definitions)	functional residual
respiratory system	capacity
pulmonary	atmospheric pressure
alveoli (alveolus)	alveolar pressure (P_{alv})
airways	intrapleural pressure (P_{ip})
inspiration	transpulmonary pressure
expiration	ventilation
pharynx	Boyle's law
larynx	lung compliance (C_L)
vocal cords	surface tension
trachea	surfactant
bronchi (bronchus)	lateral traction
bronchioles	tidal volume
conducting zone	expiratory reserve volume
respiratory zone	residual volume
type I alveolar cells	inspiratory reserve
type II alveolar cells	volume
thorax	vital capacity
diaphragm	minute ventilation
intercostal muscles	anatomic dead space
pleural sac	alveolar ventilation
pleura	alveolar dead space
intrapleural fluid	physiologic dead space

respiratory quotient (RQ)	2,3-diphosphoglycerate
Dalton's law	(DPG)
partial pressures	carbamino compounds
hypoventilation	carbonic anhydrase
hyperventilation	total blood carbon dioxide
deoxyhemoglobin (Hb)	medullary inspiratory
oxyhemoglobin (HbO$_2$)	neurons
percent hemoglobin	pulmonary stretch receptors
saturation	peripheral chemoreceptors
oxygen-carrying capacity	carotid bodies
oxygen-hemoglobin	aortic bodies
dissociation curve	central chemoreceptors

REVIEW QUESTIONS

1. List the functions of the respiratory system.

2. At rest, how many liters of air and blood flow through the lungs per minute?

3. Describe four functions of the conducting portion of the airways.

4. At functional residual capacity, in what directions are the lungs and chest wall tending to move? What prevents them from doing so?

5. What are normal values for intrapleural pressure, alveolar pressure, and transpulmonary pressure at the end of an unforced expiration?

6. Which respiration steps occur by diffusion and which by bulk flow?

7. State typical values for oxygen consumption, carbon dioxide production, and cardiac output at rest. How much oxygen (in milliliters per liter) is present in systemic venous and systemic arterial blood?

8. Write the equation relating air flow into or out of the lungs to atmospheric pressure, alveolar pressure, and airway resistance.

9. Describe the sequence of events that causes air to move into the lungs during inspiration and out of the lungs during expiration. Diagram the changes in intrapleural pressure and alveolar pressure.

10. What factors determine lung compliance? Which is most important?

11. How does surfactant increase lung compliance?

12. How is airway resistance influenced by air viscosity, airway length, and airway radii?

13. List the physical and chemical factors that alter airway resistance.

14. Contrast the causes of increased airway resistance in asthma, emphysema, and chronic bronchitis.

15. What distinguishes lung capacities, as a group, from lung volumes?

16. State the formula relating minute ventilation, tidal volume, and respiratory rate. Give representative values for each at rest.

17. State the formula for calculating alveolar ventilation. What is an average value for alveolar ventilation?

18. The partial pressure of a gas is dependent upon what two factors?

19. State the alveolar gas pressures for oxygen and carbon dioxide in a normal person at rest.

20. What factors determine alveolar gas pressures?

21. What is the mechanism of gas exchange between alveoli and pulmonary capillaries? In a normal person at rest, what are the gas pressures at the end of the pulmonary capillaries, relative to those in the alveoli?

22. Why does thickening of alveolar membranes impair oxygen movement but have little effect on carbon dioxide exchange?

23. What is the major result of ventilation-perfusion inequalities throughout the lungs? Describe one homeostatic response that minimizes mismatching.

24. What generates the diffusion gradients for oxygen and carbon dioxide in the tissues?

25. In what two forms is oxygen carried in the blood? What are the normal quantities (in milliliters per liter) in each form in arterial blood?

26. Draw an oxygen-hemoglobin dissociation curve. Put in the points that represent systemic venous and systemic arterial blood (ignore the rightward shift of the curve in systemic venous blood). What is the adaptive importance of the plateau?

27. Would breathing pure oxygen cause a large increase in oxygen carriage by the blood in a normal person? In a person with a low alveolar P_{O_2}?

28. Describe the effects of increased P_{CO_2}, H^+ concentration, and temperature on the oxygen-hemoglobin dissociation curve. How are these effects adaptive for oxygen unloading in the tissues?

29. Describe the effects of increased DPG on the oxygen-hemoglobin dissociation curve. Under what conditions does an increase in DPG occur?

30. Draw figures showing the reactions carbon dioxide undergoes entering the blood in the tissue capillaries and leaving the blood in the alveoli. What fractions are contributed by dissolved carbon dioxide, bicarbonate, and carbamino?

31. What happens to most of the hydrogen ions formed in the erythrocytes from carbonic acid? What happens to blood H^+ concentration as blood flows through tissue capillaries?

32. What are the effects of P_{O_2} on carbamino formation and H^+ binding by hemoglobin?

33. In what area of the brain does automatic control of rhythmical respirations reside?

34. Describe the function of the pulmonary stretch receptors.

35. What changes stimulate the peripheral chemoreceptors? The central chemoreceptors?

36. Why does moderate anemia or carbon monoxide exposure not stimulate the peripheral chemoreceptors?

37. Is respiratory control more sensitive to small changes in arterial P_{O_2} or in arterial P_{CO_2}?

38. Describe the pathways by which increased arterial P_{CO_2} stimulates ventilation. Which pathway is more important?

39. Describe the pathway by which a change in arterial H^+ concentration independent of altered carbon dioxide influences ventilation. What is the adaptive value of this reflex?

40. What happens to arterial P_{O_2}, P_{CO_2}, and H^+ concentration during moderate and severe exercise? List other factors that may stimulate ventilation during exercise?

41. List four general causes of hypoxic hypoxia.

42. Describe two general ways in which the lungs can alter the concentrations of substances other than oxygen, carbon dioxide, and H^+ in the arterial blood.

CLINICAL TERMS

cystic fibrosis	ventilation-perfusion
pneumothorax	inequality
respiratory-distress syndrome	shunt
of the newborn	respiratory acidosis
asthma	respiratory alkalosis
chronic obstructive	poliomyelitis
pulmonary disease	metabolic acidosis
emphysema	metabolic alkalosis
chronic bronchitis	hypoxia
Heimlich maneuver	hypoxic hypoxia
forced vital capacity (FVC)	hypoxemia
forced expiratory volume	anemic hypoxia
(FEV_1)	ischemic hypoxia
restrictive lung diseases	histotoxic hypoxia
hypoventilation	diffusion impairment
hyperventilation	hypercapnea
diffuse interstitial fibrosis	mountain sickness

THOUGHT QUESTIONS

1. At the end of a normal expiration, a person's FRC is 2 L, his alveolar pressure is 0 mmHg, and his intrapleural pressure is −4 mmHg. He then inhales 800 ml, and at the end of inspiration the alveolar pressure is 0 mmHg and the intrapleural pressure is −8 mmHg. Calculate this person's lung compliance.

2. A patient has an inability to produce surfactant. In order to inhale a normal tidal volume, will her intrapleural pressure have to be more or less subatmospheric during inspiration, relative to a normal person?

3. A patient is being artificially ventilated by a machine during surgery at a rate of 20 breaths/min and a tidal volume of 250 ml/breath. Assuming a normal anatomic dead space of 150 ml, is this patient receiving an adequate alveolar ventilation?

4. Why must a person floating on the surface of the water and breathing through a snorkel increase his tidal volume and/or breathing frequency if alveolar ventilation is to remain normal?

5. A normal person breathing room air voluntarily increases her alveolar ventilation twofold and continues to do so until new steady-state alveolar gas pressures for oxygen and carbon dioxide are reached. Are the new values higher or lower than normal?

6. A person has an alveolar P_{O_2} of 105 mmHg and an arterial P_{O_2} of 80 mmHg. Could hypoventilation, say, due to respiratory muscle weakness, produce these values?

7. A person's alveolar membranes have become thickened enough to moderately decrease the rate at which gases diffuse across them at any given partial pressure differences. Will this person necessarily have a low arterial P_{O_2} at rest? During exercise?

8. A person is breathing 100 percent oxygen. How much will the oxygen content (in milliliters per liter of blood) of the arterial blood increase compared to when the person is breathing room air?

9. Which of the following have higher values in systemic venous blood than in systemic arterial blood: plasma P_{CO_2}, erythrocyte P_{CO_2}, plasma bicarbonate concentration, erythrocyte bicarbonate concentration, plasma hydrogen-ion concentration, erythrocyte hydrogen-ion concentration, erythrocyte carbamino concentration, erythrocyte chloride concentration, plasma chloride concentration?

10. If the spinal cord were severed where it joins the brainstem, what would happen to respiration?

11. The peripheral chemoreceptors are denervated in an experimental animal, and the animal then breathes a gas mixture containing 10 percent oxygen. What changes occur in the animal's ventilation? What changes occur when this denervated animal is given a mixture of air containing 21 percent oxygen and 5 percent carbon dioxide to breathe?

12. Patients with severe uncontrolled diabetes mellitus produce large quantities of certain organic acids. Can you predict the ventilation pattern in these patients and whether their arterial P_{O_2} and P_{CO_2} increase or decrease?

C H A P T E R

16

THE KIDNEYS AND REGULATION OF WATER AND INORGANIC IONS

This chapter deals with how the water and inorganic-ion composition of the internal environment are homeostatically regulated. The kidneys play the central role in these processes, but other organs participate too, for example, bone in the regulation of calcium. Most people assume that the kidneys' sole job is to eliminate wastes and poisons from the body, but that is only one of their tasks. Indeed, their prime function is to balance the body's water and inorganic ions so as to maintain stable concentrations of these substances in the extracellular fluid. Altering urinary excretion is the means to this balancing function.

Regulation of the total-body balance of any substance can be studied in terms of the balance concept described in Chapter 7. Theoretically, a substance can appear in the body either as a result of ingestion or as a product of metabolism. On the loss side, a substance can be excreted from the body or can be metabolized. Therefore, if the quantity of any substance in the body is to be maintained at a nearly constant level over a period of time, the total amounts ingested and produced must equal the total amounts excreted and metabolized.

Reflexes that alter excretion, specifically excretion via the urine, constitute the major mechanisms that regulate the body balances of water and many of the inorganic ions determining the properties of the extracellular fluid. The extracellular concentrations of these ions are given in Chapter 6, Table 6-1. We will first describe how the kidneys work in general and then apply this information to how they process specific substances—sodium, water, potassium, and so on—and participate in reflexes that regulate these substances. It should be noted, however, that the kidneys are not important regulators of *all* inorganic substances. In particular, the body balances of many of the trace elements, such as zinc and iron, are regulated mainly by control of gastrointestinal absorption of the element or by control of its excretion in the bile by the liver, as described in Chapter 17.

FUNCTIONS OF THE KIDNEYS

The kidneys process blood by removing substances from it and, in a few cases, by adding substances to it. In so doing they perform a variety of functions, as summarized in Table 16-1. The major function is to regulate the water content, mineral composition, and acidity of the body by excreting each substance in an amount adequate to achieve total-body balance and maintain normal concentrations in the extracellular fluid.

A second renal (the adjective denoting kidney) function is the excretion of metabolic **waste products**, so termed because they serve no function. These include **urea** from protein; **uric acid** from nucleic acids; **creatinine** from muscle creatine; the end products of hemoglobin breakdown, which give urine much of its color; and many others.

A third renal function is the excretion, in the urine, of some foreign chemicals—drugs, pesticides, food additives, and so on—and their metabolites.

In addition to their excretory functions, the kidneys act as endocrine glands, secreting at least three hormones: erythropoietin (Chapter 14), renin, and the active form of vitamin D. These last two hormones are discussed in this chapter. (To avoid confusion it should be noted that renin is part of a hormonal system called the renin-angiotensin system; renin functions, as we shall see, as an enzyme in this system, but it is customary to refer to it as a "hormone.")

Finally, during prolonged fasting, the kidneys synthesize glucose from amino acids and other precursors and release it into the blood; this is termed **gluconeogenesis.** The kidneys can supply as much glucose to the blood as the liver does at such times (Chapter 18).

STRUCTURE OF THE KIDNEYS AND URINARY SYSTEM

The kidneys are paired organs that lie in the back of the abdominal wall but not actually in the abdominal cavity. They are retroperitoneal, meaning they are just behind the lining—the peritoneum—of this cavity.

Each kidney is composed of approximately 1 million functional units bound together by small amounts of connective tissue, which contains blood vessels, nerves, and lymphatics. One such unit, or **nephron**, is shown in Figure 16-1. Each nephron consists of (1) an initial filtering component called the **renal corpuscle**, and (2) a **tubule** that extends out from the renal corpuscle. The renal corpuscle forms a filtrate from blood that is free of cells and proteins. This filtrate then leaves the renal corpuscle and enters the tubule, where it is processed before exiting the kidney as urine. Let us describe the anatomy of these two structures, beginning with the renal corpuscle.

Systemic arterial blood enters each kidney via a renal artery, which then divides into progressively smaller branches. Each of the smallest arteries gives off, at right angles to itself, a series of arterioles, the **afferent arterioles**. Each of the afferent arterioles conducts blood to a compact tuft of interconnected capillary loops called the **glomerulus** (plural *glomeruli*) (also termed the **glomerular capillaries** (Figure 16-2). The glomerulus protrudes into a balloon-like hollow capsule—**Bowman's capsule**. The combination of the glomerulus and Bowman's capsule constitutes the renal corpuscle.[1]

---

[1] Until recently, renal physiologists have not used the term "renal corpuscle" but rather have used "glomerulus" to denote the combination of capillary tuft and Bowman's capsule, and the term *glomerular capillaries* to refer to the tuft alone. However, a standard nomenclature introduced in 1988 has recommended the usage adopted in this text.

TABLE 16-1   FUNCTIONS OF THE KIDNEYS

1. Regulation of water and inorganic-ion balance
2. Removal of metabolic waste products from the blood and their excretion in the urine
3. Removal of foreign chemicals from the blood and their excretion in the urine
4. Secretion of hormones:
   a. Erythropoietin, which controls erythrocyte production (Chapter 14)
   b. Renin, which controls formation of angiotensin, which influences blood pressure and sodium balance (this chapter)
   c. 1,25-Dihydroxyvitamin D_3, which influences calcium balance (this chapter)
5. Gluconeogenesis

H2O saved here

CAPILLARIES SORROUND KIDNEYS

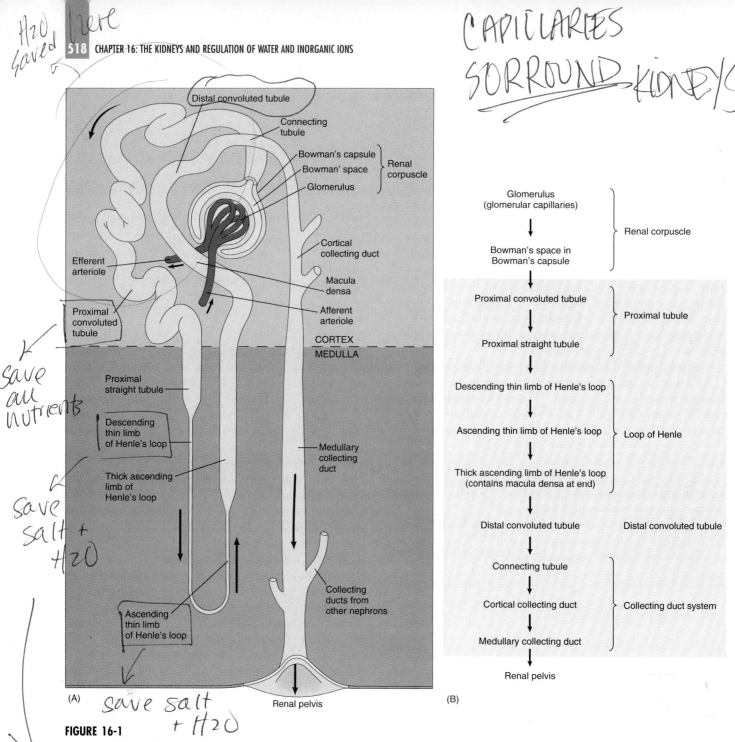

save all nutrients

save salt + H2O

save salt + H2O

(A)

Distal convoluted tubule
Connecting tubule
Bowman's capsule
Bowman' space
Glomerulus
} Renal corpuscle
Cortical collecting duct
Macula densa
Afferent arteriole
CORTEX
MEDULLA
Efferent arteriole
Proximal convoluted tubule
Proximal straight tubule
Descending thin limb of Henle's loop
Thick ascending limb of Henle's loop
Medullary collecting duct
Ascending thin limb of Henle's loop
Collecting ducts from other nephrons
Renal pelvis

(B)

Glomerulus (glomerular capillaries)
↓
Bowman's space in Bowman's capsule
} Renal corpuscle

Proximal convoluted tubule
↓
Proximal straight tubule
} Proximal tubule

Descending thin limb of Henle's loop
↓
Ascending thin limb of Henle's loop
↓
Thick ascending limb of Henle's loop (contains macula densa at end)
} Loop of Henle

Distal convoluted tubule | Distal convoluted tubule

Connecting tubule
↓
Cortical collecting duct
↓
Medullary collecting duct
} Collecting duct system

Renal pelvis

FIGURE 16-1

Basic structure of a nephron. (A) Anatomical organization. The macula densa is not a distinct segment but a plaque of cells in the ascending loop of Henle where the loop passes between the arterioles supplying its renal corpuscle of origin. The orange (outer) area is the cortex and the dark pink (inner) the medulla. (B) Consecutive segments of the nephron. All segments in the screened area are parts of the renal tubule; the terms enclosed in braces are the most commonly used combination terms for several consecutive segments.

One way of visualizing the relationships within the renal corpuscle is to imagine a loosely clenched fist—the glomerulus—punched into a balloon—Bowman's capsule. The part of Bowman's capsule in contact with the glomerulus becomes pushed inward but does not make contact with the opposite side of the capsule. Accordingly, a fluid-filled space—**Bowman's space**—exists within the capsule, and it is into this space that fluid filters from the glomerulus. Blood in the glomerulus is separated from the fluid in Bowman's space by a filtration barrier consisting of three layers: (1) the single-celled capillary endothelium, (2) the single-celled epithelial lining of Bowman's capsule,

[Handwritten annotations:]

epithelial cells not in continuum
↓
podocytes right next to cap. on and surround it

CAPILLARY TUFT

major portion of sieve = sm mw stuff thru; ↑ mw/proteins or RBC etc. kept out; go right back out

in
out

3 ~~mem~~ layers:
1. podocytes
2. basement memb
3. capillary

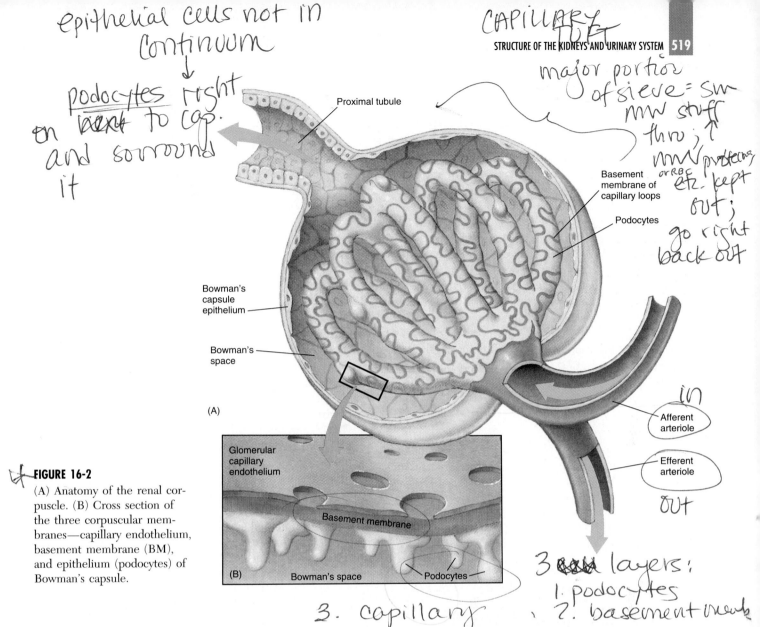

Proximal tubule

Basement membrane of capillary loops

Podocytes

Bowman's capsule epithelium

Bowman's space

(A)

Afferent arteriole

Efferent arteriole

Glomerular capillary endothelium

Basement membrane

(B) Bowman's space Podocytes

FIGURE 16-2

(A) Anatomy of the renal corpuscle. (B) Cross section of the three corpuscular membranes—capillary endothelium, basement membrane (BM), and epithelium (podocytes) of Bowman's capsule.

and (3) the noncellular proteinaceous layer of basement membrane between the endothelium and epithelium. The epithelial cells in this region are quite different from the simple flattened cells that line the rest of Bowman's capsule (the part of the "balloon" not in contact with the "fist") and are called **podocytes**. They have an octopus-like structure in that they possess a large number of extensions, or foot processes, which are embedded in the basement membrane. During filtration, fluid moves between these foot processes.

Extending out from Bowman's capsule is the nephron tubule, the lumen of which is continuous with Bowman's space. Throughout its course, the tubule is composed of a single layer of epithelial cells resting on a basement membrane. The epithelial cells differ in structure and function along the tubule's length, and 10 to 12 distinct segments are presently recognized (Figure 16-1). It is possible, however, to group two or more contiguous tubular segments when discussing function, and we shall follow this practice. Accordingly, the segment of the tubule that drains Bow-

man's capsule is the **proximal tubule** (comprising the proximal convoluted tubule and the proximal straight tubule of Figure 16-1). The next portion of the tubule is the **loop of Henle**, which is a sharp hairpin-like loop consisting of a **descending limb** coming from the proximal tubule and an **ascending limb** leading to the next tubular segment, the **distal convoluted tubule**. [In nephrons with long loops (Figure 16-1), the ascending limb is subdivided into an initial thin segment and a subsequent thick segment; in short loops there is no thin segment.] Fluid flows from the distal convoluted tubule into the **collecting duct system**, the first portion of which is the **connecting tubule**, followed by the **cortical collecting duct** and then the **medullary collecting duct**. The connecting tubule is so similar in function to the cortical collecting duct that, in subsequent discussions, we will not describe its function separately.

The many specific functions of these tubular segments will be described in the course of this chapter. We shall see that the proximal tubule is the major site for processing not only the organic constituents of the fluid filtered at the renal corpuscles but a large fraction of the water and inorganic constituents as well. The loop of Henle is involved in producing a concentrated urine. The collecting duct system is the "fine-tuning" portion of the tubule; it is the target for the major hormones that act on the kidneys, and in response to these hormones it makes the final adjustments to the urine.

From Bowman's capsule to the end of the connecting tubule, each of the nephrons is completely separate from the others. This separation ends when the tubules merge to form the cortical collecting ducts. The result of additional joining from this point on is that the completed urine drains into the kidney's central cavity, the **renal pelvis**, via only several hundred large medullary collecting ducts.

There are important regional differences in the kidney (Figures 16-1 and 16-3). The outer portion is the **renal cortex**, and the inner portion the **renal medulla**. The cortex contains all the renal corpuscles. The loops of

FIGURE 16-3

Section of a human kidney. For clarity, the nephron illustrated to show nephron orientation is not to scale—its outline would not be clearly visible without a microscope. The outer kidney, which contains all the renal corpuscles, is the cortex, and the inner kidney is the medulla. In the medulla, the loops of Henle and the collecting ducts run parallel to each other, giving the medulla a striped appearance. The medullary collecting ducts drain into the renal pelvis.

Henle extend from the cortex for varying distances down into the medulla, through which also course the medullary collecting ducts on their way to the renal pelvis. The nephrons, termed juxtamedullary nephrons, that originate in renal corpuscles near the cortex-medulla junction have long loops that extend the entire length of the medulla.

The renal pelvis is continuous with the **ureter**, the tube that passes from the kidney to the **urinary bladder**, where urine is temporarily stored. During urination urine is eliminated from the bladder via the **urethra**, the tube leading from the bladder to the external world (Figure 16-4).

To return to the kidney blood vessels: The capillaries of each glomerulus do not lead directly to a vein. Instead, they recombine to form another arteriole, the **efferent arteriole**, through which blood leaves the glomerulus. In the great majority of cases, each efferent arteriole soon divides into a second set of capillaries, the **peritubular capillaries**, which branch profusely to form a network surrounding all portions of the tubule in the cortex. The peritubular capillaries then eventually rejoin to form the veins by which blood leaves the kidney. In contrast, the blood from some efferent arterioles (those from renal corpuscles in the innermost portion of the cortex) flows into capillary-like vessels, termed the **vasa recta**, which do not supply blood to cortical structures but instead enter and supply the medulla.

One additional anatomical detail involving both the tubule and the arterioles must be mentioned. Near its end, the ascending limb of the loop of Henle passes between and contacts the afferent and efferent arterioles of its glomerulus (Figure 16-1). At this point there is a plaque of cells in the ascending limb called the **macula densa**. In the region of contact, the wall of the afferent arteriole contains secretory cells known as **juxtaglomerular (JG) cells** (also termed granular cells). The combination of macula densa and juxtaglomerular cells is known as the **juxtaglomerular apparatus (JGA)** (this term should be distinguished from the juxtaglomerular *cells* defined in the previous sentence) (Figure 16-5). The juxtaglomerular cells secrete the hormone renin; the control of this process and the participation of the macula densa in it will be described later.

BASIC RENAL PROCESSES

Urine formation begins with **glomerular filtration**, the bulk flow of protein-free plasma from the glomerular capillaries through the combined membranes of the renal corpuscle—capillary endothelium, basement membrane, and epithelial cells (podocytes) of Bowman's

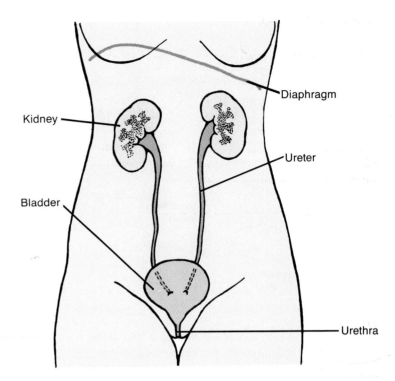

FIGURE 16-4

Urinary system in a woman. The urine, formed by the kidneys, flows from the kidneys through the ureters into the bladder, from which it is eliminated via the urethra. In the male, the urethra passes through the penis (Chapter 19).

capsule—and into Bowman's space. This fluid, now called the **glomerular filtrate**, contains all the substances, except protein, present in plasma and in virtually the same concentrations they have in plasma.

The filtrate contains almost no protein because the corpuscular membranes (specifically the basement mem-

FIGURE 16-5

Anatomy of the juxtaglomerular apparatus. The juxtaglomerular cells are specialized cells in the wall of the afferent arteriole and secrete the hormone renin. The macula densa is a group of cells located near the end of the thick ascending limb of Henle's loop as this segment passes between the arterioles supplying its renal corpuscle of origin.

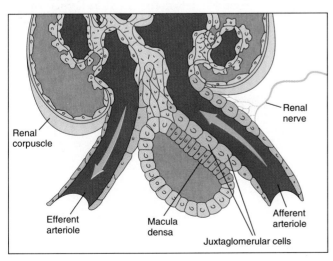

brane and podocytes) restrict the movement of such high-molecular-weight substances. Size is not the only reason for protein restriction; the filtration channels in the corpuscular membranes are negatively charged and so oppose the movement of plasma proteins, which are also negatively charged. In addition, the corpuscular membranes normally completely prevent any movement of blood cells from the glomerulus to Bowman's space.

The urine that eventually enters the renal pelvis is quite different from the glomerular filtrate because, as the filtrate flows from Bowman's space through the tubule, its composition is altered. This change occurs by two processes, tubular reabsorption and tubular secretion (Figure 16-6). The tubule is intimately associated with the peritubular capillary network, a relationship that permits transfer of materials between peritubular blood and the lumen of the tubule. When the direction of transfer is from tubular lumen to peritubular capillary plasma, the process is called **tubular reabsorption**, or simply reabsorption. Movement in the opposite direction, that is, from peritubular plasma to tubular lumen, is called **tubular secretion**, or simply secretion.

"Tubular reabsorption" and "tubular secretion" denote only the direction of the transfer, not the mechanism, which is diffusion for some substances and mediated transport for others. In the latter case the transport processes are in the plasma membranes of the tubular epithelial cells, and this explains the common use of the phrases "the tubule secretes" and "the tubule reabsorbs."

To summarize: *The amount of any substance excreted in*

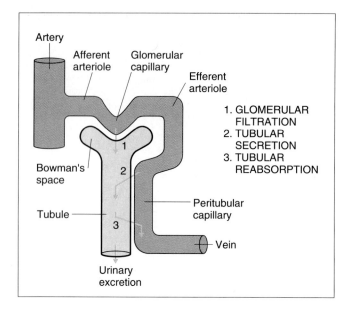

FIGURE 16-6

The three basic components of renal function. This figure is to illustrate only the directions of reabsorption and secretion, not specific sites or order of occurrence. Depending on the particular substance, reabsorption and secretion can occur at various sites along the tubule.

the urine is equal to the amount filtered plus the amount secreted minus the amount reabsorbed. Not all these processes apply to any given substance. To emphasize general principles, the renal handling of three hypothetical substances is illustrated in Figure 16-7. Approximately 20 percent of the plasma that enters the glomerular capillaries is filtered into Bowman's space. This filtrate, which contains X, Y, and Z in the same concentrations as in the plasma remaining in the capillaries, enters the proximal tubule and begins its flow through the rest of the tubule. Simultaneously, the remaining 80 percent of the plasma, with its X, Y, and Z, leaves the glomerular capillaries via the efferent arteriole and enters the peritubular capillaries.

The tubule can secrete 100 percent of the peritubular-capillary X into the tubular lumen but cannot reabsorb X. Thus, by the combination of filtration and tubular secretion, all the plasma that originally entered the renal artery loses all of its substance X, which leaves the body via the urine.

The tubule can reabsorb but not secrete Y and Z. The amount of Y reabsorption is small, so that much of the filtered material is not reabsorbed and escapes from the body. But for Z the reabsorptive mechanism is so powerful that all the filtered Z is transported back into the plasma. Therefore, no Z is lost from the body. Hence, for Z the processes of filtration and reabsorption have canceled each other out, and the net result is as though Z had never entered the kidney.

For each substance in plasma, a particular combination of filtration, tubular reabsorption, and tubular secretion applies. The critical point is that, for many substances, the rates at which the processes proceed are subject to physiological control. What would be the effect, for example, if the Y-filtration rate were increased by some physiological mechanism or its reabsorption rate decreased? Either change would mean that more Y would be lost from the body via the urine. By triggering such changes in filtration, reabsorption, or secretion whenever the plasma concentration of a substance changes from normal, homeostatic mechanisms can regulate the substance's plasma concentration.

FIGURE 16-7

Renal handling of three hypothetical substances X, Y, and Z. X is filtered and secreted but not reabsorbed. Y is filtered, and a fraction is then reabsorbed. Z is filtered and is completely reabsorbed.

Glomerular Filtration

As stated above, the glomerular filtrate, that is, the fluid in Bowman's space, is essentially protein-free and contains all other substances present in plasma in virtually the same concentrations as in plasma. The only exceptions to the last part of this generalization are certain low-molecular-weight substances that would otherwise be filterable but are bound to proteins and therefore are not filtered. For example, half of the plasma calcium and virtually all of the plasma fatty acids are bound to protein.

Forces Involved in Filtration. Glomerular filtration, like filtration across any capillary, is a bulk-flow process. As described in Chapter 14, capillary filtration is determined by opposing forces: The hydrostatic pressure difference across the capillary wall favors filtration, while the protein concentration difference across the wall creates an osmotic force that opposes filtration. This also applies to the glomerular capillaries, as summarized in Figure 16-8.

The pressure of the blood in the glomerular capillaries averages 60 mmHg.[2] This is higher than in other capillaries of the body because the nephron afferent arterioles, having relatively large diameters, offer less resistance than most arterioles, and so more of the arterial pressure is transmitted to the capillaries. This glomerular capillary hydrostatic pressure is a force favoring filtration.

The fluid in Bowman's space exerts a hydrostatic pressure of 15 mmHg, and this opposes filtration into the space. A second opposing force results from the presence of protein in the glomerular capillary plasma and its virtual absence in Bowman's space. This unequal distribution of protein (similar to that across other capillaries in the body) causes the water concentration of the plasma to be less than that of the fluid in Bowman's space. This difference in water concentration favors an osmotic flow of fluid—water plus all the low-molecular-weight solutes—from Bowman's space into the glomerular capillary, a flow equivalent to that produced by a pressure difference of 27 mmHg.

Thus, as can be seen from Figure 16-8, the **net glomerular filtration pressure**, that is, the algebraic sum of the three relevant forces, is approximately 18 mmHg. This pressure initiates urine formation by forcing an essentially protein-free filtrate of plasma out of the glomeruli and into Bowman's space and thence down the tubule into the renal pelvis.

Rate of Glomerular Filtration. The volume of fluid filtered from the glomeruli into Bowman's space per unit time is known as the **glomerular filtration rate** (**GFR**). The glomerular capillaries are so much more permeable to

---

[2]Glomerular capillary pressure cannot be directly measured in humans, and this figure is the best educated guess from work on experimental animals.

Forces	mmHg
Favoring filtration:	
Glomerular capillary blood pressure (P_{GC})	60
Opposing filtration:	
Fluid pressure in Bowman's space (P_{BS})	15
Osmotic force (due to protein in plasma) (π_{GC})	27
Net glomerular filtration pressure	18

FIGURE 16-8

Forces involved in glomerular filtration. The symbol π denotes an osmotic force due to differences in solute and hence water concentration. The difference in solute concentration is due solely to the presence of protein in plasma but not in Bowman's space, since the filtrate is essentially protein-free plasma. The rate at which fluid is filtered—the glomerular filtration rate—averages 180 L/day.

fluid than, say, a muscle or skin capillary, that the net filtration pressure of 18 mmHg causes massive filtration. In a 70-kg person, the volume filtered into Bowman's space averages 180 L/day (125 ml/min)! Contrast this figure with the net filtration of fluid across all the other capillaries in the body—4 L/day, as described in Chapter 14.

There are several implications of this remarkable filtration rate. First, in order to form such a huge volume of filtrate, the kidneys must receive a large share of the cardiac output. Each moment the kidneys receive about 20 to 25 percent of the blood pumped by the left ventricle even though the kidneys account for only about 1 percent of body weight. Second, when we recall that the total volume of plasma in the cardiovascular system is approximately 3 L, it follows that the entire plasma volume is filtered by the kidneys about 60 times a day. This opportunity to process such huge volumes of plasma enables the kidneys to regulate the constituents of the internal environment rapidly and to excrete large quantities of waste products.

It is possible to measure the total amount of any nonprotein substance (assuming also that the substance is not bound to protein) filtered into Bowman's space by multiplying the GFR by the plasma concentration of the substance. This amount is called the **filtered load** of the substance. For example, if the GFR is 180 L/day and plasma glucose concentration is 1 g/L, than 180 L/day × 1 g/L = 180 g/day is the filtered load of glucose.

Once we know the filtered load of the substance we can compare it to the amount of the substance excreted and tell whether the substance undergoes net tubular reabsorption or net secretion. Whenever the quantity of a substance excreted in the urine is less than the filtered load, tubular reabsorption must have occurred. Conversely, if the amount excreted in the urine is greater than the filtered load, tubular secretion must have occurred. Such measurements have played an important role in determining which substances undergo tubular reabsorption or tubular secretion.

Tubular Reabsorption

Many filterable plasma components are either absent from the urine or present in smaller quantities than were filtered at the renal corpuscle. This fact alone is sufficient to prove that these substances undergo tubular reabsorption. An idea of the magnitude and importance of these reabsorptive mechanisms can be gained from Table 16-2, which summarizes data for a few plasma components that that undergo filtration and reabsorption.

The values in Table 16-2 are typical for a normal person on an average diet. There are at least three important conclusions to be drawn from this table: (1) The filtered loads are enormous, generally larger than the amount of the substances in the body. For example, the body contains about 40 L of water, but the volume of water filtered each day is, as we have seen, 180 L. (2) Reabsorption of waste products is relatively incomplete, for example, only 44 percent in the case of urea, so that large fractions of their filtered loads are excreted in the urine. (3) Reabsorption of most useful plasma components, for example, water, inorganic ions, and organic nutrients, is relatively com-

plete, so that the amounts excreted in the urine represent very small fractions of the filtered loads.

In this last regard an important distinction should be made between reabsorptive processes that can be controlled physiologically and those that cannot. The reabsorption rates of most organic nutrients, for example, glucose, are always very high and are not physiologically regulated, and so the filtered loads of these substances are normally completely reabsorbed, none appearing in the urine. For these substances, like substance Z in our earlier example, it is as though the kidneys do not exist since the kidneys do not eliminate them from the body at all. Therefore, the kidneys do not help *regulate* the plasma concentrations of these organic nutrients, that is, minimize changes from their normal plasma levels. Rather, the kidneys merely maintain whatever plasma concentrations already exist, generally the result of hormonal regulation of nutrient metabolism (Chapter 18).

In contrast, the reabsorptive rates for water and many ions, although also very high, are regulatable. Consider what happens when a person drinks a lot of water. Within 1 to 2 h, all the excess water has been excreted in the urine, chiefly, as we shall see, as the result of decreased renal tubular reabsorption of water, and water balance is restored to normal. The critical point is that the rates at which water and the inorganic ions are reabsorbed, and therefore the rates at which they are excreted, are subject to physiological control.

Tubular reabsorption is a process fundamentally different from glomerular filtration. The latter occurs completely by bulk flow, with water and all low-molecular-weight solutes moving together. In contrast, there is relatively little bulk flow across the epithelial cells of the tubule from lumen to interstitial fluid, so that reabsorption is not by mass movement. Rather, the reabsorption of some substances is by diffusion, while that of others requires more-or-less distinct mediated transport systems. The phrase "more-or-less distinct" denotes the fact that, as we shall see, the reabsorption of different substances is often linked.

Reference to Figure 16-9 highlights the fact that there are two potential routes for reabsorptive movement from lumen to interstitium. The first is by diffusion *between* tubular cells, that is, across the tight junctions connecting the cells. The second route is *through* the cells: The reabsorbed substance must first cross the **luminal membrane** (separating the lumen from the cell interior), then diffuse through the cytosol of the cell, and finally cross the **basolateral membrane** (which begins at the tight junctions and constitutes the plasma membrane of the sides and base of the cell). This latter route is termed *transcellular* epithelial transport, and its mechanisms were described in Chapter 6 and should be reviewed at this time. Suffice it to point out here that if the movement across

TABLE 16-2	AVERAGE VALUES FOR SEVERAL COMPONENTS THAT UNDERGO FILTRATION AND REABSORPTION		
Substance	Amount filtered per day	Amount excreted per day	Percent reabsorbed
Water, L	180	1.8	99.0
Sodium, g	630	3.2	99.5
Glucose, g	180	0	100
Urea, g	54	30	44

FIGURE 16-9
Diagrammatic representation of tubular epithelium. The basement membrane of the tubule is a homogeneous proteinaceous structure that plays no significant role in transport and will not be shown in subsequent figures illustrating transport in this chapter.

either the luminal membrane or the basolateral membrane is active, then the entire process is termed active.

Regardless of which route the reabsorbed substance takes to reach the interstitial fluid, movement from this fluid into the peritubular capillaries is by a combination of diffusion and bulk flow.[3]

T_m-Limited Transport Mechanisms. Many of the active reabsorptive systems in the renal tubule have a limit, termed a **transport maximum (T_m)**, to the amounts of material they can transport per unit time, because the membrane proteins responsible for the transport become saturated. An important example is the active transport process for glucose, located in the proximal tubule. As noted earlier, normal persons do not excrete glucose in their urine because all filtered glucose is reabsorbed. Indeed, even by eating an extremely carbohydrate-rich meal, normal persons cannot raise their plasma glucose concentrations high enough to exceed the renal glucose T_m. In contrast, in people with diabetes mellitus, a disease in which the hormonal control of the plasma glucose concentration is defective (Chapter 18), the plasma glucose concentration and thus the filtered load become so high that

the glucose T_m is exceeded and glucose does appear in the urine (glucosuria). In other words, the kidneys' ability to reabsorb glucose is perfectly normal in diabetes, but the tubules cannot reabsorb the markedly increased filtered load.

The pattern described for glucose is also true for a large number of other organic nutrients. For example, most amino acids and water-soluble vitamins are filtered in large amounts each day, but almost all these filtered molecules are reabsorbed by the proximal tubule. If for some reason the plasma concentration becomes high enough, however, reabsorption of the filtered load will not be as complete, and the substance will appear in larger amounts in the urine. Thus, persons ingesting very large quantities of vitamin C manifest progressive increases in their plasma concentrations of vitamin C until the filtered load exceeds the tubular reabsorptive T_m for this substance, and any additional ingested vitamin C is excreted in the urine.

Reabsorption by Diffusion. Urea reabsorption provides an example of passive reabsorption by diffusion. An analysis of urea concentrations in the tubule will help elucidate the mechanism. Because the corpuscular membranes are freely filterable to urea, the urea concentration in the fluid within Bowman's space is the same as that in the plasma. Then, as this fluid flows through the proximal tubule, water reabsorption occurs (by mechanisms to be described later), increasing the concentrations of tubular-fluid solutes that, like urea, are not being reabsorbed by active transport. The result is that the tubular-fluid urea concentration becomes greater than the peritubular-plasma urea concentration. Accordingly, urea diffuses down this concentration gradient from tubular lumen to peritubular capillary. Urea reabsorption is thus a passive process dependent upon the reabsorption of water. As noted earlier, this process causes reabsorption of about 50 percent of the filtered urea.[4]

Reabsorption by diffusion is also of considerable importance for many foreign organic chemicals. The plasma membranes of the tubular epithelium, like all plasma membranes, are primarily lipid, and so lipid-soluble substances can penetrate them fairly readily. Recall from Chapter 6 that one of the major determinants of lipid solubility is the polarity of a molecule; the less polar, the more lipid-soluble. Many drugs and environmental pollutants (DDT, for example) are nonpolar and therefore highly lipid-soluble. This makes their excretion from the body via the urine difficult since they are filtered at the renal cor-

---

[3] Bulk flow occurs from interstitial fluid into peritubular capillaries because the hydrostatic pressure in the capillary is low and the protein concentration is high. This combination produces a net filtration pressure favoring bulk flow into the capillary.

[4] You might logically ask why there should be *any* reabsorption of a waste product like urea. Put another way, is there any adaptive value in not excreting the entire filtered load of this substance? The answer is probably no, and the partial reabsorption simply reflects an inevitable consequence of the easy diffusibility of urea through plasma membranes.

puscle but then reabsorbed by diffusion as water reabsorption causes their intratubular concentrations to increase. The body does have a way of making these substances more excretable, however. The liver transforms them to more polar metabolites, which, because of their reduced lipid solubility, diffuse across the tubular wall poorly and are therefore not reabsorbed but rather excreted.

Tubular Secretion

Tubular secretory processes, by which substances move from peritubular capillaries into the tubular lumen, constitute a second pathway into the tubule, the first being glomerular filtration. The most important substances secreted by the tubules are hydrogen ions and potassium, and the mechanisms by which they are secreted are described in the sections on these substances.

The kidney is also able to secrete a large number of organic ions, some of which are normally occurring metabolites such as choline and creatinine, while others are foreign chemicals, penicillin, for example.

Metabolism by the Tubules

Although renal physiologists have traditionally listed glomerular filtration, tubular reabsorption, and tubular secretion as the three basic renal processes, a fourth process—metabolism by the cells of the tubule—is of considerable importance for many substances. The cells of the renal tubules are able to synthesize certain substances, notably ammonium, which are then added to the luminal fluid and excreted. Why the cells would make something just to have it excreted will be made clear when we discuss the role of ammonium in the regulation of plasma hydrogen-ion concentration. The cells are also capable of catabolizing certain organic substances, peptides, for example, taken up from either the tubular lumen or peritubular capillaries. Catabolism eliminates these substances from the body as surely as if they had been excreted in the urine.

The Concept of Renal Clearance

A useful way of quantitating renal function is in terms of clearance. The renal **clearance** of any substance is the *volume of plasma* from which that substance is completely cleared by the kidneys per unit time. Every substance has its own distinct clearance value, but the units are always in volume of plasma per unit time. The basic clearance formula for any substance S is

$$\text{Clearance of S} = \frac{\text{mass of S excreted per unit time}}{\text{plasma concentration of S}}$$

Since the mass of S excreted per unit time is equal to the urine concentration of S multiplied by the urine volume during that time, the formula becomes

$$C_S = \frac{U_S V}{P_S}$$

where C_S = clearance of S
$\quad U_S$ = urine concentration of S
$\quad V$ = urine volume per unit time
$\quad P_S$ = plasma concentration of S

Let us take the particularly important example of a polysaccharide named **inulin** (not insulin). This substance is not normally present in the body, but we will administer it intravenously to a person at a rate sufficient to maintain plasma concentration constant at 4 mg/L. Urine collected over a 1-h period has a volume of 0.1 L and an inulin concentration of 300 mg/L; thus, inulin excretion equals 0.1 L/h × 300 mg/L, or 30 mg/h. From a variety of experiments it is known that inulin is filterable at the renal corpuscle but is not reabsorbed, secreted, or metabolized by the tubule. Therefore, the mass of inulin *excreted* in our experiment—30 mg/h—must be equal to the mass *filtered* over that same time period (Figure 16-10). How much plasma had to be completely cleared of its inulin to supply this 30 mg/h? We simply divide 30 mg/h by the plasma concentration, 4 mg/L, to obtain the volume cleared—7.5 L/h. In other words, we are calculating the inulin clearance (C_{In}) from the measured urine volume per time (V), urine inulin concentration (U_{In}), and plasma inulin concentration (P_{In}):

$$C_{In} = \frac{U_{In} V}{P_{In}}$$

$$= \frac{300 \text{ mg/L} \times 0.1 \text{ L/h}}{4 \text{ mg/L}}$$

$$= 7.5 \text{ L/h}$$

Now for the crucial point: Since inulin is filterable at the renal corpuscle but is not reabsorbed, secreted, or metabolized by the tubule, its clearance must equal the volume of plasma originally filtered; that is, C_{In} is equal to GFR.

It is important to realize that the clearance of *any* substance handled by the kidneys' in the same way as inulin—filtered, but not reabsorbed, secreted, or metabolized—would equal the GFR. Unfortunately, there are no substances normally present in the plasma that meet these criteria. Because inulin must be administered, it is usually used as a research tool rather than a routine clinical measurement. For clinical purposes, the **creatinine clearance** (C_{Cr}) is commonly used to *approximate* the GFR as

FIGURE 16-10

Example of renal handling of inulin, a substance that is filtered by the renal corpuscles, but is neither reabsorbed nor secreted by the tubule. Therefore, the mass of inulin excreted per unit time is equal to the mass filtered during the same time period, and as explained in the text, the clearance of inulin is equal to the glomerular filtration rate.

follows. The waste product creatinine produced by muscle is filtered at the renal corpuscle and does not undergo reabsorption. It does undergo a small amount of secretion, however, so that some plasma is cleared of its creatinine by secretion. Accordingly, the C_{Cr} overestimates the GFR but is close enough to be highly useful.

The leads to an important generalization: When the clearance of any substance is greater than the GFR, as measured by the inulin clearance, that substance must undergo tubular secretion. Look back now at our hypothetical substance X (page 522): X is filtered, and all the X that escapes filtration is secreted; no X is reabsorbed. Accordingly, all the plasma that enters the kidney per unit time is cleared of its X, and the clearance of X is therefore a measure of renal plasma flow. A substance that is handled like X is the organic anion para-aminohippurate (PAH), which is used for this purpose (unfortunately, like inulin, it must be administered).

One more example is needed: What is the clearance of glucose (C_G) in normal people? The answer is 0 ml/min. As stated earlier, no glucose is normally excreted in the urine; accordingly, the numerator of the clearance equation is 0 and C_G is 0. This leads to another important generalization: When the clearance of a filterable substance is less than the GFR, as measured by the inulin clearance, that substance must undergo reabsorption. For a substance that undergoes only partial reabsorption, so-

dium, for example, the clearance value will not be zero but will still be less than the inulin clearance.

MICTURITION

Urine flow through the ureters to the bladder is propelled by contractions of the ureter-wall smooth muscle. The urine is stored in the bladder and intermittently ejected during urination, termed **micturition**.

The bladder is a balloon-like chamber with walls of smooth muscle collectively termed the **detrusor muscle**, the contraction of which squeezes on the urine in the lumen to produce urination. That part of the detrusor muscle at the base (or "neck") of the bladder where the urethra begins functions as a sphincter—the **internal urethral sphincter**. Because of its anatomical orienta-

FIGURE 16-11

Micturition reflex. As the bladder fills with urine, stimulation of the stretch receptors in the bladder walls causes reflex stimulation of the parasympathetic nerves to the bladder and inhibition of the motor nerves to the external urethral sphincter. The result is bladder contraction and sphincter relaxation. Not shown in the figure is the fact that ascending pathways triggered by the stretch receptors act upon higher brain-centers to give the awareness of bladder fullness and the desire to urinate. Descending input from these higher centers acts on the efferent neurons, as described in the text, to allow voluntary initiation or delay of micturition.

tion, when the detrusor muscle is *relaxed,* the sphincter is *closed;* when the detrusor muscle actively contracts, the outlet is pulled open by the changes in the muscle's shape. Beyond the outlet the urethra is surrounded by skeletal muscle—the **external urethral sphincter**, the contraction of which can prevent urination even when the detrusor muscle contracts strongly.

The basic micturition reflex is a local spinal reflex, which can be influenced by descending pathways from the brain (Figure 16-11). We describe first the isolated reflex as it exists in infancy or in persons with spinal-cord damage that eliminates the contribution of the descending pathways. The bladder wall contains stretch receptors whose afferent fibers enter the spinal cord and stimulate the parasympathetic nerves that supply and stimulate the detrusor muscle. When the bladder contains only small amounts of urine, its internal pressure is low, there is little stimulation of the bladder stretch receptors, and the parasympathetics are relatively quiescent. As the bladder fills with urine, the pressure within it increases and the stretch receptors are stimulated, thereby reflexly eliciting stimulation of the parasympathetic neurons and contractions of the detrusor muscle. When the bladder reaches a certain volume (300 to 400 ml), the reflexly induced contraction of the detrusor muscle becomes strong enough to pull open the internal urethral sphincter. Simultaneously, the afferent input from the stretch receptors inhibits, within the spinal cord, the motor neurons that tonically stimulate the external urethral sphincter to contract. Both sphincters are now open and the contraction of the detrusor muscle is able to produce urination.

Voluntary prevention of micturition, learned during childhood, operates in the following way. As the bladder distends, the input from the bladder stretch receptors, via ascending pathways to the brain, gives rise to a sense of bladder fullness and the urge to urinate. In response to this, urination can be voluntarily prevented via descending pathways that stimulate the motor nerves to the external urethral sphincter and simultaneously inhibit the parasympathetic nerves to the detrusor muscle.

In contrast, urination can be voluntarily initiated, regardless of the degree of bladder fullness, via the descending pathways.

SECTION A SUMMARY

FUNCTIONS AND STRUCTURES OF THE KIDNEYS AND URINARY SYSTEM

I. The kidneys regulate the water and ionic composition of the body, excrete waste products and foreign chemicals, and secrete three hormones—renin, 1,25-dihydroxyvitamin D_3, and erythropoietin. The first two functions are accomplished by continuous processing of the plasma.

II. Each nephron in the kidneys consists of a renal corpuscle and a tubule.

A. Each renal corpuscle comprises a capillary tuft, termed a glomerulus, and a Bowman's capsule, into which the tuft protrudes.

B. The tubule extends out from Bowman's capsule and is subdivided into many segments, which can be combined for reference purposes into four: proximal tubule, loop of Henle, distal convoluted tubule, and collecting-duct system. Multiple tubules join at the level of the collecting ducts, which empty into the renal pelvis, from which urine flows through ureters to the bladder.

C. Each glomerulus is supplied by an afferent arteriole, and an efferent arteriole leaves the glomerulus to branch into peritubular capillaries, which supply the tubule.

BASIC RENAL PROCESSES

I. The three basic renal processes are glomerular filtration, tubular reabsorption, and tubular secretion. In addition, the kidneys synthesize and/or catabolize certain substances. The excretion of a substance is equal to the amount filtered plus the amount secreted minus the amount reabsorbed.

II. Urine formation begins with glomerular filtration—approximately 180 L/day—of essentially protein-free plasma into Bowman's capsule.

A. Glomerular filtrate contains all the plasma substances, other than protein and substances bound to protein, in virtually the same concentrations as in plasma.

B. Glomerular filtration is driven by the hydrostatic pressure in the glomerular capillaries and is opposed by both the hydrostatic pressure in Bowman's capsule and the osmotic force due to the proteins in the glomerular capillary plasma.

III. As the filtrate moves through the tubules, certain substances are reabsorbed into the peritubular capillaries.

A. Tubular reabsorption rates are generally very high for nutrients, ions, and water but are lower for waste products. Reabsorption may occur by mediated-transport mechanisms or by diffusion.

B. Many of the mediated-transport systems manifest transport maximums, so that when the filtered load of a substance exceeds the transport maximum, the substance appears in the urine.

C. Some substances to which the tubular epithelium is permeable are absorbed by diffusion because water reabsorption creates tubule-interstitium concentration gradients for them.

IV. Tubular secretion—movement from the peritubular capillaries into the tubules—is a pathway in addition to glomerular filtration for a substance to gain entry to the tubule.

V. The clearance of any substance can be calculated by dividing the mass of the substance excreted per unit time by the plasma concentration of the substance. GFR can be measured by means of the inulin clearance and estimated by means of the creatinine clearance.

MICTURITION

I. In the basic micturition reflex, bladder distention stimulates stretch receptors that trigger spinal reflexes leading to parasympathetically mediated contraction of the detrusor muscle and inhibition of the motor neurons to the external urethral sphincter.

II. Voluntary control is exerted via descending pathways to the parasympathetic nerves supplying the detrusor muscle and the motor nerves supplying the external urethral sphincter.

SECTION A KEY TERMS

waste products	tubule
urea	afferent arterioles
uric acid	glomerulus
creatinine	glomerular capillaries
gluconeogenesis	Bowman's capsule
nephron	Bowman's space
renal corpuscle	podocytes

proximal tubule	juxtaglomerular apparatus
loop of Henle	(JGA)
descending limb	glomerular filtration
ascending limb	glomerular filtrate
distal convoluted tubule	tubular reabsorption
collecting-duct system	tubular secretion
connecting tubule	net glomerular filtration
cortical collecting duct	pressure
medullary collecting duct	glomerular filtration rate
renal pelvis	(GFR)
renal cortex	filtered load
renal medulla	luminal membrane
ureter	basolateral membrane
urinary bladder	transport maximum (T_m)
urethra	clearance
efferent arteriole	inulin
peritubular capillaries	creatinine clearance
vasa recta	micturition
macula densa	detrusor muscle
juxtaglomerular (JG) cells	internal urethral sphincter
	external urethral sphincter

SECTION A REVIEW QUESTIONS

1. What are the functions of the kidneys?

2. What three hormones do the kidneys secrete?

3. Fluid flows through what sequence of structures from the glomerulus to the bladder? Blood flows through what structures from the renal artery to the renal vein?

4. What are the three basic renal processes that lead to the formation of urine?

5. How does the composition of the glomerular filtrate compare with that of plasma?

6. Describe the forces that determine the magnitude of the GFR. What is a normal value for GFR?

7. Contrast the mechanisms of reabsorption for glucose and urea. Which one shows a T_m?

8. Diagram the sequence of events leading to micturition in infants and in adults.

SECTION

REGULATION OF SODIUM, WATER, AND POTASSIUM BALANCE

TOTAL-BODY BALANCE OF SODIUM AND WATER

Table 16-3 summarizes total-body water balance. These are average values, which are subject to considerable normal variation. The two sources of body water are metabolically produced water, resulting largely from the oxidation of organic nutrients, and water ingested in liquids and so-called solid food (a rare steak is approximately 70 percent water). There are four sites from which water is lost to the external environment: skin, respiratory passageways, gastrointestinal tract, and urinary tract. Men-

TABLE 16-3 AVERAGE DAILY WATER GAIN AND LOSS IN ADULTS

Intake	
Drunk	1200 ml
In food	1000 ml
Metabolically produced	350 ml
Total	2550 ml
Output	
Insensible loss (skin and lungs)	900 ml
Sweat	50 ml
In feces	100 ml
Urine	1500 ml
Total	2550 ml

strual flow constitutes a fifth potential source of water loss in women. The loss of water by evaporation from the skin and the lining of respiratory passageways is a continuous process, often referred to as **insensible water loss**, because the person is unaware of its occurrence. Additional water can be made available for evaporation from the skin by the production of sweat. Normal gastrointestinal loss of water in feces is generally quite small but can be severe in diarrhea. Gastrointestinal loss can also be large in vomiting.

Table 16-4 is a summary of total-body balance for sodium chloride. The excretion of sodium and chloride via the skin and gastrointestinal tract is normally quite small but may increase markedly during severe sweating, vomiting, or diarrhea.

Hemorrhage can also result in loss of large quantities of both salt and water.

Under normal conditions, as can be seen from Tables 16-3 and 16-4, salt and water losses exactly equal salt and water gains, and no net change in body salt and water occurs. As we stated at the beginning of this chapter, this matching of losses and gains is primarily the result of regulation of urinary loss, which can be varied over an extremely wide range. For example, urinary water excretion can vary from approximately 0.4 L/day to 25 L/day, depending upon whether one is lost in the desert or participating in a beer-drinking contest. Similarly, some individuals ingest 20 to 25 g of sodium chloride per day, whereas a person on a low-salt diet may ingest only 50 mg. The normal kidney can readily alter its excretion of salt over this range to match loss with gain.

We will first present the basic renal processes—filtration and reabsorption—for sodium and water and then describe the homeostatic reflexes that influence these processes. The renal processing of chloride is usually coupled directly or indirectly to that of sodium, and so we shall have little more to say about chloride even though it is the most abundant anion in the extracellular fluid.

BASIC RENAL PROCESSES FOR SODIUM AND WATER

Being of low molecular weight and not bound to protein, both sodium and water freely filter from the glomerular capillaries into Bowman's space. They both undergo considerable reabsorption—normally more than 99 percent (Table 16-2)—but no secretion. Most renal energy utilization goes to accomplish this enormous reabsorptive task. The bulk of sodium and water reabsorption—about two-thirds—occurs in the proximal tubule, but the major hormonal controls of reabsorption are exerted on the collecting ducts. The mechanisms of sodium and water reabsorption can be summarized by two generalizations: (1) Sodium reabsorption is a primary active process occurring in all four major tubular segments—the proximal tubule, loop of Henle, distal convoluted tubule, and collecting duct; and (2) water reabsorption is by diffusion and is dependent upon sodium reabsorption.

Primary Active Sodium Reabsorption

The reabsorption of sodium and water occurs largely by the mechanisms of transcellular epithelial transport described in Chapter 6. The key feature throughout the tubule is the primary active transport of sodium, via basolateral-membrane Na,K-ATPase pumps, out of the cells and into the interstitial fluid (Figure 16-12). This active transport keeps the intracellular concentration of sodium low compared to the luminal concentration, and so sodium diffuses out of the lumen into the tubular epithelial cells. As summarized in Figures 16-12 and 16-13, the precise mechanism of this passive sodium movement across the luminal membrane varies from segment to segment of the tubule depending upon which channels and/or transporters are present in their luminal membranes.

Coupling of Water Reabsorption to Sodium Reabsorption

How does active sodium reabsorption lead to passive water reabsorption? The movement of sodium from the

TABLE 16-4 DAILY SODIUM CHLORIDE INTAKE AND LOSS

Intake	
Food	10.50 g
Output	
Sweat	0.25 g
Feces	0.25 g
Urine	10.00 g
Total	10.50 g

ASCENDING
LOOP OF HENLE

DISTAL CONVOLUTED TUBULE

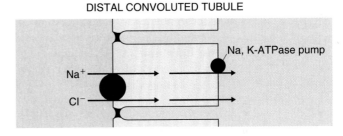

FIGURE 16-12

Mechanism of sodium reabsorption in the cortical collecting duct. The sizes of the letters for Na^+ and K^+ denote high and low concentrations of these ions. Na,K-ATPase pumps in the epithelial cell's basolateral membrane actively transport sodium out of the cell. This produces a low cytosolic sodium concentration, relative to that of the tubular lumen, and this concentration gradient causes the diffusion of Na^+ across the luminal membrane through sodium channels. (In addition to this concentration gradient favoring diffusion, there is an electrical gradient—not shown in the figure—because the cell interior is negative relative to the lumen.) Note that the K^+ pumped into the cell across the basolateral membrane diffuses into the tubular lumen through K^+ channels in the luminal membrane. Thus, as described later in the text, the *reabsorption* of sodium by the cortical collecting duct is associated with the *secretion* of potassium by this tubular segment.

FIGURE 16-13

Sodium reabsorption in tubular segments other than the cortical collecting duct. The essential points for these segments are: (1) Sodium movement across the basolateral membrane is, as in the cortical collecting duct (Figure 16-12), always via active Na,K-ATPase pumps; (2) the luminal entry step for sodium is always downhill (passive) but is via carrier-mediated transport systems rather than through channels, as is the case in the cortical collecting duct; (3) these luminal transporters simultaneously achieve *secondary active* cotransport of glucose, amino acids, potassium, and chloride into the cell or countertransport of hydrogen ion into the lumen. The cotransported substances then move passively (the mechanisms are not shown in the figure) across the basolateral membrane into the interstitial fluid and thence into peritubular capillaries. Thus, sodium reabsorption achieves the reabsorption of all these cotransported substances. This explains, for example, why the proximal tubule is the only site of glucose reabsorption—it is the only site that has the luminal-membrane Na/glucose cotransporter. The origin of the hydrogen ions countertransported with sodium is described later in the chapter.

tubular lumen to the interstitial fluid across the epithelial cells lowers the osmolarity, that is, *raises* the water concentration, of the luminal fluid (see Chapter 6 for a review of osmolarity and water concentration). It simultaneously raises the osmolarity, that is, *lowers* the water concentration, of the interstitial fluid adjacent to the epithelial cells. The difference in water concentration between lumen and interstitial fluid causes net diffusion of water from the lumen across the tubular cells' plasma membranes and/or tight junctions into the interstitial fluid. From there, water, sodium, and everything else in the interstitial fluid move together by bulk flow into peritubular capillaries as the final step in reabsorption (Figure 16-14).

Water movement across the tubular epithelium can occur, however, only if the epithelium is permeable to water. No matter how large its concentration gradient, water cannot cross an epithelium impermeable to it. Water permeability varies from tubular segment to segment. The water permeability of the proximal tubule is always very

FIGURE 16-14

Coupling of water and sodium reabsorption. (1) Reabsorption of sodium creates (2) a difference in osmolarity between lumen and interstitial fluid, which causes (3) the diffusion of water in the same direction either through the cell or across the tight junctions. (4) Movement of both solute and water from interstitial fluid into peritubular capillaries occurs by bulk flow.

high, and so water molecules are reabsorbed by this segment almost as rapidly as sodium ions. As a result, the proximal tubule always reabsorbs sodium and water in the same proportions.

We will describe the water permeability of the next tubular segments—the loop of Henle and distal convoluted tubule—later. Now for the really crucial point: The water permeability of the last portions of the tubules—the collecting ducts—can be high or low because it is subject to physiological control, the only tubular segments under such control.

The major determinant of this controlled permeability, and hence of water reabsorption in the collecting ducts, is a peptide hormone secreted by the posterior pituitary and known as **antidiuretic hormone (ADH)** or **vasopressin.**[5] ADH stimulates production of cyclic AMP in the epithelial cells of the collecting ducts, and this second messenger then induces, by a sequence of events, the insertion into the luminal membrane of proteins that function as water channels. Accordingly, in the presence of a high plasma concentration of ADH, the water permeability of the collecting ducts is very great, water reabsorption is maximal, and the final urine volume is small—less than 1 percent of the filtered water. In the absence of ADH, the water permeability of the collecting ducts is very low, and very little water is reabsorbed from these sites.[6] Therefore, a large volume of water remains behind in the tubule to be excreted in the urine, which is hypoosmotic, that is, has an osmolarity much lower than that of plasma. This increased urine excretion resulting from low

ADH is termed **water diuresis** ("**diuresis**" simply means a large urine flow from any cause). In a subsequent section we will describe the reflexes that control ADH secretion.

The disease **diabetes insipidus**, which is distinct from diabetes mellitus or "sugar diabetes," illustrates what happens when the ADH system is disrupted. People with this disease have lost the ability to produce ADH, usually as a result of damage to the hypothalamus. Thus, the permeability to water of the collecting ducts is low and unchanging regardless of the state of the body fluids, and diabetes insipidus is characterized by a constant water diuresis—as much as 25 L/day. In most cases, the flow can be restored to normal by the administration of ADH.

Note that in water diuresis, there is an increased urine flow but not an increased solute excretion. In all other cases of diuresis, termed **osmotic diuresis**, the increased urine flow (increased water excretion) is the result of a primary increase in solute excretion. For example, failure to reabsorb sodium normally will cause not only increased sodium excretion but increased water excretion as well since, as we have seen, water reabsorption is absolutely dependent on solute reabsorption. Another example of osmotic diuresis occurs in patients with uncontrolled marked diabetes *mellitus*: In this case, the glucose that escapes reabsorption because of the huge filtered load pulls out water into the urine with it. We shall talk more about the consequences of this in Chapter 18.

From what has been said so far about sodium-water coupling, one might logically, but wrongly, conclude that even in the presence of maximal amounts of ADH, the kidneys would be unable to excrete a hyperosmotic urine, that is, one with an osmolarity greater than that of plasma. For this to occur, relatively more water must be reabsorbed than sodium, but how can this happen when water reabsorption is always secondary to sodium reabsorption? The answer is given in the rest of this section.

Urine Concentration: The Countercurrent Multiplier System

The ability of the kidneys to produce hyperosmotic urine is a major determinant of one's ability to survive without

---

[5]Throughout this chapter, we use the name "antidiuretic hormone" in keeping with the action of this hormone on the kidney. Its other name, "vasopressin," which is becoming its "official" label, reflects the fact, noted in Chapter 14, that this hormone can also exert a direct vasoconstrictor action on arterioles, resulting in elevated total peripheral resistance and thereby increased arterial blood pressure.

[6]What makes the luminal plasma membranes of these tubular segments, in contrast to most plasma membranes, so impermeable to water in the absence of the water channels induced by ADH is not known.

water. The human kidney can produce a maximal urinary concentration of 1400 mOsmol/L, almost five times the osmolarity of plasma, which is 300 mOsmol/L. The typical daily excretion of urea, sulfate, phosphate, other waste products, and ions amounts to approximately 600 mOsmol. Therefore, the minimal volume of urine water in which this mass of solute can be dissolved equals

$$\frac{600 \text{ mOsmol/day}}{1400 \text{ mOsmol/L}} = 0.444 \text{ L/day}$$

This volume of urine is known as the **obligatory water loss**. The loss of this minimal volume of urine (it would be somewhat lower if no food were available) contributes to dehydration when a person is deprived of water intake.

Urinary concentration takes place as the tubular fluid flows through the medullary collecting ducts. The interstitial fluid surrounding these ducts is very hyperosmotic, and in the presence of ADH water therefore diffuses out of the ducts into the interstitial fluid and thence into the blood vessels of the medulla. The key question is: How did the medullary interstitial fluid become hyperosmotic?

The complex process that sets up this interstitial hyperosmolarity is called the **countercurrent multiplier system** and takes place in the loops of Henle. These loops, like the collecting ducts, extend into the medulla, and the long loops from the juxtamedullary nephrons extend to its very tip. The fluid in a loop flows first in one direction—down the descending limb—and then in the opposite direction—up the ascending limb; thus the name "countercurrent."

First let us explain the principle of countercurrent multiplication with a model that has some features of the loop of Henle but is simpler to visualize (Figure 16-15). Then we will move to the more complex real-life situation. Our model is a hairpin-loop tube through which flows a sodium chloride solution that enters the loop at an osmolarity of 300 mOsmol/L. The ascending limb actively cotransports sodium and chloride into the descending limb and is relatively impermeable to water, so that little water can follow the salt. The pump can achieve a maximal osmolarity difference of 200 mOsmol/L across the loop. Let us look at what occurs under conditions of tubular flow, simplifying the analysis by assuming that fluid flow along the tubule and ion pumping occur in discontinuous out-of-phase steps. Think of it as a series of snapshots of the loop.

We begin (A) by allowing the entire loop to fill with fluid having an osmolarity of 300 mOsmol/L. Then we stop the flow and allow the pumps all along the ascending loop to operate so that the osmolarity in the entire ascending limb falls to 200 mOsmol/L and that of the descending limb rises to 400 mOsmol/L (B). Then we restart the flow (C) until new 300-mOsmol/L fluid fills the top half of the descending limb; this new fluid of course pushes the entire

fluid column in front of it down, around, and up, so that an equal volume of 200-mOsmol/L fluid is forced out the top of the ascending limb. Again flow is stopped and the pumps begin operating until once again they have established a 200-mOsmol/L difference across the tubule (D). The sequence is repeated once more (E and F), this time allowing only half as much new 300-mOsmol/L fluid to enter the descending limb as in step C.

The critical point emerges after this last cycle is completed: Even though only a 200-mOsmol/L difference exists across the loop *at each level*, a 275-mOsmol/L difference exists *from the top of the descending loop to the bottom*. In other words, the 200-mOsmol/L difference generated at each level by the pumps has been *multiplied* along the length of the tubule by the countercurrent system. With continued small cycles of the system, the multiplication would have been much greater than the extra 75 mOsmol/L shown here.

We can now apply this model to the loop of Henle. Because the proximal tubule always reabsorbs sodium and water in the same proportions, the fluid entering the descending limb from the proximal tubule is the same as plasma—300 mOsmol/L. The Na,K,2Cl cotransporters in the *ascending* limb (Figure 16-13) actively cotransport sodium and chloride (we shall ignore the potassium) into the medullary interstitial fluid.[7] The ascending limb is relatively impermeable to water, so that little water follows the salt. Note the major difference between the previous model and the loop of Henle: The pumps in the ascending limb do not transport sodium and chloride into the descending limb but rather into the interstitial fluid surrounding the tubules.

The *descending* limb, in contrast to the ascending limb, does not pump sodium chloride and is highly permeable to water. Therefore, there is a net diffusion of water out of the descending limb into the more concentrated intersti-

---

[7]These transporters probably exist only in the thick segment of the ascending limb. How sodium and chloride move across the epithelial cells of the thin segment is not known with certainty. For simplicity, we have treated the entire ascending limb as though it had the characteristics of the thick portion.

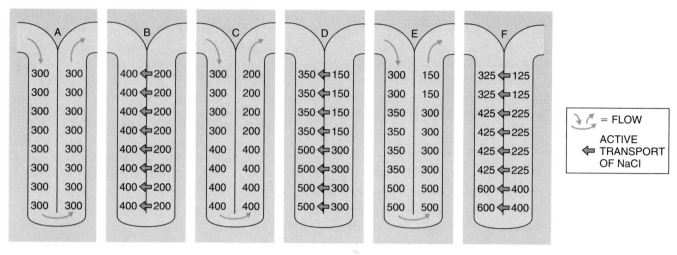

FIGURE 16-15

Model to illustrate the basic principle of countercurrent multiplication. The ascending limb actively transports sodium chloride into the descending limb. The transport process and the flow of fluid through the loop actually occur continuously but have been separated into discontinuous steps for purposes of illustration.

tial fluid until the osmolarities inside this limb and in the interstitial fluid are again equal. The interstitial osmolarity is maintained at 400 mOsmol/L during this equilibration because the ascending limb continues to pump sodium chloride to maintain the 200-mOsmol/L difference between it and the interstitial fluid.

Thus, the osmolarities of the descending limb and interstitial fluid become equal, and both are 200 mOsmol/L higher than that of the ascending limb. This is the essence of the system: The loop countercurrent multiplier causes the interstitial fluid of the medulla to become concentrated. It is this hyperosmolarity that will draw water out of the collecting ducts and concentrate the urine.

When we allow flow in this system, as in our simpler model, the result is the same (Figure 16-16): Multiplication of the osmolarity difference from 200 mOsmol/L at any given level to a much higher value—1400 mOsmol/L in this case—at the bend in the loop. It should be emphasized that the active sodium chloride transport mechanism in the ascending limb is the essential component of the

entire system. Without it, the countercurrent flow would have no effect whatever on loop and interstitial concentrations.

Now we have our concentrated medullary interstitial fluid, but we must still follow the fluid *within* the tubules from the loop of Henle through the distal convoluted tubule and into the collecting duct, using Figure 16-16 as our guide. The countercurrent multiplier system concentrates the descending-loop fluid, but then it redilutes it in the ascending loop so that the fluid entering the distal convoluted tubule is actually more dilute than the plasma (hypoosmotic). This situation persists throughout the distal convoluted tubule, since this tubular segment, like the ascending loop, actively transports sodium chloride out of the tubule but is relatively impermeable to water. Thus, hypoosmotic fluid then enters the cortical collecting duct.

As noted earlier, here in the collecting duct is where ADH increases tubular permeability to water. In other words, ADH does not influence water reabsorption in the earlier parts of the tubule and so, regardless of the plasma concentration of this hormone, the fluid entering the cortical collecting duct is always hypoosmotic. From here on, however, ADH is crucial. In the presence of high levels of ADH, water reabsorption occurs, by diffusion, from the hypoosmotic fluid in the cortical collecting duct until the fluid in this segment becomes isoosmotic to plasma, that is, until it is once again at 300 mOsmol/L.

This isoosmotic tubular fluid then enters and flows along the medullary collecting ducts. Under the influence of ADH, the medullary collecting ducts are also highly permeable to water, which diffuses out of the ducts into

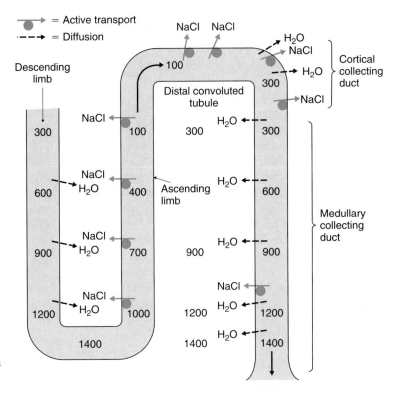

FIGURE 16-16

Generation of an interstitial fluid osmolarity gradient by the renal countercurrent multiplier system and its role in the formation of hyperosmotic urine.

the medullary interstitial fluid as a result of the high osmolarity set up there by the loop countercurrent multiplier system. This water then enters the medullary capillaries (recall that these are the vasa recta) and is carried out of the kidneys by the venous blood. Water reabsorption occurs all along the lengths of the medullary collecting ducts so that, in the presence of ADH, the fluid at the end of these ducts has essentially the same osmolarity as the interstitial fluid surrounding the bend in the loops, that is, at the bottom of the medulla. By this means, the final urine is hyperosmotic.[8] By retaining as much water as possible, the kidneys compensate for a body water deficit.

In contrast, when plasma ADH concentration is low, both the cortical and medullary collecting ducts become relatively impermeable to water. Therefore, fluid in the cortical collecting ducts does not reequilibrate with cortical peritubular plasma, and, even more important, the high medullary interstitial osmolarity set up by the loop is ineffective in inducing water movement out of the medullary collecting ducts. As a result, a large volume of hypoosmotic urine is excreted, thereby compensating for an excess of water in the body.

---

[8]We have presented here only the absolutely essential components of the countercurrent multiplier system. It is actually much more complex and includes a unique role for the vasa recta, nonhomogeneity of the thin and thick segments of the ascending loop, and a contribution from urea as well as sodium and chloride. The interested reader can consult the suggested readings for this chapter listed in Appendix G.

RENAL SODIUM REGULATION

Now we turn to the reflexes that play upon the basic renal processes for sodium and, in the next section, water to regulate their excretion. In normal individuals, urinary sodium excretion is reflexly increased when there is a sodium excess in the body and reflexly decreased when there is a sodium deficit. These reflexes are so precise that total-body sodium normally varies by only a few percent despite a wide range of sodium intakes and the sporadic occurrence of large losses via the skin and gastrointestinal tract.

Since sodium is freely filterable from the glomerular capillaries into Bowman's space and actively reabsorbed but not secreted, the amount of sodium excreted in the urine represents the resultant of two processes:

Sodium excreted = sodium filtered − sodium reabsorbed

The body is able to reflexly adjust sodium excretion by changing both processes. Thus, when total-body sodium decreases for any reason, sodium excretion is reflexly decreased below normal levels by lowering the GFR and raising sodium reabsorption.

Most of these reflexes are initiated by various cardiovascular baroreceptors, such as the carotid sinus. As described in Chapter 14, baroreceptors respond to pressure changes within the cardiovascular system and initiate reflexes that regulate these pressures. The reason that regulation of cardiovascular pressures by baroreceptors simultaneously achieves regulation of total-body sodium is that these variables are closely correlated, as described in the next paragraph.

Because sodium is the major extracellular solute, changes in total-body sodium result in similar changes in extracellular volume. Now, since extracellular volume comprises plasma volume and interstitial volume, plasma volume is also significantly affected by total-body sodium. We saw in Chapter 14 that plasma volume is in turn an important determinant of the pressures in the veins, cardiac chambers, and arteries. Thus, the chain linking total-body sodium to cardiovascular pressures is completed: Low total-body sodium leads to low plasma volume, which leads to low cardiovascular pressures, which, via baroreceptors, initiate reflexes that (1) restore the cardiovascular pressures via direct actions on the cardiovascular system (Chapter 14), and (2) simultaneously lower GFR and increase sodium reabsorption. These latter events decrease sodium excretion, thereby retaining sodium in the body and preventing further decreases in plasma volume and cardiovascular pressures. Increases in total-body sodium have the the reverse reflex effects.

Control of GFR

Figure 16-17 summarizes the major mechanisms by which a lower total-body sodium, as caused by diarrhea, for example, elicits a decrease in GFR. The key event—a reduced glomerular capillary pressure—occurs both as a direct consequence of a lowered arterial pressure in the kidneys and, more importantly, as a result of baroreceptor reflexes acting on the afferent arterioles. Note that the latter are simply the basic baroreceptor reflexes described in Chapter 14, where it was pointed out that a decrease in cardiovascular pressures causes reflex vasoconstriction in many areas of the body.

Conversely, an increased GFR is elicited when an increased total-body sodium level causes increased plasma volume, and this increased GFR contributes to the increased renal sodium loss that returns extracellular volume to normal.[9]

Control of Sodium Reabsorption

As far as long-term regulation of sodium excretion is concerned, the control of sodium reabsorption is more important than the control of GFR. The major factor determining the rate of tubular sodium reabsorption is the hormone aldosterone.

---

[9]In addition to being acted upon by this neural reflex control of GFR, the renal blood vessels are affected by several hormones. Moreover, the kidneys have the ability to self-regulate their own GFR (and blood flow). These mechanisms are described in the suggested readings for this chapter listed in Appendix G.

Aldosterone and the Renin-Angiotensin System. The adrenal cortex produces a steroid hormone, **aldosterone**, which stimulates sodium reabsorption by the cortical collecting ducts. By the time this portion of the tubule has been reached, almost all (approximately 98 percent) of the filtered sodium has already been reabsorbed by earlier tubular segments. Aldosterone then controls the reabsorption of this last remaining sodium. When this hormone is completely absent, virtually all of this sodium (equivalent to 35 g of sodium chloride per day) will not be reabsorbed but is excreted. When aldosterone is present in large quantities, essentially all of the remaining sodium will be reabsorbed and none excreted. In a normal person, the amounts of aldosterone produced and sodium excreted lie somewhere between these extremes, varying reflexly with the amount of sodium ingested.

Aldosterone, like other steroids, acts by inducing the synthesis of proteins in its target cells, in this case proteins involved in sodium transport—for example, proteins that function as sodium channels in the luminal membrane and proteins that constitute the Na,K-ATPase pumps. (By this same mechanism, aldosterone also stimulates sodium transport into the blood from the lumens of both the large intestine and the ducts carrying fluid from the sweat glands and salivary glands. In this manner, less sodium is lost in the feces and from the surface of the skin in sweat.)

The secretion of aldosterone is controlled, in part, by reflexes involving the kidneys, specifically the juxtaglomerular apparatus, and a hormonal complex called the **renin-angiotensin system**. As mentioned in the section on renal anatomy, the juxtaglomerular cells of the juxtaglomerular apparatus synthesize and secrete into the blood a protein known as **renin**. This protein acts as an enzyme to split off a small polypeptide, **angiotensin I**, from a large plasma protein, **angiotensinogen** (Figure 16-18). Angiotensin I then undergoes further cleavage to form **angiotensin II**. This conversion is mediated by an enzyme known as **angiotensin converting enzyme**, which is found in very high concentration on the luminal surface of capillary endothelial cells, particularly those in the lung. Thus, most conversion of angiotensin I to angiotensin II occurs as blood flows through the lungs. Angiotensin II is a potent stimulator of aldosterone secretion and constitutes a major input to the adrenal cortex controlling the production and release of this hormone.

FIGURE 16-17 (*opposite*)
Direct and reflex pathways by which the GFR and hence sodium and water excretion are decreased when plasma volume decreases. The reflex pathway, initiated by baroreceptors in large veins, the atria, and the carotid sinuses and aortic arch, is much more effective in lowering GFR than is the direct effect on the kidneys of the lowered arterial pressure.

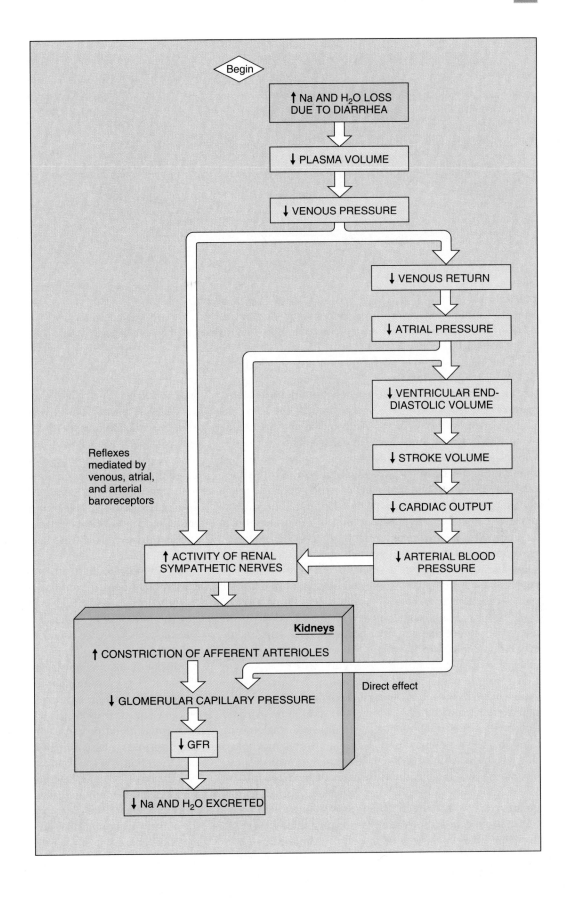

Begin

↑ Na AND H₂O LOSS DUE TO DIARRHEA

↓ PLASMA VOLUME

↓ VENOUS PRESSURE

↓ VENOUS RETURN

↓ ATRIAL PRESSURE

↓ VENTRICULAR END-DIASTOLIC VOLUME

↓ STROKE VOLUME

↓ CARDIAC OUTPUT

↓ ARTERIAL BLOOD PRESSURE

Reflexes mediated by venous, atrial, and arterial baroreceptors

↑ ACTIVITY OF RENAL SYMPATHETIC NERVES

Kidneys

↑ CONSTRICTION OF AFFERENT ARTERIOLES

Direct effect

↓ GLOMERULAR CAPILLARY PRESSURE

↓ GFR

↓ Na AND H₂O EXCRETED

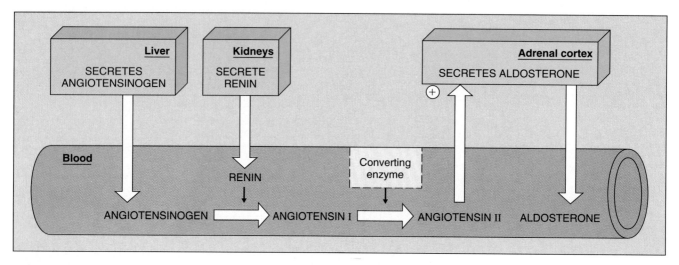

FIGURE 16-18

Summary of the renin-angiotensin-aldosterone system. Converting enzyme is located on the surface of capillary endothelial cells, particularly in the lungs. Renin is the rate-limiting factor in the system.

What determines the plasma concentration of angiotensin II? Angiotensinogen is synthesized by the liver and is always present in the blood. Angiotensin converting enzyme is also always present in amounts adequate to convert all angiotensin I to angiotensin II. Therefore, the rate-limiting factor in angiotensin II formation is the concentration of plasma renin, which in turn depends upon the rate of renin secretion by the kidneys. The critical question now becomes: What controls renin secretion?

There are at least three distinct inputs to the juxtaglomerular cells: (1) the renal sympathetic nerves, (2) *intra-renal* baroreceptors, and (3) the macula densa. That the renal sympathetic nerves constitute one important input makes excellent sense teleologically, since a reduction in body sodium and plasma volume lowers blood pressure and, via baroreceptors external to the kidneys, triggers increased sympathetic discharge to the juxtaglomerular cells, stimulating renin release (Figure 16-19).

The other two inputs for controlling renin release—intrarenal baroreceptors and the macula densa—are totally contained within the kidneys and require no external neuroendocrine input. As noted earlier, the juxtaglomerular cells are located in the walls of the afferent arterioles; they are themselves sensitive to the pressure within these arterioles, and so function as **intrarenal baroreceptors**. When renal arterial (and hence arteriolar) pressure decreases, as would occur when extracellular volume is down, these cells secrete more renin (Figure 16-19). Thus, normally, the juxtaglomerular cells respond simultaneously to the combined effects of sympathetic input, triggered by baroreceptors *external* to the kidneys, and to their own pressure sensitivity.

The second completely internal input to the juxtaglomerular cells is via the macula densa, which, as noted ear-lier, is located near the ends of the ascending loops of Henle. The macula densa senses the sodium and/or chloride concentration in the fluid flowing past it, a decreased salt concentration causing increased renin secretion. For several reasons, including a decrease in GFR and hence tubular flow rate, macula densa sodium and chloride concentrations tend to decrease when a person's arterial pressure is decreased. This input therefore also signals for increased renin release at the same time that the sympathetic nerves and intrarenal baroreceptor are doing so (Figure 16-19).[10]

By helping to regulate sodium balance, and thereby plasma volume, the renin-angiotensin system contributes to the control of arterial blood pressure. However, this is not the only way in which it influences arterial pressure. Recall from Chapter 14 that angiotensin II is a potent constrictor of arterioles and that this effect on peripheral resistance increases arterial pressure. Abnormal increases in the activity of the renin-angiotensin system (as occurs, for example, when a renal artery becomes partially occluded) can contribute to the development of **hypertension** (high blood pressure) via both the sodium-retaining and arteriole-constricting effects. It should not be surprising, therefore, that certain individuals suffering from hypertension are treated with drugs that block the renin-angiotensin system. One such group of drugs (termed ***angiotensin converting enzyme [ACE] inhibitors***) blocks the action of angiotensin converting enzyme, thus preventing the generation of angiotensin II.

---

[10]In addition to its control of renin release, the macula densa has another quite distinct function: It participates in control of its own nephron's GFR. See suggested readings listed in Appendix G.

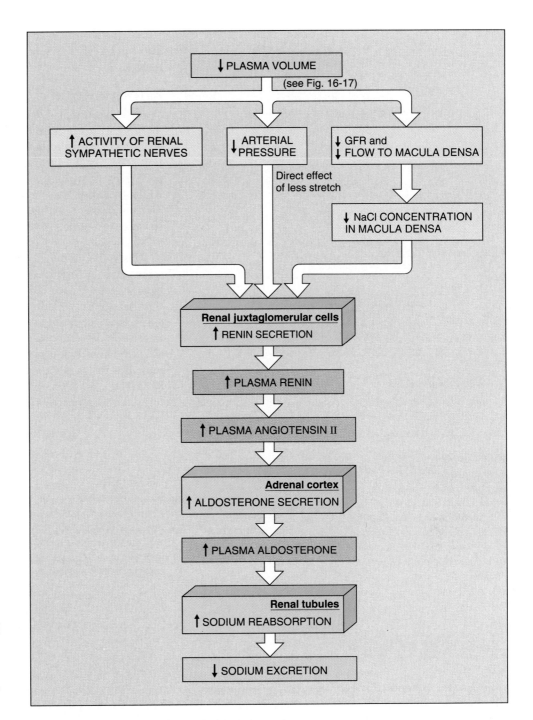

FIGURE 16-19
Pathways by which decreased plasma volume leads, via the renin-angiotensin system and aldosterone, to increased sodium reabsorption and hence decreased sodium excretion.

Atrial Natriuretic Factor. Although aldosterone is the most important controller of sodium reabsorption, a variety of other factors also play roles, including the renal nerves (which act directly on the tubules to stimulate sodium reabsorption) and a variety of other hormones. The most important of these is the peptide hormone known as **atrial natriuretic factor (ANF)**, which is synthesized and secreted by cells in the cardiac atria. ANF acts on the kidneys to inhibit sodium reabsorption. It also acts on the renal blood vessels to increase GFR, which further contributes to increased sodium excretion. As would be predicted, the secretion of ANF is increased when there is an excess of sodium in the body, the stimulus being an increase in atrial distention (Figure 16-20).

This completes our survey of the control of sodium excretion, which depends upon the control of two renal variables—the GFR and sodium reabsorption. The latter is controlled by the renin-angiotensin-aldosterone hormone system and by other factors, including atrial natriuretic factor. The reflexes that control both GFR and sodium reabsorption are essentially reflexes that regulate blood pressure since they are most frequently initiated by changes in arterial or venous pressures.

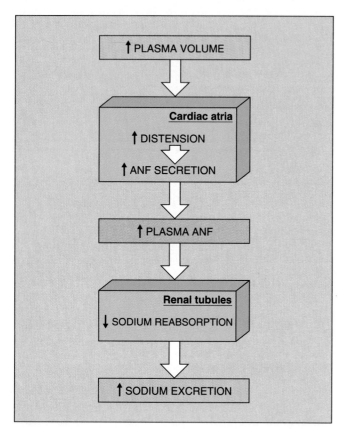

FIGURE 16-20

Atrial natriuretic factor in the *direct* control of sodium reabsorption and hence sodium excretion. ANF exerts several other effects not shown in the figure: (1) it inhibits the secretion of renin and of aldosterone and this leads *indirectly* to decreased sodium reabsorption; (2) by actions on the renal blood vessels, it also increases GFR, which further contributes to increased sodium excretion.

RENAL WATER REGULATION

W ater excretion, like sodium excretion, is the difference between the volume of water filtered (the GFR) and the volume reabsorbed. Accordingly, the baroreceptor-initiated GFR-controlling reflexes described in the previous section tend to have the same effects on water excretion as on sodium excretion. As in the case of sodium, however, the major regulated determinant of water excretion is not GFR, but instead the rate of water reabsorption. As we have seen, this is determined by ADH, and so total-body water is regulated mainly by reflexes that alter the secretion of this hormone.

As described in Chapter 10, ADH is produced by a discrete group of hypothalamic neurons whose axons termi-

nate in the posterior pituitary, from which ADH is released into the blood. The most important of the inputs to these neurons are from baroreceptors and osmoreceptors.

Baroreceptor Control of ADH Secretion

We have seen that a decreased extracellular volume, due say to diarrhea or hemorrhage, reflexly calls forth, via the renin-angiotensin system, an increased aldosterone secretion. The new fact is that decreased extracellular volume also triggers increased ADH secretion. This increased ADH increases the water permeability of the collecting ducts, more water is reabsorbed and less is excreted, and so water is retained in the body to help stabilize the extracellular volume.

This reflex is mediated by neural input to the ADH-secreting cells from several baroreceptors in the cardiovascular system (Figure 16-21). The baroreceptors decrease their rate of firing with the decreased cardiovascular pressures that occur when blood volume decreases. When fewer impulses are transmitted from the baroreceptors via afferent neurons and ascending pathways to the hypothalamus, the result is increased ADH secretion. Conversely, increased cardiovascular pressures cause more firing by the baroreceptors, resulting in a decrease in ADH secretion.

FIGURE 16-21

Baroreceptor pathway by which ADH secretion is decreased when plasma volume is increased. The greater plasma volume raises cardiovascular pressures, which stimulate baroreceptors and thereby inhibit ADH secretion. The opposite events (an increase in ADH secretion) occur when plasma volume decreases, as during hemorrhage.

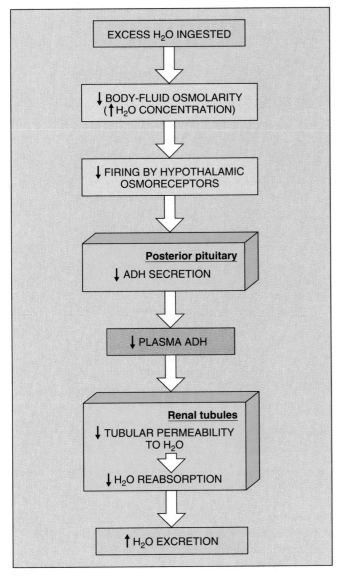

FIGURE 16-22
Osmoreceptor pathway by which ADH secretion is lowered and water excretion raised when excess water is ingested. The opposite events (a decrease in ADH secretion) occur when osmolarity increases, as during water deprivation.

Osmoreceptor Control of ADH Secretion

We have seen how changes in extracellular volume simultaneously elicit reflex changes in the excretion of *both* sodium *and* water. This is adaptive since the situations causing extracellular volume alterations are very often associated with loss or gain of both sodium and water in approximately proportional amounts. In contrast, we shall see now that changes in total-body water in which no

change in total-body sodium occurs are compensated for by altering water excretion without altering sodium excretion.

The major change caused by water loss or gain out of proportion to sodium loss or gain is a change in osmolarity of the body fluids. The reason this is a key point is that, under conditions of predominantly water gain or loss, the receptors that initiate the reflexes controlling ADH secretion are **osmoreceptors** in the hypothalamus, receptors responsive to changes in osmolarity.

Take, as an example, a person drinking 2 L of sugar-free soft drink, which contains little sodium or other solute, in a short time. The excess water lowers the body-fluid osmolarity, which reflexly inhibits ADH secretion via the hypothalamic osmoreceptors (Figure 16-22). As a result, water permeability of the collecting ducts becomes very low, water is not reabsorbed from these segments, and a large volume of hypoosmotic urine is excreted. In this manner, the excess water is eliminated.

At the other end of the spectrum, when the osmolarity of the body fluids is increased, say, because of water deprivation, ADH secretion is reflexly increased via the osmoreceptors, water reabsorption by the collecting ducts is increased, and a very small volume of highly concentrated urine is excreted. In this manner, the kidneys retain water in excess of solute and reduce the body-fluid osmolarity toward normal.

We have now described two afferent pathways controlling the ADH-secreting hypothalamic cells, one from baroreceptors and one from osmoreceptors. To add to the complexity, these cells receive synaptic input from many other brain areas, so that ADH secretion, and therefore urine volume and concentration, can be altered by pain, fear, and a variety of drugs. For example, alcohol is a powerful inhibitor of ADH release, and this probably accounts for much of the increased urine volume produced following the ingestion of alcohol, a urine volume well in excess of the volume of beverage consumed.

A SUMMARY EXAMPLE: THE RESPONSE TO SWEATING

Figure 16-23 shows the factors that control renal sodium and water excretion in response to severe sweating. Sweat is a hypoosmotic solution containing mainly water, sodium, and chloride. Therefore, sweating causes both a decrease in extracellular volume and an increase in body-fluid osmolarity. The renal retention of water and sodium helps to compensate for the water and salt lost in the sweat.

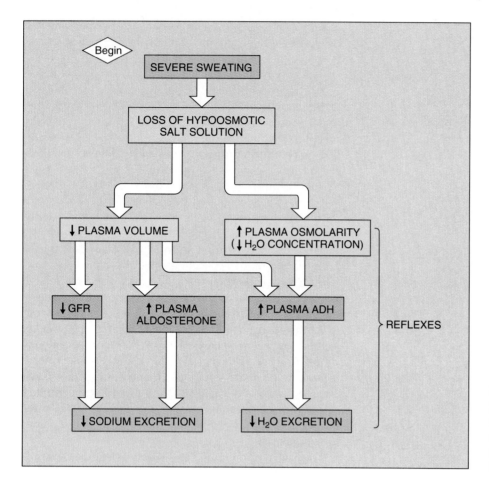

FIGURE 16-23
Pathways by which sodium and water excretion are decreased in response to severe sweating. This figure is an amalgamation of Figs. 16-17, 16-19, and the reverse of 16-21 and 16-22.

THIRST AND SALT APPETITE

Now we turn to the other component of any balance—control of intake. Deficits of salt and water must eventually be compensated for by ingestion of these substances, for the kidneys cannot create new sodium ions or water; they can only minimize their excretion until ingestion replaces the losses.

The subjective feeling of thirst, which drives one to obtain and ingest water, is stimulated both by a lower extracellular volume and a higher plasma osmolarity (Figure 16-24). Note that these are precisely the same two changes that stimulate ADH production, and the osmoreceptors and atrial baroreceptors that control ADH secretion are identical to those for thirst. The brain centers that receive input from these receptors and mediate thirst are located in the hypothalamus, very close to those areas that produce ADH.

Another influencing factor is angiotensin II, which stimulates thirst by a direct effect on the brain. Thus, the renin-angiotensin system helps regulate not only sodium balance but water balance as well and constitutes one of the pathways by which thirst is stimulated when extracellular volume is decreased.

There are still other pathways controlling thirst. For example, dryness of the mouth and throat causes profound thirst, which is relieved by merely moistening them. Some kind of "metering" of water intake by the gastrointestinal tract also occurs, but its nature remains a mystery.

Although the analog of thirst for sodium, **salt appetite**, is an important component of sodium homeostasis in most mammals, its contribution to everyday sodium homeostasis in normal human beings is probably slight.

POTASSIUM REGULATION

Potassium is, as we have seen, the most abundant intracellular ion. Although only 2 percent of total-body potassium is in the extracellular fluid, the potassium concentration in this fluid is extremely important for the function of excitable tissues, notably nerve and muscle. Recall

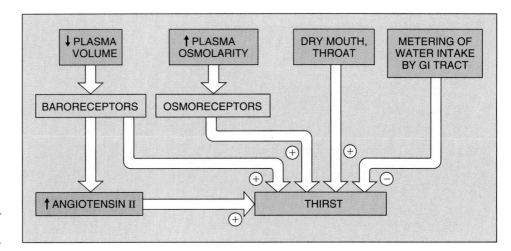

FIGURE 16-24
Inputs reflexly controlling thirst. Psychosocial factors and conditioned responses are not shown.

(Chapter 8) that the resting-membrane potentials of these tissues are directly related to the relative intracellular and extracellular potassium concentrations. An increase in extracellular potassium concentration depolarizes plasma membranes, triggering action potentials and often rendering the membrane inexcitable afterward. In the heart this may cause serious abnormalities of heart rhythm, **arrythmias**. Conversely, lowering the external potassium concentration hyperpolarizes plasma membranes. Therefore, early manifestations of potassium depletion are weakness of skeletal muscles, because of decreased firing of action potentials, and abnormalities of cardiac-muscle conduction and rhythm.

Total-body potassium balance is analogous to that of sodium in that a normal person remains in balance by daily excreting an amount of potassium in the urine equal to the amount ingested minus the amounts eliminated in the feces and sweat. Also, like sodium, potassium losses via sweat and the gastrointestinal tract are normally quite small, although large quantities can be lost during vomiting or diarrhea. The control of renal function is the major mechanism by which body potassium is regulated.

Renal Regulation of Potassium

Potassium is freely filterable from the glomerular capillaries into Bowman's space, and most of this filtered potassium is then reabsorbed by the proximal tubule and loop of Henle. In contrast, the cortical collecting ducts can *secrete* potassium, and changes in potassium *excretion* are due mainly to changes in potassium secretion by this tubular segment.

Thus, during potassium depletion, when the homeostatic response is to minimize potassium loss, there is no potassium secretion by the cortical collecting ducts, and only the small amount of filtered potassium that escaped reabsorption upstream is excreted. In all other situations, to

the small amount of potassium not reabsorbed by the proximal tubule and loop of Henle is added a variable amount of potassium secreted by the cortical collecting ducts, an amount necessary to maintain total-body balance (Figure 16-25). The mechanism of this potassium secretion was illustrated in Figure 16-12 in the context of sodium reabsorption.

FIGURE 16-25
Simplified model of the basic renal processing of potassium. Net reabsorption always occurs in the proximal tubule and loop of Henle, but the collecting ducts can show either net reabsorption or net secretion. Usually, net secretion occurs in these ducts (specifically in the cortical collecting duct), as in this figure. In a person who is potassium-depleted, however, net reabsorption occurs in the collecting ducts.

Potassium

Proximal tubule and loop of Henle

Cortical collecting duct

Excreted in urine

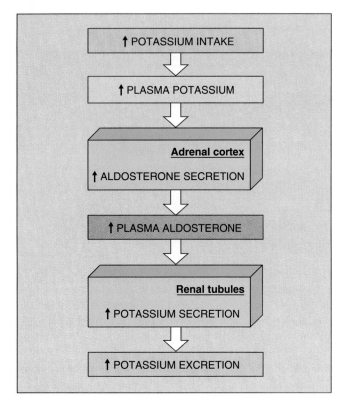

FIGURE 16-26

Pathway by which an increased potassium intake induces greater potassium excretion mediated by aldosterone.

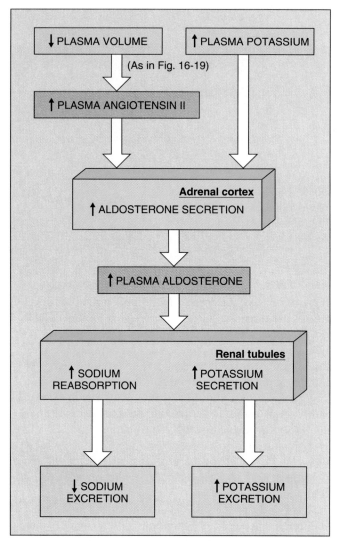

FIGURE 16-27

Summary of the control of aldosterone and its effects on sodium reabsorption and potassium secretion. The fact that a single hormone regulates both sodium and potassium excretion raises the question of potential conflicts between homeostasis of the two ions. For example, if a person were sodium-deficient and therefore secreting large amounts of aldosterone, the potassium-secreting effects of this hormone would tend to cause some potassium loss even though potassium balance were normal to start with. Normally, such conflicts cause only minor imbalances because there are a variety of other counteracting controls of sodium and potassium excretion.

One of the most important factors altering potassium secretion is aldosterone, which in addition to stimulating sodium reabsorption by the cortical collecting duct, increases potassium secretion by it. One of the major mechanisms by which it does so was mentioned earlier—recall that aldosterone stimulates the production of basolateral Na,K-ATPase pumps.

The reflex by which an excess or deficit of potassium controls aldosterone production is completely different from the reflex initiated by changes in extracellular volume. The latter constitutes the complex pathway discussed earlier involving renin and angiotensin. The former is much simpler (Figure 16-26): The aldosterone-secreting cells of the adrenal cortex are sensitive to the potassium concentration of the extracellular fluid bathing them. Thus, an increased intake of potassium leads to an increased extracellular potassium concentration, which in turn directly stimulates aldosterone production by the adrenal cortex. The resulting increased plasma aldosterone concentration increases potassium secretion and thereby eliminates the excess potassium from the body.

Conversely, a lowered extracellular potassium concentration decreases aldosterone production and thereby reduces potassium secretion. Less potassium than usual is excreted in the urine, thus helping to restore the normal extracellular concentration.

The control and major renal tubular effects of aldosterone are summarized in Figure 16-27.

SECTION B SUMMARY

TOTAL-BODY BALANCE OF SODIUM AND WATER

I. The body gains sodium and chloride by ingestion and loses them via the skin (in sweat), gastrointestinal tract, and urine.

II. The body gains water via ingestion and internal production, and it loses water via urine, the gastrointestinal tract, and evaporation from the skin and respiratory tract (as insensible loss and sweat).

III. For both water and sodium, the major homeostatic control point for maintaining a stable balance is renal excretion.

BASIC RENAL PROCESSES FOR SODIUM AND WATER

I. Sodium is freely filterable at the glomerulus, and its reabsorption is a primary active process dependent upon Na,K-ATPase pumps in the basolateral membranes of the tubular epithelium.

II. Sodium entry into the cell from the tubular lumen is always passive. Depending on the tubular segment, it is either through channels or by cotransport or countertransport with other substances.

III. Sodium reabsorption creates an osmotic difference across the tubule, which drives water reabsorption.

IV. Water reabsorption is independent of the posterior pituitary hormone antidiuretic hormone (ADH) until the collecting ducts, the water permeability of which is increased by this hormone. A large volume of dilute urine is produced when plasma ADH concentration, and hence water reabsorption by the collecting ducts, is low.

V. A small volume of concentrated urine is produced by the renal countercurrent multiplier system when plasma ADH concentration is high.

A. The active transport of sodium chloride by the ascending loop of Henle is independent of ADH and causes a progressive concentration of the interstitial fluid of the medulla but a dilution of the luminal fluid.

B. ADH increases the permeability of the cortical collecting ducts to water, and so water is reabsorbed by this segment until the luminal fluid is isoosmotic to cortical interstitial fluid.

C. The luminal fluid then enters and flows through the medullary collecting ducts, and the concentrated medullary interstitium causes water to move out of these ducts, made highly permeable to water by ADH. The result is concentration of the collecting duct fluid and the urine.

RENAL SODIUM REGULATION

I. Sodium excretion is the difference between the amount of sodium filtered and the amount reabsorbed.

II. GFR, and therefore the filtered load of sodium, are controlled by baroreceptor reflexes. Decreased vascular pressures cause decreased baroreceptor firing and hence reflexly increased sympathetic outflow to the renal arterioles, resulting in vasoconstriction and decreased GFR.

III. The major control of tubular sodium reabsorption is the adrenal cortical hormone aldosterone, which stimulates sodium reabsorption in the cortical collecting ducts.

IV. The renin-angiotensin system is one of the major controllers of aldosterone secretion.

A. Renin, the rate-limiting variable in the renin-angiotensin system, is secreted by the juxtaglomerular cells of the kidney juxtaglomerular apparatus and catalyzes, in the blood, the formation of angiotensin I from circulating angiotensinogen produced by the liver. Angiotensin I is then cleaved by angiotensin converting enzyme to yield angiotensin II, which acts on the adrenal cortex to stimulate aldosterone secretion.

B. When extracellular volume decreases, renin secretion is stimulated by three inputs: (1) stimulation of the renal sympathetic nerves to the juxtaglomerular cells by baroreceptor reflexes; (2) pressure decreases sensed by the juxtaglomerular cells, themselves acting as intrarenal baroreceptors; and (3) a signal generated by low sodium or chloride concentration in the macula densa.

V. Atrial natriuretic factor, secreted by cells in the cardiac atria in response to atrial distention, inhibits sodium reabsorption and also increases GFR.

RENAL WATER REGULATION

I. Water excretion is the difference between the amount of water filtered and the amount reabsorbed.

II. GFR regulation via the baroreceptor reflexes plays some role in regulating water excretion, but the major control is via ADH-mediated control of water reabsorption.

III. ADH secretion by the posterior pituitary is controlled by cardiovascular baroreceptors and by osmoreceptors in the hypothalamus.

A. Via the baroreceptor reflexes, a low extracellular volume stimulates ADH secretion and a high extracellular volume inhibits it.

B. Via the osmoreceptors, a high body-fluid osmolarity stimulates ADH secretion and a low osmolarity inhibits it.

THIRST AND SALT APPETITE

I. Thirst is stimulated by a variety of inputs, including baroreceptors, osmoreceptors, and angiotensin II.

II. Salt appetite is not of major regulatory importance in people.

POTASSIUM REGULATION

I. A person remains in potassium balance by excreting an amount of potassium in the urine equal to the amount ingested minus the amounts lost in the feces and sweat.

II. Potassium is freely filterable at the glomerulus and undergoes both reabsorption and secretion, the latter occurring in the cortical collecting duct and being the major controlled variable determining potassium excretion.

III. When body potassium is increased, aldosterone secretion is stimulated by an increased plasma concentration of potassium, and the increased aldosterone then stimulates potassium secretion.

SECTION B KEY TERMS

insensible water loss	renin
antidiuretic hormone (ADH)	angiotensin I
vasopressin	angiotensinogen
water diuresis	angiotensin II
diuresis	angiotensin converting
osmotic diuresis	enzyme
obligatory water loss	intrarenal baroreceptors
countercurrent multiplier system	atrial natriuretic factor (ANF)
aldosterone	osmoreceptors
renin-angiotensin system	salt appetite

SECTION B REVIEW QUESTIONS

1. What are the sources of water gain and loss in the body? What are they for sodium?

2. Describe the distribution of water and sodium between intracellular and extracellular fluids.

3. What is the relationship between body sodium and extracellular-fluid volume?

4. What is the mechanism of sodium reabsorption, and how is the reabsorption of other solutes coupled to it?

5. What is the mechanism of water reabsorption, and how is it coupled to sodium reabsorption?

6. What is the effect of ADH on the renal tubules and what are the sites affected?

7. Describe the characteristics of the two limbs of the loop of Henle with regard to their transport of sodium, chloride, and water.

8. Diagram the osmolarities in the two limbs of the loop of Henle, distal convoluted tubule, cortical collecting duct, cortical interstitium, medullary collecting duct, and medullary interstitium in the presence of ADH. What happens to the cortical and medullary collecting duct values in the absence of ADH?

9. What two processes determine how much sodium is excreted per unit time?

10. Diagram the sequence of events by which a decrease in blood pressure leads to a decreased GFR.

11. List the sequence of events leading from increased renin secretion to increased aldosterone secretion.

12. What are the three inputs controlling renin secretion?

13. Diagram the sequence of events leading from decreased cardiovascular pressures or from an increased plasma osmolarity to an increased secretion of ADH.

14. What are the stimuli for thirst?

15. Which of the basic renal processes apply to potassium, and where in the tubule do they occur? Which of them is the controlled process?

16. Diagram the reflex leading from increased plasma potassium to increased potassium excretion.

17. What are the two major controls of aldosterone secretion, and what are this hormone's major actions?

SECTION

C

CALCIUM REGULATION

Extracellular calcium concentration is also normally held relatively constant, the requirement for precise regulation stemming primarily from the effects of calcium on neuromuscular excitability. A low calcium concentration increases the excitability of nerve- and muscle-cell membranes, so that individuals with low plasma calcium suffer from **hypocalcemic tetany**, characterized by skeletal-muscle spasms. Hypercalcemia (excessive plasma cal-

cium) is life-threatening, too, in that it causes cardiac arrhythmias as well as depressed neuromuscular excitability. These effects reflect extracellular calcium's ability to bind to plasma-membrane proteins that function as ion channels. The binding alters the open or closed state of the channels. This effect of calcium on membranes is totally distinct from its role as an intracellular excitation-contraction coupler in muscle.

EFFECTOR SITES FOR CALCIUM HOMEOSTASIS

The sections in this chapter on sodium, water, and potassium homeostasis were concerned almost entirely with the *renal* handling of these substances. In contrast, the regulation of calcium depends not only on the kidneys but also on bone and the gastrointestinal tract. We will first describe how these effector sites handle calcium and then discuss how they are influenced by hormones in the homeostatic control of plasma calcium concentration.

Bone

Approximately 99 percent of total-body calcium is contained in bone. Therefore, deposition of calcium in bone or its removal very importantly influences plasma calcium concentration. Also present in bone are sodium and small amounts of magnesium and carbonate, as well as lead and some other toxic elements that are treated like calcium by the bone.

Bone has functions, summarized in Table 16-5 and discussed in various chapters, other than regulating plasma calcium concentration. It is important to recognize that its role in maintaining normal plasma calcium concentration takes precedence over the mechanical supportive role, sometimes to the detriment of the latter.

Bone is a special connective tissue made up of several cell types surrounded by a collagen matrix, called **osteoid**, upon which are deposited minerals, particularly the crystals of calcium and phosphate known as **hydroxyapatite**—$Ca_{10}(PO_4)_6(OH)_2$. In some instances bones have central marrow cavities where blood cells are formed (Chapter 14). Typically approximately one-third of a bone, by weight, is osteoid, and two-thirds is mineral (the bone cells contribute little weight).

The three types of bone cells (marrow cells are not included in this term), which occupy only 3 percent of bone volume, are osteoblasts, osteocytes, and osteoclasts (Figure 16-28). **Osteoblasts** are the bone-forming cells: They secrete collagen to form a surrounding matrix, which then becomes calcified—just how this mineralization is

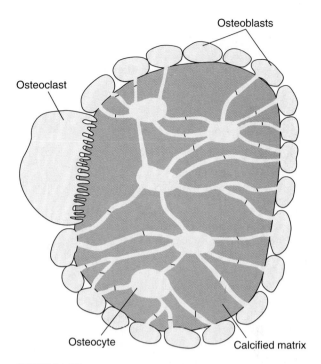

FIGURE 16-28

Cross section through a small portion of bone. The pink area is mineralized osteoid. The osteocytes have long processes that extend through small canals and connect with each other and to osteoblasts via tight junctions. (*Adapted from Goodman.*)

brought about remains controversial. Once surrounded by calcified matrix, the osteoblasts are called **osteocytes**. The osteocytes have long cytoplasmic processes that extend throughout the bone and form tight junctions with other osteocytes. **Osteoclasts** are large multinucleated cells that break down (resorb) previously formed bone by secreting hydrogen ions, which dissolve the crystals, and hydrolytic enzymes, which digest the osteoid.

The growth of bones during childhood will be discussed in Chapter 18. What is important here is that, throughout life bone is being constantly "remodeled" by the osteoblasts and osteoclasts working together. Osteoclasts resorb bone, and then osteoblasts lay down new matrix, which becomes calcified, in the same area. This process is dependent, in part, on the stresses imposed on the bones by gravity and muscle tension, both of which stimulate osteoblastic activity. It is also influenced by many hormones, as summarized in Table 16-6, and is regulated by a bewildering variety of growth factors produced locally in the bone. Of the hormones only parathyroid hormone and 1,25-dihydroxyvitamin D_3 (and possibly calcitonin) are controlled, as described below, primarily by reflexes that regulate plasma calcium concentration. When any of the other hormones listed in Table 16-6 change, for whatever

---

TABLE 16-5   FUNCTIONS OF BONE

1. Supports the body and imposed loads against gravity.
2. Provides the rigidity that permits locomotion.
3. Rib cage, vertebrae, and skull afford protection to the internal organs.
4. Serves as a reservoir for calcium, inorganic phosphate, and other mineral elements.
5. Bone marrow produces the blood cells.

**TABLE 16-6   SUMMARY OF MAJOR HORMONAL INFLUENCES
ON BONE MASS***

**Hormones that favor bone formation and
increased bone mass**
    Insulin
    Growth hormone
    Insulin-like growth factor I (IGF-I)
    Estrogen
    Testosterone
    1,25-Dihydroxyvitamin D_3 (influences only
       mineralization, not matrix)
    Calcitonin

**Hormones that favor increased bone resorption
and decreased bone mass**
    Parathyroid hormone
    Cortisol
    Thyroid hormones (T_4 and T_3)

*The effects of all hormones except 1,25-dihydroxyvitamin D_3 are ultimately due to a hormone-induced alteration of the balance between the activities of the osteoblasts and osteoclasts. This altered balance is not always the result of a *direct* action of the hormone on these cells, however, but may result *indirectly* from some other action of the hormone. For example, large amounts of cortisol depress intestinal absorption of calcium, which in turn causes reduced plasma calcium, increased parathyroid hormone secretion, and stimulation of osteoclasts by parathyroid hormone.

reason, it nonetheless has important influences on bone mass and plasma calcium concentration.

Kidneys

About 60 percent of plasma calcium is filterable at the renal corpuscle (the rest is bound to plasma protein), and most of this filtered calcium is reabsorbed. There is no tubular secretion of calcium. Accordingly, the urinary excretion of calcium is the difference between the amount filtered and the amount reabsorbed. Like that of sodium, the control of calcium excretion is exerted mainly on reabsorption; that is, reabsorption is reflexly decreased when plasma calcium concentration goes up for whatever reason, and reflexly increased when plasma calcium goes down.

In addition, as we shall see, the renal handling of phosphate plays a role in the regulation of extracellular calcium. Phosphate, too, is handled by a combination of filtration and reabsorption, the latter being hormonally controlled.

Gastrointestinal Tract

The absorption of sodium, water, and potassium from the gastrointestinal tract normally approximates 100 percent.

There is some homeostatic control of these processes, but it is relatively unimportant and so we ignored it. In contrast, a considerable amount of ingested calcium is not absorbed from the intestine and simply leaves the body along with the feces. Moreover, the active-transport system that moves this ion from intestinal lumen to blood is under important hormonal control. Accordingly, there can be large regulated increases or decreases in the amount of calcium absorbed. These changes markedly affect total-body calcium and plasma calcium concentration.

HORMONAL CONTROLS

The two major hormones that homeostatically regulate plasma calcium concentration are parathyroid hormone and the active form of vitamin D, called 1,25-dihydroxyvitamin D_3. (Another hormone, calcitonin, which is secreted by the thyroid gland, has long been thought to help regulate plasma calcium, but present evidence indicates that this hormone plays only a minor role in this regard.)

Parathyroid Hormone

All three of the effector sites described above are subject, directly or indirectly, to control by a protein hormone called **parathyroid hormone**, produced by the parathyroid glands. These glands are embedded in the surface of the thyroid gland but are distinct from it. Parathyroid hormone production is controlled by the plasma calcium concentration. Decreased plasma calcium concentration stimulates parathyroid hormone secretion, and an increased plasma calcium concentration does just the opposite. Extracellular calcium concentration acts directly upon the parathyroid glands without any intermediary hormones or nerves.

Parathyroid hormone exerts at least four distinct effects influencing calcium homeostasis (Figure 16-29):

1. It increases the resorption of bone, which results in the movement of calcium (and phosphate) from bone into extracellular fluid.
2. It stimulates the activation of vitamin D (see below), and this latter hormone then increases intestinal absorption of calcium.
3. It increases renal tubular calcium reabsorption, thus decreasing urinary calcium excretion.
4. It reduces the tubular reabsorption of phosphate, thus raising its urinary excretion and lowering its extracellular concentration.

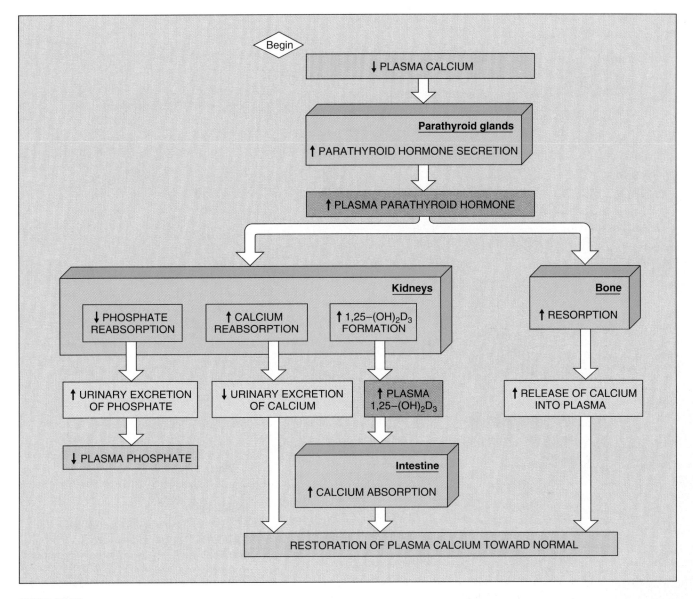

FIGURE 16-29

Reflexes by which a reduction in plasma calcium concentration is restored toward normal via the actions of parathyroid hormone. See Figure 16-30 for a description of 1,25-$(OH)_2D_3$.

The adaptive value of the first three is straightforward: They all tend to increase extracellular calcium concentration, thus compensating for the decreased concentration that originally stimulated parathyroid hormone secretion. The adaptive value of the fourth effect for calcium regulation requires further explanation as follows.

Parathyroid hormone, by stimulating bone resorption, causes both calcium and phosphate to be released from bone into the extracellular fluid. If the extracellular phosphate concentration were to increase as a result of this release, further movement of calcium from bone would be retarded because a high extracellular phosphate level causes calcium and phosphate to be deposited on bone and other tissues. Therefore, it is adaptive that parathyroid hormone also decreases tubular reabsorption of phosphate, thus permitting excess phosphate to be eliminated in the urine.

Vitamin D

The term **vitamin D** denotes a group of closely related chemicals involved in absorption of ingested calcium by the intestine. **Vitamin D_3** is formed by the action of ultraviolet radiation (from sunlight, usually) on a substance—

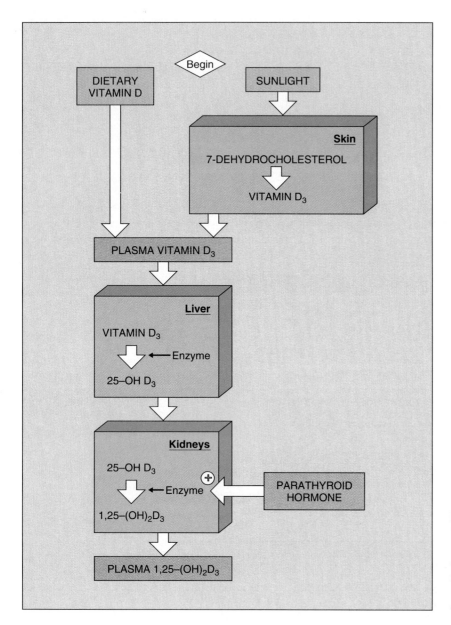

FIGURE 16-30

Metabolism of vitamin D to the active form: 1,25-$(OH)_2D_3$. The kidney enzyme that mediates the final step is activated by parathyroid hormone. The major action of 1,25-$(OH)_2D_3$ is to stimulate the absorption of calcium from the gastrointestinal tract.

7-dehydrocholesterol—found in skin. Vitamin D_3 and a closely related molecule are also ingested in food and absorbed into the blood. Because of clothing and decreased outdoor living, people are often dependent upon this dietary source of vitamin D, and for this reason it was classified as a vitamin.

Vitamin D_3 is metabolized by addition of hydroxyl groups, first in liver cells and then in kidney cells (Figure 16-30). The end result of these changes is **1,25-dihydroxyvitamin D_3** [abbreviated **1,25-$(OH)_2D_3$**], the active form of vitamin D. It should be clear from this description that 1,25-$(OH)_2D_3$ is really a hormone, not a vitamin, since it is made in the body.

The major action of 1,25-$(OH)_2D_3$ is to stimulate the

intestine to actively absorb the calcium ingested in food. Thus, the major event in vitamin D deficiency is decreased intestinal calcium absorption, resulting in decreased plasma calcium.

The blood concentration of 1,25-$(OH)_2D_3$ is subject to physiological control. The major control point is the addition of the second hydroxyl group, which occurs in kidney cells. The enzyme catalyzing this step is stimulated by parathyroid hormone. Thus, as we have seen, a low plasma calcium concentration stimulates the secretion of parathyroid hormone, which in turn enhances the production of 1,25-$(OH)_2D_3$, and both hormones contribute to restoration of the plasma calcium toward normal.

METABOLIC BONE DISEASES

Various diseases reflect abnormalies in the metabolism of bone. ***Rickets*** (in children) and ***osteomalacia*** (in adults) are conditions in which mineralization of bone matrix is deficient. In rickets, the major cause of which is deficiency of vitamin D, the soft and easily fractured bones become distorted. The child typically is severely bowlegged due to the effect of weight-bearing on the legs.

In contrast to rickets and osteomalacia, in ***osteoporosis*** both matrix and minerals are lost. The resulting decrease in bone mass and strength leads to an increased incidence of fractures. Osteoporosis occurs in people who are immobilized (disuse osteoporosis), in people who have an excessive plasma concentration of a hormone that favors bone resorption, and in people who have a deficient plasma concentration of a hormone that favors bone formation (Table 16-6). It is most commonly seen, however, with aging. Everyone loses bone as he or she ages, but frank osteoporosis is much more common in elderly women than men for several reasons: Women have a smaller bone mass to begin with, and the loss that occurs with aging occurs more rapidly, particularly after menopause removes the bone-promoting influence of estrogen. Osteoporosis in postmenopausal women causes more than 1.5 million fractures each year and is responsible for thousands of deaths, usually due to complications following surgery for hip fracture.

There is currently no effective therapy for established osteoporosis. Therefore, prevention is the focus of attention. Estrogen treatment in postmenopausal women is very effective in reducing the rate of bone loss. A regular weight-bearing exercise program (brisk walking and stair-climbing, for example) is also helpful. Adequate dietary calcium throughout life, not just after menopause, is important to build up and maintain bone mass, but the value of large dietary calcium supplements in the elderly is controversial at present. The efficacy of using calcitonin, a group of drugs (called biphosphonates) that interfere with osteoclasts, and 1,25-dihydroxyvitamin D_3 is presently being evaluated.

SECTION C SUMMARY

EFFECTOR SITES FOR CALCIUM HOMEOSTASIS

I. The effector sites for the regulation of plasma calcium concentration are bone, the gastrointestinal tract, and the kidneys.

II. Approximately 99 percent of total-body calcium is contained in bone as minerals on a collagen matrix. Bone is constantly remodeled as a result of the interaction of osteoblasts and osteoclasts, a process which determines bone mass and provides a means for raising or lowering plasma calcium concentration.

III. Calcium is actively absorbed by the gastrointestinal tract, and this process is under hormonal control.

IV. The amount of calcium excreted in the urine is the difference between the amount filtered and the amount reabsorbed, the latter process being under hormonal control.

HORMONAL CONTROLS

I. Parathyroid hormone increases plasma calcium concentration by influencing all the effector sites.

    A. It stimulates tubular reabsorption of calcium, bone resorption with release of calcium, and formation of the hormone 1,25-dihydroxyvitamin D_3, which stimulates calcium absorption by the intestine.

    B. It also inhibits the tubular reabsorption of phosphate, and the lowered plasma phosphate facilitates calcium movement out of bone.

II. Vitamin D_3 is formed in the skin or ingested and then undergoes hydroxylations in the liver and kidneys, in the latter under stimulation by parathyroid hormone, to the active form, 1,25-dihydroxyvitamin D_3.

SECTION C KEY TERMS

osteoid	parathyroid hormone
hydroxyapatite	vitamin D
osteoblasts	vitamin D_3
osteocytes	1,25-dihydroxyvitamin D_3
osteoclasts	[1,25-$(OH)_2D_3$]

SECTION C REVIEW QUESTIONS

1. List the functions of bone.
2. Describe bone remodeling.
3. Describe the handling of calcium by the kidneys and gastrointestinal tract.
4. What is the stimulus controlling the secretion of parathyroid hormone and what are this hormone's four major effects?
5. Describe the formation and action of 1,25-$(OH)_2D_3$. How does parathyroid hormone influence the production of this hormone?

SECTION

HYDROGEN-ION REGULATION

Metabolic reactions are highly sensitive to the hydrogen-ion concentration of the fluid in which they occur. This sensitivity is due to the influence on enzyme function exerted by hydrogen ions, which change the shapes of proteins. Accordingly, the hydrogen-ion concentration of the extracellular fluid is closely regulated. (At this point the reader might want to review the section on hydrogen ions, acidity, and pH in Chapter 2.)

This regulation can be viewed in the same way as the balance of any other ion, that is, as the matching of gains and losses. When loss exceeds gain, the arterial plasma hydrogen-ion concentration goes down (pH goes above 7.4), and this is termed an *alkalosis*. When gain exceeds loss, the arterial plasma hydrogen-ion concentration goes up (pH goes below 7.4), and this is termed an *acidosis*.

SOURCES OF HYDROGEN-ION GAIN OR LOSS

Table 16-7 summarizes the major routes for gains and losses of hydrogen ion. First, as described in Chapter 15, a huge quantity of CO_2 is generated daily as the result of oxidative metabolism and yields hydrogen ions via the reactions

$$CO_2 + H_2O \underset{\text{anhydrase}}{\overset{\text{Carbonic}}{\rightleftharpoons}} H_2CO_3 \rightleftharpoons HCO_3^- + H^+ \tag{16-1}$$

TABLE 16-7 SOURCES OF HYDROGEN-ION GAIN OR LOSS

Gain
1. Generation of hydrogen ions from CO_2
2. Production of phosphoric and sulfuric acids from the metabolism of protein and other organic molecules
3. Gain of hydrogen ions due to loss of bicarbonate in diarrhea or other nongastric GI fluids
4. Gain of hydrogen ions due to loss of bicarbonate in the urine

Loss
1. Loss of hydrogen ions in vomitus
2. Loss of hydrogen ions in the urine

This source does not normally constitute a net gain of hydrogen ions, however, since all the hydrogen ions generated via these reactions during passage of blood through the tissues are reincorporated into water when the reactions are reversed during passage of blood through the lungs (Chapter 15). Net retention of CO_2, however, as occurs in hypoventilation or respiratory disease, will result in a net gain of hydrogen ions. Conversely, net loss of CO_2, which occurs in hyperventilation, causes net elimination of hydrogen ions.

The body also produces acids, both organic and inorganic, from sources other than CO_2. These include phosphoric acid and sulfuric acid, generated mainly by the catabolism of proteins, and several organic acids. In the United States, where the diet is high in protein, people normally have a net daily production of 40 to 80 mmol of these acids. In addition, under certain conditions (described later) large amounts of other acids can be produced.

A third potential source of net body gain or loss of hydrogen ion is gastrointestinal secretions leaving the body. Vomitus contains a high concentration of hydrogen ions and so constitutes a source of net loss. In contrast, the other gastrointestinal secretions are alkaline, that is, contain very little hydrogen ion but a concentration of bicarbonate higher than exists in plasma. Loss of these fluids, as in diarrhea, constitutes in essence a body gain of hydrogen ions. This is an extremely important point: Given the mass action relationship shown in Equation 16-1, the loss of a bicarbonate ion from the body has virtually the same net result as gaining a hydrogen ion because loss of the bicarbonate causes the reaction to be driven to the right, thereby generating a hydrogen ion. Similarly, the gain of a bicarbonate by the body has virtually the same net result as losing a hydrogen ion.

Finally, the kidneys constitute the fourth source of net hydrogen-ion gain or loss; that is, the kidneys can either remove hydrogen ions from the plasma or add them. How they do so will be described later.

BUFFERING OF HYDROGEN IONS IN THE BODY

Any substance that can reversibly bind hydrogen ions is called a **buffer**. Between their generation in the body and their elimination, most hydrogen ions are buffered by extracellular and intracellular buffers. The normal extracellular-fluid pH of 7.4 corresponds to a hydrogen-ion concentration of only 0.00004 mmol/L. Without buffering, the daily turnover rate of the 40 to 80 mmol of H^+ produced by our diet would cause huge changes in body-fluid hydrogen-ion concentration. The general form of buffering reactions is

$$Buffer^- + H^+ \rightleftharpoons HBuffer \qquad (16\text{-}2)$$

HBuffer is a weak acid in that it can exist as the undissociated molecule (HBuffer) or can dissociate to $Buffer^-$ plus H^+. When the H^+ concentration increases for whatever reason, the reaction is forced to the right and more H^+ is bound by $Buffer^-$ to form HBuffer. For example, when H^+ concentration is increased because of increased production of lactic acid, some of the hydrogen ions combine with the body's buffers, and so the hydrogen-ion concentration does not increase as much as it otherwise would have. Conversely, when H^+ concentration decreases because of the loss of hydrogen ions or the addition of alkali, Equation 16-2 proceeds to the left and H^+ is released from HBuffer. In this manner, the body buffers stabilize H^+ concentration against changes in either direction.

The major extracellular buffer is the CO_2-HCO_3^- system summarized in Equation 16-1. This system also plays some role in buffering within cells, but the major intracellular buffers are phosphates and proteins. An example of the latter is hemoglobin, as described in Chapter 15.

You must recognize that buffering does not eliminate hydrogen ions from the body or add them to the body; it only keeps them "locked-up" until balance can be restored, which is the subject of the rest of this section.

INTEGRATION OF HOMEOSTATIC CONTROLS

The kidneys are ultimately responsible for balancing hydrogen-ion gains and losses so as to maintain plasma hydrogen-ion concentration relatively constant. Thus, they eliminate the excess hydrogen ions generated in the body during the normal catabolism of proteins and organic acids. Moreover, should there be an additional net gain of hydrogen ions due to hypoventilation or respiratory malfunction, increased metabolic production from sources other than CO_2, or loss of alkaline gastrointestinal secretions, the kidneys would increase their elimination of hydrogen ions from the body so as to restore balance. Alternatively, should there be a net loss of hydrogen ions from the body due to hyperventilation or vomiting, the kidneys would replenish these hydrogen ions.

Although the kidneys are the ultimate hydrogen-ion balancers, the respiratory system also plays a very important homeostatic role. We have pointed out that hypoventilation, respiratory malfunction, and hyperventilation can *cause* a hydrogen-ion *imbalance*; now we emphasize that when a hydrogen-ion imbalance is due to a *nonrespiratory cause*, then ventilation is *reflexly* altered so as to help compensate for the imbalance. We described this phenomenon in Chapter 15 (Figure 15-32): An elevated arterial hydrogen-ion concentration stimulates ventilation, and this reflex hyperventilation causes reduced arterial P_{CO_2}, and hence, by mass action, reduced hydrogen-ion concentration. Alternatively, a decreased plasma hydrogen-ion concentration inhibits ventilation, thereby raising arterial P_{CO_2} and therefore hydrogen-ion concentration.

Thus, the respiratory system and kidneys work together. The respiratory response to altered plasma hydrogen-ion concentration is very rapid (minutes) and keeps this concentration from changing too much until the more slowly responding kidneys (hours to days) can actually eliminate the imbalance. Of course, if the respiratory system is the actual *cause* of the hydrogen-ion imbalance, then the kidneys are the sole homeostatic responder. By the same token, malfunctioning kidneys can create a hydrogen-ion imbalance by eliminating too little or too much hydrogen ion from the body, and then the respiratory response is the only one operating.

RENAL MECHANISMS

We have spoken of the kidneys eliminating hydrogen ions from the body or replenishing them. *The kidneys perform this task by altering plasma bicarbonate concentration.* The key to understanding how altering plasma bicarbonate concentration regulates plasma hydrogen-ion concentration was stated earlier: The excretion of a bicarbonate in the urine increases the plasma hydrogen-ion concentration just as if a hydrogen ion had been added to the plasma. Similarly, the addition of a *new* bicarbonate to the plasma lowers the plasma hydrogen-ion concentration just as if a hydrogen ion had been removed from the plasma.

Thus, when there is a lowering of plasma hydrogen-ion concentration (alkalosis) for whatever reason, the kidneys' homeostatic response is to excrete large quantities of bicarbonate in the urine. This raises plasma hydrogen-ion concentration back toward normal. In contrast, in response to a rise in plasma hydrogen-ion concentration (acidosis), the kidneys do not excrete bicarbonate in the urine, but instead kidney tubular cells *produce new bicarbonate* and add it to the plasma. This lowers the plasma hydrogen-ion concentration back toward normal.

Let us now look at the basic mechanisms by which bi-

FIGURE 16-31

Reabsorption of bicarbonate is achieved by tubular hydrogen-ion secretion. Start this figure inside the cell, with the combination of CO_2 and H_2O to form H_2CO_3, a reaction catalyzed by the enzyme carbonic anhydrase. The H_2CO_3 immediately dissociates to yield H^+ and bicarbonate (HCO_3^-). The HCO_3^- moves down its concentration gradient across the basolateral membrane into the interstitial fluid and then into the blood. Simultaneously the H^+ is secreted into the lumen, *but it is not excreted.* Instead, it combines with a *filtered* HCO_3^- and generates CO_2 and H_2O (both of which can diffuse into the cell and be used for another cycle of hydrogen-ion generation). The overall result is that the bicarbonate filtered from the plasma at the renal corpuscle has disappeared but its place in the plasma has been taken by the bicarbonate that was produced inside the cell, and so no net change in plasma bicarbonate concentration has occurred. It may seem inaccurate to refer to this process as bicarbonate "reabsorption," since the bicarbonate that appears in the peritubular plasma is not the same bicarbonate ion that was filtered. Yet the overall result is, in effect, the same as if the filtered bicarbonate had been more conventionally reabsorbed like a sodium or potassium ion. These events occur in both the proximal tubule and cortical collecting duct, but the mechanisms by which hydrogen ions cross the luminal membrane differ in the two segments. In the cortical collecting duct, shown here, the hydrogen ions are transported by a primary H-ATPase pump, whereas in the proximal tubule they move mainly by Na/H countertransport (Fig. 16-13).

carbonate excretion or addition of new bicarbonate to the plasma is achieved.

Bicarbonate Excretion

Bicarbonate is completely filterable at the renal corpuscles and undergoes marked tubular reabsorption in the proxi-

mal tubules and the collecting ducts. Bicarbonate can also be secreted into the lumen of at least one tubular segment. Therefore,

$$HCO_3^-\ \text{excretion} = HCO_3^-\ \text{filtered} + HCO_3^-\ \text{secreted} - HCO_3^-\ \text{reabsorbed}$$

For simplicity, we can ignore the secretion of bicarbonate (because it is always quantitatively much less than tubular reabsorption) and treat bicarbonate excretion as the difference between filtration and reabsorption.

Bicarbonate reabsorption is an active process, but it is not accomplished in the conventional manner of simply having an active pump for bicarbonate ions at the luminal or basolateral membrane of the tubular cells. Instead, bicarbonate reabsorption requires the tubular secretion of hydrogen ions, which combine in the lumen with filtered bicarbonates. Figure 16-31 and its legend describe the sequence of events.

Addition of New Bicarbonate to the Plasma

It is essential to note in Figure 16-31 that bicarbonate reabsorption is absolutely dependent on the secretion of hydrogen ions from the tubular cells into the lumen. As long as there are still significant amounts of filtered bicarbonate in the lumen, almost all secreted hydrogen ions will combine with it. But what happens to any secreted hydrogen ions once the bicarbonate has all been reabsorbed and is no longer available in the lumen to combine with hydrogen ions?

The answer, illustrated in Figure 16-32, is that the extra secreted hydrogen ions combine in the lumen with a filtered *nonbicarbonate* buffer, usually HPO_4^{2-}. The hydrogen ion is then excreted in the urine as part of an $H_2PO_4^-$ ion (other filtered buffers can also participate but HPO_4^{2-} is the most important). Now for the critical point: Note in Figure 16-32 that, under these conditions, the bicarbonate generated within the tubular cell by the carbonic anhydrase reaction and entering the plasma constitutes a *net gain* of bicarbonate by the plasma, not merely a replacement for a filtered bicarbonate. Thus, when a secreted hydrogen ion combines in the lumen with a buffer other than bicarbonate, the overall effect is not merely one of bicarbonate conservation, as in Figure 16-31, but rather of addition to the plasma of a new bicarbonate. This raises the bicarbonate concentration of the plasma and alkalinizes it.[11]

There is a second mechanism by which the tubules con-

---

[11]Why do significant numbers of hydrogen ions combine with filtered nonbicarbonate buffers like phosphate only after the filtered bicarbonate has all been reabsorbed? The main reason is that there is such a large load of filtered bicarbonate compared to that of filtered nonbicarbonate buffers.

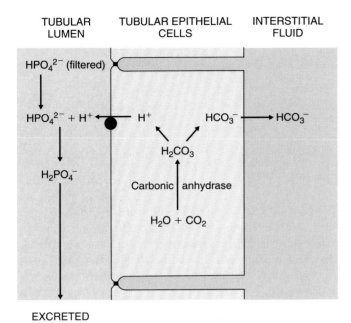

FIGURE 16-32

Renal contribution of new HCO_3^- to the plasma, as achieved by tubular secretion of H^+. The process of intracellular H^+ and HCO_3^- generation, with H^+ movement into the lumen and HCO_3^- into the plasma, is identical to that shown in Fig. 16-31. Once in the lumen, however, the H^+ combines with filtered phosphate (HPO_4^{2-}) rather than filtered HCO_3^- and is excreted. Therefore, the HCO_3^- that moves from the cell into the plasma does not merely replace "old" filtered HCO_3^-, as in Figure 16-31 but results in the addition of *new* HCO_3^- to the plasma.

tribute new bicarbonate to the plasma—one that involves not hydrogen-ion secretion but rather the renal production and secretion of ammonium (NH_4^+) (Figure 16-33). Tubular cells, mainly those of the proximal tubule, take up glutamine from both the glomerular filtrate and peritubular plasma and, by a series of steps, metabolize it. In the process, both NH_4^+ and bicarbonate are formed inside the cells. The NH_4^+ is actively secreted (via Na^+/NH_4^+ countertransport) into the lumen and excreted, while the bicarbonate moves into the peritubular capillaries and constitutes new plasma bicarbonate.[12]

---

[12]A comparison of Figures 16-32 and 16-33 demonstrates that the overall result—renal contribution of new bicarbonate to the plasma—is the same regardless of whether it is achieved by (1) H^+ secretion and excretion on nonbicarbonate buffers such as phosphate (Figure 16-32), or (2) by glutamine metabolism with NH_4^+ excretion (Figure 16-33). It is convenient, therefore, to view the latter case as representing H^+ excretion "bound" to NH_3, just as the former case constitutes H^+ excretion bound to nonbicarbonate buffers. Thus, the amount of H^+ excreted in the urine in these two forms is a measure of the amount of new bicarbonate added to the plasma by the kidneys. Indeed, "urinary H^+ excretion" and "renal contribution of new bicarbonate to the plasma" are really two sides of the same coin and are synonomous phrases.

Renal Responses to Acidosis and Alkalosis

Three events occur when the kidneys are responding homeostatically to an acidosis: (1) Enough hydrogen ions are secreted to reabsorb all the filtered bicarbonate; (2) additional hydrogen ions are secreted, and this contributes new bicarbonate to the plasma as these hydrogen ions are excreted bound to nonbicarbonate urinary buffers such as HPO_4^{2-}; and (3) tubular glutamine metabolism and ammonium excretion are enhanced, which also contributes new bicarbonate to the plasma. The net result of these three events is that plasma bicarbonate is increased, thereby compensating for the acidosis.

In contrast, when the kidneys are responding homeostatically to an alkalosis, (1) their rate of hydrogen-ion secretion is inadequate to reabsorb all the filtered bicarbonate, so that significant amounts of bicarbonate are excreted in the urine and there is little or no excretion of hydrogen ions on nonbicarbonate urinary buffers; and (2) simultaneously, tubular glutamine metabolism and ammonium excretion are decreased so that little or no new bicarbonate is contributed to the plasma from this source. The net result is that the plasma bicarbonate concentration is decreased, thereby compensating for the alkalosis.

Clearly, these homeostatic responses require that the rate of both hydrogen-ion secretion and glutamine metabolism be subject to reflex control. The specific pathways

FIGURE 16-33

Renal contribution of new HCO_3^- to the plasma, as achieved by renal metabolism of glutamine and excretion of ammonium (NH_4^+). Compare this figure to Figure 16-32. This process occurs mainly in the proximal tubule.

TABLE 16-8   CHANGES IN THE ARTERIAL CONCENTRATIONS OF HYDROGEN ION, BICARBONATE, AND CARBON DIOXIDE IN ACID-BASE DISORDERS

Primary disorder	H^+	HCO_3^-	CO_2	Cause of HCO_3^- change	Cause of CO_2 change
Respiratory acidosis	↑	↑	↑	Renal compensation	Primary abnormality
Respiratory alkalosis	↓	↓	↓		
Metabolic acidosis	↑	↓	↓	Primary abnormality	Reflex ventilatory compensations
Metabolic alkalosis	↓	↑	↑		

that bring about these rate changes are very complex and can be found in the recommended further readings listed in Appendix G.

CLASSIFICATION OF ACIDOSIS AND ALKALOSIS

To repeat, acidosis refers to any situation in which the hydrogen-ion concentration of arterial plasma is elevated; alkalosis denotes a reduction. All such situations fit into two distinct categories (Table 16-8): (1) *respiratory acidosis* or *alkalosis*, (2) *metabolic acidosis* or *alkalosis*.

Respiratory acidosis results from failure of the lungs to eliminate carbon dioxide as fast as it is produced. Respiratory alkalosis occurs when carbon dioxide is eliminated faster than it is produced. As described earlier, the imbalance of arterial hydrogen-ion concentrations in such cases is completely explainable in terms of mass action. Thus, the hallmark of a respiratory acidosis is an elevation in both arterial P_{CO_2} and hydrogen-ion concentration; that of respiratory alkalosis is a reduction in both.

Metabolic acidosis or alkalosis includes all situations other than those in which the primary problem is respiratory. Some common causes of metabolic acidosis are excessive production of lactic acid during severe exercise or

hypoxia, or of ketone bodies in uncontrolled diabetes mellitus or fasting (described in Chapter 18). Metabolic acidosis can also result from excessive loss of bicarbonate, as in diarrhea. A frequent cause of metabolic alkalosis is persistent vomiting, with its associated loss of hydrogen ions as HCl from the stomach.

What is the arterial P_{CO_2} in metabolic acidosis or alkalosis? Since, by definition, metabolic acidosis and alkalosis must be due to something other than excess retention or loss of carbon dioxide, you might have predicted that arterial P_{CO_2} would be unchanged, but such is not the case. As emphasized earlier in this chapter, the elevated hydrogen-ion concentration associated with metabolic acidosis reflexly stimulates ventilation and lowers arterial P_{CO_2}. By mass action this helps restore the hydrogen-ion concentration toward normal. Conversely, a person with metabolic alkalosis will reflexly have ventilation inhibited. The result is a rise in arterial P_{CO_2} and, by mass action, an associated restoration of hydrogen-ion concentration toward normal.

To reiterate, the plasma P_{CO_2} changes in metabolic acidosis and alkalosis are not the *cause* of the acidosis or alkalosis but are the *result* of compensatory reflex responses to nonrespiratory abnormalities. Thus, in metabolic, as opposed to respiratory conditions, the arterial plasma P_{CO_2} and hydrogen-ion concentration go in opposite directions, as summarized in Table 16-8.

SECTION D SUMMARY

SOURCES OF HYDROGEN-ION GAIN OR LOSS
I. Total-body balance of hydrogen ions is the result of both metabolic production of these ions and of net gains or losses via the gastrointestinal tract and urine (Table 16-7).
II. A stable balance is achieved by regulation of urinary losses.

BUFFERING OF HYDROGEN IONS IN THE BODY
I. Buffering is a means of minimizing changes in hy-

drogen-ion concentration by combining these ions reversibly with anions such as bicarbonate and intracellular proteins.
II. The major extracellular buffering system is the CO_2-HCO_3^- system, and the major intracellular buffers are proteins and phosphates.

INTEGRATION OF HOMEOSTATIC CONTROLS
I. The kidneys and the respiratory system are the homeostatic regulators of plasma hydrogen-ion concentration.
II. The kidneys are the ultimate balancers of body hydrogen-ion balance.

III. A decrease in arterial plasma hydrogen-ion concentration causes reflex hypoventilation, which raises arterial P_{CO_2} and, hence, raises plasma hydrogen-ion concentration toward normal. An increase in plasma hydrogen-ion concentration causes reflex hyperventilation, which lowers arterial P_{CO_2} and, hence, lowers hydrogen-ion concentration toward normal.

RENAL MECHANISMS

I. The kidneys maintain a stable plasma hydrogen-ion concentration by regulating plasma bicarbonate concentration. They can either excrete bicarbonate or contribute new bicarbonate to the blood.

II. Bicarbonate is reabsorbed when hydrogen ions, generated in the tubular cells by a process catalyzed by carbonic anhydrase, are secreted into the lumen and combine with filtered bicarbonate. The secreted hydrogen ions are not excreted in this situation.

III. In contrast, when the secreted hydrogen ions combine in the lumen with filtered phosphate or other non-bicarbonate buffer, they are excreted and the kidneys have contributed new bicarbonate to the blood.

IV. The kidneys also contribute new bicarbonate to the blood when they produce and excrete ammonium.

CLASSIFICATION OF ACIDOSIS AND ALKALOSIS

I. Acid-base disorders are categorized as respiratory or metabolic.

A. Respiratory acidosis is due to retention of carbon dioxide, and respiratory alkalosis to excessive elimination of carbon dioxide.

B. All other causes of acidosis or alkalosis are termed metabolic and reflect gain or loss, respectively, of hydrogen ions from a source other than carbon dioxide.

SECTION D KEY TERM

buffer

SECTION D REVIEW QUESTIONS

1. What are the sources of gain and loss of hydrogen ions in the body?

2. List the body's major buffer systems.

3. Describe the role of the respiratory system in the regulation of hydrogen-ion concentration.

4. How does the tubular secretion of hydrogen ions occur and how does it achieve bicarbonate reabsorption?

5. How does hydrogen-ion secretion contribute to the renal contribution of new bicarbonate to the blood. What determines whether a secreted hydrogen ion will achieve these events or will instead cause bicarbonate reabsorption?

6. How does the metabolism of glutamine by the tubular cells contribute new bicarbonate to the blood and ammonium to the urine?

7. How do the kidneys respond to the presence of an acidosis or alkalosis?

8. Classify the four types of acid-base disorders according to plasma hydrogen-ion concentration, bicarbonate concentration, and P_{CO_2}.

SECTION

DIURETICS AND KIDNEY DISEASE

DIURETICS

D rugs used clinically to increase the volume of urine excreted are known as **diuretics**. Such agents act by inhibiting the reabsorption of sodium, along with chloride and/or bicarbonate, resulting in increased excretion of these ions. Since water reabsorption is dependent upon sodium reabsorption, water reabsorption is also reduced, resulting in increased water excretion.

Diuretics are among the most commonly used medications. For one thing, they are used to treat diseases characterized by renal retention of salt and water. In normal individuals, the mechanisms for controlling total-body sodium are so precise that sodium balance does not vary by more than a few percent despite marked changes in dietary intake or in losses due to sweating, vomiting, or diarrhea. In several types of diseases, however, sodium balance becomes deranged by the failure of the kidneys to excrete sodium normally. Sodium excretion may fall virtually to zero despite continued sodium ingestion, and the person may retain huge quantities of sodium and water, leading to abnormal expansion of the extracellular fluid and formation of edema. Diuretics are used to prevent or reverse this renal retention of sodium and water.

The most common example of this phenomenon is **con-**

TABLE 16-9 CLASSES OF DIURETICS

Class	Mechanism	Major site affected
Carbonic anhydrase inhibitors	Inhibit secretion of hydrogen ion; this causes less reabsorption of sodium and bicarbonate.	Proximal tubules
Loop diuretics	Inhibit Na,K,2Cl cotransport in luminal membrane.	Ascending loops of Henle
Thiazides	Inhibit Na,Cl cotransport in luminal membrane.	Distal convoluted tubules
Potassium-sparing diuretics	Inhibit action of aldosterone.	Cortical collecting ducts
	Block sodium channels in luminal membrane.	Cortical collecting ducts

gestive heart failure (Chapter 14). A person with a failing heart manifests (1) a decreased GFR, and (2) increased aldosterone secretion, both of which contribute to the virtual absence of sodium from the urine. The net result is extracellular volume expansion and formation of edema. The sodium-retaining responses are triggered by the lower cardiac output—a result of cardiac failure—and the resulting decrease in arterial pressure.

Another disease in which diuretics are frequently employed is hypertension (Chapter 14). It is still unclear why the decrease in body sodium and water resulting from the diuretic-induced excretion of these substances brings about arteriolar dilation and a lowering of the blood pressure.

As summarized in Table 16-9, clinically used diuretics are classified according to the mechanisms by which they inhibit ion reabsorption. Figures 16-12 and 16-13 should be used in conjunction with this table to visualize the mechanisms. Except for one category, the potassium-sparing diuretics, all diuretics not only increase sodium excretion but also cause increased potassium excretion, an unwanted side effect.

KIDNEY DISEASE

The term "kidney disease" is no more specific than "car trouble," since many diseases affect the kidneys. Bacteria, allergies, congenital defects, kidney stones, tumors, and toxic chemicals are some possible sources of kidney damage. Obstruction of the urethra or a ureter may

cause injury as the result of a buildup of pressure and may predispose the kidneys to bacterial infection.

Disease can attack the kidneys at any age. Experts estimate that there are at present more than 3 million undetected cases of kidney infection in the United States and that 25,000 to 75,000 Americans die of kidney failure each year.

Although many diseases of the kidney are self-limited and produce no permanent damage, others progress if untreated. The end stage of progressive diseases, regardless of the nature of the damaging agent—bacteria, toxic chemical, and so on—is a shrunken, nonfunctioning kidney. Similarly, the symptoms of profound renal malfunction are relatively independent of the damaging agent and are collectively known as *uremia*, laterally, "urine in the blood."

The severity of uremia depends upon how well the impaired kidneys are able to preserve the constancy of the internal environment. Assuming that the person continues to ingest a normal diet containing the usual quantities of nutrients and electrolytes, what problems arise? The key fact to keep in mind is that the kidney destruction markedly reduces the number of functioning nephrons. Accordingly, the many substances that gain entry to the tubule entirely or primarily by *filtration* are excreted in diminished amounts. In addition, the excretion of potassium and hydrogen ion is impaired because there are too few nephrons capable of normal tubular *secretion*. The buildup of all these substances—water, ions, and toxic waste products—in the blood causes many of the problems of uremia.

The remarkable fact is how large the safety factor is in renal function. In general, the kidneys are still able to perform their regulatory function quite well as long as 10 percent of the nephrons are functioning. This is because these remaining nephrons undergo alterations in function—filtration, reabsorption, and secretion—so as to compensate for the missing nephrons. For example, each remaining nephron increases its rate of potassium secretion so that the total amount of potassium excreted by the kidneys can be maintained at normal levels. The limits of regulation are restricted, however. To use potassium as our example again, if someone with severe renal disease were to go on a diet high in potassium, the remaining nephrons might not be able to secrete enough potassium to prevent potassium retention.

To take another example, the diseased kidney is unable to concentrate urine normally, which should not be surprising given the complex interactions required for normal functioning of the countercurrent multiplier system. Whereas water balance can be maintained by diseased kidneys when the person is ingesting reasonable quantities of water, the kidneys may not be able to reduce urine volume adequately to avoid dehydration if the individual is water-deprived.

As noted earlier, the glomerular filtrate and, hence, the urine are essentially protein-free. Certain diseases cause the renal corpuscles to become leaky to protein, however, and considerable amounts of protein are therefore filtered. Some of this protein is reabsorbed, but much may be excreted in the urine.

Other problems arise in uremia because of abnormal secretion of the hormones produced by the kidneys. Thus, decreased secretion of erythropoietin results in anemia. Decreased ability to form 1,25-$(OH)_2D_3$ results in deficient absorption of calcium from the gastrointestinal tract, with a resulting decrease in plasma calcium and inadequate bone calcification. Both of these hormones are now available for administration to patients with uremia.

The problem with renin, the third of the renal hormones, is rarely too little secretion but rather too much secretion by the juxtaglomerular cells of the damaged kidneys. The result is increased plasma angiotensin II concentration and the development of **renal hypertension**.

Hemodialysis, Peritoneal Dialysis, and Transplantation

As described above, failing kidneys reach a point when they can no longer excrete water and ions at rates that maintain body balances of these substances, nor can they excrete waste products as fast as they are produced. Dietary alterations can minimize these problems, for example, by lowering potassium intake and thereby reducing the amount of potassium to be excreted, but such alterations

cannot eliminate the problems. The techniques used to perform the kidneys' excretory functions are hemodialysis and peritoneal dialysis. The general term "dialysis" means to separate substances using a membrane.

The artificial kidney is an apparatus that utilizes a process termed **hemodialysis** to remove excess substances from the blood. During hemodialysis, blood is pumped from one of the patient's arteries through tubing that is bathed by a large volume of fluid. The tubing then conducts the blood back into the patient by way of a vein. The tubing is generally made of cellophane that is highly permeable to most solutes but relatively impermeable to protein and completely impermeable to blood cells—characteristics quite similar to those of capillaries. The bath fluid is a salt solution with ionic concentrations similar to or lower than those in normal plasma. As blood flows through the tubing, the concentrations of nonprotein plasma solutes tend to reach diffusion equilibrium with those of the solutes in the bath fluid. For example, if the plasma potassium concentration of the patient is above normal, potassium diffuses out of the blood across the cellophane tubing and into the bath fluid. Similarly, waste products and excesses of other substances also diffuse into the bath and thus are eliminated from the body.

Patients with acute reversible renal failure may require hemodialysis for only days or weeks. Patients with chronic irreversible renal failure require treatment for the rest of their lives, however, unless they receive a renal transplant. Such patients undergo hemodialysis several times a week, often at home.

Another way of removing excess substances from the blood is **peritoneal dialysis**, which uses the lining of the patient's own abdominal cavity (peritoneum) as a dialysis membrane. Fluid is injected, via a needle inserted through the abdominal wall, into this cavity and allowed to remain there for hours, during which solutes diffuse into the fluid from the person's blood. The dialysis fluid is then removed by reinserting the needle and is replaced with new fluid. This procedure can be performed several times daily by a patient who is simultaneously doing normal activities.

The treatment of choice for most patients with permanent renal failure is kidney transplantation. Rejection of the transplanted kidney by the recipient's body is a potential problem with transplants, but great strides have been made in reducing the frequency of rejection (Chapter 20). Many people who might benefit from a transplant do not receive one because a kidney is not available. Presently, the major source of kidneys for transplanting is recently deceased persons, and improved public understanding should lead to many more individuals giving permission in advance to have their kidneys and other organs used following their death.

SECTION E SUMMARY

DIURETICS AND KIDNEY DISEASE

I. Diuretics inhibit reabsorption of sodium and water, thereby enhancing their excretion. Different diuretics act on different nephron segments (Table 16-9).

II. Many of the symptoms of uremia—general renal malfunction—are due to retention of substances because of reduced GFR and, in the case of potassium and hydrogen ion, reduced secretion. Other symptoms are due to inadequate secretion of the renal hormones.

III. Either hemodialysis or peritoneal dialysis can be used chronically to eliminate the water, ions, and waste products retained during uremia.

CHAPTER 16 CLINICAL TERMS

diabetes insipidus	respiratory acidosis
hypertension	respiratory alkalosis
angiotensin converting enzyme	metabolic acidosis
(ACE) inhibitors	metabolic alkalosis
arrythmias	diuretics
hypocalcemic tetany	congestive heart
rickets	failure
osteomalacia	uremia
osteoporosis	renal hypertension
alkalosis	hemodialysis
acidosis	peritoneal dialysis

CHAPTER 16 THOUGHT QUESTIONS

(Answers are given in Appendix A.)

1. Substance T is present in the urine. Does this prove that it is filterable at the glomerulus?

2. Substance V is not normally present in the urine. Does this prove that it is neither filtered nor secreted?

3. The concentration of glucose in plasma is 100 mg/100 ml, and the GFR is 125 ml/min. How much glucose is filtered per minute?

4. A person is found to be excreting abnormally large amounts of a particular amino acid. Just from the theoretical description of T_m-limited reabsorptive mechanisms in the text, list several possible causes.

5. The concentration of urea in urine is always much higher than the concentration in plasma. Does this mean that urea is secreted?

6. If a drug that blocks the reabsorption of sodium is taken, what will happen to the reabsorption of water, urea, chloride, glucose, and amino acids and to the secretion of hydrogen ions?

7. Compare the changes in GFR and renin secretion occurring in response to a moderate hemorrhage in two individuals: one taking a drug that blocks the sympathetic nerves to the kidneys, and the other not taking such a drug.

8. If a person is taking a drug that completely inhibits converting enzyme, what will happen to aldosterone secretion when the person goes on a low-sodium diet?

9. In the steady state, is the amount of sodium chloride excreted daily in the urine by a normal person ingesting 12 g of sodium chloride per day (a) 12 g/day or (b) less than 12 g/day? Explain.

10. A young woman who has suffered a head injury seems to have recovered but is thirsty all the time. What do you think might be the cause?

11. A patient has a tumor in the adrenal cortex that continuously secretes large amounts of aldosterone. What effects does this have on the total amount of sodium and potassium in her body?

12. A person is taking a drug that inhibits the secretion of hydrogen ion by the tubular cells. What effect does this drug have on his body's balance of sodium, water, and hydrogen ion?

CHAPTER
17

THE DIGESTION AND ABSORPTION OF FOOD

The **gastrointestinal system** (Figure 17-1) includes the **gastrointestinal tract** (mouth, pharynx, esophagus, stomach, small intestine, large intestine, and rectum) and the glandular organs (salivary glands, liver, gallbladder, and pancreas) that are not part of the tract but secrete substances into it via ducts connecting these organs to the tract. The overall function of the gastrointestinal system is to process ingested foods into molecular forms that can be transferred, along with salts and water, from the external environment to the body's internal environment, where they can be distributed to cells by the circulatory system.

The adult gastrointestinal tract is a tube approximately 15 ft long,[1] running through the body from mouth to anus. The lumen of the tract, like the hole in a doughnut, is continuous with the external environment, which means that its contents are technically outside the body. This fact is relevant to understanding some of the tract's properties. For example, the large intestine is inhabited by billions of bacteria, most of which are harmless and even beneficial

_____

[1]After death, the smooth muscles of the intestinal tract relax, and its length approximately doubles.

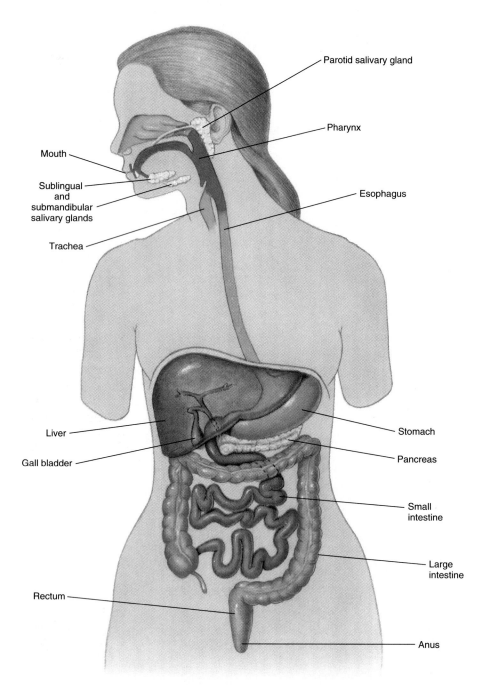

Parotid salivary gland

Pharynx

Mouth

Sublingual and submandibular salivary glands

Esophagus

Trachea

Liver

Gall bladder

Stomach

Pancreas

Small intestine

Large intestine

Rectum

Anus

FIGURE 17-1

Anatomy of the gastrointestinal system. The liver overlies the gallbladder and a portion of the stomach, and the stomach overlies part of the pancreas.

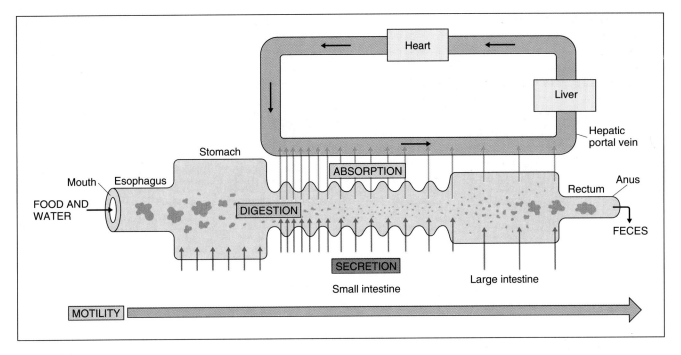

FIGURE 17-2
Four processes carried out by the gastrointestinal tract: digestion, secretion, absorption, and motility.

in this location. However, if the same bacteria enter the blood, as may happen, for example, in the case of a ruptured appendix, they may be extremely harmful and even lethal.

Most food is taken into the mouth as large particles containing macromolecules, such as proteins and polysaccharides, that are unable to cross the wall of the gastrointestinal tract. Before ingested food can be absorbed, therefore, it must be dissolved and broken down into small molecules. This dissolving and breaking-down process—**digestion**—is accomplished by the action of hydrochloric acid secreted by the stomach, bile secreted by the liver, and a variety of digestive enzymes that are released by the system's other exocrine glands, a process termed **secretion**.

The molecules produced by digestion then move from the lumen of the gastrointestinal tract across a layer of epithelial cells and enter the blood or the lymph. This process is called **absorption**.

While digestion, secretion, and absorption are taking place, contractions of smooth muscles in the gastrointestinal tract wall mix the luminal contents with the various secretions and move them through the tract from mouth to anus. These contractions are referred to as the **motility** of the gastrointestinal tract.

The functions of the gastrointestinal system can be described in terms of these four processes—digestion, secretion, absorption, and motility (Figure 17-2)—and the mechanisms controlling them.

The gastrointestinal system is designed to maximize absorption, and within fairly wide limits it will absorb as much as is ingested. With a few important exceptions, therefore, the gastrointestinal system does *not regulate* the amount of nutrients absorbed or their concentrations in the internal environment. That is primarily the function of the kidneys, as we saw in Chapter 16, and a number of endocrine systems, as will be described in Chapter 18.

Small amounts of certain metabolic end products are excreted via the gastrointestinal tract, but the elimination of most waste products from the internal environment is achieved by the lungs and kidneys. Indeed, the elimination of waste products is only a minor function of the gastrointestinal system. The material—**feces**—leaving the system at the end of the gastrointestinal tract consists almost entirely of bacteria and ingested material that was not digested and absorbed, that is, material that was never actually part of the internal environment.

OVERVIEW: FUNCTIONS OF THE GASTROINTESTINAL ORGANS

Figure 17-3 presents an overview of the secretions and functions of the gastrointestinal organs. The gastrointestinal tract begins with the **mouth**, and digestion starts there with chewing, which breaks up large pieces of food

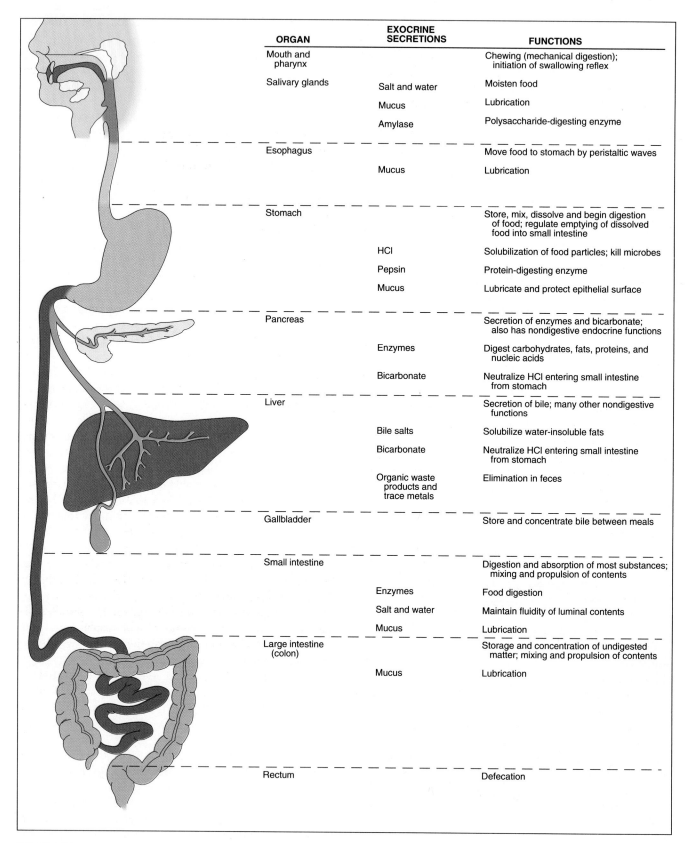

ORGAN	EXOCRINE SECRETIONS	FUNCTIONS
Mouth and pharynx		Chewing (mechanical digestion); initiation of swallowing reflex
Salivary glands	Salt and water	Moisten food
	Mucus	Lubrication
	Amylase	Polysaccharide-digesting enzyme
Esophagus		Move food to stomach by peristaltic waves
	Mucus	Lubrication
Stomach		Store, mix, dissolve and begin digestion of food; regulate emptying of dissolved food into small intestine
	HCl	Solubilization of food particles; kill microbes
	Pepsin	Protein-digesting enzyme
	Mucus	Lubricate and protect epithelial surface
Pancreas		Secretion of enzymes and bicarbonate; also has nondigestive endocrine functions
	Enzymes	Digest carbohydrates, fats, proteins, and nucleic acids
	Bicarbonate	Neutralize HCl entering small intestine from stomach
Liver		Secretion of bile; many other nondigestive functions
	Bile salts	Solubilize water-insoluble fats
	Bicarbonate	Neutralize HCl entering small intestine from stomach
	Organic waste products and trace metals	Elimination in feces
Gallbladder		Store and concentrate bile between meals
Small intestine		Digestion and absorption of most substances; mixing and propulsion of contents
	Enzymes	Food digestion
	Salt and water	Maintain fluidity of luminal contents
	Mucus	Lubrication
Large intestine (colon)		Storage and concentration of undigested matter; mixing and propulsion of contents
	Mucus	Lubrication
Rectum		Defecation

FIGURE 17-3

Functions of the gastrointestinal organs.

into smaller particles that can be swallowed without choking. **Saliva**, secreted by three pairs of **salivary glands** (Figure 17-1) located in the head, drains into the mouth though a short series of ducts. Saliva, which contains mucus, moistens and lubricates the food particles before swallowing. It also contains the enzyme **amylase**, which partially digests polysaccharides. A third function of saliva is to dissolve some of the food molecules. Only in the dissolved state can these molecules react with chemoreceptors in the mouth, giving rise to the sensation of taste (Chapter 9).

The next segments of the tract, the **pharynx** and **esophagus**, contribute nothing to digestion but provide the pathway by which ingested food and drink reach the stomach. The muscles in the walls of these segments control swallowing.

The **stomach** is a saclike organ, located between the esophagus and the small intestine. Its functions are to store, dissolve, and partially digest food, and to deliver its contents to the small intestine in amounts optimal for digestion and absorption. The glands lining the stomach's wall secrete a strong acid, **hydrochloric acid**, and several protein-digesting enzymes collectively known as **pepsin** (actually a precursor of pepsin known as pepsinogen).

The primary function of hydrochloric acid is to dissolve the particulate matter in food. The acid environment in the gastric (adjective for stomach) lumen alters the ionization of polar molecules, especially proteins, disrupting the extracellular network of connective-tissue proteins that form the structural framework of the tissues in food. The proteins and polysaccharides released by hydrochloric acid's dissolving action are partially digested in the stomach by both pepsin and amylase, the latter contributed by the salivary glands, into smaller molecular fragments. A major component of food that is not dissolved by acid is fat. As we shall see, special mechanisms must be employed to dissolve dietary fat before it can be adequately digested and absorbed.

Hydrochloric acid also kills bacteria that enter along with food. This process is not 100 percent effective, and some bacteria survive to take up residence and multiply in the intestinal tract, particularly the large intestine.

The digestive actions of the stomach reduce food particles to a solution, known as **chyme**, which contains molecular fragments of proteins and polysaccharides and droplets of fat. None of these digestion products can cross the epithelium of the gastric wall, and thus little absorption of organic nutrients occurs in the stomach.

Digestion's final stages and most absorption occur in the next section of the tract, the **small intestine**. Here molecules of intact or partially digested carbohydrates, fats, and proteins are broken down by hydrolytic enzymes into monosaccharides, fatty acids, and amino acids. Some of these enzymes are on the luminal surface of the intestinal lining cells, while others are secreted by the pancreas, as we shall see in a moment. The products of digestion cross the epithelial cells and enter the blood and/or lymph. Vitamins, minerals, and water, which do not require enzymatic digestion, are also absorbed in the small intestine.

The small intestine is a 1.5-in-diameter tube leading from the stomach to the large intestine. Its 9-ft length is divided into three segments: An initial short segment, the **duodenum**, is followed by the **jejunum** and then by the longest segment, the **ileum**. Normally, most absorption occurs in the first quarter of the small intestine, in the duodenum and jejunum. Thus, the small intestine has a considerable functional reserve.

Two major glands—the pancreas and liver—secrete substances that flow via ducts into the duodenum. The **pancreas**, a large, elongated gland located behind the stomach, has both endocrine (Chapter 18) and exocrine functions, but only the latter are directly involved in gastrointestinal function and will be described in this chapter. The exocrine portion of the pancreas secretes (1) digestive enzymes specific for each class of organic molecule, and (2) a fluid rich in bicarbonate ions. The high acidity of the chyme coming from the stomach would inactivate the pancreatic enzymes in the small intestine if the acid were not neutralized by the bicarbonate ions in the pancreatic fluid.

The **liver**, a large gland located in the upper right portion of the abdomen, has a large variety of functions which are described in various chapters. This is a convenient place to provide, in Table 17-1, a comprehensive reference list of these hepatic (pertaining to the liver) functions and the chapters in which they are described. We will be concerned here only with the exocrine functions that are directly related to the secretion of **bile**.

Bile contains bicarbonate, cholesterol, a number of organic wastes and—most important—a group of organic substances collectively termed **bile salts**. The bicarbonate ions, like those from the pancreas, help neutralize acid from the stomach, while the bile salts help solubilize dietary fat. These fats would otherwise be insoluble in water, and their solubilization increases the rates at which they are digested and absorbed.

Bile is secreted by the liver into small ducts that join to form a single duct—the common hepatic duct. Between meals, secreted bile is stored in a small sac underneath the liver, the **gallbladder**, which branches from the common hepatic duct. The gallbladder concentrates the bile by absorbing salts and water. During a meal, the smooth muscles in the gallbladder wall contract, causing a concentrated bile solution to be injected into the duodenum via the **common bile duct** (Figure 17-4), an extension of the common hepatic duct. The gallbladder can be surgically removed without impairing bile secretion by the liver or its flow into the intestinal tract. In fact, many animals that secrete bile do not have a gallbladder.

TABLE 17-1   SUMMARY OF LIVER FUNCTIONS

A. Endocrine functions
  1. In response to growth hormone, secretes insulin-like growth factor I (IGF-I), which promotes growth by stimulating mitosis in various tissues, including bone (Chapter 18).
  2. Contributes to the activation of vitamin D (Chapter 16).
  3. Forms triiodothyronine (T_3) from thyroxine (T_4) (Chapter 10).
  4. Secretes angiotensinogen, which is acted upon by renin to form angiotensin (Chapter 16).
  5. Metabolizes hormones (Chapter 10).
B. Clotting functions
  1. Produces many of the plasma clotting factors, including prothrombin and fibrinogen (Chapter 20).
  2. Produces bile salts, which are essential for the gastrointestinal absorption of vitamin K, which is, in turn, needed for production of the clotting factors (Chapter 20).
C. Plasma proteins: Synthesizes and secretes plasma albumin (Chapter 14), acute phase proteins (Chapter 20), binding proteins for steroid hormones (Chapter 10) and trace elements (Chapter 14), lipoproteins (Chapter 18), and other proteins mentioned elsewhere in this table.
D. Digestive functions (Chapter 17)
  1. Synthesizes and secretes bile acids, which are necessary for adequate digestion and absorption of fats.
  2. Secretes into the bile a bicarbonate-rich solution of inorganic ions, which helps neutralize acid in the duodenum.
E. Organic metabolism (Chapter 18)
  1. Converts plasma glucose into glycogen and triacylglycerols during absorptive period.
  2. Converts plasma amino acids to fatty acids, which can be incorporated into triacylglycerols, during absorptive period.
  3. Synthesizes triacylglycerols and secretes them as lipoproteins during absorptive period.
  4. Produces glucose from glycogen (glycogenolysis) and other sources (gluconeogenesis) during postabsorptive period and releases the glucose into the blood.
  5. Converts fatty acids into ketones during fasting.
  6. Produces urea, the major end product of amino acid (protein) catabolism, and releases it into the blood.
F. Cholesterol metabolism (Chapter 18)
  1. Synthesizes cholesterol and releases it into the blood.
  2. Secretes plasma cholesterol into the bile.
  3. Converts plasma cholesterol into bile acids.
G. Excretory and degradative functions
  1. Secretes bilirubin and other bile pigments into the bile (Chapter 17).
  2. Excretes, via the bile, many endogenous and foreign organic molecules as well as trace metals (Chapter 20).
  3. Biotransforms many endogenous and foreign organic molecules (Chapter 20).
  4. Destroys old erythrocytes (Chapter 14).

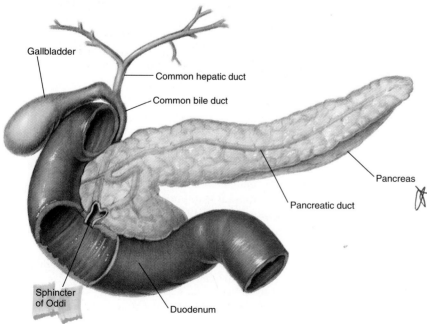

FIGURE 17-4

Bile ducts from the liver converge to form the common hepatic duct, from which branches the duct leading to the gallbladder. Beyond this branch the common hepatic duct becomes the common bile duct. The common bile duct and the pancreatic duct converge and empty their contents into the duodenum at the sphincter of Oddi.

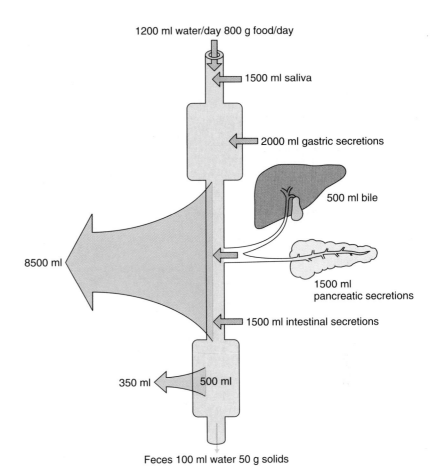

1200 ml water/day 800 g food/day

1500 ml saliva

2000 ml gastric secretions

500 ml bile

1500 ml pancreatic secretions

1500 ml intestinal secretions

8500 ml

350 ml ← 500 ml

Feces 100 ml water 50 g solids

FIGURE 17-5

Average amounts of food and fluid ingested, secreted, absorbed, and excreted from the gastrointestinal tract daily.

In the small intestine, monosaccharides and amino acids are absorbed by specific carrier-mediated transport processes in the plasma membranes of the intestinal epithelial cells, whereas fatty acids enter these cells by diffusion. Most mineral ions are actively absorbed, and water diffuses passively down osmotic gradients. Digestion and absorption have been largely completed by the middle portion of the small intestine.

The motility of the small intestine, brought about by the smooth muscles lining it, mixes the luminal contents with the various secretions, brings the contents into contact with the epithelial surface where absorption takes place, and slowly advances the luminal material toward the large intestine. Since most substances are absorbed in the early portion of the small intestine, only a small volume of water, salts, and undigested material is passed on to the next segment, the **large intestine** (or **colon**). The large intestine temporarily stores the undigested material (some of which is acted upon by bacteria) and concentrates it by absorbing salt and water. Contractile activities in the final segment of the gastrointestinal tract, the **rectum**, and associated sphincter muscles eliminate the feces by the process of **defecation**.

The average adult consumes about 800 g of food and 1200 ml of water per day, but this is only a fraction of the material entering the lumen of the gastrointestinal tract.

An additional 7000 ml of fluid from salivary glands, gastric glands, pancreas, liver, and intestinal glands is secreted into the tract each day (Figure 17-5). Only about 100 ml of water is lost in the feces, the rest being absorbed into the blood. Almost all the salts in the secreted fluids are also absorbed into the blood. The secreted digestive enzymes are themselves digested, and the resulting amino acids absorbed into the blood.

This completes our overview of the gastrointestinal system. Since its major task is digestion and absorption, we begin our more detailed description with these processes. Subsequent sections of the chapter will then describe, organ by organ, regulation of the secretions and motility that produce the optimal conditions for digestion and absorption. A prerequisite for all this physiology, however, is a knowledge of the structure of the gastrointestinal tract wall.

STRUCTURE OF THE GASTROINTESTINAL TRACT WALL

From the midesophagus to the anus, the wall of the gastrointestinal tract has the general structure illustrated in Figure 17-6. Most of the tube's luminal surface is

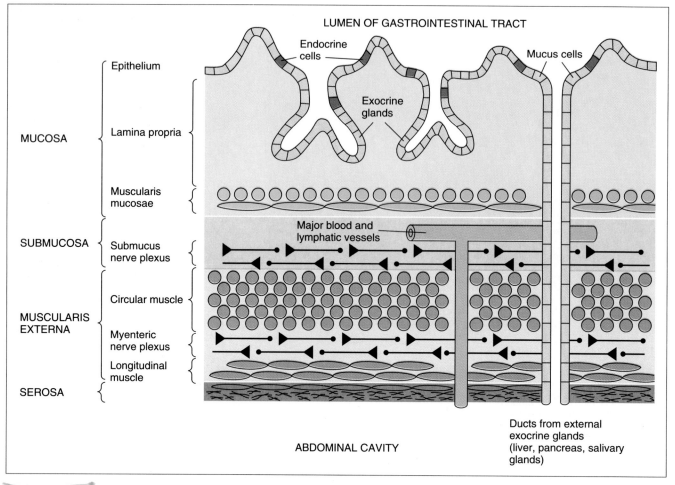

FIGURE 17-6

Structure of the gastrointestinal wall in longitudinal section. Not shown are the smaller blood vessels, neural connections between the two nerve plexuses, and neural terminations on muscles and glands.

highly convoluted, a feature that greatly increases the surface area available for absorption. From the stomach on, this surface is covered by a single layer of epithelial cells linked together along the edges of their luminal surfaces by tight junctions.

Included in this epithelial layer are exocrine cells that secrete mucus into the lumen of the tract, and endocrine cells that release hormones into the blood. Invaginations of the epithelium into the underlying tissue form exocrine glands that secrete acid, enzymes, water, and ions, as well as mucus.

Just below the epithelium is a layer of connective tissue, the lamina propria, through which pass small blood vessels, nerve fibers, and lymphatic ducts. The lamina propria is separated from underlying tissues by a thin layer of smooth muscle, the muscularis mucosae. The combination of these three layers—the epithelium, lamina propria, and muscularis mucosa—is called the **mucosa**.

Beneath the mucosa is a second connective-tissue layer, the submucosa, containing a network of nerve cells, the **submucous plexus**, and blood and lymphatic vessels whose branches penetrate into both the overlying mucosa and the underlying layers of smooth muscle called the **muscularis externa**. Contractions of these muscles provide the forces for moving and mixing the gastrointestinal contents. The muscularis externa has two layers: (1) a relatively thick inner layer of **circular muscle**, whose fibers are oriented in a circular pattern around the tube such that contraction produces a narrowing of the lumen, and (2) a thinner outer layer of **longitudinal muscle**, whose contraction shortens the tube. Between these two muscle layers is a second network of nerve cells known as the **myenteric plexus**.

Finally, surrounding the outer surface of the tube is a thin layer of cells and connective tissue called the **serosa**. Thin sheets of connective tissue connect the serosa to the

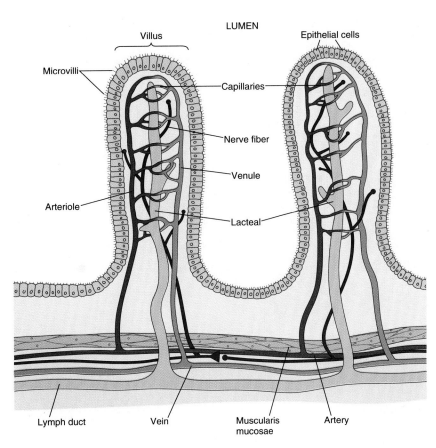

FIGURE 17-7
Structure of intestinal villi.

abdominal wall, supporting the gastrointestinal tract in the abdominal cavity. At various points along the tube, as we have seen, the secretions of exocrine glands lying outside the tract (the salivary glands, liver, and pancreas) are delivered to the lumen of the tract via ducts.

There is extensive folding of the intestinal surface. Also, extending from the surface are finger-like projections known as **villi** (Figure 17-7). The surface of each villus is covered with a single layer of epithelial cells whose surface membranes form small projections called **microvilli** (also known collectively as the brush border) (Figure 17-8). The combination of folded mucosa, villi, and microvilli increases the small intestine's surface area available for absorption about 600-fold over that of a flat-surfaced tube having the same length and diameter. The human small intestine's total surface area is about 300 m², the area of a tennis court.

Epithelial surfaces in the gastrointestinal tract are continuously being replaced by new epithelial cells. In the small intestine, new cells arise by mitosis from cells at the base of the villi. These cells differentiate as they migrate to the top of a villus, replacing older cells that disintegrate and are discharged into the intestinal lumen. These disintegrating cells release into the lumen their intracellular enzymes, which then contribute to the digestive process. About 17 billion epithelial cells are replaced each day, and the entire epithelium of the small intestine is replaced

approximately every 5 days. It is because of this rapid cell turnover that the lining of the intestinal tract is so susceptible to damage by agents, such as radiation and anticancer drugs, that inhibit cell division.

The center of each intestinal villus is occupied both by a single blind-ended lymphatic vessel termed a **lacteal** and by a capillary network (Figure 17-7). As we will see, most of the fat absorbed in the small intestine enters the lacteals, while other absorbed nutrients enter the blood capillaries. The venous drainage from the intestinal villi, as well as from the large intestine, pancreas, and portions of the stomach does not empty directly into the vena cava but passes first via the **hepatic portal vein** into the liver. There it flows through a second capillary network before leaving the liver to return to the heart. Thus, material absorbed into the intestinal capillaries, in contrast to the lacteals, can be processed by the liver before entering the general circulation.

DIGESTION AND ABSORPTION

Carbohydrate

Carbohydrate intake per day ranges from about 250 to 800 g in a typical American diet. About two-thirds of this carbohydrate is the plant polysaccharide starch, and most of the remainder consists of the disaccharides sucrose

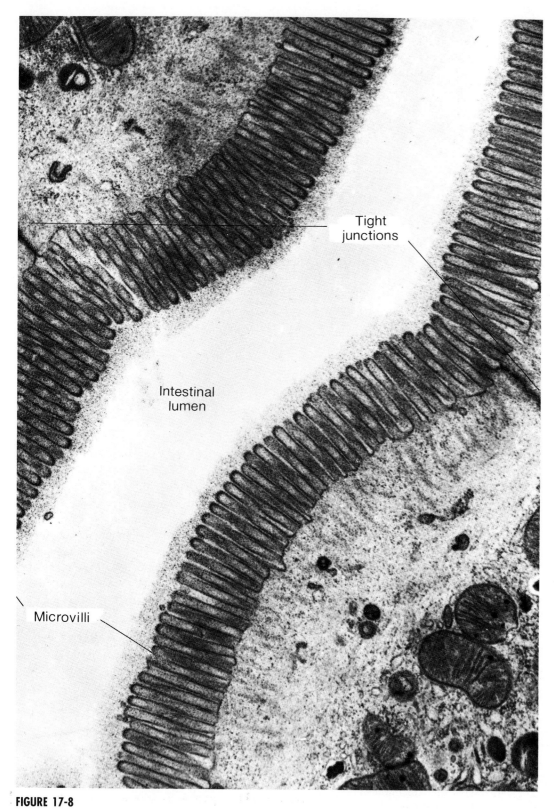

FIGURE 17-8

Microvilli on the surface of intestinal epithelial cells. [*From D. W. Fawcett, J. Histochem. Cytochem. 13:75–91 (1965). Courtesy of Susumo Ito.*]

(table sugar) and lactose (milk sugar) (Table 17-2). Only small amounts of monosaccharides are normally present in the diet. Cellulose and certain other complex polysaccharides found in vegetable matter cannot be broken down by the enzymes in the small intestine. These polysaccharides, collectively referred to as **fiber**, are passed on to the large intestine, where they are partially metabolized by bacteria.

Starch digestion by salivary amylase begins in the mouth and continues in the upper part of the stomach before amylase is destroyed by gastric acid. Starch digestion is completed in the small intestine by pancreatic amylase. The products produced by both amylases are the disaccharide maltose and a mixture of short, branched chains of glucose molecules. These products, along with ingested sucrose and lactose, are then broken down into monosaccharides—glucose, galactose, and fructose—by enzymes located on the brush-border membranes of the small-intestine epithelial cells. These monosaccharides are then transported across the intestinal epithelium into the blood. Fructose crosses the epithelium by facilitated diffusion, while glucose and galactose undergo secondary active transport coupled to sodium (page 128). Most of the ingested carbohydrate is digested and absorbed within the first 20 percent of the small intestine.

Protein

Only 40 to 50 g of protein is required by a normal adult to supply essential amino acids and replace the amino acid nitrogen converted to urea. A typical American diet contains about 125 g of protein per day. In addition, a large amount of protein, in the form of enzymes and mucus, is secreted into the gastrointestinal tract or enters it via the disintegration of epithelial cells. Regardless of source, most of the protein in the lumen is broken down into amino acids and absorbed by the small intestine.

Proteins are broken down to peptide fragments in the stomach by pepsin, and in the small intestine by **trypsin**

and **chymotrypsin**, which are secreted by the pancreas. These fragments are further digested to free amino acids by **carboxypeptidase**, secreted by the pancreas, and by **aminopeptidase**, located on the luminal epithelial membranes of the small intestine. These last two enzymes split off amino acids from the carboxyl and amino ends of the peptide chains, respectively.

The free amino acids then undergo secondary active transport coupled with sodium across the intestinal wall. Short chains of two or three amino acids are also actively absorbed.[2] This is in contrast to carbohydrate absorption, in which molecules larger than monosaccharides are not absorbed. As with carbohydrates, protein digestion and absorption are largely completed in the upper portion of the small intestine.

Small amounts of intact proteins are able to cross the intestinal epithelium and gain access to the interstitial fluid. They do so by a combination of endocytosis and exocytosis. The absorptive capacity for intact proteins is much greater in infants than in adults, and antibodies (proteins involved in the immunological defense system of the body) secreted into the mother's milk can be absorbed by the infant, providing some immunity until the infant can produce its own antibodies.

Fat

Fat intake ranges from about 25 to 160 g/day in a typical American diet; most is in the form of triacylglycerols. Fat digestion occurs almost entirely in the small intestine. The major digestive enzyme in this process is pancreatic **lipase**, which catalyzes the splitting of bonds linking fatty acids to the first and third carbon atoms of glycerol, producing two free fatty acids and a monoglyceride as products:

$$\text{Triacylglycerol} \xrightarrow{\text{Lipase}} \text{monoglyceride} + 2 \text{ fatty acids}$$

The triacylglycerols entering the small intestine are insoluble in water and aggregate into large lipid droplets. Since pancreatic lipase is a water-soluble enzyme, its digestive action can take place only at the *surface* of a lipid droplet. Therefore, if most of the ingested lipids remained in large lipid droplets, the rate of lipid digestion would be very slow. The rate of digestion is, however, substantially increased by dividing the large lipid droplets into a number of much smaller droplets, each about 1 mm in diameter, thereby increasing their surface area and accessibility to lipase action. This process is known as emulsification,

TABLE 17-2 CARBOHYDRATES IN FOOD

Class	Examples	Made up of
Polysaccharides	Starch	Glucose
	Cellulose	Glucose
	Glycogen	Glucose
Disaccharides	Sucrose	Glucose-fructose
	Lactose	Glucose-galactose
	Maltose	Glucose-glucose
Monosaccharides	Glucose	
	Fructose	
	Galactose	

[2]Amino acids are actually absorbed at a greater rate when present in small peptides than as free amino acids. This has practical applications when adequate levels of nutrients must be supplied to patients with various GI disorders.

FIGURE 17-9
Structure of bile salt. (A) Chemical formula of glycocholic acid, one of several bile salts secreted by the liver (polar groups in color). (B) Three-dimensional structure of a bile salt, showing its polar and nonpolar surfaces.

Although digestion is speeded up by emulsification, absorption of the insoluble products of the lipase reaction would still be very slow if it were not for a second action of the bile salts, the formation of **micelles**, which are similar in structure to emulsion droplets but are much smaller, 4 to 7 nm in diameter. Micelles consist of bile salts, fatty acids, monoglycerides, and phospholipids all clustered together with the polar ends of each molecule oriented toward the micelle's surface and the nonpolar portions forming the micelle's core. Also included in the core of the micelle are small amounts of nonpolar, fat-soluble vitamins.

How do micelles increase absorption? Although fatty acids and monoglycerides have an extremely low solubility in water, a few molecules do exist in solution and are free to diffuse across the plasma membranes of the epithelial cells lining the small intestine. Micelles, containing the products of fat digestion, are continuously breaking down and re-forming. When a micelle breaks down, its contents are released into the solution and become available to dif-

and the resulting suspension of small lipid droplets is an **emulsion**.

The emulsification of fat requires (1) mechanical disruption of the large fat droplets into smaller droplets; and (2) an emulsifying agent, which acts to prevent the smaller droplets from reaggregating back into large droplets. The mechanical disruption is provided by contractile activity, occurring in the lower portion of the stomach and in the small intestine, which acts to grind and mix the luminal contents. Phospholipids in food and phospholipids and bile salts secreted in the bile provide the emulsifying agents.

Phospholipids are amphiphatic molecules (Chapter 2) consisting of two nonpolar fatty acid chains attached to glycerol, with a charged phosphate group located on glycerol's third carbon. Bile salts are formed from cholesterol in the liver and are also amphiphatic (Figure 17-9). The nonpolar portions of the phospholipids and bile salts associate with the nonpolar interior of the lipid droplets, leaving the polar portions exposed at the water surface. There they repel other lipid droplets that are similarly coated with these emulsifying agents, thereby preventing their reaggregation into larger fat droplets (Figure 17-10).

FIGURE 17-10
Emulsification of fat by bile salts and phospholipids.

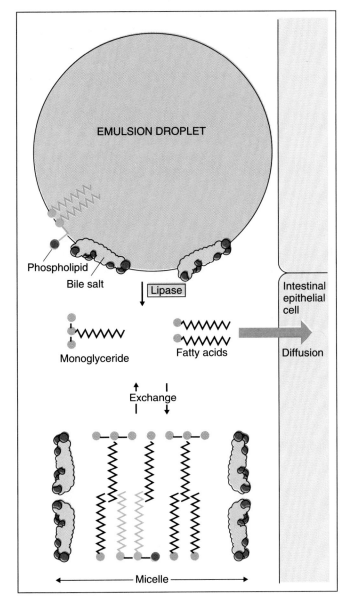

FIGURE 17-11
The products of fat digestion by lipase are held in solution in the micellar state, combined with bile salts and phospholipids. The micellar contents rapidly exchange with the free products in aqueous solution, which are able to diffuse into intestinal epithelial cells.

fuse across the intestinal lining. As the concentration of free lipids falls, because of their diffusion out of the lumen, more lipids shift out of the micelles into the free phase (Figure 17-11). Thus, the micelles provide a means of keeping most of the insoluble fat digestion products in solution, while at the same time replenishing the small amount of products that are free in solution as they diffuse into the intestinal epithelium. Note that it is not the mi-

celle that is absorbed but rather the lipids that are free in solution.

Although fatty acids and monoglycerides are the molecules that enter the epithelial cells from the intestinal lumen, it is triacylglycerol that is released on the other side of the cell into the interstitial fluid. In other words, during their passage through the epithelial cells, fatty acids and monoglycerides are resynthesized into triacylglycerols. This occurs in the agranular endoplasmic reticulum, where the enzymes for triacylglycerol synthesis are located. Within this organelle, the resynthesized fat aggregates into small droplets coated with an amphipathic protein that performs an emulsifying function similar to that of a bile salt.

The exit of these fat droplets from the cell follows the same pathway as a secreted protein (page 70). Vesicles containing the droplet pinch off the endoplasmic reticulum, are processed through the Golgi apparatus, and eventually fuse with the plasma membrane, releasing the fat droplet into the interstitial fluid. These small, extracellular fat droplets are known as **chylomicrons**. Chylomicrons contain, in addition to triacylglycerols, other lipids (including phospholipids, cholesterol, and fat-soluble vitamins) that have been absorbed by the same process that led to fatty acid and monoglyceride absorption.

The chylomicrons released from the epithelial cells pass into the lacteals rather than into the capillaries. The chylomicrons cannot enter the capillaries because a basement membrane (an extracellular glycoprotein layer) at the outer surface of the capillary provides a barrier to the large chylomicrons, which are about 1 μm in diameter. The lacteals do not have basement membranes and have very large slit pores between their endothelial cells. Thus, the chylomicrons can pass through the lacteal wall into the lymph. The lymph from the small intestine, as from everywhere else in the body, eventually empties into systemic veins. In Chapter 18 we describe how the lipids in the circulating blood chylomicrons are made available to the cells of the body.

Figure 17-12 summarizes the pathway taken by fat in moving from the intestinal lumen into the lymphatic system.

Vitamins

Most vitamins undergo little enzymatic modification during digestion and absorption. Digestion of food particles releases the vitamins, transferring them to a soluble form in which they can be absorbed.

The fat-soluble vitamins—A, D, E, and K—follow the pathway for fat absorption described in the previous section. They are solubilized in micelles. Thus, any interference with the secretion of bile or the action of bile salts in the intestine decreases the absorption of the fat-soluble vitamins.

FIGURE 17-12

Summary of fat absorption across the walls of the small intestine.

Most water-soluble vitamins are absorbed by diffusion or carrier-mediated transport. However, one—vitamin B_{12}—is a very large, charged molecule. In order to be absorbed, vitamin B_{12} must first bind to a protein, known as **intrinsic factor**, produced by the acid-secreting cells in the stomach. The resulting complex then binds to specific sites on the epithelial cells in the lower portion of the ileum, where vitamin B_{12} is absorbed. As described on page 398, vitamin B_{12} is required for erythrocyte formation, and deficiencies result in *pernicious anemia*. This form of anemia may occur when the stomach either has been removed (as, for example, to treat ulcers or gastric cancer) or fails to secrete intrinsic factor. Since the absorption of vitamin B_{12} occurs in the lower part of the ileum, removal of this segment because of disease can also result in pernicious anemia.

Water and Minerals

Water is the most abundant substance in chyme. Approximately 9000 ml of ingested and secreted fluid enters the small intestine each day, but only 1500 ml is passed on to the large intestine since 80 percent of the fluid is absorbed in the small intestine. The epithelial membranes of the small intestine are very permeable to water. Therefore, net water diffusion occurs across the epithelium whenever a water concentration difference is established by the active absorption of solutes (page 139).

Sodium ions account for much of the actively transported solutes because they constitute the most abundant solute in chyme. Sodium absorption is a primary active process, using the Na,K-ATPase pumps in a manner similar to that for renal tubular sodium reabsorption (Chapter 16).

Chloride and bicarbonate ions move with the sodium ions and contribute another large fraction of the absorbed solute. Other minerals present in smaller concentrations, such as potassium, magnesium, and calcium, are also absorbed, as are trace elements such as iron, zinc, and iodide. Consideration of the transport processes associated with all these is beyond the scope of this book, and we shall briefly consider as an example the absorption of only one of them—iron.

Only about 10 percent of ingested iron is absorbed into the blood each day. Iron ions are actively transported into intestinal epithelial cells, where most of them are incorporated into ferritin, the protein-iron complex that functions as an intracellular iron store (page 398). The absorbed iron that does not bind to ferritin is released on the blood side and bound to the plasma protein, transferrin, in which form it circulates throughout the body (page 398). Most of the iron bound to ferritin is released back into the intestinal lumen when the intestinal cells disintegrate at the tip of the villus and is excreted in the feces.

Iron absorption depends on the body's iron content. When body stores are ample, the increased concentration of free iron in the plasma and intestinal epithelial cells leads to an increased transcription of the ferritin protein and thus an increased storage of iron as ferritin. This reduces the amount of iron available for release into the blood. When the body stores drop, for example, when there is a loss of hemoglobin during hemorrhage, the production and hence the concentration of intestinal ferritin decrease; therefore, the amount of iron bound to intestinal ferritin decreases, thereby increasing the unbound iron available for release into the blood.

Once iron has entered the blood, the body has very little means of excreting it and it will accumulate in tissues. Although the control mechanisms for iron absorption just described tend to maintain the iron content of the body fairly constant, a large ingestion of iron can overwhelm them, leading to an increased deposition of iron in tissues and producing toxic effects. Some people have genetically defective control mechanisms and therefore absorb toxic amounts of iron even when ingestion is normal. This condition is termed *hemochromatosis*.

Iron absorption also depends on the type of food ingested. This is because iron binds to many negatively charged ions in food that can retard its absorption. For example, iron in ingested liver is much more absorbable than iron in egg yolk since the latter contains phosphates that bind the iron to form an insoluble complex.

The absorption of iron is typical of that of most trace metals in several respects: (1) Cellular storage proteins and plasma carrier proteins are involved; and (2) the control of absorption, rather than urinary excretion, is the major mechanism for the homeostatic control of the body's content of the trace metal.

REGULATION OF GASTROINTESTINAL PROCESSES

Unlike control systems that regulate variables in the internal environment, the control mechanisms of the gastrointestinal system regulate conditions in the lumen of the tract. With few exceptions, like those for trace metals, these control mechanisms are governed not by the nutritional state of the body, but rather by the volume and composition of the luminal contents.

Basic Principles

Gastrointestinal reflexes are initiated by a relatively small number of luminal stimuli: (1) distension of the wall by the luminal contents; (2) chyme osmolarity (total solute concentration); (3) chyme acidity; and (4) chyme concentrations of specific digestion products—monosaccharides, fatty acids, peptides, and amino acids. These stimuli act on receptors located in the wall of the tract—mechanoreceptors, osmoreceptors, and chemoreceptors—to trigger reflexes that influence the effectors—the muscle layers in the wall of the tract and the exocrine glands that secrete substances into its lumen.

Neural Regulation. The gastrointestinal tract has its own local nervous system, known as the **enteric nervous system**, in the form of two nerve networks, the myenteric plexus and the submucous plexus (Figure 17-6). These neurons either synapse with other neurons in the plexus or end near smooth muscles and glands. Many axons leave the myenteric plexus and synapse with neurons in the submucous plexus, and vice versa, so that neural activity in one plexus influences the activity in the other. Moreover, stimulation at one point in the plexus can lead to impulses that are conducted both up and down the tract. Thus, for example, stimuli in the upper part of the small intestine may affect smooth muscle and gland activity in the stomach as well as in the lower part of the intestinal tract.

The enteric nervous system contains adrenergic and cholinergic neurons as well as neurons that release other neurotransmitters, many of which are small peptides. ATP and nitric oxide have also been found to play major roles in the enteric nervous system as neurotransmitters and neuromodulators.

Many of the effectors mentioned earlier are at the ends of neurons that are part of the enteric nervous system. This permits neural reflexes that are completely within the tract, that is, independent of the central nervous system (CNS). In addition, nerve fibers from both the sympathetic and parasympathetic branches of the autonomic nervous system enter the intestinal tract and synapse with neurons in both plexuses. Via these pathways, the CNS can influence the motility and secretory activity of the gastrointestinal tract.

Thus, two types of neural reflex arcs exist (Figure 17-13): (1) **short reflexes** from receptors through the nerve plexuses to effector cells; and (2) **long reflexes** from receptors in the tract to the CNS by way of afferent nerves and back to the nerve plexuses and effector cells by way of the autonomic nerve fibers. Some controls are mediated either solely by short reflexes or solely by long reflexes, whereas other controls use both.

Finally, it should be noted that not all neural reflexes are initiated by signals *within* the tract. The sight or smell of food and the emotional state of an individual can have significant effects on the gastrointestinal tract, effects that are mediated by the CNS via autonomic neurons.

Hormonal Regulation. The hormones that control the gastrointestinal system are secreted mainly by endocrine cells scattered throughout the epithelium of the stomach and small intestine; that is, these cells are not clustered into discrete organs like the thyroid or adrenal glands. One surface of each endocrine cell is exposed to the lumen of the gastrointestinal tract. At this surface, various chemical substances in the chyme stimulate the cell to release its

hormones from the opposite, blood side of the cell. Although some of these hormones can also be detected in the lumen and may therefore be acting locally as paracrine agents, most of the gastrointestinal hormones reach their target cells via the circulation.

Several dozen substances are currently being investigated as possible gastrointestinal hormones, but only four—**secretin**, **cholecystokinin (CCK)**, **gastrin**, and **glucose-dependent insulinotropic peptide (GIP)**[3]—have met all the criteria for true hormones. They, as well as several candidate hormones, also exist in the CNS and in gastrointestinal plexus neurons, where they function as neurotransmitters or neuromodulators.

Table 17-3, which summarizes the major characteristics of the four established GI hormones, not only serves as a reference for future discussions but also illustrates two generalizations: (1) Each hormone participates in a feedback control system that regulates some aspect of the luminal environment, and (2) each hormone affects more than one type of target cell.

These two generalizations can be illustrated by CCK. The presence of fatty acids in the small intestine triggers CCK secretion from the duodenum into the blood. Circulating CCK then stimulates secretion by the pancreas of digestive enzymes, including lipase, which digests fat. CCK also causes the gallbladder to contract, delivering to the intestine the bile salts required for fat digestion and absorption. As fat is digested and absorbed, the stimulus (fatty acids in the lumen) for CCK release is removed.

In many cases, a single effector cell contains receptors for more than one hormone, as well as receptors for neu-

---

[3]GIP was originally called gastric inhibitory peptide.

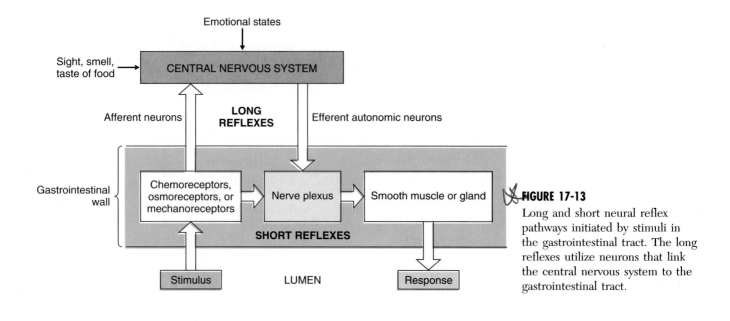

FIGURE 17-13

Long and short neural reflex pathways initiated by stimuli in the gastrointestinal tract. The long reflexes utilize neurons that link the central nervous system to the gastrointestinal tract.

TABLE 17-3   PROPERTIES OF GASTROINTESTINAL HORMONES

	Gastrin	CCK	Secretin	GIP
Structure	Peptide	Peptide	Peptide	Peptide
Endocrine cell location	Antrum of stomach	Small intestine	Small intestine	Small intestine
Stimuli for hormone release	Amino acids, peptides in stomach; parasympathetic nerves	Amino acids, fatty acids in small intestine	Acid in small intestine	Glucose, fat in small intestine
Stimuli inhibiting hormone release	Acid in stomach lumen			

(handwritten: greti receptors; acid inhibits; abnormal brain; stimulates insulin secr)

Target-Cell Responses

	Gastrin	CCK	Secretin	GIP
Stomach				
Acid secretion	Stimulates		Inhibits	
Growth	Stimulates			
Pancreas				
Bicarbonate secretion		Potentiates secretin's actions	Stimulates	
Enzyme secretion		Stimulates		
Insulin secretion				Stimulates
Growth	Stimulates	Stimulates	Stimulates	
Liver				
Bicarbonate secretion		Potentiates secretin's actions	Stimulates	
Gallbladder		Stimulates		
Sphincter of Oddi		Relaxes		
Small intestine	Stimulates ileum; inhibits ileocecal sphincter			
Growth	Stimulates			
Large intestine	Stimulates mass movement			

(handwritten: MEMORIZE IT)

rotransmitters and paracrine agents, with the result that a variety of inputs can affect the cell's response. One such group of interactions is the phenomenon known as **potentiation**, an example of which is the interaction between secretin and CCK. Secretin strongly stimulates pancreatic bicarbonate secretion, whereas the hormone CCK is a weak stimulus of bicarbonate secretion. Both hormones together, however, stimulate pancreatic bicarbonate secretion more strongly than would be predicted by the sum of the individual stimulatory effects of CCK and secretin. This is because CCK potentiates the effect of secretin. One of the consequences of potentiation is that small changes in the plasma concentration of one gastrointestinal hormone can have considerable effects on the actions of other gastrointestinal hormones.

In addition to their stimulation (or in some cases inhibition) of effector-cell functions, the gastrointestinal hormones also have tropic (growth-promoting) effects on various tissues, including the gastric and intestinal mucosa and the exocrine portions of the pancreas.

Phases of Gastrointestinal Control. The neural and hormonal control of the gastrointestinal system is, in large part, divisible into three phases—cephalic, gastric, and intestinal—according to stimulus location.

The **cephalic phase** is initiated when receptors in the head (*cephalic*, head) are stimulated by sight, smell, taste, and chewing. It is also initiated by various emotional states. The efferent pathways for these reflexes are parasympathetic fibers, most of which are in the vagus nerves, and sympathetic fibers. These fibers activate neurons in the gastrointestinal nerve plexuses, which in turn affect secretory and contractile activity.

Three stimuli in the stomach initiate the reflexes that constitute the **gastric phase** of regulation—distension, decreased acidity, and peptides formed during the digestion of ingested protein. The responses to these stimuli are mediated by short and long neural reflexes and by release of the hormone gastrin.

Finally, the **intestinal phase** is initiated by stimuli in the intestinal tract—distension, increased acidity, osmolarity, and various digestive products. Like the gastric phase, the intestinal phase is mediated by both short and long neural reflexes and by gastrointestinal hormones, but in this case secretin, CCK, and GIP.

It must be reemphasized that each of these phases is named for the site at which the various stimuli *initiate* the reflex and not for the sites of effector activity. Each phase is characterized by efferent output to virtually all organs in the gastrointestinal tract. Also, these phases do not occur in temporal sequence except at the very beginning of a meal. Rather, during ingestion and the much longer absorptive period, reflexes characteristic of all three phases may be occurring simultaneously.

Keeping in mind the neural and hormonal mechanisms available for regulating gastrointestinal activity, we can now examine the specific contractile and secretory processes that occur in each segment of the gastrointestinal system.

Mouth, Pharynx, and Esophagus

Chewing. Chewing is controlled by the somatic nerves to the skeletal muscles of the mouth and jaw. In addition to the voluntary control of these muscles, rhythmical chewing motions are reflexly activated by the pressure of food against the gums, hard palate at the roof of the mouth, and tongue. Activation of these mechanoreceptors leads to reflexive inhibition of the muscles holding the jaw closed. The resulting relaxation of the jaw reduces the pressure on the various mechanoreceptors, leading to a new cycle of contraction and relaxation.

Although chewing prolongs the subjective pleasure of taste, it does not appreciably alter the rate at which the food will be digested and absorbed from the small intestine. On the other hand, attempting to swallow a large particle of food can lead to choking if the particle lodges over the trachea, blocking the entry of air into the lungs. A number of preventable deaths occur each year from choking, the symptoms of which are often confused with those of a heart attack, so that no attempt is made to remove the obstruction from the airway. The Heimlich maneuver, described on page 485, can often dislodge the obstructing particle from the airways.

Saliva. The secretion of saliva is controlled by both sympathetic and parasympathetic neurons. Unlike their antagonistic activity in most organs, however, both systems stimulate salivary secretion, the parasympathetics producing the greater response. In the absence of ingested material, a low rate of salivary secretion keeps the mouth moist. In the presence of food, salivary secretion increases markedly. This reflex response is initiated by chemoreceptors and pressure receptors in the walls of the mouth and on the tongue.

Swallowing. Swallowing is a complex reflex initiated when pressure receptors in the walls of the pharynx are stimulated by food or drink forced into the rear of the mouth by the tongue. These receptors send afferent impulses to the **swallowing center** in the brainstem medulla oblongota. This center then elicits swallowing via efferent fibers to the muscles in the pharynx, larynx, and esophagus, as well as to the respiratory muscles.

As the ingested material moves into the pharynx, the soft palate is elevated and lodges against the back wall of the pharynx, preventing food from entering the nasal cavity (Figure 17-14B). Impulses from the swallowing center inhibit respiration, raise the larynx, and close the **glottis** (the area around the vocal cords and the space between them), keeping food from moving into the trachea. As the tongue forces the food further back into the pharynx, the food tilts a flap of tissue, the **epiglottis**, backward to cover the closed glottis (Figure 17-14C).

The next stage of swallowing occurs in the esophagus, the foot-long tube that passes through the thoracic cavity, penetrates the diaphragm, which separates the thoracic cavity from the abdominal cavity, and joins the stomach a few centimeters below the diaphragm. Skeletal muscles

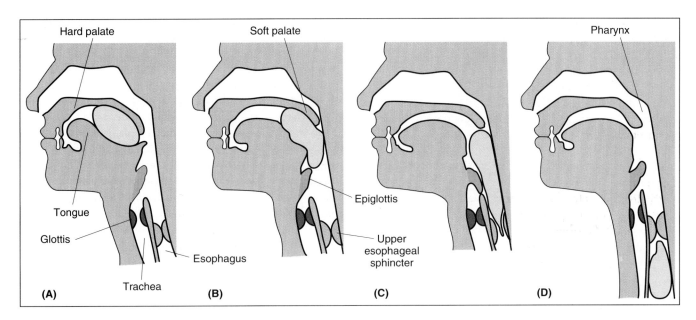

FIGURE 17-14
Movements of food through the pharynx and upper esophagus during swallowing.

surround the upper third of the esophagus, smooth muscles the lower two-thirds.

As described in Chapter 15, the pressure in the thoracic cavity is 4 to 10 mmHg less than atmospheric, and this subatmospheric pressure is transmitted across the thin wall of the intrathoracic portion of the esophagus to the lumen. In contrast, the luminal pressure in the pharynx at the opening to the esophagus is equal to atmospheric pressure, and the pressure at the opposite end of the esophagus in the stomach is slightly greater than atmospheric. Therefore, pressure differences exist that would tend to force both air (from above) and gastric contents (from below) into the esophagus. This does not occur, however, because both ends of the esophagus are normally closed by the contraction of sphincter muscles. Skeletal muscles surround the esophagus just below the pharynx, forming the **upper esophageal sphincter**, whereas the smooth muscles in the last portion of the esophagus form the **lower esophageal sphincter** (Figure 17-15).

The esophageal phase of swallowing begins with relaxation of the upper esophageal sphincter. Immediately after the food has passed, the sphincter closes, the glottis opens, and breathing resumes. Once in the esophagus, the food is moved toward the stomach by a progressive wave of muscle contractions that proceeds along the esophagus, compressing the lumen and forcing the food ahead of it. Such waves of contraction in the muscle layers surrounding a tube are known as **peristaltic waves**. One esophageal peristaltic wave takes about 9 s to reach the stomach.

Swallowing can occur even while a person is upside down since it is not primarily gravity but the peristaltic wave that moves the food to the stomach. The lower esophageal sphincter opens and remains relaxed throughout the period of swallowing, allowing the arriving food to enter the stomach. After the food has passed, the sphincter closes, resealing the junction between the esophagus and the stomach.

Swallowing is an example of a reflex in which multiple responses occur in a temporal sequence determined by the pattern of synaptic connections between neurons in a brain coordinating center. Since both skeletal and smooth muscles are involved, the swallowing center must direct efferent activity in both somatic nerves (to skeletal muscle) and autonomic nerves, specifically parasympathetic fibers (to smooth muscle). Simultaneously, afferent fibers from receptors in the esophageal wall send to the swallowing center information that can alter the efferent activity. For example, if a large food particle does not reach the stomach during the initial peristaltic wave, the distension of the esophagus by the particle activates receptors that initiate reflexes causing repeated waves of peristaltic activity (**secondary peristalsis**).

The ability of the lower esophageal sphincter to maintain a barrier between the stomach and the esophagus is aided by the fact that its last portion lies below the diaphragm and is subject to the same abdominal pressures as is the stomach. In other words, if the pressure in the abdominal cavity is raised, for example, during cycles of respiration or by contraction of the abdominal muscles, the pressures on both the gastric contents and the terminal segment of the esophagus are raised together, preventing the formation of a pressure gradient between the stomach

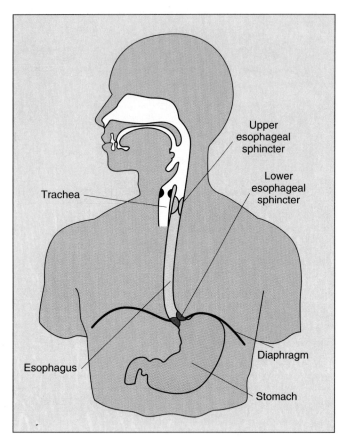

FIGURE 17-15
Location of upper and lower esophageal sphincters.

and esophagus that could force the stomach's contents into the esophagus.

During pregnancy the growth of the fetus not only increases the pressure on the abdominal contents but also pushes the terminal segment of the esophagus through the diaphragm into the thoracic cavity. The sphincter is therefore no longer assisted by changes in abdominal pressure. Accordingly, during the last half of pregnancy there is a tendency for increased abdominal pressure to force some of the gastric contents up into the esophagus. The hydrochloric acid from the stomach irritates the esophageal walls, producing pain known as **heartburn** (because the pain appears to be located over the heart). Heartburn often subsides in the last weeks of pregnancy as the uterus descends lower into the pelvis prior to delivery, decreasing the pressure on the abdominal organs.

Heartburn also occurs in nonpregnant individuals. Some people have less efficient lower esophageal sphincters, resulting in repeated episodes of refluxed gastric contents into the esophagus, heartburn, and in extreme cases, ulceration, scaring, obstruction or perforation of the lower esophagus. Heartburn can also occur after a large meal, which can raise the pressure in the stomach enough to force acid into the esophagus.

Stomach

Glands in the thin-walled upper portions of the stomach, the **body** and **fundus** (Figure 17-16), secrete mucus, hydrochloric acid, and the enzyme precursor **pepsinogen**. The lower portion of the stomach, the **antrum**, has a much thicker layer of smooth muscle. The glands in this

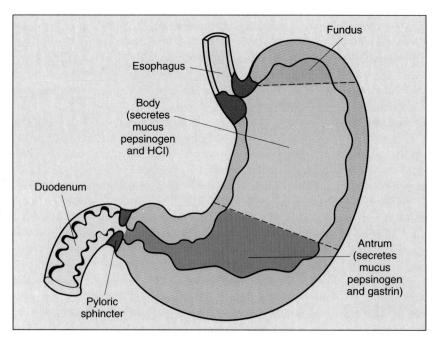

FIGURE 17-16
The three regions of the stomach: fundus, body, and antrum.

region secrete little acid, but they do contain the endocrine cells that secrete the hormone gastrin.

The epithelial layer lining the stomach invaginates into the mucosa, forming numerous tubular glands (Figure 17-17). The cells at the opening of these glands secrete mucus. In contrast, lining the walls of the glands are **parietal cells**,[4] which secrete acid (and intrinsic factor), and **chief cells**, which secrete pepsinogen. Thus, each of the three major gastric exocrine secretions—mucus, acid, and pepsinogen—is secreted by a different cell type.

HCl Secretion. The stomach secretes about 2 L of hydrochloric acid per day. The concentration of hydrogen ions in the stomach's lumen may reach 150 mM, 3 million times greater than the concentration in the blood.

A primary H,K-ATPase in the luminal membrane of the parietal cells pumps hydrogen ions into the stomach's lumen (Figure 17-18). As hydrogen ions are secreted into the lumen, bicarbonate ions are being secreted on the opposite side of the cell into the blood, lowering the acidity in the venous blood from the stomach.

During a meal, the rate of HCl secretion increases markedly. Table 17-4 summarizes the many factors controlling this secretion. The neuronal pathways and duodenal hormones involved act directly on the parietal cells and/or indirectly by influencing gastrin secretion, which in turn directly influences acid secretion by the parietal cells.

First, during the cephalic phase, the parasympathetic nerves to the stomach stimulate acid secretion. Once food has reached the stomach, the gastric phase ensues in response to distension, low H^+ concentration (why H^+ concentration is low despite increased H^+ secretion is described in the next paragraph), and peptides derived from protein digestion. The increased peptide concentration and low H^+ concentration in the stomach's lumen exert their effects on acid secretion by altering gastrin release. A high peptide concentration stimulates gastrin release, while the low H^+ removes the inhibition of acid on gastrin release. Both conditions promote increased acid secretion as a result of increased gastrin secretion.

These two responses to peptides and low acidity (H^+ concentration) explain why the greater the protein content of a meal, the greater the amount of acid secretion. This occurs for two reasons. First, the more protein ingested, the more peptides are generated in the stomach's lumen, which leads to increased gastrin secretion. The second reason is more complicated and reflects the effects of proteins on luminal acidity, as described in the rest of this paragraph. Before food enters the stomach the H^+ *concentration* in the lumen is high because there are few buffers present to bind any secreted hydrogen ions; therefore,

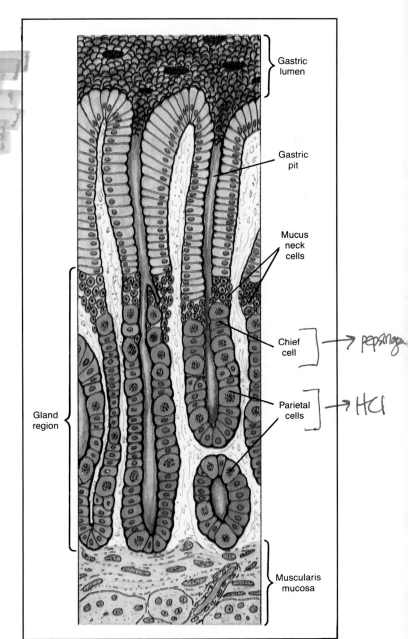

FIGURE 17-17
Gastric glands in the body of the stomach.

the rate of acid secretion is low because high acidity inhibits gastrin release. The protein in food is an excellent buffer, and so as protein enters the stomach, the H^+ concentration drops as the hydrogen ions bind to the proteins. This decrease in acidity removes the inhibition of gastrin secretion and thereby of acid secretion. The more protein in a meal, the greater the buffering of acid, the more gastrin secreted, and the more acid secreted.

Ingested substances other than protein can also stimulate acid secretion when they reach the stomach. For ex-

---

[4]Parietal cells are also known as oxyntic cells.

base out
(active)

→ HCl

FIGURE 17-18

Secretion of hydrochloric acid by parietal cells. The hydrogen ions secreted into the lumen by primary active transport are derived from the breakdown of water molecules, leaving hydroxyl ions (OH^-) behind. These hydroxyl ions are neutralized by combination with other hydrogen ions generated by the reaction between carbon dioxide and water, a reaction catalyzed by the enzyme carbonic anhydrase, which is present in high concentrations in parietal cells. The bicarbonate ions formed by this reaction move out of the parietal cell on the blood side, in exchange for chloride ions.

ample, ingestion of large amounts of calcium can stimulate acid secretion. Both regular and decaffinated coffee increase acid secretion, but the stimulatory ingredient has not been identified.[5]

We now come to the intestinal phase of acid secretion control, the phase in which stimuli in the early portion of the small intestine reflexly influence acid secretion by the stomach. First, high acidity in the duodenum triggers reflexes that inhibit gastric acid secretion. This reflex is beneficial for the following reason. The digestive activity of enzymes and bile salts in the small intestine is strongly inhibited by acidic solutions, and this reflex ensures that acid secretion by the stomach will be reduced whenever chyme entering the small intestine from the stomach contains so much acid that it cannot be rapidly neutralized by the bicarbonate-rich fluids simultaneously secreted into the intestine by the liver and pancreas.

A high acidity of duodenal chyme is not the only factor triggering reflex inhibition of gastric acid secretion. Distension, hypertonic solutions, and solutions containing amino acids, fatty acids, or monosaccharides also do so. Thus, the extent to which acid secretion is inhibited during the intestinal phase varies, depending upon the volume and composition of the meal, but the net result is the same—balancing the secretory activity of the stomach with the digestive and absorptive capacities of the small intestine.

The inhibition of gastric acid secretion during the intestinal phase is mediated by short and long neural reflexes and by hormones that inhibit either parietal-cell acid secretion or gastrin secretion. The hormones released by the intestinal tract that inhibit gastric activity are collectively called **enterogastrones** and include secretin, CCK, and additional unidentified hormones.

Pepsin Secretion. Pepsin is secreted by chief cells in an inactive precursor form known as pepsinogen. The high acidity in the stomach's lumen alters the shape of pepsinogen, exposing its active site so that this site can act on other pepsinogen molecules to break off a small chain of amino acids from their ends. This cleavage converts pepsinogen to a fully active form, pepsin (Figure 17-19). The activation of pepsin is thus an autocatalytic, positive-feedback process.

The synthesis and secretion of pepsinogen, followed by its intraluminal activation to pepsin, provides an example

[5]Acid secretion can also be altered by several paracrine agents, especially histamine and prostaglandins. Histamine, released from the stomach mucosa, can produce a marked increase in parietal-cell acid secretion (indeed, histamine is often administered clinically to measure the maximal acid-secreting capacity of the stomach), but its physiological role in the normal control of acid secretion remains unclear.

[handwritten: stomach epithelium changed every day]

[handwritten: weak enzyme (near PEPSINOGEN); intrinsic factor circled with note: most imp. thing stomach puts out; rugae crypt]

FIGURE 17-19
Conversion of pepsinogen to pepsin in the lumen of the stomach.

of a process that occurs with many other secreted enzymes in the gastrointestinal tract. Because these enzymes are synthesized in inactive forms, collectively referred to as **zymogens**, any substrates that these enzymes might be able to act upon *inside* the cell producing them are protected from digestion, thus preventing damage to the cells.

Pepsin is active only in the presence of a high H^+ concentration. It becomes inactive, therefore, when it enters the small intestine, where the hydrogen ions are neutralized by the bicarbonate ions secreted into the small intestine.

The primary pathway for stimulating pepsinogen secretion is input to the chief cells from the nerve plexuses. During the cephalic, gastric, and intestinal phases, most of the factors that stimulate or inhibit acid secretion exert the same effect on pepsinogen secretion. Thus, pepsinogen secretion parallels acid secretion.

Pepsin is not *essential* for protein digestion since in its absence, as occurs in some pathological conditions, protein can be completely digested by enzymes in the small intestine. In fact the only *absolutely required* substance produced by the stomach is intrinsic factor secreted by the parietal cells, which we saw is essential for adequate absorption of vitamin B_{12}.

Gastric Motility. An empty stomach has a volume of only about 50 ml, and the diameter of its lumen is only slightly larger than that of the small intestine. When a meal is swallowed, however, the smooth muscles in the fundus and body relax before the arrival of food, allowing the stomach's volume to increase to as much as 1.5 L with little increase in pressure. This is called **receptive relaxa-**

tion and is mediated by the parasympathetic nerves with coordination by the swallowing center in the brain.

As in the esophagus, the stomach's primary contractile activity produces peristaltic waves. Each wave begins in the body of the stomach and produces only a ripple as it proceeds toward the antrum, a contraction too weak to produce much mixing of the luminal contents with acid and pepsin. As the wave approaches the larger mass of wall muscle surrounding the antrum, however, it produces a more powerful contraction, which both mixes the luminal contents and closes the **pyloric sphincter**, a ring of smooth muscle and connective tissue between the antrum and the duodenum (Figure 17-20). The pyloric sphincter is normally relaxed and closes only upon arrival of a peristaltic wave. As a consequence of sphincter closing, only a small amount of chyme is expelled into the duodenum with each wave, and most of the antral contents are forced backward toward the body of the stomach, thereby contributing to the mixing activity of this region.

What is responsible for producing gastric peristaltic waves? Their rhythm (three per minute) is generated by pacemaker cells in the longitudinal smooth-muscle layer that undergo spontaneous depolarization-repolarization cycles (slow waves) known as the **basic electrical rhythm** of the stomach. These slow waves are conducted through gap junctions along the stomach's longitudinal muscle layer and also induce similar slow waves in the overlying circular muscle layer. In the absence of neural or hormonal input, however, these depolarizations are too small to cause the muscle membranes to reach threshold and fire action potentials. Excitatory neurotransmitters and hormones act upon the muscle to further depolarize the

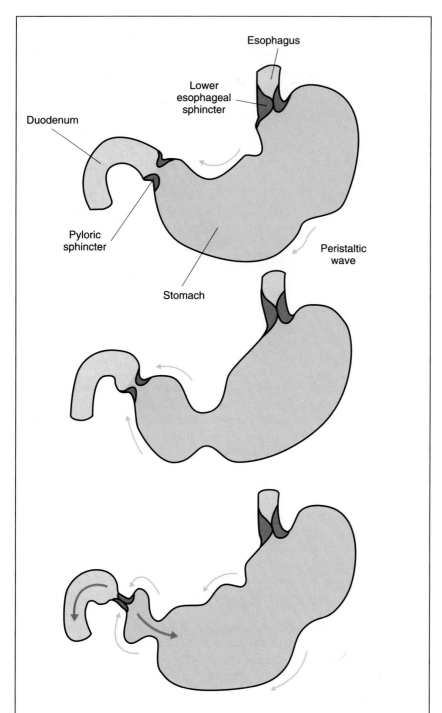

FIGURE 17-20
Peristaltic waves passing over the stomach force a small amount of luminal material into the duodenum. When a strong peristaltic wave arrives at the antrum, the pressure on the antral contents is increased, but the antral contraction also closes the pyloric sphincter, with the result that the antral contraction forces most of the antral contents back into the body of the stomach. This contributes to the mixing of the antral contents.

membrane, thereby bringing it closer to threshold. Action potentials are then generated at the peak of the slow-wave cycle (Figure 17-21). The number of spikes fired with each wave determines the strength of the muscle contraction.

Thus, whereas the *frequency* of contraction is determined by the basic electrical rhythm and remains essentially constant, the *force* of contraction and therefore the amount of gastric emptying per contraction are determined reflexly by neural and hormonal input to the antral smooth muscle.

The initiation of these reflexes depends upon the contents of both the stomach and small intestine. First, all the factors previously discussed that regulate gastrin release

FIGURE 17-21

Slow wave oscillations in the membrane potential of gastric smooth-muscle fibers trigger bursts of action potentials when threshold potential is reached at the wave peak. Membrane depolarization brings the slow wave closer to threshold, increasing the action potential frequency and thus the force of smooth-muscle contraction.

(Table 17-4) can also alter gastric motility indirectly since gastrin, in sufficiently high concentrations, increases the force of antral contractions. Distension of the stomach also increases the force of antral contractions through long and short reflexes triggered by mechanoreceptors in the stom-

ach. Therefore, the larger a meal, the faster the stomach's initial emptying rate. As the volume of the stomach decreases, the force of gastric contractions and the rate of emptying also decrease.

In contrast, distension of the *duodenum* or the presence of fat, acid, or hypertonic solutions in its lumen all inhibit gastric emptying (Figure 17-22) just as they inhibit acid and pepsin secretion. Fat is the most potent of these chemical stimuli.

Autonomic nerve fibers to the stomach can be activated independently of the reflexes originating in the stomach and duodenum and can influence gastric motility. Decreased parasympathetic or increased sympathetic activity inhibits motility. Via these pathways, pain and emotions such as sadness, depression, and fear tend to decrease motility, whereas aggression and anger tend to increase it. These relationships are not always predictable, however, and different people show different gastrointestinal responses to apparently similar emotional states.

As we have seen, a hypertonic solution in the duodenum is one of the stimuli inhibiting gastric emptying. This reflex prevents the fluid in the duodenum from becoming too hypertonic since it slows the rate of entry of chyme and thereby the delivery of large molecules that can be broken down into many small molecules. A patient who has had his stomach removed because of disease, for example, cancer, must eat a number of small meals. A large meal, in the absence of the controlled emptying by the stomach, would rapidly enter the intestine, producing a hypertonic solution. This hypertonic solution is the result of the rapid digestion of proteins and polysaccharides by the enzymes in the small intestine and can cause enough water to flow (by osmosis) into the intestine from the blood to lower the

TABLE 17-4 CONTROL OF HCL SECRETION DURING A MEAL		
Stimuli	**Pathways to the parietal cells**	**Result**
Cephalic phase Sight Smell Taste Chewing	Parasympathetic nerves directly or via stimulation of gastrin secretion	↑HCl secretion
Gastric contents (gastric phase) Distension ↑Peptides	Long and short neural reflexes, gastrin	↑HCl secretion
Intestinal contents (intestinal phase) Distension ↑H⁺ concentration ↑Osmolarity ↑Nutrient concentrations	Long and short neural reflexes; secretin, CCK, and other unspecified duodenal hormones	↓HCl secretion

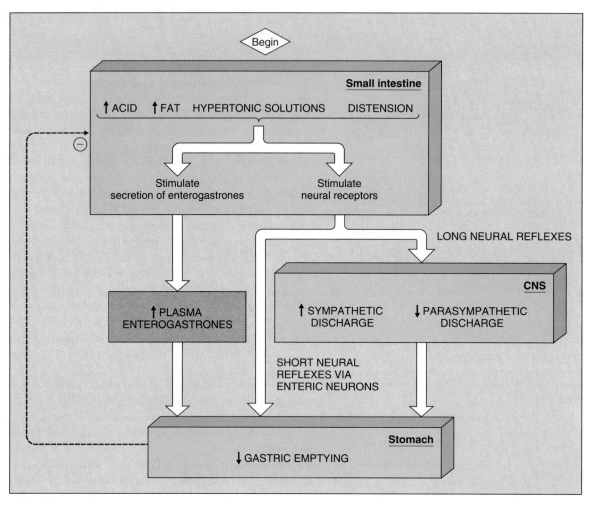

FIGURE 17-22

Intestinal-phase pathways inhibiting gastric emptying.

blood volume and produce circulatory complications. The large distension of the intestine by the entering fluid can also trigger vomiting in these patients. All these symptoms produced by the rapid entry of large quantities of ingested material into the small intestine are known as the *dumping syndrome*.

Pancreatic Secretions

The exocrine portion of the pancreas secretes bicarbonate ions and a number of digestive enzymes into ducts that converge into the pancreatic duct, the latter joining the common bile duct from the liver just before entering the duodenum (Figure 17-4). The enzymes are secreted by gland cells at the pancreatic end of the duct system, whereas bicarbonate ions are secreted by the epithelial cells lining the early portions of the duct system itself (Figure 17-23).

The mechanism of bicarbonate secretion is analogous to that of hydrochloric acid secretion by the stomach, ex-

cept that the directions of hydrogen-ion and bicarbonate-ion movement are reversed. Hydrogen ions are actively transported out of the duct cells and released into the blood, while bicarbonate ions are secreted into the duct lumen.

The enzymes secreted by the pancreas, following activation, digest fat, polysaccharides, proteins, and nucleic acids to fatty acids, sugars, amino acids, and nucleotides, respectively. A partial list of these enzymes and their activities is given in Table 17-5. Most of the proteolytic enzymes are secreted in inactive forms (zymogens) and then activated in the duodenum by other enzymes.[6] A key step in this process is mediated by **enterokinase**, which is embedded in the luminal plasma membrane of the intesti-

---

[6]Several of the pancreatic enzymes, such as amylase and lipase, are secreted in their active forms but require additional factors, such as ions and bile salts encountered in the intestinal lumen, to produce maximal activity.

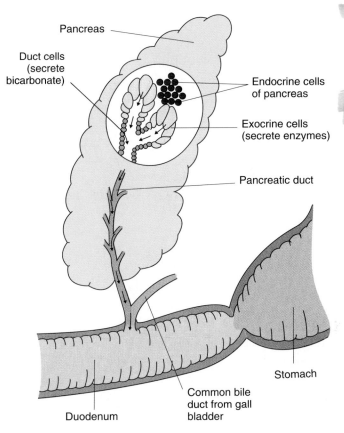

FIGURE 17-23
Structure of the pancreas. The gland areas are shown greatly enlarged relative to the entire pancreas and ducts.

nal epithelium. It is a proteolytic enzyme that splits off a peptide from pancreatic **trypsinogen**, forming the active enzyme trypsin. Trypsin is a proteolytic enzyme, and once activated, it activates the other pancreatic zymogens by splitting off peptide fragments (Figure 17-24). This func-

tion is in addition to trypsin's role in digesting ingested protein.

Pancreatic secretion increases during a meal, mainly as a result of stimulation by the hormones secretin and CCK (Table 17-3). Secretin is the primary stimulant for bicarbonate secretion, whereas CCK mainly stimulates enzyme secretion. (As noted earlier on page 577, CCK potentiates the action of secretin.)

Since the function of pancreatic bicarbonate is to neutralize the acid entering the duodenum from the stomach, it is appropriate that the major stimulus for secretin release is increased acidity in the duodenum. In analogous fashion, since CCK stimulates the secretion of digestive enzymes, including those for fat and protein digestion, it is appropriate that the stimuli for its release are fatty acids and amino acids in the duodenum. Thus, the organic nutrients in the small intestine initiate, via hormonal reflexes, the secretions involved in their own digestion.[7]

Although about 75 percent of the pancreatic exocrine secretions are controlled by stimuli arising from the intestinal phase of digestion, cephalic and gastric stimuli, by way of the parasympathetic nerves to the pancreas, also play a role. Thus, the taste of food or the distension of the stomach by food, will lead to increased pancreatic secretion. Figures 17-25 and 17-26 summarize the main factors controlling pancreatic secretion.

Bile Secretion

As stated earlier, bile is secreted by cells in the liver into a number of small ducts, the **bile canaliculi** (Figure 17-27), which converge to form the common hepatic duct (Figure

---

[7] As the amount of trypsin in the small intestine increases, the rate of CCK release decreases, and thus pancreatic enzyme secretion decreases. This negative feedback is probably the result of trypsin's digestion of a protein required for CCK secretion.

lots enzymes secreted into beg. of small intestine

TABLE 17-5	PANCREATIC ENZYMES	
Enzyme	**Substrate**	**Action**
Trypsin, chymotrypsin, elastase	Proteins	Breaks peptide bonds in proteins to form peptide fragments
Carboxypeptidase	Proteins	Splits off terminal amino acid from carboxyl end of protein
Lipase	Fat	Splits off two fatty acids from triacylglycerols, forming free fatty acids and monoglycerides
Amylase	Polysaccharide	Splits polysaccharides into glucose and maltose
Ribonuclease, deoxyribonuclease	Nucleic acids	Splits nucleic acids into free mononucleotides

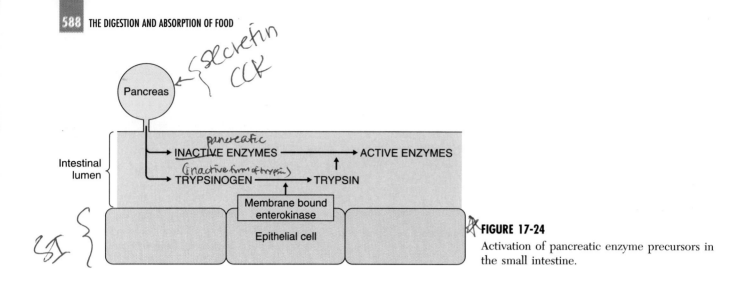

Secretin CCK (handwritten)

Pancreas

Intestinal lumen

INACTIVE ENZYMES ——————→ ACTIVE ENZYMES

pancreatic (handwritten)

(inactive form of trypsin) (handwritten)

TRYPSINOGEN ——————→ TRYPSIN

Membrane bound enterokinase

Epithelial cell

SI (handwritten)

FIGURE 17-24

Activation of pancreatic enzyme precursors in the small intestine.

FIGURE 17-26

Hormonal regulation of pancreatic enzyme secretion.

FIGURE 17-25

Hormonal regulation of pancreatic bicarbonate secretion.

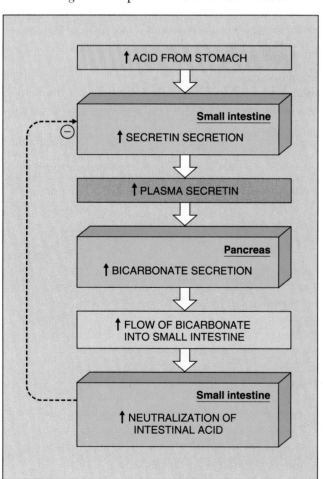

↑ ACID FROM STOMACH

Small intestine
↑ SECRETIN SECRETION

↑ PLASMA SECRETIN

Pancreas
↑ BICARBONATE SECRETION

↑ FLOW OF BICARBONATE INTO SMALL INTESTINE

Small intestine
↑ NEUTRALIZATION OF INTESTINAL ACID

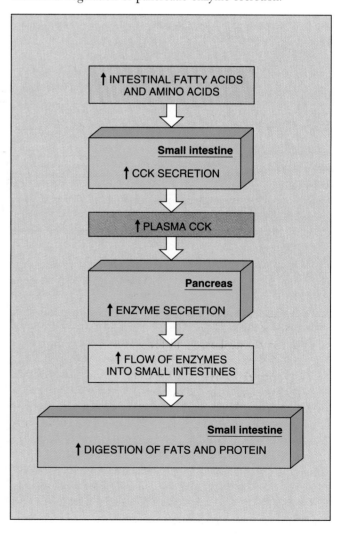

↑ INTESTINAL FATTY ACIDS AND AMINO ACIDS

Small intestine
↑ CCK SECRETION

↑ PLASMA CCK

Pancreas
↑ ENZYME SECRETION

↑ FLOW OF ENZYMES INTO SMALL INTESTINES

Small intestine
↑ DIGESTION OF FATS AND PROTEIN

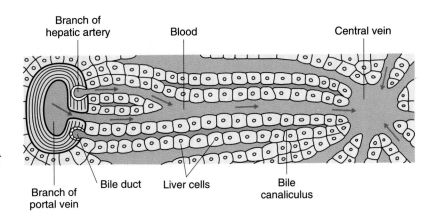

FIGURE 17-27

A small section of the liver showing location of bile canaliculi and ducts with respect to blood and liver cells. (*Adapted from Kappas and Alvares.*)

17-4). Bile contains six major ingredients: (1) bile salts, (2) cholesterol, (3) lecithin (a phospholipid), (4) bicarbonate ions and other salts, (5) bile pigments and small amounts of other metabolic end products, and (6) trace metals. The first three ingredients are synthesized in the liver and help solubilize fat in the small intestine. Bicarbonate ions neutralize acid in the duodenum, and the fifth and sixth categories represent substances extracted from the blood by the liver and excreted via the bile.

From the standpoint of gastrointestinal function, the most important components of bile are the bile salts. During the digestion of a fatty meal, most of the bile salts entering the intestinal tract via the bile are absorbed in the ileum (the last segment of the small intestine) and returned via the portal vein to the liver, where they are once again secreted into the bile. This recycling pathway from the intestine to the liver and back to the intestine via the bile duct is known as the **enterohepatic circulation** (Figure 17-28). A small amount of the bile salts are not recycled, however, but are lost in the feces. The liver synthesizes new bile salts from cholesterol to replace them.

In addition to synthesizing bile salts from cholesterol, the liver also secretes cholesterol into the bile. [This process, followed by excretion of cholesterol in the feces, is one of the mechanisms by which cholesterol homeostasis is maintained (Chapter 18).] Cholesterol is insoluble in water, and its solubility in the bile is achieved by its incorporation into micelles. (Gallstones, consisting of precipitated cholesterol, will be discussed at end of the chapter.)

The **bile pigments** are substances formed when the heme portions of hemoglobin are broken down during the destruction of old or damaged erythrocytes in the spleen and liver. The predominant bile pigment is **bilirubin**. Hepatic cells extract bilirubin from the blood and actively secrete it into the bile. It is bilirubin that gives bile its yellow color. After entering the intestinal tract via the bile, bilirubin is modified by bacterial enzymes to form the brown pigments that give feces their characteristic color. During their passage through the intestinal tract some of

the bile pigments are absorbed into the plasma and are eventually excreted in the urine, giving urine its yellow color.

Like pancreatic secretions, the components of bile are secreted by two different cell types. The bile salts, cholesterol, lecithin, and bile pigments are secreted by **hepatocytes** (liver cells), whereas most of the bicarbonate-rich salt solution is secreted by the epithelial cells lining the bile ducts. The salt solution secreted by the bile ducts, just like that secreted by the pancreas, is stimulated by secretin in response to the presence of acid in the duodenum.

FIGURE 17-28

Enterohepatic circulation of bile salts.

HEPATIC PORTAL VEIN

LIVER

Bile salts

Synthesis

Bile salts

Venous blood

COMMON BILE DUCT

GALL BLADDER

DUODENUM

Bile salts

ILEUM

5% lost in feces

Bile salts → Bile salts

SMALL INTESTINE

Although bile secretion is greatest during and just after a meal, some bile is always being secreted by the liver. Surrounding the bile duct at the point where it enters the duodenum is a ring of smooth muscle known as the **sphincter of Oddi**. When this sphincter is closed, the dilute bile secreted by the liver is shunted into the gallbladder and becomes concentrated as salt and water are absorbed. During a meal, the gallbladder contracts, emptying concentrated bile into the small intestine. The higher plasma concentration resulting from increased absorption of the bile salts from the intestine leads to an increased rate of bile salt secretion by the liver. Bile salt secretion is controlled by the concentration of bile salts in the blood—the greater the plasma concentration of bile salts, the greater their secretion into the bile canaliculi.

Shortly after the beginning of a fatty meal, the sphincter of Oddi relaxes, and the smooth muscles in the wall of the gallbladder contract, discharging concentrated bile into the duodenum. The signal for gallbladder contraction and sphincter relaxation is the intestinal hormone CCK—appropriately so, since a major stimulus for this hormone's release is the presence of fat in the duodenum. (It is from this ability to cause contraction of the gallbladder that cholecystokinin received its name: *chole*, bile; *cysto*, bladder; *kinin*, to move). Figure 17-29 summarizes the factors controlling the entry of bile into the small intestine.

FIGURE 17-29

Regulation of bile entry into the small intestine.

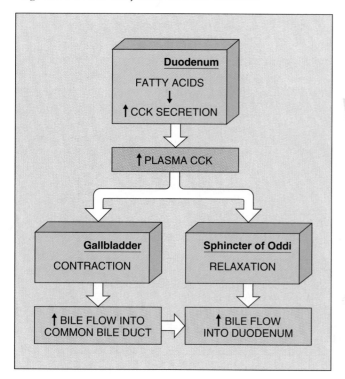

Small Intestine

Secretions. Approximately 2000 ml of fluid is *secreted* from the blood into the lumen by the walls of the small intestine each day. A much larger volume, contributed by the salivary, gastric, hepatic, and pancreatic secretions as well as ingested water, is simultaneously absorbed—from the lumen into the blood—so that normally there is an overall net absorption of water from the small intestine.

One of the reasons for water movement into the lumen is that the intestinal epithelium secretes a number of mineral ions, notably sodium, chloride, and bicarbonate ions into the lumen, and water moves with these ions. As stated earlier, another reason for water movement into the lumen is that the chyme entering the small intestine from the stomach may be hypertonic because of a high concentration of solutes in the meal and because digestion breaks down large molecules into many more small molecules. This hypertonicity causes the osmotic movement of water from the isotonic plasma into the intestinal lumen.

As noted above, the intestinal epithelium secretes not only water but also a number of mineral ions. The continuous disintegration of the intestinal epithelium and the secretion of mucus provide additional sources of material entering the lumen of the small intestine.

Motility. In contrast to the peristaltic waves that sweep over the stomach, the most common motion of the small intestine during a meal is a stationary contraction and relaxation of intestinal segments, with little apparent net movement toward the large intestine (Figure 17-30). Each contracting segment is only a few centimeters long, and the contraction lasts a few seconds. The chyme in the lumen of a contracting segment is forced both up and down the intestine. This rhythmical contraction and relaxation of the intestine, known as **segmentation**, produces a continuous division and subdivision of the intestinal contents, thoroughly mixing the chyme in the lumen and bringing it into contact with the intestinal wall.

These segmenting movements are initiated by electrical activity generated by pacemaker cells in the longitudinal smooth-muscle layer. Like the slow waves in the stomach, this intestinal basic electrical rhythm produces oscillations in smooth-muscle membrane potential that, if threshold is reached, trigger action potentials causing muscle contraction. The frequency of segmentation is set by the frequency of the intestinal basic electrical rhythm, but unlike the stomach, which normally has a single rhythm, the intestinal rhythm varies along the length of the intestine, each successive region having a slightly lower frequency than the one above. For example, segmentation in the duodenum occurs at a frequency of about 12 contractions/min, whereas in the terminal portion of the ileum the rate is only 9 contractions/min. Segmentation produces, there-

FIGURE 17-30
Segmentation movements of the small intestine in which segments of the intestine contract and relax in a rhythmical pattern but do not undergo peristalsis. This is the pattern encountered during a meal which mixes the luminal contents.

fore, a slow migration of the intestinal contents toward the large intestine because more chyme is forced downward, on the average, than upward.

The intensity of segmentation can be altered by hormones, the enteric nervous system, and autonomic nerves; parasympathetic activity increases the force of contraction, and sympathetic stimulation decreases it. As is true for the stomach, these inputs produce changes in the force of smooth-muscle contraction but do not significantly change the frequencies of the basic electrical rhythms.

After most of a meal has been absorbed, the segmenting contractions cease and are replaced by a pattern of peristaltic activity known as the **migrating motility complex**. Beginning in the lower portion of the stomach, repeated waves of peristaltic activity travel only a short distance (about 2 ft) along the small intestine and then die out. This short segment of peristaltic activity slowly migrates down the small intestine, taking about 2 h to reach the large intestine. By the time the migrating motility complex reaches the end of the ileum, new waves are beginning in the upper portion of the intestinal tract and the process is repeated. Upon the arrival of a meal in the stomach, the migrating motility complex rapidly ceases and is replaced by segmentation.

The migrating motility complex moves into the large

intestine any undigested material still remaining in the small intestine and also prevents bacteria from remaining in the small intestine long enough to grow and multiply. In diseases in which there is an aberrant migrating motility complex, bacterial overgrowth in the small intestine can become a major problem.

A rise in the plasma concentration of a candidate intestinal hormone, called **motilin**, is thought to initiate the migrating motility complex, while the patterns of contractile activity during segmentation and peristalsis are coordinated by the enteric nervous system. The mechanisms of motilin action and the control of its release are unclear.

Mild distension of the intestine produces a contraction of the smooth muscle on the oral side of the distension and relaxation of the smooth muscle on the anal side. This pattern of activity, known as the **law of the intestine**, is mediated by neurons in the myenteric plexus and promotes movement of the luminal contents toward the large intestine.

The contractile activity in various regions of the small intestine can be altered by reflexes initiated at different points along the gastrointestinal tract. For example, segmentation intensity in the ileum increases during periods of gastric emptying, and this is known as the **gastroileal reflex**. Large distensions of the intestine, injury to the intestinal wall, and various bacterial infections in the intestine lead to a complete cessation of motility, the **intestino-intestinal reflex**.

A person's emotional state can also affect the contractile activity of the intestine, and therefore the rate of chyme propulsion and mixing. Fear tends to decrease motility, whereas hostility increases it, although, as with gastric motility, these intestinal responses vary greatly in different individuals. They are mediated via autonomic nerves to the intestine.

As much as 500 ml of air may be swallowed during a meal. Most of this air travels no farther than the esophagus, from which it is eventually expelled by belching. Some of the air reaches the stomach, however, and is passed on to the intestines, where its percolation through the chyme as the intestinal contents are mixed produces gurgling sounds that are often quite loud.

Large Intestine

The large intestine is a tube 2.5 in. in diameter and about 4 ft long. Its first portion, the **cecum**, forms a blind-ended pouch from which extends the **appendix**, a small finger-like projection having no known function (Figure 17-31). The colon consists of three relatively straight segments—the ascending, transverse, and descending portions. The terminal portion of the descending colon is S-shaped, forming the sigmoid colon, which empties into a relatively straight segment, the **rectum**, which ends at the anus.

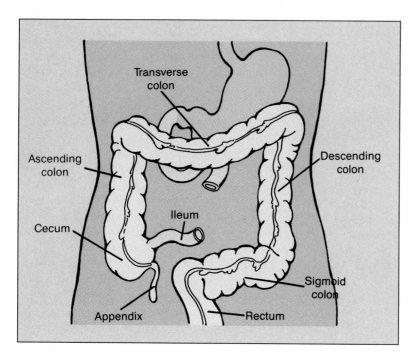

FIGURE 17-31
The large intestine (colon) and rectum.

Although the large intestine has a greater diameter than the small intestine, its epithelial surface area is far less than that of the small intestine, since the colon is about half as long as the small intestine, its surface is not convoluted, and its mucosa lacks villi. The secretions of the colon are scanty, lack digestive enzymes, and consist mostly of mucus. The primary function of the large intestine is to store and concentrate fecal material before defecation.

Chyme enters the colon through the **ileocecal sphincter**. This sphincter is normally closed, but after a meal, when the gastroileal reflex increases ileal contractions, it relaxes each time the terminal portion of the ileum contracts, allowing chyme to enter the large intestine. Distension of the colon, on the other hand, produces a reflex contraction of the sphincter, preventing fecal material from moving back into the small intestine.

About 1500 ml of chyme enters the colon from the small intestine each day. This material is derived largely from the secretions of the lower small intestine since most of the ingested food has been absorbed before reaching the large intestine. Absorption by the colon accounts for only about 4 percent of the material entering the gastrointestinal tract.

The primary absorptive process in the large intestine is the active transport of sodium from lumen to blood, with the accompanying osmotic absorption of water. If fecal material remains in the large intestine for a long time, almost all the water is absorbed, leaving behind hard fecal pellets. There is normally a net movement of potassium from blood into the colon lumen, and severe depletion of total-body potassium can result when large volumes of fluid are excreted in the feces. There is also net movement of bicarbonate ions into the lumen, and loss of this bicarbonate in patients with prolonged diarrhea can cause the blood to become acidic.

The large intestine also absorbs some of the products (vitamins, for example) synthesized by the bacteria inhabiting this region. Although this source of vitamins generally provides only a small part of the normal daily requirement, it may make a significant contribution when dietary vitamin intake is low. An individual who depends on colonic absorption of vitamins may become vitamin-deficient if treated with antibiotics that inhibit many species of colonic bacteria as well as disease-causing bacteria.

Other bacterial products include gas (**flatus**), which is a mixture of nitrogen and carbon dioxide, with small amounts of hydrogen, methane, and hydrogen sulfide. Bacterial fermentation of undigested polysaccharides produces these gases in the colon at the rate of about 400 to 700 ml/day. Certain foods, beans, for example, contain large amounts of carbohydrates that cannot be digested by intestinal enzymes but are readily metabolized by bacteria in the large intestine, producing large amounts of gas.

Motility and Defecation. Contractions of the circular smooth muscle in the colon produce a segmentation motion with a rhythm considerably slower (one every 30 min) than that in the small intestine. Because of the slow propulsion of the colonic contents, material entering the colon from the small intestine remains for about 18 to 24 h. This provides time for bacteria to grow and multiply. Three to four times a day, generally following a meal, a wave of intense contraction, known as a **mass movement**, spreads rapidly over the colon toward the rectum. This usually coincides with the gastroileal reflex. Unlike a peristaltic wave, in which the smooth muscle at each point relaxes after the wave of contraction has passed, the smooth muscle of the colon remains contracted for some time after a mass movement.

The **anus,** the exit from the rectum, is normally closed by the **internal anal sphincter**, which is composed of smooth muscle, and the **external anal sphincter**, composed of skeletal muscle under voluntary control. The sudden distension of the walls of the rectum produced by the mass movement of fecal material into it initiates the **defecation reflex**, which is mediated primarily by the external nerves to the terminal end of the large intestine. The reflex response consists of a contraction of the rectum, relaxation of the internal anal sphincter, contraction initially of the external anal sphincter, and increased peristaltic activity in the sigmoid colon. Eventually, a pressure is reached in the rectum that triggers *relaxation* of the external anal sphincter, allowing the feces to be expelled.

The conscious urge to defecate, mediated by stretched mechanoreceptors, accompanies distension of the rectum. Brain centers can, however, via descending pathways to somatic nerves to the external anal sphincter, override the reflexive signals that eventually would relax the sphincter, thereby keeping the external sphincter closed and allowing a person to delay defecation. In this case the smooth muscle in the walls of the rectum relaxes, and the urge to defecate subsides until the next mass movement propels more feces into the rectum, increasing its volume and again initiating the defecation reflex. Voluntary control of the external anal sphincter is learned during childhood. Spinal-cord damage can lead to a loss of voluntary control over defecation.

Defecation is normally assisted by a deep inspiration, followed by closure of the glottis and contraction of the abdominal and thoracic muscles, producing an increase in abdominal pressure that is transmitted to the contents of the large intestine and rectum. This maneuver also causes a rise in intrathoracic pressure, which leads to a transient rise in blood pressure followed by a fall in pressure as the venous return to the heart is decreased. The cardiovascular changes resulting from excessive strain during defecation may precipitate a stroke or heart attack in individuals with cardiovascular disease.

About 150 g of feces, consisting of about 100 g of water and 50 g of solid material, is normally eliminated each day. The solid matter is mostly bacteria, undigested polysaccharides, bile pigments, cholesterol, and small amounts of electrolytes, particularly potassium.

PATHOPHYSIOLOGY OF THE GASTROINTESTINAL TRACT

Since the end result of gastrointestinal function is the absorption of nutrients, salts, and water, most malfunctions of this organ system affect either the nutritional state of the body or its salt and water content. The following provide a few examples of disordered gastrointestinal function.

Ulcers

Considering the high concentration of acid and pepsin secreted by the stomach, it is natural to wonder why the stomach does not digest itself. Several of the factors that protect the walls of the stomach from being digested are: (1) The surface of the mucosa is lined with cells that secrete a slightly alkaline mucus, which forms a thin layer over the luminal surface. Both the protein content of mucus and its alkalinity neutralize hydrogen ions in the immediate area of the epithelium. Thus, mucus forms a chemical barrier between the highly acid contents of the lumen and the cell surface. (2) In addition, the tight junctions between the epithelial cells lining the stomach restrict the diffusion of hydrogen ions into the underlying tissues. (3) Also, these epithelial cells are replaced every few days by new cells arising by the division of cells within the gastric pits.

Yet these protective mechanisms can prove inadequate, and erosions (*ulcers*) of the gastric surface occur. Ulcers can occur not only in the stomach but also in the lower part of the esophagus and in the duodenum. Indeed, duodenal ulcers are about 10 times more frequent than gastric ulcers, affecting about 10 percent of the U.S. population. Damage to blood vessels in the tissues underlying the ulcer may cause bleeding into the gastrointestinal lumen. On occasion, the ulcer may penetrate the entire wall, resulting in leakage of the luminal contents into the abdominal cavity.

Ulcer formation involves breaking the mucosal barrier and exposing the underlying tissue to the corrosive action of acid and pepsin, but it is not always clear what produces the initial damage to the barrier. Although acid is essential for ulcer formation, it is not necessarily the primary factor that breaks the mucosal barrier. Many patients with ulcers have normal or even subnormal rates of acid secretion. However, reducing the level of acid and pepsin secretion, either by the use of drugs that inhibit acid secretion or by cutting the parasympathetic (vagus) nerves to the stomach, promotes healing and tends to prevent the reoccurrence of ulcers.

Many factors—genetic susceptibility, drugs, alcohol, bile salts, and excessive secretion of acid and pepsin—

may contribute to ulcer formation. The major factor, however, may be the presence of a bacterium, *Helicobacter pylori,* that is present in the stomachs of a majority of patients with ulcers or **gastritis** (inflammation of the stomach's walls). Suppression of this bacterium with antibiotics often leads to healing of the damaged mucosa.

Despite popular notions that ulcers are due to emotional stress and despite the existence of a pathway (the parasympathetic nerves) for mediating stress-induced increases in acid secretion, the role of stress in producing ulcers remains unclear. Once the ulcer has been formed, however, emotional stress can aggravate it by increasing acid secretion.

Vomiting

Vomiting is the forceful expulsion of the contents of the stomach and upper intestinal tract through the mouth. Like swallowing, vomiting is a complex reflex coordinated by a region in the brainstem medulla oblongata, in this case known as the **vomiting center**. Neural input to this center from receptors in many different regions of the body can initiate the vomiting reflex. For example, excessive distension of the stomach or small intestine, various substances acting upon chemoreceptors in the intestinal wall or in the brain, increased pressure within the skull, rotating movements of the head (motion sickness), intense pain, and tactile stimuli applied to the back of the throat can all initiate vomiting.

What is the adaptive value of this reflex? Obviously, the removal of ingested toxic substances before they can be absorbed is of benefit. Moreover, the nausea that usually accompanies vomiting may have the adaptive value of conditioning the individual to avoid the future ingestion of foods containing such toxic substances. Why other types of stimuli, such as those producing motion sickness, have become linked to the vomiting center is not clear.

Vomiting is usually preceded by increased salivation, sweating, increased heart rate, pallor, and feelings of nausea. The events leading to vomiting begin with a deep inspiration, closure of the glottis, and elevation of the soft palate. The abdominal muscles then contract, raising the abdominal pressure, which is transmitted to the stomach's contents. The lower esophageal sphincter relaxes, and the high abdominal pressure forces the contents of the stomach into the esophagus. This initial sequence of events can occur repeatedly without expulsion via the mouth and is known as **retching**. Vomiting occurs when the abdominal contractions become so strong that the increased intrathoracic pressure forces the contents of the esophagus through the upper esophageal sphincter.

Vomiting is also accompanied by strong contractions in the upper portion of the small intestine, contractions that tend to force some of the intestinal contents back into the stomach from which they can be expelled. Thus, some bile may be present in the vomitus.

Excessive vomiting can lead to large losses of the water and salts that normally would be absorbed in the small intestine. This can result in severe dehydration, upset the body's salt balance, and produce circulatory problems due to a decrease in plasma volume. The loss of acid from vomiting lowers blood acidity.

Gallstones

As described earlier, bile contains not only bile salts but also cholesterol and phospholipids, which are water-insoluble and are maintained in soluble form in the bile as micelles. When the concentration of cholesterol in the bile becomes too high in relation to the concentrations of phospholipid and bile salts, cholesterol crystallizes out of solution, forming **gallstones**. This can occur if the liver secretes excessive amounts of cholesterol or if the cholesterol becomes overly concentrated in the gallbladder as a result of salt and water absorption. Although cholesterol gallstones are the most frequently encountered gallstones in the Western world, the precipitation of bile pigments can also occasionally be responsible for gallstone formation.

Why some individuals develop gallstones and others do not is still unclear. Women, for example, have about twice the incidence of gallstone formation as men, and Native Americans have a very high incidence compared with other ethnic groups in the United States.

If a gallstone is small, it may pass through the common bile duct into the intestine with no complications. A larger stone may become lodged in the opening of the gallbladder, causing contractile spasms of the smooth muscle and pain. A more serious complication arises when a gallstone lodges in the common bile duct, thereby preventing bile from entering the intestine. The absence of bile in the intestine decreases the rate of fat digestion and absorption, so that approximately half of ingested fat is not digested and passes on to the large intestine and eventually appears in the feces. Furthermore, bacteria in the large intestine convert some of this fat into fatty acid derivatives that alter salt and water movements, leading to a net flow of fluid into the large intestine. The result is diarrhea and increased fluid loss.

Since the duct from the pancreas joins the common bile duct just before it enters the duodenum, a gallstone that becomes lodged at this point prevents both bile and pancreatic secretions from entering the intestine. This results in failure both to neutralize acid and to digest most organic nutrients, not just fat, adequately. The end result is severe nutritional deficiencies.

The buildup of pressure in a blocked common bile duct inhibits further secretion of bile. As a result, bilirubin, which is normally secreted into the bile from the blood, accumulates in the blood and diffuses into tissues, where it produces the yellowish coloration of the skin and eyes known as *jaundice*.

It should be emphasized, however, that bile duct obstruction is not the only cause of jaundice. Bilirubin accumulation in the blood can occur if hepatocytes are damaged by liver disease and therefore fail to secrete bilirubin into the bile. It can also occur if the level of bilirubin in the blood exceeds the capacity of the normal liver to secrete it, as in diseases that result in an increased breakdown of red blood cells—hemolytic jaundice. At birth, the liver's capacity to secrete bilirubin is not fully developed. This may result in jaundice during the first few days of life, but the jaundice normally clears spontaneously. Excessive accumulation of bilirubin during the neonatal period, as occurs, for example, with hemolytic disease of the newborn (Chapter 20), carries a risk of bilirubin-induced neurological damage at a time when a critical consolidation of the nervous system is occurring.

Lactose Intolerance

Lactose is the major carbohydrate in milk. It cannot be absorbed directly but must first be digested into its components—glucose and galactose—which are readily absorbed by active transport. Lactose is digested by the enzyme **lactase**, which is embedded in the plasma membranes of intestinal epithelial cells. Lactase is present at birth, but in approximately 25 percent of white Americans and in most northern Europeans its concentration then declines when the child is between 18 and 36 months old. In those individuals with decreased lactase, ingested lactose is not completely digested and some remains in the small intestine, leading to a condition known as *lactose intolerance*.

Since the absorption of water requires prior absorption of solute to provide an osmotic gradient, the unabsorbed lactose in persons with lactose intolerance prevents some of the water from being absorbed. This lactose-containing fluid is passed on to the large intestine, where bacteria digest the lactose. They then metabolize the released monosaccharides, producing large quantities of gas (which distends the colon, producing pain) and organic products that inhibit active ion absorption. This causes fluid movement into the lumen of the large intestine, producing diarrhea. The response to milk ingestion by adults whose lactase levels have diminished during development varies from mild discomfort to severely dehydrating diarrhea,

according to the volume of milk and milk products ingested and the amount of lactase present in the intestine.

Constipation and Diarrhea

Many people have a mistaken belief that, unless they have a bowel movement every day, the absorption of toxic substances from fecal material in the large intestine will somehow poison them. Attempts to identify such toxic agents in the blood following prolonged periods of fecal retention have been unsuccessful, and there appears to be no physiological necessity for having bowel movements at frequent intervals. Whatever maintains a person in a comfortable state is physiologically adequate, whether this means a bowel movement after every meal, once a day, or only once a week.

On the other hand, there often are symptoms—headache, loss of appetite, nausea, and abdominal distension—that may arise when defecation has not occurred for several days or even weeks, depending on the individual. These symptoms of *constipation* are caused not by toxins but by distension of the rectum. In addition, the longer fecal material remains in the large intestine, the more water is absorbed and the harder and drier the feces become, making defecation more difficult and sometimes painful. Thus, constipation tends to promote constipation.

Decreased motility of the large intestine is the primary factor causing constipation. This often occurs in the elderly or may result from damage to the colon's enteric nervous system. Emotional stress can also decrease the motility of the large intestine.

One of the factors increasing colonic motility, and thus opposing the development of constipation, is distension of the large intestine. As noted earlier, dietary fiber (cellulose and other complex polysaccharides) is not digested by the enzymes in the small intestine and is passed on to the large intestine, where its bulk produces distension and thereby increases motility. Bran and most fruits and vegetables are examples of foods that have a relatively high fiber content.

Laxatives, agents that increase the frequency or ease of defecation, act through a variety of mechanisms. Thus, fiber provides a natural laxative. Some laxatives, such as mineral oil, simply lubricate the feces, making defecation easier and less painful. Others contain magnesium and aluminum salts, which are poorly absorbed and therefore lead to water retention in the intestinal tract. Still others, such as castor oil, stimulate the motility of the colon and alter ion transport across the wall, thus indirectly affecting water movement.

Excessive use of laxatives in an attempt to maintain a preconceived notion of regularity leads to a decreased responsiveness of the colon to normal defecation-promoting signals. In such cases, a long period without defecation may occur following cessation of laxative intake, appearing to confirm the necessity of taking laxatives to promote regularity.

Diarrhea is characterized by an increased fecal water content and weight (greater than 200 g/day) and may be accompanied by an increased frequency of defecation. Diarrhea results from decreased fluid absorption, increased fluid secretion, or both. The increased motility that accompanies diarrhea probably does not cause the diarrhea (by decreasing the time available for fluid absorption) but rather is a result of the distension produced by increased luminal fluid.

A number of bacterial, protozoan, and viral diseases of the intestinal tract cause diarrhea. In many cases they do so by releasing substances that either alter ion-transport processes in the epithelial membranes or damage the epithelial barriers by direct penetration into the mucosa. As described earlier, the presence of unabsorbed solutes in the lumen, resulting from decreased digestion or absorption, also results in retained fluid and diarrhea.

The major consequences of severe diarrhea are decreased blood volume, potassium depletion, and metabolic acidosis, resulting from the excessive fecal loss of water and sodium, potassium, and bicarbonate ions. Untreated diarrhea is a major cause of death in children in underdeveloped countries. In most cases of childhood diarrhea prevention of severe dehydration can be achieved by ingesting a simple solution containing salt and glucose. The active absorption of these solutes is accompanied by absorption of water, which replaces the fluid lost by diarrhea.

SUMMARY

I. The gastrointestinal system transfers organic nutrients, minerals, and water from the external environment to the internal environment. The four processes used to accomplish this function are (a) digestion, (b) secretion, (c) absorption, and (d) motility.
   A. The system is designed to maximize the absorption of most nutrients, not to regulate the amount absorbed.
   B. The system does not play a major role in the removal of waste products from the internal environment.

OVERVIEW: FUNCTIONS OF THE GASTROINTESTINAL ORGANS

I. The names and functions of the gastrointestinal organs are summarized in Figure 17-3.
II. Each day the gastrointestinal tract secretes about 3.5 times more fluid into the lumen than is ingested. Only about 1 percent of the luminal contents is excreted in the feces.

STRUCTURE OF THE GASTROINTESTINAL TRACT WALL

I. The structure of the wall of the gastrointestinal tract is summarized in Figure 17-6.
   A. The area available for absorption in the small intestine is greatly increased by the folding of the intestinal wall, the presence of villi, and microvilli on the surface of the epithelial cells.
   B. The epithelial cells lining the intestinal tract are continuously replaced by new cells arising from mitosis.
   C. The venous blood from the small intestine, containing absorbed nutrients other than fat, passes to the liver via the hepatic portal vein before returning to the heart. Fat is absorbed into the lymphatic vessels (lacteals) in each villus.

DIGESTION AND ABSORPTION

I. Starch is digested by amylases secreted by the salivary glands and pancreas, and the resulting products, as well as ingested disaccharides, are digested to monosaccharides by enzymes in the membranes of epithelial cells in the small intestine.
   A. The monosaccharides are then absorbed by secondary active transport.
   B. Some polysaccharides, such as cellulose, cannot be digested and pass to the large intestine, where they are metabolized by bacteria.
II. Proteins are broken down into small peptides and amino acids, which are absorbed by secondary active transport in the small intestine.
   A. The breakdown of proteins to peptides is catalyzed by pepsin in the stomach and primarily by the pancreatic enzymes trypsin and chymotrypsin in the small intestine.
   B. Peptides are broken down into amino acids by pancreatic carboxypeptidase and intestinal aminopeptidase.
III. The digestion and absorption of fat by the small intestine requires mechanisms that solubilize the fat and its digestion products.
   A. Large fat globules leaving the stomach are emulsified in the small intestine by bile salts and phospholipids secreted by the liver.
   B. Lipase from the pancreas digests fat at the surface of the emulsion droplets, forming fatty acids and monoglycerides.
   C. These water-insoluble products of lipase action,

when combined with bile salts, form micelles that are in equilibrium with the free molecules.

   D. Free fatty acids and monoglycerides diffuse across the luminal membranes of epithelial cells, within which they are enzymatically recombined to form triacylglycerol, which is released as chylomicrons from the blood side of the cell by exocytosis.

   E. The released chylomicrons enter lacteals in the intestinal villa and pass, by way of the lymphatic system, to the venous blood returning to the heart.

   IV. Fat-soluble vitamins are absorbed by the same pathway used for fat absorption. Most water-soluble vitamins are absorbed in the small intestine by diffusion or carrier-mediated transport. Vitamin B_{12} is absorbed in the ileum after combining with intrinsic factor secreted by the stomach.

   V. Water is absorbed from the small intestine by osmosis following the active absorption of solutes, primarily sodium chloride.

REGULATION OF GASTROINTESTINAL PROCESSES

   I. Most gastrointestinal reflexes are initiated by luminal stimuli: (a) distension, (b) osmolarity, (c) acidity, and (d) digestion products.

   A. Neural reflexes are mediated by short reflexes in the enteric nervous system and by long reflexes involving afferent and efferent neurons to and from the CNS.

   B. Gastrin, secretin, CCK, and GIP are secreted by endocrine cells scattered throughout the epithelium of the stomach (gastrin) and small intestine (secretin, CCK, and GIP). Their properties are summarized in Table 17-3.

   C. The three phases of gastrointestinal regulation—cephalic, gastric, and intestinal—are named for the location of the stimulus that initiates the response.

   II. Chewing breaks up food into particles suitable for swallowing but is not essential for the eventual digestion and absorption of food.

   III. Salivary secretion is stimulated by food in the mouth acting reflexly via chemoreceptors and pressure receptors. Both sympathetic and parasympathetic stimulation increase salivary secretion.

   IV. Food moved into the pharynx by the tongue initiates swallowing, which is coordinated by the swallowing center in the brainstem medulla oblongata.

   A. Food is prevented from entering the trachea by inhibition of respiration and by closure of the glottis.

   B. The upper esophageal sphincter relaxes as food is moved into the esophagus and then closes.

   C. Food is moved through the esophagus toward the stomach by peristaltic waves. The lower esophageal sphincter remains open throughout swallowing.

   D. If food does not reach the stomach with the first peristaltic wave, distension of the esophagus will initiate secondary peristalsis.

   V. The factors controlling acid secretion by parietal cells in the stomach are summarized in Table 17-4.

   VI. Pepsinogen, secreted by the gastric chief cells in response to most of the same reflexes that control acid secretion, is converted to the active proteolytic enzyme pepsin in the stomach's lumen by acid and by pepsin itself.

   VII. Peristaltic waves sweeping over the stomach become stronger in the antrum, where most mixing occurs. With each wave, only a small portion of the stomach's contents are expelled into the small intestine through the pyloric sphincter.

   A. The basic electrical rhythm generated by gastric smooth muscle determines gastric peristaltic wave frequency. Contraction strength depends on the frequency of action potentials triggered by the slow waves.

   B. The larger a meal, the faster the stomach empties initially. Distension of the small intestine, and fat, acid, or hypertonic solutions in the intestinal lumen inhibit gastric emptying.

   VIII. The exocrine portion of the pancreas secretes digestive enzymes and bicarbonate ions, which reach the duodenum through the pancreatic duct.

   A. The bicarbonate ions neutralize acid entering the small intestine from the stomach.

   B. Most proteolytic enzymes, including trypsin, are secreted by the pancreas in inactive forms. Trypsin is activated by enterokinase located on the membranes of the small intestine cells and in turn activates the other inactive enzymes.

   C. The hormone secretin, released from the small intestine in response to increased luminal acidity, stimulates bicarbonate secretion. CCK is released from the small intestine in response to the products of fat and protein digestion, and stimulates pancreatic enzyme secretion.

   IX. The liver secretes bile, the major ingredients of which are bile salts, cholesterol, lecithin, bicarbonate ions, bile pigments, and trace metals.

   A. Bile salts undergo continuous enterohepatic recirculation. The liver also synthesizes new bile salts to replace those lost in the feces.

   B. The greater the bile salt concentration in the hepatic portal blood, the greater the rate of bile secretion.

   C. Bilirubin, the major bile pigment, is a breakdown product of hemoglobin and is absorbed from the blood by the liver and secreted into the bile.

D. Secretin stimulates bicarbonate secretion by the cells lining the bile ducts in the liver.

E. Bile is concentrated in the gallbladder by the absorption of salt and water.

F. Following a meal, the release of CCK from the small intestine causes the gallbladder to contract and the sphincter of Oddi to relax, thereby injecting concentrated bile into the intestine.

X. In the small intestine, the digestion of polysaccharides and proteins increases the osmolarity of the luminal contents, producing water flow into the lumen.

XI. Small amounts of sodium, chloride, bicarbonate, and water are secreted by the small intestine. However, most of these secreted substances, as well as those entering the small intestine from other sources, are absorbed back into the blood.

XII. Intestinal motility is coordinated by the enteric nervous system and modified by long and short reflexes and hormones.

A. During and shortly after a meal, the intestinal contents are mixed by segmenting movements of the intestinal wall.

B. After most of the food has been digested and absorbed, segmentation is replaced by the migrating motility complex, which moves the undigested material into the large intestine.

XIII. The primary function of the large intestine is to store and concentrate fecal matter before defecation.

A. Water is absorbed from the large intestine secondary to the active absorption of sodium, leading to the concentration of fecal matter.

B. Flatus is produced by bacterial fermentation of undigested polysaccharides.

C. Three to four times a day, mass movements in the large intestine move its contents into the rectum.

D. Distension of the rectum initiates defecation, which is assisted by a forced expiration against a closed glottis.

E. Defecation can be voluntarily controlled through somatic nerves to the skeletal muscles of the external anal sphincter.

PATHOPHYSIOLOGY OF THE GASTROINTESTINAL TRACT

I. The factors that normally prevent breakdown of the mucosal barrier and ulcers are (1) secretion of an alkaline mucus, (2) tight junctions between epithelial cells, and (3) rapid replacement of epithelial cells.

II. Vomiting is coordinated by the vomiting center in the medulla oblongata. Contractions of abdominal muscles force the contents of the stomach into the esophagus (retching), and if the contractions are strong enough, they force the contents of the esophagus through the upper esophageal sphincter into the mouth (vomiting).

III. Precipitation of cholesterol or, less often, bile pigments in the gallbladder forms gallstones, which can block the exit of the gallbladder or common bile duct. In the latter case, the failure of bile salts to reach the intestine causes decreased digestion and absorption of fat, and the accumulation of bile pigments in the blood and tissues causes jaundice.

IV. In the absence of lactase, lactose cannot be digested, and its presence in the small intestine results in diarrhea and increased flatus production.

V. Constipation is primarily the result of decreased colonic motility. The symptoms of constipation are produced by overdistension of the rectum, not by the absorption of toxic bacterial products.

VI. Diarrhea can be caused by decreased fluid absorption, increased fluid secretion, or both.

KEY TERMS

gastrointestinal system	colon
gastrointestinal tract	rectum
digestion	defecation
secretion	mucosa
absorption	submucous plexus
motility	muscularis externa
feces	circular muscle
mouth	longitudinal muscle
saliva	myenteric plexus
salivary glands	serosa
amylase	villi
pharynx	microvilli
esophagus	lacteal
stomach	hepatic portal vein
hydrochloric acid	fiber
pepsin	trypsin
chyme	chymotrypsin
small intestine	carboxypeptidase
duodenum	aminopeptidase
jejunum	lipase
ileum	emulsion
pancreas	micelles
liver	chylomicrons
bile	intrinsic factor
bile salts	enteric nervous system
gallbladder	short reflexes
common bile duct	long reflexes
large intestine	secretin

cholecystokinin (CCK)
gastrin
glucose insulinotropic
   peptide (GIP)
potentiation
cephalic phase
gastric phase
intestinal phase
swallowing center
glottis
epiglottis
upper esophageal
   sphincter
lower esophageal
   sphincter
peristaltic waves
secondary peristalsis
body (of stomach)
fundus
pepsinogen
antrum
parietal cells
chief cells
enterogastrones
zymogens
receptive relaxation
pyloric sphincter
basic electrical rhythm

enterokinase
trypsinogen
bile canaliculi
enterohepatic circulation
bile pigments
bilirubin
hepatocytes
sphincter of Oddi
segmentation
migrating motility
   complex
motilin
law of the intestine
gastroileal reflex
intestino-intestinal reflex
cecum
appendix
rectum
ileocecal sphincter
flatus
mass movement
anus
internal anal sphincter
external anal sphincter
defecation reflex
vomiting center
lactase

REVIEW QUESTIONS

1. List the four processes that accomplish the functions of the gastrointestinal system.

2. List the primary functions performed by each of the organs in the gastrointestinal system.

3. Approximately how much fluid is secreted into the gastrointestinal tract each day, compared with the amount of food and drink ingested? How much of this appears in the feces?

4. What structures are responsible for the large surface area of the small intestine?

5. Where does the venous blood go after leaving the small intestine?

6. Identify the enzymes involved in carbohydrate digestion and the mechanism of carbohydrate absorption in the small intestine.

7. List three ways in which proteins or their digestion products can be absorbed from the small intestine.

8. Describe the process of fat emulsification.

9. What is the role of micelles in fat absorption?

10. Describe the movement of fat across the wall of the small intestine.

11. How does the absorption of fat-soluble vitamins differ from that of water-soluble vitamins?

12. Specify two conditions that may lead to failure to absorb vitamin B_{12}.

13. How are salts and water absorbed in the small intestine?

14. Describe the role of ferritin in the absorption of iron.

15. List the four types of stimuli that initiate most gastrointestinal reflexes.

16. Describe the location of the enteric nervous system and its role in both short and long reflexes.

17. Name the four gastrointestinal hormones and state their major functions.

18. Describe the neural reflexes leading to increased salivary secretion.

19. Describe the sequence of events that occur during swallowing.

20. List the cephalic, gastric, and intestinal phase stimuli that stimulate or inhibit acid secretion by the stomach.

21. Describe the function of gastrin and the factors controlling its secretion.

22. By what mechanism is pepsinogen converted to pepsin in the stomach?

23. Describe the factors that control gastric emptying.

24. Describe the mechanisms controlling pancreatic secretion of bicarbonate and enzymes.

25. How are pancreatic enzymes activated in the small intestine?

26. List the major constituents of bile.

27. Describe the recycling of bile salts by the enterohepatic circulation.

28. What determines the rate of bile secretion by the liver?

29. Describe the effects of secretin and CCK on the bile ducts and gallbladder.

30. What causes water to move from the blood to the lumen of the duodenum following gastric emptying?

31. Describe the type of intestinal motility found during and shortly after a meal and the type found several hours after a meal.

32. Describe the production of flatus by the large intestine.

33. Describe the factors that initiate and control defecation.

34. Why is the stomach's wall normally not digested by the acid and digestive enzymes in the lumen?

35. Describe the process of vomiting.

36. What are the consequences of the blocking of the common bile duct with a gallstone?

37. What are the consequences of the failure to digest lactose in the small intestine?

38. Contrast the factors that cause constipation with those that produce diarrhea.

CLINICAL TERMS

pernicious anemia   hemochromatosis

heartburn
dumping syndrome
ulcers
gastritis
retching
gallstones

jaundice
lactose intolerance
constipation
laxatives
diarrhea

THOUGHT QUESTIONS

(Answers are given in Appendix A.)

1. If the salivary glands were unable to secrete amylase, what effect would this have on starch digestion?

2. Whole milk or a fatty snack consumed before the ingestion of alcohol decreases the rate of intoxication. By what mechanism may fat be acting to produce this effect?

3. A patient brought to a hospital after a period of prolonged vomiting has an elevated heart rate, decreased blood pressure, and below-normal blood acidity. Explain these symptoms in terms of the consequences of excessive vomiting.

4. Can fat be digested and absorbed in the absence of bile salts? Explain.

5. How might damage to the lower portion of the spinal cord affect defecation?

6. One of the procedures used in the treatment of ulcers is vagotomy, surgical cutting of the vagus (parasympathetic) nerves to the stomach. By what mechanism will this procedure help ulcers to heal and decrease the incidence of new ulcers?

CHAPTER

18

REGULATION OF ORGANIC METABOLISM, GROWTH, AND ENERGY BALANCE

hapter 5 introduced the concepts of energy and of organic metabolism at the level of the individual cell. This chapter deals with a variety of topics that are concerned in one way or another with those same concepts, but for the entire body. First we describe how the metabolic pathways for carbohydrate, fat, and protein are controlled so as to provide a continuous source of energy to the various tissues and organs at all times. The next topic is how the metabolic changes that underlie body growth occur and are controlled. Finally, we describe the determinants of total-body energy balance in terms of energy intake and output and how the body temperature—a measure of the heat content of the body—is regulated.

SECTION

CONTROL AND INTEGRATION OF CARBOHYDRATE, PROTEIN, AND FAT METABOLISM

EVENTS OF THE ABSORPTIVE AND POSTABSORPTIVE STATES

echanisms have evolved for survival during alternating periods of plenty and fasting. We speak of two functional states or periods: the **absorptive state**, during which ingested nutrients are entering the blood from the gastrointestinal tract, and the **postabsorptive state**, during which the gastrointestinal tract is empty of nutrients and energy must be supplied by the body's own stores. Since an average meal requires approximately 4 h for complete absorption, our usual three-meals-a-day pattern places us in the postabsorptive state during the late morning and afternoon and almost the entire night. We shall refer to going more than 24 h without eating as fasting.

During the absorptive period, some of the ingested nutrients supply the energy needs of the body, and the remainder are added to the body's energy stores, to be called upon during the next postabsorptive period. Total-body energy stores are adequate for the average person to easily withstand a fast of many weeks (provided that water is available).

Figures 18-1 and 18-2 summarize the major pathways to be described in this chapter. Although they may appear formidable at first glance, they should present little difficulty after we have described the component parts, and

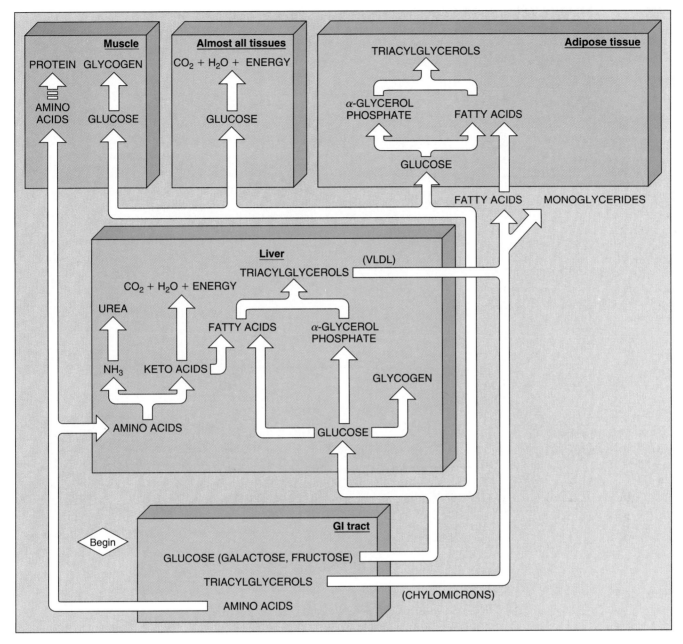

FIGURE 18-1

Major metabolic pathways of the absorptive state. The monoglycerides formed by the action of lipoprotein lipase in the adipose-tissue capillaries are not taken up by the adipose-tissue cells but circulate to the liver for further metabolism. The arrow from amino acids to protein in muscle is dashed to denote the fact that excess amino acids are not *stored* as protein (see text). Urea, formed in the liver, enters the blood and is excreted by the kidneys. All arrows between boxes denote carriage of the substance via the blood. VLDL = very low density lipoproteins.

these figures should be referred to constantly during the following discussion.

Absorptive State

We shall assume, for this discussion, that an average meal contains all three of the major nutrients—carbohydrate, protein, and fat, the carbohydrate constituting most of the meal's energy content (calories). Recall from Chapter 17 that carbohydrate and protein are absorbed primarily as monosaccharides and amino acids, respectively, into the blood supplying the gastrointestinal tract. The blood leaves the gastrointestinal tract to go directly to the liver

FIGURE 18-2

Major metabolic pathways of the postabsorptive state. The central focus is regulation of the blood glucose concentration. All arrows between boxes denote carriage of the substance via the blood. Urea, formed in the liver, enters the blood and is excreted by the kidneys.

by way of the hepatic portal vein, allowing the liver to alter the nutrient composition of the blood before it returns to the heart to be pumped to the rest of the body. In contrast to carbohydrate and amino acids, fat is absorbed into the lymph, as triacylglycerols in chylomicrons; the lymph then drains into the systemic venous system. Thus, the liver does not get first crack at absorbed fat.

Absorbed Glucose. Some of the carbohydrate absorbed from the gastrointestinal tract is galactose and fructose, but since these sugars are either converted to glucose by the liver or enter essentially the same metabolic pathways

as does glucose, we shall simply refer to absorbed carbohydrate as glucose.

As shown in Figure 18-1, a fraction of the absorbed glucose enters the liver cells. This is a very important point: During the absorptive period there is net *uptake* of glucose by the liver. We shall describe the fate of this glucose in a moment.

Of the absorbed glucose that does not enter liver cells, a very large fraction enters most other body cells and is catabolized to carbon dioxide and water, providing the energy for ATP formation (Chapter 5). Indeed, and this is a key point, glucose is the body's major energy source during the absorptive state. In this regard, it should be recognized that skeletal muscle makes up the majority of body mass and is the major consumer of metabolic fuel, even at rest.

Skeletal muscle not only catabolizes glucose during the absorptive phase but converts some of the glucose to the polysaccharide glycogen, which is then stored in the muscle.

Yet another fraction of absorbed glucose enters adipose-tissue cells (adipocytes) where some, as in muscle, is catabolized for energy. The most important fate, however, of glucose in adipocytes during the absorptive phase is its transformation to both α-glycerol phosphate and fatty acids, which are then linked together to form triacylglycerols.

We now return to the absorbed glucose that enters the liver: As shown in Figure 18-1, it is either stored as glycogen, as in skeletal muscle, or transformed to α-glycerol phosphate and fatty acids, which are then used to synthesize triacylglycerols, as in adipose tissue. Some of this fat synthesized from glucose in the liver is stored there, but most is packaged, along with specific proteins, into molecular aggregates of lipids and proteins. These aggregates are secreted by the liver cells and enter the blood. They are called **very-low-density lipoproteins (VLDL)** because they contain much more fat than protein, and fat is less dense than protein. The synthesis of VLDL by liver cells occurs by processes similar to those for synthesis of chylomicrons by intestinal mucosal cells, as described in Chapter 17.

Once in the bloodstream, VLDL complexes, being quite large, do not readily penetrate capillary walls. Instead, their triacylglycerols are hydrolyzed mainly to monoglycerides (glycerol linked to one fatty acid chain) and fatty acids by the enzyme **lipoprotein lipase** located on the blood-facing surface of the capillary endothelium. The capillaries of most tissues and organs contain lipoprotein lipase, but those in adipose tissue are particularly rich in this enzyme. The fatty acids generated by this enzyme's action in adipose tissue diffuse across the capillary wall and into the adipocytes. There they combine with α-glycerol phosphate, supplied by glucose metabolites, to form triacylglycerols once again. Thus, most of the fatty acids in the VLDL triacylglycerol originally synthesized from glucose by the *liver* end up being stored in triacylglycerol in *adipose tissue*. (The monoglycerides released into the blood by the action of lipoprotein lipase in adipose tissue do not enter the adipocytes but circulate to the liver where they are metabolized.)

To summarize, the major fates of glucose during the absorptive phase are utilization for energy, storage as glycogen in liver and skeletal muscle, and storage as fat in adipose tissue.

Absorbed Triacylglycerols. As noted earlier, almost all ingested fat is absorbed as chylomicrons into the lymph, which flows into the systemic circulation. The biochemical processing of these chylomicron triacylglycerols in plasma is quite similar to that just described for VLDL produced by the liver. The fatty acids of plasma chylomicrons are released, mainly within adipose tissue capillaries, by the action of endothelial lipoprotein lipase, and the released fatty acids then enter adipocytes and combine with α-glycerol phosphate, synthesized from glucose metabolites, to form triacylglycerols.

The importance of glucose for triacylglycerol synthesis in adipocytes cannot be overemphasized. Adipocytes do not have the enzyme required for phosphorylation of glycerol, and so α-glycerol phosphate can be formed in these cells only from glucose metabolites and not from glycerol or any other fat metabolites.

In contrast, there are three major sources of the fatty acids found in adipose-tissue triacylglycerol: (1) glucose that enters adipose tissue and is converted to fatty acids; (2) glucose that is converted in liver to VLDL triacylglycerols, which are transported via the blood to the adipose tissue; and (3) ingested triacylglycerols transported to adipose tissue in chylomicrons. Sources 2 and 3 require the action of lipoprotein lipase to release the fatty acids from the circulating triacylglycerols.

This description has emphasized the *storage* of ingested fat. For simplicity, we have not shown in Figure 18-1 that a fraction of the ingested fat is not stored but is oxidized during the absorptive state by various organs to provide energy. The relative amounts of carbohydrate and fat used for energy during the absorptive period depend largely on the content of the meal.

Absorbed Amino Acids. A minority of the absorbed amino acids enter liver cells. They are used to synthesize a variety of proteins, including liver enzymes and plasma proteins, or they are converted to carbohydrate-like intermediates known as **keto acids** by removal of the amino group (deamination, Chapter 5). The amino groups are used to synthesize urea, which is excreted by the kidneys.

The keto acids generated by deamination are *not* converted to glucose during the absorptive phase, unlike the situation to be described for the postabsorptive phase. However, they can enter the Krebs tricarboxylic acid cycle and be catabolized to provide energy for the liver cells, or they can be converted to fatty acids, thereby participating in fat synthesis by the liver.

Most ingested amino acids are not taken up by the liver cells but enter other cells (Figure 18-1), where they may be used to synthesize proteins. We have simplified the diagram by showing "nonliver" amino acid uptake only by muscle, because muscle contains by far the largest amount of body protein. It should be emphasized, however, that all cells require a constant supply of amino acids for protein synthesis and participate in the dynamics of protein metabolism.

Protein synthesis is represented by a *dashed* line in the muscle box in Figure 18-1 to call attention to an important fact: There is a net synthesis of protein during the absorptive period, but this basically just replaces the proteins catabolized during the postabsorptive period. In other words, excess amino acids are not *stored* as protein in the sense that glucose is stored as glycogen or that both glucose and fat are stored as fat. Rather, ingested amino acids in excess of those needed to maintain a stable protein turnover are merely converted to carbohydrate or fat. Therefore, eating large amounts of protein does not in itself cause increases in body protein. This discussion does not apply to growing children, who manifest a continuous increase in body protein, or to adults who are actively building body mass as, for example, by weightlifting.

Nutrient metabolism during the absorptive period is summarized in Table 18-1.

Postabsorptive State

As the absorptive period ends, net synthesis of glycogen, fat, and protein ceases, and net catabolism of all these substances begins to occur. The overall significance of these events can be understood in terms of the essential problem during the postabsorptive period: No glucose is being absorbed from the intestinal tract, yet the plasma glucose concentration must be maintained because the brain normally utilizes only glucose for energy. Too low a plasma glucose concentration can result in alterations of neural activity ranging from subtle impairment of mental function to coma and even death.

The events that maintain plasma glucose concentration fall into two categories: (1) reactions that provide sources of blood glucose, and (2) glucose sparing because of fat utilization.

TABLE 18-1   SUMMARY OF NUTRIENT METABOLISM DURING THE ABSORPTIVE PERIOD

1. Energy is provided primarily by absorbed carbohydrate.
2. There is net uptake of glucose by the liver.
3. Some carbohydrate is stored as glycogen in liver and muscle, but most carbohydrate and fat in excess of that utilized for energy are stored mainly as fat in adipose tissue.
4. There is some synthesis of body proteins, but much dietary protein is utilized for energy or converted to fat.

Sources of Blood Glucose.   The sources of blood glucose during the postabsorptive period are as follows (Figure 18-2):

1. **Glycogenolysis**, the hydrolysis of glycogen stores, occurs in the liver and skeletal muscle. In the liver, glucose is formed by this process and enters the blood. Hepatic glycogenolysis, a rapidly occurring event, is the first line of defense maintaining plasma glucose concentration. Its role, however, is relatively short-lived for the following reason: After the absorptive period is completed, the normal liver contains less than 100 g of glycogen; at 4 kcal/g, the subsequent breakdown of all this glycogen would provide 400 kcal, enough to fulfill an average person's total caloric need for only 4 h. Moreover, this is an overestimate since liver glycogen stores never become fully depleted even during prolonged fasting.

   Glycogenolysis also occurs in skeletal muscle, which contains approximately the same amount of glycogen as the liver. However, muscle, unlike liver, lacks the enzyme necessary to form glucose from the glucose 6-phosphate formed during glycogenolysis (Chapter 5). The glucose 6-phosphate undergoes glycolysis within the muscle to yield pyruvate and lactate. These substances are liberated into the blood, circulate to the liver, and are converted into glucose, which can then leave the liver cells to enter the blood. Thus, muscle glycogen contributes to the blood glucose indirectly via the liver.

2. The catabolism of triacylglycerols, a process termed **lipolysis**, yields glycerol and fatty acids. The major site of lipolysis is adipose tissue, and the glycerol and fatty acids then enter the blood. The glycerol reaching the liver is converted to glucose. Thus, an important source of glucose during the postabsorptive period is the glycerol released when adipose-tissue triacylglycerol is broken down.

3. A few hours into the postabsorptive period protein becomes the major source of blood glucose. Large quantities of protein in muscle and, to a lesser extent, other tissues can be catabolized without serious cellular malfunction. There are, of course, limits to this process, and continued protein loss during a prolonged fast ultimately means functional disintegration, sickness, and death. Before this point is reached, however, protein breakdown can supply large quantities of amino acids, particularly alanine, that enter the blood and are picked up by the liver, which converts them, via the keto acid pathway, to glucose.

We have now described the synthesis of glucose from pyruvate, lactate, glycerol, and amino acids. Synthesis from any of these precursors is known as **gluconeogene-**

sis, that is, new formation of glucose. During a 24-h fast, gluconeogenesis provides approximately 180 g of glucose. The liver is not the only organ capable of gluconeogenesis; the kidneys also perform gluconeogenesis, but mainly during a prolonged fast. In such a fast the kidneys may contribute as much glucose as the liver.

Glucose Sparing (Fat Utilization). The 180 g of glucose per day produced by gluconeogenesis in the liver and kidneys during fasting supplies 720 kcal: 180 g/day × 4 kcal/g = 720 kcal/day. As described later in this chapter, normal total energy expenditure for an average adult equals 1500 to 3000 kcal/day. Accordingly, gluconeogenesis cannot supply all the body's energy needs. The following essential adjustment must therefore take place during the transition from the absorptive to the postabsorptive state: Most organs and tissues markedly reduce their glucose catabolism and increase their fat utilization, the latter becoming the major energy source. This metabolic adjustment, termed **glucose sparing,** "spares" the glucose produced by the liver for use by the nervous system.

The essential step in this adjustment is lipolysis, the catabolism of adipose-tissue triacylglycerol, which liberates glycerol and fatty acids into the blood. We described lipolysis in the previous section in terms of its importance in providing *glycerol* to the liver for conversion to glucose. Now, we focus on the liberated *fatty acids,* which circulate bound to plasma albumin. (Despite this binding to protein, they are known as free fatty acids in that they are "free" of glycerol.) The circulating fatty acids are metabolized by almost all tissues, excluding the nervous system. They enter the Krebs cycle by way of acetyl CoA and are catabolized to carbon dioxide and water (Chapter 5), thereby providing energy.

The liver also catabolizes fatty acids to acetyl CoA. The liver is unique, however, in that most of the acetyl CoA it forms from fatty acids during the postabsorptive state, particularly during prolonged fasting, does not enter the Krebs cycle but is processed into three compounds collectively called **ketones** (or ketone bodies). The reader should distinguish ketones from keto acids, which are metabolites of amino acids. Ketones are released into the blood and provide an important energy source during prolonged fasting for the many tissues capable of oxidizing them via the Krebs cycle. One of the ketones is acetone, some of which is exhaled and accounts for the distinctive breath odor of individuals undergoing prolonged fasting or, as we shall see, suffering from severe untreated diabetes mellitus.

The net result of fatty acid and ketone utilization during fasting is provision of energy for the body and sparing of glucose for the brain. Moreover, an important change in brain metabolism with prolonged fasting also occurs. Many areas of the brain are capable of utilizing ketones for

energy, and so as these substances begin to build up in the blood after the first few days of a fast, the brain begins to utilize them, as well as glucose, for its energy source. The survival value of this phenomenon is very great; when the brain greatly reduces its glucose requirement by utilizing ketones, much less protein breakdown is required to supply the amino acids for gluconeogenesis. Accordingly the protein stores will last longer, and the ability to withstand a long fast without serious tissue disruption is enhanced.

Table 18-2 summarizes the events of the postabsorptive period. The combined effects of glycogenolysis, gluconeogenesis, and the switch to fat utilization are so efficient that, after several days of complete fasting, the plasma glucose concentration is reduced by only a few percent. After 1 month, it is decreased only 25 percent.

ENDOCRINE AND NEURAL CONTROL OF THE ABSORPTIVE AND POSTABSORPTIVE STATES

We now turn to the endocrine and neural factors that control and integrate these metabolic pathways and transformations. As before, the reader should constantly refer to Figures 18-1 and 18-2. We shall focus primarily on the following questions, summarized in Figure 18-3, raised by the previous discussion: (1) What controls net anabolism of protein, glycogen, and triacylglycerol in the absorptive phase, and net catabolism in the postabsorptive phase? (2) What induces primarily glucose utilization by cells for energy during the absorptive phase, but fat utilization during the postabsorptive phase?

TABLE 18-2 SUMMARY OF NUTRIENT METABOLISM DURING THE POSTABSORPTIVE PERIOD

1. Glycogen, fat, and protein syntheses are curtailed, and net breakdown occurs.
2. Glucose is formed in the liver both from the glycogen stored there and by gluconeogenesis from blood-borne lactate, pyruvate, glycerol, and amino acids. The kidneys also perform gluconeogenesis during a prolonged fast.
3. The glucose produced in the liver (and kidneys) is released into the blood, but its utilization for energy is greatly reduced in muscle and other nonneural tissues.
4. Lipolysis releases adipose-tissue fatty acids into the blood, and the oxidation of these fatty acids and of ketones produced from them by the liver provides most of the body's energy supply.
5. The brain continues to use glucose but also starts using ketones as they build up in the blood.

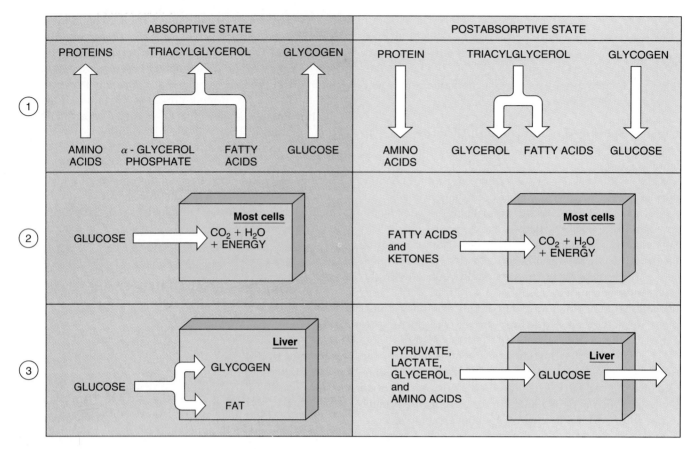

FIGURE 18-3

Summary of critical points in transition from absorptive state to postabsorptive state. The phrase "absorptive state" could be replaced with "actions of insulin," "postabsorptive state" with "results of decreased insulin."

(3) What drives net glucose uptake by the liver during the absorptive phase, but gluconeogenesis and glucose release during the postabsorptive phase?

The most important controls of these transitions from feasting to fasting, and vice versa, are two pancreatic hormones—insulin and glucagon. Also playing a role are the hormone epinephrine, from the adrenal medulla, and the sympathetic nerves to liver and adipose tissue.

Insulin and glucagon are peptides secreted by the **islets of Langerhans**, clusters of endocrine cells in the pancreas. Appropriate histological techniques reveal four distinct types of islet cells, termed A (or alpha), B (or beta), D (or delta), and F (or PP) cells, each of which secretes a different hormone. The **beta cells** are the source of insulin, and the **alpha cells** of glucagon. There are two other pancreatic hormones, somatostatin and pancreatic polypeptide, secreted by the delta cells and the PP cells, respectively, but the functions of these two pancreatic hormones are not known.

Insulin

Insulin is the most abundant hormone secreted by the islets and is the single most important controller of organic metabolism. Its secretion, and hence plasma concentration, are increased during the absorptive state and decreased during the postabsorptive state. For simplicity, insulin's many actions are often divided into two broad categories: (1) metabolic effects on carbohydrate, lipid, and protein synthesis; and (2) growth-promoting effects on DNA synthesis, cell division, and cell differentiation. This section deals with the metabolic effects; the growth-promoting effects are described later in this chapter in the section on growth.

Insulin's major targets are muscle (both cardiac and skeletal), adipose tissue, and liver, and the most important responses of these targets are summarized in Figure 18-4. Compare this figure to Figure 18-1 and you will see that these responses to insulin are the same as the events of the absorptive-state pattern. Conversely, the effects of a reduction in plasma insulin are the same as the events of the postabsorptive pattern in Figure 18-2.

What are the biochemical sequences of events that lead to the responses summarized in Figure 18-4? The first step in all the sequences is the binding of insulin to specific receptors on the outer surface of the plasma membrane of its target cells. As noted in Chapter 7, the insulin-

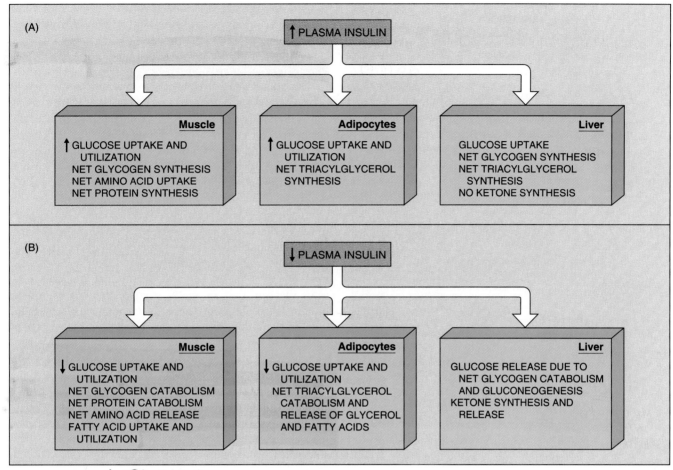

★ FIGURE 18-4   LEARN iT

Summary of overall target-cell responses to an increase (A) or decrease (B) in the plasma concentration of insulin. The biochemical events that underlie these responses are given in Figure 18-5.

activated receptor is a tyrosine kinase enzyme, which catalyzes its own phosphorylation using ATP. This autophosphorylation is necessary for the insulin receptor to trigger the next steps in the sequences leading to the cell's responses, that is, to initiate the signal transduction mechanisms (Chapter 7).[1] In some cases, the insulin receptor inhibits adenylyl cyclase, thereby reducing the intracellular cyclic AMP concentration, but in most cases the signal transduction mechanisms remain unclear, involving as yet unidentified second messengers.

Whatever the signal transduction mechanisms are, the final steps of the sequences leading to the cell's responses are changes in the target-cell's membrane transport and/or enzymes, to which we now turn. It is important here not to lose sight of the forest for the trees: The essential information (the "forest") to understand about insulin's actions is

the target cells' ultimate responses, that is, the material summarized in Figure 18-4; the following sections, summarized in Figure 18-5, attempt merely to show some of the specific biochemical reactions (the "trees") that underlie these ultimate responses.

Effects on Muscle and Adipose Tissue. Glucose enters most cells of the body by the carrier-mediated mechanism that we described in Chapter 6 as facilitated diffusion. Glucose transport is unique in muscle and adipocytes (and a few other cell types), however, in that the glucose transporter is responsive to insulin. This hormone causes glucose-transport proteins stored in the cytoplasm to be inserted in the plasma membranes of these cells. This causes greater glucose entry, which then increases this sugar's availability for all the reactions in which it participates in these cells (Figure 18-5): In muscle, the most important are glycolysis and glycogen synthesis; in adipose tissue, they are syntheses of fatty acids and α-glycerol phosphate, which then combine to form triacylglycerol.

---

[1]There is still controversy, however, as to whether all biological responses to insulin require activation of insulin receptor tyrosine kinase and receptor autophosphorylation.

[handwritten: liver produce globular proteins that carry hormones]

[handwritten: phosphorylation, so glucose not go out cell]

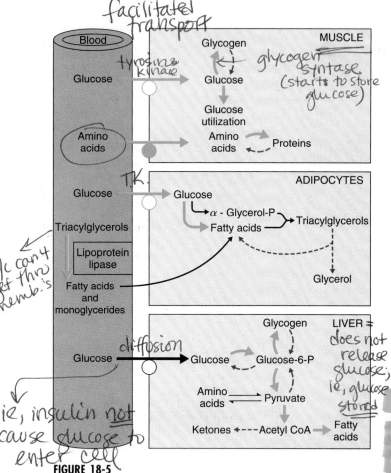

[handwritten annotations on figure: facilitated transport; tyrosine kinase; glycogen syntase (starts to store glucose); TK; b/c can't get thru memb.'s; diffusion; ie, insulin not cause glucose to enter cell; LIVER = does not release glucose; ie, glucose stored]

FIGURE 18-5

Key biochemical events that underlie the responses of target cells to insulin summarized in Figure 18-4. Each green arrow denotes a process stimulated by insulin, whereas a dashed red arrow denotes inhibition by insulin. All these effects, except for those exerted on the transport of glucose and amino acids, are mediated by insulin-dependent enzymes. The bowed arrows, as described in Chapter 5, denote pathways whose reversibility is mediated by different enzymes. For simplicity we do not show the multiple steps in liver between pyruvate and glucose by which insulin inhibits gluconeogenesis while stimulating glucose utilization (see Chapter 5 for a review of the biochemical steps in these pathways).

But insulin favors glycolysis and net synthesis of glycogen and triacylglycerol not just by its effects on glucose *transport*. Insulin can also alter the activities and/or concentrations of the *enzymes* involved in the metabolic pathways of these substances. (For simplicity in these descriptions, when we refer to stimulation and inhibition we will not specify whether it is enzyme activity or enzyme concentration that is being altered.)

Glycogen synthesis in muscle provides an excellent example (Figure 18-5, top right): Increased glucose transport stimulates glycogen synthesis by increasing glucose availability, but in addition insulin increases the activity of

the enzyme (glycogen synthase) catalyzing the rate-limiting step in glycogen synthesis and inhibits the enzyme (glycogen phosphorylase) that catalyzes glycogen catabolism. Thus, insulin favors glucose transformation to glycogen in muscle by a triple-barreled effect!

The situation for triacylglycerol metabolism in adipocytes is analogous to that for carbohydrate (Figure 18-5): The stimulation by insulin of glucose transport into adipocytes provides precursors for the synthesis of triacylglycerols, but insulin also stimulates the intracellular enzymes that catalyze fatty acid synthesis, and very importantly, it inhibits the intracellular lipase that catalyzes triacylglycerol breakdown. Again there is a triple-barreled effect favoring, in this case, triacylglycerol storage in adipocytes. Actually there is a four-barreled effect, for insulin also stimulates lipoprotein lipase in the endothelial cells of adipose-tissue capillaries; recall that this enzyme catalyzes the breakdown of plasma triacylglycerols and releases fatty acids that can then enter the adipose-tissue cells and be built into triacylglycerol there. The reader must remember to distinguish lipoprotein lipase, which is on the surface of endothelial cells and promotes fat *storage*, from the completely different intracellular lipase that mediates lipolysis, thereby favoring fat *mobilization*.[2]

And similarly for protein in muscle (Figure 18-5): First, insulin stimulates the active transport system that moves amino acids into muscle cells, thereby making more amino acids available for protein synthesis. But this hormone also stimulates some of the ribosomal enzymes that mediate the synthesis of protein from these amino acids and inhibits the enzymes that mediate protein catabolism.

Effects on Liver. Some of insulin's effects on carbohydrate and lipid metabolism in liver are the same as those seen in muscle and adipocytes. Thus, in liver insulin favors both net glycogen synthesis and net triacylglycerol synthesis through the same profile of enzyme stimulation and inhibition described above for muscle and adipocytes.

There are, however, several aspects of insulin's actions on liver that are different from those on the other targets and determine whether the liver will take up or release glucose. First, glucose production—gluconeogenesis—is an activity limited to the liver (and the kidneys), and it is abolished by insulin, which inhibits critical enzymes that mediate the gluconeogenic pathways. Thus, the insulin-stimulated liver does not release glucose but rather takes it up. Indeed, it takes it up in very large quantities despite a second important difference between liver and insulin's

---

[2]The intracellular lipase that is affected by insulin (and other hormones) is often called hormone-sensitive lipase. This can be confusing because, as we have seen, endothelial-cell lipoprotein lipase is also sensitive to hormones.

other two major targets: The facilitated-diffusion glucose transporter in liver, unlike that in muscle and adipocytes, is *not* influenced by insulin.

How, then, does insulin cause the marked uptake of glucose? First, recall two facts from previous chapters: (1) Facilitated diffusion into a cell, although carrier-mediated, is downhill transport and is dependent upon a concentration difference across the plasma membrane (Chapter 6); and (2) the first step in the intracellular metabolism of glucose is its phosphorylation to glucose 6-phosphate (Chapter 5). Insulin stimulates the enzyme (glucokinase) in liver that catalyzes this first metabolic step and inhibits the enzyme (glucose-6-phosphatase) that removes the phosphate, and this keeps the cytosolic glucose concentration low, resulting in a large concentration gradient favoring glucose movement into the liver cells.

Finally, recall that ketone formation is another process limited to the liver. Insulin inhibits this process in a variety of ways.

Effects of Decreases in Plasma Insulin Concentration. A decrease in plasma insulin concentration, by eliminating or reducing insulin's effects, will bring about results just opposite those described in the previous two sections: (1) net protein catabolism in muscle due to less entry of amino acids into muscle cells, decreased activity of the enzymes mediating protein synthesis, and less inhibition of the enzymes mediating protein catabolism; (2) net glycogen catabolism in all target cells due to less glucose entry into cells, decreased activity of the enzyme mediating glycogen synthesis, and less inhibition of the enzyme mediating glycogen catabolism; (3) net fat catabolism in adipose tissue due to less entry of glucose into adipose-tissue cells, decreased activity of the enzymes mediating fat synthesis, and less inhibition of the enzyme mediating lipolysis; (4) decreased glycolysis due to less entry of glucose into muscle and adipose tissue (and several other tissues) and decreased activity of the glycolytic enzymes; (5) increased utilization of fatty acids and ketones by many cells due to increased availability of these substances secondary to lipolysis and to ketone synthesis by the liver; and (6) gluconeogenesis and release of glucose by the liver due to less inhibition of the gluconeogenic enzymes.

We have now given a major part of the answers to the three questions posed on page 607 in that a *decrease* in plasma insulin concentration is largely (but not solely, as we shall see) responsible for the metabolic transformations that occur in going from the absorptive phase to the postabsorptive phase: Thus, effects 1, 2, and 3 in the above paragraph help explain the shift from net anabolism to net catabolism, effects 4 and 5 help explain the shift from glucose utilization to fatty acid and ketone utilization for en-

ergy,[3] and effect 6 helps explain the appearance of gluconeogenesis. With the next meal, the plasma insulin concentration increases as a result of increased insulin secretion and plays an important role in reversing all these transformations, that is, helps restore the metabolic profile of the absorptive phase.

Control of Insulin Secretion. The most important control of insulin secretion is the glucose concentration of the blood flowing through the pancreas, a system requiring no participation of nerves or of other hormones. An increase in blood glucose concentration stimulates insulin secretion, whereas a decrease inhibits secretion. The feedback nature of this system is shown in Figure 18-6: The rise in plasma glucose concentration following a meal stimulates insulin secretion, and the insulin stimulates entry of glucose into muscle and adipose tissue, as well as net uptake, rather than net output, of glucose by the liver. These effects reduce the blood concentration of glucose, thereby removing the stimulus for insulin secretion, which returns to its previous level.

There are numerous insulin-secretion controls other than plasma glucose concentration (Figure 18-7). One is the plasma concentration of certain amino acids, an elevated amino acid concentration causing enhanced insulin secretion. This is another negative-feedback control: Amino acid concentrations increase after ingestion of a protein-containing meal, and the increased plasma insulin stimulates uptake of these amino acids by muscle (and other cells as well).

There are also important hormonal controls over insulin secretion. For example, one of the hormones—glucose-dependent insulinotropic peptide (GIP, also termed gastric inhibitory peptide)—secreted by the gastrointestinal tract (Chapter 17) in response to eating stimulates the release of insulin. This provides an "anticipatory" (or feedforward) component to glucose regulation during ingestion of a meal; that is, insulin secretion will rise earlier and to a greater extent than it would if plasma glucose were the only controller.

Finally, the autonomic neurons to the islets of Langerhans also influence insulin secretion. Activation of the parasympathetic neurons, which occurs during ingestion of a meal, stimulates secretion of insulin and constitutes a second type of anticipatory regulation. In contrast, activa-

[3]The decreased glycolysis in muscle associated with a low plasma insulin concentration is only partly due to the loss of insulin's *direct* actions on glucose uptake and glycolytic enzymes. A second important contributor is the interaction called the glucose-fatty acid cycle: As fatty acid utilization increases in muscle, metabolites generated in the process themselves inhibit glycolysis and, ultimately, glucose uptake. Thus, muscle glucose utilization is controlled by insulin both directly and indirectly, the latter via insulin's actions on adipose tissue.

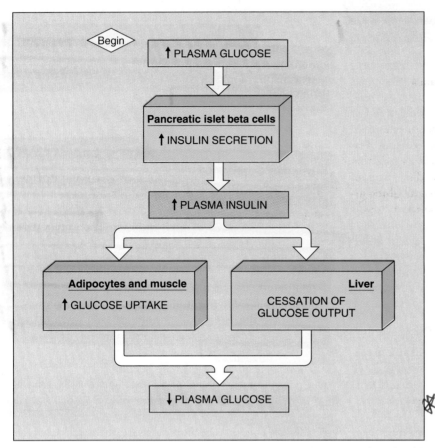

FIGURE 18-6
Negative-feedback nature of plasma glucose control over insulin secretion.

FIGURE 18-7
Major controls of insulin secretion. GIP = glucose-dependent insulinotropic peptide, a gastrointestinal hormone.

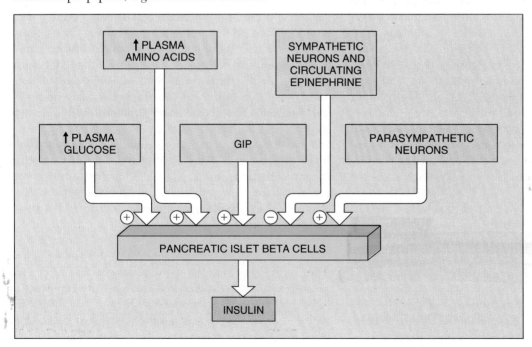

tion of the sympathetic neurons to the islets or an increase in the plasma concentration of epinephrine (the hormone secreted by the adrenal medulla) inhibits insulin secretion. The significance of this relationship for the body's response to low plasma glucose (**hypoglycemia**), stress, and exercise—all situations in which sympathetic activity is increased—will be described later in this chapter.

To repeat, insulin unquestionably plays the primary role in controlling the metabolic adjustments required for feasting or fasting, but other hormonal and neural factors also play significant roles. They all oppose the action of insulin in one way or another and are known as **glucose-counterregulatory controls**. Of these, the most important is glucagon.

Glucagon

As noted earlier, **glucagon** is the peptide hormone produced by the alpha cells of the pancreatic islets. The major physiological effects of glucagon are all on the liver.[4] Glucagon binds to receptors in the plasma membrane of liver cells, leading to the activation of adenylyl cyclase and generation of cyclic AMP in the cells. Cyclic AMP in turn activates cAMP-dependent protein kinase, which phosphorylates enzymes that mediate the effects of glucagon. All these effects on the liver are opposed to those of insulin (Figure 18-8): (1) increased glycogen breakdown; (2) increased gluconeogenesis; and (3) synthesis of ketones. Thus, the overall results of glucagon's effects are to increase the plasma concentrations of glucose and ketones, which are important for the postabsorptive period.

From a knowledge of these effects, one would logically suppose that glucagon secretion should increase during the postabsorptive period and prolonged fasting, and such is the case because a major stimulus for glucagon secretion is hypoglycemia. The adaptive value of such a reflex is obvious: A decreasing plasma glucose concentration induces increased release of glucagon which, by its effects on metabolism, serves to restore normal blood glucose concentrations by glycogenolysis and gluconeogenesis while at the same time supplying (if the fast is prolonged) ketones for cell utilization. Conversely, an increased plasma glucose concentration inhibits glucagon's secretion, thereby helping to return the plasma glucose concentration toward normal.[5]

---

[4]Glucagon in very large concentrations also acts on adipose tissue to stimulate lipolysis, but this effect probably does not occur physiologically.
[5]The mechanism by which changes in plasma glucose concentration act on the islets to alter glucagon secretion is controversial. It has been proposed that the A cells are controlled not by glucose per se but by insulin, that is, that an increase in insulin directly inhibits glucagon secretion, whereas a decrease in insulin removes the inhibition, resulting in increased secretion. Another proposal is that some substance other than insulin—possibly GABA—is coreleased with insulin from the B cells and acts locally to inhibit glucagon secretion. Pancreatic somatostatin, released from nearby D cells, may also inhibit glucagon secretion.

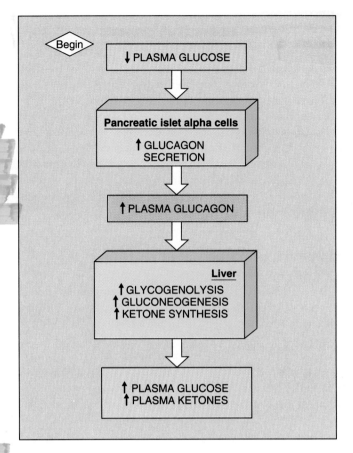

FIGURE 18-8

Negative-feedback nature of plasma glucose control over glucagon secretion.

Thus, during the postabsorptive state plasma insulin concentration is low and plasma glucagon concentration is high, and this combined change accounts almost entirely for the transition from the absorptive to the postabsorptive state. Said in a different way, this shift is best explained by a rise in the glucagon/insulin ratio in the plasma.

Thus far, the story is quite uncomplicated: The beta cells and alpha cells of the pancreatic islets constitute a push-pull system for regulating plasma glucose by producing two hormones—insulin and glucagon—whose actions and major controlling input are just the opposite of each other. However, we must now point out a complicating feature: A second major control of glucagon secretion is the plasma amino acid concentration acting directly on the alpha cells, and in this regard the effect is identical to rather than opposite that for insulin: Glucagon secretion, like insulin secretion, is stimulated by a rise in plasma amino acid concentration. Therefore, absorption of a mixed protein-carbohydrate meal is accompanied by a rise in the plasma concentrations of both insulin and glucagon. However, the insulin rise is relatively much larger than the glucagon rise because the postingestion increases in blood glucose and amino acids work together to stimulate insulin secretion, whereas they tend to counteract each other so far as glucagon secretion is concerned.

The secretion of glucagon, like that of insulin, is controlled not only by the plasma concentrations of glucose and amino acids but also by neural and hormonal inputs to the islets (Figure 18-9). For example, the sympathetic nerves to the islets stimulate glucagon secretion—just the opposite of their effect on insulin secretion. The adaptive significance of this relationship for exercise and stress will be described subsequently. Interestingly, the parasympathetic nerves also stimulate glucagon secretion.

Epinephrine and Sympathetic Nerves to Liver and Adipose Tissue

As noted earlier, epinephrine and the sympathetic nerves to the pancreatic islets inhibit insulin secretion and stimulate glucagon secretion. In addition, epinephrine also affects nutrient metabolism directly (Figure 18-10). Its major direct effects include stimulation of (1) glycogenolysis in both the liver and skeletal muscle, (2) gluconeogenesis in the liver, and (3) lipolysis in adipocytes. Activation of the sympathetic nerves to the liver and adipose tissue elicits essentially the same responses by these organs as does circulating epinephrine.

Thus, enhanced sympathetic nervous system activity exerts effects on organic metabolism—increased plasma concentrations of glucose, glycerol, and fatty acids—that are opposite those of insulin.

As might be predicted from these effects, hypoglycemia leads reflexly to increases in both epinephrine secretion and sympathetic-nerve activity to the liver and adipose tissue. This is the same stimulus that, as described above, leads to increased secretion of glucagon, although the receptors and pathways are totally different. When the plasma glucose concentration decreases, glucose receptors in the central nervous system initiate the reflexes that lead to increased activity in the sympathetic pathways to the adrenal medulla, liver, and adipose tissue. The adaptive value of the response is the same as that for the glucagon response to hypoglycemia: Blood glucose returns toward normal, and fatty acids are supplied for cell utilization.

How important is the sympathetic nervous system in the acute compensatory response to hypoglycemia? The present view is that this system is less important than glucagon but nevertheless contributes to bringing plasma glucose back toward normal.

In contrast to its increase during *acute* hypoglycemia, sympathetic nervous system activity decreases during prolonged fasting or ingestion of low-calorie diets; the adaptive significance of this change is discussed later in this chapter.

FIGURE 18-9

Major controls of glucagon secretion. Note that the sympathetic and parasympathetic nerves to the pancreatic alpha cells both stimulate glucagon secretion.

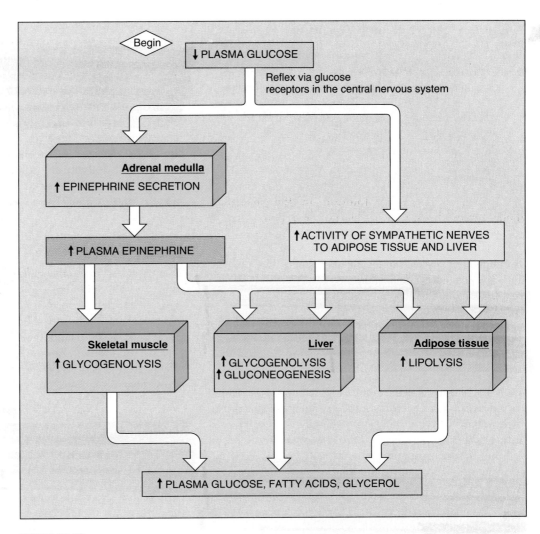

FIGURE 18-10

Participation of the sympathetic nervous system in the response to a low plasma glucose concentration (hypoglycemia). Glucose receptors in the liver (not shown) may also participate in this reflex. (Glycogenolysis in skeletal muscle contributes to increased plasma glucose by releasing lactate and pyruvate, which are converted to glucose in the liver.)

Other Hormones

In addition to the three hormones already described in this section, there are many others—cortisol, growth hormone, thyroid hormones, sex steroids, vasopressin, angiotensin, and still more—that have various effects on organic metabolism. The secretion of these hormones, however, is not primarily keyed to the transitions between the absorptive and postabsorptive states.[6] Instead, their secretion is controlled by other factors, and these hormones are for the most part involved in homeostatic processes described elsewhere in this book. Nonetheless, the effects of cortisol and growth hormone on nutrient metabolism warrant description here for two reasons: (1) Though the plasma concentrations of these two hormones do not usually change in accord with the absorptive and postabsorptive states, their *basal* plasma concentrations play physiological roles in determining the body's normal responses to these states; (2) an excess of either hormone produces important abnormalities in nutrient metabolism.

Cortisol. Cortisol, the major glucocorticoid produced by the adrenal cortex, plays an essential "permissive" role in the adjustments to fasting. We have described how fasting is associated with stimulation of both gluconeogenesis and lipolysis; however, neither of these critical metabolic transformations occurs to the usual degree in a person deficient in cortisol. In other words, the plasma cortisol

---

[6]Some people do show a small burst of growth hormone secretion several hours after a meal, but it is unlikely that this change contributes significantly to postabsorptive adaptations.

TABLE 18-3   EFFECTS OF CORTISOL ON ORGANIC METABOLISM

1. Basal concentrations are permissive for stimulation of gluconeogenesis and lipolysis in the postabsorptive state
2. Increased plasma concentrations cause:
   a. Increased protein catabolism
   b. Increased gluconeogenesis
   c. Decreased glucose uptake by cells
   d. Increased triacylglycerol breakdown

Net result: Increased plasma concentrations of amino acids, glucose, and free fatty acids

level need not *rise* during fasting and usually does not, but the presence of even small amounts of cortisol in the blood somehow maintains the concentrations of the key liver and adipose-tissue enzymes required for gluconeogenesis and lipolysis. Therefore, in response to fasting, people with a cortisol deficiency develop hypoglycemia serious enough to interfere with brain function.

Moreover, cortisol can play more than a permissive role when its plasma concentration does increase, as occurs during stress (Chapter 20). In high concentration, cortisol elicits many metabolic events ordinarily associated with fasting (Table 18-3). Clearly, here is another hormone, in addition to glucagon and epinephrine, that can exert actions opposite those of insulin. Indeed, persons with very high plasma levels of cortisol, due either to abnormally high secretion or to cortisol administration for medical reasons (Chapter 20), develop symptoms similar to those seen in individuals with insulin deficiency.

Growth Hormone. The primary physiological effects of growth hormone are to stimulate both growth and protein anabolism. Compared to these effects, those it exerts on carbohydrate and lipid metabolism are minor. Nonetheless, as is true for cortisol, either severe deficiency or marked excess of growth hormone does produce significant abnormalities in lipid and carbohydrate metabolism. Growth hormone's effects on these nutrients are similar to those of cortisol and opposite those of insulin. Growth hormone (1) renders adipocytes more responsive to lipolytic stimuli; (2) increases gluconeogenesis by the liver; and (3) reduces the ability of insulin to cause glucose uptake by peripheral tissues. These are often termed growth hormone's "anti-insulin effects."

Summary

To a great extent insulin may be viewed as the "hormone of plenty." Its secretion and plasma concentration are increased during the absorptive period and decreased during postabsorption, and these changes are adequate to cause most of the metabolic changes associated with these periods. In addition, opposed in various ways to insulin's effects are the actions of four major glucose-counterregulatory controls—glucagon, epinephrine and the sympathetic nerves to the liver and adipose tissue, cortisol, and growth hormone (Table 18-4). Glucagon and the sympathetic nervous system are activated during the postabsorptive period (or in any other situation with hypoglycemia) and definitely play roles in preventing hypoglycemia, glucagon being the more important. The rates of secretion of cortisol and growth hormone are not usually coupled to the absorptive-postabsorptive pattern; nevertheless, their presence in the blood at basal concentrations is necessary for normal adjustment of lipid and carbohydrate metabolism to the postabsorptive period, and excessive amounts of either hormone cause abnormally elevated plasma glucose concentrations.

TABLE 18-4   SUMMARY OF GLUCOSE-COUNTERREGULATORY CONTROLS*

	Glucagon	Epinephrine	Cortisol	Growth hormone
Glycogenolysis	X	X		
Gluconeogenesis	X	X	X	X
Lipolysis		X	X	X
Inhibition of glucose uptake			X	X

*All the processes listed on the left—glycogenolysis, gluconeogenesis, lipolysis, and inhibition of glucose uptake—are opposed to insulin's actions and are stimulated by one or more of the glucose-counterregulatory hormones in the table. An X indicates that the hormone stimulates the process; no X indicates that the hormone has no major physiological effect on the process. Epinephrine stimulates glycogenolysis in both liver and skeletal muscle, whereas glucagon does so only in liver.

FUEL HOMEOSTASIS IN EXERCISE AND STRESS

During exercise large quantities of fuels must be mobilized to provide the energy required for muscle contraction. As described in Chapter 11, these fuels include plasma glucose and fatty acids, as well as the muscle's own glycogen.

The plasma glucose used during exercise is supplied by the liver, both by breakdown of its glycogen stores and by gluconeogenesis—conversion of pyruvate, lactate, glycerol, and amino acids into glucose. The glycerol is made available to the liver by a marked increase in adipose-tissue lipolysis with a resultant release of glycerol and fatty acids into the blood, the fatty acids serving along with glucose as a fuel source for the exercising muscle.

What happens to blood glucose concentration during exercise? It changes very little in short-term, mild to moderate exercise and may increase slightly with strenuous short-term activity. However, during prolonged exercise (Figure 18-11), more than 90 min, plasma glucose concentration decreases, sometimes by as much as 25 percent. These relatively minor changes in blood glucose in the presence of marked increases in glucose utilization clearly demonstrate that glucose output by the liver must increase approximately in proportion to the increased utilization, at least until the later stages of exercise when it begins to lag somewhat.

The metabolic profile seen in an exercising individual—increases in hepatic glucose production, triacylglycerol breakdown, and fatty acid utilization—is similar to that seen in a fasting person, and the controls are also the same: Exercise is characterized by a fall in insulin secretion and a rise in glucagon secretion (Figure 18-11), plus increased activity of the sympathetic nervous system. In addition, cortisol and growth hormone are also secreted in increased amounts. All these events tend to increase plasma glucose, balancing the glucose-lowering effect caused by increased muscle glucose utilization.

What triggers increased glucagon secretion and decreased insulin secretion during exercise? One signal during prolonged exercise is the modest decrease in plasma glucose that occurs; this is the same signal that controls the secretion of these hormones in fasting. A second input—independent of plasma glucose concentration—is increased circulating epinephrine and enhanced activity of the sympathetic neurons supplying the pancreatic islets; this output is mediated by the central nervous system as part of the neural response to exercise. Thus, the increased sympathetic nervous system activity characteristic of exercise not only contributes directly to fuel mobilization by acting on the liver and adipose tissue but contributes indirectly by inhibiting the secretion of insulin and stimulating that of glucagon.

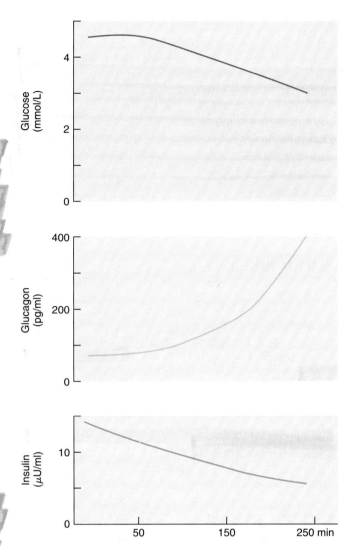

FIGURE 18-11

Plasma concentrations of glucose, glucagon, and insulin during prolonged (250 min) moderate exercise at a fixed intensity. (*Adapted from Felig and Wahren.*)

One component of the response to exercise is quite different from fasting: In exercise glucose uptake and utilization by the muscles is increased, whereas in fasting it is markedly reduced. How is it that, during exercise, the movement of glucose, via facilitated diffusion, into muscle can remain high in the presence of reduced plasma insulin and increased plasma concentrations of cortisol and growth hormone, all of which decrease glucose uptake by skeletal muscle? By an as yet unidentified mechanism, muscle contraction causes, as does insulin, migration of intracellular stores of glucose transporters to the plasma membrane.

Exercise is not the only situation characterized by the neuroendocrine profile of decreased insulin and increased glucagon, sympathetic activity, cortisol, and growth hormone. This profile also occurs in response to a variety of nonspecific stresses, both physical and emotional. The adaptive value of these neuroendocrine responses to stress is that the resulting shifts in metabolism prepare the body for exercise ("fight or flight") in the face of real or threatened injury. In addition, the amino acids liberated by catabolism of body protein stores, because of decreased insulin and increased cortisol, not only provide energy via gluconeogenesis but also constitute a potential source of amino acids for tissue repair should injury occur. The subject of stress and the body's responses to it are further described in Chapter 20.

DIABETES MELLITUS

The name "diabetes," meaning "syphon" or "running through," was used by the Greeks over 2000 years ago to describe the increased urinary volume excreted by people suffering from this disease. "Mellitus," meaning "sweet," distinguishes this urine from the large quantities of nonsweet ("insipid") urine produced by persons suffering from vasopressin deficiency. As described in Chapter 16, the latter disorder is known as diabetes insipidus, and the unmodified word "diabetes" is often used as a synonym for *diabetes mellitus*, a disease that affects nearly 15 million people in the United States.

Diabetes can be due to a deficiency of insulin or to a hyporesponsiveness to insulin, for it is not one but several diseases with different causes. Classification of these diseases rests on how much insulin the person is secreting and whether therapy requires the administration of insulin. In *insulin-dependent diabetes mellitus* (IDDM, also termed type 1 diabetes), the hormone is completely or almost completely absent from the islets of Langerhans and the plasma, and therapy with insulin is essential (this protein hormone cannot be given orally but must be injected because gastrointestinal enzymes would digest it). In *non-insulin-dependent diabetes mellitus* (NIDDM, also termed type 2 diabetes), the hormone is often present in plasma at near-normal or even above-normal levels, and therapy does not require administration of insulin.[7]

IDDM is less common, affecting 15 percent of diabetic patients. It is due to the total or near-total destruction of the pancreatic beta cells by the body's own white blood cells (autoimmune disease, Chapter 20). The triggering events for this autoimmune response are unknown.

Largely because of their insulin deficiency (we'll see

later that glucagon also plays a role), untreated patients with IDDM always have elevated plasma glucose concentrations. This occurs both because glucose fails to enter insulin's target cells normally and because the liver continuously makes glucose—via glycogenolysis and gluconeogenesis—and releases it into the blood. Another result of the insulin deficiency is marked lipolysis with resultant elevation of plasma glycerol and fatty acids. Marked ketone formation by the liver is also present.

If extreme, these metabolic changes culminate in the acute life-threatening emergency called *diabetic ketoacidosis (DKA)* (Figure 18-12). Some of the problems are due to the effects a markedly elevated plasma glucose produces on renal function. In Chapter 16, we pointed out that a normal person does not excrete glucose because all glucose filtered at the renal corpuscle is reabsorbed by the tubules. However, the elevated plasma glucose of diabetes may so increase the filtered load of glucose that the maximum tubular reabsorptive capacity is exceeded and large amounts of glucose may be excreted. For the same reasons, large amounts of ketones may also appear in the urine. These urinary losses aggravate the situation by depleting the body of nutrients and leading to weight loss. Far worse, however, is the effect of these solutes on sodium and water excretion. The osmotic force exerted by unreabsorbed glucose and ketones holds water in the tubule, thereby preventing its reabsorption. Sodium reabsorption is also retarded, and the net result is marked excretion of sodium and water, which can lead, by the sequence of events shown in Figure 18-12, to hypotension, brain damage, and death.

The other serious abnormality in diabetic ketoacidosis is the increased plasma hydrogen-ion concentration caused by the accumulation of ketones, two of which are weak acids. This increased hydrogen-ion concentration causes brain dysfunction that can contribute to the development of coma and death.[8]

Diabetic ketoacidosis is seen only in patients with untreated IDDM, that is, those with almost total inability to secrete insulin. However, 85 percent of diabetics are in the NIDDM category and never develop metabolic derangements severe enough to go into diabetic ketoacidosis. NIDDM is a disease mainly of overweight adults, typically starting in middle life. Given the earlier mention of progressive weight loss in IDDM as a symptom of diabetes, it may seem contradictory that most people with NIDDM are overweight. The paradox is resolved when one realizes that people with NIDDM, in contrast to those with IDDM, do not excrete enough glucose in the urine to cause weight loss.

---

[7]Some people with NIDDM are in fact treated with insulin to help control their blood glucose levels, but they do not require this for day-to-day survival.

[8]The acidosis also leads, in a positive-feedback manner, to worsening of the diabetes and the acidosis because acidosis decreases the affinity of insulin receptors for insulin.

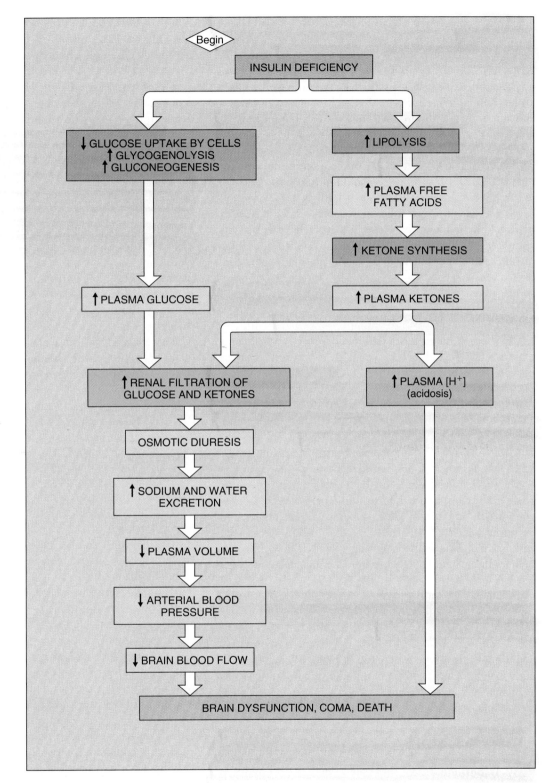

FIGURE 18-12

Effects of severe untreated insulin deficiency (diabetic ketoacidosis).

There are several factors that combine to cause NIDDM. One major problem is target-cell hyporesponsiveness to insulin, termed *insulin resistance*. Insulin's target cells do not respond adequately to circulating insulin because of alterations either in the insulin receptors and/or some intracellular process occurring after receptor activation. Obesity accounts for much of this insulin resistance in NIDDM, for obesity in any person—diabetic or not—induces some degree of insulin resistance, particularly in adipose tissue cells. However, additional components of insulin resistance, not related to obesity and not yet understood, also usually occur with NIDDM.

As a result of target-cell hyporesponsiveness to insulin, plasma glucose increases. Note, however, that this rise will stimulate the pancreatic beta cells to secrete additional insulin, and the resulting increase in plasma insulin concentration will tend to overcome the target-cell hyporesponsiveness. Thus, significant NIDDM emerges only when the insulin resistance exceeds the ability of the beta cells to compensate by secreting more insulin. Until recently it was thought that the beta cells were entirely normal in NIDDM unless they became "exhausted" by their persistent hypersecretion of insulin. Recently, however, it has become clear that most people with NIDDM not only have insulin hyporesponsiveness but also have a defect in the ability of their beta cells to secrete insulin in response to a rise in plasma glucose concentration.

Thus, NIDDM is a multifactorial disease: Insulin resistance is the primary factor inducing hyperglycemia, but an as yet unidentified defect in beta-cell function prevents these cells from responding to the hyperglycemia in normal fashion. In contrast, other persons who are obese (and therefore have some degree of insulin resistance) but who have normal beta cells do not develop NIDDM because their beta cells are able to secrete enough insulin to get the job done.

The major therapy for obese persons with NIDDM is dietary—caloric reduction, which eliminates the insulin resistance caused by obesity. An exercise program also is useful, because insulin responsiveness is increased by frequent endurance-type exercise, independent of changes in body weight. This may reflect the fact that training causes a substantial increase in the total number of plasma-membrane glucose transporters in both muscles and adipocytes.

If plasma glucose concentration is not adequately controlled by a program of diet and exercise, then the use of drugs is warranted. The most commonly used family of orally active agents is the *sulfonylureas*, which lower plasma glucose mainly by acting on the beta cells to stimulate insulin secretion.

Unfortunately, people with either IDDM or NIDDM tend to develop a variety of chronic abnormalities, including atherosclerosis, small-vessel and nerve disease, suscep-tibility to infection, and blindness. The factors responsible are still unclear, but it is hypothesized that elevated plasma glucose contributes directly or indirectly to some, if not all, of these abnormalities.

This discussion of diabetes has focused on insulin, but it is now clear that the hormones that elevate plasma glucose concentration may contribute to the severity of the disease. Glucagon is quite important in this regard. Since glucagon secretion is inhibited by an elevated plasma glucose level, one would expect to find a low plasma glucagon concentration in diabetic persons. However, most diabetics, particularly those with IDDM, have plasma glucagon concentrations that are either increased or unchanged.[9] This absolute or relative glucagon excess contributes to the metabolic dysfunction typical of diabetes.

Finally, as we have seen, all the systems that raise plasma glucose concentration are activated during stress, which explains why stress exacerbates the symptoms of diabetes. Since diabetic ketoacidosis itself constitutes a severe stress, a positive-feedback cycle is triggered in which a marked lack of insulin induces ketoacidosis, which elicits activation of the glucose-counterregulatory systems, which worsens the ketoacidosis.

HYPOGLYCEMIA AS A CAUSE OF SYMPTOMS

As we have seen, "hypoglycemia" means a low plasma glucose concentration. Plasma glucose concentration can drop to very low values during fasting in individuals with several types of disorders. This is termed *fasting hypoglycemia*, and the relatively uncommon disorders responsible for it can be understood in terms of the regulation of blood glucose concentration. They include (1) an excess of insulin due to an insulin-producing tumor, a drug that stimulates insulin secretion, or the taking of too much insulin by a diabetic; and (2) a defect in one or more of the glucose-counterregulatory systems, for example, inadequate glycogenolysis and/or gluconeogenesis due to liver disease, glucagon deficiency, or cortisol deficiency.

Fasting hypoglycemia causes many symptoms, some of which—hunger, increased heart rate, tremulousness, weakness, nervousness, and sweating—are accounted for by activation of the sympathetic nervous system caused reflexly by the hypoglycemia. Other symptoms, such as headache, confusion, uncoordination, and slurred speech are direct consequences of too little glucose reaching the

---

[9]From the material given in footnote 5 the most likely explanation can be deduced: If hypoglycemia stimulates glucagon secretion *indirectly* via insulin or some substance coreleased with insulin, then one would expect the defect in insulin secretion associated with diabetes to result in less inhibition of glucagon secretion.

brain. More serious brain effects, including convulsions and coma, can occur if the plasma glucose concentration becomes low enough.

In contrast, low plasma glucose concentration has *not* been shown to routinely produce either acute or chronic symptoms of fatigue, lethargy, loss of libido, depression, or many other symptoms for which the lay press frequently holds it responsible. Despite this, a large number of persons who suffer from such symptoms, particularly several hours after eating, have been told or have assumed that the symptoms are due to "reactive" hypoglycemia. Few of these people have ever had their blood glucose concentrations measured at the time of the symptoms, and the blood sugar is usually within the normal range in those cases where measurements have been made. For all these reasons, most experts believe that most of the symptoms popularly ascribed to reactive hypoglycemia have other causes.

REGULATION OF PLASMA CHOLESTEROL

n the previous sections, we described the flow of lipids to and from adipose tissue in the form of fatty acids and triacylglycerols complexed with proteins. One very impor-

tant lipid—**cholesterol**—was not mentioned earlier because it, unlike the fatty acids and triacylglycerols, serves not as a metabolic fuel but rather as a precursor for plasma membranes, bile salts, steroid hormones, and other specialized molecules. Thus, cholesterol has many important functions in the body. Unfortunately, it can also cause problems. Specifically, high plasma concentrations of cholesterol enhance the development of **atherosclerosis**, the arterial thickening that leads to heart attacks, strokes, and other forms of cardiovascular damage (Chapter 14).

A schema for cholesterol metabolism is illustrated in Figure 18-13. The two sources of cholesterol are synthesis within the body and dietary intake. Almost all cells can synthesize some of the cholesterol required for their own plasma membranes, but most cannot do so in adequate amounts and depend upon receiving cholesterol from the blood. This is also true of the endocrine cells that produce steroid hormones from cholesterol. Thus, most cells *remove* cholesterol from the blood. In contrast, the liver and cells lining the gastrointestinal tract can produce large amounts of cholesterol, most of which *enters* the blood. Dietary cholesterol comes from animal sources, egg yolk being by far the richest in this lipid (a single egg contains about 250 mg of cholesterol). Not all ingested cholesterol is absorbed into the blood, however, much of it simply

FIGURE 18-13

Metabolism of cholesterol.

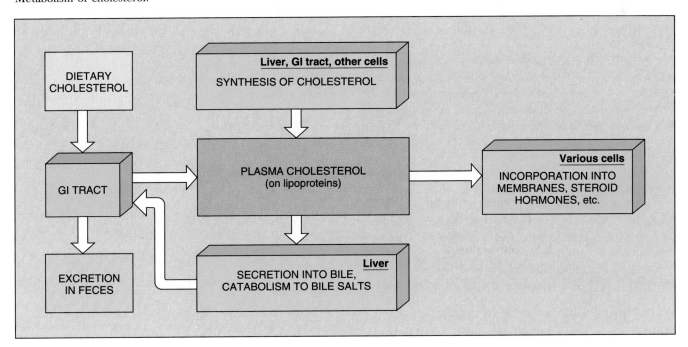

moving the length of the gastrointestinal tract to be excreted in the feces.

Now for the other side of cholesterol balance—the pathways, involving the liver, for net cholesterol loss from the body. First of all, some plasma cholesterol is picked up by liver cells and secreted into the bile, which carries it to the intestinal tract. Here it is treated much like ingested cholesterol, some being absorbed back into the blood and the remainder being excreted in the feces. Second, much of the cholesterol picked up by the liver cells is metabolized into bile salts (Chapter 17). After their production by the liver, these bile salts, like secreted cholesterol, flow through the bile duct into the small intestine. (As described in Chapter 17, many of these bile salts are then reclaimed by absorption back into the blood across the wall of the lower small intestine.)

The liver is clearly the center of the cholesterol universe, for it can add newly synthesized cholesterol to the blood or it can remove cholesterol from the blood, secreting it into the bile or metabolizing it to bile salts. The homeostatic control mechanisms that keep plasma cholesterol relatively constant operate on all of these hepatic processes, but the single most important response involves cholesterol production: The synthesis of cholesterol by the liver is inhibited whenever dietary cholesterol is increased. This is because cholesterol inhibits the enzyme critical for cholesterol synthesis by the liver.

Thus, as soon as the plasma cholesterol level starts rising because of increased cholesterol ingestion, hepatic synthesis is inhibited, and the plasma concentration remains close to its original value. Conversely, when dietary cholesterol is reduced and plasma cholesterol begins to fall, hepatic synthesis is stimulated (released from inhibition), and this increased production opposes any further fall. The sensitivity of this negative-feedback homeostatic control of synthesis differs greatly from person to person, but it is the major reason why, for most people, it is difficult to change plasma cholesterol very much in either direction by altering only dietary cholesterol. (A remarkable example of this is the documented case of a man who, due to a compulsion, had been eating 25 eggs a day for 15 years and yet had a relatively low plasma cholesterol; his intestinal absorption and hepatic synthesis of cholesterol were markedly below normal, and his conversion of cholesterol to bile salts was markedly elevated.)

Thus far, the relative constancy of plasma cholesterol has been emphasized. However, there are environmental and physiological factors that can alter plasma cholesterol concentrations considerably by influencing one or more of the metabolic pathways for cholesterol. Perhaps the most important of these factors are the quantity and type of dietary fatty acids. Ingesting saturated fatty acids, the dominant fatty acids of animal fat, raises plasma cholesterol. Eating either polyunsaturated fatty acids, the dominant plant fatty acids, or monounsaturated fatty acids such as those in olive or peanut oil, lowers plasma cholesterol.[10] The various fatty acids exert their effects by altering cholesterol synthesis, excretion, and metabolism to bile salts. A variety of drugs now in common use also are capable of lowering plasma cholesterol by influencing one or more of the metabolic pathways or by interfering with intestinal absorption of bile salts.

Based on studies of the relationship between plasma cholesterol levels and cardiovascular diseases, recent recommendations from the National Institutes of Health call a total plasma cholesterol below 200 mg/deciliter (dl, 100 ml) "desirable," 200 to 239 mg/dl "borderline high," and 240 mg/dl or greater "high."

The story is more complicated than this, however, since not all plasma cholesterol has the same function or significance for disease. Like most other lipids, cholesterol circulates in the plasma as part of various lipoprotein complexes. These include chylomicrons (Chapter 17), VLDL (this chapter, page 605), **low-density lipoproteins (LDL)** and **high-density lipoproteins (HDL)**. LDL are the main cholesterol carriers, and they deliver cholesterol *to* cells. LDL bind to plasma-membrane receptors specific for a protein component of the LDL, and the LDL are taken up by the cell. In contrast to LDL, HDL serve as acceptors of cholesterol *from* various tissues. They promote the removal of cholesterol from cells and its secretion into the bile by the liver. For these reasons, LDL cholesterol is "bad" cholesterol with regard to enhancing the deposition of cholesterol in arterial walls, whereas HDL cholesterol is "good" cholesterol.

The best single indicator of the likelihood of developing atherosclerotic heart disease is, therefore, not *total* plasma cholesterol but rather the *ratio* of plasma LDL cholesterol to plasma HDL cholesterol—the lower the ratio, the lower the risk. Cigarette smoking, a known risk factor for heart attacks, lowers plasma HDL, whereas weight reduction (in overweight persons) and regular exercise increase it. Estrogen not only lowers total cholesterol and LDL but raises HDL, which may explain why premenopausal women have so much less coronary artery disease than men. After menopause, the cholesterol values and coronary artery disease rates become similar to those in men.

In summary, dietary and life-style changes, in combination with drug therapy if necessary, can result in significant lowering of plasma cholesterol concentration and a decrease in the LDL/HDL ratio, with important consequences for reducing cardiovascular disease.

---

[10]Although grouping of fatty acids into the major categories of saturated and unsaturated is very useful, it is now clear that specific fatty acids within these two categories actually differ markedly in their effects on cholesterol; for example, stearic acid is a saturated fatty acid but does not raise plasma cholesterol. Such information will facilitate the devising of better cholesterol-lowering diets.

SECTION A SUMMARY

EVENTS OF THE ABSORPTIVE AND POSTABSORPTIVE STATES

I. During absorption, energy is provided primarily by absorbed carbohydrate, and net synthesis of glycogen, triacylglycerol, and protein occurs.

   A. Some absorbed carbohydrate not used for energy is converted to glycogen, mainly in the liver and skeletal muscle, but most is converted, in liver and adipocytes, to α-glycerol phosphate and fatty acids, which then combine to form triacylglycerol. The liver releases its triacylglycerols in very-low-density lipoproteins, the fatty acids of which are picked up by adipocytes.

   B. The fatty acids of some absorbed triacylglycerol are used for energy, but most are rebuilt into fat in adipose tissue.

   C. Some absorbed amino acids are converted to proteins, but excess amino acids are converted to carbohydrate and fat.

   D. There is net uptake of glucose by the liver.

II. In the postabsorptive state, blood glucose is maintained by a combination of glucose production by the liver and a switch from glucose utilization to fatty acid and ketone utilization by most tissues.

   A. Synthesis of glycogen, fat, and protein is curtailed, and net breakdown of these molecules occurs.

   B. The liver forms glucose by glycogenolysis of its own glycogen and by gluconeogenesis from lactate and pyruvate (from breakdown of muscle glycogen), glycerol (from adipose-tissue lipolysis), and amino acids (from protein catabolism).

   C. Glycolysis is decreased, and most of the body's energy supply comes from the oxidation of fatty acids released by adipose tissue lipolysis and of ketones produced from fatty acids by the liver.

   D. The brain continues to use glucose but also starts using ketones as they build up in the blood.

ENDOCRINE AND NEURAL CONTROL OF THE ABSORPTIVE AND POSTABSORPTIVE STATES

I. The major hormones secreted by the pancreatic islets of Langerhans are insulin by the beta cells and glucagon by the alpha cells.

II. Insulin is the most important hormone controlling metabolism.

   A. In muscle, it stimulates glucose uptake, glycolysis, and net synthesis of glycogen and protein; in adipose tissue, it stimulates glucose uptake and net synthesis of triacylglycerol; in liver, it inhibits gluconeogenesis and glucose release and stimulates the net synthesis of glycogen and triacylglycerols.

   B. The major stimulus for insulin secretion is an increased plasma glucose concentration, but se-

cretion is also influenced by many other factors summarized in Figure 18-7.

III. Glucagon, epinephrine, cortisol, and growth hormone all exert effects on carbohydrate and lipid metabolism that are opposed, in one way or another, to those of insulin. They raise plasma concentrations of glucose, glycerol, and fatty acids.

   A. Glucagon's physiological actions are all on the liver, where it stimulates glycogenolysis, gluconeogenesis, and ketone synthesis.

   B. The major stimulus for glucagon secretion is hypoglycemia, but secretion is also stimulated by plasma amino acids and by both the sympathetic and parasympathetic nerves to the islets.

   C. Epinephrine released from the adrenal medulla in response to hypoglycemia stimulates glycogenolysis in the liver and muscle, gluconeogenesis in liver, and lipolysis in adipocytes. The sympathetic nerves to liver and adipose tissue exert effects similar to those of epinephrine.

   D. Cortisol is permissive for gluconeogenesis and lipolysis; in higher concentrations, it stimulates gluconeogenesis and blocks glucose uptake. These last two effects are also exerted by growth hormone.

FUEL HOMEOSTASIS IN EXERCISE AND STRESS

I. During exercise, the muscles use as their energy sources plasma glucose, plasma fatty acids, and their own glycogen.

   A. Glucose is produced by the liver, and fatty acids are provided by adipose-tissue lipolysis.

   B. The changes in plasma insulin, glucagon, and epinephrine are similar to those that occur during the postabsorptive period and are mediated mainly by the sympathetic nervous system.

II. Stress causes hormonal changes similar to those caused by exercise.

DIABETES MELLITUS

I. Insulin-dependent diabetes is due to absolute insulin deficiency and can lead to diabetic ketoacidosis.

II. Non-insulin-dependent diabetes is usually associated with obesity and is caused by a combination of insulin resistance and a defect in beta-cell responsiveness to elevated plasma glucose concentration. Plasma insulin concentration is usually normal or elevated.

REGULATION OF PLASMA CHOLESTEROL

I. Plasma cholesterol is a precursor for the synthesis of plasma membranes, bile salts, and steroid hormones.

II. Cholesterol synthesis by the liver is controlled so as to homeostatically regulate plasma cholesterol concentration; it varies inversely with ingested cholesterol.

III. The liver also secretes cholesterol into the bile and converts it to bile salts.

IV. Plasma cholesterol is carried mainly by low-density lipoproteins, which deliver it to cells; high-density lipoproteins carry cholesterol from cells to the liver. The LDL/HDL ratio correlates with the incidence of coronary heart disease.

SECTION A KEY TERMS

absorptive state	beta cells
postabsorptive state	alpha cells
very-low-density	insulin
lipoproteins (VLDL)	hypoglycemia
lipoprotein lipase	glucose-counterregulatory
keto acids	controls
glycogenolysis	glucagon
lipolysis	cholesterol
gluconeogenesis	low-density lipoproteins
glucose sparing	(LDL)
ketones	high-density lipoproteins
islets of Langerhans	(HDL)

SECTION A REVIEW QUESTIONS

1. Using a diagram, summarize the events of the absorptive period.

2. In what two organs does major glycogen storage occur?

3. How do the liver and adipose tissue metabolize glucose during the absorptive period?

4. How does adipose tissue metabolize absorbed triacylglycerol, and what are the three major sources of the fatty acids in adipose tissue triacylglycerol?

5. What happens to most of the absorbed amino acids when a high-protein meal is ingested?

6. Using a diagram, summarize the events of the postabsorptive period; include the four sources of blood glucose and the pathways leading to ketone formation.

7. Distinguish between the roles of glycerol and free fatty acids during fasting.

8. List the overall responses of muscle, adipose tissue, and liver to insulin. What effects occur when plasma insulin concentration decreases?

9. List five inputs controlling insulin secretion and state the physiological significance of each.

10. List the effects of glucagon on the liver and their consequences.

11. List three inputs controlling glucagon secretion and state the physiological significance of each.

12. List four metabolic effects of epinephrine and the sympathetic nerves to the liver and adipose tissue and state the net results of each.

13. List the permissive effects of cortisol and the effects that occur when plasma cortisol concentration increases.

14. List three effects of growth hormone on carbohydrate and lipid metabolism.

15. Which hormones stimulate gluconeogenesis? Glycogenolysis in liver? Glycogenolysis in skeletal muscle? Lipolysis? Inhibition of glucose uptake?

16. Describe how plasma glucose, insulin, glucagon, and epinephrine levels change during exercise and stress. What causes the changes in the concentrations of the hormones?

17. Describe the metabolic disorders of severe insulin-dependent diabetes.

18. How does obesity contribute to non-insulin-dependent diabetes?

19. Hypersecretion of which hormones can induce a diabetic state?

20. Using a diagram, describe the sources of cholesterol gain and loss. Include three roles of the liver in cholesterol metabolism and state the controls over these processes.

21. What are the effects of saturated and unsaturated fatty acids on plasma cholesterol?

22. What is the significance of the LDL cholesterol/HDL cholesterol ratio?

SECTION

CONTROL OF GROWTH

Growth is a complex process influenced by genetics, endocrine function, and a variety of environmental factors, including nutrition and the presence of infection. The process involves cell division and net protein synthesis throughout the body, but a person's height is determined specifically by bone growth, particularly of the vertebral column and legs.

BONE GROWTH

A s described in Chapter 16, bone is a living tissue consisting of a protein (collagen) matrix upon which calcium salts, particularly calcium phosphates, are deposited. A growing long bone is divided, for descriptive purposes, into the ends, or **epiphyses**, and the remainder, the **shaft**. The portion of each epiphysis that is in contact with the shaft is a plate of actively proliferating cartilage, the **epiphyseal growth plate** (Figure 18-14). **Osteoblasts**, the bone-forming cells (Chapter 16), at the shaft edge of the epiphyseal growth plate convert the cartilaginous tissue at this edge to bone while new cartilage is simultaneously being laid down in the interior of the plate by cells called **chondrocytes**. In this manner, the epiphyseal growth plate remains intact (indeed, actually widens) and is gradually pushed away from the center of the bony shaft as the latter lengthens.

Linear growth of the shaft can continue as long as the epiphyseal growth plates exist but ceases when the plates are themselves ultimately converted to bone as a result of hormonal influences at puberty. This is known as **epiphyseal closure** and occurs at different times in different bones. Accordingly, a person's **bone age** can be determined by x-raying the bones and determining which ones have undergone epiphyseal closure.

As shown in Figure 18-15, children manifest two periods of rapid body growth, one during the first 2 years of life and the second during puberty. Note in this figure that linear growth is not necessarily correlated with the rates of growth of specific organs.

The pubertal growth spurt lasts several years in both sexes, but growth during this period is greater in boys. This, plus the fact that boys grow more before puberty because they begin puberty approximately 2 years later than girls, accounts for the differences in average height between men and women.

FIGURE 18-14
Anatomy of a long bone during growth.

ENVIRONMENTAL FACTORS INFLUENCING GROWTH

A dequacy of nutrient supply and freedom from disease are the primary environmental factors influencing growth. Lack of sufficient amounts of any of the essential amino acids, essential fatty acids, vitamins, or minerals interferes with growth. Total protein and sufficient nutrients to provide energy must also be adequate. No matter how much protein is ingested, growth cannot be normal if the intake of all energy-providing nutrients is too low since the protein is simply catabolized for energy.

The growth-inhibiting effects of *malnutrition* can be seen at any time of development but are most profound when they occur very early in life. Thus, maternal malnutrition may cause growth retardation in the fetus. Since low birth weight is strongly associated with increased infant mortality, prenatal malnutrition causes increased numbers of prenatal and early postnatal deaths. Moreover, irreversible stunting of brain development may be caused by prenatal malnutrition.

Malnutrition during infancy can also result in stunting of both brain development and total-body growth. The individual seems locked into a younger developmental age.

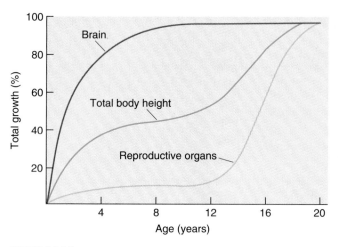

FIGURE 18-15

Relative growth in brain, total body height (a measure of long bone and vertebral growth), and reproductive organs. Note that brain growth is nearly complete by the age 5, whereas maximal height and reproductive-organ size are not reached until the late teens.

On the other hand, the final height a child reaches cannot be increased beyond the genetically determined maximum by the child eating more than adequate vitamins, protein, or total calories. Overfeeding produces obesity, not growth.

Sickness can also stunt growth, but if the illness is temporary, the recovered child manifests a remarkable growth spurt ("catch-up" growth) that rapidly brings him or her up to the normal height expected for his or her age.

HORMONAL INFLUENCES ON GROWTH

The hormones most important to human growth are growth hormone, thyroid hormones, insulin, testosterone, and estrogens, all of which exert widespread effects. In addition to all these hormones, there is a huge group of peptide **growth factors** (for example, nerve growth factor), each of which is highly effective in stimulating differentiation and/or cell division of certain cell types. The general term for a chemical that stimulates cell division is a **mitogen**. There are also peptide **growth-inhibiting factors** that modulate growth by inhibiting cell division in specific tissues. Numbering more than 60 at present, these growth factors and growth-inhibiting factors are usually produced by multiple cell types rather than by discrete endocrine glands. Indeed, many of them are produced and released in the immediate vicinity of their sites of action and so are categorized as paracrine and autocrine agents. Some, however, may enter the blood and function as hormones. In any case, their secretion is often controlled by hormones.

The physiology of growth factors and growth-inhibiting factors is important not just for understanding control of normal growth but also because these factors may be involved in the development of **cancer**. Thus, some **oncogenes** (genes involved in the induction of cancer, page 79) code for proteins that are identical to or very similar to growth factors, growth factor receptors, or postreceptor components of growth factor signal transduction pathways. The problem is that these proteins have lost important regulatory constraints on their activity. For example, one oncogene codes for a version of the receptor for epidermal growth factor that is always in the activated state even in the absence of the growth factor. This activated receptor imparts a continuous growth signal to the cells containing it.

The various hormones and growth factors do not all stimulate growth at the same periods of life. For example, fetal growth is largely independent of the major hormones that stimulate growth during childhood—growth hormone, the thyroid hormones, and the sex steroids.

Growth Hormone

Although growth hormone, secreted by the anterior pituitary, has little or no effect on fetal growth, it is the single most important hormone for postnatal growth. Its major growth-promoting effect is stimulation (indirect, as we shall see) of cell division in its many target tissues. Thus, growth hormone promotes bone lengthening by stimulating maturation and cell division of the chondrocytes in the epiphyseal plates, thereby continuously widening the plates and providing more cartilaginous material for bone formation.

Growth hormone excess during childhood produces **giantism**, whereas a deficiency produces **dwarfism**. However, when excess growth hormone is secreted in adults after epiphyseal closure, it cannot lengthen the bones further, but it does produce the disfiguring bone thickening and overgrowth of other organs known as **acromegaly**.

Importantly, growth hormone exerts its mitosis-stimulating (mitogenic) effect not *directly* on cells but rather *indirectly* through the mediation of a chemical messenger whose synthesis and release are induced by growth hormone. This messenger is called **insulin-like growth factor I (IGF-I)** (also known as **somatomedin C**). Under the influence of growth hormone, IGF-I is secreted by the liver and many other types of cells, and it is thought to act at these sites as a paracrine or autocrine agent. It remains controversial as to whether IGF-I also exerts some functions as a hormone, that is, as a blood-borne messenger.[11]

---

[11]The problem is that virtually all the IGF-I in plasma is tightly bound to a specific binding protein and so is unable to pass through capillaries and act on target cells. A likely hormonal effect of IGF-I is its negative-feedback inhibition of GH secretion by the anterior pituitary, as presented in Chapter 10.

Current concepts of how growth hormone and IGF-I interact on the epiphyseal plates of bone are as follows: (1) Growth hormone stimulates the chondrocyte precursor cells (prechondrocytes) and/or young differentiating chondrocytes in the epiphyseal plates to differentiate into chondrocytes; (2) during this differentiation, the cells begin both to secrete IGF-I and to become responsive to IGF-I; (3) this produced IGF-I then acts as an autocrine or paracrine agent to stimulate the differentiating chondrocytes to undergo cell division.

It is likely that a similar interplay between growth hormone and IGF-I underlies the ability of growth hormone to stimulate growth in target tissues other than bone; that is, growth hormone stimulates precursor cells to differentiate and to secrete IGF-I, and IGF-I stimulates the newly differentiated cells to undergo cell division.

The importance of IGF-I mediating the major growth-promoting effect of growth hormone is illustrated by the fact that dwarfism can be due not only to decreased secretion of growth hormone but also to decreased production of IGF-I or failure of the tissues to respond to IGF-I. For example, the short stature of Pygmies is probably due to a genetic defect in the ability to produce IGF-I in response to growth hormone.

The secretion and activity of IGF-I can be influenced by several hormones other than growth hormone and by the nutritional status of the individual. For example, malnutrition during childhood inhibits the production of IGF-I even though plasma growth hormone concentration is elevated and should be stimulating IGF-I secretion.

In addition to its specific growth-promoting effect on cell division via IGF-I, growth hormone directly stimulates protein synthesis in various tissues and organs. It does this by increasing amino acid uptake by cells, as well as by the synthesis of RNA and ribosomes. All these events are essential for protein synthesis.[12] This anabolic effect on protein metabolism facilitates the ability of tissues and organs to enlarge. Table 18-5 summarizes the multiple effects of growth hormone, all of which have been described in this chapter.

The hypothalamic hypophysiotropic hormones controlling growth hormone secretion were described in Chapter 10 (Figure 10-23). Briefly, growth hormone secretion is stimulated by growth hormone releasing hormone (GHRH) and inhibited by hypothalamic somatostatin. As a result of changes in these two signals, which are virtually 180 degrees out of phase with each other (that is, one is high when the other is low), growth hormone secretion

TABLE 18-5 MAJOR EFFECTS OF GROWTH HORMONE

1. Promotes growth: Induces precursor cells to differentiate and secrete insulin-like growth factor I (IGF-I), which stimulates cell division
2. Stimulates protein synthesis
3. Anti-insulin effects:
   a. Renders adipocytes more responsive to lipolytic stimuli.
   b. Stimulates gluconeogenesis
   c. Reduces the ability of insulin to stimulate glucose uptake

occurs in episodic bursts and manifests a striking diurnal rhythm. During most of the day, there is little or no growth hormone secreted, although bursts may be elicited by certain stimuli, including stress,[13] hypoglycemia, and exercise. In contrast, 1 to 2 h after a person falls asleep, one or more larger, prolonged bursts of secretion may occur.

In addition to the hypothalamic controls, a variety of hormones—notably the sex hormones and thyroid hormones, as described below—influence secretion of growth hormone. The net result of all these inputs is that the total 24-h secretion rate of growth hormone is highest during adolescence—the period of most rapid growth—next highest in children, and lowest in adults. Indeed, there is evidence that the decreased growth hormone secretion associated with aging is responsible, in part, for the decrease in lean-body mass, the expansion of adipose tissue, and the thinning of the skin that occur at that time.

The availability of large quantities of human growth hormone produced by recombinant-DNA technology has greatly facilitated the treatment of children with short stature due to deficiency of growth hormone. Controversial at present are the questions of whether growth hormone should be given to healthy short children who do not have growth hormone deficiency or to athletes to increase muscle mass. In addition to the ethical questions they pose, such usages are dangerous because the large amounts required can cause insulin resistance and produce diabetes.

Thyroid Hormones

The thyroid hormones (TH)—thyroxine (T_3) and triiodothyronine (T_4)—are essential for normal growth because they are required for both the synthesis of growth hormone and the growth-promoting effects of that hormone. Accordingly, infants and children with **hypothyroidism** (deficient thyroid function) manifest retarded growth due

---

[12]The similarity of growth hormone's effect on *protein* synthesis to that exerted by insulin may seem puzzling when one recalls our earlier description of the anti-insulin effects of growth hormone on *carbohydrate* and *lipid* metabolism. It has been postulated that these varied actions of growth hormone may be mediated by different receptors responding to different amino acid sequences on the large growth hormone molecule.

[13]In contrast, during childhood severe prolonged psychosocial stress may inhibit growth hormone secretion and lead to diminished growth.

to slowed bone growth. Because epiphyseal closure is delayed, bone age is decreased (that is, the bone age lags behind the child's chronological age). Growth can be restored to normal by administration of physiological quantities of thyroid hormone.

Quite distinct from its growth-promoting effect, TH is permissive for normal development of the central nervous system during fetal life and the first few months after birth. Hypothyroid infants are mentally retarded, a defect that can be completely repaired by early treatment with TH. However, if the infant is untreated for more than several months, the developmental failure is largely irreversible.

This effect on brain *development* must be distinguished from other stimulatory effects TH exerts on the nervous system throughout life, not just during infancy. A hypothyroid person exhibits sluggishness and poor mental function, and these effects are completely reversible at any time with administration of TH. Conversely, a person with an excessive secretion of TH, **hyperthyroidism,** is jittery and hyperactive.

Insulin

It should not be surprising that adequate amounts of insulin are necessary for normal growth since insulin is, in all respects, an anabolic hormone. Its stimulatory effects on amino acid uptake and protein synthesis are particularly important with regard to growth.

In addition to this general anabolic effect, however, insulin exerts specific growth-promoting effects on cell differentiation and cell division during fetal life. Insulin may also exert this effect during childhood since it can stimulate the secretion of IGF-I.

Sex Hormones

As will be described in Chapter 19, sex hormone secretion (testosterone in the male and estrogen in the female) begins in earnest at about the age of 8 to 10 and progressively increases to reach a plateau over the next 5 to 10 years. A normal pubertal growth spurt, which reflects growth of the long bones and vertebrae, requires this increased production of the sex hormones. The major growth-promoting effect of the sex hormones is to stimulate the secretion of growth hormone.

Unlike growth hormone, however, the sex hormones ultimately *stop* bone growth by inducing epiphyseal closure. The dual effects of the sex hormones explain the pattern seen in adolescence—rapid lengthening of the bones culminating in complete cessation of growth for life.

In addition to these dual effects on bone, testosterone, but not estrogen, exerts a direct anabolic effect on protein synthesis in many nonreproductive organs and tissues of the body. This accounts, at least in part, for the increased muscle mass of men compared with women.

This also is why synthetic testosterone-like agents termed **anabolic steroids** are used by athletes in an at-

---

TABLE 18-6 MAJOR HORMONES INFLUENCING GROWTH

Hormone	Principal actions
Growth hormone	Major stimulus of postnatal growth: Induces precursor cells to differentiate and secrete insulin-like growth factor I (IGF-I), which stimulates cell division Stimulates protein synthesis
Insulin	Stimulates fetal growth ? Stimulates postnatal growth by stimulating secretion of IGF-I Stimulates protein synthesis
Thyroid hormones	Permissive for growth hormone's secretion and actions Permissive for development of the central nervous system
Testosterone	Stimulates growth at puberty, at least in part by stimulating the secretion of growth hormone Causes eventual epiphyseal closure Stimulates protein synthesis
Estrogen	Stimulates the secretion of growth hormone at puberty Causes eventual epiphyseal closure
Cortisol	Inhibits growth Stimulates protein catabolism

tempt to increase their muscle mass and strength. However, it remains controversial as to how much, if at all, these agents, in men who are not testosterone-deficient to start with, increase muscle mass or improve athletic performance. Moreover, the steroids generally used have multiple toxic side effects (for example, liver damage). Although these drugs definitely have a positive effect on muscle mass and strength in women, they produce masculinization as well as the same toxic side effects as in men.

Cortisol

Cortisol, the major hormone secreted by the adrenal cortex in response to stress, can have potent antigrowth effects under certain conditions. When present in high concentration, it inhibits DNA synthesis and stimulates protein catabolism in many organs, and it inhibits bone growth. Indeed, it causes bone breakdown by inhibiting osteoblasts and stimulating osteoclasts (Chapter 16). In children, the elevation in plasma cortisol that accompanies infections and other stresses is, at least in part, responsible for the retarded growth that occurs with illness.

As we shall see in Chapter 20, cortisol and very similar steroids are commonly used medically in persons with arthritis or other inflammatory disorders. A side effect of such treatment is increased protein catabolism and bone breakdown. One must carefully distinguish cortisol-type steroids (glucocorticoids) from testosterone-type steroids (anabolic steroids).

This completes our survey of the major hormones that affect growth. Their actions are summarized in Table 18-6.

COMPENSATORY GROWTH

We have dealt thus far only with growth during *childhood*. During adult life, a specific type of regenerative organ growth, known as **compensatory growth**, can occur in many human organs. For example, after the surgical removal of one kidney, the cells of the other begin to manifest increased cell division, and the kidney ultimately grows until its total mass approaches the initial mass of the two kidneys combined. Many growth factors are known to participate in compensatory growth, but the precise signals that trigger the process are not known.

SECTION B SUMMARY

BONE GROWTH

 I. A bone lengthens as osteoblasts at the shaft edge of the epiphyseal growth plates convert cartilage to bone while new cartilage is being laid down in the plate.
 II. Growth ceases when the plates are completely converted to bone.

ENVIRONMENTAL FACTORS INFLUENCING GROWTH

 I. The major environmental factors influencing growth are nutrition and disease.
 II. Malnutrition during in utero life and infancy may produce irreversible stunting.

HORMONAL INFLUENCES ON GROWTH

 I. Growth hormone is the major stimulus of postnatal growth.
   A. It stimulates the release of IGF-I from the liver and many other cells, and IGF-I then acts locally to stimulate cell division.
   B. Growth hormone also acts directly on cells to stimulate protein synthesis.
   C. Growth hormone secretion is highest during adolescence.

 II. Because thyroid hormones are required for growth hormone synthesis and the growth-promoting effects of this hormone, they are essential for normal growth during childhood and adolescence. They also are permissive for brain development during infancy.
 III. Insulin stimulates growth mainly during in utero life.
 IV. Mainly by stimulating growth hormone secretion, testosterone and estrogen promote bone growth during adolescence, but they also cause epiphyseal closure. Testosterone also stimulates protein synthesis.
 V. Cortisol in a high concentration inhibits growth and stimulates protein catabolism.

SECTION B KEY TERMS

epiphyses
shaft
epiphyseal growth plate
osteoblasts
chondrocytes
epiphyseal closure
bone age

growth factors
mitogen
growth-inhibiting factors
insulin-like growth factor I
   (IGF-I, somatomedin C)
compensatory growth

SECTION B REVIEW QUESTIONS

1. Describe the process by which bone is lengthened.
2. What are the effects of malnutrition on growth?
3. List the major hormones that control growth.
4. Describe the relationship between growth hormone and IGF-I and the roles of each in growth.
5. What are the effects of growth hormone on protein synthesis?
6. What is the status of growth hormone secretion at different stages of life?
7. State the effects of the thyroid hormones on growth and development.
8. Describe the effects of testosterone on growth, cessation of growth, and protein synthesis. Which of these effects are shared by estrogen?
9. What is the effect of cortisol on growth?

SECTION

REGULATION OF TOTAL-BODY ENERGY BALANCE AND TEMPERATURE

BASIC CONCEPTS OF ENERGY EXPENDITURE AND CALORIC BALANCE

The breakdown of organic molecules liberates the energy locked in their molecular bonds. This is the energy cells use to perform the various forms of biological work—muscle contraction, active transport, and molecular synthesis. As described in Chapter 5, the first law of thermodynamics states that energy can be neither created nor destroyed but can be converted from one form to another. Thus, internal energy liberated (ΔE) during breakdown of an organic molecule can either appear as heat (H) or be used to perform work (W):

$$\Delta E = H + W$$

During metabolism, about 60 percent of the energy released from organic molecules appears immediately as heat, and the rest is used for work. The energy used for work must first be incorporated into molecules of ATP, the subsequent breakdown of which serves as the immediate energy source for the work. It is essential to realize that the body is not a heat engine since it is totally incapable of converting heat to work, but the heat released in its chemical reactions is valuable for maintaining body temperature. Biological work can be divided into two general categories: (1) **external work**—movement of external objects by contracting skeletal muscles; and (2) **internal work**—all other forms of work, including skeletal-muscle activity not used in moving external objects. As just stated, much of the energy liberated from nutrient catabolism appears immediately as heat. What may not be obvious is that all internal work, too, is ultimately transformed to heat except during periods of growth. Several examples will illustrate this essential point.

1. Internal work is performed during cardiac contraction, but this energy appears ultimately as heat generated by the friction of blood flow through the blood vessels.
2. Internal work is performed during secretion of HCl by the stomach and $NaHCO_3$ by the pancreas, but this work appears as heat when the H^+ and HCO_3^- combine in the small intestine.
3. The internal work performed during synthesis of a plasma protein is recovered as heat during the inevitable catabolism of the protein since with few exceptions all body constituents are constantly being built up and broken down. During periods of net synthesis of protein, fat, and other molecules, however, energy is stored in the bonds of these molecules and does not appear as heat.

Thus, the total energy liberated when organic nutrients are catabolized by cells may be transformed into body heat, appear as external work, or be stored in the body in the form of organic molecules. The **total energy expenditure** of the body is therefore given by the equation

Total energy expenditure = heat produced by the body + external work done + energy stored

Metabolic Rate

The unit for energy is the **kilocalorie (kcal)**,[14] which is the amount of heat required to raise the temperature of one liter of water one degree Celsius. Total energy expenditure per unit time is called the **metabolic rate**, which can be measured directly or indirectly. In either case, the measurement is much simpler if the person is fasting and at rest. Total energy expenditure then becomes equal to heat production since energy storage and external work are eliminated.

The direct method of measuring the metabolic rate is simple to understand but difficult to perform. The subject is placed in a chamber known as a calorimeter, and his or her heat production is measured by the temperature changes in water flowing through the calorimeter. This is an excellent method in that it measures heat production directly, but calorimeters are found in only a few research laboratories. Accordingly, a simple, indirect method has been developed for widespread use.

In the indirect procedure (Figure 18-16), one simply measures the subject's oxygen uptake per unit time by measuring total ventilation and the oxygen content of both inspired and expired air. From this value one calculates heat production based on the fundamental principle that the energy liberated by the catabolism of foods inside the body must be the same as that liberated when the foods are catabolized to the same products outside the body. We know precisely how much heat is liberated when 1 L of oxygen is utilized in the oxidation of fat, protein, or carbohydrate outside the body; this same quantity of heat must be produced when 1 L of oxygen is utilized in the body. Fortunately, we do not need to know precisely which type of nutrient is being oxidized internally because the quantities of heat produced per liter of oxygen utilized are reasonably similar for the oxidation of fat, carbohydrate, and protein, and average 4.8 kcal/L of oxygen. When more exact calculations are required, additional techniques are used to estimate the relative quantity of each nutrient.

Determinants of Metabolic Rate

Basal Metabolic Rate. Since many factors cause the metabolic rate to vary (Table 18-7), the test used clinically to evaluate it specifies certain standardized conditions and measures what is known as the **basal metabolic rate (BMR)**. The subject is at mental and physical rest in a room at a comfortable temperature and has not eaten for at least 12 h. These conditions are arbitrarily designated "basal," even though the metabolic rate during sleep may be less than the BMR. For the following discussion, it

FIGURE 18-16

Indirect method for measuring metabolic rate. When 1 L of oxygen is utilized in the oxidation of organic nutrients, approximately 4.8 kcal of energy is liberated as heat. In the example, the metabolic rate is (15.2 L of O_2/h) (4.8 kcal/L) = 73 kcal/h, a typical value for a normal, fasted, resting adult. This rate of energy expenditure is approximately equal to that of a 100-watt bulb.

must be emphasized that the term "BMR" can be applied to a person's metabolic rate only when the specified conditions are met; thus, a person who has recently eaten or is exercising has a metabolic rate but not a *basal* metabolic rate.

The BMR is often termed the "metabolic cost of living," and most of it is expended by the heart, liver, kidneys, and brain. The magnitude of a person's BMR is related not only to physical size but to age and sex as well. The growing child's BMR, expressed on a per-weight basis, is considerably higher than the adult's, in part because the child expends a great deal of energy in net synthesis of new tissue (much of this energy remains in the body as stored energy). On the other end of the age scale, the BMR gradually decreases with advancing age. A woman's BMR is generally less than that of a man, even taking

---

[14] In the field of nutrition, the three terms "Calorie" (with a capital C), "large calorie," and "kilocalorie" are synonyms.

TABLE 18-7 SOME FACTORS AFFECTING THE METABOLIC RATE

Age
Sex
Height, weight, and body surface area
Growth
Pregnancy, menstruation, lactation
Infection or other disease
Body temperature
Recent ingestion of food
Prolonged alteration in amount of food intake
Muscular activity
Emotional state
Sleep
Environmental temperature
Circulating levels of various hormones, especially
  epinephrine and thyroid hormone

into account size differences, but increases markedly during pregnancy and lactation. Greater demands upon the body made by infection or other disease generally increase the BMR. However, when a person suffers wasting because of infection, the BMR may decrease below normal.

Thyroid Hormones. The thyroid hormones are the single most important determinant of BMR for any given size, age, and sex. Indeed, the BMR test was once commonly used for evaluation of thyroid hormone status but has now been superseded by more specific tests. TH increases the oxygen consumption and heat production of most body tissues, a notable exception being the brain.

This ability to increase BMR is termed a **calorigenic effect**. The mechanism of the TH calorigenic effect is presently uncertain, but the plasma concentration of TH is the major factor that "sets" the body's BMR.

Long-term excessive TH, as in persons with hyperthyroidism, induces a host of effects secondary to the calorigenic effect. For example, the increased metabolic demands markedly increase hunger and food intake; the greater intake frequently remains inadequate to meet the metabolic needs, and net catabolism of protein and fat stores leads to loss of body weight. Also, the greater heat production activates heat-dissipating mechanisms (skin vasodilation and sweating), and the person suffers from marked intolerance to warm environments. In contrast, the hypothyroid individual complains of cold intolerance.

The calorigenic effect of TH is only one of a bewildering variety of effects exerted by these hormones. With one exception—facilitation of the activity of the sympathetic nervous system (described in Chapter 10)—the functions of the thyroid hormones have all been described earlier in this chapter and are listed for reference in Table 18-8. Control of the secretion of these hormones, as well as their metabolism, is described in Chapter 10.

Epinephrine. Epinephrine is another hormone that exerts a calorigenic effect. This effect may be related to the hormone's stimulation of glycogen and triacylglycerol catabolism, since ATP splitting and energy liberation occur in both the breakdown and subsequent resynthesis of these molecules. Regardless of the mechanism, when epinephrine secretion by the adrenal medulla is stimulated, the metabolic rate rises. This accounts for part of the

TABLE 18-8 FUNCTIONS OF THE THYROID HORMONES (TH)

1. Required for normal maturation of the nervous system in the fetus and infant
   Deficiency: Mental retardation (cretinism)

2. Required for normal bodily growth because they facilitate the secretion of and response to growth hormone
   Deficiency: Deficient growth in children

3. Required for normal alertness and reflexes at all ages
   Deficiency: Mentally and physically slow and lethargic
   Excess: Restless, irritable, anxious, wakeful

4. Major determinant of the rate at which the body produces heat during the basal metabolic state.
   Deficiency: Low BMR, sensitivity to cold, decreased food appetite
   Excess: High BMR, sensitivity to heat, increased food appetite, increased catabolism of nutrients

5. Facilitates the activity of the sympathetic nervous system by stimulating the synthesis of one class of receptors (beta receptors) for epinephrine and norepinephrine
   Excess: Symptoms similar to those observed with activation of the sympathetic nervous system (for example, increased heart rate)

greater heat production associated with emotional stress, although increased muscle tone also contributes.

Food-Induced Thermogenesis. The ingestion of food acutely increases the metabolic rate by 10 to 20 percent for a few hours after eating. This effect is known as **food-induced thermogenesis**. Ingested protein produces the greatest effect, carbohydrate and fat, less. Most of the increased heat production is secondary to processing of the absorbed nutrients by the liver, not to the energy expended by the gastrointestinal tract in digestion and absorption. It is to avoid the contribution of food-induced thermogenesis that BMR is performed in the postabsorptive state.

To reiterate, food-induced thermogenesis is the *rapid* increase in energy expenditure in response to ingestion of a meal. As we shall see, *prolonged* alterations in food intake (either increased or decreased total calories) also have significant effects on metabolic rate but are not termed food-induced thermogenesis.

Muscle Activity. The factor that can increase metabolic rate most is altered skeletal-muscle activity. Even minimal increases in muscle contraction significantly increase metabolic rate, and strenuous exercise may raise heat production more than fifteenfold (Table 18-9). Thus, depending on the degree of physical activity, total energy expenditure may vary for a normal young adult from a value of approximately 1500 kcal/24 h to more than 7000 kcal/24 h (for a lumberjack). Changes in muscle activity also account in part for the changes in metabolic rate that occur during sleep (decreased muscle contraction), during exposure to a low environmental temperature (increased muscle contraction and shivering), and with strong emotions.

Total-Body Energy Balance

The laws of thermodynamics dictate that the total energy expenditure (metabolic rate) of the body must equal the total energy intake. We have already identified the ultimate forms of energy expenditure: internal heat production, external work, and net molecular synthesis (energy storage). The source of input is the energy contained in ingested food. Therefore:

Energy from food intake = internal heat produced
+ external work + energy stored

Our equation includes no term for loss of fuel from the body via excretion of nutrients because, in normal persons, only negligible losses occur via the urine, feces, and as sloughed hair and skin. In certain diseases, however, the most important being diabetes, urinary losses of organic molecules may be quite large and would have to be included in the equation.

Let us now rearrange the equation to focus on energy storage:

Energy stored = energy from food intake
− (internal heat produced + external work)

Thus, whenever energy intake differs from the sum of internal heat produced and external work, changes in energy storage occur; that is, the total-body energy content increases or decreases (Table 18-10).

Total-body energy content in adults is usually regulated around a relatively constant operating point. Theoretically, this constancy can be achieved through (1) adjusting metabolic energy expenditure to compensate for randomly occurring food intake, (2) adjusting food intake to changing metabolic expenditures, or (3) both. There is no question that (2) is the major means of regulating total-body energy content.

Nevertheless, there is some contribution from method 1, that is, adjustment of metabolic expenditure when food intake changes. A striking experiment documenting this phenomenon was the reduction of caloric intake in normal male volunteers from 3492 kcal/day to 1570 kcal/day for 24 weeks. These men were soldiers performing considerable physical activity, and weight loss was initially very rapid and ultimately averaged 24 percent of original body weight. However, the important fact is that the weights did stabilize at this point; that is, energy balance was reestablished despite the continued caloric intake of only 1570 kcal/day. Clearly, the metabolic rate must have decreased to the same value. The decrease was due partly to a reduction in physical activity as the men became apa-

TABLE 18-9   ENERGY EXPENDITURE DURING DIFFERENT TYPES OF ACTIVITY FOR A 70-KG (154-LB) PERSON

Form of activity	Energy kcal/h
Lying still, awake	77
Sitting at rest	100
Typewriting rapidly	140
Dressing or undressing	150
Walking on level, 4.3 km/h (2.6 mi/h)	200
Bicycling on level, 9 km/h (5.5 mi/h)	304
Walking on 3 percent grade, 4.3 km/h (2.6 mi/h)	357
Sawing wood or shoveling snow	480
Jogging, 9 km/h (5.3 mi/h)	570
Rowing, 20 strokes/min	828

TABLE 18-10   THREE POSSIBLE STATES OF ENERGY BALANCE

State	Result
1. Energy intake = (internal heat production + external work)	Body energy content remains constant (body fat content remains constant).
2. Energy intake > (internal heat production + external work)	Body energy content increases (body fat content increases).
3. Energy intake < (internal heat production + external work)	Body energy content decreases (body fat content decreases).

thetic and reluctant to engage in any activity, but the BMR was also decreased.[15]

Experiments have also been done at the other end of the spectrum to see whether prolonged deliberate over-feeding of volunteers would induce an increased metabolic rate adequate to reestablish caloric balance despite the continued high-calorie diet. In many subjects, a compensatory increase in metabolic rate did in fact occur, and the weight gains of these subjects were less than those expected from the degree of overfeeding.

To summarize these studies, after several weeks of dietary alteration in either direction, the resulting deviations in an individual's total-body energy content trigger significant, although generally relatively small, counteracting changes in metabolism. This helps explain why some dieters lose about 10 lb of fat fairly easily and then become stuck at a plateau, losing additional weight at a much slower rate. It may also help explain why some very thin people have difficulty trying to gain much weight.

We now turn to the control of food intake, the more important mechanism for keeping body energy content constant.

Control of Food Intake

The control of food intake can be analyzed in the same way as any other biological control system, that is, in terms of its various components—regulated variable, receptor sensitive to this variable, afferent pathway, and so on. As our previous description emphasized, the variable being maintained relatively constant in this system is total-body energy content. Here we have a problem similar to that described in Chapter 16 for total-body sodium balance: What kind of receptors could possibly detect the *total-*body content of a particular variable, in this case calories?

It is very unlikely that any such receptors exist, and so instead the system depends on signals that are intimately correlated to food intake and total energy storage. These include the plasma concentrations of glucose and the hormones that regulate organic metabolism. These inputs are thought to constitute **satiety signals** that cause the person to cease feeling hungry and set the time period before hunger returns once again.

Figure 18-17 presents one hypothesized model for satiety: Plasma glucose concentration and the rate of cellular glucose utilization rise during eating as the ingested carbohydrate is digested and absorbed. Detection of this increase by glucose receptors in the brain could constitute a signal to those portions of the brain that control eating behavior and lead to cessation of hunger. Conversely, in the postabsorptive period, plasma glucose and glucose utilization decrease, the signal to the brain glucose receptors would be removed, and the individual once again would become hungry.[16]

Similarly, changes in plasma concentrations of the hormones that regulate carbohydrate and fat metabolism could be important satiety signals to the brain's integrating centers. For example, insulin, which increases during food absorption, has been shown to suppress hunger. Glucagon, which may also increase after consumption of a high-protein or mixed-nutrient meal, also suppresses hunger.

A nonchemical correlate of food ingestion—body temperature—is yet another possible satiety signal. The increase in metabolic rate induced by eating tends to raise body temperature slightly, and this probably constitutes a signal inhibitory to hunger.

All the satiety signals described above reflect events occurring as a result of nutrient *absorption,* but there are also important signals initiated by the presence of food within the gastrointestinal tract. These include neural signals triggered by stimulation of both stretch receptors and

---

[15]A decreased total-body mass contributed to the decrease in BMR (a smaller body utilizes less energy), but there was also a decrease in metabolism by the liver and other organs out of proportion to their changes in weight. The mechanism of this latter effect was a decrease in the activity of the sympathetic nervous system.

---

[16]Despite extensive evidence from other species that such glucose receptors exist for the control of food appetite, it is not certain that they are present in humans.

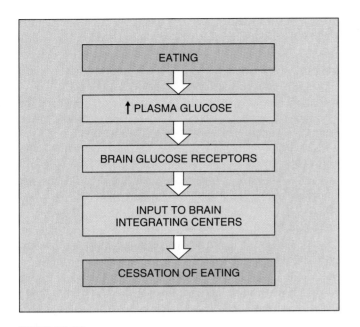

FIGURE 18-17

Hypothesized mechanism by which plasma glucose acts as a satiety signal to shut off eating.

chemoreceptors in the stomach and duodenum, as well as by several of the hormones (cholecystokinin, for example) released from the stomach and duodenum during eating.

Thus far we have been dealing with those inputs that would help to control meal size and frequency. To be effective over long periods of time in regulating total caloric intake and matching it to energy expenditure, however, the magnitude of these signals must reflect not merely meal-eating patterns but the total-body energy content itself. The identities of such long-term regulators remain unknown.

It is presently not possible to quantify the contributions of the many signals postulated to control food intake—summarized in Figure 18-18—and to describe the location and nature of the receptors stimulated by each. Moreover, there appear to be multiple brain areas, in addition to the hypothalamus, that integrate all these afferent inputs and cause the individual either to feel hungry or not. The ways in which these various areas interact remain to be determined.

Although food intake is very likely reflexly controlled by the input from some combination of glucose receptors, thermoreceptors, and so on, it also is strongly influenced by the reinforcement, both positive and negative, of such things as smell, taste, and texture. For example, rats given a "cafeteria-style" choice of foods highly palatable to people overeat by 70 to 80 percent and soon become obese.

FIGURE 18-18

Inputs controlling food intake. The minus signs denote hunger suppression, and the plus signs denote hunger stimulation.

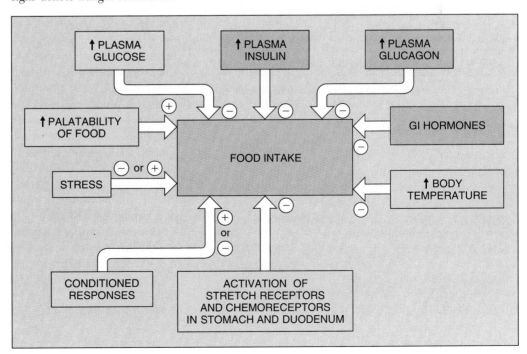

An analogous (but reverse) experiment has shown that obese people lose weight when they must obtain all their food from a monotonous diet delivered via a tube in response to lever pressing. Thus, the behavioral concepts of reinforcement, drive, and motivation, described in Chapter 13, must be incorporated into any comprehensive theory of food-intake control. So must factors such as stress. For example, repeated tail-pinching will cause rats to overeat, and this response can be blocked by drugs that antagonize endogenous opiates.

Obesity

Obesity has been defined, by a 1985 Consensus Development Conference at the National Institutes of Health, as an excess of body fat resulting in a significant impairment of health from a variety of diseases, notably hypertension, atherosclerotic heart disease, and diabetes. The conference concluded that a level of 20 percent or more above "desirable" body weight qualifies as obesity and is associated with sufficient risk to health to justify clinical intervention.

How does one determine desirable weight? The most commonly used ideal or desirable weight tables are those put out by the Metropolitan Life Insurance Company and are based on mortality data. However, there is considerable controversy over the fact that the tables issued in 1983 indicate that weights approximately 12 to 14 pounds higher than those of the 1959 tables are safe and in fact may be associated with a *lower* mortality risk. Most experts believe, however, that the 1959 tables (Table 18-11) are more accurate predictors of health consequences.

In any case, the presently preferred simple method for assessing degree of obesity is the **body mass index (BMI)**, calculated as weight in kilograms divided by the square of height in meters. For example, a 70-kg person with a height of 180 cm would have a BMI of 21.6 (70/1.8^2). This method correlates quite well with body fat measurement techniques such as skinfold thickness. Normal BMI ranges for adults are 19 to 25; a BMI of more than 27.8 for men and 27.3 for women is defined as obesity.

The bad news about the causes of obesity is that hereditary influences are quite strong. For example, identical twins who have been separated soon after birth and raised in different households manifest strikingly similar body weights as adults. The good news is that studies on animal models and human populations indicate that environmental factors, which should in theory be alterable, can also play important roles. Human studies indicate that the prevalence of obesity in industrialized countries is related to social conditions, economic circumstances, or both. For example, in the United States obesity is six times more common among members of the lowest socioeconomic class than among those of the highest class. In nonindustrialized countries, this relationship does not hold because the poor cannot obtain adequate food.

The methods and goals of treating obesity are presently undergoing extensive rethinking. An increase in fat must be due to an excess of food intake over the metabolic rate, and low-calorie diets have long been the mainstay of therapy. However, it is now clear that such diets alone have limited effectiveness in many obese people partly because, as described earlier, the person's metabolic rate drops, sometimes falling low enough to prevent further weight loss on as little as 1000 calories a day. Related to this, studies have also shown that many obese people get fat or stay fat on a caloric intake no greater than, and sometimes less than, the amount consumed by people of normal weight. These persons must either be less active than normal or have lower basal metabolic rates. Finally, at least half of definitely obese people—those who are more than 20 percent overweight—who try to diet down to desirable weights suffer medically, physically, and psychologically.

Exercise has proven to be a valuable element in any weight-loss program. The exercise itself utilizes calories, though depressingly few, and usually does not stimulate appetite in obese persons. More importantly, exercise partially offsets the tendency for the metabolic rate to decrease during long-term caloric restriction and weight loss.

TABLE 18-11 METROPOLITAN LIFE INSURANCE "DESIRABLE-WEIGHT" TABLE (1959), MEDIUM FRAME*

Men		Women	
Height	Weight, lb	Height	Weight, lb
5'2"	114–126	4'9"	94–106
5'3"	117–129	4'10"	97–109
5'4"	120–132	4'11"	100–112
5'5"	123–136	5'0"	103–115
5'6"	127–140	5'1"	106–118
5'7"	131–145	5'2"	109–122
5'8"	135–149	5'3"	112–126
5'9"	139–153	5'4"	116–131
5'10"	143–158	5'5"	120–135
5'11"	147–163	5'6"	127–140
6'0"	151–168	5'7"	128–143
6'1"	155–173	5'8"	132–147
6'2"	160–178	5'9"	136–151
6'3"	165–183	5'10"	140–155

*Height is without shoes, and weight is without clothes.

Also, the combination of exercise and diet causes the person to lose more fat and less protein than with diet alone.

Finally, as an exercise in energy balance, let us calculate how rapidly a person can expect to lose weight on a reducing diet. Suppose an individual whose steady-state metabolic rate per 24 h is 2000 kcal goes on a 1000 kcal/day diet. How much of the person's own body fat will be required to supply this additional 1000 kcal/day? Since fat contains 9 kcal/g:

$$\frac{1000 \text{ kcal/day}}{9 \text{ kcal/g}} = 111 \text{ g/day, or } 777 \text{ g/week}$$

Approximately another 77 g of water is lost from the adipose tissue along with this fat (adipose tissue is 10 percent water), so that the grand total for 1 week's loss equals 854 g, or 1.8 lb. Thus, during a long-term diet, the person can reasonably expect to lose approximately this amount of weight per week, assuming no decrease in metabolic rate occurs. Actually, the amount of weight loss during the first week will probably be considerably greater since a large amount of water may be lost early in the diet, particularly when the diet contains little carbohydrate. This early loss, which is associated with a depletion of glycogen stores in liver and skeletal muscle, is really of no value so far as elimination of excess fat is concerned and often underlies the claims made for fad diets.

Eating Disorders: Anorexia Nervosa and Bulimia

The two major eating disorders are found almost exclusively in adolescent girls and young women. The typical person with *anorexia nervosa* becomes pathologically afraid of gaining weight and reduces her food intake so severely that she may die of starvation. It is not known whether the cause of anorexia nervosa is primarily psychological or biological. There are many other abnormalities associated with it—loss of menstrual periods, low blood pressure, low body temperature, altered secretion of many hormones—but it is not clear whether these are simply the result of starvation or whether they represent signs, along with the eating disturbances, of primary hypothalamic malfunction.

Bulimia is recurrent episodes of binge eating. It is associated with regular employment of self-induced vomiting, laxatives, or diuretics, as well as strict dieting, fasting, or vigorous exercise to prevent weight gain. Like individuals with anorexia nervosa, those with bulimia manifest a persistent overconcern with body weight, although they are generally within 10 percent of their ideal weight. It, too, is accompanied by a variety of physiological abnormalities, but it is unknown whether they are causal or secondary.

REGULATION OF BODY TEMPERATURE

Animals capable of maintaining their body temperatures within very narrow limits are termed **homeothermic**. The relatively constant and high body temperature frees biochemical reactions from fluctuating with the external temperature. However, the maintenance of a relatively high body temperature imposes a requirement for precise regulatory mechanisms, since further large elevations of temperature cause nerve malfunction and protein denaturation. Some people suffer convulsions at a body temperature of 41°C (106°F), and 43°C is the absolute limit for survival of most people.

Several important generalizations about normal human body temperature should be stressed at the outset: (1) Oral temperature averages about 0.5°C less than rectal, which is generally used as an estimate of internal temperature; thus, not all parts of the body have the same temperature. (2) Internal temperature varies several degrees in response to activity pattern and external temperature.

FIGURE 18-19

Circadian changes in core (measured as rectal) body temperature in normal males and in normal females in the first half of the menstrual cycle. (*Adapted from Scales et al.*).

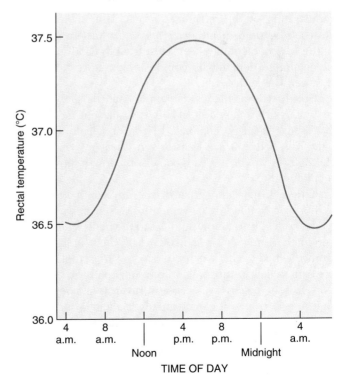

(3) There is a characteristic circadian fluctuation (Figure 18-19), so that temperature is lowest during sleep and highest during the awake state even if the person remains relaxed in bed. (4) An added variation in women is a higher temperature during the last half of the menstrual cycle.

If temperature is viewed as a measure of heat "concentration," temperature regulation can be studied by our usual balance methods. In this case, the total heat content of the body is determined by the *net difference* between heat produced and heat lost. Maintaining a constant body temperature means that, in the steady state, heat production must equal heat loss. The basic principles of heat production were described earlier in this chapter in the section on metabolic rate, and those of heat loss are described next. Then we will present the reflexes that play upon these processes specifically to regulate body temperature.

Mechanisms of Heat Loss or Gain

The surface of the body can lose heat to the external environment by radiation, conduction, and convection (Figure 18-20) and by the evaporation of water. Before defining each of these processes, however, it must be emphasized that radiation, conduction, and convection can under certain circumstances lead to heat *gain*, not heat loss.

Radiation is the process by which the surfaces of all objects constantly emit heat in the form of electromagnetic waves. The rate of emission is determined by the temperature of the radiating surface. Thus, if the body surface is warmer than the *average* of the various surfaces in the environment, net heat is lost from the body, the rate being directly dependent upon the temperature difference between the surfaces.

Conduction is the loss or gain of heat transfer of thermal energy during collisions between adjacent molecules. In essence, heat is "conducted" from molecule to molecule. The body surface loses or gains heat by conduction through direct contact with cooler or warmer substances, including the air or water.

Convection is the process whereby conductive heat loss or gain is aided by movement of the air or water next to the body. For example, air next to the body is heated by conduction, moves away, and carries off the heat just taken from the body. The air that moved away is replaced by cool air, which in turn follows the same pattern. Convection is always occurring because warm air is less dense and therefore rises, but it can be greatly facilitated by external forces such as wind or fans. Thus, convection aids conductive heat exchange by continuously maintaining a supply of cool air. Henceforth we shall also imply convection when we use the term "conduction."

Because of the great importance of air movement in aiding heat loss, attempts have been made to quantify the cooling effect of combinations of air speed and tempera-

FIGURE 18-20

Mechanisms of heat transfer. In radiation, heat is transferred by electromagnetic waves. In conduction, heat moves by direct transfer of thermal energy from molecule to molecule. Here, the thermal energy from the water molecules is being transferred to the molecules of the foot. Convection moves warm air away from the body to be replaced by cooler air.

ture. The most useful tool is called the **windchill index**, which states the hypothetical temperature with *no* wind that would provide the same cooling effect as the actual temperature and wind velocity. For example, the wind chill index would be $-10°C$ if an object in a $5°C$ windy environment cooled as fast as if the temperature were actually $-10°C$ and there were no wind at all.

Evaporation of water from the skin and membranes lining the respiratory tract is the other major process for loss of body heat. A very large amount of energy—600 kcal/L—is required to transform water from the liquid to the gaseous state. Thus, whenever water vaporizes from the body's surface, the heat required to drive the process is conducted from the surface, thereby cooling it.

Temperature-Regulating Reflexes

Temperature regulation offers a classic example of a biological control system (we used it as our example of such systems in Chapter 7, Figure 7-2). The balance between heat production and heat loss is continuously being disturbed, either by changes in metabolic rate (exercise being the most powerful influence) or by changes in the external environment that alter heat loss or gain. The resulting changes in body temperature are detected by thermoreceptors, which initiate reflexes that change the output of various effectors so that heat production and/or loss are changed and body temperature is restored toward normal.

Figure 18-21 summarizes the specific components of these reflexes. There are two categories of thermoreceptors, one in the skin (**peripheral thermoreceptors**, described in Chapter 9) and the other (**central thermoreceptors**) in deep body structures, including the hypothalamus, spinal cord, and abdominal organs. Since it is the internal temperature, not the skin temperature, that is being maintained relatively constant, the central chemoreceptors provide the essential negative-feedback component of the reflexes. The peripheral chemoreceptors provide feedforward information, as described in Chapter 7

and also account for one's ability to identify a hot or cold area of the skin.

An area of the hypothalamus serves as the primary overall integrator of the reflexes, but other brain centers (not shown in Figure 18-21) also exert some control over specific components of the reflexes.

Output from the hypothalamus and the other brain areas to the effectors is via (1) sympathetic nerves to the sweat glands, skin arterioles, and the adrenal medulla; and (2) motor neurons to the skeletal muscles.

Control of Heat Production. Changes in muscle activity constitute the major control of heat production for temperature regulation. The first muscle changes in response to cold are a gradual and general increase in skeletal-muscle contraction. This may lead to shivering, the characteristic muscle response to cold, which consists of oscillating rhythmical muscle tremors occurring at the rate of

FIGURE 18-21

Summary of temperature-regulating mechanisms beginning with (A) peripheral thermoreceptors and (B) central thermoreceptors. The dashed arrow from the adrenal medulla indicates that this hormonal pathway is of minor importance in human beings. The solid arrows denote neural pathways. For simplicity, other nonhypothalamic integrating areas are not shown.

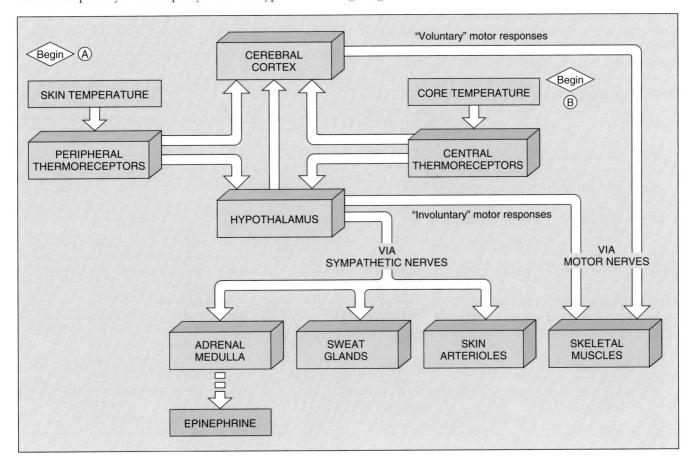

about 10 to 20 per second. During shivering, the efferent motor nerves to the skeletal muscles are controlled by descending pathways under the primary control of the hypothalamus. So effective is shivering that body heat production may be increased severalfold within seconds to minutes. Because no external work is performed by shivering, all the energy liberated by the metabolic machinery appears as internal heat and is known as **shivering thermogenesis**. People also use their muscles for voluntary heat production activities such as foot stamping and hand clapping.

Thus far, our discussion has focused primarily on the muscle response to *cold;* the opposite muscle reactions occur in response to heat. Basal muscle contraction is reflexly decreased, and voluntary movement is also diminished. These attempts to reduce heat production are relatively limited, however, both because basal muscle contraction is quite low to start with and because increased body temperature acts directly on cells to increase metabolic rate.

Muscle contraction is not the only process controlled in temperature-regulating reflexes. In most experimental animals, chronic cold exposure induces an increase in metabolic rate, that is, heat production, that is not due to increased muscle activity and is termed **nonshivering thermogenesis**. Its cause is an increased secretion of epinephrine, with some contribution by thyroid hormone as well. Nonshivering thermogenesis is quite minimal, if present at all, in adult human beings, and there is no increased secretion of thyroid hormone in response to cold. Nonshivering thermogenesis does occur in infants.

Control of Heat Loss by Radiation and Conduction. For purposes of temperature control, it is convenient to view the body as a central core surrounded by a shell consisting of skin and subcutaneous tissue; we shall refer to this complex outer shell simply as skin. It is the temperature of the central core that is being regulated at approximately 37°C. As we shall see, the temperature of the outer surface of the skin changes markedly.

If the skin were a perfect insulator, no heat would ever be lost from the core. The temperature of the outer skin surface would equal the environmental temperature, and net conduction and radiation would be zero. The skin is not a perfect insulator, however, and so the temperature of its outer surface generally is somewhere between that of the external environment and that of the core.

The skin's effectiveness as an insulator is subject to physiological control by a change in the blood flow to it. The more blood reaching the skin from the core, the more closely the skin's temperature approaches that of the core. In effect, the blood vessels diminish the insulating capacity of the skin by carrying heat to the surface (Figure 18-22) to be lost to the external environment. These vessels are controlled largely by vasoconstrictor sympathetic nerves, the firing rate of which is increased in response to cold and decreased in response to heat.[17] There is also a population of sympathetic neurons to the skin whose neurotransmitters (as yet unidentified) cause active *vasodilation* in association with sweating. Certain areas of skin participate much more than others in all these vasomotor responses, and so skin temperatures vary with location.

Three *behavioral* mechanisms for altering heat loss by radiation and conduction remain to be described: changes

---

[17]In addition, the affinity of alpha-adrenergic receptors for norepinephrine, the sympathetic neurotransmitter, is increased directly by cold, and so the ability of any given rate of nerve firing to cause vasoconstriction is increased when the skin is cold.

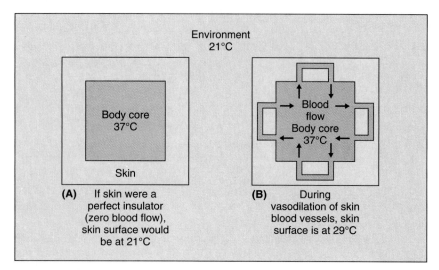

(A) If skin were a perfect insulator (zero blood flow), skin surface would be at 21°C

(B) During vasodilation of skin blood vessels, skin surface is at 29°C

FIGURE 18-22
Relationship of skin's insulating capacity to skin blood flow. (A) If skin were a perfect insulator—in other words, if there were zero blood flow (a situation never reached in a normal person even during maximal vasoconstriction)—the temperature of its outer surface would equal that of the external environment. (B) The skin blood vessels dilate, and the increased blood flow carries heat to the body surface. In this way, the insulating capacity of the skin is reduced, and its surface temperature becomes intermediate between that of the core and that of the external environment.

in surface area, in clothing, and choice of surroundings. Curling up into a ball, hunching the shoulders, and similar maneuvers in response to cold reduce the surface area exposed to the environment, thereby decreasing heat loss by radiation and conduction. In human beings, clothing is also an important component of temperature regulation, substituting for the insulating effects of feathers in birds and fur in other mammals. The outer surface of the clothes forms the true "exterior" of the body surface. The skin loses heat directly to the air space trapped by the clothes, which in turn pick up heat from the inner air layer and transfer it to the external environment. The insulating ability of clothing is determined primarily by the thickness of the trapped air layer.

Clothing is important not only at low temperatures but also at very high temperatures. When the environmental temperature is greater than body temperature, radiation and conduction favor heat *gain* rather than heat loss. People therefore insulate themselves against such temperatures by wearing clothes. The clothing, however, must be loose so as to allow adequate movement of air to permit evaporation (see below). White clothing is cooler since it reflects more radiant energy, which dark colors absorb. Loose-fitting, light-colored clothes are far more cooling than going nude during direct exposure to the sun.

The third behavioral mechanism for altering heat loss is to seek out warmer or colder surroundings, as for example by moving from a shady spot into the sunlight. Raising or lowering the thermostat of a house or turning on an air conditioner also fits this category.

Control of Heat Loss by Evaporation. Even in the absence of sweating, there is loss of water by diffusion through the skin, which is not waterproof. A similar amount is lost from the respiratory lining during expiration. These two losses are known as **insensible water loss** and amount to approximately 600 ml/day in human beings. Evaporation of this water accounts for a significant fraction of total heat loss. In contrast to this passive water loss, sweating requires the active secretion of fluid by **sweat glands** and its extrusion into ducts that carry it to the skin surface.

Production of sweat is stimulated by the sympathetic nerves. Sweat is a dilute solution containing sodium chloride as its major solute. There are an estimated 2.5 million sweat glands spread over the adult human body, and sweating rates of over 4 L/h have been reported. The evaporation of 4 L of water would eliminate almost 2400 kcal from the body!

It is essential to recognize that sweat must evaporate in order to exert its cooling effect. The most important factor determining evaporation is the water vapor concentration of the air, that is, the relative humidity. The discomfort suffered on humid days is due to the failure of evapora-

tion; the sweat glands continue to secrete, but the sweat simply remains on the skin or drips off.

Integration of Effector Mechanisms. Table 18-12 summarizes the effector mechanisms regulating temperature, none of which is an all-or-none response but a graded, progressive increase or decrease in activity. Changes in skin blood flow alone can regulate body temperature, by altering heat loss, over a range of environmental temperatures (approximately 25 to 30°C or 75 to 86°F) known as the **thermoneutral zone**. At temperatures lower than this, even maximal vasoconstriction cannot prevent heat loss from exceeding heat production, and the body must increase its heat production to maintain temperature. At environmental temperatures above the thermoneutral zone, even maximal vasodilation cannot eliminate heat as fast as it is produced, and another heat-loss mechanism—sweating—is therefore brought strongly into play. Indeed, at environmental temperatures above that of the body, heat is actually added to the body by radiation and conduction, and evaporation is the sole mechanism for heat loss. A person's ability to tolerate such temperatures is determined by the humidity and by the maximal sweating rate. For example, when the air is completely dry, an individual can tolerate a temperature of 130°C (255°F) for 20 min or longer, whereas very moist air at 46°C (115°F) is bearable for only a few minutes.

Temperature Acclimatization

Acclimatization to Heat. Changes in sweating onset, volume, and composition determine people's chronic adaptation to high temperatures. A person newly arrived in a hot environment has poor ability to do work initially; body temperature rises, and severe weakness and illness may occur. After several days, there is a great improvement in work tolerance, with little increase in body temperature, and the person is said to have acclimatized to the heat (see Chapter 7 for a discussion of the concept of acclimatization). Body temperature does not rise as much because sweating begins sooner and the volume of sweat produced is greater.

There is also an important change in the composition of the sweat, namely, a marked reduction in its sodium concentration. This adaptation, which minimizes the loss of sodium from the body via sweat, is due to increased secretion of the mineralocorticoid hormone aldosterone. The sweat-gland secretory cells produce a solution with a sodium concentration similar to that of plasma, but some of the sodium is absorbed back into the blood as the secretion flows along the sweat-gland ducts toward the skin surface. Aldosterone stimulates this absorption in a manner identical to its stimulation of sodium reabsorption in the

TABLE 18-12 SUMMARY OF EFFECTOR MECHANISMS IN TEMPERATURE REGULATION

Desired effect	Mechanism
	Stimulated by Cold (see also Figure 7-2)
Decrease heat loss	1. Vasoconstriction of skin vessels 2. Reduction of surface area (curling up, etc.) 3. Behavioral response (put on warmer clothes, raise thermostat setting, etc.)
Increase heat production	1. Increased muscle tone 2. Shivering and increased voluntary activity 3. Increased secretion of thyroid hormone and epinephrine 4. Increased food appetite
	Stimulated by Heat
Increase heat loss	1. Vasodilation of skin vessels 2. Sweating 3. Behavioral response (put on cooler clothes, turn on fan, etc.)
Decrease heat production	1. Decreased muscle tone and voluntary activity 2. Decreased secretion of thyroid hormone and epinephrine 3. Decreased food appetite

renal tubules. The reflexes that activate the renin-angiotensin-aldosterone system were described in Chapter 16.

Acclimatization to Cold. Cold acclimatization has been less studied than heat acclimatization because of the difficulty of subjecting individuals to total-body cold stress sufficient to produce acclimatization. The best-studied group was the Korean women who, wearing only cotton garments, used to dive for shellfish and edible seaweed in the middle of winter when the seawater temperature was as low as 10°C. Moreover, the fact that the characteristics, to be described, disappeared within several years after the women began using wet suits is strong evidence that these characteristics really represented acclimatization, not genetic differences.

The major components of their acclimatization were (1) an increase in metabolic rate, (2) an increase in the insulating ability of a given amount of skin fat, and (3) an ability to withstand a colder water temperature without shivering.

A different kind of adaptation is exhibited by Eskimos and various groups of fishermen who manifest less vasoconstriction of finger blood vessels during exposure of the hands to cold water. This is an adaptation that permits these individuals to do work with their hands despite intense cold. The Eskimos and fishermen, unlike the diving women, normally expose only their hands to the cold and use warm clothing to protect the rest of the body.

Fever

The term **hyperthermia** denotes an elevation of body temperature regardless of cause. The specific type of hyperthermia termed **fever** is due to a "resetting of the thermostat" in the hypothalamus; that is, fever is a hyperthermia in which the person still regulates body temperature in response to heat or cold but at a higher set point. The most common cause of fever is infection, but physical trauma and stress can also induce fever.

The onset of fever during infection is frequently gradual, but it is most striking when it occurs rapidly in the form of a chill. The brain thermostat is suddenly raised, the person feels cold, and marked vasoconstriction and shivering occur (Figure 18-23). The person also curls up and puts on more blankets. This combination of decreased heat loss and increased heat production serves to drive body temperature up to the new set point, where it stabilizes. It will continue to be regulated at this new value until the thermostat is reset to normal and the fever "breaks." The person then feels hot, throws off the covers, and manifests profound vasodilation and sweating.

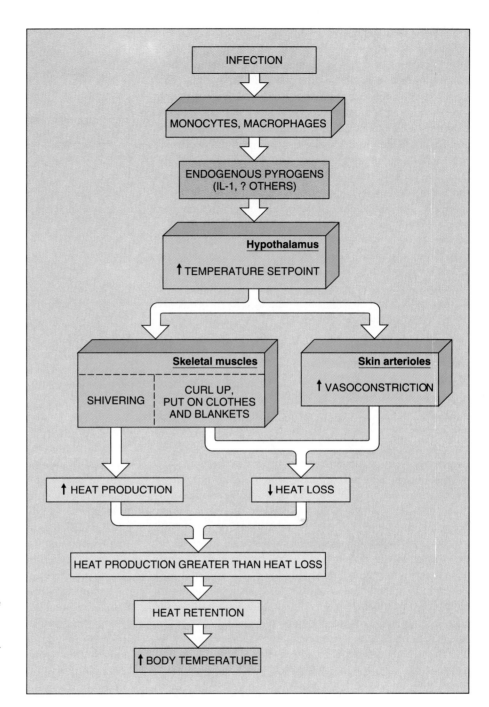

FIGURE 18-23

Pathway by which infection causes fever. IL-1 = interleukin 1. Compare this figure to Figure 7-2: The effector responses are identical but they serve to keep body temperature *relatively constant* when one is exposed to cold (Figure 7-2) and *raise* body temperature during an infection.

What is the basis for the thermostat resetting? A chemical messenger originally called **endogenous pyrogen (EP)** is released from monocytes and macrophages in the presence of infection or inflammation. EP acts upon the thermoreceptors in the hypothalamus (and perhaps other brain areas), altering their rate of firing and their input to the integrating centers. It is likely that the action of EP is mediated via local release of prostaglandins, which then directly alter central thermoreceptor function. Aspirin reduces fever by inhibiting prostaglandin synthesis.

The term EP was coined at a time when the specific identity of EP was not known, and it is still not clear whether there is only one such substance. At least one peptide, **interleukin 1 (IL-1)**, is now known to function as an EP, but other peptides [for example, tumor necrosis factor (TNF) and interleukin 6 (IL-6)] also released from monocytes and macrophages in response to infection or inflammation may also play a role. In addition to their effects on temperature, IL-1 and the other peptides have many other effects—to be described in Chapter 20—that have the common denominator of enhancing resistance to infection and promoting the healing of damaged tissue.

One would expect fever, which is such a consistent concomitant of infection, to play some important protective role, and most evidence suggests that such is the case. Increased body temperature stimulates a large number of the body's defensive responses to infection. The likelihood that fever is a beneficial response raises as yet unanswered questions concerning the use of aspirin and other drugs to suppress fever during infection. It must be emphasized that these questions apply to the usual modest fevers. There is no question that an extremely high fever can be harmful, particularly in its effects on the central nervous system, and must be vigorously opposed with drugs and other forms of therapy.

Other Causes of Hyperthermia

To reiterate, fever is a hyperthermia caused by an elevation of the thermal set point. There are a variety of situations other than a change in set point in which hyperthermia occurs.

Exercise. The most common cause of hyperthermia in normal people is exercise, during which body temperature rises and is maintained as long as the exercise continues. It is possible that a small fraction of this rise represents a new set point, and some IL-1 may be released during sustained exercise, perhaps because of slight tissue damage. However, most of the rise in body temperature is not a fever but is simply a physical consequence of the internal heat generated by the exercising muscles. As shown in Figure 18-24, heat production rises immediately during the initial stage of exercise and exceeds heat loss, causing heat storage in the body and a rise in the core temperature. This rise in core temperature triggers reflexes, via the central thermoreceptors, for increased heat loss—increased skin blood flow and sweating—and the discrepancy between heat production and heat loss starts to diminish but does not disappear. Therefore core temperature continues to rise, albeit more slowly. Ultimately, core temperature will be high enough to drive, via the central thermoreceptors, the heat-loss reflexes at a rate such that heat loss equals heat production, and core temperature stabilizes at this elevated value despite continued exercise.

Heat Exhaustion and Heat Stroke. *Heat exhaustion* is a state of collapse, often taking the form of fainting, due to hypotension brought on by (1) depletion of plasma volume secondary to sweating, and (2) extreme dilation of

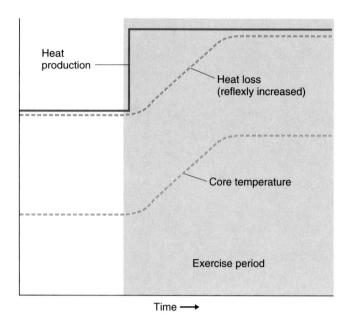

FIGURE 18-24

Thermal changes during exercise. Heat loss is reflexly increased, and when it once again equals heat production, core temperature stabilizes.

skin blood vessels. Thus, decreases in both cardiac output and peripheral resistance contribute to the hypotension. Heat exhaustion occurs as a direct consequence of the activity of heat-loss mechanisms, and because these mechanisms have been so active, the body temperature is only modestly elevated. In a sense, heat exhaustion is a safety valve that, by forcing cessation of work in a hot environment when heat-loss mechanisms are overtaxed, prevents the larger rise in body temperature that would precipitate the far more serious condition of heat stroke.

In contrast to heat exhaustion, *heat stroke* represents a complete breakdown in heat-regulating systems so that body temperature keeps going up and up. It is an extremely dangerous situation, characterized by collapse, delirium, seizures, or prolonged unconsciousness—all due to marked elevation of body temperature. It almost always occurs in association with exposure to or overexertion in hot and humid environments. In some individuals, particularly the elderly, heat stroke may appear with no apparent prior period of severe sweating, but in most cases it comes on as the end stage of prolonged untreated heat exhaustion. Exactly what triggers the transition to heat stroke is not clear—impaired circulation to the brain due to dehydration is one factor—but the striking finding is that even in the face of a rapidly rising body temperature, the person fails to sweat. This sets off a positive-feedback situation in which the rising body temperature directly stimulates metabolism, that is, heat production, which further raises body temperature.

SECTION C SUMMARY

BASIC CONCEPTS OF ENERGY EXPENDITURE AND CALORIC BALANCE

I. The energy liberated during a chemical reaction appears either as heat or work.

II. Total energy expenditure = heat produced + external work done + energy stored.

III. Metabolic rate is influenced by the many factors summarized in Table 18-7.

IV. Basal metabolic rate is increased by the thyroid hormones and epinephrine. The other functions of the thyroid hormones are summarized in Table 18-8.

V. Energy storage, as fat, can be positive or negative when the metabolic rate is less than or greater than, respectively, the energy content of ingested food.
   A. Energy storage is regulated mainly by reflex adjustment of food intake to the metabolic rate.
   B. In addition, the metabolic rate increases or decreases, to some extent, when food intake is chronically increased or decreased, respectively.

VI. Food appetite is controlled by the many factors summarized in Figure 18-18.

VII. Obesity, the result of an imbalance between food intake and metabolic rate, increases the incidence of many diseases.

REGULATION OF BODY TEMPERATURE

I. Body temperature, measured as rectal temperature, shows a circadian rhythm, being highest during the day and lowest at night.

II. The body exchanges heat with the external environment by radiation, conduction, convection, and evaporation of water from the body surface.

III. The hypothalamus and other brain areas are the integrating centers for temperature-regulating reflexes, and both peripheral and central thermoreceptors participate in these reflexes.

IV. Body temperature is regulated by altering heat production and/or heat loss so as to change total-body heat content.
   A. Heat production is altered by increasing muscle tone, shivering, and voluntary activity.
   B. Heat loss by radiation, conduction, and convection depends on the difference in temperature between the skin surface and the environment.
   C. In response to cold, skin temperature is decreased by decreasing skin blood flow through reflex stimulation of the sympathetic nerves to the skin. In response to heat, skin temperature is increased by inhibiting the nerves.
   D. Behavioral responses such as putting on more clothes also influence heat loss.
   E. Evaporation of water occurs all the time as insensible loss from the skin and respiratory lining.

Additional water for evaporation is supplied by sweat, stimulated by the sympathetic nerves to the sweat glands.
   F. Increased heat production is essential for temperature regulation at environmental temperatures below the thermoneutral zone, and sweating is essential at temperatures above this zone.

V. Temperature acclimatization to heat is achieved by an earlier onset of sweating, an increased volume of sweat, and a decreased sodium concentration of the sweat.

VI. The most common causes of hyperthermia are fever and exercise.
   A. Fever is due to a resetting of the temperature set point so that heat production is increased and heat loss is decreased in order to raise body temperature to the new set point and keep it there. The stimulus is endogenous pyrogen, which is interleukin 1 and possibly other peptides as well.
   B. The hyperthermia of exercise is not due to a changed set point but to the increased heat produced by the muscles.

SECTION C KEY TERMS

external work	evaporation
internal work	peripheral
total energy expenditure	thermoreceptors
kilocalorie (kcal)	central thermoreceptors
metabolic rate	shivering thermogenesis
basal metabolic rate (BMR)	nonshivering
calorigenic effect	thermogenesis
food-induced thermogenesis	insensible water loss
satiety signals	sweat glands
body mass index (BMI)	thermoneutral zone
homeothermic	hyperthermia
radiation	fever
conduction	endogenous pyrogen
convection	(EP)
windchill index	interleukin 1 (IL-1)

SECTION C REVIEW QUESTIONS

1. State the formula relating total energy expenditure, heat produced, external work, and energy storage.

2. What two hormones alter the basal metabolic rate?

3. State the equation for total-body energy balance. Describe the three possible states of balance with regard to energy storage.

4. What happens to the basal metabolic rate after a person has either lost or gained weight?

5. List five satiety signals.

6. List three beneficial effects of exercise in a weight-loss program.

7. Compare and contrast the four mechanisms for heat loss.

8. Describe the control of skin blood vessels during exposure to cold or heat.

9. With a diagram, summarize the reflex responses to heat or cold. What are the dominant mechanisms for temperature regulation in the thermoneutral zone and in temperatures below and above this range?

10. What changes are exhibited by a heat-acclimatized person?

11. Summarize the sequence of events leading to a fever and contrast this to the sequence leading to hyperthermia during exercise.

CHAPTER 18 CLINICAL TERMS

diabetes mellitus	giantism
insulin-dependent diabetes mellitus (IDDM)	dwarfism
	acromegaly
non-insulin-dependent diabetes mellitus (NIDDM)	hypothyroidism
	hyperthyroidism
diabetic ketoacidosis	anabolic steroids
insulin resistance	obesity
sulfonylureas	anorexia nervosa
fasting hypoglycemia	bulimia
atherosclerosis	hyperthermia
malnutrition	fever
cancer	heat exhaustion
oncogenes	heat stroke

CHAPTER 18 THOUGHT QUESTIONS

1. What happens to the triacylglycerol concentrations in the plasma and in adipose tissue after administration of a drug that blocks the action of lipoprotein lipase?

2. A resting, unstressed person has increased plasma concentrations of free fatty acids, glycerol, amino acids, and ketones. What situations might be responsible, and what additional plasma measurement would distinguish among them?

3. A normal volunteer is given an injection of insulin. The plasma concentrations of which hormones increase?

4. If the sympathetic preganglionic fibers to the adrenal medulla were cut in an animal, would this eliminate the sympathetically mediated component of increased gluconeogenesis and lipolysis during exercise? Explain.

5. A patient with insulin-dependent diabetes suffers a broken leg. Would you advise this person to increase or decrease his dosage of insulin?

6. A person has a defect in the ability of her small intestine to absorb bile salts. What effect will this have on her plasma cholesterol concentration?

7. A well-trained athlete is found to have a moderately elevated plasma cholesterol concentration. What additional measurement would you advise this person to have done?

8. A full-term newborn infant is abnormally small. Is this most likely due to deficient growth hormone, deficient thyroid hormones, or deficient in utero nutrition?

9. Why might the administration of androgens to stimulate growth in a small 12-year-old male turn out to be counterproductive?

10. What are the sources of heat loss for a person immersed up to the neck in a 40°C bath?

11. Lizards can regulate their body temperatures only through behavioral means. Can you predict what they do when they are injected with bacteria?

CHAPTER

19

REPRODUCTION

SECTION

A

GENERAL TERMINOLOGY AND CONCEPTS

Before we begin detailed descriptions of male and female reproductive systems, it is worthwhile to summarize some general terminology and concepts. This brief description is for orientation, and the specifics of these processes will be dealt with in subsequent sections.

The primary reproductive organs are known as the **gonads**: the **testes** (singular *testis*) in the male and the **ovaries** in the female. In both sexes, the gonads serve dual functions: (1) **gametogenesis**, the production of the reproductive cells, termed **gametes**—**spermatozoa** (singular *spermatozoan*, usually shortened to **sperm**) by males and **ova** (singular **ovum**) by females; and (2) secretion of particular steroid hormones, often termed **sex hormones**. The primary sex hormones are **testosterone** in the male and **estradiol** and **progesterone** in the female.

Several comments about sex hormone terminology are useful at this point. As described in Chapter 10, testosterone belongs to a group of steroid hormones that have similar masculinizing actions and are collectively called **androgens**. Only the testes secrete significant amounts of testosterone. Other circulating androgens are produced by the adrenal cortex, but they are much less potent than testosterone and are unable to maintain male reproductive function should testosterone secretion be inadequate. Accordingly, we shall ignore them in discussing male reproduction. Estradiol—secreted in large amounts only by the ovaries—is also one of several steroid hormones, in this case hormones that have similar actions on the female reproductive tract and are collectively termed estrogens or, more commonly, simply **estrogen**. In the remainder of this chapter we shall follow the common practice of using this generic term rather than "estradiol," pointing out where relevant the situations in which an estrogen other than estradiol is produced by an extraovarian source and becomes important in the female.

The systems of ducts through which the sperm or ova are transported and the glands lining or emptying into the ducts are termed the **accessory reproductive organs**. In the female the breasts are also usually included in this category. The **secondary sexual characteristics** comprise the many external differences—hair distribution and body contours, for example—between males and females. The secondary sexual characteristics are not directly involved in reproduction.

Reproductive function is largely controlled by a chain of hormones (Figure 19-1). The first hormone in the chain is **gonadotropin releasing hormone (GnRH)**. As described in Chapter 10, GnRH is one of the hypophysiotropic hormones; that is, it is a hormone secreted by neuroendocrine cells in the hypothalamus and reaches the anterior pituitary via the hypothalamo-pituitary portal blood vessels. Accordingly, the brain is the primary regulator of the reproductive process.

Secretion of GnRH, like that of all the hypophysiotropic hormones, is triggered by action potentials in GnRH-producing hypothalamic neuroendocrine cells. These occur periodically in brief bursts, with virtually no secretion in between.[1] It is not yet known what underlies the rhythmical nature of the hypothalamic GnRH "pulse generator." This pattern of GnRH secretion is important because the anterior pituitary will not sustain a response to GnRH if the plasma concentration of this hormone remains elevated over time. The reason is that down-regulation of GnRH receptors occurs under such circumstances.

---

[1]The secretion pattern of GnRH has not been directly measured in humans because blood cannot be obtained from the hypothalamo-pituitary blood vessels in intact unanesthetized people. Its pattern has been inferred from the pattern of LH and FSH secretion from the anterior pituitary, since GnRH controls the secretion of these two hormones.

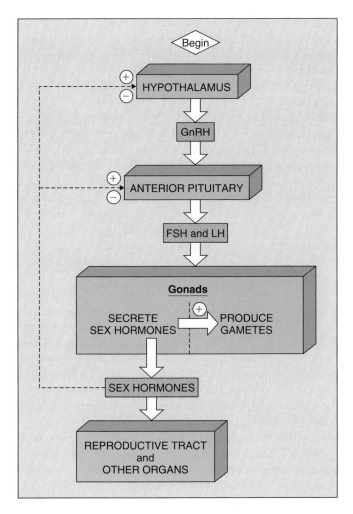

FIGURE 19-1

General pattern of reproduction control in both males and females. GnRH, like all hypothalamic hypophysiotropic hormones, reaches the anterior pituitary via the hypothalamo-pituitary portal vessels (Chapter 10). The arrow within the gonads denotes the fact that the sex hormones act locally, as paracrine agents, to stimulate gamete formation. Not shown in this introductory figure but described later is another hormone, inhibin, that is secreted by the gonads.

In the anterior pituitary, GnRH stimulates the release of the pituitary **gonadotropins—follicle-stimulating hormone (FSH)** and **luteinizing hormone (LH)**. These two protein hormones, which are produced by a single pituitary cell type, were named for their effects in the female, but their molecular structures are the same in both sexes. The two hormones act together upon the gonads, the result being gametogenesis and sex hormone secretion. In turn, the sex hormones exert many effects on all portions of the reproductive system, including the gonads from which they come and other parts of the body as well.

In addition, the steroidal sex hormones exert feedback effects on the secretion of GnRH, FSH, and LH. One other gonadal hormone—**inhibin**, which is a protein hormone—also exerts feedback effects on the anterior pituitary.

It must be emphasized that each link in this hormonal chain is essential, and malfunction of either the hypothalamus or the anterior pituitary can result in failure of sex hormone secretion and gametogenesis as surely as if the gonads themselves were diseased.

As a result of changes in the amount and pattern of hormonal secretions, reproductive function changes markedly during a person's lifetime and may be divided into the stages summarized in Table 19-1.

GENERAL PRINCIPLES OF GAMETOGENESIS

All cells at any point in gametogenesis are termed **germ cells**. These cells undergo either mitosis or the type of cell division known as meiosis. Because the general principles of gametogenesis are essentially the same in males and females, they are treated in this section, and features specific to the male or female are described later.

The first stage in gametogenesis is proliferation of the primordial germ cells by mitosis. Recall from our discussion of cell division in Chapter 4 that each nucleated human cell, *except the gametes*, contains 46 chromosomes, 23 from each parent. The two corresponding chromosomes in such a pair are said to be homologous to each other. In mitosis all the dividing cell's 46 chromosomes are replicated, and each of the two cells, termed daughter

---

TABLE 19-1 STAGES IN THE CONTROL OF REPRODUCTIVE FUNCTION

1. During the initial stage, which begins during fetal life and ends in the first year of life (infancy), GnRH, the gonadotropins, and gonadal sex hormones are secreted at relatively high levels.

2. From infancy to puberty, the secretion rates of these hormones are very low, and reproductive function in general is quiescent.

3. Beginning at puberty, hormonal secretion rates increase markedly, being stable in men but varying greatly in women during the menstrual cycle, and this ushers in the period of active reproduction.

4. Finally, reproductive function diminishes later in life as the gonads become less responsive to the gonadotropins, the ability to reproduce ceasing entirely in women.

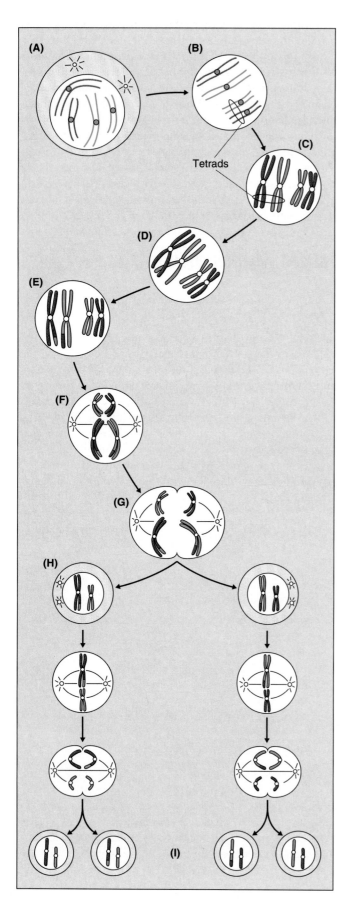

cells, resulting from the division receives a full set of 46 chromosomes—22 pairs of homologous chromosomes and 2 sex chromosomes (described later, in the section on sex determination)—identical to those of the original cell. Thus each daughter cell receives identical genetic information.

Mitosis of primordial germ cells, the first stage of gametogenesis, provides a supply of identical germ cells for the next stages. The timing of mitotic activity in germ cells differs greatly in females and males. In the female, mitosis of germ cells occurs exclusively during the individual's embryonic development. In the male, some mitosis occurs in the embryo to generate the population of germ cells present at birth, but mitosis really begins in earnest at puberty and usually continues throughout life.

The second stage of gametogenesis is **meiosis**, in which each resulting gamete receives only 23 chromosomes from a 46-chromosome germ cell, 1 chromosome from each homologous pair. Because a mature sperm and ovum each has only 23 chromosomes, their union at fertilization results in a cell with a full complement of 46 chromosomes.

Let us see how meiosis works, using Figure 19-2 in which the letters are keyed to the text. Meiosis consists of two cell divisions in succession, and the events preceding the first meiotic division are identical to those preceding a mitotic division (Chapter 4). During the interphase preceding this division, the DNA of the chromosomes was replicated. Thus the resting interphase cell still has 46 chromosomes, but each chromosome consists of two identical strands of DNA termed sister chromatids and joined together by a centromere (A).

As the first meiotic division begins, homologous chromosomes, each consisting of two identical sister chromatids, come together and line up point for point along their entire lengths. Thus, 23 four-chromatid groupings, called tetrads, are formed (B). The sister chromatids of each chromosome condense into thick rodlike structures and become highly visible (C). Then, within a tetrad, corresponding segments of homologous chromosomes come to overlap one another (D). At these points, portions of the homologous chromosomes break off and exchange with each other in a process known as **crossing-over** (E). Thus, crossing-over results in the recombination of genes on homologous chromosomes. Although crossing-over usually occurs, it is not required for meiosis to continue.

FIGURE 19-2

Stages of meiosis in a generalized germ cell. For simplicity, the initial cell (A), which is in interphase, is given only four chromosomes rather than 46, the human number. Also, cytoplasm is shown only in (A), (H), and (I). Chromosomes from one parent are red and those from the other parent are blue. The letters are keyed to descriptions in the text. (*Adapted from Carlson.*)

In the following manner the dividing cell's maternal and paternal chromosomes, partially scrambled because of crossing-over, are then distributed randomly to the two daughter cells, which will contain 23 chromosomes, each still consisting of two sister chromatids. Following crossing-over, the tetrads line up in the center of the cell so the maternal sister chromatids are on one side of the equatorial plain and the paternal on the other (F). The orientation of the tetrads on the equator is random, meaning that sometimes the maternal portion points "north" and sometimes the paternal portion points "north." The cell then divides (the first division of meiosis), with the two maternal sister chromatids of any tetrad going to one of the two cells resulting from the division, and the two paternal sister chromatids going to the other (G). Because of the random orientation at the equator, it is extremely unlikely that all 23 maternal chromosomes will end up in one cell and all 23 paternal chromosomes in the other. Over 8 million (2^{23}) different combinations of maternal and paternal chromosomes can result during this division.

The second division of meiosis occurs without any further replication of DNA. The two chromatids of each chromosome separate and move apart into the new daughter cells (H). The daughter cells resulting from the second meiotic division, therefore, contain 23 one-chromatid chromosomes (I).

To summarize, meiosis produces daughter cells having only 23 chromosomes, and two events during the first meiotic division contribute to the enormous genetic variability of the daughter cells: (1) crossing-over and (2) the random distribution of maternal chromatid pairs and paternal chromatid pairs between the two daughter cells.

SECTION A SUMMARY

GENERAL PRINCIPLES OF GAMETOGENESIS

I. The first stage of gametogenesis is mitosis of primordial germ cells.

II. This is followed by meiosis, a sequence of two cell divisions resulting in each gamete receiving 23 chromosomes.

III. Crossing-over and random distribution of maternal and paternal chromatids to the daughter cells during meiosis cause genetic variability in the gametes.

SECTION A KEY TERMS

gonads	gametogenesis
testes	gametes
ovaries	spermatozoa

sperm	secondary sexual
ova	characteristics
ovum	gonadotropin-releasing
sex hormones	hormone (GnRH)
testosterone	gonadotropins
estradiol	follicle-stimulating
progesterone	hormone (FSH)
androgens	luteinizing hormone (LH)
estrogen	inhibin
accessory reproductive	germ cells
organs	meiosis
	crossing-over

SECTION A REVIEW QUESTION

1. Describe the stages of gametogenesis and how meiosis results in genetic variability.

SECTION

B

MALE REPRODUCTIVE PHYSIOLOGY

ANATOMY

The male reproductive system includes the two testes, the system of ducts that store and transport sperm to the exterior, the glands that empty into these ducts, and the penis. The duct system, glands, and penis constitute the male accessory reproductive organs.

The testes are suspended outside the abdomen in the **scrotum**, which is an outpouching of the abdominal wall and is divided internally into two sacs, one for each testis. During embryonic development, the testes are located in the abdomen, but during the seventh month of intrauterine development, they descend into the scrotum. This descent is essential for normal sperm production during adulthood, since sperm formation requires a temperature

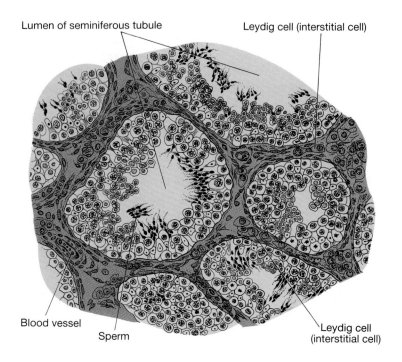

Lumen of seminiferous tubule

Leydig cell (interstitial cell)

Blood vessel

Sperm

Leydig cell (interstitial cell)

FIGURE 19-3

Cross section of an area of testis. The blue areas are the seminiferous tubules, the sites of sperm production. Mature sperm from each tubule are found in the tubular lumen. This low-power magnification is only for general orientation, and the positions of the other cells in the tubules are shown in a later figure (Figure 19-8). The tubules are separated from each other by interstitial space (colored pink) that contains Leydig cells and blood vessels.

several degrees lower than normal internal body temperature. This is achieved by air circulating around the scrotum and by a heat-exchange mechanism in the blood vessels supplying the testes. In contrast to spermatogenesis, testosterone secretion can usually occur normally at internal body temperature, and so failure of testes descent does not impair testosterone secretion.

The sites of sperm formation (**spermatogenesis**) in the testes are the many tiny, convoluted **seminiferous tubules** (Figure 19-3), the combined length of which is 250 m. Each seminiferous tubule is bounded by a basement membrane and a layer of smooth-muscle cells that are responsible for peristaltic movements of the tubules. In the center of each tubule is a fluid-filled lumen containing spermatozoa. The tubular wall is composed of developing germ cells and another cell type, to be described later, called Sertoli cells.

The **Leydig cells** (also called interstitial cells), which lie in small connective tissue spaces *between* the tubules, are the cells that secrete testosterone. Thus, the sperm-producing and testosterone-producing functions of the testes are carried out by different structures.

The seminiferous tubules from different areas of a testis unite to form a network of interconnected tubes, the rete testis (Figure 19-4). Small ducts termed efferent ductules leave the rete testis, pierce the fibrous covering of

FIGURE 19-4

Section of a testis. The upper portion of the testis has been removed to show its interior. On the right, the scrotal sac covering the epididymis and vas deferens has also been removed to show these structures.

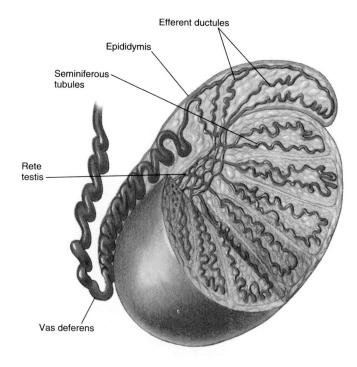

Efferent ductules

Epididymis

Seminiferous tubules

Rete testis

Vas deferens

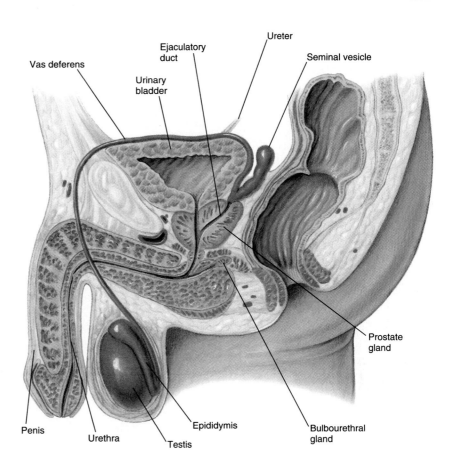

FIGURE 19-5

Anatomic organization of the male reproductive tract. This figure shows the testis, epididymis, vas deferens, ejaculatory duct, seminal vesicle, and bulbourethral gland on only one side of the body, but they are all paired structures. With the exception of the testes (the primary reproductive organs), these structures along with the prostate gland and penis constitute the accessory reproductive organs in the male. The urinary bladder and a ureter are shown for orientation but are not part of the reproductive tract. Once the ejaculatory ducts join the urethra in the prostate, the urinary and reproductive tracts have merged.

the testis, and empty into a single duct within a structure called the **epididymis** (plural *epididymides*). The epididymis is loosely attached to the outside of the testis, and the duct of the epididymis is so convoluted that, when straightened out at dissection, it measures 6 m. In turn, the epididymis draining each testis leads to a **vas** (or ductus) **deferens**, a large thick-walled tube. The vas deferens and the blood vessels and nerves supplying the testis are bound together in the **spermatic cord**, which passes through a slitlike passage, the inguinal canal, in the abdominal wall.

After entering the abdomen, the two vas deferens—one from each side—course to the back of the urinary bladder base (Figure 19-5) and become the **ejaculatory ducts**. Just at this transition, two large glands, the **seminal vesicles**, which lie behind the bladder, drain into the two vas deferens. The ejaculatory ducts then enter the substance of the **prostate gland** and join the urethra, coming from the bladder. The prostate gland is a single donut-shaped gland below the bladder and surrounding the upper part of the urethra, into which it secretes fluid through hundreds of tiny openings in the side of the urethra. The urethra leaves the prostate gland to enter the penis. The paired **bulbourethral glands**, lying below the prostate, drain into the urethra just after it leaves the prostate.

The prostate gland and seminal vesicles secrete the bulk of the fluid in which ejaculated sperm are suspended. This fluid, plus the sperm cells, constitute **semen**, the sperm contributing only a few percent of the total volume. The glandular secretions contain a large number of different chemical substances, including nutrients, buffers for protecting the sperm against the acidic vaginal secretions, and prostaglandins.[2] The function of the prostaglandins in semen is still not clear. The bulbourethral glands contribute a small volume of mucoid secretions.

In addition to providing a route for sperm from the seminiferous tubules to the exterior, several of the duct system segments perform additional functions to be described in the section on sperm transport.

SPERMATOGENESIS

The various stages of spermatogenesis are summarized in Figure 19-6. The undifferentiated germ cells, which are termed **spermatogonia** (singular *spermatogonium*) begin to divide mitotically at puberty. The daughter

---

[2]So named because it was originally thought that the prostaglandins in semen were produced by the prostate rather than at the actual site—the seminal vesicles.

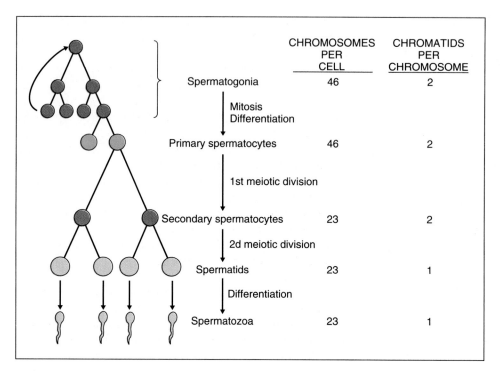

	CHROMOSOMES PER CELL	CHROMATIDS PER CHROMOSOME
Spermatogonia	46	2
Mitosis Differentiation		
Primary spermatocytes	46	2
1st meiotic division		
Secondary spermatocytes	23	2
2d meiotic division		
Spermatids	23	1
Differentiation		
Spermatozoa	23	1

FIGURE 19-6

Summary of spermatogenesis beginning at puberty. Each spermatogonium yields, by mitosis, a clone of spermatogonia. For simplicity, the figure shows only two such cycles, with a third mitotic cycle generating two primary spermatocytes. Each primary spermatocyte then yields two secondary spermatocytes, each of which yields two spermatids. Each of the spermatids contains 23 chromosomes and differentiates into a mature spermatozoan. Thus, each primary spermatocyte yields four sperm. The arrow from one of the spermatogonia back to an original spermatogonium denotes the fact that one cell of the clone does not go on to generate primary spermatocytes, but reverts to being an undifferentiated spermatogonium that gives rise to a new clone.

cells of this first division then divide, and so on for a specified number of division cycles so that a clone of spermatogonia is produced from each original spermatogonium. Some differentiation occurs as well as mitosis. The cells that result from the final mitotic division and differentiation in the series are called **primary spermatocytes**, and these are the cells that will undergo the first meiotic division of spermatogenesis.

It should be emphasized that if all the cells in the clone produced by each original spermatogonium followed this pathway, the spermatogonia would all disappear, that is, would all be converted to primary spermatocytes. This does not occur because, at an early point, one of the cells of each clone "drops out" of the mitosis-differentiation cycle and reverts to being a primitive spermatogonium that, at a later time, will enter into its own full sequence of divisions. In turn, one cell of the clone it produces will do likewise, and so on. Thus, the supply of spermatogonia does not decrease.

Each primary spermatocyte increases markedly in size

and undergoes the first meiotic division (Figure 19-2G) to form two **secondary spermatocytes**, each of which in turn undergoes the second meiotic division (Figure 19-2H) into two **spermatids**. Thus, each primary spermatocyte, containing 46 chromosomes, gives rise to four spermatids, each containing 23 chromosomes.

The final phase of spermatogenesis is the differentiation of the spermatids into spermatozoa. This process involves extensive cell remodeling, including elongation, but no further cell divisions. The head of a sperm (Figure 19-7) consists almost entirely of the nucleus, containing the DNA that bears the sperm's genetic information. The tip of the nucleus is covered by the **acrosome**, a protein-filled vesicle containing several enzymes that play an important role in the sperm's penetration of the ovum. Most of the tail is a flagellum—a group of contractile filaments that produce whiplike movements capable of propelling the sperm at a velocity of 1 to 4 mm/min. The sperm's mitochondria form the midpiece of the tail and provide the energy for the sperm's movement.

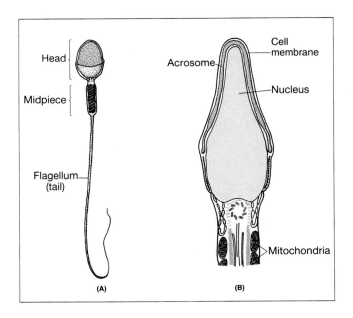

FIGURE 19-7

(A) Diagram of a human mature sperm. (B) A close-up of the head, The acrosome contains enzymes required for fertilization of the ovum.

In any small segment of each seminiferous tubule, spermatogenesis proceeds in a regular sequence. For example, at any given time, virtually all the primary spermatocytes in one portion of the tubule are undergoing division, whereas in an adjacent segment, all the secondary spermatocytes may be dividing. The entire process, from primary spermatocyte to sperm, takes approximately 64 days. The normal human male manufactures approximately 30 million sperm per day.

Thus far, we have described spermatogenesis without regard to its orientation within the seminiferous tubules or the participation of the second seminiferous-tubule cell type, the **Sertoli cell**, with which the developing germ cells are intimately associated. As noted earlier, each seminiferous tubule is surrounded by a basement membrane. Each Sertoli cell extends from the basement membrane all the way to the lumen in the center of the tubule and is joined to adjacent Sertoli cells by means of tight junctions (Figure 19-8). Thus, the Sertoli cells form an unbroken ring around the outer circumference of the seminiferous tubule, and the tight junctions divide the tubule into two compartments—a basal compartment between the basement membrane and the tight junctions, and a central compartment beginning at the tight junctions and including the lumen.

This arrangement has several very important results: (1) The ring of interconnected Sertoli cells forms a **blood-testis barrier**, which prevents the movement of many chemicals from the blood into the lumen of the seminifer-

ous tubule; and (2) different stages of spermatogenesis take place in different compartments and, hence, in different environments.

Mitosis of spermatogonia to yield primary spermatocytes takes place entirely in the basal compartment. The primary spermatocytes then move through the tight junctions of the Sertoli cells, which open in front of them while at the same time new tight junctions form behind them, to gain entry into the central compartment. In this central compartment, the meiotic divisions of spermatogenesis occur, and the spermatids are remodeled into spermatozoa while contained in recesses formed by invaginations of the Sertoli-cell plasma membranes. When sperm formation is completed, the Sertoli-cell cytoplasm around the sperm retracts, and the sperm are released into the lumen to be bathed by the luminal fluid.

Sertoli cells serve as the route by which nutrients reach developing germ cells, and they also secrete most of the fluid of the tubule lumen. This fluid has a highly characteristic ionic composition and contains **androgen-binding protein**, which binds testosterone that has been secreted by the Leydig cells and crossed the blood-testis barrier to enter the tubule. This maintains a high concentration of testosterone in the lumen of the duct system.

Thus far we have emphasized how Sertoli cells influence the ionic and nutritional environment of the germ cells, but they do more than this: They act as the "middleman" between the germ cells and the hormones that stimulate spermatogenesis. In other words, these hormones—FSH and testosterone, as we shall see—do not act directly on the germ cells but rather on the Sertoli cells, which in response secrete a variety of chemical messengers that function as paracrine agents to stimulate proliferation and differentiation of the germ cells. In addition, the Sertoli cells are the testicular cells that secrete the protein hormone inhibin. The many functions of Sertoli cells are summarized in Table 19-2.

TABLE 19-2 FUNCTIONS OF SERTOLI CELLS

1. Provide blood-testis barrier to chemicals
2. Nourish developing sperm
3. Secrete luminal fluid, including androgen-binding protein
4. Receive stimulation by testosterone and FSH to secrete paracrine agents that stimulate sperm production and maturation
5. Secrete the protein hormone inhibin, which inhibits FSH secretion
6. Phagocytize defective sperm
7. Secrete, during embryonic life, Müllerian inhibiting factor, which causes the primordial female duct system to regress

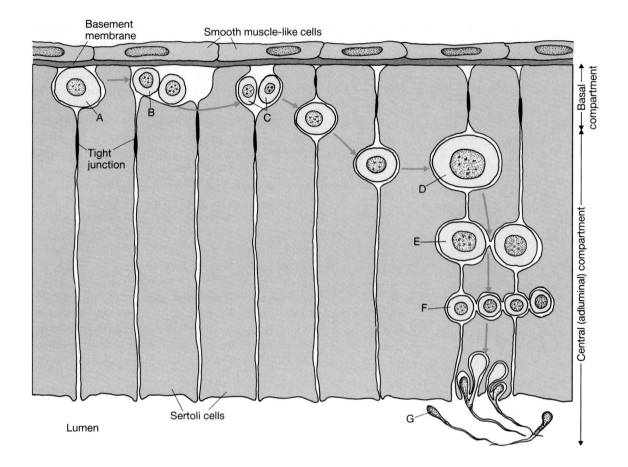

Basement membrane

Smooth muscle-like cells

Basal compartment

Tight junction

Sertoli cells

Lumen

Central (adluminal) compartment

FIGURE 19-8

Relation of the Sertoli cells (green) and germ cells (yellow). The Sertoli cells form a ring around the entire tubule. For convenience of presentation, the various stages of spermatogenesis are shown as though the germ cells move down a line of adjacent Sertoli cells. In reality, all stages beginning with any given spermatogonium take place between the same two Sertoli cells. Spermatogonia (A and B) are found only in the basal compartment (between the tight junctions of the Sertoli cells and the basement membrane of the tubule). After several mitotic cycles (A to B), the spermatogonia (B) give rise to primary spermatocytes (C). Each of the latter crosses a tight junction, enlarges (D), and divides into two secondary spermatocytes (E), which divide into spermatids (F), which in turn differentiate into spermatozoa (G). This last step involves loss of cytoplasm by the spermatids. (*Adapted from Tung.*)

TRANSPORT OF SPERM

From the seminiferous tubules, the sperm pass through the rete testis and efferent ductules into the epididymis and thence into the vas deferens. The vas deferens and the portion of the epididymis closest to it serve as a storage reservoir for sperm, holding them until sexual arousal leads to ejaculation.

Movement of the sperm as far as the epididymis results from the pressure created both by the continuous forma-tion of fluid by the Sertoli cells back in the seminiferous tubules and by peristalsis of the tubules. The sperm themselves are nonmotile at this time. During passage through the epididymis there occurs a hundredfold concentration of the sperm by fluid absorption from the lumen of the epididymis. Therefore, as the sperm pass from the end of the epididymis into the vas deferens, they are a densely packed mass whose transport is no longer a result of fluid movement but is due to peristaltic contractions of the smooth muscle in the epididymis and vas deferens. The absence of a large quantity of fluid accounts for the fact that ***vasectomy***—surgical tying-off and removal of a segment of each vas deferens—does not cause the accumulation of much fluid behind the tied-off point. (The sperm do build up, however, and eventually dissolve, their chemical components being absorbed into the bloodstream.) Vasectomy has no effect on testosterone secretion.

The next step in sperm transport is ejaculation, usually preceded by erection, which permits entry of the penis into the vagina.

Erection

The penis's becoming rigid—**erection**—is a vascular phenomenon. The penis consists almost entirely of three cylindrical vascular compartments running its entire length. Normally the small arteries supplying the vascular compartments are constricted so that the compartments contain little blood and the penis is flaccid. During sexual excitation, the small arteries dilate, the three vascular compartments become engorged with blood at high pressure, and the penis becomes rigid. The vascular dilation is accomplished by stimulation of the parasympathetic nerves and inhibition of the sympathetic nerves to the small arteries of the penis (Figure 19-9). (Note that these blood vessels are one of the exceptional cases that receive parasympathetic as well as sympathetic innervation.)

Moreover, as the vascular compartments expand, the veins emptying them are passively compressed, thus contributing to the engorgement. This entire process occurs rapidly, complete erection sometimes taking only 5 to 10 s.

Which receptors and afferent pathway initiate these reflexes? The primary tactile input comes from highly sensitive mechanoreceptors in the genital region, particularly in the head of the penis. The afferent fibers carrying the impulses synapse in the lower spinal cord on interneurons which trigger the efferent outflow.

It must be stressed, however, that higher brain centers, via descending pathways from the hypothalamus, may also exert profound stimulatory or inhibitory effects upon the autonomic neurons to the small arteries of the penis. Thus, mechanical stimuli from areas other than the penis as well as thoughts, emotions, sight, and odors, can induce erection in the complete absence of penile stimulation.

Impotence, the consistent inability to achieve or sustain an erection of sufficient rigidity for sexual intercourse, is a common disorder, affecting an estimated 10 million Americans. It is very much age-dependent, increasing from an incidence of 2 percent at age 40 to 25 percent at age 65. The organic causes are multiple and include damage to the efferent nerves or descending pathways, endocrine disorders, various therapeutic and "recreational"

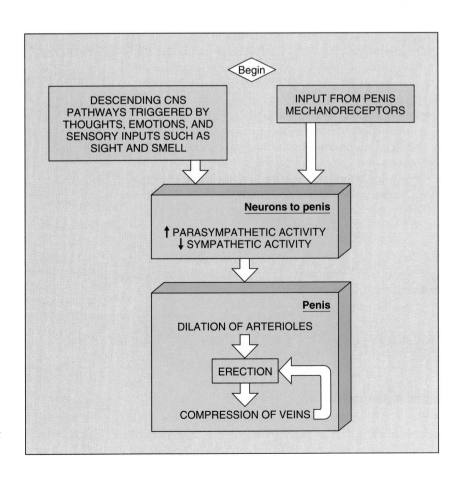

FIGURE 19-9

Reflex pathways for erection. The reflex can be initiated by mechanoreceptors in the penis and/or by input from the brain. Nitric oxide is an important vasodilator of the arterioles in this reflex.

drugs (alcohol, for example), and certain diseases, particularly diabetes. Impotence can also be due to psychological factors, which influence the brain and, hence, the descending pathways.

Ejaculation

The discharge of semen from the penis—**ejaculation**—is also basically a spinal reflex, the afferent pathways from penile mechanoreceptors being identical to those described for erection. When the level of stimulation produces sufficient summation of synaptic potentials, there is elicited a patterned automatic sequence of efferent discharge that can be divided into two phases: (1) The smooth muscles of the epididymus, vas deferens, ejaculatory ducts, prostate, and seminal vesicles contract as a result of sympathetic stimulation, emptying the sperm and glandular secretions into the urethra (**emission**); and (2) the semen (average volume 3 ml, containing 300 million sperm) is then expelled from the urethra by a series of rapid contractions of the urethral smooth muscle as well as the skeletal muscle at the base of the penis. During ejaculation, the sphincter at the base of the bladder is closed so that sperm cannot enter the bladder nor can urine be expelled from it. It is worth noting that although *erection* involves *inhibition* of sympathetic nerves (to the small arteries of the penis), *ejaculation* involves *stimulation* of sympathetic nerves (to the smooth muscles of the duct system).

The rhythmical muscular contractions that occur during ejaculation are associated with intense pleasure and many systemic physiological changes, the entire event being termed an **orgasm**. Marked skeletal muscle contractions occur throughout the body, and there is a large increase in heart rate and blood pressure. This is followed by the rapid onset of muscular and psychological relaxation.

Once ejaculation has occurred, there is a latent period during which a second erection is not possible. The latent period is quite variable but may last from minutes to hours.

As is true of erection, premature ejaculation, failure to ejaculate, or lack of a generalized orgasm at the time of ejaculation can be the result of influence by higher brain centers.

HORMONAL CONTROL OF MALE REPRODUCTIVE FUNCTIONS

Control of the Testes

Figure 19-10 summarizes the control of the testes. In a normal adult man, the GnRH-secreting neuroendocrine cells fire a brief burst of action potentials approximately

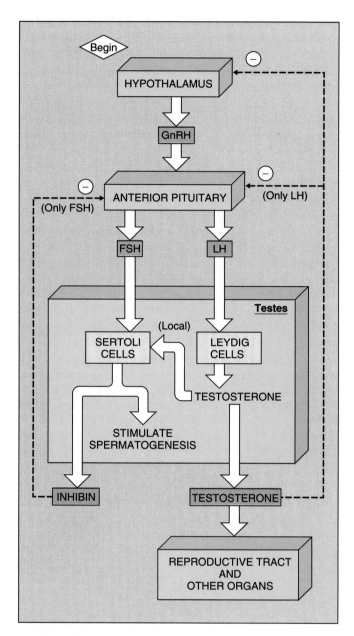

FIGURE 19-10

Summary of hormonal control of male reproductive function. GnRH reaches the anterior pituitary via the hypothalamo-pituitary portal vessels. Note that FSH acts only on the Sertoli cells, and its secretion is inhibited by inhibin, a protein hormone secreted by the Sertoli cells. LH acts only on the Leydig cells, and its secretion is inhibited by testosterone, the hormone secreted by the Leydig cells. Testosterone, acting locally, is essential for spermatogenesis.

every 2 h, secreting GnRH at these times. The GnRH reaching the anterior pituitary during each periodic pulse triggers the release from the anterior pituitary of both LH and FSH, although not necessarily in equal amounts. Accordingly, systemic plasma concentrations of FSH and LH also show rhythmical episodic changes—rapid increases during the pulse followed by slow decreases over the next 90 min or so as the hormones are slowly removed from the plasma.

There is a clear separation of the actions of FSH and LH within the testes (Figure 19-10): FSH acts on the Sertoli cells to stimulate the production of paracrine agents that stimulate spermatogenesis and other Sertoli cell functions; in contrast, LH acts on the Leydig cells to stimulate testosterone secretion. Recall that the Leydig cells lie in the small triangular interstitial spaces between the seminiferous tubules. In addition to its many important systemic effects as a hormone, the testosterone secreted by these cells also acts locally, as a paracrine agent, on spermatogenesis by moving from the interstitial spaces into the seminiferous tubules. There, testosterone enters Sertoli cells, and it is via these cells that it facilitates spermatogenesis. It must be emphasized that, despite the absence of any *direct* effect of LH on spermatogenesis, this hormone exerts an essential *indirect* effect because the testosterone secretion stimulated by LH is required for spermatogenesis.[3]

The last components of the hypothalamo-pituitary control of male reproduction that remain to be discussed are the negative feedbacks exerted by testicular hormones. That such inhibition exists is evidenced by the fact that **castration** (removal of the gonads) results in marked increases in the secretion of both LH and FSH. For this discussion it is important to realize that even though FSH and LH are produced by a single cell, their secretion rates can be altered to different degrees by negative-feedback inputs.

Testosterone inhibits mainly LH secretion. It does so in two ways (Figure 19-10): (1) It acts on the hypothalamus to decrease the frequency of GnRH bursts, thereby resulting in less GnRH reaching the pituitary over any given period of time; and (2) it acts on the anterior pituitary to cause less LH secretion, but not less FSH secretion, in response to any given level of GnRH. This direct action on the pituitary helps explain why testosterone inhibits LH secretion so much more than it does FSH secretion.[4]

How does the presence of functioning testes reduce FSH secretion if not via testosterone? The major inhibitory signal, exerted directly on the anterior pituitary, is the protein hormone inhibin secreted by the Sertoli cells (Figure 19-10). That the Sertoli cells, via inhibin, are the major source of feedback inhibition of FSH secretion makes sense since, as pointed out above, the facilitatory effect of FSH on spermatogenesis is exerted via the Sertoli cells. Thus, these cells are in all ways the link between FSH and spermatogenesis.

Despite these complexities, one should not lose sight of the fact that the total amounts of GnRH, LH, FSH, and testosterone secreted and of sperm produced are relatively constant from day to day in the adult male.[5] This is completely different from the large cyclical swings of activity so characteristic of the female reproductive processes.

Testosterone

In addition to its essential paracrine action within the testes on spermatogenesis and its negative-feedback effects on the hypothalamus and anterior pituitary, testosterone exerts a large number of other effects, as summarized in Table 19-3.

Accessory Reproductive Organs. The fetal differentiation, growth, and function of the entire male duct system, glands, and penis all depend upon testosterone. Following castration in the adult, all the accessory reproductive or-

---

[3]It is an unsettled question whether the hormonal requirements for maintenance of spermatogenesis in adult men differ from those needed for its initiation at puberty. It is possible that once FSH and testosterone, acting together, have initiated spermatogenesis at puberty, only testosterone is required for maintaining it. This question has important implications for the development of a male contraceptive.

[4]There is now good evidence that the testes secrete estrogen as well as testosterone and that this estrogen also inhibits LH secretion.

[5]However, this is not to say that the interplay among GnRH, LH, FSH, testosterone, and inhibin results in absolutely unchangeable levels of these hormones. The GnRH-secreting cells in the hypothalamus receive much synaptic input from other neurons, some excitatory and some inhibitory. This input can cause changes in the frequency at which the GnRH pulses occur and, hence, changes in the average rates at which FSH, LH, and testosterone are secreted. For example, watching sexually arousing movies causes a marked increase in the secretion of all these hormones.

TABLE 19-3 EFFECTS OF TESTOSTERONE IN THE MALE

1. Required for spermatogenesis (acts via Sertoli cells)
2. Decreases GnRH secretion via an action on the hypothalamus
3. Inhibits LH secretion via an action on the anterior pituitary
4. Induces and maintains differentiation of male accessory reproductive organs and maintains their function
5. Induces male secondary sex characteristics
6. Stimulates protein anabolism, bone growth, and cessation of bone growth
7. Maintains sex drive and may enhance aggressive behavior

gans decrease in size, the glands markedly reduce their secretion rates, and the smooth-muscle activity of the ducts is diminished. Erection and ejaculation may be deficient. These defects disappear upon the administration of testosterone.

Secondary Sex Characteristics and Growth. Virtually all the male secondary sex characteristics are dependent on testosterone. For example, a male castrated before puberty does not develop a beard or either underarm or pubic hair. Other testosterone-dependent secondary sexual characteristics are deepening of the voice resulting from growth of the larynx, thick secretion of the skin oil glands (this predisposes to acne), and the masculine pattern of fat distribution. As described in Chapter 18, testosterone also stimulates bone growth, largely indirectly through its stimulation of growth hormone secretion, but ultimately shuts off bone growth by causing closure of the bones' epiphyseal plates. Also as described in Chapter 18, testosterone is an "anabolic steroid" in that it exerts a direct stimulatory effect on protein synthesis in muscle. Interestingly, testosterone is necessary for expression of the gene that determines the common type of baldness ("male pattern") in men.

Behavior. Testosterone is essential in males for the development of sex drive at puberty. It also plays an important role in maintaining sex drive in the adult male, although men often remain sexually active, albeit usually at a reduced level, for years after castration.

A controversial question is whether testosterone influences other human behaviors in addition to sexual behavior; that is, are there any other inherent male-female behavior differences, or are any observed differences all socially conditioned? It has proven very difficult to answer such questions with respect to human beings, but there is little doubt that behavioral differences based on gender do exist in other mammals. For example, aggression is clearly greater in males and is testosterone-dependent.

Mechanism of Action. Like other steroid hormones, testosterone crosses plasma membranes readily and, within target cells, combines with specific receptors for it. In the cell's nucleus the activated receptor influences the transcription of certain genes into messenger RNA. The result is a change in the rate at which the target cell synthesizes the proteins for which these genes code. It is the changes in the concentrations of these proteins that underlie the cell's overall response to the hormone. For example, testosterone induces in the prostate gland increased synthesis of enzymes that catalyze formation of the gland's secretions.

In Chapter 10 we mentioned that hormones sometimes must undergo transformation in their target cells in order to be effective, and this is true of testosterone in many (but not all) of its target cells. In some, for example those of the prostate, after its entry into the cytoplasm, testosterone undergoes an enzyme-mediated conversion to another steroid, **dihydrotestosterone**, and it is mainly this molecule that then induces effects. In still other target cells, including brain, testosterone is transformed not to dihydrotestosterone but to estradiol, which is the active hormone in these cells. Note in this latter case that the male sex hormone must be converted to the female sex hormone to be active.

Prolactin

Another anterior pituitary hormone, **prolactin**, probably has significant functions in men (again, as we shall see, its name—"for lactation"—reflects its long-recognized major function in women). It may potentiate the stimulatory effects of LH on Leydig cells and of testosterone on many of its target cells.

SECTION B SUMMARY

SPERMATOGENESIS

I. The male gonads, the testes, produce sperm in the seminiferous tubules and secrete testosterone from the Leydig cells.

II. The meiotic divisions of spermatogenesis result in each sperm containing 23 chromosomes, compared to the original 46 of the spermatogonia.

III. The developing germ cells are intimately associated with the Sertoli cells, which perform many functions, as summarized in Table 19-2.

TRANSPORT OF SPERM

I. From the seminiferous tubules, the sperm pass through the epididymis, where they are concentrated.

II. The epididymis and vas deferens store the sperm, and the seminal vesicles and prostate secrete the bulk of the semen.

III. Erection of the penis occurs because of vascular engorgement accomplished by relaxation of the small arteries and passive occlusion of the veins.

IV. Ejaculation includes emission—emptying of semen into the urethra—followed by expulsion of the semen from the urethra.

HORMONAL CONTROL OF MALE REPRODUCTIVE FUNCTIONS

I. Hypothalamic GnRH stimulates the anterior pituitary to secrete FSH and LH, which then act on the testes: FSH on the Sertoli cells to stimulate spermatogenesis and inhibin secretion, and LH on the Leydig cells to stimulate testosterone secretion.

II. Testosterone, acting locally on the Sertoli cells, is essential for maintaining spermatogenesis.

III. Testosterone exerts a negative-feedback inhibition on both the hypothalamus and the anterior pituitary to reduce LH secretion. Inhibin exerts a negative-feedback inhibition on FSH secretion.

IV. Testosterone maintains the accessory reproductive organs and male secondary sex characteristics and stimulates growth of muscle and bone. In many of its target cells it must first undergo transformation to dihydrotestosterone or to estrogen.

SECTION B KEY TERMS

scrotum	vas deferens
spermatogenesis	spermatic cord
seminiferous tubules	ejaculatory ducts
Leydig cells	seminal vesicles
epididymis	prostate gland
bulbourethral glands	blood-testis barrier
semen	androgen-binding protein
spermatogonia	erection
primary spermatocytes	ejaculation
secondary spermatocytes	emission
spermatids	orgasm
acrosome	dihydrotestosterone
Sertoli cell	prolactin

SECTION B REVIEW QUESTIONS

1. Describe the sequence of events leading from spermatogonia to sperm.

2. List the functions of the Sertoli cells.

3. Describe the path taken by sperm from the seminiferous tubules to the urethra.

4. State the roles of the prostate gland, seminal vesicles, and bulbourethral glands in the formation of semen.

5. Describe the neural control of erection and ejaculation.

6. Diagram the hormonal chain controlling the testes. Contrast the effects of FSH and LH.

7. What are the feedback controls from the testes to the hypothalamus and pituitary?

8. List the effects of testosterone on accessory reproductive organs, secondary sex characteristics, growth, protein metabolism, and behavior.

SECTION

C

FEMALE REPRODUCTIVE PHYSIOLOGY

Unlike the continuous sperm production of the male, the production of the female gamete, followed by its release from the ovary—**ovulation**—is cyclical. This cyclical pattern is also true for the function and structure of virtually the entire female reproductive system. In human beings, these cycles are called **menstrual cycles**. The length of a menstrual cycle varies considerably from woman to woman and in any particular woman, but averages about 28 days. The first day of menstrual bleeding **(menstruation)** is termed day 1.

The events of the menstrual cycle are complex, and some orientation to our approach at this point may be useful. The most obvious event of a menstrual cycle in which pregnancy does not occur is, of course, menstruation, which is the result of events occurring in the uterus—

the source of menstrual bleeding. However, the uterine events of the menstrual cycle are due entirely to cyclical changes in hormone secretion by the ovaries. Moreover, the ovaries, as we have stated, are the sites of gamete production, normally one per menstrual cycle. For these reasons, after summarizing the anatomy of the female reproductive tract, we begin our discussion of the menstrual cycle with the ovaries and their interactions with the anterior pituitary and hypothalamus. It is these interactions that produce the cyclical changes in the ovaries that result in (1) generation of a gamete each cycle, and (2) hormone secretions that cause cyclical changes in the entire female reproductive tract, including the uterus. The uterine changes ready this organ to receive and nourish the gamete, and only when pregnancy does not occur does menstruation occur. After describing the full menstrual cycle as it occurs in the absence of pregnancy, we then describe the events of pregnancy, delivery, and lactation.

ANATOMY

The female reproductive system includes the two ovaries and the female reproductive tract—two uterine tubes, a uterus, and a vagina. These structures are also termed the **female internal genitalia** (Figure 19-11A and B). In the female, unlike in the male, the urinary and reproductive duct systems are entirely separate from each other.

The ovaries are almond-sized organs in the upper pelvic cavity, one on each side of the uterus. The ends of the **uterine tubes** (also known as oviducts or fallopian tubes) are not directly attached to the ovaries but open into the abdominal cavity close to them. The opening of each uterine tube is funnel-shaped and surrounded by long, finger-like projections (the fimbriae) lined with ciliated epithe-

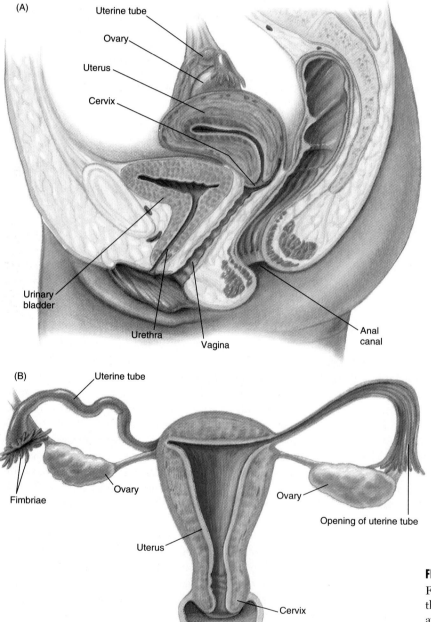

(A)

Uterine tube
Ovary
Uterus
Cervix
Urinary bladder
Urethra
Vagina
Anal canal

(B)

Uterine tube
Fimbriae
Ovary
Uterus
Vagina
Ovary
Opening of uterine tube
Cervix

FIGURE 19-11

Female reproductive system. (A) Section through a female pelvis. (B) Diagram cut away on the right to show the continuity between the organs of the reproductive duct system—uterine tubes, uterus, and vagina.

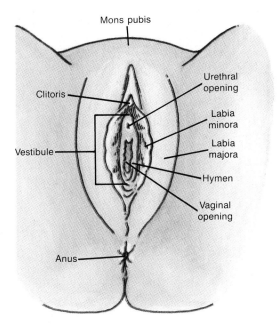

FIGURE 19-12
Female external genitalia.

lium. The other ends of the uterine tubes are attached to the uterus and empty directly into its cavity. The **uterus** is a hollow, thick-walled muscular organ lying between the urinary bladder and rectum. It is the source of bleeding during menstruation and it houses the fetus during pregnancy. The lower portion of the uterus is the **cervix**. A small opening in the cervix leads to the **vagina**, the canal leading from the uterus to the outside.

The **female external genitalia** (Figure 19-12) include the mons pubis, labia majora, labia minora, clitoris, vestibule of the vagina, and vestibular glands. The term **vulva** is another name for all these structures. The mons pubis is the rounded fatty prominence over the junction of the pubic bones. The labia majora, the female analog of the scrotum,[6] are two prominent skin folds that form the outer lips of the vulva. The labia minora are small skin folds lying between the labia majora. They surround the urethral and vaginal openings, and the area thus enclosed is the vestibule, into which the vestibular glands empty. The vaginal opening lies behind that of the urethra. Partially overlying the vaginal opening is a thin fold of mucous membrane, the **hymen**. The **clitoris**, the female analog of the penis, is an erectile structure located at the front of the vulva.

---

[6]The term "analog" or "homolog" used frequently in this chapter does not imply that one structure is dominant and its analog somehow an inferior imitation. It simply means that the two structures are derived embryologically from the same source and/or have similar functions.

OVARIAN FUNCTION

As noted at the beginning of this chapter, the ovary, like the testis, serves a dual purpose: (1) **oogenesis**, the production of gametes—the ova; and (2) secretion of the female steroidal sex hormones, estrogen and progesterone, as well as the peptide hormone inhibin. Before ovulation, the gametogenic and endocrine functions take place in a single structure—the follicle—and after ovulation the follicle, now without an ovum, differentiates into a corpus luteum, which has only an endocrine function. For comparison, recall that in the testes the production of gametes and the secretion of sex steroids take place in different compartments—in the seminiferous tubules and in the Leydig cells, respectively.

This section will describe the events that occur in the ovary during a menstrual cycle, and the next section will replay these events, adding the controls.

Oogenesis

First, a word about terminology is appropriate: As we shall see, the female germ cells, like those of the male, have different names at different stages of development; it is helpful to use the term **egg** to refer to the germ cells at any stage.

At birth, a female's ovaries contain an estimated total of 2 to 4 million eggs, and no new ones appear after birth. Thus, in marked contrast to the male, the newborn female already has all the germ cells she will ever have. Only a few, perhaps 400, are destined to be ovulated. All the others degenerate at some point in their development so that few, if any, remain by the time a woman reaches approximately 50 years of age. One result of this developmental pattern is that the eggs that are ovulated near age 50 are 35 to 40 years older than those ovulated just after puberty. It has been suggested that certain defects more common among children born to older women are the result of aging changes in the egg.

During early fetal development, the primitive germ cells, or **oogonia** (singular *oogonium*), a term analogous to spermatogonia in the male, undergo numerous mitotic divisions (Figure 19-13). Around the third month of fetal life, the oogonia cease dividing, and from this point on no new germ cells are generated. In the fetus, all the oogonia develop into **primary oocytes** (analogous to primary spermatocytes), which then begin a first meiotic division by replicating their DNA. They do not, however, complete the division. Accordingly, all the germ cells present at birth are primary oocytes containing 46 chromosomes, each with two sister chromatids. The cells are said to be in a state of **meiotic arrest**.

This state continues until puberty and the onset of re-

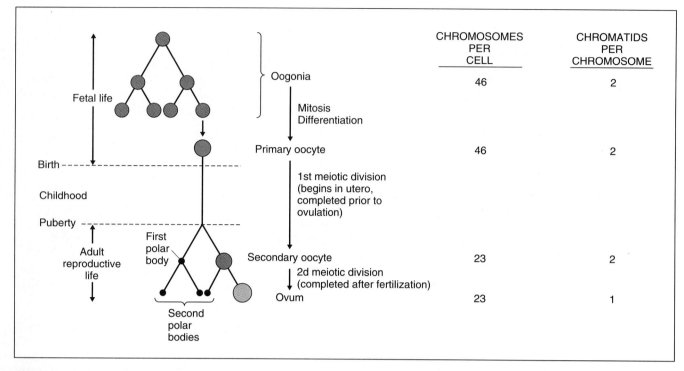

	CHROMOSOMES PER CELL	CHROMATIDS PER CHROMOSOME
Oogonia	46	2
Primary oocyte	46	2
Secondary oocyte	23	2
Ovum	23	1

FIGURE 19-13

Summary of oogenesis. Compare with the male pattern of Figure 19-6. The secondary oocyte is ovulated and does not complete its meiotic division unless it is penetrated (fertilized) by a sperm. Thus, it is a semantic oddity that the egg is not termed an ovum until after fertilization occurs. Note that each primary oocyte yields only one secondary oocyte, which can yield only one ovum.

newed activity in the ovaries. Indeed, only those primary oocytes destined for ovulation will ever complete the first meiotic division, for it occurs just before the egg is ovulated. This division is analogous to the division of the primary spermatocyte, and each daughter cell receives 23 chromosomes, each with two chromatids. In this division, however, one of the two daughter cells, the **secondary oocyte**, retains virtually all the cytoplasm. The other, termed the **first polar body**, is very small and adheres to the secondary oocyte. Thus, the primary oocyte, which is already as large as the ovum will be, passes on to the secondary oocyte half of its chromosomes but almost all of its nutrient-rich cytoplasm.

The second meiotic division occurs, in a uterine tube, *after ovulation* but only if the secondary oocyte is fertilized, that is, penetrated by a sperm. As a result of this division the daughter cells each receive 23 chromosomes, each with a single chromatid. Once again, one daughter cell, now termed an ovum, retains nearly all the cytoplasm, whereas the other, termed the **second polar body**, is very small and nonfunctional. Interestingly, the first polar body also undergoes a second meiotic division at the same time

the secondary oocyte does. However, as far as is known, neither of the resulting cells nor the second polar body is fertilized, and they all eventually disintegrate. The net result of oogenesis is that each primary oocyte produces only one ovum (Figure 19-13).[7] In contrast, each primary spermatocyte produces four viable spermatozoa.

Follicle Growth

Throughout their life in the ovaries, the eggs exist in structures known as **follicles**. Follicles begin as **primordial follicles**, which consist of one primary oocyte surrounded by a single layer of cells called **granulosa cells**. Further development from the primordial follicle stage (Figure 19-14) is characterized by an increase in the size of the oocyte, a proliferation of the granulosa cells into mul-

---

[7]Since the final stage of gametogenesis—formation of the ovum—occurs only after fertilization and since fertilization occurs *outside* the ovary (in a uterine tube, as we shall see), technically the *ovaries* do not themselves produce the fully mature gametes—the ova—but only secondary oocytes; this technicality is universally ignored in talking about the ovarian function of gamete production.

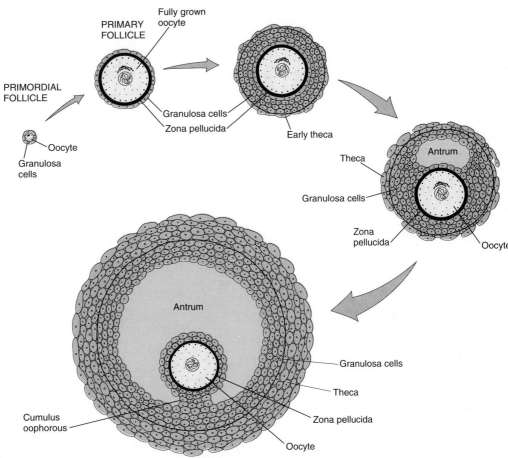

FIGURE 19-14

Development of a human oocyte (yellow) and ovarian follicle. (*Adapted from Erickson et al.*)

tiple layers, and the separation of the oocyte from the inner granulosa cells by a thick layer of material, the **zona pellucida**. The granulosa cells secrete estrogen, small amounts of progesterone just before ovulation, and the peptide hormone inhibin.

Despite the presence of a zona pellucida, however, the inner layer of granulosa cells remains intimately associated with the oocyte by means of cytoplasmic processes that traverse the zona pellucida and form gap junctions with the oocyte. Through these gap junctions, nutrients and chemical messengers are passed to the oocyte. For example, the granulosa cells produce one or more factors that act on the oocyte to maintain it in meiotic arrest. Granulosa cells also have gap junctions with each other so the entire structure functions as a syncitium.

As the follicle grows by mitosis of granulosa cells, connective-tissue cells surrounding the granulosa cells differentiate and form layers known as the **theca**, which plays an important role in estrogen secretion by the granulosa cells, as we shall see. Shortly after this, the primary oocyte reaches full size (115 μm in diameter), and a fluid-filled space, the **antrum**, begins to form in the midst of the granulosa cells as a result of fluid they secrete.

The progression of some primordial follicles to the preantral stage occurs continuously, so that at any moment most of the follicles present are still primordial but there are always present a relatively constant number of preantral follicles. At the beginning of each menstrual cycle, 10 to 25 of these preantral follicles begin to develop into antral follicles; what causes these particular follicles to be selected is unknown. About 1 week into the cycle, a further selection process occurs: Only one follicle, the **dominant follicle**, continues to develop, and the others that had begun to enlarge undergo a degenerative process called **atresia**. The eggs in these follicles also die.

Atresia is not limited just to antral follicles, however, for follicles can undergo atresia at all stages of development. Indeed, this process begins in utero so that the 2 to 4 million follicles and eggs present at birth represent only a small fraction of those present at an earlier time in the fetus. Atresia then continues all through prepubertal life so that only 200,000 to 400,000 follicles remain when active reproductive life begins.

As the dominant follicle enlarges, mainly as a result of its expanding antrum, the granulosa cell layers surrounding the egg form a mound that projects into the antrum and is termed the cumulus oophorous (the cumulus cells immediately surrounding the egg are termed the corona radiata). As ovulation approaches, the egg completes its first meiotic division to become a secondary oocyte. The cumulus separates from the follicle wall so that it and the oocyte it surrounds float free in the antral fluid. The mature follicle (also termed a graafian follicle) becomes so large (diameter about 1.5 cm) that it balloons out on the surface of the ovary.

Ovulation occurs when the thin walls of the follicle and ovary at the site where they are joined rupture and the secondary oocyte, surrounded by its tightly adhering zona pellucida and the cumulus of granulosa cells, are carried out of the ovary and onto the ovarian surface by the antral fluid. All this happens on approximately day 14 of the menstrual cycle.

On occasion (1 to 2 percent of all cycles), two or more follicles reach maturity, and more than one egg may be ovulated. This is the commonest cause of multiple births. In such cases the siblings are fraternal, not identical, because the eggs carry different sets of genes.

Formation of the Corpus Luteum

After the mature follicle discharges its antral fluid and egg, its remnant in the ovary collapses around the antrum and undergoes a rapid transformation. The granulosa cells enlarge greatly, newly formed capillaries move into the interior, and the entire glandlike structure is known as the **corpus luteum**, which secretes estrogen, progesterone, and inhibin. If the discharged egg, now in the uterine tube, is not fertilized, the corpus luteum reaches its maximum development within approximately 10 days and then rapidly degenerates. As we shall see, it is the loss of corpus luteum function that leads to menstruation and the beginning of a new menstrual cycle.

In terms of ovarian function, therefore, the menstrual cycle may be divided into two phases approximately equal in length and separated by ovulation (Figure 19-15): (1) the **follicular phase**, during which a single mature follicle and secondary oocyte develop; and (2) the **luteal phase**, beginning after ovulation and lasting until the demise of the corpus luteum.

Sites of Secretion of Ovarian Hormones

This is a good place to review the sites of ovarian hormone secretion. Estrogen is secreted during the follicular phase mainly by the granulosa cells; following ovulation, it is secreted by the corpus luteum. Progesterone, the other major ovarian steroid hormone, is secreted in very small amounts by the granulosa and theca cells just before ovulation, but its major source is the corpus luteum.

Inhibin, a peptide hormone, is secreted by both the granulosa cells and corpus luteum.[8]

The actions of these ovarian hormones will be described in the next sections of this chapter where we take up the control of female reproduction.

CONTROL OF OVARIAN FUNCTION

The basic factors controlling ovarian function are analogous to the controls described for testicular function in that they constitute a hormonal series made up of GnRH, the anterior pituitary gonadotropins FSH and LH, and gonadal sex hormones—estrogen and progesterone. We say "basic" factors because these hormones are not the exclusive regulators of ovarian function. Several other hormones (insulin, for example) and growth factors (for example, the insulin-like growth factors) may play important but still poorly understood roles. The growth factors are produced by granulosa and theca cells and function as paracrine and autocrine agents.

[8]Another peptide hormone, relaxin, is also produced by the corpus luteum, but the function of this hormone in humans is uncertain.

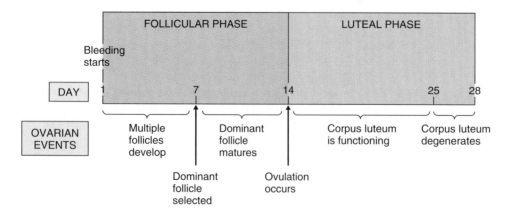

FIGURE 19-15

Summary of ovarian events during a menstrual cycle. The first day of the cycle, the onset of menstrual bleeding, is named for a uterine event even when ovarian events are used to denote the cycle phases.

As in the male, the entire sequence of basic controls depends upon the secretion of GnRH from hypothalamic neuroendocrine cells in episodic pulses. In the female, however, the frequency of these pulses and hence the total amount of GnRH secreted during a 24-h period change in a patterned manner over the course of the menstrual cycle. So does the responsiveness both of the anterior pituitary to GnRH and of the ovaries to FSH and LH.

For purposes of orientation, let us look first, in Figure 19-16, at the patterns of plasma hormone concentrations in systemic venous plasma during a normal menstrual cycle (GnRH is not shown since its important concentration is in the hypothalamo-pituitary plasma). It should be understood that each value is an *average daily concentration*; that is, the rises and falls during a single day stemming from episodic secretion have been averaged to yield a single value. For now, ignore both the legend and circled numbers in this figure since we are concerned here only with hormonal patterns, not the explanations of these patterns.

Note that FSH is slightly elevated in the early part of the follicular phase and then steadily decreases throughout

FIGURE 19-16

Summary of plasma hormone concentrations and ovarian events during the menstrual cycle. The events marked by the circled numbers are described later in the text and are listed here to provide a summary. The arrows in this legend denote causality. There are no arrows preceding numbers 4 and 14 because the causes of these events are not yet known. (1) FSH and LH secretion increase (because plasma estrogen concentration is low and exerting little negative feedback).→(2) Multiple follicles begin to enlarge and secrete estrogen.→(3) Plasma estrogen concentration begins to rise. (4) One follicle becomes dominant (? cause) and secretes very large amounts of estrogen.→(5) Plasma estrogen level increases markedly.→(6) FSH secretion and plasma FSH concentration decrease, but then (7) plasma estrogen reaches levels high enough to exert a positive feedback on gonadotropin secretion.→(8) An LH surge is triggered.→(9) The egg completes its first meiotic division and cytoplasmic maturation while the follicle secretes less estrogen accompanied by some progesterone, (10) ovulation occurs, and (11) the corpus luteum forms and begins to secrete large amounts of both estrogen and progesterone.→(12) Plasma estrogen and progesterone increase.→(13) FSH and LH secretion are inhibited and their plasma concentrations progressively fall. (14) The corpus luteum begins to degenerate (? cause) and decrease its hormone secretion.→ (15) Plasma estrogen and progesterone concentrations fall.→(16) FSH and LH secretion begin to increase, and a new cycle begins.

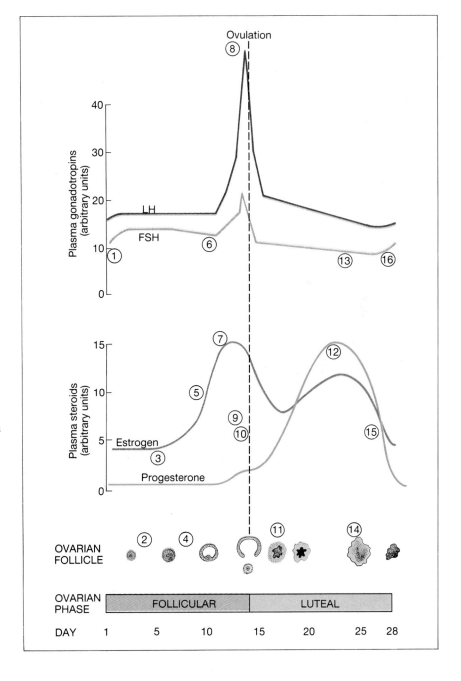

the remainder of the cycle except for a midcycle peak. The average daily concentration of LH is constant during most of the follicular phase but then shows a large midcycle rise—the **LH surge**—peaking approximately 18 h before ovulation, followed by a rapid return to presurge values and then a further slow decline during the luteal phase.

The estrogen pattern is more complex. After remaining fairly low and stable for the first week, it rises rapidly during the second week as the ovarian follicle grows and secretes it. Estrogen then starts falling shortly after LH has peaked. This is followed by a second rise, due to secretion by the corpus luteum, and finally, a rapid decline during the last days of the cycle. The progesterone pattern is simplest of all: Virtually no progesterone is secreted by the ovaries during the follicular phase until just before ovulation, but very soon after ovulation, the developing corpus luteum begins to secrete large amounts of progesterone, and from this point the progesterone pattern is similar to that for estrogen. Not shown in Figure 19-6 is the plasma concentration of inhibin; its pattern remains uncertain but is thought to be similar to that of estrogen.

The following discussion will explain how these changes are all interrelated to yield a self-cycling pattern. The numbers in Figure 19-16 are keyed to the text. The feedback effects of the ovarian hormones to be described in the text are summarized for reference in Table 19-4.

Follicle Development and Estrogen Secretion During the Early and Middle Follicular Phases

As mentioned earlier, there are always a number of preantral follicles in the adult ovary. Further development requires stimulation by FSH and LH. The increase in gonadotropin secretion that occurs as one cycle ends and the next begins (number 1 in Figure 19-16) provides this stimulation, and the follicle begins to enlarge (2). (The explanation of what causes gonadotropin secretion to increase at this time is best delayed until we discuss the events at the end of a cycle.) During the next week or so, there is a separation of function of FSH and LH on the follicle: FSH acts on the granulosa cells, and LH acts on the theca cells.

FSH stimulates the granulosa cells to multiply and produce estrogen, and it also stimulates formation and enlargement of the antrum. Some of the estrogen produced diffuses into the blood and maintains a relatively stable plasma concentration (3), and some estrogen functions as a paracrine or autocrine agent in the follicle, where, along with FSH, it stimulates the granulosa cells to increase still further their proliferation and their production of estrogen.[9]

---

[9]In humans, as opposed to experimental animals, a role for estrogen in the control of granulosa cell function is presently controversial. We have chosen to present the time-honored concept of dual control by estrogen and FSH.

TABLE 19-4   SUMMARY OF MAJOR FEEDBACK EFFECTS OF ESTROGEN, PROGESTERONE, AND INHIBIN

1. Estrogen, in *low* plasma concentrations, causes the anterior pituitary to secrete less FSH and LH in response to GnRH and also may inhibit the hypothalamic neurons that secrete GnRH.
   Result: Negative-feedback inhibition of FSH and LH secretion during the early and middle follicular phase.

2. Inhibin acts on the pituitary to inhibit the secretion of FSH.
   Result: Negative-feedback inhibition of FSH secretion throughout the cycle.

3. Estrogen, in *high* plasma concentrations, causes the anterior pituitary cells to secrete more LH (and FSH) in response to GnRH and also may stimulate the hypothalamic neurons that secrete GnRH.
   Result: Positive-feedback stimulation of the LH surge, which triggers ovulation.

4. High plasma concentrations of progesterone, in the presence of estrogen, inhibit the hypothalamic neurons that secrete GnRH.
   Result: Negative-feedback inhibition of FSH and LH secretion and prevention of LH surges during the luteal phase and pregnancy.

The granulosa cells, however, require help to produce estrogen because they are deficient in the enzymes required to produce the androgens that are the precursors of estrogen. This aid is supplied by the theca cells. As shown in Figure 19-17, LH acts upon the theca cells, stimulating them not only to proliferate but to synthesize androgens. The androgens diffuse into the granulosa cells and are converted to estrogen. Thus, the secretion of estrogen by the granulosa cells requires the interplay of both types of follicle cells and both pituitary gonadotropins. In addition, the theca and granulosa cells communicate with each other in other ways by means of paracrine agents, particularly peptide growth factors, that they secrete.

At this point it is worthwhile to emphasize the similarities the two follicle cell types bear to cells of the testes: The granulosa cell is similar to the Sertoli cell in that it controls the microenvironment in which the germ cell develops and matures, and it is stimulated by both FSH and the major gonadal sex hormone. The thecal cell is similar to the Leydig cell in that it produces mainly androgens and is stimulated to do so by LH.

By the beginning of the second week, one follicle has become dominant (4 in Figure 19-6), and it becomes the major producer of estrogen. So much estrogen is secreted that the plasma concentration of this steroid begins to rise

FIGURE 19-17
Control of estrogen secretion during the early and middle follicular phase.

markedly (5). Note that this occurs even though FSH—a crucial stimulus for estrogen secretion—is *decreasing* during this second week. The explanation is that, by this time, the number of granulosa cells in the dominant follicle and their sensitivity to FSH have markedly increased. Thus the *quantitative* response of the ovaries to any given level of FSH and LH can vary during the cycle as the number and sensitivity of responding ovarian cells change.

What about hormonal feedbacks throughout this part of the cycle? For about the first 11 days of the cycle, plasma estrogen exerts a negative-feedback inhibition over the secretion of gonadotropins (Figure 19-18). One important site of its action is the anterior pituitary, where it reduces the amount of FSH and LH secreted in response to any given amount of GnRH. It may also act on the hypothalamus to decrease the amplitude of GnRH pulses and, hence, the total amount of GnRH secreted over any time period.

Therefore, as expected from this negative feedback, the plasma concentration of FSH begins to fall as a result of the rising level of estrogen as the follicular phase continues (6 in Figure 19-16). It falls more than LH because the granulosa cells also secrete inhibin which, as in the male, preferentially inhibits secretion of FSH (Figure 19-18).

LH Surge and Ovulation

The inhibitory effect estrogen exerts on the pituitary and hypothalamus occurs only when plasma estrogen concen-

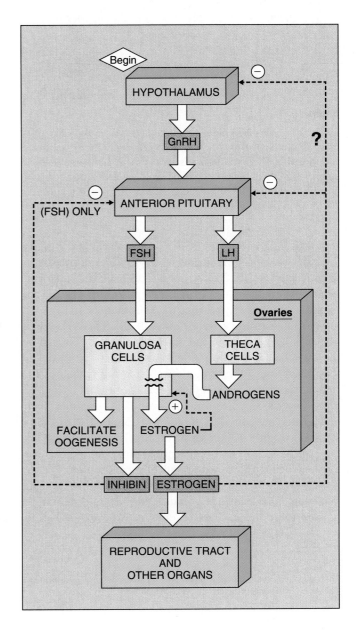

FIGURE 19-18
Summary of hormonal control of ovarian function during the early and middle follicular phases. Compare with the analogous pattern of the male (Figure 19-10). Inhibin is a protein hormone that inhibits FSH secretion. The wavy broken arrows in the granulosa cells denote the conversion of androgens to estrogen in these cells, as in Figure 19-17.

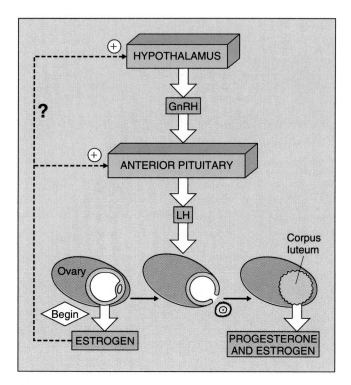

FIGURE 19-19
In the late follicular phase, the dominant follicle secretes large amounts of estrogen, which acts on the anterior pituitary and, possibly, the hypothalamus, to cause an LH surge. The increased plasma LH then triggers both ovulation and formation of the corpus luteum. These actions of LH are mediated via the granulosa cells.

tration is relatively *low*, as during the early and middle follicular phases. In contrast, high plasma concentrations of estrogen for 1 to 2 days, as occurs during the estrogen peak of the late follicular phase (7 in Figure 19-16), act upon the pituitary to *enhance* the sensitivity of LH releasing mechanisms to GnRH (Figure 19-19). The high estrogen may also stimulate increased secretion of GnRH by the hypothalamus. These effects are termed the positive-feedback effects of estrogen. The net result is that, as estrogen secretion rises rapidly during the late follicular phase, its blood concentration eventually becomes high enough to cause the LH surge (8 in Figure 19-16).[10] (As shown in Figure 19-16, an FSH surge also occurs at the time of the LH surge, but it is not known whether this has a physiological role in the regulation of the cycle.)

The midcycle surge of LH is the event that induces ovulation. One more important piece of information is needed to understand how it does so. We emphasized in

the previous section that, during the early and middle follicular phases, FSH acts on the granulosa cells and LH acts on the thecal cells. As the dominant follicle matures, however, this situation changes. LH receptors, induced by FSH with the assistance of estrogen, begin to appear in large numbers on the granulosa cells, and this sets the stage for the LH surge to act upon the granulosa cells to cause the events, presented in Table 19-5, that culminate in ovulation (9 and 10).

The function of the granulosa cells in mediating the effects of the LH surge is the last in the series of these cells' functions described in this chapter. They are all summarized in Table 19-6.

The Corpus Luteum

The LH surge not only induces ovulation by the mature follicle but also stimulates the reactions that transform the remaining granulosa and theca cells of that follicle into a corpus luteum (11 in Figure 19-16). Even though its plasma concentration becomes relatively low, LH continues to stimulate the corpus luteum throughout the luteal phase.

During its short life in the nonpregnant woman, the corpus luteum secretes large quantities of progesterone and estrogen (12). In the presence of estrogen, the high plasma concentration of progesterone acts on the hypo-

---

[10]The small increase in the plasma concentration of progesterone that exists during the late follicular phase may facilitate the estrogen-induced LH surge by an effect on the hypothalamus.

TABLE 19-5 EFFECTS OF THE LH SURGE ON OVARIAN FUNCTION

1. The primary oocyte completes its first meiotic division and undergoes cytoplasmic changes that prepare the ovum for implantation after fertilization. These LH effects on the oocyte are mediated by messengers from the granulosa cells.

2. Antrum size and blood flow to the follicle increase markedly.

3. The granulosa cells begin secreting progesterone and decrease their secretion of estrogen, which accounts for the midcycle drop in plasma estrogen concentration and the small rise in plasma progesterone just before ovulation.

4. Enzymes and prostaglandins, synthesized by the granulosa cells, break down the follicular-ovarian membranes. These weakened membranes rupture, allowing the oocyte and its surrounding granulosa cells to be carried out onto the surface of the ovary.

5. The remaining granulosa cells of the ruptured follicle (along with the theca cells of that follicle) are transformed into the corpus luteum, which begins to secrete progesterone and estrogen.

TABLE 19-6 FUNCTIONS OF GRANULOSA CELLS

1. Nourish oocyte
2. Secrete chemical messengers that influence the oocyte and the thecal cells
3. Secrete antral fluid
4. Are the site of action for estrogen and FSH in the control of follicle development during early and middle follicular phases
5. Secrete estrogen from the androgens reaching them from the theca cells
6. Secrete inhibin, which inhibits FSH secretion via an action on the pituitary
7. Are the site of action for LH induction of changes in the oocyte and follicle culminating in ovulation and formation of the corpus luteum

thalamus to *suppress* the secretion of GnRH by reducing the frequency of GnRH pulses. The decrease in GnRH secretion results in a decrease in the secretion of the gonadotropins by the pituitary. Accordingly, during the luteal phase of the cycle, plasma concentrations of the gonadotropins are very low (13), which explains why no new follicles can develop beyond the preantral or small-antral stage during the second half of the cycle. Inhibin, secreted by the corpus luteum, is also elevated in the luteal phase and contributes to the suppression of FSH secretion.

Recall from page 666 that the corpus luteum degenerates within 2 weeks if pregnancy does not occur (14). What causes this? The most likely hypothesis at present is that the corpus luteum "self-destructs" after 10 to 14 days by producing large quantities of a paracrine agent, probably a prostaglandin, that interferes locally with the corpus luteum's activities.

With degeneration of the corpus luteum, plasma progesterone and estrogen concentrations decrease (15). GnRH, FSH, and LH secretions increase (16 and 1) as a result of being relieved from the inhibiting effects of high concentrations of progesterone, and a new group of follicles is stimulated to mature. The cycle then begins anew.

This completes our description of the control of ovarian function. It should be emphasized that, although the hypothalamus and anterior pituitary are essential links in the chain, events within the ovary are the real sources of *timing* for the cycle. When the ovary secretes enough estrogen, the LH surge is induced, which in turn causes ovulation. When its corpus luteum self-destructs, the decrease in sex hormone secretion permits the gonadotropin level to rise enough to start another group of follicles developing. Thus, ovarian events, via hormonal feedbacks, "instruct" the hypothalamus and anterior pituitary.

UTERINE CHANGES IN THE MENSTRUAL CYCLE

Because we have been describing ovarian function, we have so far referred to the phases of the menstrual cycle in terms of ovarian events—follicular and luteal phases separated by ovulation. However, the phases of the menstrual cycle can also be named in terms of uterine events (Figure 19-20). Day 1 is, as noted earlier, the first day of menstrual bleeding, and the entire period of menstruation is known as the **menstrual phase**, which is generally about 3 to 5 days in a typical 28-day cycle. During this period the epithelial lining of the uterus—the **endometrium**—degenerates, resulting in the menstrual flow. The menstrual flow then ceases, and the endometrium begins to thicken as it regenerates. This period of growth, the **proliferative phase**, lasts for the 10 days or so between cessation of menstruation and occurrence of ovulation. Soon after ovulation, the endometrium begins to secrete various substances, and so the part of the menstrual cycle between ovulation and the onset of the next menstruation is called the **secretory phase**.

The ovarian follicular phase includes the uterine menstrual and proliferative phases, whereas the ovarian luteal phase is the same as the uterine secretory phase.

The uterine changes during a menstrual cycle are caused by changes in the plasma concentrations of estrogen and progesterone (Figure 19-20). During the proliferative phase, a rising plasma estrogen level stimulates growth of both the endometrium and the underlying uterine smooth muscle (**myometrium**). In addition, it induces the synthesis of receptors for progesterone in endometrial cells. Then, following ovulation and formation of the corpus luteum, during the secretory phase progesterone acts upon this estrogen-primed endometrium to convert it to an actively secreting tissue: Its glands become coiled and filled with glycogen, the blood vessels become more numerous, and various enzymes accumulate in the glands and connective tissue. These changes are essential to make the endometrium a hospitable environment for an embryo.

Progesterone also inhibits myometrial contractions, in large part by opposing the stimulatory actions of estrogen and locally generated prostaglandins. This is very important to ensure that the fertilized egg, once it arrives in the uterus, will not be swept out by uterine contractions before it can implant in the wall. This uterine quiescence is maintained by progesterone throughout pregnancy and is essential to prevent premature delivery.

Estrogen and progesterone also have important effects on mucus secretion by the cervix. Under the influence of estrogen alone, this mucus is abundant, clear, and nonviscous. All these characteristics are most pronounced at ovulation and allow sperm deposited in the vagina to move

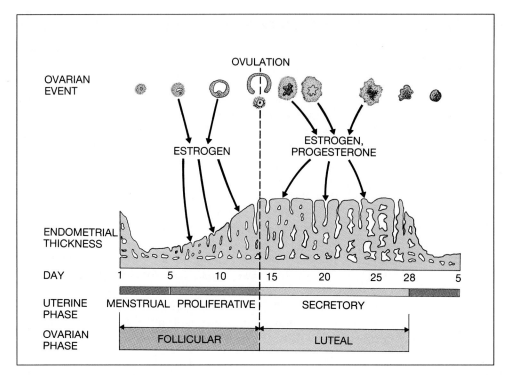

FIGURE 19-20

Relationships between ovarian and uterine changes during the menstrual cycle.

easily through the mucus on their way to the uterus and on to the uterine tubes. In contrast, progesterone, present in significant concentrations only after ovulation, causes the mucus to become thick and sticky—in essence a "plug" that prevents bacteria from entering the uterus from the vagina. The antibacterial blockade protects the fetus if conception has occurred.

The fall in plasma progesterone and estrogen levels that results from degeneration of the corpus luteum deprives the highly developed endometrium of its hormonal support and causes menstruation. The immediate result is profound constriction of the uterine blood vessels, which leads to a diminished supply of oxygen and nutrients to the endometrial cells. Disintegration starts, and the entire lining, except for a thin, underlying layer that will regenerate the endometrium in the next cycle, begins to slough. Also, the uterine smooth muscle begins to undergo rhythmical contractions.

Both the vasoconstriction and uterine contractions are mediated by prostaglandins produced by the endometrium. The major cause of menstrual cramps, ***dysmenorrhea***, is overproduction of these prostaglandins, leading to excessive uterine contractions. The prostaglandins also affect smooth muscle elsewhere in the body, which accounts for the systemic symptoms—nausea, vomiting, and headache—that sometimes accompany the cramps.

After the initial period of vascular constriction, the endometrial arterioles dilate, resulting in hemorrhage through the weakened capillary walls. The menstrual flow consists of this blood mixed with endometrial debris. Typical blood loss per menstrual period is about 50 to 150 ml.

This completes our description of the menstrual cycle, the major events of which are summarized in Table 19-7. This table, in essence, combines the information in Figures 19-16 and 19-20.

OTHER EFFECTS OF ESTROGEN AND PROGESTERONE

Estrogen, in addition to its paracrine function within the ovaries, its effects on the anterior pituitary (and, possibly, the hypothalamus), and its uterine actions, exerts a large number of other effects, as summarized in Table 19-8.

It maintains the uterine tubes, vagina, external genitalia, and breasts. Estrogen is also responsible for the general female body configuration: narrow shoulders, broad hips, and the characteristic female fat deposition on the hips, abdomen, and breasts. Estrogen does not have testosterone's anabolic effect on skeletal muscle but, as described in Chapter 18, it does cause bone growth as well as eventual cessation of growth by closure of the bones' epiphyseal plates.

Progesterone (Table 19-8) also exerts important effects on the breasts and uterine tubes, the significance of which

TABLE 19-7 SUMMARY OF THE MENSTRUAL CYCLE

Day(s)	Major events
1–5	Estrogen and progesterone are low because the previous corpus luteum has completely regressed. *Therefore*: (a) Endometrial lining sloughs. (b) Secretion of FSH and LH is released from inhibition, and their plasma concentrations rise. *Therefore*: Several follicles are stimulated to enlarge.
7	Dominant follicle is selected.
7–12	Plasma estrogen rises because of secretion by the dominant follicle. *Therefore*: Endometrium is stimulated to proliferate.
12–13	LH surge is induced by high plasma estrogen. *Therefore*: (a) Oocyte is induced to complete its first meiotic division and undergo cytoplasmic maturation. (b) Follicle is stimulated to secrete lytic enzymes and prostaglandin.
14	Ovulation is mediated by follicular enzymes and prostaglandin.
15–25	Corpus luteum forms and, under the influence of LH, secretes estrogen and progesterone, and so plasma concentrations of these hormones increase. *Therefore*: (a) Secretory endometrium develops. (b) Secretion of FSH and LH is inhibited, lowering their plasma concentrations. *Therefore*: No new follicles develop.
25–28	Corpus luteum degenerates. *Therefore*: Plasma estrogen and progesterone concentrations decrease. *Therefore*: Endometrium begins to slough at conclusion of day 28, and a new cycle begins.

will be described later. In addition, progesterone inhibits proliferation of the cells lining the vagina, and the microscopic examination of these cells provides an indicator that ovulation has or has not occurred.

Another indicator that ovulation has occurred is a small rise (approximately 0.5 C°) in body temperature that usually occurs at this time and persists throughout the luteal phase. This change is probably due to an action of progesterone on temperature regulatory centers in the brain.

Note that in its myometrial and vaginal effects, as well as several others in Table 19-8, progesterone exerts an "antiestrogen effect," probably by decreasing the number of estrogen receptors. In contrast, the synthesis of progesterone receptors is stimulated by estrogen in many tissues (for example, the endometrium), and so responsiveness to

progesterone usually requires the presence of estrogen.

As is true for testosterone, both estrogen and progesterone act on the cell nucleus, and their biochemical mechanism of action is at the level of gene transcription.

In closing this section, brief mention should be made of the *premenstrual syndrome (PMS)* because it is often ascribed to estrogen excess or progesterone deficiency. However, the cause of this syndrome is not known. PMS, which is distinct from dysmenorrhea, is a cluster of distressing physical and psychological symptoms that occur during the week or so preceding menstruation and that are relieved at the onset of menstruation or within the first few days. The symptoms may include painful or swollen breasts, bloating, headache, backache, depression, anxiety, irritability, and other behavioral and motor changes. These

TABLE 19-8   EFFECTS OF FEMALE SEX STEROIDS

Estrogen

1. Stimulates growth of ovary and follicles.
2. Stimulates growth of smooth muscle and proliferation of epithelial linings of reproductive tract. In addition:
   a. Uterine tubes: Increases contractions and ciliary activity.
   b. Uterus: Increases myometrial contractions and responsiveness to oxytocin. Stimulates secretion of abundant, clear cervical mucus. Prepares endometrium for progesterone's actions by inducing progesterone receptors.
   c. Vagina: Increases layering of epithelial cells.
3. Stimulates external genitalia growth.
4. Stimulates breast growth, particularly ducts and fat deposition.
5. Stimulates female body configuration development: narrow shoulders, broad hips, female fat distribution.
6. Stimulates a more-fluid sebaceous gland secretion ("antiacne" effect).
7. Stimulates development of female pubic hair pattern (growth of pubic and axillary hair is androgen-stimulated).
8. Stimulates bone growth and ultimate cessation of bone growth (closure of epiphyseal plates); protects against osteoporosis.
9. Vascular effects (deficiency produces "hot flashes").
10. Has feedback effects on hypothalamus and anterior pituitary (Table 19-4).
11. Stimulates retention of fluid.
12. Stimulates prolactin secretion but inhibits prolactin's milk-inducing action on the breasts.
13. Protects against atherosclerosis.

Progesterone

1. Stimulates endometrial glands to secrete.
2. Induces thick, sticky cervical mucus.
3. Decreases contractions of uterine tubes and myometrium.
4. Decreases proliferation of vaginal epithelial cells.
5. Stimulates breast growth, particularly glandular tissue.
6. Inhibits milk-inducing effects of prolactin.
7. Has feedback effects on hypothalamus and anterior pituitary (Table 19-4).

symptoms may occur singly or in varying combinations. Estimates of the incidence of this syndrome depend on what criteria are used and vary from as low as 2 to 5 percent of adult women to as high as 30 to 40 percent.

ANDROGENS IN WOMEN

Testosterone is not a uniquely male hormone but is found in very low concentration in the blood of normal women as a result of production by the ovaries and adrenal glands as well as peripheral conversion of adrenal androgens. Of greater importance is the fact that androgens other than testosterone are found in quite significant concentrations in the blood of women. The sites of production are mainly the adrenal glands, which contribute these same androgens in the male.

The adrenal androgens have little significance in the male because testosterone is so much more potent, but they do play several important roles in the female, notably maintenance of sex drive (as discussed below). In several disease states, the female adrenals may secrete abnormally large quantities of androgen, which produce virilism: The female fat distribution disappears, a beard appears along with the male body-hair distribution, the voice lowers in pitch, the skeletal-muscle mass enlarges, the clitoris enlarges, and the breasts diminish in size.

FEMALE SEXUAL RESPONSE

The female response to sexual intercourse is characterized by marked vasocongestion and muscular contraction in many areas of the body. For example, increasing sexual excitement is associated with vascular engorgement of the breasts and erection of the nipples, resulting from contraction of smooth-muscle fibers in them. The clitoris, which is endowed with a rich supply of sensory nerve endings, also becomes erect as a result of vascular congestion. During intercourse, the vaginal epithelium becomes highly congested and secretes a mucus-like lubricant.

Orgasm in the female, as in the male, is accompanied by intense pleasure and many physical events. There is a sudden increase in skeletal-muscle activity involving almost all parts of the body; the heart rate and blood pressure increase; the female counterpart of male genital contraction is a transient rhythmical contraction of the vagina and uterus. Orgasm seems to play no essential role in ensuring fertilization since conception can occur in the absence of an orgasm.

A question related to the female sexual response concerns sex drive. Incongruous as it may seem, sexual desire in women is probably more dependent upon androgens, secreted by the adrenal glands, than estrogen, and sex drive is maintained beyond menopause when estrogen levels become very low.

This completes our survey of normal reproductive physiology in the nonpregnant female. In weaving one's way through this maze, it is all too easy to forget the prime function subserved by this entire system, namely, reproduction. Accordingly, we must now return to the egg we left free on the surface of the ovary, obtain a sperm for it, and carry the fertilized egg through pregnancy and delivery.

PREGNANCY

Following their ejaculation into the vagina, sperm remain fertile approximately 48 h. After ovulation, the egg remains fertile for 10 to 15 h. The net result is that for pregnancy to occur, sexual intercourse must be performed no more than 48 h before or 15 h after ovulation. These are only average figures, and there is probably considerable variation in the survival time of both sperm and egg.

Ovum Transport

At ovulation, the egg is extruded from the ovary, and its first mission is to gain entry into a uterine tube. The fimbriae at the end of the uterine tubes are lined with ciliated epithelium. At ovulation, the fimbriae smooth muscle causes them to pass over the ovary while the cilia beat in waves toward the interior of the duct. These ciliary motions sweep the egg into the uterine tube as it emerges onto the ovarian surface.

Once in the uterine tube, the egg moves rapidly for

several minutes, propelled by cilia and by contractions of the tube's smooth-muscle coating. The muscular contractions soon diminish, and egg movement, driven almost entirely by the cilia, becomes so slow that the egg takes about 4 days to reach the uterus. Thus, if fertilization is to occur, it must do so in the uterine tube because of the short life span of the unfertilized egg.

Sperm Transport and Capacitation

Within a minute or so after intercourse, some sperm can be detected in the uterus. The act of intercourse itself provides some impetus for transport of sperm out of the vagina through the cervix and into the uterus because of the fluid pressure of the ejaculate and the pumping action of the penis in the vagina during ejaculation. In addition, beating of the cilia on the inner surface of the cervix probably wafts the sperm toward the uterus. Passage through the cervical mucus by the swimming sperm is dependent on the estrogen-induced changes in consistency of the mucus described earlier. Transport of the sperm the length of the uterus and into the uterine tube probably is via the sperm's own propulsions and the currents set up by the beating of uterine cilia. Uterine smooth-muscle contractions may also play a role.

The mortality rate of sperm during the trip is huge. One reason for this is that the vaginal environment is acidic, a protection against yeast and bacterial infections. Another is the length and energy requirements of the trip. Of the several hundred million sperm deposited in the vagina, only a few hundred reach the uterine tube. This is one of the major reasons there must be so many sperm in the ejaculate for fertilization to occur.

Sperm are not able to fertilize the egg until they have resided in the female tract for several hours. This effect, termed **capacitation**, causes: (1) the previously regular wavelike beats of the sperm's tail to be replaced by a more whiplike action that propels the sperm forward in strong lurches, and (2) the sperm's plasma membrane to become altered so that it will be capable of fusing with the surface membrane of the egg.

Fertilization

Fertilization is the fusion of a sperm and egg. Many sperm, after moving between the cumulus of granulosa cells still surrounding the egg, bind to the zona pellucida. This is a species-specific binding between sperm receptors in the zona pellucida's outer surface and complementary proteins in the plasma membrane of the sperm's head. The sperm head has many of these proteins and so becomes bound simultaneously to many sperm receptors on the zona pellucida.

This binding triggers what is termed the **acrosome reaction** in the bound sperm: The plasma membrane of the sperm head alters so that the underlying membrane-bound acrosomal enzymes become exposed to the outside, that is, to the zona pellucida. The enzymes digest a path through the zona as the sperm, using its tail, advances through this coating. The first sperm to penetrate the entire zona and reach the narrow space between the zona and the egg's plasma membrane fuses with this membrane. This sperm then slowly passes into the egg's cytoplasm, penetration being achieved not by the sperm's motility but as a result of contractile elements in the egg, which draw the sperm in.

Viability of the newly fertilized egg, now termed a **zygote**, depends upon preventing the fusion and entry of additional sperm. The mechanism of this "block to polyspermy" is as follows: The initial fusion of the sperm and egg plasma membranes triggers a reaction in which secretory vesicles located around the egg's periphery release their contents, by exocytosis, into the space between the plasma membrane and the zona pellucida. Some of these molecules are enzymes that enter the zona pellucida and cause both inactivation of its sperm-binding sites and hardening of the entire zona. This prevents additional sperm from binding to the zona and those sperm already advancing through it from continuing.

The fertilized egg completes its second meiotic division over the next few hours, and the one daughter cell with practically no cytoplasm—the second polar body—is extruded and disintegrates. The two sets of chromosomes—23 from the egg and 23 from the sperm—each become surrounded by distinct membranes and are known as pronuclei, which migrate to the center of the cell. During this period of a few hours, the DNA of the chromosomes in

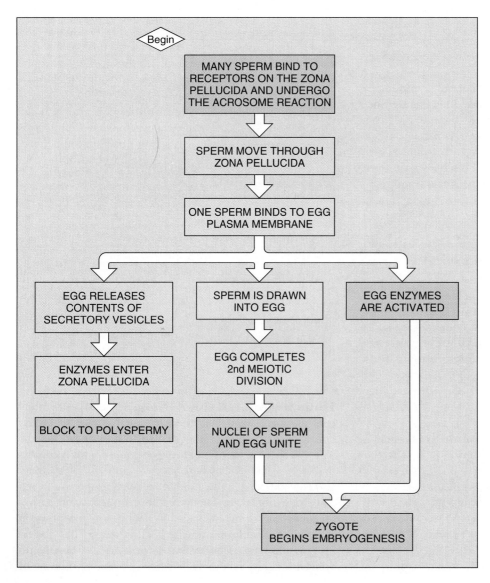

FIGURE 19-21

Events leading to fertilization, block to polyspermy, and the beginning of embryogenesis.

both pronuclei is replicated, the pronuclear membranes break down, the cell is ready to undergo a mitotic division, and fertilization, the major events of which are summarized in Figure 19-21, is complete. Fertilization also triggers activation of the ovum enzymes required for the ensuing cell divisions and embryogenesis.

If fertilization had not occurred, the egg would have slowly disintegrated and been phagocytized by cells lining the uterus. Rarely, a fertilized egg remains in the uterine tube and embeds itself in the tube wall. Such tubal pregnancies cannot succeed because of lack of space for the fetus to grow, and surgery will be necessary, unless there is spontaneous abortion, because of the risk of maternal hemorrhage. Even more rarely a fertilized egg may be expelled into the abdominal cavity where implantation may take place and proceed to term, the infant being delivered surgically. Tubal and abdominal pregnancies are termed *ectopic pregnancies*.

Early Development, Implantation, and Placentation

During its 3- to 4-day stay in the uterine tube, the **conceptus**—a collective term for the fertilized egg and all its derivatives throughout pregnancy—undergoes a number of mitotic cell divisions, a process known as **cleavage**. These divisions are unusual for mitosis in that no cell growth occurs before each division. Thus, the 16- to 32-cell conceptus that reaches the uterus is essentially the same size as the original fertilized egg.

Identical or monozygotic twins result when, at some point during cleavage, the dividing cells become com-

pletely separated into two independently growing cell masses. In contrast, as we have seen, dizygotic (fraternal) twins result from two eggs being ovulated and fertilized.

After reaching the uterus, the conceptus floats free in the intrauterine fluid, from which it receives nutrients, for approximately 3 days, all the while undergoing further cell divisions. Soon the conceptus reaches the stage known as a **blastocyst**, consisting of an outer layer of cells, the **trophoblast**, an **inner cell mass**, and a central fluid-filled cavity (Figure 19-22). During subsequent development, the inner cell mass will give rise to the developing human—termed an **embryo** during the first 2 months and a **fetus** after that—and some of the membranes associated with it. The trophoblast will surround the embryo and fetus throughout development and be involved in its nutrition as well as in the secretion of several important hormones.

The period during which the zygote develops into a blastocyst corresponds with days 14 to 21 of the typical menstrual cycle. During this period the uterine lining is being prepared by estrogen and progesterone, secreted by the corpus luteum, to receive the blastocyst. By approximately the twenty-first day of the cycle, that is, 7 days after ovulation, **implantation**—the embedding of the blastocyst in the endometrium—begins. The trophoblast cells are quite sticky, particularly in the region overlying the inner cell mass, and it is this portion of the blastocyst that adheres to the endometrium and initiates implantation.

The initial contact between blastocyst and endometrium induces rapid proliferation of the trophoblast, the cells of which penetrate between endometrial cells. Proteolytic enzymes secreted by the trophoblast allow the blastocyst to bury itself in the endometrial layer. The endometrium, as well, is undergoing changes at the site of contact as the result of hormone stimulation: Increased vascularization and vascular permeability, edema, and compositional changes in the intercellular matrix and in the endometrial cells all occur. Implantation is soon completed (Figure 19-23), and the nutrient-rich endometrial cells provide the metabolic fuel and raw materials required for early growth of the embryo.

This simple nutritive system, however, is adequate to provide for the embryo only during the first few weeks, when it is very small. The structure taking over this function is the **placenta**, a combination of interlocking fetal and maternal tissues that serves as the organ of exchange between mother and fetus for the remainder of the pregnancy. The fetal portion of the placenta is supplied by the outermost layer of trophoblast cells, termed the **chorion**, and the maternal portion by the endometrium underlying the chorion. Finger-like projections, **chorionic villi**, extend from the chorion into the endometrium (Figure 19-24). The villi contain a rich network of capillaries linked to the embryo's circulatory system. The endometrium around the villi is altered by enzymes secreted from the

FIGURE 19-22
Photomicrograph showing the beginning implantation of a 9-day monkey blastocyst. [*From C. H. Heuser and G. L. Streeter, Carnegie Contrib. Embryol, 29:15 (1941).*]

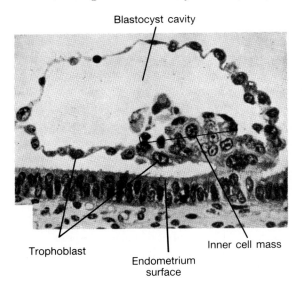

Blastocyst cavity

Trophoblast

Endometrium
surface

Inner cell mass

Endometrium—

Trophoblast—

Inner cell mass—

Endometrial surface

FIGURE 19-23
Eleven-day human embryo completely embedded in the uterine lining. [*From A. T. Hertig and J. Rock, Carnegie Contrib. Embryol., 29:127 (1941).*]

cells of the villi so that each villus comes to be completely surrounded by a pool, or sinus, of maternal blood.

The maternal blood enters these placental sinuses via the uterine artery, percolates through them, and then exits via the uterine veins. Simultaneously, blood flows from the fetus into the capillaries of the chorionic villi via the **umbilical arteries** and out of the capillaries back to the fetus via the **umbilical vein**. All these umbilical vessels are contained in the **umbilical cord**, a long ropelike structure that connects the fetus to the placenta.

Five weeks after implantation, the placenta has become well established, the fetal heart has begun to pump blood, and the entire mechanism for nutrition of the fetus and excretion of its waste products is in operation. Waste products move from blood in the fetal capillaries across the cells lining the villi into the maternal blood, and nutrients move in the opposite direction. Many substances, such as oxygen and carbon dioxide, move by simple diffusion, whereas others are carried by mediated-transport mechanisms in the lining. It must be emphasized that there is an *exchange of materials* between the two bloodstreams but no actual *mingling* of the fetal and maternal blood.

Meanwhile, a space called the **amniotic cavity** has formed between the inner cell mass and the trophoblast. The epithelial layer lining the cavity is derived from the inner cell mass and is called the **amnion** (or **amniotic sac**). It eventually fuses with the inner surface of the chorion so that only a single combined membrane surrounds the fetus. The fluid in the amniotic cavity, the **amniotic fluid**, resembles the fetal extracellular fluid, and it buffers mechanical disturbances and temperature variations.

The fetus, floating in the amniotic cavity and attached by the umbilical cord to the placenta (Figure 19-25), develops into a viable infant during the next 8 months. (A description of intrauterine development is beyond the scope of this book but can be found in any standard textbook of human embryology.) Note in Figure 19-25 that only the amniotic sac separates the fetus from the uterine lumen.

Amniotic fluid can be sampled (*amniocentesis*) as early as the fourth month by inserting a needle into the amniotic cavity. A large number of genetic diseases can be diagnosed by the finding of certain chemicals either in the fluid or in cells suspended in the fluid. The chromosomes

Gland in
endometrium

Endometrium

Myometrium

Branch of
umbilical
artery and
vein

Yolk
sac

Umbilical
vein

Umbilical
arteries

Umbilical cord
to fetus

Main stem of
chorionic villus

Chorionic villi

Uterine
artery
and vein

Pool of
maternal
blood

PLACENTA

AMNIOTIC
CAVITY

FIGURE 19-24

Interrelations of fetal and maternal tissues in formation of placenta. See Figure 19-25 for orientation of the placenta. *(From B. M. Carlson, "Patten's Foundations of Embryology," 5th ed., McGraw-Hill, New York, 1988.)*

of these cells can also be examined for diagnosis of certain disorders as well as to determine the sex of the fetus. Another technique for fetal diagnosis is ***chorionic villus sampling***. This technique, which can be performed as early as the beginning of the third month of pregnancy, involves obtaining tissue from a chorionic villus of the placenta. A third technique for fetal diagnosis is ultrasound, which provides a "picture" of the fetus without the use of x-rays.

Maternal nutrition is crucial for the fetus. ***Malnutrition*** early in pregnancy can cause certain congenital abnormalities and/or the formation of an inadequate placenta. Malnutrition retards fetal growth and results in infants with higher-than-normal death rates, reduced

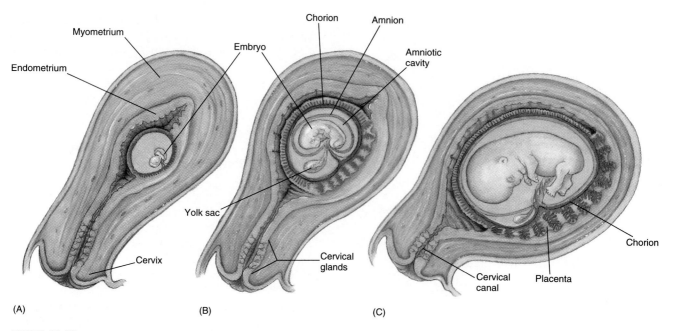

FIGURE 19-25
The uterus at (A) 3, (B) 5, and (C) 8 weeks after fertilization. Embryos and their membranes are drawn to actual size. Uterus is within actual size range. *(From B. M. Carlson, "Patten's Foundations of Embryology," 5th ed., McGraw-Hill, New York, 1988.)*

growth after birth, and an increased incidence of learning disabilities. The developing embryo and fetus are also subject to considerable influence by a host of other factors (noise, radiation, chemicals, viruses, and so on) to which the mother may be exposed. For example, drugs taken by the mother can reach the fetus via the placenta and impair fetal growth and development. In this regard, it must be emphasized that aspirin, alcohol, and the chemicals in cigarette smoke are very potent agents, as are "street drugs" such as cocaine.

It should also be recognized that, since half of the fetal genes differ from those of the mother, the fetus is in essence a foreign transplant in the mother. Why the fetus is not rejected (Chapter 20) is still not well understood.

Finally, recent evidence has suggested that approximately half of all pregnancies end in spontaneous abortion, most so early that the woman is unaware of having been pregnant.

Hormonal and Other Changes During Pregnancy

Throughout pregnancy, plasma concentrations of estrogen and progesterone remain high (Figure 19-26). Estrogen stimulates growth of the uterine muscle mass which will eventually supply the contractile force needed to deliver the fetus. Progesterone inhibits uterine motility so that the fetus is not expelled prematurely. During approximately the first 2 months of pregnancy, almost all the estrogen

and progesterone are supplied by the extremely active corpus luteum.

Recall that if pregnancy had not occurred, this gland-like structure would have degenerated within 2 weeks after its formation. The persistence of the corpus luteum during pregnancy is due to a hormone called **chorionic gonadotropin (CG),** which starts to be secreted by the trophoblast cells around the time they start their endometrial invasion. The CG gains entry to the maternal blood via the endometrial blood vessels of the placenta. The detection of CG in the mother's plasma and/or urine is used as a test of pregnancy and is positive before the next expected menstruation. This protein hormone is very similar to but not identical to LH, and it maintains the corpus luteum and strongly stimulates steroid secretion by it. Thus, the signal that preserves the corpus luteum comes from the conceptus (everything derived from the fertilized egg), not the mother's tissues.

The secretion of CG reaches a peak 60 to 80 days after the last menstrual period (Figure 19-26). It then falls just as rapidly, so that by the end of the third month it has reached a low, but definitely detectable, level that remains relatively constant for the duration of the pregnancy. Associated with this falloff of CG secretion, the placenta begins to secrete large quantities of estrogen and progesterone. The very marked increases in plasma concentrations of estrogen and progesterone during the last 6 months of pregnancy are due entirely to their secretion by the trophoblast cells of the placenta, and the corpus luteum re-

FIGURE 19-26

Urinary excretion of estrogen, progesterone, and chorionic gonadotropin during pregnancy. Urinary excretion rates are an indication of blood concentrations of these hormones.

gresses after about 3 months. Indeed, surgical removal of the ovaries during the last 7 months of pregnancy, as opposed to the first 2 months, has no effect at all upon the pregnancy.

Recall that secretion of GnRH and, hence, of LH and FSH is powerfully inhibited by high concentrations of progesterone in the presence of estrogen. Since both these steroid hormones are present in high concentration throughout pregnancy, the secretion of the pituitary gonadotropins remains extremely low. In addition, the trophoblast cells secrete large amounts of inhibin, which further contributes, via its action on the anterior pituitary, to reduced FSH secretion. The low gonadotropin levels prevent further follicle development and ovulation for the duration of the pregnancy.

An important aspect of placental steroid secretion is that the placenta has the enzymes required for the synthesis of progesterone but not those for the formation of androgens, which are the precursors of estrogen. The placenta is supplied with these androgens by the *fetal* adrenal glands via the fetal circulation, and it converts them mainly into **estriol,** the major estrogen of pregnancy.

The trophoblast cells of the placenta produce not only CG, steroids, and inhibin, but many other hormones as well, all examples of hormones produced by the conceptus (everything derived from the fertilized egg) and influencing the mother. Some of these (for example, thyroid-

stimulating hormone) are identical to hormones normally produced by other endocrine glands, whereas some are unique. One unique hormone that is secreted in very large amounts has effects similar to those of both prolactin and growth hormone. This protein hormone, **placental lactogen** (also called chorionic somatomammotropin), may play several roles in the mother—mobilizing fat for energy and stabilizing plasma glucose at relatively high levels (growth-hormone-like effects) and facilitating development of the breasts (a prolactin-like effect). In the fetus, this hormone may exert growth-promoting effects.

Some of the numerous other physiological changes, hormonal and nonhormonal, in the mother during pregnancy are summarized in Table 19-9.

One comment about fluid balance during pregnancy is necessary: Some women retain abnormally large amounts of fluid and manifest both protein in the urine and hypertension. These are the symptoms of the disease known as *toxemia of pregnancy* or eclampsia, a condition that can sometimes be controlled by salt restriction. The factors responsible for the disease are unknown.

Pregnancy Sickness. The majority of women suffer from *pregnancy sickness* (popularly called morning sickness)—nausea and vomiting—during the first three months (first trimester) of pregnancy. The exact cause is unknown, but high concentrations of estrogen, progesterone, and other substances secreted at this time are thought to act on the vomiting center (Chapter 17) in the brain. Pregnancy sickness is also associated with changes in the perception of food palatability and the presence of taste aversions.

Parturition

A normal human pregnancy lasts approximately 40 weeks. Safe survival of premature infants is now possible at about the twenty-seventh week of pregnancy, but treatment of these infants often requires heroic efforts at great costs. Delivery of the infant, followed by the placenta, the entire process being termed **parturition,** is produced by strong rhythmical contractions of the myometrium. Actually, weak and infrequent uterine contractions begin at approximately 30 weeks and gradually increase in both strength and frequency. During the last month, the entire uterine contents shift downward so that the baby is brought into contact with the cervix. In over 90 percent of births, the baby's head is downward and acts as the wedge to dilate the cervical canal when labor begins (Figure 19-27).

This dilation can occur because, during the last few weeks of pregnancy, the cervix becomes soft and flexible. The cervical softening (often termed "ripening") is largely the result of a breakup of collagen fibers. These biochemi-

TABLE 19-9 MATERNAL RESPONSES TO PREGNANCY

	Response
Placenta	Secretion of estrogen, progesterone, chorionic gonadotropin, inhibin, placental lactogen, and other hormones.
Anterior pituitary	Increased secretion of prolactin and ACTH. Secretes very little FSH and LH.
Adrenal cortex	Increased secretion of aldosterone and cortisol.
Posterior pituitary	Increased secretion of vasopressin.
Parathyroids	Increased secretion of parathyroid hormone.
Kidneys	Increased secretion of renin, erythropoietin, and 1,25-dihydroxyvitamin D_3. Retention of salt and water. *Cause:* Increased aldosterone, vasopressin, and estrogen
Breasts	Enlarge and develop mature glandular structure. *Cause:* Estrogen, progesterone, prolactin, and placental lactogen
Blood volume	Increases. *Cause:* Erythrocyte volume is increased by erythropoietin, and plasma volume by salt and water retention.
Calcium balance	Positive. *Cause:* Increased parathyroid hormone and 1,25-dihydroxyvitamin D_3.
Body weight	Increases by average of 12.5 kg, 60 percent of which is water.
Circulation	Cardiac output increases, total peripheral resistance decreases (vasodilation in uterus, skin, breasts, GI tract, and kidneys), mean arterial pressure stays constant.
Respiration	Hyperventilation (arterial P_{CO_2} decreases).
Organic metabolism	Metabolic rate increases. Plasma glucose, gluconeogenesis, and fatty acid mobilization all increase. *Cause:* Hyporesponsiveness to insulin due to insulin antagonism by placental lactogen and cortisol.
Appetite and thirst	Increase.
Nutritional RDAs	Increase.

cal changes are mediated by a variety of messengers, including estrogen and prostaglandins.

At the onset of labor or before, the amniotic sac ruptures and the amniotic fluid escapes through the vagina. When labor begins in earnest, the uterine contractions become coordinated and quite strong (although usually painless at first) and occur at approximately 10- to 15-min intervals. The contractions begin in the upper portion of the uterus and sweep downward. This coordination is made possible by the fact that the uterine smooth-muscle cells are connected to each other by gap junctions. These junctions increase markedly in number near the end of pregnancy.

As the contractions increase in intensity and frequency, the cervical canal is gradually forced open to a maximum diameter of approximately 10 cm. Until this point, the contractions have not moved the fetus out of the uterus but have served only to dilate the cervix. Now the contractions move the fetus through the cervix and vagina. At this time the mother, by bearing down to increase abdominal pressure, can help the uterine contractions to deliver the baby. The umbilical vessels and placenta are still functioning, so that the baby is not yet on its own, but within minutes of delivery both the umbilical vessels and the placental vessels completely constrict, stopping blood flow to the placenta. The entire placenta becomes separated from

(A)

Uterus

Urinary bladder

Pubic bone

Urethra

Vagina

Placenta

Cervix

Rectum

(B)

Amniotic sac

Cervix

Vagina

Placenta

(C)

Ruptured
amniotic sac

(D)   Placenta

(E)

Placenta
(partially detached)

Uterus

Umbilical cord

FIGURE 19-27

Stages of parturition. (A) Parturition has not yet begun. (B) The cervix is dilating. (C) The cervix is completely dilated and the fetus's head is entering the cervical canal. (D) The fetus has moved through the vagina. (E) The placenta is coming loose from the uterine wall preparatory to its expulsion.

the underlying uterine wall, and a wave of uterine contractions delivers the placenta as the **afterbirth.**

Ordinarily, parturition proceeds automatically from beginning to end and requires no significant medical intervention. In a small percentage of cases, however, the position of the baby or some maternal defect can interfere with normal delivery. The headfirst position of the fetus is important for several reasons: (1) If the baby is not oriented headfirst, another portion of its body is in contact with the cervix and is generally a far less effective wedge. (2) Because of the head's large diameter compared with the rest of the body, if the body were to go through the cervical canal first, the canal might obstruct the passage of the head, leading to problems when the partially delivered baby attempts to breathe. (3) If the umbilical cord becomes caught between the canal wall and the baby's head or chest, mechanical compression of the umbilical vessels can result. Despite these potential problems, however, many babies who are not oriented headfirst are born normally.

What mechanisms control the events of parturition? Let us consider a set of fairly well established facts:

1. The autonomic neurons to the uterus are of little importance in parturition since anesthetizing them does not interfere with delivery.
2. The smooth-muscle cells of the myometrium have inherent rhythmicity and are capable of autonomous contractions, which are facilitated as the muscle is stretched by the growing fetus.
3. The pregnant uterus near term and during labor secretes a prostaglandin that is a profound stimulator of uterine smooth-muscle contraction.
4. **Oxytocin**, one of the hormones released from the posterior pituitary, is an extremely potent uterine-muscle stimulant. It not only acts directly on uterine smooth muscle but also stimulates it to synthesize prostaglandins. Oxytocin is reflexly released as a result of input to the hypothalamus from receptors in the uterus, particularly the cervix. During pregnancy the concentration of oxytocin receptors in the uterus markedly and progressively increases as a result of estrogen stimulation and, possibly, uterine distention near term.
5. Progesterone exerts a powerful inhibitory effect upon uterine contractions by decreasing the sensitivity to estrogen, oxytocin, and prostaglandins. Shortly before delivery, the ratio of progesterone to estrogen in plasma often decreases.

These facts can now be put together in a unified pattern, as shown in Figure 19-28. Once started, the uterine contractions exert a positive-feedback effect upon themselves via both local facilitation of inherent uterine contractions and reflex stimulation of oxytocin secretion. But

what *starts* the contractions? The most tenable hypothesis at present involves both oxytocin and prostaglandin: Even though these is no dramatic change in circulating oxytocin just before the onset of labor, the increased number of oxytocin receptors in the myometrium makes the uterus so sensitive to oxytocin that contractions become coordinated and strong. The decrease in progesterone/estrogen ratio further increases responsiveness to oxytocin. Simultaneously, the increased sensitivity to oxytocin results in an increased oxytocin-induced local synthesis of uterine prostaglandin, which further stimulates uterine contractions.

The action of prostaglandin on parturition is the last in a series of prostaglandin effects on the female reproductive system we have described. They are summarized in Table 19-10.

Lactation

The secretion of milk by the breasts, or **mammary glands**, is termed **lactation**. The breasts contain ducts that branch all through the tissue and converge at the nipples (Figure 19-29). These ducts arise in saclike glands called **alveoli** (the same term is used to denote the lung air sacs). The breast alveoli, which are the sites of milk secretion, look like bunches of grapes with stems terminating in the ducts. The alveoli and the ducts immediately adjacent to them are surrounded by specialized contractile cells called **myoepithelial cells**.

Before puberty, the breasts are small with little internal glandular structure. With the onset of puberty in females, the increased estrogen causes a marked enhancement of duct growth and branching but relatively little development of the alveoli, and much of the breast enlargement at this time is due to fat deposition. Progesterone secretion also commences at puberty during the luteal phase of each cycle, and this hormone contributes to breast growth by stimulating growth of alveoli.

During each menstrual cycle, the breasts undergo fluctuations in association with the changing blood concentrations of estrogen and progesterone, but these changes are small compared with the marked breast enlargement that occurs during pregnancy as a result of the stimulatory effects of high plasma concentrations of estrogen, progesterone, prolactin, and placental lactogen. This last hormone, as described earlier, is secreted by the placenta, whereas prolactin is secreted by the anterior pituitary. Under the influence of all these hormones, both the ductal and the alveolar structures become fully developed.

As described in Chapter 10, the anterior-pituitary cells that secrete prolactin are influenced by many hormones. They are inhibited by **dopamine**, which is secreted by both the hypothalamus and the posterior pituitary. They are stimulated by one or more **prolactin releasing factors (PRF)** also secreted by both the hypothalamus and

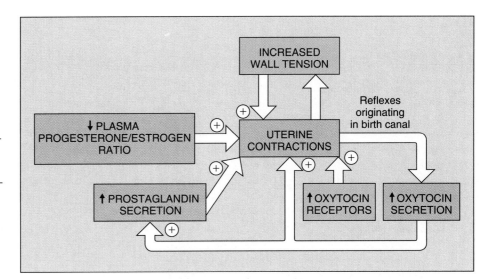

FIGURE 19-28

Factors stimulating uterine contractions during parturition. Note the positive-feedback nature of several of the inputs. Not shown in the figure is the fact that estrogen (or a decrease in the progesterone to estrogen ratio) and, possibly, uterine distention, are the cause of the increased number of oxytocin receptors in the myometrium.

the posterior pituitary. The dopamine and PRF secreted by the hypothalamus (hypophysiotropic hormones) reach the anterior pituitary by way of the hypothalamo-pituitary portal vessels, while those from the posterior pituitary arrive by way of a group of short portal vessels connecting the two lobes of the pituitary. Finally, estrogen also acts on the anterior pituitary to stimulate prolactin secretion.

Under the dominant inhibitory influence of dopamine, prolactin secretion is low before puberty. It then increases considerably at puberty in girls but not in boys, stimulated by the increased plasma estrogen concentration that occurs at this time. During pregnancy, there is a marked further increase in prolactin secretion due to stimulation by estrogen. Despite the fact that prolactin is elevated and the breasts are markedly enlarged and fully developed as pregnancy progresses, there is no secretion of milk. This is because estrogen and progesterone, in large concentrations, prevent milk production by inhibiting this particular action of prolactin on the breasts. Thus, although estrogen causes an increase in the secretion of prolactin and acts with prolactin in promoting breast growth and differentiation, it (along with progesterone) is antagonistic to prolactin's ability to induce milk secretion. Delivery removes the source—the placenta—of the large amounts of sex steroids and thereby the inhibition of milk production.

The drop in estrogen following parturition also causes

TABLE 19-10	SOME EFFECTS OF PROSTAGLANDINS* ON THE FEMALE REPRODUCTIVE SYSTEM	
Site of production	**Action**	**Result**
Late-antral follicle	Stimulate production of lytic enzymes	Rupture of follicle
Corpus luteum	Interfere with corpus luteum's hormone secretion and function	Death of corpus luteum
Uterus	Constrict blood vessels in endometrium	Onset of menstruation
	Cause changes in endometrial blood vessels and cells early in pregnancy	Facilitates implantation
	Increase contraction of myometrium	Helps initiate both menstruation and parturition

*The term "prostaglandins" is used loosely here, as is customary in reproductive physiology, to include all the eicosanoids (Chapter 7).

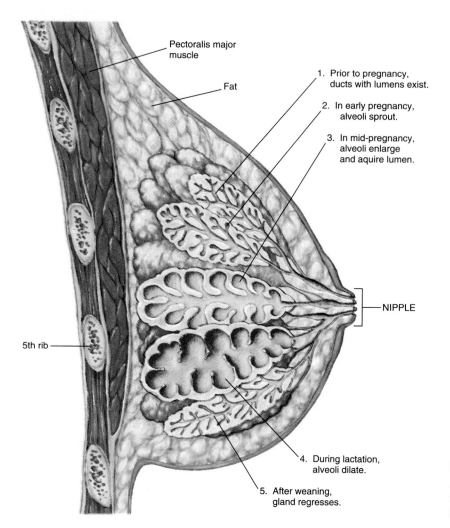

Pectoralis major
muscle

Fat

1. Prior to pregnancy,
ducts with lumens exist.

2. In early pregnancy,
alveoli sprout.

3. In mid-pregnancy,
alveoli enlarge
and aquire lumen.

NIPPLE

5th rib

4. During lactation,
alveoli dilate.

5. After weaning,
gland regresses.

FIGURE 19-29

Anatomy of the breast. The numbers refer to
the sequential changes that occur over time.
(Adapted from Elias et al.).

basal prolactin secretion to decrease from its peak late-pregnancy levels and after several months to return to pre-pregnancy levels even though the mother continues to nurse. Superimposed upon this basal level, however, are large secretory bursts of prolactin during each nursing period. The episodic pulses of prolactin are signals to the breasts for maintenance of milk production, which ceases several days after the mother completely stops nursing her infant but continues uninterrupted for years if nursing is continued.

The reflexes mediating the prolactin bursts (Figure 19-30) are initiated by afferent input to the hypothalamus from nipple receptors stimulated by suckling. This input's major effect is to stimulate the posterior pituitary neurons that secrete PRF.

One other reflex process is essential for nursing. Milk is secreted into the lumen of the alveoli, but the infant cannot suck the milk out of the alveoli. It must first be moved into the ducts, from which it can be sucked. This movement is called the **milk ejection reflex** (formerly called milk let-down) and is accomplished by contraction of the myoepithelial cells surrounding the alveoli. The contraction is under the control of oxytocin, which is reflexly released from posterior pituitary neurons in response to suckling (Figure 19-30), just like PRF. Higher brain centers can also exert an important influence over oxytocin release: A nursing mother may actually leak milk when she hears her baby cry or even thinks about nursing.

Another neuroendocrine reflex triggered by suckling (it may be mediated, in part, by prolactin) is inhibition of the hypothalamic-pituitary-ovarian chain at a variety of steps, with a resultant block of ovulation. If suckling is continued at high frequency, ovulation can be delayed for years. When supplements are added to the baby's diet and the frequency of suckling is decreased, however, most women will resume ovulation even though they continue to lactate. Failure to recognize this fact may result in an unplanned pregnancy.

Milk contains four major constituents: water, protein, fat, and the carbohydrate lactose (milk sugar). The alveolar

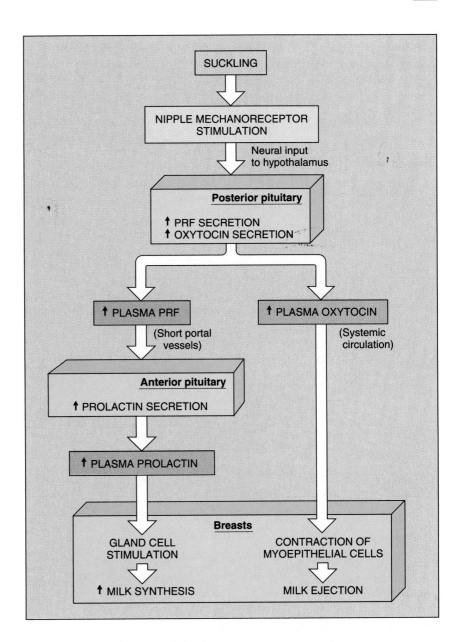

FIGURE 19-30

Major controls of the secretion of prolactin and oxytocin during nursing. In addition, the neural input to the hypothalamus may also inhibit the neurons that release dopamine from the posterior pituitary, and this would further stimulate prolactin secretion.

cells must be capable of extracting the raw materials—amino acids, fatty acids, glycerol, glucose, and so on—from the blood and building them into the higher-molecular-weight substances. Although prolactin is the single most important hormone controlling these synthetic processes, insulin, growth hormone, cortisol, and still other hormones also participate.

Milk also contains antibodies that are important for the newborn, as described in Chapter 20. Unfortunately, infectious agents, including the virus that causes AIDS (Chapter 20), can be transmitted through breast milk, as can some drugs. For example, the concentration of alcohol in breast milk is approximately the same as in maternal plasma.

Breast feeding for the first 3 to 6 months of an infant's life is advocated by the medical community. In less developed countries, where alternative formulas are often either contaminated or nutritionally inadequate because of improper dilution or refrigeration, breast feeding significantly reduces infant sickness and mortality. In the United States, effects on infant survival are not usually apparent, but the practice is economical, may reduce the severity of gastrointestinal infections, and has positive effects on the mother-infant interaction.

Contraception

About two-thirds of all American women between the ages of 15 and 44 use some method of fertility control (***contra-***

TABLE 19-11 SUMMARY OF CONTRACEPTIVE METHODS IN THE UNITED STATES*

Type and estimated percentage of use	First-year failure rate†	Advantages	Disadvantages	Comments
Surgical sterilization (vasectomy in male; tubal ligation in female) (33%)	0%	Safe, highly effective, and inexpensive over long term. Frees couples from concern associated with the use of other methods.	Requires surgery. May not be reversible.	Vasectomy is performed under local anesthesia. Tubal ligation is performed vaginally or abdominally under local or general anesthesia.
Birth control pill (oral contraceptive) (32%)	2%	Most effective reversible contraceptive. Results in lighter, more regular periods. Protects against cancer of the ovaries and uterine lining. Decreases risk of pelvic inflammatory disease, fibrocystic breast disease, and benign ovarian cysts.	Minor side effects similar to early pregnancy (nausea, breast tenderness, fluid retention) during first 3 months of use. Major complications (blood clots, hypertension) may occur in a very small number of smokers and those over 35. Controversial as to whether breast cancer is increased. Must be taken on a regular daily schedule.	Combination types contain both synthetic estrogen and progestagen. Minipill contains only progestagen and may produce irregular bleeding. Available by prescription only.
Injectable progestagens (Norplant) (Depo-Provera) (?)	1%	Long-lasting (5 yr for Norplant; 3 months for Depo-Provera).	Norplant: Prolonged menstruation; spotting. Headaches and mood changes also reported. Depo-Provera: Menstrual irregularities; ?increased risk of osteoporosis and breast cancer.	Most recently approved methods.
Intrauterine device (IUD) (3%)	5%	Once inserted, usually stays in place. Remains effective for 1–4 years.	May cause bleeding and cramping. Increased risk of pelvic inflammatory disease. If pregnancy occurs, increased risk that it may be ectopic. Must check for placement after each period. Requires annual replacement.	Available by prescription only.

ception[11]) (Table 19-11). Some forms—vasectomy, tubal ligation, vaginal diaphragms, vaginal caps, spermicides, and condoms—prevent sperm from reaching the egg. In addition, condoms significantly reduce the risk of *sexually transmitted diseases (STDs)* such as AIDS, syphilis, gonorrhea, chlamydia, and herpes.

In contrast, *oral contraceptives* are based on the fact that estrogen and progesterone can inhibit pituitary gonadotropin release, thereby preventing ovulation. One type is a combination of a synthetic estrogen and a progesterone-like substance (a progestagen or progestin). Another type is the so-called minipill, which contains only the progesterone-like substance. In actuality, oral contracep-

---

[11]In some usages, the term "contraception" is restricted to fertility control by the prevention of conception, that is, the union of the egg and sperm, and "abortifacient" is used to denote fertility control by interference with the pregnancy at any point beyond conception.

TABLE 19-11 SUMMARY OF CONTRACEPTIVE METHODS IN THE UNITED STATES* *(continued)*

Type and estimated percentage of use	First-year failure rate†	Advantages	Disadvantages	Comments
Condom (rubber, prophylactic, sheath) (17%)	10%	Protects against sexually transmitted diseases, including AIDS and herpes. May protect against cervical cancer.	Must be applied immediately before intercourse. Rare cases of allergy to rubber. May break. Blunting of sensation.	More effective when the woman uses a spermicide.
Vaginal spermicide (foams, jellies) (2%)	18% (used alone)	Available over the counter as jellies, foam, creams, and suppositories.	Messiness. Must be applied no more than 1 h before intercourse.	Best results occur when used with a condom or diaphragm.
Diaphragm (5%)	15% (with spermicide)	Can be inserted up to 6 h before intercourse.	Increased risk of urinary tract infection. Rare cases of allergy to rubber.	Use with spermicide is recommended. Available by prescription only and must be fitted. Must be left in for 6–8 h after intercourse.
Cervical cap (?)	15% (with spermicide)	Can be inserted several days before intercourse. Is smaller than a diaphragm.	Some women find it difficult to insert. Can cause an unpleasant odor.	Must be left in place for 6–8 h after intercourse but not more than 48 h.
Vaginal sponge (3%)	15%	Easy to use because spermicide is self-contained. May be inserted as much as (but no more than) 24 h before intercourse.	May be hard to remove; may fragment. May irritate vaginal lining. Higher failure rate in women who have given birth.	Must be left in for 6 h after intercourse.

*Coitus interruptus (withdrawal) and periodic abstinence from sexual intercourse around the time of ovulation (rhythm method) are not included because of their high failure rate.
†For all methods, most of the failures are due to improper or inconsistent use. It is likely that oral contraceptives, the IUD, and condoms are 99 to 100 percent effective when properly used; the others are 90 to 95 percent effective.
Source: Table adapted from University of California, Berkeley, *Wellness Letter,* 1987, and *New England Journal of Medicine,* 320:777–786, 1989.

tives, particularly the minipill, do not always prevent ovulation yet still are effective because they have other antifertility effects. For example, the progestagen component inhibits the estrogen-induced proliferation of the endometrium, making it inhospitable for implantation. In addition, the progestagen affects the composition of the cervical mucus, preventing passage of sperm through the cervix.

A newer method of delivering contraceptive progesterone-like steroids is via tiny capsules (Norplant) that are implanted beneath the skin and last for 5 years. Still more recent is the injection of yet another progesterone-like substance (Depo-Provera) every 3 months.

Not available in the United States but widely used in France and China is the drug RU 486, which has anti-progesterone activity because it binds competitively to progesterone receptors but does not activate them. Administration of RU 486, followed by a prostaglandin derivative, is an extremely effective and safe method for terminating pregnancy within 7 weeks of conception. Antagonism of progesterone's effects causes the endometrium to erode and the myometrial contractions to increase, thereby expelling the embryo.

The ***intrauterine device (IUD)***, like RU 486, also works beyond the point of fertilization. The presence of one of these small objects in the uterus somehow interferes with the endometrial preparation for acceptance of the blastocyst.

The rhythm method uses abstention from sexual intercourse near the time of ovulation. Unfortunately, it is difficult to time ovulation precisely even with laboratory techniques. For example, the small rise in body temperature or change in cervical mucus and vaginal epithelium, all of which are indicators of ovulation, occur only *after* ovulation. This problem, combined with the marked variability of the time of ovulation in many women—from day 5 to day 15 of the cycle—explains why this technique has a high failure rate (19 percent).

There are still no effective chemical agents for male contraception.

Infertility

Approximately 12 percent of the married couples in the United States are infertile, the number of infertile men and women being approximately equal. Careful investigation permits, in 85 percent of cases, diagnosis and successful therapy with drugs, artificial insemination, and corrective surgery.

When the basic defect cannot be treated, it can sometimes be circumvented by the technique of *in vitro fertilization*. First, the woman is injected with drugs that stimulate multiple egg production. Immediately before ovulation, at least one egg is then removed from the ovary via a needle inserted into the ovary through the top of the vagina or the lower abdominal wall. The egg is placed in a dish for several days with sperm from the male partner. After the fertilized egg has developed into a cluster of two to eight cells, it is transferred to the woman's uterus. The most extensive national study of this technique, in 1988, showed a success rate of 12 percent, but recent developments are greatly increasing this number.

Increasing numbers of women are choosing to delay childbearing until well into their thirties. It is known that fertility in women peaks in their twenties and declines gradually after the age of 30. Also, the incidence of Down's syndrome increases with advancing maternal age as do various other chromosomal abnormalities and the risk of spontaneous abortion. On the other hand, recent studies have documented that women over 35 had no increased risk of having a preterm delivery or of having an infant who was small for gestational age, had a low Apgar score (a measure of the condition of the infant at birth), or died in the perinatal period.

SECTION C SUMMARY

OVARIAN FUNCTION

I. The female gonads, the ovaries, produce eggs and secrete estrogen, progesterone, and inhibin.

II. The two meiotic divisions of oogenesis result in each ova having 23 chromosomes, in contrast to the 46 of the original oogonia.

III. The follicle cells consist of inner layers of granulosa cells and outer layers of theca cells.

IV. At the beginning of each menstrual cycle, a group of follicles begins to develop into antral follicles, but soon only the dominant follicle continues its development to full maturity and ovulation.

V. Following ovulation the remaining cells of that follicle are transformed into a corpus luteum, which lasts about 10 to 14 days if pregnancy does not occur.

VI. The menstrual cycle can be divided, according to ovarian events, into a follicular phase and a luteal phase, which are approximately 14 days each and are separated by ovulation.

CONTROL OF OVARIAN FUNCTION

I. The menstrual cycle results from a finely tuned interplay of hormones secreted by the ovaries, the anterior pituitary, and the hypothalamus.

II. During the early and middle follicular phases, FSH stimulates the granulosa cells to proliferate and secrete estrogen, and LH stimulates the theca cells to proliferate and produce the androgens that the granulosa cells use to make estrogen.

A. During this period, estrogen exerts a negative feedback on the anterior pituitary to inhibit the secretion of the gonadotropins.

B. Estrogen may also inhibit secretion of GnRH by the hypothalamus.

C. Inhibin preferentially inhibits FSH secretion.

III. During the late follicular phase, plasma estrogen becomes high enough to elicit a surge of LH, which then causes, via the granulosa cells, completion of the egg's first meiotic division and cytoplasmic maturation, ovulation, and formation of the corpus luteum.

IV. During the luteal phase, under the influence of small amounts of LH, the corpus luteum secretes progesterone and estrogen. Regression of the corpus luteum results in a cessation of the secretion of these hormones.

V. Secretion of GnRH and the gonadotropins is inhibited during the luteal phase by the combination of progesterone, estrogen, and inhibin.

UTERINE CHANGES IN THE MENSTRUAL CYCLE

I. The ovarian follicular phase is equivalent to the uterine menstrual and proliferative phases, the first day of menstruation being the first day of the cycle. The ovarian luteal phase is equivalent to the uterine secretory phase.

  A. Menstruation occurs when the plasma progesterone and estrogen levels fall as a result of regression of the corpus luteum.

  B. During the proliferative phase, estrogen stimulates growth of the endometrium and myometrium and causes the cervical mucus to be readily penetrable by sperm.

  C. During the secretory phase, progesterone converts the estrogen-primed endometrium to a secretory tissue and makes the cervical mucus relatively impenetrable to sperm. It also inhibits uterine contractions.

OTHER EFFECTS OF ESTROGEN AND PROGESTERONE

  I. The many effects of estrogen and progesterone are summarized in Table 19-8.

PREGNANCY

  I. After ovulation, the egg is swept into a uterine tube, where a sperm, having undergone capacitation and the acrosome reaction, fertilizes it.

  II. Following fertilization the egg undergoes its second meiotic division, and the nuclei of the ovum and sperm fuse. Reactions in the ovum block penetration by other sperm and trigger cell division and embryogenesis.

  III. The conceptus undergoes cleavage, becoming a blastocyst, which implants in the endometrium on approximately day 7 after ovulation.

   A. The trophoblast gives rise to the fetal part of the placenta, whereas the inner cell mass develops into the embryo proper.

   B. Although they do not mix, fetal blood and maternal blood both flow through the placenta, exchanging gases, nutrients, and waste products.

   C. The fetus is surrounded by amniotic fluid in the amniotic sac.

  IV. The progesterone and estrogen required to maintain the uterus during pregnancy come from the corpus luteum for the first 2 months of pregnancy, their secretion stimulated by chorionic gonadotropin produced by the trophoblast.

  V. During the last 7 months of pregnancy, the corpus luteum regresses and the placenta itself produces large amounts of progesterone and estrogen.

  VI. The high levels of progesterone, in the presence of estrogen, inhibit the secretion of GnRH and thereby that of the gonadotropins, so that menstrual cycles are eliminated.

  VII. Parturition occurs by rhythmical contractions of the uterus, which first dilate the cervix and then move the infant, followed by the placenta, through the vagina. The contractions are stimulated by a decrease in the progesterone/estrogen ratio (progesterone inhibits and estrogen stimulates contractions), by oxytocin released from the posterior pituitary in a reflex triggered by uterine mechanoreceptors, and by uterine prostaglandins.

  VIII. The breasts develop markedly during pregnancy as a result of the combined influences of estrogen, progesterone, prolactin, and placental lactogen.

   A. Prolactin secretion is stimulated during pregnancy by estrogen acting on the anterior pituitary, but milk is not synthesized because high concentrations of estrogen and progesterone inhibit the milk-producing action of prolactin on the breasts.

   B. As a result of the suckling reflex, large bursts of prolactin and oxytocin occur during nursing, the prolactin stimulating milk production and the oxytocin causing milk ejection.

SECTION C KEY TERMS

ovulation	LH surge
menstrual cycles	menstrual phase
menstruation	endometrium
female internal genitalia	proliferative phase
uterine tubes	secretory phase
uterus	myometrium
cervix	capacitation
vagina	fertilization
female external genitalia	acrosome reaction
vulva	zygote
clitoris	conceptus
oogenesis	cleavage
egg	blastocyst
oogonia	trophoblast
primary oocytes	inner cell mass
meiotic arrest	embryo
secondary oocytes	fetus
first polar body	implantation
second polar body	placenta
follicles	chorion
primordial follicles	chorionic villi
granulosa cells	umbilical arteries
zona pellucida	umbilical vein
theca	umbilical cord
antrum	amniotic cavity
dominant follicle	amnion
atresia	amniotic sac
corpus luteum	amniotic fluid
follicular phase	chorionic gonadotropin
luteal phase	(CG)

estriol
placental lactogen
parturition
afterbirth
oxytocin
mammary glands
lactation

alveoli
myoepithelial cells
dopamine
prolactin releasing factor
  (PRF)
milk ejection reflex

SECTION C REVIEW QUESTIONS

1. Draw the female reproductive tract.
2. Describe the various stages from oogonium to mature ovum.
3. Describe the progression from a primordial follicle to a dominant follicle.
4. Name three hormones produced by the ovaries and name the cells that produce them.
5. Diagram the changes in plasma concentrations of estrogen, progesterone, LH, and FSH during the menstrual cycle.
6. What are the analogies between the granulosa cells and the Sertoli cells and between the theca cells and the Leydig cells?
7. List the effects of FSH and LH on the follicle.
8. Describe the effects of estrogen and inhibin on gonadotropin secretion during the early, middle, and late follicular phases.
9. List the effects of the LH surge on the egg and the follicle.
10. What are the effects of the sex steroids and inhibin on gonadotropin secretion during the luteal phase?
11. Describe the hormonal control of the corpus luteum and its history in a nonpregnant cycle.
12. What happens to the sex steroids and the gonadotropins as the corpus luteum degenerates?
13. Compare the phases of the menstrual cycle according to uterine and ovarian events.

14. Describe the effects of estrogen and progesterone on the endometrium, cervical mucus, and myometrium.
15. Describe the uterine events associated with menstruation.
16. List the effects of estrogen on the accessory sex organs and secondary sex characteristics.
17. List the effects of progesterone on the breasts and body temperature.
18. What are the source and effects of androgens in women?
19. How does the egg get from the ovary to a uterine tube?
20. Where does fertilization normally occur?
21. Describe the events that occur during fertilization.
22. How many days after ovulation does implantation occur, and in what stage is the conceptus at that time?
23. Describe the components of the placenta and the mechanisms of exchange between maternal and fetal blood.
24. State the sources of estrogen and progesterone during different stages of pregnancy. What is the dominant estrogen of pregnancy, and how is it produced?
25. What is the state of gonadotropin secretion during pregnancy, and what is the cause?
26. What anatomical feature permits coordinated contractions of the myometrium?
27. Describe the mechanisms and messengers that contribute to parturition.
28. List the effects of prostaglandins on the female reproductive system.
29. Describe the development of the breasts after puberty and during pregnancy and list the hormones responsible.
30. Describe the effects of estrogen on the secretion and actions of prolactin during pregnancy.
31. Diagram the suckling reflex for prolactin release.
32. Diagram the milk ejection reflex.

SECTION

THE CHRONOLOGY OF REPRODUCTIVE FUNCTION

This section treats a variety of topics that have to do, in one way or another, with sequential changes in reproductive development or function. Thus, genetic inheritance, which sets the sex of the individual—**sex determination**—is established at the moment of fertilization. This is followed by **sex differentiation**, the multiple processes in which development of the reproductive system occurs in the fetus. Then there is the maturation of the system at puberty and the eventual decline that occurs with aging.

SEX DETERMINATION

One's sex is determined by genetic inheritance of two chromosomes called the **sex chromosomes**. The larger of the sex chromosomes is called the **X chromosome** and the smaller, the **Y chromosome**. Males possess one X and one Y, whereas females have two X chromosomes. Thus, the *genetic* difference between male and female is simply the difference in one chromosome.

The reason for the approximately equal sex distribution of the population should be readily apparent: The ovum can contribute only an X chromosome, whereas half of the sperm produced during meiosis are X and half are Y. When the sperm and egg join, 50 percent should have XX and 50 percent XY. Interestingly, however, sex ratios at birth are not exactly 1:1; rather, for unclear reasons, there tends to be a slight preponderance of male births.

An easy method exists for determining whether a person's cells contain two X chromosomes, the normal female pattern. When two X chromosomes are present, only one functions; the nonfunctional X chromosome condenses to form a nuclear mass, termed the **sex chromatin**, that is readily observable with a light microscope (scrapings from the cheek mucosa are a convenient source of cells to be examined). The single X chromosome in male cells rarely condenses to form sex chromatin.

A more exacting technique for determining sex chromosome composition employs tissue culture visualization of all the chromosomes—a **karyotype**. This technique has revealed a group of genetic sex abnormalities characterized by such unusual chromosomal combinations as XXX, XXY, X, and others. The end result of such combinations is usually the failure of normal anatomical and functional sexual development.

SEX DIFFERENTIATION

It is not surprising that people with abnormal genetic endowment manifest abnormal sexual development, but careful study has also revealed individuals with normal chromosomal combinations but abnormal sexual appearance and function. In these people, sex differentiation has been abnormal, and their appearance may even be at odds with their genetic sex, that is, the presence of XX or XY chromosomes.

It will be important to bear in mind during the following description one essential generalization: The genes directly determine only whether the individual will have testes or ovaries. All the rest of sex differentiation depends upon the presence or absence of substances, such as the sex hormones, produced by the genetically determined gonads.

Differentiation of the Gonads

The male and female gonads derive embryologically from the same site in the body. Until the sixth week of uterine life, there is no differentiation of this site. In the genetic male the testes begin to develop during the seventh week. A single gene (the **SRY gene**) on the Y chromosome determines this development. In the absence of a Y chromosome and, hence, the SRY gene, testes do not develop and, instead, ovaries begin to develop at about 11 weeks.

Differentiation of Internal and External Genitalia

As far as its internal duct system and external genitalia are concerned, the fetus is capable of developing into either sex. Before the functioning of the fetal gonads, the primitive reproductive tract includes a double genital duct system—**Wolffian ducts** and **Müllerian ducts**—and a common opening for the genital ducts and urinary system to the outside. Normally, most of the reproductive tract develops from only one of these duct systems: In the male, the Wolffian ducts persist and the Müllerian ducts regress, whereas in the female, the opposite happens. The external genitalia in the two sexes and the vagina do not develop from these duct systems but from other structures at the body surface.

Which of the two duct systems and types of external genitalia develops depends on the presence or absence of fetal testes. If testes are present, they secrete (1) testosterone, from the Leydig cells under stimulation by chorionic gonadotropin secreted by the placenta; and (2) a protein called **Müllerian inhibiting factor (MIF)**, from the Sertoli cells. MIF acts as a paracrine agent to cause the Müllerian duct system to degenerate, and testosterone causes the Wolffian ducts to differentiate into the epididymis, vas deferens, ejaculatory duct, and seminal vesicle. Externally and somewhat later, under the influence of testosterone, after conversion to dihydrotestosterone, a penis forms and the tissue near it fuses to form the scrotum, into which the testes will ultimately descend, stimulated to do so by both MIF and testosterone (Figure 19-31A).

In contrast, the female fetus, lacking testes and thus testosterone and MIF, develops uterine tubes and a uterus from the Müllerian system as well as a vagina and female external genitalia from the structures at the body surface (Figure 19-31B). A female gonad need not be present for the female organs to develop; in other words, female development will occur automatically unless stopped from doing so by the presence of secretions from functioning testes.

There is a variety of conditions in which normal sex differentiation does not occur. For example, in the syn-

FIGURE 19-31

Sex differentiation. (A) Male. (B) Female.

drome known as *testicular feminization* (or androgen insensitivity syndrome), the person's genetic endowment is XY and testes are present, but he has female external genitalia, a vagina, and no internal duct system at all. The problem causing this is a lack of androgen receptors due to a genetic defect. The fetal testes differentiate as usual, and they secrete both MIF and testosterone. MIF causes the Müllerian ducts to regress, but the inability of the Wolffian ducts to respond to testosterone also causes them to regress, and so no duct system develops. The tissues that give rise to external genitalia (and the vagina, in the female) are also unresponsive to testosterone, and so female external genitalia and a vagina develop rather than male structures.

Sexual Differentiation of the Central Nervous System

In humans and other primates there are no inherent male-female differences in the ability of the hypothalamus to secrete GnRH in response to neuronal or hormonal inputs. For example, administration of large amounts of estrogen to castrated male monkeys elicits LH surges indistinguishable from those shown by females.

The situation may be different for sexual *behavior*, however, in that differences in the brain may be formed during development. For example, genetic female monkeys given testosterone during late fetal life manifest evidence of masculine sex behavior (mounting, for example) as adults.

In this regard, a potentially important difference in brain anatomy has recently been reported for people: The size of a particular nucleus (neuronal cluster) in the hypothalamus is more than twice as large in men as in women. Interest in this difference soared when a subsequent study showed that the nucleus is also more than twice as large in heterosexual men as in homosexual men. A similar sexually dimorphic area exists in rats, in which it is known to be involved in male-type sexual behavior and is influenced during development by testosterone. Evaluation of the meaning of these findings for the genetics and hormone dependency of sexual behavior and gender preference will await much more research. Another relevant human study that has gained much attention reported that 52 percent of identical twin brothers of gay men also were gay, compared to 22 percent of fraternal twins and 11 percent of genetically unrelated (adoptive) brothers.

PUBERTY

Puberty is the period, usually occurring sometime between the ages of 10 and 14, during which the reproductive organs, having differentiated many years earlier in utero, mature and reproduction becomes possible.

In the female, GnRH, the pituitary gonadotropins, and estrogen are all secreted at very low levels during childhood. Accordingly, follicle maturation and menstrual cycles do not occur, the female accessory sex organs remain small and nonfunctional, and there are minimal secondary sex characteristics. The onset of puberty is caused, in large part, by an alteration in brain function that raises secretion of GnRH. This hypophysiotropic hormone in turn stimulates secretion of pituitary gonadotropins, which stimulate follicle development and estrogen secretion. Estrogen, in addition to its critical role in follicle development, induces the striking changes in the accessory sex organs and secondary sex characteristics associated with puberty.

The picture for the male is analogous to that for the female. Increased GnRH secretion at puberty causes increased secretion of pituitary gonadotropins, which stimulate the seminiferous tubules and testosterone secretion. Testosterone, in addition to its critical role in spermatogenesis, induces the pubertal changes in the accessory reproductive organs, secondary sex characteristics, and sex drive.

The mechanism of the brain change that results in increased GnRH secretion at puberty remains unknown.[12] Whatever the mechanism, the process is not abrupt but develops over several years, as evidenced by slowly rising plasma concentrations of the gonadotropins and testosterone or estrogen.

It should be recognized that the maturational events of puberty usually proceed in an orderly sequence but that the ages at which they occur may vary among individuals. In girls, the onset of breast development is usually the first event, beginning at an average age of 11, although pubic hair may, on occasion, appear first. **Menarche**, the first menstrual period, is a later event (average of 12.3 years) and occurs almost invariably after the peak of the total-body growth spurt has passed.

In boys, the first sign of puberty is accelerated growth of testes and scrotum. Pubic hair appears a trifle later, and axillary and facial hair still later. Acceleration of penis growth begins on the average at 13 years and is complete by 15.

Some children with brain tumors or other lesions of the hypothalamus may undergo precocious puberty, that is, sexual maturation at an unusually early age, sometimes within the first 5 years of life. The youngest mother on record gave birth to a full-term, healthy infant by caesarean section (abdominal incision) at 5 years, 8 months.

---

[12]One proposed candidate for the trigger is a decrease in secretion of the hormone melatonin by the pineal gland, but there is no convincing evidence for this hypothesis in humans. Another theory is that the brain becomes less sensitive to the negative feedback effects of gonadal hormones at the time of puberty.

MENOPAUSE

A round the age of 50, on the average, menstrual cycles become less regular. Ultimately they cease entirely, and this cessation is known as the **menopause**. The phase of life beginning with menstrual irregularity and culminating in menopause is known as the **climacteric**, the counterpart of puberty. It involves numerous physical and emotional changes as sexual maturity gives way to cessation of reproductive function.

Menopause and the irregular function leading to it are caused by ovarian failure. The ovaries lose their ability to respond to the gonadotropins, partly because of a decreasing number of follicles and partly because the remaining follicles are hyporesponsive. That the hypothalamus and anterior pituitary are functioning relatively normally is evidenced by the fact that the gonadotropins are secreted in greater amounts in response to the decreasing plasma estrogen levels.

Although some ovarian secretion of estrogen generally continues beyond menopause, as does peripheral conversion of adrenal androgens to estrogen, plasma estrogen gradually diminishes until it is inadequate to maintain the estrogen-dependent tissues. The breasts and genital organs gradually atrophy to a large degree. Thinning and dryness of the vaginal epithelium can cause sexual intercourse to be painful. Marked decreases in bone mass and strength, termed *osteoporosis*, may occur because of bone resorption and can result in bone fractures (Chapter 16). Sex drive frequently stays the same and may even increase. The hot flashes so typical of menopause are accompanied by dilation of the skin arterioles, a feeling of warmth, and marked sweating, but why estrogen deficiency causes this is unknown. Another aspect of menopause is its relationship to cardiovascular diseases. Women have much less coronary artery disease than men until after the menopause, when the incidence becomes similar in both sexes (see Chapter 18 for estrogen's effects on plasma cholesterol).

Most of the symptoms associated with menopause, as well as the increases in osteoporosis and coronary artery disease, can be reduced by the administration of estrogen. The desirability of such administration is controversial, however, because of the fact that estrogen administration definitely increases the risk of developing uterine (endometrial) cancer and, possibly, breast cancer as well. This risk of cancer can be reduced, however, by administration of a progestagen along with estrogen, but there is some question as to whether the progestagen might eliminate some of estrogen's protective effect against coronary artery disease. Because of these complexities, quantitation of the competing risks and benefits of estrogen replacement therapy, with and without added progestagen, must await the completion of the large controlled studies presently underway in postmenopausal women.

Changes in the male reproductive system with aging are less drastic than those in women. Once testosterone and pituitary gonadotropin secretions are initiated at puberty, they continue, at least to some extent, throughout adult life. There is a steady decrease, however, in testosterone secretion, beginning at about the age of 40, which apparently reflects slow deterioration of testicular function and, as in the female, failure of the gonads to respond to the pituitary gonadotropins. Along with the decreasing testosterone levels, both sex drive and capacity diminish, although many men continue to be fertile in their seventies and eighties.

With aging, some men manifest increased emotional problems, such as depression, and this is sometimes referred to as "male menopause" (or male climacteric). It is not clear, however, what role hormone changes play in this phenomenon.

SECTION D SUMMARY

SEX DETERMINATION AND SEX DIFFERENTIATION

  I. Sex is determined by the two sex chromosomes: Males are XY, and females are XX.
 II. A gene on the Y chromosome is responsible for the development of testes. In the absence of a Y chromosome, testes do not develop and ovaries do instead.
III. When a functioning male gonad is present to secrete testosterone and MIF, a male reproductive tract and external genitalia develop. In the absence of testes, the female system develops.

PUBERTY

  I. At puberty, the hypothalamic-anterior-pituitary-gonadal chain of hormones becomes active as the result of a change in brain function that permits increased secretion of GnRH.
 II. In girls the first sign of puberty is either the beginning of breast development or appearance of pubic hair. In boys it is acceleration of growth of the testes and scrotum.

MENOPAUSE

  I. Around the age of 50, a woman's menstrual periods

become less regular and ultimately disappear—menopause.

A. The cause of menopause is a decrease in the number of ovarian follicles and their hyporesponsiveness to the gonadotropins.

B. The symptoms of menopause are largely due to the marked decrease in plasma estrogen concentration.

II. Men show a steady decrease in testosterone secretion after age 40 but generally no complete cessation of reproductive function.

SECTION D KEY TERMS

sex determination	Wolffian ducts
sex differentiation	Müllerian ducts
sex chromosomes	Müllerian inhibiting factor (MIF)
X chromosome	puberty
Y chromosome	menarche
sex chromatin	menopause
karyotype	climacteric
SRY gene	

SECTION D REVIEW QUESTIONS

1. State the genetic difference between males and females and a method for identifying genetic sex.
2. Describe the sequence of events, the timing, and the control of the development of the gonads and the internal and external genitalia.
3. What is the state of gonadotropin and sex hormone secretion before puberty?
4. What is the state of estrogen and gonadotropin secretion after menopause?
5. List the hormonal and anatomical changes that occur after menopause.

CHAPTER 19 CLINICAL TERMS

vasectomy	malnutrition
castration	toxemia of pregnancy
impotence	pregnancy sickness
dysmenorrhea	contraception
premenstrual syndrome (PMS)	sexually transmitted diseases (STDs)
ectopic pregnancies	
amniocentesis	oral contraceptives
chorionic villus sampling	intrauterine device

in vitro fertilization   testicular feminization
osteoporosis

CHAPTER 19 THOUGHT QUESTIONS

(Answers are given in Appendix A.)

1. What symptom will be common to a person whose Leydig cells have been destroyed and to a person whose Sertoli cells have been destroyed? What symptom will not be common?
2. A male athlete taking large amounts of an androgenic steroid becomes sterile (unable to produce sperm capable of causing fertilization). Explain.
3. A man who is sterile is found to have no evidence of demasculinization. He has an increased blood concentration of FSH and a normal plasma concentration of LH. What is the most likely basis of his sterility?
4. If you were a scientist trying to develop a male contraceptive acting on the anterior pituitary, would you try to block the secretion of FSH or that of LH? Explain the reason for your choice.
5. A 30-year-old man has very small muscles, a sparse beard, and a high-pitched voice. His plasma concentration of LH is elevated. Explain the likely cause of all these findings.
6. There are disorders of the adrenal cortex in which excessive amounts of androgens are produced. If this occurs in a woman, what will happen to her menstrual cycles?
7. Women with inadequate secretion of GnRH are often treated for their sterility with drugs that mimic the action of this hormone. Can you suggest a possible reason that such treatment often is associated with multiple births?
8. Which of the following would be a signal that ovulation is soon to occur: the cervical mucus becoming thick and sticky, an increase in body temperature, a marked rise in plasma LH?
9. The absence of what phenomenon would interfere with the ability of sperm obtained by masturbation to fertilize an egg in a test tube?
10. If a woman 7 months pregnant is found to have a marked decrease in plasma estriol but a normal plasma progesterone for that time of pregnancy, what would you conclude?
11. What types of drugs might you work on if you were trying to develop one to stop premature labor?
12. If a genetic male failed to produce MIF during in utero life, what would the result be?
13. Could the symptoms of menopause be treated by injections of FSH and LH?

C H A P T E R
20

DEFENSE MECHANISMS OF THE BODY

SECTION

IMMUNOLOGY: DEFENSES AGAINST FOREIGN MATTER

Immunology is the study of the physiological responses by which the body destroys or neutralizes foreign matter, both living and nonliving. In distinguishing "self" from "nonself," immune responses (1) protect against infection by *microbes*—viruses, bacteria, fungi, and parasites; (2) isolate or remove nonmicrobial foreign substances; and (3) destroy cancer cells that arise in the body, a function known as **immune surveillance**.

Immune defenses (also termed simply immunity) can be classified into two categories—nonspecific and specific—which interact with each other. **Nonspecific immune defenses** protect against foreign substances or cells without having to recognize their specific identities. **Specific immune defenses** depend upon recognition of the substance or cell to be attacked.

Before introducing the cells that participate in immune defenses, let us first look at the microbes we shall be most concerned with in this chapter—bacteria and viruses. These are the dominant infectious organisms in the United States and other industrialized nations. On a global basis, however, infection with parasitic protozoans (malaria, for example) or worms are responsible for considerable illness and mortality. For example, over 600 million people presently suffer from malaria.

Bacteria are unicellular organisms (prokaryocytes, Chapter 3) that have an outer coating, the cell wall, in addition to a plasma membrane, but no intracellular membrane-bound organelles. Infectious bacteria may replicate at their initial site of entry or they may travel via the blood or lymph to other areas before significant replication occurs. Bacteria can damage tissues at their sites of replication, or they can release into the extracellular fluid toxins that are carried by the blood and disrupt physiological functions in other parts of the body.

Viruses are essentially nucleic acids surrounded by a protein coat. Unlike bacteria, which can carry out metabolic activity and replicate independent of other cells, viruses lack both the enzyme machinery for energy production and the ribosomes essential for protein synthesis. Thus, they cannot multiply by themselves but must "live" inside other cells whose biochemical apparatus they make use of. The viral nucleic acid directs the host cell to synthesize the proteins required for viral replication, with the required nucleotides and energy sources also being supplied by the host cell.

The effect of viral habitation and replication within a cell depends on the type of virus. Some viruses (the common cold virus, for example), after entering a cell, multiply rapidly, kill the cell, and then move on to other cells. Others, such as the virus that causes genital herpes, can lie dormant in infected cells before suddenly undergoing the rapid replication that causes cell damage. Still others, termed slow viruses, replicate inside their host cells very slowly, and the viral nucleic acid may even become associated with the cell's own DNA molecules, replicating along with them and being passed on to the daughter cells during cell division. Such a virus [the one that causes AIDS (acquired immune deficiency syndrome), for example] may remain in the cell or the cell's offspring for many years, replicating very slowly until it reaches numbers that cause disease. Finally, certain viruses cause transformation of their host cells into cancer cells.

CELLS MEDIATING IMMUNE DEFENSES

The cells that carry out immune responses are collectively termed the **immune system**, but they do not constitute a "system" in the sense of anatomically connected organs like the gastrointestinal or urinary system. Rather, they are a diverse collection of cells found both in the blood and in tissues throughout the body. The major cell types are listed in Table 20-1, along with their sites of production. Because of the large number of cells and the far larger number of chemical messengers that participate in immune responses, a miniglossary defining the cells and messengers discussed in this chapter is given at the end of Section A (Table 20-12).

The most numerous of the immune-system cells are the **leukocytes**. Their anatomy, origin in the bone marrow, and distribution in blood were described in Chapter 14, Section A, and should be reviewed at this time. Unlike erythrocytes, the leukocytes use the blood mainly for transportation and leave the circulatory system to enter the tissues and function there. In this regard, the lymphocytes are the most complex of the leukocytes, and we shall delay until a subsequent section the description of the var-

TABLE 20-1   CELLS MEDIATING IMMUNE RESPONSES

Name	Site produced
Leukocytes (white blood cells)	
Neutrophils	Bone marrow
Basophils	Bone marrow
Eosinophils	Bone marrow
Monocytes	Bone marrow
Lymphocytes	Bone marrow, thymus, and peripheral lymphoid organs
B cells	
T cells	
Cytotoxic T cells	
Helper T cells	
Suppressor T cells	
NK cells	
Plasma cells	Peripheral lymphoid organs; differentiate from B lymphocytes during immune responses
Macrophages	Almost all tissues and organs; differentiate from monocytes
Mast cells	Almost all tissues and organs; differentiate from bone marrow cells

ious classes and subclasses of lymphocytes, their origins, migrations, and major organs of residence—the lymphoid organs.

Plasma cells are not a distinct cell line but differentiate from a particular set of lymphocytes (the B lymphocytes) during immune responses. Despite their name, plasma cells are not usually found in the blood but rather in the tissues in which they have differentiated from lymphocytes. The major function of plasma cells is to synthesize and secrete antibodies.

Macrophages are large cells found in virtually all organs and tissues, their structures varying somewhat from location to location. They are derived from monocytes that pass out of blood vessels to enter the tissues and become transformed into macrophages. By the time of birth, this process has already supplied the tissues with a large number of tissue macrophages that occupy fixed positions, but the migration of monocytes continues throughout life. In keeping with one of their major functions, the engulfing of particles, including microbes, macrophages are strategically placed where they will encounter their targets. For example, they are found in large numbers in the various epithelia in contact with the external environment, and in several organs they line the vessels through which blood or lymph flows.

Mast cells are also found scattered throughout many organs and tissues. They are derived from the differentiation of as yet unidentified bone marrow cells that have entered the blood and then left the blood vessels to enter the tissues, where they can undergo cell division. The most striking anatomical feature of mast cells is a very large number of secretory vesicles, and these cells secrete many locally acting chemical messengers.

The functions of all these cells are briefly listed in Table 20-2 for reference and will be described in subsequent sections.

NONSPECIFIC IMMUNE DEFENSES

The nonspecific immune defenses—those that protect against foreign matter without having to recognize its identity—include defenses at the body surfaces, the response to injury known as inflammation, and a family of antiviral proteins called interferons. Another nonspecific defense—the lymphocytes called natural killer (NK) cells—is best described later in the context of the specific immune defenses that commonly mobilize them.

TABLE 20-2 MAJOR FUNCTIONS OF CELLS MEDIATING IMMUNE RESPONSES

Neutrophils	1. Phagocytosis 2. Release chemicals involved in inflammation (vasodilators, chemotaxins, etc.)
Basophils	Have functions in blood similar to those of mast cells in tissues (see below)
Eosinophils	1. Destroy parasitic worms 2. Participate in immediate hypersensitivity reactions
Monocytes	1. Have functions in blood similar to those of macrophages in tissues (see below) 2. Enter tissues and are transformed into macrophages
B cells	1. Initiate antibody-mediated immune responses by binding specific antigens to their plasma-membrane receptors, which are immunoglobulins 2. During activation are transformed into plasma cells, which secrete antibodies 3. Present antigen to helper T cells
Cytotoxic T cells	Bind to antigens on plasma membrane of target cells (virus-infected cells, cancer cells, and tissue transplants) and directly destroy the cells
Helper T cells	Secrete cytokines that activate B cells, cytotoxic T cells, NK cells, and macrophages
Suppressor T cells	Inhibit B cells and cytotoxic T cells
NK cells	1. Bind directly and nonspecifically to virus-infected cells and cancer cells and kill them 2. Function as killer cells in antibody-dependent cellular cytotoxicity (ADCC)
Plasma cells	Secrete antibodies
Macrophages	1. Phagocytosis and intracellular killing 2. Extracellular killing via secretion of toxic chemicals 3. Process and present antigens to helper T cells 4. Secrete cytokines involved in inflammation, activation of helper T cells, and systemic responses to infection or injury (the acute phase response)
Mast cells	Release histamine and other chemicals involved in inflammation

Defenses at Body Surfaces

The body's first lines of defense against microbes are the barriers offered by surfaces exposed to the external environment. Very few microorganisms can penetrate the intact skin, and the sweat, sebaceous, and lacrymal glands all secrete antimicrobial chemicals.

The mucus secreted by the epithelial linings of the respiratory and upper gastrointestinal tracts also contains antimicrobial chemicals, but more important, mucus is sticky. Particles that adhere to it are prevented from entering the blood. They are either swept by ciliary action up into the pharynx and then swallowed, as occurs in the upper respiratory tract, or are engulfed by macrophages in the various linings.

Other specialized surface defenses are the hairs at the entrance to the nose, the cough and sneeze reflexes, and the acid secretion of the stomach, which kills microbes. Finally, a major defense against infection are the many relatively innocuous microbes normally found on the skin and other linings exposed to the external environment. These microbes suppress the growth of other potentially more dangerous ones.

Inflammation

Inflammation is the body's local response to infection or injury. Although we will concentrate mainly on the nonspecific inflammation induced by the invasion of *microbes,* most of the same responses can be elicited by a variety of other injuries—cold, heat, and trauma, for example. Regardless of cause, inflammation is relatively stereotyped since a major trigger is cell or tissue injury. The function of inflammation is to destroy or inactivate foreign invaders and/or set the stage for tissue repair.

The key actors in inflammation are **phagocytes.** This term denotes any cell capable of the form of endocytosis termed **phagocytosis,** whereby particulate matter is engulfed (Chapter 6). The engulfed matter is then usually destroyed inside the phagocyte. The most important phagocytes are neutrophils, monocytes, and macrophages.

In this section, we describe inflammation as it occurs in a *nonspecific* response. We shall see later that inflammation is also an important component of many specific immune responses, in which the inflammation becomes amplified and made more effective.

The sequence of local events in a typical nonspecific inflammatory response to a bacterial infection, due say to cutting oneself with a bacteria-covered knife, is summarized in Table 20-3. The familiar manifestations of tissue injury and inflammation are local redness, swelling, heat, and pain. The events of inflammation that underlie these manifestations are induced and regulated by a large number of chemical mediators produced by the body, as summarized in Table 20-4. Any given event of inflammation, vasodilation for example, may be induced by multiple

TABLE 20-3 SEQUENCE OF EVENTS IN A LOCAL INFLAMMATORY RESPONSE TO BACTERIA

1. Initial entry of bacteria into tissue
2. Vasodilation of the microcirculation in the infected area, leading to increased blood flow
3. Marked increase in protein permeability of the capillaries and venules in the infected area, with resulting diffusion of protein and filtration of fluid into the interstitial fluid, causing swelling
4. Exit of neutrophils and, later, of monocytes from the capillaries and venules into the interstitial fluid of the infected area
5. Destruction of bacteria in the tissue either through phagocytosis or by mechanisms not requiring prior phagocytosis
6. Tissue repair

mediators, and any given mediator may induce more than one event. Based on their origins, the mediators fall into two general categories: (1) substances released into the extracellular fluid from cells that either already exist in the infected area (mast cells, for example) or enter it during inflammation (neutrophils, for example); and (2) peptides (kinins, for example) generated in the infected area by the enzymatic splitting of proteins that circulate in the plasma. The stimuli for the release or generation of the mediators are microbial chemical substances or chemicals released by tissue cells that have interacted with and/or been damaged by the microbes.

Let us now go step by step through the process summarized in Table 20-3, assuming that the bacterial infection is localized to the tissue just beneath the skin and that the bacteria have not entered the blood. If entry into the blood or lymph were to occur, then similar inflammatory responses would take place in any other tissue or organ invaded by the blood-borne or lymph-borne bacteria. Also, microbes can be phagocytized by neutrophils and monocytes in the blood itself.

Vasodilation and Increased Permeability to Protein.
A variety of chemical mediators dilate most of the microcirculation vessels in an infected and/or damaged area. The mediators also cause the local capillaries to become quite permeable to proteins by inducing the capillary endothelial cells to contract, opening spaces between them.

The adaptive value of these vascular changes is twofold: (1) The increased blood flow to the inflamed area—which accounts for the redness—increases the delivery of leukocytes; and (2) the increased capillary permeability to protein ensures that the plasma proteins that participate in

TABLE 20-4 SOME IMPORTANT LOCAL INFLAMMATORY MEDIATORS

Mediator	Source
Kinins	Plasma proteins
Complement	Plasma proteins
Products of blood clotting	Plasma proteins
Histamine	Mast cells
Eicosanoids	Many cell types
Platelet-activating factor	Many cell types
Interleukin 1, tumor necrosis factor, interleukin 6, and other cytokines	Monocytes, macrophages, lymphocytes, and several nonimmune cell types
Lysosomal enzymes, nitric oxide, and other oxygen-derived substances	Neutrophils and macrophages

inflammation—many of which are normally restrained by the intact capillary endothelium—can gain entry to the area.

As described in Chapter 14, the vasodilation and increased permeability to protein cause net filtration of plasma into the interstitial fluid and the formation of edema. This accounts for the swelling in an inflamed area, which is simply a consequence of the changes in the microcirculation and has no known adaptive value of its own.

Chemotaxis. Within 30 to 60 min of the onset of inflammation, circulating neutrophils begin to stick to the luminal surface of the endothelium of the capillaries and venules in the infected area. This occurs because several inflammatory mediators stimulate the endothelial cells to express on their surface "adhesion molecules," which can bind to other adhesion molecules displayed on the surface of the circulating neutrophils. A narrow projection of the neutrophil is then inserted into the space between two endothelial cells, and the entire neutrophil squeezes through the capillary wall and into the interstitial fluid. In this way, huge numbers of neutrophils migrate into the inflamed area and move toward the microbes.

But movement of leukocytes from the blood into the damaged area is not limited to neutrophils. Monocytes follow later and once in the tissue undergo the anatomical and functional changes that transform them to macrophages. Meanwhile, some of the macrophages already present in the tissue may become active.

The entire process whereby various phagocytes are attracted to the vicinity of invading microbes is known as **chemotaxis**, and any chemical mediator that can cause it is termed a **chemotaxin**.

Killing by Phagocytes. The initial step in phagocytosis is contact between the surfaces of the phagocyte and microbe. Such contact is not itself always sufficient to trigger engulfment, particularly with those bacteria that are surrounded by a thick polysaccharide capsule. As we shall see, chemical factors produced by the body can bind the phagocyte tightly to the microbe and markedly enhance phagocytosis. Any substance that does this is known as an **opsonin**, from the Greek word that means "to prepare for eating."

As the phagocyte engulfs the microbe (Figure 20-1), the internal, microbe-containing sac formed in this step is called a **phagosome**. The microbe remains in the phagosome, a layer of plasma membrane separating it from the phagocyte's cytosol. The phagosome membrane then makes contact with one of the phagocyte's lysosomes, which are filled with a variety of hydrolytic enzymes, the membranes of the two structures fuse, and the combined vesicles are now called the **phagolysosome**. Inside the phagolysosome, the microbe's macromolecules are broken down by the lysosomal enzymes. In addition, enzymes found in the phagolysosome membrane produce **nitric oxide** (from the amino acid arginine, Chapter 8), as well as hydrogen peroxide and other oxygen derivatives, all of which are extremely destructive toward macromolecules.

Intracellular destruction is not the only way phagocytes can kill microbes. The phagocytes also release their antimicrobial hydrolytic enzymes and oxygen derivatives into the *extracellular* fluid, where these chemicals can destroy the microbes without prior phagocytosis. (As we shall discuss later, these chemicals can also damage normal tissue.)

The phagocytes also secrete still other substances into the extracellular fluid (Figure 20-2), which function as in-

such tiny pieces that not antigenic, filtered out in kidney

FIGURE 20-1

Phagocytosis and intracellular digestion of a microbe. The microbe is taken into the cell by endocytosis, and a membrane-bound phagosome is formed inside the phagocyte. The phagosome then merges with a lysosome, which brings together the digestive enzymes of the lysosome and the contents of the phagosome. After digestion has taken place in the phagolysosome, the end products are released to the outside of the cell by exocytosis or used by the cell for its own metabolism.

flammatory mediators. Thus, positive feedback occurs such that when more phagocytes enter the area and encounter microbes, more inflammatory mediators are released to bring in more phagocytes.

Complement. The family of proteins known as **complement** provides another means for killing microbes without prior phagocytosis. Certain of the complement proteins always circulate in the blood in an inactive state. Upon activation of one of the group in response to infection or damage, there occurs a cascade in which this active protein activates a second complement protein, which activates a third, and so on. In this way, multiple complement proteins are generated in the extracellular fluid of the infected areas from inactive precursors that have entered from the blood. Since this system consists of at least 20 distinct proteins, it is extremely complex, and we shall identify the roles of only a few of the individual proteins.

Five of the active proteins generated in the complement cascade form a complex, the **membrane attack complex (MAC)**, which embeds itself in the microbial plasma membrane. In this manner, channels are created in the membrane, making it leaky. Water and salts enter the

microbe, which disrupts the intracellular ionic environment and kills the microbe.

In addition to supplying a means for direct killing of microbes, the complement system serves other important functions in inflammation (Figure 20-3). Some of the activated complement molecules along the cascade cause, either directly or indirectly by stimulating the release of other inflammatory mediators, vasodilation, increased capillary permeability to protein, and chemotaxis. Also, one of the complement molecules—C3b—acts as an opsonin to attach the phagocyte to the microbe (Figure 20-4).

As we shall see later, antibodies, a class of proteins secreted by lymphocytes, are required to activate the first protein (C1) in the full sequence known as the classical complement pathway, but lymphocytes are not involved in nonspecific inflammation. How, then, is the complement sequence initiated during nonspecific inflammation? The answer is that there is an **alternate complement pathway**, one that is not antibody-dependent and bypasses C1. The alternate pathway is initiated as the result of complex interactions between complement molecules beyond C1, several other plasma proteins, and polysaccharides on the surface of the foreign particles. The alternate pathway

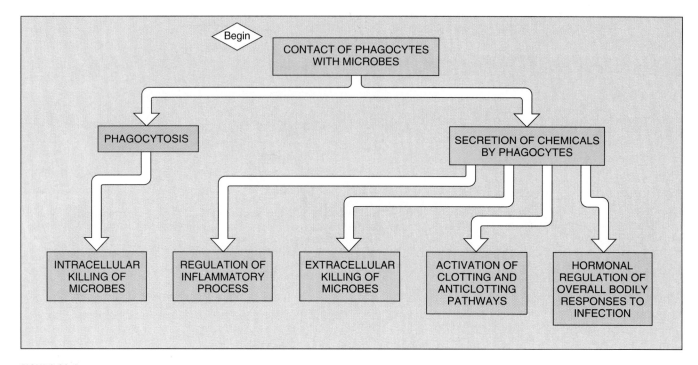

FIGURE 20-2

Role of phagocytes in nonspecific immune responses.

plugs into the classical pathway at the point of formation of C3b. Not all microbes have a surface conducive to initiating the alternate pathway.

Tissue Repair. The final stage of inflammation is tissue repair. Depending upon the tissue involved, multiplication of organ-specific cells by cell division may or may not occur during this stage. For example, liver cells multiply but neurons do not. In any case, fibroblasts (a type of connective-tissue cell) in the damaged area divide rapidly and begin to secrete large quantities of collagen. These events are brought about by chemical mediators, particularly a group of locally produced growth factors, for example, fibroblast growth factor.

FIGURE 20-3

Functions of complement proteins. The effects on blood vessels and chemotaxis are exerted both directly by complement molecules and indirectly via other inflammatory mediators (for example, histamine) whose release the complement molecules stimulate.

[handwritten note at top of page:] bacteria= vanilla ice cream w/ CHOCOLATE SPRINKLES = opsonin ← phagocytosis

EXTRACELLULAR FLUID

BACTERIUM

C3b receptor

C3b

PHAGOCYTE

FIGURE 20-4

Function of complement C3b as an opsonin. One portion of this complement molecule binds nonspecifically to the surface of the microbe, whereas another portion binds to specific receptor sites for it on the plasma membrane of the phagocyte. The structures are not drawn to scale.

Interferon

Interferon refers collectively to a family of three proteins that *nonspecifically* inhibit viral replication inside host cells. In response to infection by a virus, various cell types secrete interferon into the extracellular fluid. Interferon then binds to plasma membrane receptors on nearby cells, whether they are infected or not (Figure 20-5). It also enters the circulation and reaches cells at far-removed sites. Thus cells that can synthesize interferon provide it to cells that cannot.

How does interferon prevent viral replication? Its binding to the plasma membrane triggers the synthesis of several enzymes by the cell. If the cell is infected or eventually becomes infected, these enzymes block the synthesis of proteins the virus requires for replication. It must be reemphasized that interferon is not specific. Many, but not all, viruses induce interferon synthesis, and interferon in turn can inhibit the multiplication of many kinds of viruses.

SPECIFIC IMMUNE DEFENSES

Overview

Lymphocytes mediate specific immune defenses. Unlike nonspecific defense mechanisms, lymphocytes must recognize the specific foreign matter to be attacked. Any foreign molecule that can trigger a specific immune response against itself or the cell bearing it is termed an **antigen**.[1] Most antigens are either proteins or very large polysaccharides. The term "antigen" does not denote a specific struc-

---

[1]Terminology can be confusing here. Technically, a molecule that induces a specific immune response is an *immunogen*, whereas "antigen" refers to the ability of a molecule to react with the products of the response, particularly antibodies. Despite this, "antigen" is commonly used interchangeably with "immunogen," and we have adopted this practice.

FIGURE 20-5

Role of interferon in preventing viral replication. (A) Several cell types, when infected with virus, secrete interferon, which enters the interstitial fluid and blood and binds to interferon receptors on adjacent or far-removed cells (B). This induces synthesis of proteins (C) that inhibit viral replication should virus enter the cell (D). We have shown two cells acted upon by interferon to denote the amplification effect here: The interferon secreted by a single cell can stimulate many cells to produce antiviral proteins.

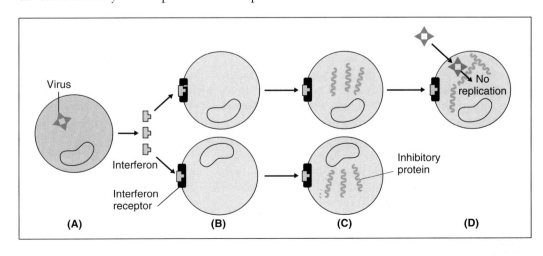

Virus

No replication

Interferon

Interferon receptor

Inhibitory protein

(A)   (B)   (C)   (D)

ture in the way that anatomical terms like "microtubule" and "integral membrane protein" do. Rather it is a functional term; that is, any molecule, no matter what its function may otherwise be, that can induce a specific immune response is by definition an antigen. It is the ability of lymphocytes to distinguish one antigen from another that confers specificity upon the immune responses in which they participate.

A common example of an antigen is ragweed pollen, the antigen that causes the specific immune response we know as hay fever. In other cases the antigen is part of the surface of a cell—microbe, virus-infected body cell, tumor cell, or transplanted cell—that appears in the body. The reason for saying "appears in" rather than "enters" is that, as we shall see, body cells, themselves, produce the "foreign" molecules that act as antigens on tumor cells and virus-infected cells. These molecules are foreign in the sense that they are not present in normal cells. As we shall see, normal cells can be transformed in still other ways and, as a result, possess components that can serve as antigens.

A typical specific immune response can be divided into three stages: (1) antigen encounter and recognition by lymphocytes, (2) lymphocyte activation, and (3) the attack.

1. A lymphocyte programmed during its development to "recognize" a specific antigen encounters it, and the antigen becomes bound to receptors specific for that antigen on the outer surface of the lymphocyte's plasma membrane. This binding is the physicochemical meaning of the word "recognize." Accordingly, the ability of lymphocytes to distinguish one antigen from another is determined by the nature of the plasma-membrane receptors the lymphocytes have.
2. Binding of antigen by receptor is the trigger for lymphocyte activation. The lymphocyte undergoes a cell division, and the two resulting daughter cells then also divide, even though only one of them still has the antigen combined with it, and so on. In other words, the original binding of antigen by a single lymphocyte specific for that antigen triggers multiple cycles of cell divisions to occur. As a result, many lymphocytes are formed that are identical to the one that started the cycles and can recognize the antigen. These progeny then differentiate into cells that serve multiple functions, depending upon the lymphocyte type. With few exceptions, this process of cell division and differentiation, termed **lymphocyte activation**, requires interaction, via chemical messengers, between one type of lymphocyte—helper T cells—and the "effector" lymphocytes—B cells and cytotoxic T cells—that continue the responses into the attack phase.
3. The activated effector lymphocytes launch an attack against all antigens of the kind that initiated the im-

mune response. B cells do so indirectly by secreting antibodies, which then recruit and guide other molecules and cells to perform the actual attack. In contrast, cytotoxic T cells directly attack and kill the cells bearing the antigens. It is essential to understand that, theoretically, it takes only one or two antigen molecules to *initiate* the specific immune response that will then result in an attack on all of the other antigens of that specific kind in the body.

Lymphoid Organs and Lymphocyte Types

Our first task is to describe how lymphocytes arise and the organs and tissues in which they come to reside. Then we describe the various types alluded to in the overview and summarized in Tables 20-1 and 20-2.

Lymphoid Organs. Like all leukocytes, lymphocytes circulate in the blood. At any moment, however, the great majority of lymphocytes are not in the blood but in a group of organs and tissues collectively termed the **lymphoid organs**. These are subdivided into primary lymphoid organs and peripheral lymphoid organs.

The **primary lymphoid organs** are the bone marrow and thymus. These organs supply the peripheral lymphoid organs with mature lymphocytes already programmed to perform their functions. The bone marrow and thymus are not normally sites at which specific immune responses occur.

The **peripheral lymphoid organs** are the lymph nodes, spleen, tonsils, and lymphocyte accumulations in the linings of the intestinal, respiratory, genital, and urinary tracts. It is in the peripheral lymphoid organs that lymphocytes are stimulated to participate in specific immune responses.

We have stated that the bone marrow and thymus supply lymphocytes to the peripheral lymphoid organs. Most of the lymphocytes in the peripheral organs are not, however, cells that originated in the primary lymphoid organs. The explanation is that, once in the peripheral organ, a lymphocyte can undergo cell division to produce additional identical lymphocytes, which in turn undergo cell division, and so on. In other words, all lymphocytes are *descended* from ancestors that were produced in the bone marrow or thymus but may not themselves have arisen in these organs.

(A distinction must be made between the "lymphoid organs" and the "lymphatic system," described in Chapter 14. The latter is a network of lymphatic vessels and the lymph nodes found along these vessels. Of all the lymphoid organs, only the lymph nodes also belong to the lymphatic system.)

There are no anatomical links, other than via the cardiovascular system, between the various lymphoid organs.

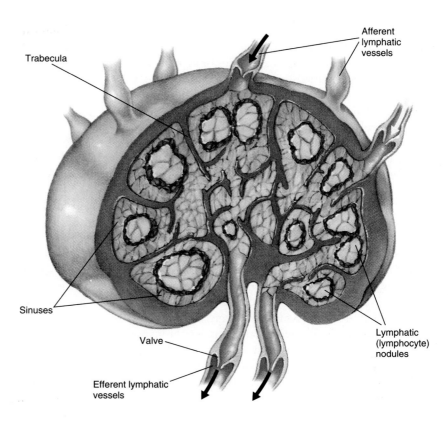

Trabecula

Afferent lymphatic vessels

Sinuses

Valve

Efferent lymphatic vessels

Lymphatic (lymphocyte) nodules

FIGURE 20-6
Anatomy of a lymph node.

Let us look briefly at these organs excepting the bone marrow, which was described in Chapter 14.

The **thymus** lies in the upper part of the chest. Its size varies with age, being relatively large at birth and continuing to grow until puberty, when it gradually atrophies and is replaced by fatty tissue. Before its atrophy, the thymus consists mainly of lymphocytes that will eventually migrate via the blood to the peripheral lymphoid organs. It also contains endocrine cells that secrete a group of hormones that exert a still poorly understood regulatory effect on the peripheral lymphocytes of thymic origin.

Recall from Chapter 14 that the fluid flowing along the lymphatic vessels is called lymph, which is interstitial fluid that has entered the lymphatic capillaries and is being routed to the large lymphatic vessels that drain into systemic veins. During this trip, the lymph flows through **lymph nodes** scattered along the vessels. Lymph, therefore, is the route by which lymph-node cells encounter the materials that trigger their immune responses. Each node is a honeycomb of lymph-filled sinuses (Figure 20-6) with large clusters of lymphocytes between the sinuses. There are also many macrophages and, as is the case with other peripheral lymphoid organs, cells that are distinguishable from macrophages but carry out macrophage-like functions. For simplicity, these cells are included in our use of the term "macrophages."

The **spleen** is the largest of the lymphoid organs and lies in the left part of the abdominal cavity between the stomach and the diaphragm. In essence, the spleen is to the circulating blood what the lymph nodes are to the lymph. Blood percolates through the vascular meshwork of the spleen's interior, and large collections of lymphocytes and macrophages are found in the spaces of the meshwork. The macrophages of the spleen, in addition to interacting with lymphocytes, also phagocytize aging or dead erythrocytes.[2]

The **tonsils** are a group of small, rounded organs in the pharynx. They are filled with lymphocytes and macrophages and have openings ("crypts") to the surface of the pharynx. Their lymphocytes respond to microbes that arrive by way of ingested food as well as inspired air. Similarly, the lymphocytes in the linings of the various tracts exposed to the external environment respond to infectious agents that penetrate into these linings from the lumen of the tract.

Finally, we must describe the source of the lymphocytes in blood. Some are cells on their way from the bone marrow or thymus to the peripheral organs, but the vast majority are cells that are participating in lymphocyte traffic between the peripheral lymphoid organs, blood, lymph, and all the tissues of the body. Lymphocytes from the peripheral lymphoid organs constantly enter the lymph and

---

[2]In the fetus, the spleen is an important organ for forming all types of blood cells, but in the adult only lymphocytes are formed there.

are carried, via lymphatic vessels, to the blood. Simultaneously, some blood lymphocytes are pushing through the endothelium of blood-vessel capillaries or venules all over the body to enter the interstitial fluid. From there, they move into lymphatic capillaries and along the lymphatic vessels to lymph nodes. They may then leave the lymphatic vessels to take up residence in the node. This recirculation is going on all the time, not just during an infection. It greatly increases the likelihood that any given lymphocyte will encounter the target it is specifically programmed to recognize.

Lymphocyte Origins. The multiple populations and subpopulations of lymphocytes are summarized in Tables 20-1 and 20-2. The **B lymphocytes**, or simply **B cells**, mature in the bone marrow and then are carried by the blood to the peripheral lymphoid organs. This overall process of maturation and migration continues throughout a person's life. All generations of lymphocytes that subsequently arise from these cells by cell division in the peripheral lymphoid organs will be identical to the parent cells, that is, will also be B cells.

In contrast to the B cells, other lymphocytes leave the bone marrow in an immature state during fetal and early neonatal life. They are carried to the thymus and mature in this organ before heading on to the peripheral lymphoid organs. They constitute the second major class of lymphocytes, the **T lymphocytes** or **T cells**. Like B cells, T cells also undergo cell division in peripheral lymphoid organs, the offspring being identical to the original T cells.

In addition to the B and T cells, there is a third population of lymphocytes that are large and granular and include the **natural killer cells (NK cells)**. These cells arise in the bone marrow, but their precursors and life history are still unclear. As we shall see, NK cells, unlike B and T cells, do not manifest specificity for antigens.

Functions of B Cells and T Cells

B cells, upon activation by antigen, differentiate into plasma cells, which secrete **antibodies**. These proteins then travel all over the body to reach antigens of the kind that stimulated that particular immune response. They combine with the antigens and guide an attack (by phagocytes, complement, or NK cells, as we shall see) that eliminates the antigens or the cells bearing them. Antibody-mediated responses are also called humoral responses, the adjective "humoral" denoting communication by way of soluble chemical messengers, antibodies in this case, in the blood.

There are multiple functional subsets of T cells, termed **cytotoxic, helper**, and **suppressor T cells**.[3] Cytotoxic T cells are, themselves, "attack" cells. They travel to the location of antigen-bearing cells, bind to them via the antigen and directly kill them, via secreted chemicals, without the intermediation of antibodies.[4] It is worth emphasizing the important geographical difference in antibody-mediated responses and responses mediated by cytotoxic T cells. In the former case, the B cells remain in whatever location the recognition and activation steps occurred and send their antibodies forth, via the blood, to seek out antigens or antigen-bearing cells identical to those that triggered the response. In the responses mediated by cytotoxic T cells, the cells themselves must enter the blood and seek out the targets.

Antibody-mediated responses have an extremely wide diversity of targets and are the major defense against bacteria, viruses, and other microbes in the extracellular fluid, and against toxic molecules (toxins). In contrast, the direct killing of cells carried out by cytotoxic T cells occurs with a more limited number of targets, specifically the body's own cells that have become cancerous or infected with viruses.

We have now assigned roles to the B cells and cytotoxic T cells. What roles do the other two classes of T cells perform? Suppressor T cells inhibit the function of both B cells and cytotoxic T cells. Suppressor T cells are still poorly understood, and thus we shall have relatively little to say about them in this chapter. Helper T cells help activate both B cells and cytotoxic T cells. The helper T cells go through the usual first two stages of the immune response in that they must combine with antigen and then undergo activation. Once activated, however, they do not direct an attack against antigens but instead secrete protein messengers that act on B cells and cytotoxic T cells that have also bound antigen. This is a very important point: With only a few exceptions, the binding of antigen by a B cell or T cell is usually not enough to cause activation of the cell; a second signal—messengers secreted by helper T cells—is also required.

One important note on terminology is appropriate: Protein chemical messengers secreted by lymphocytes are **lymphokines**, and those secreted by monocytes and mac-

---

[3]Another way to categorize T cells is not by function but rather by the presence of certain proteins, particularly those called CD4 and CD8, in their plasma membranes. Cytotoxic T cells and suppressor T cells have CD8 and so are also commonly called CD8 cells; helper T cells have CD4 and so are also commonly called CD4 cells.

[4]Responses mediated by cytotoxic T cells are sometimes termed cell-mediated responses. Unfortunately this can be confusing since the term is also used to refer to a particular category of immune response—delayed hypersensitivity—in which mainly helper T cells and macrophages participate.

rophages are termed **monokines**. However, because certain of these messengers are secreted by both lymphocytes and monocytes or macrophages, as well as by several other nonimmune cell types—notably fibroblasts and endothelial cells—the term **cytokines** is generally used to include all protein messengers that regulate immune responses.[5] We shall use this term exclusively. (To avoid confusion, it should be recognized that antibodies are not classified as cytokines.)

---

[5]The suffix-*kine*, derived from the Greek word for "action," indicates the function of these proteins in activating cells of the immune system. The prefix used indicates the cell that secretes the protein, the prefix *cyto*-denoting any cell.

The cytokines exert many local effects on the cells of the immune system, and some also circulate in the blood to have hormone-like effects on organs and tissues involved in host defenses. They are also important inflammatory mediators. There are presently more than 20 known cytokines [including 12 interleukins, 4 colony-stimulating factors (Chapter 14), 3 interferons, and 2 tumor necrosis factors], and each usually has multiple target cells and actions. We will, of necessity, limit our discussions in the rest of this chapter to only a few of them.

Figure 20-7 summarizes the basic interactions among B, cytotoxic T, and helper T cells presented in this section.

Lymphocyte Receptors

As stated earlier, the ability of lymphocytes to distinguish

FIGURE 20-7

Summary of roles of B, cytotoxic T, and helper T cells in immune responses. Suppressor T cells, not shown in the figure, can inhibit B-cell and cytotoxic T-cell responses.

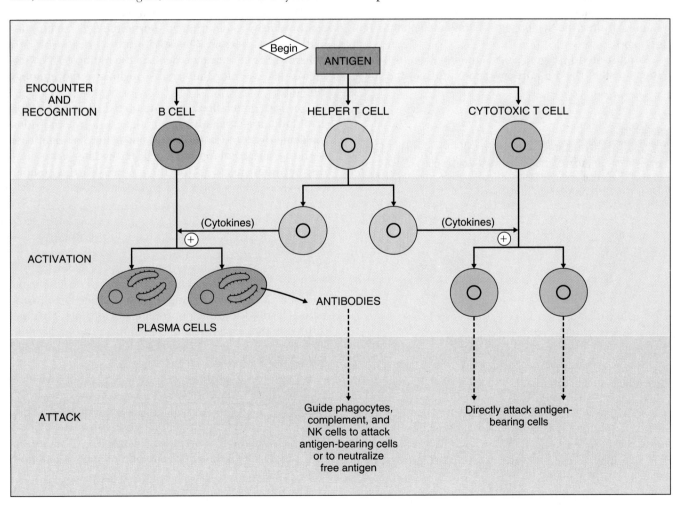

one antigen from another is determined by the lymphocytes' receptors.

B-Cell Receptors. We need to restate one fact and add a new one before describing B-cell receptors. The old fact is that after activation, B cells proliferate and differentiate into plasma cells, which secrete antibodies. The new one is that the plasma cells derived from a particular B cell can secrete only one particular antibody. Now for the receptor: Each B cell always displays on its plasma membrane copies of the particular antibody its plasma cell progeny are able to produce. This surface protein (glycoprotein, to be more accurate) acts as the receptor for the antigen specific to it. Since all antibodies are categorized as **immunoglobulins**, B-cell receptors are immunoglobulins. (The receptors are technically not themselves antibodies since only *secreted* immunoglobulins are termed antibodies.)

Each immunoglobulin molecule is composed of four interlinked polypeptide chains (Figure 20-8). The two long chains are called heavy chains, and the two short ones, light chains. There are five major classes of immunoglobulins, determined by the amino acid sequences in the heavy chains. The classes are designated by the letters A, D, E, G, and M after the symbol Ig for immunoglobulin: IgA, IgD, and so on.

As illustrated in Figure 20-8, immunoglobulins have a "stem," called the **Fc** portion and comprising the lower

half of the two heavy chains, and two "prongs," each containing one **antigen binding site** (also termed antibody combining site)—the amino acid sequences that bind antigen. The amino acid sequences of the Fc portion are identical for all immunoglobulins of a single class (IgA, IgD, and so on). In contrast, the amino acid sequences of the antigen binding sites vary from immunoglobulin to immunoglobulin in a given class (and are termed the "variable regions"). Thus, each class contains thousands, or even millions, of unique immunoglobulins, each capable of combining with only one specific antigen or, in some cases, several antigens whose structures are very similar. The interaction between an antigen and an immunoglobulin is analogous to the lock-and-key interactions that apply generally to the binding of ligands by proteins.

Any given B cell or clone of identical B cells produces receptors—plasma membrane immunoglobulins—with unique antigen binding sites. Thus, the body has armed itself with small clones of millions of different B cells in order to ensure that receptors will exist that are specific for the vast number of different antigens the organism *might* encounter during its lifetime. The immunoglobulin that any given B cell (and all of its plasma-cell progeny) can produce was determined during the cell's maturation in the bone marrow. Diversity arose as the result of a unique series of rearrangements in the multiple DNA segments that code for the variable regions of the immunoglobulins.

One last point should be mentioned: B-cell receptors can bind antigen whether the antigen is a free individual molecule dissolved in the extracellular fluid or whether it is on the surface of a foreign cell. In the later case, the B cell becomes linked to the foreign cell via the complex between B-cell receptor and surface antigen.

T-Cell Receptors. T cells do not produce immunoglobulins, and so T-cell surface receptors for antigen are not immunoglobulins. Rather they are two-chained proteins that, like immunoglobulins, have specific regions that differ from one T cell to another. As in B-cell development, multiple DNA transformations occur during T-cell maturation, leading to clones of millions of distinct T cells—distinct in that each cell and its offspring possess receptors of a single specificity. For T cells, this maturation occurs during their residence in the thymus.

In addition to their general structural differences, the B- and T-cell receptors differ in a much more important way: The T-cell receptor cannot combine with antigen unless the antigen is first complexed with certain of the body's own plasma-membrane proteins. The T-cell receptor combines with the entire complex of antigen and body (self) protein.

The self plasma-membrane proteins that must be complexed with the antigen in order for T-cell recognition to

FIGURE 20-8

Immunoglobulin (antibody) structure. The Fc portions are the same for all immunoglobulins of a particular class. Each "prong" contains a single antigen-binding site. The links between chains represent disulfide bonds.

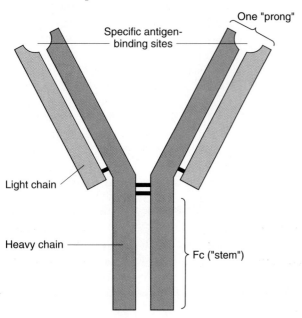

Specific antigen-binding sites

One "prong"

Light chain

Heavy chain

Fc ("stem")

TABLE 20-5   MHC RESTRICTION OF THE LYMPHOCYTE RECEPTORS

Cell type	MHC restriction
B	None
Helper T	Class II, found only on macrophages, B cells, and several other cell types (dendritic cells and keratinocytes)
Cytotoxic T and suppressor T	Class I, found on all nucleated cells of the body
NK	None

occur are a group of proteins coded for by genes known as the **major histocompatibility complex (MHC)** and therefore called **MHC proteins**.[6] Since no two persons other than identical twins have the same MHC genes,[7] no two individuals have the same MHC proteins on the plasma membranes of their cells. MHC proteins are, in essence, cellular "identity tags," that is, genetic markers of biological individuality.

The MHC proteins are often termed "restriction elements" since, as we have seen, the ability of a T cell's receptor to recognize an antigen is restricted to situations in which the antigen is complexed with an MHC protein. There are two classes of MHC proteins: I and II. Class I proteins are found on the surface of virtually all nucleated cells of a person's body, that is, virtually all cells but erythrocytes. Class II proteins are found only on the surface of macrophages, B cells, and several macrophage-like cells—dendritic cells, which are found in virtually all tissues but the brain, and keratinocytes, a common cell in the skin. The different subsets of T cells do not all have the same MHC requirements (Table 20-5): Cytotoxic and suppressor T cells require antigen to be associated with class I proteins, whereas helper T cells require class II proteins.

At this point you might well ask: How do antigens, which are foreign, end up on the surface of the body's own cells complexed with MHC proteins? The answer is provided by the process known as **antigen presentation**, to which we now turn.

Antigen Presentation to T Cells

To repeat, T cells can bind antigen only when the antigen appears on the plasma membrane of a host cell complexed with the cell's MHC proteins. Cells bearing these complexes therefore function as **antigen-presenting cells (APCs)** for T cells.

Presentation to Helper T Cells. Since helper T cells require class II MHC proteins and since these proteins are found only on macrophages, B cells, and the macrophage-like dendritic cells and keratinocytes, only these cells can function as APCs for helper T cells. The function of the macrophage as an APC for helper T cells is easiest to visualize (Figure 20-9A) since the macrophage forms, in essence, a link between nonspecific and specific responses. After a microbe or noncellular antigen has been phagocytized or pinocytized by a macrophage in a *nonspecific* response, it is partially broken down into smaller peptide fragments by proteolytic enzymes. The resulting fragments then bind *inside* the cell to class II MHC proteins synthesized there. The fragments actually fit into a groove in the center of the MHC proteins. The fragment-MHC complex is then transported to the cell surface where it is displayed in the plasma membrane. It is to this entire complex on the cell surface that a specific helper T cell can bind.

It is presently thought that antigen hydrolysis and binding of the fragments to the class II MHC proteins occur in the endocytosed vesicles. Note that it is not the intact antigen but rather the peptide fragments, termed antigenic determinants or **epitopes**, of the antigen that are complexed to the MHC proteins and presented to the T cell. Despite this, it is customary to refer simply to "antigen" presentation. More than one epitope can be formed from a given antigen.

---

[6]The term "histocompatibility" means "tissue compatibility." It refers to the fact that the likelihood that a tissue transplant from one person to another will be compatible is often evaluated by testing how closely the two individuals' MHC proteins match. In humans, the MHC proteins are termed HLA proteins, for "human leukocyte antigens," because they were first discovered on leukocytes. We prefer to use the term "MHC proteins" because of its universal biological applicability, as well as to avoid the incorrect impression that the proteins are found only on leukocytes.

[7]The MHC system of genes is extremely polymorphic, having multiple alternative forms or alleles (Chapter 4) of each gene. For example, there are at least 50 distinct alleles of one of the genes.

FIGURE 20-9

Sequence of events by which antigen is processed and presented to a helper T cell by (A) a macrophage or (B) a B cell. In both cases the antigen is internalized and broken down to fragments, which are then complexed to the cell's Class II MHC proteins inside the cell. The antigenic fragment fits into a groove in the center of the MHC protein. The complex is then shuttled to the membrane surface and inserted in the plasma membrane. Note that the helper T cell binds to the entire complex. The compartments—probably endosomes—in which the intracellular events occur are simply indicated by clear circles since the details of the process are not completely understood. In addition to presenting the antigen to the helper T cell, the macrophage or B cell also secretes the cytokine interleukin 1 (IL-1), which provides the additional signal required to activate the helper T cell. (*Adapted from Gray, Sette, and Buus.*)

How B cells process antigen and present it to helper T cells is similar to the story we just described for macrophages (Figure 20-9B). An intact antigen binds to the B-cell receptor (recall that these are immunoglobulins), and this triggers off receptor-mediated endocytosis, so that the antigen-receptor complex is internalized. Inside the B cell, the antigen is hydrolyzed to peptide fragments, which are complexed with class II MHC proteins. The complex is then shuttled to the cell surface where a helper T cell specific for the complex can bind to it. It must be emphasized that the ability of B cells to present antigen to helper T cells is a *second* function of B cells in response to antigenic stimulation, the other being the differentiation of the B cells into antibody-secreting plasma cells.

Regardless of whether the APC is a macrophage, B cell, or macrophage-like cell, it not only processes and presents the antigen to the helper T cell but also secretes a cytokine—**interleukin 1 (IL-1)**—that is required for activation of the antigen-bound T cell.[8]

Presentation to Cytotoxic T Cells. Because class I MHC proteins are synthesized by virtually all nucleated cells, any such cell—not just macrophages or B cells—can act as an APC for a cytotoxic T cell. This distinction helps explain the major function of cytotoxic T cells—destruction of *any* of the body's own cells that have become cancerous or infected with viruses. The key point is that the antigens that complex with class I MHC proteins arise *within* body cells. They are "endogenous" antigens—foreign proteins synthesized by a body cell.

---

[8]There are actually two distinct interleukin 1 molecules—interleukin 1α and interleukin 1β. For simplicity we shall simply refer to them collectively as interleukin 1.

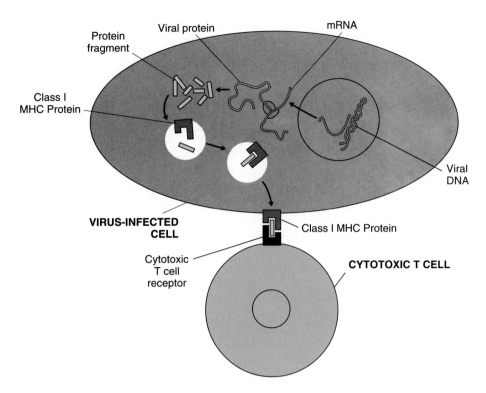

FIGURE 20-10

Processing and presentation of viral antigen to a cytotoxic T cell by an infected cell. The virus induces the production by the cell of viral protein, which is then hydrolyzed and the fragments complexed to the cell's Class I MHC proteins, probably in the endoplasmic reticulum. These complexes are then shuttled to the plasma membrane. Note that the cytotoxic T cell binds to the entire complex. *(Adapted from Gray, Sette, and Buus.)*

How can such antigens arise? In the case of viruses, once a virus has taken up residence inside a host cell, the viral nucleic acid causes the host cell to manufacture viral proteins, which of course are foreign proteins (Figure 20-10). A cancerous cell, as described in Chapter 4, has had one or more of its genes altered by chemicals, radiation, or other factors; the altered genes—*oncogenes*—code for proteins that are either unique or are normally present beyond embryonic life only in very small concentrations. Such proteins can act as antigens.

In both cases, some of the proteins are hydrolyzed by enzymes into peptide fragments, complexed with the host cell's class I MHC proteins, and then shuttled by exocytosis to the plasma-membrane surface, where a cytotoxic T cell specific for the complex can bind to it. (In contrast to APC processing by macrophages and B cells, the hydrolysis of endogenous antigens and the complexing of the peptide fragments to class I MHC proteins probably occurs in the endoplasmic reticulum.)

NK Cells

As noted earlier, NK cells constitute a distinct class of lymphocytes. They have several functional similarities to cytotoxic T cells: (1) Their major targets are virus-infected cells and cancer cells; and (2) they attack and kill these target cells directly, after binding to them. However, unlike cytotoxic T cells, NK cells are not antigen-specific; that is, each NK cell is able to attack virus-infected cells or cancer cells without any specific recognition on the part of the NK cell. They have neither T-cell receptors nor the immunoglobulin receptors of B cells, and the nature of the NK-cell surface receptors that permits the cells to identify their targets is unknown (one exception to this statement will be given later). Also, they manifest no MHC restriction, and they require neither antigen presentation nor any previous exposure to antigen.

All these characteristics have suggested that NK cells are lymphocytic "Minutemen," which can be mobilized quickly and go into action *nonspecifically* without the prolonged period of exposure and activation required by B cells and cytotoxic T cells. Why then do we deal with them in the context of *specific* immune responses? Because, as we shall see, their participation in an immune response is greatly enhanced by cytokines secreted by helper T cells activated during specific responses.

Development of Immune Tolerance

Our basic framework for understanding specific immune responses requires consideration of one more crucial question: How does the body develop what is called **immune tolerance**—lack of immune responsiveness to *self-components*? This may seem to be a strange question given our definition of an antigen as a *foreign* molecule that can generate an immune response. In essence, however, we are now asking how it is that the body "knows" that its own molecules—particularly proteins—are not foreign.

Recall that the huge diversity of lymphocyte receptors is ultimately the result of multiple random DNA recombination processes. It is virtually certain, therefore, that in each person clones of lymphocytes would have emerged with receptors that could bind to that person's own proteins. The existence and functioning of such lymphocytes would, of course, be disastrous because such binding would launch an immune attack against the cells expressing these proteins; that is, the person's own (self) proteins would act as antigens. There are at least two mechanisms, termed clonal deletion and clonal inactivation, that explain why *normally* there are no active lymphocytes that respond to self-components.

First, during in utero and early postnatal life, T cells are exposed to a potpourri of self proteins in the thymus. There, those T cells that have receptors capable of binding self proteins are destroyed by an unknown mechanism. This process is termed **clonal deletion** (also called negative clonal selection).

But clonal deletion does not fully explain immune tolerance. It is very likely, for example, that some proteins in the body do not make their way to the thymus during development, and so T cells capable of binding to these proteins would not be destroyed. A second process, termed **clonal inactivation** (or clonal anergy) acts not in the thymus but in the periphery and somehow *inactivates* potentially self-reactive lymphocytes instead of killing them.

To summarize, the body normally does not launch a specific immune attack against its own proteins because it has no T cells able to bind to these proteins. Such lymphocytes did exist in the body at one time but were either destroyed or inactivated.

This completes our framework for understanding specific immune responses. The next two sections utilize this framework in presenting typical responses from beginning to end, fleshing out the interactions between lymphocytes and describing the attack mechanisms used by the various pathways.

Antibody-Mediated Immune Responses: Defenses Against Bacteria, Extracellular Viruses, and Toxins

A classical antibody-mediated response is one that results in the destruction of bacteria. The sequence of events, which would be quite similar to the response to a virus in the extracellular fluid, is summarized in Table 20-6 and Figure 20-11.

B-Cell Recognition and Activation. The story starts in the same way as for nonspecific responses, with the bacteria penetrating one of the body's linings and entering the interstitial fluid. The bacteria then enter the lymphatic system and/or bloodstream and are carried to the lymph nodes and/or the spleen, respectively. There a B cell specific for an antigen on the bacterial surface binds to the antigen via the B cell's plasma membrane immunoglobulin receptor.[9]

In a few cases (notably bacteria with polysaccharide capsules), this binding is all that is needed to trigger B-cell activation. For the great majority of antigens, however, binding is not enough, and signals in the form of cytokines released into the interstitial fluid by helper T cells near the antigen-bound B cells are also needed.

But for helper T cells to be brought into play and secrete cytokines, they must bind to a complex of antigen and class II MHC protein on an antigen-presenting cell (APC). Let us assume that in this case the APC is a macrophage that has phagocytized one of the bacteria, hydrolyzed its proteins into peptide fragments, complexed them with class II MHC proteins, and displayed the complexes on its surface. A helper T cell specific for the complex then binds to it, beginning the activation of the helper T cell. Moreover, the macrophage helps this activation process in a second way: It secretes IL-1.

So far this has all been review. Now we begin new material. IL-1 stimulates the helper T cell to enlarge, to secrete another cytokine named **interleukin 2 (IL-2)**, and to express the receptor for IL-2. This messenger, acting as an autocrine agent, then further stimulates the helper T cell (Figure 20-11). The cell divides, beginning the mitotic cycles that lead to formation of a clone of activated helper T cells, and these cells then release not only IL-2 but sev-

---

[9]In our scenario, B cells bind directly to antigen with no intermediation of macrophages. It is likely that, in many cases, a macrophage first phagocytizes the antigen-bearing foreign cell, processes the antigen, and presents it on the surface of the macrophage. But, unlike the story for antigen presentation to T cells, any antigen presentation to B cells by macrophages would not involve complexing of the antigen to MHC proteins.

TABLE 20-6 SUMMARY OF EVENTS IN ANTIBODY-MEDIATED IMMUNITY AGAINST BACTERIA

1. In peripheral lymphoid organs, bacterial antigen binds to specific receptors on the plasma membrane of B cells.
2. Simultaneously, antigen-presenting cells (for example, macrophages) (APCs) present to helper T cells processed antigen complexed to MHC Class II proteins on the APCs and secrete IL-1, which acts on the helper T cells.
3. In response, the helper T cells secrete IL-2, which activates the helper T cells to proliferate and secrete IL-2 and other cytokines. These activate the antigen-bound B cells to proliferate and differentiate into plasma cells. Certain B cells differentiate into memory cells rather than plasma cells.
4. The plasma cells secrete antibodies specific for the antigen that initiated the response, and the antibodies circulate all over the body via the blood.
5. Antibodies combine with antigen on the surface of the bacteria anywhere in the body.
6. Presence of antibody bound to antigen facilitates phagocytosis of the bacteria by neutrophils and macrophages. It also activates the complement system, which further enhances phagocytosis and can directly kill the bacteria by the membrane attack complex.

eral other cytokines (for example, **interleukin 6**) as well.

It is these cytokines, along with IL-2, that provide the additional signals required to activate nearby antigen-bound B cells to proliferate and differentiate into plasma cells, which then secrete antibodies.

Thus, as shown in Figure 20-11, we are dealing with a series of protein messengers interconnecting the various cell types, the helper T cells serving as the central coordinator. The macrophage releases IL-1, which acts on the helper T cell to stimulate release of IL-2, which stimulates the helper T cell to multiply, the activated progeny then releasing still other cytokines that, along with IL-2, activate antigen-bound B cells. Some of the B-cell progeny do not differentiate into plasma cells but instead become **memory cells** (Figure 20-11), ready to respond vigorously should the antigen ever reappear at a future time. In other words, the proliferation triggered by a first exposure to an antigen results in a long-lasting expansion of the clone of B cells specific for that antigen.

The example we have been using employed a macrophage as the APC to helper T cells. Recall, however, that this role can also be served by B cells. Moreover, B cells can also secrete the IL-1 required for activation of the helper T cells. The binding of the helper T cell to the antigen-bound B cell ensures maximal stimulation of the B cell by the cytokines secreted by that helper T cell and any of its progeny that remain nearby.[10]

---
[10]Some experts believe that even when a macrophage acts as the APC, the helper T cells activated by this process then bind to antigen-bound B cells, thereby reducing the distance over which the cytokines secreted by the helper T cell must act.

Antibody Secretion. Plasma cells produce thousands of antibody molecules per second before they die in a day or so. We mentioned earlier that there are five major classes of antibodies. The most abundant are the **IgG** antibodies, also commonly called **gamma globulin**. They and **IgM** provide the bulk of specific immunity against bacteria and viruses in the extracellular fluid. **IgE** antibodies mediate allergic responses and participate in defenses against multicellular parasites. **IgA** antibodies are secreted by plasma cells in the linings of the gastrointestinal, respiratory, and genitourinary tracts. IgA antibodies generally do not circulate but act locally in the linings or on their surfaces. They are also secreted by the mammary glands and hence are the major antibodies in milk. The functions of **IgD** are still unclear.

In the kind of infection we've been describing, the secreted antibodies—mostly IgG and IgM—enter the blood, which carries them from the peripheral lymphoid organ in which recognition and activation occurred to all tissues and organs of the body. At sites of infection, the antibodies leave the blood (recall that nonspecific inflammation has already made capillaries leaky at these sites) and combine with the type of bacterial surface antigen that initiated the immune response (Figure 20-11). These antibodies then direct the attack against the bacteria to which they are now bound.

Thus, immunoglobulins play two distinct roles in immune responses: (1) During the initial recognition step, those on the surface of B cells bind to antigen brought to them; and (2) those secreted by the plasma cells seek out and bind to bacteria bearing the same antigens, "marking" them as the targets to be attacked.

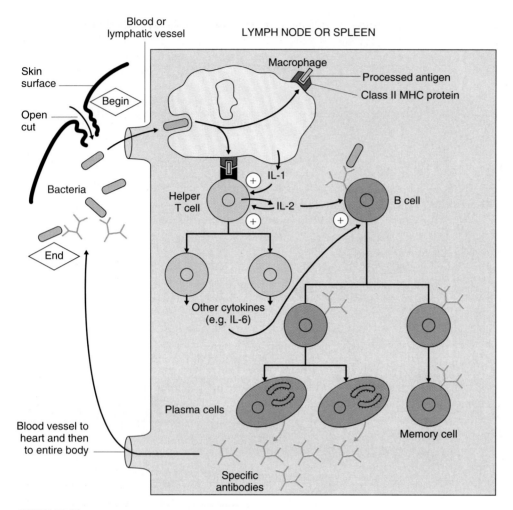

FIGURE 20-11

Summary of events by which a bacterial infection leads to antibody synthesis in peripheral lymphoid organs and the secreted antibodies travel by the blood to the site of infection where they bind to bacteria of the type that induced the response. A B cell binds directly to antigen on the bacterial surface, but the helper T cell can only bind to antigen that has been processed and presented, in this case by a macrophage. For simplicity, the intracellular processing of the antigen by the macrophage is not shown (see Figure 20-9A). As described in the text and illustrated in Figure 20-9B, an antigen-bound B cell, rather than a macrophage, can function as the antigen-presenting cell to the helper T cell.

The Attack: Effects of Antibodies. The antibodies bound to antigen on the microbial surface do not directly kill the microbe but instead link up the microbe physically to the actual killing mechanism—complement, macrophages, or NK cells. This linkage not only activates the mechanism but ensures that the killing effects take place only in the immediate vicinity of the microbe. This protects adjacent normal structures from toxic effects of the chemicals employed by the mechanisms.

Activation of the complement system As described on page 705, the complement system is activated in *nonspecific* inflammatory responses via the alternate complement pathway. In *specific* immune responses, the presence of antibody belonging to the IgG or IgM class bound to antigen is a powerful activator of the **classical complement pathway**. The first molecule in this pathway, C1, binds to the Fc portion of an antibody that has combined with antigen. This results in activation of the enzymatic portions of

C1, thereby initiating the entire classical pathway. The end product of this cascade, the membrane attack complex (MAC), can kill the cells to which the antibody is bound by making their membranes leaky. In addition, as we saw earlier, another activated complement molecule—C3b—functions as an opsonin to enhance phagocytosis of the microbe by neutrophils and macrophages, and still others stimulate the steps of inflammation leading to phagocytosis.

It is important to note that C1 binds not to the unique antigen binding sites in the antibody's prongs but rather to complement binding sites in the Fc portion. Since the latter are the same in virtually all antibodies of the IgG and IgM classes, the complement molecule will bind to *any* antigen-bound antibodies belonging to these classes. In other words, there is only one set of complement molecules, and once activated, they do essentially the same thing regardless of the specific identity of the invader.

Direct enhancement of phagocytosis
Activation of complement is not the only mechanism by which antibodies enhance phagocytosis. Merely the presence of an IgG antibody attached to antigen on the microbe's surface has some enhancing effect on phagocytosis. In other words, antibodies can act directly as opsonins in addition to their indirect action via complement.

The mechanism is analogous to that for complement in that the antibody links the phagocyte to the antigen. As shown in Figure 20-12, the phagocyte has membrane receptors that bind to the Fc portion of antibodies. This linkage promotes attachment of the antigen to the phagocyte and the triggering of phagocytosis.

Antibody-dependent cellular cytotoxicity
We have seen that both a particular complement molecule (C1) and a phagocyte can bind nonspecifically to the Fc portion of antibodies. NK cells can also do this (just substitute a NK cell for the phagocyte in Figure 20-12). Thus, antibodies can link target cells to NK cells, which then kill the targets directly by secreting toxic chemicals. This is termed **antibody-dependent cellular cytotoxicity (ADCC)** because the killing (cytotoxicity) is carried out by cells (NK cells) but the process depends upon the presence of antibody. Note that it is the antibodies that confer specificity upon ADCC, just as they do on antibody-dependent complement activation and phagocytosis. As we shall see, antibodies are not the only mechanism for bringing NK cells into play, but the antibody mechanism provides the one qualification, promised earlier, to the generalization that NK cells identify their targets by an unknown mechanism.

Direct neutralization of bacterial toxins and viruses
Toxins secreted by bacteria into the extracellular fluid can act as antigens to induce antibody production. The antibodies then combine with the free toxins, thus preventing interaction of the toxin with susceptible cell-membrane sites. Since each antibody has two binding sites for combination with antigen, clumplike chains of antibody-antigen complexes are formed (Figure 20-13), and these clumps can then be phagocytized.

A similar binding process is the major antibody-mediated mechanism for eliminating viruses in the extracellular fluid. Certain of the viral surface molecules serve as antigens, and the antibodies produced against them combine with them, preventing attachment of the virus to plasma

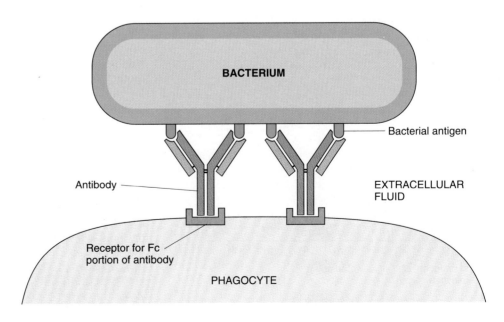

FIGURE 20-12

Direct enhancement of phagocytosis by antibody. The antibody links the phagocyte to the bacterium.

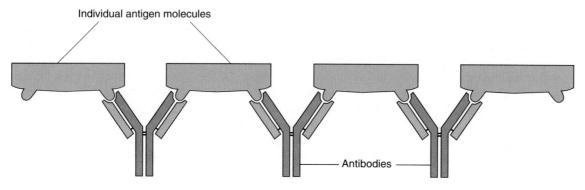

FIGURE 20-13

A chain of interlocking antigen-antibody complexes.

membranes of potential host cells. This prevents the virus from entering a cell. As with bacterial toxins, chains of antibody-virus complexes are formed and can be phagocytized.

Active and Passive Humoral Immunity. We have been discussing antibody formation without regard to the course of events in time. The response of the antibody-producing machinery to invasion by a foreign antigen varies enormously, depending upon whether the machinery has previously been exposed to that antigen. Antibody production responds slowly over several days to the first contact with a microbial antigen, but any subsequent infection by the same invader elicits an immediate and marked outpouring of additional specific antibody (Figure 20-14).

FIGURE 20-14

Rate of specific antibody production following initial contact with an antigen and subsequent contact with the same antigen.

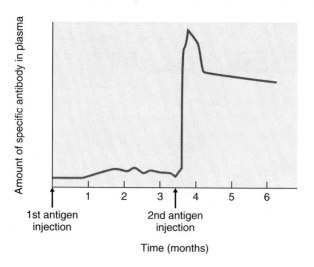

This response, which is mediated by the memory B cells described earlier, confers a greatly enhanced resistance toward subsequent infection with that particular microorganism. Resistance built up as a result of the body's contact with microorganisms and their toxins or other antigenic components is known as **active immunity**.

Until this century, the only way to develop active immunity was to suffer an infection, but now the injection of microbial derivatives in vaccines is used. A *vaccine* may consist of small quantities of living or dead microbes, small quantities of toxins, or harmless antigenic molecules derived from the microorganism or its toxin. The general principle is always the same: Exposure of the body to the agent results in induction of the memory cells required for rapid, effective response to possible future infection by that particular organism.

A second kind of immunity, known as **passive immunity,** is usually simply the direct transfer of actively formed antibodies from one person (or animal) to another, the recipient thereby receiving preformed antibodies. Such transfers normally occur between mother and fetus since IgG is selectively transported across the placenta. Breast-fed children also receive IgA antibodies in the mother's milk. These are important sources of protection for the infant during the first months of life, when the antibody-synthesizing capacity is relatively poor. Monoclonal antibodies produced by genetic engineering can also be used for passive immunity.

The same principle is used clinically when specific antibodies or pooled gamma globulin is given to patients exposed to or suffering from certain infections such as measles, hepatitis, and tetanus. The protection afforded by this transfer of antibodies is relatively short-lived, usually lasting only a few weeks or months.

Summary. We can now summarize the interplay between nonspecific and specific humoral immune mechanisms in resisting a bacterial infection. When we encounter particular bacteria for the first time, *nonspecific* defense mechanisms resist their entry and, if entry is gained, attempt to eliminate them by phagocytosis and nonphagocytic killing in the inflammatory process. Simultaneously, the bacterial antigens induce the specific B-cell clones to differentiate into plasma cells capable of antibody production. If the nonspecific defenses are rapidly successful, these slowly developing *specific* immune responses may never play an important role. If the nonspecific responses are only partly successful, the infection may persist long enough for significant amounts of antibody to be produced. The presence of antibody leads to both enhanced phagocytosis and direct destruction of the foreign cells, as well as to neutralization of toxins secreted by the bacteria. All subsequent encounters with that type of bacteria will be associated with the same sequence of events, with the crucial difference that the specific responses may be brought into play much sooner and with greater force; that is, the person may have active immunity against that type of bacteria.

The defenses against viruses in the extracellular fluid are similar, resulting in destruction or neutralization of the virus.

Defenses Against Virus-Infected and Cancer Cells

The previous section described how antibody-mediated immune responses constitute the major defenses against "exogenous antigens"—bacteria, viruses, and individual foreign molecules that enter the body and are encountered by the immune system in the extracellular fluid. This section now details how cytotoxic T cells, NK cells, and activated macrophages, all working with helper T cells, destroy the body's own cells that have become infected by viruses or transformed into cancer cells.

What is the value of destroying virus-infected cells? Such destruction results in release of the viruses into the extracellular fluid where they can then be directly neutralized by circulating antibody, as just described. Generally, only a few host cells must be sacrificed in this way, but once viruses have had a chance to replicate and spread from cell to cell, so many virus-infected host cells may be killed by the body's own defenses that organ malfunction may occur.

Role of Cytotoxic T Cells. Figure 20-15 summarizes a typical cytotoxic T-cell response triggered by viral infection of body cells. The response triggered by a cancer cell would be very similar. As described earlier, a virus-infected cell or a cancer cell itself produces foreign proteins—"endogenous antigens"—which are processed and presented on the plasma membrane of the cell complexed with class I MHC proteins. Cytotoxic T cells specific for

the particular antigen can bind to the complex, but just as with B cells, binding to antigen alone does not cause activation of the cytotoxic T cell. Cytokines from adjacent activated helper T cells are also needed.

How the helper T cells are brought into play in these cases, however, is not fully understood. Since helper T cells manifest class II MHC restriction, they cannot bind to the complex of antigen and class I MHC proteins on the target cell the way cytotoxic T cells can. Figure 20-15 illustrates one likely way to get the helper T cells involved: Macrophages probably phagocytize free extracellular virus (or, in the case of cancer, antigens released from the surface of the transformed cells) and then process and present antigen, in association with class II MHC proteins, to the helper T cells. The macrophages also secrete IL-1, in response to which the antigen-bound helper T cell releases IL-2. This cytokine then acts as an autocrine agent, as we have mentioned, to stimulate the proliferation of helper T cells.

The IL-2 also acts on the cytotoxic T cell bound to the surface of the virus-infected or cancer cell, stimulating this attack cell to proliferate. Why is proliferation important if a cytotoxic T cell has already found and bound to its target? The answer is that there is rarely just one infected cell or one cancer cell. By increasing the pool of cytotoxic T cells capable of recognizing the particular antigen, proliferation increases the likelihood that the other virus-infected or cancer cells will be encountered by the specific type of cytotoxic T cell.

In addition to IL-2, helper T cells secrete at least one other cytokine, **gamma interferon**, that promotes the killing ability of cytotoxic T cells. Gamma interferon belongs to the family of interferon proteins whose ability to prevent viral replication was described in the section on nonspecific immune defenses. Their promotion of killer cells is completely distinct from their antiviral properties.

There are several mechanisms of target-cell killing by cytotoxic T cells, but the best-defined one is as follows. The cytotoxic T cell releases, by exocytosis, the contents of its secretory vesicles into the extracellular space between itself and the target cell to which it is bound. These vesicles contain molecules of a protein, **perforin** (also termed pore-forming protein), which is similar in structure to the proteins of the complement system's membrane attack complex. Perforin inserts into the target cell's membrane and forms channels through the membrane. In this manner, it causes the attacked cell to become leaky and die. The fact that perforin is released into an enclosed space between the tightly attached attacking cell and the target ensures that innocent bystander cells will not be killed since perforin is not at all specific.

Some cytotoxic T cells generated during proliferation following an initial antigenic stimulation do not complete their full activation at this time but remain as memory

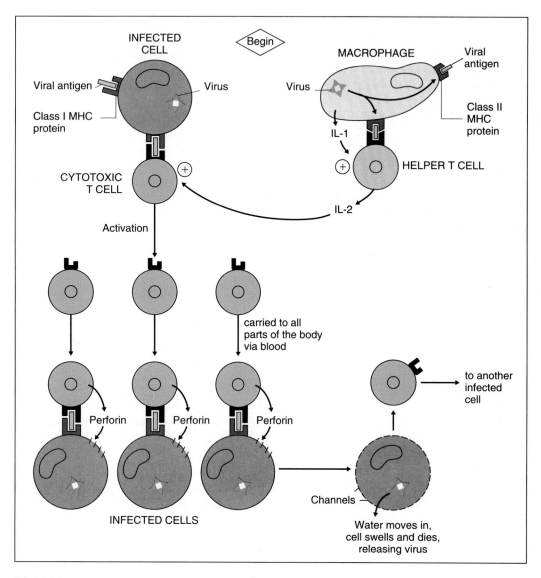

FIGURE 20-15

Summary of events in the killing of virus-infected cells by cytotoxic T cells. The sequence would be similar if the inducing cell were a cancer cell rather than a virus-infected cell. Specific cytotoxic T cells bind to viral antigen complexed to class I MHC protein on the infected cell. Simultaneously, macrophages have processed and presented antigen to helper T cells in association with the macrophage's class II MHC proteins, and they have also secreted IL-1. The helper T cell becomes activated by these events and proliferates (not shown in the figure). Under stimulation by the IL-2 secreted by the activated helper T cells, the antigen-bound cytotoxic T cell proliferates, and many of its progeny enter the blood to reach other cells infected with the same virus. They bind to the infected cell's antigen–class I MHC complexes and kill by releasing perforin, which inserts into the membrane of the infected cells and makes them leaky. The infected cell swells and dies, releasing virus into the extracellular fluid, where it can be attacked by antibodies. The cytotoxic T cell is not damaged in the process but can move on to another infected cell.

cells. Thus, active immunity exists for cytotoxic T cells just as for B cells.

Role of NK Cells and Activated Macrophages. Cytotoxic T cells are the most important attack cells against virus-infected and cancer cells, but not the only ones. NK cells and "activated macrophages" also destroy such cells by secreting toxic chemicals.

In the section on antibody-dependent cellular cytotoxicity (ADCC) we pointed out that NK cells can be linked to target cells by antibodies, and this certainly constitutes one potential method of bringing them into play against virus-infected or cancer cells. In most cases, however, antibody responses are not triggered by virus-infected cells or cancer cells,[11] and the NK cell must bind *directly* to its target, without the intermediation of antibodies. As noted earlier, NK cells do not have antigen specificity or MHC restrictions; they nonspecifically bind to virus-infected and cancer cells, but how they do so is not really understood.

Why do we describe NK cells, given their nonspecificity, in the context of "specific" responses? Because the major signals for NK cells to proliferate and secrete their toxic chemicals are cytokines secreted by the helper T cells that have been activated specifically by the targets. These are the same cytokines—IL-2 and gamma interferon, among others—that perform the identical function for cytotoxic T cells (Figure 20-16). Thus, the attack by the NK cells is nonspecific, but a specific immune response on the part of the helper T cells is required to bring the NK cells into play.

Similarly, IL-2 and gamma interferon act on *macrophages* in the vicinity to enhance their ability to kill cancer cells and cells infected with viruses (and other microbes). Macrophages stimulated in this way are termed **activated** (or effector) **macrophages** (Figure 20-16). They secrete large amounts of many chemicals, particularly the cytokine **tumor necrosis factor (TNF)**, that are capable of killing cells by a variety of mechanisms.

In the course of this chapter, we have mentioned several cytokines secreted by helper T cells. Table 20-7 summarizes this information.

Table 20-8 summarizes the multiple defenses against viruses described in this chapter.

Immunotherapy Against Cancer. Several methods are being developed at present to strengthen the innate ability

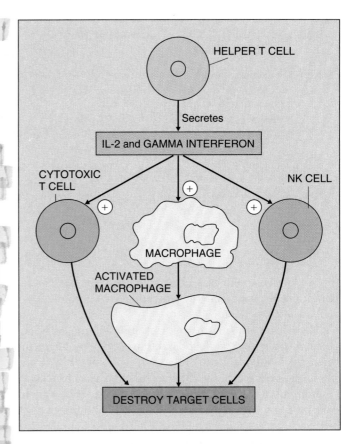

FIGURE 20-16

Role of IL-2 and gamma interferon, secreted by helper T cells, in stimulating the killer ability of cytotoxic T cells, NK cells, and macrophages.

of the immune system to fight cancer. The most hopeful approach obtains tumor-specific cytotoxic T cells from a person's tumor, treats the cells with IL-2 to cause their proliferation and enhanced tumoricidal ability, and then injects the now-enlarged pool of cells back into the person.

SYSTEMIC MANIFESTATIONS OF INFECTION

There are many *systemic* responses to infection, that is, responses of organs and tissues distant from the site of infection or immune response. These responses are collectively known as the **acute phase response**. It is natural to think of them as part of the disease, but the fact is that most of them actually represent adaptive responses to the disease.

Probably the single most common and striking systemic sign of infection is fever, the mechanism of which is described in Chapter 18. Present evidence suggests that

---

[11]Until recently, it had been thought that antibodies were relatively unimportant in the response to virus-infected cells and cancer cells. Some evidence indicates, however, that certain cancer cells may exhibit antigen on their plasma membranes not complexed with MHC proteins. Such antigen could trigger an antibody response, and the subsequent killing of the cancer cell would then be mediated by complement or, more likely, NK cells functioning in the process of ADCC.

TABLE 20-7 SOME IMPORTANT CYTOKINES SECRETED BY HELPER T CELLS AND THEIR LOCAL ACTIONS

1. Interleukin 2
   a. Acts as an autocrine agent to stimulate its cells of origin, helper T cells, to proliferate and secrete other cytokines.
   b. Stimulates the proliferation and differentiation of B cells and cytotoxic T cells.
   c. Activates macrophages and enhances the killing properties of cytotoxic T cells and NK cells.
2. Interleukin 6 and several other cytokines stimulate B-cell proliferation and differentiation into antibody-secreting plasma cells.
3. Gamma interferon activates macrophages and enhances the killing properties of cytotoxic T cells and NK cells.

---

fever is often beneficial, in that an increase in body temperature enhances many of the protective responses described in this chapter.

Decreases in the plasma concentrations of iron and zinc occur in response to infection and are due to changes in the uptake and/or release of these trace elements by liver, spleen, and other tissues. The decrease in plasma iron concentration has adaptive value since bacteria require a high concentration of iron to multiply. The role of the decrease in zinc is not known. The decrease in appetite characteristic of infection may also deprive the invading organisms of nutrients—particularly minerals—they require to proliferate.

Another adaptive response to infection is the secretion by the liver of a group of proteins known collectively as **acute phase proteins**. These proteins exert a large array of adaptive effects on the inflammatory process, immune cell function, and tissue repair.

Another response to infection, release of neutrophils and monocytes by the bone marrow, is of obvious value. Finally, there is release of amino acids from muscle, and these amino acids provide the building blocks for the synthesis of proteins required to fight the infection and for tissue repair.

All these responses and many others not listed are elicited by one or more of the cytokines released from stimulated macrophages. Thus, IL-1, TNF, and IL-6, all of which serve *local* roles in immune responses, also serve as

---

TABLE 20-8 SUMMARY OF HOST RESPONSES TO VIRUSES

	Main cells involved	Comment on action
Nonspecific defenses		
Anatomical barriers	Body surface linings	Physical barrier; antiviral chemicals
Inflammation	Tissue macrophages	Phagocytosis of extracellular virus
Interferon	Multiple cell types after viruses enter them	Interferon nonspecifically prevents viral replication inside host cells
Specific defenses		
Antibody-mediated	Plasma cells derived from B cells secrete antibodies	Antibodies neutralize virus and thus prevent viral entry into cell
		Antibodies activate complement, which leads to enhanced phagocytosis of extracellular virus
Direct cell killing	Cytotoxic T cells, NK cells, and activated macrophages	Via secreted chemicals, destroy host cell and thus induce release of virus into extracellular fluid where it can be phagocytized

hormones to elicit far-flung responses such as fever (Figure 20-17).[12] This is a good place to review the various functions of macrophages in immune responses (Table 20-9).

Several other cytokines also participate. For example, **colony-stimulating factors**, which are secreted by macrophages, lymphocytes, endothelial cells, and fibroblasts, provide the stimulus to the bone marrow to produce more neutrophils and monocytes (Chapter 14).

FACTORS THAT ALTER THE BODY'S RESISTANCE TO INFECTION

There are many factors that determine the body's capacity to resist infection. We offer here only a few examples.

Protein-calorie malnutrition is, worldwide, the single greatest contributor to decreased resistance to infection. Deficits of specific nutrients other than protein can also lower resistance to infection.

A preexisting disease, infectious or noninfectious, can also predispose the body to infection. People with diabetes, for example, have a propensity to numerous infections, at least partially explainable on the basis of defective leukocyte function. Moreover, any injury to a tissue lowers its resistance, perhaps by altering the chemical environment or interfering with the blood supply.

A growing body of evidence has also documented that

both stress and a person's state of mind can either enhance or reduce resistance to infection (and cancer). The physiological links among stress, state of mind, and resistance are only now being determined, and the entire question is being given great impetus by the emerging field of psychoneuroimmunology. Until recently, the tendency was to treat the immune system, on the one hand, and the nervous and endocrine systems, on the other, as entirely separate. It is now clear, however, that lymphoid tissue is innervated and that the cells mediating immunity possess receptors for many neurotransmitters and hormones. Conversely, many of the cytokines released by immune cells have important effects on the brain and endocrine system. Moreover, lymphocytes secrete several of the same hormones produced by endocrine glands. It seems certain, therefore, that the nervous and endocrine systems interact with the immune system in important ways. For example, it has been shown that the production of antibodies can be altered by psychological conditioning in much the same way as other body functions. Some possible mediators of the effects of stress on immune responses are discussed in Section C of this chapter.

Resistance to infection will also be impaired if one of the basic resistance mechanisms itself is deficient, as, for example, in people having a genetic deficiency in antibody synthesis. These individuals experience frequent and sometimes life-threatening infections that can be prevented by regular replacement injections of gamma globulin. Another genetic defect is combined immunodeficiency, which is an absence of both B and T cells. If untreated, infants with this disorder usually die within their first year of life from overwhelming infections. Combined immunodeficiency can be cured by a bone-marrow transplantation which supplies both B cells and cells that will migrate to the thymus and become T cells.

---

[12]A remarkable recent finding is that certain bacteria known to be highly virulent respond to IL-1 with increased proliferation. Thus, the bacteria have "captured" a host defense mechanism for their own purposes.

TABLE 20-9 ROLE OF MACROPHAGES IN IMMUNE RESPONSES

1. In nonspecific inflammation, phagocytize particulate matter, including microbes. Also secrete antimicrobial chemicals and protein messengers (cytokines) that function as local inflammatory mediators. The inflammatory cytokines include IL-1 and TNF.
2. Process and present antigen to helper T cells.
3. Secrete IL-1, which stimulates helper T cells to secrete IL-2 and to express the receptor for IL-2.
4. During specific immune responses, perform same killing and inflammation-inducing functions as in (1) but are more efficient because antibodies act as opsonins and because the cells are transformed into activated macrophages by IL-2 and gamma interferon, both secreted by helper T cells.
5. Secrete IL-1, TNF, and another cytokine, IL-6, which mediate many of the systemic responses to infection or injury.

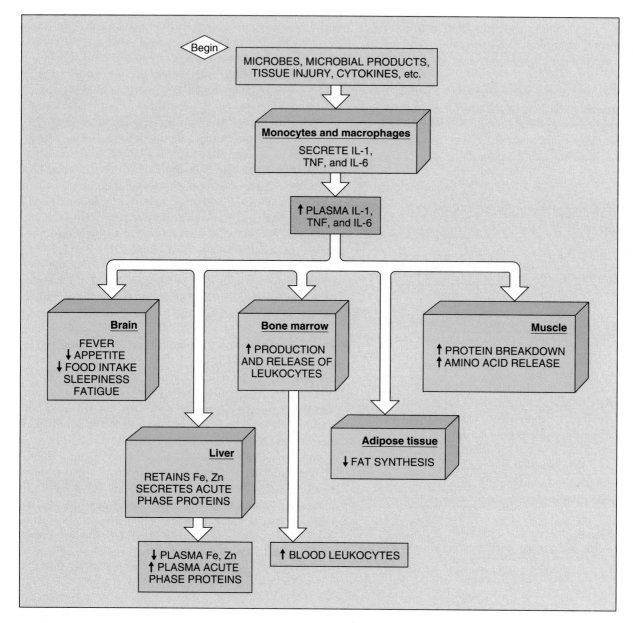

FIGURE 20-17

Systemic responses to infection or injury (the acute phase response). Cytokines other than IL-1, TNF, and IL-6 probably also participate. This figure does not include all the components of the acute phase response; for example, IL-1 and several other cytokines also stimulate secretion of various hormones, including insulin, glucagon, and ACTH (the significance of this last hormone increasing is described in Section C).

An environmentally induced decrease in the production of leukocytes is also an important cause of lowered resistance, as, for example, in patients given drugs specifically to inhibit rejection of tissue or organ transplants (see section on graft rejection).

AIDS

The most striking example of the lack of a basic resistance mechanism is the disease called *acquired immune defi-* *ciency syndrome (AIDS)*. This disease is caused by the *human immunodeficiency virus (HIV)*, which incapacitates the immune system. HIV belongs to the retrovirus family, whose nucleic acid core is RNA rather than DNA. Retroviruses possess an enzyme that, once the virus is inside a host cell, transcribes the virus's RNA into DNA, which is then integrated into the host cell's chromosomes. Replication of the virus inside the cell causes the cell's death.

Unfortunately, the cells that HIV preferentially enters and resides in are helper T cells,[13] and so the disease causes depletion of these cells, with catastrophic consequences. Without adequate numbers of helper T cells, neither B cells nor cytotoxic T cells can function normally. Thus the AIDS patient dies from infections and cancers that ordinarily would be readily handled by the immune system.

AIDS was first described in 1981, but it has since reached epidemic proportions. The World Health Organization estimates that, worldwide, over 12 million adults and 1 million children have been infected with HIV. By October 1992, over 200,000 cases (the great majority in men) of AIDS had been reported in the United States alone, and two-thirds of these people had already died. It is estimated, based on the finding of antibodies against HIV in the blood, that an additional 1 to 2 million more Americans are infected with HIV (that is, are HIV-positive) but have no symptoms of AIDS as yet. This is an important point: One must distinguish between the presence of the symptomatic disease—AIDS—and asymptomatic infection with HIV. It is presently thought, however, that all infected persons will eventually develop AIDS.

The path from HIV infection to AIDS commonly takes about 10 years. Typically, the virus slowly multiplies during the first 5 years after HIV infection, the person is asymptomatic, and the number of helper T cells stays normal (at about 1000 cells per cubic millimeter of blood). During the next 5 years, the number of helper T cells drops to about half the normal level, although many people remain asymptomatic. As the helper T-cell count continues to fall, the symptoms of AIDS begin—infections with bacteria, viruses, fungi, and parasites, accompanied by systemic symptoms of weight loss, lethargy, and fever.

The transmission of HIV is known to occur only through (1) transfer of contaminated blood or blood products from one person to another; (2) sexual intercourse with an infected partner; and (3) transmission from an infected mother to her offspring either across the placenta during pregnancy and delivery, or via breast milk. Transfusion of blood is no longer a significant source of AIDS in the United States since blood is now tested and discarded if found to be positive for the presence of antibody to HIV.[14] Infection with HIV among intravenous drug users is related to exposure to contaminated blood through the

practice of sharing needles. The major reason that homosexual men are a high risk group is that anal intercourse is often associated with small tears in anal blood vessels, which allows HIV-containing semen from an infected person to pass into the blood of the partner.

HIV can definitely be transmitted during heterosexual intercourse. Such transmission occurs mainly during vaginal intercourse and can be male to female or female to male. In the United States, where most cases of AIDS are in homosexual males and intravenous drug users, 5 to 6 percent of all AIDS cases are presently attributed to heterosexual transmission. In contrast, in sub-Saharan Africa (where an estimated 8 to 12 million people are infected) and parts of the Caribbean and Asia, most cases of AIDS occur among heterosexuals, and the reasons for this are not completely clear. One hypothesis is that the high incidence of other venereal diseases in these parts of the world makes transmission during heterosexual intercourse much more likely because of the presence of open genital sores that permit entry of HIV from infected semen.

There is no evidence that HIV is transmitted through intact skin or via food, saliva, tears, sweat, feces, urine, vomit, insects, toilet seats, or swimming pools. Even prolonged close contact with persons infected with HIV does not lead to infection in the absence of the transmission routes described above. Nor is there any risk in *donating* blood.

Evidence indicates that the use of condoms markedly reduces (but does not completely eliminate) the risk of transmission of HIV during sexual intercourse.[15] At present, zidovudine (formerly called AZT) is the primary drug for the treatment of HIV infections. Zidovudine acts by blocking the action of the enzyme that converts the viral RNA into the host cell's DNA. At first used only in patients with advanced symptoms of AIDS, zidovudine is now known to delay progression of the disease in HIV-infected persons who are completely asymptomatic or suffering from only mild symptoms. It is not a cure but it does extend life expectancy significantly. The ultimate hope for prevention of AIDS is development of a vaccine. For a variety of reasons related to the nature of the virus and the fact that it infects a cell crucial for immune responses, this is not an easy task.

Antibiotics

The most important of the drugs we employ in altering resistance to microbes—mainly bacteria—are called ***antibiotics***, such as penicillin. With few exceptions (for exam-

---

[13]HIV specifically infects these cells because the CD4 protein on the plasma membrane of helper T cells acts as a high-affinity receptor for one of the HIV's surface proteins.

[14]There is an extremely slight possibility that a blood donor might have become infected with HIV so recently that the antibodies would not have become evident at the time of blood giving. This possibility is further minimized by careful screening of prospective donors to avoid those who might be in a high-risk group.

---

[15]The condom should be made of latex, and a water-based, not oil-based, lubricant, preferably one containing the antiviral drug nonoxynol-9, should be used with it.

ple, zidovudine in HIV infections), there are no antibiotics presently in common use against viruses.

Antibiotics exert a wide variety of effects, but the common denominator is interference with the synthesis of one or more of the bacterium's essential macromolecules. Antibiotics must not be used indiscriminately. For one thing, they may exert toxic effects on the body's cells as well as the bacteria. A second reason for judicious use is the problem of drug resistance. Most large bacterial populations contain a few mutants that are resistant to the drug. These few are capable of multiplying into large populations resistant to the effects of that particular antibiotic. Perhaps even more important, resistance can be transferred from one microbe directly to another previously nonresistant microbe by means of genes ("resistance genes") passed between them. A third reason for the judicious use of antibiotics is that these agents may actually contribute to a new infection by eliminating certain species of relatively harmless bacteria that ordinarily prevent growth of more dangerous ones.

HARMFUL IMMUNE RESPONSES

Until now, we have focused on the mechanisms of immune responses and their *protective* effects. In this section we shall see that immune responses can be harmful to the body.

Graft Rejection

The major obstacle to successful transplantation of tissues and organs is that the immune system, of course, recognizes the transplants, called grafts, as foreign and launches an attack against them. This is termed *graft rejection*. Although antibodies play some role, cytotoxic T cells are mainly responsible for graft rejection.

Except in the case of identical twins, the class I MHC proteins on the cells of a graft differ from the recipient's. So do the class II molecules present on the macrophages present in the graft (recall that virtually all organs and tissues have macrophages). Accordingly, the MHC proteins of both classes are recognized as foreign, and the cells bearing them are destroyed by the recipient's cytotoxic T cells with the aid of helper T cells.[16]

Some of the tools aimed at reducing graft rejection are radiation and drugs that kill actively dividing lymphocytes

and thereby decrease the host's T-cell population. The single most effective drug, however, is *cyclosporin,* which does not kill lymphocytes but rather blocks the production of IL-2 and other cytokines by helper T cells. This eliminates a critical signal for proliferation of the cytotoxic T cells.

Adrenal corticosteroids (Chapter 10) in large doses are also used to reduce the rejection. Their possible mechanisms of action are described in Section D.

Transfusion Reactions

Transfusion reactions, the illness caused when erythrocytes are destroyed during blood transfusion, are a special example of tissue rejection, one that illustrates the fact that antibodies rather than cytotoxic T cells can sometimes be the major factor in rejection. Erythrocytes do not have MHC proteins, but they do have plasma-membrane proteins and carbohydrates that can function as antigens when exposed to another person's blood. There are more than 400 erythrocyte antigens, but the ABO system of carbohydrates is the most important for transfusion reactions.

As described in the section on blood types in Chapter 14, some people have the gene that results in synthesis of the A antigen,[17] some have the gene for the B antigen, some have both genes, and some have neither gene. The erythrocytes of those with neither gene are said to have O-type erythrocytes. Accordingly, the possible blood types are A, B, AB, and O (Table 20-10).

Type A individuals always have anti-B antibodies in their plasma. Similarly, type B individuals have plasma anti-A antibodies. Type AB individuals have neither anti-A nor anti-B antibody, and type O individuals have both. These antierythrocyte antibodies are called **natural antibodies**. It is thought that they are induced early in life by antigens very similar to A and B on the surface of intestinal bacteria.

With this information as background, we can predict what happens when a type A person is given type B blood. There are two incompatibilities: (1) The recipient's anti-B antibody causes the transfused cells to be attacked, and (2) the anti-A antibody in the transfused plasma causes the recipient's cells to be attacked. The latter is generally of little consequence, however, because the transfused antibodies become so diluted in the recipient's plasma that they are ineffective in inducing a response. It is the destruction of the transfused cells by the recipient's antibodies that produces the problems.

Similar analyses show that the following situations

---

[16]There is an interesting problem here concerning antigen presentation. To be recognized by the host's cytotoxic T cells, the *graft's* MHC proteins should theoretically by complexed with the *host's* MHC proteins on *host* antigen-presenting cells. It is not clear whether (and how) this really occurs or whether foreign MHC proteins are so strongly antigenic that they can be recognized without such complexing.

[17]Genes, of course, do not code directly for carbohydrates; rather they code for the particular enzymes that catalyze formation of the carbohydrates.

TABLE 20-10 HUMAN ABO BLOOD GROUPS

Blood group	Percent°	Antigen on RBC	Genetic possibilities Homozygous	Heterozygous	Antibody in blood
A	42	A	AA	AO	Anti-B
B	10	B	BB	BO	Anti-A
AB	3	A and B	—	AB	Neither anti-A nor anti-B
O	45	Neither A nor B	OO	—	Both anti-A and anti-B

°In the United States.

would result in an attack on the transfused erythrocytes: a type-B person given either A or AB blood; a type A person given either type B or AB blood; a type O person given A, B, or AB blood. Type O people are, therefore, sometimes called universal donors, whereas type AB people are universal recipients. These terms are misleading, however, since besides those of the ABO type, there are a host of other erythrocyte antigens and plasma antibodies against them. Therefore, except in a dire emergency, the blood of donor and recipient must be tested for incompatibilities directly by the procedure called **cross-matching**. The recipient's serum is combined on a glass slide with the prospective donor's erythrocytes (a "major" cross-match), and the mixture observed for rupture (hemolysis) or clumping (agglutination) of the erythrocytes. In addition, the recipient's erythrocytes can be combined with the prospective donor's serum (a "minor" cross-match).

Another group of erythrocyte membrane antigens of medical importance is the Rh system of proteins. There are more than 40 such antigens, but the most strongly antigenic one is termed Rh_o (also called D), known commonly as the **Rh factor** because it was first studied in rhesus monkeys. Human erythrocytes either have the antigen (Rh-positive) or lack it (Rh-negative). About 85 percent of the United States population is Rh-positive.

The Rh system follows the classical immunity pattern in that no one has anti-Rh antibodies unless exposed to Rh-positive cells from another person. This can be a problem if an Rh-negative person is subjected to multiple transfusions with Rh-positive blood, but its major importance is in the mother-fetus relationship. When an Rh-negative mother carries an Rh-positive fetus, some of the fetal erythrocytes may cross the placental barriers into the maternal circulation, inducing her to synthesize anti-Rh antibodies. Because this occurs mainly during separation of the placenta at delivery, a first Rh-positive pregnancy rarely offers any danger to the fetus since delivery occurs before the antibodies are made by the mother. In future pregnancies, however, these antibodies will already be present in the mother and can cross the placenta to attack and hemolyze the erythrocytes of an Rh-positive fetus. This condition, which can cause an anemia severe enough to cause death of the fetus in utero or of the newborn, is called **hemolytic disease of the newborn**. The risk increases with each Rh-positive pregnancy as the mother becomes more and more sensitized.

Fortunately, this disease can be prevented by giving an Rh-negative mother human gamma globulin against Rh-positive erythrocytes within 72 h after she has delivered an Rh-positive infant. These antibodies bind to the antigenic sites on any Rh-positive erythrocytes that might have entered the mother's blood during delivery and prevent them from inducing antibody synthesis by the mother. The administered antibodies are eventually catabolized.

You may be wondering whether ABO incompatibilities are also a cause of hemolytic disease of the newborn. For example, a woman with type O blood has natural antibodies to both the A and B antigens. If her fetus is type A or B, this theoretically should cause a problem. Fortunately, it usually does not, partly because the A and B antigens are not strongly expressed in fetal erythrocytes and partly because the natural antibodies are of the IgM type, which do not readily cross the placenta.

Allergy (Hypersensitivity)

Allergy or **hypersensitivity** refers to certain diseases in which immune responses to environmental antigens cause inflammation and damage to the body itself. Antigens that cause allergy are termed **allergens**, common examples of which include those in ragweed pollen and poison ivy. Most allergens themselves are relatively or completely harmless, and it is the immune responses to them that cause the damage. In essence, then, allergy is immunity gone wrong, for the response is inappropriate to the stimulus.

To develop a particular allergy, a genetically predisposed person must first be exposed to the allergen. This initial exposure causes "sensitization," and it is the subsequent exposures that elicit the damaging immune responses we recognize as the disease. The diversity of allergic responses reflects the different immunological effector pathways elicited, and the classification of allergic diseases is based on these mechanisms.

In one type of hypersensitivity, the inflammatory response is independent of antibodies. It is due to marked secretion of cytokines by sensitized helper T cells in the area. These cytokines themselves act as inflammatory mediators and also activate macrophages to secrete their potent mediators. Because it takes several days to develop, this type is known as *delayed hypersensitivity*. The skin rash that appears after contact with poison ivy is an example.

In contrast to these are the various types of antibody-mediated hypersensitivity responses. One important type is termed *immune-complex hypersensitivity*. It occurs when so many antibodies combine with free antigens that a large number of antigen-antibody complexes precipitate out on the surface of endothelial cells or are trapped in capillary walls, particularly the renal corpuscles. These immune complexes activate complement, which then induces an inflammatory response that damages the tissues immediately surrounding the complexes. Allergy to penicillin is an example.

The most common type of antibody-mediated allergic responses, however, are those termed *immediate hypersensitivity* because they are usually very rapid in onset. They are also called IgE-mediated hypersensitivity because they involve IgE antibodies.

Immediate Hypersensitivity. In immediate hypersensitivity, initial exposure to the antigen leads to some antibody synthesis and, more important, to the production of memory B cells that mediate active immunity. Upon reexposure, the antigen elicits a more powerful antibody response. So far, none of this is unusual, but the difference is that the particular antigens that elicit immediate-hypersensitivity reactions stimulate, in genetically susceptible persons, the production of type IgE antibodies. Production of IgE requires the participation of a particular subset of helper T cells which are activated by the allergens and then release cytokines that preferentially stimulate IgE-producing B cells.

Upon their release from plasma cells, IgE antibodies circulate to various parts of the body and become attached to connective-tissue mast cells (Figure 20-18). When subsequently an antigen enters the body and combines with the mast-cell IgE, this triggers release of the mast cell's secretory vesicles, which contain many inflammatory mediators, including **histamine**. In addition to releasing these preformed inflammatory mediators stored in mast-cell vesicles, the binding of antigen to IgE triggers the mast cell to synthesize prostaglandins and leukotrienes as well as a substance called **platelet-activating factor**. All these mediators then initiate a local inflammatory response.

Thus, the symptoms of antibody-mediated allergy reflect the various effects of these mediators and the body site in which the antigen-IgE-mast cell combination occurs. For example, when a previously sensitized person inhales ragweed pollen, the antigen combines with IgE on mast cells in the respiratory passages. The mediators released cause increased mucus secretion, increased blood flow, swelling of the epithelial lining, and contraction of the smooth muscle surrounding the airways. Thus, there follow the symptoms of congestion, running nose, sneezing, and difficulty in breathing that characterize hay fever.

Allergic symptoms are usually localized to the site of entry of the antigen. If very large amounts of the chemicals released by the mast cells enter the circulation, however, systemic symptoms may result and cause severe hypotension and bronchiolar constriction. This sequence of events *(anaphylaxis)* can cause death due to circulatory and respiratory failure. It can be elicited in some sensitized people by the antigen in a single bee sting.

The very rapid component of immediate hypersensitivity often proceeds to a *late-phase reaction* lasting many hours or days, during which large numbers of leukocytes, particularly eosinophils, migrate into the inflamed area. The chemotaxins that attract them are mediators released by a number of cells in the inflamed area, including the mast cells. The eosinophils, once in the area, secrete mediators that prolong the inflammation and sensitize the tissues so that less stimulation is needed the next time to evoke a response.

Given the inappropriateness of most immediate hypersensitivity responses, how did such a system evolve? The normal physiological function of the IgE-mast-cell-eosinophil pathways is to repel invasion by multicellular parasites. The mediators released by the mast cells stimulate the inflammatory response against the parasites, and the eosinphils serve as the major killer cells against them. How this system also came to be inducible by harmless agents is not clear.

Autoimmune Disease

To repeat, allergy is due to an inappropriate response to an *environmental* antigen. *Autoimmune disease*, in contrast, is due to an immune attack triggered by the body's own proteins, acting as antigens, and is therefore directed specifically against the body's own cells that contain these proteins.

We explained earlier how the body normally is in a state of immune tolerance toward its own cells. Unfortunately, there are situations in which this tolerance breaks down and the body does in fact launch antibody- or cell-medi-

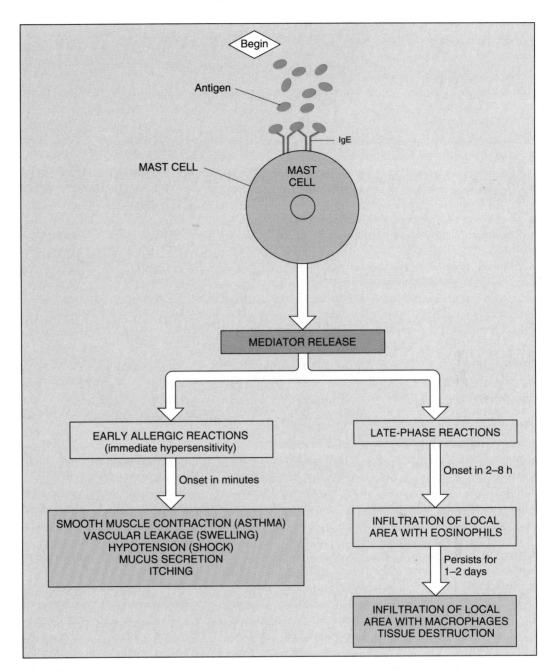

FIGURE 20-18
Sequence of events in an immediate-hypersensitivity allergic response. The mediators include substances stored in vesicles, such as histamine, and substances synthesized upon stimulation, such as leukotrienes.

ated attacks against its own cells and tissues, the result being damage and/or alteration of function. A growing number of human diseases are being recognized as auto-immune in origin. Examples are multiple sclerosis, in which myelin is attacked; myasthenia gravis, in which the receptors for acetylcholine on skeletal muscle cells are the target; rheumatoid arthritis, in which joints are damaged; and insulin-dependent diabetes mellitus, in which the insulin-producing cells of the pancreas are destroyed. Some possible causes for the body's failure to recognize its own cells are summarized in Table 20-11.

Finally, another important unsolved question in the field of autoimmunity concerns the relationship between mother and fetus: Why does the mother's immune system

---

TABLE 20-11   SOME POSSIBLE CAUSES OF AUTOIMMUNE ATTACK

1. There may be failure of negative clonal selection in the thymus or of clonal inactivation in the periphery.
2. Normal body proteins may be altered by combination with drugs or environmental chemicals. This leads to an attack on the cells bearing the now-"foreign" protein.
3. In cell-mediated immune attacks on virus-infected bodily cells, so many cells may be destroyed that disease results.
4. Genetic mutations in the body's cells may yield new proteins that serve as antigens.
5. The body may encounter microbes whose antigens are so close in structure to certain of the body's own proteins that the antibodies or cytotoxic T lymphocytes produced against these microbial antigens also attack cells bearing the self proteins.
6. Proteins normally never encountered by lymphocytes may become exposed as a result of some other disease.
7. A deficiency of suppressor T cells could contribute to the development of autoimmunity.

---

not reject the fetus, since half of the fetal proteins are paternal and therefore foreign to the mother?

Excessive Inflammatory Responses to Microbes

Recall that complement, other inflammatory mediators, and the toxic chemicals secreted by neutrophils and macrophages are not specific in their targets. Accordingly, sometimes during an inflammatory response directed against microbes there can be so much generation or release of these substances that adjacent normal tissues may be damaged. These substances can also cause potentially lethal systemic responses. For example, the release of large amounts of IL-1 and TNF in response to an infection with certain types of bacteria can cause profound vasodilation throughout the body, precipitating hypotension and shock, termed **septic shock**. Moreover, prolonged secretion of TNF can cause marked catabolism of fat and protein so as to lead to general wasting of the body. In other words, it is not the bacteria themselves that cause septic shock and general wasting but rather the cytokines released in response to the bacteria.

Thus, the various mediators of inflammation and immunity are a double-edged sword: In usual amounts they are essential for normal resistance, but in excessive amounts they can cause illness. Thus, at the same time that some scientists are studying how to enhance resistance to microbes and cancer by *administering* IL-1 and TNF, other scientists are developing drugs to *block* the action of these same cytokines in situations associated with excessive secretion.

This completes the section on immunology. Table 20-12 presents a summary of immune mechanisms in the form of a miniglossary of cells and chemical mediators involved in immune responses. All the material in this table has been covered in this chapter.

TABLE 20-12   A MINIGLOSSARY OF CELLS AND CHEMICAL MEDIATORS INVOLVED IN IMMUNE FUNCTIONS

Cells

Activated macrophages Macrophages whose killing ability has been enhanced by cytokines, particularly IL-2 and gamma interferon.

Antigen-presenting cells Cells that present antigen, complexed with MHC proteins, on their surface to T cells.

B cells Lymphocytes that, upon activation, proliferate and differentiate into antibody-secreting plasma cells; provide major defense against bacteria, viruses in the extracellular fluid, and toxins; can function as antigen-presenting cells for helper T cells.

TABLE 20-12   A MINIGLOSSARY OF CELLS AND CHEMICAL MEDIATORS INVOLVED IN IMMUNE FUNCTIONS (*continued*)

Cells (*continued*)

Cytotoxic T cells (also sometimes called killer T cells) The class of T lymphocytes that, upon activation by specific antigen, directly attack the cells bearing that type of antigen; are major killers of virus-infected cells and tumor cells; bind antigen associated with class I MHC proteins.

Eosinophils Granulocytic leukocytes involved in immediate hypersensitivity responses and destruction of parasites.

Helper T cells The class of T cells that, via secreted cytokines, play a stimulatory role in the activation of B cells and cytotoxic T cells; also can activate NK cells and macrophages; bind antigen associated with class II MHC proteins.

Lymphocytes The type of leukocyte responsible for specific immune defenses; categorized mainly as B cells and T cells (NK cells is another category).

Macrophages Cell type that (1) functions as a phagocyte, (2) processes and presents antigen to helper T cells, and (3) secretes cytokines involved in inflammation, activation of lymphocytes, and the systemic acute phase response to infection or injury.

Mast cells Tissue cell that binds IgE and releases inflammatory mediators in immediate hypersensitivity reactions.

Memory cells B cells and cytotoxic T cells that differentiate during an initial immune response and respond rapidly during a subsequent exposure to the same antigen.

Monocytes A type of leukocyte; leaves the bloodstream and is transformed into a macrophage; has functions similar to those of macrophages.

Natural killer (NK) cells Class of lymphocytes that bind to cells bearing foreign antigens without MHC restriction and kill them directly; major targets are virus-infected cells and cancer cells; participate in antibody-dependent cellular cytotoxicity (ADCC).

Neutrophils Granulocytic leukocytes which function as phagocytes and also release chemicals involved in inflammation.

Plasma cells Cells that differentiate from activated B lymphocytes and that secrete antibodies.

Suppressor T cells The class of T cells that inhibit antibody production and cytotoxic T-cell function.

T cells Lymphocytes derived from precursors that differentiated in the thymus; see cytotoxic T cells, helper T cells, and suppressor T cells.

Chemical Mediators

Acute phase proteins Group of proteins secreted by the liver during systemic response to injury or infection; stimulus for their secretion is IL-1 and other cytokines.

Antibodies Immunoglobulins that are secreted by plasma cells; combine with the type of antigen that stimulated their production and direct an attack against the antigen or a cell bearing it.

C1 The first protein in the classical complement pathway.

Chemotaxin A general name given to any chemical mediator that stimulates chemotaxis (chemical attraction) of neutrophils or other phagocytes.

Complement A group of plasma proteins that, upon activation, kill microbes directly and facilitate the various steps of the inflammatory process, including phagocytosis; the classical complement pathway is triggered by antigen-antibody complexes, whereas the alternate pathway can operate independently of antibody.

Cytokines General term for protein messengers that regulate immune responses; secreted by macrophages and monocytes (monokines), lymphocytes (lymphokines), and several other cell types.

Eicosanoids General term for products of arachidonic acid metabolism (prostaglandins, thromboxanes, leukotrienes); function as important inflammatory mediators.

Gamma interferon (See interferon.)

Histamine An inflammatory mediator secreted mainly by mast cells; acts on microcirculation to cause vasodilation and increased permeability to protein.

IgA The class of antibodies secreted by the lining of the body's various "tracts."

IgD A class of antibodies whose function is unknown.

IgE The class of antibodies that mediate immediate hypersensitivity and resistance to parasites.

IgG The most abundant class of plasma antibodies.

IgM A class of antibodies that, along with IgG, provide the bulk of specific humoral immunity against bacteria and viruses.

TABLE 20-12 A MINIGLOSSARY OF CELLS AND CHEMICAL MEDIATORS INVOLVED IN IMMUNE FUNCTIONS (*continued*)

Chemical Mediators (*continued*)

Immunoglobulin (Ig) Proteins that function as B-cell receptors and antibodies; the five major classes are IgA, IgD, IgE, IgG, and IgM.

Interferon Class of proteins that nonspecifically inhibit viral replication; also stimulate the killing ability of cytotoxic T cells, NK cells, and macrophages.

Interleukin 1 (IL-1) Cytokine secreted by macrophages (and other cells) that activates helper T cells, exerts many inflammatory effects, and mediates many of the systemic acute phase responses, including fever.

Interleukin 2 (IL-2) Cytokine secreted by activated helper T cells that causes helper T cells, B cells, cytotoxic T cells, and NK cells to proliferate.

Interleukin 6 (IL-6) Cytokine secreted by macrophages (and other cells) that helps activate B cells and exerts multiple effects on inflammation and the acute phase response.

Kinins Peptides that split from kininogens in inflamed areas and facilitate the vascular changes associated with inflammation; they also activate neuronal pain receptors.

Leukotrienes A class of eicosanoids that are generated by the lipoxygenase pathway and function as inflammatory mediators.

Lymphokines Cytokines secreted by lymphocytes.

Membrane attack complex (MAC) Group of complement proteins that form channels in the surface of a microbe, making it leaky and killing it.

Monokines Cytokines secreted by macrophages and monocytes.

Natural antibodies Antibodies to the erythrocyte antigens (of the A or B type) not present in a person's blood.

Opsonin General name given to any chemical mediator that promotes phagocytosis.

Perforin Protein secreted by cytotoxic T cells and NK cells that forms channels in the plasma membrane of the target cell, making it leaky and killing it; its structure and function are similar to that of the MAC in the complement system.

Platelet-activating factor Mediator synthesized and released by mast cells that stimulates inflammation.

Prostaglandins A class of eicosanoids that are generated by the cyclooxygenase pathway and function as inflammatory mediators.

Tumor necrosis factor Cytokine that kills cells outright, stimulates inflammation, and mediates many of the systemic acute phase responses.

SECTION A SUMMARY

CELLS MEDIATING IMMUNE DEFENSES

I. Immune defenses may be nonspecific, in which the identity of the target is not recognized, or specific, in which it is.

II. The cells of the immune system are leukocytes (neutrophils, eosinophils, basophils, monocytes, and lymphocytes), plasma cells, macrophages, and mast cells. The leukocytes use the blood for transportation but function mainly in the tissues.

NONSPECIFIC IMMUNE DEFENSES

I. External barriers to infection are the skin, the linings of the respiratory and GI tracts, the cilia of these linings, and antimicrobial chemicals in glandular secretions.

II. Inflammation, the local inflammatory response to injury or infection, includes vasodilation, increased vascular permeability to protein, phagocyte chemotaxis, destruction of the invader via phagocytosis or extracellular killing, and tissue repair.

A. The mediators controlling these processes, summarized in Table 20-4, are either released from cells in the area or generated extracellularly from plasma proteins.

B. The main cells that function as phagocytes are the neutrophils, monocytes, and macrophages. They also secrete many mediators.

C. One group of inflammatory mediators—the complement family of plasma proteins activated during nonspecific inflammation by the alternate pathway—not only stimulates many of the steps of inflammation but mediates extracellular killing via its membrane attack complex.

D. The end result of infection or tissue damage is tissue repair.

III. Interferon stimulates the production of intracellular proteins that nonspecifically inhibit viral replication.

SPECIFIC IMMUNE DEFENSES

I. Lymphocytes mediate specific immune responses.

II. Specific immune responses occur in three stages.

    A. A lymphocyte programmed to recognize a specific antigen encounters it and binds to it via plasma-membrane receptors specific for the antigen.

    B. The lymphocyte is activated to undergo mitosis and further differentiation.

    C. The activated cells launch an attack against antigens of that kind all over the body.

III. The lymphoid organs are categorized as primary (bone marrow and thymus) or peripheral (lymph nodes, spleen, tonsils, and lymphocyte collections in the linings of the body's tracts).

    A. The primary lymphoid organs are the sites of maturation of lymphocytes that will then be carried to the peripheral lymphoid organs, which are the major sites of lymphocyte mitosis and specific immune responses.

    B. Lymphocytes undergo a continuous recirculation among the peripheral lymphoid organs, lymph, blood, and all the body's organs and tissues.

IV. The three broad populations of lymphocytes are B, T, and NK cells.

    A. B cells mature in the bone marrow and are carried to the peripheral lymphoid organs; there, additional B cells arise by mitosis.

    B. T cells leave the bone marrow in an immature state, are carried to the thymus, and undergo maturation there. These cells are then carried to the peripheral lymphoid organs, and new T cells arise from them by mitosis.

    C. The origin of NK cells is in the bone marrow.

V. B cells and T cells have different functions.

    A. B cells, upon activation, differentiate into plasma cells, which secrete antibodies. Antibody-mediated responses constitute the major defense against bacteria, viruses, and toxins in the extracellular fluid.

    B. Cytotoxic T cells directly attack and kill virus-infected cells and cancer cells, without the participation of antibodies.

    C. Suppressor T cells inhibit the function of both B cells and cytotoxic T cells. Helper T cells stimulate B cells and cytotoxic T cells via chemical messengers they secrete. With few exceptions, this help is essential for activation of the B cells and cytotoxic T cells.

VI. B-cell surface plasma-membrane receptors are copies of the specific antibody (immunoglobulin) the cell is capable of producing.

    A. Any given B cell or clone of B cells produces unique antibodies, that is, ones that have a unique antigen-binding site.

    B. Antibodies are composed of four interlocking polypeptide chains; the variable regions of the antibodies are the sites that bind antigen.

VII. T-cell surface plasma-membrane receptors are not immunoglobulins, but they do have specific antigen binding sites which differ from one T-cell clone to another.

    A. The T-cell receptor binds antigen only when the antigen is complexed to one of the body's own plasma-membrane MHC proteins.

    B. Class I MHC proteins are found on all nucleated cells of the body, whereas class II MHC proteins are found only on macrophages, B cells, and several macrophage-like cells. Cytotoxic T cells require antigen to be complexed to class I proteins, whereas helper T cells require class II proteins.

VIII. Immune tolerance is the result of clonal deletion and clonal activation.

IX. Antigen presentation is required for T cells.

    A. Only macrophages, B cells, and several macrophage-like cells function as antigen-presenting cells (APCs) for helper T cells. The antigen is internalized by the APC and hydrolyzed to peptide fragments, which are complexed with class II MHC proteins. This complex is then shuttled to the plasma membrane of the APC, which also secretes interleukin 1.

    B. A virus-infected cell or cancer cell can function as an APC for cytotoxic T cells. The viral antigen or cancer-associated antigen is synthesized by the cell itself and hydrolyzed to peptide fragments, which are complexed to class I MHC proteins. The complex is then shuttled to the plasma membrane of the cell.

X. NK cells have the same targets as cytotoxic T cells, but they are not antigen-specific, have no MHC requirement, and do not require antigen presentation.

XI. In antibody-mediated responses, the membrane receptors of a B cell bind antigen, and at the same time a helper T cell also binds antigen in association with a class II MHC protein on a macrophage or other APC.

    A. The helper T cell, activated both by the antigen and by IL-1 secreted by the APC, secretes IL-2, which then causes the helper T cell to proliferate into a clone of cells that secrete additional cytokines.

B. These cytokines, with IL-2, then stimulate the antigen-bound B cell to proliferate and differentiate into plasma cells, which secrete antibodies. Some of the activated B cells become memory cells, which are responsible for active immunity.

C. There are five major classes of secreted antibodies: IgG, IgM, IgA, IgD, and IgE. The first two are the major antibodies against bacterial and viral infection.

D. The secreted antibodies are carried throughout the body by the blood and combine with antigen. The antigen-antibody complex enhances the inflammatory response mainly by activating the complement system. Complement proteins mediate many steps of inflammation, act as opsonins, and directly kill antibody-bound cells via the membrane attack complex.

E. Antibodies of the IgG class act directly as opsonins and also link target cells to NK cells which directly kill the target cells.

F. Antibodies also neutralize toxins and extracellular viruses.

XII. Virus-infected cells and cancer cells are killed by cytotoxic T cells, NK cells, and activated macrophages.

A. A cytotoxic T cell binds, via its membrane receptor, to cells bearing a viral antigen or cancer-associated antigen in association with a class I MHC protein.

B. Activation of the cytotoxic T cell also requires cytokines, particularly IL-2 and gamma interferon, secreted by helper T cells, themselves activated by antigen presented by a macrophage. The cytotoxic T cell then releases perforin, which kills the attached target cell by making it leaky.

C. NK cells and macrophages are also stimulated by helper T-cell cytokines to attack and kill virus-infected or cancer cells.

SYSTEMIC MANIFESTATIONS OF INFECTION

I. The acute phase response is summarized in Figure 20-17.

II. The major mediators of this response are IL-1, TNF, and IL-6.

FACTORS THAT ALTER THE BODY'S RESISTANCE TO INFECTION

I. The body's capacity to resist infection is influenced by nutritional status, the presence of other diseases, psychological factors, and the intactness of the immune system.

II. AIDS is caused by a retrovirus that destroys helper T cells and therefore reduces the ability to resist infection and cancer.

III. Antibiotics interfere with the synthesis of macromolecules by bacteria.

HARMFUL IMMUNE RESPONSES

I. Rejection of tissue transplants is initiated by MHC proteins on the transplanted cells and is mediated mainly by cytotoxic T cells.

II. Transfusion reactions are mediated by antibodies.

A. Transfused erythrocytes will be destroyed if the recipient has natural antibodies against antigens—type A or type B—on the cells.

B. Antibodies against Rh-positive erythrocytes can be produced following exposure of an Rh-negative person to such cells.

III. Allergies (hypersensitivity reactions), caused by allergens, are of several types.

A. In delayed hypersensitivity, the inflammation is due to the interplay of helper T-cell cytokines and macrophages. Immune complex hypersensitivity is due to complement activation by antigen-antibody complexes.

B. In immediate hypersensitivity, antigen binds to IgE antibodies, themselves bound to mast cells. The mast cells then release inflammatory mediators such as histamine that produce the symptoms of the allergy. The late phase of immediate hypersensitivity is mediated by eosinophils.

IV. Autoimmune attacks are directed against the body's own proteins, acting as antigens. Reasons for the failure of immune tolerance are summarized in Table 20-12.

V. Normal tissues can be damaged by excessive inflammatory responses to microbes.

SECTION A KEY TERMS

immunology	phagosome
immune surveillance	phagolysosome
nonspecific immune	nitric oxide
defenses	complement
specific immune defenses	membrane attack complex
immune system	(MAC)
leukocytes	alternate complement
plasma cells	pathway
macrophages	interferon
mast cells	antigen
inflammation	lymphocyte activation
phagocytes	lymphoid organs
phagocytosis	primary lymphoid organs
chemotaxis	peripheral lymphoid
chemotaxin	organs
opsonin	thymus

lymph nodes
spleen
tonsils
B lymphocytes (B cells)
T lymphocytes (T cells)
natural killer cells
   (NK cells)
antibodies
cytotoxic T cells
helper T cells
suppressor T cells
lymphokines
monokines
cytokines
immunoglobulins
Fc
antigen binding site
major histocompatibility
   complex (MHC)
MHC proteins (class I
   and class II)
antigen presentation
antigen-presenting cells
   (APCs)
epitopes
interleukin 1 (IL-1)
immune tolerance
clonal deletion

clonal inactivation
interleukin 2 (IL-2)
interleukin 6 (IL-6)
memory cells
IgG
gamma globulin
IgM
IgE
IgA
IgD
classical complement
   pathway
antibody-dependent cellular
   cytotoxicity (ADCC)
active immunity
passive immunity
gamma interferon
perforin
activated macrophages
tumor necrosis factor (TNF)
acute phase response
acute phase proteins
colony-stimulating factors
natural antibodies
Rh factor
histamine
platelet-activating factor

SECTION A REVIEW QUESTIONS

1. What are the major cells of the immune system and their general functions?
2. Describe the major anatomical and biochemical barriers to infection.
3. Name the three cell types that function as phagocytes.
4. List the sequence of events in an inflammatory response and describe each.
5. Name the sources of the major inflammatory mediators.
6. What triggers the alternate pathway for complement activation? What roles does complement play in inflammation and cell killing?

7. Describe the antiviral role of interferon.
8. Name the lymphoid organs. Contrast the functions of the bone marrow and thymus with those of the peripheral lymphoid organs.
9. Name the various populations and subpopulations of lymphocytes and state their roles in specific immune responses.
10. Contrast the major targets of antibody-mediated responses and responses mediated by cytotoxic T cells and NK cells.
11. How do the Fc and antigen-combining site portions of antibodies differ?
12. What are the differences between B-cell receptors and T-cell receptors? Between cytotoxic T-cell receptors and helper T-cell receptors?
13. What two processes contribute to immune tolerance?
14. Compare and contrast antigen presentation to helper T cells and cytotoxic T cells.
15. Compare and contrast cytotoxic T cells and NK cells.
16. Diagram the sequence of events in an antibody-mediated response, including the role of helper T cells, interleukin 1, and interleukin 2.
17. Contrast the general functions of the different antibody classes.
18. How is complement activation triggered in the classical complement pathway, and how does complement "know" what cells to attack?
19. Name two ways in which the presence of antibodies enhances phagocytosis.
20. How do NK cells "know" what cells to attack in ADCC?
21. Diagram the sequence of events by which a virus-infected cell is attacked and destroyed by cytotoxic T cells. Include the roles of cytotoxic T cells, helper T cells, interleukin 1, and interleukin 2.
22. Contrast the extracellular and intracellular phases of immune responses to viruses, including the role of interferon.
23. List the systemic responses to infection or injury and the mediators responsible for them.
24. What factors influence the body's resistance to infection?
25. What is the major defect in AIDS, and what causes it?
26. What is the major cell type involved in graft rejection?
27. Diagram the sequences of events in immediate hypersensitivity.

SECTION

NONIMMUNE METABOLISM OF FOREIGN CHEMICALS

The body is exposed to a huge number of nonmicrobial foreign chemicals. Many are products of the natural world, but many are man-made. There are now more than 10,000 foreign chemicals being commercially synthesized, and over 1 million have been synthesized at one time or another. They find their way into the body either because they are purposely taken, as drugs, or simply because they are in the air, water, and food we use.

As described in Section A of this chapter, foreign materials can induce inflammation and specific immune responses. These defenses do not, however, constitute the major defense mechanisms against foreign chemicals. Rather, metabolism—molecular alteration (**biotransformation**) and excretion—does.

The body's metabolism of foreign chemicals is summarized in Figure 20-19. First, the chemical gains entry to the body through the gastrointestinal tract, lungs, skin, or placenta in the case of a fetus. Once in the blood, the chemical may become bound reversibly to plasma proteins or to erythrocytes. Such binding lowers its free concentration and thereby its ability to alter cell function. It may accumulate in storage depots—for example, DDT in fat tissue—or it may undergo enzyme-mediated biotransformation in various organs and tissues. The metabolites resulting from biotransformation may enter the blood and are subject to the same fates as the parent molecules. Finally, the foreign chemical and its metabolites may be eliminated from the body in the urine, expired air, skin secretions, or feces.

The blood concentration of any foreign chemical is determined by the interplay of all these metabolic pathways. For example, kidney function and biotransformation both tend to decrease with age, and this explains why a particular dose of a drug often produces much higher blood concentrations in elderly people than in young people.

ABSORPTION

In practice, most foreign molecules move through the lining of some portion of the gastrointestinal tract fairly readily, either by diffusion or by carrier-mediated transport. This should not be surprising since the gastrointestinal tract evolved to favor absorption of the wide variety of nutrient molecules in the environment. Nonnutrient

chemicals are the beneficiaries of these relatively nondiscriminating transport mechanisms.

The lung alveoli are highly permeable to most foreign chemicals and therefore offer an easy entrance route for those that are airborne. Lipid solubility is all-important for entry through the skin, so that this route is of little importance for charged molecules but can be used by oils, steroids, and other lipids.

The penetration of the placental membranes by foreign chemicals is important since the effects of environmental agents on the fetus during critical periods of development may be quite marked and, in many cases, irreversible. Diffusion across the placenta is an important mechanism for lipid-soluble substances, and carrier-mediated systems, which evolved for the carriage of endogenous nutrients, may be usurped by foreign chemicals to gain entry into the fetus.

STORAGE SITES

The major storage sites for foreign chemicals are cell proteins, bone, and fat. The chemical bound to cell proteins or bone or dissolved in the fat is in equilibrium with the free chemical in the blood, so that an increase in blood concentration causes more movement into storage, up to the point of saturation. Conversely, as the chemical is eliminated from the body and its blood concentration falls, movement occurs out of storage sites.

These storage sites are a source of protection, but it sometimes happens that the storage sites accumulate so much chemical that they become damaged.

EXCRETION

As described in Chapter 16, to appear in the urine, a chemical must either be filtered through the renal corpuscle or secreted across the tubular epithelium. Glomerular filtration is a bulk-flow process, so that all low-molecular-weight substances in plasma undergo filtration. Accordingly, there is considerable filtration of most foreign chemicals, except those bound to plasma proteins or

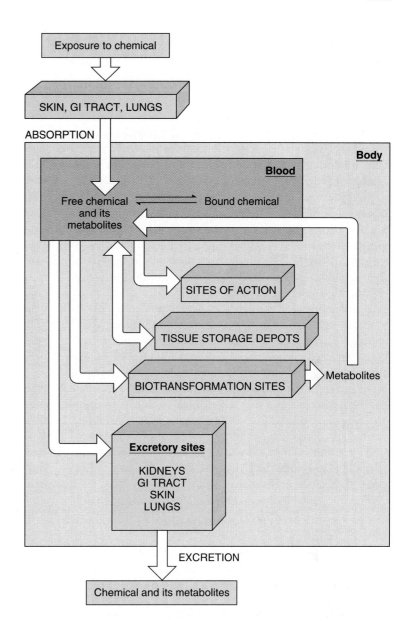

FIGURE 20-19
Metabolic pathways for foreign chemicals.

erythrocytes. In contrast, tubular secretion is by discrete transport processes, and many foreign chemicals—penicillin, for example—utilize the mediated transport systems available for naturally occurring substances.

Once in the tubular lumen, via either filtration or tubular secretion, the foreign chemical will still not be excreted if it is reabsorbed across the tubular epithelium into the blood. As the filtered fluid moves along the renal tubules, molecules that are lipid-soluble passively diffuse along with reabsorbed water through the tubular epithelium and back into the blood. The net result is that little is excreted in the urine, and the chemical is retained in the body. If

these chemicals could be transformed into more polar and therefore less lipid-soluble molecules, their passive reabsorption from the tubule would be retarded and they would be excreted more readily. This type of transformation is precisely what occurs in the liver, as described in the next section.

An analogous problem exists for foreign molecules secreted in the bile. Many of these substances, having reached the lumen of the small intestine, are absorbed back into the blood, thereby escaping excretion in the feces. This cyclic enterohepatic circulation is described in Chapter 17.

BIOTRANSFORMATION

The metabolic alteration—biotransformation—of foreign molecules occurs mainly in the liver but to some extent also in kidney, skin, placenta, and other organs. A large number of distinct enzymes and pathways are involved, but the common denominator of most of them is that they transform chemicals into more polar, less lipid-soluble substances. One consequence of this transformation is that the chemical may be rendered less toxic, but this is not always so. The second, more important, consequence is that the chemical's tubular reabsorption is diminished and urinary excretion facilitated. Similarly, for substances handled by biliary secretion, gut absorption of the metabolite is less likely so that fecal excretion is also enhanced.

The hepatic enzymes that perform these transformations are called the **microsomal enzyme system (MES)** and are located mainly in the smooth endoplasmic reticulum. One of the most important facts about this enzyme system is that it is easily inducible; that is, the number of these enzymes can be greatly increased by exposure to a chemical that acts as a substrate for the system. For example, chronic overuse of alcohol results in an increased rate of alcohol catabolism because of induction of the microsomal enzymes. This accounts for much of the tolerance to alcohol, that is, the fact that increasing doses must be taken to achieve a given magnitude of effect.

The hepatic biotransformation mechanisms vividly demonstrate how an adaptive response may, under some circumstances, turn out to be maladaptive. These enzymes all too frequently "toxify" rather than "detoxify" a drug or pollutant. In fact, many foreign chemicals are quite nontoxic until the liver enzymes biotransform them. Of particular importance is the fact that many chemicals that cause cancer do so only after biotransformation. For example, a major component of cigarette smoke is transformed by the MES into a carcinogenic compound. Individuals with a particularly highly inducible MES have a twenty- to fortyfold higher risk of developing lung cancer from smoking.

The MES can also cause problems in another way because it evolved primarily not to defend against foreign chemicals, which were much less prevalent during our evolution, but rather to metabolize *endogenous* substances, particularly steroids and other lipid-soluble molecules. Therefore, the induction of these enzymes by a drug or pollutant increases metabolism not only of that drug or pollutant but of the endogenous substances as well. The result is a decreased concentration in the body of the normal substance, resulting in its possible deficiency.

Another fact of importance concerning the MES is that whereas certain chemicals induce it, others inhibit it. The presence of such chemicals in the environment could have deleterious effects on the system's capacity to protect against those chemicals that it transforms. Just to illustrate how complex this picture can be, note that any chemical that inhibits the microsomal enzyme system may actually confer protection against those other chemicals that must undergo transformation in order to become toxic.

SECTION B SUMMARY

I. The concentration of a foreign chemical in the body depends upon degree of exposure to the chemical, its rate of absorption across the GI tract, lung, skin, or placenta, and its rates of storage, biotransformation, and excretion.

II. Biotransformation occurs in the liver and other tissues and is mediated by multiple enzymes, notably the microsomal enzyme system (MES). Its major function is to make lipid-soluble substances more polar (less lipid-soluble), thereby decreasing renal tubular reabsorption and increasing excretion.

   A. This system can be induced or inhibited by the chemicals it processes and by other chemicals.

   B. It detoxifies some chemicals but toxifies others, notably carcinogens.

SECTION B KEY TERMS

biotransformation   microsomal enzyme system (MES)

SECTION B REVIEW QUESTIONS

1. Why is the urinary excretion of lipid-soluble substances generally very low?

2. What are two functions of biotransformation mechanisms?

3. What are two ways in which activation of biotransformation mechanisms may actually cause malfunction?

HEMOSTASIS: THE PREVENTION OF BLOOD LOSS

Elimination of bleeding is known as **hemostasis** (don't confuse this word with "homeostasis"). Physiological hemostatic mechanisms are most effective in dealing with injuries in small vessels—arterioles, capillaries, venules—which are the most common source of bleeding in everyday life. In contrast, the bleeding from a medium or large artery is not usually controllable by the body. Venous bleeding is less dangerous because veins have low blood pressure. Indeed, the drop in pressure induced by raising the bleeding part above the heart level may stop hemorrhage from a vein. In addition, if the venous bleeding is into the tissues, the accumulation of blood may increase interstitial pressure enough to eliminate the pressure gradient required for continued blood loss. Accumulation of blood in the tissues can occur as a result of bleeding from any vessel type and is termed a *hematoma*.

When a blood vessel is severed or otherwise injured, its immediate inherent response is to constrict (the mechanism is unclear). This short-lived response slows the flow of blood in the affected area. In addition, this constriction presses the opposed endothelial surfaces of the vessel together, and this contact induces a stickiness capable of keeping them "glued" together against high pressures.

Permanent closure of the vessel by constriction and contact stickiness occurs only in the very smallest vessels of the microcirculation, however, and the staunching of bleeding ultimately is dependent upon two other processes that are interdependent and occur in rapid succession: (1) formation of a platelet plug, and (2) blood coagulation (clotting). The blood platelets are involved in both processes.

FORMATION OF A PLATELET PLUG

The involvement of platelets in hemostasis requires their adhesion to a surface. Although platelets have a propensity for adhering to surfaces, they do not adhere to the normal endothelial cells lining the blood vessels. However, injury to a vessel disrupts the endothelium and exposes the underlying connective-tissue collagen molecules—fibrous proteins that constitute a major component of the interstitial matrix. Platelets adhere to collagen, an event facilitated by **von Willebrand factor (vWF)**, a plasma protein secreted by endothelial cells and platelets. This protein forms a bridge between the damaged vessel wall and the platelets: It binds to collagen, and then platelets bind to it.[18]

Adhesion triggers the platelets to release the contents of their secretory vesicles ("granules"), which contain a variety of chemical agents. Many of these agents, including adenosine diphosphate (ADP) and serotonin, then act locally to induce changes in the surface of the platelets, causing new platelets to adhere to the old ones. Termed **platelet aggregation**, this self-perpetuating (positive-feedback) process rapidly creates a **platelet plug** inside the vessel.

Chemical agents in the platelets' secretory granules are not the only stimulator of platelet aggregation. In addition, adhesion of the platelets to collagen induces the synthesis, from arachidonic acid in the platelet plasma membrane, of **thromboxane A$_2$**, a member of the eicosanoid family (Chapter 7). This substance is released into the extracellular fluid and acts locally to further stimulate platelet aggregation and secretion of platelet granules (Figure 20-20).

Fibrinogen, a plasma protein whose crucial role in blood clotting is described in the subsequent section, also participates in the formation of platelet plugs. It does so by forming bridges between platelets. The binding sites for fibrinogen on the platelet plasma membrane somehow become exposed as platelet aggregation proceeds.

The platelet plug can completely seal small breaks in blood vessel walls. Its effectiveness is further enhanced by another property of platelets—contraction. Platelets contain a very high concentration of actin and myosin, which are stimulated to contract in aggregated platelets. This results in a compression and strengthening of the platelet plug.[19]

While the plug is being built up and compacted, the vascular smooth muscle in the vessels around it is being stimulated to contract (Figure 20-20), thereby decreasing the blood flow to the area and the pressure within the damaged vessel. This vasoconstriction is the result of platelet activity, for it is mediated by thromboxane A$_2$ and by several chemicals contained in the secreted platelet granules.

---

[18]vWF serves a second function in clotting: It acts as a binding protein for one of the other proteins—factor VIII—involved in clotting and described later in the text.

[19]In a test tube this contraction and compression are termed clot retraction.

FIGURE 20-20

Sequence of events leading to vasoconstriction and formation of a platelet plug following damage to a blood-vessel wall. Note the two positive feedbacks in the pathways.

FIGURE 20-21

Platelets produce thromboxane A_2 (TXA$_2$), whereas normal endothelium adjacent to a platelet plug produces prostaglandin I_2 (PGI$_2$) from platelet and endothelial-cell arachidonic acid, and this eicosanoid inhibits platelet aggregation. Nitric oxide, NO, also secreted by the endothelial cells, does the same thing as PGI$_2$. Thus, PGI$_2$ and NO prevent spread of platelet aggregation from the damaged site.

Once started, why does the platelet plug not continuously expand, spreading away from the damaged endothelium along intact endothelium in both directions? One important reason involves the ability of the adjacent intact endothelial cells to synthesize and release the eicosanoid known as **prostacyclin** (also termed prostaglandin I_2, **PGI$_2$**), which is a profound inhibitor of platelet aggregation. Thus, whereas stimulated *platelets* possess the enzymes that produce thromboxane A_2 from arachidonic acid, normal *endothelial cells* contain a different enzyme, one that converts intermediates formed from arachidonic acid not to thromboxane A_2 but to PGI$_2$ (Figure 20-21). In addition to PGI$_2$, the endothelial cells also release **nitric oxide**, which is not only a vasodilator (recall that nitric oxide is endothelium-derived relaxing factor) but also an inhibitor of platelet aggregation.

To reiterate, the platelet plug is built up extremely rapidly and is the primary sealer of breaks in vessel walls. In the following section, we shall see that platelets are also absolutely essential for the next, more slowly occurring, hemostatic event, blood coagulation.

BLOOD COAGULATION: CLOT FORMATION

Blood coagulation (clotting) is the transformation of blood into a solid gel termed a **clot** or **thrombus** and consisting mainly of a protein polymer known as **fibrin**. Clotting occurs locally around the original platelet plug and is the dominant hemostatic defense. Its function is to support and reinforce the platelet plug and to solidify blood that remains in the wound channel.

The events leading to clotting are summarized, in very simplified form, in Figure 20-22. These events, like plate-

[handwritten margin notes:] produced by endothelial cell (and sticks onto cell); keeps plugs where belong / not spread; when constriction plug gets degrade but not latch on anywhere b/c of PGI2

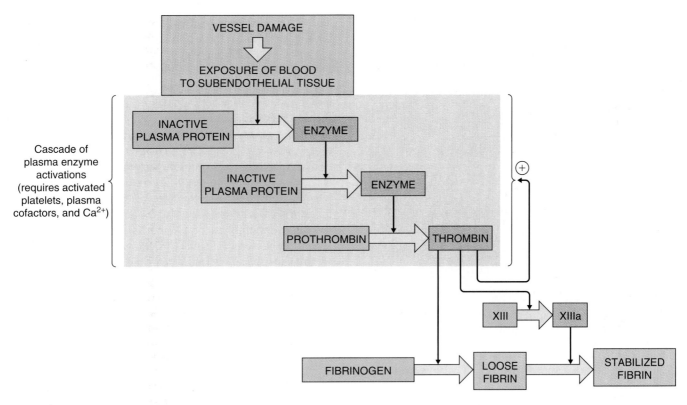

FIGURE 20-22

Simplified diagram of the clotting pathway. The pathway leading to thrombin is denoted by two enzyme activations, but the story is actually much more complex (as will be shown in Figures 20-24 and 20-25). Note that thrombin has three different effects—generation of fibrin, activation of factor XIII, and positive-feedback on the cascade leading to itself.

let aggregation, are initiated when injury to a vessel disrupts the endothelium and permits the blood to contact the underlying tissue. This contact initiates a locally occurring sequence or "cascade" of chemical activations. At each step of the cascade, an inactive plasma protein, or "factor," is converted (activated) to a proteolytic enzyme, which then catalyzes the generation of the next enzyme in the sequence. Each of these activations results from the splitting of a small peptide fragment from the inactive plasma protein precursor, thus exposing the active site of the enzyme. It should be noted, however, that several of the plasma protein factors, following their activation, function not as enzymes but rather as cofactors for the enzymes.

To reduce the risk that you might "lose sight of the forest for the trees" immediately, Figure 20-22 gives no specifics about the cascade until the point at which a plasma protein, **prothrombin**, is converted to an enzyme called **thrombin**. Thrombin then catalyzes a reaction in which several polypeptides are split from molecules of the large rod-shaped plasma protein **fibrinogen**. The still large fibrinogen remnants then bind to each other to form fibrin. The fibrin, initially a loose mesh of interlacing

strands, is rapidly stabilized and strengthened by enzymatically mediated formation of covalent cross-linkages. This chemical linking is catalyzed by an enzyme known as factor XIIIa, which is formed from the plasma protein inactive factor XIII in a reaction also catalyzed by thrombin.

Thus, thrombin catalyzes not only the formation of loose fibrin but also the activation of factor XIII, which will stabilize the fibrin network. But thrombin does even more than this: It exerts a profound positive-feedback effect on its own formation. It does this by activating several proteins in the cascade and also by activating platelets. (We'll talk about platelet activation and its significance for clotting in the next paragraph). Therefore, once thrombin formation has begun, reactions leading to much more thrombin generation are brought into play by this initial thrombin. We will make use of this crucial fact later when we describe the specifics of the cascade leading to thrombin.

In the process of clotting, many erythrocytes and other cells are trapped in the fibrin meshwork (Figure 20-23), but the essential component of the clot is fibrin, and clotting can occur in the absence of all cellular elements except platelets. Platelets are essential because some of the

FIGURE 20-23
Scanning electron micrograph of an erythrocyte enmeshed in fibrin. (*Courtesy of Elia Kairinen, Gillett Research Institute.*)

cascade reactions take place mainly on the surface of platelets. To participate, the platelets themselves must be activated, which occurs very early in the clotting response; as noted above, thrombin is an important stimulator of this activation. The activation causes the platelets to display specific plasma-membrane receptors that bind several of the clotting factors. The activated platelets also display particular phospholipids, called **platelet factor (PF)**, which functions as a cofactor in the steps mediated by the bound factors.

One more generalization about the clotting cascade should be noted: Plasma calcium is required at various steps. However, calcium concentration in the plasma can never get low enough to cause clotting defects because death would occur from muscle paralysis or cardiac arrythmias before such low concentrations were reached.

Now we present the specifics of the early portions of the clotting cascade, those leading from vessel damage to the prothrombin-thrombin reaction. Until very recently, it had been thought that there were *two* mechanisms by which exposure of the blood to subendothelial tissue could initiate the cascade and that these mechanisms gave rise to two completely independent, parallel pathways which merged at the step before the prothrombin-thrombin reaction. These are called (1) the **intrinsic pathway**, so named because everything necessary for it is *in* the blood;

and (2) the **extrinsic pathway**, so named because a cellular element *outside* the blood is needed. We will first present this "classical" dual view (many tests of clinical bleeding disorders require an understanding of it) and then describe how, in fact, the two pathways function in an integrated way. Figure 20-24 will be an essential reference for this entire discussion. Also, Table 20-13 is a reference list of the names of and synonyms for the substances in these pathways.

The first plasma protein in the classical intrinsic pathway (upper left of Figure 20-24) is called factor XII. It can become activated to factor XIIa when it contacts certain types of surfaces, including the collagen fibers underlying damaged endothelium.[20] Factor XIIa then catalyzes the activation of factor XI to factor XIa, which activates factor IX to factor IXa. This last factor then activates factor X to factor Xa, which is the enzyme that converts prothrombin to thrombin. Note in Figure 20-24 that another plasma protein—factor VIIIa, the activated form of factor VIII— serves as a cofactor (not an enzyme) in the factor IXa-mediated activation of factor X. The importance of factor VIII is emphasized by the fact that the disease *hemophilia,* in which excessive bleeding occurs, is usually due to a genetic absence of this factor. In a smaller number of cases hemophilia is due to an absence of factor IX.

Now we turn to the extrinsic pathway for initiating the clotting cascade (upper right of Figure 20-24). This pathway begins with a protein called **tissue factor**, which is *not* a plasma protein. It is located instead on the outer plasma membrane of various tissue cells, including fibroblasts and other cells in the walls of blood vessels below the endothelium (tissue factor is *not* normally found on endothelial cells or blood cells). The blood is exposed to subendothelial cells when vessel damage disrupts the endothelial lining, and tissue factor then binds a plasma protein, factor VII, which becomes activated to factor VIIa. The complex of tissue factor and factor VIIa on the plasma membrane of the cell then catalyzes the activation of factor X. In addition, it catalyzes the activation of factor IX, which can then help activate more factor X by plugging into the intrinsic pathway.

In summary, theoretically clotting can be initiated either by the activation of factor XII or by the appearance of the tissue factor-factor VIIa complex. The two paths merge at factor Xa, which then catalyzes the conversion of

---

[20]The contact activation of factor XII is a complex process that requires not only collagen but also the participation of several other plasma proteins. Contact activation also explains why blood coagulates when it is taken from the body and put in a glass tube. This has nothing whatever to do with exposure to air, as popularly supposed, but happens because the glass surface induces the activation of factor XII and aggregation of platelets, as does a damaged vessel surface. A silicone coating markedly delays clotting by reducing the activating effects of the glass surface.

TABLE 20-13 OFFICIAL INTERNATIONAL COMMITTEE DESIGNATIONS FOR CLOTTING FACTORS ALONG WITH SYNONYMS MORE COMMONLY USED AT PRESENT

Factor I (fibrinogen)

Factor Ia (fibrin)

Factor II (prothrombin)

Factor IIa (thrombin)

Factor III (tissue factor, tissue thromboplastin)

Factor IV (Ca^{2+})

Factors V, VII, VIII, IX, X, XI, XII, and XIII are the inactive forms of these factors; the active forms add an "a" (for example, factor XIIa). There is no factor VI.

Platelet factor

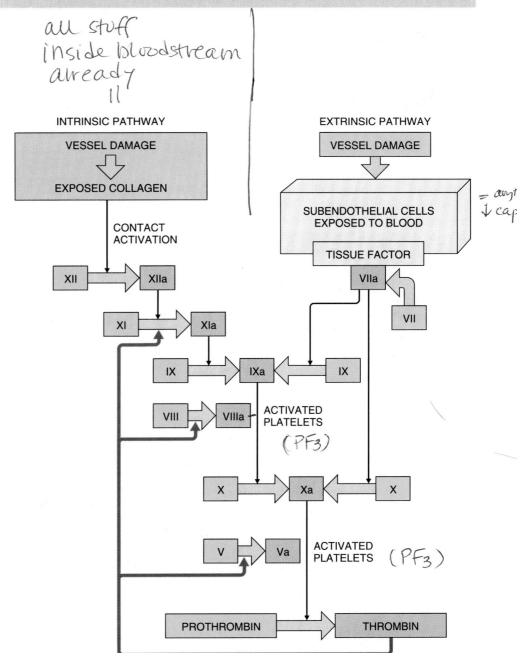

FIGURE 20-24

Classical view of two independent pathways—called intrinsic and extrinsic—leading to the generation of thrombin. In the extrinsic pathway, tissue factor is a receptor for plasma factor VII, which becomes activated after binding to it. Factors VIIIa and Va act as cofactors, not enzymes. Activated platelets participate in the formation of factor Xa and thrombin. You might think that factors IX and X were accidentally transposed in the intrinsic pathway, but such is not the case; the order of activation really is XI, IX, and X. For the sake of clarity, the roles of calcium are not shown. As described in the text (and illustrated in Figure 20-25), factor XII and the contact activation step probably play little, if any, role in blood clotting in the body. The extrinsic pathway is usually the initiator, and the thrombin generated initially by it then recruits the intrinsic pathway by activating factors XI, VIII, and V, as well as platelets (not shown).

prothrombin to thrombin, which catalyzes the formation of fibrin. As shown in Figure 20-24, thrombin also activates two factors—XI and VIII—in the intrinsic pathway, as well as factor V, which serves as a cofactor for factor X. Thrombin also activates platelets.

We implied earlier that this classical view of two independent, parallel pathways is in the process of being revised. Recent evidence indicates that both pathways are indeed involved, but that they come into play *sequentially*. The most likely present hypothesis for how this works can be understood by turning again to Figure 20-24; hold your hand over the first part of the intrinsic pathway so that you eliminate the contact activation of factor XII and then begin the next paragraph's description at the top of the extrinsic pathway.

(1) The *extrinsic pathway,* with its tissue factor, is the usual way of *initiating* clotting *in the body,* and factor XII— the beginning of the full intrinsic pathway—probably plays little if any role (in contrast to its role in test-tube clotting).[21] Accordingly, thrombin is *initially* generated only by the extrinsic pathway. The amount of thrombin is too small, however, to produce good, sustained coagulation. (2) It *is* large enough, though, to trigger thrombin's positive feedback effects on the *intrinsic pathway*— activation of factors XI and VIII and of platelets. (3) This is all that is needed to trigger the intrinsic pathway, which then generates the large amounts of thrombin required for adequate coagulation. Thus, the extrinsic pathway, via its initial generation of small amounts of thrombin, provides the means for recruiting the more potent intrinsic pathway without the participation of factor XII. In essence, thrombin eliminates the need for factor XII. Moreover, thrombin not only recruits the intrinsic pathway but facilitates the prothrombin-thrombin step itself by activating factor V and platelets.

Figure 20-25 summarizes the stages of the coagulation pathway. It emphasizes how the surface of activated platelets serves as a station for several of the reactions in which assemblies of factor complexes are formed.

Finally it should be noted that the liver plays several important indirect roles in clotting (Figure 20-26), and persons with liver disease frequently have serious bleeding problems. First, the liver is the site of production for many of the plasma clotting factors. Second, the bile salts produced by the liver (Chapter 17) are important for normal intestinal absorption of the lipid-soluble substance **vitamin K**, which the liver requires to produce prothrombin and three other clotting factors. Thus, the liver produces bile salts, which help in the absorption of vitamin K, which helps in the liver's production of clotting factors.

[21]It has been found that patients genetically missing factor XII do not display clotting defects.

ANTICLOTTING SYSTEMS

Factors That Oppose Clot Formation

There are at least three different mechanisms that oppose clot formation once underway, thereby helping to limit this process and prevent it from spreading excessively. The first mechanism acts during the initiation phase and utilizes the plasma protein called **tissue factor pathway inhibitor (TFPI)**. This substance binds to tissue factor-factor VIIa complexes and partially inhibits the ability of these complexes to generate factor X. This explains why the extrinsic pathway by itself can generate only small amounts of thrombin.

The second inhibitory mechanism is triggered by thrombin. As illustrated in Figure 20-27, thrombin activates a plasma protein, **protein C** (distinguish this from protein kinase C), which then inactivates factors VIII and V.[22] Thus, we saw earlier that thrombin *directly activates* factors VIII and V, and now we see that it *indirectly inactivates* them via protein C.[23] Table 20-14 summarizes all the effects—both stimulatory and inhibitory—of thrombin on the clotting pathways.

A third naturally occurring anticoagulant is a plasma protein called **antithrombin III**, which inactivates thrombin and several of the other clotting factors. (To do so, circulating antithrombin III must itself be activated, and this occurs when it binds to **heparin**, a substance that is present on the surface of endothelial cells.) Antithrombin III prevents spread of a clot by rapidly inactivating clotting factors that are carried away from the immediate site of the clot by the flowing blood.

The Fibrinolytic System

TFPI, protein C, and antithrombin III all function to *limit* clot formation. The system to be described now, however, *dissolves* a clot *after* it is formed.

A fibrin clot is not designed to last forever. It is a transitory device until permanent repair of the vessel occurs. The **fibrinolytic** (or thrombolytic) **system** is the principal effector of clot removal. The physiology of this system (Figure 20-28) is analogous to that of the clotting system: It constitutes a plasma proenzyme, **plasminogen**, which can be activated to the active enzyme **plasmin** by protein **plasminogen activators**. Once formed, plasmin digests fibrin, thereby dissolving the clot.

[22]Another plasma protein, termed protein S, is required for the action of protein C, and the two proteins together are often termed the protein C–protein S system.

[23]Thrombin, in order to activate protein C, must first bind to a thrombin receptor, called thrombomodulin, in the plasma membrane of endothelial cells. This binding also eliminates all of thrombin's clot-producing effects. Thus, the binding of thrombin to thrombomodulin converts thrombin from a procoagulant to an anticoagulant.

FIGURE 20-25
The clotting cascade can be divided into three parts, which occur sequentially. This is basically a reworking of Figure 20-24, one that begins with the extrinsic pathway and clearly illustrates the effects of thrombin to recruit the intrinsic pathway and the role of platelets. (*Adapted from Roberts and Lozier*).

The fibrinolytic system is proving to be every bit as complicated as the clotting system, with multiple types of plasminogen activators and pathways for generating them, as well as several inhibitors of these plasminogen activators. In describing how this system can be set into motion, we restrict our discussion to one example—the particular plasminogen activator known as **tissue plasminogen activator (t-PA)**, which is secreted by endothelial cells. During clotting, both plasminogen and t-PA bind to fibrin and become incorporated throughout the clot. The binding of t-PA to fibrin is crucial because t-PA is a very weak enzyme in the absence of fibrin. The presence of fibrin profoundly

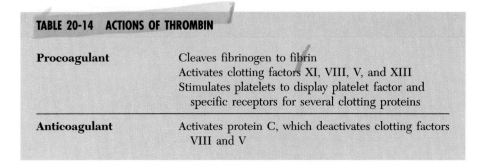

TABLE 20-14   ACTIONS OF THROMBIN

Procoagulant	Cleaves fibrinogen to fibrin
	Activates clotting factors XI, VIII, V, and XIII
	Stimulates platelets to display platelet factor and specific receptors for several clotting proteins
Anticoagulant	Activates protein C, which deactivates clotting factors VIII and V

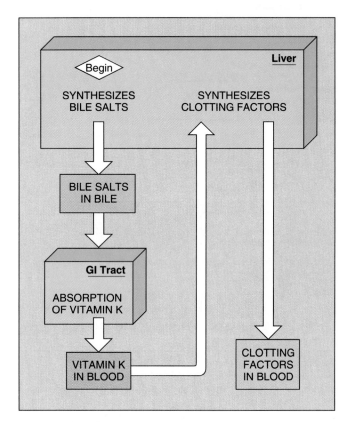

FIGURE 20-26
Roles of the liver in clotting.

increases the ability of t-PA to generate plasmin from plasminogen. Thus, fibrin is an important initiator of the fibrinolytic process that leads to its own dissolution.[24]

The secretion of t-PA is the last of the various anticlotting functions exerted by endothelial cells that we have mentioned in this chapter. They are summarized in Table 20-15.

ANTICLOTTING DRUGS

Various drugs are used clinically to prevent or reverse clotting, and a brief description of these actions serves as a review of key clotting mechanisms. One of the most common uses of these drugs is in the prevention and treatment of myocardial infarction (heart attacks), which,

---

[24]Plasminogen activators are normally involved not only in fibrinolysis but also in a host of other physiological processes, including tissue repair, ovulation, fertilization, and cell proliferation.

TABLE 20-15   ANTICLOTTING ROLES OF ENDOTHELIAL CELLS

Action	Result
Synthesize and release PGI_2 and nitric oxide	These inhibit platelet aggregation
Bind thrombin, which then activates protein C	Active protein C inactivates clotting factors VIII and V
Display heparin molecules on the surfaces of their plasma membranes	Heparin binds antithrombin III, and this molecule then inactivates thrombin and several other clotting factors
Secrete tissue plasminogen activator	Tissue plasminogen activator catalyzes the formation of plasmin, which dissolves clots

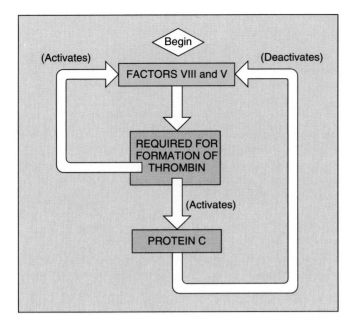

FIGURE 20-27
Thrombin activates factors VIII and V directly but deactivates them indirectly via protein C. Thus, it exerts both stimulatory and inhibitory effects on its own formation. (To activate protein C, thrombin must first bind to a thrombin-receptor, thrombomodulin, on endothelial cells, and this binding eliminates thrombin's procoagulant effects.)

FIGURE 20-28
Basic fibrinolytic system. There are many different plasminogen activators and many different pathways for bringing them into play.

as described in Chapter 14, is often the result of abnormal clotting in an atherosclerotic coronary vessel.

Aspirin inhibits the cyclooxygenase enzyme in the eicosanoid pathways that generate prostaglandins and thromboxanes (Chapter 7). Since thromboxane A_2, produced by the platelets, is important for platelet aggregation, aspirin reduces both platelet aggregation and the ensuing coagulation. Importantly, low doses of aspirin inhibit platelet cyclooxygenase but not endothelial-cell cyclooxygenase, and so the formation of prostacyclin—the prostaglandin that opposes platelet aggregation—is not impaired. It has been demonstrated that the taking of one aspirin every other day for several years by men with no previous history of heart disease reduces the incidence of heart attacks by 50 percent.

Drugs that interfere with the action of vitamin K, which is required for synthesis of clotting factors by the liver, are collectively termed **oral anticoagulants**.

Heparin, the naturally occurring endothelial-cell cofactor for antithrombin III, can also be administered as a drug, which then binds to endothelial cells. In addition to its role in the action of antithrombin III, heparin also inhibits platelet function.

In contrast to aspirin, the oral anticoagulants, and heparin, all of which *prevent* clotting, the fourth type of drug—plasminogen activators—dissolves a clot *after* it is formed and is termed **thrombolytic therapy**. Intravenous administration of recombinant t-PA or a proteolytic drug called streptokinase within a few hours after myocardial infarction significantly reduces myocardial damage and mortality.

SECTION C SUMMARY

I. The initial response to blood-vessel damage is vasoconstriction and the sticking together of the opposed endothelial surfaces.

II. The next events are formation of a platelet plug followed by blood coagulation (clotting).

FORMATION OF A PLATELET PLUG

I. Platelets adhere to exposed collagen in a damaged vessel and release the contents of their secretory vesicles.

A. These substances help cause platelet aggregation.

B. This process is also enhanced by von Willebrand

factor, secreted by the endothelial cells, and by thromboxane A_2, produced by the platelets.
 C. Contractile elements in the platelets compress and strengthen the plug.
II. The platelet plug does not spread along normal endothelium because the latter secretes prostacyclin and nitric oxide, both of which inhibit platelet aggregation.

BLOOD COAGULATION: CLOT FORMATION

 I. Blood is transformed into a solid gel when, at the site of vessel damage, plasma fibrinogen is converted into fibrin molecules, which bind to each other to form a mesh.
 II. This reaction is catalyzed by the enzyme thrombin, which also activates factor XIII, a plasma protein that stabilizes the fibrin meshwork.
 III. The formation of thrombin from the plasma protein prothrombin is the end result of a cascade of reactions in which an inactive plasma protein is activated and then enzymatically activates the next protein in the series.
  A. Thrombin exerts a positive-feedback stimulation of the cascade by activating platelets and several clotting factors.
  B. Activated platelets, which display platelet factor and binding sites for several activated plasma factors, are essential for the cascade.
 IV. In the body, the cascade usually begins via the extrinsic clotting pathway when tissue factor forms a complex with factor VIIa. This complex activates factor X, which then catalyzes the conversion of small amounts of prothrombin to thrombin. This thrombin then recruits the intrinsic pathway by activating factor XI and factor VIII, as well as platelets, and this pathway generates large amounts of thrombin.
 V. Vitamin K is required by the liver for normal production of prothrombin and other clotting factors.

ANTICLOTTING SYSTEMS

 I. Clotting is limited by three events: (1) Tissue factor pathway inhibitor inhibits the tissue factor–factor VIIa complex; (2) protein C, activated by thrombin, inactivates factors VIII and V; and (3) antithrombin III inactivates thrombin and several other clotting factors.

II. Clots are dissolved by the fibrinolytic system.
 A. A plasma proenzyme, plasminogen, is activated by plasminogen activators to plasmin, which digests fibrin.
 B. Tissue plasminogen activator is secreted by endothelial cells and is activated by fibrin in a clot.

SECTION C KEY TERMS

hemostasis	intrinsic pathway
von Willebrand factor (vWF)	extrinsic pathway
platelet aggregation	tissue factor
platelet plug	vitamin K
thromboxane A_2	tissue factor pathway
prostacyclin (PGI_2)	inhibitor (TFPI)
nitric oxide	protein C
blood coagulation	antithrombin III
clotting	heparin
clot	fibrinolytic system
thrombus	plasminogen
fibrin	plasmin
prothrombin	plasminogen activators
thrombin	tissue plasminogen
fibrinogen	activator (t-PA)
platelet factor (PF)	

SECTION C REVIEW QUESTIONS

1. Describe the sequence of events leading to platelet aggregation and the formation of a platelet plug. What helps keep this process localized?
2. Diagram the clotting pathway beginning with prothrombin.
3. What is the role of platelets in clotting?
4. List all the procoagulant effects of thrombin.
5. How is the clotting cascade initiated? How does the extrinsic pathway recruit the intrinsic pathway?
6. Describe the roles of the liver and vitamin K in clotting.
7. List three ways in which clotting is limited.
8. Diagram the fibrinolytic system.
9. How does fibrin help initiate the fibrinolytic system?

SECTION

RESISTANCE TO STRESS

Much of this book has been concerned with the body's response to stress in its broadest meaning of an environmental change that must be adapted to if health and life are to be maintained. Thus, any change in external temperature, water intake, and so on, sets into motion mechanisms designed to prevent a significant change in some physiological variable. In this section, however, we describe the basic stereotyped response to **stress** in the more limited sense of noxious or potentially noxious stimuli. These stimuli comprise an immense number of situations, including physical trauma, prolonged exposure to cold, prolonged heavy exercise, infection, shock, decreased oxygen supply, pain, fright, and other emotional stresses.

It is obvious that the overall response to cold exposure is very different from that to infection or fright, but in one respect the response to all these situations is the same: Invariably, secretion of the glucocorticoid hormone **cortisol** by the adrenal cortex is increased. Indeed, the term "stress" has come to mean to physiologists any event that elicits increased cortisol secretion. Activity of the sympathetic nervous system, including release of the hormone **epinephrine** from the adrenal medulla, is also usually increased in stress.

The increased cortisol secretion of stress is mediated mainly by the hypothalamo-anterior pituitary system described in Chapter 10. As illustrated in Figure 20-29, neural input to the hypothalamus from portions of the nervous system responding to a particular stress induces secretion of **corticotropin releasing hormone (CRH)**. This hormone is carried by the hypothalamo-pituitary portal vessels to the anterior pituitary and stimulates **adrenocorticotropic hormone (ACTH)** release. The ACTH in turn circulates to the adrenal cortex and stimulates cortisol release.

It has recently become clear that the secretion of ACTH, and therefore of cortisol, is stimulated by several hormones in addition to hypothalamic CRH. These include vasopressin and epinephrine, both of which are usually increased in stress. But the most interesting recent finding, mentioned in Section A, is that several of the cytokines, including interleukin 1, also stimulate ACTH secretion. These cytokines provide a means for eliciting a classical stress response when the immune system is stimulated. The possible significance of this relationship for immune function is described below.

FUNCTIONS OF CORTISOL IN STRESS

The major effects of increased cortisol during stress are summarized in Table 20-16. The effects on organic metabolism, as described in Chapter 18, are to mobilize fuels—to increase the plasma concentrations of amino acids, glucose, glycerol, and free fatty acids. These effects are ideally suited to meet a stressful situation. First, an animal faced with a potential threat is usually forced to forego eating, and these metabolic changes are essential for survival during fasting. Second, the amino acids liberated by catabolism of body protein stores not only provide a source of glucose, via gluconeogenesis, but also constitute a potential source of amino acids for tissue repair should injury occur.

A few of the medically important implications of these cortisol-induced effects on organic metabolism are as follows: (1) Any patient who is ill or is subjected to surgery catabolizes considerable quantities of body protein; (2) a diabetic who suffers an infection requires more insulin than usual; and (3) a child subjected to severe stress of any kind manifests retarded growth.

Cortisol has important effects during stress other than those on organic metabolism. It enhances vascular reactivity; that is, it increases the ability of vascular smooth muscle to contract in response to stimuli such as norepinephrine. A patient with insufficient cortisol faced with even a moderate stress may develop hypotension, due primarily to a marked decrease in total peripheral resistance.

As denoted by item 3 in Table 20-16, we still do not know the other reasons increased cortisol is so important for the body's optimal response to stress, that is, for its ability to resist the damaging influences of stress. What is clear is that animals and people exposed to severe stresses can die if their plasma cortisol concentration does not increase above basal levels.

Effect 4 in the table is controversial. It stems from the known fact that administration of very large amounts of cortisol profoundly reduces the inflammatory response to injury or infection. Such doses of cortisol inhibit phospholipase A_2 and hence block the production of all the eicosanoids, important mediators of inflammation. Such doses also inhibit the release or action of other inflammatory mediators and hence can block almost every step of inflammation—vasodilation, increased vascular permeability, and phagocytosis. Cortisol can also reduce the

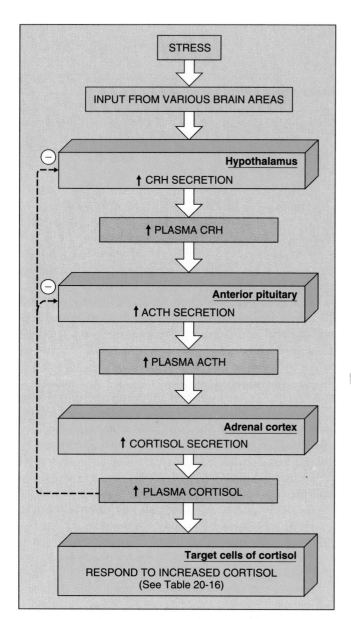

FIGURE 20-29
Pathway by which stressful stimuli elicit increased cortisol secretion. Additional stimuli, not shown in the figure, for ACTH release are vasopressin, epinephrine, and several cytokines, including IL-1, released from immune cells.

number of circulating lymphocytes and decrease both antibody production and the activity of helper T cells and cytotoxic T cells. Because of these effects, cortisol is an invaluable tool in the treatment of allergy, arthritis, other inflammatory diseases, and graft rejection.

These anti-inflammatory effects have generally been classified among the various *pharmacological* effects of cortisol because such large doses are required to achieve them. Until recently, it has been assumed by physiologists that these effects do not occur at the usual plasma concentrations of cortisol. Now, however, that view is being questioned, and it is likely that the plasma concentrations achieved during stress are, in fact, anti-inflammatory. Thus, the increased cortisol typical of infection or trauma is probably exerting a dampening effect on the body's immune responses, protecting against possible damage from excessive inflammation.

This also explains the significance of the fact that several cytokines, including interleukin 1, stimulate the secretion of ACTH and thereby cortisol. Such stimulation is part of a negative-feedback system in which the increased cortisol then partially blocks the inflammatory processes in which the cytokines participate.

TABLE 20-16   EFFECTS OF INCREASED PLASMA CORTISOL CONCENTRATION DURING STRESS

1. Effects on organic metabolism
   a. Stimulation of protein catabolism
   b. Stimulation of liver uptake of amino acids and their conversion to glucose (gluconeogenesis)
   c. Inhibition of glucose uptake and oxidation by many body cells ("insulin antagonism") but not by the brain
   d. Stimulation of triacylglycerol catabolism in adipose tissue, with release of glycerol and fatty acids into the blood
2. Enhanced vascular reactivity, that is, increased ability to maintain vasoconstriction in response to norepinephrine and other stimuli
3. Unidentified protective effects against the damaging influences of stress
4. Inhibition of inflammation and specific immune responses

It should not be assumed, however, that all the effects of stress on immune responses are due to cortisol. Many of the other hormones released in increased quantities during stress (see below) have important effects, both inhibitory and stimulatory, on the immune system.

One more point about the ACTH-cortisol system should be mentioned: Until recently, it was assumed that the only role of ACTH in stress was to stimulate the secretion of cortisol. It is now known, however, that ACTH, independent of its stimulation of cortisol secretion, is one of the peptides that facilitates learning and memory (Chapter 13). Thus, it may well be that the rise in ACTH secretion induced by psychosocial stress helps one to cope with the stress by facilitating the learning of appropriate responses to it.

FUNCTIONS OF THE SYMPATHETIC NERVOUS SYSTEM IN STRESS

Activation of the sympathetic nervous system during stress is often termed the **fight-or-flight response**, and the name is appropriate. A list of the major effects of increased sympathetic activity, including secretion of epinephrine, almost constitutes a guide to how to meet emergencies in which physical activity may by required and bodily damage may occur. Most of these actions have been discussed in other sections of the book, and they are listed in Table 20-17 with little or no comment. Actions 6 and 7 have not been mentioned before; they reflect stimulation by epinephrine of the brain respiratory centers and of platelet aggregation.

The adaptive value of these responses in a fight-or-

flight situation is obvious. But what purpose do they serve in the psychosocial stresses so common to modern life, when neither fight nor flight is appropriate? A question yet to be answered is whether these effects, if prolonged, might enhance the development of certain diseases, particularly atherosclerosis and hypertension. For example, one can easily imagine that the increased blood lipid concentration and cardiac work could contribute to the former disease. Considerable work remains to be done to evaluate such possibilities.

OTHER HORMONES RELEASED DURING STRESS

Other hormones that are usually released during many kinds of stress are aldosterone, vasopressin (ADH), growth hormone, and glucagon. Insulin secretion is usually decreased. The increases in vasopressin and aldosterone ensure the retention of water and sodium within the body, an important adaptation in the face of potential losses by hemorrhage or sweating. Vasopressin also stimulates the secretion of ACTH, as we have seen, and may influence learning. As described in Chapter 18, the overall effects of the changes in growth hormone, glucagon, and insulin are, like those of cortisol and epinephrine, to mobilize energy stores.

This list of hormones whose secretion rates are altered by stress is by no means complete. It is likely that the secretion of almost every known hormone may be influenced by stress. For example, prolactin and thyroid hormone are often increased, whereas the pituitary gonadotropins and the sex steroids are decreased. The adaptive significance of many of these changes is unclear.

TABLE 20-17 ACTIONS OF THE SYMPATHETIC NERVOUS SYSTEM, INCLUDING EPINEPHRINE SECRETED BY THE ADRENAL MEDULLA, IN STRESS

1. Increased hepatic and muscle glycogenolysis (provides a quick source of glucose)
2. Increased breakdown of adipose tissue triacylglycerol (provides a supply of glycerol for gluconeogenesis and of fatty acids for oxidation)
3. Decreased fatigue of skeletal muscle
4. Increased cardiac output secondary to increased cardiac contractility and heart rate
5. Shunting of blood from viscera to skeletal muscles by means of vasoconstriction in the former beds and vasodilation in the latter
6. Increased ventilation
7. Increased coagulability of blood

SECTION D SUMMARY

I. Classical responses to stress, whether physical or psychological, are increased secretion of cortisol from the adrenal cortex and activation of the sympathetic nervous system, including release of epinephrine by the adrenal medulla.

II. The functions of these responses, summarized in Tables 20-16 and 20-17, can be viewed as a preparation both for fight or flight and for coping with new situations.

III. Other hormones released during stress include aldosterone, vasopressin, glucagon, growth hormone, and prolactin. Insulin secretion is usually decreased.

SECTION D KEY TERMS

stress
cortisol
epinephrine

corticotropin releasing hormone (CRH)
adrenocorticotropic hormone (ACTH)
fight-or-flight response

SECTION D REVIEW QUESTIONS

1. Diagram the CRH-ACTH-cortisol pathway.
2. List the functions of cortisol in stress.
3. List the major effects of activation of the sympathetic nervous system during stress.
4. List four hormones other than those listed in previous questions that increase during stress and one that decreases.

CHAPTER 20 CLINICAL TERMS

(Because of the subject matter of this chapter it is difficult to distinguish between "physiological" key terms and "clinical" terms. This list is limited largely to disease processes.)

microbes
bacteria
viruses
oncogenes
active immunity

vaccine
acquired immune deficiency
  syndrome (AIDS)
human immunodeficiency
  virus (HIV)

antibiotics
graft rejection
cyclosporin
transfusion reactions
cross-matching
hemolytic disease of the
  newborn
allergy (hypersensitivity)
allergens
delayed hypersensitivity
immune-complex
  hypersensitivity

immediate hypersensitivity
anaphylaxis
late-phase reaction
autoimmune disease
septic shock
hematoma
hemophilia
oral anticoagulants
thrombolytic therapy

CHAPTER 20 THOUGHT QUESTIONS

(Answers are given in Appendix A.)

1. If an individual failed to develop a thymus because of a genetic defect, what would happen to the immune responses mediated by antibodies and those mediated by cytotoxic T cells?

2. What abnormalities would a person with a neutrophil deficiency display? A person with a monocyte deficiency?

3. An experimental animal is given a drug that blocks phagocytosis. Will this drug prevent the animal's immune system from killing foreign cells via the complement system?

4. If the Fc portion of a patient's antibodies is abnormal, what effects could this have on antibody-mediated responses?

5. Would you predict that patients with AIDS would develop fever in response to an infection? Explain.

6. A patient with symptoms of hyperthyroidism is found to have circulating antibodies against the receptors for the thyroid hormones. Can you deduce the cause of the hyperthyroidism?

7. Barbiturates and alcohol are normally metabolized by the MES. Can you deduce why the actions of an administered barbiturate last for a shorter time than normal in persons who chronically consume large quantities of alcohol?

APPENDIX
A

ANSWERS TO THOUGHT QUESTIONS

Chapter 4

4-1. A drug could inhibit acid secretion by (1) binding to the membrane sites that inhibit acid secretion, which could produce the same effect as the body's compounds, that is, inhibition of acid secretion; (2) binding to membrane proteins that normally cause acid secretion but without triggering acid secretion, thereby preventing the body's natural messengers from binding (competition); or (3) having an allosteric effect upon the binding sites, which would increase the affinity of the sites that bind inhibitors or decrease the affinity of the sites that bind stimulating compounds.

4-2. The reason for a lack of insulin effect could be either a decrease in the number of available binding sites to which insulin can bind or a decrease in the affinity of the binding sites for insulin so that less insulin is bound. A third possibility, which does not involve the process of insulin binding, would be a defect in the way in which the binding site triggers a cell response once it has bound insulin (see Chapter 7).

4-3. An increase in the concentration of compound A will lead to a decrease in the concentration of compound H by the route shown below. Sequential activations and inhibitions of proteins of this general type are frequently encountered in physiological control systems.

4-4. (a) Acid secretion could be increased to 20 mmol/h by (1) increasing the concentration of compound X from 2 pM to 8 pM, thereby increasing the number of binding sites occupied; or (2) increasing the affinity of the binding site for compound X, thereby increasing the amount bound without changing the concentration of compound X. (b) Increasing the concentration of compound X from 18 pM to 28 pM will not increase acid secretion because, at 18 pM, all the binding sites are occupied (the system is saturated) and there are no further binding sites available.

4-5. Phosphoprotein phosphatase removes the phosphate group from proteins that have been covalently modulated by protein kinase. Without phosphoprotein phosphatase, the protein could not return to its unmodulated state and would remain in its activated state. The ability to decrease as well as increase protein activity is essential to the regulation of physiological processes.

4-6. Nucleotide bases in DNA pair, A to T, and G to C. Given the base sequence of one DNA strand as

A-G-T-G-C-A-A-G-T-C-T

the corresponding strand of DNA would be

T-C-A-C-G-T-T-C-A-G-A

and the sequence in mRNA transcribed from the first strand would be

U-C-A-C-G-U-U-C-A-G-A

(Recall that uracil U replaces thymine T in RNA.)

4-7. The triplet code GTA will be transcribed into mRNA as CAU, and the anticodon in tRNA corresponding to CAU will be GUA.

4-8. If the gene were composed only of the triplet exon code words, it would be 300 nucleotides in length since a triplet of 3 nucleotides codes for one amino acid. However, because of the presence of intron segments, which account for 75 to 90 percent of the nucleotides in a gene, the gene would be between 900 and 2700 nucleotides long. Thus, the exact size of a gene cannot be determined by knowing the number of amino acids in the protein coded by the gene.

4-9. Tubulin is the protein that polymerizes to form microtubules. Tubulin monomers become linked together in a spiral that forms the walls of the hollow microtubule. Without microtubules to form the spindle apparatus, the chromosomes will not separate during mitosis. There are chemical agents in the cell that control the polymerization of tubulin at the time of mitosis and cause it to depolymerize following cell division.

4-10. A drug that inhibits DNA replication will inhibit mitosis since a duplicate set of chromosomes is necessary for cell division. Since one of the characteristics of cancer cells is their ability to undergo unlimited division, a drug that inhibits DNA replication will inhibit the multiplication of cancer cells. Unfortunately, such drugs also inhibit the division of normal cells, and this effect is particularly serious in cells that divide quickly. These include the cells that give rise to blood cells and the epithelial lining of the gastrointestinal tract. The use of such drugs must be carefully monitored to balance the damage done to normal tissues against the inhibition of tumor growth.

Chapter 5

5-1. The reactant molecules have a combined energy content of $55 + 93 = 148$ kcal/mol, and the combined energy content of the products is $62 + 87 = 149$. Thus, the energy content of the products exceeds that of the reactants by 1 kcal/mol, and this amount of energy must be added to A and B to form the products C and D.

The reaction is a reversible reaction since the difference in energy content between the reactants and products is small. When the reaction reaches chemical equilibrium, there will be a slightly higher concentration of reactants than products.

5-2. The maximum rate at which the end product E can be formed is 5, the rate of the slowest—rate-limiting—reaction in the pathway.

5-3. Under normal conditions, the concentration of oxygen at the level of the mitochondria is sufficient to saturate the enzyme that combines oxygen with hydrogen to form water. In the electron-transport chain, the rate-limiting reactions depend on the available concentrations of ADP and P_i, which are combined to form ATP.

If ADP and P_i concentrations are low, the rate of oxygen consumption will be low and will not be increased by increasing the oxygen concentration. In certain types of lung and circulatory diseases in which the transfer of oxygen from normal air to the blood and the delivery of blood to the tissues is impaired, the concentration of oxygen at the level of the mitochondria can become rate-limiting, and increasing the concentration of oxygen in the inhaled air will result in the delivery of more oxygen to the tissues and increase the rate of ATP formation.

5-4. During starvation, in the absence of ingested glucose, the body's stores of glycogen are rapidly depleted. Glucose, which is the major fuel used by the brain, must now be synthesized from other types of molecules. The major source of this newly formed glucose comes from the breakdown of proteins into amino acids and their conversion to glucose. To a lesser extent, the glycerol portion of fat is converted to glucose. The fatty acid portion of fat cannot be converted to glucose.

5-5. Since the Krebs cycle can function only during aerobic conditions, the catabolism of fat is dependent on the presence of oxygen. Fatty acids are broken down to acetyl coenzyme A during beta oxidation, and acetyl coenzyme A enters the Krebs cycle to be converted to carbon dioxide. In the absence of oxygen, acetyl coenzyme A cannot be converted to carbon dioxide and its increased concentration will inhibit the further beta oxidation of fatty acids.

5-6. Since the liver is the site at which ammonia is converted to urea, diseases that damage the liver can lead to an accumulation of ammonia in the blood, which is especially toxic to nerve cells. Note that it is not the liver that produces the ammonia. Ammonia is formed in most cells during the oxidative deamination of amino acids and then travels to the liver via the blood. The function of the liver is then to detoxify the ammonia by converting it to the nontoxic compound urea.

Chapter 6

6-1. (a) During diffusion, the net flux always occurs from high to low concentration. Thus it will be from 2 to 1 in A and from 1 to 2 in B. (b) At equilibrium the concentrations of solute in the two compartments will be equal: 4 mM in case A and 31 mM in case B. (c) Both will reach diffusion equilibrium at the same rate since the difference in concentration across the membrane is the same in each case, 2 mM $(3 - 5) = -2$, and $(32 - 30) = 2$. The two one-way fluxes will be much larger in B than in A, but the net fluxes are the same in both cases, although oriented in opposite directions.

6-2. The ability of one amino acid to decrease the flux of a second amino acid across a plasma membrane is an example of the competition between two molecules for the same binding site, as explained in Chapter 4. The binding site for alanine on the transport protein can also bind leucine. The higher the concentration of alanine, the greater the number of binding sites occupied by it, and the fewer available for binding leucine. Thus, less leucine will be moved into the cell.

6-3. The net transport will be out of the cell, in the direction from the higher-affinity site on the intracellular surface to the lower-affinity site on the extracellular surface. More molecules will be bound to the transporter on the high-affinity side of the membrane, and thus more will move out of the cell than into it, until the concentration in the extracellular fluid becomes large enough so that the number of bound proteins at the extracellular surface is equal to the number of bound proteins at the intracellular surface.

6-4. Although ATP is not used directly in secondary active transport, it is necessary for the primary active transport of sodium out of cells. Since it is the sodium concentration gradient across the plasma membrane that provides the energy for most secondary-active-transport systems, a decrease in ATP production, by decreasing primary active sodium transport, leading to a decrease in the sodium concentration gradient, will decrease secondary active transport.

6-5. The solution with the greatest osmolarity will have the lowest water concentration. The osmolarities are

A: $20 + 30 + 2(150) + 3(10) = 380$ mOsm
B: $10 + 100 + 2(20) + 3(50) = 300$ mOsm
C: $100 + 200 + 2(10) + 3(20) = 380$ mOsm
D: $30 + 10 + 2(60) + 3(100) = 460$ mOsm

Solution D thus has the lowest water concentration. (Recall that NaCl forms two ions in solution, and $CaCl_2$, three.)

Solutions A and C are isoosmotic since they have the same osmolarity.

6-6. Initially the osmolarity of compartment 1 is $(2 \times 200) + 100 = 500$ mOsm, and that of 2 is $(2 \times 100) + 300 = 500$ mOsm. The two solutions are thus isoosmotic, and there is no difference in water concentration across the membrane. Since the membrane is permeable to urea but not to NaCl, urea will diffuse from compartment 2 into compartment 1, producing an increase in the osmolarity of compartment 1, lowering its water concentration and thus causing a net flow of water into compartment 1, increasing its volume. This net movement of urea and water into compartment 1 will continue until (a) urea reaches diffusion equilibrium at a concentration of 200 mM in each compartment, and (b) the movement of water has lowered the concentration of NaCl in compartment 1 to 150 mM and raised that of NaCl in compartment 2 to 150 mM. Note that the same volume change would have occurred if there had been no urea pres-

ent in either compartment. It is only the concentration of nonpenetrating solutes, NaCl in this case, that determines the volume change, regardless of the concentration of any penetrating solutes that are present.

6-7. The osmolarities and nonpenetrating solute concentrations are:

Solution	Osmolarity, mOsm	Nonpenetrating solute concentration, mM
A	$(2 \times 150) + 100 = 400$	$2 \times 150 = 300$
B	$(2 \times 100) + 150 = 350$	$2 \times 100 = 200$
C	$(2 \times 200) + 100 = 500$	$2 \times 200 = 400$
D	$(2 \times 100) + 50 = 250$	$2 \times 100 = 200$

Only the concentration of nonpenetrating solutes, NaCl in this case, will determine the change in cell volume. Since the intracellular concentration of nonpenetrating solute is 300 mOsm, solution A will produce no change in cell volume. Solutions B and D will cause cells to swell since they have a lower concentration of nonpenetrating solutes than the intracellular fluid. Solution C will cause cells to shrink because it has a higher concentration of nonpenetrating solutes than the intracellular fluid.

6-8. Solution A is isotonic—having the same concentration of nonpenetrating solutes as the intracellular fluid (300 mM). Solution A is also hyperosmotic since its total osmolarity is greater than 300 mOsm, as is true also for solutions B and C. Solution B is hypotonic since its concentration of nonpenetrating solutes is less than 300 mM. Solution C is hypertonic since its concentration of nonpenetrating solutes is greater than 300 mM. Solution D is hypotonic (less than 300 mM of nonpenetrating solutes) and also hypoosmotic (having a total osmolarity of less than 300 mOsm).

6-9. Exocytosis is triggered by an increase in intracellular calcium concentration. Calcium ions can be actively transported out of cells by secondary countertransport coupled to the entry of sodium ions on the same transport protein. If the intracellular concentration of sodium ions were increased, the sodium concentration gradient across the membrane would be decreased, and this would decrease the secondary active transport of calcium out of the cell. This would lead to an increase in intracellular calcium concentration, which would trigger increased exocytosis.

Chapter 7

7-1. 4.4 mM. If you answered 8 mM, you ignored the fact that plasma potassium concentration is homeostatically regulated so that the doubling of input will lead to negative-feedback reflexes that oppose an equivalent increase in plasma concentration. If you answered 4 mM, you ignored the fact that homeostatic control systems cannot *totally* prevent changes in the regulated variable when a perturbation occurs. Thus, there must be *some* rise in plasma potassium concentration in this situation (to serve as the error signal for the compensating reflexes), and this is consistent with the answer 4.4 mM. (The actual rise would have to be experimentally determined. There is no way you could have predicted that the rise would be 10 percent. All you could predict is that it would neither double nor stay absolutely unchanged.)

7-2.   No. There may in fact be one, but there is another possibility—that the altered skin blood flow in the cold represents an *acclimatization* undergone by each Eskimo during his or her lifetime as a result of performing such work repeatedly.

7-3.   Patient A's drug very likely acts to block phospholipase A$_2$, whereas patient B's drug blocks lipoxygenase. (See Figure 7-9.)

7-4.   The chronic loss of exposure of the heart's receptors to norepinephrine causes an up-regulation of this receptor type, that is, more receptors in the heart for norepinephrine. The drug, being an agonist of norepinephrine, that is, able to bind to norepinephrine's receptors and activate them, is now more effective since there are more receptors for it to combine with.

7-5.   None. Since you are told that all six responses are mediated by the cAMP system, then blockade of any of the steps listed in the question would eliminate all six of the responses. This is because the cascade for all six responses is identical from the receptor through the formation of cAMP and activation of cAMP-dependent protein kinase. Thus, the drug must be acting at a point beyond this kinase, for example, at the level of the phosphorylated protein mediating this response.

7-6.   Not in most cells, since there are other physiological mechanisms by which signals impinging on the cell can increase cytosolic calcium concentration. These include IP$_3$-induced release of calcium from the endoplasmic reticulum and voltage-sensitive calcium channels.

7-7.   Cyclic AMP itself. All three substances activate one or more protein kinases.

Chapter 8

8-1.   Little change in the resting potential would occur when the pump first stops because the pump's direct contribution to charge separation (recall that the pump is electrogenic) is very small. With time, however, the membrane potential would depolarize progressively toward zero because the concentration gradients, which depend on the Na,K-ATPase pumps and which give rise to the diffusion potentials that constitute most of the membrane potential, would have run down.

8-2.   The resting potential would decrease, that is, become less negative, because the concentration gradient causing net diffusion of this positively charged ion out of the cell would be smaller. The action potential would fire more easily, that is, with smaller stimuli, because the resting potential would be closer to threshold. It would repolarize more slowly because repolarization depends on net potassium diffusion from the cell, and the concentration gradient driving this diffusion would be smaller.

8-3.   The hypothalamus was probably damaged. It plays a critical role in appetite, thirst, and sexual activity.

8-4.   The drug probably blocks cholinergic muscarinic receptors. These receptors on effector cells mediate the actions of the parasympathetic nerves. Therefore, the drug would remove the

slowing effect of these nerves on the heart, allowing the heart to speed up. Blocking their effect on the salivary glands would cause the mouth to become dry. The drug is not blocking cholinergic nicotinic receptors because the skeletal muscles are not affected.

8-5.   Since the membrane potential of the cells in this question depolarizes, that is, becomes less negative, when chloride channels are blocked, one can predict that there was net chloride diffusion into the cells through these channels prior to the drug. Therefore, one can also predict that this passive inward movement was being exactly balanced by active chloride transport out of the cells.

8-6.   Without acetylcholinesterase, acetylcholine would remain bound to the receptors and all the actions normally caused by acetylcholine would be accentuated. Thus, there would be marked narrowing of the pupil, airway constriction, stomach cramping and diarrhea, sweating, salivation, slowing of the heart, and a fall in blood pressure. On the other hand, in skeletal muscle, which must repolarize after excitation in order to be excited again, there would be weakness, fatigue, and finally inability to contract. In fact, poisoning by high doses of cholinesterase inhibitors occurs because of paralysis of the muscles involved in respiration. Low doses of these compounds are used therapeutically.

8-7.   These potassium channels, which open after a short delay following the initiation of the action potential, increase potassium diffusion out of the cell, hastening repolarization. They also account for the increased potassium permeability that causes the afterhyperpolarization. Therefore, the action potential would be broader (that is, longer in duration), returning to its resting level more slowly, and the afterhyperpolarization would be absent.

Chapter 9

9-1.   (a) Block synaptic transmission in the pathways that convey information about pain to the brain. For example, if substance P is the neurotransmitter at the central endings of the nociceptor afferent fibers, give a drug that blocks the substance P receptors. (b) Cut the dorsal root at the level of entry of the nociceptor fibers to prevent transmission of their action potentials into the central nervous system. (c) Give a drug that activates receptors in the descending pathways that block transmission of the incoming or ascending pain information. (d) Stimulate the neurons in these same descending pathways to increase their blocking activity (stimulation-produced analgesia or, possibly, acupuncture). (e) Cut the ascending pathways that transmit information from the nociceptor afferents. (f) Deal with the emotions, attitudes, memories, and so on, to decrease the sensitivity to the pain. (g) Stimulate nonpain, low-threshold afferent fibers to block transmission through the pain pathways (TENS). (h) Block transmission in the afferent nerve with a local anesthetic such as Novacaine or Lidocaine.

9-2.   Damage to the spinal cord on the side of the body opposite the stimulus would interfere with awareness of a heat stimulus, but only if the damage occurs between the entry of the afferent fibers from the stimulated receptors into the spinal cord and the brainstem. Damage to the somatosensory cortex of the cerebral hemisphere opposite the stimulus would also interfere with awareness of the stimulus. Injury to the brainstem at the point at which fibers from the lateral spinothalamic tracts of the two halves of the spinal cord cross to the opposite side would interfere with the awareness of heat applied to either side of the body.

9-3. Vision would be restricted to the rods; therefore, it would be normal at very low levels of illumination (when the cones would not be stimulated anyway), but at higher levels of illumination clear vision of fine details would be lost, and everything would appear in shades of gray. There would be no color vision.

9-4. (a) The individual lacks a functioning primary visual cortex. (b) The individual lacks a functioning visual association cortex.

Chapter 10

10-1. Epinephrine falls to very low levels during rest and fails to increase during stress. The sympathetic preganglionics provide the only major control of the adrenal medulla.

10-2. The increased concentration of binding protein causes more TH to be bound, thereby lowering the plasma concentration of *free* TH. This causes less negative-feedback inhibition of TSH by the anterior pituitary, and the increased TSH causes the thyroid to secrete more TH until the free concentration has returned to normal. The end result is an increased *total* plasma TH—most bound to the protein—but a normal free TH. There is no hyperthyroidism because it is only the free concentration that exerts effects on TH's target cells.

10-3. Destruction of the anterior pituitary or hypothalamus. These symptoms reflect the absence of, in order, growth hormone, the gonadotropins, and ACTH (the symptom is due to the resulting decrease in the secretion of cortisol). One cannot tell from these data alone whether the problem is primary hyposecretion of the anterior pituitary hormones or secondary hyposecretion because the hypothalamus is not secreting hypophysiotropic hormones normally.

10-4. Vasopressin and oxytocin, that is, the major posterior pituitary hormones. The anterior pituitary hormones would not be affected because the influence of the hypothalamus on these hormones is exerted not by connecting nerves but via the hypophysiotropic hormones in the hypothalamo-pituitary portal vessels.

10-5. The secretion of both GH and TSH would increase. Somatostatin, coming from the hypothalamus, normally exerts an inhibitory effect on the secretion of these two hormones.

10-6. Norepinephrine and many other neurotransmitters are released by neurons that terminate on the hypothalamic neurons that secrete the hypophysiotropic hormones. Therefore, manipulation of these neurotransmitters will alter secretion of the hypophysiotropic hormones and thereby the anterior pituitary hormones.

10-7. The high dose of the cortisol-like substance inhibits the secretion of ACTH by feedback inhibiton of (1) hypothalamic corticotropin releasing hormone, and (2) the response of the anterior pituitary to this hypophysiotropic hormone. The lack of ACTH causes the adrenal to atrophy and decrease its secretion of cortisol.

10-8. The hypothalamus. The low basal TSH indicates either that the pituitary is defective or that it is receiving inadequate stimulation (TRH) from the hypothalamus. If the thyroid itself were defective, basal TSH would be elevated because of less negative-feedback inhibition by TH. The TSH increase in response to TRH shows that the pituitary is capable of responding to a stimulus and so is unlikely to be defective. Therefore, the problem is that the hypothalamus is secreting too little TRH.

Chapter 11

11-1. (a) Under resting conditions, the myosin has already bound and hydrolyzed a molecule of ATP, resulting in an energized molecule of myosin ($M^* \cdot ADP \cdot P_i$). (b) Since ATP is necessary to detach the myosin cross bridge from actin at the end of cross-bridge movement, the absence of ATP will result in rigor mortis, in which the cross bridges become bound to actin but do not detach, leaving myosin bound to actin ($A \cdot M$).

11-2. The transverse tubules conduct the muscle action potential from the plasma membrane into the interior of the fiber, where it can trigger the release of calcium from the sarcoplasmic reticulum. If the transverse tubules were not attached to the plasma membrane, an action potential would not be conducted to the sarcoplasmic reticulum and there would be no release of calcium to initiate contraction.

11-3. As a muscle shortens, the thick and thin filaments slide past each other, and thus the amount of overlap changes, changing the number of cross bridges that can bind to actin and thus the maximal force of contraction. This gives rise to the length-tension relation. As the sarcomere length becomes shorter than the optimal length, the maximum tension that can be generated decreases. With a light load, the muscle will continue to shorten until its maximal tension just equals the load. No further shortening is possible since at shorter sarcomere lengths the tension would be less than the load and the load would have the effect of stretching the sarcomere. The heavier the load, the less the distance shortened before entering the isometric state since maximum tension decreases as the muscle shortens below l_o.

11-4. Maximum tension is produced when the fiber is (1) stimulated by a frequency of action potentials that is high enough to produce a maximal tetanic tension, and (2) at its optimum length l_o, where the thick and thin filaments have maximal overlap and thus provide the greatest number of cross bridges for tension production.

11-5. Moderate tension—for example, 50 percent of maximal tension—is accomplished by recruiting sufficient numbers of motor units to produce this degree of tension. (For example, if all motor units were the same size, which they are not, this would mean recruiting 50 percent of the motor units in the muscle.) If activity is maintained at this level for prolonged periods, some of the active fibers will begin to fatigue and their contribution to the total tension will decrease. The same level of total tension can be maintained, however, by recruiting additional motor units as some of the others fatigue. At this point, one might have 50 percent of the fibers active, 25 percent fatigued, and 25 percent still unrecruited. Eventually the whole muscle will fatigue when all the fibers have fatigued and there are no additional motor units to recruit.

11-6. The oxidative motor units, both fast and slow, will be affected first by a decrease in blood flow since they depend on it to provide both the fuel—glucose and fatty acids—and the oxygen required to metabolize the fuel. The fast-glycolytic motor units will be affected more slowly by the decreased blood flow since they rely predominantly on internal stores of glycogen, the glucose molecules of which are anaerobically metabolized by glycolysis.

11-7. Two factors lead to recovery of muscle force. (1) Some new fibers can be formed by the fusion and development of undifferentiated satellite cells. This will replace some, but not all, of the fibers that were damaged. (2) Some of the restored force is the result of hypertrophy of the surviving fibers. The undamaged fibers must produce more force to move a given load because of the loss of supporting fibers in the accident, and these fibers are stimulated to undergo increased synthesis of actin and myosin, resulting in increases in fiber diameter and thus their force of contraction.

11-8. In the absence of extracellular calcium ions, skeletal muscle contracts normally in response to an action potential in its plasma membrane because the calcium required to trigger contraction comes entirely from the sarcoplasmic reticulum within the muscle fibers. If the motor neuron to the muscle is stimulated in a calcium-free medium, however, the muscle will not contract because the influx of calcium from the extracellular fluid into the motor nerve terminal is necessary to trigger the release of acetylcholine that in turn triggers an action potential in the muscle.

The response of smooth muscle in a calcium-free medium depends on the type of smooth muscle. Smooth muscles that depend primarily on calcium released from the sarcoplasmic reticulum will behave like skeletal muscle and respond to direct stimulation but not to nerve stimulation in the absence of extracellular calcium. Smooth muscles that rely on an influx of calcium from the extracellular fluid to trigger contraction will fail to contract in response to both types of stimuli.

11-9. The simplest model to explain the experimental observations is as follows: Upon parasympathetic stimulation, a neurotransmitter is released that binds to receptor sites on the membranes of smooth-muscle cells and triggers contraction. The substance released is not acetylcholine and does not act on ACh receptors. (Not ruled out by these observations is the possibility that the neurotransmitter acts upon some nonmuscle cells that in turn release a substance that acts upon the smooth muscle to produce contraction.)

Action potentials in the parasympathetic nerves are essential for initiating nerve-induced contraction. When the nerves were prevented from generating action potentials by blocking their voltage-sensitive sodium channels, there was no response to nerve stimulation. However, the muscle still responded to the nonmetabolized form of ACh because smooth-muscle action potentials depend on opening voltage-sensitive calcium channels, not voltage-sensitive sodium channels. ACh is the neurotransmitter released from most, but not all, parasympathetic endings. The observation that the muscle could be contracted by injecting a nonmetabolized form of ACh indicates that the smooth muscle probably has receptors for ACh and this response can be blocked by a drug that specifically blocks ACh at muscarinic receptors, the receptors for ACh on smooth muscle. When the muscarinic receptors were blocked, however, stimulation of the parasympathetic nerves still produced a contraction, providing evidence that some substance other than ACh was producing contraction. This indicates that postganglionic parasympathetic nerve endings release a substance other than ACh. It is also possible that the ending releases ACh, which acts on nicotinic receptors (these are not blocked by muscarinic drugs) located on another neuron, which then releases the non-ACh neurotransmitter that acts upon the smooth muscle.

Chapter 12

12-1. None. The gamma motor neurons are important in preventing the muscle-spindle stretch receptors from going slack, but when testing this reflex, the intrafusal fibers are not flaccid. The test is performed with a bent knee, which stretches the extensor muscles in the thigh (and the intrafusal-muscle fibers within them). The stretch receptors are therefore responsive.

12-2. The efferent pathway of the reflex arc (the alpha motor neurons) would not be activated, the effector organ (the extrafusal muscle fibers) would not be activated, and there would be no reflex response.

12-3. The drawing must have excitatory synapses on the motor neurons of both ipsilateral extensor and ipsilateral flexor muscles. Thus, there will be no reciprocal innervation.

12-4. A toxin that interferes with the inhibitory synapses on motor neurons would leave unbalanced the normal excitatory input to these neurons. Thus, the motor neurons would fire excessively, which would result in increased muscle contraction. This is exactly what happens in lockjaw as a result of the toxin produced by the tetanus bacillus.

Chapter 13

13-1. Dopamine is depleted in the basal ganglia of people having Parkinson's disease, and they are therapeutically given dopamine agonists, usually L-dopa. This treatment raises dopamine levels in other parts of the brain, however, where the dopamine levels were previously normal. Schizophrenia is associated with increased brain dopamine levels, and symptoms of this disease appear when dopamine levels are high. The converse therapeutic problem can occur during the treatment of schizophrenics with dopamine-lowering drugs when the symptoms of Parkinson's disease sometimes show as side effects.

13-2. Experiments done on anesthetized animals often involve either stimulating a brain part to observe the effects of increased neuronal activity or damaging ("lesioning") an area to observe resulting deficits. Such experiments on animals, which lack the complex language mechanisms of people, cannot help with language studies. Diseases sometimes mimic these two experimental situations, and behavioral studies of the resulting language deficits in people with aphasia, coupled with study of their brains after death, have provided a wealth of information.

Chapter 14

14-1. No. Decreased erythrocyte volume is certainly one possible explanation, but there is a second: The person might have a normal erythrocyte volume but an abnormally increased plasma volume. Convince yourself of this by writing the hematocrit equation as erythrocyte volume/(erythrocyte volume + plasma volume).

14-2. A halving of tube radius. Resistance is directly proportional to blood viscosity but inversely proportional to the *fourth power* of tube radius.

14-3. The plateau of the action potential and the contraction would be absent. You might think that contraction would persist since most calcium in excitation-contraction coupling in the heart comes from the sarcoplasmic reticulum. However, the major signal for the release of this calcium is the calcium entering across the plasma membrane.

14-4. The SA node is not functioning, and the ventricles are being driven by a pacemaker in the vicinity of the AV Node.

14-5. The person has a narrowed aortic valve. Normally, the resistance across the aortic valve is so small that there is only a tiny pressure difference between the left ventricle and the aorta during ventricular ejection. In the example given here, the large pressure difference indicates that resistance across the valve must be very high.

14-6. This question is analogous to question 14-5 in that the large pressure difference across a valve while the valve is open indicates an abnormally narrowed valve—in this case the left AV valve.

14-7. Decreased heart rate and contractility. These are effects mediated by the sympathetic nerves on the beta-adrenergic receptors in the heart.

14-8. 120 mmHg. $MAP = DP + \frac{1}{3}(SP - DP)$.

14-9. The drug must have caused the arterioles in the kidneys to dilate enough to reduce their resistance by 50 percent. Blood flow to an organ is determined by mean arterial pressure and the organ's resistance to flow. Another important point can be deduced here: If mean arterial pressure has not changed even though renal resistance has dropped 50 percent, then either the resistance of some other organ or the cardiac output has gone up.

14-10. The experiment suggests that acetylcholine causes vasodilation by releasing EDRF or some other vasodilator from endothelial cells.

14-11. A low plasma protein concentration. Capillary pressure is, if anything, lower than normal and so cannot be causing the edema. Another possibility is that capillary permeability to plasma proteins has increased, as occurs in burns.

14-12. 20 mmHg/L per minute. $TPR = MAP/CO$.

14-13. Nothing. Cardiac output and TPR have remained unchanged, and so their product, MAP, has also remained unchanged. This question emphasizes that MAP depends on cardiac output but not upon the combination of heart rate and stroke volume that produces the cardiac output.

14-14. It increases. There are a certain number of impulses traveling up the nerves from the arterial baroreceptors. When these nerves are cut, the number of impulses reaching the medullary cardiovascular center goes to zero, just as it would physiologically if the mean arterial pressure were to decrease markedly. Accordingly, the medullary cardiovascular center responds to the absent impulses by reflexly increasing arterial pressure.

14-15. It decreases. The hemorrhage causes no immediate change in hematocrit since erythrocytes and plasma are lost in the same proportion. As interstitial fluid starts entering the capillaries, however, it expands the plasma volume and decreases the hematocrit. (This is too soon for any new erythrocytes to be synthesized.)

Chapter 15

15-1. 200 ml/mmHg.

$$
\begin{aligned}
\text{Lung compliance} &= \frac{\Delta \text{ lung volume}}{\Delta (P_{alv} - P_{ip})} \\
&= \frac{800 \text{ ml}}{[0 - (-8)] \text{ mmHg} - [0 - (-4)] \text{ mmHg}} \\
&= \frac{800 \text{ ml}}{4 \text{ mmHg}} = \frac{200 \text{ ml}}{\text{mmHg}}
\end{aligned}
$$

15-2. More subatmospheric than normal. A decreased surfactant level causes the lungs to be less compliant, that is, more difficult to expand. Therefore, a greater transpulmonary pressure $(P_{alv} - P_{ip})$ is required to expand them a given amount.

15-3. No.

$$
\begin{aligned}
\text{Alveolar ventilation} &= (\text{tidal volume} - \text{dead space}) \\
&\qquad\qquad\qquad\quad \times \text{ breathing rate} \\
&= (250 \text{ ml} - 150 \text{ ml}) \times (20 \text{ breaths/min}) \\
&= 2000 \text{ ml/min}
\end{aligned}
$$

whereas normal alveolar ventilation is approximately 4000 ml/min.

15-4. The volume of the snorkel constitutes an additional dead space, and so total pulmonary ventilation must be increased if alveolar ventilation is to remain constant.

15-5. The alveolar P_{O_2} will be higher than normal, and the alveolar P_{CO_2} will be lower. If you do not understand why, review the factors that determine the alveolar gas pressures.

15-6. No. Hypoventilation reduces arterial P_{O_2} but only because it reduces alveolar P_{O_2}. That is, in hypoventilation, both alveolar and arterial P_{O_2} are decreased to essentially the same degree. In this problem, alveolar P_{O_2} is normal, and so the person is not hypoventilating. The low arterial P_{O_2} must therefore represent a defect that causes a discrepancy between alveolar P_{O_2} and arterial P_{O_2}. Possibilities include impaired diffusion, a shunting of blood from the right side of the heart to the left through a hole in the heart wall, and mismatching of air flow and blood flow in the alveoli.

15-7. Not at rest, if the defect is not too severe. Recall that equilibration of alveolar air and pulmonary capillary blood is normally so rapid that it occurs well before the end of the capillaries. Therefore, even though diffusion may be retarded, as in this problem, there may still be enough time for equilibration to be reached. In contrast, the time for equilibration is decreased during exercise, and failure to equilibrate is much more likely to occur, resulting in a lowered arterial P_{O_2}.

15-8. Only a few percent (specifically, from approximately 200 ml O_2/L blood to approximately 215 ml O_2/L blood). The reason the increase is so small is that almost all the oxygen in blood is carried bound to hemoglobin and hemoglobin is almost 100 percent saturated at the arterial P_{O_2} achieved by breathing room air. The high arterial P_{O_2} achieved by breathing 100 percent oxygen does cause a directly proportional increase in the amount of oxygen *dissolved* in the blood, but this still remains a small fraction of the total oxygen in the blood. Review the numbers given in the text.

15-9. All except plasma chloride concentration. The reasons are all given in the text.

15-10. It would cease. Respiration depends upon descending input from the medulla oblongata to the nerves supplying the diaphragm and the inspiratory intercostal muscles.

15-11. The 10 percent oxygen mixture will markedly lower alveolar and thus arterial P_{O_2}, but no increase in ventilation will occur because the reflex response to hypoxia is initiated solely by the peripheral chemoreceptors. The 5 percent carbon dioxide mixture will markedly increase alveolar and arterial P_{CO_2}, and a large increase in ventilation will be elicited reflexly via the central chemoreceptors. The increase will not be as large as in a normal animal because the peripheral chemoreceptors do play a role, albeit minor, in the reflex response to elevated P_{CO_2}.

15-12. These patients have profound hyperventilation, with marked increases in both the depth and rate of ventilation. The stimulus, mainly via the peripheral chemoreceptors, is the marked increase in their arterial hydrogen-ion concentration due to the acids produced. The hyperventilation causes an increase in their arterial P_{O_2} and a decrease in their arterial P_{CO_2}.

Chapter 16

16-1. No. It is a possibility, but there is another. Substance T may be secreted by the tubules.

16-2. No. It is a possibility, but there is another. Substance V may be filtered and/or secreted, but the V entering the lumen via these routes may be completely reabsorbed.

16-3. 125 mg/min. The amount of any substance filtered per unit time is given by the product of the GFR and the filterable plasma concentration of the substance, in this case (125 ml/min) $\times$ (100 mg/100 ml) = 125 mg/min.

16-4. The plasma concentration might be so high that the T_m for the amino acid is exceeded, and so all the filtered amino acid is not reabsorbed. A second possibility is that there is a specific defect in the tubular transport for this amino acid. A third possibility is that some other amino acid is present in the plasma in high concentration and is competing for reabsorption.

16-5. No. Urea is filtered and then partially reabsorbed. The reason its concentration in the tubule is higher than in the plasma is that relatively more water is reabsorbed than urea. Therefore, the urea in the tubule becomes concentrated. Despite the fact that urea concentration in the urine is greater than in the plasma, the amount excreted is less than the filtered load; that is, net reabsorption has occurred.

16-6. They would all be decreased. The transport of all these substances is coupled, in one way or another, to that of sodium.

16-7. GFR would not go down as much, and renin secretion would not go up as much as in a person not receiving the drug. The sympathetic nerves are a major pathway for both responses during hemorrhage.

16-8. There would be little if any increase in aldosterone secretion. The major stimulus for increased aldosterone secretion is angiotensin II, but this substance is formed from angiotensin I by the action of angiotensin converting enzyme, and so blockade of this enzyme would block the entire pathway.

16-9. (B). Urinary excretion in the steady state must be less than ingested sodium chloride by an amount equal to that lost in the sweat and feces. This is normally quite small, less than 1 g/day, so that urine excretion in this case equals approximately 11 g/day.

16-10. If the hypothalamus had been damaged, there might be inadequate secretion of ADH. This would cause loss of a large volume of urine, which would tend to dehydrate the person and make her thirsty. Of course, the area of the brain involved in thirst might itself have suffered damage.

16-11. Because aldosterone stimulates sodium reabsorption and potassium secretion, there will be total-body retention of sodium and loss of potassium. Interestingly, the person in this situation actually retains very little sodium because urinary sodium excretion returns to normal despite the continued presence of the high aldosterone. One hypothesized explanation for this is that GFR and atrial natriuretic hormone both go up.

16-12. Sodium and water balance would become negative because of increased excretion of these substances in the urine. The person would also develop a decreased plasma bicarbonate concentration and metabolic acidosis because of increased bicarbonate excretion. The effects on acid-base status are explained by the fact that hydrogen-ion secretion—blocked by the drug—is needed both for bicarbonate reabsorption and for the excretion of hydrogen ion (contribution of new bicarbonate to the blood). The increased sodium excretion reflects the fact that much sodium reabsorption by the proximal tubule is achieved by Na/H countertransport. By blocking hydrogen-ion secretion, therefore, the drug also partially blocks sodium reabsorption. The increased water excretion occurs because the failure to reabsorb sodium and bicarbonate decreases water reabsorption (remember that water reabsorption is secondary to solute reabsorption).

Chapter 17

17-1. If the salivary glands fail to secrete amylase, the undigested starch that reaches the small intestine will still be digested by the amylase secreted by the pancreas. Thus, starch digestion is not affected by the absence of salivary amylase.

17-2. Alcohol can be absorbed across the stomach wall, but absorption is much more rapid from the small intestine with its larger surface area. Ingestion of foods containing fat releases enterogastrones from the small intestine, and these hormones inhibit gastric emptying and thus prolong the time alcohol spends in the stomach before reaching the small intestine. This delay decreases the rate at which alcohol enters the blood. Milk, contrary to popular belief, does not "protect" the lining of the stomach by coating it with a fatty layer. Rather, the fat content of milk decreases the absorption of alcohol by decreasing the rate of gastric emptying.

17-3. Vomiting results in the loss of fluid and acid from the body. The fluid comes from the luminal contents of the stomach and duodenum, most of which was secreted by the gastric glands, pancreas, and liver and thus is derived from the blood. The cardiovascular symptoms of this patient are the result of the decrease in blood volume that accompanies vomiting.

The secretion of acid by the stomach produces an equal number of bicarbonate ions, which are released into the blood. Normally these bicarbonate ions would be neutralized by hydrogen ions released by the pancreas when bicarbonate ions are secreted into the small intestine to neutralize the acid from the stomach. Because gastric acid is lost during vomiting, the pancreas is not stimulated to secrete bicarbonate, and the corresponding hydrogen ions that would be formed are not available in the blood to neutralize the bicarbonate released by the stomach into the blood. As a result, the acidity of the blood decreases.

17-4. Fat can be digested and absorbed in the absence of bile salts but in greatly decreased amounts. Without adequate emulsification of fat by bile salts and phospholipids, only the fat at the surface of large lipid droplets is available to pancreatic lipase, and the rate of fat digestion is very slow. Without the formation of micelles with the aid of bile salts, the products of fat digestion become dissolved in the large lipid droplets, where they are not readily available for diffusion into the epithelial cells. In the absence of bile salts, only about 50 percent of the ingested fat is digested and absorbed. The undigested fat is passed on to the large intestine, where the bacteria produce compounds that increase colonic motility and promote the secretion of fluid into the lumen of the large intestine, leading to diarrhea.

17-5. Damage to the lower portion of the spinal cord produces a loss of voluntary control over defecation as a result of disruption of the somatic nerves to the skeletal muscle of the external anal sphincter. Damage to the somatic nerves leaves the external sphincter in a continuously relaxed state. Under these conditions, defecation occurs whenever the rectum becomes distended and the defection reflex is initiated.

17-6. Vagotomy decreases the secretion of acid by the stomach. Impulses in the parasympathetic nerves directly stimulate acid secretion by the parietal cells and also cause the release of gastrin, which in turn stimulates acid secretion. Impulses in the vagus nerves are increased during both the cephalic and gastric phases of digestion. Vagotomy, by decreasing the amount of acid secreted decreases irritation of existing ulcers, which promotes

healing and decreases the probability of acid contributing to the production of new ulcers.

Chapter 18

18-1. The concentration in plasma would increase, and the amount stored in adipose tissue would decrease. Lipoprotein lipase cleaves plasma triacylglycerols, so its blockade would decrease the rate at which these molecules were cleared from plasma and would decrease the availability of the fatty acids in them for synthesis of intracellular triacylglycerols. However, this would only reduce but not eliminate such synthesis, since the adipose tissue cells could still synthesize their own fatty acids from glucose.

18-2. The person might be an insulin-dependent diabetic or might be a normal fasting person; plasma glucose would be increased in the first case but decreased in the second. Plasma insulin concentration would not be useful because it would be decreased in both cases. The fact that the person was resting and unstressed was specified because severe stress or exercise could also produce the plasma changes mentioned in the question. Plasma glucose would be increased in the former and decreased in the latter.

18-3. Glucagon, epinephrine, and growth hormone. The insulin will produce hypoglycemia, which then induces reflex increases in these hormones.

18-4. It might reduce it but not eliminate it. The sympathetic effects on organic metabolism during stress are mediated not only by circulating epinephrine but also by sympathetic nerves to the liver (glycogenolysis and gluconeogenesis), to the adipose tissue (lipolysis), and to the islets (inhibition of insulin secretion and stimulation of glucagon secretion).

18-5. Increase. The stress of the accident will elicit increased activity of all the glucose-counterregulatory controls and will therefore necessitate more insulin to oppose these influences.

18-6. It will lower plasma cholesterol concentration. Bile salts are formed from cholesterol, and losses of these bile salts in the feces will be replaced by the synthesis of new ones from cholesterol. Chapter 17 describes how bile salts are normally absorbed from the small intestine so that very few of those secreted into the bile are normally lost from the body.

18-7. Plasma concentration of HDL. It is the ratio of LDL cholesterol to HDL cholesterol that best correlates with the development of atherosclerosis; that is, HDL cholesterol is "good" cholesterol. The answer to this question would have been the same regardless of whether the person was an athlete or not, but the question was phrased this way to emphasize that people who exercise generally have increased HDL cholesterol.

18-8. In utero malnutrition. Neither growth hormone nor the thyroid hormones influence in utero growth.

18-9. Androgens stimulate growth but also cause the ultimate cessation of growth by closing the epiphyseal plates. Therefore, there might be a rapid growth spurt in response to the androgens but a subsequent premature cessation of growth. Estrogens exert similar effects.

18-10. Heat loss from the head, mainly via convection and sweating, is the major route for loss under these conditions. The rest of the body is *gaining* heat by conduction, and sweating is of no value in the rest of the body because the sweat cannot evaporate. Heat is also lost via the expired air (insensible loss), and some people actually begin to pant under such conditions. The rapid shallow breathing increases air flow and heat loss without causing hyperventilation.

18-11. They seek out warmer places, if available, so that their body temperature increases. That is, they use behavior to develop a fever. This is excellent evidence that the hyperthermia of infection is a fever, that is, a set-point change.

Chapter 19

19-1. Sterility due to lack of spermatogenesis would be the common symptom. The Sertoli cells are essential for spermatogenesis, and so is testosterone produced by the Leydig cells. The person with Leydig cell destruction, but not the person with Sertoli cell destruction, would also have other symptoms of testosterone deficiency.

19-2. The androgens act on the hypothalamus and anterior pituitary to inhibit the secretion of the gonadotropins. Therefore, spermatogenesis is inhibited. Importantly, even if this man were given FSH, the sterility would probably remain since the lack of LH would cause deficient testosterone secretion and locally produced testosterone is needed for spermatogenesis (that is, the exogenous androgen cannot do this job).

19-3. Impaired function of the seminiferous tubules, notably of the Sertoli cells. The increased plasma FSH concentration is due to the lack of negative-feedback inhibition of FSH secretion by inhibin, itself secreted by the Sertoli cells. The Leydig cells seem to be functioning normally in this person, since the lack of demasculinization and the normal plasma LH indicate normal testosterone secretion.

19-4. FSH secretion. Since FSH acts on the Sertoli cells and LH acts on the Leydig cells, the answer to this question is essentially the same as that for question 19-1—sterility would result in either case, but the loss of LH would also cause an undesirable elimination of testosterone and its effects.

19-5. These findings are all due to testosterone deficiency. You would also expect to find that the testes and penis were small.

19-6. They will be eliminated. The androgens act on the hypothalamus to inhibit the secretion of GnRH and on the pituitary to inhibit the response to GnRH. The result is inadequate secretion of gonadotropins and therefore inadequate stimulation of the ovaries. In addition to the loss of menstrual cycles, the woman will suffer some degree of masculinization of the secondary sex characteristics because of the combined effects of androgen excess and estrogen deficiency.

19-7. Such treatment may cause so much secretion of FSH that multiple dominant follicles are stimulated to develop simultaneously and have their eggs ovulated during the LH surge.

19-8. An increased plasma LH. The other two are due to increased plasma progesterone and so do not occur until *after* ovulation and formation of the corpus luteum.

19-9. The absence of sperm capacitation. When test-tube fertilization is performed, special techniques are used to induce capacitation.

19-10. The fetus is in difficulty. The placenta produces progesterone entirely on its own, whereas estriol secretion requires participation of the fetus, specifically, the fetal adrenal cortex.

19-11. Prostaglandin antagonists, oxytocin antagonists, and drugs that lower cytosolic calcium concentration. You may not have thought of the last category since calcium in not mentioned in this context in the text, but as in all muscle, calcium is the immediate cause of contraction in the myometrium.

19-12. This person would have normal male external genitals and testes, although the testes may not have descended fully, but would also have some degree of development of uterine tubes, a uterus, and a vagina. These female structures would tend to develop because no MIF was present to cause degeneration of the Müllerian duct system.

19-13. No. These two hormones are already elevated in menopause, and the problem is that the ovaries are unable to respond to them with estrogen secretion. Thus, the treatment must be with estrogen itself.

Chapter 20

20-1. Both would be impaired because T cells would not differentiate. The absence of cytotoxic T cells would eliminate responses mediated by these cells. The absence of helper T cells would impair antibody-mediated responses because most B cells require cytokines from helper T cells to become activated.

20-2. Neutrophil deficiency would impair nonspecific inflammatory responses to bacteria. Monocyte deficiency, by causing macrophage deficiency, would impair both nonspecific inflammation and specific immune responses.

20-3. The drug might reduce but would not eliminate the action of complement, since this system destroys cells directly (via the membrane attack complex) as well as by facilitating phagocytosis.

20-4. Antibodies would bind normally to antigen but might not be able to activate complement, act as opsonins, or recruit NK cells in ADCC. The reason for these defects is that the sites to which complement C1, phagocytes, and NK cells bind are all located in the Fc portion of antibodies.

20-5. They do develop fever, although often not to the same degree as normal. They can do so because IL-1 and other cytokines secreted by macrophages cause fever, whereas the defect in AIDS is failure of helper T-cell function.

20-6. This person is suffering from an autoimmune attack against the receptors. The antibodies formed then bind to the receptors and activate them just as the thyroid hormones would have.

20-7. Alcohol over time induces a high level of MES activity, which causes an administered barbiturate to be metabolized more rapidly than normal.

APPENDIX
B

GLOSSARY

A cell *see* alpha cell

absolute refractory period time during which an excitable membrane cannot generate an action potential in response to any stimulus

absorption movement of materials across an epithelial layer from body cavity or compartment toward the blood

absorptive state period during which nutrients enter bloodstream from gastrointestinal tract

accessory reproductive organ duct through which sperm or eggs are transported, or a gland emptying into such a duct (in the female the breasts are usually included)

acclimatization (ah-climb-ah-ti-ZA-shun) environmentally induced improvement in functioning of a genetically based physiological system

accommodation adjustment of eye for viewing various distances by changing lens's shape

acetone (ASS-ih-tone) ketone body produced from acetyl CoA during prolonged fasting or untreated severe diabetes mellitus

acetyl coenzyme A (acetyl CoA) (ASS-ih-teal koh-EN-zime A, koe-A) metabolic intermediate that transfers acetyl groups to Krebs cycle and various synthetic pathways

acetyl group —$COCH_3$

acetylcholine (ACh) (ass-suh-teal-KOH-lean) a particular neurotransmitter released by pre- and postganglionic parasympathetic neurons, preganglionic sympathetic neurons, somatic neurons, and some CNS neurons

acetylcholinesterase (ass-suh-teal-koh-lin-ES-ter-ase) enzyme that breaks down acetylcholine into acetic acid and choline

acid molecule capable of releasing a hydrogen ion; solution having H^+ concentration greater than that of pure water, that is, pH less than 7; *see also* strong acid, weak acid

acidity concentration of free, unbound hydrogen ion in a solution; the higher the H^+ concentration, the greater the acidity

acidosis (ass-ih-DOUGH-sis) any situation in which arterial H^+ concentration is elevated; *see also* metabolic acidosis, respiratory acidosis

acrosome (AK-roh-sohm) cytoplasmic vesicle containing digestive enzymes and located at head of a sperm

actin (AK-tin) globular contractile protein to which myosin cross-bridges bind; located in muscle thin filaments and in microfilaments of cytoskeleton

action potential electric signal propagated by nerve and muscle cells; an all-or-none depolarization of membrane polarity; has a threshold and refractory period and is conducted without decrement

activated macrophage macrophage whose killing ability has been enhanced by cytokines, particularly IL-2 and gamma interferon; also called effector macrophage

activation *see* lymphocyte activation

activation energy energy necessary to disrupt existing chemical bonds during a chemical reaction

active hyperemia (hi-per-EE-me-ah) increased blood flow through a tissue due to increased metabolic activity

active immunity resistance to reinfection acquired by contact with microorganisms, their toxins, or other antigenic material; *compare* passive immunity

active site region of enzyme to which substrate binds

active transport energy-requiring system that uses transporters to move ions or molecules across a membrane against an electrochemical difference; *see also* primary active transport, secondary active transport

activity *see* enzyme activity

acute (ah-CUTE) lasting a relatively short time; *compare* chronic

acute phase protein one of a group of proteins secreted by liver during systemic response to injury or infection

acute phase response responses of tissues and organs distant from site of infection or immune response

adaptation (evolution) a biological characteristic that favors survival in a particular environment; (neural) decrease in action-potential frequency in a neuron despite constant stimulus

adenosine diphosphate (ADP) (ah-DEN-oh-seen die-FOS-fate) two-phosphate product of ATP breakdown

adenosine monophosphate (AMP) monophosphate derivative of ATP

adenosine triphosphate (ATP) major molecule that transfers energy from metabolism to cell functions during its breakdown to ADP and P_i

adenylyl cyclase (ah-DEN-il-il SIGH-klase) enzyme that catalyzes transformation of ATP to cyclic AMP

adipocyte (ah-DIP-oh-site) cell specialized for triacylglycerol synthesis and storage; fat cell

adipose tissue (ADD-ah-poss) tissue composed largely of fat-storing cells

adrenal cortex (ah-DREE-nal KOR-tex) endocrine gland that forms outer shell of each adrenal gland; secretes mainly cortisol, aldosterone, and androgens; *compare* adrenal medulla

adrenal gland one of a pair of endocrine glands above each kidney; each gland consists of outer *adrenal cortex* and inner *adrenal medulla*

adrenal medulla (mah-DULL-ah) endocrine gland that forms inner core of each adrenal gland; main secretion is epinephrine; *compare* adrenal cortex

adrenaline (ah-DREN-ah-lyn) British name for epinephrine

adrenergic (ad-ren-ER-jik) pertaining to norepinephrine or epinephrine; compound that acts like norepinephrine or epinephrine

adrenocorticotropic hormone (ACTH) (ad-ren-oh-kor-tih-koh-TROH-pik) polypeptide hormone secreted by anterior pituitary; stimulates adrenal cortex to secrete cortisol; also called corticotropin

aerobic (air-OH-bik) with oxygen

affect (AF-fect, not af-FECT) external expression of inner emotions

afferent (AF-er-ent) carrying toward

afferent arteriole vessel in kidney that carries blood from artery to renal corpuscle

afferent neuron neuron that carries information from receptors at its peripheral endings to CNS; cell body lies outside CNS

afferent pathway component of reflex arc that transmits information from receptor to integrating center

affinity strength with which ligand binds to its binding site

afterbirth placenta and associated membranes expelled from uterus after delivery of infant

agonist (AG-ah-nist) chemical messenger that binds to receptor and triggers cell's response; often refers to drug that mimics action of chemical normally in the body

airway tube through which air flows between external environment and lung alveoli

albumin (al-BU-min) most abundant plasma protein

aldosterone (al-doe-stir-OWN or al-DOS-stir-own) mineralocorticoid steroid hormone secreted by adrenal cortex; regulates electrolyte balance

alkaline having H^+ concentration lower than that of pure water, that is, having a pH greater than 7

alkalosis (alk-ah-LOW-sis) any situation in which arterial blood H^+ concentration is reduced; *see also* metabolic alkalosis, respiratory alkalosis

all-or-none pertaining to event that occurs maximally or not at all

allele (al-EEL) one nucleotide sequence in a given gene different from other sequences of that same gene; can be classified as *dominant* or *recessive*

allosteric modulation (al-low-STAIR-ik) control of protein binding-site properties by modulator molecules that bind to regions of the protein other than the binding site altered by them

allosteric protein protein whose binding-site characteristics are subject to allosteric modulation

alpha cell glucagon-secreting cell of pancreatic islet of Langerhans

alpha-adrenergic receptor plasma membrane receptor for epinephrine and norepinephrine that utilizes phospholipase C second-messenger system or directly affects potassium and calcium channels in the membrane; *compare* beta-adrenergic receptor; also called alpha adrenoceptor

alpha-gamma coactivation simultaneous, or near simultaneous, activation of alpha and gamma motor neurons

alpha-glycerol phosphate three-carbon molecule; combines with fatty acids to form mono-, di-, and triacyl-glycerols; also called glycerol 3-phosphate

alpha-helix coiled conformation of polypeptide chain found in many proteins

alpha motor neuron motor neuron that innervates extrafusal muscle fibers

alpha rhythm prominent 8- to 13-Hz oscillation on the electroencephalograms of awake, relaxed adults with their eyes closed

alternate complement pathway sequence for complement activation that bypasses first steps in classical pathway and is not antibody-dependent

alveolar dead space (al-VEE-oh-lar) volume of inspired air that reaches alveoli but cannot undergo gas exchange with blood

alveolar pressure air pressure in pulmonary alveoli

alveolar ventilation volume of atmospheric air entering alveoli each minute

alveolus (al-VEE-oh-lus) thin-walled, air-filled "outpocketing" from terminal air passageways in lungs; cell cluster at end of duct in secretory gland

amine hormone (ah-MEAN) hormone

derived from amino acid tyrosine; includes thyroid hormone, epinephrine, norepinephrine, and dopamine

amino acid (ah-MEAN-oh) molecule containing amino group, carboxyl group, and side chain attached to a carbon; molecular subunit of protein

amino group —NH$_2$; ionizes to —NH$_3^+$

aminoacyl-tRNA synthetase (ah-MEAN-oh-ACE-il tee-RNA SIN-the-tase) general name for 20 enzymes each of which catalyzes covalent linkage of a specific amino acid to its particular tRNA during protein synthesis

aminopeptidase (ah-mean-oh-PEP-tih-dase) one of a family of enzymes located in the intestinal epithelial membrane; breaks peptide bond at amino end of polypeptide

ammonia NH$_3$; produced during amino acid breakdown; converted in liver to urea; ionized form is ammonium

amnesia memory loss; *see also* retrograde amnesia

amniotic membrane (am-nee-AHT-ik) membrane surrounding fetus in utero

amphetamine drug that increases transmission at catecholamine-mediated synapses in brain

amphipathic molecule (am-fuh-PATH-ik) molecule containing polar or ionized groups at one end and nonpolar groups at the other

amplitude height, how much, magnitude of change

amylase (AM-ih-lase) enzyme that partially breaks down polysaccharides

anabolic steroid (an-ah-BOL-ik STEAR-oid) testosterone-like agent that increases protein synthesis

anabolism (ah-NAB-oh-lizm) cellular synthesis of organic molecules

anaerobic (an-ih-ROW-bik) in absence of oxygen

analgesia (an-al-JEE-zee-ah) removal of pain without loss of consciousness

anatomic dead space space in respiratory tract airways whose walls do not permit gas exchange with blood

androgen (AN-dro-jen) any chemical with testosterone-like actions

androstenedione (an-dro-steen-die-OWN) androgen hormone secreted by adrenal cortex; intermediary in sex hormone synthetic pathway

anemia (ah-KNEE-me-ah) reduction in total blood hemoglobin

anemic hypoxia (ah-KNEE-mik hi-POK-see-ah) hypoxia with normal arterial O$_2$ pressure but reduced total blood oxygen content

angina pectoris (an-JI-nah PEK-tor-iss) chest pain associated with inadequate blood flow to heart muscle

angiotensin I peptide generated in plasma by renin's action on angiotensinogen

angiotensin II hormone formed by action of angiotensin converting enzyme on angiotensin I; stimulates aldosterone secretion from adrenal cortex, vascular smooth-muscle contraction, and thirst

angiotensin converting enzyme enzyme on capillary endothelial cells that catalyzes removal of two amino acids from angiotensin I to form angiotensin II

angiotensinogen (an-gee-oh-ten-SIN-oh-jen) plasma protein precursor of angiotensin I

anion (AN-eye-on) negatively charged ion; *compare* cation

antagonist (muscle) muscle whose action opposes intended movement; (drug) molecule that competes with another for a receptor and binds to the receptor but does not trigger the cell's response

anterior toward or at the front

anterior pituitary anterior portion of pituitary gland; synthesizes, stores, and releases ACTH, GH, TSH, prolactin, FSH, and LH

antibody (AN-tih-bah-dee) immunoglobulin that is secreted by plasma cell; combines with type of antigen that stimulated its production; directs attack against antigen or cell bearing it; *see also* natural antibody

anticodon (an-tie-KOE-don) three-nucleotide sequence in tRNA able to base-pair with complementary codon in mRNA during protein synthesis

antidiuretic hormone (ADH) (an-tie-die-your-ET-ik) *see* vasopressin

antigen (AN-tih-jen) any foreign molecule that stimulates a specific immune response

antigen-presenting cell cell that presents antigen, complexed with MHC proteins on its surface, to T cells

antithrombin III (an-tie-throm-bin THREE) plasma anticlotting protein that inactivates thrombin

antrum (AN-trum) (gastric) lower portion of stomach, that is, region closest to pyloric sphincter; (ovarian) fluid-filled cavity in maturing ovarian follicle

aorta (a-OR-tah) largest artery in body; carries blood from left ventricle of heart to thorax and abdomen

aortic arch baroreceptor (a-OR-tik) *see* arterial baroreceptor

aortic body chemoreceptor chemoreceptor located near aortic arch; sensitive to arterial blood O$_2$ pressure and H$^+$ concentration

aortic valve valve between left ventricle of heart and aorta

aphasia (ah-FAY-see-ah) specific language deficit not due to mental retardation or muscular weakness

apnea (AP-nee-ah) cessation of breathing

appendix small finger-like projection from cecum of large intestine

aqueous (A-kwee-us) watery; prepared with water

arachidonic acid (ah-rak-ah-DON-ik) polyunsaturated fatty acid and precursor of eicosanoids

arrhythmia (a-RYTH-me-ah) any variation from normal heartbeat rhythm

arterial baroreceptor nerve endings sensitive to stretch or distortion produced by arterial blood pressure changes; located in carotid sinus or aortic arch; also called carotid sinus and aortic arch baroreceptors

arteriole (are-TEER-ee-ole) blood vessel between artery and capillary; surrounded by smooth muscle; primary site of vascular resistance

artery (ARE-ter-ee) thick-walled, elastic vessel that carries blood away from heart to arterioles

ascending limb portion of Henle's loop of renal tubule leading to distal convoluted tubule

ascending pathway neural pathways that go to the brain; also called sensory pathways

aspartate (ah-SPAHR-tate) a major excitatory neurotransmitter in CNS; ionized form of the amino acid aspartic acid

association cortex *see* cortical association areas

asthma (AS-muh) disease characterized by severe airway constriction and plugging of the airways with mucus

atmospheric pressure air pressure surrounding the body (760 mmHg at sea level)

atom smallest unit of matter that has unique chemical characteristics; has no net charge; combines with other atoms to form all chemical substances

atomic mass relative value that indicates an atom's mass relative to the mass of other types of atoms, based on the assignment of a value of 12 to carbon

atomic nucleus dense region, consisting of protons and neutrons, at center of atom

atomic number number of proteins in nucleus of atom

atomic weight relative value that indicates an atom's mass relative to mass of other types of atoms based on the assignment of a value of 12 to carbon

ATPase enzyme that breaks down ATP to ADP and inorganic phosphate; *see* Na,K-ATPase, Ca-ATPase

atrial natriuretic factor (ANF) (nat-rye-your-ET-ik) peptide hormone secreted by cardiac atrial cells in response to atrial distension; causes increased renal sodium excretion

atrioventricular (AV) node (a-tree-oh-ven-TRIK-you-lar) region at base of right atrium near interventricular septum, containing specialized cardiac muscle cells through which electrical activity must pass to go from atria to ventricles

atrioventricular (AV) valve valve between atrium and ventricle of heart; AV valve on right side of heart is the *tricuspid valve*, and that on left side is the *mitral valve*

atrium (ATE-ree-um) chamber of heart that receives blood from veins and passes it on to ventricle on same side of heart

atrophy (AT-row-fee) wasting away; decrease in size; *see also* disuse atrophy, denervation atrophy

auditory (AW-dih-tor-ee) pertaining to sense of hearing

auditory cortex region of cerebral cortex that receives nerve fibers from auditory pathways

autocrine agent (AW-toe-crin) chemical messenger that is secreted into extracellular fluid and acts upon cell that secreted it

automaticity (aw-toe-mah-TISS-ih-tee) capable of rhythmical self-excitation

autonomic nervous system (aw-toe-NAHM-ik) component of efferent division of peripheral nervous system that consists of sympathetic and parasympathetic subdivisions; innervates cardiac muscle, smooth muscle, and glands; *compare* somatic nervous system

autoreceptors receptors on a cell affected by a chemical messenger released from the same cell

autoregulation (aw-toe-reg-you-LAY-shun) ability of an individual organ to control (self-regulate) its vascular resistance independent of neural and hormonal influence

aversive motivation goal-directed quality of behavior that is related to avoidance, escape, or aggression

axon (AXE-own) extension from neuron cell body; propagates action potentials away from cell body; also called a nerve fiber

axon terminal end of axon; forms synaptic or neuroeffector junction with postjunctional cell

axon transport process involving intracellular filaments by which materials are moved from one end of axon to other

axon-axon synapse *see* presynaptic synapse

B cell (immune system) lymphocyte that, upon activation, proliferates and differentiates into antibody-secreting plasma cell; (endocrine cell) *see* beta cell

B lymphocyte *see* B cell

bacteria unicellular organisms that have outer cell wall and a plasma membrane

balance concept if quantity of any substance in body is to be maintained constant over time, amount ingested and produced must equal amount excreted and metabolized

barometric pressure *see* atmospheric pressure

baroreceptor receptor sensitive to pressure and to rate of change in pressure; *see also* arterial baroreceptor, intrarenal baroreceptor

basal (BAY-sul) resting level

basal ganglia nuclei deep in cerebral hemispheres that code and relay information associated with control of body movements; specifically, caudate nucleus, globus pallidus, and putamen

basal metabolic rate (BMR) metabolic rate when one is at mental and physical rest but not sleeping, at comfortable temperature, and has fasted at least 12 h; also called metabolic cost of living

base (acid-base) any molecule that can combine with H$^+$; (nucleotide) molecular ring of carbon and nitrogen which, with a phosphate group and a sugar, constitutes a nucleotide; *see also* purine base, pyrimidine base

basement membrane thin proteinaceous layer of extracellular material upon which epithelial and endothelial cells sit

basic electrical rhythm spontaneous depolarization-repolarization cycles of pacemaker cells in longitudinal smooth-muscle layer of stomach and intestines; coordinates repetitive muscular activity of GI tract

basilar membrane (BAS-ih-lar) membrane that separates cochlear duct and scala tympani in inner ear; supports organ of Corti

basolateral membrane (bay-so-LAH-ter-al) sides of epithelial cell facing away from lumen; also called serosal or blood side of cell

basophil (BAY-so-fill) polymorphonuclear granulocytic leukocyte whose granules stain with basic dyes; enters tissues and becomes mast cell

beta-adrenergic receptor (BAY-ta adren-ER-jik) plasma membrane receptor for epinephrine and norepinephrine that utilizes cAMP second-messenger system; *compare* alpha-adrenergic receptor; also called beta adrenoceptor

beta cell insulin-secreting cell in pancreatic islet of Langerhans; also called B cell

beta oxidation (ox-ih-DAY-shun) series of reactions that generate hydrogens (for oxidative phosphorylation) from fatty acid breakdown to acetyl CoA

beta rhythm low, fast EEG oscillations in alert, awake adults who are paying attention to (or thinking hard about) something

bicarbonate (by-CAR-bah-nate) HCO$_3^-$

bile fluid secreted by liver; contains bicarbonate, bile salts, cholesterol, lecithin, bile pigments, metabolic end products, and certain trace metals

bile canaliculi (can-al-IK-you-lee) small ducts adjacent to liver cells into which bile is secreted

bile pigment colored substance, derived from breakdown of heme group of hemoglobin, secreted in bile

bile salt one of a family of steroid molecules secreted in bile by the liver; promotes solubilization and digestion of fat in small intestine

bilirubin (bill-eh-RUE-bin) yellow substance resulting from heme breakdown; excreted in bile as a bile pigment

binding site region of protein to which a specific ligand binds

biogenic amine (by-oh-JEN-ik ah-MEAN) one of family of neurotransmitters having basic formula R—NH$_2$; includes dopamine, norepinephrine, epinephrine, serotonin, and histamine

"biological clock" neurons that function in absence of apparent external stimulation and drive body rhythms

biotransformation (by-oh-trans-for-MAY-shun) alteration of foreign molecules by an organism's metabolic pathways

bipolar cell retinal neuron postsynaptic to rod or cone

bladder *see* urinary bladder

blastocyst (BLAS-toe-cyst) early embryonic stage consisting of ball of developing cells surrounding central cavity

blood-brain barrier group of anatomical barriers and transport systems that controls kinds of substances entering brain extracellular space from blood and their rates of entry

blood coagulation (koh-ag-you-LAY-shun) blood clotting

blood sugar glucose

blood-testis barrier barrier that limits chemical movements between blood and lumen of seminiferous tubules

blood type blood classification according to presence of A, B, or O antigens

body mass index (BMI) method for assessing degree of obesity calculated as weight in kilograms divided by square of height in meters

bone marrow highly vascular, cellular substance in central cavity of some bones; site of erythrocyte, leukocyte, and platelet synthesis

Bowman's capsule blind sac at beginning of tubular component of kidney nephron

Boyle's law (boils) pressure of a fixed amount of gas in a container is inversely proportional to container's volume

bradykinin (braid-ee-KI-nin) protein formed by action of the enzyme kallikrein on precursor; dilates vessels, increases capillary permeability, and probably stimulates pain receptors

brainstem brain subdivision consisting of medulla oblongata, pons, and midbrain and located between spinal cord and forebrain

Broca's area (BRO-kahz) region of left frontal lobe associated with speech production

bronchiole (BRON-key-ole) small airways distal to bronchus

bronchus (BRON-kus) large-diameter air passage that enters lung; located between trachea and bronchioles

buffer weak acid or base that can exist in undissociated (Hbuffer) or dissociated (H$^+$ + buffer) form

buffering reversible hydrogen-ion binding by anions when H$^+$ concentration changes; tends to minimize changes in acidity of a solution when acid is added or removed

bulbourethral gland (bul-bo-you-WREATH-ral) one of paired glands in male that secretes fluid components of semen into the urethra

bulk flow movement of fluids or gases from region of higher pressure to one of lower pressure

C1 first protein activated in classical complement pathway

C3 first protein activated in alternate complement pathway

C3b complement protein that functions as an opsonin

Ca-ATPase primary active-transport carrier protein for calcium in plasma membrane and in several organelle membranes

calcitonin (kal-sih-TOE-nin) peptide hormone secreted by thyroid gland; may play a role in regulation of plasma calcium

calmodulin (kal-MOD-you-lin) intracellular calcium-binding protein that mediates many of calcium's second-messenger functions

calorie (cal) unit of heat energy measurement; amount of heat needed to raise temperature of 1 g of water 1°C; *compare* kilocalorie

calorigenic effect (kah-lor-ih-JEN-ik) increase in metabolic rate caused by epinephrine or thyroid hormones

candidate hormone substance sus-pected of being a hormone but not yet proven to be one

capacitation *see* sperm capacitation

capillary smallest blood-vessel type

carbamino compound (car-bah-ME-no) compound resulting from combination of carbon dioxide and protein amino groups, particularly in hemoglobin

carbohydrate substance composed of carbon, hydrogen, and oxygen according to general formula C$_n$(H$_2$O)$_n$, where n is any whole number

carbon monoxide CO; gas that reacts with hemoglobin and decreases blood oxygen-carrying capacity; possible neurotransmitter

carbonic acid (car-BAHN-ik) H$_2$CO$_3$; an acid formed from H$_2$O and CO$_2$

carbonic anhydrase (an-HI-drase) enzyme that catalyzes the reaction CO$_2$ + H$_2$O $\rightleftharpoons$ H$_2$CO$_3$

carboxyl group (car-BOX-il) —COOH; ionizes to carboxyl ion (—COO$^-$)

carboxypeptidase (car-box-ee-PEP-tih-dase) enzyme secreted into small intestine by exocrine pancreas as precursor, procarboxypeptidase; breaks peptide bond at carboxyl end of protein

carcinogen (car-SIN-oh-jen) any agent that can induce cancerous transformation of cells

cardiac (CAR-dee-ak) pertaining to the heart

cardiac cycle one contraction-relaxation sequence of heart

cardiac muscle heart muscle

cardiac output blood volume pumped by each ventricle per minute (not total output pumped by both ventricles)

cardiovascular center neuron cluster in brainstem medulla oblongata that serves as a major integrating center for reflexes affecting heart and blood vessels

cardiovascular system heart and blood vessels

carotid (ka-RAH-tid) pertaining to two major arteries (carotid arteries) in neck that convey blood to head

carotid body chemoreceptor chemoreceptor near main branching of carotid artery; sensitive to blood O$_2$ pressure and H$^+$ concentration

carotid sinus dilatation of internal carotid artery just above main carotid branching; location of carotid baroreceptors

carotid sinus baroreceptor *see* arterial baroreceptor

carrier *see* transporter

cascade (KAS-kade) multiplicative sequence of events in which the number of reaction products increases at one or more steps

catabolism (kah-TAH-bowl-ism) cellular breakdown of organic molecules

catalyst (CAT-ah-list) substance that accelerates chemical reactions but does not itself undergo any net chemical change during the reaction

catecholamine (cat-eh-COLE-ah-mean) dopamine, epinephrine, or norepinephrine, all of which have similar chemical structures

catechol-*O*-methyl transferase (CAT-eh-cole oh METH-il) enzyme that degrades catecholamine neurotransmitters

cation (CAT-eye-on) ion having net positive charge; *compare* anion

cecum (SEE-come) dilated pouch at beginning of large intestine into which open the ileum, colon, and appendix

cell adhesion molecule (CAM) glycoprotein important in nervous system development

cell body in cells with long extensions, the part that contains the nucleus

cell differentiation *see* differentiation

cell organelle (or-guh-NELL) membrane-bound compartment, nonmembranous particle, or filament that performs specialized functions in cell

cellulose polysaccharide composed of glucose subunits; found in plant cells

center of gravity point in a body at which body mass is in perfect balance; if the body were suspended from a string attached to this point, there would be no movement

central chemoreceptor receptor in brainstem medulla oblongata that responds to H^+ concentration changes of brain extracellular fluid

central command fatigue fatigue due to failure of appropriate regions of cerebral cortex to excite motor neurons

central nervous system (CNS) brain plus spinal cord

central pattern generator cluster of brainstem or spinal neurons that activates skeletal muscle in cyclical manner for repetitive behavior

central thermoreceptor temperature receptor in hypothalamus, spinal cord, abdominal organ, or other internal location

centriole (SEN-tree-ole) small cytoplasmic body having nine fused sets of microtubules; participates in nuclear and cell division

cephalic phase (seh-FAHL-ik) (of gastrointestinal control) initiation of the neural and hormonal reflexes regulating gastrointestinal functions by stimulation of receptors in head, that is, cephalic receptors—sight, smell, taste, and chewing—as well as by emotional states

cerebellum (ser-ah-BELL-um) brain subdivision lying behind forebrain and above brainstem; deals with muscle movement control

cerebral cortex (SER-ah-brul or sah-REE-brul) cellular layer covering the cerebrum

cerebrospinal fluid (CSF) (sah-ree-broh-SPY-nal) fluid that fills cerebral ventricles and the subarachnoid space surrounding brain and spinal cord

cerebrum (SER-ah-brum or sah-REE-brum) part of brain which, with diencephalon, forms the forebrain

cervix (SIR-vix) lower portion of uterus; cervical opening connects uterine and vaginal lumens

channel small passage in plasma membrane formed by integral membrane proteins and through which certain small-diameter molecules and ions can diffuse; *see also* voltage-sensitive channel, mechanosensitive channel

channel gating process of opening and closing ion channels

chaperone protein that guides the folding of large segments of a newly formed protein

charge *see* electric charge

chemical bond interaction between electric forces of subatomic particles of adjacent atoms; holds atoms together in a molecule

chemical element specific type of atom

chemical equilibrium state when rates of forward and reverse components of a chemical reaction are equal, and no net change in reactant or product concentration occurs

chemical reaction breaking of some chemical bonds and formation of new ones, which changes one type of molecule to another; *see also* reversible reaction, irreversible reaction

chemical specificity *see* specificity

chemical synapse (SIN-apse) synapse at which neurotransmitters released by one neuron diffuse across an extracellular gap to influence a second neuron's activity

chemoreceptor afferent nerve ending (or cell associated with it) sensitive to concentrations of certain chemicals

chemotaxin (key-moh-TAX-in) any chemical that causes chemotaxis

chemotaxis (key-moh-TAX-iss) movement of cells, particularly phagocytes, in a specific direction in response to a chemical stimulus

chief cell gastric gland cell that secretes pepsinogen, precursor of pepsin

cholecystokinin (CCK) (koh-lee-sis-toe-KI-nin) peptide hormone secreted by duodenum that regulates gastric motility and secretion, gall bladder contraction, and pancreatic enzyme secretion; possible satiety signal

cholesterol particular steroid molecule; precursor of steroid hormones and bile salts and a component of plasma membranes

cholinergic (koh-lyn-ER-jik) pertaining to acetylcholine; a compound that acts like acetylcholine

chondrocyte (KON-droh-site) cell type that forms new cartilage

chorionic gonadotropin (CG) (kor-ee-ON-ik go-NAD-oh-troh-pin) protein hormone secreted by trophoblastic cells of blastocyst and placenta; maintains secretory activity of corpus luteum during first 3 months of pregnancy

choroid plexus (KOR-oid) highly vascular epithelial structure lining portions of cerebral ventricles; responsible for much of cerebrospinal fluid formation

chromatid (KROME-ah-tid) one of two identical strands of chromatin resulting from DNA duplication during mitosis or meiosis

chromatin (KROM-ih-tin) combination of DNA and nuclear proteins that is the principal component of chromosomes

chromophore retinal component of a photopigment

chromosome highly coiled, condensed form of chromatin formed in cell nucleus during mitosis and meiosis

chronic (KRON-ik) persisting over a long time; *compare* acute

chylomicron (kye-low-MY-kron) small droplet consisting of lipids and protein that is released from intestinal epithelial cells into the lacteals during fat absorption

chyme (kyme) solution of partially digested food in stomach and intestinal lumens

chymotrypsin enzyme secreted by exocrine pancreas; breaks certain peptide bonds in proteins and polypeptides

cilia (SILL-ee-ah) hairlike projections from specialized epithelial cells; sweep back and forth in a synchronized way to propel material along epithelial surface

circadian (sir-KAY-dee-an) recurring once approximately every 24 h

circular muscle smooth-muscle layer in stomach and intestinal walls and having muscle fibers circumferentially oriented around these organs

citric acid cycle *see* Krebs cycle

classical complement pathway antibody-dependent system for activating complement; begins with complement molecule C1

clearance volume of plasma from which a particular substance has been completely removed in a given time

climacteric (kli-MAK-ter-ik) phase involving physical and emotional changes as sexual maturity gives way to cessation of reproductive function

clitoris (KLIT-or-iss) small body of erectile tissue in female external genitalia; homologous to penis

clone genetically identical molecules, cells, or organisms

CO₂ carbon dioxide

coactivation *see* alpha-gamma coactivation

coagulation (coe-ag-you-LAY-shun) blood clotting

cochlea (COCK-lee-ah) inner ear; fluid-filled spiral-shaped compartment that contains cochlear duct

cochlear duct (COCK-lee-er) fluid-filled membranous tube that extends length of inner ear, dividing it into compartments; contains organ of Corti

code word three-nucleotide sequence in DNA that signifies a given amino acid in a synthesized protein

codon (KOH-don) three-base sequence in mRNA that corresponds to given code word in DNA

coenzyme (koh-EN-zime) organic cofactor; generally serves as a carrier that transfers atoms or small molecular fragments from one reaction to another; is not consumed in the reaction and can be reused

coenzyme A (koh-en-zime A) coenzyme that transfers acetyl groups from one reaction to another

cofactor (KOH-fact-or) organic or inorganic substance that binds to specific region of an enzyme and is necessary for the enzyme's activity

collagen (COLL-ah-jen) strong, fibrous protein that functions as extracellular structural element in connective tissue

collecting duct system portion of renal tubules between distal convoluted tubules and renal pelvis; comprises *connecting tubule, cortical collecting duct,* and *medullary collecting duct*

colloid (KAH-loid) large molecule, mainly protein, to which capillaries are relatively impermeable

colon (KOH-lon) large intestine, specifically that part extending from cecum to rectum; *see also* sigmoid colon

colony-stimulating factor (CSF) collective term for several cytokines that stimulate production of neutrophils and monocytes

color blindness defect in color vision often due to absence of one or even two cone photopigments

coma deep, prolonged unconsciousness not fulfilling all the criteria for brain death; thus, there may be spontaneous movement and some intact reflexes

"command" neuron neuron or one of a group of neurons whose activity initiates series of neural events resulting in a voluntary action

commissure (KOM-iss-sure) bundle of nerve fibers linking right- and left-brain halves

common bile duct carries bile from liver and gall bladder to small intestine

compensatory growth type of regeneration present in many organs after tissue damage

competition ability of similar molecules to combine with the same binding site or receptor

complement (KOM-plih-ment) one of a group of plasma proteins that, upon activation, kill microbes directly and facilitate the inflammatory process, including phagocytosis

compliance stretchability; *see also* lung compliance

concentration amount of material per unit volume of solution

concentration gradient gradation in concentration that occurs between two regions having different concentrations

conducting system network of cardiac muscle fibers specialized to conduct electrical activity to different areas of heart

conducting zone air passages that extend from top of trachea to beginning of respiratory bronchioles and have walls too thick for gas exchange between air and blood

conduction heat exchange by transfer of thermal energy during collisions of adjacent molecules

conductor material having low resistance to charge flow

cone one of two retinal receptor types for photic energy; gives rise to color vision

conformation three-dimensional shape of a molecule

congestive-heart failure set of signs and symptoms associated with decreased contractility of heart and engorgement of heart, veins, and capillaries

connective tissue cell cell specialized to form extracellular elements that connect, anchor, and support body structures

conscious experience things of which a person is aware; thoughts, feelings, perceptions, ideas, and reasoning during any state of consciousness

consciousness *see* conscious experience, state of consciousness

contractility (kon-trak-TIL-ity) force of heart contraction that is independent of fiber length

contraction operation of the force-generating process in a muscle

contraction time time between a muscle action potential and development of peak twitch tension by the muscle

contralateral on the opposite side of the body

control system collection of interconnected components that keeps a physical or chemical parameter within predetermined range of values

convection (kon-VEK-shun) process by which air or water next to a warm body is heated by conduction, moves away, and is replaced by colder air that in turn follows the same cycle

convergence (neuronal) many presynaptic neurons synapsing upon one postsynaptic neuron; (of eyes) turning of eyes inward, that is, toward nose, to view near objects

cooperativity interaction between functional binding sites in a multimeric protein

core temperature temperature of inner body

cornea (KOR-nee-ah) transparent structure covering front of eye; forms part of eye's optical system and helps focus an object's image on retina

cornification (kor-nif-ih-KAY-shun) process by which outer epithelial layer is converted to dead, horny cells

coronary pertaining to blood vessels of the heart

coronary blood flow blood flow to heart muscle

corpus callosum (KOR-pus kal-LOW-sum) wide band of nerve fibers connecting the two cerebral hemispheres; a brain commissure

corpus luteum (LOO-tee-um) ovarian structure formed from the follicle after ovulation; secretes estrogen and progesterone

cortex (CORE-tex) outer layer of organ; *see also* adrenal cortex, cerebral cortex; *compare* medulla

cortical association area region of parietal and frontal cerebral cortex; receives input from various sensory types, memory stores, and so on, and performs further perceptual processing

corticobulbar pathway (kor-tih-koh BUL-bar) descending pathway having its neuron cell bodies in cerebral cortex; its axons pass without synapsing to region of brainstem motor neurons

corticospinal pathway descending pathway having its neuron cell bodies in cerebral cortex; its axons pass without synapsing to region of spinal motor neurons; also called the pyramidal tract; *compare* noncorticospinal pathway, corticobulbar pathway

corticosteroid (kor-tih-koh-STEAR-oid) steroid produced by adrenal cortex or drug that resembles one

corticotropin releasing hormone (CRH) (kort-ih-koh-TROH-pin) hypothalamic hormone that stimulates ACTH (corticotropin) secretion by anterior pituitary

cortisol (KORT-ih-sol) main glucocorticoid hormone secreted by adrenal cortex; regulates various aspects of organic metabolism

cotransmitter chemical messenger released with a neurotransmitter from synapse or neuroeffector junction

cotransport form of secondary active transport in which net movement of actively transported substance and "downhill" movement of molecule supplying the energy are in the same direction

countercurrent multiplier system mechanism associated with loops of Henle that creates in renal medulla a region having high interstitial-fluid osmolarity

countertransport form of secondary active transport in which net movement of actively transported molecule is in direction opposite "downhill" movement of molecule supplying the energy

covalent bond (koh-VAY-lent) chemical bond between two atoms in which each atom shares one of its electrons with the other

covalent modulation alteration of a protein's shape and therefore its function by covalent binding of various chemical groups to it

cranial nerve one of 24 peripheral nerves (12 pairs) that join brainstem or forebrain

creatine phosphate (KREE-ah-tin) molecule that transfers phosphate and energy to ADP to generate ATP

creatinine (kree-AT-ih-nin) waste product derived from muscle creatine

creatinine clearance plasma volume from which creatinine is removed by kidneys per unit time; approximates glomerular filtration rate

critical period time during development when a system is most readily influenced by environmental factors, sometimes irreversibly

cross-bridge myosin projection extending from muscle thick filament and capable of exerting force on thin filament, causing the filaments to slide past each other

cross-bridge cycle sequence of events between binding of a cross-bridge to actin, its release, and reattachment

crossed-extensor reflex increased activation of extensor muscles contralateral to a limb flexion

crossing-over process in which segments of maternal and paternal chromosomes exchange with each other during chromosomal pairing in meiosis

crystalloid low-molecular-weight solute

cumulus oophorous (QUUM-you-lus oh-oh-FOR-us) granulosa cells surrounding egg where egg projects into ovarian follicle antrum

current movement of electric charge; in biological systems, this is achieved by ion movement

cutaneous (cue-TAY-nee-us) pertaining to skin

cyclic AMP (cAMP) cyclic 3′,5′-adenosine monophosphate; cyclic nucleotide that serves as a second messenger for many chemical messengers

cyclic AMP-dependent protein kinase (KI-nase) enzyme that is activated by cyclic AMP and then phosphorylates specific proteins, thereby altering their activity; also called protein kinase A

cyclic endoperoxide eicosanoid formed from arachidonic acid by cyclo-oxygenase

cyclic GMP (cGMP) cyclic 3′,5′-guanosine monophosphate; cyclic nucleotide that acts as second messenger in some cells

cyclooxygenase (cy-klo-OX-ah-jen-ase) enzyme that acts on arachidonic acid and leads to production of cyclic endoperoxides, prostaglandins, and thromboxanes

cytochrome (SIGH-toe-krome) one of a series of enzymes that couples energy to ATP formation during oxidative phosphorylation

cytokine (SIGH-toe-kine) general term for protein intercellular messengers that influence cells of the immune system; secreted by macrophages and monocytes (monokine), lymphocytes (lymphokine), and other cells

cytokinesis (sigh-toe-kin-EE-sis) stage of cell division during which cytoplasm divides to form two new cells

cytoplasm (SIGH-toe-plasm) region of cell interior outside the nucleus

cytosine (C) (SIGH-toe-seen) pyrimidine base in DNA and RNA

cytoskeleton cytoplasmic filamentous network associated with cell shape and movement

cytosol (SIGH-toe-sol) intracellular fluid that surrounds cell organelles and nucleus

cytotoxic T cell (sigh-toe-TOX-ik) T lymphocyte that, upon activation by specific antigen, directly attacks a cell bearing that type of antigen and destroys it; major killer of virus-infected and tumor cells

daughter cell one of the two new cells formed when a cell divides

dead space volume of inspired air that cannot be exchanged with blood; *see* *also* anatomic dead space, alveolar dead space, total dead space

deamination (dee-am-in-A-shun) removal of amino (—NH$_2$) group from a molecule

decremental decreasing in amplitude

defecation (deaf-ih-KAY-shun) expulsion of feces from rectum

dehydroepiandrosterone (dee-hydro-epi-andro-stir-OWN) androgen hormone secreted by adrenal cortex

delta wave oscillation on electroencephalogram slower than 4 Hz; associated with sleep

dendrite (DEN-drite) highly branched extension of neuron cell body; receives synaptic input from other neurons

denervation atrophy (AT-row-fee) decrease in size of muscle fiber whose nerve supply is destroyed

dense body cytoplasmic structure to which thin filaments of a smooth-muscle fiber are anchored

deoxyhemoglobin (Hb) (dee-ox-see-HE-mo-glo-bin) hemoglobin not combined with oxygen; reduced hemoglobin

deoxyribonucleic acid (DNA) (dee-ox-see-rye-bow-new-CLAY-ik) nucleic acid that stores and transmits genetic information; consists of double strand of nucleotide subunits that contain deoxyribose

depolarize to change membrane potential value toward zero, so that cell interior becomes less negative than resting level

depression disturbance in mood characterized by pervasive sadness or loss of interest or pleasure

descending limb (of Henle's loop) segment of renal tubule into which proximal tubule drains

descending pathway neural pathways that go from the brain down to the spinal cord

desmosome (DEZ-moe-zome) cell junction that holds two cells together; consists of plasma membranes of adjacent cells linked by fibers yet separated by a 20-nm extracellular space filled with a cementing substance

diacylglycerol (DAG) (die-ace-ill-GLIS-er-all) second messenger that activates protein kinase C, which then phosphorylates a large number of other proteins

dialysis (die-AL-ih-sis) process of altering the concentration of substances in the blood by using concentration differences between plasma and a bathing solution separated by a semipermeable membrane

diaphragm (DIE-ah-fram) dome-shaped skeletal muscle sheet that separates the abdominal and thoracic cavities; principal muscle of respiration

diastole (die-ASS-toe-lee) period of cardiac cycle when ventricles are not contracting

diastolic pressure (die-ah-STAL-ik) minimum blood pressure during cardiac cycle

diencephalon (die-en-SEF-ah-lon) core of anterior part of brain; lies beneath cerebral hemispheres and contains *thalamus* and *hypothalamus*

differentiation (dif-fer-en-she-A-shun) process by which cells acquire specialized structural and functional properties

diffusion (dif-FU-shun) random movement of molecules from one location to another because of random thermal molecular motion; net diffusion always occurs from a region of higher concentration to a region of lower concentration

diffusion equilibrium state during which diffusion fluxes in opposite directions are equal; that is, net flux equals zero.

diffusion potential voltage difference created by net diffusion of ions

digestion process of breaking down large particles and high-molecular-weight substances into small molecules

dihydrotestosterone (die-hi-droh-tes-TOS-ter-own) steroid formed by enzyme-mediated alteration of testosterone; active form of testosterone in certain of its target cells

1,25-dihydroxyvitamin D$_3$ (1-25-die-hi-DROX-ee-vie-tah-min DEE-3) hormone that is formed by kidneys and is active form of vitamin D

2,3-diphosphoglycerate (DPG) (2-3-die-fos-foe-GLISS-er-ate) substance produced by erythrocytes during glycolysis; binds reversibly to hemoglobin, causing it to release oxygen

disaccharide (die-SAK-er-ide) carbohydrate molecule composed of two monosaccharides

disinhibition removal of inhibition from a neuron, thereby allowing its activity to increase

dissociation separation from

distal (DIS-tal) farther from reference point; *compare* proximal

distal convoluted tubule portion of kidney tubule between loop of Henle and collecting duct

disulfide bond R—S—S—R

disuse atrophy (AT-row-fee) decrease in size of muscle fibers that are not used for a long time

diuresis (die-u-REE-sis) increased urine excretion

diuretic (die-u-RET-ik) substance that inhibits fluid reabsorption in renal tubule, thereby increasing urine excretion

diurnal (die-URN-al) daily; occurring in a 24-h cycle

divergence (die-VER-gence) (neuronal) one presynaptic neuron synapsing upon many postsynaptic neurons; (of eyes) turning of eyes outward to view distant objects

dl deciliter; 0.1 L

DNA polymerase enzyme that, during DNA replication, forms new DNA strand by joining together nucleotides already base-paired with an existing DNA strand

dopamine (DOPE-ah-mean) biogenic amine (catecholamine) neurotransmitter and hormone; precursor of epinephrine and norepinephrine

dopamine hypothesis theory that schizophrenia is due to increased activity in dopaminergic pathways

dorsal (DOR-sal) toward or at the back

dorsal root group of afferent nerve fibers that enters dorsal region of spinal cord

double bond two covalent chemical bonds formed between same two atoms; symbolized by =

double helix molecular conformation in which two strands of molecules are coiled around each other; conformation of DNA

down-regulation decrease in number of target-cell receptors for a given messenger in response to a chronic high concentration of that messenger

dual innervation (in-ner-VAY-shun) innervation of an organ or gland by both sympathetic and parasympathetic nerve fibers

duodenum (due-oh-DEE-num) first portion of small intestine (between stomach and jejunum)

eardrum *see* tympanic membrane

ectopic focus (ek-TOP-ik) region of heart other than SA node that assumes role of cardiac pacemaker

ectopic pregnancy implantation and development of a fetus at a site other than the uterus

edema (eh-DEE-mah) accumulation of excess fluid in interstitial space

EEG arousal transformation of EEG pattern from alpha to beta rhythm during increased levels of attention

effector (ee-FECK-tor) cell or cell collection whose change in activity constitutes the response in a control system

effector macrophage *see* activated macrophage

effector protein plasma membrane protein that serves as ion channel or enzyme in signal transduction sequence; intracellular protein altered in response to activated receptor

efferent (EF-er-ent) carrying away from

efferent arteriole renal vessel that conveys blood from glomerulus to peritubular capillaries

efferent neuron neuron that carries information away from CNS

efferent pathway component of reflex arc that transmits information from integrating center to effector

egg female germ cell at any of its stages of development

eicosanoid (eye-KOH-sah-noid) general term for modified fatty acids that are products of arachidonic acid metabolism (cyclic endoperoxides, prostaglandins, thromboxanes, and leukotrienes); function as paracrine or autocrine agents

ejaculation (ee-jak-you-LAY-shun) discharge of semen from penis

ejaculatory duct (ee-JAK-you-lah-tory) continuation of vas deferens after it is joined by seminal vesicle duct; joins urethra in prostate gland

electric charge particle having excess positivity or negativity

electric force force that causes charged particles to move toward regions having an opposite charge and away from regions having a like charge

electric potential (E) (or electric potential difference) *see* potential

electric signal graded potential or action potential

electric synapse (SIN-apse) synapse at which local currents resulting from electrical activity flow between two neurons through gap junctions joining them

electrocardiogram (ECG, EKG) (ee-lek-tro-CARD-ee-oh-gram) record-

ing at skin surface of the electric currents generated by cardiac muscle action potentials

electrochemical difference force determining direction and magnitude of net charge movement; combination of electrical and chemical gradients

electrode (ee-LEK-trode) probe used to stimulate electrically, or record from, the body surface or a tissue

electroencephalogram (EEG) (eh-lek-tro-en-SEF-ah-low-gram) recording of brain electrical activity from scalp

electrogenic pump (elec-tro-JEN-ik) active-transport system that directly separates electric charge, thereby producing a potential difference

electrolyte (ee-LEK-tro-lite) substance that dissociates into ions when in aqueous solution

electromagnetic radiation radiation composed of waves with electrical and magnetic components; includes gamma rays, x-rays, and ultraviolet, light, infrared, and radio waves

electron (ee-LEK-tron) subatomic particle that carries one unit of negative charge

embryo (EM-bree-oh) organism during early stages of development; in human beings, the first 2 months of intrauterine life

emission (ee-MISH-un) movement of male genital duct contents into urethra prior to ejaculation

emotion *see* inner emotion, emotional behavior

emotional behavior outward expression and display of inner emotions

emulsification (eh-mul-sih-fih-KAY-shun) fat-solubilizing process in which large lipid droplets are broken into smaller ones

end-diastolic volume (EDV) (die-ah-STAH-lik) amount of blood in ventricle just prior to systole

endocrine gland (EN-doe-krin) group of cells that secrete into the extracellular space hormones that then diffuse into bloodstream; also called a ductless gland

endocrine system all the body's hormone-secreting glands

endocytosis (en-doe-sigh-TOE-sis) process in which plasma membrane folds into the cell, forming small pockets that pinch off to produce intracellular, membrane-bound vesicles; *see also* phagocytosis

endogenous opioid (en-dodge-en-ous OH-pea-oid) certain neuropeptides—endorphin, dynorphin, and enkephalin

endogenous pyrogen (EP) (en-DAHJ-en-us PIE-row-jen) cytokines (including interleukin 1 and probably interleukin 6 and tumor necrosis factor) that act physiologically in the brain to cause fever

endometrium (en-dough-ME-tree-um) glandular epithelium lining uterine cavity

endoperoxide *see* cyclic endoperoxide

endoplasmic reticulum (en-doe-PLAS-mik ree-TIK-you-lum) cell organelle that consists of interconnected network of membrane-bound branched tubules and flattened sacs; two types are distinguished—*granular*, with ribosomes attached, and *agranular*, which is smooth-surfaced

β-endorphin (en-DOR-fin) opioid peptide secreted by anterior pituitary; synthesized as part of pro-opiomelanocortin and cosecreted with ACTH; *see also* endorphin

endorphin an endogenous opioid; functions as neurotransmitter at synapses activated by opiate drugs and as paracrine agent and hormone

endothelium (en-doe-THEE-lee-um) thin layer of cells that lines heart cavities and blood vessels

endothelium-derived relaxing factor (EDRF) nitric oxide; secreted by vascular endothelium, it relaxes vascular smooth muscle and causes arteriolar dilation

end-plate potential (EPP) depolarization of motor end plate of skeletal-muscle fiber in response to acetylcholine; initiates action potential in muscle plasma membrane

end-product inhibition inhibition of a metabolic pathway by final product's action upon allosteric site on an enzyme (usually the rate-limiting enzyme) in the pathway

end-systolic volume (ESV) (sis-TAH-lik) amount of blood remaining in ventricle after ejection

energy ability to produce change; measured by amount of work performed during a given change

enkephalin (en-KEF-ah-lyn) peptide neurotransmitter at some synapses activated by opiate drugs; an endogenous opioid

enteric nervous system (en-TAIR-ik)

neural network residing in and innervating walls of gastrointestinal tract

enterogastrones (en-ter-oh-GAS-tronez) collective term for hormones that are released by intestinal tract and inhibit stomach activity

enterohepatic circulation (en-ter-oh-hih-PAT-ik) reabsorption of bile salts (and other substances) from intestines, passage to liver (via hepatic portal vein), and secretion back to intestines (via bile)

enterokinase (en-ter-oh-KI-nase) an enzyme in luminal plasma membrane of intestinal epithelial cells; converts pancreatic trypsinogen to trypsin

entrainment (en-TRAIN-ment) adjusting biological rhythm to environmental cues

enzyme (EN-zime) protein catalyst that accelerates specific chemical reactions but does not itself undergo net change during the reaction

enzyme activity measure of the properties of enzyme's active site as altered by allosteric or covalent modulation; affects rate of enzyme-mediated reaction

eosinophil (ee-oh-SIN-oh-fil) polymorphonuclear granulocytic leukocyte whose granules take up red dye eosin; involved in allergic responses and parasite destruction

epididymis (ep-ih-DID-eh-mus) portion of male reproductive duct system located between seminiferous tubules and vas deferens

epiglottis (ep-ig-GLOT-iss) thin cartilage flap that folds down, covering trachea, during swallowing

epinephrine (ep-ih-NEF-rin) hormone secreted by adrenal medulla and involved in regulation of organic metabolism; a biogenic amine (catecholamine) neurotransmitter; also called adrenaline

epiphyseal closure (eh-pif-ih-SEE-al) conversion of epiphyseal growth plate to bone

epiphyseal growth plate actively proliferating cartilage near bone ends; region of bone growth

epiphysis (eh-PIF-ih-sis) end of long bone

epithelial cell (ep-ih-THEE-lee-al) cell at surface of body or hollow organ; specialized to secrete or absorb ions and organic molecules; with other epithelial cells, forms an epithelium

epithelial transport molecule movement from one extracellular compartment across epithelial cells into a second extracellular compartment

epithelium (ep-ih-THEE-lee-um) tissue that covers all body surfaces, lines all body cavities, and forms most glands

equilibrium (ee-qua-LIB-rium) no net change occurs in a system; requires no energy

equilibrium potential voltage gradient across a membrane that is equal in force but opposite in direction to concentration force affecting a given ion species

erection penis or clitoris becoming stiff due to vascular congestion

error signal steady-state difference between level of regulated variable in a control system and set point for that variable

erythrocyte (eh-RITH-row-site) red blood cell

erythropoiesis (eh-rith-row-poy-EE-sis) erythrocyte production

erythropoietin (eh-rith-row-POY-ih-tin) hormone secreted mainly by kidney cells; stimulates red blood cell production; one of the hematopoietic growth factors

esophagus portion of digestive tract that connects throat (pharynx) and stomach

essential amino acid amino acid that cannot be formed by the body at all (or at rate adequate to meet metabolic requirements) and must be obtained from diet

essential element chemical substance that must be present for normal growth and function of the body

essential nutrient substance required for normal or optimal body function but synthesized by the body either not at all or in amounts inadequate to prevent disease

estradiol (es-tra-DIE-ol) steroid hormone of estrogen family; major female sex hormone

estriol (ES-tree-ol) steroid hormone of estrogen family; major estrogen secreted by placenta during pregnancy

estrogen group of steroid hormones that have effects similar to estradiol on female reproductive tract

euphorigen (you-FOR-ih-jen) drug that elevates mood

excitability ability to produce electric signals

excitable membrane membrane capable of producing action potentials

excitation-contraction coupling mechanism in muscle fibers linking plasma membrane depolarization with cross-bridge force generation

excitatory postsynaptic potential (EPSP) (post-sin-NAP-tic) depolarizing graded potential in postsynaptic neuron in response to activation of excitatory synapse

excitatory synapse (SIN-apse) synapse that, when activated, increases likelihood that postsynaptic neuron will undergo action potentials or increases frequency of existing action potentials

excretion appearance of a substance in urine or feces

exocrine gland (EX-oh-krin) cluster of epithelial cells specialized for secretion and having ducts that lead to an epithelial surface

exocytosis (ex-oh-sigh-TOE-sis) process in which intracellular vesicle fuses with plasma membrane, the vesicle opens, and its contents are liberated into the extracellular fluid

exon (EX-on) gene region containing code words for an amino acid sequence in a protein

expiration (ex-pur-A-shun) movement of air out of lungs

expiratory reserve volume (ex-PIE-ruh-tor-ee) volume of air exhaled by maximal contraction of expiratory muscles after normal expiration

extension straightening a joint

extensor muscle muscle whose activity straightens a joint

external anal sphincter ring of skeletal muscle around lower end of rectum

external environment environment surrounding external surfaces of an organism

external genitalia (jen-ih-TAH-lee-ah) (female) mons pubis, labia majora and minora, clitoris, vestibule of the vagina, and vestibular glands; (male) penis and scrotum

external work movement of external objects by skeletal muscle contraction

extracellular fluid fluid outside cell; interstitial fluid and plasma

extrafusal fiber primary muscle fiber in skeletal muscle, as opposed to modified (intrafusal) fibers in muscle spindle; also called skeletomotor fiber

extrapyramidal system *see* multineuronal pathway

extrinsic (ex-TRIN-sik) coming from outside

extrinsic clotting pathway formation of fibrin clots by pathway using tissue factor on cells in interstitium; once activated, it also recruits the intrinsic clotting pathway below factor XII

facilitated diffusion (fah-SIL-ih-tay-ted) system using a transporter to move molecules from high to low concentration across a membrane; energy not required

facilitation (fah-sil-ih-TAY-shun) general depolarization of a neuron when excitatory synaptic input exceeds inhibitory input

factor XII initial factor in complete intrinsic pathway sequence of reactions that results in blood clotting

factor XIIIa activated plasma protein that catalyzes cross-link formation between fibrin molecules to strengthen blood clot

farsighted vision defect that occurs because eyeball is too short for the lens so that near objects are focused behind the retina

fast fiber skeletal-muscle fiber that contains myosin having high ATPase activity

fat mobilization increased breakdown of triacylglycerols and release of glycerol and fatty acids into blood

fat-soluble vitamin a vitamin that is soluble in nonpolar solvents and insoluble in water; vitamin A, D, E, or K

fatty acid carbon chain with carboxyl group at one end through which chain can be linked to glycerol to form triacylglycerol; *see also* polyunsaturated fatty acid, saturated fatty acid, unsaturated fatty acid

Fc portion "stem" part of antibody

feces (FEE-sees) material expelled from large intestine during defecation

feedback characteristic of control systems in which output response influences input to system; *see also* negative feedback, positive feedback

feedforward aspect of some control systems that allows system to anticipate changes in a regulated variable

ferritin (FAIR-ih-tin) iron-binding protein that stores iron in body

fertilization union of sperm and egg

fetus (FEE-tus) period of human development from second month of intrauterine life until birth

fever increased body temperature due to setting of "thermostat" of temperature-regulating mechanisms at higher-than-normal level

fiber *see* nerve fiber, muscle fiber

fibrillation (fib-rih-LAY-shun) rapid, unsynchronized cardiac muscle contractions that prevent effective pumping of blood

fibrin (FYE-brin) protein polymer resulting from enzymatic cleavage of fibrinogen; can turn blood into gel (clot)

fibrinogen (fye-BRIN-oh-jen) plasma protein precursor of fibrin

fibrinolytic system (fye-brin-oh-LIT-ik) cascade of plasma enzymes that breaks down clots; also called thrombolytic system

fight-or-flight response activation of sympathetic nervous system during stress

filtered load amount of any substance filtered from renal glomerular capillaries into Bowman's capsule

filtration movement of essentially protein-free plasma out across capillary walls due to a pressure gradient across the wall

first messenger extracellular chemical messenger or electric message that arrives at a cell's plasma membrane

flatus (FLAY-tus) intestinal gas or gas expelled through anus

flavine adenine dinucleotide (FAD) coenzyme derived from the B vitamin riboflavin; transfers hydrogen from one substrate to another

flex (FLEKS) bend a joint

flexion reflex bending of those joints that withdraw an injured part away from a painful stimulus

flow autoregulation ability of individual arteries and arterioles to alter their resistance in response to changing blood pressure so that relatively constant blood flow is maintained

fluid mosaic model (mo-ZAY-ik) cell membranes consist of proteins embedded in bimolecular lipid that has the physical properties of a fluid, allowing membrane proteins to move laterally within it

flux movement of a substance across a surface in a unit of time; *see also* net flux

folic acid (FOE-lik) vitamin of B-complex group; essential for nucleotide formation

follicle *see* ovarian folllicle, primary follicle

follicle-stimulating hormone (FSH) protein hormone secreted by anterior pituitary in males and females; a gonadotropin

follicular phase (foe-LIK-you-lar) that portion of menstrual cycle during which follicle and egg develop to maturity prior to ovulation

forced vital capacity (FVC) maximal expiration as fast as possible following maximal inspiration

forebrain large, anterior brain subdivision consisting of right and left cerebral hemispheres (the cerebrum) and diencephalon

fovea centralis (FO-vee-ah) area near center of retina where cones are most concentrated; gives rise to most acute vision

free-running rhythm cyclical activity driven by biological clock in absence of environmental cues

frequency number of times an event occurs per unit time

frontal lobe region of anterior cerebral cortex where motor cortex, Broca's speech center, and some association cortex are located

fructose (FRUK-tose) five-carbon sugar; present in sucrose (table sugar)

functional residual capacity lung volume after relaxed expiration

functional site binding site on allosteric protein which, when activated, carries out protein's physiological function; also called active site

functional unit organ subunit; all subunits of a given organ have similar structural and functional properties

fused-vesicle channel endocytotic or exocytotic vesicles that have fused to form a continuous water-filled channel through capillary endothelial cell

G protein family of regulatory membrane proteins that in response to receptor activation bind guanosine nucleotides and interact with membrane ion channels or enzymes; for the G proteins that regulate adenylyl cyclase, subscript "i" (G_i protein) denotes inhibitory action, and "s" (G_s protein) denotes stimulatory action

galactose (gah-LAK-tose) six-carbon monosaccharide; present in lactose (milk sugar)

gallbladder small sac under the liver; concentrates bile and stores it between meals; contraction of gallbladder ejects bile into small intestine

gallstone precipitate of cholesterol (and

occasionally other substances) in gallbladder or common bile duct

gamete (GAM-eat) germ cell or reproductive cell; sperm in male and egg in female

gametogenesis (gam-ee-toe-JEN-ih-sis) gamete production

gamma-aminobutyric acid (GABA) major inhibitory neurotransmitter in CNS

gamma globulin immunoglobulin G (IgG), most abundant class of plasma antibodies

gamma interferon *see* interferon

gamma motor neuron small motor neuron that controls intrafusal muscle fibers

ganglion (GANG-glee-on) (pl. ganglia); generally reserved for cluster of neuron cell bodies outside CNS

ganglion cell retinal neuron that is postsynaptic to bipolar cells; axons of ganglion cells form optic nerve

gap junction protein channels linking cytoplasm of adjacent cells; allows ions and small molecules to flow between cytoplasms of the cells

gastric (GAS-trik) pertaining to the stomach

gastric phase (of gastrointestinal control) initiation of neural and hormonal gastrointestinal reflexes by stimulation of stomach wall

gastrin (GAS-trin) peptide hormone secreted by antral region of stomach; stimulates gastric acid secretion

gastroileal reflex (gas-tro-ILL-ee-al) reflex increase in contractions of ileum during gastric emptying

gastrointestinal system (gas-tro-in-TES-tin-al) gastrointestinal tract plus salivary glands, liver, gallbladder, and pancreas

gastrointestinal tract mouth, pharynx, esophagus, stomach, and small and large intestines

gating opening or closing ion channels

gene unit of hereditary information; portion of DNA containing information required to determine a protein's amino acid sequence

gene cloning process of forming identical DNA sequences using genetic engineering techniques

genetic code three-nucleotide sequence in a gene; indicates a particular amino acid in the protein specified by that gene

genome complete set of an organism's genes

germ cell cell that gives rise to male or female gametes (sperm and eggs)

GI gastrointestinal

gland group of epithelial cells specialized for secretion; *see also* endocrine gland, exocrine gland

glial cell (GLEE-al) nonneuronal cell in CNS; helps regulate extracellular environment of CNS; also called neuroglial cell

globin (GLOW-bin) polypeptide chains of hemoglobin molecule

globulin (GLOB-you-lin) one of a family of proteins found in blood plasma

glomerular filtration (glow-MER-you-lar) bulk flow of an essentially protein-free plasma from renal glomerular capillaries into Bowman's capsule

glomerular filtration rate (GFR) volume of fluid filtered from renal glomerular capillaries into Bowman's capsule per unit time

glomerulus (glow-MER-you-lus) tufts of glomerular capillaries at beginning of kidney nephrons

glottis opening between vocal cords and surrounding area through which air passes

glucagon (GLUE-kah-gahn) peptide hormone secreted by alpha cells of pancreatic islets of Langerhans; leads to rise in plasma glucose

glucocorticoid (glue-koh-KORT-ih-coid) steroid hormone produced by adrenal cortex and having major effects on nutrient metabolism

gluconeogenesis (glue-koh-nee-oh-JEN-ih-sis) formation of glucose by the liver or kidneys from pyruvate, lactate, glycerol, or amino acids

glucose major monosaccharide (carbohydrate) in the body; a six-carbon sugar, $C_6H_{12}O_6$; also called blood sugar

glucose-counterregulatory control neural or hormonal factor that opposes insulin's actions; glucagon, epinephrine and sympathetic nerves to liver and adipose tissue, cortisol, and growth hormone

glucose-dependent insulinotropic hormone (GIP) intestinal hormone; stimulates insulin secretion in response to glucose and fat in small intestine; also called gastric inhibitory peptide

glucose 6-phosphate (FOS-fate) first intermediate in glycolytic pathway

glucose sparing switch from glucose to

fat utilization by most cells during postabsorptive state

glutamate (GLU-tah-mate) anion formed from the amino acid glutamic acid; a major excitatory CNS neurotransmitter

glutamine (GLUE-tah-mean) glutamate having an extra NH_3

glycerol (GLIS-er-ol) three-carbon carbohydrate; forms backbone of triacylglycerol

glycine (GLY-seen) an amino acid; a neurotransmitter at some inhibitory synapses in CNS

glycogen (GLY-koh-jen) highly branched polysaccharide composed of glucose subunits; major carbohydrate storage form in body

glycogenolysis (gly-koh-jen-NOL-ih-sis) glycogen breakdown to glucose

glycolysis (gly-KAHL-ih-sis) metabolic pathway that breaks down glucose to two molecules of pyruvate (aerobically) or two molecules of lactate (anaerobically)

glycolytic fiber skeletal-muscle fiber that has a high concentration of glycolytic enzymes and large glycogen stores; white muscle fiber

glycoprotein protein containing covalently linked carbohydrates

Golgi apparatus (GOAL-gee) cell organelle consisting of membranes and vesicles; usually near nucleus; processes newly synthesized proteins for secretion and distribution to other organelles

Golgi tendon organ tension-sensitive mechanoreceptor ending of afferent nerve fiber; wrapped around collagen bundles in tendon

gonad (GO-nad) gamete-producing reproductive organ, that is, testes in male and ovaries in female

gonadotropic hormone (go-nad-oh-TROH-pik) hormone secreted by anterior pituitary; controls gonadal function; FSH or LH

gonadotropin releasing hormone (GnRH) hypothalamic hormone that stimulates LH and FSH secretion by anterior pituitary in males and females

graded potential membrane potential change of variable amplitude and duration that is conducted decrementally; has no threshold or refractory period

gradient (GRAY-dee-ent) continuous increase or decrease of a variable over distance

gram atomic mass amount of element

in grams equal to the numerical value of its atomic weight

granulosa cell (gran-you-LOW-sah) cell that surrounds egg and antrum in ovarian follicle; secretes estrogen and inhibin and has many other functions

gray matter area of brain and spinal cord that appears gray in unstained specimens and consists mainly of cell bodies and unmyelinated portions of nerve fibers

ground substance material surrounding cells and fibers in connective tissue

growth cone specialized enlargement at tip of growing neuron process

growth factor one of a group of peptides that is highly effective in stimulating cell division and/or differentiation of certain cell types

growth hormone (GH) peptide hormone secreted by anterior pituitary; stimulates insulin-like growth factor I release; enhances body growth by stimulating protein synthesis

growth hormone release inhibiting hormone see somatostatin

growth hormone releasing hormone (GHRH) hypothalamic hormone that stimulates growth hormone secretion by anterior pituitary

growth-inhibiting factor one of a group of peptides that modulate growth by inhibiting cell division in specific tissues

guanine (G) (GWA-neen) purine base of DNA and RNA

guanosine triphosphate (GTP) (GWA-no-seen tri-FOS-fate) energy-transporting molecule similar to ATP except that it contains the base guanine rather than adenine

H zone one of transverse bands making up striated pattern of cardiac and skeletal muscle; light region that bisects A band

habituation (hah-bit-you-A-shun) reversible decrease in response strength upon repeatedly administered stimulation

hair cell mechanoreceptor in organ of Corti and vestibular apparatus

HCO_3^- bicarbonate

H_2CO_3 carbonic acid

heart attack damage to or death of cardiac muscle; also called myocardial infarction

heart failure see congestive heart failure

heart murmur abnormal heart sound caused by turbulent blood flow through narrowed or leaky valves or through hole in interventricular or interatrial septum

heart rate number of heart contractions per minute

heart sound noise that results from vibrations due to closure of atrioventricular valves (first heart sound) or pulmonary and aortic valves (second heart sound)

heartburn pain that seems to occur in region of heart but is due to pain receptors in esophageal wall stimulated by acid refluxed from stomach

heat exhaustion state of collapse due to hypotension because of plasma volume depletion, secondary to sweating, and extreme skin blood-vessel dilation; thermoregulatory centers still function

heat stroke positive-feedback situation in which heat gain exceeds heat loss, which causes body temperature to become so high that brain thermoregulatory centers do not function, allowing temperature to rise even higher

Heimlich maneuver (HEIM-lik) forceful elevation of diaphragm produced by rescuer's fist against choking victim's abdomen; causes sudden sharp increase in alveolar pressure to expel obstructing material that is causing choking

helper T cell T cell that, via secreted cytokines, enhances the activation of B cells and cytotoxic T cells; can also activate NK cells and macrophages; binds antigen associated with MHC class II proteins

hematocrit (he-MAT-oh-krit) percentage of total blood volume occupied by blood cells

heme (heem) iron-containing organic molecule bound to each of the four polypeptide chains of hemoglobin or to cytochromes

hemodialysis see dialysis

hemoglobin (HE-mo-glo-bin) protein composed of four polypeptide chains and heme; located in erythrocytes and transports most blood oxygen

hemoglobin saturation percent of hemoglobin molecules combined with oxygen

hemorrhage (HEM-or-age) bleeding

hemostasis (he-mo-stay-sis) stopping blood loss from a damaged vessel

Henle's loop see loop of Henle

heparin (HEP-ah-rin) anticlotting agent found on endothelial-cell surfaces; binds antithrombin III to tissues; an anticoagulant drug

hepatic (hih-PAT-ik) pertaining to the liver

hepatic portal vein vein that conveys blood from capillaries in the intestines and portions of the stomach and pancreas to capillaries in the liver

hertz (Hz) cycles per second; measure used for wave frequencies

heterozygous (het-er-oh-ZIE-gus) condition of having maternal and paternal copies of a gene with slightly different nucleotide sequences; compare homozygous

high-density lipoprotein lipid-protein aggregate having low proportion of lipid; promotes removal of cholesterol from cells

hippocampus (hip-oh-KAM-pus) portion of limbic system associated with learning

histamine (HISS-tah-mean) inflammatory chemical messenger secreted mainly by mast cells; monoamine neurotransmitter

histotoxic hypoxia (hiss-toe-TOKS-ik hi-POK-see-ah) hypoxia in which cell cannot utilize oxygen because a toxic agent has interfered with its metabolic machinery

homeostasis (home-ee-oh-STAY-sis) relatively stable condition of extracellular fluid that results from regulatory system actions

homeostatic control system (home-ee-oh-STAT-ik) interconnected components that keep a physical or chemical parameter of internal environment relatively constant

homeothermic (home-ee-oh-THERM-ik) capable of maintaining body temperature within very narrow limits

homologous (ho-MAHL-oh-gus) corresponding in origin, structure, and position

homozygous (hoe-moe-ZIE-gus) condition of having maternal and paternal copies of a gene with identical nucleotide sequences; compare heterozygous

hormone chemical messenger synthesized by specific endocrine gland in response to certain stimuli and secreted into the blood, which carries it to target cells

hydrochloric acid (hi-dro-CLOR-ik) HCl; strong acid secreted into stomach lumen by parietal cells

hydrogen bond weak chemical bond

between two molecules or parts of the same molecule, in which negative region of one polarized substance is electrostatically attracted to a positively polarized hydrogen atom in the other

hydrogen ion (EYE-on) H^+; single proton; H^+ concentration of a solution determines its acidity

hydrogen peroxide H_2O_2; chemical produced by phagosome and highly destructive to the macromolecules within it

hydrolysis (hi-DRAHL-ih-sis) breaking of chemical bond with addition of elements of water (—H and —OH) to the products formed; also called hydrolytic reaction

hydrophilic (hi-dro-FILL-ik) attracted to, and easily dissolved in, water

hydrophobic (hi-dro-FOE-bik) not attracted to, and insoluble in, water

hydrostatic pressure (hi-dro-STAT-ik) pressure exerted by fluid

hydroxyl group (hi-DROX-il) —OH

hyper- increased

hypercalcemia increased plasma calcium

hypercapnea increased arterial P_{CO_2}

hyperemia (hi-per-EE-me-ah) increased blood flow; *see also* active hyperemia

hyperosmotic (hi-per-oz-MAH-tik) having total solute concentration greater than plasma

hyperpolarize to change membrane potential so cell interior becomes more negative than its resting state

hypertension chronically increased arterial blood pressure

hyperthermia increased body temperature regardless of cause

hypertonia (hi-per-TOE-nee-ah) abnormally high muscle tone

hypertonic (hi-per-TAH-nik) solution containing a higher concentration of effectively membrane-impermeable solute particles than cells contain

hypertrophy (hi-PER-tro-fee) enlargement of a tissue or organ due to increased cell size rather than increased cell number

hyperventilation increased ventilation without similar increase in CO_2 production

hypo- too little

hypocalcemic tetany (hi-po-kal-SEE-mik TET-ah-nee) skeletal-muscle spasms due to a low extracellular calcium concentration

hypoglycemia (hi-po-glye-SEE-me-ah) low blood sugar (glucose) concentration

hypoosmotic (hi-po-oz-MAH-tik) having total solute concentration less than that of plasma

hypophysiotropic hormone (hi-poe-fiz-ee-oh-TRO-pic) hormone secreted by hypothalamus that controls secretion of an anterior pituitary hormone

hypotension low blood pressure

hypothalamic releasing hormone (hi-po-thah-LAM-ik) *see* hypophysiotropic hormone

hypothalamus (hi-po-THAL-ah-mus) brain region below thalamus; responsible for integration of many basic behavioral patterns involving correlation of neural and endocrine functions, especially those concerned with regulation of internal environment

hypotonia (hi-po-TOE-nee-ah) abnormally low muscle tone

hypotonic (hi-po-TAH-nik) solution containing a lower concentration of effectively nonpenetrating solute particles than cells contain

hypoventilation decrease in ventilation without similar decrease in O_2 consumption or CO_2 production

hypoxia (hi-POK-see-ah) deficiency of oxygen at tissue level; *see also* hypoxic hypoxia, anemic hypoxia, ischemic hypoxia, histotoxic hypoxia

hypoxic hypoxia (hi-POK-sik hi-POK-see-ah) hypoxia due to decreased arterial P_{O_2}; also called hypoxemia

I band one of transverse bands making up repeating striations of cardiac and skeletal muscle; located between A bands of adjacent sarcomeres and bisected by Z line

IgA class of antibodies secreted by, and acting locally in, lining of gastrointestinal, respiratory, and urinary tracts

IgD class of antibodies whose function is unknown

IgE class of antibodies that mediate immediate hypersensitivity and resistence to parasites

IgG gamma globulin; most abundant class of antibodies

IgM class of antibodies that, along with IgG, provide major specific humoral immunity against bacteria and viruses

ileocecal sphincter (ill-ee-oh-SEE-kal) ring of smooth muscle separating small and large intestines, that is, ileum and cecum

ileum (ILL-ee-um) final, longest segment of small intestine

immune response *see* nonspecific immune response, specific immune response

immune surveillance (sir-VAY-lence) recognition and destruction of cancer cells that arise in body

immunity physiological mechanisms that allow body to recognize materials as foreign or abnormal and to neutralize or eliminate them; *see also* active immunity, passive immunity

immunoglobulin (Ig) (im-mun-oh-GLOB-you-lin) synonym for antibody; five classes are IgG, IgA, IgD, IgM, and IgE

implantation (im-plan-TAY-shun) event during which fertilized egg becomes embedded in uterine wall

inferior vena cava (VEE-nah CAVE-ah) large vein that carries blood from lower half of body to right atrium of heart

inflammation (in-flah-MAY-shun) local response to injury or infection characterized by local swelling, pain, heat, and redness

inhibin (in-HIB-in) protein hormone secreted by seminiferous-tubule Sertoli cells and ovarian granulosa cells; inhibits FSH secretion

inhibitory postsynaptic potential (IPSP) hyperpolarizing graded potential that arises in postsynaptic neuron in response to activation of inhibitory synaptic endings upon it

inhibitory synapse (SIN-apse) synapse that, when activated, decreases likelihood that postsynaptic neuron will fire an action potential (or decreases frequency of existing action potentials)

initial segment first portion of axon plus part of cell body where axon joins

inner ear cochlea; contains organ of Corti

inner emotion emotional feelings that are entirely within a person

innervate to supply with nerves

inorganic pertaining to substances that do not contain carbon; *compare* organic

inorganic phosphate (P_i) (FOS-fate) $H_2PO_4^-$, HPO_4^{2-}, or PO_4^{3-}

inositol trisphosphate (IP_3) (in-OS-ih-tol tris-FOS-fate) second messenger that causes calcium release from endoplasmic reticulum into cytosol

insensible water loss water loss of which a person is unaware, that is, loss by evaporation from skin and respiratory-passage lining

inspiration air movement from atmosphere into lungs

inspiratory muscles those muscles whose contraction contributes to inspiration

inspiratory neuron neuron in medulla oblongata that fires in synchrony with inspiration and ceases firing during expiration

inspiratory reserve volume maximal air volume that can be inspired above resting tidal volume

insulin (IN-suh-lin) peptide hormone secreted by B cells of pancreatic islets of Langerhans; has metabolic and growth-promoting effects; stimulates glucose and amino acid uptake by most cells and stimulates protein, fat, and glycogen synthesis

insulin-like growth factor one of a group of peptides that have growth-promoting effects

insulin-like growth factor I (IGF-I) insulin-like growth factor that mediates mitosis-stimulating effect of growth hormone on bone and possibly other tissues; also known as somatomedin C

integral protein protein embedded in membrane lipid layer; may span entire membrane or be located at only one side

integrating center cells that receive one or more signals, compare them to a physiological set point, and send out appropriate response; also called an integrator

intercalated disk (in-TER-kah-lay-ted) thickened end of cardiac muscle cell where cell is connected to adjacent cell

intercellular cleft a narrow, water-filled space between capillary endothelial cells

intercellular fluid fluid that lies between cells; also called interstitial fluid

intercostal muscle (in-ter-KOS-tal) skeletal muscle that lies between ribs and whose contraction causes rib cage movement during breathing

interferon (in-ter-FEAR-on) family of proteins that nonspecifically inhibit viral replication inside host cells; gamma interferon also activates macrophages and enhances killing ability of cytotoxic T cells and NK cells

interleukin (in-ter-LEW-kin) a family of cytokines with many effects on immune responses and host defenses

interleukin 1 (IL-1) cytokine secreted by macrophages and other cells that activates helper T cells, exerts many inflammatory effects, and mediates many of the systemic acute phase responses, including fever

interleukin 2 (IL-2) cytokine secreted by activated helper T cells that causes antigen-activated helper T, cytotoxic T, and NK cells to proliferate and increase their activity

interleukin 6 (IL-6) cytokine secreted by macrophages and other cells that increases plasma cell formation and activity; also mediates some of the acute phase responses, including probably fever

internal anal sphincter smooth-muscle ring around lower end of rectum

internal energy energy present in intramolecular bonds of organic molecules

internal environment extracellular fluid (interstitial fluid and plasma)

internal genitalia (jen-ih-TALE-ee-ah) (female) ovaries, uterine tubes, uterus, and vagina

internal urethral sphincter (you-REETH-ral) part of smooth muscle of urinary bladder wall that opens and closes the bladder outlet

internal work energy-requiring activities in body; *see also* work; *compare* external work

interneuron neuron whose cell body and axon lie entirely in CNS

interphase period of cell division cycle between end of one division and visible signs of beginning of next

interstitial cell stimulating hormone (ICSH) *see* luteinizing hormone

interstitial fluid extracellular fluid surrounding tissue cells; excludes plasma, which is extracellular fluid surrounding blood cells

interstitium (in-ter-STISH-um) interstitial space; fluid-filled space between tissue cells

interventricular septum (in-ter-ven-TRIK-you-lar) partition in heart separating right and left ventricles

intestinal phase (of gastrointestinal control) initiation of neural and hormonal gastrointestinal reflexes by stimulation of intestinal-tract walls

intestino-intestinal reflex reflex cessation of contractile activity of intestines in response to various stimuli in intestine

intracellular fluid fluid in cells; cytosol plus fluid in cell organelles, including nucleus

intrafusal fiber modified skeletal-muscle fiber in muscle spindle; also called spindle fiber

intrapleural fluid (in-tra-PLUR-al) thin fluid film in thoracic cavity between pleura lining the inner wall of thoracic cage and pleura covering lungs

intrapleural pressure pressure in pleural space; also called intrathoracic pressure

intrarenal baroreceptor pressure-sensitive juxtaglomerular cells of afferent arterioles, which respond to decreased renal arterial pressure by secreting renin

intrathoracic pressure *see* intrapleural pressure

intrinsic (in-trin-sik) situated entirely within a part

intrinsic clotting pathway intravascular sequence of fibrin clot formation initiated by factor XII or, more usually, by the initial thrombin generated by the extrinsic clotting pathway

intrinsic factor glycoprotein secreted by stomach epithelium and necessary for absorption of vitamin B_{12} in the ileum

intron (IN-trahn) region of noncoding base sequences in gene

inversely proportional relationship in which, as one factor increases by a given amount, the other decreases by a given amount

ion (EYE-on) atom or small molecule containing unequal number of electrons and protons and therefore carrying a net positive or negative electric charge

ionic bond (eye-ON-ik) strong electrical attraction between two oppositely charged ions

ionization (eye-on-ih-ZAY-shun) process of removing electrons from or adding them to an atom or small molecule to form an ion

ipsilateral (ip-sih-LAT-er-al) on the same side of the body

iris ringlike structure surrounding pupil of eye

irreversible reaction chemical reaction that releases large quantities of energy and results in almost all the reactant molecules being converted to product; *compare* reversible reaction

ischemia (iss-KEY-me-ah) reduced blood supply

ischemic hypoxia (iss-KEY-mik hi-POK-see-ah) too little blood flow to tissues to deliver adequate amounts of oxygen

islet of Langerhans (EYE-let of LAN-ger-hans) cluster of pancreatic endocrine cells; distinct islet cells secrete insulin, glucagon, somatostatin, and pancreatic polypeptide

isometric contraction (ice-so-MET-rik) contraction of muscle under conditions in which it develops tension but does not change length

isoosmotic (ice-oh-oz-MAH-tik) having the same osmotic pressure, thus the same solute particle concentration

isotonic (ice-oh-TAH-nik) containing the same number of effectively nonpenetrating solute particles as cells; *see also* isotonic contraction

isotonic contraction contraction of muscle under conditions in which load on muscle remains constant but muscle shortens

isovolumetric ventricular contraction (iso-vol-you-MET-rik) early phase of systole when atrioventricular and aortic valves are closed

isovolumetric ventricular relaxation early phase of diastole when atrioventricular and aortic valves are closed

isozyme (EYE-so-zime) one of two or more enzymes that catalyze the same reaction but have slightly different structures and therefore slightly different affinities for substrate

jejunum (je-JEW-num) middle segment of small intestine

juxtaglomerular apparatus (JGA) (juxtah-glow-MER-you-lar) renal structure consisting of macula densa and juxtaglomerular cells; site of renin secretion and sensors for renin secretion and control of glomerular filtration rate

keto acid (KEY-toe) molecule formed from amino acid metabolism and containing carbonyl (—CO—) and carboxyl (—COOH) groups

ketone (KEY-tone) product of fatty acid metabolism that accumulates in blood during starvation and in untreated diabetes mellitus; acetoacetic acid, acetone, or β-hydroxybutyric acid; also called ketone body

kilocalorie (kcal) (KILL-oh-kal-ah-ree) amount of heat required to heat 1 L water 1°C; calorie used in nutrition; also called Calorie and large calorie

kinase (KIE-nase) enzyme that transfers a phosphate (usually from ATP) to another molecule

kinesthesia (kin-ess-THEE-zee-ah) sense of movement derived from movement at a joint

kinin (KI-nin) peptide split from kininogen in inflamed area; facilitates vascular changes associated with inflammation; may also stimulate pain receptors

kininogen (ki-NIN-og-jen) plasma protein from which kinins are generated

Krebs cycle mitochondrial metabolic pathway that utilizes fragments derived from carbohydrate, protein, and fat breakdown and produces carbon dioxide, hydrogen, and small amounts of ATP; also called tricarboxylic acid cycle or citric acid cycle

L-dopa dopamine precursor; administered to patients with Parkinson's disease

lactase (LAK-tase) small-intestine enzyme that breaks down lactose (milk sugar) into glucose and galactose

lactate *see* lactic acid

lactation (lak-TAY-shun) production and secretion of milk by mammary glands

lacteal (lak-TEAL) blind-ended lymph vessel in center of each intestinal villus

lactic acid (LAK-tic) three-carbon molecule formed by glycolytic pathway in absence of oxygen; dissociates to form lactate and hydrogen ions

lactose (LAK-tose) disaccharide composed of glucose and galactose; also called milk sugar

lactose intolerance inability to digest lactose because of lack of intestinal lactase; leads to accumulation of large amounts of gas and fluid in large intestine, which causes pain and diarrhea

larynx (LAIR-inks) part of air passageway between pharynx and trachea; contains the vocal cords

latent period (LAY-tent) period lasting several milliseconds between action potential initiation in a muscle fiber and beginning of mechanical activity

lateral position farther from the midline

lateral inhibition method of refining sensory information in afferent neurons and ascending pathways whereby fibers inhibit each other, the most active fibers causing the greatest inhibition of adjacent fibers

lateral sac enlarged region at end of

each sarcoplasmic reticulum segment; adjacent to transverse tubule

law of mass action maxim that an increase in reactant concentration causes a chemical reaction to proceed in direction of product formation; the opposite occurs with decreased reactant concentration

lecithin (LESS-ih-thin) a phospholipid

lengthening contraction contraction as a load pulls a muscle to a longer length despite opposing forces generated by the active cross-bridges

lens adjustable part of eye's optical system, which helps focus object's image on retina

leukocyte (LEW-ko-site) white blood cell

leukotriene (LOO-koe-treen) type of eicosanoid that is generated by lipoxygenase pathway

Leydig cell (LIE-dig) testosterone-secreting endocrine cell that lies between seminiferous tubules of testes; also called interstitial cell

LH surge large rise in luteinizing-hormone secretion by anterior pituitary about day 14 of menstrual cycle

ligand (LIE-gand) any molecule or ion that binds to protein surface by noncovalent bonds

limbic system (LIM-bik) interconnected brain structures in cerebrum; involved with emotions and learning

lipase (LIE-pase) *see* pancreatic lipase, lipoprotein lipase

lipid (LIP-id) molecule composed primarily of carbon and hydrogen and characterized by insolubility in water

lipid bilayer a sheet consisting of two layers of phospholipid

lipolysis (lie-POL-ih-sis) triacylglycerol breakdown

lipoprotein (lip-oh-PRO-teen) lipid aggregate partially coated by protein; involved in lipid transport in blood

lipoprotein lipase capillary endothelial enzyme that hydrolyzes triacylglycerol to monoglyceride and fatty acids

lipoxygenase (lie-POX-ih-jen-ase) enzyme that acts on arachidonic acid and leads to leukotriene formation

load force acting on muscle due to weight of an object

local current flow movement of positive ions toward more negative membrane region and simultaneous movement of negative ions in opposite direction

local homeostatic response (home-ee-oh-STAH-tik) response acting in immediate vicinity of a stimulus, without nerves or hormones, and having net effect of counteracting stimulus

local potential small, graded potential difference between two points that is conducted decrementally and has no threshold or refractory period

locus coeruleus (sih-RUE-lee-us) brainstem nucleus that projects to many brain parts and is implicated in directed attention

long-loop negative feedback inhibition of anterior pituitary and/or hypothalamus by hormone secreted by another endocrine gland

long-term memory memory that has a relatively long lifespan

long-term potentiation process by which certain synapses undergo long-lasting increase in effectiveness when heavily used

loop of Henle (HEN-lee) hairpin-like segment of kidney nephron with *descending* and *ascending limbs;* situated between proximal and distal tubules

low-density lipoprotein (lip-oh-PRO-teen) protein-lipid aggregate that is major carrier of plasma cholesterol to cells

lower esophageal sphincter smooth muscle of lowest 4 cm of esophagus; closes off esophageal opening into the stomach

lumen (LOO-men) space in hollow tube or organ

luminal (LOO-min-ul) pertaining to lumen

luminal membrane (LOO-min-al) portion of plasma membrane facing the lumen; also called apical or mucosal membrane

lung compliance (come-PLY-ance) change in lung volume caused by given change in transpulmonary pressure; the greater the lung compliance, the more stretchable the lung wall

luteal phase (LOO-tee-al) last half of menstrual cycle; corpus luteum is active ovarian structure

luteinizing hormone (LH) (LOO-tea-en-iz-ing) peptide hormone secreted by anterior pituitary; gonadotropin whose sudden increase in females at mid-menstrual cycle initiates ovulation; also called interstitial cell stimulating hormone (ICSH) in male

lymph (limf) fluid in lymphatic vessels

lymph node small organ, containing lymphocytes, located along lymph vessel; a site of lymphocyte formation and storage and initiation of specific immune responses

lymphatic system (lim-FAT-ik) network of vessels that conveys lymph from tissues to blood, and lymph nodes along these vessels

lymphocyte (LIMF-oh-site) type of leukocyte that is responsible for specific immune defenses; B cells, T cells, and NK cells

lymphocyte activation cell division and differentiation of lymphocytes

lymphoid organ (LIMF-oid) lymph node, spleen, thymus, tonsil, or aggregate of lymphoid follicles; *see also* primary lymphoid organ, peripheral lymphoid organ; *compare* lymphatic system

lymphokine (LIMF-oh-kine) cytokine secreted by lymphocytes

lysosome (LIE-so-zome) membrane-bound cell organelle containing digestive enzymes that break down bacteria, large molecules that have entered cell, and damaged components of cell

macrophage (MAK-ro-faje) cell that phagocytizes, processes, and presents antigen to lymphocytes, and secretes cytokines (monokines) involved in inflammation, activation of lymphocytes, and systemic acute phase response to infection or injury; *see also* effector macrophage

macula densa (MAK-you-lah DEN-sah) specialized sensor cells of renal tubule at end of loop of Henle; component of juxtaglomerular apparatus

major histocompatibility complex (MHC) group of genes that code for major histocompatibility complex proteins, which are important for immune function

malignant (mah-LIG-nant) tending to become worse and result in death; *compare* benign

mammary gland milk-secreting gland in breast

mass fundamental property of an object equivalent to the amount of matter in the object

mass movement contraction of large segments of colon; propels fecal material into rectum

mast cell tissue cell that releases histamine and other chemicals involved in inflammation

maximal tubular capacity (T_m) maximal rate of mediated transport of substance across renal tubule wall

mean arterial pressure (MAP) average blood pressure during cardiac cycle; approximately diastolic pressure plus one-third pulse pressure

mechanoreceptor (meh-CAN-oh-re-sep-tor) sensory receptor that responds preferentially to mechanical stimuli such as bending, twisting, or compressing

mechanosensitive channel membrane ion channel that transduces membrane deformation or stretch into electric signal

median eminence (EM-ih-nence) region at base of hypothalamus containing capillary tufts into which hypophysiotropic hormones are secreted

mediate (MEE-dee-ate) bring about

mediated transport movement of molecules across membrane by binding to protein transporter; characterized by specificity, competition, and saturation; includes facilitated diffusion and active transport

medulla (meh-DULL-ah or meh-DUEL-ah) innermost portion of an organ; *compare* cortex; *see* adrenal medulla and medulla oblongata

medullary cardiovascular center *see* cardiovascular center

medullary inspiratory neuron *see* inspiratory neuron

megakaryocyte (meg-ah-CARE-ee-oh-site) large bone marrow cell that gives rise to platelets

meiosis (my-OH-sis) process of cell division leading to gamete (sperm and egg) formation; daughter cells receive only half the chromosomes present in original cell

melatonin (mel-ah-TOE-nin) candidate hormone secreted by pineal gland; suspected role in puberty onset

membrane structural barrier composed of lipids and proteins; provides selective barrier to molecule and ion movement and structural framework to which enzymes, fibers, and ligands are bound

membrane attack complex (MAC) group of complement proteins that form channels in microbe surface and destroy microbe

membrane potential voltage difference between inside and outside of cell

memory *see* working memory, long-term memory

memory cell B cell or T cell that differentiates during an initial infection and responds rapidly during subsequent exposure to same antigen

memory consolidation processes by which memory is transferred from working to long-term form

memory trace neural substrate of memory

menarche (MEN-ark-ee) onset, at puberty, of menstrual cycling

meninges (men-IN-gees) protective membranes that cover brain and spinal cord

menopause (MEN-oh-pause) cessation of menstrual cycling

menstrual cycle (MEN-stru-al) cyclical rise and fall in female reproductive hormones and processes

menstruation (men-stroo-A-shun) flow of menstrual fluid from uterus; also called menstrual period

messenger RNA (mRNA) ribonucleic acid that transfers genetic information from DNA to ribosome

metabolic acidosis (met-ah-BOL-ik ass-ih-DOE-sis) acidosis due to build up of acids other than carbonic acid (from carbon dioxide)

metabolic alkalosis (al-kah-LOW-sis) alkalosis resulting from removal of hydrogen ions by mechanisms other than respiratory removal of carbon dioxide

metabolic end product final molecule produced by a metabolic reaction or series of reactions

metabolic pathway sequence of enzyme-mediated chemical reactions by which molecules are synthesized and broken down in cells

metabolic rate total body energy expenditure per unit time

metabolism (meh-TAB-ol-izm) chemical reactions that occur in a living organism

metabolite (meh-TAB-oh-lite) substance produced by metabolism

metabolize change by chemical reactions

metarteriole (MET-are-tier-ee-ole) blood vessel that directly connects arteriole and venule

methyl group —CH_3

MHC protein plasma-membrane protein coded for by a major histocompatibility complex; restricts T-cell receptor's ability to combine with antigen on a cell; categorized as class I and class II

micelle (MY-cell) soluble cluster of amphipathic molecules in which molecules' polar regions line surface and nonpolar regions are oriented toward center; formed from fatty acids, 2-monoglycerides, and bile salts during fat digestion in small intestine

microbe bacterium, virus, fungus, or other parasite

microcirculation blood circulation in arterioles, capillaries, and venules

microfilament rodlike cytoplasmic actin filament that forms major component of cytoskeleton

microsomal enzyme system (MES) (my-kro-ZOME-al) enzymes, found in smooth endoplasmic reticulum of liver cells, that transform molecules into more polar, less lipid-soluble substances

microtubule tubular cytoplasmic filament that provides internal support for cells; allows change in cell shape and organelle movement in cell

microvilli (my-kro-VIL-eye) small finger-like projections from epithelial-cell surface; greatly increase surface area of cell; characteristic of epithelium lining small intestine and kidney nephrons

micturition (mik-tu-RISH-un) urination

middle-ear cavity air-filled space in temporal bone contains three ear bones that conduct sound waves from tympanic membrane to cochlea

migrating motility complex pattern of peristaltic waves that pass over small segments of intestine after absorption of meal

milk ejection reflex process by which milk is moved from mammary gland alveoli into ducts, from which it can be sucked; due to oxytocin; formerly called milk let-down

milliliter (ml) (MIL-ih-lee-ter) volume equal to 0.001 L

millimole (mmol) (MIL-lee-mole) amount equal to 0.001 mol

millivolt (mV) (MIL-ih-volt) electric potential equal to 0.001 V

mineral inorganic substance, that is, without carbon; major minerals in body are calcium, phosphorus, potassium, sulfur, sodium, chloride, and magnesium

mineralocorticoid (min-er-al-oh-KORT-ih-coid) steroid hormone produced by adrenal cortex; has major effect on sodium and potassium balance; major mineralocorticoid is aldosterone

minute ventilation total ventilation per minute; equals tidal volume times respiratory rate

mitochondrion (my-toe-KON-dree-un) rod-shaped or oval cytoplasmic organelle that produces most of cell's ATP; site of Krebs cycle and oxidative-phosphorylation enzymes

mitogen (my-toe-JEN) chemical that stimulates cell division

mitosis (my-TOE-sis) process in cell division in which DNA is duplicated and an identical set of chromosomes is passed to each daughter cell; nuclear division

mitral valve (MY-tral) valve between left atrium and left ventricle of heart

modality (moe-DAL-ih-tea) type of sensory stimulus

modulation *see* allosteric modulation and covalent modulation

modulator molecule ligand that, by acting at an allosteric regulatory site, alters properties of other binding site on a protein and thus regulates its functional activity

molarity (mo-LAR-ih-tee) number of moles of solute per liter of solution

mole (mol) number of molecules of substance; number of moles = weight in grams/molecular weight; 1 mol = 6 × 10^{23} molecules

molecular weight sum of atomic weights of all atoms in molecule

molecule chemical substance formed by linking atoms together

monoamine (mah-no-ah-MEAN) class of neurotransmitters having the structure R—NH_2, where R is molecule remainder; by convention, excludes peptides and amino acids

monoamine oxidase enzyme that inactivates catecholamine neurotransmitters and serotonin

monocyte (MAH-no-site) type of leukocyte; leaves bloodstream and is transformed into a macrophage

monoglyceride (mah-no-GLISS-er-ide) glycerol linked to one fatty acid side chain

monokine (MAH-no-kine) cytokine secreted by a monocyte or macrophage

monosaccharide (mah-no-SAK-er-ide) carbohydrate consisting of one sugar molecule, which generally contains five or six carbon atoms

monosynaptic reflex (mah-no-sih-NAP-tik) reflex in which the afferent neuron directly activates the motor neuron

motivation *see* primary motivated behavior, secondary motivated behavior

motor having to do with muscles and movement

motor control hierarchy brain areas having a role in skeletal muscle control are rank-ordered in three functional groups

motor control system CNS parts that contribute to control of skeletal-muscle movements

motor cortex strip of cerebral cortex along posterior border of frontal lobe; gives rise to many axons descending in corticospinal and multineuronal pathways; also called primary motor cortex

motor end plate specialized region of muscle-cell plasma membrane that lies directly under axon terminal of a motor neuron

motor neuron somatic efferent neuron, which innervates skeletal muscle

motor neuron pool all the motor neurons for a given muscle

motor potential electrical activity that can be recorded over motor cortex about 50 to 60 ms before movement begins

motor program pattern of neural activity required to perform a certain movement

motor unit motor neuron plus the muscle fibers it innervates

mucosa (mu-KO-sah) three layers of gastrointestinal tract wall nearest lumen, that is, *epithelium, lamina propria,* and *muscularis mucosa*

mucus highly viscous solution secreted by mucous membranes

Müllerian duct (mul-AIR-ee-an) part of embryo that, in a female, develops into reproductive system ducts, but in a male, degenerates

Müllerian inhibitiory factor (MIF) protein secreted by fetal testes that causes Müllerian ducts to degenerate

multineuronal pathway pathway made up of chains of neurons functionally connected by synapses; also called multisynaptic pathway

multiunit smooth muscle smooth muscle that exhibits little, if any, propagation of electrical activity from fiber to fiber and whose contractile activity is closely coupled to its neural input

muscarinic receptor (mus-cur-IN-ik) acetylcholine receptor that responds to the mushroom poison muscarine; located on smooth muscle, cardiac muscle, some CNS neurons, and glands

muscle number of muscle fibers bound together by connective tissue

muscle fatigue decrease in mechanical response of muscle with prolonged stimulation

muscle fiber muscle cell

muscle-spindle stretch receptor capsule-enclosed arrangement of afferent nerve fiber endings around specialized skeletal muscle fibers; sensitive to stretch

muscle tension force exerted by contracting muscle on object

muscle thick filament *see* thick filament

muscle tone degree of resistance of muscle to passive stretch while attempting to relax; *see also* smooth-muscle tone

mutagen factor in the environment that increases mutation rate

mutation (mu-TAY-shun) any change in base sequence of DNA that changes genetic information

myelin (MY-ah-lin) insulating material covering axons of many neurons; consists of layers of myelin-forming-cell plasma membrane wrapped around axon

myenteric plexus (my-en-TER-ik PLEX-us) nerve cell network between circular and longitudinal muscle layers in esophagus, stomach, and intestinal walls

myo- (MY-oh) pertaining to muscle

myoblast (MY-oh-blast) embryological cell that gives rise to muscle fibers

myocardial infarction *see* heart attack

myocardium (my-oh-CARD-ee-um) cardiac muscle, which forms heart walls

myoepithelial cell (my-oh-ep-ih-THEE-lee-al) specialized contractile cell in certain exocrine glands; contraction forces gland's secretion through ducts

myofibril (my-oh-FI-bril) bundle of thick or thin contractile filaments in cytoplasm of striated muscle; myofibrils exhibit a repeating sarcomere pattern along longitudinal axis of muscle

myogenic (my-oh-JEN-ik) originating in muscle

myoglobin (my-oh-GLOW-bin) muscle-fiber protein that binds oxygen

myometrium (my-oh-ME-tree-um) the uterine smooth muscle

myosin (MY-oh-sin) contractile protein that forms thick filaments in muscle fibers

myosin ATPase enzymatic site on globular head of myosin that catalyzes ATP breakdown to ADP and P_i, releasing the chemical energy used to produce force of muscle contraction

myosin light-chain kinase smooth-muscle protein kinase; when activated by Ca-calmodulin, phosphorylates myosin

myotatic reflex *see* stretch reflex

Na,K-ATPase pump primary active-transport protein that splits ATP and releases energy used to transport sodium out of cell and potassium in

natural antibody antibody to erythrocyte antigens A or B; are present without prior exposure to antigen

natural killer (NK) cell type of lymphocyte that binds nonspecifically to virus-infected and cancer cells and kills them directly; no prior exposure to the antigen is required

nearsighted vision defect because eyeball is too long for lens, so that images of distant objects are focused in front of retina

negative balance substance loss from body exceeds gain, and total amount in body decreases; also used for physical parameters such as body temperature and energy; *compare* positive balance

negative feedback aspect of control systems in which system's response opposes input to system; *compare* positive feedback

nephron (NEF-ron) functional unit of kidney; has vascular and tubular component

nerve group of many nerve fibers traveling together in peripheral nervous system

nerve cell one of two principal types of cells in the nervous system; cell specialized to initiate, integrate, and conduct electric signals; also called neuron

nerve fiber *see* axon

nerve growth factor protein that stimulates growth and differentiation of some neurons

net amount remaining after deductions have been made; final amount

neuroeffector junction "synapse" between a neuron and muscle or gland cell

neuroglia *see* glial cell

neurohormone chemical messenger that is released by a neuron and travels in bloodstream to its target cell

neuromodulator chemical messenger that acts on neurons, usually by a second-messenger system, to alter response to a neurotransmitter

neuromuscular junction synapse-like junction between an axon terminal of an efferent nerve fiber and a skeletal muscle fiber

neuron (NUR-on) *see* nerve cell

neuropeptide family of more than 50 neurotransmitters composed of 2 or more amino acids; often also functions as chemical messenger in nonneural tissues

neurotransmitter chemical messenger used by neurons to communicate with each other or with effectors

neutrophil (NEW-tro-fil) polymorphonuclear granulocytic leukocyte whose granules show preference for neither eosin nor basic dyes; functions as phagocyte and releases chemicals involved in inflammation

NH₃ ammonia

NH₄⁺ ammonium ion

nicotinamide adenine dinucleotide (NAD⁺) coenzyme derived from the B vitamin niacin; transfers hydrogen from one substrate to another

nicotinic receptor (nik-oh-TIN-ik) acetylcholine receptor that responds to nicotine; primarily, receptors at motor end plate and on postganglionic autonomic neurons

nitric oxide gas molecules that function as intercellular messengers; destroys intracellular microbes; is endothelium-derived relaxing factor

nociceptor (NO-sih-sep-tor) sensory receptor whose stimulation causes pain

node of Ranvier (RAHN-vee-a) space between adjacent myelin-forming cells along myelinated axon where axonal plasma membrane is exposed to extracellular fluid; also called neurofibril node

noncorticospinal pathway descending pathway having its cells of origin in brainstem; *compare* corticospinal pathway

nonpolar pertaining to molecule or region of molecule containing predominantly chemical bonds in which electrons are shared equally between atoms; having few polar or ionized groups

nonspecific ascending pathway chain of synaptically connected neurons in CNS that are activated by sensory units of several different types; signal general information; *compare* specific ascending pathway

nonspecific immune defense response that nonselectively protects against foreign material without having to recognize its specific identity

norepinephrine (nor-ep-ih-NEF-ryn) biogenic amine (catecholamine) neurotransmitter released at most sympathetic postganglionic endings, from adrenal medulla, and in many CNS regions

nuclear envelope double membrane surrounding cell nucleus

nuclear pore opening in nuclear envelope through which molecular messengers pass between nucleus and cytoplasm

nucleic acid nucleotide polymer in which phosphate of one nucleotide is linked to the sugar of the adjacent one; stores and transmits genetic information; includes DNA and RNA

nucleolus (new-KLEE-oh-lus) densely staining nuclear structure containing DNA that codes for rRNA; site of ribosome assembly

nucleotide (NEW-klee-oh-tide) molecular subunit of nucleic acid; purine or pyrimidine base, sugar, and phosphate

nucleus (NEW-klee-us) (pl. nuclei) (cell) large membrane-bound organelle that contains cell's DNA; (neural) cluster of neuron cell bodies in CNS

occipital lobe posterior region of cerebral cortex where primary visual cortex is located

Ohm's law (omz) current (I) is directly proportional to voltage (E) and inversely proportional to resistance (R) such that $I = E/R$

olfaction sense of smell

olfactory (ol-FAK-tor-ee) pertaining to sense of smell

olfactory mucosa (mu-KO-sah) mucous membrane in upper part of nasal cavity containing receptors for sense of smell

olfactory nerve cranial nerve I; relays information about sense of smell

oligodendroglia (oh-lih-go-den-dro-GLEE-ah) type of glial cell; responsible for myelin formation in CNS

oncogene (ON-ko-jean) altered gene associated with cancer

oogenesis (oh-oh-JEN-ih-sis) gamete production in female

oogonium (oh-oh-GO-nee-um) primitive germ cell that, upon mitotic division, gives rise to primary oocyte

operating point steady-state value maintained by homeostatic control system; also called set point

opioid (OH-pea-oid) *see* endogenous opioid

opsin (OP-sin) protein component of photopigment

opsonin (op-SO-nin) any substance that binds a microbe to a phagocyte and promotes phagocytosis

optic nerve cranial nerve II; relays information about vision

optimal length (l_o) length at which muscle fiber develops maximal tension

organ collection of tissues joined in structural unit to serve common function

organ of Corti (KOR-tee) structure in inner ear capable of transducing sound wave energy into action potentials

organ system organs that together serve an overall function

organelle *see* cell organelle

organic pertaining to carbon-containing substances; *compare* inorganic

orgasm (OR-gazm) inner emotions and systemic physiological changes that mark apex of sexual intercourse, usually accompanied in the male by ejaculation

orienting response behavior in response to a novel stimulus; that is, the person stops what he or she is doing, looks around, listens intently, and turns toward stimulus

osmolarity (oz-mo-LAIR-ih-tee) total solute concentration of a solution; measure of water concentration in that the higher the solution osmolarity, the lower the water concentration

osmole 1 mol of solute particles

osmoreceptor (OZ-mo-ree-sep-tor) receptor that responds to changes in osmolarity of surrounding fluid

osmosis (oz-MO-sis) net diffusion of water across a selective barrier from region of low solute concentration (high water concentration) to region of high solute concentration (low water concentration)

osmotic pressure (oz-MAH-tik) pressure that must be applied to a solution on one side of a membrane to prevent osmotic flow of water across the membrane from a compartment of pure water

osteoblast (OS-tee-oh-blast) cell type responsible for laying down protein matrix of bone; called osteocyte after calcified matrix has been set down

otolith (OH-toe-lith) calcium carbonate "stone" in gelatinous mass of utricle and saccule of vestibular apparatus

oval window membrane-covered opening between middle-ear cavity and scala vestibuli of inner ear

ovarian follicle (oh-VAR-ee-an FOL-ih-kle) egg and its encasing follicular, granulosa, and theca cells prior to ovulation

ovary (OH-vah-ree) gonad in female

ovulation (ov-you-LAY-shun) release of egg, surrounded by its zona pellucida and cumulus, from ovary

ovum (pl. ova) gamete of female; egg

oxidation (ox-ih-DAY-shun) combining, or causing a substance to combine, with oxygen

oxidative (OX-ih-day-tive) using oxygen

oxidative deamination (dee-am-ih-NAY-shun) reaction in which an amino group from an amino acid is replaced by oxygen to form a keto acid

oxidative fiber muscle fiber that has numerous mitochondria and therefore a high capacity for oxidative phosphorylation; red muscle fiber

oxidative phosphorylation (fos-for-ih-LAY-shun) process by which energy derived from reaction between hydrogen and oxygen to form water is transferred to ATP during its formation

oxyhemoglobin (ox-see-HEE-mo-glow-bin) HbO_2; hemoglobin combined with oxygen

oxytocin (ox-see-TOE-sin) peptide hormone synthesized in hypothalamus and released from posterior pituitary; stimulates mammary glands to release milk and uterus to contract

P wave component of electrocardiogram reflecting atrial depolarization

pacemaker neurons that set rhythm of biological clocks independent of external cues; any nerve or muscle cell that has an inherent autorhythmicity and determines activity pattern of other cells

pacemaker potential spontaneous depolarization to threshold of some nerve and muscle cell's plasma membrane

pancreas (PAN-kree-us) gland in abdomen near stomach; connected by duct to small intestine; contains *endocrine* gland cells which secrete insulin, glucagon, and somatostatin into bloodstream, and *exocrine* gland cells which secrete digestive enzymes and bicarbonate into intestine

pancreatic lipase (LIE-pase) enzyme secreted by exocrine pancreas; acts on triacylglycerols to form 2-monoglycerides and free fatty acids

paracrine agent (PEAR-ah-krin) chemical messenger that exerts its effects on cells near its secretion site; by convention, excludes neurotransmitters

paradoxical sleep sleep state associated with small, rapid EEG oscillations, complete loss of tone in postural muscles, and dreaming; also called rapid eye movement, or REM, sleep

parasympathetic nervous system (pear-ah-sim-pah-THET-ik) portion of autonomic nervous system whose preganglionic fibers leave CNS from brainstem and sacral portion of spinal cord; most of its postganglionic fibers release acetylcholine; *compare* sympathetic nervous system

parathyroid gland one of four parathyroid-hormone secreting glands on thyroid gland surface

parathyroid hormone (PTH) peptide hormone secreted by parathyroid glands; regulates calcium and phosphate concentrations of extracellular fluid

parietal cell (pah-RYE-ih-tal) gastric gland cell that secretes hydrochloric acid and intrinsic factor

parietal lobe region of cerebral cortex containing sensory cortex and some association cortex

Parkinson's disease disease characterized by tremor, rigidity, and delay in initiation of movement; due in part to deficit of dopamine in basal ganglia

parotid (pah-ROT-id) one of the three pairs of salivary glands

partial pressure (P) that part of total gas pressure due to molecules of one gas species; measure of concentration of a gas in a gas mixture

parturition (par-tu-RISH-un) birth; delivery of infant and placenta

passive immunity resistance to infection resulting from direct transfer of antibodies or sensitized T cells from one person (or animal) to another; *compare* active immunity

pathway group of nerve fibers in CNS

pelvic diaphragm (PEL-vik DIE-ah-fram) sheet of skeletal muscle that forms floor of pelvis and helps support abdominal and pelvic viscera

pepsin (PEP-sin) family of several protein-digesting enzymes formed in the stomach; breaks protein down to peptide fragments

pepsinogen (pep-SIN-oh-jen) inactive precursor of pepsin; secreted by chief cells of gastric mucosa

peptide (PEP-tide) short polypeptide chain; by convention, having less than 50 amino acids

peptide bond polar covalent chemical bond joining two amino acids; forms protein backbone

peptidergic neuron that releases peptides

percent hemoglobin saturation *see* hemoglobin saturation

perception understanding of objects and events of external world that we acquire from neural processing of sensory information

perforin protein secreted by cytotoxic T cells; forms channels in plasma membrane of target cell, which destroys it

perfusion capillary blood flow

pericardium (pear-ah-CAR-dee-um) connective-tissue sac surrounding heart

peripheral chemoreceptor carotid or aortic body; responds to changes in blood O_2 and CO_2 pressures and H^+ concentration

peripheral lymphoid organ (LIM-foid) lymph node, spleen, tonsil, or lymphocyte accumulation in gastrointestinal, respiratory, urinary, or reproductive tract; site of stimulation of lymphocyte response

peripheral nervous system nerve fibers extending from CNS

peripheral protein protein that is bound to surface of plasma membrane and does not associate with lipid bilayer

peripheral thermoreceptor cold or warm receptor in skin or certain mucous membranes

peristaltic wave (per-ih-STALL-tik) progressive wave of muscle contraction that proceeds along wall of a tube, compressing the tube and causing its contents to move

peritoneum (per-ih-toe-NEE-um) membrane lining abdominal and pelvic cavities and covering organs there

peritubular capillary capillary closely associated with renal tubule

permissiveness situation whereby small quantities of one hormone are required in order for a second hormone to exert its full effects

peroxisome (per-OX-ih-zome) cell organelle that destroys certain toxic products of oxidative reactions

pH expression of a solution's acidity; negative logarithm to base 10 of H^+ concentration; pH decreases as acidity increases

phagocyte (FAH-go-site) any cell capable of phagocytosis

phagocytosis (fah-go-sigh-TOE-sis) engulfment of particles by a cell

pharmacological effect effect produced by much larger amounts of hormone than are normally present

pharynx (FARE-inks) throat; passage common to routes taken by food and air

phasic (FASE-ik) intermittent; *compare* tonic

phosphate group (FOS-fate) —PO_4^{2-}

phosphatidylinositol bisphosphate (PIP₂) (fos-fa-tid-il-in-OS-ih-tol bis-FOS-fate) plasma membrane phospholipid that forms inositol trisphosphate and diacylglycerol when catalyzed by phospholipase C

phosphodiesterase (fos-foe-die-ES-terase) enzyme that catalyzes cyclic AMP breakdown to AMP or cyclic GMP to GMP

phospholipase A₂ (fos-fo-LIE-pace A-two) enzyme that splits arachidonic acid from plasma membrane phospholipid

phospholipase C receptor-controlled plasma-membrane enzyme that catalyzes phosphatidyl bisphosphate breakdown to inositol trisphosphate and diacylglycerol

phospholipid (fos-foe-LIP-id) lipid subclass similar to triacylglycerol except that a phosphate group (—PO_4^{2-}) and small nitrogen-containing molecule are attached to third hydroxyl group of glycerol; major component of cell membranes

phosphoprotein phosphatase (FOS-fah-tase) enzyme that removes phosphate from protein, restoring protein's original shape

phosphoric acid (fos-FOR-ik) acid generated during catabolism of phosphorus-containing compounds; dissociates to form inorganic phosphate and hydrogen ions

phosphorylation (fos-for-ah-LAY-shun) addition of phosphate group to an organic molecule

photopigment light-sensitive molecule altered by absorption of photic energy of certain wavelengths; consists of opsin bound to a chromophore

photoreceptor receptor sensitive to light (photic energy)

physiology branch of biology dealing with the mechanisms by which the body functions

pitch degree of how high or low a sound is perceived

pituitary (pih-TWO-ih-tair-ee) endocrine gland that lies in bony pocket below hypothalamus; constitutes anterior and posterior pituitary

pituitary gonadotropin *see* gonadotropic hormone

placenta (plah-SEN-tah) interlocking fetal and maternal tissues that serve as organ of molecular exchange between fetal and maternal circulations

placental lactogen (plah-SEN-tal LAK-toe-jen) hormone that is produced by placenta and has effects similar to those of growth hormone and prolactin

plasma (PLAS-muh) liquid portion of blood; component of extracellular fluid

plasma cell cell that differentiates from activated B lymphocytes and secretes antibodies

plasma membrane membrane that forms outer surface of cell and separates cell's contents from extracellular fluid

plasma protein albumins, globulins, and fibrinogen

plasmin (PLAZ-min) proteolytic enzyme able to decompose fibrin and thereby to dissolve blood clots

plasminogen (plaz-MIN-oh-jen) inactive precursor of plasmin

plasminogen activator any plasma protein that activates proenzyme plasminogen

plasticity (plas-TISS-ih-tee) ability of neural tissue to change its responsiveness to stimulation because of its past history of activation

platelet (PLATE-let) cell fragment present in blood; plays several roles in blood clotting

platelet-activating factor mediator secreted by mast cells; promotes inflammation

platelet aggregation (ag-reh-GAY-shun) positive-feedback process resulting in platelets sticking together

platelet factor (PF) phospholipid exposed in membranes of aggregated platelets; important in activation of several plasma factors in clot formation

pleura (PLUR-ah) thin cellular sheet attached to thoracic cage interior (*parietal pleura*) and, folding back upon itself, is attached to lung surface (*visceral pleura*); forms two enclosed pleural sacs in thoracic cage

pluripotent stem cells (plur-ih-poe-tent STEM) single population of bone marrow cells from which all blood cells are descended

polar pertaining to molecule or region of molecule containing polar covalent bonds or ionized groups; part of molecule to which electrons are drawn becomes slightly negative, and region from which they are drawn becomes slightly positive; molecule is soluble in water

polar body small cell resulting from unequal distribution of cytoplasm during division of primary or secondary oocyte

polar covalent bond covalent chemical bond in which two electrons are shared unequally between two atoms; atom to which the electrons are drawn becomes slightly negative, and other atom slightly positive; also called polar bond

polarized (PO-lar-izd) having two electric poles, one negative and one positive

polymer (POL-ih-mer) large molecule formed by linking together smaller similar subunits

polymorphonuclear granulocyte (pol-ee-morf-oh-NUK-lee-er GRAN-you-low-site) subclass of leukocytes; *see also* eosinophil, basophil, neutrophil

polypeptide (pol-ee-PEP-tide) polymer consisting of amino acid subunits joined by peptide bonds; also called peptide or protein

polysaccharide (pol-ee-SAK-er-ide) large carbohydrate formed by linking monosaccharide subunits together

polysynaptic reflex (pol-ee-sih-NAP-tik) reflex employing one or more interneurons in its reflex arc

polyunsaturated fatty acid fatty acid that contains more than one double bond

pool body's readily available quantity of a substance; often equals amount in extracellular fluid

portal vein blood vessel that links two capillary networks

positive balance gain of substance exceeds loss, and amount of that substance in body increases; *compare* negative balance

positive feedback aspect of control systems in which an initial disturbance sets off train of events that increases the disturbance even further; *compare* negative feedback

postabsorptive state (post-ab-SORP-tive) period during which nutrients are not absorbed by gastrointestinal tract and energy must be supplied by body's endogenous stores

posterior toward or at the back

posterior pituitary portion of pituitary from which oxytocin and vasopressin are released

postganglionic (post-gang-glee-ON-ik) autonomic-nervous-system neuron or nerve fiber whose cell body lies in ganglion and whose axon terminals form neuroeffector junctions; conducts impulses away from ganglion toward periphery; *compare* preganglionic

postsynaptic neuron (post-sin-NAP-tik) neuron that conducts information away from a synapse

postsynaptic potential local potential that arises in postsynaptic neuron in response to activation of synapses upon it; *see also* excitatory postsynaptic potential, inhibitory postsynaptic potential

postural reflex reflex that maintains or restores upright, stable posture

potential (or potential difference) voltage difference between two points; *see also* graded potential, action potential

potentiation (po-ten-she-A-shun) presence of one agent enhances response to a second such that final response is greater than sum of the two individual responses

precapillary sphincter (SFINK-ter) smooth muscle ring around capillary where it exits from thoroughfare channel or arteriole

preganglionic autonomic-nervous-system neuron or nerve fiber whose cell body lies in CNS and whose axon terminals lie in a ganglion; conducts

action potentials from CNS to ganglion; *compare* postganglionic

presynaptic neuron (pre-sin-NAP-tic) neuron that conducts action potentials toward a synapse

presynaptic synapse relation between two neurons in which axon terminal of one neuron ends on axon terminal of second neuron; action potentials in first neuron alter neurotransmitter release from second, altering effectiveness of synapse second neuron makes with a third

primary active transport active transport in which chemical energy is transferred directly from ATP to transporter protein

primary cortical receiving area region of cerebral cortex where specific ascending pathways end; somatosensory, visual, auditory, or taste cortex

primary lymphoid organ organ that supplies peripheral lymphoid organs with mature lymphocytes; bone marrow and thymus

primary motivated behavior behavior related directly to achieving homeostasis

primary motor cortex *see* motor cortex

primary oocyte (OH-oh-site) female germ cell that undergoes first meiotic division to form secondary oocyte and polar body

primary spermatocyte (sper-MAH-toe-site) male germ cell derived from spermatogonia; undergoes meiotic division to form two secondary spermatocytes

primordial follicle (FAH-lick-el) cell cluster in ovaries that consists of one primary oocyte surrounded by single layer of granulosa cells

process long extension from neuron cell body

product molecule formed in enzyme-catalyzed chemical reaction

progestagen (pro-JES-tah-jen) progesterone-like substance

progesterone (pro-JES-ter-own) steroid hormone secreted by corpus luteum and placenta; stimulates uterine gland secretion, inhibits uterine smooth-muscle contraction, and stimulates breast growth

program related sequence of neural activity preliminary to motor act

prohormone peptide precursor from which are cleaved one or more active peptide hormones

prolactin (pro-LAK-tin) peptide hor-

mone secreted by anterior pituitary; stimulates milk secretion by mammary glands

prolactin inhibiting hormone (PIH) dopamine, which serves as a hypothalamic and posterior pituitary hormone to inhibit prolactin secretion by anterior pituitary

prolactin releasing factor (PRF) one or more hypothalamic and posterior pituitary hormones that stimulate prolactin release from anterior pituitary

proliferative phase (pro-LIF-er-ah-tive) stage of menstrual cycle between menstruation and ovulation during which endometrium repairs itself and grows

promoter specific nucleotide sequence at beginning of gene; determines which of the paired strands of DNA is transcribed into mRNA

pro-opiomelanocortin (pro-oh-pee-oh-mel-an-oh-KOR-tin) large protein precursor for ACTH, endorphin, and several other hormones

propagation (prop-ah-GAY-shun) transmission by reproduction of self

prostacyclin eicosanoid that inhibits platelet aggregation in blood clotting; also called prostaglandin I_2 (PGI_2)

prostaglandin (pros-tah-GLAN-din) one of a group of modified unsaturated fatty acids (eicosanoids) that functions mainly as paracrine or autocrine agents

prostate gland (PROS-tate) large gland encircling urethra in the male; secretes fluid into urethra

protein large polymer consisting of one or more sequences of amino acid subunits joined by peptide bonds

protein binding site *see* binding site

protein C plasma protein that inhibits clotting

protein kinase (KI-nase) one of family of enzymes that phosphorylate certain other proteins by transferring to them a phosphate group from ATP

protein kinase C enzyme that phosphorylates certain intracellular proteins when activated by diacylglycerol

proteolytic (pro-tee-oh-LIT-ik) breaks down protein

prothrombin (pro-THROM-bin) inactive precursor of thrombin; produced by liver and normally present in plasma

proton (PRO-tahn) positively charged subatomic particle

proximal (PROX-sih-mal) nearer; closer to reference point; *compare* distal

proximal tubule first tubular component of a nephron after Bowman's capsule; comprises *convoluted* and *straight segments*

psychoactive drug drug that affects the mind or behavior

puberty attainment of sexual maturity when conception becomes possible; as commonly used, refers to 3 to 5 years of sexual development that culminates in sexual maturity

pulmonary (PULL-mah-nair-ee) pertaining to lungs

pulmonary circulation circulation through lungs; portion of cardiovascular system between pulmonary trunk, as it leaves the right ventricle, and pulmonary veins, as they enter the left atrium

pulmonary stretch receptor afferent nerve ending lying in airway smooth muscle and activated by lung inflation

pulmonary surfactant *see* surfactant

pulmonary trunk large artery that carries blood from right ventricle of heart to lungs

pulmonary valve valve between right ventricle of heart and pulmonary trunk

pulmonary ventilation *see* total pulmonary ventilation

pulse pressure difference between systolic and diastolic arterial blood pressures

pupil opening in iris of eye through which light passes to reach retina

purine base (PURE-ene) double-ring, nitrogen-containing subunit of nucleotide; adenine or guanine

Purkinje fiber (purr-KIN-jee) specialized myocardial cell that constitutes part of conducting system of heart; conveys excitation from bundle branches to ventricular muscle

pyloric sphincter (pie-LOR-ik) ring of smooth muscle between stomach and small intestine

pyramidal tract *see* corticospinal pathway

pyrimidine base (pur-RIM-ih-dean) single-ring, nitrogen-containing subunit of nucleotide; cytosine, thymine, or uracil

pyrogen *see* endogenous pyrogen

pyruvate (PIE-rue-vate) anion formed when pyruvic acid loses a hydrogen ion

pyruvic acid (pie-RUE-vik) three-carbon intermediate in glycolysis that, in absence of oxygen, forms lactic acid or, in presence of oxygen, enters Krebs cycle

QRS complex component of electrocardiogram corresponding to ventricular depolarization

R— in chemical formula, signifies remaining portion of molecule

radiation emission of heat from object's surface in form of electromagnetic waves

rapid eye movement sleep *see* paradoxical sleep

rate-limiting enzyme enzyme in metabolic pathway most easily saturated with substrate; determines rate of entire metabolic pathway

rate-limiting reaction slowest reaction in metabolic pathway; catalyzed by rate-limiting enzyme

reactant (re-AK-tent) molecule that enters a chemical reaction; called the substrate of enzyme-catalyzed reactions

reaction *see* chemical reaction

reactive hyperemia (hi-per-EE-me-ah) transient increase in blood flow following release of occlusion of blood supply

readiness potential electrical activity recorded over parts of brain during "decision-making period," about 0.8 s before movement begins

receptive field (of neuron) part of body which, if stimulated, results in activity in that neuron

receptive relaxation reflex decrease in smooth-muscle tension in walls of hollow organs in response to distension

receptor (in sensory system) specialized peripheral ending of afferent neuron, or separate cell intimately associated with it, that detects changes in some aspect of environment; (in chemical communication) specific binding site in plasma membrane or interior of target cell with which a chemical messenger combines to exert its effects

receptor activation change in receptor conformation caused by combination of messenger with receptor

receptor potential graded potential that arises in afferent-neuron ending, or a specialized cell intimately associated with it, in response to stimulation

reciprocal innervation inhibition of motor neurons activating muscles whose contraction would oppose an intended movement

recognition binding of antigen to receptor on lymphocyte surface specific for that antigen

recombinant DNA (re-KOM-bih-nent) DNA formed by joining portions of two DNA molecules previously fragmented by a restriction enzyme

recruitment activation of additional cells in response to increased stimulus strength

rectum short segment of large intestine between sigmoid colon and anus

red muscle fiber muscle fiber having high oxidative capacity and large amount of myoglobin

reflex (REE-flex) unlearned biological control system linking stimulus with response and mediated by a reflex arc

reflex arc neural or hormonal components that mediate a reflex; usually includes receptor, afferent pathway, integrating center, efferent pathway, and effector

reflex response final change due to action of stimulus upon reflex arc; also called effector response

refractory period (re-FRAK-tor-ee) time during which an excitable membrane does not respond to a stimulus that normally causes response; *see also* absolute refractory period, relative refractory period

regulatory site site on protein that interacts with modulator molecule; alters functional-site properties

relative refractory period time during which excitable membrane will produce action potential but only to a stimulus of greater strength than the usual threshold strength

relaxin (re-LAX-in) polypeptide hormone secreted mainly by corpus luteum; softens cervix prior to parturition

releasing hormone hormone secreted by hypothalamic neuron; controls hormone release by anterior pituitary

REM sleep (rem) *see* paradoxical sleep

renal (REE-nal) pertaining to kidneys

renal corpuscle combination of *glomerulus* and *Bowman's capsule*

renal pelvis large cavity at base of each kidney; receives urine from collecting ducts and empties it into ureter

renin (REE-nin) hormone secreted by kidneys; acts as an enzyme that catalyzes splitting off of angiotension I from angiotensinogen in plasma

replicate (REP-lih-kate) duplicate

repolarize return transmembrane potential to its resting level

residual volume air volume remaining in lungs after maximal expiration

resistance (R) hindrance to movement through a particular substance or tube

respiration (cellular) oxygen utilization in metabolism of organic molecules; (respiratory system) oxygen and carbon dioxide exchange between organism and external environment

respiratory acidosis increased arterial H^+ concentration due to carbon dioxide retention

respiratory alkalosis decreased arterial H^+ concentration when carbon dioxide elimination from lungs exceeds its production

respiratory pump effect on venous return of changing intrathoracic and intraabdominal pressures associated with respiration

respiratory quotient (RQ) (KWO-shunt) ratio of carbon dioxide produced to oxygen consumed during metabolism

respiratory rate number of breaths per minute

respiratory zone portion of airways from beginning of respiratory bronchioles to alveoli; contains alveoli across which gas exchange occurs

resting membrane potential voltage difference between inside and outside of cell in absence of excitatory or inhibitory stimulation; also called resting potential

restriction element *see* MHC protein

restriction nuclease (NEW-clee-ase) bacterial enzyme that splits DNA into fragments, acting at different loci on the two DNA strands

retching strong involuntary attempt to vomit but without anything coming up

reticular formation extensive neuron network extending through brainstem core; receives and integrates information from many afferent pathways and from other CNS regions

retina thin layer of neural tissue lining back of eyeball; contains receptors for vision

retinal (ret-in-AL) form of vitamin A that forms chromophore component of photopigment

retrograde opposite the usual course of events

retrograde amnesia (RET-row-grade am-NEE-jha) loss of memory for events immediately preceding a memory-disturbing trauma such as a blow to the head

retrovirus (RET-ro-vi-rus) virus with RNA core and enzyme capable of tran-

scribing that RNA to DNA, which is then incorporated into host's DNA

reversible reaction chemical reaction in which reactants are converted to products and, simultaneously, products are converted to reactants; *compare* irreversible reaction

reward system brain structures, including locus coeruleus and nucleus accumbens, that provide pleasurable inner emotions in response to certain behaviors and drugs

Rh factor group of erythrocyte plasma-membrane antigens that may (Rh+) or may not (Rh−) be present

rhodopsin (ro-DOP-sin) photopigment in rods

ribonucleic acid (RNA) (rye-bo-new-CLAY-ik) single-stranded nucleic acid involved in transcription of genetic information and translation of that information into protein structure; contains the sugar ribose; *see also* messenger RNA, ribosomal RNA, and transfer RNA

ribosomal RNA (rRNA) (rye-bo-ZOME-al) type of RNA used in ribosome assembly; becomes part of ribosome

ribosome (RYE-bo-zome) cytoplasmic particle that mediates linking together of amino acids to form proteins; attached to endoplasmic reticulum as bound ribosome, or suspended in cytoplasm as free ribosome

rickets disease in which new bone matrix is inadequately calcified due to 1,25-dihydroxyvitamin D_3 deficiency

rigidity (rih-JID-ih-tee) hypertonia with normal muscle reflexes; *compare* spasticity

rigor mortis (RIG-or MORE-tiss) stiffness of skeletal muscles after death resulting from ATP loss

RNA polymerase (POL-ih-mer-ase) enzyme that forms RNA by joining together appropriate nucleotides after they have base-paired to DNA

RNA processing enzymatic removal of intron sequences from newly formed RNA

rod one of two receptor types for photic energy; contains the photopigment rhodopsin

round window membrane-covered opening between scala tympani of inner ear and middle-ear cavity

saccade (sah-KADE) short, jerking eyeball movement

saliva watery solution of salts and pro-

teins, including mucins and amylase, secreted by salivary glands

sarcomere (SAR-ko-mere) repeating structural unit of myofibril; composed of thick and thin filaments; extends between two adjacent Z lines

sarcoplasmic reticulum (sar-ko-PLAS-mik re-TIK-you-lum) endoplasmic reticulum in muscle fiber; site of storage and release of calcium ions

satiety signal (sah-TIE-ih-tee) input to food control centers that causes hunger to cease and sets time period before hunger returns

saturated fatty acid fatty acid all of whose carbon atoms are linked by single covalent bonds

saturation degree to which protein binding sites are occupied by ligands

scala tympani (SCALE-ah TIM-pah-nee) fluid-filled inner-ear compartment that receives sound waves from basilar membrane and transmits them to round window

scala vestibuli (ves-TIB-you-lee) fluid-filled inner-ear compartment that receives sound waves from oval window and transmits them to basilar membrane and cochlear duct

schizophrenia (skit-zo-FREE-nee-ah) disease, or family of diseases, characterized by altered motor behavior, distorted perceptions, disturbed thinking, altered mood, and abnormal interpersonal behavior

Schwann cell nonneural cell that forms myelin sheath in peripheral nervous system

scrotum (SKRO-tum) sac that contains testes and epididymides

second messenger intracellular substance that serves as relay from plasma membrane to intracellular biochemical machinery, where it alters some aspect of cell's function

secondary active transport active transport in which energy released during transmembrane movement of one substance from higher to lower concentration is transferred to the simultaneous movement of another substance from lower to higher concentration

secondary motivated behavior behavior not directed toward achieving homeostasis

secondary peristalsis (pear-ih-STALL-sis) esophageal peristaltic waves not immediately preceded by pharyngeal phase of swallow

secondary sexual characteristics external differences between male and female not directly involved in reproduction

secondary spermatocyte (sper-MAH-toe-site) male germ cell derived from primary spermatocyte as a result of the first meiotic division

secretin (SEEK-reh-tin) peptide hormone secreted by upper small intestine; stimulates pancreas to secrete bicarbonate into small intestine

secretion (sih-KREE-shun) elaboration and release of organic molecules, ions, and water by cells in response to specific stimuli

secretory phase (SEEK-rih-tor-ee) stage of menstrual cycle following ovulation during which secretory type of endometrium develops

secretory vesicle membrane-bound vesicle produced by Golgi apparatus; contains protein to be secreted by cell

section cut surface; slice

segmentation (seg-men-TAY-shun) series of stationary rhythmical contractions and relaxations of rings of intestinal smooth muscle; mixes intestinal contents

semen (SEE-men) sperm-containing fluid of male ejaculate

semicircular canal passage in temporal bone; contains sense organs for equilibrium and movement

seminal vesicle pair of exocrine glands in males that secrete fluid into vas deferens

seminiferous tubule (sem-ih-NIF-er-ous) tubule in testis in which sperm production occurs; contains Sertoli cells

semipermeable membrane (sem-eye-PER-me-ah-ble) membrane permeable to some substances but not to others

sensor first component of control system; detects specific environmental changes; also called receptor

sensorimotor cortex (sen-sor-ee-MO-tor) all areas of cerebral cortex that play a role in skeletal-muscle control

sensory information information that originates in stimulated sensory receptors

sensory system part of nervous system that receives, conducts, or processes information that leads to perception of a stimulus

sensory unit afferent neuron plus receptors it innervates

serosa (sir-OH-sah) connective-tissue layer surrounding outer surface of stomach and intestines

serotonin (sair-oh-TONE-in) biogenic amine neurotransmitter; paracrine agent in blood platelets and digestive tract; also called 5-hydroxytryptamine, or 5-HT

Sertoli cell (sir-TOE-lee) cell intimately associated with developing germ cells in seminiferous tubule; creates blood-testis barrier, secretes fluid into seminiferous tubule, and mediates hormonal effects on tubule

serum (SEER-um) blood plasma from which fibrinogen and other clotting proteins have been removed as result of clotting

sex chromatin (CHROM-ah-tin) nuclear mass not usually found in cells of males; of condensed X chromosome

sex chromosome X or Y chromosome

sex determination genetic basis of individual's sex, XY determining male, and XX, female

sex differentiation (dif-er-en-she-A-shun) development of male or female reproductive organs

sex hormone estrogen, progesterone, testosterone, or related hormones

shock decrease in blood flow severe enough to damage tissues and organs

short-loop negative feedback inhibition of hypothalamus by an anterior pituitary hormone

sickle-cell anemia disease in which an amino acid in hemoglobin is abnormal, and at low oxygen concentrations erythrocytes assume sickle shapes or other bizarre forms that block capillaries

sigmoid colon (SIG-moid) S-shaped terminal portion of colon

signal sequence initial portion of newly synthesized protein (if protein is destined for secretion)

signal transduction mechanism sequence of events that relay information from plasma-membrane receptor to cell's response mechanism; *see also* transduction

single-unit smooth muscle smooth muscle that responds to stimulation as single unit because gap junctions join fibers, allowing electrical activity to pass from cell to cell

sinoatrial (SA) node (sigh-no-A-tree-al) region in right atrium of heart containing specialized cardiac-muscle cells that depolarize spontaneously faster than other cells in the conducting system; determines heart rate

sister chromatid (CHROM-ah-tid) one of two identical DNA threads joined together during meiosis

skeletal muscle striated muscle attached to bones or skin and responsible for skeletal movements and facial expression; controlled by somatic nervous system

skeletal muscle "pump" pumping effect of contracting skeletal muscles on blood flow through underlying vessels

skeletomotor fiber *see* extrafusal fiber

sleep *see* paradoxical sleep, slow-wave sleep

sliding-filament mechanism process of muscle contraction in which shortening occurs by thick and thin filaments sliding past each other

slow channel voltage-sensitive calcium channel in myocardial-cell plasma membrane; opens, after a short delay, upon depolarization

slow fiber muscle fiber whose myosin has low ATPase activity

slow-wave sleep sleep state associated with large, slow EEG waves and considerable postural-muscle tone but not dreaming

smooth muscle nonstriated muscle that surrounds hollow organs and tubes; controlled by autonomic nervous system, hormones, and paracrine agents; *see also* single-unit smooth muscle, multiunit smooth muscle

smooth-muscle tone smooth muscle tension due to low-level cross-bridge activity in absence of external stimuli

sodium inactivation turning off of increased sodium permeability at action-potential peak

soft palate (PAL-et) nonbony region at back of roof of mouth

solute (SOL-ute) substances dissolved in a liquid

solution liquid (solvent) containing dissolved substances (solutes)

solvent liquid in which substances are dissolved

somatic (so-MAT-ik) pertaining to the body; related to body's framework or outer walls, including skin, skeletal muscle, tendons, and joints

somatic nervous system component of efferent division of peripheral nervous system; innervates skeletal muscle; *compare* autonomic nervous system

somatic receptor neural receptor in the framework or outer wall of the body that responds to mechanical stimulation of skin or hairs and underlying tissues, rotation or bending of joints, temperature changes, or painful stimuli

somatomedin C *see* insulin-like growth factor I

somatosensory cortex (so-mat-oh-SEN-so-ree) strip of cerebral cortex in parietal lobe in which nerve fibers transmitting somatic sensory information synapse

somatostatin (SS) (so-mat-oh-STAT-in) hypothalamic hormone that inhibits growth hormone and TSH secretion by anterior pituitary; possible neurotransmitter; also in stomach and pancreatic islets

sound wave air disturbance due to variations between regions of high air molecule density (compression) and low density (rarefaction)

spasm (SPAH-zm) brief involuntary muscle contraction

spasticity (spaz-TISS-ih-tee) hypertonia with increased responses to motor reflexes; *compare* rigidity

spatial summation (spaysh-al) adding together effects of simultaneous inputs to different places on a neuron to produce potential change greater than that caused by single input

specific ascending pathway chain of synaptically connected neurons in CNS, all activated by sensory units of same type

specific immune defense response that depends upon recognition of specific foreign material for reaction to it

specificity selectivity; ability of binding site to react with only one, or a limited number of, types of molecules

sperm *see* spermatozoa

sperm capacitation (kah-pas-ih-TAY-shun) process by which sperm in female reproductive tract gains ability to fertilize egg

spermatid (SPER-mah-tid) immature sperm

spermatogenesis (sper-mah-toe-JEN-ih-sis) sperm formation

spermatogonium (sper-mah-toe-GO-nee-um) undifferentiated germ cell that gives rise to primary spermatocyte

spermatozoon (spur-ma-toe-ZOE-in) male gamete; also called sperm

sphincter (sfink-ter) smooth-muscle ring that surrounds a tube, closing tube as muscle contracts

sphincter of Oddi (OH-dee) smooth-muscle ring surrounding common bile duct at its entrance into duodenum

sphygmomanometer (sfig-mo-mah-NOM-eh-ter) device consisting of inflatable cuff and pressure gauge for measuring arterial blood pressure

spinal nerve one of 86 peripheral nerves (43 pairs) that join spinal cord

spinal reflex reflex whose afferent and efferent components are in spinal nerves; can occur in absence of brain control

spindle fiber (muscle) modified skeletal muscle fiber in muscle spindle; also called intrafusal fiber; (mitosis) microtubule that connects chromosome to centriole during mitosis

spleen largest lymphoid organ; located between stomach and diaphragm

SRY gene gene on the Y chromosome that determines development of testes in genetic male

stable balance net loss of substance from body equals net gain, and body's amount of substance neither increases nor decreases; *compare* positive balance, negative balance

starch moderately branched plant polysaccharide composed of glucose subunits

Starling force factor that determines direction and magnitude of fluid movement across capillary wall

Starling's law of the heart within limits, increased end-diastolic volume of heart (increased muscle-fiber length) increases force of cardiac contraction

state of consciousness degree of mental alertness, that is, whether awake, drowsy, asleep, and so on

steady state no net change occurs; continual energy input to system is required, however, to prevent net change; *compare* equilibrium

stem cell cell that in adult body divides continuously and forms supply of cells for differentiation

steroid (STEER-oid) lipid subclass; molecule consists of four interconnected carbon rings to which polar groups may be attached

stimulus detectable change in internal or external environment

stress environmental change that must be adapted to if health and life are to be maintained; event that elicits increased cortisol secretion

stretch receptor afferent nerve ending that is depolarized by stretching; *see also* muscle-spindle stretch receptor

stretch reflex monosynaptic reflex, mediated by muscle-spindle stretch receptor, in which muscle stretch causes contraction of that muscle; also called myotatic reflex

striated muscle (STRI-ate-ed) muscle having transverse banding pattern due to repeating sarcomere structure; *see also* skeletal and cardiac muscle

stroke brain damage due to blood stoppage because of occlusion or rupture of cerebral vessel

stroke volume blood volume ejected by a ventricle during one heartbeat

strong acid acid that ionizes completely to form hydrogen ions and corresponding anions when dissolved in water; *compare* weak acid

subcortical nucleus neuron cluster deep in brain; includes basal ganglia

submucosa (sub-mu-KO-sah) connective-tissue layer under mucosa in gastrointestinal tract

submucous plexus (sub-MU-kus PLEX-us) nerve-cell network in submucosa of esophageal, stomach, and intestinal walls

substance P neuropeptide neurotransmitter released by afferent neurons in pain pathway as well as other sites

substrate (SUB-straight) reactant in enzyme-mediated reaction

substrate level phosphorylation (fos-for-ih-LAY-shun) direct transfer of phosphate group from metabolic intermediate to ADP to form ATP

subsynaptic membrane (sub-sih-NAP-tik) part of postsynaptic neuron's plasma membrane under synapse

subthreshold potential (sub-THRESH-old) depolarization less than threshold potential

subthreshold stimulus stimulus capable of depolarizing membrane but not by enough to reach threshold

sucrose (SUE-krose) disaccharide composed of glucose and fructose; also called table sugar

sulfate SO_4^{2-}

sulfhydryl group (sulf-HI-dral) —SH

sulfuric acid (sulf-YOUR-ik) acid generated during catabolism of sulfur-containing compounds; dissociates to form sulfate and hydrogen ions

summation (sum-MAY-shun) increase in muscle tension or shortening in response to rapid, repetitive stimulation relative to single twitch

superior vena cava (VEE-nah CAVE-ah) large vein that carries blood from upper half of body to right atrium of heart

supersensitivity increased responsiveness of target cell to given messenger due to up-regulation

suppressor T cell T cell that inhibits antibody production and cytotoxic T-cell function

suprathreshold stimulus (soup-ra-THRESH-old) any agent capable of depolarizing membrane more than its threshold potential, that is, closer to zero

surface tension attractive forces between water molecules at an air-water interface resulting in net force that acts to reduce surface area

surfactant (sir-FACT-ant) detergent-like phospholipid produced by pulmonary type II alveolar cells; reduces surface tension of fluid film lining alveoli

sympathetic nervous system portion of autonomic nervous system whose preganglionic fibers leave CNS at thoracic and lumbar portions of spinal cord; *compare* parasympathetic

sympathetic trunk one of paired chains of interconnected sympathetic ganglia that lie on either side of vertebral column

sympathomimetic (sym-path-oh-mih-MET-ik) produces effects similar to those of sympathetic nervous system

synapse (SIN-apse) anatomically specialized junction between two neurons where electrical activity in one neuron influences excitability of second; term also used for junction between neuron and effector cell; *see also* chemical synapse, electric synapse, excitatory synapse, inhibitory synapse

synaptic cleft narrow extracellular space separating pre- and postsynaptic neurons at chemical synapse

synaptic potential *see* postsynaptic potential

synergistic muscle (sin-er-JIS-tik) muscle whose action aids intended motion

systemic circulation (sis-TEM-ik) circulation from left ventricle through all organs except lungs and back to heart

systole (SIS-toe-lee) period of ventricular contraction

systolic pressure (sis-TAHL-ik) maximum arterial blood pressure during cardiac cycle

T cell lymphocyte derived from precursor that differentiated in thymus; *see*

also cytotoxic T cell, helper T cell, suppressor T cell

T lymphocyte *see* T cell

T tubule *see* transverse tubule

T wave component of electrocardiogram corresponding to ventricular repolarization

target cell cell influenced by a certain hormone

taste bud sense organ that contains chemoreceptors for taste

tectorial membrane (tek-TOR-ee-al) structure in organ of Corti in contact with receptor-cell hairs

teleology (teal-ee-OL-oh-gee) explanation of events in terms of ultimate purpose served by them

template (TEM-plit) pattern

temporal lobe region of cerebral cortex where primary auditory cortex and Wernicke's speech center are located

temporal summation membrane potential produced as two or more inputs, occurring at different times, are added together; potential change is greater than that caused by single input

tendon (TEN-don) collagen fiber bundle that connects skeletal muscle to bone and transmits muscle contractile force to the bone

tension force; *see also* muscle tension

termination code word three-nucleotide sequence in DNA that signifies gene end

testis (TES-tiss) (pl. testes) gonad in male

testosterone (tes-TOS-ter-own) steroid hormone produced in interstitial cells of testes; major male sex hormone; essential for spermatogenesis and maintains growth and development of reproductive organs and secondary sexual characteristics of male

tetanus (TET-ah-nus) maintained mechanical response of muscle to high-frequency stimulation; also the disease lockjaw

tetrad (TET-rad) grouping of two homologous chromosomes, each with its sister chromatid, during meiosis

thalamus (THAL-ah-mus) subdivision of diencephalon; integrating center for sensory input on its way to cerebral cortex; also contains motor nuclei

theca (THEE-kah) cell layer that surrounds ovarian-follicle granulosa cells

thermogenesis (ther-mo-JEN-ih-sis) heat generation

thermoneutral zone temperature

range over which changes in skin blood flow alone can regulate body temperature

thermoreceptor sensory receptor for temperature and temperature changes, particularly in low (cold receptor) or high (warm receptor) range

theta wave (THAY-tah) slow 4- to 8-Hz oscillation on electroencephalogram; associated with sleep

thick filament myosin filament in muscle cell

thin filament filament in muscle cell; consists of actin; may contain troponin and tropomyosin

thoracic cavity (thor-ASS-ik) chest cavity

thoracic wall chest wall

thorax (THO-raks) closed body cavity between neck and diaphragm; contains lungs, heart, thymus, large vessels, and esophagus; also called the chest

threshold (THRESH-old) (or threshold potential) membrane potential to which excitable membrane must be depolarized to initiate an action potential

threshold stimulus stimulus capable of depolarizing membrane to threshold

thrombin (THROM-bin) enzyme that catalyzes conversion of fibrinogen to fibrin; has multiple other actions

thrombolytic system *see* fibrinolytic system

thrombosis (throm-BO-sis) clot formation in body

thromboxane (throm-BOX-ain) cyclooxygenase-pathway eicosanoid closely related to prostaglandins

thromboxane A_2 thromboxane that, among other effects, stimulates platelet aggregation in blood clotting

thrombus (THROM-bus) blood clot

thymine (T) (THIGH-mean) pyrimidine base in DNA but not RNA

thymus (THIGH-mus) lymphoid organ in upper part of chest; site of T-lymphocyte differentiation and thymosin secretion

thyroglobulin (thigh-ro-GLOB-you-lin) large protein to which thyroid hormones bind in thyroid gland; storage form of thyroid hormones

thyroid gland paired endocrine gland in neck; secretes thyroid hormones and calcitonin

thyroid hormones (TH) collective term for amine hormones released from thyroid gland, that is, thyroxine (T_4) and triiodothyronine (T_3)

thyroid-stimulating hormone (TSH) glycoprotein hormone secreted by anterior pituitary; induces secretion of thyroid hormone; also called thyrotropin

thyrotropin (thigh-roe-TRO-pin) *see* thyroid-stimulating hormone

thyrotropin releasing hormone (TRH) hypothalamic hormone that stimulates thyrotropin and prolactin secretion by anterior pituitary

thyroxine (T₄) (thigh-ROCKS-in) tetra-iodothyronine; iodine-containing amine hormone secreted by thyroid gland

tidal volume air volume entering or leaving lungs with single breath during any state of respiratory activity

tight junction cell junction in epithelial tissues; extends around cell and restricts molecule diffusion through space between cells

tissue aggregate of single type of specialized cell; also denotes general cellular fabric of a given organ

tissue factor extravascular plasma-membrane protein capable of initiating clot formation

tissue plasminogen activator (t-PA) plasma protein produced by endothelial cells; after binding to fibrinogen, activates the proenzyme plasminogen

tolerance condition in which increasing drug doses are required to achieve effects that initially occurred in response to a smaller dose

tone *see* muscle tone

tonic (TAH-nik) continuous activity; *compare* phasic

tonsil one of several small lymphoid organs in pharynx

total carbon dioxide sum total of dissolved carbon dioxide, bicarbonate, and carbamino-CO₂

total dead space alveolar and anatomic dead space; *see also* alveolar dead space, anatomic dead space

total energy expenditure sum of external work done plus heat produced plus energy stored by body

total peripheral resistance (TPR) total resistance to flow in systemic blood vessels from beginning of aorta to end of venae cavae

toxemia of pregnancy (tox-EE-me-ah) disease occurring in pregnant women and associated with fluid retention, urinary protein, hypertension, and possibly convulsions; also called eclampsia

toxin (TOX-sin) poison

trace element mineral present in body in extremely small quantities

trachea (TRAY-key-ah) single airway connecting larynx with bronchi; windpipe

tract large, myelinated nerve-fiber bundle in CNS

transamination (trans-am-ih-NAY-shun) reaction in which an amino acid amino group (—NH₂) is transferred to a keto acid, the keto acid thus becoming an amino acid

transcription formation of mRNA containing, in linear sequence of its nucleotides, genetic information in specific gene; first stage of protein synthesis

transduction process by which stimulus energy is transformed into a response

transepithelial transport *see* epithelial transport

transfer RNA (tRNA) type of RNA; different tRNAs combine with different amino acids and with codon on mRNA specific for that amino acid, thus arranging amino acids in sequence to form specified protein

transferrin (trans-FAIR-in) iron-binding protein carrier for iron in plasma

translation assembly of amino acids in correct order during protein synthesis, according to genetic instructions in mRNA; occurs on ribosomes

transmural pressure pressure difference exerted on the two sides of a wall

transport maximum (Tₘ) upper limit to amount of material that carrier-mediated transport can move across the renal tubule

transporter integral membrane protein that mediates passage of molecule through membrane; also called carrier

transpulmonary pressure difference between alveolar and intrapleural pressures; force that holds lungs open

transverse tubule (T tubule) tubule extending from striated-muscle plasma membrane into the fiber, passing between opposed sarcoplasmic-reticulum segments; conducts muscle action potential into muscle fiber

triacylglycerol (tri-ace-il-GLISS-er-ol) subclass of lipids composed of glycerol and three fatty acids; also called fat, neutral fat, or triglyceride

tricarboxylic acid cycle *see* Krebs cycle

tricuspid valve (try-CUS-pid) valve between right atrium and right ventricle of heart

triglyceride *see* triacylglycerol

triiodothyronine (T₃) (try-eye-oh-doe-THIGH-ro-neen) iodine-containing amine hormone secreted by thyroid gland

triplet code three-base sequence in DNA and RNA that specifies particular amino acid

trophoblast (TRO-fo-blast) outer layer of blastocyst; gives rise to placental tissues

tropic (TRO-pic) growth-promoting

tropic hormone hormone that stimulates the secretion of another hormone and, often, growth of hormone-secreting gland

tropomyosin (tro-po-MY-oh-sin) regulatory protein capable of reversibly covering binding sites on actin; associated with muscle thin filaments

troponin (tro-PO-nin) regulatory protein bound to actin and tropomyosin of striated-muscle thin filaments; site of calcium binding that initiates contractile activity

trypsin (TRIP-sin) enzyme secreted into small intestine by exocrine pancreas as precursor trypsinogen; breaks certain peptide bonds in proteins and polypeptides

trypsinogen (trip-SIN-oh-jen) inactive precursor of trypsin; secreted by exocrine pancreas

tryptophan (TRIP-toe-fan) essential amino acid; serotonin precursor

tubular reabsorption transfer of materials from kidney tubule lumen to peritubular capillaries

tubular secretion transfer of materials from peritubular capillaries to kidney tubule lumen

tumor necrosis factor (TNF) (neh-CROW-sis) cytokine that stimulates inflammation and mediates many systemic acute phase responses

twitch mechanical response of muscle to single action potential

tympanic membrane (tim-PAN-ik) membrane stretched across end of ear canal; also called ear drum

type II cell pulmonary alveolar cell that produces surfactant

tyrosine (TIE-ro-seen) amino acid; precursor of catecholamines and thyroid hormones

tyrosine kinase protein kinase that is part of receptor and is activated upon ligand binding to the receptor; phosphorylates tyrosine portion of proteins

ulcer an erosion, or sore, as on stomach or intestinal wall

ultrafiltrate (ul-tra-FILL-trate) essentially protein-free fluid formed from plasma as it is forced through capillary walls by pressure gradient

umbilical vessel (um-BIL-ih-kal) artery or vein transporting blood between fetus and placenta

unsaturated fatty acid fatty acid containing one or more double bonds

upper esophageal sphincter (ih-sof-ih-JEE-al SFINK-ter) skeletal-muscle ring surrounding esophagus just below pharynx that, when contracted, closes entrance to esophagus

up-regulation increase in number of target-cell receptors for given messenger in response to chronic low extracellular concentration of that messenger; *see also* supersensitivity; *compare* down-regulation

uracil (U) (YOUR-ah-sil) pyrimidine base; present in RNA but not DNA

urea (you-REE-ah) major nitrogenous waste product of protein breakdown and amino acid catabolism

uremia (you-REE-me-ah) general term for symptoms of profound kidney malfunction

ureter (YUR-ih-ter) tube that connects kidney to urinary bladder

urethra (you-REE-thrah) tube that connects urinary bladder to outside of body

uric acid (YUR-ik) waste product derived from nucleic acid catabolism

urinary bladder thick-walled sac composed of smooth muscle; stores urine prior to urination

uterine tube (YOU-ter-in) one of two tubes that carries egg from ovary to uterus; also called fallopian tube, oviduct

uterus (YOU-ter-us) hollow organ in pelvic region of females; houses fetus during pregnancy; also called womb

vagina (vah-JI-nah) canal leading from uterus to outside of body; also called birth canal

vagus nerve (VAY-gus) cranial nerve X; major parasympathetic nerve

valence (VAY-lence) number of hydrogen atoms (or its equivalent) that an ion can hold in combination or displace in a reaction

van der Waals forces (walls) weak attracting forces between nonpolar regions of molecules

varicosity (vair-ih-KOS-ih-tee) swollen region of axon; contains neurotransmitter-filled vesicles; analogous to presynaptic ending

vas deferens (vahz DEF-er-enz) one of paired male reproductive ducts that connect epididymis of testis to urethra; also called ductus deferens

vasectomy (vay-SEK-toe-me) cutting and tying off of both vas deferens, which results in sterilization of male without loss of testosterone

vasoconstriction (vay-zoh-kon-STRIK-shun) decrease in blood-vessel diameter due to vascular smooth-muscle contraction

vasodilation (vaz-oh-die-LAY-shun) increase in blood-vessel diameter due to vascular smooth-muscle relaxation

vasopressin (vaz-oh-PRES-sin) peptide hormone synthesized in hypothalamus and released from posterior pituitary; increases water permeability of kidneys' collecting ducts; also called antidiuretic hormone (ADH)

vein any vessel that returns blood to heart; but see portal vein

vena cava (VEE-nah CAVE-ah) (pl. venae cavae) one of two large veins that returns systemic blood to heart; *see also* superior vena cava, inferior vena cava

venous return (VR) blood volume flowing to heart per unit time

ventilation air exchange between atmosphere and alveoli; alveolar air flow

ventral (VEN-tral) toward or at the front of body

ventral root one of two groups of efferent fibers that leave ventral side of spinal cord

ventricle (VEN-trick-il) cavity, as in cerebral ventricle or heart ventricle

venule (VEEN-ule) small vessel that carries blood from capillary network to vein

very-low-density lipoprotein (VLDL) (lip-oh-PRO-teen) lipid-protein aggregate having high proportion of fat

vesicle (VES-ik-il) small, membrane-bound organelle

vestibular apparatus *see* vestibular system

vestibular receptor hair cell in semicircular canal, utricle, or saccule

vestibular system sense organ in temporal bone of skull; consists of *three semicircular canals,* a *utricle,* and a *saccule;* also called vestibular apparatus, sense organ of balance

villi (VIL-eye) finger-like projections from highly folded surface of small intestine; covered with single-layered epithelium

virilism (VIR-il-ism) development of masculine physical characteristics in a woman

virus nucleic acid core surrounded by protein coat; lacks enzyme machinery for energy production and ribosomes for protein synthesis; thus cannot survive or reproduce except inside other cells whose biochemical apparatus it uses

viscera (VISS-er-ah) organs in thoracic and abdominal cavities

viscoelastic (viss-ko-ee-LAS-tik) having viscous and elastic properties

viscosity (viss-KOS-ih-tee) measure of friction between adjacent layers of a flowing liquid; property of fluid that makes it resist flow

visual field part of world being viewed at a given time

vital capacity maximal amount of air that can be expired, regardless of time required, following maximal inspiration

vitalism (VI-tal-ism) view that life processes require a "life force" rather than physicochemical processes alone

vitamin organic molecule that is required in trace amounts for normal health and growth but is not manufactured by metabolic pathways in the body and must be supplied by diet; classified as *water-soluble* (vitamins C and the B complex) and *fat-soluble* (vitamins A, D, E, and K)

vocal cord one of two elastic-tissue bands stretched across laryngeal opening and caused to vibrate by air movement past them, producing sounds

volt (V) unit of measurement of electric potential between two points

voltage measure of potential of separated electric charges to do work; measure of electric force between two points

voltage-sensitive channel cell-membrane ion channel opened or closed by electric signals

vomiting center neurons in brainstem medulla oblongata that coordinate vomiting reflex

von Willebrand factor (vWF) (von-

VILL-ih-brand) plasma protein secreted by endothelial cells; facilitates adherence of platelets to damaged vessel wall

vulva (VUL-vah) female external genitalia; mons pubis, labia majora and minora, clitoris, vestibule of vagina, and vestibular glands

Wallerian degeneration after injury of neuron, degeneration of those parts separated from cell body by the injury

waste product product from a metabolic reaction or series of reactions that serves no function

wavelength distance between two successive wave peaks in oscillating medium

weak acid acid whose molecules do not completely ionize to form hydrogen ions when dissolved in water; *compare* strong acid

white matter portion of CNS that appears white in unstained specimens and contains primarily myelinated nerve fibers

white muscle fiber muscle fiber lacking appreciable amounts of myoglobin

withdrawal reflex *see* flexion reflex

Wolffian duct (WOLF-ee-an) part of embryonic duct system that, in male, remains and develops into reproductive-system ducts, but in female, degenerates

work measure of energy required to produce physical displacement of matter; *see also* external work, internal work

working memory short-term, limited-capacity memory storage process serving as initial depository of information from which memory may be transferred to long-term storage or forgotten

X chromosome *see* sex chromosome

Y chromosome *see* sex chromosome

Z line structure running across myofibril at each end of striated muscle sarcomere; anchors one end of thin filaments

zona pellucida (ZO-nah peh-LEW-sih-dah) thick, clear layer separating egg from surrounding granulosa cells

APPENDIX

C

ENGLISH AND METRIC UNITS

	English	**Metric**
Length	1 foot = 0.305 meter	1 meter = 39.37 inches
	1 inch = 2.54 centimeters	1 centimeter (cm) = 1/100 meter
		1 millimeter (mm) = 1/1000 meter
		1 micrometer (μm) = 1/1000 millimeter
		1 nanometer (nm) = 1/1000 micrometer
		°[1 angstrom (Å) = 1/10 nanometer]
Mass	†1 pound = 433.59 grams	1 kilogram (kg) = 1000 grams = 2.2 pounds
	1 ounce = 27.1 grams	1 gram (g) = 0.037 ounce
		1 milligram (mg) = 1/1000 gram
		1 microgram (μg) = 1/1000 milligram
		1 nanogram (ng) = 1/1000 microgram
		1 picogram (pg) = 1/1000 nanogram
Volume	1 gallon = 3.785 liters	1 liter = 1000 cubic centimeters = 0.264 gallon
	1 quart = 0.946 liter	1 liter = 1.057 quarts
		1 deciliter (dl) = 1/10 liter
		1 milliliter (ml) = 1/1000 liter
		1 microliter (μl) = 1/1000 milliliter

°The angstrom unit of length is not a true metric unit, but has been included because of its frequent use, until recently, in the measurement of molecular dimensions.

†A pound is actually a unit of force, not mass. The correct unit of mass in the English system is the slug. When we write 1 kg = 2.2 pounds, this means that one kilogram of *mass* will have a *weight* under standard conditions of *gravity* at the earth's surface of 2.2 pounds *force*.

APPENDIX
D

ELECTROPHYSIOLOGY EQUATIONS

I. The **Nernst equation** describes the equilibrium potential for any ion species, that is, the electric potential necessary to balance a given ionic concentration gradient across a membrane so that the net passive flux of the ion is zero. The Nernst equation is

$$E = \frac{RT}{zF} \ln \frac{C_o}{C_i}$$

where E = equilibrium potential for the particular ion in question
C_i = intracellular concentration of the ion
C_o = extracellular concentration of the ion
z = valence of the ion (+1 for sodium and potassium, +2 for calcium, −1 for chloride)
R = gas constant [8314.9 J/(kg · mol · K)]
T = absolute temperature (temperature measured on the Kelvin scale: degrees centigrade + 273)
F = Faraday (the quantity of electricity contained in 1 mol of electrons: 96,484.6 C/mol of charge)
$\ln$ = logarithm taken to the base e

II. A membrane potential depends on the intracellular and extracellular concentrations of potassium, sodium, and chloride (and other ions if they are in sufficient concentrations) and on the relative permeabilities of the membrane to these ions. The **Goldman equation** is used to calculate the value of the membrane potential when the potential is determined by more than one ion species. The Goldman equation is

$$V_m = \frac{RT}{F} \ln \frac{P_K \times K_o + P_{Na} \times Na_o + P_{Cl} \times Cl_i}{P_K \times K_i + P_{Na} \times Na_i + P_{Cl} \times Cl_o}$$

where V_m = membrane potential
R = gas constant [8314.9 J/(kg · mol · K)]
T = absolute temperature (temperature measured on the Kelvin scale: degrees centigrade + 273)
F = Faraday (the quantity of electricity contained in 1 mol of electrons: 96,484.6 C/mol of charge)
$\ln$ = logarithm taken to the base e
$P_K, P_{Na},$ and P_{Cl} = membrane permeabilities for potassium, sodium, and chloride, respectively
$K_o, Na_o,$ and Cl_o = extracellular concentrations of potassium, sodium, and chloride, respectively
$K_i, Na_i,$ and Cl_i = intracellular concentrations of potassium, sodium, and chloride, respectively

APPENDIX

E

OUTLINE OF EXERCISE PHYSIOLOGY

APPENDIX
F

CLINICAL TERMS IN TEXT

APPENDIX
G

SUGGESTED READING

Like all scientists, physiologists report the results of their experiments in scientific journals. Approximately 1300 such journals in the life sciences publish more than 300,000 papers each year. Every physiologist must be familiar with the ever-increasing number of articles in his or her own specific field of research.

Another type of scientific writing is the review article, a summary and synthesis of the relevant research reports on a specific subject. Such reviews, which are published in many different journals, are extremely useful. Also, the American Physiological Society has a massive program of publishing comprehensive reviews in almost all fields of physiology. These reviews are gathered into a series of ongoing volumes known collectively as the "Handbook of Physiology." Another important series is the *Annual Review of Physiology,* which publishes yearly reviews of the most recent research articles in specific fields and provides the most rapid means of keeping abreast of developments in physiology.

Another type of review that is of value to the nonexpert is the *Scientific American* article. Written in a manner usually intelligible to the layperson, these articles, in addition to reviewing a topic, often present experimental data so that the reader can obtain some insight into how the experiments were done and the data interpreted. Many articles published in *Scientific American* can be obtained individually as inexpensive offprints from W. H. Freeman and Company, San Francisco, CA, 94104, which also publishes collections of *Scientific American* articles in a specific area, for example, psychobiology. Two other magazines that frequently publish excellent reviews of physiology for the nonexpert are *New England Journal of Medicine* and *Hospital Practice.* The New York Times (particularly in its Tuesday "Science" section) provides excellent coverage of physiology-related health news. Finally, in the realm of nutrition, fitness, and stress management, The University of California at Berkeley Wellness Letter, published by that university's School of Public Health, is superb; the mailing address is P.O. Box 420149, Palm Coast, FL 32142-9821.

Another level of scientific writing is the monograph, an extended review of a subject area that is broader than the review articles described above. Monographs are usually in book form and generally do not attempt to cover all the relevant literature on the topic; rather they analyze and synthesize the most important data and interpretations. At the last level is the textbook, which deals with a much larger field than the monograph or review article. Its depth of coverage of any topic is accordingly much less complete and is determined by the audience to which it is aimed.

We have restricted our suggested readings to textbooks and monographs because they are usually available in college and university libraries. Their bibliographies will serve as a further entry into the scientific literature. We list first a group of books that cover wide areas of physiology.

BOOKS COVERING WIDE AREAS OF PHYSIOLOGY

Cell Physiology

Alberts, Bruce, Dennis Bray, Julian Lewis, Martin Raff, Keith Roberts, and James D. Watson: "Molecular Biology of the Cell," 2d edn., Garland Publishing, New York, 1989.

Avers, C. J.: "Molecular Cell Biology," Addison-Wesley, Reading, Mass., 1986.

Darnell, James, Harvey Lodish, and David Baltimore: "Molecular Cell Biology," 2d edn., Scientific American Books, New York, 1990.

DeRobertis, E. D. P., and E. M. F. DeRobertis, Jr.: "Essentials of Cell and Molecular Biology," Lea & Febiger, Philadelphia, 1987.

Macleod, Alexander, and Karol Sikora: "Molecular Biology and Human Disease," Blackwell Scientific Publications, St. Louis, Mo., 1984.

Organ-System Physiology

Berne, R. M., and M. N. Levy: "Physiology," 3d edn., Mosby, St. Louis, 1992.

Ganong, W. F.: "Review of Medical Physiology," 16th ed., Lange, Los Altos, Calif., 1993.

Guyton, A. C.: "Textbook of Medical Physiology," 8th edn., Saunders, Philadelphia, 1991.

Patton, H. D., A. F. Fuchs, B. Hille, A. M. Scher, and R. Steiner (eds.): "Textbook of Physiology: Volume 1 Excitable Cells and Neurophysiology, Volume 2 Circulation, Respiration, Body Fluids, Metabolism, and Endocrinology," 21st edn., Saunders, Philadelphia, 1989.

West, John B. (ed.): "Best and Taylor's Physiological Basis of Medical Practice," 12th edn., Williams & Wilkins, Baltimore, 1991.

Anatomy

Basmajian, J. V.: "Grant's Method of Anatomy," 11th edn., Williams & Wilkins, Baltimore, 1988.

Bloom, W., and D. W. Fawcett: "A Textbook of Histology," 11th edn., Saunders, Philadelphia, 1986.

Carlson, B. M.: "Patten's Foundations of Embryology," 5th edn., McGraw-Hill, New York, 1988.

Clemente, C. D.: "Gray's Anatomy of the Human Body," 30th American edn., Lea & Febiger, Philadelphia, 1984.

Hollinshead, W. Henry, and Cornelius Rosse: "Textbook of Anatomy," 4th edn., Harper and Row, Philadelphia, 1985.

Woodburne, R. T.: "Essentials of Human Anatomy," 8th edn., Oxford, New York, 1988.

SUGGESTIONS FOR INDIVIDUAL CHAPTERS

Chapter 1

Bernard, C.: "An Introduction to the Study of Experimental Medicine," Dover, New York, 1957 (paperback).

Brooks, C. McC., and P. F. Cranefield (eds.): "The Historical Development of Physiological Thought," Hafner, New York, 1959.

Butterfield, H.: "The Origins of Modern Science," Macmillan, New York, 1961 (paperback).

"The Excitement and Fascination of Science: A Collection of Autobiographical and Philosophical Essays," Annual Reviews, Palo Alto, Calif., 1966.

Fulton, J. F., and L. C. Wilson (eds.): "Selected Readings in the History of Physiology," 2d edn., Charles C Thomas, Springfield, Ill., 1966.

Harvey, W.: "On the Motion of the Heart and Blood in Animals," Gateway, Henry Regnery, Chicago, 1962 (paperback).

Leake, Chauncey: "Some Founders of Physiology," American Physiological Society, Washington, D.C., 1961.

Chapter 2

Creighton, Thomas E.: "Proteins: Structures and Molecular Principles," Freeman, New York, 1984.

Devlin, Thomas M.: "Textbook of Biochemistry With Clinical Correlations," 3d edn., Wiley-Liss, New York, 1992.

Lehninger, Albert L.: "Principles of Biochemistry," 2d edn., Worth, New York, 1982.

Stryer, Lubert: "Biochemistry," 3d edn., Freeman, San Francisco, 1989.

Chapter 3

Berns, Michael W.: "Cells," 2d edn., Holt, Rinehart, and Winston, New York, 1983.

Bloom, W., and D. W. Fawcett: "A Textbook of Histology," 11th edn., Saunders, Philadelphia, 1986.

Fawcett, D. W.: "The Cell," 2d edn., Saunders, Philadelphia, 1981.

Schliwa, M.: "The Cytoskeleton: An Introductory Survey," Springer-Verlag, New York, 1986.

Weiss, Leon, et. al (eds.): "Cell and Tissue Biology: A Textbook of Histology," 6th edn., Urban & Schwarzenberg, Baltimore, 1988.

Chapter 4

Alberts, Bruce, Dennis Bray, Julian Lewis, Martin Raff, Keith Roberts, and James D. Watson: "Molecular Biology of the Cell," 2d edn., Garland, New York, 1989.

Darnell, James, Harvey Lodish, and David Baltimore: "Molecular Cell Biology," 2d edn., Scientific American Books, New York, 1990.

Creighton, Thomas E.: "Proteins: Structures and Molecular Principles," Freeman, New York, 1984.

Gelehrter, Thomas D., and Francis S. Collins: "Principles of Medical Genetics," Williams & Wilkins, Baltimore, Maryland, 1990.

Mange, Arthur P., and Elaine Johnson Mange: "Genetics: Human Aspects," Sinauer Associates, Sunderland, Mass., 1990.

Ross, D. W.: "Introduction to Molecular Medicine," Springer-Verlag, New York, 1992.

Ruddon, Raymond W.: "Cancer Biology," 2d edn., Oxford, New York, 1987.

Sirica, Alphonse E. (ed.): "The Pathobiology of Neoplasia," Plenum, New York, 1989.

Watson, James D., Nancy H. Hopkins, Jeffrey W. Roberts, Joan Argetsinger Steitz, and Alan M. Weiner: "The Molecular Biology of the Gene," 4th edn., Benjamin, New York, 1987.

——, Michael Gilman, Jan Witkowski, and Mark Zoller: "Recombinant DNA," Freeman, New York, 1992.

Chapter 5

Baker, Jeffrey J. W., and Garland E. Allen: "Matter, Energy, and Life," 4th edn., Addison-Wesley, Reading, Mass., 1981.

Bittar, E. Edward (ed.): "Chemistry of the Living Cell," JAI Press, Greenwich, Conn., 1992.

Devlin, Thomas M.: "Textbook of Biochemistry With Clinical Correlations," 3d edn., Wiley-Liss, New York, 1992.

Fersht, A.: "Enzyme Structure and Mechanism," 2d edn., Freeman, New York, 1984.

Hunt, Sara M., and James L. Groff: "Advanced Nutrition and Human Metabolism," West Pub., St. Paul, Minn., 1990.

Kinney, John M., and Hugh N. Tucker: "Energy Metabolism: Tissue Determinants and Cellular Corollaries," Raven, New York, 1992.

Newsholme, E. A., and A. R. Leech: "Biochemistry for Medical Science," Wiley, New York, 1984.

Stryer, Lubert: "Biochemistry," 3d edn., Freeman, San Francisco, 1988.

Wills, Eric D.: "Biochemical Basis of Medicine," Wright, Bristol, 1985.

Chapter 6

Alberts, Bruce, Dennis Bray, Julian Lewis, Martin Raff, Keith Roberts, and James D. Watson: "Molecular Biology of the Cell," 2d edn., Garland, New York, 1989.

Andreoli, T. E., J. F. Hoffman, and D. D. Fanestil (eds.): "Membrane Physiology," 2d edn., Plenum, New York, 1987.

Byrne, John. H., and Stanely G. Schultz: "An Introduction to Membrane Transport and Bioelectricity," Raven, New York, 1988.

Darnell, James, Harvey Lodish, and David Baltimore: "Molecular Cell Biology," 2d edn., Scientific American Books, New York, 1990.

Finkelstein, Alan: "Water Movement Through Lipid Bilayers, Pores, and Plasma Membranes: Theory and Reality," Wiley, New York, 1987.

Chapter 7

Arendt, J., D. S. Minors, and J. M. Waterhouse: "Biological Rhythms in Clinical Practice," Wright, London, 1990.

Bernard, C.: "An Introduction to the Study of Experimental Medicine," Dover, New York, 1957 (paperback).

Cannon, W. B.: "The Wisdom of the Body," Norton, New York, 1939 (paperback).

Goodman, H. M.: "Basic Medical Endocrinology," Raven, New York, 1988.

Griffin, J. E., and S. R. Ojeda: "Textbook of Endocrinology," Oxford, New York, 1988.

Langley, L. L. (ed.): "Homeostasis: Origin of the Concept," Dowden, Hutchinson, and Ross, Stroudsburg, Pa., 1973.

Mrosovksy, N.: "Rheostasis: The Physiology of Change," Oxford, New York, 1991.

Wilson, J. D. and D. W. Foster (eds.): "Williams Textbook of Endocrinology," 7th edn., Saunders, Philadelphia, 1987.

Chapter 8

Aidley, D. J.: "The Physiology of Excitable Cells," 3d edn., Cambridge, New York, 1989.

Brown, A. G.: "Nerve Cells and Nervous Systems: An Introduction to Neuroscience," Springer-Verlag, London, 1991.

Byrne, J. H., and S. G. Shultz: "An Introduction to Membrane Transport and Bioelectricity," Raven, New York, 1988.

Carpenter, M. B.: "Core Text of Neuroanatomy," 3d edn., Williams and Wilkins, Baltimore, 1985.

Kandel, E. R., J. H. Schwartz, and T. M. Jessell: "Principles of Neural Science," 3d edn., Elsevier/North-Holland, New York, 1991.

Kelner, K. L., and D. E. Koshland (eds.): "Molecules to Models: Advances in Neuroscience," American Association for the Advancement of Science, Washington, D.C., 1989.

Levitan, I. B., and L. K. Kaczmarek: "The Neuron: Cell and Molecular Biology," Oxford, New York, 1991.

Martin, J. H.: "Neuroanatomy: Text and Atlas," Elsevier, New York, 1989.

Nauta, W. J. H., and M. Feirtag: "Fundamental Neuroanatomy," Freeman, New York, 1986.

Patton, H. D., A. F. Fuchs, B. Hille, A. M. Scher, and R. Steiner (eds.): "Textbook of Physiology: Volume 1 Excitable Cells and Neurophysiology," 21st edn., Saunders, Philadelphia, 1989.

Chapter 9

Aidley, D. J.: "The Physiology of Excitable Cells," 3d edn., Cambridge, New York 1989.

Gregory, R. L.: "Eye and Brain: The Psychology of Seeing," 4th edn., Princeton, Princeton, N.J., 1979.

Kandel, E. R., J. H. Schwartz, and T. M. Jessell: "Principles of Neural Science," 3d edn., Elsevier/North-Holland, New York, 1991.

Patton, H. D., A. F. Fuchs, B. Hille, A. M. Scher, and R. Steiner (eds.): "Textbook of Physiology: Volume 1 Excitable

Cells and Neurophysiology," 21st edn., Saunders, Philadelphia, 1989.

Pickles, J. O.: "An Introduction to the Physiology of Hearing," 2d edn., Academic, San Diego, 1988.

Spillman, L., and J. S. Warner (eds.): "Visual Perception: The Neurophysiological Foundations," Academic, San Diego, 1990.

Chapter 10

Bailieue, E.-E., and P. A. Kelly: "Hormones: From Molecules to Disease," Herman, New York, 1991.

Bolander, F. F.: "Molecular Endocrinology," Academic, San Diego, 1989.

Goodman, H. M.: "Basic Medical Endocrinology," Raven, New York, 1988.

Griffin, J. E., and S. R. Ojeda: "Textbook of Endocrinology," Oxford, New York, 1988.

Greenspan, F. S.: "Basic and Clinical Endocrinology," 3d edn., Appleton and Lange, E. Norwalk, Conn. 1991.

Hedge, G. A., H. D. Colby, and R. L. Goodman: "Clinical Endocrine Physiology," Saunders, 1987.

Tepperman, J.: "Metabolic and Endocrine Physiology," 5th edn., Year Book, Chicago, 1987.

Wilson, J. D., and D. W. Foster (eds.): "Williams Textbook of Endocrinology," 7th edn., Saunders, Philadelphia, 1987.

Chapter 11

Bulbring, Edith, Alison F. Brading, Allan W. Jones, and Tadao Tomita (eds.): "Smooth Muscle," University of Texas, Austin, 1981.

Hoyle, C.: "Muscles and Their Neural Control," Wiley-Interscience, New York, 1983.

Jones, D. A., and J. M. Round: "Skeletal Muscle in Health and Disease: A Textbook of Muscle Physiology," Manchester University, Manchester, England, 1990.

Keynes, R. D., and D. J. Aidley: "Nerve and Muscle," 2d edn., Cambridge, Cambridge, 1992.

Peachy, Lee D., and Richard H. Adrian (eds.): "Handbook of Physiology: Section 10, Skeletal Muscle," American Physiological Society, Bethesda, Md., 1983.

Shepard, Roy J.: "Exercise Physiology," Decker, Philadelphia, 1987.

Squire, John: "The Structural Basis of Muscle Contraction," Plenum, New York, 1981.

———: "Muscle Design and Disease," Benjamin/Cummings, Menlo Park, Calif., 1986.

Twarog, Betty M., Rhea J. C. Levine, and Maynard M. Dewey (eds.): "Basic Biology of Muscles: A Comparative Approach," Raven, New York, 1982.

Walton, John: "Disorders of Voluntary Muscle," 5th edn., Churchill Livingstone, New York, 1988.

Woledge, Roger C., Nancy A. Curtin, and Earl Homsher: "Energetic Aspects of Muscle Contraction," Academic, New York, 1985.

Chapter 12

Brooks, V. B.: "The Neural Basis of Motor Control," Oxford, New York, 1986.

Evarts, E. V., S. P. Wise, and D. Bousfield (eds.): "The Motor System in Neurobiology," Elsevier, New York, 1985.

Kandel, E. R., J. H. Schwartz, and T. M. Jessell: "Principles of Neural Science," 3d edn., Elsevier/North-Holland, New York, 1991.

Patton, H. D., A. F. Fuchs, B. Hille, A. M. Scher, and R. Steiner (eds.): "Textbook of Physiology: Volume 1 Excitable Cells and Neurophysiology," 21st edn., Saunders, Philadelphia, 1989.

Rosenbaum, D. A.: "Human Motor Control," Academic, San Diego, 1991.

Chapter 13

Gregory, R. L.: "Odd Perceptions," Routledge, New York, 1986.

Kandel, E. R., J. H. Schwartz, and T. M. Jessell: "Principles of Neural Science," 3d edn., Elsevier/North-Holland, New York, 1991.

Kaplan, H. I., and B. J. Sadock: "Synopsis of Psychiatry: Behavioral Sciences and Clinical Psychiatry," 6th edn., Williams & Wilkins, Baltimore, 1991.

Kelner, K. L., and D. E. Koshland (eds.): "Molecules to Models: Advances in Neuroscience," American Association for the Advancement of Science, Washington, D.C., 1989.

Levitan, I. B., and L. K. Kaczmarek: "The Neuron: Cell and Molecular Biology," Oxford, New York, 1991.

Martinez, J. L., Jr., and R. P. Kesner: "Learning and Memory: A Biological View," 2d edn., Academic, 1991.

Patton, H. D., A. F. Fuchs, B. Hille, A. M. Scher, and R. Steiner (eds.): "Textbook of Physiology: Volume 1 Excitable Cells and Neurophysiology," 21st edn., Saunders, Philadelphia, 1989.

Scientific American (entire issue), "Brain and Mind," September, 1992.

Chapter 14

Beck, W. S.: "Hematology," 5th edn., MIT, Cambridge, 1991.

Berne, R. M., and M. N. Levy: "Cardiovascular Physiology," 6th edn., Mosby, St. Louis, 1992.

Mohrman, D. E., and L. J. Heller: "Cardiovascular Physiology," 3d edn., McGraw-Hill, New York, 1991.

Honig, C. R.: "Modern Cardiovascular Physiology," 2d edn., Little, Brown, Boston, 1988.

Little, R. C., and W. C. Little: "Physiology of the Heart and Circulation," 4th edn., Year Book, Chicago, 1989.

Williams, W. J., E. Beutler, A. J. Erslev, and M. A. Lichtman: "Hematology," 4th edn., McGraw-Hill, New York, 1990.

Chapter 15

Davenport, H. W.: "The ABC of Acid-Base Chemistry," 7th edn., University of Chicago, Chicago, 1978.

Levitzky, M. G.: "Pulmonary Physiology," 3d edn., McGraw-Hill, New York, 1991.

Mines, A. H.: "Respiratory Physiology," 3d edn., Raven, New York, 1992.

Staub, N. C.: "Basic Respiratory Physiology," Churchill, Livingstone, New York, 1990.

Taylor, A. E., K. Rehder, R. E. Hyatt, and J. C. Parker: "Clinical Respiratory Physiology," Saunders, Philadelphia, 1989.

West, J. B.: "Respiratory Physiology: The Essentials," 4th edn., Williams & Wilkins, Baltimore, 1989.

Crystal, R. G., and J. B. West (eds.): "The Lung: Scientific Foundations," Raven, New York, 1991.

Chapter 16

Brenner, B. M., and F. C. Rector (eds.): "The Kidney," 4th edn., Saunders, Philadelphia, 1991.

Davenport, H. W.: "The ABC of Acid-Base Chemistry," 7th edn., University of Chicago, Chicago, 1978.

Selden, D. W., and G. H. Giebisch (eds.): "The Kidney: Physiology and Pathophysiology," 2d edn., Raven, New York, 1992.

Koepen, B. M., and B. A. Stanton: "Renal Physiology," Mosby Year Book, St. Louis, 1992.

Rose, B. D.: "Clinical Physiology of Acid-Base and Electrolyte Disorders," 3d edn., McGraw-Hill, New York, 1989.

Smith, H. W.: "From Fish to Philosopher," Anchor Books, Doubleday, Garden City, N.Y., 1961.

Vander, A. J.: "Renal Physiology," 4th edn., McGraw-Hill, New York, 1991.

Chapter 17

Brooks, Frank P. (ed.): "Gastrointestinal Pathophysiology," 2d edn., Oxford, New York, 1978.

Davenport, Horace W.: "Physiology of the Digestive Tract," 5th edn., Year Book Medical Publishers, Chicago, 1982.

Granger, D. N., J. A. Barrowman, and P. R. Kvietys: "Clinical Gastrointestinal Physiology," Saunders, Philadelphia, 1985.

Johnson, L. R. (ed.): "Gastrointestinal Physiology," 3d edn., Mosby, St. Louis, 1985.

————, J. Christensen, E. D. Jacobson, and J. H. Walsh (eds.): "Physiology of the Gastrointestinal Tract," 2d edn., Raven, New York, 1987 (two volumes).

Chapter 18

Adolph, E. F.: "Physiology of Man in the Desert," Interscience, New York, 1947.

Bailieue, E.-E., and P. A. Kelly: "Hormones: From Molecules to Disease," Herman, New York, 1991.

Falkner, F., and Tanner, J. M. (eds.): "Human Growth," Plenum, New York, 1986.

Goodman, H. M.: "Basic Medical Endocrinology," Raven, New York, 1988.

Griffin, J. E., and S. R. Ojeda: "Textbook of Endocrinology," Oxford, New York, 1988.

Greenspan, F. S.: "Basic and Clinical Endocrinology," 3d edn., Appleton and Lange, E. Norwalk, Conn., 1991.

MacKowiak, P. A. (ed.): "Fever: Basic Mechanisms and Management," Raven, New York, 1991.

Vander, A. J.: "Nutrition, Stress, and Toxic Chemicals: An Approach to Environmental Health Controversies," University of Michigan, Ann Arbor, 1981.

Wilson, J. D., and D. W. Foster (eds.): "Williams Textbook of Endocrinology," 7th edn., Saunders, Philadelphia, 1987.

Chapter 19

Bailieue, E.-E., and P. A. Kelly: "Hormones: From Molecules to Disease," Herman, New York, 1991.

Carlson, B. M.: "Patten's Foundations of Embryology," 5th edn., McGraw-Hill, New York, 1988.

Goodman, H. M.: "Basic Medical Endocrinology," Raven, New York, 1988.

Griffin, J. E., and S. R. Ojeda: "Textbook of Endocrinology," Oxford, New York, 1988.

Johnson, M., and B. Everett: "Essential Reproduction," 2d edn., Blackwell, Oxford, 1985.

Tepperman, J.: "Metabolic and Endocrine Physiology," 5th edn., Year Book, Chicago, 1987.

Wilson, J. D., and D. W. Foster (eds.): "Williams Textbook of Endocrinology," 7th edn., Saunders, Philadelphia, 1987.

Yen, S. S. C., and Jaffee, R. B.: "Reproductive Endocrinology," 3d edn., Saunders, 1991.

Chapter 20

Asterita, M. E.: "The Physiology of Stress," Sciences Press, 1985.

Barrett, J. T.: "Textbook of Immunology," 5th edn., Mosby, St. Louis, 1988.

————: "Medical Immunology," F. A. Davis, Philadelphia, 1991.

Beck, W. S.: "Hematology," MIT, 5th edn., Cambridge, 1991.

Plotnikoff, N., A. Murgo, R. Faith, and J. Wybran: "Stress and Immunity," CRC, Boca Raton, La., 1991.

Roit, I.: "Essential Immunology," 6th edn., Blackwell, St. Louis, 1988.

————: "Immunology," 2d edn., Mosby, St. Louis, 1989.

Stites, D. P., and A. I. Terr: "Basic and Clinical Immunology," 7th edn., Lange, Norwalk, Conn., 1991.

Vander, A. J.: "Nutrition, Stress, and Toxic Chemicals: An Approach to Environmental Health Controversies," University of Michigan, Ann Arbor, 1981.

Williams, W. J., E. Beutler, A. J. Erslev, and M. A. Lichtman: "Hematology," 4th edn., McGraw-Hill, New York, 1990.

PART AND CHAPTER OPENING PHOTO CREDITS

Part One   Scanning electron micrograph of a human lymphocyte. *(CNRI/Science Photo Library/Photo Researchers.)*

Part Two   Computer-enhanced MRI of a normal brain. *(Scott Camazine/Photo Researchers.)*

Part Three   Bone scan of entire human body. *(Alexander Tsiaras/Science Source/Photo Researchers.)*

Chapter 1   Scanning electron micrograph of cells in an organ (the thymus). CNRI/Science Photo Library/Photo Researchers.)

Chapter 2   Molecular graphics image of hydrogen-bonding between a benzene molecule and a water molecule. *(Image provided by Prof. G. A. Blake/Division of Geological and Planetary Sciences/California Institute of Technology.)*

Chapter 3   Electron micrograph of a mast cell. *(Dr. Brian Eyden/Science Photo Library/Photo Researchers.)*

Chapter 4   Computer model of DNA molecules. *(R. Langridge/ D. McCoy/Rainbow.)*

Chapter 5   Computer graphic of an enzyme (lysozyme) and its substrate. *(Science Photo Library/Photo Researchers.)*

Chapter 6   Model for the structure of the plasma membrane. *(Francis Leroy/Biocosmos/Science Photo Library/ Photo Researchers.)*

Chapter 7   Increase in cytosolic calcium concentration (indicated by the yellow) of pancreatic exocrine gland cells during stimulation by the hormone cholecystokinin. *(Courtesy D. I. Yule and J. A. Williams.)*

Chapter 8   Scanning electron micrograph of nerve cells from cerebral cortex. *(CNRI/Science Photo Library/Photo Researchers.)*

Chapter 9   Fluorescein dye angiogram of the eye. *(Alexander Tsiaras/Photo Researchers.)*

Chapter 10   Light micrograph of a thyroid gland. *(John Burbidge/Science Photo Library/Photo Researchers.)*

Chapter 11   Electron micrograph of skeletal muscle. *(Don W. Fawcett/Photo Researchers.)*

Chapter 12   Visualization of brain activity preceding rotation of a limb; each line represents the directional preference of a population of neurons in the motor cortex. *(Apostokos P. Georgopoulos, M.D.)*

Chapter 13   Computer-digitized image of the brain (top view). *(T. Porett/Photo Researchers.)*

Chapter 14   Angiogram (x-ray examination after prior injection of a radio-opaque contrast medium) of the heart (coronary) blood vessels. *(Science Photo Library/ Science Source/Photo Researchers.)*

Chapter 15   Resin cast of the pulmonary arteries and bronchi. *(Science Photo Library/Science Source/Photo Researchers.)*

Chapter 16   Resin cast of the kidneys' blood vessels and outflow system. *(John Watney/Photo Researchers.)*

Chapter 17   X-ray of the abdomen showing the large intestine (after infusion of radio-opaque contrast medium into the rectum). *(CNRI/Science Photo Library/ Photo Researchers.)*

Chapter 18   Light micrograph of pancreas showing exocrine glands and (top left of center) an islet of Langerhans. *(Astrid and Hans-Frieder Michler/ Science Photo Library/Photo Researchers.)*

Chapter 19   Scanning electron micrograph of sperm on the surface of an egg. *(David M. Phillips/Photo Researchers.)*

Chapter 20   Scanning electron micrograph of a macrophage (larger cell) and a lymphocyte (smaller cell). *(Don Fawcett/E. Shelton/Science Source/Photo Researchers.)*

INDEX

Androgen-binding protein, 655
Androgens, 648
  adrenal, 274
  secretion of, by adrenal cortex, 279
  in women, 674
Androsterone, 279
Anemia, 399–400
  deficiency of vitamin B_{12}, 574
Anemic hypoxia, 508
ANF (*see* Atrial natriuretic factor)
Angina pectoris, 469
Angiogenesis, 437–438
Angiogenic factors, 439
Angiotensin (*see* Angiotensin I;
    Angiotensin II)
Angiotensin converting enzyme, 536,
    538
  blockers, in hypertension, 467–468
  inhibitors, 538
Angiotensin I, 536, 538
Angiotensin II, 275, 536, 538
  in baroreceptor reflex, 456
  in control of antidiuretic hormone
      secretion, 541
  as a neurotransmitter, 209
  production of, by lung capillaries,
      509
  as stimulus for aldosterone secretion,
      536
  and thirst, 542
  as vasoconstrictor, 436, 538
Angiotensinogen, 536, 538
  secretion of, by liver, 538
Anions, 17
Anorexia nervosa, 637
Antagonists, 162, 163
  skeletal muscle, 333
Antagonists and receptors, 207
Anterior pituitary, 274, 286
  hormones of, 274, 288–289
  in pregnancy, 682
Anterolateral system, 246, 248
Antibiotics, 727–728
Antibodies, 733
  classes of, 717
  effects of, 718–720
  in milk, 687
  secreted by plasma cells, 710
  secretion of, 717
Antibody-dependent cellular cytotoxicity
    (ADCC), 719
Antibody-mediated responses, 710, 716–
    721
Anticlotting drugs, 748–749
Anticoagulants (*see* Oral anticoagulants)
Anticodon, 67, 68, 69
Antidiuretic hormone (ADH), 274, 286,
    432
  control of secretion of, 540–541

effects of, on collecting ducts, 534–
    535
(*See also* Vasopressin)
Antigen, 707–708
  binding site, 712
  presentation of, 713–715, 732
Antigen-presenting cells (APCs), 713,
    732
  secretion of interleukin 1 by, 714
  (*See also* B cells; Macrophages)
Anti-inflammatory drugs in asthma, 485
Antithrombin III, 746, 748
Antrum:
  of follicle, 665
  of stomach, 580
Anus, 562
Aorta, 405
Aortic arch baroreceptor, 455
Aortic bodies, 500
Aortic pressure, 419
Aortic valves, 409
Apgar score, 690
Aphasia, 386–387
Appendix, 591–592
Appetite:
  in infection, 724, 726
  in pregnancy, 682
Aqueous humor, 250, 252
Arachidonic acid, 25, 160
  role of, in learning, 385
Arachnoid, 214
Arrhythmias, cardiac:
  and calcium, 546
  and plasma potassium, 543
Arterial baroreceptors, 455
  (*See also* Baroreceptors)
Arterial blood pressure, 430–432
  measurement of, 431–432
  in pregnancy, 682
  regulation of, 450–460
  relation of, to blood volume, 458–459
  (*See also* Mean arterial pressure)
Arteries, 404, 430–432
  and endothelium-derived natriuretic
      factor, 437
  function of, 408
Arterioles, 405, 432–437
  control of, in specific organs, 437, 438
  extrinsic controls of, 435–436
  functions of, 408, 432–434
  innervation of, 227
  local control of, 434–435
  response of, to injury, 435
  summary of controlling factors of, 437
Ascending limb of Henle's loop, 518,
    519
Ascending pathways, 236
  central control of, 244–245, 361–362
  nonspecific, 238

for somatic sensation, 245–246
  specific, 236–238
Ascending thin limb of Henle's loop,
    518
Aspartate, 209, 211
Aspirin, 161–162, 248
  as anticlotting drug, 479
  and fever, 643
Association cortex, 238–239
  role of, in motor control, 358
Asthma, 484–485, 731
Astigmatism, 252
Astroglia, 185
Atherosclerosis, 470
  and plasma cholesterol, 621
Atmospheric air, 490
Atmospheric pressure, 478
Atomic nucleus, 14–15
Atomic number, 14–15
Atomic weight, 15
Atoms, 14–15
ATP (*see* Adenosine triphosphate)
Atresia, 665
Atria:
  function of, 408
  secretion of atrial natriuretic factor
      by, 538, 539
Atrial contraction, 417, 418, 419
Atrial fibrillation, 420
Atrial natriuretic factor (ANF), 275,
    538, 539
  as vasodilator, 436
Atriopeptin (*see* Atrial natriuretic factor)
Atrioventricular (AV) node, 413, 414
Atrioventricular (AV) valves, 409
Atrium, 403
Atrophy of skeletal muscle, 331
Auditory cortex, 237, 238
Auriculin (*see* Atrial natriuretic factor)
Autocrine agents, 159, 160
Autoimmune disease, 730–732
Automaticity in cardiac conducting
    system, 412
Autonomic nervous system, 222–228
  dual innervation in, 226
  effects of, on heart, 427
  in exercise, 463–464
  ganglia of, 222
  neurotransmitters of, 223–226
  (*See also* Parasympathetic nerves;
      Parasympathetic nervous system;
      Sympathetic nerves; Sympathetic
      nervous system)
Autoreceptors, 206
AV conduction disorders, 414, 415
Axon, 181
Axon terminal, 181, 184
Axon transport, 182
AZT (*see* Zidovudine)

ABBREVIATIONS USED IN THE TEXT

A actin, adenine
A surface area
Acetyl CoA acetyl coenzyme A
ACh acetylcholine
ACTH adrenocorticotropic hormone
  (adrenocorticotropin, corticotropin)
ADCC antibody-dependent cellular
  cytotoxicity
ADH antidiuretic hormone (vasopressin)
ADP adenosine diphosphate
AIDS acquired immune deficiency syndrome
ANF atrial natriuretic factor
AP action potential
APC antigen-presenting cell
ATP adenosine triphosphate
AV atrioventricular

BMI body mass index
BMR basal metabolic rate

C Celsius (centigrade), creatine, cytosine
Ca calcium
cal calorie
CAM cell adhesion molecule
cAMP cyclic 3',5'-adenosine monophosphate
CCK cholecystokinin
cdc genes cell division cycle genes
CG chorionic gonadotropin
cGMP cyclic 3',5'-guanosine monophosphate
CGRP calcitonin gene-related peptide
C_i intracellular concentration
C_L lung compliance
Cl chlorine (Cl^- chloride ion)
cm centimeter
CNS central nervous system
CO carbon monoxide, cardiac output
C_o extracellular concentration
CoA coenzyme A
CP creatine phosphate
CPK creatine phosphokinase
CPR cardiopulmonary resuscitation
Cr creatinine

CRH corticotropin releasing hormone
CSF colony stimulating factor
C_x clearance of substance x
cyclic AMP cyclic 3',5'-adenosine
  monophosphate

DA dopamine
DAG diacylglycerol
Δ change
ΔP pressure difference
DKA diabetic ketoacidosis
dl deciliter
DNA deoxyribonucleic acid
DP diastolic pressure
DPG 2,3-diphosphoglycerate

E electric potential difference, voltage
E epinephrine (also Epi), internal energy
ECF extracellular fluid
ECG, EKG electrocardiogram
ECT electroconvulsive therapy
EDRF endothelium-derived relaxing factor
EDV end-diastolic volume
EEG electroencephalogram
EF ejection fraction
EP endogenous pyrogen
Epi epinephrine (also E)
EPP end-plate potential
EPSP excitatory postsynaptic potential
η fluid viscosity

F flow
F net flux
FAD flavine adenine dinucleotide
Fe iron
FEV_1 forced expiratory volume in 1 s
FSH follicle-stimulating hormone
f_i influx
f_o efflux
FRC functional residual capacity
FVC forced vital capacity

G guanine

g gram
G_0 phase "time out" phase of cell cycle
G_1 phase first gap phase of cell cycle
G_2 phase second gap phase of cell cycle
GABA gamma-aminobutric acid
GDP guanosine diphosphate
GFR glomerular filtration rate
GH growth hormone
GHRH growth hormone releasing hormone
GI gastrointestinal
GIP glucose-dependent insulinotropic peptide
GnRH gonadotropin releasing hormone
GTP guanosine triphosphate

H heat, hydrogen
h hour
Hb deoxyhemoglobin
HbH deoxyhemoglobin
HbO_2 oxyhemoglobin
HDL high-density lipoprotein
HGF hematopoietic growth factor
HIV human immunodeficiency virus
HR heart rate
5-HT serotonin, 5-hydroxytryptamine
Hz hertz (cycle/s)
I current
IDDM insulin-dependent diabetes mellitus
Ig immunoglobulin
IGF-I insulin-like growth factor I,
  somatomedin C
IL-1 interleukin 1
IL-2 interleukin 2
IL-6 interleukin 6
In inulin
IP_3 inositol trisphosphate
IPSP inhibitory postsynaptic potential
IUD intrauterine device

JG juxtaglomerular
JGA juxtaglomerular apparatus

K potassium
kcal kilocalorie